Terra/Wattel – European Tax Law

Ninth Edition

Terra/Wattel – European Tax Law

Ninth Edition

Volume I
General Topics and Direct Taxation

Edited by
Sjoerd Douma
Otto Marres
Hein Vermeulen
Dennis Weber

Wolters Kluwer

Published by:
Kluwer Law International B.V.
PO Box 316
2400 AH Alphen aan den Rijn
The Netherlands
E-mail: lrs-sales@wolterskluwer.com
Website: www.wolterskluwer.com/en/solutions/kluwerlawinternational

Sold and distributed by:
Wolters Kluwer Legal & Regulatory U.S.
920 Links Avenue
Landisville, PA 17538
United States of America
E-mail: customer.service@wolterskluwer.com

ISBN 978-94-035-4145-7

e-Book: ISBN 978-94-035-2026-1
web-PDF: ISBN 978-94-035-2036-0

PREFACE

This book is intended as a reference book for EU law and tax law practitioners, administrators, academics, the judiciary, and tax law or Union law policy makers. For students, an abridged textbook edition is available.

The present Volume I on general topics and direct taxation offers a systematic survey of the implications of the EU Treaties and of EU tax harmonization policy for national tax law, tax treaties and third State tax relations, a thorough and critical discussion of the EU Court's case law in direct tax matters, as well as a thorough discussion of the Union's direct tax rules in force and pending. Volume II of this book, on indirect taxation, was published in 2021 and covers the Union Customs Code, the Recast VAT directive, Excises and Energy taxation directives, as well as administrative cooperation in the field of indirect taxation.

The present Volume I is divided into four parts:
1. General EU Law and Taxation
2. Negative Integration of Direct Taxation;
3. Positive Integration of Corporate Taxes, and
4. Exchange of Information and Recovery Assistance.

In addition to all relevant substantive aspects of taxation, also matters of cross-border administrative cooperation, procedural matters and judicial protection are covered, including tax implications of the EU Charter of Fundamental Rights.

Apart from some last-minute additions, copy was closed in March 2025.

OVERVIEW

TABLE OF CONTENTS

CHAPTER 5

Third States and External Tax Relations / 163

Ana Paula Dourado and Peter Wattel

PART 2 INTEGRATION OF DIRECT TAXATION

CHAPTER 6

Conceptual Background of the CJEU Case Law in Direct Tax Matters / 205

Peter Wattel and Dennis Weber

CHAPTER 12

Exit Taxes / 431

Servaas van Thiel

CHAPTER 13

Individual Income Taxation / 453

Peter Wattel

CHAPTER 18

The Interest and Royalties Directive / 661

Peter Wattel

LIST OF ABBREVIATIONS

ACE	Allowance for corporate equity
ACR	Advance Cross-Border Rulings
ACT	Advance Corporation Tax
AD	Accounting Directive
AML	Anti-Money Laundering
AMLD	Anti-Money Laundering Directive
APA	Advance Pricing Agreement
Art.	Article
ATAD	Anti-tax avoidance Directive
ATR	Advance tax ruling
BEPS	Base Erosion and Profit Shifting
Bull.	Bulletin
C-	Case Number Court of Justice of the EU
CARF	Crypto-Asset Reporting Framework
CbC	country-by-country
CbCR	country by country reporting
CCC	Community Customs Code
CCCTB	Common Consolidated Corporate Tax Base
CCN	Common Communication Network
CCT	Common Customs Tariff
CCTB	Common Corporate Tax Base
CEN	Capital Export Neutrality
Cf.	Conform
CFA	Committee on Fiscal Affairs
CFC	Controlled Foreign Corporation
CFI	Court of First Instance
CIN	Capital Import Neutrality
CJEU	Court of Justice of the European Union
CMLRep.	Common Market Law Reports
CMLR	Common Market Law Review
CoE	Council of Europe
COM	Document of the European Commission
CRS	Common Reporting Standard
CRS MCAA	Multilateral Competent Authority Agreement for the Common Reporting Standard
CUP	Comparable Uncontrolled Price
DAC	Directive on Administative Cooperation in Tax Matters
Dfl.	Netherlands guilders
DPD	Data Protection Directive
EC	European Community/Communities
ECHR	European Convention for the Protection of Human Rights and Fundamental Freedoms
ECtHR	European Court for the Protection of Human Rights and Fundamental Freedoms (Strasbourg)
ECOFIN	Council of Ministers for Economic affairs and Finance
ECR	Reports of Cases before the Court
ECSC	European Coal and Steel Community

ECU	European Currency Unit
EEA(A)	European Economic Area (Agreement)
EEC	European Economic Community
EEIG	European Economic Interest Grouping
EFTA	European Free Trade Association
EMU	Economic and Monetary Union
EP	European Parliament
ESC	Economic and Social Committee
ET	European Taxation
et seq.	*et sequitur*
EU	European Union
EUA	European Unit of Account
EU TDP	EU Transfer Pricing Documentation
FASTER	Faster and Safer Relief of Excess Withholding Taxes
FATCA	Foreign Account Tax Compliance Act
FF	French francs
FII	Franked Investment Income
FSR	Foreign Subsidies Regulation
FTT	Financial Transactions Tax
GAAR	General anti-avoidance rule
GATT	General Agreement on Tariffs and Trade
GATS	General Agreement on Trade in Services
GDP	Gross Domestic Product
GDPR	General Data Protection Regulation (EU) 2016/679
GNP	Gross National Product
HMRC	Her Majesty's Revenue and Customs (UK)
HS	Harmonized System
i.e.	*id est*
IBFD	International Bureau of Fiscal Documentation
ICT	Information and Communication Technology
IFA	International Fiscal Association
IGA	Intergovernmental Agreement
IMF	International Monetary Fund
JTPF	EU Joint Transfer Pricing Forum
l.c.	*locus citandi*
LDCs	Least Developed Countries
Lit	Italian lira
LOB	Limitation on Benefits
Ltd	Private Limited Company
M&S II	Case C-446/03, *Marks & Spencer v David Halsey*
MAP	Mutual Agreement Procedure
MCMAATM	Multilateral Convention on Mutual Administrative Assistance in Tax Matters
MFN	Most Favoured Nation
MLI	Multilateral Instrument
MNEs	Multinational enterprises
NATO	North Atlantic Treaty Organization
NID	National interest deduction
o.c.	*opus citandi*
OCT	Overseas countries and territories
OECD	Organization for Economic Cooperation and Development
OECD-MC	OECD Model Double Taxation Convention on Income and on Capital
O.J.	Official Journal of the European Union
Plc	Public Limited Company
RAD	Recovery Assistance Directive
SAAR	Specific anti-avoidance rule
SCE	European Cooperative Society
SE	Societas Europaea (European company)
SME	Small and medium sized enterprises
RT	Registration Tax

T-	Case Number General Court of the EU
TEU	Treaty on European Union
TFEU	Treaty on the Functioning of the European Union
Thin cap	Thin Capitalization
TIEA	Tax information exchange agreement
UBO	Ultimate beneficial owner
UK	United Kingdom of Great Britain and Northern Ireland
UNCTAD	United Nations Conference on Trade and Development
US	United States of America
VAT	Value added tax
VIES	VAT Information Exchange System
Vol.	Volume
WCO	World Customs Organization
WTO	World Trade Organization

PART 1 GENERAL EU LAW AND TAXATION

CHAPTER 1

Introduction

Peter Wattel[1]

Update and elaboration by Otto Marres, Sjoerd Douma, Hein Vermeulen, Dennis Weber

Articles 2-6 of the Treaty on European Union (TEU) state the mission of the European Union. They enumerate, *inter alia*, the founding values of the Union, notably freedom, democracy, equality, the rule of law, respect for human rights, etc. They further state Union objectives, notably the realization or at least promotion of these values, as well as peace, the well-being of the peoples, cohesion and solidarity, and an area of freedom, security and justice without internal frontiers. More mundane objectives are a balanced and sustainable growth, price stability, full employment, social protection, competitiveness, etc. The Articles 3 and 4 TEU also mention two means to realize especially these more mundane objectives: the establishment of an internal market and of an economic and monetary union whose currency is the Euro.

An internal European market having the characteristics of one single national market requires, in particular, the free movement of goods, services, persons and capital, irrespective of national borders (Art. 26(2) TFEU), undistorted conditions of competition within that internal market (a level playing field; Arts. 101-109 TFEU), as well as harmonization of national laws insofar as disparities between national laws and administrative practices impede the functioning of that internal market (Art. 114 TFEU). The most manifest tax obstacles to the proper functioning of an internal EU market are:

- taxes on cross-border transactions, i.e. on the border-crossing of goods and services;
- differential tax treatment of domestic and imported goods and services;
- compulsory and current tax settlement of unrealized gains and other tax latencies upon the emigration of legal persons and individuals (exit taxes);
- substantial differences (disparities) between national tax laws, leading to market distortions, especially excessive tax competition between Member States facilitating tax avoidance by mobile capital;
- especially for EU-wide businesses: having to comply with up to 27 different tax administrations and 27 different sets of substantive and procedural tax law, including differences in tax accounting rules and tax timing;
- differential tax treatment of resident and nonresident taxpayers;
- differential tax treatment of domestic and foreign investment;
- differential tax treatment of domestic and foreign source income;

1 Professor emeritus of EU Tax Law, ACTL, University of Amsterdam; Advocate-General, Supreme Court of the Netherlands; State Councillor extraordinary, Netherlands Council of State.

- international economic double taxation (same tax base; different taxpayer), i.e. as a result of profit distributions by a company in one Member State to a shareholder in another Member State;
- International juridical double taxation (same tax base; same taxpayer) as a result of parallel exercise of taxing power by the source State and the residence State of the taxpayer (e.g. uncreditable source taxation: 'excess foreign tax credit'), or as a result of mismatches, e.g. transfer pricing differences, income characterization mismatches, tax accounting differences, etc.

Since the financial crises of 2008-2010, attention of politics has also turned to the drawbacks of free movement of capital and the freedom of establishment, especially to the resulting tax avoidance opportunities for mobile capital, and the drawbacks of not harmonizing direct taxes, especially corporate income taxes. The main drawbacks are distortive disparities (mismatches between tax systems) producing opportunities to exploit these mismatches (BEPS: base erosion and profit shifting, notably (i) double deduction, (ii) deduction without inclusion and (iii) non-taxation without inclusion) and excessive tax competition between Member States leading to 'tax degradation' (sponging on other Member States' tax revenue). Such competition may even result in prohibited State aid for multinational companies. It produces unacceptable undertaxation of mobile capital at the cost of public services.

These drawbacks obviously need to be addressed, but that does not take away the fact that tax obstacles as the ones listed cause market fragmentation along national borders which may impel (smaller) economic operators to stay on their home markets to avoid international double taxation or excessive administrative burdens, and thus may improperly affect the decisions of undertakings, employees, and (portfolio) investors as to where to trade, where to accept a job, where to establish an undertaking, where to incorporate, and where to invest. Therefore, integration of the tax systems of the EU Member States is necessary to a certain extent. Such integration may be 'negative' (market integration, *i.e.* integration through prohibitions: the abolition of restrictive national tax measures which are incompatible with the TFEU) or 'positive' (policy integration, *i.e.* integration through legislation, coordination and cooperation at Union level: harmonization of national tax laws, or at least policy coordination between Member States).

This book discusses both negative and positive tax integration in the EU. Negative integration mostly consists of case-by-case – and therefore rather unorganized – case law of the Court of Justice of the EU (CJEU, or: Court) on the (in)compatibility of national tax measures with EU free movement rights or the State aid prohibition. The discussion of positive integration of tax law covers the current harmonizing tax measures taken at Union level and pending proposals for Union action in the area of taxation, as well as EU soft law in that area.

This edition is divided into two volumes. Volume 2 covers indirect taxation and administrative cooperation in that field. The present Volume 1 covers (i) general Union law issues of importance for direct taxation, (ii) negative integration of direct taxation, (iii) harmonization of corporate taxation and (iv) administrative cooperation as regards direct taxation.

Part I (Chapters 1-5) deals with general issues of EU law, (international) tax law and (external) EU policy and the way in which general (principles of) EU law and (international) tax law interact;

Part II (Chapters 6-15) covers negative integration of direct taxes, especially the extensive body of CJEU case law – more than 350 cases – on the (in)compatibility of national tax measures and bilateral tax treaties with free movement rights and the State aid prohibition contained in the TFEU.

Part III (Chapters 16-26) discusses the current and pending EU Directives on corporate taxation, including the minimum harmonization of national and bilateral anti-abuse legislation, dispute settlement rules, soft law on tax competition and tax aspects of the European Company, the European Cooperative Company and the European Economic Interest Grouping;

Part IV, finally, covers cross-border administrative assistance in the levying and collecting of taxes, notably (automatic) exchange of tax information and recovery assistance between Member States.

Positive integration (harmonization measures and coordination at EU level) only modestly contributes to the abolition of tax impediments to the proper functioning of the internal market. Whereas most of the extensive integration of indirect taxes, especially of customs duties, turnover taxes and excises has been achieved by way of positive integration measures (EU regulations and directives), most of the integration of direct taxes is a result of prohibitions, *i.e.* case law of the CJEU holding national tax measures incompatible with primary EU law. Generally speaking, indirect taxes have been harmonized at EU level because they are a conspicuous and immediate obstacle to free trade as they are taxes on transactions: taxes on trade in, or the border-crossing of, goods and services. If one is to have free trade, there is no choice but to either abandon such taxes altogether, as is the case with taxes on the intra-EU border-crossing of goods and services (customs duties), or to harmonize them to make them internationally neutral. Direct taxes, by contrast, are taxes on the income or wealth of (legal) persons, having a less direct and less visible effect on trade and services, although one may argue they distort trade just as much as transaction taxes: unlike indirect taxes, they are not refunded upon exportation, but remain locked in the price of the goods and services exported by the economic operators.

Direct taxation is viewed by most Member States as the last hardcore part of their sovereignty within the Union, which implies little political enthusiasm for positive integration of direct taxes, as that would entail relinquishing budgetary and therefore core sovereignty. The consequence is, however, a large and rapidly expanding body of case-by-case and therefore unorganized and inconsistent case law of the Court, often fatal for the national direct tax measure at issue because it violates a free movement right or the State aid prohibition.

Because of these marked differences in legal basis (see Chapter 2) and in degree of integration between indirect and direct taxes, the CJEU's case law in indirect tax matters is different in character from its case law in direct tax matters. For indirect taxation, comprehensive and technically detailed secondary EU law has been enacted and implemented. The indirect tax cases brought before the Court therefore mostly concern implementation problems, *i.e.* the interpretation of these detailed, technical EU rules on indirect taxation. They are hardly ever on the consequences of free movement rights or the State aid prohibition. This part of EU tax law is *tax* law rather than *EU* law: the rules to be interpreted and applied are detailed and technical rules of indirect taxation, and to a much lesser extent Union law principles such as, notably, free movement, non-discrimination, proportionality, etc.

In the field of *direct* taxes, it is the other way around. Direct tax cases still rarely concern the implementation of dedicated EU legislation, although since 2017 an increase in cases on the application of the few EU corporate tax directives has been notable, as there still is little such legislation. Rather, direct tax cases before the CJEU concern the clash between the TFEU free movement rights and EU law principles on the one hand, and detailed, unharmonized domestic tax legislation and bilateral tax treaties on the other. Consequently, direct tax issues before the Court do not so much concern interpretation of *tax* law (as the Court is not competent to interpret national law or bilateral tax treaties) as they concern (principles of) *general EU* law, *i.e.* the general, sweeping Treaty rules of principle, such as free movement, market access, market equality, subsidiarity, proportionality, abuse of rights, level playing field (undistorted competition), Union loyalty, effectiveness of EU law, etc. In direct tax cases, the Court is a balancing artist between the interests of the internal market and the legitimate interests of 27 Member States to protect their separate national tax bases against base erosion, profit shifting, fiscal incoherence and (hybrid) mismatches. The national direct tax rules the Court is called upon to assess in the light of these very general principles of EU law are often extremely technical and detailed. This extreme difference in abstraction level of the two bodies of law clashing, makes negative integration of direct taxes complex and chaotic, more so because of a sophisticated third set of rules in between involved: the bilateral tax treaty network between the Member States which itself is complicated by the OECD Multilateral Convention to Implement Tax Treaty Related Measures to Prevent BEPS (multilateral instrument or MLI) into existing bilateral tax treaties.

The TFEU contains principles which must be respected in all areas affecting the objectives of the Union, therefore also in the tax area. One of these principles is the prohibition of discrimination against goods, services, workers, undertakings and capital from other Member States, of any other discrimination directly or indirectly based on nationality of persons or on origin of goods, capital and services, and even of nondiscriminatory measures hindering free movement. This principle – and other principles, such as Union loyalty and undistorted competition – have significant consequences for national tax sovereignty. They considerably limit Member States' freedom to arrange their national tax systems in the way they see fit. The far-reaching impact on national taxation of these general (non-tax) TFEU provisions will be discussed in Chapters 2-5 (general EU law principles and concepts) and 6-15 (negative integration of direct taxation). They are especially important in direct tax matters because of the scarcity of substantive harmonization in that area and the fact that national direct tax systems tend to distinguish between domestic-source income and foreign-source income and between resident taxpayers and nonresident taxpayers, whereas the TFEU in principle prohibits differential (less favorable) taxation of cross-border investment, establishment and employment than purely domestic investment, establishment and employment. Even non-discriminatory measures (national measures not distinguishing between cross-border and domestic cases) which nonetheless make cross-border market access excessively difficult, may be incompatible with the TFEU Freedoms.

Another harmonizing factor more important in direct tax matters than positive integration, is regulatory competition between Member States. All Member States court the favors of foreign investors to attract economic activity, employment, and growth, from both third States and other Member States, *inter alia* by offering competitive company taxation legislation, individual tax rulings and advance pricing agreements (APAs) to international business. Such tax competition produces spontaneous harmonization, especially of corporate tax rates, since neighboring States with a comparable level of economic opportunity, infrastructure, social security and public services, cannot afford to diverge significantly in tax burdens, less so as the (other) obstacles to individual or corporate emigration and to cross-border economic activity have been removed. This is more so since the introduction of the Euro as a common currency, taking away currency risks of cross-border investment and employment. If Member States diverge significantly in tax burdens without offering corresponding levels of public service and economic opportunity, then mobile economic activity will move to more tax-efficient Member States. The ensuing economic and social necessity for less tax-efficient Member States to keep up with the rest of the Union is usually a more convincing argument for national tax policy makers than abstract ideas, lofty objectives, or legal principles. It is striking to see how the levels of corporation tax in the 'old' fifteen Member States in a relatively short period came down from around 40% or higher to nowadays around 20% or lower (12,5% in Ireland), especially since the accession of the twelve eastern European Member States. At the same time – as the effective tax burden is the product of the tax base (corporate income) and the tax rate – most Member States broadened their tax base (fewer deductions, fewer exemptions and fewer credits) to compensate for the lower rate, overall possibly implying only a modest reduction in effective tax burden. If most Member States are forced by each other's regulatory competition to follow this pattern, the result is a more homogeneous corporate fiscal landscape throughout the Union.

Excessive ('unfair') tax competition, however, may lead to base erosion and fiscal degradation: Member States outbidding each other to attract foreign investors, sponging on each other's tax bases. The result may be an unjustified and economically dysfunctional EU-wide loss of tax revenue, benefiting mainly those who were already very capable of looking after themselves (internationally mobile capital), at the cost of less mobile tax bases like wages, the cost of which was already higher than in the US and Asia. In order to prevent both the exploitation of mismatches by internationally mobile capital, especially big tech, and excessive tax competition between States, the OECD designed a 'Two-Pillar Solution to Address the Tax Challenges Arising from the Digitalisation of the Economy': Pillar 1 re-allocates taxing rights over MNEs from their home countries to their market jurisdictions, regardless of whether they have a physical presence there. Pillar 2 introduces a global minimum effective corporate tax rate of 15%. This two-pillar approach has been adopted by the OECD/G20 'Inclusive Framework', comprising 137 countries representing more than 90% of global gross domestic product (GDP). The EU Commission aimed to implement it as fast as possible in the EU; in December 2021, it tabled proposals for a Directive to prevent the misuse of shell entities for tax purposes ('Unshell'), to be effective from 1 January 2024, and for a Directive on ensuring a global minimum level of taxation for multinational groups in the Union, to be effective from 1 January 2023 (see Section 25.3). Both met with quite some political opposition. The Unshell Directive proposal is still pending; the Pillar 2 Directive is adopted on 14 December 2022 and applicable in respect of the fiscal years beginning from 31 December 2023 (see Chapter 22). Implementation of Pillar 1 will take longer (if adopted at all), as it is politically even more controversial.

Harmonization of taxes, especially of direct taxes, is politically highly sensitive. Tax sovereignty is a fundamental part of national sovereignty. One of the most basic rights of a national parliament is its budget right: the right to vote on taxes. The European Parliament cannot, as yet, be considered an adequate substitute for national democratic parliamentary control, as there are, precisely, no European taxes, *i.e.* taxes levied at EU level by an EU tax administration on the spending of which the European Parliament votes. Taxation is the most important economic and social policy instrument for national governments. It may be used to redistribute income or wealth, to encourage investments or savings, to discourage the consumption or the use of certain goods (sin taxes; Pigouvian taxes), to protect the environment, etc. Therefore, the TFEU still provides for unanimity voting on tax matters, implying that each Member State has a veto right. The more unavoidable the harmonization and, with that, the loss of national sovereignty as regards *indirect* taxation is, the less Member States are inclined to forego their remaining tax sovereignty in the field of *direct* taxation. No Member State wants its tax base to be determined by the EU, let alone its tax rate. The adoption of the Pillar 2 Directive, resulting in a minimum *effective* corporate income taxation of 15%, is a major political achievement, because it implies, to a certain extent, harmonization of the corporate tax base. Pillar 1 (partial re-allocation of MNE's tax bases to market jurisdictions) is even more controversial, as it, precisely, interferes even more with tax base determination *and* allocation and looks like a first step towards an EU system of formula apportionment of tax base to Member States.

As observed, a genuine *European* tax does not exist yet. There is no tax administrated, levied and collected at Union level by a Union tax authority – except the payroll tax on the salaries of the EU civil servants, the 'Eurocrats' – on the spending of which the European Parliament votes. A Belgian proposal in 2000 to introduce a Eurotax met with skepticism and irony. Other Member States referred to historical examples of new taxes which led to war, such as the Spanish Duke of Alva's 'tenth penny', which led to the eighty-year Dutch-Spanish war, and the British tax on tea, which through the Boston Tea Party lead to the American War of Independence. But little did they know in 2000 that it was precisely the *absence* of a fiscal and political union – to complete and bolster the monetary union – which in 2011-2012 almost lead to a budgetary war, which almost destroyed the monetary union and the Euro. The successive credit crisis, bank crisis, Euro crisis and public debt crisis revealed a serious and dangerous lack of fiscal and political integration in the hitherto very successful Euro-area. Measures have been taken to prevent such crises from happening again, but among these was not an EU tax.

For the time being, the Union will have to make do with two categories of own revenue sources. Its most important traditional 'own resources' are (i) a percentage of the national bases of value added tax, capped to a percentage of GDP, (ii) the customs duties levied at the outside borders of the EU (minus perception costs), and (iii) agricultural levies. Since the budgetary and euro crises in the first decade of the 21st century, an *ad hoc* intergovernmental stability mechanism was added, funded by national revenue contributions of which every one of the 17 Euro Member States' parliaments had to approve (leading to government changes in four of the Member States in those crisis years). In December 2021, the Commission proposed to add three own resources to the EU budget: (i) 15% of the additional tax base to be allocated to Member States by the upcoming Pillar 1 reallocation of residual profits of in-scope MNE's to EU markets; (ii) 25% of Member States' revenue from the EU CO2-emissions trading system (ETS), and (iii) the revenue from the proposed EU carbon border adjustment mechanism (CBAM) which will put a carbon price on imports from third States corresponding to what would have been paid, had the goods been produced in the EU. The Commission completed its proposal in June 2023 (see Section 25.3.4).

All of these own resources are not genuine EU taxes, however, as they are levied and collected by national tax administrations, and the revenue is transmitted to the EU. That revenue is relatively small as compared to the percentage of Member States' GDP taken by national taxation. At Union level, taxation thus plays a limited role as a policy instrument. Consequently, at present the Union hardly has a tax policy of its own. The Commission policy is one of aligning national taxes and tax policies in so far as necessary for the functioning of the internal market, eliminating discriminatory, restrictive, and protective national taxation, but also excessive tax competition and fiscal State aid, if necessary by taking Member States to Court (see Art. 258 TFEU), and encouraging Member States to use taxation as a means to further economic development, especially of small and medium-sized enterprises (SMEs) and of research and development. Since the EU 'Green Deal', environmental policy objectives have been added, to be financed by the ETS and CBAM revenues mentioned above.

To date, the largest EU law impacts on national tax systems have been, for indirect taxation, the abolition of intra-EU customs duties, the concomitant introduction of common outside border customs duties (the customs union), and the introduction of the value added tax (VAT) system with a harmonized base for all national turnover taxes. For direct taxation, they were the CJEU's case law prohibiting national tax measures which make it less attractive to work, establish or invest abroad than at home, and the adoption of a series of directives greatly extending the automatic exchange of tax information between the Member States (see Chapters 25-29). Also, for the first time in more than 20 years, the Member States in 2017 adopted substantive EU direct tax measures. Anti-abuse measures were inserted in the existing Parent-Subsidiary Directive (PSD; see Chapter 16) and adopted in a new separate Anti-Tax Avoidance Directive (ATAD; see Chapter 19). A proposal for a common consolidated corporate tax base (CCCTB) has never been adopted, however, but is now rebranded as BEFIT: the Commission's decades-long ambition to achieve a harmonized corporate income tax is still burning (see Section 25.3.6).

CHAPTER 2

Constitutional Foundations: EU Tax Competences; Treaty Basis for Tax Integration; Sources and Enactment of EU Tax Law

Peter Wattel

Update and elaboration by Rita Szudoczky[1] and Dennis Weber[2]

2.1 Division of (Tax) Competences Between the Union and the Member States

Union competence is based on the principle of conferral: the Union has only the competences conferred on it by the Member States in the founding treaties, i.e. the Treaty on the European Union (TEU) and the Treaty on the Functioning of the European Union (TFEU) (see Article 5 TEU). The competences conferred upon the Union may be divided into three categories: (i) exclusive competences (Member States are not competent any more), listed in Article 3 TFEU; (ii) shared competences with 'preemption' (both the Union and the Member States are competent, but whenever the Union exercises its competence, the Member States lose their competence in the field on which the Union has exercised its competence), listed in Article 4 TFEU; and (iii) shared competences without preemption, meaning that the Union is only competent to support, coordinate or supplement, without superseding the competence of the Member States, listed in Article 6 TFEU.

Taxation is not expressly mentioned amongst the competences listed under Articles 3 to 6 TFEU. This does not mean that the Union does not have competences in the field of taxation. On the contrary, the customs union is listed as the first area in which the Union has exclusive competence (Article 3(1)(a) TFEU). A customs union is the mundane basis of the Union's genesis. In fact, the most basic idea of the European Union is a fiscal idea. Article 28 TFEU states that 'the Union shall comprise a customs union (...).' Indeed, custom duties at the border and discriminatory taxation of foreign goods and services are blunt and conspicuous restrictions of free trade. They are flagrantly incompatible with free movement of goods and services. Therefore, elimination of trade barriers within the (then) 'Community' began with the abolition of customs duties and other import restrictions, and the harmonization of indirect taxes. A customs union implies the total prohibition,

1 Associate professor, Vienna University of Economics and Business (WU).
2 Professor of European Corporate Tax Law, University of Amsterdam, of counsel, Loyens & Loeff, Amsterdam.

between the Member States, of import and export duties, of any charges having an effect equivalent to a customs duty (Article 30 TFEU), and of all quantitative restrictions on imports and all measures having equivalent effect (Article 34 TFEU). Obviously, it also implies a common customs tariff at the *outside* borders of the Union (Article 31). That common customs tariff came into force on 1 July 1968.

Furthermore, since taxation affects intra-Union cross-border trade, investment, service provision and employment, it is clearly an internal market issue. Hence, both indirect taxation – other than customs duties – and direct taxation are caught under the competence heading 'internal market' in Article 4(2)(a) TFEU, which is a shared competence with preemption: as soon as and to the extent in which the Union has exercised its competence to regulate a tax matter by way of a regulation or a directive, the Member States have, to that extent, lost their individual competences to regulate that tax matter.

The Union, incited by Article 113 TFEU (see Section 2.3.2.) to harmonize indirect taxes, has done so extensively in respect of customs duties, excise duties and turnover tax. It has used its competence as regards direct taxation to a much lesser extent, but the Anti-Tax-Avoidance Directive (see Chapter 19), the implementation of the global minimum tax in the EU (the EU Pillar Two Directive; see Chapter 22) and the reinvigoration of the idea of a common EU corporate tax system (Business in Europe: Framework for Income Taxation, BEFIT)[3] may bring the degree of – at least – corporate income tax harmonization closer to that of indirect taxation. Nevertheless, the Court of the EU (Court or CJEU) persistently emphasizes in its case law that direct taxation falls 'within the competence of the Member States,' to which it invariably adds: but they 'must none the less exercise that competence consistently with Union law,' meaning that they should respect the internal market free movement rights of taxpayers, and observe the State aid prohibition.[4]

Where the principle of conferral delimits the competences of the Union vis-à-vis Member States' sovereignty ("competences not conferred upon the Union in the Treaties remain with the Member States"), the principles of subsidiarity and of proportionality, also laid down in Article 5 TEU, regulate the *exercise* of the competences which have been conferred upon the Union. According to the principle of subsidiarity (Article 5(3) TEU):

> "...the Union shall act only if and in so far as the objectives of the proposed action cannot be sufficiently achieved by the Member States, either at central level or at regional and local level, but can rather, by reason of the scale or effects of the proposed action, be better achieved at Union level."

This unclear language and the lack of substantive interpretation by the Court makes constitutional subsidiarity a rather elusive concept.[5] The principle governs the scope of

3 Communication from the Commission to the European Parliament and the Council, Business Taxation for the 21st Century COM (2021) 251 final, Brussels 18 May 2021.

4 In the context of the free movement provisions, see for example, Case C-446/03, *Marks & Spencer*, EU:C:2005:763, point 29; Case C-196/04, *Cadbury Schweppes*, EU:C:2006:544, point 40; Case C-279/93, *Schumacker*, EU:C:1995:31, point 21. In the context of the State aid prohibition, see for example: Case C-501/00, *Spain v Commission*, EU:C:2004:438, point 123. In the context of various general EU rules and principles, see Case C-417/10, *3M Italia*, EU:C:2012:184, point 25.

5 Out of the abundant literature for a critical view, see for example Gareth Davies, Subsidiarity: The wrong idea, in the wrong place, at the wrong time, 43 *Common Market Law Review* 1 (2006), pp. 63-84.

Union action only in areas where the Union has a shared competence with the Member States or a complementary competence to Member States' actions. As a constitutional principle, subsidiarity is meant to be a safeguard of the present division of powers in the Union, whether one wishes to call that federalism or not.[6] It is aimed at containment of the exercise of Union competence – in particular legislation[7] – by allowing the Union to act/ legislate only when the objectives concerned (i) cannot be realized by the Member States on their own (absolute test) and (ii) could better be realized at Union level (relative test). The principle of proportionality (Article 5(4) TEU) sets forth that Union action should not go beyond what is necessary to achieve the objectives of the Treaties. When the Commission proposes Union legislation, it has to give reasons for considering the proposed Union act in line with the principles of subsidiarity and proportionality.[8] The Court has jurisdiction to review the compatibility of Union legislative acts with these principles and to 'annul' Union acts which are in breach of them (Article 263 TFEU) or to declare them 'invalid' (Article 267 TFEU). Despite these checks, the principles of subsidiarity and proportionality are not very effective in halting the 'competence creep', i.e. the slow but steady expansion of the Union's competence. In practice, it is often enough that a measure has transnational aspects or is aimed at the harmonization of national laws in order to consider its objective unattainable by the Member States themselves, making Union action in line with the principle of subsidiarity. The Court is reluctant to exercise effective judicial review in this respect, as it would mean substituting its own judgement for that of the Union legislature as to the question of whether Union action is necessary in a certain field with regard to a certain issue. As a result, the Court has until now never annulled any Union act for non-compliance with the principle of subsidiarity.[9]

To reinforce the principle of subsidiarity as a constitutional limit on Union action and at the same time involve national parliaments in the Union's legislative process – thus remedying the Union's lamented democratic deficit – the Treaty of Lisbon granted monitoring rights to national parliaments in respect of compliance of Union legislative proposals with the principle of subsidiarity. The monitoring procedure is set out in a Protocol attached to the treaties[10] and has become known as the 'yellow card procedure'. Any national parliament or, in a bicameral system, any chamber of a national parliament may submit a 'reasoned opinion' to the Union institutions within eight weeks from notification of a draft legislative act if it considers that draft a breach of the principle of

6 Schütze discusses two lines of interpretation of subsidiarity, i.e. a political and a judicial safeguard of federalism, see R. Schütze, European Union Law (Cambridge University Press 2015), pp. 252-259.

7 Although Article 5(3) TEU refers generally to 'acts of the Union', Protocol (No 2) to the TEU and TFEU on the application of the principles of subsidiarity and proportionality only applies to 'draft legislative acts'.

8 This follows from Article 296 TFEU which lays down a duty to give reasons for legislative acts. Article 5 of Protocol (No 2) to the TEU and TFEU on the application of the principles of subsidiarity and proportionality specifies this obligation.

9 See for example, Case C-84/94 *United Kingdom v Council (Working Time Directive)*, EU:C:1996:431; Case C-377/98 *Netherlands v European Parliament and Council (Biotechnology Directive)*, EU:C:2001:523; Case C-491/01 *British American Tobacco*, EU:C:2002:741; Joined Cases C-154/04 and C-155/04 *Alliance for Natural Health*, EU:C:2005:449; Case C-58/08 *Vodafone*, EU:C:2010:321.

10 Protocol (No 2) on the application of the principles of subsidiarity and proportionality.

subsidiarity. Each national parliament is allocated two votes[11] (therefore, there are 54 votes). For a 'yellow card' at least one third of all 54 votes must be cast against the draft. The consequence of a 'yellow card' is that the Commission must review its legislative proposal. The Commission may maintain, amend or withdraw the draft. National parliaments cannot, therefore, compel the Commission to abandon its plans; they cannot block the adoption of the Union act by the Council and the European Parliament. The mechanism is called 'yellow card procedure' because national parliaments may shout 'foul' at the Union institutions, but they cannot send the impugned proposal 'off the field'; they cannot draw a 'red card'. Some national parliaments issued yellow cards for the Commission's proposals for a Common Consolidated Tax Base (CCCTB), in respect of both the 2011 proposal[12] and the 2016 proposal,[13] but the requisite one third of all votes was not reached; to our knowledge, it has never been reached yet.

2.2 Sources of EU Tax Law

2.2.1 Primary and Secondary EU Law

The sources of European law can be divided into primary and secondary sources.[14] Primary EU law originates directly from the Member States. These primary sources are the founding treaties, presently the Treaty on the Functioning of the European Union (TFEU)[15] and the Treaty on European Union (TEU) (Treaty of Maastricht).[16] In addition, primary Union law includes the treaties amending the founding treaties, such as the treaties of Amsterdam,[17] Nice[18] and Lisbon,[19] and the accession treaties with new Member States.

11 In Member States that have a bicameral parliamentary system the two votes are shared between the two houses of the parliament each house being entitled to one vote.

12 See R. Szudoczky, Is the CCCTB Proposal in line with the Principle of Subsidiarity?: Negative Opinions Submitted by National Parliaments in the 'Yellow Card Procedure', in: CCCTB: Selected Issues, EUCOTAX Series (D. Weber ed., Kluwer Law International 2012), pp. 93 – 126.

13 See www.ipex.eu.

14 See A. Schrauwen, Sources of EU law for integration in taxation, in: Traditional and alternative routes to European Tax Integration, editor Dennis Weber, GREIT, IBFD 2010, p. 15 and E.C.C.M. Kemmeren, Sources of EU law for European tax integration: well-know and alternative legal instruments, in: Traditional and alternative routes to European Tax Integration, editor Dennis Weber, GREIT, IBFD 2010, p. 29.

15 This treaty was originally called Treaty establishing the European Economic Community (1957) (EEC Treaty or Treaty of Rome). It was renamed by the Maastricht Treaty to the Treaty establishing the European Community (EC Treaty). Finally, the Lisbon Treaty renamed it to its current name. For the latest consolidated version see Consolidated versions of the Treaty on European Union and the Treaty on the Functioning of the European Union OJ C 202 of 7.6.2016, p. 1-388.

16 Treaty on European Union (1992), OJ C 191 of 29.07.1992, p. 1-112. For the latest consolidated version see Consolidated versions of the Treaty on European Union and the Treaty on the Functioning of the European Union OJ C 202 of 7.6.2016, p. 1-388.

17 Treaty of Amsterdam amending the Treaty on European Union, the Treaties establishing the European Communities and certain related acts (1997), OJ C 340 of 10.11.1997, p. 1-184.

18 Treaty of Nice amending the Treaty on European Union, the Treaties establishing the European Communities and certain related acts (2001), OJ C 80 of 10.3.2001, p. 1–87.

19 Treaty of Lisbon amending the Treaty on European Union and the Treaty Establishing the European Community (2007), OJ C 306 of 13.12.2007, p. 1-17.

The Charter of Fundamental Rights of the European Union,[20] albeit not incorporated in the text of the founding treaties, has the same legal value as the founding treaties.[21] Therefore, it is primary Union law. So are the general principles of EU law developed by the Court and those mentioned in Article 6(3) TEU, and so are international agreements concluded by the EU.

In contrast to primary law, acts adopted by the EU institutions are the secondary sources of Union law. Secondary Union law is derived from and based on primary Union law in the sense that secondary law can only come into existence if a legal basis in the founding treaties authorizes the Union legislature to adopt such law. Article 288 TFEU provides that "[t]o exercise the Union's competences, the institutions shall adopt regulations, directives, decisions, recommendations and opinions."[22] The adoption, at EU level, of these acts, is the most important part of the process called 'positive integration', i.e. integration by agreeing on common rules and policies and coordination of national policies. Integration on the basis of prohibitions (especially the non-discrimination principle and the State aid prohibition; see 2.2.2.1) is called 'negative integration'.

The often-used term *acquis communautaire* means 'what has been achieved by the Union' at a certain moment, i.e. the entire body of EU law, both written and unwritten, in force at that time.

2.2.2 Primary law

2.2.2.1 Treaty Provisions Relevant for Direct Taxation

The founding treaties contain very few provisions which are relevant for direct tax law. The most important of those are the fundamental treaty freedoms incorporated in the TFEU, namely, (i) the right of Union citizens to move and reside freely within the EU (Article 21(1)); (ii) the free movement of goods, comprising a prohibition of customs duties and charges having equivalent effect (Article 30) and a prohibition of quantitative restrictions and measures having equivalent effect on imports (Article 34) and exports (Article 35); (iii) the free movement of persons, comprising the free movement of workers (Article 45) and the freedom of establishment (Article 49); (iv) the freedom to provide services (Article 56) and (v) the free movement of capital and payments (Article 63). The Court has been called upon in hundreds of cases to assess whether national direct tax measures restricted the free movement of persons, capital or services and if they did, whether they could be justified for mandatory public interest reasons. The declaration of unharmonized national law as incompatible with the EU free movement rights of Union citizens and companies is a part of a phenomenon called negative integration. The Court's 'prohibition' of national tax measures incompatible with the Treaty freedoms has had a far-reaching influence on the design of the direct tax systems of the Member States (see Chapters 3-15).

---

20 Charter of Fundamental Rights of the European Union (2007), OJ C 303 of 14.12.2007. For the latest consolidated version see Charter of Fundamental Rights of the European Union OJ C 202 of 7.6.2016, p. 391-407.

21 Article 6(1) first subparagraph TEU.

22 This list is not complete, as there are many other forms of acts that the EU institutions and bodies use to carry out their tasks and competences.

Other EU norms with increasing importance for direct tax law stem from EU competition law namely, the State aid prohibition (Articles 107-108 TFEU). As State aid law is in principle a prohibition (to distort competition), it is also part of the mechanism of 'negative integration' of national laws. State aids are in principle prohibited, unless they serve certain enumerated purposes of (Union) public interest (Article 107 TFEU). This is also true for tax measures favouring certain undertakings or the production of certain goods (selectivity). Such non-horizontal but selectively benefiting (tax) measures are in principle prohibited because they tilt the 'level playing field' of competition. Examples are tax breaks for shipping companies or airlines, interest-free extension of payment of taxes for companies in cash-flow problems, lower tax rates for certain activities or companies in certain regions, beneficial advance tax rulings for certain multinationals, etc. The reach of the State aid rules is expanding in the area of tax due to the evolving interpretation of the notion of 'selectivity' of State financed advantages by the Commission and the Union Courts. As a result, not only tax advantages benefitting a certain sector, region or type of activity are within the scope of State aid control, but also transfer pricing agreements at variance with the arm's length principle, certain anti-abuse measures (or the lack of them) and advantages caused by mismatches between different tax systems (see Chapter 15).

2.2.2.2 Treaty Provisions Relevant for Indirect Taxation

The treaty freedoms (with the exception of Article 30 TFEU on the prohibition of customs duties and charges having equivalent effect) and the rules on the prohibition of State aid are general internal market rules which apply to all policy areas including taxation, but the TFEU also contains provisions which refer expressly and specifically to taxation, in its chapter on 'Tax provisions' (Title VII, Chapter 2, Articles 110-113 TFEU). All of these address only indirect taxation, i.e. taxes on transactions. Article 110 TFEU prohibits discriminatory and protective taxes on products. To the extent there are no (exhaustive) Union measures on the matter (as far as the Recast VAT Directive and the General Arrangements Excise Directive allow), Member States remain free to organize their product tax systems in the way they see fit, and to impose the rates they consider appropriate. However, they may not tax products of other Member States less favourably. Article 110 only allows product taxation as part of a general internal consumption tax which is levied indiscriminately on both domestic and foreign products, such as turnover taxes (the VAT), excise duties and taxes on the registration of new motor cars. Article 110 has direct effect: it can be relied on by individuals and undertakings before their national courts, to invalidate national tax law incompatible with it. In addition to the prohibition of discriminatory and protective taxes, the chapter on 'Tax provisions' includes the legal basis for the harmonisation of indirect taxes (Article 113 TFEU).

2.2.2.3 *Remaining Treaty Provisions Relevant for Taxation*

For the rest, the TFEU contains only three, rather subordinate, references to taxation, in Article 65(1) (free movement of capital), Article 179(2) (Research & Development and Space), and Article 191(2) *juncto* Article 194(3) (Environment and Energy, respectively).[23]

Article 65(1) allows an exception to the free movement of capital (Article 63 TFEU) as it retains for the Member States the rights:

> 'to apply the relevant provisions of their tax law which distinguish between taxpayers who are not in the same situation with regard to their place of residence or with regard to the place where their capital is invested'

and:

> 'to take all requisite measures to prevent infringements of national law and regulations, in particular in the field of taxation (... etc.)'.

Although these provisions seem to legitimize, to a certain extent, differential tax treatment of resident and nonresident taxpayers, and of domestic and foreign-source investment income, Article 65(3) specifies that such differential treatment:

> 'shall not constitute a means of arbitrary discrimination or a disguised restriction on the freedom of movement of capital and payments as defined in Article 63'.

The case law of the Court shows, however, that it treats Article 65(1)(a) and (3) as a mere codification of its rule of reason (see Chapter 3) in the field of capital movement.[24] Article 65(1)(a) therefore does not add to the possibilities which the Member States already have, under the Court's rule of reason, to distinguish between domestic and foreign taxpayers and between domestic and foreign investment. Hence, Article 65 does not bestow a special status on the free movement of capital as compared to the other treaty freedoms (see Chapter 3.2.6).

Article 179(2) is part of the Title on Research and Technological Development and Space, and provides, *inter alia*, that the Union shall support the efforts of undertakings to cooperate with each other, in particular through measures such as the removal of legal and fiscal barriers to such cooperation, to serve the Union's aim of strengthening the scientific and technological basis of European industry. This statement does not add anything which specifically relates to tax matters, and is in any case too vague to have direct effect in any (tax) litigation. Slightly more concrete is Article 191(2), in combination with Article 192(2) (a) (both in the Title on Environment), and with Article 194(3) (in the Title on Energy), which provides that the Union's environmental policy shall be based, *inter alia*, on the principle that the polluter should pay, and that the Council shall take fiscal action

---

23 For completeness sake, Article 173(3) (Industry) may also be mentioned, but it only states that the title on Industry 'shall not provide a basis for the introduction by the Union of any measure which (...) contains tax provisions (...).'

24 Case C-35/98, *Verkooijen*, EU:C:2000:294, point 43; Case C-319/02, *Manninen*, EU:C:2004:484, point 29.

in that field only by unanimous acts. These provisions do not change the rule that all tax matters, even the smallest,[25] must be decided by unanimity (see Articles 113, 114(2), 115, 192(2)(a), and 194(3) TFEU) – on the contrary; they reiterate that rule – but they provide a specific legal basis for EU-driven environmental ('green') and energy taxation. Nevertheless, these provisions may also be used or misused to avoid the unanimity requirement for fiscal measures (see sec. 2.3.1. below), as demonstrated by certain recent legislative acts that lay down provisions of a fiscal nature while having been adopted based on the legal basis provisions envisaged for acts of a general, i.e. non-fiscal, nature in the area of environmental or energy policy. Specifically, the Regulation establishing a carbon border adjustment mechanism (CBAM)[26] was adopted based on Article 192(1) TFEU which provides for the ordinary legislative procedure for deciding on action to be taken to achieve the environmental objectives laid down in Article 191 TFEU. Article 192(2)(a) TFEU explicitly excludes fiscal measures from the scope of this provision.[27] While the CBAM may not be a tax in the strict sense of the term, it would be rather difficult to maintain that it lacks fiscal nature altogether. Similarly, the regulation that introduced a solidarity contribution with regard to high energy prices, which arguably showed all the characteristics of a tax, has been proposed by the Commission and eventually adopted based on Article 122(1) TFEU.[28] The latter provision allows the introduction of measures through the ordinary legislative procedure in case of severe difficulties in the supply of products, in particular, in the energy sector while reserving that it is "*without prejudice to any other procedures provided in the Treaties*". As for fiscal measures the Treaties consistently prescribe another procedure, i.e. the special legislative procedure with unanimity, the basis of the regulation on the solidarity contribution appears to be rather wobbly.[29]

Differently from these more recent legislative acts, the Directive on energy taxation[30] does not refer to Articles 191, 192 or 194 or any other legal basis within a specific policy field, but only to Article 113 (harmonization of indirect taxes in general).

2.2.2.4 *General Principles of EU law*

General principles of EU law are unwritten principles recognized by the Court as fundamental to the Union legal order and as common to the constitutional and legal traditions of

25 See Article 223(2)(last sentence) TFEU.
26 Regulation (EU) 2023/956 of the European Parliament and of the Council of 10 May 2023 establishing a carbon border adjustment mechanism, OJ L 130 of 16.5.2023, p. 52–104.
27 "By way of derogation from the decision-making procedure provided for in paragraph 1 and without prejudice to Article 114, the Council acting unanimously in accordance with a special legislative procedure and after consulting the European Parliament, the Economic and Social Committee and the Committee of the Regions, shall adopt: (a) provisions primarily of a fiscal nature [...]."
28 Council Regulation (EU) 2022/1854 of 6 October 2022 on an emergency intervention to address high energy prices, OJ L 261I of 7.10.2022, p. 1–21.
29 An action for annulment has been brough against the Regulation in which the applicants claim, *inter alia*, that it was adopted on an incorrect legal basis, see Case T-775/22 TJ and Others v Council. For a more detailed discussion on these issues, see S. Hemels, Tax Autonomy From a Member State Perspective: Are we Faced with a Democratic Deficit?, in R. Luja (ed.), National Tax Autonomy and the European Union, IBFD 2024, sec. 1.5.1.
30 Council Directive 2003/96/EC of 27 October 2003 restructuring the Community framework for the taxation of energy products and electricity, OJ L 283 of 31.10.2003, p. 51-70.

the Member States. Not only do they have the status of primary law but, like the founding treaties, they also have constitutional status.[31] This means that secondary Union law (and, within certain jurisdictional limits, also national law[32]) is subject to judicial review for compatibility with the general principles of EU law. In addition to serving as a standard for legality review of Union (and national) legislation, a further important function of the general principles is that they aid the interpretation of Union law, as well as national law falling within the scope of Union law. Finally, they enable the Court to fill normative gaps in the treaties or in Union legislation thereby ensuring the autonomy and coherence of the Union legal system.[33]

An important category of general principles of EU law are fundamental rights. The Court acknowledged as early as the beginning of the 1970's that "respect for fundamental rights forms an integral part of the general principles of law protected by the Court of Justice".[34] These fundamental rights were drawn from the constitutional tradition common to the Member States and from international agreements on which the Member States have collaborated or to which they are signatories.[35] In 2000, they were codified in the EC Charter of Fundamental Rights which had a murky legal status for some time, but gained the same legally binding force as the founding Treaties in December 2009 due to the Lisbon amendments (see Chapter 4).

Another category of general principles, which are sometimes referred to as 'systemic principles',[36] the Court has based on the objectives of Union law. They govern the relationship between Union law and national law. These are notably the principles of primacy and direct effect of Union law, making sure Union law is substantively effective by trumping national law and bilateral treaty law between Member States (see Chapter 3.5.1.) and the combination of the principle of procedural autonomy of the Member States (EU law does not provide itself for procedural law to enforce it within the national legal orders, which implies that in principle, national procedural law is applicable) and the procedural EU principles of equivalence (procedural law available for enforcement of EU law may not be less favourable than procedural law available for enforcement of purely domestic law) and of effectiveness (even if the procedural possibilities are comparable, they may not be such as to make effectuation of substantive EU law excessively difficult or virtually impossible)[37] (see Chapter 3.5.2.1.).

31 Case C-101/08 *Audiolux*, EU:C:2009:626, point 63; Case C-174/08 *NCC Construction*, EU:C:2009:669, points 42, 45.

32 National law can be tested for its compliance with the general principles of EU law only when the situation at hand falls within the scope of Union law, which is the case when the Member States enact national law in order to *implement Union law* (see for example, Case 5/88 *Wachauf*, EU:C:1989:321; Joined Cases 201/85 and 202/85 *Klensch and others*, EU:C:1986:439; Case C-292/97 *Karlsson*, EU:C:2000:202; Case C-313/99 *Mulligan*, EU:C:2002:386) or where they *derogate from Union law* (see for example, C-260/89 *ERT*, EU:C:1991:254, point 43; Case C-368/95 *Familiapress Zeitungsverlags*, EU:C:1997:325; Case C-60/00 *Carpenter*, EU:C:2002:434).

33 K. Lenaerts and J. A. Gutiérrez-Fons, *The Role of General Principles of EU Law*, in: A Constitutional Order of States? Essays in EU Law in Honour of Alan Dashwood (A. Arnull, C. Barnard, M.Dougan and E. Spaventa eds., Hart Publishing 2011), pp. 179-197, at p. 179.

34 Case 11/70 *Internationale Handelsgesellschaft*, EU:C:1970:114, point 4.

35 Case 4/73 *Nold*, EU:C:1974:51, point 13; Case 44/79 *Hauer*, EU:C:1979:290, point 15.

36 T. Tridimas, The General Principles of EU Law, Second Edition, Oxford University Press 2006, p. 2.

37 See for example, Case C-291/03 *MyTravel*, EU:C:2005:591, point 17; Case C-35/05 *Reemtsma*, EU:C:2007:167, point 37.

Some general principles have been laid down in the founding treaties. As observed above, this is the case with the principles of subsidiarity and proportionality (see Section 2.1). The same is true, since 2009, for the fundamental rights codified in the EU Charter (see Chapter 4).

For taxation several (still) unwritten principles of EU law are important. These are the principle of proportionality,[38] the principle of prohibition of abuse,[39] the principles of legal certainty and legitimate expectations,[40] the principle of legality in taxation,[41] the (procedural) principles of equivalence and effectiveness referred to above, the general principle of equality and a specific aspect of that principle in the field of VAT[42] namely, the principle of fiscal neutrality.[43]

As regards their legal effects, the general principles of EU law are capable of having direct effect provided that they fulfil the condition of being clear, precise and unconditional enough in a specific case to be applied by a Court to decide the case put before it.[44]

2.2.3 Secondary Law

2.2.3.1 Characteristics of Regulations, Directives and Decisions

As observed, the Union institutions can adopt, on the basis of Article 288 TFEU, regulations, directives, decisions, recommendations and opinions. Pursuant to Article 288 TFEU, a regulation is binding in its entirety and directly applicable in all Member States.[45] Member States, therefore, do not need to transpose regulations into national law. On the contrary, they should directly apply it and should not interfere with its direct effect in the national legal order. Regulation are intended and perfectly suited to impose prohibitions or to introduce a uniform rule within the EU. The Union Customs Code (see Chapter 25 in the other Volume of this book), for example, takes the form of a regulation.[46]

---

38 The usually decisive part of the rule of reason which the Court applies to test the compatibility of national tax measures with the Treaty freedoms (see Section 3) is a proportionality assessment. In this regard, the principle of proportionality is the most frequently applied general principle in the area of taxation. The principle of proportionality is also sometimes applied as a *sui generis* standard to review the legality of secondary Union law or of national law (see for example, Case C-409/04 *Teleos*, EU:C:2007:548, point 45; Case C-25/07 *Sosnowska*, EU:C:2008:395, point 23).

39 Case C-255/02 *Halifax*, EU:C:2006:121, point 70 et seq., Case C-425/06 *Part Service*, EU:C:2008:108, point 54-55; Case C-321/05 *Kofoed*, EU:C:2007:408, point 38; Joined Cases C-115/16, C-118/16, C-119/16 and C-299/16 *N Luxembourg et al.*, EU:C:2019:134, points 96, 101; Joined Cases C-116/16 and C-117/16, *T Danmark*, EU:C:2019:135, point 70 et seq.

40 See for example, Case C-201/08 *Plantanol*, EU:C:2009:539, point 43.

41 Joined Cases C-885/19 P and C-898/19 P *Fiat Chrysler Finance Europe*, EU:C:2022:859, point 97.

42 For a comprehensive analysis, see J. Englisch, VAT and General Principles of EU Law, in: Traditional and Alternative Routes to European Tax Integration (D. Weber ed., IBFD 2010), pp. 231-266.

43 See for example, Case C-309/06 *Marks & Spencer*, EU:C:2008:211, points 47 and 49; Case C-460/07 *Puffer*, EU:C:2009:254, point 53.

44 M. Dougan, In Defence of Mangold?, in: A Constitutional Order of States? Essays in EU Law in Honour of Alan Dashwood (A. Arnull, C. Barnard, M. Dougan and E. Spaventa eds., Hart Publishing 2011), pp. 219-244, at p. 227.

45 See for example, Joined cases C-4/10 and C-27/10 *Bureau national interprofessionnel du Cognac*, EU:C:2011:484, point 40.

46 Regulation (EU) No 952/2013 of the European Parliament and of the Council of 9 October 2013 laying down the Union Customs Code, OJ L 269 of 10.10.2013.

By contrast, a directive is only binding as to the result to be achieved, but leaves to the national legislator the choice of form and methods to achieve that result. A directive, therefore, must be transposed into national law. Directives are often used to introduce legislation that needs elaboration and detail in the national legal orders; they are in particular an effective instrument when a part of the laws of the Member States has to be harmonised. The Member States can then, to the extent necessary, adjust their legislation on the relevant points. In tax law, mostly directives are used. Examples are the many VAT directives (see Chapter 26), the Excise directives (see Chapter 27) and the directives in the area of corporate taxation (see Chapters16-23) and of exchange of tax information (see Chapter 25).

The EU institutions can also take 'decisions'. A decision is in principle addressed to specific parties and is binding in its entirety to whom it is addressed (Article 288 TFEU). An example is the decision by which the European Commission prohibits a national tax scheme or tax ruling as an illegal State aid measure. The Commission then determines in that decision that the Member State involved must withdraw or amend this measure within a period determined by the Commission[47] and that it should recover any aid possibly already extended. Another example is the decision of the Council authorizing a Member State to take special measures in deviation from, for example, the VAT directives.[48]

2.2.3.2 Legislative, Delegated and Implementing acts

Acts of the Union institutions may also be categorised in another manner. As most constitutional orders, the Union's legal order recognizes not only law-making by the legislature but also executive law-making. Accordingly, first, a distinction has to be drawn between (i) 'legislative acts' adopted by the Union's legislature (i.e. in most cases, the European Parliament and the Council acting jointly, see Section 2.3.1. below) through formalized legislative procedures[49] and (ii) executive acts adopted by the executive branch (i.e. in most cases, the Commission) exercising powers delegated to it by the Union legislator. Since the Treaty of Lisbon, executive acts are further divided into two categories namely, 'delegated acts' and 'implementing acts'. Delegated acts are the result of a delegation of *legislative* power, i.e. the power to *supplement* or *amend* legislative acts (on non-essential issues), from the legislature to the executive. The TFEU provides that:

47 See for example, Commission Decision of 11 July 2001 concerning the aid scheme implemented by Spain in favour of certain enterprises recently incorporated in Vizcaya (Spain) 2002/806/EC, OJ L 279 of 17.10.2017, p. 35-49; Commission Decision of 17 February 2003 concerning an aid scheme implemented by the Netherlands in favour of international financing activities 2003/515/ EC (notified under document number C(2003) 568), OJ L 180 of 18.7.2003, p. 52-66; Commission Decision (EU) 2017/1283 of 30 August 2016 on State aid SA.38373 (2014/C) (ex 2014/NN) (ex 2014/ CP) implemented by Ireland to Apple (notified under document C(2017) 5605), OJ L 187 of 19.7.2017, p. 1-110.

48 See for example, Council Implementing Decision (EU) 2018/1904 of 4 December 2018 authorising the Netherlands to introduce a special measure derogating from Article 285 of Directive 2006/112/ EC on the common system of value added tax, OJ L 310 of 4.12.2018.

49 As defined by the TFEU, legislative acts are legal acts adopted by legislative procedure (Article 289(3)).

> A legislative act may delegate to the Commission the power to adopt non-legislative acts of general application to supplement or amend certain non-essential elements of the legislative act (Article 290 TFEU).

Thus, a delegated act can modify the basic (legislative) act but only with regard to non-essential elements.

Implementing acts, by contrast, are a result of a delegation of *executive* power, i.e. the power to *implement* legislative acts. Where uniform conditions for implementing legally binding Union acts are needed, those acts can confer implementing powers on the Commission (or in specific cases on the Council) (Article 291 TFEU). Especially in the field of (automatic) exchange of tax information, there are tax relevant implementing Commission acts.

The main constitutional difference between delegated and implementing acts lies in the control mechanism over the Commission's exercise of the delegated power. In the case of delegated acts, the European Parliament and the Council have the right to control the Commission's exercise of delegated powers pursuant to Article 290 TFEU. By contrast, the control of implementing acts is entrusted to the Member States instead of the Union legislature (Article 291(3) TFEU). This control mechanism is called 'comitology' because it takes place in committees of civil servants representing their Member States which report via the so-called CoRePer (*comité des représentants permanents*, a diplomatic body) to the Council. Comitology thus stands for a set of procedures through which the Commission adopts implementing measures working together with a committee of representatives of national governments whose role is to oversee the adoption of these measures.[50]

Legislative, delegated and implementing acts can all take the form of a regulation, a directive or a decision. The TFEU stipulates that the adjectives 'delegated' or 'implementing' must be added to the title of the acts concerned. Hence, when an act is simply called 'regulation' 'directive' or 'decision' without any addition, it is always a legislative act.

2.2.4 International Agreements Concluded by the Union

The EU as a quasi-federal union of states has not only internal but also external competences in the exercise of which the Union can conclude international agreements as an international actor with legal personality.[51] International agreements concluded by the Union are located in the hierarchy of sources of EU law between primary law and secondary law, meaning that they are inferior to primary law but superior to secondary law.

In line with the principle of conferral, the Union is endowed with specific external powers by the TFEU (Part V, Titles II-IV),[52] each of which involve treaty-making powers

50 The Comitology Regulation currently in force (i.e. Regulation (EU) No 182/2011 of the European Parliament and of the Council of 16 February 2011 laying down the rules and general principles concerning mechanisms for control by Member States of the Commission's exercise of implementing powers, (OJ L55, 28.02.2011)) establishes two procedures for controlling the Commission's exercise of implementing powers namely, the advisory and the examination procedures. The examination procedure, which applies to the area of taxation, gives a more influential role to the committee of the Member States' representatives.

51 Article 47 TEU.

52 At the same time, the Common Foreign and Security Policy (CFSP) represents a general competence for the Union in foreign affairs which is set out in the TEU (Title V).

as well. Apart from these specific treaty-making powers, the TFEU also grants the Union a residual competence to conclude international agreements across the board through all Union policies laid down in the TFEU. In particular, Article 216 provides:

> "The Union may conclude an agreement with one or more third countries or international organisations where the Treaties so provide or where the conclusion of an agreement is necessary in order to achieve, within the framework of the Union's policies, one of the objectives referred to in the Treaties, or is provided for in a legally binding Union act or is likely to affect common rules or alter their scope."

To the extent this provision refers to the situation "where the conclusion of an agreement is necessary in order to achieve, within the framework of the Union's policies, one of the objectives referred to in the Treaties," it is a codification of the already existing, Court-made doctrine of implied treaty-making powers.[53]

The agreements concluded by the Union are binding on the Union institutions and on the Member States (Article 216(2)). The treaty-making procedure – in which the central role is for the Council – is set out under Article 218 TFEU.

Union competence to conclude international agreements is exclusive in three situations: (i) where the conclusion of an agreement is provided for in a legislative act of the Union; (ii) where such external competence is necessary to enable the Union to exercise its internal competence; or (iii) where their conclusion may affect common rules or alter the scope of EU rules (Article 3(2)). In areas of shared competence, international agreements are customarily concluded in the form of mixed agreements to which both the Union and the Member States are contracting parties. Although taxation is an internal market matter which is a shared competence area (see Section 2.1.), we are strangely enough not aware of any such mixed agreements. Tax treaties with third States are concluded solely by the Member States separately and autonomously, within their exclusive competence. By contrast, certain clearly tax related international agreements with third countries are concluded exclusively by the Union, such as the Savings Taxation Agreement with Switzerland[54] which ensured that Switzerland applied measures equivalent to those in the Savings Directive[55] and its Amending Protocol[56] which provides for automatic exchange of financial account information between Switzerland and the EU in order to conform

53 See Case 22/70 *Commission v Council (ERTA)*, EU:C:1971:32. See on this, R. Schütze, European Union Law (Cambridge University Press 2015), pp. 270-273.

54 2004/911/EC: Council Decision of 2 June 2004 on the signing and conclusion of the Agreement between the European Community and the Swiss Confederation providing for measures equivalent to those laid down in Council Directive 2003/48/EC on taxation of savings income in the form of interest payments and the accompanying Memorandum of Understanding, OJ L 385 of 29.12.2004, p. 28–29.

55 Council Directive 2003/48/EC of 3 June 2003 on taxation of savings income in the form of interest payments, OJ L 157 of 26.6.2003, p. 38-48, repealed on 10 November 2015.

56 Amending Protocol to the Agreement between the European Community and the Swiss Confederation providing for measures equivalent to those laid down in Council Directive 2003/48/EC on taxation of savings income in the form of interest payments, OJ L 333 of 19.12.2015, p. 12–49. Similar Agreements and Amending Protocols were concluded with Andorra, Lichtenstein, Monaco and San Marino.

to the standard of the intra-Union exchange of tax information under Council Directive 2011/16/ EU[57] (see Chapter 25).

2.2.5 *Soft Law*

2.2.5.1 *Recommendations, Opinions and Communications*

The EU institutions can also adopt recommendations or opinions. This is called 'soft law'.[58] This law, as opposed to 'hard law', is not legally binding.[59] Article 288 TFEU provides recommendations and opinions have no binding force. The *Grimaldi* case,[60] however, shows that recommendations may have some 'legal effect:' national judicial authorities are, according to the Court, 'bound to take recommendations into consideration in order to decide disputes submitted to them, in particular where they cast light on the interpretation of national measures adopted in order to implement them or where they are designed to supplement binding Community provisions'.

Under Article 398 of the VAT Directive, an advisory committee has been established for VAT (VAT Committee). In *Finanzamt T/S*[61], the Court ruled that while the guidelines of the VAT Committee do not have binding effect, they 'nevertheless constitute an aid to the interpretation' of the VAT directive.

Examples of recommendations to the Member States as regards taxation are those on the taking into consideration of tax reliefs for non-residents,[62] and the Commission recommendations on aggressive tax planning[63] and on tax treaty abuse.[64]

The Commission also regularly issues 'communications' addressed to the Council, the European Parliament and the European Economic and Social Committee, on all kinds of tax matters. In the past, the Commission used communications to unfold its views on the implications for national tax regimes of the case law of the Court and to encourage the Member States to remove restrictions to free movement in their tax legislation (or else) and

57 Council Directive 2011/16/EU of 15 February 2011 on administrative cooperation in the field of taxation and repealing Directive 77/799/EEC, OJ L 64 of 11.3.2011, p. 1–12.

58 See *D. Sarmiento*, The function of EU soft law, EU soft-law instrument, in: Traditional and alternative routes to European Tax Integration, editor Dennis Weber, GREIT, IBFD 2010, p. 53. See for the relationship between EU law and the OECD Model Treaty: *T. Dubut*, The Court of Justice and the OECD Model Tax Conventions or the Uncertainties of the Distinction between Hard Law, Soft Law, and No Law in the European Case Law, Intertax 2012/1, p. 2.

59 See on this: J.L.M. Gribnau, Improving the legitimacy of soft law in EU tax law, Intertax 2007/1, p. 30 and L. Senden, Soft law in European Community law, Hart Publishing, Oxford, 2004.

60 Case C-322/88, *Grimaldi*, ECLI:EU:C:1989:646, para. 18.

61 *Case C-184/23, Finanzamt T/S, H&I 2024/238 (comments by Stapperfend).*

62 See Commission Recommendation of 21 December 1993 on the taxation of certain items of income received by non-residents in a Member State other than that in which they are resident (94/79/EC), OJ L 39 of 10.2.1994, p. 22–28.

63 2012/772/EU: Commission Recommendation of 6 December 2012 on aggressive tax planning, *H&I 2013/1.3 (comments by Nouwen)*; see also: 2012/771/EU: Commission Recommendation of 6 December 2012 regarding measures intended to encourage third countries to apply minimum standards of good governance in tax matters, *H&I 2013/1.4 (comments by Nouwen).*

64 Commission Recommendation (EU) 2016/136 of 28 January 2016 on the implementation of measures against tax treaty abuse, OJ L25 of 2.2.2016, p. 67-68.

thus facilitate the coordination of the tax systems of the Member States.[65] The Commission has not issued such coordinative communications for a long while. Nowadays, it seems to 'communicate' to announce its tax policy priorities and the actions and legislative proposals on its tax agenda which may be expected in the short, medium and long-term.[66]

The Council and the European Parliament often adopt 'resolutions', which are not mentioned in the EU Treaties either. An example is the European Parliament's resolution on the necessary reform of the EU policy on harmful tax practices.[67]

To date, however, the influence of EU soft law on national tax law is limited. The Court refers to OECD soft law (the OECD Model Tax Convention and the Commentaries relating thereto) much more often in its reasoning than to EU soft law.[68] More importantly, recent EU Directives and EU Commission proposals for directives that implement global tax standards developed by the OECD tend to mandate the use of OECD interpretive materials in the interpretation and application of their rules.[69] Some of these references are dynamic in the sense that they mandate the use of subsequent OECD materials that do not exist at the time of the adoption of the EU Directive. This may raise questions as regards the implications of this practice on the legitimacy and legality of these pieces of EU legislation.[70]

As far as EU soft law instruments are concerned, they remain important in the area of fiscal State aid where the Commission regularly issues various 'guidelines', 'notices' and 'frameworks' to provide guidance on the conditions under which various types of aid are considered compatible with the internal market under Article 107(3) TFEU.

2.2.5.2 Codes of Conduct

A specific form of 'soft law' are codes of conduct. Although legally no more than a gentlemen's agreement, these codes may politically be *de facto* binding. In the area of taxation, three codes of conduct have been adopted by the Council. The best known is the Code of

---

65 See, for example, Communication from the Commission to the Council, the European Parliament and the European Economic and Social Committee: Co-ordinating Member States' direct tax systems in the Internal Market COM (2006) 823 final, Brussels 19 December 2006; Communication from the Commission to the Council, the European Parliament and the European Economic and Social Committee: Exit taxation and the need for co-ordination of Member States' tax policies COM (2006) 825 final, Brussels 19 December 2006.

66 See, for example, Communication from the Commission to the European Parliament and the Council, Business Taxation for the 21st Century COM (2021) 251 final, Brussels 18 May 2021.

67 European Parliament resolution of 7 October 2021 on reforming the EU policy on harmful tax practices (including the reform of the Code of Conduct Group), and the underlying Council Resolution on the Code of Conduct for business taxation (see chapter 23).

68 *F. Roccatagliata*, The European Commission's soft law approach and its possible impact on EC law interpretation, in: Legal Remedies in European Tax Law, editor P. Pistone, GREIT, IBFD 2009, p. 85.

69 Council Directive (EU) 2022/2523 of 14 December 2022 on ensuring a global minimum level of taxation for multinational enterprise groups and large-scale domestic groups in the Union, Preamble, Recital 24; Council Directive (EU) 2018/822 of 25 May 2018 amending Directive 2011/16/EU as regards mandatory automatic exchange of information in the field of taxation in relation to reportable cross-border arrangements, Preamble, Recital 13; Proposal for a Council Directive on transfer pricing, COM(2023) 529 final, Strasbourg, 12.9.2023, Preamble, Recital 15.

70 See, J. Englisch, Dynamic References to International Soft Law Agreements: Flexibility with Limits, EC Tax Review 2024/1, pp. 2-7.

Conduct for Business Taxation that targets harmful tax competition, discussed in Chapter 23.[71] In essence, it establishes a taxer's cartel. It has been successful in curbing the 'tax race to the bottom', i.e. in making Member States repeal harmful tax competitive measures ("rollback" commitment) and in making Member States more cautious in introducing measures which could cause harmful tax competition ("standstill" commitment).[72] Originally, the Code of Conduct covered only preferential tax regimes, that is, measures that lead to an effective level of taxation that is significantly lower than the general level of taxation in a given Member State. In 2022, the ECOFIN Council approved a revised Code of Conduct with an extended scope.[73] As a result of the broadening of the scope, the Code now encompasses 'tax features of a general application', which create opportunities for double non-taxation or can lead to the double or multiple use of tax benefits. The reform however did not affect the field of application of the Code of Conduct, which remained limited to business taxation. As personal income tax measures are increasingly being used by the Member States as means of tax competition,[74] this limitation severely affects the effectiveness of the Code of Conduct in constraining harmful tax competition in the Union and thus, prompts further revision of the Code. See for elaboration Chapter 23.

Two codes of conduct have further been adopted in the area of transfer pricing. The first is the code of conduct for an effective implementation of the EU Arbitration Convention[75] (see Chapter 21), which provides for uniform (soft law) interpretations of a number of provisions of that Convention.[76] The second is the code of conduct on transfer pricing documentation describing a standardised and coherent EU transfer pricing documentation (EU TPD).[77]

In general, codes of conduct are political commitments that do not *legally* affect the Member States' rights and obligations or the respective spheres of competence of the Member States and the Union resulting from the treaties,[78] but they may be very committal politically and therefore in fact.

71 Resolution of the Council and the representatives of the Governments of the Member States, meeting within the Council of 1 December 1997 on a code of conduct for business taxation. OJ C 2 of 6.1.1998, p. 2–6. When reference is made in practice to the 'code of conduct', this often refers to this code of conduct.

72 See further: *J.L.M. Gribnau*, The Code of Conduct for Business Taxation as soft law-instrument, *TFB* 2008/2, p. 19 and *H. Gribnau*, The code of conduct for business taxation: an evaluation EU soft-law instrument, in: Traditional and alternative routes to European Tax Integration, editor Dennis Weber, GREIT, IBFD 2010, p. 67.

73 Council conclusions on the reform of the Code of Conduct for Business Taxation, ECOFIN 1131, Brussels, 8 November 2022.

74 R. Szudoczky, C. Rodrígues Peña, Preferential Personal Income Tax Regimes in the European Union: A New Form of Permitted (Harmful) Tax Competition?, WTJ 2024/2, p. 245.

75 Convention 90/436/EEC on the elimination of double taxation in connection with the adjustment of transfers of profits between associated undertakings, OJ L 225 of 20.8.1990, p. 10-16.

76 Revised Code of Conduct for the effective implementation of the Convention on the elimination of double taxation in connection with the adjustment of profits of associated enterprises, OJ C 322 of 30.12.2009, p. 1–10.

77 Resolution of the Council and of the representatives of the governments of the Member States, meeting within the Council, of 27 June 2006 on a code of conduct on transfer pricing documentation for associated enterprises in the European Union (EU TPD), OJ C 176 of 28.7.2006, p. 1–7.

78 See also AG Léger in para. 57 of his Opinion in Case C-196/04, *Cadbury Schweppes*, EU:C:2006:278.

2.2.6 Relationship Between Primary and Secondary Law

In a substantive, functional sense, the Union's legal order is a constitutional order in which the founding treaties function as a constitution.[79] Secondary law which is enacted by the Union institutions derives its existence from the treaties and must accord to the treaties. Decades ago already, the Court emphasized that secondary Union law is subject to a constitutional review in the light of the provisions of the founding treaties:

> The European Economic Community is a Community based on the rule of law, inasmuch as neither its Member States nor its institutions can avoid a review of the question whether the measures adopted by them are in conformity with the basic constitutional charter, the Treaty.[80]

As observed above, apart from the founding treaties, also the general principles of EU law, including fundamental rights, have a constitutional status and as such secondary Union law must comply also with these principles. The CJEU has exclusive jurisdiction for such review and to annul or declare secondary law invalid whilst national courts lack such competence.[81] In fact, however, the CJEU is reluctant to exercise an effective legality review over Union legislation. This is evident from the very low number of cases in which secondary Union law or a provision thereof has been invalidated by the Court on the ground of infringement of higher ranking norms of a substantive nature (i.e. not on the basis of violation of a procedural requirement or conditions of the legislative process). The Court's reluctance to interfere with the result of the Union institution's legislative process may be explained by respect for the institutional balance in the Union or by the recognition of the difficulties inherent in the supranational legislative process where, specifically in tax matters, the unanimity requirement in those matters, leads to hard-fought political compromises and concessions.

In the *RPO* case[82], a case about VAT, the Court (Grand Chamber) made it clear that the EU legislator has a broad discretion:

> "(...), it is understood that, when the EU legislature adopts a *tax measure*, it is called upon to make political, economic and social choices, and to rank divergent interests or to undertake complex assessments.
>
> Consequently, it should, in that context, be accorded a *broad discretion*, so that judicial review of compliance with the conditions set out in the previous paragraph of this judgment [i.e. proportionality; author] must be limited to review as to *manifest error* (...)." (italics author)

---

79 See for example, K. Lenaerts, The Basic Constitutional Charter of a Community Based on the Rule of Law, in: The Past and Future of EU Law. The Classics of EU Law Revisited on the 50th Anniversary of the Rome Treaty (M.P. Maduro and L. Azoulai eds., Hart Publishing 2010), pp. 293-333, at 298.

80 Case 294/83 *Les Verts*, EU:C:1986:166, point 23.

81 See for example, Case 314/85 *Foto-Frost*, EU:C:1987:452, point 15; Case C-461/03 *Gaston Schul Douane-expediteur*, EU:C:2005:742, point 17.

82 Case C-390/15, *Rzecznik Praw Obywatelskich (RPO)*, EU:C:2017:174.

Thus, the Court, when it reviews whether a tax measure which introduces, *e.g.*, a difference in tax treatment between a cross-border case and a purely domestic case, does so to achieve a legally permitted objective in a proportional manner, limits itself to manifest errors assessment.

The Grand Chamber recently emphasized in *Poland v EU Parliament and Council*[83] that the EU legislature's broad discretion "implies limited judicial review of its exercise".

It is important that the Court in *Czech Republic v EU Parliament and Council*[84] points out that in this context:

> 'the criterion to be applied is *not* whether a measure adopted in such an area *was the only or the best possible measure*, since its legality can be affected only if the measure is manifestly inappropriate having regard to the objective which the competent institution is seeking to pursue' (italics authors)

Of importance is also that in *British American Tobaccco*[85] the Court with regard to the principle of proportionality decided that:

> 'the Community legislature did not overstep the bounds of its discretion when it considered that such a prohibition nevertheless constitutes a measure *likely* to make an *effective contribution to limiting the risk* of growth in the illegal trafficking of cigarettes and to preventing the consequent undermining of the internal market' (italics authors).

The Court applies a light test by requiring that it is sufficient if an EU measure will 'likely' make an 'effective contribution' to its aim. The Court has not yet applied such a light test in tax matters, but given that the Member States in principle have sovereignty in tax matters and transfer (part of) this sovereignty by means of EU measures, it is not to be expected that the Court in tax matters will introduce a much stricter test.

That being said, in *Belgian Association of Tax Lawyers*[86] the Court limited the "broad discretion' of the EU legislature to the question of whether the EU legislature has respected the principle of equal treatment. Only when tested against this principle is a measure unlawful if it is 'manifestly inappropriate'. In such cases, the Court does not require that the EU measure is the 'only or best possible measure', but only that this rule can contribute 'effectively' to the objective.

When testing against *other* principles or rights, the EU legislature therefore has no broad discretion. Examples include the principle of legal certainty, the principle of legality of penalties and the right to respect for private life (Article 7 EU Charter).

In *Belgian Association of Tax Lawyers* the validity of the DAC6 directive (mandatory automatic exchange of information with regard to reportable cross-border arrangements)

83 Case C-626/18, *Poland v EU Parliament and Council*, EU:C:2020:1000, point 97.
84 Case C-482/17, *Czech Republic v EU Parliament and Council*, EU:C:2019:1035, point 77.
85 Case C-491/01, *British American Tobacco*, EU:C:2002:741, point 129.
86 Case C-623/22, *Belgian Association of Tax Lawyers, H&I 2024/198 (comments by Thomas).*

was tested by the Court against the aforementioned rights and was declared not to be in conflict with them.

In *Orde van Vlaamse Balies*[87] the Court did declare a specific provision of the DAC6 Directive invalid because it conflicted with the right to respect for communications between lawyers and their clients guaranteed by Article 7 of the Charter. The Court did not grant he EU legislator a broad discretion in this regard.

In *F SCS/Ordre des avocats du Barreau de Luxembourg*[88] which, among other things, concerned the Directive on administrative cooperation in the field of taxation (DAC Directive) the Court found no indication that could affect the validity of the DAC Directive in the light of respect for private and family life (Article 7 EU Charter). However, the Court ruled that the Luxembourg national legislation implementing this Directive infringed the right to respect for communications between lawyers and their clients guaranteed by Article 7 of the Charter.

In any case, it is clear that since 2022 the Court has taken the assessment of secondary EU law against the Charter very seriously, as in the *WM-case*[89] a provision of the Money Laundering Directive was declared invalid because it conflicted with respect for privacy (etc.) and with the protection of personal data (Articles 7 and 8 of the Charter) and in the *VYSOCINA WIND*-case[90] a provision of Directive 2012/19/EU on waste electrical and electronic equipment was declared invalid due to retroactive application contrary to the principle of legal certainty (a general principle of EU law). In case T-143/23, *Fugro*, the issue was whether the carve-out for shipping in Directive EU 2022/2523 (Global minimum tax – pillar 2) was invalid. However, for procedural reasons, the General Court did not have to answer the (substantive) question. An appeal was lodged in this case with the Court (C-146/24 P).

A tension between primary and secondary EU law can be resolved by declaring a provision of secondary law invalid, but this tension can also be resolved in other ways. The Court has developed in this regard various techniques. One of this is the principle of reconciliatory (or consistent) interpretation according to which:

> [w]hen the wording of secondary Community law is open to more than one interpretation, preference should be given to the interpretation which renders the provision consistent with the Treaty rather than the interpretation which leads to its being incompatible with the Treaty.[91]

---

87 Case C-694/20, *Orde van Vlaamse Balies.*

88 Case C-432/23, *F SCS/Ordre des avocats du Barreau de Luxembourg, H&I 2024/294 (comments by Thomas).*

89 Joined Cases C-37/20 and C-601/20, *WM*, ECLI:EU:C:2022:912.

90 Case C-181/20, *VYSOCINA WIND*, ECLI:EU:C:2022:51.

91 See for example, Joined Cases C-90/90 and C-91/90 *Jean Neu and others*, EU:C:1991:303, point 12; Case C-90/92 *Dr Tretter*, EU:C:1993:264, point 11; Case C-135/93 *Spain v Commission*, EU:C:1995:201, point 37.

Furthermore, in cases where a directive grants options to the Member States or leaves a broad scope of discretion in transposing it, the options or the discretion must be exercised by the Member States in compliance with primary law, including the Treaty freedoms.[92]

See also, on judicial review of secondary EU law by the Court, Chapters 19.3 and 7.2.

2.3 Enactment of EU Measures as Regards Taxation

2.3.1 Different Legislative Procedures

Of the seven Union institutions,[93] as a main rule three participate in the legislative process: the Commission, the Council, and the European Parliament. The Commission[94] has the (almost) exclusive right to propose Union legislation. Because of this, the Commission, although formally not adopting laws, controls the Union's legislative agenda. Hence its designation as "the engine of integration". The European Parliament[95] – representing the Union citizens and directly elected by them – and the Council[96] – representing the Member States – usually co-decide on the adoption of Union legislative acts proposed by the Commission.

There are two types of legislative procedures in the Union's constitutional order: an ordinary legislative procedure and special legislative procedures. Article 289 TFEU defines them in the following terms:

1. The ordinary legislative procedure shall consist in the joint adoption by the European Parliament and the Council of a regulation, directive or decision on a proposal from the Commission. This procedure is defined in Article 294.
2. In the specific cases provided for by the Treaties, the adoption of a regulation, directive or decision by the European Parliament with the participation of the Council, or by the latter with the participation of the European Parliament, shall constitute a special legislative procedure.

Thus, in the ordinary legislative procedure the European Parliament and the Council act as co-legislators with equal rights. By contrast, in the special legislative procedures one of these two institutions has a dominant role, i.e. it decides on adoption of the act, and the other party is only consulted or has only a right of consent. These roles change depending on the specific form of the special legislative procedure. When the European Parliament adopts the legislative act in question, the Council participates in the process through its consent. When the Council adopts the act, the European Parliament contributes either through its consent or by way of consultation. In the former case (consent procedure) the

---

92 Case C-386/14 *Groupe Steria*, EU:C:2015:524, point 39; Case C-168/01 *Bosal*, EU:C:2003:479, points 25, 26; Case C-471/04 *Keller Holding*, EU:C:2006:143, point 45; Case C-446/04 *Test Claimants in the FII Group Litigation*, EU:C:2006:774, point 46.

93 The TEU sets up seven institutions for the Union: the European Parliament, the European Council, the Council, the European Commission, the Court of Justice of the European Union, the European Central Bank and the Court of Auditors (Article 13 TEU).

94 See Article 17 TEU and Articles 244-250 TFEU.

95 See Article 14 TEU and Articles 223-234 TFEU.

96 See Article 16 TEU and Articles 237-243 TFEU.

European Parliament must approve of the act but it cannot influence its content. In the latter case (consultation procedure) the European Parliament has even weaker rights as the Council is merely required to ask its opinion but not to follow that opinion.

The question of whether the ordinary or one of the special legislative procedures applies, is answered by the legal basis provision which authorizes the adoption of the act concerned. In line with the principle of conferral, for the Union to adopt a legislative act a specific authorization is necessary which is granted in the founding treaties. Specific legal basis provisions can be found with regard to each policy area provided for in the treaties. Apart from specific legal basis provisions, the treaties also contain some general legal basis provisions which authorize the Union to legislate in any of the policy areas regulated in the treaties.

The ordinary legislative procedure is defined in a separate provision of the TFEU (Article 294). There is no such general definition of the special legislative procedures. They are defined in the specific legal basis provisions which provide for their use in the areas concerned.

To the area of taxation, a special legislative procedure applies in which the Council adopts the act after consulting the European Parliament and the Economic and Social Committee. Hence this is a consultation procedure in which the European Parliament has a limited role. Nevertheless, even in this procedure the voice of Parliament has to be heard.[97] In addition, besides the European Parliament, the Economic and Social Committee also has to be consulted.[98] Each time the finally adopted text differs substantially in essence from the text on which the European Parliament has been consulted, a new consultation of Parliament and of the Economic and Social Committee must follow. Examples are the Merger Directive and the Parent-Subsidiary Directive (see Chapters 16 and 17) which were adopted by the Council after many points had been changed as compared to the original directive proposals on which Parliament was consulted. Those changes were not re-submitted to the European Parliament and the Economic and Social Committee, and in *Océ van der Grinten*[99] the question was raised whether Article 7(2) of the Parent-Subsidiary Directive was invalid due to this. The Court considered the provision valid, because it did not concern a 'substantial change'.

Legislative acts must be sufficiently reasoned and must refer to the proposals, initiatives, recommendations, requests and opinions which are required by the treaties (Article 296 TFEU). Furthermore, the legislative procedure must be followed precisely. In the absence

97 The European Parliament's involvement through consultation "represents an essential factor in the institutional balance intended by the Treaty" and therefore, it is an essential procedural requirement the disregard of which leads to the annulment of the legislative act, see Case 138/79 *Roquette Frères*, EU:C:1980:249, point 33.

98 Apart from the Union institutions, the treaties also acknowledge the existence of other 'bodies'. The Economic and Social Committee (together with the Committee of Regions) is an advisory body which is aimed at assisting the European Parliament, the Council and the Commission (Article 13(4) TEU). The composition and powers of the Economic and Social Committee are laid down in Articles 301-304 TFEU.

99 Case C-58/01, *Océ van der Grinten*, EU:C:2003:495. See also Case C-390/15 *RPO*, EU:C:2017:174.

of sufficient substantiation, or if the legislative procedure has not been followed correctly, the legal act may later be declared invalid by the Court.[100]

2.3.2 *Treaty Bases for Tax Integration*

As observed, Article 28 TFEU called for a customs union, which implies the total prohibition, between the Member States, of import and export duties, of any charges having an effect equivalent to a customs duty (Art. 30 TFEU), and of quantitative restrictions on imports and all measures having equivalent effect (Art. 34 TFEU). This prohibition (*negative* integration, therefore) means the following. A 'charge having equivalent effect' to a customs duty is any pecuniary charge, under whatever name or scheme, for whatever purpose, however small, which is levied by a Member State on the occasion of the border-crossing of products. Therefore, charges like 'statistics duties' are prohibited, even if they cannot be considered to protect national productions.[101] Charges on the occasion of the border-crossing of goods are allowed only if they do not exceed the cost of the service individually rendered to economic operators by the Member State charging them (reimbursements, such as the cost of bonded warehouse). The CJEU applies a substantive interpretation of 'customs duties' and 'charges having equivalent effect', as obviously, covert import charges are prohibited just as much as straightforward tariff walls. Even an *internal* levy charged indiscriminately on both domestic and imported products may be prohibited if the revenue raised is used to finance schemes that benefit only domestic products and fully compensate for the charge borne by domestic production.[102] And even if the revenue is only partially used for reimbursing domestic producers, who are thus not entirely compensated for the charge, the levy may still be prohibited – not under Article 30, but under Article 110 TFEU, which prohibits discriminatory and protective internal taxes. Indeed, if domestic producers are only partially compensated for the charge, it may not be *equivalent* to a customs duty, but it still indirectly discriminates against foreign producers, who are not compensated for the charge at all. Article 110 only allows product taxation as part of a general internal consumption tax which is levied indiscriminately on both domestic and foreign products, such as turnover taxes (the VAT), excise duties and taxes on the registration of new motor cars.

The prohibitions of Articles 30 (customs duties and charges with equivalent effect) and 110 (discriminatory or protective product taxation) never apply simultaneously,[103] because they concern different subject matters: whereas Article 30 prohibits charges on imports from other Member States (and on exports to other Member States), Article 110 allows taxes on imported products, provided that similar domestic products bear the exact same tax burden. Article 110 *grants* Member States the competence to levy product taxes within the limits set by the EU harmonization rules ex Article 113, and within the

100 See for an example of a case in which the Court examines whether the obligation to provide reasons was violated: Case C-508/13, *Estonia/European Parlement*, EU:C:2015:403.

101 Case 24/68 *Commission v. Italy*, EU:C:1969:29.

102 See for example, Case C-17/91 *Lornoy v. Belgium*, EU:C:1992:514; Case C-266/91 *Celulosa Beira Industrial (CELBI)*, EU:C:1993:334; Case C-517/04 *Koornstra*, EU:C:2006:375.

103 Case 57/65 *Lütticke*, EU:C:1966:34; Case C-347/95 *Fazenda Pública v. UCAL*, EU:C:1997:411; Case C-28/96 *Fazenda Pública v. Fricarnes*, EU:C:1997:412. See also the Lornoy and Celulosa Beira cases mentioned above.

limits set by Article 110 itself, whereas Article 30, by contrast, *eliminates* all Member State competence to levy any charge that has the effect of a customs duty, however small or indirect. See for elaboration on discriminatory or protective product taxation Chapter 3.1.0.

As observed, a harmonisation mandate (*positive* integration, therefore) is laid down in Article 113 TFEU, to adopt provisions for the harmonisation of legislation concerning turnover taxes, excise duties and other forms of indirect taxation, 'to the extent that such harmonisation is necessary to ensure the establishment and the functioning of the internal market and to avoid distortion of competition'. The decision-making takes place on the basis of the special legislative procedure which entails that the Council – after consulting the European Parliament and the Economic and Social Committee – must adopt the act proposed by the Commission by unanimous decision.

The TFEU does not provide for a harmonisation mandate for direct taxation, which explains why by far the most integration of direct taxes is negative integration, notably on the basis of the free movement rights prohibiting hindrances to the functioning of the internal market and of the State aid prohibition. The only legal basis for harmonization of direct taxes thus is the general harmonization provisions aimed at establishing and ensuring the functioning of the internal market (Articles 114 and 115 TFEU *juncto* Article 26 TFEU).[104] Article 114(1) provides for the 'ordinary legislative procedure', which entails qualified majority voting, on matters concerning the establishment and the functioning of the internal market. Article 114(2) stipulates, however, that Article 114(1) is not applicable 'to fiscal provisions'. In *Commission v Council*, the Court held that 'those words cover not only all areas of taxation, without drawing any distinction between the types of duties or taxes concerned, but also all aspects of taxation, whether material rules or procedural rules'[105] and that 'the words 'fiscal provisions' contained in Article 95(2) EC [now Article 114(2) TFEU] must be interpreted as covering not only the provisions determining taxable persons, taxable transactions, the basis of imposition, and rates of and exemptions from direct and indirect taxes, but also those relating to arrangements for the collection of such taxes'.[106] Therefore, directives adopted in the area of direct taxation are based on the general legal basis provision for the internal market of Article 115 TFEU. On the basis of this provision, directives can be adopted unanimously under the special legislative procedure "for the approximation of such laws, regulations or administrative provisions

104 Possibly, the complementary provision of Article 352 TFEU (also called 'flexibility clause') could also be a legal basis. This provision permits 'appropriate measures' to be taken unanimously by the Council 'if action by the Union should prove necessary, within the framework of the policies defined in the Treaties, to attain one of the objectives set out in the Treaties, and the Treaties have not provided the necessary powers (...)'. This provision served as the legal basis for the EU Regulation on the European Economic Interest Grouping (EEIG) (Council Regulation (EEC) No 2137/85 of 25 July 1985 on the European Economic Interest Grouping, OJ L 199 of 31.7.1985, p. 1-9) which contains one provision on the tax treatment of an EEIG. It was also the legal basis for the Statute for a European Company (Societas Europaea) (Council Regulation (EC) No 2157/2001 of 8 October 2001 on the Statute for a European company (SE), OJ L 294 of 10.11.2001, p. 1-21) that Statute however contains no tax provision.

105 Case C-338/01, *Commission v Council*, EU:C:2004:253, para. 63.

106 Case C-338/01, *Commission v Council*, EU:C:2004:253, para. 65.

of the Member States as directly affect the establishment or functioning of the internal market"[107].

To date, seven direct tax directives have been adopted on the basis of Article 115:[108] the Parent-Subsidiary Directive, on intra-group cross-border dividends (see Chapter 10),[109] the Merger Directive, on the tax consequences of mergers of companies of different Member States and on the transfer of seat of an SE or SCE (see Chapter 20),[110] the Interest and Royalty Directive, on intra-group cross-border payments of interest and royalties (see Chapter 18),[111] the Anti-Tax Avoidance Directive, laying down compulsory anti-avoidance measures that the Member States must implement into their domestic laws as a minimum standard[112] (see Chapter 19), the Tax Dispute Resolution Directive (see Chapter 21)[113]. the Pillar 2 (minimum taxation) Directive[114] (see Chapter 22) and the so-called FASTER Directive on Faster and Safer Relief of Excess Withholding Taxes[115] (see Chapter 23).

In sum, therefore, acts in the area of indirect taxation (Article 113 TFEU) and in the area of direct taxation (Article 115 TFEU) are adopted by means of the special legislative

107 See the public country-by-country reporting Directive (Directive (EU) 2021/2101 of the European Parliament and of the Council of 24 November 2021 amending Directive 2013/34/EU as regards disclosure of income tax information by certain undertakings and branches), which is based on Article 114(1) TFEU. The preamble of this Directive seems to be adjusted to circumvent Article 114(2) and the unanimity requirement. Very critical about this: W. Schon, Public Country-by-Country Reporting: Corporate Law, Fiscal Law and the Principle of Unanimity, Max Planck Institute for Tax Law and Public Finance, Working paper 2021-14, August 2021.

108 The directives concerning administrative assistance in the assessment and recovery of taxes (Council Directive 2011/16/EU of 15 February 2011 on administrative cooperation in the field of taxation and repealing Directive 77/799/EEC, OJ L 64 of 11.3.2011, p. 1–12 and Council Directive 2010/24/EU of 16 March 2010 concerning mutual assistance for the recovery of claims relating to taxes, duties and other measures, OJ L 84 of 31.3.2010, p. 1–12) are based on both Articles 113 and 115 TFEU, as they concern both direct and indirect taxes.

109 Council Directive 2011/96/EU of 30 November 2011 on the common system of taxation applicable in the case of parent companies and subsidiaries of different Member States, OJ L 345 of 29.12.2011, p. 8–16 (original directive: Council Directive 90/435/EEC of 23 July 1990 on the common system of taxation applicable in the case of parent companies and subsidiaries of different Member States, OJ L 225 of 20.8.1990, p. 6).

110 Council Directive 2009/133/EC of 19 October 2009 on the common system of taxation applicable to mergers, divisions, partial divisions, transfers of assets and exchanges of shares concerning companies of different Member States and to the transfer of the registered office of an SE or SCE between Member States, OJ L 310 of 25.11.2009, p. 34–46 (original directive: Council Directive 90/434/EEC of 23 July 1990 on the common system of taxation applicable to mergers, divisions, partial divisions, transfers of assets and exchanges of shares concerning companies of different Member States and to the transfer of the registered office, of an SE or SCE, between Member States, OJ L 225 of 20.8.1990, p. 1).

111 Council Directive 2003/49/EC of 3 June 2003 on a common system of taxation applicable to interest and royalty payments made between associated companies of different Member States, OJ L 157 of 26.6.2003, p. 49–54.

112 Council Directive (EU) 2016/1164 of 12 July 2016 laying down rules against tax avoidance practices that directly affect the functioning of the internal market, OJ L 193 of 19.7.2016, p. 1–14.

113 Council Directive (EU) 2017/1852 of 10 October 2017 on tax dispute resolution mechanisms in the European Union, OJ L 265 of 14.10.2017, p. 1-14.

114 Council Directive (EU) 2022/2523 of 14 December 2022 on ensuring a global minimum level of taxation for multinational enterprise groups and large-scale domestic groups in the Union; 2022, L 328/1.

115 Council Directive on Faster and Safer Relief of Excess Withholding Taxes, H&I 2024/315.

procedure and by unanimous vote in the Council. On the basis of Article 115 TFEU, only *directives* (i.e. no regulations) can be adopted. Article 113 TFEU uses the term 'provisions' thus permitting the adoption of all kinds of measures for the harmonization of indirect taxes including regulations.

2.3.3 Escapes From the Unanimity Requirement: Enhanced Cooperation, Market Distortion Provisions, Curbing Fraud, Comitology and Passerelle

The fact that tax measures can be adopted only by means of unanimity significantly restricts further harmonisation of national tax legislation within the Union, as all 27 Member States thus effectively have the power to veto any proposal in that field. For this reason, the Commission endeavoured in the approach to the Treaty of Nice to introduce the qualified majority rule for certain tax measures (i.e. for direct tax obstacles, in the case of fraud and tax avoidance, for VAT, excise duties and capital tax and for measures which protect the environment).[116] This proposal, however, never made it into the Treaty of Nice. The Commission also failed, in *Commission v Council*,[117] to make the Court decide that Article 114(1) TFEU (qualified majority) instead of Articles 113 and 115 TFEU (unanimity) should be the legal basis for amending the Recovery Assistance Directive.[118] Therefore, tax law remains a stronghold of unanimity voting, as regards both direct and indirect taxation and in the area of both substantive and procedural tax law (such as the exchange of tax information and tax recovery procedure).

The unanimity requirement can be 'circumvented' by using the market distortion provisions (Articles 116 and 117 TFEU; see below) or the provisions on 'enhanced cooperation' in Article 20 TEU and Articles 326-334 TFEU[119]. At least nine Member States can enter into a closer cooperation on the basis of the latter provisions whereby the measures so adopted are only applicable in those Member States. The Commission should, to that end, submit a proposal to the Council to authorise enhanced cooperation. The Council – after obtaining the consent of the European Parliament – may approve enhanced cooperation by a qualified majority. Enhanced cooperation thus offers a way out of the unanimity deadlock. For tax law, enhanced cooperation was first proposed to introduce a financial

116 Communication from the Commission - Supplementary contribution of the Commission to the Intergovernmental Conference on institutional reforms - Qualified majority voting for Single Market aspects in the taxation and social security fields, Brussels, 14 March 2000, COM(2000) 114 def. See further on this proposal: *D.M. Weber*, Noodzakelijke institutionele hervormingen in het Europese belastingrecht door uitbreiding EU, *TFB* 2000/6, p. 11.

117 Case C-338/01 *Commission/Council*, EU:C:2004:253.

118 Council Directive 2001/44/EC of 15 June 2001 amending Directive 76/308/EEC on mutual assistance for the recovery of claims resulting from operations forming part of the system of financing the European Agricultural Guidance and Guarantee Fund, and of agricultural levies and customs duties and in respect of value added tax and certain excise duties, OJ L 175 of 28.6.2001, p. 17–20.

119 See: C. Heber, Enhanced cooperation and European Tax Law, Oxford Studies in European Law, 2021.

transaction tax,[120] as several Member States are very much against it, but even under an enhanced cooperation approach, the plan seems to have been bogged down by practical difficulties (especially the problem of the ease with which the tax may be circumvented and the market and trade shifts it would entail, especially if not all Member States participate). It does not seem likely either that the Commission proposal for a Common Consolidated Corporate Tax Base (CCCTB) will be adopted under any unanimity voting procedure; only under the rules of enhanced cooperation it may stand a chance.

Furthermore, there is a legal basis provision in the TFEU which allows the adoption of directives by qualified majority, in theory, also in the area of taxation. Article 116 TFEU provides that the Council and the European Parliament adopt directives to eliminate market distortions caused by disparities between national laws or practices where those distortions cannot be eliminated through consultation with the Member States. Notably, such directives are to be adopted through the ordinary legislative procedure, which entails qualified majority voting.[121] Article 116 could be seen as a safety valve which enables the Union to handle market crises without being paralysed by the unanimity rule of Article 115. In the past, the Commission has threatened the Member States with the use of the procedure in Articles 116 in tax matters, but it has never done so to date. In fact, the provision has not played any significant role in Union policy up till now.

For completeness sake, it is observed that Article 325 (combating fraud) might also provide a legal basis for qualified majority decision-making in tax fraud matters, as it calls for measures, under the ordinary legislative procedure, necessary for combating fraud and all other illegal activities affecting the financial interests of the Union. Since customs duties and a part of VAT are own resources of the Union, customs and VAT fraud manifestly affect the financial interests of the Union.

A rather marginal (subordinate) means of avoiding cumbersome unanimous decision-making at Council level is delegation of power to the Commission to adopt delegated or implementing acts. As described above (Section 2.2.3.2), such acts can be used for (tax) law-making, as delegated acts can amend or add non-essential elements to the basic act, and implementing acts can provide for supplementary rules necessary for practical application of the basic act. Although delegated and implementing acts are adopted by the Commission, the Council or the Member States still participate in the process, as they exercise control over the adoption of such acts. However, in the case of delegated acts, the Council exercises its rights of control by qualified majority (Article 290(2) TFEU). In the case of implementing acts, the control is in the hands of committees of Member States' representatives ('comitology') cooperating with and overseeing the Commission

120 See Council Decision of 22 January 2013 authorising enhanced cooperation in the area of financial transaction tax (2013/52/EU), H&I 2013/3.7. The UK, being fiercely opposed to the financial transaction tax, challenged the Decision before the Court which, however, rejected the challenge, see Case C-209/13 *UK v Council*, EU:C:2014:283. See further on the issue, A. Cédelle, Enhanced Cooperation: A Way Forward for Tax Harmonization in the European Union? in: International Tax Law: New Challenges to and from Constitutional and Legal Pluralism, editor Joachim Englisch, GREIT, IBFD 2016, p. 165-206.

121 In addition, Article 117 TFEU provides that Member States planning to introduce national measures which may be expected to cause distortions, must consult the Commission, which may make recommendations for appropriate measures, to be taken by the States concerned, to avoid the distortion.

and adopting Commission proposals for implementing measures by qualified majority.[122] As observed, delegated and implementing acts have entered the area of taxation through recent and proposed legislative acts, but due to their limitations as regards substantive scope (they can only concern non-essential elements of the legislative act), they cannot significantly ease the unanimity requirement prevailing in the tax area.

In the field of VAT, the Commission proposed to set up a comitology committee that would assist the Commission in drawing up binding implementation measures in the field of VAT[123]. These measures can then be adopted by qualified majority[124]. This would enable the Union legislator to take more efficient decisions[125]. So far this proposal has not been adopted by the Member States, presumably because Member States are hesitant to give up their sovereignty.

A last possibility to escape the unanimity rule is the procedure laid down in Article 48(7) TEU, the so-called general *passerelle* clause.[126] This clause enables the Council to switch from unanimous voting to qualified majority voting[127] with the significant constraint, however, that for such switch the unanimous decision of the European Council (this is not the regular 'Council', but the gathering of the heads of State) is required (after obtaining the consent of the European Parliament). Therefore, the hurdle of unanimity is not eliminated, it is merely brought forward in the procedure and to the highest political institution of the Union.[128] In addition, even if unanimity could be achieved in the European Council, each national parliament has the right to object and to prevent the general passerelle clause from being activated. With these strict procedural safeguards, the general passerelle clause does not seem to offer a real alternative to the unanimity requirement applicable to all fiscal decisions in the Union. Nevertheless, the Commission suggested the use of this clause in a communication envisaging the progressive phasing out of the unanimity rule on matters of taxation by the end of 2025 and its replacement with qualified majority voting.[129]

122 See Regulation No 182/2011, Articles 5-6.

123 Proposal for a Council Directive amending Directive 2006/112/EC as regards conferral of implementing powers to the Commission to determine the meaning of the terms used in certain provisions of that Directive, COM/2020/749 final, 18.12.2020.

124 See: J. Gruson & M. Merkx, The Comitology proposal shifting the legistative balances in EU VAT, EC Tax Review 2021-3, p. 99.

125 See: ECOFIN Report to the European Council on Taxation, 21 June 2021, point 47.

126 'Passerelle' is French for gangplank. 'General' because there are also specific *passerelles*.

127 The provision also permits a switch from the special legislative procedure to the ordinary legislative procedure, under the same strict conditions.

128 The European Council consists of the heads of state or government of the Member States, the President of the European Council and the President of the Commission, see Article 15 TEU.

129 Communication from the Commission to the European Parliament, the European Council and the Council Towards a more efficient and democratic decision making in EU tax policy, COM (2019) 8 final, Strasbourg 15 January 2019, and Passerelle clauses in the EU treaties, Study, EPRS, December 2020, para. 7.2.

CHAPTER 3

General EU Law Concepts and Tax Law

Peter Wattel[1]

Update and elaboration by Sjoerd Douma[2]

3.1 Introduction

This Chapter will be on (basic) Union law rather than on tax law. It describes the most important general principles and internal market rules of Union law relevant for (unharmonised, i.e. direct) taxation (except State aid; for that, see Chapter 15) and the transmission mechanisms by which EU law penetrates the national legal orders. Tax issues will be discussed mainly as examples to illustrate the functioning of EU law, especially internal market law and the principle of effectiveness of EU law, in the national legal order. To slightly contradict the previous sentence, we will first discuss the Treaty prohibition on discriminatory and protective product taxation (Article 110 TFEU) and of import restrictions (Art. 34 TFEU), using car taxation to illustrate its effects, also to acquire the taste of the concepts of 'discrimination' and 'protective taxation'.

This Chapter will only deal with negative integration and with the transmission mechanisms by which EU law functions in the national legal order; not on positive integration (harmonisation). For harmonisation of direct taxes, see Part 3, Chapters 16-23, and for harmonisation of indirect taxes, see the second Volume of this book. For a detailed discussion of the implications of negative integration in specific areas of direct taxation, see Part 2, Chapters 6-15.

3.1.0 Prohibition of Discriminatory and Protective Product Taxation and of Import Restrictions; Small Phenomenology of International Car Taxation

Article 110 TFEU, prohibiting discriminatory and protective product taxation, does not in itself affect national tax sovereignty. To the extent there are no (exhaustive) EU measures on the matter (i.e. as far as the Recast VAT Directive and the General Arrangements Excise Directive allow), Member States remain free to organize their product tax systems in the way they see fit, and to impose the rates they consider appropriate. However, they may not tax products of other Member States less favourably. Article 110 only allows product taxation as part of a general domestic consumption tax levied indiscriminately on both

1 Professor of EU Tax Law, ACTL, University of Amsterdam; Advocate-General, Supreme Court of the Netherlands; State Councillor extraordinary, Netherlands Council of State.

2 Professor of International and European Procedural Tax Law, ACTL, Director of the Adv LLM Program in International Tax Law, University of Amsterdam; Partner, Lubbers, Boer & Douma, The Hague.

domestic and foreign products, such as general turnover taxes and excise duties. Article 110 has direct effect: it can be relied on by individuals and undertakings before their national courts, to invalidate national tax law incompatible with it. It is for the national court within the framework of its own legal system to decide whether the whole of any internal taxation which is discriminatory or only that part of it which exceeds the tax assessed on the domestic product is to be regarded as not payable.[3]

Application of the first paragraph of Article 110 ('similar products') requires a comparison of foreign and domestic products (are they similar?), and a comparison of the fiscal burdens on these similar products. Similarity is mainly determined on the basis of whether the products serve similar consumer needs and have similar characteristics, placing them in a competitive (potential substitution) relation.[4] Even if a national tax measure on that basis escapes the prohibition of the first paragraph, it may still be caught under the second paragraph: even if the domestic and the imported products are not similar, or if the effective tax burdens are equal, the tax may still have the indirect effect of protecting domestic production.

The *Humblot* case[5] illustrates the effect of Article 110. French Monsieur Humblot liked powerful cars. He purchased a German brand. In France the use of a car was subject to a road tax at a progressive rate depending on the power rating of the car. However, the rate was progressive only up to 16 CV (*chevaux* = horsepower for tax purposes). Cars powered in excess of 16 CV were taxed at a flat rate of FF 5000 *per annum*. The highest progressive rate (for a car under 16 CV) was only FF 1100 *per annum*. As a result, the tax on a 16-CV car was 4.5 times as high as the tax on a 15-CV car. Monsieur Humblot surmised it could hardly be a coincidence that all cars produced in France fell within the power rating band of up to and including 15 CV. Only imported (German) cars were subject to the very high flat rate. The Court found that, as EU law stood at the time (no harmonization, except for VAT and customs duties), Member States were free to subject products like cars to a system of road tax which increases progressively depending on an objective criterion. However, although embodying no formal distinction based on the origin of the car, the French levy was manifestly discriminatory and protective, setting the high rate at a level only catching imported cars. Moreover, the difference between the highest progressive rate and the flat rate (FF 3900, or 450% of the highest progressive rate) was excessive compared to the rate steps within the progressive rate structure. Consumers would be discouraged from buying non-French automobiles. France proved to be hard-headed, as it was convicted again by the Court for maintaining car taxation which penalized buyers of imported cars fitted with certain (then) innovative technologies, such as five-speed automatic transmissions and six-speed manual transmissions.[6]

In another case of a progressive car taxation, by contrast, the Commission could not convince the Court of a protective effect. Case 132/88[7] concerned a Greek tax on new cars in three categories: moderate (up to 1600 cc cylinder capacity), high (between 1600 and 1800 cc), and very high (above 1800 cc). The Commission objected to the rate jump

3 Case 74/76, *Ianelli v Meroni*, EU:C:1977:51, [1977] ECR 00557.
4 See, for example, for a comparison between (innovative) imported cars and (non-innovative) domestic cars, Case C-265/99, *Commission v. France*, EU:C:2001:169, [2001] ECR I-2301.
5 Case 112/84, *Michel Humblot v. Directeur des services fiscaux*, EU:C:1985:185, [1985] ECR 1376.
6 Case C-265/99, *Commission v. France*, EU:C:2001:169, [2001] ECR I-2301.
7 Case 132/88, *Commission v. Hellenic Republic*, EU:C:1990:165, [1990] ECR I-1567.

from the second category to the third, not unlike the rate jump in *Humblot*. The Court considered, however, that a car taxation system is not discriminatory solely because only imported products fall into the highest tax category. Member States remain free to tax certain luxury goods heavily for social policy reasons. All cars in the medium rate class of 1600 to 1800 cc were also non-Greek. The consumer thus had a choice between medium and high which differed entirely from the choice between domestic and foreign make, as it was a choice between two foreign products (in the low rate category, were both Greek and foreign cars). Therefore, the Commission had not demonstrated that the Greek system was biased against cars manufactured abroad or protective of the Greek manufacturers.

The Commission struck back in two cases on Greek taxation of imported second-hand cars.[8] As cars newly sold in Greece bore the Greek special sales tax described above, Greece also levied a tax on imported used cars. In order not to be discriminatory, that tax should not be higher than the residual tax in the price of second-hand cars originally sold new in Greece. The tax on imported used cars was calculated on the basis of a 5% reduction on the original sales price for each year of use, but for only four years, meaning that always at least 80% of the new price would be taxed, irrespective of the real value. Obviously, the Court held that car value does not decrease in a linear way, let alone with just 5% per year, that it does not stop decreasing after four years, and that value decrease certainly does not stop at 80% of the original price. The Greek system manifestly overtaxed imported used cars. The Greek plea that the tax was meant to discourage the marketing of old, polluting cars was dismissed; such policy may be applauded, but it may not be applied discriminately only to *imported* old and polluting cars. Subsequent to this judgment, Greece introduced a degressive depreciation scale for imported second-hand cars, reducing the tax base (the value) with a decreasing percentage of the original market price for each year of use (7% in the first two years, decreasing to 1% in the fifteenth year). The car purchaser could rebut rebut this valuation by demonstrating a lower value. The Commission was not satisfied, and took Greece to Court again.[9] The Court was not satisfied either, because (i) in the first year, no depreciation was allowed if mileage remained below 6000 km., and (ii) after the first year, the depreciation scale did not take account of mileage at all. Therefore, the system still did not ensure that "the taxable value imputed to the imported second-hand vehicle by the revenue authorities (...) faithfully reflect(s) the value of a similar second-hand vehicle already registered on the domestic market".

The difference between discriminatory and protective product taxation (Art. 110) and measures having the effect of a quantitative import restriction (Art. 34), is illustrated by a Danish tax on the registration of both new cars and imported used cars.[10] The tax on *new* cars was very high, so high that the Commission considered it a protective measure under Article 110(2). The Court, however, held that Article 110 cannot be relied on if there is no similar or competing domestic production. Since Denmark did not manufacture cars itself, Article 110 could not be applied. However, Article 34 might apply, since a very high tax on imported new cars, even if not discriminatory or protective for lack of competing national production, may still have the effect of restricting importation of new cars (but the Commission had not invoked Article 34). The Danish registration tax on imported

8 Case C-375/95, *Commission v. Hellenic Republic*, EU:C:1997:505, [1997] ECR I-5981.
9 Case C-74/06, *Commission v. Hellenic Republic*, EU:C:2007:534, [2007] ECR I-7585.
10 Case C-47/88, *Commission v. Denmark*, EU:C:1990:449, [1990] ECR I-4509.

second-hand cars was similar to the Greek tax described above. Denmark had fixed the tax base for imported second-hand cars at 90% of the original price, manifestly favouring the purchase of domestic second-hand cars, the price of which included only residual registration tax.

In two Hungarian cases,[11] the CJEU held that Article 110 opposes a registration tax on imported used cars which takes into account technical and environmental characteristics only, disregarding value decrease, if this leads to a higher tax on imported used cars than the residual tax in the value of comparable domestic used cars.

Had Denmark, Greece and Hungary designed their taxes on imported used cars such that they decreased with the factual decrease in value of the car (thus approximating the residual domestic tax in the second-hand price of comparable domestic used cars), the Court would not have objected.[12]

Still, even under a non-discriminatory system of taxation of imported used cars, market distortion persists, as imported second-hand cars were already subject to registration tax when they were originally marketed in their country of origin. That tax component in the second-hand value of the car is not refunded by the country of origin upon exportation. Therefore, there is still residual foreign first-registration tax in the import value of imported second-hand cars. An additional tax levied by the importing State, even if it is strictly commensurate with value depreciation, thus leads to double taxation of the second-hand value. Does EU law provide a remedy? A comparable issue was considered by the Court for VAT purposes in the *Gaston Schul* case,[13] concerning intra-EU importation of a second-hand yacht by an end-consumer (at that time still a taxable event). The Court required the State of importation to prevent cumulation of VAT, relying on both the (neutrality principle of the) VAT-system and on (now) Article 110. Apart from an old directive exempting temporary importation,[14] there is no harmonising EU Directive on car taxation, however, let alone a neutrality principle contained therein. Double registration tax on imported used cars therefore does not seem contrary to existing EU Law as long as neither of the two States discriminates against imported cars or exported cars, respectively.[15]

That is illustrated by two cases, one on a Danish charge on the slaughter of pigs[16] and one on a Netherlands charge on the landing of shrimps.[17] For compatibility of these charges with Article 110 TFEU the Court did not consider relevant that after transportation to another Member State, that other Member State levied a similar charge, provided both the exporting and the importing State did not distinguish between pigs/shrimps domestically produced/consumed and pigs/shrimps exported/imported.

If one wishes to have an internal market, however, such double taxation should obviously be avoided. As regards the double registration tax on second-hand cars, one of the two

11 Joined Cases C-290/05 and C-333/05, *Nádasdi* and *Németh*, EU:C:2006:652, [2006] ECR I-10115.
12 See Case C-101/00, *Tulliasiamies and Siilin*, EU:C:2002:505, [2002] ECR I-7487.
13 Case 15/81, *Gaston Schul I*, EU:C:1982:135, [1982] ECR 1409.
14 Council Directive 83/182/EEC of 28 March 1983 on tax exemptions within the Community for certain means of transport temporarily imported into one Member State from another, O.J. L 105 of 23 April 1983, p. 59 – 63.
15 Compare Case C-365/02, *Lindfors*, EU:C:2004:449, [2004] ECR I-07183, Case C-105/22, *P.M.*, EU:C:2023:414.
16 Case C-234/99, *Nygård*, EU:C:2002:244, [2002] ECR I-3657.
17 Case C-517/04, *Koornstra*, EU:C:2006:375, [2006] ECR I-5015.

Member States involved should prevent it, either the origin State by refunding residual tax upon exportation, or the destination State by refraining from taxing second-hand cars imported from other Member States already having been subject to a similar tax (mutual recognition). In 2005, the Commission tabled a Directive proposal[18] to that end, based on (now) Article 113, calling for a refund of residual tax by the Member State of origin upon the exportation or permanent transfer of a car to another Member State. The proposal contained two other elements: (i) eventual abolition of car registration taxes over a transitional period of five to ten years, and (ii) replacement by introduction of a CO2-element into the tax base of annual circulation taxes and – pending their abolition – of registration taxes.[19]

Article 110 TFEU also implies a prohibition of excessive penalties for tax offences connected with cross-border trade as compared to penalties for similar domestic tax offences. A much higher criminal or administrative fine for failure to pay VAT on an intra-Community transaction than for failure to pay VAT on domestic supplies may be incompatible with Article 110, because obviously, those higher penalties affect only imported goods.[20] This does not prevent penalty differentiation on the basis of objective factual differences. Member States may take into account that cross-border tax fraud may be more difficult to detect and to curb, and that it may be more profitable than tax fraud within only one jurisdiction, provided the penalty differentiation is commensurate with the different risk of being caught and/or the different profitability of the offences.

As already appeared from the Greek car tax case 132/88 cited above, Article 110 does not forbid Member States to pursue a legitimate (industrial) policy by way of objective differential taxation of similar products. *Vinal*[21] concerned an Italian charge on alcohol. Llt. 12000 was levied per hectolitre of synthetic alcohol (manufactured from petroleum derivates), but only Llt. 1000 was levied per hectolitre of alcohol obtained through fermentation (manufactured from agricultural products). Italy hosted scarcely any production of synthetic alcohol. The high rate therefore applied almost exclusively to imports of synthetic alcohol. The Court nonetheless accepted the rate differentiation, because (i) imports from other Member States of agricultural alcohol qualified for the same low tax as Italian agricultural alcohol and (ii) although the charge on synthetic alcohol restricted importation of synthetic alcohol, it had an equivalent domestic economic effect in that it also prevented the establishment of profitable production of synthetic alcohol by Italian industry, whilst (iii) a national policy of discouraging synthetic alcohol production (promoting agricultural alcohol production) was not at odds with EU law. Therefore, no discrimination against foreign agricultural alcohol was present and domestic production was not being protected as the virtual absence of national synthetic alcohol production was a result, precisely, of that high charge on synthetic alcohol. Therefore, Member States may levy a 'discouragement tax' (a sin tax) on products, services or behaviour

18 Commission proposal of 5 July 2005, COM(2005)261 final.

19 In its Communication 'Removing cross-border tax obstacles for EU citizens' of 20 December 2010 COM(2010)769 (see section 4.2.1(iii)), the Commission promised to come forward in 2011 with new suggestions to end double car taxation, but we are not aware of any legislative initiatives.

20 See Case 299/86, *Drexl*, EU:C:1988:103, [1988] ECR 1228 and Case C-276/91, *Commission v. France*, EU:C:1993:336, [1993] ECR I-4413.

21 Case 46/80, *SpA Vinal v. SpA Orbat*, EU:C:1981:4, [1981] ECR 90.

they consider contrary to the general interest, provided it is levied indiscriminately and does not protect domestic production.

3.1.1 An Internal Market[22]

As observed (Chapter 1), one of the means to reach the Union goals is the establishment of an internal market (Art. 3(3) TEU). The concept of an 'internal market' has gradually taken over from the concept of a 'common market', contained in the EEC and EC Treaties which preceded the TFEU. A common market entails, in the words of the Court of Justice of the EU (CJEU) in 1982:[23]

> 'the elimination of all obstacles to intra-Community trade in order to merge the national markets into a single market bringing about conditions as close as possible to those of a genuine internal market'.

Article 26(2) TFEU now states that the 'internal' market 'shall comprise:'

> 'an area without internal frontiers in which the free movement of goods, persons, services and capital is ensured in accordance with the provisions of the Treaties.'

These are the traditional 'four freedoms'; well ... five, actually,[24] since the introduction of the citizenship of the Union (Article 20), which includes the right for EU citizens to move and reside within the territory of the Union (Article 21 TFEU).

Although not mentioned in Article 26, the internal market also comprises undistorted conditions of competition and approximation of national laws (see Protocol No 27 to the TFEU). Indeed, the free movement rights and the rules on State aid have a common purpose, namely to ensure free movement between Member States under normal conditions of competition.[25]

In the area of direct taxation, the four freedoms are the most important agents of what is called 'negative' integration (market integration; see Chapter 1): they prohibit in principle all differences in taxation between cross-border situations and comparable domestic situations.

The second, also 'negative,' main feature of the internal market is the prohibition on cartel agreements, abuse of a dominant market position and State aid to undertakings. The State aid prohibition is about to become also in direct taxation an important negative market integrator (see Chapter 15).

---

22 A recent handbook on the EU internal market is: Panos Koutrakos and Jukka Snell (ed.), *Research Handbook on the Law of the EU's Internal Market*, Elgar, 2017. See, for a recent exposé on the internal market concept in direct taxation: Eric C.C. M. Kemmeren, The CJEU and the Internal Market Concept in Direct Taxation', i: Werner Haslehner, Georg Kofler and Alexander Rust, EU Tas Law and Policy in the 21st Century, Wolters Kluwer 2017 (Eucotax Series).

23 Case 15/81, *Gaston Schul I*, EU:C:1982:135, [1982] ECR 1409.

24 If one wants to honour tradition (*four* freedoms), one may consider the freedom to move and reside to be encompassed in the free movement of persons, which after all already includes two separable freedoms: free movement of workers and the freedom of establishment.

25 Case C-518/16, *ZPT AD*, EU:C:2018:126, point 47.

The third main feature of the internal market is 'positive' integration (policy integration; see Chapter 1) through (i) approximation of laws of the Member States (Art. 114(1)) and (ii) common agricultural, fishery, and transport policies. In matters of direct taxation, positive integration has traditionally played a modest role (see Chapter 1), but things have been changing under the political pressure and the budgetary and economic consequences (especially austerity measures) of the Euro-crisis and the budgetary crises, the public and political outrage against tax avoidance by multinationals and tax evasion by rich individuals, intolerable tax competition between the Member States leading to – precisely – tax avoidance and 'tax degradation'and increasing Commission scrutiny of tax rulings for multinationals.

3.1.2 Interaction of Positive and Negative Integration; Direct and Indirect Taxation; Limits to Negative Integration in Tax Matters

Positive integration (policy integration) and negative integration (market integration) interact. As long as no positive integration (EU legislation or coordination) has been brought about in a certain field, such as direct taxation, Member States remain in principle free to regulate that field as they consider appropriate, except for matters for which competence has exclusively been conferred upon the Union, such as (see Art. 3(1) TFEU) in the areas of customs union, competition law, and the common trade, agricultural and fishery policies. National (tax) sovereignty is restricted, however, by negative integration, *i.e.* by the TFEU prohibitions, especially the free movement rules (Arts. 28-37 and 45-66) and the competition rules, of which the ban on State aid to undertakings (Arts. 107-109) is the most important for taxation. It follows that although in the absence of EU legislation the design of direct taxation is a prerogative of the Member States, they may not enact or maintain tax laws or administrative practices which offend these general Treaty rules. Specifically, they may not tax cross-border establishment, investment or employment less favorably than comparable domestic establishment, investment or employment, nor may they enact or maintain selective tax incentives.

For *indirect* taxation, far-reaching harmonization or even uniformity has been reached at Union level, such as (see Volume II of this book) the Union Customs Code,[26] the Recast VAT Directive,[27] and the General Arrangements for Excise Duty Directive,[28] leaving Member States little or no tax sovereignty. Therefore, the CJEU's case law in indirect tax matters is different in character from its case law in direct tax matters. For *indirect* taxation, a large body of very technical, very detailed secondary EU law has been enacted (positive integration). The indirect tax cases brought before the CJEU therefore mainly concern implementation problems, *i.e.* the interpretation of these very detailed, very technical EU rules on indirect taxation. They concern the question of whether the national detailed implementing measures fully correspond with the detailed indirect tax directives and regulations at EU level. Application of the Treaty Freedoms or the State aid prohibition

26 Regulation (EU) No. 952/2013 of the European p\Parliament and of the Council of 9 October 2013 laying down the Union Customs Code (recast), O.J. L 269/1 of 10 October 2013.

27 Council Directive 2006/112/EC of 28 November 2006 on the common system of value added tax, OJ L 347, 11.12.2006, p. 1–118.

28 Council Directive 2008/118/EC of 16 December 2008 concerning the general arrangements for excise duty and repealing Directive 92/12/EEC, OJ L 9, 14.1.2009, p. 12–30.

is hardly ever an issue in indirect taxation. This part of EU tax law is really *tax* law rather than *EU* law: the rules to be interpreted and applied are mainly detailed and technical rules of taxation, and to a much lesser extent Union law principles such as, notably, free movement rights, proportionality, and level competition.

In the field of *direct* taxes, it is the other way around. Because of the lack of legal basis for positive integration (see Chapter 2) and because of the Member States' reluctance to give up sovereignty in respect of direct taxation, there is traditionally little secondary EU law on direct taxation, although the fight against tax avoidance has recently given more impetus to direct tax harmonization. Direct tax cases before the CJEU thus often concern the clash between the EU free movement right, general principles of EU law and the State aid prohibition on the one hand, and detailed unharmonized domestic tax legislation or bilateral tax treaties on the other. Consequently, direct tax issues before the Court do not so much concern interpretation of *tax* law (as the Court is not competent to interpret national law or bilateral tax treaties) as they concern (principles of) general *EU* law. The rules to be interpreted and applied are not rules on taxation, let alone detailed rules. Rather, they are the general, sweeping Treaty rules of principle, such as market access, market equality, market distortions, subsidiarity, proportionality, the prohibition of abuse of rights, non-discrimination, non-restriction, the prohibition of State aid, etc. In direct tax cases, the Court is a balancing artist between the interests of the internal market and the 27 separate interests of the Member States to protect their tax bases, rather than Montesquieu's *bouche qui prononce les paroles de la loi (Européenne)*. By contrast, the national direct tax rules the Court is called upon to assess in the light of these general rules and principles of EU law are often excessively technical and detailed. This extreme difference in abstraction level of the two bodies of law having to cohabit, and the fact that the Court is only competent to interpret EU law, not national, bilateral or multilateral tax law, makes the (negative) integration of direct taxes complex and chaotic, more so because there is a third, sophisticated set of rules involved: the tax treaty network between the Member States, based on the extremely successful OECD Model Double Taxation Convention and its official commentary and on authoritative OECD reports, e.g. on transfer pricing (soft law).

Negative integration thus has its limitations. First, the Court cannot simply strike down every national measure which restricts free trade or free movement. A restrictive national measure may be unavoidable to protect a mandatory requirement of public interest enumerated in the EU Treaty or developed by the Court. The Court must assess, in the absence of dedicated secondary EU law, whether the national measure, although possibly restricting the exercise of the EU free movement rights, serves a legitimate purpose of overriding public interest and if so, whether it restricts the Treaty Freedoms no more than necessary to serve that purpose (proportionality). This unwritten escape from the Treaty prohibitions on national measures distinguishing between cross-border and comparable domestic cases is called the 'rule of reason' (see section 3.2.1).

Second, the judiciary cannot solve political problems. It cannot – and should not – make policy and budget division choices which should be left to elected political decision-making bodies. The Court should not, *e.g.*, allocate or divide taxing power, nor prescribe which of two concurring jurisdictions should take away resulting double taxation, let alone in which detailed manner,[29] provided neither of them is discriminating against nonresidents, nor against foreign-source income, but still double taxation persists. The Court can only do away with tax impediments caused by the unilateral behavior of one jurisdiction, *i.e.* impediments for which (only) one jurisdiction can be held responsible because that jurisdiction treats cross-border situations less favorably than comparable internal situations. Two-jurisdiction problems can only be solved by making jurisdictional priority choices, *i.e.* political choices. Two-jurisdiction problems arise from (i) disparities (differences between the (tax) laws and administrative practices of Member States) of and (ii) dislocations (exposure of persons or of their income to two instead of only one taxing jurisdiction: parallel exercise of taxing power). The most important disparities in the area of direct taxation are differences in tax rates, in assumption of taxing power (differences in connecting factors for subjection of (legal) persons to tax, such as source, residence, territory or nationality), in transfer pricing rules, in attribution of income to persons, and mismatches in income characterization (interest or dividend; business profit or freelance income; deductible or nondeductible) and in respect of rules on legal personality or fiscal transparency (hybrid entity mismatches). Dislocations are problems resulting from the division of the tax base over more than one jurisdiction, leading to double taxation. The Court is not competent to prohibit disparities (differences) between national laws (see section 3.2.7), or the 'exercise in parallel'[30] of two taxing powers (see section 3.2.7.1).

Third, even though the TFEU precludes Member States from maintaining discriminatory and protective national laws, the Court can do no more than establish just that; it cannot prescribe which national measure should replace the disqualified measure. Its power in direct tax matters is primarily destructive (*negative* integration), not constructive.

Another example of the interaction between positive and negative integration is the phenomenon of the Court turning to available positive integration to be inspired on how to approach a negative integration problem. Indeed, why should the Court invent the wheel from scratch if there are already well-functioning wheels? A clear example of this interaction is Case C-446/04, *Test Claimants in the FII Group Litigation*, in which the Court allowed the UK to apply a credit for underlying tax to prevent economic double taxation of foreign group dividends, although domestic group dividends were exempt, apparently because Article 4 of the EU Parent-Subsidiary Directive (see Chapter 16) leaves the Member States a choice between these two methods. Conforming to existing positive integration is not limited to EU law. The Court also takes leads from settled international tax law, as represented by the OECD Model Double Taxation Convention and its Official Commentary. Thus, the Court (unfortunately, in our view) accepted that residents and nonresidents are not, as a rule, comparable for income taxation purpose (Case C-279/93, *Schumacher*): it allowed source taxation for nonresidents and worldwide taxation for residents, probably presuming that source taxation (limited tax liability) can hardly be less favorable than worldwide taxation (unlimited tax liability), but that is a fallacy in case of negative home State income (home State losses) of the nonresident. It further accepted the OECD Model Tax Treaty as a standard in Case C-336/96, *Gilly*, holding that when they are dividing taxing power, it is 'not unreasonable' for the Member States to base

29 See, e.g. Case C-385/00, *De Groot v. Inspecteur van belastingen*, EU:C:2002:750, [2002] ECR I-11819.
30 A term first used by the Court in Case C-513/04, *Kerckhaert-Morres*, EU:C:2006:713, [2006] ECR I-10967.

their agreements on international practice, especially the OECD Model. In Case *Amurta*,[31] the Court made acceptability of a discriminatory withholding tax in the source State (negative integration) dependent on the 'neutralization' of that discriminatory taxation by creditability of the withholding tax in the residence State of the taxpayer on the basis of a bilateral tax treaty between the two States involved (positive integration). In *Thin Cap*,[32] it accepted as *prima facie* evidence of abusive tax avoidance the derogation of the OECD's arm's length principle for transfer pricing (provided the taxpayer may rebut that presumption by showing business purpose).

3.1.3 Access to the Four Freedoms

3.1.3.1 Treaty Standing; Cross-Border Element; Internal Situations; EU Citizenship

To be able to rely on any of the TFEU Freedoms, a person needs to have a capacity coming within the ambit of the provisions on free movement, *e.g.* frontier worker, provider or consumer of cross-border supplies or services, entrepreneur establishing abroad, investor investing abroad, etc. The Four Freedoms do not address purely domestic situations within just one Member State. Therefore, in principle, two tests must be passed for 'Treaty standing': (i) capacity (worker, undertaking, investor, etc.) and (ii) an intra-EU (or EEA[33]) cross-border element. Apart from the free movement rights, the TFEU also contains a general prohibition on discrimination directly or indirectly based on nationality (Art. 18), for the application of which no specific economic capacity (worker, undertaking, investor, etc.) is required, but it applies 'without prejudice to any special provisions,' and only 'within the scope of application of this Treaty.' Because of these limitations, Article 18 is not often applied on its own merits. Mostly, a 'special provision' takes priority, notably one of the free movement rights (of persons, goods, services and capital). These leave little scope for Article 18, as they cover almost the entire 'scope of application of this Treaty', *i.e.* almost all cross-border *economic* activity (employment, self-employment, establishment of undertakings, subsidiaries, branches and agencies, active and passive (portfolio) investment, provision and purchase of goods and services, payments for all of these, etc.). Article 18 applies independently only to situations which are within the ambit of the TFEU, but for which the TFEU lays down no specific prohibition of discrimination.[34] Where a national provision is compatible with the four freedoms, it is also compatible with Article 18.

Until 1993, the limitation 'within the scope of application of this Treaty' excluded all cases lacking a cross-border *economic* element, especially the frequent and simple case of an EU citizen taking up residence abroad without changing economic activity. The

31 Case C-379/05, *Amurta*, EU:C:2007:655.

32 Case C-524/04, *Test Claimants in the Thin Cap Group Litigation*, EU:C:2007:161, [2007] ECR I-2107. Compare also Case C-484/19, *Lexel*, EU:C:2021:34.

33 European Economic Area: the EU plus Iceland, Liechtenstein and Norway.

34 Case 305/87, *Commission v. Greece*, EU:C:1989:218, [1989] ECR 1461; Case C-1/93 *Halliburton Services*, EU:C:1994:127, [1994] ECR I-1137; Case C-311/97, *Royal Bank of Scotland*, EU:C:1999:216, [1999] ECR I-2651.

Maastricht Treaty[35] changed that. It introduced EU citizenship and the right to freely move and reside in the Union (Articles 20 and 21).[36] The case law of the CJEU since then has shown a gradual relaxation of the conditions for individuals for access to the European discrimination prohibitions. A cross-border economic aspect is not necessary any more for Treaty standing. The Right of residence has become an autonomous TFEU entrance for persons who are not economically active, such as, notably, pensioners moving to another Member State for better climate, nature or taxes, rather than for taking up a business or a job ('grey panthers'). For legal persons, by contrast, some commercial activity is still required for treaty freedom access, as these are not EU citizens within the meaning of Article 20 TFEU and have therefore no access to the right to move and reside ex Article 21, while Article 54 TFEU (right of establishment) excludes companies and firms 'which are non-profit-making.' The *Baumbast* Case[37] made clear that the right to move and to reside has direct effect and can therefore relied on by EU citizens directly before their national courts.

3.1.3.2 Treaty Access in Direct Tax Cases

For direct-tax purposes, two cases still deserve attention, even though the introduction of the Right to move and reside did away with the requirement of cross-border economic activity and therefore made Treaty standing much easier.

The *Pusa* case,[38] concerning a Finnish pensioner moving to Spain, put beyond doubt that economic activity was not required anymore for an emigrant to have treaty standing. It shows that the right of residence of EU citizens avails also the economically inactive of a right to national treatment in the State of destination and of a right of non-restriction in the State of origin. Mr Pusa was a retired Finnish national, receiving a Finnish disability pension, who had moved to Spain without taking up any economic activity there. As he failed to repay a Finnish bank loan, an attachment order was issued to his pension fund to withhold part of his pension benefits, to be paid to his creditor. Finnish law provided that part of his monthly pension must be left free of attachment (a failing debtor should still have minimum means of subsistence) and that the part subject to attachment was to be calculated on a net basis, *i.e.* after deduction of the Finnish wage withholding tax on Mr Pusa's pension (as Mr Pusa could dispose of only a net amount, precisely because of the withholding tax). However, Mr Pusa lived in Spain, and the Spanish-Finnish tax treaty allocated the right to tax the pension benefits to Spain. Therefore, Finland did not withhold any tax. Consequently, the pension part subject to attachment was calculated on a gross basis, having the effect that a larger part of Mr Pusa's pension benefits went to the bank, despite the fact that Mr Pusa, instead of paying the Finnish withholding tax, had to pay a 19% income tax on his benefits in Spain. The question was whether Finland should take into account the Spanish tax as if it were Finnish for the calculation of the pension benefits part subject to attachment. The Court answered that question in the affirmative

35 Treaty on the European Union (TEU), signed on 7 February 1992 in Maastricht, entered into force on 1 November 1993.

36 See, on the implications of EU citizenship especially for direct taxation: Erik Ros, *EU Citizenship and Direct Taxation*, Wolters Kluwer 2017 (Eucotax Series).

37 Case C-413/99, *Baumbast*, EU:C:2002:493, [2002] ECR I-7091.

38 Case C-224/02, *Heikki Antero Pusa*, EU:C:2004:273, [2004] ECR I-5763.

(an example of mutual recognition of taxation) after deciding that Mr Pusa enjoyed free movement rights even though he showed no cross-border economic activity whatsoever:

> '16. (...), Union citizenship is destined to be the fundamental status of nationals of the Member States, enabling those who find themselves in the same situation to enjoy within the scope *ratione materiae* of the Treaty the same treatment in law irrespective of their nationality, subject to such exceptions as are expressly provided for (see, *inter alia*, Case C-184/99 *Grzelczyk* [2001] ECR I-6193, paragraph 31; Case C-224/98 *D'Hoop* [2002] ECR I-6191, paragraph 28, and Case C-148/02 *Garcia Avello* (...), paragraphs 22 and 23).
> 17. The situations falling within the scope of Community law include those involving the exercise of the fundamental freedoms guaranteed by the Treaty, in particular those involving the freedom to move and reside within the territory of the Member States, as conferred by Article 18 EC [now 21 TFEU; *authors*] (see, *inter alia*, as cited above, *Grzelczyk*, paragraph 33; *D'Hoop*, paragraph 29, and *Garcia Avello*, paragraph 24).
> 18. In that a citizen of the Union must be granted in all Member States the same treatment in law as that accorded to the nationals of those Member States who find themselves in the same situation, it would be incompatible with the right of freedom of movement were a citizen, in the Member State of which he is a national, to receive treatment less favourable than he would enjoy if he had not availed himself of the opportunities offered by the Treaty in relation to freedom of movement (*D'Hoop*, paragraph 30).
> 19. Those opportunities could not be fully effective if a national of a Member State could be deterred from availing himself of them by obstacles raised to his residence in the host Member State by legislation of his State of origin penalising the fact that he has used them (see, by analogy, *D'Hoop*, paragraph 31).'

This considerably widened the scope of the prohibition on free movement hindrance as compared to the situation before the entry into force of the right of residence, and correspondingly limited national (tax) sovereignty, especially as regards relocating pensioners.

Substantively, the *Pusa* case was interesting because if Finland had *not* prevented international double taxation (if it had not concluded a tax treaty with Spain allocating the taxing right exclusively to the residence State), then full double taxation of the pension would have ensued (Spain applying the residence principle and Finland the source principle) and the Spanish tax could not have been taken into account when calculating the attachment free amount. Nevertheless, in that case the Court could have done nothing for Mr Pusa, as in neither State he would have been taxed less favourably than a resident. Indeed, as the Court has recognized, EU law does not require Member States to conclude bilateral tax treaties,[39] nor to prevent double taxation,[40] nor to adapt their tax system to that of the other State,[41] nor to ensure that the relocation of a taxpayer will be neutral tax-wise,[42] as long as they do not treat the cross-border position less favorable than the comparable domestic position. If Finland had taxed Mr Pusa as if he were a resident, then the Finnish withholding tax would have been levied and only that tax would have

39 See Case C-336/96, *Gilly*, EU:C:1998:221, [1998] ECR I-2793.

40 See, a.o. Case C-513/04, *Kerckhaert and Morres*, EU:C:2006:713, [2006] ECR I-10967, Case C-128/08 *Damseaux*, EU:C:2009:471, [2009] ECR I-6823, and Case C-67/08, *Block*, EU:C:2009:92, [2009] ECR I-883.

41 Case C-298/05, *Columbus Container Services*, EU:C:2007:754, [2007] ECR I-10451.

42 Case C-403/03, *Schempp*, EU:C:2005:446, [2005] ECR I-6421, and Case C-365/02, *Lindfors*, EU:C:2004:449, [2004] ECR I-7183.

been taken into account. Finland in fact treated Mr Pusa *more* favorable than a resident by exempting him from the withholding tax payable by residents. Thus, the Court's interpretation would seem to *penalize* Finland for its laudable, internal market-friendly preventing of double taxation.

Be that as it may, the subsequent Case C-520/04, *Turpeinen*[43] reiterated that pensioners of EU nationality emigrating to another Member State to do nothing there but live well, may rely on Articles 20 and 21 TFEU to ward off, *inter alia*, current exit taxation of unrealized capital gains in their assets and of the value of pension rights for which the contributions were deducted from departure State income. The *N. v. Inspecteur* case[44] was expected to confirm this implication, but the Court surprisingly decided that case on the basis of the right of establishment rather than the right of residence. It concerned a retired Dutchman emigrating to the UK. At the date of his emigration in 1997, he held all shares in three passive limited liability companies, the tax seat of which was transferred on the same day to the Netherlands Antilles by entrusting the management of the three companies (consisting only of portfolio and pension investment) to a local trust office. The Antilles are not a part of EU territory. Mr N. did not pursue any economic activity in the UK. The referring Court explicitly asked the CJEU whether Mr N. could rely on Article (now) 21 or on Article (now) 49. The Court, however, did not go into the reach of Article 21, as it considered the right of establishment applicable:

> '28. The situation here is that of a Community national who, since the transfer of his residence, has been living in one Member State and holding all the shares of companies established in another. It follows that, since that transfer, N has fallen within the scope of Article 43 EC [now Article 49 TFEU; *authors*] (see, to that effect, Case C-152/03 *Ritter-Coulais* [2006] ECR I-1711, paragraph 32).'

This implies that the private emigration (for whatever non-economic reasons) of any person holding a majority in any company (whether or not showing economic substance or just bank accounts and portfolio investment) originally incorporated anywhere within the Union, falls within the scope of the Right of establishment of self-employed persons and undertakings. Apparently, it was even irrelevant that the companies' real seats were outside the Union. For tax purposes, the three companies were not established in 'another Member State,' as they were effectively managed in the Netherlands Antilles, which are not part of the Union (see Articles 52 TEU and 355 TFEU). The European part of the Netherlands had no taxing jurisdiction anymore, as no permanent establishment had remained in the Netherlands; the jurisdiction of effective management of the companies (Curaçao) had exclusive taxing jurisdiction. The *N.* judgment seems to imply that for Treaty Freedoms purposes, a company remains 'established in a Member State' if it has (once) been incorporated under the law of a Member State (not applying the real seat system). At any rate, despite (i) Mr N's total lack of economic activity after emigration, (ii) the companies' passive character, and (iii) the extra-Union location of the effective management (the real seat) of the companies, Article 49 (freedom of establishment) was applied rather than Article 21 (right of residence). Possibly Article 21 was applicable *as well* (we would suppose it would, given the *Pusa* case), but the Court may have considered

43 Case C-520/04, *Turpeinen*, EU:C:2006:703, [2006] ECR I-10685.
44 Case C-470/04, *N. v. Inspecteur*, EU:C:2006:525, [2006] ECR I-7409.

'establishment' of an undertaking to have been preponderant, and Article 21 does not apply if any of the other Treaty freedoms applies.

The above case law shows that the Court is doing its best to give economic and non-economic operators going across an intra-EU border access to the Treaty's free movement rights in one way or another.

3.1.3.3 *Abuse of Rights Does Not Bar Treaty Access, but May Justify a Restriction*

On many occasions Member States have argued before the CJEU that no recourse to the Treaty freedoms should be available for economic operators improperly using them for internal-market-alien and unacceptable purposes, such as malicious avoidance of national rules on social security, on creditor protection, on broadcasting, or on taxation. Persons trying to abuse the Treaty, should not be given Treaty standing. The Court has consistently held, however, that subjective intent is irrelevant for the question of whether the Treaty Freedoms are engaged. Only objective circumstances are decisive as to whether or not a person is a 'worker' or 'establishing' himself and as to whether or not he is/does so within the range of the treaty freedoms. If a Union national takes up a job, starts a commercial activity, invests abroad or uses a legal form incorporated in another Member State, it is irrelevant – for the mere activation of the Treaty Freedoms – whether he does so for commercial reasons, to avoid arrest, to be close to his kids after a divorce, or to avoid taxation. Case C-212/97, *Centros*,[45] concerned the use of a UK legal form for Danish commercial activities by a Danish couple. It was common ground that the UK legal form was used *solely* to circumvent Danish minimum capitalization requirements. The Court not only granted access to the Right of Establishment, but did not see any improper use of it either:

> '18. That Mrs and Mrs Bryde formed the company Centros in the United Kingdom for the purpose of avoiding Danish legislation requiring that a minimum amount of share capital be paid up (...) does not, however, mean that the formation by that British company of a branch in Denmark is not covered by freedom of establishment for the purposes of Article 52 [now 49] and 58 [now 54] of the Treaty. The question of the application of those Articles of the Treaty is different from the question whether or not a Member State may adopt measures in order to prevent attempts by certain of its nationals to evade domestic legislation by having recourse to the possibilities offered by the Treaty.'

(Tax) avoiders thus in principle have access to the four freedoms. This does not mean that Member States may not fight abuse of (EU) rights. Even if a person or situation comes within the scope of free movement rights, the actual exercise of that freedom may still be restricted where that is necessary and proportionate for a mandatory reason of public interest like the prevention of abuse of (EU) law for tax avoidance purposes (the *rule of reason*; see section 3.2.1). Chapter 7 of this Volume is entirely devoted to the Court's case law and secondary EU law on the prevention of abuse of law. The general message of that case law is that abuse of free movement rights may be considered present only if either the taxpayer has set up 'wholly artificial arrangements', lacking 'economic reality' (meaning that no genuine exercise of the Treaty freedoms is present, but merely

45 Case C-212/97, *Centros*, EU:C:1999:126, [1999] ECR I-1459.

artifices), or objective and relevant facts justify a presumption of abuse, which, however, the taxpayer must be given an opportunity to rebut.

The distinction between the question of (objective) engagement of the free movement rights and the (subsequent) question of whether their exercise may be limited or denied to prevent abuse of them, cannot be upheld in all cases, however. This is due to the fact that abuse may entail lack of reality. Both the right of 'establishment' and the free movement of 'workers' presuppose real 'establishment' or 'employment', respectively. In Case C-196/04, *Cadbury Schweppes*,[46] *e.g.*, the Court observed that 'establishment' within the meaning of Article (now) 49 TFEU requires 'the actual pursuit of an economic activity through a fixed establishment in that State for an indefinite period.' Disregarding the circularity of this description, it would seem clear that a 'wholly artificial arrangement' not 'reflecting economic reality', such as a 'letterbox' or 'front' subsidiary or a 'fictitious establishment' (all quotes from *Cadbury Schweppes*), does *not* constitute 'the actual pursuit of an economic activity' and therefore does not amount to any 'establishment' within the meaning of Article 49. This implies that the artificiality of the abusive arrangement already prevented it from entering the scope of the Treaty Freedoms in the first place, meaning that we do not need to bother with the subsequent question of whether there is a justification to limit the exercise of them. In such cases, the first question (do we enter the scope?) and the second question (is there a 'wholly artificial arrangement'?) seem to coincide.

See Chapter 7 for more on abuse of rights, anti-abuse measures in secondary EU tax law and the relationship between the abuse doctrine and other justifications for restricting free movement rights in tax matters.

3.1.4 *The Rule of Law; Human Rights; General Principles of EU Law; Effective Legal Remedy*

Although in some political circles one cannot use the f-word, Article 4(3) TEU may be attributed a federal character. It may be compared to the German constitutional concept of *Bundestreue* (federation loyalty). It lays down the principle of sincere cooperation, requiring Member States (i) to assist each other and the Union to carry out the tasks flowing from the European Treaties, (ii) to take any appropriate measure to ensure fulfilment of the obligations arising out of primary and secondary EU law and to facilitate the achievement of the Union's task, and (iii) to refrain from any measures which could jeopardize the attainment of the Union's objectives. The Court has based several far-reaching judicial doctrines on this provision, such as the obligation for national courts to interpret national law in conformity with EU law as much as national law allows (or even further), as well as Member State liability for serious breaches of EU law by institutions of a Member State, including its judiciary (see section 3.4).

Further, Articles 2 and 19 TEU establish the rule of law in the Union. Article 2 TEU founds the Union on the values of, *inter alia*, 'equality, the rule of law and respect for human rights,' and Article 19(1) TEU provides that:

46 Case C-196/04, *Cadbury Schweppes*, EU:C:2006:544, [2006] ECR I-7995.

> 'The Court of Justice (....) shall ensure that in the interpretation and application of the Treaties the law is observed.'

The recognition of 'the law' in general as a source of EU law provided the legal basis for the Court to develop general principles of EU law, such as, in the first place, the principle of protection of fundamental rights common to the legal traditions and constitutions of the Member States and as enshrined in the European Convention for the Protection of Human Rights and Fundamental Freedoms (ECHR), such as the principles of *lex certa*, of a fair hearing, of the rights of the defense and of equality of arms in (quasi-)criminal matters like competition (fine) cases, and the respect for family life in cases concerning free movement of persons. It furthermore developed more mundane legal principles which are also common to the legal traditions of the Member States, such as the prohibition of abuse of rights, the principles of proportionality, legal certainty, *res iudicata*, protection of legitimate expectations, prevention of unjust enrichment, legal privilege of communication with legal counsel, the right to be heard prior to a negative administrative decision, etc. Also, it developed some genuinely autonomous and very general EU law concepts, such as, notably, the opponent principles of procedural autonomy of the Member States (see section 3.5.2.1), and of effectiveness of EU law.

In its widest sense, the principle of effectiveness of EU law encompasses EU law's direct effect in and precedence over national law,[47] as well as principles designed to ensure that national procedural law, which EU law is dependent on for enforcement, enables individuals and undertakings to effectuate rights conferred upon them by EU law (see sections 3.4 and 3.5).

Human rights were formally recognized as EU law by the Member States with the proclamation, at the 2000 Nice summit, of the EU Charter of Fundamental Rights.[48] This Charter had a murky legal status until the coming into force of the Lisbon Treaty in 2009. Article 6(1) TFEU since then lays down that the Charter has the same legal status as the Treaties. It is, therefore, primary EU law. On the basis of Article 6(2) TEU, the Union intended to accede to the European Convention for the Protection of human Rights and Fundamental Freedoms (ECHR), but that process has for the time being come to a halt for constitutional reasons (see Chapter 4). Article 6(3) TEU further provides that the fundamental rights guaranteed by the ECHR and as they result from the constitutional traditions of the Member States, are also general principles of EU law.

Long before the proclamation of the Charter in 2000 and its rise to primary EU law in 2009, the Court already protected fundamental rights, more or less forced to do so by national constitutional courts, especially the German *Bundesverfassungsgericht*. The latter court is only prepared to recognize precedence of EU law over national (constitutional) law '*so lange*' (as long as) EU law respects fundamental rights at least at a level comparable

47 This was not entirely new, as direct effect and precedence of treaty law already existed in a less permeating form in public international law in Member States entertaining a monistic constitutional system. Especially in international tax law, priority and direct effect in the national legal order was already widely known, as the distributive and prevention rules in tax treaties are precise, clear and unconditional and are therefore self-executing, and have direct effect, in countries with a monistic constitutional tradition.

48 Charter of Fundamental Rights of the European Union, O.J. of 14 December 2007, C 303/1, and O.J. 2010, C 83, p. 2.

to that of the German Constitution and only to the extent that competence has been transmitted to the Union by the German parliament (the so-called *ultra virus* supervision).[49]

An example of a general principle of EU law protected by the Court which is very relevant for tax law is the *administrative* principle of the rights of the defense, postulated for tax law in the *Sopropé* Case.[50] That case concerned the question whether a Portuguese company had been given enough time by Portuguese Customs (8 days) to be heard prior to the intended recovery from it of € 249 462 for incorrect clearing of shoes imported from Cambodia. Sopropé submitted its observations on the eighth day. Five days later, Customs informed Sopropé that its submissions contained no new information and that payment had to be completed within ten days. Sopropé refused to pay and went to court, complaining that – in summary – it had not seriously been (given an opportunity to be) heard. Upon the preliminary questions on the issue asked by the Portuguese court, the CJEU referred to a general principle of observance of the rights of the defense, and held:

> '33. Fundamental rights form an integral part of the general principles of law the observance of which the Court ensures. For that purpose, it draws inspiration from the constitutional traditions common to the Member States and from the guidelines supplied by international treaties for the protection of human rights on which the Member States have collaborated or to which they are signatories (see, inter alia, Case C-274/99 P *Connolly v Commission* [2001] ECR I-1611, paragraph 37).
> 34. It also follows from the settled case-law of the Court that, where national legislation comes within the scope of Community law, the Court, when requested to give a preliminary ruling, must provide all the criteria of interpretation required by the national court to determine whether those rules are compatible with the fundamental rights the observance of which the Court ensures (see, inter alia, Case C-260/89 *ERT* [1991] ECR I-2925, paragraph 42, and Case C-159/90 *Society for the Protection of Unborn Children Ireland* [1991] ECR I-4685, paragraph 31).
> 35. Since the questions referred for a preliminary ruling concern the procedures to be followed by national authorities when applying the Community Customs Code, the Court has jurisdiction to provide the national court with all the criteria of interpretation required by that court to determine whether the national rules at issue are compatible with the fundamental rights the observance of which the Court ensures.
> 36. Observance of the rights of the defence is a general principle of Community law which applies where the authorities are minded to adopt a measure which will adversely affect an individual.
> 37. In accordance with that principle, the addressees of decisions which significantly affect their interests must be placed in a position in which they can effectively make known their views as regards the information on which the authorities intend to base their decision. They must be given a sufficient period of time in which to do so (see, inter alia, *Commission v Lisrestal and Others*, paragraph 21, and *Mediocurso v Commission*, paragraph 36).
> 38. The authorities of the Member States are subject to that obligation when they take decisions which come within the scope of Community law, even though the Community legislation applicable does not expressly provide for such a procedural requirement. As regards the implementation of that principle and, in particular, the periods within which the rights of the defence must be exercised, it must be stated that, where those periods are

49 See for an example as regards the reach of the competence of the European Central Bank to resort to OMT (outright monetary transactions): BVerfG, *Zweite Senat*, 21 June 2016, 2 BvR 2728/13.

50 Case C-349/07, *Sopropé v Fazenda Pública*, EU:C:2008:746, [2008] ECR I-10369.

> not, as in the main proceedings, fixed by Community law, they are governed by national law on condition, first, that they are the same as those to which individuals or undertakings in comparable situations under national law are entitled and, secondly, that they do not make it impossible in practice or excessively difficult to exercise the rights of defence conferred by the Community legal order.'

Although in principle, a period of 8 to 15 days was acceptable for submitting observations on a customs debt effecting post-clearance recovery of import duties from an importer suspected of a customs offence, the national court had to ascertain whether, having regard to the specific circumstances of the case, the period actually allowed made it possible for the importer to be given a proper hearing by Customs.

Thus, EU law requires that national tax administrations, in all cases where 'they take decisions which come within the scope of Community law' and 'which significantly affect (the) interests' of the taxpayer, must hear the taxpayer prior to deciding, and must allow him enough time and opportunity to challenge the information on which the intended decision is based. It should be noted that the right to challenge the data the tax administration intends to base its decision on, presupposes the right to be informed of those data timely.[51] We further observe that in the last paragraph quoted, the Court impresses on the national court the principle of effectiveness of EU law (see section 3.5.2).

The Court's recognition of the principles of legal certainty and of legitimate expectations as general principles of EU law does not exclude retro-active tax legislation. To prevent taxpayers from setting up on a massive scale, during the legislative process, avoidance schemes which the legislator precisely aims to curb, Member States may, in exceptional circumstances, enact with retro-active effect anti-avoidance legislation, provided that such retro-actively effective ant-abuse legislation was foreseeable for the affected taxpayers.[52]

One consequence of the enactment of the EU Charter on Human Rights is that via Article 47 of the Charter (the right to an effective remedy and to a fair trial) the fair hearing requirements enshrined in Art. 6 ECHR now also apply to all national litigation in which EU rights and freedoms are at issue. This implies, *inter alia*, that the absolute exclusion of pure tax disputes from the scope of Article 6 ECHR (fair hearing) by the European Court of Human Rights (ECtHR; Strasbourg) in the *Ferrazzini* case,[53] has been nullified within the Union for all tax disputes entering the scope of EU law, i.e. in all tax cases in which EU law is in some way (co-)decisive for the outcome of the case. That is notably the case if one of the parties relies on the Treaty freedoms, or on Article 30, 34, 35, or 119 TFEU, or on secondary EU legislation on taxation, such as a VAT Directive or a corporate tax Directive. Thus, the CJEU has become competent to decide on the fairness of national tax proceedings within the scope of application of (any) EU law.[54] The Court has therefore also become competent to assess whether a national tax dispute involving EU law has been adjudicated 'within a reasonable time' (Art. 47 of the Charter), although we imagine the Court is not looking forward to questions on that issue. In *Ferrazzini*, the ECtHR probably did not categorically exclude tax litigation from the scope of Art. 6

51 Case C-189/18, *Glencore*, EU:C:2019:861.
52 Case C-376/02, *Goed Wonen*, EU:C:2005:251, [2005] ECR I-3445.
53 ECtHR 12 July 2001, Case 44759/98, *Ferrazzini v Italy*.
54 See Case C-617/10, *Åkerberg Fransson*, EU:C:2013:105.

ECHR because it was bored with too small a workload. Case C-279/09, *DEB*,[55] concerning a bankrupt legal person which applied for legal aid in order to sue Germany for State liability under EU law, shows that Article 47 of the Charter (effective legal remedy) also addresses legal persons, meaning, *inter alia*, that also legal persons which cannot afford it – such as DEB, in liquidation – may, depending on the circumstances be entitled to free legal counsel and to a waiver of the obligation to make an advance payment of court fees. Legal persons therefore also may complain about undue delay or lack of a fair hearing, etc., under the Charter in cases involving EU law issues.

The Charter applies to the EU institutions and to the Member States in so far as they are implementing Union law (Article 51(1)). This raised the question of what 'implementing Union law' means. One of the first tax cases to reach the Court on the Charter of Human Rights concerned that fundamental question. Obviously, the wider that scope, the wider the competence of the Court and with that, of the EU. The reach of EU competence is a politically extremely sensitive area. The Member States explicitly included in Article 5 TEU that the EU institutions have no other competences than attributed to them by the Treaties and that exercise of such competences by the EU is subject to the principle of subsidiarity, meaning that outside the area of its exclusive competences, the EU may act only if the goal envisaged cannot be reached by the member States themselves at national or regional level and will be better served at EU level. The Court's development and application of its general principles of (EU) law already stretched the EU's competences, the so-called 'competence creep',[56] a phenomenon of which most Member States are quite wary. In the landmark case *Åkerberg Fransson*,[57] the Grand Chamber of the CJEU clearly and tersely decided that "(t)he applicability of EU law entails applicability of the fundamental rights guaranteed by the Charter." This means that the Charter is applicable irrespective of whether the Member State involved is acting as an 'agent' of EU law (implementing EU Directives and Regulations) or EU law is relied on by an economic operator to ward off application of incompatible national law (e.g. a taxpayer relying on the freedom of establishment to challenge a national exit tax). The Charter thus has the exact same scope as the general principles of EU law developed by the Court and recognized by Article 6(3) TEU, which have the exact same scope as EU law itself. *Åkerberg Fransson* concerned VAT fraud committed by a Swedish fisherman who was made subject, first, to imposition of a punitive administrative surcharge, and subsequently to a criminal prosecution for the same tax offence. The question referred to the CJEU was whether this was compatible with Article 50 of the Charter (the right not to be tried or punished twice in criminal proceedings for the same criminal offence (*ne bis in idem*)). See Chapter 4.

In the *J. McB. Case*,[58] the CJEU pointed out that Article 52 (3) of the Charter provides that in so far as the Charter contains rights corresponding to rights guaranteed by the ECHR, their meaning and scope are to be the same as those laid down by the ECHR, but that this provision explicitly does not preclude the grant of wider protection by European Union law.

55 Case C-279/09, *DEB GmbH v Bundesrepublik Deutschland*, EU:C:2010:811.

56 See on this phenomenon: S. Prechal, 'Competence Creep and General Principles of Law,' *Review of European Administrative Law* 2010. p. 5-22.

57 See Case C-617/10, *Åkerberg Fransson*, EU:C:2013:105, discussed in Chapter 4.

58 Case C-400/10 PPU (urgent preliminary procedure; *procédure préliminaire urgent*), J. McB. v L.E., EU:C:2010:582.

We stress that the Court only assesses the compatibility of national measures with fundamental rights in cases which come within the scope of application of Union law: the case must involve application of TEU or TFEU provisions, implementation or application of EU directives or EU regulations, or have some other link with EU law.[59] This means that in most indirect tax cases, the Charter and EU principles of law are applicable, as these taxes have been harmonized or regulated at EU level, and in most direct tax cases, the Charter and EU principles of law are not applicable, as there is very little EU legislation on direct taxes and apart from that, direct taxes in principle only come within the scope of EU law if free movement or State aid aspects are at issue.[60] Obviously, the Court also assesses all Union Acts and actions in the light of the Charter and the general principles of law, *e. g.* Commission investigative or enforcement actions in the field of competition law, but also the Union's implementation of anti-terrorist measures on the basis of UN security council resolutions, such as the secret blacklisting of individuals and organizations.[61]

See Chapter 4 for elaboration on the EU Charter of Fundamental Rights.

3.2 The Four Freedoms

3.2.1 *'Discriminations' and 'Obstacles'; Market access and Market Equality; the Rule of Reason*

3.2.1.1 *Discrimination and Restriction Concepts*

The four freedoms (free movement of goods, services, persons and capital) encompass two basic rights: a right of cross-border circulation (market *access*, including the freedom to leave the State of departure unhindered) and a prohibition of discrimination on grounds of nationality or origin on the market (market *equality*). Since the introduction of the right of residence (Art. 21; see section 3.1.3), which is not connected to any economic activity, the use of the term 'market' is not entirely adequate any more for the free movement of individuals and should maybe be replaced for 'jurisdiction' or 'territory', or simply be deleted: access and equality. For direct tax purposes, by far the most important free movement rights are the free movement of persons (to be divided in free movement of workers and free movement of undertakings (the right of establishment)) and the free movement of capital and payments. As observed in section 3.1.3.3, the right of residence is crucial for non-economic relocation, such as emigration of pensioners. For *indirect* taxation, obviously the free movements of goods and services are the most important Treaty freedoms, but there is much less need for Treaty freedoms in the indirect tax area than there is in the direct tax area, as the TFEU contains many specific provisions on indirect taxation, notably on the Community customs union, harmonization of indirect taxes and a ban on discriminatory and protective product taxation (see Chapter 2), and an impressive body of dedicated secondary EU legislation on indirect taxes has been based on these specific treaty provisions. There is very little purely national indirect tax law

59 See, *e.g.*, Case C-309/96, *Annibaldi*, EU:C:1997:631, [1997] ECR I-7493, and Case C-299/95, *Kremzow*, EU:C:1997:254, [1997] ECR I-2629, Case C-617/10, *Åkerberg Fransson*, EU:C:2013:105.

60 Case C-257/20, *Viva Telecom Bulgaria*, EU:C:2022:125, point 129.

61 Cases C-402/05 P and C-415/05 P, *Kadi and Al Barakaat Foundation*, EU:C:2008:461, [2008] ECR I-6351.

left: transaction taxes are regulated at EU level. Therefore, national indirect tax law is primarily implementation of secondary EU law (e.g. the recast VAT Directive), and most EU law problems in respect of indirect taxation are implementation problems. In principle, the Court does not assess national law implementing EU secondary law (such as VAT and excise duties) in the light of primary EU law (such as the free movement rights), but only in the light of the secondary EU law it implements (the recast VAT Directive or the Excise Duties Directive).[62] Below, we therefore concentrate on direct taxes, as these are, for lack of harmonization, still largely governed by primary Union law (if a cross-border aspect can be discerned).

Obviously, distinctions in national (or bilateral) law covertly or indirectly based on nationality or origin are just as prohibited by the four freedoms as direct discrimination against goods, services, workers, undertakings or capital of other Member States. Distinctions based on criteria other than nationality of persons or origin of goods and therefore appearing neutral, such as the place of residence or being subject to limited or unlimited tax liability, but mainly disadvantaging foreigners, imported goods and services or foreign investment, are just as detrimental to free movement as direct discrimination. The market *access* rights imply that even measures without distinction (obstacles) may be prohibited if they block free movement and no justification is available. For instance, the *Bosman* case[63] shows that the Court prohibits measures which have the same domestic as cross-border effect, if that effect makes it virtually impossible to accept a job abroad. The case concerned a Belgian professional football player who signed a contract with a French club after the expiry of his contract with a Belgian club, but was unable to actually be employed by the French club because of the UEFA transfer fee regulations. The same obstacle would have obtained if Mr Bosman had signed a contract with another *Belgian* football club. Therefore, no distinction between the domestic and the cross-border situation was present. Nonetheless, the CJEU held the transfer fee regulations to be incompatible with the free movement of workers, as it blocked both Mr. Bosman's departure from the Belgian labour market and his access to another EU labour market, thus virtually blocking his market access altogether.

Another example of a nondiscriminatory but nevertheless prohibited obstacle, this time on the destination State side of the border, also frustrating market access, is Case C-442/02, *Caixa*.[64] It concerned a French measure prohibiting banks to pay interest on sight accounts. The idea behind this rule was, according to the French government, that in return for not receiving interest, bank clients would not need to pay for basic bank services such as bank transfers, cheque issuance and debit card services. The measure applied indiscriminately to any bank operating on the French market. Still, the Court considered the interest prohibition incompatible with the freedom of establishment, as it seriously impeded foreign bank access to the French consumer market, interest rates on sight accounts at that time being the primary means of competition on that market.

62 See, e.g. Case C-97/09, *Ingrid Schmelz*, EU:C:2010:632, Case C-154/04, *Alliance for Natural Health*, EU:C:2005:449, and Case C-14/16, *Euro Park Service*, EU:C:2017:177.

63 Case C-415/93, *UEFA and others v. Jean-Marc Bosman*, EU:C:1995:463, [1995] ECRI-4921, points 98 and 99.

64 Case C-442/02, *Caixa-Bank France*, EU:C:2004:586, [2004] ECR 1-8961.

Similar principles were applied in *Berlington*, a case concerning taxes on the operation of slot machines in amusement arcades.[65] The Court held that a tax which is so high that the profit remaining after the deduction of those taxes and expenses would have been non-existent or, at most, minimal, causes a restriction on, in this case, the freedom to provide services. This would in particular be the case if the tax at issue does not apply to other actors on the same market.

A further variation on this theme is provided by *Van der Weegen*,[66] concerning a Belgian exemption for savings interest of individuals applicable without distinction to domestic and foreign savings interest, but requiring compliance with conditions which were *de facto* specific to the Belgian savings accounts market and consequently amounted to an obstacle to foreign service providers offering their banking services in Belgium.[67]

This case law amounts to application, also in substantive matters, of the Court's procedural doctrine of effectiveness of EU law (see section 3.5.2): it should not be made impossible or excessively difficult to access another Member State's market. For the tax area, this case law could imply that internationally restrictive tax rules, such as cumbersome transfer pricing documentation requirements, cannot always be made EU-proof by applying them also domestically if they make it excessively difficult to successfully go abroad, regardless of whether the same obstacle exists domestically, or where they, although not making market access excessively difficult, do not have comparably restrictive effects domestically.[68]

Because the concept of 'discrimination' in the case law of the CJEU on the free movement of persons and of capital has shifted over time, it has conceptually become difficult to imagine restrictive tax measures without distinction (obstacles: nondiscriminatory restrictions), apart from tax measures such as the Belgian exemption in the *Van der Weegen* Case, which are *framed* neutrally, but which *de facto* discriminate against foreign banking service providers, or tax measures like the one in *Berlington* which are so burdensome that they render the exercise of a free movement right almost impossible.[69]

Because of the Court's wide concept of 'discrimination', nationality and origin do not matter much anymore as a comparison criterion. Decisive has become the comparison between the cross-border position and a comparable domestic position, irrespective of the nationality of the economic operator or emigrant or the origin of the capital. Origin (source, territoriality) does, however, play an important role at the stage of justifying discriminatory tax measures: Member States may take measures to protect their tax base. i.e. to ensure that income generated within their territory can be taxed by them. For instance, if one were to judge exit taxes upon emigration of taxpayers on the basis

65 Compare outside the area of taxation Case C-384/93, *Alpine Investments*, EU:C:1995:126, [1995] ECR I-1141; Case C-110/05, *Commission v Italy*, EU:C:2009:66, [2009] ECR I-519; and Case 107/83, *Klopp*, EU:C:1984:270, [1984] ECR 2791.

66 Case C-580/15, *Van der Weegen a.o. v Belgium*, EU:C:2017:429.

67 Compare also Case C-342/20, *A SCPI*, EU:C:2022:276, points 54 et seq; Case C-156/17, *Köln-Aktienfonds Deka*, EU:C:2020:51, points 55-56; Case C-18/23, *Dyrektor Krajowej Informacji Skarbowej (Mode de gestion d'un OPC)*, EU:C:2025:119, points 65 et seq.

68 Compare Case C-250/95, *Futura Participations and Singer*, on non-discriminatory bookkeeping requirements.

69 Case C-98/14, Berlington, EU:C:2015:386, points 39-41. Compare outside the area of taxation Case C-384/93, *Alpine Investments*, EU:C:1995:126, [1995] ECR I-1141; Case C-110/05, *Commission v Italy*, EU:C:2009:66, [2009] ECR I-519; and Case 107/83, *Klopp*, EU:C:1984:270, [1984] ECR 2791.

of a nationality or origin criterion, then one would conclude that such taxes are not discriminatory, as they mostly affect own nationals rather than nationals of other Member States. Still, exit taxes manifestly divide the internal market into national parts, directly hindering emigration, and therefore restrict free movement. Consequently, where a Greek resident wishes to leave Athens in order to establish herself in Barcelona, the Court does not look at nationality (except to ensure that she has some EU nationality), but compares her tax position, both under Greek law and under Spanish/Catalan law, with a comparable domestic position: in Greece, the exit tax connected to her emigration will be compared to the Greek tax position of someone moving from Athens to Chania, and in Spain, her tax position will be compared to that of an (economic) operator already resident and subject to tax there. On the basis of *that* comparison, there *is* a discrimination in Greece, as a person moving within Greece is not required to pay, or to provide security for, a tax on unrealized capital gains and pension rights. Greece might argue that for Greek taxation purposes, an Athens-Chania move is not comparable to an Athens-Barcelona move; that a taxpayer leaving the Greek taxing jurisdiction is in a different tax position from a taxpayer staying within the reach of the Greek taxing power, as for the latter there is no necessity for a final tax settlement. But the very idea of an internal market is that moving across an accidental national border within that single internal market should not be taxed less favorably than moving within the same national jurisdiction. In many direct tax cases the Court therefore simply ignores the change in taxing jurisdiction as a relevant difference, at least for its discrimination analysis, and it considers subject-to-tax and not-subject-to-tax (*i.e.* subject to tax in *another* jurisdiction) as comparable. Although a *discrimination* is thus found very easily to exist, this does not mean there is no *justification* for it. Greece may legitimately protect tax claims emanating in its jurisdiction, but it needs to justify its fiscal restrictions on emigration (in this case, it can put forward the need to ensure a balanced allocation of taxing powers), and it may impose only a proportional, that is the least restrictive measure possible to protect its taxing rights as regards the tax claims threatening to disappear from its jurisdiction. In this case, that would be a precautionary exit assessment, with extension of payment until realization of the unrealized gains, and without requiring security for payment (see Case C-470/04, *N. v. Inspecteur*, discussed in Chapter 12). Thus, in its *justification* and *proportionality* analysis, the Court recognizes that to a certain extent, someone moving from Athens to Barcelona is different from someone moving from Athens to Chania, as the former is still fully taxable in Greece for unrealized capital gains and pension rights, whereas the latter has left the Greek taxing jurisdiction for good, disconnecting all tax connecting factors. This is either an objective difference capable of explaining a difference in tax treatment or a justification for such different treatment. See the Case C-371/10, *National Grid Indus*, discussed in Chapter 12.

The Court's wide concept of 'discrimination' in direct tax matters thus leaves little room to prohibit restrictive tax measures without distinction, as prohibiting restrictive but indiscriminate tax measures could lead to prohibiting taxation itself. In principle, *every* tax is restrictive (see section 3.2.7.1). Viewing taxation itself as an in principle prohibited measure – after all, it clearly restricts economic activity – may appeal to some, but implies that Member States should *justify* before the Court of Justice *every* tax they wish to levy. That is arguably not what was intended by the drafters of the Treaty Freedoms. Taxation itself cannot be considered as a restriction of free movement within the meaning of the Treaty Freedoms.[70] That being so, only a Pigouvian tax (German: *Erdrosselungssteuer*: a prohibitively high tax on certain goods or services), such as the one in *Berlington*, discussed above, would seem comparable to the examples provided above of indiscriminate measures nonetheless in principle prohibited for their market access-barring effects. Such taxes would be *in*direct taxes, for that matter. An excessively high (expropriating) *income* tax would already be prohibited by Article 1 Protocol I ECHR[71] (and, if within the scope of EU law, also by Article 17 of the EU Charter).

By contrast, it is very easy to imagine nondiscriminatory direct tax measures which cause double burdens: most of international tax law is concerned with the undoing of international juridical and economical double taxation. If both the source State of the income and the residence State of the recipient tax that income, there clearly is a double burden impeding cross-border work, investment or establishment, but there is no discrimination, as the source State also taxes such income in the hands of its residents, and the residence State also taxes such income if sourced domestically. Such *double burden* problem, although clearly restricting the functioning of the internal market, cannot be solved by the Court on the basis of primary EU law, as it is not attributable to just one of the States, but to parallel exercise of neutrally defined taxing rights, and primary EU law does not contain any indication which of the two States' taxing rights should take priority over the other (see section 3.2.7). Mutual recognition (the consumer State should not impose a second regulatory burden on goods and services that have satisfactorily been regulated in the origin State; see sections 3.2.1.2 and 6.5.2) does not work for taxation, as the division of taxing power between the source and the residence State is far from univocal, and it is object of both bilateral (tax treaty) negotiation and unilateral delineation of jurisdiction. Even if the Court would like to give priority to the source principle over the nationality principle, the territoriality principle or the residence principle (for which there is, however, no legal basis in primary EU law), it is not always easy and sometimes impossible to clearly point out the source, especially as regards passive income from mobile capital and derivates.

The only possibility for the Court to reduce such remaining international double tax burden (which, for that matter, has already been reduced very considerably by the division of taxing power in bilateral tax treaties between the Member States) is to adopt – on the basis of the nondiscrimination rule embodied in the free movement rights of the TFEU – the 'internal consistency' requirement which the US Supreme Court applies on the basis of the (dormant) 'interstate commerce clause' in the US Constitution. That clause represents a comparable concept as the EU free movement rights. In *Comptroller v Wynne*,[72] a heavily divided US Supreme Court required the US States to apply the same system as a *residence* State as they apply in their capacity as a *source* State and *vice*

70 Case C-134/03, *Viacom Outdoor*, EU:C:2005:94, [2005] ECR I-01167.

71 See the ECtHR cases of 14 May 2013, No. 66529/11, *N.K.M. v. Hungary*, ECLI:CE:ECHR:2017:1114DEC004618416, 2 July 2013, No. 41838/11, *R.Sz. v. Hungary*, ECLI:CE:ECHR:2013:0702JUD004183811, and 25 juni 2013, No. 49570/11, *Gáll v. Hungary* ECLI:CE:ECHR:2013:0625JUD004957011.

72 US Supreme Court, *Comptroller (Maryland) v. Wynne*, 18 May 2015, *docket no.* 13-485.

versa ('internal consistency'):[73] they may apply, as a source State, the source principle, and therefore tax nonresidents' income sourced within their territory, but if they do, they will have to acknowledge the source principle also in their capacity as residence State, meaning that they will have to prevent double taxation in respect of out-of-State income of their residents (by crediting the source State's tax). Inversely, if they do not wish to credit the source tax on their residents' out-of-State income because they feel the residence principle prevails, then they will have to refrain from taxing nonresidents' income sourced within their territory, as they will then need to recognize the priority of the residence State which they claim themselves as well in their capacity of residence State. The Swiss federal court secures single taxation among the Swiss cantons on the basis of the territoriality principle: it divides taxing rights between the cantons on the basis of the question which territory has the strongest links with the income to be taxed. In contrast to the CJEU and the USSC, however, the Swiss federal court can rely on an explicit prohibition of inter-cantonal double taxation in the Swiss Constitution (which does not, however, provide the necessary allocation criteria, necessitating the federal court to develop its own criterion: territoriality).[74] The CJEU has not ventured into any such daring approach, however. It allows Member States to apply worldwide taxation to residents and source taxation to nonresidents – probably reasoning that source taxation is not less favourable than worldwide taxation – and it considers possibly ensuing international double taxation to be a result (nondiscriminatory) 'parallel exercise of taxing power' by two different Member States (see Chapters 6.2 and 8.1.2).

For elaboration on the discrimination and obstacle approaches in tax matters, see section 3.2.7.1.

3.2.1.2 Permissible Restrictions on Free Movement; the Rule of Reason

Given the origins of the Union as a free *trade* area, the foremost important Treaty Freedom was the free movement of goods (Arts. 28-37). Especially the customs union is a cornerstone of the Union. The free movement of goods encompasses:

- Abolition of all tariff barriers at intra-EU borders; a total prohibition of customs duties and of any charges having an effect equivalent to a customs duty (Arts. 28-33) (see section 2.2.2.2); and
- Abolition of all non-tariff barriers at intra-EU borders: abolition of quantitative import restrictions and all measures having an effect equivalent to import restrictions (Arts. 34-37).

These prohibitions have direct effect and can therefore be relied on by individuals and undertakings before national courts in order to invalidate incompatible domestic legislation and administrative practice. The first prohibition outlaws all unilateral pecuniary

73 Ruth Mason already in 2008 recommended the internal consistency test for the EU: Ruth Mason, 'Made in America for European Tax: the Internal Consistency Test', 5 Boston College law Review XLIX (November 2008), p. 1277-1326.

74 See, for a comparison of the judicial policies as regards double taxation of the USSC, the Swiss federal court and the CJEU, Anne van de Vijver, 'International Double Taxation in the European Union: Comparative Guidelines from Switzerland and the United States', EC Tax Review 2017/1, p. 10-22.

charges, however small, on the border-crossing of goods. It is immaterial whether or not the charge has the goal or the effect of protecting domestic production. The decisive question is whether there is, in fact or potentially, a restrictive effect on intra-Union trade, however small. For example, the levying of 'statistics duties' at the border is not permitted, not even if they are levied indiscriminately on imported and exported goods, and not even if the proceeds are used solely to pay for the cost of drawing up import and export statistics. Such costs, made for public interest reasons, should be paid out of general public resources.[75] The ban on quantitative restrictions and measures having the same effect, in principle prohibits:

> 'all trading rules enacted by Member States which are capable of hindering, directly or indirectly, actually or potentially, intra-Community trade.'[76]

That is a very broad prohibition. Too broad, really, as the Court recognized. Obviously, a national campaign like 'Buy Irish!' is prohibited,[77] but the Court's prohibition went much further. It pussyfooted around the unmanageable consequences of its unlimited prohibition for some time. It hesitated for years, *e.g.*, about national rules prohibiting shops to open on Sundays. Obviously, mandatory shop closure one non-working day a week restricts trade, and therefore also intra-Union trade, but the measure is neutral, and its rationale has no relation whatsoever with trade conditions, competition or market access. Finally, in the landmark *Keck* and *Mithouard* case,[78] the Court held that national selling arrangements (such as mandatory shop closure on Sundays, or restricted sale of certain goods, *e.g.* alcohol only in government shops, pornography only in certain areas, petrol sales only outside city centres, etc.) fall outside the ambit of Article 34 if the prescribed mode of sale has exactly the same effect on trade in imported goods as it has on trade in domestic products. The trade effect of such neutral modes of sale was too general and remote to be covered by the Treaty Freedoms (*rule of remoteness*).[79] A fiscal example is the *Krantz* case discussed in section 3.2.3. The Court subsequently slightly changed its language, however, in *Ker-Optika*,[80] holding that in general, any market access hindrance, also selling arrangements, is within the ambit of Article 34 TFEU, unless it is shown that they have the same effect on domestic and cross-border trade. The evidential presumption was thus reversed:[81] instead of the economic operator having to show adverse effects, the Member State concerned must demonstrate neutrality.

Apart from this *Keck*-rule, there are two other escapes from the prohibition on restrictions on the free movement of goods: Article 36 TFEU and the CJEU-made *rule of reason*. Article 36 allows restrictions on intra-Union trade, even if they distinguish between imported goods and domestic goods, if one of the justification grounds listed therein

75 Case 24/68, *Commission v. Italy*, EU:C:1969:29, [1969] ECR 193.

76 Case 8/74, *Dassonville*, EU:C:1974:82, [1974] ECR 837.

77 Case 249/81, *Commission v. Ireland*, EU:C:1982:402, [1982] ECR 4005.

78 Joined Cases C-267 and 268/91, *Keck and Mithouard*, EU:C:1993:905, [1993] ECR I-6097.

79 See, for a more straightforward application of this remoteness rule, *e.g.* Case C-93/92, *CMC Motorradcenter*, EU:C:1993:838, [1993] ECR I-5009.

80 Case C-108/09, *Ker-Optika*, EU:C:2010:725.

81 See: Gareth Davies, 'Between market access and discrimination: free movement as a right to fair conditions of competition', in: Panos Koutrakos/Jukka Snell (eds.), *Research Handbook on the Law of the EU's Internal Market*, Edward Elgar Publishing, 2017, p. 19.

applies: public morality, public policy, public security, protection of life and health of humans, animals or plants, protection of national artistic, historic or archaeological treasures, and protection of industrial and commercial property. Trade restrictions are justified on these grounds if they are necessary for these goals and do not go any further than necessary (proportionality), and only as long as no (exhaustive) Union measures have come into force protecting these interests. For instance, a restrictive rule on food safety may in itself be justified in the interest of public health, but it may not be an unnecessary duplication of an adequate safety measure already taken in the Member State of origin of the foodstuffs. It is unlikely, for instance, Estonians would fall ill of imported *pasta di grano duro* if the Italians have been eating that same pasta for centuries without any apparent health drawbacks. In such cases, the concept of *mutual recognition* is applied: if foodstuffs have been legally produced and checked for human consumption in one Member State, then the other Member States must in principle accept the origin State's approval. Destination State superimposition of duplicating rules and checks is disproportionate. Similarly, if a dentist has been educated, qualified and practicing in Germany, then France must recognize his professional skills and qualifications and may not require him to go to dental school all over again in France if he wishes to open practice in France. France may require him to demonstrate that his skills are comparable to the skill required in France, and it may require him to show that his French is good enough to communicate adequately with patients, however. If a company meets all legal requirements imposed by its Member State of incorporation, then the host State must recognize its legal personality and *locus standi* (see the *Überseering* Case[82] discussed in section 12.3).

The Court seems to apply mutual recognition sometimes also in tax matters. In the VAT case *Gaston Schul I*[83] it held that although the Member State of import of a second-hand boat may levy VAT to equalize the tax burden on imported and domestic second-hand goods, it must credit the residual foreign VAT still present in the second-hand value of the boat. In *Lenz* and *Manninen* (see Chapter 11.2.5), the Court *de facto* required Member States to recognize and credit foreign corporation tax as if it were their own. In *Futura Participations*,[84] it required Luxembourg to recognize the accounts of a French company with a Luxembourg branch as a valid basis to calculate losses attributable to the Luxembourg branch. See also section 6.5.2. As observed, however, mutual recognition is not very helpful in direct tax matters, as there is no origin State and destination State, but rather a source State and a residence State, and EU law contains no clue on whether the source jurisdiction or the residence jurisdiction has the prior right to tax income.

The CJEU applies Article 36 strictly. In principle, it does not accept justifications not mentioned, especially not justifications of an economic nature. However, recognizing that Article 36 (and also the escapes in the Treaty provisions on the other free movement rights) is framed too narrowly to simply prohibit all public interest restrictions not mentioned therein, the Court also allows unwritten reasons of public interest for restricting free movement rights under its so-called *rule of reason*, a concept first developed by the Court in its *Cassis de Dijon* judgment.[85] Under the rule of reason, a restrictive national

82 Case C-208/00, *Überseering*, EU:C:2002:632.
83 Case 15/81, *Gaston Schul I*, EU:C:1982:135, [1982] ECR 1409.
84 Case C-250/95, *Futura Participations SA and Singer*, EU:C:1997:239.
85 Case 120/78, *Rewe Zentrale AG v. Bundesmonopolverwaltung für Branntwein*, EU:C:1979:42, [1979] ECR 649, commonly called *Cassis de Dijon*.

measure not mentioned in the Treaty, is nonetheless acceptable if (i) it is necessary to protect a legitimate public interest, (ii) it does not distinguish between domestic and comparable imported goods and (iii) its restrictive effects do not go any further than necessary to protect that legitimate interest (proportionality). The reason for the strict non-discrimination requirement is that if a Member State does not consider its own products to be harmful to, *e.g.*, the environment, then it is difficult to see what reasonable grounds that same Member State could have for considering identical or similar products from other Member States to be so harmful to the environment as to justify a restriction on their importation.

3.2.2 *Rule of Reason Justifications for (Fiscal) Market Restrictions*

The Court usually calls acceptable reasons for trade restrictions 'mandatory (or 'imperative') requirements of public interest.' The Court's rule of reason test – in its most extensive configuration, *i.e.* in the field of free movement of goods – consists of eight steps:

i. Does the person relying on the free movement rights have access to them? Does he have sufficient Treaty status (see section 3.1.3 above)?
ii. Has the object of the impugned national measure been (exhaustively) harmonized at EU level? If so, individual Member States are no longer permitted to impose other rules, and the Treaty freedoms are in principle not relevant, as the national measure will then be assessed in the light of the secondary EU law (the EU Directive): is the national measure correct implementation of the Directive? If there is no such (exhaustive) harmonisation:
iii. Does the impugned national measure restrict cross-border trade by distinguishing between domestic and imported goods? If so, it cannot be upheld (except possibly under Article 36 or another Treaty-based escape). If not:
iv. Does the national measure, despite being applicable without distinction (therefore providing for national treatment (nondiscrimination)), restrict trade by creating 'obstacles' to trade (e.g. nondiscriminatory, but different product safety, diploma or certification requirements from the ones in the origin State, causing a double regulatory or administrative burden)? If so:
v. Does the legislation of the origin State, despite being different from the domestic rules, provide equivalent protection of the public interest at stake (public health, consumer protection, the environment, etc.)? If so, the Member State of destination may not impose its own different and hindering measure (mutual recognition). In direct tax matters, this test is not relevant, and is replaced by:
vi. Is the aim of the restrictive measure legitimate? Is the policy goal of the measure a 'mandatory requirement of public interest', which can in principle outweigh free movement rights? The Court has accepted as sufficiently vital a number of public interests not listed in the free movement provisions, such as consumer protection, prevention of unfair competition, protection of the environment, improvement of working conditions, road safety, product safety, the promotion of culture, the safeguarding of political diversity of the media and freedom of speech, the protection of (other) fundamental rights, etc. Mere economic and budgetary policy goals are generally not accepted as mandatory requirements of public interest. As regards free

movement restricting tax measures, until now five justifications seem to have been accepted. Conceptually, these may be reduced to two or even to one single justification: the need for safeguarding ***tax base integrity*** (see for elaboration Chapter 7):

- the need for effective fiscal supervision (national tax administrations must be enabled to be effective) was accepted, a.o., in *Cassis de Dijon*,[86] and *Passenheim-Van Schoot*[87] for restrictive checks necessary for the *assessment* of taxes. A similar justification was accepted in *Scorpio*:[88] 'the need to ensure the effective *collection* of income tax.' The latter justification may have lost scope after the inclusion of tax claims in the Recovery Assistance Directive[89] (see Chapter 30), although *Truck Center*[90] and *National Grid Indus*[91] seem to reiterate it;
- the need to protect fiscal (territorial) coherence (or 'cohesion'):[92] the need to match, within the same taxing jurisdiction, tax base reductions and corresponding tax base increases, such as loss relief and taxation of the corresponding profits, deduction of annuity contributions and future taxation of the annuity benefits, taxation of income and deduction of the expenses incurred in earning it, untaxed accrual of capital gains and taxation of those gains upon realization, etc. In recent cases, the Court also refers to the principle of 'symmetry',[93] and to the fiscal 'territoriality' principle.[94] This justification is often difficult to distinguish from the balanced allocation of taxing power (see below).[95]
- 'the fiscal principle of territoriality',[96] *i.e.* the right of a Member State to tax income generated by economic activity within its territory. Possibly, however, the Court refers to the international public law principle of territoriality (which differs from the international tax law territoriality concept of *source* taxation), i.e. to effectuation of the usual (OECD) nexuses of international taxation, i.e. *worldwide* jurisdiction as regards residents and source jurisdiction only as regards nonresidents. Clearly, advocate-general Bobek understands 'territoriality' in this

86 See the previous footnote.

87 Joined Cases C-155/08 and C-157/08, *X. and Passenheim-Van Schoot*, EU:C:2009:368, [2009] ECR I-5093.

88 Case C-290/04, *FKP Scorpio Konzertproduktionen GmbH*, EU:C:2006:630, [2006] ECR I-9461.

89 See paragraph 36 of *Scorpio* and paragraphs 35 and 37 of Case C-520/04, *Pirkko Marjatta Turpeinen*, EU:C:2006:703, [2006] ECR I-10685.

90 Case C-282/07, *Truck Center*, EU:C:2008:762, [2008] ECR I-10767, point 47.

91 Case C-371/10, *National Grid Indus BV*, EU:C:2011:785.

92 Recognized for the first time in Case C-204/90, *Bachmann v. Belgium*, EU:C:1992:35, [1992] ECR I-249.

93 Case C-157/07, *Krankenheim Ruhesitz am Wannsee-Seniorenheimstatt*, EU:C:2008:588, [2008] ECR I-8061.

94 Case C-470/04, *N. v. Inspecteur*, EU:C:2006:525, [2006] ECRI-7409, and Case C-157/07, *Krankenheim Ruhesitz am Wannsee-Seniorenheimstatt*, EU:C:2008:588, [2008] ECR I-8061.

95 See Peter J. Wattel: 'Fiscal Cohesion, Fiscal territoriality and preservation of the (Balanced) Allocation of taxing Power; What is the Difference?', in Dennis Weber (ed.), *The Influence of European Law on Direct Taxation; Recent and Future Developments*, Kluwer Law international, 2007, p. 139-156.

96 Recognized by the Court in. a.o., Case C-250/95, *Futura*, EU:C:1997:239, [1997] ECR I-2471, and Case C-446/03, *Marks & Spencer II*, EU:C:2005:763, [2005] ECR I-10837.

non-tax way.[97] Like advocate-general Bobek, we find it difficult to distinguish this territoriality principle from:

- the need to protect a balanced allocation of taxing power.[98] This justification seems to be the most important one, not only overlapping with the need for fiscal coherence, but especially with what the Court calls the fiscal principle of territoriality. Apparently, it refers to what has been coined 'BEPS' in OECD circles (base erosion and profit shifting), i.e. to the need to prevent that tax base generated within a jurisdiction is eroded or shifted elsewhere through, *e.g.*, loss trafficking, hybrid mismatches, interest and royalty deductions, etc.;
- the need to prevent abuse of rights, especially 'wholly artificial arrangements', which 'do not reflect economic reality.'[99] We believe this justification to be encompassed by the wider category(ies) of fiscal coherence and/or a balanced allocation of taxing rights (and/or the fiscal territoriality principle), as abusive tax avoidance mostly consists of the *intentional* and *artificial* creating or benefiting of fiscal incoherences and imbalances (BEPS: base erosion and profit shifting). See Chapter 7 for elaboration. In *Felixtowe*,[100] the Court referred to 'the objective of fighting tax havens' as a justification for restricting free movement, but we consider that a specimen of the abuse type justification.

All other attempted justifications for discriminatory tax measures have been rejected. Unsuccessful were, amongst others, the need to prevent gambling addiction, divorces and suicides,[101] administrative difficulties in obtaining information from abroad (the Member States should use the Directive on Administrative Assistance),[102] alleged or real compensating advantages for disadvantage suffered by nonresidents (the Treaty freedoms require *equal* treatment),[103] the *de minimis* argument (the Treaty Freedoms prohibit all discriminations, also minor ones),[104] and loss of tax revenue (as observed: economic policy goals are not recognized as mandatory requirements of public interest);

vii. Is the restrictive measure at issue suitable (appropriate) for the protection of the public interest stated? Is it effective; does it make sense or is it (hopelessly) underinclusive (ineffective)? If it is not suitable, then it is arbitrary and therefore disproportionate. If it is suitable to reach the legitimate aim envisaged:

viii. Is the measure proportionate stricto sensu in its restrictive effects in relation to the legitimate aim pursued? Are there no equally effective measures to attain the legitimate aim which would be less restrictive to free movement? Is it overinclusive (overkill)?

97 Opinion of 14 December 2017 in Case C-382/16, *Hornbach-Baumarkt AG*, EU:C:2017:974.

98 See, a.o., Case C-231/05, *Oy AA*, EU:C:2007:439, [2007] ECR I-6373, and Case C-470/04, *N. v. Inspecteur*, EU:C:2006:525, [2006] ECR I-7409.

99 *E.g.* Case C-196/04, *Cadbury Schweppes*, EU:C:2006:544, [2006] ECR I-7995.

100 Case C-80/12, *Felixstowe Dock and Railway Company Ltd a.o.*, EU:C:2014:200, point 32.

101 Case C-42/02, *Diana Elisabeth Lindman*, EU:C:2003:613, [2003] ECR I-13519, concerning a Swedish tax on foreign lottery prizes.

102 *E.g.* Case 204/90, *Bachmann*, EU:C:1992:35, [1992] ECR I-249.

103 *E.g.* the Avoir Fiscal Case 270/83, *Commission v France*, EU:C:1986:37, [1986] ECR 273; and Case C-330/91, *The Queen v Inland Revenue Commissioners, ex parte Commerzbank AG*, EU:C:1993:303, [1993] ECR I-4017.

104 *E.g.*, again, the *Avoir Fiscal* Case 270/83, *Commission v. French Republic*, EU:C:1986:37. [1986] ECR 273.

Here, the Court is most at risk to take political decisions rather than political ones, but it is the test most flunked by discriminatory national direct tax measures, which often succeed in passing the justifiability test and the suitability test.

Despite their different wordings, the Court applies all four Treaty Freedoms in the same manner (converging interpretation), as they all serve the same overall goal (free movement; a level internal market), as well as for practicability and legal certainty reasons. Therefore, for daily use, the Court summarized its *rule of reason* test for all Treaty Freedoms in four criteria in its *Gebhard* judgment[105] (on the free movement of persons, but in this respect relating to all fundamental freedoms) (indents added):

> '37. It follows [...] from the Court's case law that national measures liable to hinder or make less attractive the exercise of fundamental freedoms guaranteed by the Treaty must fulfil four conditions:
> – they must be applied in a non-discriminatory manner;
> – they must be justified by imperative requirements in the general interest;
> – they must be suitable for securing the attainment of the objective which they pursue; and
> – they must not go beyond what is necessary in order to attain it (...).'

The Rule of reason in Direct Tax Matters

For (direct) tax purposes, the Court's rule of reason may be summarized in a slightly different four-step test (well ..., three-step, really, as the first two steps are part of one comparability analysis):

(1a) A *prima facie* comparability test: does the national tax measure *prima facie* distinguish between cross-border investment/work/establishment and comparable domestic investment/establishment/work (resident/nonresident; emigrant/non-emigrant; domestic-source income/foreign-source income, etc.)?[106] If it does not, then – and this is important – in principle the analysis stops here: the Court does not seem to require justifications (anymore) for tax measures, much as they may be restrictive, if they are nondiscriminatory. If the measure falls foul of this test, the Court applies:

(1b) A teleological comparability test: is there an objective difference between the cross-border and the internal case which explains the difference in tax treatment of the cross-border case? Conceptually, this test coincides with the test of whether the two positions are still comparable when judged in the light of *object* and *purpose* of the impugned tax measure (e.g. avoiding economic double taxation, or consolidating profits and losses of companies which form a group, or bureaucratic simplicity of administration). For instance, in *Timac Agro*,[107] the Court accepted different treatment of foreign and domestic secondary establishment in respect of branch loss relief, as domestic branches were subject to tax domestically and foreign branches were

105 Case C-55/94, *Reinhard Gebhard*, EU:C:1995:411, [1995] ECR I-4165.

106 Note that a *prima facie* discrimination may also be present if two cross-border situations are treated differently (Case C-194/06, *Orange European Smallcap Fund*, EU:C:2008:289, point 56; Case C-512/13, *Sopora* EU:C:2015:108, point 25 or when a subsidiary is treated worse than a permanent establishment (Case C-436/23, *Volvo Group Belgium*, EU:C:2024:1023, points 22 et seq.).

107 Case C-388/14, *Timac Agro Deutschland GmbH*, EU:C:2015:829.

not (from a corporate income tax point of view, subject-to-tax is not comparable to not-subject-to-tax), and in *SGI*,[108] it accepted that Belgian anti-BEPS measures were only applied cross-border, as the BEPS-effect could only occur cross-border. Another example concerns case law on the taxation of investment funds, where the Court examines comparability in the light of the objective of treating direct and indirect investment equally.[109] On a closer look, therefore, despite a *prima facie* discrimination against cross-border investment/work being present, the measure is eventually not discriminatory, meaning – and this is important again – that no justification is required and the analysis stops here, as internationally neutral tax measures will not be repudiated for being merely restrictive (as *every* tax is restrictive in respect of the economic activity taxed. It is true, however, that the Court is notorious for mixing up this step (objective comparability) and the next step (justifiability of the – discriminatory – measure.

If there still is a discrimination present, viewed in light of the aim of the national tax measure at issue, the Court applies:

(2) A justification test: is there a mandatory requirement of public interest (a legitimate aim) justifying the discriminatory measure, *e.g.* curbing abuse, safeguarding tax base integrity, or ensuring effective fiscal supervision? If so, the Court applies:
(3) A proportionality test: is the discriminatory, but justifiable tax measure effective (appropriateness subtest) and does it not restrict free movement beyond what is necessary to attain its legitimate aim (proportionality *stricto sensu*)?

As observed, the Court wanders between steps 1b and 2, often presenting incomparability as a justification for (in our view) non-existent discrimination. This may be the echo of the Court's reflex in trade (free movement of goods and services) to consider *every* measure which hinders the exercise of Treaty freedoms as in principle prohibited, irrespective of whether it distinguishes between domestic and cross-border trade. Sometimes the Court realizes in time that in direct tax matters, nondiscriminatory measures are best steered clear from; sometimes it does not. But there may also be judicial policy reasons behind the Court's ostensible confusion of the discrimination analysis and the justification analysis.

Restrictive/discriminatory national measures, whether fiscal or otherwise, are most of the times disqualified not on the absence of a legitimate aim, but on the disproportionateness of their restrictive effects. Usually, a Member State can put forward quite laudable reasons for its restrictive measure, such as consumer protection, prevention of gaming or alcohol addiction, prevention of abuse of rights or affordability of public health insurance, but often, closer scrutiny reveals that the measure is either not the most suitable for the stated purpose (and therefore, sometimes other motives may be surmised), or it has (much) more restrictive effects on cross-border trade/investment/work than necessary for the stated legitimate aim.

For instance, a *general* requirement that the entire ship's crew be UK resident and that all ship surveys be carried out in the UK (also for vessels *not* fishing for quota-assigned

108 Case C-459/17, *Société de Gestion Industrielle (SGI)*, EU:C:2010:26.
109 See for instance Case C-156/17, *Deka*, EU:C:2020:51, points 76 et seq.

fish), is unsuitable for protecting fish quota in respect of only *specific types of fish.*[110] And an exit tax on unrealized capital gains upon emigration of a shareholder is in itself an appropriate measure to serve the legitimate aim of fiscal territorial coherence between the untaxed accrual of the gain and taxation of the future realization of the gain (and, therefore, of curbing tax avoidance by emigration), but it is disproportionate to require immediate cash payment at the border, as the gain has not been realized yet. *N. v. Inspecteur*[111] shows that even if the exit State grants extension of payment, but requires security for payment upon later realization, the measure is still considered disproportionate, as the exit State may rely on the Recovery Assistance Directive (see Chapter 30) to request the immigration State to collect the deferred tax upon later realization of the capital gain. That case may, however, have been overtaken on this point by *National Grid Indus*[112] and *DMC,*[113] accepting a security requirement upon emigration of companies if it is proportionate to the risk of non-payment, and C-503/14, *Commission v Portugal,*[114] in which the Court stated that there should be no difference (anymore) between exit taxation of natural persons and exit taxation of legal persons (see for elaboration Chapter 12).

3.2.3 (Rare) Examples of Direct Tax Measures Affecting Free Trade in Goods; French Newspapers and Krantz

For direct taxes, the free movement of capital and of persons (workers, entrepreneurs, and economically inactive (especially pensioners)) are by far the most important, but the free movement of goods may affect national direct tax measures as well. Two cases to illustrate this: Case 18/84, *Commission v France,*[115] concerned a French tax measure allowing political opinion publishers to form a tax-free reserve for the acquisition of equipment or buildings necessary for such publishing, or to deduct from their tax base payments for that purpose. National law also provided that 'publishing houses shall not benefit (from such tax relief) in respect of any part of their publications printed abroad'. The civil servant drafting this clause probably missed his EU law classes. Obviously, the CJEU found the French measure urged French publishing houses to have their printing done in France rather than abroad, manifestly obstructing intra-Union trade. No justification being present, the measure was prohibited for being effectively equivalent to a quantitative import restriction.

The *Krantz* case[116] concerned the Netherlands Tax Recovery Act, which empowers the Tax Collector to seize moveable business equipment used on the business premises of a defaulting taxpayer, even if those goods are not the taxpayer's property (the 'right of soil'). The German company *Krantz GmbH* had sold machines to a Dutch company on instalment terms under reservation of its property title to secure payment. The Dutch company

110 See, e.g. Case C-213/89, *Factortame I*, EU:C:1990:257, [1990] ECR I-2433.

111 Case C-470/04, *N. v. Inspecteur*, EU:C:2006:525, [2006] ECR I-7409.

112 Case C-371/10, *National Grid Indus BV*, EU:C:2011:785.

113 Case C-164/12, *DMC Beteiligungsgesellschaft mbH*, EU:C:2014:20.

114 Case C-503/14, *Commission v Portugal* (exit tax), EU:C:2016:979.

115 Case 18/84, *Commission v. France* (Tax advantages for newspaper publishers), EU:C:1985:175, [1985] ECR 1339.

116 Case C-69/88, *H. Krantz GmbH & Co. v. Ontvanger der directe belastingen*, EU:C:1990:97, [1990] ECR I–583.

went bankrupt, leaving the Tax Collector, Krantz and other creditors unpaid. Ignoring Krantz's reservation of title, the Collector seized and sold the machines. Krantz argued that this measure (potentially) hampered intra-Union trade, as foreign suppliers would be reluctant to sell equipment on instalment terms to undertakings in the Netherlands as their reservation of title would be worthless *vis-à-vis* the tax authorities. The Court considered that the Collector's 'right of soil' applied without distinction to both domestic and imported moveable business assets, that it did not seek to control trade with other Member States, and that a noticeable restrictive effect on intra-Union trade was unlikely. The possibility that foreign suppliers would be reluctant to sell equipment on instalment terms to purchasers in the Netherlands because of the risk of attachment by the Tax Collector in case of non-payment of tax due by the purchaser was too uncertain and indirect to consider the right of soil liable to render trade with Netherlands' purchasers less attractive (*rule of remoteness;* see also section 3.2.1.2).

3.2.4 Direct Taxation and the Freedom to Provide (and Purchase) Services

The freedom of services (Arts 56–62 TFEU) can be distinguished from the free movement of goods in that services are intangible. From the text of Article 57 it appears that the freedom of services is complemental to the free movement of goods, persons and capital: if one of the latter freedoms is applicable, the freedom to provide services in principle is not, but the Court is not always consistent in the order of application or the four freedoms. The freedom to provide services is needed as a separate category because cross-border provision of services may take place without goods being moved, without relocation of capital and without any (secondary) establishment of an undertaking across the border. This includes such services as banking and insurance, data transmission, booking and other tourism services, broadcasting services, internet mail order services, telephone, television and the provision, via the internet, of digitalized 'goods' (or services?), such as (big) data, software, music, film and, with 3D-printing, even physical objects. With e-commerce, the digitalization of the economy and the possibility of 3D-printing, the distinctions between goods, capital and services is being blurred.

The freedom to *provide* services encompasses a right, for the service provider, to enter the markets of other Member States (market *access*; this may encompass mutual recognition) and a right to be treated in the same manner as domestic service providers on that market (market *equality*). It has direct effect and can therefore be relied on before national courts. The freedom has a wide ambit. It extends to the *purchaser* of services: it includes the rights to move to the Member State of the service provider in order to collect the service there, and to national treatment in that other State. Tourists from other Member States may not be treated differently from national tourists, as they are consumers of the freedom to provide services. Unacceptable therefore are, *e.g.*, reduced museum admittance fees only for domestic students or domestic elderly,[117] or the refusal, by a national violence victims' relief fund, to pay damages to an uninsured foreign tourist falling victim of a traffic accident or a subway mugging on the grounds that he is not a resident.[118] National direct tax measures falling foul of Article 56 are mostly in the area

117 See, *e.g.* Case C-388/01, *Commission v Italy*, EU:C:2003:30, [2003] ECR I-721.

118 See Case 186/87, *Cowan*, EU:C:1989:47, [1989] ECR 195.

of life insurance services and pensions. Examples of such direct tax cases in which the Court considered the freedom of (insurance) services to be violated are the *Bachmann*,[119] *Safir*,[120] *Danner*[121] and *Skandia and Ramstedt*[122] cases, concerning the (non)deductibility of contributions to foreign annuity or pension contracts, or the taxability of the benefits once the policy expires or the pension becomes payable. The national tax measures in those cases disadvantaged cross-border annuity or pension contracts as compared to domestic contracts, either by refusing or restricting deduction of the contributions or by taxing the contract value before expiration of the policy. See Chapter 20. Other examples of cases in which national direct tax measures were considered incompatible with the freedom of services are the *Eurowings* case,[123] on the unfavourable tax treatment of leasing aircrafts abroad instead of domestically, and the *Svensson and Gustavsson* case[124] on unfavourable treatment of a cross-border mortgage contract (refusal of deduction of the mortgage interest).

3.2.5 The Free Movement of Persons and the Right of Residence

(i) Introduction

The Free Movement of Persons (Arts. 45–55) is the most important free movement right in direct tax matters. The large majority of direct tax cases before the CJEU concerns the compatibility of national tax measures with the free movement of persons. This freedom includes both the freedom for employees to apply for and accept jobs in other Member States, and the right of undertakings, including the self-employed professions, to set themselves up or to open branches, subsidiaries or agencies in other Member States. In respect of employees, the TFEU refers to 'free movement of workers' (Art. 45(1)) and in respect of undertakings and the self-employed to 'the right of establishment' (Arts. 49 and 54). In 1993, also the right of residence of EU citizens was introduced (Arts 20 and 21), producing access to the Treaty freedoms also for individuals of EU nationality whose cross-border move ments are not connected to an economic activity (see Section 3.1.3). The freedom of establishment encompasses equal rights for nationals of other Member States to participate in the capital of companies or firms (Art. 55).

(ii) Free Movement of Workers

This freedom includes both freedom of migration, *i.e.* the right to accept employment abroad, the right to leave one's Member State of origin, the right to enter the job State and the right to live in that other Member State (market access; see Article 45(3)), and a prohibition on discrimination, *i.e.* a prohibition on differential treatment of workers from other Member States in respect of employment, remuneration and other conditions of work (market equality; see Article 45(2)). Regulation (EU) 492/2011 on freedom of

119 Case 204/90, *Bachmann*, EU:C:1992:35, [1992] ECR I-249.
120 Case C-118/96, *Jessica Safir*, EU:C:1998:170, [1998] ECR I-1897.
121 Case C-136/00, *Rolf Dieter Danner*, EU:C:2002:558, [2002] ECR I-8147.
122 Case C-422/01, *Skandia and Ola Ramstedt v. Riksskatteverket*, EU:C:2003:380, [2003] ECR I-6817.
123 Case C-294/97, *Eurowings Luftverkehrs AG*, EU:C:1999:524, [1999] ECR I-7447.
124 Case C-484/93, *Peter Svensson and Lena Gustavsson*, EU:C:1995:379, [1995] ECR I-3955.

movement for workers,[125] which is an elaboration of the equal treatment principle for employees, explicitly states (Art. 7(2)) that workers from other Member States have a right to equal treatment as regards social security benefits *and taxation*. This freedom addresses both the job State and the home State, and, in case of a relocation for taking up a job in another Member State, both the emigration State and the immigration State. like the job State and the immigration State, also the home State and the emigration State are precluded from hindering cross-border employment, *e.g.* by denying personal tax allowances after having taken up employment abroad, or by charging an exit tax upon emigration. The Court interprets the term 'worker' widely: the German student Wallentin, spending his three-week holiday on a work experience with the Church of Sweden, could rely on the free movement of workers to claim a refund of the Swedish wage withholding tax.[126] Article 45 TFEU has direct effect and can therefore be relied on before national courts by individuals to invalidate incompatible national law. Like Article 36 in respect of the circulation of goods, Article 45(3) allows unilateral restrictions on the free movement of workers on grounds of public policy, public security and public health (public morality is not repeated). As with respect to all Treaty Freedoms, the Court's *rule of reason* (see Sections 3.2.1. and 3.2.2. above) further allows restrictions necessary to – proportionally – serve mandatory requirements of public interest not enumerated in the TFEU. However, the Court does not easily accept arguments put forward by Member States to justify differential tax treatment of workers from other Member States or of cross-border employment in comparison to employment within one jurisdiction. In *Renneberg*,[127] for instance, the Court even required the job State to accept deduction of home State mortgage interest financing the home State dwelling of the nonresident employee, even though (i) the applicable tax treaty unequivocally allocated the taxing power as regards real estate exclusively to the home State, meaning that the job State was unable to tax the corresponding (cadastral) income from the house (which *was* taxed in case of residents) and (ii) Mr. Renneberg had not been disadvantaged as a result of working abroad, as his home State did not allow any mortgage interest deduction from employment income, meaning that the Court was *favouring* him as compared to his identical neighbour with the same job in the home State. We believe this case may have been decided wrongly; see Section 3.2.7.3(iv) below.

(iii) The Right of Establishment

This freedom includes the right to take up and carry on activities as a self-employed person and to set up and manage undertakings (market access), as well as the right to treatment as a domestic entrepreneur in the Member State of establishment (market equality). It encompasses both the right to set up a new undertaking (primary establishment) and the right to set up agencies, branches or subsidiaries of existing undertakings (secondary establishment). It addresses both the departure or head office State and the State to which the undertaking or the company seat is transferred or in which a primary or secondary establishment is set up. The right of establishment is conferred upon both individuals

125 Regulation (EU) No 492/2011 of the European Parliament and of the Council of 5 April 2011 on freedom of movement for workers within the Union, O.J. 2011 L 141, p. 1.

126 Case C-169/03, *Florian W. Wallentin v. Riksskatteverket*, EU:C:2004:403, [2004] ECR I-6443.

127 Case C-527/06, *Renneberg*, EU:C:2008:566, [2008] ECR I-7735.

(EU citizens) (Arts 49-53 TFEU) and companies or firms, including all for-profit public or private legal entities, having their registered office, central administration or principal place of business within the Union (Art. 54). The right of establishment has direct effect and may therefore be relied on before national courts in derogation of incompatible national provisions. Nonetheless, in non-harmonized fields Member States retain the power to (proportionally) protect national public interests, especially through professional qualification requirements (*e.g.* diplomas), solvability requirements, etc. (Arts. 52 and 53). These differences in conditions for market access must gradually be eliminated through coordination of national law and administrative practice and through mutual recognition of diplomas and certificates (Art. 53). A general system of mutual recognition of professional qualifications obtained in another Member State has been put in place by Directive 2005/36.[128] For the establishment of, and service provision by lawyers, two specific directives applies.[129] For the banking and insurance sector, a 'single licence' system was introduced, and since the financial crises, much of the banking and insurance (supervision) regulation has been Europeanised.

Such regulation at EU level is positive integration (harmonisation). In this Chapter, however, we are concerned with negative integration by way of the prohibition of restricting free movement. Mutual recognition is at the basis of free movement in the internal market in that the Court requires the Member State of destination to have a very good reason in the general interest (the rule of reason; see Sections 3.2.1.2 and 3.2.2) to hinder market access of products, service providers and undertakings which are legally marketed or operating on their home State market.[130] The Member State of destination will have to recognize the regulatory system of the origin State and grant market access if it is not *necessary* and *proportionate* in the general interest to restrict access.[131] This is the case not only in respect of goods and services, but also in respect of persons, i.e. in respect of diplomas, certificates and licenses issued in another Member State.[132] Member State A may not, *e.g.*, require a dentist trained in State B, wishing to open practice in State A, to start all over again in a State A dental school as if his training in State B had been for plumbing. It may, however, require that they speak the language enough to understand the patient explaining which tooth hurts. Thus, if the destination State sees gaps in the qualifications, skills or experience acquired abroad, it may set additional requirements, but only to the extent these are necessary for protecting weighty reasons of public interest, such as public health. It must accept the foreign regulatory system in so far as it maintains standards which are equivalent to its own. The clearest example of mutual recognition in a field relevant for direct taxation, especially exit taxation (see Chapter 12), is mutual recognition of foreign legal entities. Member States of destination cannot require

128 Directive 2005/36/EC of the European Parliament and of the Council of 7 September 2005 on the recognition of professional qualifications, O.J. 2005, L 255, p. 22.

129 Directives 98/5/EC of 16 February 1998, O.J. 1998, L77, p. 36 (establishment), and 77/249/EEC of 22 March 1077, O.J. 1977, L 78, p. 17 (services).

130 See on mutual recognition in the internal market in general: Wulf-Henning Roth, 'Mutual recognition', in Panos Koutrakos, Jukka Snell (ed.), *Research Handbook on the Law of the EU's Internal Market*, Edward Elgar Publishing, 2017, p. 427-459.

131 See Case 120/78, *Rewe-Zentral*, EU:C:1979:42, Case C-110/05, *Commission v Italy*, EU:C:2009:66, and Case C-108/09, *Ker-Optika*, EU:C:2010:725.

132 See e.g. Case C-442/02, *CaixaBanque France*, EU:C:2004:586 and Case C-340/89, *Vlassopoupou*, EU:C:1991:193.

companies to reincorporate in their jurisdiction if the original jurisdiction of incorporation allows companies to transfer their seat without losing their legal personality, and origin States cannot terminate the legal personality of their companies on the occasion of a seat transfer abroad if the jurisdiction of destination recognises their legal personality and accepts its continuation under local law (cross-border transformation), unless there are weighty reasons in the general interest for doing so.[133]

It is not always clear whether a (cross-border) shareholding in a company is covered by the right of establishment or by the free movement of capital or by both. That distinction is not very relevant within the Union, as capital movement and payments have been fully liberalized since 1994, and as the Court interprets the four Treaty Freedoms in the same manner because they serve the same goal. However, the distinction between establishment and capital may be crucial in relation to third States, as the free movement of capital is the only Treaty Freedom which also extends to third States (see Article 63(2)). If an economic operator is merely making a portfolio investment, the free movement of capital applies, whereas the right of establishment is involved if he is in a position to exert definite influence on the management of the company involved. 'Definite influence' as understood by the Court does not necessarily require a majority interest, but a controlling interest in a company of another Member State is in any event 'establishment'. The Court considered in *Baars*:[134]

> '22. (...) So, a national of a Member State who has a holding in the capital of a company established in another Member State which gives him definite influence over the company's decisions and allows him to determine its activities is exercising his right of establishment.'

As observed, Case C-470/04, *N. v. Inspecteur*, implies that the mere holding of a majority interest in a passive (cash box) company incorporated in another Member State activates the right of establishment, even if the company has its real seat outside the EU.

For elaboration on the distinction between Capital and Establishment, especially as regards relations with third States, where that distinction is of the utmost importance, see Chapter 5.

As regards the distinction between Establishment and Workers, the *Asscher* case (see Section 3.1.3.2) shows that the Court regards a company director (*i.e.* a company employee) who also holds the majority of shares in the company he directs, not as an employee, but as a self-employed person if he is in fact his own boss (if there is no real subordination), and therefore as within the scope of the right of establishment rather than the free movement of workers. Again, the distinction is not very relavent, because, as the Court observed in *Asscher*, point 29, both freedoms are based on the same principles and have the same goal.

(iv) Fiscal Significance

The freedom of movement of workers and the right of establishment of undertakings has had a huge impact on the design of national tax law, by far the largest impact of the four freedoms, although the free movement of capital has been catching up since the full

133 See, e.g. Case C-208/00, *Überseering*, EU:C:2002:632, [2002] ECR I-9919, Case C-210/06, *Cartesio*, EU:C:2008:723, [2008] ECR I-9641, and Case C-106/16, *Polbud*, EU:C:2017:804.

134 Case C-251/98, *Baars v. Inspecteur der belastingen*, EU:C:2000:205, [2000] ECR I-2787.

liberalization of capital movement in 1994. A very large number of national tax provisions, which (international) tax law specialists used to consider perfectly legitimate, have been found incompatible with the requirements of the free movement of persons. Especially the – until 30 years ago – usual distinctions between residents and non-residents, between domestic-source income and foreign-source income, and between domestic payments and cross-border payments in traditional (inter)national tax law had to be rewritten after coming face to face with the EU Treaty Freedoms. The Chapters 6-15 of Part II of this book are devoted to the multiple hundreds of cases before the CJEU on the confrontation of unharmonised tax law and the EU free movement rights of persons (and capital) and the ensuing rewriting of (international) tax law within the EU.

3.2.6 Freedom of Capital and Payments; Extending to Third States

Within an internal market not only labour and entrepreneurship must be able to move freely. Obviously, the same is true for the other production factor: capital. Undertakings must be free to borrow money or issue shares where they think the cost of capital is lowest. Investors must be free to invest their money where they consider the risk/yield ratio best, although since the financial crisis the Member States may regret their total liberalization of capital movement. Moreover, the right of establishment of undertakings implies the need for free movement of capital, as cross-border establishment of undertakings usually entails cross-border capital (assets) movement. Therefore, Articles 63–66 TFEU ensure free movement of capital and freedom of payments. Article 63 has direct effect since the liberalization of the capital market, first by way of Directive 88/361/EEC,[135] later by the TEU (the Maastricht Treaty).[136] In principle, all restrictions to the free movement of capital and payments were abolished on 1 January 1994, not only between Member States, but also between Member States and third States. This is remarkable, as this is a unilateral move by the EU Member States as regards the rest of the world, which did not need to liberalize anything in return.

Article 63(1) TFEU prohibits all restrictions on the movement of capital between Member States and between Member States and third countries. Paragraph 2 prohibits all restrictions on payments between Member States and between Member States and third countries. Capital movements were listed in Annex I of Directive 88/361/EEC, which became obsolete after the 1992 Maastricht Treaty, but it is settled case law that the nomenclature of capital movements in that Annex I retained its indicative value for defining "movement of capital"[137] in the absence of a definition of capital movement in the Treaty. The Annex did not contain a definition either, but rather an enumeration. In general terms, any right concerning movable or immovable assets is 'capital' for purposes of the TFEU, and 'movement' of capital is the transfer of rights concerning assets, also, e.g., because of inheriting them. In *X v Staatssecretaris*,[138] the Court considered, on the

135 Council Directive of 24 June 1988 on the Implementation of Article 67 of the Treaty, 88/361/EEC, OL 178/5, 8 July 1988.

136 See Joined Cases C-163/94, C-1 65/94 and C-250/94, *Sanz de Lera and others*, EU:C:1995:451, [1995] ECR I-4821.

137 Case C-513/03, *van Hilten-van der Heijden*, EU:C:2006:131, point 35.

138 Case C-317/15, *X v Staatssecretaris*, EU:C:2017:119.

substance of the free movement of capital in a case in which the question was referred whether the opening of a bank account constituted 'capital movement':

> "27. (...), in the absence of a definition of 'movement of capital' in the TFEU, the Court has recognised the nomenclature that constitutes Annex I to Directive 88/361 as having indicative value, it being understood that, as pointed out in the introduction to that annex, the list which it contains is not exhaustive (...). Nevertheless, (...), that annex makes reference, under Heading VI, to 'operations in current and deposit accounts with financial institutions', which include 'operations carried out by residents with foreign financial institutions'. Accordingly, the opening of a securities account with a banking institution, such as that at issue in the main proceedings, comes within the concept of 'movement of capital'."

The free movement of capital was a bit of a wallflower for lack of sufficient direct effect until its liberalization in 1990 (Directive) and 1994 (TEU). By now, it has convincingly caught up with the other Treaty Freedoms. Many tax cases on foreign-source capital income or on outbound capital remuneration were decided by the CJEU in favour of the taxpayer on the basis of Article 63, especially cases on discriminatory taxation of inbound and outbound dividends, such as the cases C-35/98 *Verkooijen*, C-334/02 *Commission v. France*, C-315/02 *Lenz*, C-319/02, *Manninen*, and C-292/04, *Meilicke*, C-521/07 *Commission v Netherlands* and C-575/17 *Sofina*. Among others, the Court's tax case law on the basis of Article 63 made the previously widespread imputation systems of taxation of distributed company profits disappear almost completely within the EU. See Chapter 11.

The freedom of payments is complemental to the four main freedoms (goods, services, persons and capital). Free movement is of little use to a frontier worker if he is unable to transfer his wages home from his job State. Similarly, free establishment and provision of services would have little meaning if restrictions or prohibitions could be placed on the cross-border payment of dividends, interest, lease installments, billing of goods supplied or services rendered, etc.

Genuine free movement of capital and freedom of payments, at least between the Member States which joined 'Euroland,' has come into being with the introduction of the economic and monetary union (EMU), especially the single European currency, as of 1 January 2002, although the financial crisis showed that something is still missing: political and budgetary and therefore fiscal integration.

Probably because they were not entirely comfortable with the *Avoir Fiscal* judgment of the CJEU and the total prohibition of restrictions under Article 63 within the Union, the Member States included Article (now) 65 TFEU in 1993 (the Maastricht Treaty). Probably, they hoped to protect imputation systems of taxation of distributed company profits from discrimination analysis by the Court. Article 65(1)(a) empowers Member States to apply national tax provisions which distinguish between resident and nonresident investors and between domestic and foreign-source capital income. Such provisions may not, however, amount to arbitrary discrimination or covert restriction of the free movement of capital and payments (Art. 65(3)). The Court's case law, especially *Bachmann*, *Verkooijen*, *Lenz* and *Manninen*, showed that Article 65(1)(a) is superfluous, as the Court regards it as no more than a codification, in the field of capital movement, of its rule of reason test for restrictions on free movement (see section 3.2.2). That case law shows that it does not provide Member States with any tax sovereignty in the field of capital movement they did not already possess without that provision, under the Court's rule of reason. As observed, Article 65(1)(a) did not save Member States' imputation systems of taxation of dividends.

Free movement of capital and payments extends, unlike the other Treaty Freedoms, also to non-Member States. It is essential, therefore, to distinguish between capital and payment operations and all other operations. When a national measure concerns several of the freedoms of movement guaranteed by the Treaties, the Court will in principle examine the measure in dispute in relation to only one of those freedoms if it appears, in the light of the subject matter of that measure, that the other freedoms are entirely secondary in relation to that freedom and may be considered together with it.[139] It is, therefore, decisive whether the objective of the tax measure is to regulate capital movements (possibly in addition to the movement of goods, services and persons). We refer to Chapter 5 for explanation and for elaboration on the distinction between free capital movement and the other Treaty freedoms.

Still, third State capital movement is not quite as free as within the Union. In the first place, Article 64 TFEU contains a standstill or 'grandfather' clause as regards four categories of capital movement in respect of which Member States may maintain restrictions as regards third States which already existed on 31 December 1993: (i) direct investment (including real estate), (ii) establishment, (iii) provision of financial services and (iv) admission of securities to capital markets. Many restrictive tax measures as regards third States are thus still permitted. Article 63 has grandfathered, *e.g.*, an Austrian measure denying the Austrian half rate for domestic (and EU) dividends to taxpayers receiving third State (Swiss) sourced dividends on a substantial interest in a Swiss company.[140] Further, Articles 64(3), 65(4), and 66 TFEU allow certain restrictions in specific situations. Lastly, the Court recognizes that third State capital movement takes place in a 'different legal context' from intra-Union capital movement, as third States are not bound by EU law such as, especially, Union loyalty and the Directives on Administrative Cooperation and on Recovery Assistance in tax matters (see Chapter 27). The Court therefore accepts that taxation of third State capital operations may not always be comparable to taxation of intra-EU capital operations, and also that in third State situations justifications may be acceptable which would not be accepted intra-EU, because of this 'different legal context' of third State capital movement.

Chapter 5 deals in general with external (tax) relations, and therefore also with the relationship between EU Member States and their associated and dependent territories (OCT: overseas countries and territories) and between the EU and associated third States, as well as with the European Economic Area (EEA) agreement between the EU and three EFTA-Member States (Norway, Iceland and Liechtenstein) and Brexit. It also deals with EU-BEPS vis-à-vis third States, e.g. with the recently drawn up blacklist of non-cooperative tax havens outside the EU.

139 Case C-788/19, *Commission v Spain*, EU:C:2022:55, point 11.
140 Case C-157/05, *Winfried Holböck*, EU:C:2007:297, [2007] ECR I-4051.

3.2.7 Discriminations, Restrictions, Disparities and Dislocations

3.2.7.1 Measures With and Without Distinction; From an Obstacle-Approach to a Discrimination-Approach; Exercise in Parallel of Taxing Power

The concept of discrimination[141] refers to measures directly or in effect distinguishing between domestic and foreign economic operators, capital or goods. The provisions on the free movement of persons still refer to 'discrimination based on nationality' (Art. 45(2) for workers) and to the concept of national treatment (Art. 48 (2nd indent) for undertakings), which suggests that they do not prohibit hindering measures without distinction on the basis of nationality or origin, but only discriminatory measures on that basis. At first, the Court did confine itself to a discrimination analysis in respect of free movement of *persons*, but from the outset it was clear that a discrimination analysis would not do for free movement of *goods* and *services*, and that the treaty provisions called for review of all 'restrictions' to trade (see Arts. 34, 35 and 56 TFEU): nondiscriminatory measures may also have protective effects, such as an indiscriminate prohibition on certain economic activities (e.g. on 'cold calling,' or on the sale of certain goods) or a 'single office' requirement for lawyers or physicians (see section 3.2.1.1). Also, the exercise in parallel of two regulatory systems, even if they apply in themselves indiscriminately to domestic and cross-border economic activity, such as product safety requirements or diploma requirements, cause double regulatory burdens which may seriously hinder free movement. The Court therefore requires the destination State to justify imposition of a second regulatory burden especially where the regulatory system of the origin State provides equivalent regulation (mutual recognition). Since the diverging wording of the different Treaty freedoms did not seem to express any difference in intention (they all have the same goal: establishing free movement within an internal market) and diverging scopes of the various freedoms would create unnecessary legal uncertainty, the CJEU eventually interpreted all four freedoms in the same manner (converging interpretation).[142] In particular, cases such as *Bosman*[143] and *Gebhard* (quoted in section 3.2.2) show that measures without distinction which nonetheless restrict free movement are in principle prohibited under all four freedoms, also under the free movement of persons, and will be accepted only if they pass the *rule of reason* test.

As *Gebhard* (point 37) states, the treaty Freedoms prohibit in principle any national measure 'which is liable to hinder' free movement, unless it is justified for mandatory

141 See, on the EU law concept of discrimination, applied to taxation: Jan Wouters, 'The principle of non-discrimination in European Community law', *EC Tax Review* 1999-2, p. 98 ff., and Axel Cordewener, 'Is there a difference in the way in which the principle of non-discrimination and the principle of non-restriction operate?' and Moris Lehner, 'Is there a distinction in the application of the non-restriction principle between rules regulating purely domestic situations, rules regulating domestic and cross-border situations and rules regulating exclusively cross-border situations?', the latter two both in: Frans Vanistendael (ed.): 'EU Freedoms and Taxation,' EATLP International Tax Series, IBFD, Amsterdam, 2006.

142 See, in particular, Case 143/87, *Stanton*, EU:C:1988:378, [1988] ECR 3877; Case 81/87, *Daily Mail*, EU:C:1988:456, [1988] ECR 5483; Case C-10/90, *Masgio*, EU:C:1991:107, [1991] ECR I-1119; Case C-415/93, *VZW Koninklijke Belgische Voetbalbond and others v Jean-Marc Bosman*, EU:C:1995:463, [1995] ECR I-4921; and Case C-55/94, *Reinhard Gebhard*, EU:C:1995:411, [1995] ECR I-4165.

143 See the previous footnote.

reasons of public interest and proportionate in its restricting effects. Taken at face value, this would mean that national taxes are prohibited unless the Court considers them justified and proportionate. Indeed, every form of taxation is 'liable to hinder' the economic activity subject to it. Obviously, the Treaty drafters never intended to confer upon the Court any such absurdly wide budgetary competence. On the other hand, it is clear that especially income taxation is a paradigm example of a regulatory double burden. Even if parallel taxation of the same cross-border income by two national systems (the source State and the residence State) may be in itself nondiscriminatory, the resulting international double taxation still is a formidable hindrance to cross-border economic activity. As the Treaty freedoms do not contain any guidance on which of the two jurisdictions has the prior right to tax the income, there is no basis for mutual recognition.

According to old case law, discriminatory (tax) measures can only be justified by public interests listed in the TFEU itself, such as public health and public security,[144] whereas measures without distinction may also be saved by the Court's unwritten *rule of reason* test. The Court has not at all been consistent in this respect, however, regularly testing and accepting discriminatory tax measures under its rule of reason.[145] Since the rule of reason has been applied by the Court in virtually every direct tax case of the last two decades in which the Court found a discrimination to be present, we conclude that for justifiability, it is immaterial whether a (tax) measure is discriminatory of merely restrictive. Apparently, any restrictive measure, whether discriminatory or nondiscriminatory) may be justified by either a Treaty justification or an unwritten rule of reason justification. Indeed, in Case C-446/04, *Test Claimants in the FII Group Litigation*, and in the joined Cases C-436/08 and C-437/08, *Haribo and Österreichische Salinen*, the Court even accepted a *direct* discrimination on the basis of origin under an unwritten rule of reason exception (a balanced allocation of taxing rights). It thus accepted an overtly discriminatory treatment of foreign group dividends (credit for underlying tax) as compared to domestic group dividends (exempted).

Another development in the case law especially in tax matters is that, despite still often using 'restriction' and 'obstacle' language, the Court more or less consistently steers clear from nondiscriminatory tax measures. It seems to consider these in principle outside its scrutiny under the Treaty freedoms, and therefore as in principle not prohibited. The Court has not vocalised this policy, but it is apparent in its case law: in tax matters, it looks for a discrimination before engaging the free movement rights. See, especially, Chapter 6.4.

---

144 *E.g.* in Case 270/83, *Commission v France (Avoir Fiscal)*, EU:C:1986:37, and Case C-311/97, *Royal Bank of Scotland*, EU:C:1999:216.

145 There are very many examples. In Case C-204/90, *Hans Martin Bachmann v. Belgium*, EU:C:1992:35, [1992] ECR I-249, the Court accepted fiscal coherence as a justification for a tax measure it held to be discriminatory. In Case C-446/04, *Test Claimants in the FII Group Litigation*, EU:C:2006:774, and joined cases C-436/08 and C-437/08, *Haribo and Österreichische Salinen*, EU:C:2011:61, the Court allowed overtly discriminatory treatment of foreign group dividends. In Case C-379/05, *Amurta*, EU:C:2007:655, [2007] ECR I-9569, concerning discriminatory withholding taxation of outbound dividends, and in the joined cases C-155/08 and C-157/08, *X and Passenheim-van Schoot*, EU:C:2009:368, [2009] ECR I-5093, concerning a statute of limitations overtly discriminating against foreign portfolio investment, the national rules were assessed under the rule of reason and partly accepted on the basis of unwritten justification grounds.

In cases such as *Kerckhaert-Morres*,[146] *Damseaux*,[147] and *Block*,[148] international juridical double taxation as a result of 'the exercise in parallel by two Member States of their fiscal sovereignty' (worldwide taxation by the residence State and source taxation by the source State) although obviously a major obstacle to free movement, could not be remedied by relying on free movement rights. In *Damseaux*, concerning a dividend payment by a French company to a Belgian resident on which France had withheld dividend tax and Belgium levied income tax, the Court put it as follows:

> '30. In the absence of any unifying or harmonising Community measures, Member States retain the power to define, by treaty or unilaterally, the criteria for allocating their powers of taxation, particularly with a view to eliminating double taxation (....). It is for the Member States to take the measures necessary to prevent (...) double taxation by applying, in particular, the criteria followed in international tax practice (...).
> 31. (...).
> 32. In a situation where both the Member State in which the dividends are paid and the Member State in which the shareholder resides are liable to tax those dividends, to consider that it is necessarily for the Member State of residence to prevent that double taxation would amount to granting a priority with respect to the taxation of that type of income to the Member State in which the dividends are paid.
> 33. Even though such an attribution of powers complied, in particular, with the rules of international legal practice as reflected in the model tax convention on income and on capital drawn up by the (...) (OECD), in particular Article 23B thereof, it is not in dispute that Community law, in its current state and in a situation such as that at issue in the main proceedings, does not lay down any general criteria for the attribution of areas of competence between the Member States in relation to the elimination of double taxation within the Community (see Kerckhaert and Morres, paragraph 22, and Columbus Container Services, paragraph 45).
> 34. (...), the fact that both the Member State in which the dividends are paid and the Member State in which the shareholder resides are liable to tax those dividends does not mean that the Member State of residence is obliged, under Community law, to prevent the disadvantages which could arise from the exercise of competence thus attributed by the two Member States.'

The adverse effect of simultaneous source taxation and residence taxation of the same tax base is not caused by *one* of the two jurisdictions, therefore not by any discrimination, but by the parallel existence of *two* jurisdictions. Both States may delineate their taxing jurisdictions on the basis of residence, source, asset location, even nationality, or any other objective criterion. In doing so, neither of them can be accused of taxing foreign-sourced income or nonresidents less favourably than domestic income. As neither State is discriminating against the cross-border situation, it is thus indeterminable, at least on the basis of EU law, which of the two States should yield to the taxing power of the other State. The Treaty freedoms do not require Member States to adapt their tax systems to fit the tax systems of other Member States,[149] nor do they guarantee

146 Case C-513/04, *Kerckhaert-Morres*, EU:C:2006:713, [2006] ECR I-10967.
147 Case C-128/08, *Damseaux*, EU:C:2009:471, [2009] ECR I-6823.
148 Case C-67/08, *Block*, EU:C:2009:92, [2009] ECR I-883.
149 Case C-298/05, *Columbus Container Services*, EU:C:2007:754, [2007] ECR I-10451.

that changing jurisdictions will always be neutral from a tax point of view.[150] As will be elaborated in Chapter 6, the Court's case law shows that disadvantages arising from differences in scope of subjection to tax between residents and nonresidents (the latter only for sourced income) and between foreign-source and domestic income (*e.g. exclusion* of foreign-source income *and therefore also of foreign losses*) are in principle outside the scope of the free movement rules, provided nonresidents and foreign-source income are not subject to tax on a *wider* basis than residents and domestic income, respectively, nor, *within* the scope of subjection to tax, to less favourable tax treatment.

The Court's case law in direct tax matters has thus moved away from its regular 'obstacle'-based approach applied in other areas than direct taxation, especially in the area of free movement of goods and services, to a 'distinction' approach, similar to the Court's shift from an obstacle approach to discrimination-analysis in its case law on levies for public services.[151] In that area, the Court at first seemed to ignore whether domestic and cross-border positions were treated differently or alike. The *Sea-Land Service* cases,[152] *e.g.*, concerned a Netherlands tariff for public vessel traffic services in ports and waterways, payable only by sea-going vessels longer than 41 metres, although also inland waterway vessels – to a lesser extent – used the service. These inland waterway vessels were mostly operated by Netherlands undertakings. Nevertheless, the Court explicitly did not consider the exemption for inland waterway vessels shorter than 41 metres indirectly discriminatory, as (i) the traffic services used by the two categories were different and (ii) the markets served by inland waterway vessels and sea-going vessels were different: the two categories were not comparable and not in competition with each other. Additional cost for one of them thus would not affect their respective market positions. Therefore, no unequal treatment (discrimination) whatsoever was present. The Court then found it necessary to go on:

> '38. None the less, the VTS system at issue (...), in that it requires the payment of a tariff by sea-going vessels longer than 41 metres, is liable to impede or render less attractive the provision of those services and therefore constitutes a restriction on their free circulation'.

This finding was rather startling, but a logical consequence of an obstacle-based approach ('liable to hinder'). It would imply that the Treaty freedoms in principle prohibit *every* tax, levy or fee which makes it less attractive to use or undertake the activity triggering such tax, levy or fee. Taxation could thus only be justified if the Court considers it justified. The further reasoning in *Sea-Land Services* supported that uneasy conclusion: on the basis of self-designed – at least not Treaty-based – criteria for proper retributioning, the Court assessed the *reasonableness* of the tariff. It observed that the tariff was charged to all operators in a comparable position (the horizontality requirement for fair taxation), that vessel traffic services were essential to public security, and that the charge contributed to the general interest of public security in the waters concerned. Finally, the Court was

150 Case C-403/03, *Schempp*, EU:C:2005:446, [2005] ECR I-6421, and Case C-365/02, *Lindfors*, EU:C:2004:449, [2004] ECR I-7183.

151 See: Karen Banks, 'The application of the fundamental freedoms to Member State tax measures: Guarding against protectionism or second-guessing national policy choices?', 33 *European Law Review*, August 2008, p. 482-506.

152 Joined Cases C-430/99 and C-431/99, *Sea-Land Service*, EU:C:2002:364, [2002] ECR I-5235.

satisfied that the level of the charge corresponded to the cost of the traffic services. One would expect, however, the Court not to see any role for itself after establishing the absence of any discrimination, protectionist effect or distortion of competition. Given that absence, it was not for the Court to develop any views on how a Member State should finance a completely neutral vessel traffic services system.[153]

The Court's advocates-general pointed this out to it, arguing that an obstacle-based approach does not make sense in case of (neutral) taxation and charges, and subsequently, in a *Keck*-like judgment, it changed its analysis. The *Mobistar* and *Belgacom* cases[154] concerned two Belgian local taxes on transmission pylons, masts and antennae for GSM telephony services. The Court first used 'obstacle'-language, reiterating that all restrictions on the free provision of services are prohibited, including measures without distinction but making the cross-border provision of services more burdensome, but then considered:

> '31. By contrast, measures, the only effect of which is to create additional costs in respect of the service in question and which affect in the same way the provision of services between Member States and that within one Member State, do not fall within the scope of Article 59 [now 56; *authors*] of the Treaty.
> 32. As regards the question whether the levy by municipal authorities of taxes such as those in question (...) amounts to a restriction incompatible with Article 59, it is necessary to point out that such taxes apply without distinction to all owners of mobile telephone installations within the commune in question, and that foreign operators are not, either in fact or in law, more adversely affected by those measures than national operators.
> 33. Nor do the tax measures in question make cross-border service provision more difficult than national service provision. Admittedly, introducing a tax on pylons, masts and antennae can make tariffs for mobile telephone communications to Belgium from abroad and vice versa more expensive. However, national telephone service provision is, to the same extent, subject to the risk that the tax will have an impact on tariffs.
> 34. It is appropriate to add that there is nothing in the file to suggest that the cumulative effect of the local taxes compromises freedom to provide mobile telephony services between other Member States and the Kingdom of Belgium'.

This looks like an exclusion altogether, from the scope of free movement rights, of indiscriminate modes of taxation, comparable to the exclusion of indiscriminate modes of sale in *Keck*. Although the Court's language is confusing ('... even if it applies without distinction ...'), this implies that tax measures which do not in fact *discriminate* against the cross-border provision of services, are not only justified, they are entirely *outside the scope* of the free movement provisions (see point 31 of the judgment), unless the tax is so high as to render the exercise of a fundamental freedom practically impossible on a certain market (*Berlington*). As observed in Section 3.1.0, the Court drew the same conclusion as regards the prohibition, in Article 110, of discriminatory *or protective* product taxation, in two cases of manifest international double taxation, concerning (duplicating)

153 See Karen Banks, *l.c.*

154 Joined Cases C-544/03, *Mobistar*, and C-545/03, *Belgacom Mobile*, EU:C:2005:518, [2005] ECR I-7723.

charges levied by Denmark on the slaughter of pigs[155] and by the Netherlands on the landing of shrimps.[156]

The Court probably moved away from 'obstacle' analysis in tax matters because, as Kingston observed,[157] it is impossible to levy a tax which is *not* liable to hinder free movement in some respect. In any event, the Court cannot take away nondiscriminatory double tax burdens, as the Treaty contains no legal basis for choosing between two competing taxing jurisdictions. It may have helped that two of the Court's advocates-general explicitly invited the Court to limit itself to discrimination-analyses in direct tax matters.[158] Still, the Court has never actually *said* it has done so, and in the pending *Hornbach* case,[159] advocate-general Bobek tried again to persuade the Court "to clearly articulate which is the approach to freedom of establishment in the area of direct taxation. (...), it ought to be, from my point of view, the discrimination approach."

Notwithstanding conceptual wandering and confusing language, we infer (see also Section 3.2.1.1 and Chapter 6.4.1) that the Court more or less consistently assesses direct tax cases under the Treaty freedoms only on the basis of a discrimination analysis, *i.e.* by comparing the cross-border position to the comparable internal position (resident - nonresident, foreign-source income - domestic income, emigrant - non-emigrant; foreign investment - domestic investment, foreign service provider - domestic service provider, etc.).

Banks[160] analysed the Court's case law in (para)fiscal matters, and concluded that the Court has never in fact found a nondiscriminatory tax measure to be contrary to EU law, although it often uses justification-language to accept the measure, rather than to accept it already at the stage of the (non)comparability analysis. We observe, however, that in *Deutsche Shell*, the Court explicitly used an obstacle-based approach as regards the nondeductibility of a currency loss on a foreign branch ('constitutes an obstacle'; 'increases the economic risk'[161]) and considered nondeductibility to be a violation of the freedom of establishment, and that in *Bosal*, the Court condemned a perfectly neutral measure connecting deductibility to taxability,[162] as it did in Marks & Spencer II in respect of final foreign subsidiary losses.[163] Moreover, in *De Groot*, it condemned the wrong State, *i.e.* the State which was *not* doing the discriminating (it incorrectly relieved from its Treaty obligations the other State, which overtly discriminated against nonresident

155 Case C-234/99, *Nygård*, EU:C:2002:244, [2002] ECR I-3657.

156 Case C-517/04, *Koornstra*, EU:C:2006:375, [2006] ECR I-5015.

157 Suzanne Kingston, 'A light in the darkness: Recent developments in the CJEU's Direct Tax Juris-prudence,' 2007 *Common Market Law Review* 44, p. 1321-1359, at 1331.

158 Opinions of A.-G. Geelhoed in Cases C-374/04, *Test Claimants in Class IV of the ACT Group Litigation*, EU:C:2006:773, [2006] ECR I-11673, and C-446/04, *Test Claimants in the FII Group Litigation*, EU:C:2006:774, [2006] ECR I-11753, and Opinion of A.-G. Poiares Maduro in Case C-446/03, *Marks & Spencer* II, EU:C:2005:763, [2005] ECR I-10837.

159 Opinion of 14 December 2017 in Case C-382/16, *Hornbach-Baumarkt AG*, EU:C:2017:974.

160 Karen Banks, *l.c.*

161 Case C-293/06, *Deutsche Shell*, EU:C:2008:129, [2008] ECR I-1129, paras. 28, 30 and 32.

162 Cf: Suzanne Kingston, 'The Boundaries of Sovereignty: The CJEU's Controversial Role Applying Internal Market Law to Direct Tax Measures,' in: Cambridge Yearbook on European Legal Studies 2006-2007, at 301-302.

163 Case C-446/03, *Marks & Spencer II*, EU:C:2005:763, [2005] ECR I-10837.

employees; see Chapter 13.4). But these cases may be mistakes or at least cases the Court would possibly not decide in the same manner any more.

In *D. v Inspecteur*[164] and *Truck Center*,[165] the Court explicitly used a discrimination analysis, and stopped already at the first step of its rule of reason (is there a restriction/ discrimination?), because the measure did not discriminate. This approach (no discrimination, no breach) is, as observed, a *Keck*-like exception for indiscriminate modes of taxation from free movement scrutiny. In *D. v Inspecteur*, the Court articulated that Member States are free to determine the connecting factors for allocating taxing powers, and that it accepts 'that a difference in treatment between nationals of the two Contracting States that results from that allocation cannot constitute discrimination.' In *Truck Center* (point 47), it did not see any 'restriction' (let alone a discrimination) in different treatment of foreign creditors (withholding at source) as compared to domestic creditors (taxed by assessment in the corporation tax), because that difference in treatment reflected (i) the accepted difference between source taxation by the source State (in respect of nonresident creditors) and residence taxation by the residence State (in respect of domestic creditors) and (ii) a difference in recovery possibilities for the source State,[166] and because the different treatment did not 'necessarily procure an advantage for domestic recipient companies.' This *Keck*-like approach puts disadvantages resulting from indiscriminate taxation outside Court scrutiny. However, in *Marks & Spencer II*,[167] the Court used another approach, which seemed since to become standard practice: it accepted indiscriminate taxation not yet at the first step of the rule of reason, but only at the second step (justifications). It *in fact* applied a discrimination test, but presented the fact that the tax measure at issue was not discriminatory as a *justification* for the 'restriction' found at the first step. Maybe, the Court (i) did not want to derogate too visibly from its restriction-based approach in non-tax cases, keeping its hands free to use its traditional 'obstacle' approach in the area of free movement of goods and services,[168] and (ii) ealized that placing indiscriminate direct tax measures, like the indiscriminate modes of sale in *Keck*, entirely outside the scope of the Treaty freedoms, would sideline the Court: presenting indiscriminateness not as a *Keck*-like exception, but as a 'justification' for the 'restriction' found, keeps the Member States virtuous, and enables the Court to continue to keep an eye on them. Nevertheless, in the recent *Timac Agro* Case,[169] it accepted territoriality (base exemption) for residents with foreign source income as *nondiscriminatory* and therefore as not needing justification, because under base exemption, foreign and domestic branches are not objectively comparable, the latter being subject to tax and the former not being subject to tax. This does not square with *Marks & Spencer II*.

The most compelling support for the conclusion that the Court does not apply an 'obstacle'-based approach in direct tax matters (anymore), we consider the fact that it accepts full double taxation in cases such as *Kerckhaert-Morres*, *Damseaux*, *Columbus*

164 Case C-376/03, *D. v Inspecteur*, EU:C:2005:424, [2005] ECR I-5821.
165 Case C-282/07, *Truck Center*, EU:C:2008:762, [2008] ECR I-10767.
166 We observe that until then, this had only been accepted as a *justification* for a restriction (second step of the rule of reason).
167 Case C-446/03, *Marks & Spencer II*, EU:C:2005:763, [2005] ECR I-10837.
168 See Karen Banks, l.c. Compare also the Opinion of advocate-general Hogan in Joined Cases C-478/19 and C-479/19, *UBS Real Estate*, EU:C:2021:148, point 52.
169 Case C-388/14, *Timac Agro Deutschland GmbH*, EU:C:2015:829.

Container Services and *Block*, despite the fact that it is difficult to think of a more effective obstacle to free movement than double taxation.

We observe that discrimination arises not only from the application of different rules to comparable situations, but also from the application of the same rule to different situations,[170] especially from the application of the same administrative rules to both domestic and foreign-source income or to both residents and nonresidents where that same rule is significantly more burdensome for foreign-source income or for nonresidents than it is for domestic income or for residents. Examples are Case C-250/95, *Futura*, and Case C-262/09, *Meilicke (II)*. In *Futura*, rules of evidence of a Member State could not be indiscriminately applied to the permanent establishment of a nonresident, as the same treatment as residents would put the nonresident company at a disadvantage: it was significantly easier for residents to meet the domestic evidence requirement than for nonresidents, while other means of evidence existed. In this case, the Court in fact required mutual recognition of foreign bookkeeping. In *Meilicke (II)*, Germany required from shareholders receiving foreign dividends the same certificate ascertaining the amount of foreign corporation tax on inbound dividends as from shareholders receiving domestic dividends, but the latter received such certificate already from the domestic distributing company, whereas in the source countries of the foreign dividends obviously no such German certificate existed, especially where that source country did not apply an imputation system.

3.2.7.2 Disparities

Discriminations and restrictions have their origin in one single jurisdiction. They are one-country-problems, They occur where a disadvantage is caused by (the rules of) one single jurisdiction, by one Member State maintaining domestic law which directly or indirectly distinguishes between domestic and comparable cross-border situations or which otherwise hinders the exercise of the Treaty freedoms. Such single-jurisdiction obstacles to intra-Union economic activity may be dealt with through negative integration. They may be prohibited under the Treaty freedoms if they cannot be justified or have disproportionate effects.

Disparities, on the other hand, are two-country problems. They are obstacles to intra-Union free movement caused by differences between the legal systems of two or more different Member States. If a company established in a Member State levying corporation tax at 28% opens up a branch in another Member State levying 36%, it cannot complain in the branch State that the tax level is higher than at home, because the branch is given national treatment in the branch State: domestic companies of that State also pay 36%. It cannot complain in its home State either, since the home State is not discriminating either and can hardly be required to refund tax levied by another State on profits taxable in that other State.[171]

170 For tax cases, see Cases C-279/93, *Schumacker*, EU:C:1995:31, point 30; C-80/94, *Wielockx*, EU:C:1995:271, point 17; C-107/94, *Asscher*, EU:C:1996:251, point 40; C-311/97, *Royal Bank of Scotland*, EU:C:1999:216, point 26; and C-655/13, *Mertens*, EU:C:2002:492, point 32.

171 In Case C-336/96, *Gilly*, the Court held that it would be a breach of tax sovereignty of the Member States not provided for in the Treaty if the home State of a frontier worker would be required to credit more wages tax levied by the job State than it would levy itself on that wage.

The Court reiterated many times that disparities are outside the scope of the prohibitions of the Treaty freedoms, e.g. in *Perfili*:[172]

> '17. (...), the Court has consistently held that, in prohibiting every Member State from applying its law differently on the ground of nationality, within the field of application of the Treaty, Articles [now 18, 49, and 56; *authors*] are not concerned with any disparities in treatment which may result, between Member States, from differences existing between the laws of the various Member States, so long as they affect all persons subject to them in accordance with objective criteria and without regard to their nationality (....).'

A tax example of a disparity, unremediable under free movement rights, is the *Schempp* case,[173] concerning a German resident who paid alimony to his ex-spouse, who after their divorce moved to Austria. Because of that move, Mr Schempp's alimony payments were not deductible any more, as under the German tax system, such payments were deductible only if they were taxable in the hands of the recipient, whereas under the Austrian system, they were non-deductible and non-taxable. Therefore, the Court could not help Mr Schempp. See, for elaboration, Chapter 6.4.1.

If it is difficult to decide whether a certain disadvantageous tax effect of doing business or working abroad is caused by a (unilateral and therefore in principle prohibited) discrimination or by a disparity between two or more legal systems, one should imagine that both States involved were to have exactly the same legal system. If within such thought experiment the disadvantage disappears, then it was a disparity effect; if it is still there, then either we are looking at a unilateral discrimination (or restriction), or at a dislocation effect caused by *both* States applying the same *in*consistent national tax law. The Court calls this this latter phenomenon 'exercise in parallel by two Member States of their fiscal sovereignty' (see 3.2.7.1), comparable to two Member States both applying their (diverging) diploma requirements or product safety requirements. There is a difference, however, between the concept of 'parallel exercise' in tax matters and the parallel exercise of market access requirements in the area of trade: in the area of trade, the market access impediment is caused by parallel exercise of *different* (diploma or safety) requirements, whereas in tax, the double burden is caused by parallel exercise of *identical* tax systems, which are, however, in themselves inconsistent, as they treat residents and nonresidents differently (worldwide taxation and source taxation, respectively).

Already in 1994, the Court hinted at the fact that exercise in parallel of taxing power by two States – which term it only used for the first time in 2004 (*Kerckhaert-Morres*) to explain that EU law cannot remedy juridical double taxation – could be conceived as a sort of disparity, for which there is no EU remedy other than harmonization of national tax laws. It considered, in *Peralta*[174] (*italics* added):

> '34. In the absence of Community harmonization, a Member State may certainly impose, directly or indirectly, technical rules which are specific to it and which are not necessarily to be found in the other Member States on maritime transport undertakings which, like the undertaking employing Mr Peralta, are established on its territory and which operate

172 Case C-177/94, *Criminal proceedings against Gianfranco Perfili*, EU:C:1996:24, [1996] ECR I-161.
173 Case C-403/03, *Schempp*, EU:C:2005:446, [2005] ECR I-6421.
174 Case C-379/92, *Criminal proceedings against Matteo Peralta*, EU:C:1994:296, [1994] ECR I-3453.

> vessels flying its flag. But the difficulties which might arise for those undertakings from that situation do not affect freedom of establishment within the meaning of (...) the Treaty. Fundamentally, those difficulties are no different in nature from those which may originate in disparities between national laws governing, for example, labour costs, social security costs *or the tax system.*'

This, however, still refers to 'rules which are specific to' each Member State, whereas the special feature of the 'exercise in parallel' in tax matters is that both States have identical systems, but nevertheless a double burden ensues.

3.2.7.3 Dislocations (Tax Base Compartmentalization); Source Taxation and EU-Wide Taxation; National Tax Treatment of Nonresidents?

(i) Dislocations

Apart from discriminations, indiscriminate obstacles and disparities, there is a fourth category of tax impediments to the functioning of the internal market. This fourth category probably exists only in direct tax matters, as a consequence of the Court's acceptance that (i) Member States are not limited by EU law in choosing a connecting factor for the delineation of their taxing jurisdiction (residence, source, nationality, territoriality, asset location, internet sales, or any other objective connecting factor), and that (ii) residents and nonresidents are not, as a rule, comparable for taxation purposes, meaning that Member States may apply these connecting factors asymmetrically: they may use worldwide taxation for residents or nationals and source or *situs* taxation for nonresidents or non-nationals. Obviously, simultaneous source taxation of nonresidents and worldwide taxation of residents leads to double taxation of the foreign-sourced income. This is not due to a disparity, because both States apply the same system: worldwide for residents and source for nonresidents. Even if both States apply the same system for residents and nonresidents, a double taxation problem persists, because income may be negative (losses): source taxation by both the residence and the source States for both residents and nonresidents (territoriality principle[175]) has the consequence of splitting up one single tax base over two taxing jurisdictions, which is disadvantageous to the taxpayer if his income is positive in one State, but negative in the other. Worldwide taxation by both States for both residents and nonresidents, although in itself consistent and nondiscriminatory as well, obviously leads to complete double taxation of the entire worldwide income in both States. If both States use nationality or asset location as a connecting factor, then in principle no double taxation arises, except for persons with two or more nationalities (bilocation seems improbable to us).

This evasive fourth category of tax impediments to free movement emanates from the division of the tax base (the income) over two jurisdictions, leading to a double burden or to the separation of the positive part from the negative part of the income in the other jurisdiction, incapable of canceling each other out, as they would in a one-country situation. In cross-border (two-country) situations, the tax base is located simultaneously in two separate, unharmonised and uncoordinated tax systems which in principle ignore each

175 We observe that the Court may understand 'the fiscal principle of territoriality' in a different manner, i.e. in the meaning international public law attaches to it. For sure, its advocate-general Bobek uses 'territoriality' in tax matters in a non-tax meaning. See Section 14.3.

other's existence. It is important to realise that this is a situation for which by definition no comparable internal situation is conceivable, except where a Member State would be a federation consisting of separate sub-states or provinces with autonomous income tax powers not coordinated at federal level. This situation may be illustrated by *AURES Holdings*.[176] In this case, the Court held that a Member State of arrival does not have to import losses suffered in the Member State of departure of a migrating company. This makes sense, because the losses in the first-mentioned Member State have been suffered completely outside of the tax jurisdiction of the last-mentioned Member State.

Although the disadvantageous tax effect (double burden or compartmentalisation of positive and negative income) occurs because of the border-crossing of the taxpayer or of his income, neither of the two jurisdiction involved can be blamed for it, as neither of them distinguishes between national and international positions (no discrimination), and both States apply the same tax system (no disparity). One might then be inclined to call it a 'restriction', as, indeed, the taxpayer is dissuaded from using his free movement rights, but (i) the disadvantage does *not* occur in a comparable one-country situation (which raises the question of whether the domestic and the cross-border situation are comparable in the first place), and (ii) it is impossible to say who is doing the restricting, as only the simultaneous exercise of two sovereign taxing rights creates the disadvantage. No single culprit and no comparable internal situation being available, we are not looking at a 'restriction' (obstacle) in the usual meaning. We call these situations 'dislocations.' Advocate-general Geelhoed called them 'quasi-restrictions.'[177] The Court calls them 'exercise in parallel of taxing power'. We elaborate on an example in subsection (ii) below.

In *Schumacker*[178] and *Futura*,[179] the Court accepted that residents and nonresidents are not, as a rule, comparable for direct taxation purposes, and it accepted different tax connecting factors for residents and nonresidents. It probably did so because

i. EU law provides no guidance how Member States should delineate, divide or coordinate their taxing jurisdictions,
ii. source taxation for nonresidents, although derogating from worldwide taxation for residents, does not – at first sight – subject nonresidents to less favourable taxation than residents, as it subjects them to tax on a smaller tax base than residents: only for sourced income (the Court probably did not realise at first that income may also be negative, in which case it is disadvantageous not to be subject to tax), and
iii. at the basis of established international tax law, especially the extremely successful OECD Model Double Taxation Convention (around 3000 bilateral tax treaties are based on it; all tax treaties between Member States are based on it) is the distinction between residence taxation for residents and source taxation for nonresidents.

(ii) Compartmentalization of the Tax Base; Territorial Matching of Positive and Corresponding Negative Elements of the Tax Base

From an (international) tax law point of view, it is essential to have a rule providing that if certain income or capital gains are exempt within a jurisdiction, then the connected

176 Case C-405/18, *AURES Holdings*, EU:C:2020:127.
177 Opinion in Case C-374/04, *Test Claimants in Class IV of the ACT Group Litigation*, EU:C:2006:773.
178 Case C-279/93, *Schumacker*, EU:C:1995:31, [1994] ECR I-5535.
179 Case C-250/95, *Futura Participations*, EU:C:1997:239, [1997] ECR I-2471.

expenses or corresponding capital losses are also exempt, *i.e.* also excluded from the tax base in that jurisdiction. If a Member State exempts foreign subsidiary dividends and capital gains on holdings in foreign subsidiaries in the hands of a domestic parent company, then it is fair, consistent and coherent to disallow deduction of costs incurred by the parent to finance the subsidiary and to disallow deduction of capital losses upon the disposal of the holding. The CJEU incorrectly decided otherwise in *Bosal*,[180] probably because it could not accept that losses may fall between two stools, *i.e.* between two jurisdictions (as it did accept later, in *Krankenheim Ruhesitz*). Just like exercise in parallel of taxing jurisdiction may lead to nondiscriminatory double taxation, parallel *non*-exercise of taxing power may lead to nondiscriminatory double nondeductibility of charges or losses. If a Member State does not exercise taxing power in respect of income from and gains on foreign real estate, then it is entirely fair, consistent and coherent to also disallow deduction from the domestic tax base of financing costs for and losses on such foreign real estate. The Court correctly decided accordingly in the Finnish case *K.*,[181] and it correctly decided accordingly in *Timac Agro*[182] as regards exemption of both positive and negative foreign *business* income, but it incorrectly decided otherwise in *Renneberg*[183] in respect of deduction of expenses for Belgian real estate from Netherlands *employment* income, possibly because of an incorrect understanding of the facts, of the applicable tax treaty and of its own *Schumacker*-doctrine. We will discuss the *Renneberg* Case in subsection (iv) below as it is very instructive in respect of the uneasy relationship between international tax law and internal market law.

Although fundamentally fair, neutral and coherent viewed from one single taxing jurisdiction, such tax base tracing and matching rules aimed at connecting deductibility to taxability and nondeductibility to exemptions, produce obstacles viewed from an internal market point of view. The territorial compartmentalization of the tax base, especially of loss relief possibilities, is a problem, *e.g.*, for multinational groups of companies based in small home markets (small home tax base), but also for frontier workers earning employment income in one State and having a negative income from a private dwelling in the other and for people like K., who made a loss on the sale of his French holiday home he could not deduct from his home State (Finland) investment income.

Let us calculate. An employee, resident and employed in Home State, takes out a mortgage loan to buy a house in Home State. The interest is deductible from Home State taxable income. She subsequently accepts a job in another Member State (Job State) and finds out that her interest deduction in Home State is lost for lack of Home State tax base to deduct the interest from: the applicable OECD-conform tax treaty allocates her employment income to Job State, and her (negative) income from real estate to the State of location. Let us assume that (i) in both States mortgage interest is deductible from income from real estate financed with the mortgaged loan, (ii) in both States home owners are taxed for a deemed rental income from their dwellings, (iii) in both States a negative balance between such deemed income and the mortgage interest paid is deductible from other income, and (iv) both States tax residents for worldwide income, with double tax relief,

180 Case C-168/01, *Bosal Holding BV*, EU:C:2003:479, [2003] ECR I-9409.
181 Case C-322/11, *K.*, EU:C:2013:716.
182 Case C-388/14, *Timac Agro Deutschland GmbH*, EU:C:2015:829.
183 Case C-527/06, *Renneberg*, EU:C:2008:566, [2008] ECR I-7735.

and tax nonresidents only for income sourced within their territory without double tax relief. Since the two tax systems are thus identical, a disadvantageous tax effect of the border-crossing is not a result of any disparity. As the employment income is exempt in Home State to prevent double taxation, our employee has no Home State income to absorb the negative income from real estate in Home State. Her employment income in Job State could easily absorb the loss, but the loss is not within the taxing jurisdiction of Job State. Therefore, there is a significant tax disadvantage as compared to an identical situation within one single jurisdiction. Probably, Home State applies worldwide taxation for residents and therefore reserved, in the tax treaty, the right to include the employment income in its taxable base for the purpose of determining progression of the tax rate on the income allocated to Home State, but that does not help the taxpayer: although Home State taxes her for worldwide income, including both the Job State employment income and the negative income from her private dwelling, it will subsequently grant her obviously no more double tax relief than for the income taxable in Home State, *i.e.* only for the employment income *less* the negative income from real estate. In figures:

- Employment income Job State	50 000	
Income tax in Job State 50% =		25 000
- Negative net real estate income Home State	(7 000)	
- Worldwide income, taxed in Home State	43 000	
Income tax in Home State 50% =		21 500
- Double tax relief by Home State (also at 50%)		21 500
- Remaining double tax		3 500

The taxpayer may carry over, in Home State, the unused double tax relief of 3500 to subsequent tax years (or her domestic real estate loss of 7000, depending on the legislative technique applied), but that does not help her if there is no positive domestic-source income to absorb it in those subsequent years either.

This disadvantageous result as compared to taking a job in Home State could be avoided if both States were to adopt worldwide taxation for both residents and nonresidents (their tax treaty allowing), and both were to provide double tax relief. Job State would then 'import' the negative Home State real estate income and would levy only 21 500 (instead of 25 000) on a tax base of 43 000 (instead of 50 000). The overtaxation would disappear. However, under current international tax law, job States – source States in general – do not import foreign losses of nonresidents, as they consistently do not import foreign profits of nonresidents either. Traditionally, source States were not in a position to apply worldwide taxation to nonresidents, as they lacked the information to assess worldwide income, the possibilities to get that information, and possibilities to recover tax outside its territory.

Obviously, the tax base compartmentalisation described is a major hindrance to cross-border economic activity. EU law does not tell us, however, which of the two States is responsible. Their tax systems are identical, neither of them discriminates against either nonresidents or foreign source income, and their tax connecting factors (source and residence) are objective and nondiscriminatory. It is therefore impossible to say which of the two is to blame for the disadvantage. The choice between worldwide taxation (with double tax relief) and source taxation (territoriality) for residents or for nonresidents or for both is a political choice which cannot be made by a Court. Even if the Court were competent to force Member States to choose symmetrically (worldwide taxation with double tax relief for both residents and nonresidents, or source taxation for both), then the problem would still not go away if one State would symmetrically choose Worldwide and the other would symmetrically chooses Source (but then we could call it a disparity). The disadvantage would not even go away if both States would choose for territoriality taxation for both residents and nonresidents, thus also eliminating disparities: although in a territoriality system, double taxation of *positive* income is automatically eliminated because both States refrain from taxing income not sourced within their territory (presuming both States define domestic and foreign source income in the same manner), the total tax base is still split up over two jurisdictions, which in the example above still causes the loss from real estate to be allocated to Home State and the positive employment income to Job State, still resulting in a significant disadvantage for our cross-border employee as compared to her colleague with the same house, the same loan and the same job within one single jurisdiction.

(iii) The Court's Acceptance of Territoriality (Source) Taxation

For business income of companies, the Court has accepted that both the Home State and the Source State limit their jurisdiction to profits and losses sourced within their territory, with the disadvantageous compartmentalization effect described above if profit is made in one State but a loss is suffered in the other. It did so in *Lidl Belgium*[184] and *Marks & Spencer II.*[185] The first case concerned a Luxembourg branch loss of a German company. The German-Luxembourg tax treaty eliminated foreign-sourced business results from the German tax base altogether, whether positive or negative (territoriality principle). The problem was not, therefore in the *source* (branch) State applying territoriality (as it is in the example above), but in the *home* State of the company, which (also) applied the source (territoriality) principle, resulting in nondeductibility of the Luxembourg branch loss from the company's German profits. By contrast, domestic branch losses could be deducted from domestic profits (but, obviously, domestic branch *profits* would also be taxed by Germany). The Court found the exclusion of foreign-source losses to be discriminatory, but it considered symmetric exclusion of both foreign profits and foreign losses justified by 'the need to preserve the allocation of the power to impose taxes.' In our view, there was no discrimination in the first place, as foreign branches (*not* subject to tax) were not comparable to domestic branches (subject to tax). The Court seems to have accepted that view in *Timac Agro.*[186]

Marks & Spencer II concerned not foreign branch losses, but nonresident subsidiary losses of a UK-based group of companies. As nonresident subsidiaries were not subject to tax in the UK, also their losses were excluded from the UK group relief scheme. By contrast, domestic subsidiaries – subject to UK tax – could transfer their losses to profitable domestic group companies. Again the Court considered exclusion of foreign (subsidiary)

184 Case C-414/06, *Lidl Belgium*, EU:C:2008:278, [2008] ECR I-3601.
185 Case C-446/03, *Marks & Spencer II*, EU:C:2005:763, [2005] ECR I-10837.
186 Case C-388/14, *Timac Agro Deutschland GmbH*, EU:C:2015:829.

losses discriminatory, but again it accepted that a balanced allocation of taxing power (plus two overlapping similar justifications) justified the UK's limitation of taxing power to (profits and losses of) *subject-to-tax* group companies (at least as long as the foreign losses could still be offset abroad in subsequent years if the subsidiary would return to profit; see Chapter 10 on that issue). Also in this case, in our view the Court incorrectly saw a discrimination, even though it considered it justified: entities subject to tax are not comparable to entities not subject to tax.

This case law shows that Member States may choose source taxation (territoriality) not only for nonresidents, but also for residents. The residence State may delineate its taxing jurisdiction so as to cover only domestic-source results. That certainly does not help the employee in the example above. She would only be helped if symmetrical taxation of residents and nonresidents were sought in the opposite direction: both States applying worldwide (at least EU-wide) taxation of both residents and nonresidents and both applying a – preferably the same – double tax relief mechanism. In the example, Job State would thus import Home State loss from real estate, reducing the taxpayer's tax exposure in Job State. Job State may be less than enthusiastic about this, as it will see less tax revenue because of losses alien to economic activity on its territory. In many cases, however, that is only a matter of time: if in a subsequent year the taxpayer derives positive income in Home State, then Job State will also import and tax such positive income, and it will not grant double tax relief, as there will be no double tax: indeed, the taxpayer will not be paying any Home State tax on the subsequent positive income: the previous losses will be offset against the positive income in Home State. In this way, all involved will get what is coming to them, although not in the same fiscal year.

The only trouble with the specific example above (with only a dwelling in the home State, the entire employment income being earned in Job State) is that Job State may not be able to recapture the loss deduction in future, as it may be facing loss imports every year. As long as the employee has no other Home State income than a loss from real estate (and does not redeem the mortgaged loan), the real estate losses will persist, and will be transferred from Home State to Job State indefinitely. This would force the Job State to accept foreign losses forever. That is one of the reasons why source States do not extend their jurisdiction outside their territory. For final foreign subsidiary losses, the CJEU has nevertheless forced a similar system upon the Member States in *Marks & Spencer II*: if a parent company in one Member State demonstrates that the losses of its subsidiary in another Member State cannot be offset any more in the subsidiary jurisdiction (because the subsidiary has been wound up), the parent company State is required to absorb that foreign subsidiary loss even though it had symmetrically (also for profits) *not* extended its taxing jurisdiction to nonresident subsidiaries. This Case seems incompatible with *K.* (C-322/11), *Lidl Belgium* and *Timac Agro*, and the Court rightly seems to regret it in *Marks and Spencer III* (*Commission v UK*).[187] But then again, the Court held in *Bevola* that as regards losses attributable to a non-resident permanent establishment which has ceased activity and whose losses could not, and no longer can, be deducted from its taxable profits in the Member State in which it carried on its activity, the situation of a resident company possessing such an establishment is not different from that of a resident company possessing a resident permanent establishment, from the point of view of the

187 Case C-172/13, *Commission v UK* ('Marks & Spencer III'), EU:C:2015:50.

objective of preventing double deduction of the losses. Thus, the Court has confirmed Marks & Spencer II for head offices with a foreign permanent establishment. In addition, the Court observed that the ability to pay tax of a company possessing a non-resident permanent establishment which has definitively incurred losses is affected in the same way as that of a company whose resident permanent establishment has incurred losses. The Court held that the two situations are thus comparable in this respect too.[188]

(iv) But: the Renneberg Case[189]

The income split-up problem in the employee example above has been addressed by the Court. First, in *Ritter-Coulais*[190] and *Lakebrink*,[191] it held that negative income from a personal dwelling in one State must be taken into account for the calculation of the (progressive) tax *rate* on the employment income in the other State. That was unsurprising, as for residents, negative income is also taken into account for rate progression purposes. These cases did not concern the taking into account of foreign negative tax *base*. That issue was tackled in *Renneberg*.[192] Mr Renneberg lived in Belgium and had taken out a mortgaged loan in Belgium to finance his Belgian home. In Belgium, mortgage interest was only deductible from income from real estate (in this case: a deemed low rental income: 'cadastral income'). The greater part of the interest was thus not deductible in Belgium. He wished to deduct the interest from his employment income, which was earned entirely in the Netherlands. It is important to see that if he had not used his free movement right and had earned his employment income in Belgium, he would *not* have been able to deduct most the interest. In the Netherlands, by contrast, mortgage interest was deductible from income in general. Clearly, that is a ***disparity***. Like Belgium, the Netherlands added a low rental income from private dwellings to taxable income, but obviously only for residents, as by definition only residents have a personal dwelling in the Netherlands. Obviously, the Netherlands had *not* assumed any taxing jurisdiction in respect of *foreign* dwellings occupied by *non*residents, and obviously, the applicable tax treaty allocated taxing rights as regards (positive or negative) income from real estate exclusively to the State of location of the real estate.

The case seemed quite clear therefore. The presence of a disparity, the Court's 'exercise in parallel' doctrine, and its *Lidl Belgium* and *Marks & Spencer II* cases all pointed in the same direction: the mortgage interest was exclusively connected to the taxing jurisdiction assumed by the State taxing the positive income from real estate (Belgium); the mortgage interest was not in any way in the Netherlands' jurisdiction, and therefore not deductible in the Netherlands (possibly – given the curious *Marks & Spencer II* ruling on final losses – unless Mr Renneberg could show that nondeductibility in Belgium was forever, but even then: he had chosen to reside in a jurisdiction *not* allowing deduction of mortgage interest from employment income, and the Treaty freedoms do not guarantee

188 Case C-650/16, *Bevola*, EU:C:2018:424, points 38-39.

189 See for a comment on the case: Eric Kemmeren, 'Renneberg Endangers the Double Tax Convention System or Can a Second Round Bring Recovery?', 18 *EC Tax Review* 1 (2009).

190 Case C-152/03, *Ritter-Coulais*, EU:C:2006:123, [2006] ECR I -1711.

191 Case C-182/06, *Lakebrink*, EU:C:2007:452, [2007] ECR I-6705.

192 Case C-527/06, *Renneberg*, EU:C:2008:566, [2008] ECR I-7735.

tax neutrality of relocation[193] (see Chapter 6.4.1(ii)), nor do they require the job State to adapt its legislation to protect a migrant taxpayer from disadvantageous effects of disparities[194] (see Chapter 6.4.1(iii)).

The Court, however, ignored all that and applied its *Schumacker* reasoning.[195] It observed that Mr Renneberg earned almost all of his income in the Netherlands, making him, according to the Court, comparable to a resident. That is a mistake, as (i) Mr Renneberg did not earn almost his entire income in the Netherlands: he earned a significant amount of – on balance negative – income in Belgium, distinguishing him from *Schumacker*, (ii) the Netherlands was *neither* residence State *nor* source State (both Mr Renneberg's residence *and* the source of his negative income – his real estate – were in Belgium), and (iii) residents by definition do not live in foreign real estate, but in domestic real estate. The Court further observed that the Netherlands had retained, in its tax treaty with Belgium, the right to include items of income allocated to Belgium in the income *of its residents* for purposes of determining the progression of the tax rate on the domestic income (exemption with progression). It is important to see that this rate progression rule obviously only applies to *residents* as only residents are subject to worldwide progressive taxation (the Court accepts that nonresidents are only subject to *source* taxation; and the source (the real estate) was *not* in the Netherlands) and that even for residents, this rule does not imply that foreign-source income is *taxed*, but only that rate progression is calculated on the basis of worldwide income. Eventually, *also* for residents (positive or negative) income from foreign real estate was exempt in the Netherlands. But residence taxation was anyhow irrelevant, as Mr Renneberg was a *non*resident, solely subject to tax for *sourced* income. The Court further observed that this inclusion had the effect that Netherlands residents with a *second* (holiday) house in Belgium could deduct mortgage interest financing such a second house. Finally, the Court concluded that Mr Renneberg, as he was a *Schumacker*-case, should be treated in the same way as residents in respect of all factors determining his personal ability to pay. He was therefore entitled to deduction in the Netherlands.

Even if one compares Mr Renneberg to a Netherlands resident – which does not make sense, as neither his residence nor the source of his negative income from real estate had anything to do with the Netherlands taxing jurisdiction – we observe that the Court also missed that the deduction for *residents* (which Mr Renneberg was not) was only temporary: the treaty and national law contained a reintegration mechanism which excluded double tax relief for residents for *positive* income from foreign real estate in subsequent years. Thus, the deduction of foreign losses was taken back in later years. It is precisely this reintegration mechanism which the Court itself called, in *Krankenheim Ruhesitz*,[196] 'the logical complement of the deduction previously granted,' 'perfectly symmetrical', 'entirely proportional', and a 'indissociable and logical complement' of

193 Case C-403/03, *Schempp*, EU:C:2005:446, [2005] ECR I-6421, and Case C-365/02, *Lindfors*, EU:C:2004:449, [2004] ECR I-7183.

194 Case C-298/05, *Columbus Container Services*, EU:C:2007:754, [2007] ECR I-10451, Case C-293/06, *Deutsche Shell*, EU:C:2008:129, [2008] ECR I-1129, and Case C-157/07, *Krankenheim Ruhesitz am Wannsee-Seniorenheimstatt*, EU:C:2008:588, [2008] ECR I-8061.

195 See section 21.4; C-279/93, *Schumacker*, EU:C:1995:31, [1994] ECR I-5535.

196 Case C-157/07, *Krankenheim Ruhesitz am Wannsee-Seniorenheimstatt*, EU:C:2008:588, [2008] ECR I-8061.

previous deduction of foreign losses (in the *residence* State, which the Netherlands was not). The Court therefore also missed that this mechanism by definition cannot apply to *non*residents, as the treaty obviously does not entitle them to any double tax relief in the *source* State, but only in their *home* State (we again stress that the Netherlands was neither residence nor source State). See Chapter 10 for technical background on the interaction of loss relief and double tax relief. Income from Belgian real estate was, by virtue of both the applicable tax treaty and domestic law – *also* in the case of residents – eventually *not* taxed in the Netherlands, but in Belgium. In *Krankenheim* and *Timac Agro*, this fact justified the residence State *not* having to accept deduction of foreign losses. One might argue that nothing prevented the Netherlands from applying the reintegration mechanism also to nonresidents like Mr Renneberg, but as the tax treaty allocated income from Belgian real estate earned by a Belgian resident exclusively to Belgium, the Netherlands was unable to correct the Court's asymmetrical extension of the Netherlands taxing jurisdiction to a selected negative item of extraterritorial income of a nonresident. It would be in contravention of the tax treaty to still assume (moreover retro-actively) taxing power in respect of income from Belgian real estate earned by Belgian residents to gain access to a reintegration mechanism. Thus, the Netherlands, being neither source State nor residence State, was forced to accept forever deduction of foreign losses on a foreign fixed asset of a nonresident to which it had *not* extended its jurisdiction and to which in any event the applicable tax treaty prohibited it to extend its jurisdiction.

We therefore consider the *Renneberg* judgment to be inconsistent with other case law, such as *Lidl Belgium*, *Marks & Spencer II*, *Krankenheim Ruhesitz*, *K.* and *Timac Agro*, although it may be consistent with *Bevola*. Moreover, as mortgage interest was not deductible in Belgium, Mr Renneberg did not lose any advantage as a result of working abroad. Had Mr Renneberg had two jobs, one of which in Belgium, then the Netherlands could not have been required to accept deduction, as there would have been sufficient Belgian income for a deduction. However, Belgium simply did not allow any deduction, and only Belgium can be held responsible for Belgium's tax system. The Court clearly discriminated against Mr Renneberg's neighbour having the same house, the same loan, the same mortgage interest, the same job and the same income in Belgium. This entirely equal neighbour can *not* deduct his mortgage interest, and is therefore encouraged by this judgment to be employed in the Netherlands rather than in Belgium.

Possibly, the clear difference between on the one hand the *Lidl Belgium*, *Marks & Spencer II* and *Timac Agro* line of case law and on the other the *Schumacker* line may be explained by the fact that in the first line of cases (concerning companies), the Court seems to look at territorial and jurisdictional comparability, whereas in the latter line of cases (concerning individuals) it seems to focus on ability to pay. The K. case is the odd one out then, because that case concerned an individual and nevertheless he could not deduct his capital loss anywhere. Nevertheless, the general approach of the Court could be that individuals have personal and family circumstances and a personal ability to pay, whereas companies do not, being plain objective profit vehicles. It seems the Court wants to ensure that for individuals, all personal ability to pay factors are always taken into account, in whichever jurisdiction there is tax base to take personal deductions into account. The recent *Bechtel* case[197] concerning an individual, which contradicts (point

197 Case C-20/16, *Bechtel*, EU:C:2017:488.

68) the *Timac Agro* case concerning a corporate entity, again seems to confirm that. If that is the policy goal, we believe it is for the EU legislator, not for the Court, because it presupposes (i) that all Member States take into account personal ability to pay factors, which may not be the case (they may apply a *flat tax*), and (ii) that they all do so in more or less the same manner, which is most certainly *not* the case (the German tax free amounts, personal deductions and marital splitting of income differ greatly from the very frugal personal allowances in some other Member States, as do – of course – the average and marginal income tax rates). National tax systems differ widely in (not) taking into account personal circumstances, as they can make the political choice to have a flat tax (one single low rate and no deductions) or to have many personal deductions but – as a consequence – a progressive rate increasing to a high marginal level. The *Renneberg* case itself is a good illustration: Belgium did not allow mortgage interest deduction, whereas the Netherlands did. See also Section 13.4.6.

For elaboration on the issue of territoriality or EU-wide taxation, see Chapter 6.3.

(v) (No) National Tax Treatment of Nonresidents

Nevertheless, the *Renneberg* case is a – probably inadvertent – step in the direction of national tax treatment of nonresidents, at least for individuals. Different taxation of nonresidents (only for sourced income) and residents (worldwide taxation) is not national treatment, especially not as regards losses. Articles 45 and 49 TFEU require Member States to grant at least national treatment to nonresidents. Article 7 of Regulation (EU) 492/2011 on freedom of movement for workers,[198] requires national tax treatment of employees. We draw the not very daring conclusion that Member States must provide national treatment. This means that States applying worldwide taxation for residents, should also apply worldwide (or at least EU-wide) taxation for EU-nonresidents. Not only is this an EU law imperative, it would solve a lot of problems, inconsistencies and anomalies. It would end both the base fragmentation problems discussed above, as well as some inconsistencies – to be discussed in Chapters 6.3 and 13.4.3 – in interjurisdictional attribution of personal tax allowances and in progressive taxation of foreign-source income. Several States – Ireland, Switzerland, the Netherlands apply or have applied it.

Apart from *Renneberg*, the Court does not seem to require national tax treatment of nonresidents. It has accepted, regrettably, that (i) residents and nonresidents are not, as a rule, comparable for taxation purposes (the *Schumacher* line of case law; see Chapter 13.4), (ii) the 'fiscal principle of territoriality' (source taxation) is applied as regards nonresidents (Case C-250/95, *Futura*), and (iii) the job State may simply deny national treatment of nonresidents in respect of personal tax allowances (Case C-385/00, *De Groot*).

Especially *De Groot*,[199] *Bosal*,[200] *N. v. Inspecteur*[201] and *Marks & Spencer II*[202] suggest that the Court does not consider correct jurisdictional matching of positive and corresponding negative items of income a mandatory requirement of public interest if that would lead to allowances, losses or expenses not being deductible anywhere. It seems focused on

198 Regulation (EU) No 492/2011 of the European Parliament and of the Council of 5 April 2011 on freedom of movement for workers within the Union, O.J. 2011 L 141, p. 1.

199 Case C-385/00, *De Groot v. Inspecteur van belastingen*, EU:C:2002:750, [2002] ECR I-11819.

200 Case C-168/01, *Bosal Holding BV*, EU:C:2003:479, [2003] ECR I-9409.

201 Case C-470/04, *N. v. Inspecteur*, EU:C:2006:525, [2006] ECR I -7409.

202 Case C-446/03, *Marks & Spencer II*, EU:C:2005:763, [2005] ECR I-10837.

trying to ensure that a taxpayer operating cross-border is able, like taxpayers operating in one single jurisdiction, to deduct expenses, losses, allowances and credits *somewhere* in the internal market, in whichever State there is enough tax base (the always-somewhere approach; see Chapter 6.5.1). In *Schumacker*, the Court held that

> 'discrimination arises from the fact that his personal and family circumstances are taken into account neither in the State of residence nor in the State of employment.'

With all due respect, this is incomprehensible. One cannot define discrimination by reference to something *another* State is *not* doing. This discrimination concept says that, no matter how or by whom, a migrating taxpayer's personal and family circumstances must always be taken into account *some*where. Clearly, the Court's statement fails to designate *who* is doing the discriminating. Moreover, as observed, this approach in any event starts from a fallacy: if one of the two States involved applies a flat tax, then personal circumstances are *not* taken into account for anyone; not for residents either. It is difficult to see why another Member State should be required to provide allowances the home State does not care to extend itself to its residents. This approach therefore also ignores and contradicts two findings the Court emphasizes regularly: the Treaties do not guarantee that a change of jurisdiction will be neutral in respect of taxation[203] and do not require a Member State to adapt its tax rules to the other State's system such as to ensure fiscal neutrality of going across the border.[204]

We conclude that it is a clear violation of the Treaty freedoms – and that the Court should never have accepted, in *De Groot* – that source States deny national treatment to nonresidents by refusing to take into account their personal and family circumstances in the same way as for residents. The Court may have realized that *De Groot* was a mistake, as in recent case law, *Kieback*[205] and *X v Staatssecretaris*,[206] it required *proportional* allocation of ability-to-pay factors to the two source States involved, according to the extent in which they tax the total income of the taxpayer. But then again, these two cases were different from *De Groot*, which may therefore still stand, unfortunately; see Chapter 13.4.9.

3.2.7.4 Derivative (Second-Tier) Discrimination

The Court's case law shows that not only unequal treatment of nonresidents is prohibited, but also unfavourable treatment of residents if that indirectly affects nonresidents.

The *Halliburton* case[207] concerned the Netherlands transfer tax on the alienation of immovable property, which is levied from the purchaser. An exemption applied for transfers as part of a reorganization of a group of companies. However, Netherlands law required both the transferring and the acquiring company to be incorporated under

203 Case C-403/03, *Schempp*, EU:C:2005:446, [2005] ECR I-6421, and C-365/02, *Lindfors*, EU:C:2004:449, [2004] ECR I-7183.
204 Case C-298/05, *Columbus Container Services*, EU:C:2007:754, [2007] ECR I-10451, Case C-293/06, *Deutsche Shell*, EU:C:2008:129, [2008] ECR I-1129, and Case C-157/07, *Krankenheim Ruhesitz am Wannsee-Seniorenheimstatt*, EU:C:2008:588, [2008] ECR I-8061.
205 Case C-9/14, *Kieback*, EU:C:2015:406.
206 Case C-283/15, *X v Staatssecretaris*, EU:C:2017:102.
207 Case C-1/93, *Halliburton Services BV*, EU:C:1994:127, [1994] ECR I-1137.

Netherlands law. Halliburton was a US group of companies with subsidiaries, *inter alia*, in the Netherlands and Germany. In the course of a reorganization of the European activities, the German subsidiary (Halliburton *GmbH*; not a Netherlands legal form) transferred its Netherlands branch to a Netherlands subsidiary of the group, Halliburton *BV*. Part of the branch's assets consisted of Netherlands immovable property. Halliburton *BV* was denied the exemption from transfer tax because the transferring company did not have the requisite legal form. The Netherlands argued that Halliburton *BV* had no access to the Treaty, as the case was a purely internal one: the tax was levied from a Netherlands company acquiring Netherlands immovable property. The Court held, however, that the transferor, a nonresident *GmbH*, was derivatively discriminated against *via* its Netherlands transaction partner *BV*. Although the *GmbH* was not required to pay the tax, the tax levied from the *BV* disadvantaged the *GmbH's* conditions of sale: the property would have fetched a higher price had there been no transfer tax on the account of the *BV*. Also, it was clear that if the *GmbH* had invested in Netherlands immovable property through a Netherlands subsidiary rather than through a branch, the exemption would have been granted. The freedom of establishment also prohibits unjustified restrictions on the choice between a subsidiary and a branch. The Court also dismissed the Netherlands' argument that the Netherlands tax administration was unable to ascertain whether companies incorporated under foreign law were sufficiently comparable to Netherlands legal forms capable of being part of a group for reorganization purposes. It referred the Netherlands to the Directive on administrative cooperation (see Chapter 13) for obtaining the necessary information from the foreign tax administration.

The *Schempp* case, discussed in Section 3.2.7.3 and in Chapter 6.4.1(ii), is another example of a person not exercising any free movement right himself but nonetheless entitled to rely on the free movement rights because another person (his ex-wife) exercised her right to move and reside.

3.3 Normal Conditions of Competition (a 'Level Playing Field')

An internal market presupposes accessibility and unity of the market. Accessibility and unity may be distorted by public-law impediments and by private-law impediments. Cartel agreements between undertakings, product dumping and abuse of a dominant position are private-law market distortions. The main public-law impediments to normal conditions of competition are national measures discriminating against foreign products, services, workers and capital. The Treaty freedoms may be relied on to challenge that kind of measures. But public-law measures may restrict free competition in other manners as well: through the selective aiding of certain economic activity out of State resources, and through State monopolies. State monopolies are subject to the same competition rules as private monopolies (see Article 106(1) TFEU). Further, like private undertakings, public undertakings are subject to the Treaty provisions prohibiting restrictions to competition (the prohibitions on cartel agreements or practices, on abuse of a dominant position, and on dumping practices; Articles 101 and 102).

In *ZPT*, the Court held that the free movement rights and the rules on State aid have a common purpose, namely to ensure free movement between Member States under normal conditions of competition.[208] Indeed, Articles 107–109 TFEU are aimed against distortions of competition through State aid to certain undertakings or to certain productions. The form of the aid is irrelevant. It may take the form of subsidies, low-interest loans, cheap energy supply, tax breaks, extension of payment, etc. In a case concerning tax incentives for the Italian textile industry,[209] the Court held that neither the fiscal character nor the possible social objective of a State aid measure could protect it from the applicability of the State aid prohibition. A rebate on energy consumption taxes only benefiting undertakings manufacturing goods constitutes State aid.[210] Lenience in the recovery of tax claims and social security contributions from undertakings may constitute State aid, especially if the State's policy as a creditor of the undertakings is at variance with the normal receivables policy of a private creditor such as a bank.

For a national measure to constitute State aid, four conditions must be met: (i) the measure confers upon addressees an advantage; (ii) at the cost of State resources; this includes foregoing tax revenue which, but for the special scheme or administrative practice, would normally have been collected;[211] (iii) it (potentially) affects competition and trade between Member States, and (iv) it is selective in that it favours 'certain undertakings or the production of certain goods'.

State aid has recently become quite an issue in direct tax matters, due to the Commission's prohibitions of tax rulings extended to many multinational undertakings by several Member States. Like the Treaty Freedoms have proven to be formidable fiscal market integrators, the State aid prohibition as well is beginning to develop itself as a negative integration instrument of great importance, not so much – as the Treaty Freedoms – in respect of doing away with tax measures discriminating *against* cross-border economic operators, but rather in respect of doing away with market distortive tax competition in the form of selectively *benefiting* cross-border players by offering them tax breaks in exchange for inbound (re)location of economic activity.

Chapter 15 is entirely devoted to the increasing significance of the State aid prohibition in (international) tax law and, with that, in the area of policy competition between the Member States. (Unfair) tax competition itself is the subject of Chapter 23.

3.4 Sincere Cooperation and Effectiveness of EU Law

Article 4(3) TEU contains two (sets of) overarching obligations for Member States, a positive obligation (to assist each other and the Union to carry out the tasks flowing from the Treaties, to take any appropriate measure to ensure fulfilment of the obligations arising out of primary and secondary EU law and to facilitate the achievement of the Union's task), and a negative obligation (to refrain from any measures which could jeopardize the attainment of the Union's objectives). Article 4(3), together with Articles 2 and 19 TEU, establishing the rule of law in the Union and in the application of the Treaties, and together with general principles of law common to the legal traditions of the Member States, forms the legal basis on which the Court relies for the establishment and development of an

208 Case C-518/16, *ZPT AD*, EU:C:2018:126, point 47.
209 Case 173/73, *Italy v. Commission*, EU:C:1974:71, [1974] ECR 709.
210 See Case C-143/99, *Adria-Wien Pipeline GmbH*, EU:C:2001:598, [2001] ECR I-8365.
211 See, for example, Case C-156/98, *Germany v. Commission*, EU:C:2000:467, [2000] ECR I-6857.

autonomous Union legal order and for developing general EU law principles. See Chapter 2 for elaboration on the constitutional aspects and the sources of EU law.

Article 4(3) has been used by the Court to fill various gaps in Union law. It has served as a legal basis for, *inter alia*, the following very important and fundamental developments, which all may be summarized in one principle: the principle of substantive and procedural effectiveness of EU law in all national legal orders:

- The Court's prohibition on Member States' measures which may frustrate the useful effect ('*effet utile*') of EU measures[212] or even proposed measures;
- The case law requiring national authorities and courts to interpret national law in such a way that it accords with relevant Union law ('consistent interpretation'). This is especially important where EU Directives have not, or not correctly, been transposed into national law;[213]
- The Court's *Rewe* and *Comet* rules[214] stating that the national procedural autonomy of the Member States to effectuate EU law in their national legal orders is limited by the principles of equivalence and of effectiveness of EU law in the national legal order.[215] For its enforcement, EU law is almost entirely dependent on national procedural law. Exercise of rights based on EU law may not be more cumbersome than exercise of similar domestic law rights, nor may it be virtually impossible or excessively difficult to exercise EU law rights (see Section 3.5 below);
- The case law holding Member States liable for damages suffered by individuals or undertakings caused by serious breaches of EU law by Member States, such as the non-implementation or manifestly incorrect implementation of EU directives, or the levying of taxes in manifest breach of Treaty freedoms (*Francovich* liability; see Section 3.5.4); this liability may extend to the Member States' judiciaries in case of 'manifest' misapplication of EU law by a highest national court (*Köbler* liability; see Section 3.5.4);
- The Court's finding that if national administrative or judicial authorities have the power – but not the obligation – to apply the law *ex officio* (without the applicant or the parties having relied on it), then they are *required* to apply EU law of their own motion: a national procedural *power* becomes an EU law *obligation*. The also means that if national law allows reconsideration of definitive administrative decisions, national administrative authorities are required to reconsider final decisions if, although such decision has become irrevocable by decision of the highest national court, subsequent CJEU case law shows that that decision was in hindsight incompatible with EU law. A discretionary power to review final decisions thus becomes a mandatory obligation where the effectiveness of EU law is at issue. See the *Kühne & Heitz* case in Section 3.5.3.2. This has become a general procedural rule: an internal law *discretion* implies an EU law *obligation*;

212 See, for instance, Case 199/82, *San Giorgio*, EU:C:1983:318, [1983] ECR 3595.

213 See, for instance, Case 14/83, *Von Colson and Kamann*, EU:C:1984:153, [1984] ECR 1891; Case *80/86, Kolpinghuis, EU:C:1987:431*, [1987] ECR 3969; and Case C-106/89, *Marleasing*, EU:C:1990:395, [1990] ECR I-4135.

214 Cases 33/76, *Rewe*, EU:C:1976:188, [1976] ECR 1989; and 45/76, *Comet*, EU:C:1976:191, [1976] ECR 2043.

215 See also Case 199/82, *San Giorgio*, EU:C:1983:318, [1983] ECR 3595; Case C-208/90, *Emmott*, EU:C:1991:333, [1991] ECR I-4269; and Joined Cases C-6/90 and C-9/90, *Francovich v. Italy* and *Bonifaci v. Italy*, EU:C:1991:428, [1991] ECR I-5403, and [1993] 2 CMLR 66, p. 107.

- The recognition of so-called implied powers of the Union in the field of external relations (with third States; see Chapter 5).

Article 4(3) must be observed by every part and level of the Member States' constitutional, legislative, executive, administrative and judicial organization, therefore not only by the central government and its (tax) administration, but also by local and regional governments, by autonomous regions, as well as by the judiciary, including tax courts.

Obviously, the requirements ensuing from the principles of sincere cooperation and from the rule of law also affect national tax law. We quote four examples. The first concerns refund of overpaid tax not due on the basis of EU law. According to the Court, the substantive right to be refunded where tax has been levied in breach of EU law flows directly, 'as a matter of principle,' from the principle of sincere cooperation and the rule of law.[216] Such refund of overpaid tax may not be subject to a shorter time-limit than a refund based on purely domestic law,[217] nor may the procedural conditions set by national law render a refund based on EU law virtually impossible or excessively difficult[218] (see, for elaboration, Section 3.5.2.2).

A second example is Case C-129/00, *Commission v. Italy*,[219] in which the Court held invalid an onerous presumption of fact that indirect taxes are passed on to customers, to the detriment of undertakings claiming a refund of indirect taxes levied in contravention of EU law.

The principles of effectiveness of EU law and the rule of law may also work to the disadvantage of taxpayers. Third example: tax deductibility of competition fines imposed by the Commission on undertakings for violating EU competition law reduces their effectiveness as an instrument to correct illegal market behaviour of undertakings, unless the Commission takes account of their possible deductibility in fixing their amount, but the Commission does not have the necessary information on the tax position of the culprit. Deductibility is therefore probably incompatible with the principle of sincere cooperation.[220] The CCCTB proposal excludes deductibility of all penalties for breaches of law (see Chapter 22).

The fourth example also concerns effectiveness of EU law to the detriment of taxpayers. Illegal State aid must be recovered in principle ten years back, with interest (see Chapter 15). Obviously, this is also the case in respect of State aid in the form of tax breaks such as selectively advantageous tax rulings for multinationals, even if national tax law or even

216 See, a.o., Case C-62/00, *Marks & Spencer I*, EU:C:2002:435, [2002] ECR I-6325, quoted in section 3.5.2.2.

217 Case 240/87, *Deville v Administration des impôts*, EU:C:1988:349, [1988] ECR 3524.

218 Case 199/82, *San Giorgio*, EU:C:1983:318, [1983] ECR 3595. See also the *Metallgesellschaft and Hoechst* cases C-397/98 en C-410/98 and the *Thin Cap* case C-524/07).

219 Case C-129/00, *Commission v. Italy*, EU:C:2003:656, [2003] ECR I-4637.

220 See Case C-429/07, *X BV v Inspecteur*, EU:C:2009:359, [2009] ECR I-4833. The preliminary referral only concerned the question of whether the Commission has procedural standing (on the basis of Article 15(3) of Council Regulation (EC) No 1/2003 of 16 December 2002 on the implementation of the rules on competition (...), O.J. 2003 L 1, p. 1), to submit written observation of its own motion in national proceedings on the tax deductibility of a competition fine (it has), but both the advocate-general's opinion and the Court's judgment suggest that the referring court is not supposed to allow deduction (that was also the drift of the written submission of the Commission in the national proceedings).

constitutional law does not allow additional tax assessments further back than, *e.g.*, five years for reasons of legal certainty.

Although national administrations and courts are required to apply national law in conformity with relevant EU law, this obligation of consistent interpretation itself finds its limitation in general principles of law, especially in the principle of legitimate expectations: a totally new application of national law to conform it to EU law, but which could not reasonably be expected by the parties to the dispute is unacceptable as it offends legal certainty and legitimate expectations. Individuals must be able, in their mutual relations, to rely on national law as long as their Member States have not clearly and correctly implemented contrary EU directives. We observe that individuals and undertakings, like everyone in the Union, are directly bound by EU *Regulations*, which do not need to be transposed into national law to have full binding effect in the national legal order, although some practical implementation measures may be necessary.

'First generation' general concepts of EU law, such as direct effect in the national legal order and primacy of EU law over national and bilateral law, seem to have converged into a general 'second generation' and overarching concept of EU law: the principle of effectiveness of EU law. All public institutions of Member States must ensure, effectively and if necessary of their own motion, that EU law is applied and enforced in their national legal order as fully as possible. National administrations and courts must apply EU law provisions even if they are not unconditional, but the case is nonetheless justiciable on the basis of EU law provisions: if EU law can be applied to the case before them without having to make discretionary policy choices which should be left to democratically chosen legislators, they must do so.

3.5 Implications of the Principle of Effectiveness of EU Law in the National Legal Order[221]

The realization of EU law within the national legal orders has been secured by the CJEU through several permeating or transmission mechanisms, which together may be referred to as the principle of effectiveness of EU law in the wide sense (the *effet utile* doctrine). These transmission mechanisms are:

- primacy of EU law over any level of national or bilateral law of the Member States,
- direct effect (self-execution) of all provisions of primary EU law and of EU Directives which are unconditional and precise enough for justiciability of individual cases (EU Regulations have direct effect of themselves; see Chapter 2), – the requirement that national law be interpreted in conformity with EU law (consistent interpretation), – the principle of State liability for damages caused by serious breaches of EU law by any public authority, and
- the procedural principle of effectiveness: national procedural law must be applied such that for individuals relying on EU law, effective access to court and judicial protection is provided, as well as adequate procedural possibilities for them to enforce their rights derived from EU law. Their possibilities to that end may not be more limited than the

221 See on this subject: J.H. Jans, S. Prechal and R.J.G.M. Widdershoven: 'Europeanisation of Public Law', Europa Law Publishing, 2nd edition 2015, and Michael Lang e.a. (eds.), 'Procedural Rules in Tax Law in the Context of European Union and domestic Law,' Kluwer Law International, 2010.

possibilities available for individuals relying on national law (principle of equivalence), nor may they be so limited as to render effectuation of EU rights excessively difficult or virtually impossible (principle of effectiveness in the narrow sense).

What all this means, is that EU law, if judicially practicable, always jumps the queue: it trumps national and bilateral treaty law; it sets aside any provisions of national (procedural) law, even national constitutional law, and any provision of (tax) treaties between Member States which thwart the full effect of EU law.

The principle of effective judicial protection does not imply, however, that national law must provide for a free-standing legal action against national legislation possibly at odds with EU law. EU law does not require that without factual basis and without individually being affected, any individual or undertaking may ask a national court to nullify a national law possibly at odds with EU law, but then there should be individual legal protection offering adequate possibilities to assess the EU-compatibility of the impugned national measure, *e.g.* in the form of appeal against individual decisions, or of a damages suit against the State for tort.[222] Taxpayers will thus in principle have to await a tax assessment or will have to request an administrative decision as an admission ticket to legal remedies. They cannot simply go to Court and ask it to nullify national law they consider incompatible with EU law, unless their national law provides for such a free-standing action. We observe that Article 263(4) TFEU provides for a semi-free-standing action of natural or legal persons against 'a regulatory act' of an EU institution 'which is of direct concern to them and does not entail implementing measures.'[223]

3.5.1 *Direct Effect and Primacy of EU Law; Consistent Interpretation; Effects of Directives*

As early as 1964, the CJEU considered that if a common market was to be, European law must take precedence over the national laws of the Member States.[224] Without such precedence, EU law would be largely inconsequential as it would be entirely dependent on the scope the various national constitutions would allow it and on the question of whether national law would accord with it or contradict it. Individuals and undertakings would, in any event in Member States with a dualistic constitutional system, be unable to effectuate their EU rights. For such effectuation, not only precedence over contrary national law is needed, but also direct effect: EU law should be 'self-executing' as far as possible, meaning that economic operators should be able to rely on it in court as against their administrations, otherwise they would be dependent on the (lack of) discipline of national governments, parliaments and administrators in (not) implementing EU directives into national law. The Court therefore also borrowed from regular international public law, and further developed, the concept of direct applicability. European Treaty and Directive provisions which are sufficiently precise, clear and unconditional to be applied by the administration and in court without prior transformation into national law, must be applied directly, i.e. independently of whether they have been (correctly)

222 Case C-432/05, *Unibet v. Justitiekanslern*, EU:C:2007:163, [2007] ECR I-2271.

223 See on this issue Stephan Balthasar, 'Locus Standi Rules for Challenges to regulatory Acts by Private Applicants: the New Article 263(4) TFEU,' *European Law Review* 2010/4, p. 542-550.

224 Case 6/64, *Costa/ENEL*, EU:C:1964:66, [1964] ECR 614.

transposed.[225] Economic operators may therefore in proceedings against his Member State, rely on such EU Treaty and Directive provisions to trump any incompatible domestic provisions, even constitutional provisions. As observed, a provision is in principle clear, precise and unconditional enough if a case is justiciable on the basis of it: if the national administration or court can decide the case before it on the basis of that EU law provision without having to make political or policy choices.

Regulations have direct binding effect in all national legal orders by definition (Art. 288 TFEU). There are few EU regulations on tax law, except in the field of customs duties (the Community Customs Code; see Chapter 25 of the other Volume of this book). Directives are more important tools of harmonization in the field of taxes. Directives are binding only on the Member States and only as regards the result to be achieved, not as regards specific means to reach that result (Art. 288). They are addressed to the Member States rather than to individuals and undertakings, and direct effect of their provisions is therefore not obvious, but dependent on their framing. See Chapter 2 for elaboration on these legal instruments within the EU constitutional order.

Article 114 TFEU, which is the legal basis for the harmonization of direct taxes (see Chapter 2), only provides for EU measures in the form of directives. Although Article 113, concerning indirect taxes, refers to 'provisions' and therefore also encompasses regulations and other measures, most of the harmonization of indirect taxes, except customs duties, has also been realized through directives, the most important one being the Recast VAT Directive. Directive implementation discipline of Member States is therefore of major importance for the effectiveness of EU tax rules. Direct effect and precedence ensure that if a directive is not implemented timely or incorrectly, that does not leave individuals and undertakings deriving rights from it empty-handed. The Court found it unacceptable and incompatible with the binding character of directives for Member States that an implementation failure of a Member State would benefit that same defaulting Member State (*estoppel* principle). We cite the seminal *Becker* case,[226] concerning a self-employed credit negotiator relying, before her national tax court, on a provision of the Sixth VAT Directive requiring Member States to exempt from VAT, *inter alia*, 'the granting and the negotiation of credit.' Germany was late in transposing this exemption into national law. Under Germany's dualist constitutional system, in principle application and enforcement of international law is only possible after its transposition by national Act of Parliament into a national law. Becker wanted – but was denied – the exemption for the period between the ultimate implementation date and the date on which the German implementing provisions finally came into force, without retroactive effect. The Court held:

> 'According to the third paragraph of Article 189 [now 288; *authors*] of the Treaty, "a directive shall be binding, as to the result to be achieved, upon each Member State to which it is addressed, but shall leave to the national authorities the choice of form and methods". (...) Wherever a directive is correctly implemented, its effects extend to individuals through the medium of the implementing measures adopted by the Member State concerned (...). However, special problems arise where a Member State has failed to implement a directive correctly and, more particularly, where the provisions of the directive have not been implemented by the end of the period prescribed for that purpose. It follows from the

225 Case 26/62, *Van Gend & Loos*, EU:C:1963:1, [1963] ECR 1.
226 Case 8/81, *Ursula Becker v. Finanzamt Münster-Innenstadt*, EU:C:1982:7, [1982] ECR 69.

> well-established case law of the Court (...) that whilst under Article [288] regulations are directly applicable and, consequently, by their nature capable of producing direct effects, that does not mean that other categories of measures covered by that Article can never produce similar effects. It would be incompatible with the binding effect which Article [288] ascribes to directives to exclude in principle the possibility of the obligations imposed by them being relied on by persons concerned. (...) [A] Member State which has not adopted the implementing measures required by the directive within the prescribed period may not plead, as against individuals, its own failure to perform the obligation which the directive entails. Thus, wherever the provisions of a directive appear, as far as their subject matter is concerned, to be unconditional and sufficiently precise, those provisions may, in the absence of implementing measures adopted within the prescribed period, be relied upon as against any national provision which is incompatible with the directive in so far as the provisions define rights which individuals are able to assert against the State (...).'

Much on the same grounds, but obviously also on the basis of the requirements of legal certainty, a directive does *not* have direct effect in the opposite direction (no inverse vertical direct effect): a Member State which failed to implement a directive, cannot rely on that unimplemented directive in proceedings against individuals or undertakings, less so if the Directive calls for penalization of certain conduct of individuals or undertakings.[227] That would be incompatible with basic requirements of legal certainty: individuals must be able to rely on their national (criminal) law. A Directive cannot, therefore, of itself (without implementation) impose obligations on individuals. This means, a.o., that where a Member State has not properly implemented an EU directive calling for, *e.g.*, a specific environmental tax, it cannot legally levy that tax directly on the basis of the Directive. It also implies that individuals and undertakings have a choice: where national law does not conform to a directly applicable directive provision, they may rely, depending on which suits their interest best, either on that Directive provision or on the contrary national law provision. This invites 'provision shopping,' but that is an inherent consequence of the one-way vertical direct effect of directives and of the fact that the Member State involved failed to implement without discrepancies between the directive provision and the national implementation. As the Court considered in the VAT case *GMAC UK*,[228] a Member State cannot prevent a taxable person from relying on the direct effect of a directive provision by arguing that that person is at the same time relying on a national law provision concerning the same transaction with the cumulative effect of producing an overall beneficial fiscal result (a windfall profit) which neither national law nor the Sixth VAT Directive if applied separately would produce or are intended to produce, as that effect was a result of incorrect implementation by the Member State involved.

This is not to say, that directives cannot have adverse effects for individuals. National authorities and courts are required to interpret national law as much as possible such that it accords with relevant EU law (consistent interpretation), especially where directives have not, incompletely or ambiguously been transposed into national law.[229] This obligation arises after the implementation period of the Directive has expired but even before

227 Case 80/86, *Kolpinghuis*, EU:C:1987:431, [1987] ECR 3969.

228 Case C-589/12, *GMAC UK plc*, EU:C:2014:2131.

229 See, for instance, Case 14/83, *Von Colson and Kamann*, EU:C:1990:153, [1984] ECR 1891; Case 80/86, *Kolpinghuis*, EU:C:1987:431, [1987] ECR 3969; and Case C-106/89, *Marleasing*, EU:C:1990:395, [1990] ECR I-4135.

that date, national Courts must avoid an interpretation of national law (we submit: or bilateral treaty law between Member States) which could seriously undermine the later effectiveness of the adopted Directive.[230] The requirement of EU consistent application of national law extends to all provisions of national law (whether predating or postdating the relevant provision of EU law and whether or not intended as implementation of an EU directive) and to all provisions of EU law, not only directive provisions. Moreover, national courts must assume, when applying national implementation measures, that the national legislator had the intention of giving full effect to its legislative obligations ensuing from EU law, especially from directives it had to implement.[231] When a directive confers rights on individuals, this duty of consistent interpretation benefits these individuals, but this also means that if the result prescribed by the directive is not favourable to the taxpayer (*e.g.* a denial of participation exemption under Article 4 PSD (see Chapter 16) or an exchange of tax information to another Member State on the basis of the DAC (see Chapter 25)), that result must also be pursued with all interpretative means available to the national court.

The duty of consistent interpretation may thus come close to inverse vertical direct effect, i.e. direct effect against a taxpayer. In the VAT Case *Italmoda*,[232] the Court denied restitution, deduction and exemption rights to a company on the basis of a combination of the general prohibition on abuse of rights and the fact that one of the objectives of the Recast VAT Directive is to curb fraud and evasion, even though according to national law, all conditions for such restitution, deduction or exemption were met. In this case, therefore, even though national law offered no possibilities to deny the tax benefit, it was nevertheless denied on the basis of a Directive consistent and abuse-of-law-principle-consistent interpretation of the VAT Directive. The difference with inverse vertical direct effect is difficult to see.

Since a directive cannot of itself impose obligations on private parties, it cannot be applied directly either in horizontal relationships (between two private parties). Although many commentators as well as advocates-general argued it would be appropriate for directives to have horizontal direct effect as well, the Court explicitly rejected that possibility[233] because directives are addressed to Member States and should therefore, again in the light of the requirements of legal certainty, not of themselves be capable of creating obligations for individuals or undertakings not reckoning with such obligations on the basis of their national law. The Court regularly reiterates[234] that the principle of legal certainty opposes directives creating obligations for individuals without prior implementation into national law. Again, this is not to say that directives may not have horizontal effects. For instance, in the *Delena Wells* case,[235] the UK was required, on the basis of a directive on mandatory assessment of environmental effects of projects,[236] to withdraw a permit it had already granted to a mining company, because an individual

230 Case C-212/04, *Konstantinos Adeneler*, EU:C:2006:443.
231 Case C-334/92, *Wagner Miret*, EU:C:1993:945, [1993] ECR I-6 911.
232 Joined Cases C-131/13, C-163/16 and C-164/16, Italmoda a.o., EU:C:2014:2455.
233 Case C-91/92, *Faccini Dori*, EU:C:1994:292, [1994] ECR I-3325.
234 *E.g.* in Case C-201/02, *the Queen, ex parte Delena Wells*, EU:C:2004:12, [2004] ECR I-723.
235 See the previous footnote.
236 Directive 85/337/EEC on the assessment of the effects of certain public and private projects on the environment, O.J. No. L175 of 5 July 1985, p. 40-48.

living close to the site rightly complained that the environmental assessment required by the directive had not taken place. Directive consistent interpretation of national law may produce drastic horizontal effects of directives as well. The *Pfeiffer a.o.* cases[237] concerned a German collective employment contract which tallied with German labour law, but not quite with EU Directive 93/104, prohibiting a working week for employees of more than 48 hours. That directive had not been transposed properly into German law. The case thus raised the question of how lack of horizontal direct effect of directives relates to the obligation of national courts to apply national law consistent with EU law, especially how far consistent interpretation reaches. The Court explained:

> '114. The requirement for national law to be interpreted in conformity with Community law is inherent in the system of the Treaty, since it permits the national court, for the matters within its jurisdiction, to ensure the full effectiveness of Community law when it determines the dispute before it (...).
> 115. Although the principle that national law must be interpreted in conformity with Community law concerns chiefly domestic provisions enacted in order to implement the directive in question, it does not entail an interpretation merely of those provisions but requires the national court to consider national law as a whole in order to assess to what extent it may be applied so as not to produce a result contrary to that sought by the directive (...).
> 116. In that context, if the application of interpretative methods recognised by national law enables, in certain circumstances, a provision of domestic law to be construed in such a way as to avoid conflict with another rule of domestic law or the scope of that provision to be restricted to that end by applying it only in so far as it is compatible with the rule concerned, the national court is bound to use those methods in order to achieve the result sought by the directive.
> 117. In such circumstances, the national court, when hearing cases which, like the present proceedings, fall within the scope of Directive 93/104 and derive from facts postdating expiry of the period for implementing the directive, must, when applying the provisions of national law specifically intended to implement the directive, interpret those provisions so far as possible in such a way that they are applied in conformity with the objectives of the directive (...).
> 118. In this instance, the principle of interpretation in conformity with Community law thus requires the referring court to do whatever lies within its jurisdiction, having regard to the whole body of rules of national law, to ensure that Directive 93/104 is fully effective, in order to prevent the maximum weekly working time laid down in Article 6(2) of the directive from being exceeded (...).'

National courts are thus required to apply all methods of interpretation available to them for avoiding conflicts of law in order to attain a result consistent with EU law. The only limitation seems to be the principle of legal certainty. Consistent interpretation may not lead to unforeseeable results which the Court, precisely, wished to preclude by rejecting horizontal and inverse vertical direct effect.

The obligation to interpret national law in conformity with EU law will for direct taxation purposes be most relevant in two instances: (i) the application of national tax law provisions affecting issues covered by one of the EU Direct Tax directives, and (ii)

237 Joined Cases C-397/01 to C-403/01, *Pfeiffer a.o.*, EU:C:2004:584, [2004] ECR I-8835.

cases in which according to national law two interpretations of a tax law provision are possible; even if that tax law provision is not in any way an implementation or application of EU law, and even if both interpretations are tenable under the EU free movement provisions or State aid rules, the tax administration and the tax courts are required to choose the interpretation which serves *best* object and purpose of the Treaty Freedoms and State aid rules.

As observed, from *Adeneler*[238] it follows that the obligation to interpret national law consistent with EU directives in principle only applies after their implementation period has expired, but that (courts of) Member States obviously also before that time are bound by the obligation in Article 4(3) TEU to refrain from interpretations or courses of action which could frustrate the later effectuation of object and purpose of the directive. Moreover, if a directive (also) expresses a fundamental right which is protected by general principles of EU law, such as non-discrimination in respect of age, sex, religion or race, then the national courts must guarantee the full effectiveness of the directive provisions concerned already in the period *before* its implementation date, setting aside any conflicting national law provisions.[239] Probably, since 2009, this already follows from Article 6 TEU *juncto* the Charter on Fundamental Rights (see Chapter 4).

3.5.2 Enforcement of EU Law: Procedural Equivalence and Effectiveness

3.5.2.1 National Procedural Autonomy on Two Conditions; Procedural Rule of Reason

Many matters have not been regulated at Union level. Especially the enforcement of EU law within the national jurisdictions is largely left to the national judicial systems. The CJEU recognizes that, in the absence of EU procedural rules, it is for the Member States to designate the courts and tribunals having jurisdiction and to lay down the detailed procedural rules governing actions for safeguarding rights which individuals derive from EU law. This implies that the enforcement of EU law may differ from Member State to Member State (national procedural autonomy). However, the Court limited this autonomy by setting two general conditions, called the *Rewe/Comet* rule:[240]

i. the national procedural rules governing the exercise of rights derived from EU law may not be less favourable than those governing the exercise of similar purely domestic rights (principle of *equivalence*) and
ii. they may not render practically impossible or excessively difficult the exercise of rights conferred by EU law (principle of *effectiveness*).

The principle of effectiveness also implies the right to effective judicial protection, especially access to a competent court. As the Court explained in *Pontin*:[241]

238 Case C-212/04, *Konstantinos Adeneler*, EU:C:2006:443, [2006] ECR I-6057.

239 Case C-144/04, *Werner Mangold*, EU:C:2005:709, [2005] ECR I-9981.

240 See, in particular, Case 33/76, *Rewe*, EU:C:1976:188, [1976] ECR 1989; Case 45/76, *Comet*, EU:C:1976:191, [1976] ECR 2043; Case C-231/96, *Edis*, EU:C:1998:401, [1998] ECR I-4951, points 19 and 34; Case C-260/96, *Spac*, EU:C:1998:402, [1998] ECR I-4997, point 18; and Case C-228/96, *Aprile*, EU:C:1998:544, [1998] ECR I-7141, point 18.

241 Case C-63/08, *Pontin*, EU:C:2009:666, [2009] ECR I-10467.

> '44. Those requirements of equivalence and effectiveness embody the general obligation on the Member States to ensure judicial protection of an individual's rights under Community law. They apply both as regards the designation of the courts and tribunals having jurisdiction to hear and determine actions based on Community law and as regards the definition of detailed procedural rules (...).'
> 45. The principle of equivalence requires that the national rule at issue be applied without distinction, whether the infringement alleged is of Community law or national law, where the purpose and cause of action are similar (...).'

Since the entering into force of the Treaty of Lisbon, Article 19(1)(2nd indent) TEU explicitly requires Member States to provide 'remedies sufficient to ensure effective legal protection in the fields covered by Union law.'

The rule of law and the principle of effectiveness also affect national procedural autonomy as regards the right to be heard, in matters involving EU law, by the authorities *before* they impose ad adverse decision: in the *Sopropé* Case[242] (quoted in Section 3.1.3), the Court required national tax administrations to observe the (administrative) 'rights of the defence'. It required those authorities, in all cases where 'they take decisions which come within the scope of Community law' and 'which significantly (adversely) affect (the) interests' of the taxpayer (e.g. a tax assessment), to hear the taxpayer *prior* to deciding, and to allow him enough time and opportunity to challenge the information on which the intended tax assessment is based, a.o. to avoid irreparable damage but also mistakes. If a prior hearing and access to the relevant documents are omitted, then the rights of defence of the taxpayer are infringed even if he can give his views during a subsequent administrative objection stage, unless (i) immediate action by the authorities was required (e.g. the taxpayer is minded to disappear)[243] or (ii) national law suspends collection of the assessment until the authorities have duly taken account of his views during the objection stage.[244] The consequence of an infringement of the rights of the defense, in particular the right to be heard, do not need to be annulment of the tax assessment. That should be the consequence, however, if the outcome of the procedure might have been different without the infringement of the right to be heard.[245] The rights of the defence are also included in the EU Charter of fundamental rights, but only in respect of criminal charges and, in case of administrative decisions, only addressed at the EU institutions.

Compulsory prior mediation by a regional committee before being able to go to (tax) court need not be detrimental to the effectiveness of the remedy, but if such prior mediation is only possible via the internet or otherwise limited itself in access, it may fall foul of the effectiveness principle.[246]

The effectiveness principle also affects national law on judiciary organization and appeals: a lower court must lay aside binding instructions from the court of appeal which quashed its judgment if it considers those instructions to be incompatible with EU law: a national rule providing that lower courts are bound by the judgment of the higher court

242 Case C-349/07, *Sopropé*, EU:C:2008:746.
243 See, e.g. Case 28/05, *Dokter*, EU:C:2006:408, concerning the necessity for immediate action to stop a cattle plague from spreading and which could therefore be put into place without giving the farmer involved a prior say in the matter.
244 Joined Cases 129/13 and 130/13, *Kamino* and *Datema Hellman*, EU:C:2014:2041.
245 Joined Cases 129/13 and 130/13, *Kamino* and *Datema Hellman*, EU:C:2014:2041.
246 See Case C-317-320/08, *Alassini a.o. v Telecom Italia Spa a.o.*, EU:C:2010:146, [2010] ECR I-2213.

is trumped by EU law providing that also lower courts are competent to ask preliminary questions if they doubt the correctness of the interpretation of EU law.[247]

The principle of effectiveness did not oppose an Italian tax amnesty which also curtailed the competence of the Italian *Corte Suprema di Cassazione* in tax matters. Case *3M Italia*[248] concerned not only procedural autonomy in tax matters, but also State aid, non-discrimination and abuse of rights. Italy had enacted a tax amnesty involving, *inter alia*, the termination of pending direct tax disputes which started more than 10 years ago and in which the tax administration had been unsuccessful in the first two instances, on the condition of payment of 5% of the contested amount of tax (which raised questions of equal treatment and of possible State aid), as well as a temporary procedural rule which removed the power to review legality from the *Corte Suprema di Cassazione*, implying that that court could not review the correct interpretation and application of EU law in the cases covered by the tax amnesty, although a highest court is under an obligation ex Art. 267 TFEU to refer questions of validity under EU law to the Court of Justice of the EU. The Court held, however, that Article 4(3) TEU, the TFEU freedoms, the principle of non-discrimination, the rules on State aid and the obligation to ensure the effective application of EU did not preclude this Italian tax amnesty, at least not for unharmonised direct taxes (which are not, unlike VAT and customs duties, an own resource of the EU). In *Taricco*,[249] the Court did not accept limitation periods for criminal offences which made it impossible to successfully prosecute serious VAT-fraud, entailing *de facto* impunity of VAT evasion amounting to several million euros, or which were longer where the financial interests of the Member State involved were at issue than where the financial interests of the Union were involved.[250]

The *Rewe/Comet* rule (equivalence; effectiveness) further implies, *inter alia*, that time-limits for bringing objections or appeal may not distinguish between actions based on domestic law and actions based on EU law, nor may they be extremely short (see section 3.5.3 below), and that national procedural law may not excessively hinder access to court or preclude national courts from considering claims based on EU law.[251] The CJEU case law on effectiveness advances two mutually reinforcing goals: (i) ensuring that individuals are able to effectively exercise subjective rights conferred upon them by EU law, and (ii) objective effectiveness and enforcement of EU law in all Member States alike, at least at the level of domestic judicial protection, but if that level is too low, at a level consistent with Article 47 of the EU Charter on Fundamental Rights (and with that, with Article 6 of the European Convention on the Protection of Human Rights and Fundamental Freedoms; see Chapter 4). If necessary to that end, the CJEU requires national courts to disapply national procedural rules hindering access to court and even to apply remedies which

247 Case C-173/09, *Elchinov*, EU:C:2010:581. See also Joined Cases C-188 and 189/10, *Melki and Abdeli*, EU:C:2010:363, [2010] ECR I-5667.

248 Case C-417/10, *3M Italia*, EU:C:2012:184.

249 Case C-105/14, *Taricco*, EU:C:2015:555.

250 In Case C-42/17, M.A.S. and M.B., EU:C:2017:936, the Court clarified that the limitation period cannot be disapplied if that would infringe the principle of legality.

251 See, *e.g.*, Case C-97/91, *Oleificio Borelli Spa v. Commission*, EU:C:1992:491, [1992] ECR I-6313, points 13-14.

do not seem to be available under national law,[252] thus harmonizing national remedies and procedural law at a minimum level necessary for the effectiveness of EU law and effective legal protection of individuals within the national jurisdictions.

Presumptions of fact under national procedural law must be disapplied if they render excessively difficult the repayment of tax to which an undertaking is entitled under EU law. For example, a legal presumption that overpaid indirect tax levied in contravention of EU law has been passed on to customers, may not be excessively difficult to rebut for undertakings claiming repayment of the overpaid tax.[253] *Meilicke II*[254] shows that the question of which kind and force of evidence is required for obtaining an imputation credit for foreign corporation tax is in principle left to national procedural autonomy, but that even if formally *equivalence* is guaranteed, that does not necessarily mean that also *effective* access to EU law rights has been guaranteed: requiring a (non-existent) foreign certificate identical to the domestic certificate required for crediting domestic corporation tax, may formally ensure equivalence, but is in substance discriminatory and disproportionate. According to the Court, it would moreover 'breach the principle of sound administration.'[255] This is typically a case in which mutual recognition may be read in the Treaty freedoms: there is no overriding reason of public interest why the German authorities would not accept foreign other means of evidence.

The equivalence and effectiveness rules also apply as regards interest calculation on successful tax refund claims based on EU law: if national law provides for interest on tax refunds, it must also provide for interest on tax refunds based on EU law.[256] But that is not enough: if national law does not provide for any interest on repayment of tax not due in cases involving only domestic law, then, although the principle of equivalence is not violated if no interest is calculated on a VAT refund either, still the effectiveness principle is infringed, as no compensation at all does not take away the damages for not having available money illegally levied by the tax administration. The principle of effectiveness of EU law therefore not only entails a right to refund of tax charged in contravention of EU law which directly flows from EU law (see Section 3.5.2.2 below), but also a right to interest calculation on such refund. As the Court considered in *Irimie*:[257]

> "21. (…), where a Member State has levied taxes in breach of the rules of European Union law, individuals are entitled to reimbursement not only of the tax unduly levied but also of the amounts paid to that State or retained by it which relate directly to that tax. That

252 See, *e.g.*, Case 222/86, *Heylens*, EU:C:1987:442, [1987] ECR 1651, point 14; Joined Cases C-87/90, C-88/90 and C-89/90, *Verholen and others*, EU:C:1991:314, [1991] ECR I-3757; Case C-226/99, *Siples Sri v Ministero delle Finanze c.s.*, EU:C:2001:14, [2001] ECR I-227; C-213/89, *Factortame III*, EU:C:1990:257, [1990] ECR I-2433, point 19; Case C-187/00, *Kutz-Bauer v Hamburg*, EU:C:2003:168, [2003] ECR I-2741; and Case C-462/99, *Connect Austria GmbH*, EU:C:2003:297, [2003] ECR I-5197.

253 See, *e.g.*, Case C-147/01, *Weber's Wine World a.o.*, EU:C:2003:533, [2003] ECR I-11365.

254 Case C-262/09, *Meilicke II*, EU:C:2011:438.

255 Case C-262/09, *Meilicke II*, EU:C:2011:438.

256 See Case C-330/91, *The Queen/Inland Revenue Commissioners, ex parte Commerzbank*, EU:C:1993:303, [1993] ECR I-4017.

257 Case C-565/11, *Irimie*, EU:C:2013:250.

> also includes losses constituted by the unavailability of sums of money as a result of a tax being levied prematurely (....).
> 22. Accordingly, the principle of the obligation of Member States to repay with interest amounts of tax levied in breach of European Union law follows from that law (*Littlewoods Retail and Others*, paragraph 26, and *Zuckerfabrik Jülich and Others*, paragraph 66).
> 23. (...), in the absence of European Union legislation, it is for the internal legal order of each Member State to lay down the conditions in which such interest must be paid, particularly the rate of that interest and its method of calculation. Those conditions must comply with the principles of equivalence and effectiveness; that is to say that they must not be less favourable than those concerning similar claims based on provisions of national law or arranged in such a way as to render the exercise of rights conferred by the European Union legal order impossible in practice or excessively difficult (see, to that effect, *Littlewoods Retail and Others*, paragraphs 27 and 28 and the case-law cited)."

The *Rewe/Comet* rule also applies to deduction or reimbursement of the cost of legal counsel in proceedings concerning EU rights: if these exist for proceedings based on internal law, they must also exist for proceedings based on EU law.[258] A taxpayer winning a case against on the basis of EU law must at least receive the same principal repayment, the same interest on repayment of overpaid tax, the same compensation for or deduction of the cost of legal counsel, and the same refund of a possible court fee, as a taxpayer winning a case on the basis of purely internal law.

The principle of effectiveness of EU law also prohibits Member States from enacting legislation specifically aimed at limiting the financial effects of an CJEU judgment holding national tax law in breach of EU law,[259] because the rule of EU law explained in the judgment is deemed to have meant what the Court said it means from the moment of its coming into force.

The principle of effectiveness does not require, however, that claimants who did not use their procedural rights within reasonable time-limits for bringing actions, be granted the possibility to still bring an action beyond the national reasonable time-limits. Claimants may be required to limit their potential damages by using their procedural rights to oppose the decision causing the damages and considered illegal by them (see section 3.5.3.2). On the other hand, if exceeding the time-limit for refunds was excusable because the national authorities confused the claimant about his (procedural) rights or sent him into the wrong procedure,[260] a late action will have to be admitted.

On the basis of the principle of effectiveness of EU law, the Court thus has established a *procedural* rule of reason (see for the *substantive* rule of reason sections 3.2.1 and 3.2.2): Member States may restrict national procedural possibilities to exercise (repayment) rights derived from EU law, including ancillary rights such as interest calculation, compensation for cost of legal counsel, and refund of court fees, but they must do so indiscriminately and there must be a general interest justification for the restriction, such as legal certainty for both taxpayers and the tax administration, the prevention of unjust enrichment, the principle of *litis finiri oportet*, or other interests of good procedure.

258 See Case C-346/04, *Conijn*, EU:C:2006:445, [2006] ECR I-6137.
259 Case C-231/96, *Edis*, EU:C:1998:401, [1998] ECR I-4951.
260 See Case C-208/90, *Emmott*, EU:C:1991:333, [1991] ECR I-4269.

3.5.2.2 Illustration: Restrictions on Restitution of Overpaid Tax

To illustrate the effect of the *Rewe/Comet* rule in practice, we discuss a number of cases, which are of particular interest in the field of taxation. They concern different types of national procedural rules restricting the effectiveness of claims for restitutions of tax paid in breach of EU law. To set the stage, we cite Case C-62/00, *Marks & Spencer I*[261] (not to be mixed up with Case C-446/03, *Marks & Spencer II*, on cross-border loss relief). *Marks & Spencer I* concerned a retroactive reduction, from six years to three years, of the UK time-limit for bringing claims for repayment of VAT paid but not due because of incompatibility with EU law. This curtailing of the time-limit had the effect of voiding claims and law suits already pending on tax periods further back than three years. The UK's aim was to protect the public budget against unforeseen large repayment obligations. It applied for all VAT repayment claims, irrespective of their legal basis (internal law or EU law). It thus agreed with the principle of equivalence. The Court held, however, on the basis of the principle of effectiveness:

> '33. (...), the question must be construed as asking essentially whether national legislation retroactively curtailing the period within which repayment may be sought of sums paid by way of VAT collected in breach of provisions of the Sixth Directive with direct effect, (...), is compatible with the principles of effectiveness and of the protection of legitimate expectations.
>
> *The principle of effectiveness*
> 34. (...) in the absence of Community rules on the repayment of national charges wrongly levied it is for the domestic legal system of each Member State to designate the courts and tribunals having jurisdiction and to lay down the detailed procedural rules governing actions for safeguarding rights which individuals derive from Community law, provided, first, that such rules are not less favourable than those governing similar domestic actions (the principle of equivalence) and, second, that they do not render virtually impossible or excessively difficult the exercise of rights conferred by Community law (...).
> 35. As regards the latter principle, the Court has held that in the interests of legal certainty, which protects both the taxpayer and the administration, it is compatible with Community law to lay down reasonable time-limits for bringing proceedings (...). Such time-limits are not liable to render virtually impossible or excessively difficult the exercise of the rights conferred by Community law. In that context, a national limitation period of three years which runs from the date of the contested payment appears to be reasonable (...).
> 36. Moreover, it is clear from the judgments in *Aprile* (paragraph 28) and *Dilexport* (paragraphs 41 and 42) that national legislation curtailing the period within which recovery may be sought of sums charged in breach of Community law is, subject to certain conditions, compatible with Community law. First, it must not be intended specifically to limit the consequences of a judgment of the Court to the effect that national legislation concerning a specific tax is incompatible with Community law. Secondly, the time set for its application must be sufficient to ensure that the right to repayment is effective. In that connection, the Court has held that legislation which is not in fact retrospective in scope complies with that condition.
> 37. It is plain, however, that that condition is not satisfied by national legislation (...) which reduces from six to three years the period within which repayment may be sought of VAT

261 Case C-62/00, *Marks & Spencer I*, EU:C:2002:435, [2002] ECR I-6325.

wrongly paid, by providing that the new time-limit is to apply immediately to all claims made after the date of enactment of that legislation and to claims made between that date and an earlier date, being that of the entry into force of the legislation, as well as to claims for repayment made before the date of entry into force which are still pending on that date.
38. Whilst national legislation reducing the period within which repayment of sums collected in breach of Community law may be sought is not incompatible with the principle of effectiveness, it is subject to the condition not only that the new limitation period is reasonable but also that the new legislation includes transitional arrangements allowing an adequate period after the enactment of the legislation for lodging the claims for repayment which persons were entitled to submit under the original legislation. Such transitional arrangements are necessary where the immediate application to those claims of a limitation period shorter than that which was previously in force would have the effect of retroactively depriving some individuals of their right to repayment, or of allowing them too short a period for asserting that right.
39. In that connection it should be noted that Member States are required as a matter of principle to repay taxes collected in breach of Community law (Joined Cases C-192/95 to C-218/95 *Comateb and Others*, paragraph 20, and *Dilexport*, paragraph 23), and whilst the Court has acknowledged that, by way of exception to that principle, fixing a reasonable period for claiming repayment is compatible with Community law, (…). (…), in order to serve their purpose of ensuring legal certainty limitation periods must be fixed in advance (Case 41/69 *ACF Chemiefarma v. Commission*, paragraph 19).
40. Accordingly, legislation such as that at issue in the main proceedings, the retroactive effect of which deprives individuals of any possibility of exercising a right which they previously enjoyed with regard to repayment of VAT collected in breach of provisions of the Sixth Directive with direct effect must be held to be incompatible with the principle of effectiveness.
41. That applies notwithstanding the argument of the United Kingdom Government to the effect that the enactment of the legislation at issue in the main proceedings was motivated by the legitimate purpose of striking a due balance between the individual and the collective interest and of enabling the State to plan income and expenditure without the disruption caused by major unforeseen liabilities.
42. Whilst such a purpose may serve to justify fixing reasonable limitation periods for bringing claims, as was noted in paragraph 35, it cannot permit them to be so applied that rights conferred on individuals by Community law are no longer safeguarded.'

We draw attention to paragraph 39, stating that repayment of taxes collected in breach of EU law is 'a matter of principle.' The right to repayment of tax levied in violation of EU law is thus, apparently, another general principle of EU law, as is the right to calculation of interest on that repayment: see the *Irimie* case mentioned in Section 3.5.2.1).

The UK was stubborn to try again and was taken to Court again by the Commission in infringement proceedings on a new retroactive and without adequate transitional provisions curtailing of limitation period for remedies to recover tax paid in contravention of EU law. The Court again found that such retroactive limitation of taxpayers' EU rights offends the principles of sincere cooperation, of effectiveness of EU law and of protection of legitimate expectations.[262]

262 See Case C-640/13, Commission v UK, EU:C:2014:2457.

Another example of a procedural restriction of the right to repayment of tax levied in breach of EU law is the *Paolo Speranza* case,[263] concerning a claim for restitution of payment of capital duty not due under Directive 69/335 (see Chapter 29 of the other Volume of this book) in a case where the capital contribution had not effectively taken place. Italian procedural law restricted the possibilities of the taxpayer to prove that no contribution was in fact effected: only a final civil court judgment declaring the capital registration null and void, or annulling it, was considered acceptable in evidence. This meant that capital duty had in any event to be paid and that reimbursed was only possible by means of a cumbersome filing for a civil judgment, even though other means of evidence could be just as convincing. Although this evidential rule agreed with the principle of equivalence (it applied to claims based on internal law as well), the Court considered it to violate the principle of effectiveness, as it made exercise of the right of reimbursement conferred by EU law excessively difficult. In terms of the (procedural) rule of reason: Italy had shown no mandatory requirement of public (procedural) interest to justify such extreme restriction of the possibility to claim an EU right.

The third example resembles Case 129/00, *Commission v. Italy*,[264] cited in section 3.4. It is the case of *Accor*,[265] concerning the discriminatory effects of the (former) French imputation system (no imputation credit for foreign dividends), which were incompatible with the right of establishment. Accor therefore claimed the imputation credit to offset it against the *précompte* it had to pay upon redistribution of foreign subsidiary dividends received by Accor. France argued that the *précompte* charged on Accor's redistribution had been passed on to Accor's shareholders, who had simply received a lower net dividend. According to France, Accor had not borne the *précompte* and would unjustly be enriched by repayment. France thus in fact tried to place on Accor the burden of proving that it had *not* shifted the *précompte* to its shareholders. The Court held that although it is conceivable that the *précompte* had reduced the amount of the redistributed dividend, it was just as conceivable that Accor had been impelled to increase its redistribution in order to be able to pay the same net amount. Thus, the onus of proof of any passing on of the tax burden was placed on the tax administration.

In Case C-398/09, *Lady & kid*, on restitution of a Danish social security levy levied in breach of VAT rules, the Court[266] considered that recovery of sums wrongly paid under EU law can give rise to unjust enrichment only when the amounts wrongly paid by the taxpayer have been passed on 'direct to the purchaser.' Neither could Denmark argue that the amounts wrongly levied had been set off by the simultaneous abolition of the former social security contribution system, since such a set-off cannot be regarded, from the point of view of EU law, as an unjust enrichment as regards the tax wrongfully levied.

3.5.2.3 Application of EU Law ex officio; Public Policy Provisions

The principle of effectiveness and the principle of sincere cooperation require national authorities, especially administrative authorities such as the revenue service, to apply EU

263 Case C-35/09, *Paolo Speranza*, EU:C:2010:393.

264 Case C-129/00, *Commission v. Italy*, EU:C:2003:656, [2003] ECR I-4637.

265 Case C-310/09, *Accor SA*, EU:C:2011:581, point 75.

266 Case C-398/09, *Lady & Kid A/S a.o.*, EU:C:2011:540.

law as if it were national law, therefore also *ex officio*. It does not go so far, however, as to oblige a national court to apply EU law of its own motion if that would require having to go beyond the limits of the dispute brought before it or having to gather and examine facts not submitted by the parties.[267] EU law does not require national courts to look beyond the dispute as defined by the parties, as in general, EU law provisions are not public policy (*ordre public*) provisions which have to be applied irrespective of the views of the litigating parties. However, if a national court has the discretionary power to raise points of national law of its own motion *within* the boundaries of the dispute defined by the parties (i.e. without stealing the dispute from the parties), it is *required* to raise relevant EU law of its own motion. This rule based on the principle of effectiveness of EU law may be summarized in the maxim *internal law discretion implies EU law obligation*: a national court is *required* to use its *discretion* any way possible to effectuate EU law relevant to the dispute, also where it might not use that discretion as regards points of internal law in an otherwise similar procedural situation. In this respect, EU law is positioned beyond equivalence, as it is placed in a systemic better procedural position than internal law, probably to avoid as much as possible merely accidental activation of EU law *ex officio*.

Under national law, often certain specific procedural rules and sometimes also certain substantive rules are considered too important to be left to the discretion of the parties. These rules of public policy or *ordre public* provisions comprise rules on the competence of the administrative body which issued the contested administrative decision, on the court's own competence to adjudicate the case, and on the admissibility of the appeal, usually especially as regards time limits. As far as substantive law is concerned, national law may in exceptional circumstances designate rules so fundamental that no restrictions of a procedural nature should prevent their application. Under national law, courts thus may be required to apply such rules *ex officio, e.g.* rules that prevent law suits aiming at a criminal or otherwise illegal result, such as a client claiming observance of a contract concluded with a contract killer. This raises the question of whether such substantive public policy provisions also exist in EU law, because if they do, they must also be applied *ex officio* by the national court (principle of equivalence). In *Van der Weerd a.o.*,[268] the CJEU held that in general, provisions of EU law – which are usually of a substantive nature – do not take a comparable place in the legal order as national public policy provisions. Courts therefore are not, as a rule, required to apply EU law of their own motion if that would mean changing the dispute. An exception applies, however, on the basis of the effectiveness principle, where the parties themselves had no genuine opportunity to raise points of EU law and the national court is not at liberty to raise pleas of law of its own motion other than public policy provisions. Indeed, the effectiveness principle also requires adequate access to judicial review, so EU law should have at least one chance to be brought up. If the parties could have raised it, but did not do so, then the national court is not required to do so if under its national law it cannot raise points of law other than public policy points. The Court considered in *Van der Weerd a.o.*:

> '41. (…) the principle of effectiveness does not, (…), impose a duty on national courts to raise a plea based on a Community provision of their own motion, irrespective of the

267 Joined Case C-430 and 431/93, *Van Schijndel and Van Veen*, EU:C:1995:441, [1995] ECR I-4705.
268 Joined Cases C-222/05 through C-225/05, *Van der Weerd a.o.*, EU:C:2007:318, [2007] ECR I-4233.

importance of that provision to the Community legal order, where the parties are given a genuine opportunity to raise a plea based on Community law before a national court. Since the appellants in the main proceedings have had a genuine opportunity to raise pleas based on Directive 85/511, the principle of effectiveness does not require the national court to examine of its own motion a plea based on Articles 11 and 13 of that directive.'

National courts are in particular not required to raise points of EU law *ex officio* where national procedural law prohibits *reformatio in peius, i.e.* the situation in which a contested administrative decision would be revised not to the benefit of the appellant, but to his detriment if the court would apply EU law of its own motion.[269] This is not to say that the tax administration may not change its position during litigation and argue on new grounds and new evidence that the taxpayer should be denied a deduction or an exemption because he should have known he was involved in a VAT carrousel fraud. As the Court held in *Maks Penn OEED*,[270] a case which also illustrate the far-reaching duty of national courts to interpret national law consistent with EU law, in particular with the general principle of EU law that abuse of rights is prohibited:

"36. (...) it is for the national court to interpret the national law, so far as possible, in the light of the wording and the purpose of the directive concerned in order to achieve the result sought by the directive, which requires that it does whatever lies within its jurisdiction, taking the whole body of domestic law into consideration and applying the interpretative methods recognised by that law (...). It is therefore for the national court to ascertain whether the rules of national law on which it is relying and which, in its view, might be contrary to the requirements of European Union law, can be interpreted in accordance with the objective of preventing tax evasion on which those requirements are based.
37. (...), admittedly, European Union law cannot oblige a national court to apply European Union legislation of its own motion where this would have the effect of disregarding the principle, enshrined in its national procedural law, of the prohibition of reformatio in peius (Case C-455/06 Heemskerk and Schaap (...), paragraph 46). However, it is not obvious, in any event, that, in a dispute such as that in the main proceedings which, from its origin, concerns the right to deduct the VAT included in a number of specific invoices, such a prohibition can apply to the submission by the tax authorities during court proceedings of new evidence which, concerning those same invoices, cannot be regarded as adversely affecting the situation of the taxable person who is relying on that right to deduct.
(...).
39. (...), where the national courts must or may raise of their own motion points of law based on binding rules of national law, they must do so in relation to a binding rule of European Union law such as that which requires that national courts and authorities refuse entitlement to the right to deduct VAT where it is established, in the light of objective evidence, that that right is being relied on for fraudulent or abusive ends. It is incumbent on those courts, in the assessment of whether that right to deduct was relied on for fraudulent or abusive ends, to interpret the national law, so far as possible, in the light of the wording and the purpose of Directive 2006/112, in order to achieve the result sought by that directive, which requires that they do whatever lies within their jurisdiction, taking the whole body of domestic law into consideration and applying the interpretative methods recognised by that law."

269 Case C-455/06, *Heemskerk en Schaap*, EU:C:2008:650, [2008] ECR I-8763.
270 Case C-18/13, *Maks Pen OEED*, EU:C:2014:49.

The respect for a national principle which prohibits *reformatio in peius* does not withstand, however, that there are two specific types of substantive EU law which do take a similar position as public policy provisions, meaning that they must be applied *ex officio* even if both parties had ample opportunity to rely on them but did not do so and even if the position of one or both of the parties is negatively affected as compared to not having litigated at all. The first category is not very interesting in the tax field, as it regards consumer protection: national courts are required to protect consumers of their own motion against unfair terms in consumer contracts on the basis of the EU directives on consumer protection.[271] We infer the Court regards consumer protection as a fundamental right. The second category, by contrast, may be relevant for tax cases: in the *Eco Swiss* case,[272] the Court considered the prohibition on private distortion of competition (Art. 101 TFEU) to be a rule of public policy, to be applied the national court of its own motion. The case law is not very clear, however, as this case can also be read as an application of the equivalence principle in that the Court may have considered that if binding arbitral awards could be set aside in certain circumstances on national grounds of public policy, the national court should also be able to set it aside, notwithstanding that it was binding, on grounds of EU law. *If* competition law as regards private parties has to a certain extent the character of public policy law, then this may also be relevant for public distortions of competition, especially for tax measures constituting State aid. The prohibition on illegal State aid may then have a mandatory public policy character as well, to be applied *ex officio* in tax litigation if the tax court finds that the taxpayer is relying on a selectively advantageous national scheme or ruling which has not been notified to the Commission and which clearly falls foul of the State aid prohibition. For the effectiveness of the State aid prohibition, this may be very helpful, as usually, neither the taxpayer nor the national tax administration – although possibly quarrelling on the precise application of the benificial tax scheme – has any interest whatsoever in raising the point that the entire scheme may be illegal and prohibited.

3.5.3 National Time-Limits, Final Decisions and Res Iudicata

3.5.3.1 The Length of National Time-Limits; Again Equivalence and Effectiveness

Time-limits for appealing administrative decisions are a paradox: on the one hand they seek to make administrative decisions final in a relatively short period after issuance (one month, six weeks, two months) to serve legal certainty, but precisely because expiry of that period will bar any future possibility to challenge the invalidity of the decision, the addressee may feel compelled to bring – possibly systematically – *pro forma* objections or appeals within that short period to safeguard his access to legal remedies. Short time limits thus also encourage bringing objections and appeals and therefore also jeopardize the legal certainty they seek to serve.

Time-limits for appealing administrative (tax) decisions are the most concrete obstacle to the effectiveness of any law. The CJEU therefore assesses their reasonableness where

271 See, *e.g.*, Case C-168/05, *Mostaza Claro*, EU:C:2006:675, [2006] ECR I-10421, and Case C-40/08, *Asturcom Telecomunicaciones*, EU:C:2009:615, [2009] ECR I-9579.

272 Case C-126/97, *Eco Swiss China Time*, EU:C:1999:269, [1999] ECR I-3055.

access to EU law is involved. Initially, it took a rather extreme position, but it subsequently followed a more relaxed approach. In *Emmott*[273] (1991), it held that a Member State which has failed to transpose a directive (correctly) into national law cannot rely on its national time-limits to bar proceedings by individuals claiming their EU rights under a (directly applicable) provision of that directive. The case concerned Irish Mrs. Emmott, claiming social security benefits under a directly applicable provision of the Equal Treatment Directive[274] not correctly transposed into Irish law. The CJEU dismissed the Irish authorities' reliance on the national time-limit, ostensibly solely because Ireland had failed to transpose the directive. It held that appeals based on a directive cannot be time-barred as long as the Member State involved has not discharged its obligation to correctly transpose that directive into national law. This judgment was a potential budgetary disaster for Member States, as it may be only after decades before it transpires that a Member State possibly has not transposed a directive correctly twenty or thirty years ago.

To the relief of the Member States, the Court in later cases[275] paid heed to the principle of legal certainty, and gradually reduced the scope of *Emmott*, limiting that case to its facts. Those facts were that when Mrs Emmott first (timely) applied, the Irish authorities told her to await the outcome of two similar cases (*McDermott* and *Cotter*) which had been referred to the CJEU. After these cases had been decided in favour of McDermott and Cotter, obviously Mrs Emmott reported to the authorities again, only to be told that – alas – she was too late.[276] With the benefit of hindsight, the Court in later cases explained that the facts and reasoning in this case must be understood as meaning that the Irish authorities had made it excessively difficult or virtually impossible for Mrs Emmott to exercise her rights under EU law (a violation of the effectiveness principle, therefore). In these subsequent cases the Court emphasized the importance of legal certainty and the virtue of reasonable time-limits. It may not have had much choice, as the Member States did not cease to point out to that the Court is rather strict itself in applying the short time-limits contained in EU law for direct appeals to the Court itself, *e.g.* appeals against negative Commission competition or State aid decisions. The CJEU thus integrated – and disarmed – the budgetary frightening *Emmott* case into its concepts of, on the one hand, procedural autonomy and the principle of legal certainty, and on the other hand the principle of effectiveness of EU law. Provided national time-limits apply indiscriminately and are in themselves reasonable, they may be relied on by Member States to bar proceedings.

That raised the question of what a 'reasonable' time-limit is. In *Recheio Cash & Carry*,[277] the taxpayer argued that it was unreasonable to allow the tax administration a (much) longer period for (re)assessing his tax liability (several years) than he was allowed to

273 Case C-208/90, *Emmott*, EU:C:1991:333, [1991] ECR I-4269.

274 Council Directive 79/7/EEC of 19 December 1978 on the progressive implementation of the principle of equal treatment for men and women in matters of social security, O.J. 1979 No. L 6, p. 24.

275 See, for instance, Case C-338/91, *Steenhorst-Neerings*, EU:C:1993:857, [1993] ECR I-5475, and Case C-30/02, *Recheio Cash & Carry*, EU:C:2004:373, [2004] ECR I-6051, which disarmed *Emmott* for good.

276 For a similar case of wrong-footing or even deceit in a horizontal situation (employer misleading employee on the inequality of the salary levels for men and women), see Case C-326/96, *Levez v Jennings Ltd*, EU:C:1998:577, [1998] ECR I-7835.

277 Case C-30/02, *Recheio Cash & Carry*, EU:C:2004:373, [2004] ECR I-6051.

challenge his tax assessment (90 days). *Se non è vero, è ben trovato.* The Court held that the period for appeal for the taxpayer and the period to impose assessments for the tax administration do not need to be identical, because (i) a longer assessment period does not in itself make a 90-day appeals period insufficient in terms of effectiveness of EU law, and (ii) the period available to the tax authorities to assess tax liability serves other goals than the period available for the introduction of an action for annulment of a charge to tax. The Court considered 90 days sufficient to enable Recheio to decide whether or not to litigate, and to gather and consider the relevant points of facts and of law.

In contrast with *Emmott*, the CJEU rejected Recheio's argument that Portugal had not yet transposed the Capital Duty Directive into national law at the time Recheio paid the disputed fees and had thus left Recheio ignorant of its EU rights. EU law does not preclude a Member State which has not properly transposed a directive from resisting actions for repayment of charges levied in breach of that directive by relying on a national time-limit. Thus, the fact that a directive has not been (properly) implemented, does not make it impossible or excessively difficult to know its directly applicable provisions and to rely on them in an appeal against an administrative decision incompatible with it or in a civil law action for damages as a result of the non-implementation. *Ius unione vigilantibus scriptum est.*

Recheio overturned the *Grundig Italiana* case,[278] in which the CJEU had held that if Italy wished to reduce an appeals period of ten or five years to three years, a transitional period was required to ensure that rights conferred by EU law could be effectively exercised, and that this transitional period should be six months instead of 90 days, as Italy had eacted. Indeed, in *Recheio*, an *entire* appeals period of 90 days was sufficient, whereas in *Grundig Italiana* even a *transitional* period of 90 days had been considered too short, and had been doubled by the Court. Apparently, the Court realised that it is a Court and not a legislator.

In the very old *Comet* case,[279] which introduced the *Rewe/Comet* rules of equivalence and effectiveness, a period for bringing objections of only one month was applicable, to which the Court did not object, but in that case the time limit was not in dispute. The more recent joined Cases *Arcor* and *i-21*[280] concerned two German telephone companies which had not contested but simply paid considerable license fees which later proved to be incompatible with EU law in proceedings brought by other telephone companies. The appeals period as regards the licence fees was, as in *Comet*, only one month, but again the (in)acceptability of that period in the circumstances of the case did not seem to have been explicitly contested.

In *Santex*,[281] the Court accepted in principle a 60-day period for opposing a public procurement award, but did not accept, in that particular case, that the public authority calling for the tender had created uncertainty as regards the starting point of that period for the undertakings not awarded. Similarly, in *Uniplex*,[282] the Court did not accept a UK time-limit requiring a public tender award to be challenged "promptly and in any event within three months from the date when grounds for the bringing of the proceedings first arose unless the [UK] court considers that there is good reason for extending the period

278 Case C-255/00, *Grundig Italiana*, EU:C:2002:525, [2002] ECR I-8003.
279 Case 45/76, *Comet*, EU:C:1976:191, [1976] ECR 2043.
280 Joined Cases C-392/04 and C-422/04, *Arcor* and *i-21*, EU:C:2006:586, [2006] ECR I-8559.
281 Case C-327/00, *Santex Spa*, EU:C:2003:109, [2003] ECR I-1877.
282 Case C-406/08, *Uniplex*, EU:C:2010:45, [2010] ECR I-817.

within which proceedings may be brought." This time-limit violated the principle of effectiveness as 'promptly' was too vague, and the national court had too much discretion in appreciating promptness or the lack of it. Interested parties thus had no clarity nor certainty on the period available to them for challenging the award.

In *Bulicke*,[283] the Court in principle accepted a two month period for claiming damages from a potential employer for rejecting a job applicant because of her age, provided the principles of equivalence and of effectiveness were respected, which was for the national court to ascertain. The judgment indicates that two months is acceptable if the period starts not only from the moment of notification of rejection, but also (restarts) from the moment it dawns on the worker that she has been discriminated against.

In sum, it may be inferred that the Court largely respects national time-limits, provided they are (i) not less favourable than in proceedings based on purely internal law (equivalence), (ii) nondiscretionary and clear for interested parties, and (iii) such as to allow interested parties a genuine opportunity to raise pleas based on EU law. If those conditions are met, a one month time limit may be enough from an EU law point of view.

It should be borne in mind that, as explained in Sections 3.1.3 and 3.5.2.1, the rule of law and the principle of effectiveness also entail the right to be heard by the authorities in any matter within the scope of EU law *prior* to the decision one might want to oppose. The *Sopropé* case requires national tax administrations, in all cases where 'they take decisions which come within the scope of Community law' and 'which significantly affect (the) interests' of the taxpayer, to hear the taxpayer prior to deciding, and to allow him enough time and opportunity to contest the information on which the intended decision is based.

3.5.3.2 (No) Revision of Final Administrative Decisions and Final Judgments

Closely related to the subject of the preceding section is the question of whether and to what extent the principle of effectiveness of EU law requires revision of final tax assessments or of judgments which have become final, if a subsequent CJEU judgment reveals that the decision or the judgment was wrong. Given that not only the principle of legal certainty, but also the principles of *litis finiri oportet* and *res iudicata* are a general principle of EU law, there is in principle no reason to reconsider final decisions and judgments, provided that decisions and judgments based on internal law are not reconsidered either after the domestic highest court hands down a judgment from which it appears that a decision or judgment which has become final was wrong. But there are exceptional circumstances in which an EU obligation exists to reconsider final decisions or judgments exists.

Final Administrative Decisions

First, a case will be discussed showing the main rule (final is final) and subsequently some – exceptional – exceptions (final is not always final). The case of Dr *Barth*[284] concerned the same Austrian length-of-service salary increments for professors as in the *Köbler* case to be discussed in section 3.5.4.4. Those rules did not take into account periods of service in universities outside Austria. Because his first twelve years of service had been performed in Germany, Dr Barth did not receive that increment. After the *Köbler* judgment of the

283 Case C-246/09, *Susanne Bulicke*, EU:C:2010:418.
284 Case C-542/08, *Barth*, EU:C:2010:193, [2010] ECR I-3189.

CJEU of 30 September 2003 (see 3.5.4.4), Austria changed its legislation, after which Dr Barth on 2 March 2004 still applied for the increment, requesting his German years to be taken into account. That request was granted, implying that he would have been entitled to the special increment from 1994 onward, but the Austrian legislation provided for a limitation period of three years, meaning that Dr Barth's salary adjustment would take effect only for remunerations as from 1 October 2000. Dr Barth considered this to frustrate his EU free movement rights by frustrating the CJEU's *Köbler* judgment. The Court however, noted that the time-limit for application applied indiscriminately and that an application had to be made by all professors whose increment had not been calculated correctly (principle of equivalence). As to effectiveness, Dr Barth in substance argued that he was in a Catch-22: at the time he should have applied in order to get the full increment EU law entitled him to, the *Köbler* judgment had not been handed down yet, so he could not have known his EU rights. At the time he should, in hindsight, have applied for the increment, there was unambiguous national Austrian law explicitly *not* granting him the increment, and anyway, the authorities would have rejected his application, had he made it then, as the *Köbler* case showed. Nevertheless, the CJEU upheld the principle of legal certainty: the Austrian authorities had not misled Dr Barth in any way (as was the case in *Emmott* and *Levez*; see section 3.5.3.1), and he was not altogether deprived of the right to obtain an increment. The mere existence of unambiguous national legislation which in hindsight proved to be in contravention of EU law could not be equated to misrepresentation or deception by the authorities, such as in *Emmott* and *Levez*, as that would make application of reasonable time limits impossible. We infer that Dr Barth should have applied anyway (should not have let national law discourage him) and should have challenged a surely negative decision on his application, invoking his EU rights before the competent national administrative court.

In exceptional circumstances, however, final decisions must be reconsiderd. The *Kühne & Heitz* case[285] concerned EU export restitutions for poultry meat exports to third States, based on an EU customs union regulation. The restitutions were denied to the Kühne & Heitz company by the competent Netherlands Commodity Board. The Netherlands Administrative Court for Trade and Industry dismissed Kühne & Heitz's action against that decision in 1991. However, in the subsequent *Voogd* case[286] of 5 October 1994, the CJEU gave an interpretation of the EU customs nomenclature supporting Kühne & Heitz's views. On the basis of that posterior CJEU judgment, Kühne & Heitz in December 1994 again filed for export restitutions with the Commodity Board, That request was again dismissed as it called into question a prior decision which had become final by the dismissal of the company's appeal against it (principle of *res judicata*). Kühne & Heitz again brought an action before the administrative court, pointing out that under Netherlands administrative law, administrative bodies in principle have the discretionary power to review final decisions. The administrative court considered that, in general, amending final decisions of any age to make them consistent with later case law would give rise to administrative chaos, would seriously impair legal certainty and could therefore not

285 Case C-453/00, *Kühne & Heitz NV v. Productschap voor pluimvee en eieren*, EU:C:2004:17, [2004] ECR I-837.

286 Case C-151/93, *Criminal proceedings against Voogd Vleesimport en-export*, EU:C:1994:365, [1994] ECR I-4915.

be accepted. However, Kühne & Heitz's case was special in that the company (i) had previously exhausted all legal remedies available to it, (ii) had been dismissed by the highest national court, which (iii) had not referred preliminary questions to the CJEU because it considered the case an *acte clair*, but which (iv) in hindsight had interpreted EU law incorrectly, and the company (v) had immediately brought a new action after the *Voogd* judgment. The Netherlands administrative court therefore referred the case to Luxembourg.

The CJEU first reiterated that its interpretation of a rule of EU law is purely declaratory, *i.e.* it clarifies and defines the meaning and scope of that rule as it ought to have been understood and applied from the time of its coming into force. Such rule must therefore be applied by an administrative body within the sphere of its competence even to legal relationships which arose or were formed before the CJEU gave its ruling. Nevertheless, finality of an administrative decision upon expiry of reasonable time-limits for legal remedies or by exhaustion of those remedies, contributes to legal certainty, which is also a principle of EU law, and EU law therefore in principle does not require that administrative bodies reopen an administrative decision which has become final in that way. Therefore, provided that sufficient legal remedy was available, there is no need for the administration to reopen cases which have become final.

Secondly, however, the CJEU listed the particular circumstances of Kühne & Heitz:

i. national law conferred on the administrative body the discretionary competence to reconsider the decision despite its finality,
ii. the decision had become final only as a result of a judgment of a national court against whose decisions there was no judicial remedy,
iii. that judgment was based on an interpretation of EU law which, in the light of a subsequent judgment of the Court, was incorrect and which was adopted without a question having been referred to the Court for a preliminary ruling, and
iv. the person concerned had complained to the administrative body 'immediately' after becoming aware of that subsequent judgment of the Court.

It considered that in these specific circumstances, EU loyalty (now: the principle of sincere cooperation; Art. 4(3) TEU) required the administrative body to review the final decision to take account of the correct CJEU interpretation of EU law now available. On the basis of the outcome of that review, the administrative body must determine to what extent it is under an obligation to amend its decision, without, however, adversely affecting the interests of third parties who relied on the definitive character of the decision.

We stress that this exception to the principle of *res judicata* and to the definitive character of upheld administrative decisions solely applies for addressees who used and exhausted all their legal remedies (but to no avail), and only if they take 'immediate' action following a CJEU judgment which reveals that their national highest court got it wrong in their case. If a taxpayer did not appeal an unfavourable decision or an unfavourable judgment of a lower court, then he has no case if subsequently a new CJEU judgment proves him right after all. It is a general principle, also of EU law, that interested parties have an obligation to limit their damages and therefore to use all legal possibilities available to them to effectuate their rights, especially legal remedies, also because lower courts do not have an obligation ex Article 267 TFEU to refer preliminary questions on the interpretation of EU law. That obligation rests only on courts against whose judgments no appeal is possible.

It must also be stressed that *Kühne & Heitz* does not create a new legal remedy and does not mean that the administration has to change its mind. It may after review still come to the same decision, considering insufficient grounds for amending to be present. EU law does not provide a legal remedy against that *ex officio* finding. It depends on national law whether there is such legal remedy. If national law does not provide for one, then that is probably the end of the story. At most, the frustrated addressee could in that case sue the authorities before a civil law court only if they manifestly did not seriously reconsider their decision in the light of the relevant EU law, which could amount to tort.

The CJEU's reference to the peculiarity that the administrative body had discretion to reopen an otherwise final decision, implies that in Member State where administrative bodies have no such power, a company in an otherwise comparable situation cannot successfully apply for a review. The absence of EU procedural law implies that the procedural protection of EU rights in Member States depends – above the minimum level of the principle of effectiveness *stricto sensu* – on national procedural law. It is on the same level as the procedural protection of rights in general in that State, unless that level below the minimum. Especially time-limits may vary widely among Member States.

As observed, *Kühne & Heitz* does not mean that a taxpayer who failed to appeal a tax assessment, gets another chance upon posterior contrary CJEU case law. This is confirmed by the joined Cases *Arcor* and *i-21*,[287] cited in Section 3.5.3.1, concerning German telephone companies which had not contested license fees which later proved to be incompatible with EU law in proceedings initiated by other telephone companies. Arcor and i-21 subsequently tried, relying on *Kühne & Heitz*, to get the same treatment as their competitors who timely appealed the license fee notices, but in vain:

> '53. The case giving rise to the judgment in Kühne & Heitz, (...), was entirely different from those at issue in the main proceedings. Whilst the undertaking Kühne & Heitz NV had exhausted all legal remedies available to it, i-21 and Arcor did not avail themselves of their right to appeal against the fee assessments issued to them.
> 54. Accordingly, (...), the judgment in Kühne & Heitz is not relevant for the purpose of determining whether, in a situation such as that in the main proceedings, an administrative body is under an obligation to review decisions which have become final.'

Another example of a national law peculiarity which leads to the obligation to reconsider – in this case – VAT (self)assessments, is offered by the *Transportes Urbanos* case.[288] It concerned an undertaking which claimed a VAT refund of € 1 228 366.39 after the CJEU had held, in a Commission action against Spain,[289] that the Spanish limitations on deduction of VAT violated the Sixth VAT Directive. As the undertaking had not requested deduction in its VAT self-assessments, nor rectification of its self-assessments within the statutory period for rectification, her restitution request was time-barred, and it would have remained so forever, if it were not for a peculiarity in Spanish constitutional law. The case law of the Spanish *Tribunal Supremo* allowed for actions for damages against the State – *without*

287 Joined Cases C-392/04 and C-422/04, *Arcor* and *i-21*, EU:C:2006:586, [2006] ECR I-8559.
288 Case C-118/08, *Transportes Urbanos*, EU:C:2010:39, [2010] ECR I-635.
289 Case C-204/03, *Commission* v *Spain*, EU:C:2005:588, [2005] ECR I-8389.

prior exhaustion of all legal remedies – in respect of adverse administrative measures which in hindsight – after a subsequent ruling of the *Tribunal Supremo* – appeared to be based on legislation in breach of the Spanish constitution. Final decisions in hindsight offending the Spanish constitution could therefore still be challenged. By contrast, if a final administrative measure in hindsight – after a subsequent ruling of the CJEU – appeared to be based on national legislation violating EU law, then the *Tribunal Supremo did* require prior exhaustion of all administrative and judicial remedies against that measure. As was to be expected, the CJEU held that this distinction in admissibility of actions against final administrative measures according to whether they offended the Spanish constitution or EU law, was incompatible with the principle of equivalence.

Much as the Court pays respect to the principle of legal certainty and accepts that if reasonable time limits have expired without the taxpayer having used legal remedies, that is in principle the end of it, it does not accept the finality of unappealed administrative decisions if that would make it impossible forever to reopen them even though they keep violating EU law also in the future. *Byankov*[290] concerned a coercive administrative measure imposed on Mr Byankov, prohibiting him for an indefinite period and without regular review to leave Bulgarian territory and preventing him from being issued with a passport, solely because he owed a considerable debt to a private law legal person and he had not provided adequate security. The order had no other aim than to protect creditors, *i.e.* no (other) mandatory requirement of public interest was involved. Mr Byankov had not challenged the order in court and it had become final. Obviously, it flagrantly frustrated Mr Byankov's EU free movement rights. He applied for the reopening of the administrative procedure, to obtain annulment of the prohibition, but it was rejected, and apart from repaying the sum claimed or providing adequate security no possibilities were available to Mr Byankov for obtaining a review. The Court first established that *Kühne & Heitz* was not relevant, as Mr Byankov had not challenged the order before the courts. It went on to consider that the order and the unavailability of reopening possibilities perpetuated an infringement of the right of Article 21(1) TFEU to move and reside freely within the EU; that is was in fact the antithesis of this freedom conferred by Union citizenship. To the extent that a national measure (i) prevents EU citizens from asserting free movement rights against absolute territorial prohibitions for an unlimited period, (ii) prevents administrative bodies from acting upon case-law of the CJEU confirming the illegality of such prohibitions, and (iii) cannot reasonably be justified by the principle of legal certainty, the Court considers it contrary to the principle of effectiveness and to Article 4(3) TEU. The Court's main objection was that such a prohibition keeps producing, indefinitely, legal effects contrary to fundamental EU law with regard to its addressee. We surmise that a similar administrative (or court) order aimed at recovering unpaid tax or at coercing an economic operator into providing information to the tax administration, must also be susceptible to appeal if it indefinitely keeps frustrating free movement, even where the taxpayer could have objected or appealed but failed to do so and the administrative or court order became final.

290 Case C-249/11, *Byankov*, EU:C:2012:608.

Res Iudicata
The *Kapferer* case[291] shows that *Kühne & Heitz* does not mean that national courts of appeal should review lower court judgments of their own motion on points which have become final for lack of appeal on those points. *Kühne & Heitz* concerns only reconsideration competence of administrative authorities and is not aimed at calling into question the principle of *res judicata*. If one looks at the four *Kühne & Heitz* critera for review of final decisions, than one must conclude that none of them is satisfied in case of a late appeal against a judgment of a lower court which has become final for lack of timely appeal.

This is not to say that the principle of effectiveness of EU law never supersedes the principle of *res judicata*. The *Lucchini Siderurgica* case,[292] *e.g.*, shows that a national *res judicata* rule will be set aside if it stands in the way of the recovery of illegal State aid, the illegality of which appeared from a subsequent Commission decision. Another example of EU law overriding national *res iudicata* rules is the VAT case of *Fallimento Olimpiclub*,[293] concerning an Italian procedural rule[294] providing that a court judgment on a certain issue for a certain period between two parties which has become final, also bars proceedings on the same issue for other periods between the same parties. In the case of *Fallimento Olimpiclub*, this rule would result in the Italian courts being prevented from taking into consideration the rules of EU law on abusive practices in the field of VAT, because there were already two judgments of the *Commissione tributaria regionale del Lazio*, which had become final and concerned VAT adjustment notices issued as part of the same tax inspection of *Fallimento Olimpiclub*, but relating to other tax years. The Court noted that if the principle of *res judicata* were to be applied in this manner, the effect would be that, if ever a judicial decision that had become final were based on incorrect interpretation of EU law on abusive VAT practice, those rules would continue to be misapplied for each new tax year, without it being possible to rectify that incorrect interpretation. That would make the application of EU law impossible for tax years not yet adjudicated and for an indefinite period, and was therefore found to be incompatible with EU law. In essence, this case is for the judicial (*res iudicata*) stage what the *Byankov* case cited above is for the administrative (final decision) stage.

These two cases again show that, like the obligation to apply national law consistently with EU law, the principles of equivalence and effectiveness of EU law work both ways, *i.e.* also to the detriment of the taxpayer.

3.5.4 State Liability for 'Serious' Breaches of EU Law; Penalty Payments

3.5.4.1 Introduction; Conditions for Liability

Member States are liable for damages of individuals and undertakings caused by serious breaches of EU law by their institutions, including their judiciaries. The case law of the CJEU on this part of the *effet utile* (effectiveness) of EU law started in respect of the

291 See Case C-234/04, *Rosmarie Kapferer*, EU:C:2006:178, [2006] ECR I-2585.
292 Case C-119/05, *Lucchini Siderurgica Spa*, EU:C:2007:434, [2007] ECR I-6199.
293 Case C-2/08, *Fallimento Olimpiclub*, EU:C:2007:434, [2009] ECR I-7501.
294 Article 2909 *Code civile*, as interpreted by the *Corte suprema di cassazione*.

incorrect, late or non-implementation of EU directives by Member States, but it applies to all breaches of all categories of primary and secondary EU law.

The landmark *Francovich and Bonifaci* judgment[295] concerned the Italian failure to implement directive 80/987/EEC which conferred rights on individual workers in case of employer insolvency, such as the right to back wages. Mr Francovich and Mr Bonifaci were dismissed by the receiver in charge of the insolvency of their employer. National law did not give them the rights contained in the Directive and they could not rely directly on the relevant directive provisions as these had no direct effect: they were unspecific as to who should fund a wages guarantee fund, the employees, the employer, public funds, or any combination thereof. Thus, no fund having been formed and no funder being known, there was no fund or funder to address. The ex-employees therefore instead sued the Italian Republic for damages, arguing that its failure to transpose the directive amounted to a State tort, inflicting damages on them which should be compensated.

Referring to Article (now) 4(3) TFEU (sincere cooperation) and to its case law on precedence of EU law, notably its *Van Gend & Loos, Costa/ENEL, Simmenthal* and *Factortame* judgments,[296] the Court postulated a principle of State liability to be inherent in the system of the Treaty for harm caused to individuals by breaches of EU law for which the State is responsible. The possibility of compensation by the responsible Member State is particularly indispensable where the full effectiveness of EU law is subject to prior action on the part of the State and consequently individuals cannot, in the absence of such action, enforce their EU law rights before the national courts. Among the Member States' obligations ensuing from Article (now) 4(3) TFEU the Court identified 'the obligation to nullify the unlawful consequences of a breach of Community law'. It set three conditions for Member State liability for breaches of EU law:

- The result prescribed by the directive implies the granting of rights to individuals;
- It must be possible to identify the content of those rights on the basis of the provisions of the directive;
- There must be a causal link between the breach of the Member State's obligations and the harm suffered by the injured parties.

Later, the Court added a fourth requirement: the breach of EU law must be sufficiently 'serious' (see *Brasserie du Pêcheur* below).

In the case at issue it was evident that EU law had been violated, as in previous infringement proceedings against Italy the Court had already held Italy in default of its Treaty obligation to transpose Directive 80/987. Such prior infringement proceeding brought by the Commission is not a prerequisite for State liability, however. The national courts are competent themselves to find a serious breach of EU law and to hold their States liable for damages. Obviously, they may, if they are in doubt, refer the case for a preliminary ruling of the CJEU. The Court pointed out, in *Francovich*, that it is a matter for the national legal orders to determine the competent national courts and to lay down the procedural rules for adjudicating *Francovich* claims. However, the substantive and

295 Joined Cases C-6/90 and C-9/90, *Francovich v. Italy* and *Bonifaci v. Italy*, EU:C:1991:428, [1991] ECR I-5403, and [1991] ECR I-5403, [1993] 2 CMLR 66, p. 107.

296 Case 26/62, *Van Gend & Loos*, EU:C:1963:1, [1963] ECR 3; Case 6/64, *Costa v ENEL*, EU:C:1964:66, [1964] ECR 1203; Case 106/77, *Simmenthal*, EU:C:1978:49, [1978] ECR 643; and Case C-213/89, *Factortame I*, EU:C:1990:257, [1990] ECR I-2433.

procedural conditions in the national law on compensation for damages may not (there we go again: the *Rewe/ Comet* rule) be less favourable than those relating to similar claims based on internal law (equivalence), and may not be so framed as to make it virtually impossible or excessively difficult to obtain compensation (effectiveness).[297]

Whether or not a provision of EU law confers rights on individuals, is not always evident. It seems clear that, *e.g.*, the substantive provisions of the Parent-Subsidiary Directive (see Chapter 16), the Merger Directive (see Chapter 17) and the Interest and Royalty Directive (see Chapter 18) confer rights on individual taxpayers, but these provisions are also clear und unconditional enough to have direct effect, meaning that they can be enforced directly before the national tax courts, making a claim for damages in principle superfluous: the tax charge will be annulled by the court. Only for ancillary damages, such as *lucrum cessans* or the cost of litigation, State liability could be relevant where direct effect already prevents or takes away *damnun emergens* (see Section 3.5.4.3). A case such as *Peter Paul v. Germany*[298] shows that directives on the supervision of financial institutions, even though explicitly having as one of their objectives the protection of depositors, do not necessarily confer individual rights on individuals which engage State liability where national bank supervision was failing. This latter judgment would seem to have been a very fortunate one, considering the later financial crises, even though many Member States during the credit crunch saw themselves forced to provide a State guarantee of € 100.000 per individual saver to avoid an EU-wide bank run.

We observe that, *vice versa*, economic operators, even if they are resident in other Member States, may be held liable by Member States on the basis of *national* (tort) law for tortious violation of EU law to the detriment of (the financial interests of) the Member State concerned, *e.g.* for VAT fraud. See, for instance, case *HMRC v Sunico ApS a.o.*[299]

3.5.4.2 A 'Sufficiently Serious' Breach of EU Law

From the subsequent *Brasserie du Pêcheur II, Factortame III* and *British Telecom* cases,[300] it followed that for Member State liability to arise, a 'sufficiently serious' breach of EU law is required. In the tax case *Test Claimants in the FII Group Litigation*,[301] the CJEU summarized what a 'sufficiently serious breach' is. A breach of EU law is sufficiently serious where, in the exercise of its legislative power, a Member State has manifestly and gravely disregarded the limits on its discretion. Where the Member State at the time when it committed the infringement had only a very reduced or even no discretion in the implementation or application of EU law, the mere infringement of EU law may be sufficient to establish the required seriousness of the infringement.[302] In determining whether a breach of EU law is sufficiently serious, the national court must take account of all the factors which characterise the situation brought before it, including, in particular, the clarity and

297 Case C-278/20, *Commission v Spain (Violation du droit de l'Union par le législateur)*, EU:C:2022:503.
298 Case C-222/02, *Peter Paul a.o. v Germany*, EU:C:2004:606, [2004] ECR I-9425.
299 Case C-49/12, *HMRC v Sunico ApS a.o.*, EU:C:2013:545.
300 Joined Cases C-46/93 and C-48/93, *Brasserie du Pêcheur SA and Factortame Ltd and others*, EU:C:1996:79, [1996] ECR I-1029; and Case C-392/93, *British Telecom*, EU:C:1996:131, [1996] ECR I-1631.
301 Case C-446/04, *Test Claimants in the FII Group Litigation*, EU:C:2006:774, [2006] ECR I-11753.
302 Case C-5/94, *Hedley Lomas*, EU:C:1996:205.

precision of the rule infringed, whether the infringement and the damage caused were intentional or involuntary, whether any error of law was excusable or inexcusable, as well as possible legitimate expectations, as the position taken by EU institutions such as the Council or the Commission or the Court itself may have contributed to the adoption or maintenance of national measures or practices which prove to be contrary to EU law. On any view, a breach of EU law is clearly sufficiently serious if it has persisted despite a CJEU judgment clearly establishing the infringement or a preliminary ruling or settled case-law of the CJEU on the matter from which it is clear that the conduct in question constituted an infringement of EU law.

As Article 288 TFEU provides that directives are binding upon Member States as to the result to be achieved, the failure to implement a directive altogether implies a serious breach. If, on the other hand, the directive was implemented, but incorrectly, then liability for damages does not necessarily ensue, since directive obligations may be unclear and ambiguous, as they often are, especially in tax matters, political compromises. A directive may also extend a wide substantive discretion to Member States, as seems the case, for instance, with the anti-abuse reservations in the Merger, Parent-Subsidiary and Interest and Royalty Directives (see Chapters 16, 17 and 18) and with the minimum harmonisation contained in the Anti-tax avoidance Directive (ATAD; see Chapter 19). Liability for wrongful assessment of the limit of Member State discretion will in such cases generally not ensue, unless the CJEU finds that the national anti-abuse measure taken was manifestly outside the scope of the reservation of competence. The *Denkavit, VITIC* and *Voormeer* cases[303] illustrate this: although the Court held that Article 5 of the Parent-Subsidiary Directive has direct effect and Germany had failed to implement it correctly, it did not hold Germany liable for (additional) damages as a result of the incorrect interpretation, because the mistake made by Germany was understandable and was moreover also made by almost all other Member States.

Complex international direct tax cases, especially those also involving application of tax treaties, in general will not easily lead to State liability where ultimately an infringement is found, as there is little or no guidance from secondary EU law, the tax consequences of the Treaty freedoms as interpreted by the CJEU are often difficult to predict, and the Court's case law on direct taxes is inconsistent, ambiguous and sometimes plainly erroneous (such as the *De Groot, Bosal, Deutsche Shell, Renneberg*, and *Marks and Spencer II* (C-172/13) cases) (which raises the question of whether the EU should be held liable for the budgetary consequences of erroneous ECJ judgments).

Case C-446/04, *Test Claimants in the FII Group Litigation*,[304] shows the Court's restraint in finding 'serious' breaches in complex direct tax cases:.

> '215. In the present case, in order to determine whether a breach of Article 43 EC [now 49 TFEU; authors] committed by the Member State concerned was sufficiently serious, the national court must take into account the fact that, in a field such as direct taxation, the consequences arising from the freedoms of movement guaranteed by the Treaty have been only gradually made clear, in particular by the principles identified by the Court since delivering judgment in Case 270/83 *Commission v. France*. Moreover, as regards the

303 Joined Cases C-283/94, C-291/94 and C-292/94, *Denkavit Internationaal BV, VITIC Amsterdam BV and Voormeer BV*, EU:C:1996:387 [1996] ECR I-5063.

304 Case C-446/04, *Test Claimants in the FII Group Litigation*, EU:C:2006:774, [2006] ECR I-11753.

> taxation of dividends received by resident companies from non-resident companies, it was only in *Verkooijen, Lenz* and *Manninen* that the Court had the opportunity to clarify the requirements arising from the freedoms of movement, in particular as regards the free movement of capital.
> 216. Apart from cases to which Directive 90/435 applied, Community law gave no precise definition of the duty of a Member State to ensure that, as regards mechanisms for the prevention or mitigation of the imposition of a series of charges to tax or economic double taxation, dividends paid to residents by resident companies and those paid by non-resident companies were treated in the same way. It follows that, until delivery of the judgments in *Verkooijen, Lenz* and *Manninen*, the issue raised by the order for reference in the present case had not yet been addressed as such in the case-law of the Court.
> 217. It is in the light of those considerations that the national court should assess the matters referred to in paragraph 213 of this judgment, in particular the clarity and precision of the rules infringed and whether any errors of law were excusable or inexcusable.'

An example of a sufficiently serious breach in a tax case is offered by *Stockholm Lindöpark*,[305] concerning a VAT exemption which Sweden should have known was incompatible with EU VAT law:

> "40. As the Court found in answering the first two questions, it is evident from the provisions of the VAT Law at issue (...) that the general exemption enacted by the Swedish legislature has no basis in the Sixth Directive and therefore became clearly incompatible with the directive as from the date of (...) Sweden's accession to the European Union. Given the clear wording of the Sixth Directive, the Member State concerned was not in a position to make any legislative choices and had only a considerably reduced, or even no, discretion. In those circumstances, the mere infringement of Community law may be sufficient to establish the existence of a sufficiently serious breach (....). Furthermore, the fact that the national legislation at issue in the main proceedings was repealed with effect from 1 January 1997, two years after Sweden's accession, indicates that the Swedish legislature had become aware that it was incompatible with Community law."

3.5.4.3 Interaction with Direct Effect; Incidental Damages

If the EU law provision involved has direct effect, as the free movement rights, there may be no damages to be claimed, because the tax issue may be solved by simply granting the taxpayer the tax benefit sought on the basis of the direct effect of the EU law provision. In the *Denkavit, VITIC* and *Voormeer* cases, *e.g.*, the taxpayers could rely on the direct effect of Article 5 of the Parent-Subsidiary Directive, granting them an exemption of dividend withholding tax. The German tax court could therefore simply grant them the exemption, automatically leading to a refund if the tax had already been paid. However, there may be additional damages, such as the interest cost of not having available the money incorrectly withheld for a number of years, court fees, costs of legal counsel and *lucrum cessans*. Having to pay tax which was not due may even cause a bankruptcy, but the causal link may be difficult to prove.

Therefore, even if direct effect of an EU law provision will usually prevent or nullify the damages consisting of the amount of unduly charged tax itself, the *Francovich* case law may

305 Case C-150/99, *Stockholm Lindöpark*, EU:C:2001:34.

still be relevant where Treaty freedoms were violated. *Metallgesellschaft*[306] (points 87 and 88) and *Test Claimants in the FII Group Litigation*[307] (point 205) suggest that interest cost for wrongfully withheld sums must be reimbursed, apparently irrespective of the interest regime of claims based on domestic law. From the latter case (point 207) it also appears that in general, EU law does not confer a right of compensation for indirect consequences of positions wrongfully taken by the tax administration, such as opportunity costs as a result of entrepreneurial decisions taken on the basis of – in hindsight – wrongful positions of the tax administration, where these entrepreneurial decisions were not an inevitable consequence of that wrongful position. Such consequences of entrepreneurial decisions are apparently to be considered as a normal entrepreneurial risk.

3.5.4.4 State Liability for Wrongful Supreme Court Judgments

In Case C-224/01, *Köbler*,[308] the CJEU extended its *Francovich* case law to the (highest) judiciary of the Member States, holding Member States liable for damages of individuals caused by 'manifest infringements' of EU law by their highest courts. It considered:

> '54. (...) the national court hearing a claim for reparation must take account of all the factors which characterise the situation put before it.
> 55. Those factors include, in particular, the degree of clarity and precision of the rule infringed, whether the infringement was intentional, whether the error of law was excusable or inexcusable, the position taken, where applicable, by a Community institution and non-compliance by the court in question with its obligation to make a reference for a preliminary ruling under the third paragraph of Article [now 267 TFEU; *authors*].
> 56. In any event, an infringement of Community law will be sufficiently serious where the decision concerned was made in manifest breach of the case-law of the Court in the matter (...).
> 59. (...) the principle that Member States are obliged to make good damage caused to individuals by infringements of Community law for which they are responsible is also applicable where the alleged infringement stems from a decision of a court adjudicating at last instance where the rule of Community law infringed is intended to confer rights on individuals, the breach is sufficiently serious and there is a direct causal link between that breach and the loss or damage sustained by the injured parties. In order to determine whether the infringement is sufficiently serious when the infringement at issue stems from such a decision, the competent national court, taking into account the specific nature of the judicial function, must determine whether that infringement is manifest. It is for the legal system of each Member State to designate the court competent to determine disputes relating to that reparation.'

We emphasize that this liability only exists for erroneous judgments of national courts adjudicating at last instance (where no appeal is possible). That is explained by the fact that only last-instance courts are under an obligation (Art. 267 TFEU) to refer preliminary questions on EU law to the CJEU if doubt exists as to its interpretation. Against judgments of lower courts, one may appeal, and, as was shown in Section 3.5.3, individuals and

306 Case C-397/98, *Metallgesellschaft a.o.*, EU:C:2001:134, [2001] ECR I-1727.
307 Case C-446/04, *Test Claimants in the FII Group Litigation*, EU:C:2006:774, [2006] ECR I-11753.
308 Case C-224/01, *Köbler v. Austria*, EU:C:2003:513, [2003] ECR I-10239.

undertakings who wish to retain the right to claim damages, are required to take all reasonable measures to limit their damages, especially to use all legal remedies available to them to challenge administrative decisions and lower court judgments they consider in breach of EU law.

The *Köbler* judgment has been criticised,[309] the main drift being that (i) cases should be final after adjudication in highest instance (*litis finiri oportet*), as the national court hearing claims based on 'manifest infringements' of EU law by its highest national court will again make mistakes, on which yet another court will have to hear claims, which court will again make mistakes, which will again have to be heard by yet another court, etc.; (ii) it is not evident that an undertaking claiming some pecuniary right under some very technical EU directive,[310] concerning in substance no more than a mundane entrepreneurial risk, should be better protected against judicial errors than, *e.g.* individuals who seek protection against violation of (much) more fundamental legal interests but who happen not to be able to rely on some provision of EU law (the Court overestimates the importance of technocratic secondary EU law); (iii) especially in direct tax cases, the CJEU itself makes at least as many 'manifest' errors of law as national highest courts do, sometimes with huge budgetary effects affecting many individuals who have never been able to vote on the Court's case law: if Member States are liable for erroneous judgments of their highest courts, then by the same standard the Union should be liable for manifest mistakes of the CJEU on the basis of Article 340(2) TFEU (non-contractual liability of the Union); and (iv) the CJEU is setting a standard it is unable to meet itself and which is manifestly incompatible with its *CILFIT* judgment,[311] given its inconsistent and sometimes puzzling judgments, especially in tax matters.

On the other hand, *Köbler* may help convince the tax courts of Member States which as yet have asked few or no preliminary questions on direct taxes and Treaty freedoms to ask such questions and to help negative integration. It is extremely unlikely that in, *e.g.*, Spain, Greece, Ireland, Latvia, Estonia, Bulgaria, Slovakia and the Czech Republic *every* national rule of direct taxation affecting cross-border situations is in conformity with EU law, given the facts that infringement proceedings brought by the Commission against Member States in direct tax matters are usually successful and that many preliminary referrals by other Member States' courts result in the CJEU finding the national tax measure at issue incompatible with EU law.

More or less simultaneously to the *Köbler* case, the CJEU was seized of a Commission action[312] against Italy for Treaty infringement consisting of a dominant line in the Italian case law, including the case law of the *Corte Suprema di Cassazione*, which made it excessively difficult for undertakings to obtain repayment of tax levied contrary to EU law. This case required the CJEU to consider issues analogous to those raised in *Köbler*, and, like in *Köbler*, it held the Member State involved responsible for frustration of the effectiveness of EU law by its national courts. The case did not (yet) involve a liability issue, but taxpayers in Italy may, on the basis of the infringement judgment, have started

309 Peter J. Wattel: 'Köbler, CILFIT and Welthgrove: We Can't Go On Meeting Like This', *41 Common Market Law Review 1* (February 2004), p. 177-190.

310 The *Kühne & Heitz* case, *e.g.*, concerned the export restitution classification of chicken legs (or wings; that was the question).

311 Case 283/81, *CILFIT*, EU:C:1982:335, [1982] ECR 3415.

312 Case C-129/00, *Commission v. Italy*, EU:C:2003:656, [2003] ECR I-4637.

actions for damages against the State, especially where the Italian judiciary was slow in coming round or the Italian legislator did not change the law of evidence.

Obviously, in order for State liability to be an effective deterrent, it must not be limited by onerous conditions. *Traghetti del Mediterraneo*,[313] concerned Italian legislation virtually excluding State liability for the judicial functions of (i) interpretation of legal provisions or (ii) assessment of facts or evidence (*i.e.* for almost the entire judicial function, therefore), and moreover limiting State liability to cases of 'intentional fault or serious misconduct' of a judge. Obviously, if these exclusions and limitations were accepted, the *Köbler* judgment would be robbed of all significance. The CJEU held that, although national law may define the criteria relating to the nature or degree of the infringement to be met for State liability for an infringement of EU law by a national court adjudicating at last instance, under no circumstances may such criteria impose requirements stricter than that of a manifest infringement of EU law, as set out in *Köbler.*

Ferreira da Silva e Brito a.o.,[314] concerned an incorrect application of Directive 2001/23 on the safeguarding of employees rights in the event of transfers of undertakings by the highest Portuguese court, which refused to refer a preliminary question on its interpretation to the CJEU. The employees suffering damages from the incorrect interpretation sued the Portuguese State before a civil law court. Portuguese law did provide for a possibility to hold the State liable for wrongful judgments of the highest court, but only if that judgment had previously been set aside, *i.e.* only if first the *res iudicata* was lifted. However, in practice, it was virtually impossible under national law to lift a *res iudicata* from the highest national court. The CJEU noted that there were conflicting decisions of lower courts on the interpretation of a 'transfer of a business' within the meaning of Directive 2001/23 and that that concept frequently gives rise to difficulties of interpretation in various other Member States as well, indicating that the Portuguese highest court could not reasonably have thought that the case was an *acte clair* for which no preliminary reference was needed, and held, as was to be expected, that EU law precludes national law requiring as a precondition for liability the setting aside of the decision of the highest court which caused the loss or damage, when such setting aside is, in practice, impossible.

3.5.4.5 Penalty Payments for Breaches of EU Law

Where the Court, in a Commission-initiated infringement procedure, has found a Member State to have failed its treaty obligations and that State still does not comply, it may be taken to Court again by the Commission on the basis of Article 260 TFEU, making it liable to penalty payments and/or lump sum fines for noncompliance. For instance, the Commission filed a claim against Spain for not complying with a Directive against pollution of bathing areas, which was sustained by the Court (€ 624 150 per year and per 1% of inshore bathing area, *i.e.* € 62.4 million per year maximum).[315] In 2011, the Court confirmed a lump sum fine for Greece *ad* € 3 million for not complying with an earlier Court judgment condemning Greece for not implementing Directive 2004/80/EC on compensation for

313 Case C-173/03, *Traghetti del Mediterraneo Spa*, EU:C:2006:391.
314 Case C-160/14, *Ferreira da Silva e Brito a.o.*, EU:C:2015:565.
315 Case C-278/01, *Commission v. Spain*, EU:C:2003:635, [2003] ECR I-14141.

crime victims.[316] The Court went even further in Case C-304/02, *Commission v. France*:[317] for not complying with an earlier finding of serious non-compliance with EU fish stock protection regulations, the Court imposed on France both a penalty payment of € 58 million per half year, *and* a lump sum fine of € 20 million, the latter of its own motion, as the Commission had sued only for penalty payments. The Commission has published a Communication on its policy as regards application of its competence on the basis of Article 260.[318] We are not aware of penalty payments having been imposed on Member States for continuous violation of EU law in direct tax matters.

316 Case C-407/09, Commission v Greece, EU:C:2011:196.

317 Case C-304/02, *Commission v. France*, [2005] ECR I-6263.

318 Communication from the Commission on the application of Article 228 of the EC Treaty [now Article 260 TFEU; authors], SEC(2005) 1658.

CHAPTER 4

The EU Charter of Fundamental Rights, General Principles of EU Law and Taxation

Pasquale Pistone[1]

4.1 Legal value, classification and relation with EU law principles

Human rights were formally recognized as EU law by the Member States with the proclamation, at the 2000 Nice summit, of the EU Charter of Fundamental Rights, which had a murky legal status until the coming into force of the Lisbon Treaty in 2009. Article 6(1) TEU since then lays down that the EU Charter of Fundamental Rights has the same legal status as the Treaties. It is, therefore, primary EU law. Many of the rights and principles codified in the Charter had already been recognized long before by the Court of Justice of the EU (CJEU) as general principles of EU law, common to the legal traditions of the Member States.

The EU Charter of Fundamental Rights (hereinafter: the Charter)[2] is in our view a successful compromise that overcomes the problems resulting from the failure to ratify the European Constitution.[3] It can be seen as a model for pursuing fairness and justice at the supranational level.[4]

The CJEU has expressed a negative opinion[5] on the accession of the European Union to the Convention for the Protection of Human Rights and Fundamental Freedoms (ECHR), which Article 6(2) TEU calls for, as that might, in the view of the Court, jeopardize the

1 IBFD Academic Chairman. Holder of a Jean Monnet *ad Personam* Chair in European Tax Law and Policy at WU Vienna and Full Professor of Tax Law at the University of Salerno.

2 For a comprehensive discussion of the EU Charter, see, a.o., Peers, P. , Hervey, T., Kenner, J. and Ward, A., The EU Charter of Fundamental Rights, Beck-Hart-Nomos, 2014; De Vries, S., Bernitz, U., and Weatherill, S., The EU Charter of Fundamental Rights as a Binding Instrument, Bloomsbury, 2015.

3 The Convention on the Future of Europe (composed by members of the European Parliament, national Parliaments, representatives of national governments and the European Commission, plus representatives from applicant countries) drafted an EU Constitution and its text was agreed unanimously in the Convention on 13 June 2003. The EU Constitution was meant to replace the existing European treaties, but was voted down in plebiscites in France and the Netherlands, after which it was not even put to the vote any more in other Member States such as the UK. Part II of the EU Constitution included the provisions on the Charter of Fundamental Rights.

4 On the concept of unwritten global supranational tax law see R. Avi-Yonah, International Tax as International Law, in 57 Tax Law Review 4 (2003-2004), p. 483 ff.

5 Opinion 2/13, EU:C:2014:2454.

competences of the Court and the supremacy of EU law.[6] However, Article 6(3) TEU provides that the fundamental rights guaranteed by the ECHR and as they result from the constitutional traditions of the Member States, are general principles of EU law.

In line with its preamble, the Charter links up, on the one hand, fundamental rights of European Union law with principles and rules resulting from the constitutional traditions and international obligations common to the Member States,[7] and, on the other hand, principles and rules contained in the European Convention of Human Rights.

This has two important implications. First, the Charter harmoniously gives most national constitutional principles an EU dimension, thus reducing the potential for interpretative theories of national Constitutional Courts, especially the German *Bundesverfassungsgericht*,[8] that keep questioning the full supremacy of European over national law in order to preserve an effective protection of core fundamental principles in national Constitutions.[9] Second, it anchors EU fundamental rights to the ones protected by the European Convention of Human Rights. This enhances the substantive validity of the EU standards of protection of rights and gives European human rights a supranational dimension within the legal order of the European Union, which allows for their immediate and effective protection under the jurisdiction of the Court of Justice of the European Union and in national courts.

Settled case law of the Court of Justice indicates that the Charter reaffirms many already existing principles of European Union law.[10] Accordingly, the Charter neither constitutes the immediate legal source of all of the rights it enshrines, nor excludes the existence of rights that are not contained in it. Yet, the inclusion of a fundamental right in the Charter proves its existence and relevance for EU law purposes.

In general, the declaratory function of the Charter in respect of the rights that it enshrines implies that such rights have the legal value that European Union law attributes to them. Usually, such value is linked with the general principles of European Union law. For this reason, Article 51 of the Charter requires EU Member States to secure an effective protection of such rights whenever they implement EU law. However, in some cases, the Charter narrows its scope to the relations with EU institutions, such as in the case of Articles 41 – 44 of the Charter.

---

6 See further on this Ackermann, T., The EU's accession to the ECHR: a "NO" from ECJ!, in Common Market Law Review, 2015, pp. 1-15 and Douglas-Scott, S., The Relationship between the EU and the ECHR Five Years on from the Treaty of Lisbon, in de Vries, S., Bernitz, U., Weatherill, S., Five Years Binding EU Charter of Fundamental Rights, cit., available at https://ssrn.com/abstract=2533207.

7 Case C-349/07, *Sopropé*, EU:C:2008:746, point 33; Joined Cases 129/13 and 130/13, *Kamino* and *Datema Hellman*, EU:C:2014:2041, point 69.

8 The German Constitutional Court closely monitors the compliance with the German Constitution, which it considers as a prerequisite for the legality of Germany's participation in the European integration. This was particularly problematic for the *Bundesverfassungsgericht*, on which see BVerfG, 5 May 2020, 2 BvR 859/15, 2 BvR 1651/15, 2 BvR 2006/15 and 2 BvR 980/16, ECLI:DE:BVerfG:2020:rs20200505.2bvr085915. When addressing the same issues, the Court of Justice had held that the compliance with national Constitutions may not go as far as undermining the effective supremacy of European Union law and the exclusive jurisdiction of the Court of Justice to interpret its own supranational law. See CJEU, C-62/14, *Gauweiler et al.*, EU:C:2015:400.

9 See Case C-399/11, *Melloni*, EU:C:2013:107. For this reason, we consider the link with common constitutional traditions of EU Member States as a qualitatively more advanced solution than the one that could be reached in the late 1960's at the interpretative level in Case 11/70, *Internationale Handelsgesellschaft*, EU:C:1970:114.

10 See, e.g., Joined Cases C-402/05 P and C-415/05 P, *Kadi et aa.*, EU:C:2008:461, point 335.

After addressing its legal value, content, relations with EU law principles and general provisions, this chapter will provide an overview of the Charter provisions that may affect taxation by Member States.

The main impact of the Charter in matters of taxation is on the rights of taxpayers. Taxpayers are persons, thus holders of rights in the European Union legal order, rather than mere objects of the exercise of taxing powers. The predominant interest in securing the general support of the community to collect taxes has often overshadowed that of protecting taxpayers' rights, especially in cross-border situations. Our view is that the European Union legal order is a model for protecting both interests in line with the rule of law and the fundamental principles of EU law.

The Charter provisions relevant in tax matters can be grouped in three categories, namely substantive (or material) rights, procedural (or formal) rights and rights related to penalties.

Some substantive rights are subject to limitations that preserve the state's interest to exercise its taxing sovereignty in line with the rule of law. By contrast, procedural rights should in our view apply in tax matters – and thus protect taxpayers – exactly the same as in other matters and to all persons in other capacities.[11] Finally, a more intensive protection should apply to fundamental rights connected with the imposition of administrative penalties and criminal sanctions, since in such circumstances the personal sphere of the person concerned is more severely affected.

Substantive rights relevant for taxpayers include the rights to privacy (Article 7 of the Charter), data protection (Article 8 of the Charter), property (Article 17 of the Charter), equality before the law (Article 20 of the Charter), non-discrimination (Article 21 of the Charter), and free movement and residence (Article 45 of the Charter).

Procedural rights include the right to an effective remedy and to fair trial (Article 47 of the Charter), to presumption of innocence, and the rights of the defence (Article 41(2) of the Charter, as regards administrative decisions by the EU institutions, and Article 48 of the Charter, as regards criminal charges). In this cluster, the Charter enshrines additional rights geared at the sole EU institutions, such as the right to good administration (Article 41 of the Charter), of access to documents (Article 42 of the Charter) and to refer a case to the EU Ombudsman (Article 43 of the Charter).

Rights related to the imposition of penalties include the prohibition of double jeopardy (*ne bis in idem*), which Article 50 of the Charter lays down in both its substantive aspect (not to be punished twice) and its procedural dimension (not to be tried twice), the rights of the defence of a charged person already mentioned (Article 48 of the Charter), as well as the right to have criminal offences and penalties governed by the principles of legality and proportionality (Article 49 of the Charter).

11 In Case C-682/15, *Berlioz*, EU:C:2017:373, point 51, the CJEU has held that Article 47 Charter reaffirms a general principle of EU law in order to protect taxpayers against arbitrary or disproportionate interventions by public authorities in the sphere or the private activities of any natural or legal person.

4.2 General provisions

4.2.1 *Scope and requirements for protection: in which cases does the Charter apply?*[12]

4.2.1.1 *"Only when they are implementing Union law"*

Although the object and purpose of the Charter is to secure a common standard of effective protection of fundamental rights within the territory of the European Union, Article 51 (1) Charter admits the Charter's general application only for *EU institutions and bodies*, whilst *EU Member States* are only required to comply with the Charter 'when they are implementing Union law'. The latter limitation, contained in Article 51 (1) Charter stems from the Member States' wish, expressed in Article 51 (2), not to extend the Union's competences through the Charter.

It is therefore of paramount importance for the reach of the Charter in the national legal orders to establish the meaning of the term 'when they are implementing Union law'. The Court did so in point 21 of *Åkerberg Fransson*:[13] it held clearly and tersely that "(t)he applicability of EU law entails applicability of the fundamental rights guaranteed by the Charter". The Court thus does not interpret the phrase "implementing Union Law" narrowly as "only when Member States are acting as agents of EU Law", but more broadly, as "in all situations governed by EU law".[14] As soon as one enters the scope of applicability of EU law, one therefore also automatically enters the scope of applicability of the Charter. It applies to every instance in which an EU law based obligation for Member States can be identified, whether positive (e.g. implementation of EU Directives) or negative (e.g. the obligation to respect EU free movement rights and the EU State aid prohibition). The Court thus ensured that (i) EU law will be applied uniformly in all Member States, independent of possible differences between Member States in the level of protection of fundamental rights, and (ii) the scope of the Charter coincides with the scope of the rights and general principles of EU law developed in the Court's case law.

This is especially important in tax matters. In this area, it would be difficult to explain why, in a dispute before a national court on *harmonized indirect* taxation, the right of property in Article 17 of the Charter must be respected if, in a dispute before the same national court on *unharmonized direct* taxation violating the EU free movement rights, the property and other rights protected by the Charter could be ignored. It would be just as strange and contradictory to apply the general EU prohibition of abuse of rights only as regards harmonized taxes, such as VAT, and *not* to allow that general principle as a justification for fiscal restrictions of the Treaty freedoms.[15]

---

12 See, on the scope of the Charter: van Bockel, B. and Wattel, P. J., New Wine into Old Wineskins: The scope of the Charter of fundamental rights of the EU after *Åklagaran v Hans Åkerberg Fransson, European Law Review*, Issue 6, 2013, p. 866-883.

13 Case C-617/10, *Åkerberg Fransson*, EU:C:2013:105.

14 When a Member State acts "within the scope of Union law"; see points 19 and 20 of the judgment.

15 *Conform* van Bockel, B. and Wattel, P. J., New Wine into Old Wineskins: The scope of the Charter of fundamental rights of the EU after *Åklagaran v Hans Åkerberg Fransson, in European Law Review*, cit.

The problems connected with securing the compliance with EU law standards of protection of fundamental rights in the absence of an actual link with EU law are possibly hard to address at the level of legal interpretation and thus require intervention with the issuing of secondary law, which could comprehensively address the protection of taxpayers' fundamental rights.

Meanwhile, there are some areas in which legal interpretation could already address such issues even in the absence of a relevant degree of tax harmonisation. Two of them are worth a mention hereby. First, the settlement of cross-border tax disputes when the taxpayer requests protection under the EU Directive. Second, tax procedures involving joint audits regulated by the DAC system.

CJEU tax case law on Article 51 Charter generally acknowledges that all national measures connected with EU directives amount to implementation of EU law,[16] including the ones aimed at securing their effective implementation, such as the imposition of penalties for violations of the requirements of the said directives.[17] Indeed, in such cases, the Member States act as 'agents of EU law'. However, since *Åkerberg Fransson*, it is clear that the Charter also applies where no implementation *stricto sensu* is at issue, *e.g.*, where a retired person wishes to migrate to another Member State and is confronted with a restrictive or discriminatory exit tax.

The Court's case law specifically excludes the applicability of the Charter as regards national measures not implementing EU law, though not specifying until present the boundaries of 'implementation of Union law'.[18]

In our view, EU Member States are also 'implementing Union law' when they give a (tax) directive effect in their national legal orders beyond the requirements of the directive to the extent this contributes to achieving the goals of the directive. By contrast, if they do so to ensure that domestic situations are treated according to the same legal regime as the cross-border situations covered by the directive,[19] i.e. if they voluntarily *add* to rights granted by a directive, then in principle, the Charter is not applicable. In Case C-198/13, *Hernández*,[20] concerning voluntary national widening of employee protection

16 Case C-349/07, *Sopropé*,:EU:C:2008:746, point 34; Case C-617/10, *Åkerberg Fransson*, EU:C:2013:105, points 19-20.

17 Case C-617/10, *Åkerberg Fransson*, EU:C:2013:105, points 24-27; Case C-105/14, *Taricco et aa.*, EU:C:2015:555, points 49, 52-53; Case C-419/14, *WebMindLicences*,:EU:C:2015:832, point 67; Joined Cases C-217/15 and C-350/15, *Orsi and Baldetti*,:EU:C:2017:264, point 16; Case C-682/15, *Berlioz*,:EU:C:2017:373, point 41.

18 Case C-617/10, *Åkerberg Fransson*, EU:C:2013:105, point 22 and Case C-497/14, *Burzio*, EU:C:2015:251, point 31. However, Jakab, A., Application of the EU Charter by National Courts in Purely Domestic Cases, in Jakab, A., Kochenov, D. (eds.), The Enforcement of EU Law and Values: Ensuring Member States' Compliance, Oxford, 2017, p. 255, argues in favour of a re-interpretation of Article 51(1) EU Charter, in order to make it applicable also in purely domestic situations. As the author indicates, "if we aim for a fully-fledged value community which benefits all its citizens equally, then the Charter as such should gain full applicability in every case, even in purely domestic cases in domestic courts and even if there is no systemic failure of fundamental rights protection on a domestic level."

19 Since the Case C-28/95, *Leur-Bloem*, EU:C:1997:369, point 44, the CJEU has stated its jurisdiction to interpret domestic tax legislation applicable to purely domestic situations when the object and purpose of such legislation is to match the one enshrined in an EU Directive that the Member State has the obligation to implement.

20 Case C-198/13, *Hernández*, EU:C:2014:2055, points 45-47.

in insolvency cases beyond what was required by EU law, the Court held that the Member State concerned was only implementing EU law to the extent its measures were required by the Directive, and that the Charter therefore did not apply as regards its voluntary national overimplementation. We submit that this result was due to the circumstance that the national legislation pursued a completely different goal from that of the Directive. By contrast, in the *Alemo-Herron* case[21] the Court took a different view, namely that when a Member State is providing greater protection under the directive, it should do so while abiding by the rules of Chapter.[22] Therefore, if a member state 'overimplements' the ATAD in the sense that it goes beyond what is required by such directive, for that part of national anti-abuse law the Charter does not apply, unless that 'overimplementation' violates free movement rights[23] or the prohibition of state aids.[24]

One important change the Charter has made for tax matters as regards the scope of fundamental rights is the following: unlike Article 6 ECHR (right to a fair hearing), whose scope is limited to cases in which a 'criminal charge' or the 'determination of civil rights and obligations' is at issue, and which therefore excludes tax cases,[25] the scope of Article 47 of the Charter (the rights to an effective legal remedy and a fair hearing) is not in any way substantively limited, but only by the requirement that some aspect of EU law must (also) be involved.[26]

4.2.1.2 *The level of fundamental rights protection; interaction of the Charter, the European Convention and national constitutional law*

A reading of the *Åkerberg Fransson* case mentioned in 4.2.1.1 together with the *Melloni* judgment[27] of the same day also clarifies what level of fundamental rights protection national Courts may or must offer in situations within the scope of EU Law where the Charter, the ECHR, and national (constitutional) law interact. As regards national law: national courts may offer a higher level of protection than the Charter and the ECHR provide for (only) if EU law leaves national authorities room for discretion, and the primacy, unity, and effectiveness of EU law are not jeopardized. On the other hand, in all cases with an EU law aspect, national courts must always guarantee the minimum level of protection guaranteed by the Charter.[28] Article 53 ('level of protection') prohibits interpreting the

21 Case C-426/11, *Alemo Herron*, EU:C:2013:521.

22 See, *Alemo-Herron*, point 36. Conform Bertl, M., Leone, C., Minimum Harmonization after *Alemo-Herron*: the Janus Face of EU Fundamental Rights Review, in European Constitutional Law Review, Vol. 11, 2015, pp. 140-154.

23 This could be the case if it restricts the exercise of fundamental freedoms in a way that is not compatible with primary law of the European Union, as interpreted by the CJEU.

24 This could for instance occur insofar as one considers that the absence of a GAAR in purely domestic situations creates a selective advantage for such situations, as compared to the cross-border ones.

25 ECtHR, *Ferrazzini v. Italy* (Grand Chamber), Application No. 44759/98, CE:ECHR:2001:0712JUD004475998.

26 See section 4.3.5.below.

27 Case C-399/11, *Melloni*, EU:C:2013:107 concerned a Spanish constitutional provision, which offered better protection than the EU rules on the European arrest warrant.

28 See van Bockel, B. and Wattel, P. J., New Wine into Old Wineskins: The scope of the Charter of fundamental rights of the EU after *Åklagaran v Hans Åkerberg Fransson*, *European Law Review*, Issue 6, 2013, pp. 866-883.

Charter as restricting or adversely affecting any human rights and fundamental freedoms as recognised by EU law, international law, agreements to which the EU or all Member States are a party (e.g. the ECHR) or Member States' constitutions.

The distinction between (tax) cases within the scope of EU law and with that also within the scope of the Charter and (tax) cases outside the scope of EU law Charter may create a two-speed system of legal protection of fundamental rights of taxpayers within the European Union.

The first category may be much faster to reach the CJEU (Luxembourg) than the last category is in reaching the ECtHR (Strasbourg), as for a complaint under the European Convention to be admissible, national legal remedies must have been exhausted, whereas for a claim based on the EU Charter, already a first instance national (tax) court may refer the case directly to the CJEU. Also, Article 52(3) of the Charter makes it explicit that the level of protection may be higher in Luxembourg than it is in Strasbourg.

4.2.2 Limitations of Rights and the link with the Community and Union Treaties

According to settled CJEU case law, the protection of EU fundamental rights applies insofar as there is a genuine link with Union law.

However, even when there is such link, Article 52 (1) of the Charter admits limitations to the Charter rights and freedoms. These limitations are subject to four cumulative requirements: (i) the limitations must be provided for by law, (ii) they must respect the essence of those rights and freedoms, (iii) they must be necessary and must genuinely meet objectives of general interest recognised by the Union or the need to protect the rights and freedoms of others, and (iv) their implementation must comply with the principle of proportionality.

Article 52 (2) of the Charter provides that the rights recognised by the Charter which relate to provisions enshrined in European Treaties (such as, e.g. free movement rights), shall be exercised under the conditions and within the limits defined by those Treaties. This has various important corollaries, two of which are worth mentioning here.

In cases of overlap between the provisions contained in the Charter and in European treaties, the latter determine the conditions under which a given right operates. The effects of this relationship can be clearly perceived in the wording of Article 21 (2) of the Charter, which prohibits discrimination based on grounds of nationality 'within the scope of application of the Treaties and without prejudice to any of their specific provisions', among which, most notably, the free movement rights regulated in the Treaty on the Functioning of the European Union.

Furthermore, secondary EU law may not limit the scope of rights established by primary EU law, thus preventing for instance that directives fighting abusive tax practices may undermine the effectiveness of rights guaranteed by the Treaty on the Functioning of the European Union.[29]

Article 52 (3) of the Charter sets a general correspondence between the Charter and the ECHR as to the meaning and scope of fundamental rights which are protected both under the Charter and the European Convention on Human Rights, but, as observed, it allows for stronger protection of such rights under European Union law. This has several implications that section 4.2.3 will address.

Finally, when fundamental rights enshrined in the Charter result from the common constitutional traditions of EU Member States, Article 52 (4) Charter requires their interpretation to be in harmony with such traditions. By acknowledging the relevance of national constitutional values in the European Union legal order, this provision establishes an obligation to reconciliatory interpretation with the common constitutional dimension of such rights, thus structurally limiting the possibility of open clashes between national constitutional law and supranational law, without making the interpretation of European Union law subject to the constitutional tradition of any single Member State. National constitutional traditions are generally comparable as regards across the European Union, e.g. 'no taxation without representation', taxation according to the ability to pay and no taxation with retroactive effect. However, sometimes they present significant discrepancies. This is for instance the case of the protection of tax secrecy, which is much higher in, e.g., Austria and Luxembourg than it is in, e.g. Finland and Sweden. Article 52 (4)of the Charter secures the protection of such right under European law in a way that neither prevents tax authorities from gathering all relevant information, nor allows for disclosure of personal data, i.e. sensitive information covered by Article 2 of the Data Protection Regulation,[30] to the public.[31]

The second requirement (respect for the essence of the rights and freedoms) can be particularly problematic in practice, as indicated by CJEU case law on the prohibition of double jeopardy.[32]

Some additional considerations are necessary on how the four cumulative requirements operate.

---

29 Even if Article 3 of Directive 2016/1164/EC – the Anti-Tax Avoidance Directive (ATAD) – allows EU Member States to exceed the minimum standards established by the Directive, it may not be interpreted as giving them *carte blanche* to counter tax avoidance in a way that could undermine the effectiveness of the rights protected by primary EU law, especially the rights of establishment and of free movement of capital. The CJEU concretely applied this line of reasoning to mutual assistance in tax matters and, in particular, to mandatory disclosure under DAC 6. In *Orde van Vlaamse Balies* (case C-667/18, *Orde van Vlaamse Balies*, ECLI:EU:C:2020:372) the Court of Justice indicated that such disclosure could not be interpreted as to oblige lawyers to publicly reveal confidential information concerning their clients, nor to reveal them to other intermediaries obliged to such disclosure. In later judgments (see case C-623/22, Belgian Association of Tax Lawyers, ECLI:EU:C:2024:639; case C-432/23, Ordre des avocats du Barreau de Luxembourg, ECLI:EU:C:2024:791) the Court of Justice was more explicit in saying that the obligations under DAC 6 may not be exercised in a way that undermines data protection, striking down Article 8ab (5) of the DAC for its impact on the client-attorney privilege. See further on this in Chapter 29.

30 Regulation EU 2016/679 of 27 April 2016.

31 In Case C-201/14, *Smaranda Bara et aa.*, EU:C:2015:638, point 29, concerning the data protection directive, the CJEU acknowledged the right of data subjects to prior information in respect of a transfer of data from national tax to social security authorities.

32 See below under 4.3.9. in this book.

In particular, the implications of the second and third requirements for limitations of fundamental rights (respect for the essence and necessity with a view to the need to secure either the protection of an objective of general Union interest, or of the rights and freedoms of others) in tax matters are quite evident in connection with the limitation of rights with a view to curbing abusive practices. In such context, European Union law justifies restrictions to taxpayer rights to preserve the overall consistency of its legal order and that of its Member States, but also with a view to limiting possible negative repercussions on how other persons exercise their own rights. Article 54 of the Charter addresses such issues connected with the abuse of rights, by stating that the Charter may not be interpreted in a way that allows acts aimed at the frustration of Charter rights, or at further limitation than provided for in the Charter itself.[33]

The fourth requirement expresses the principle of proportionality,[34] a cornerstone of European Union law that measures the ability of a rights-limiting measure to achieve its purported justified goals and to apply the limitation in a way that does not exceed what is strictly needed to reach such goals. The application of this principle requires a case-by-case analysis of any limitation and prevents overkill effects, which are a recurrent feature of tax systems and which are thus often denounced by the Court of Justice.

4.2.3 Interaction between the Charter and the European Convention

Articles 52 (3) and 53 of the Charter regulate the relevance of the European Convention for the Protection of Human Rights and Fundamental Freedoms (ECHR) within the legal order of the European Union.[35]

In particular, Article 52 (3) of the Charter states the binding value of the ECHR for the interpretation of corresponding provisions of the EU Charter; it sets the scope and meaning of the ECHR rights as a minimum standard of protection of the corresponding rights within the EU, allowing Union law to provide a more extensive protection.

Article 52 (3) of the Charter may have two important corollaries for our purposes. First, setting the ECHR as a minimum standard of protection may mean a stronger protection of taxpayers' rights than under national law. Accordingly, the *Berlioz* judgment of the CJEU on the right to judicial review of penalties for not complying with a request for information in the framework of an exchange of tax information between Member States comes as no surprise.[36] Likewise, one may expect the CJEU's *Schrems* judgment to have implications also in tax matters, by prohibiting cross-border exchange of information with

33 On the prohibition of abusive practices, see Chapters 12 and 15.

34 For case law applying this requirement of Article 52 (1) of the EU Charter see *inter alia Nordzucker*, cit., para. 50.

35 On the relations between the EU Charter and the ECHR see further Lenaerts, K., Exploring the Limits of the EU Charter of Fundamental Rights, in 8 *European Constitutional Law Review* 2012, pp. 375-403; Timmermans, C., Will the Accession of the EU to the European Convention on Human Rights fundamentally change the relationship between the Luxemburg and the Strasbourg Court?, in Centre for Judicial Cooperation, CJC DL 2014/01, pp. 1-19; Brittain, S., The Relationship Between the EU Charter of Fundamental Rights and the European Convention on Human Rights: an Originalist Analysis, in 11 *European Constitutional Law Review, 2015*, pp. 482-511.

36 Case C-682/15, *Berlioz*, EU:C:2017:373.

countries that have low standards of data protection as compared to the ones applicable within the European Union.[37]

Second, the existence of an ECtHR precedent declaring an application manifestly ill-founded on a (tax) matter submitted to the CJEU does not in any way prevent the latter Court from judging it on the basis of European Union law. It should be observed that the ECtHR in fact uses inadmissibility as a *certioriari* tool because it drowns in the number of applications. That is not the case in Luxembourg.

Article 53 of the Charter adds that the interpretation of the Charter must conform with human rights and international agreements to which the Union or all the Member States are party, including a specific reference to ECHR.

The wording of the latter provision is possibly explained by Article 6(2) TEU, which provides for the accession of the European Union to the ECHR. That accession was blocked, however, by the negative opinion of the CJEU in 2014. Consequently, the CJEU denies in its (tax) case law that the ECHR is legally a part of EU law.[38]

Yet, Articles 52 (3) and 53 of the Charter – especially if read in with the light of the Preamble to the Charter (in particular of its fifth recital,[39]) – are sufficiently specific to let legal values from the ECHR, as interpreted by the ECtHR, flow into the EU legal system, subject to the filter of the CJEU, which secures their interpretation consistently with EU law.

The flow of legal values between the two Courts is not uncommon,[40] as witnessed also by tax case law of CJEU, which includes quotation of case law of ECtHR in its judgments,[41] and *vice versa*, e.g. in the *Dangeville* judgment[42] of the ECtHR. In the *Roquette Frères* judgment of 2002, the CJEU invoked the development of ECtHR case law to support its own position.[43] Furthermore, the ECtHR has developed the so-called *Bosphorus*[44] doctrine, which starts from (i) a rebuttable presumption of equivalence in the protection of fundamental rights between the EU Charter and the ECHR in the absence of any margin of manoeuvre on the part of domestic authorities implementing an EU law obligation and (ii) the deployment of the full potential of the supervisory mechanism provided for under EU law.[45]

Issues that are more complex may nevertheless arise when the CJEU decides a case in the absence of any precedent from the ECtHR. In such circumstances, the ECtHR may

37 Case C-362/14, *Schrems*, EU:C:2015:650.

38 After Opinion 2/13, CJEU has confirmed this view in Joined Cases C-217/15 and 350/15, *Orsi and Baldetti*, EU:C:2017:264, point 15.

39 The fifth recital to the EU Charter states that "This Charter reaffirms...the rights as they result... from the constitutional traditions and international obligations common to the Member States, the European Convention for the Protection of Human Rights and Fundamental Freedoms...and the *case-law of the Court of Justice of the European Union and of the European Court of Human Rights*".

40 On the relations between ECHR and CJEU see further Cruz Villalón, P., Rights in Europe: the Crowded House, Working Paper 01/2012, Centre of European Law, King's College, London.

41 See Case C-98/14, *Berlington Hungary*, EU:C:2015:386, point 85; Case C-105/14, *Taricco*, EU:C:2015:555, point 57; Case C-419/14, *WebMindLicences*, EU:C:2015:832, points 70-72, 77-78, 81.

42 ECtHR, *Dangeville v. France*, Application no. 36677/97, CE:ECHR:2002:0416JUD003667797.

43 Case C-94/00, *Roquette Frères*, EU:C:2002:603.

44 ECtHR, *Bosphorus Hava Yollari Turizm*, Application no. 45036/98, CE:ECHR:2005:0630JUD004503698, points 155-156.

45 The ECtHR has confirmed this doctrine in ECtHR, Michaud v France, Application no. 12323/11, CE:ECHR:2012:1206JUD001232311, points 102-104, and, after the CJEU Opinion 2/13 that denied the access of the EU to the ECHR, in ECtHR, *Avotins v Latvia*, Application no. 17502/07, CE:ECHR:2016:0523JUD001750207.

take into account the arguments developed by the earlier CJEU pronouncement, but it is not legally bound by it. Insofar as the ECtHR takes a view different from that of the CJEU, the question arises whether the latter Court must adjust its case law correspondingly. Although a literal interpretation of Article 53 Charter could suggest so, we believe the CJEU could find reasons to keep its own interpretation, especially in the presence of arguments that duly explain the differences between the two contexts, or the existence of a more extensive protection under European Union law.[46]

However, if the interpretation of the ECtHR yields in fact a stronger protection than that resulting from the interpretation provided by the CJEU, it would be hard for the latter Court to stick to its interpretation. In principle, that would infringe the obligation to comply with the ECHR as a minimum standard for the protection of human rights. However, in cases of non-blatant violations of fundamental rights, the CJEU may in fact tolerate lower standards of protection within the European Union than those secured by the ECtHR as a consequence of the principle of mutual trust and the rebuttable presumption that Member States comply with such rights.[47]

4.3 Tax Aspects of EU fundamental rights

4.3.1 Right to privacy and data protection

Data protection is regulated within the European Union by the General Data Protection Regulation, signed on 8 April 2016 and in force since 25 May 2018. The object and purpose of such rules is to prevent public disclosure of confidential information without an express authorization of the interested person. The Data Protection Regulation grants rights to all individuals in the European Union, and applies to all data controllers and data processors, even those not established within the EU, establishing onerous obligations on data controllers and limiting the transfer of data without consent of the data subject in order to secure accuracy and effective protection, which in turn facilitates the free flow of data within the EU: if the level of protection is up to standard in all Member States, then there is less reason for Member States to limit cross-border data processing.

The overall framework for data protection is established by two separate provisions of the Charter, namely Articles 7 and 8, which regulate the rights to privacy and data protection, respectively, Charter. For three reasons we shall analyse these rights jointly. First, unlike the Charter, the ECHR contains no specific provision on data protection, but frames that right within the more general context of Article 8 ECHR on the right to

46 A good example of this is the position held by CJEU on the prohibition of double jeopardy, on which see *supra* 4.2.2.

47 The interpretation of fundamental rights in respect of asylum seekers offers example of this situation between the CJEU (Case C-411/10, N.S., EU:C:2011:865, points 80, 104 and 106), and the ECtHR (*Sufi and Elmi vs United Kingdom*, Application Nos. 8319/07 and 11449/07, CE:ECHR:2011:0628JUD000831907, and *M.S.S. vs Belgium and Greece*, Application No. 30696/09, CE:ECHR:2011:0121JUD003069609).

respect for private and family life.[48] Second, both rights are the object of secondary EU legislation establishing a European standard for legal protection of individuals as to the processing of personal data and the free movement of data'[49] which are partially the basis for the substance of Article 8 of the Charter[50] Third, insofar as CJEU protects data of legal persons also by applying the right to privacy,[51] it shows that the possible narrower scope of data protection under Article 8 of the Charter may be subsumed within the broader boundaries of Article 7 of the Charter.

The comparison between the wording of Articles 7 and 8 of the Charter, on the one hand, and Article 8 ECHR, on the other, shows an apparent higher standard of protection of confidentiality within the European Union, since the latter provision expressly admits exceptions, which do not appear in the Charter provisions.

ECtHR case law has endorsed a wide margin of appreciation for States to admit limitations to data protection in the interest of national security.[52] CJEU case law admits instead a stronger protection, which excludes data retention[53] and limiting transfer of personal data.

The latter position reflects the wording of Article 8 (2) 1st sentence of the Charter, which imposes for fair data processing either the consent of the person concerned, or a legal basis for processing. In the *Smaranda Bara* case[54] the CJEU held that the transfer of personal data by the Romanian tax administration to the Romanian social security authorities violated the EU standard of data protection.

---

48 See among others ECtHR, *Leander v. Sweden*, Application No. 9248/81, CE:ECHR:1987:0326JUD000924881, point 48; ECtHR, *Amann v. Switzerland*" Application no. 27798/95, CE:ECHR:2000:0216JUD002779895, points 65 and 69-70; ECtHR, *Rotaru v. Romania*, Application 28341/95, CE:ECHR:2000:0504JUD002834195, point 43; ECtHR, *S. and Marper v. The United Kingdom*, Application Nos. 30562/04 and 30566/04, CE:ECHR:2008:1204JUD003056204, point 67; *ECtHR, Khelili v. Switzerland*, Application No. 16188/07, CE:ECHR:2011:1018JUD001618807, point 55; ECtHR, *M.M. v. The United Kingdom*, Application No. 24029/07, CE:ECHR:2012:1113JUD002402907, point 187. On 28 January 1981, a convention was signed in Strasbourg for the protection of individuals with regard to automatic processing of personal data. This convention forms part of the legal rules of the Council of Europe and is currently in force in fifty-one countries (four of which non-members of the Council of Europe).

49 Directive 95/46/EC, repealed by the EU General Data Protection Regulation, with effect from 25 May 2018.

50 Both the EU Data Protection Directive and the EU Data Protection Regulation only concern data protection in respect of individuals. By contrast, Article 8 of the Charter seems to have a broader subjective scope, since it extends such rights to "everyone". The English language version of Article 8 (1) and (2) Charter includes a reference to data concerning 'him" or "her". This could be interpreted as narrowing down the meaning of the expression "everyone" only to individuals. This nuance is missing in other official languages, including Dutch, French, German, Italian, Portuguese and Spanish. Therefore, the interpretation of the wording of this provision would be compatible with the conclusion that it also applies to persons other than individuals. However, the explanations to the EU Charter indicate otherwise, specifying that "the right to protection of personal data is to be exercised under the conditions laid down in the directive".

51 See C-450/06, *Varec*, ECLI:EU:C:2008:91.

52 ECtHR, *Big Brother Watch and Others v The United Kingdom*, nos 58170/13, 62322/14 and 24960/15 (25 May 2021), paras 338 and 424.

53 See C-293/12, *Digital Rights Ireland*, ECLI:EU:C:2014:238; C-203/15, *Tele2 Sverige*, ECLI:EU:C:2016:970.

54 Case C-201/14, *Smaranda Bara*, EU:C:2015:638.

The access of tax authorities to confidential information concerning taxpayers does not per se require their public disclosure. For this reason, there is no intrinsic conflict between data protection and the right of tax authorities to obtain such information.

However, not even the general obligation for taxpayers to cooperate with tax authorities should imply for the latter ones the right to be free to dispose of such information without any limit, or to make it publicly available in the form of the so-called naming and shaming.[55]

Moreover, the existence of a prior law making data collection, processing or transfer in principle legitimate, should not allow any disclosure of data that could unnecessarily undermine the general respect for private and family life under Article 7 of the Charter. Furthermore, Article 18 of the Data Protection Regulation establishes four specific limitations for data processing that would be hard to reconcile with any public disclosure.[56]

Accordingly, we do not see any major issue in connection with the lifting of tax secrecy as long as the data use remains protected by the confidentiality obligations of the tax authorities, except for the fact that mandatory disclosure should not undermine the client-attorney privilege.[57] This means any exchange of tax information within the European Union is not in principle the source of a potential violation of Articles 7 and 8, especially considering that all EU Member States are bound to comply with both these human rights standards and the EU Directives on Administrative Cooperation in Tax Matters (DAC).[58]

However, the same may not hold true in respect of transfer of tax information to third countries that do not comply with the standards of data protection. Such situation should be addressed in the light of the *Schrems* judgment,[59] which could have far-reaching repercussions on automatic exchange of information in the framework of mechanisms like FATCA with the US.[60] Likewise, problems will in our view arise, also within the European Union, in connection with the adoption of public country-by-country reporting by multinationals.[61] The latter mechanism forces enterprises to make confidential information available not just to tax authorities with a secrecy obligation (as instead the BEPS Project requires), but also to the public at large. As indicated earlier, even though the EU Charter does not protect the confidentiality of data of such enterprises under Article 8 of the EU

55 However, ECtHR, *L.B. v. Hungary*, nos 36345/16 (12 January 2021) indicated that such practice could be accepted in the specific context that was submitted to the attention of the Court.

56 Article 18 (1) of the Data Protection Regulation allows the data subject to obtain from the controller restriction of processing where one of the following applies (a) the accuracy of personal data is contested by the data subject, (b) the processing is unlawful and the data subject opposes the erasure, (c) the controller no longer needs the personal data for the purposes of processing and (d) the data subject has objected to processing pending the verification.

57 See CJEU, case C-623/22, Belgian Association of Tax Lawyers, ECLI:EU:C:2024:639; case C-432/23, Ordre des avocats du Barreau de Luxembourg, ECLI:EU:C:2024:791.

58 See EU Directives 2011/16/EU (as amended by Directive 2014/107/EU), 2015/2376/EU and 2016/881/ EU.

59 Case C-362/14, *Schrems*, ECLI:EU:C:2015:650.

60 Foreign Accounts Tax Compliance Act (US).

61 See Directive 2021/2101 of the European Parliament and of the Council of 24 November 2021, amending Directive 2013/34/EU as regards disclosure of income tax information by certain undertakings and branches. This Directive has introduced Chapter 10a on report on income tax information.

Charter, such disclosure could have an indirect impact on the individuals related to them,[62] or anyway be protected under the right of privacy.[63]

Furthermore, Article 8 (2) 2nd sentence of the Charter provides for a general right to access data concerning him or her, as well as a right to have it rectified.[64] This provision, also known in some legal systems as *habeas data*, may have important implications in tax matters, especially where the national legal system does not yet provide for this standard. Such right extends to tax information gathered in the framework of cross-border exchange of information,[65] except in the presence of an overriding general interest that could prevent this. In the *Sabou* case[66] – in which no taypayer rights were recognized in respect of cross-border exchange of information – the request from the national Court exclusively focused on the existence of rights of taxpayers in connection with the mutual assistance directives in tax matters (now DAC[67]), and the facts of the case predated the entry into force of the Treaty of Lisbon.

4.3.2 *Right to property*

The right to property in Article 17 of the Charter (peaceful enjoyment) partially reflects the wording of the general provision contained in Article 1, 1st ECHR Protocol. In particular, both provisions protect this right for all persons, but differ in at least two aspects, which may suggest a stronger protection of this right in the European Union legal order as compared to the European Human Rights Convention.

First, Article 17 of the Charter, apart from stating the entitlement to the peaceful enjoyment of possessions, also recognizes the right of all persons to own, use, dispose of and bequeath of lawfully acquired possessions. This wording may facilitate the protection of the right to property also in connection with transfers of property, such as the ones related to taxes on the transfer of property (also *mortis causa*).

Furthermore, Article 17 of the Charter does not include the limitation to this right included in Article 1, 1st ECHR Protocol, explicitly safeguarding the "right of a State to enforce such laws as it deems necessary to...secure the payment of taxes...".[68] However, as object and purpose of this limitation are that when States require and enforce the payment of taxes in line with the rule of law, they do not infringe the right to property, no significant difference should arise between Luxembourg and Strasbourg as regards this provision: taxation is a justified regulation of property, as long as it is provided for by law

62 CJEU, judgment of 17 December 2015, *WebMindLicences*, case C-419/14, ECLI:EU:C:2015:832, [2015], cited, paras 79 and ff.
63 CJEU, judgment of 14 February 2008, *Varec*, case C-450/06, ECLI:EU:C:2008:91.
64 See C-189/18, *Glencore Agriculture Hungary*, ECLI:EU:C:2019:861.
65 See C-682/15, *Berlioz Investment Fund*, ECLI:EU:C:2017:373. Until present there has been no judgment acknowledging this right in connection with mutual agreement procedures, but in our view such right should exist in no different way as it applies to any other administrative procedure of taxation, in line with the criteria indicated in C-349/07, *Sopropé*, ECLI:EU:C:2008:746.
66 In the Case C-276/12, *Sabou*, ECLI:EU:C:2013:678, the CJEU held that EU law does not provide for access to the request or to the exchanged information as long as no assessment has been issued to the taxpayer on the basis of that request/information, concerned this type of issue.
67 Directive on Administrative Cooperation; see Chapter 13.
68 This limitation is also absent in Article 8 of the Inter-American Charter of Human Rights.

(lawfulness test), serves a legitimate aim (general interest test) and respects a fair balance between the general interest and the protection of individual rights (fair balance test).

Although the CJEU has so far never applied Article 17 of the Charter in tax matters, ECtHR case law – which provides the minimum standard of protection under the Charter (see Article 52(3)) – can help determining two main implications of the protection of the right to property in this domain.

First, since the levying of taxes may not deprive the taxpayer of his possessions, taxes may not be confiscatory. The link with the ECHR and the common constitutional traditions of EU Member States may help identify some criteria for characterizing taxes as confiscatory under Article 17 Charter. Whilst the ECtHR acknowledged the confiscatory nature of taxation in extreme cases,[69] national constitutional courts have admitted it also in respect of lower levels of taxation.[70] The CJEU has until now never acknowledged the possible confiscatory effects resulting from the parallel exercise of taxing jurisdiction by two Member States,[71] perhaps also because national Courts have never raised this specific issue in connection with Article 17 of the Charter. However, the overkill effects of international tax coordination aimed at countering the exploitation of unintended tax advantages resulting from cross-border disparities could soon be a good reason to address this issue.

Second, even if the national legislator has wide powers to determine the applicable rates and the division of the tax burden if there is sufficient nexus within its taxing jurisdiction,[72] tax authorities must collect and enforce taxes in line with the rule of law. Any departure from such standard in administrative and judicial tax procedures falls

69 See the cases on the Hungarian severance pay tax for former civil servants, rising to a 98% marginal rate: ECtHR, *N.K.M. v. Hungary*, Application No. 66529/11, CE:ECHR:2013:0514JUD006652911 and ECtHR, *Gáll v. Hungary*, Application no. 49570/11, CE:ECHR:2013:0625JUD004957011.

70 In recent years, national constitutional courts have qualified a 90% rate (the top Walloon inheritance tax rate in Belgium) and a 75% rate (the top income tax rate in France) as confiscatory. Furthermore, the German constitutional court has first developed the *Halbteilungsgrundsatz*, which regards as confiscatory any tax on capital income at rates above 50%, since this would represent the maximum for allowing a joint use of property for private purposes and for the welfare of the community. However, it later raised the threshold to 60%. National Parliaments have taken similar action, such as for instance in the case of Slovakia, where Parliament repealed in 2012 the 80% income tax rate for its confiscatory nature that could conflict with European Union law.

71 This type of problems is rather frequent in the field of income (see Case C-513/04, *Kerckhaert Morres*, EU:C:2006:713; Case C-128/08, *Damseaux*, EU:C:2009:471; Case C-194/15, *Baudinet*, EU:C:2016:81) and inheritance taxes (see Case C-67/08, Block, EU:C:2009:92).

72 This conclusion is drawn from a combined reading of the principle stated in ECtHR *Ferrazzini*, Application no. 44759/98, cit., point 29 and the later assessment of compatibility of tax policy mensuren with Article 1, 1st ECHR Protocol made by ECtHR in various other occasions. See ECtHR *Koufaki and ADEDY v. Greece*, Application Nos. 57665/12 and 57657/12, CE:ECHR:2013:0507DEC005766512; *N.K.M. Hungary*, Application no. 66529/11, cit., *Da Conceição Mateus v. Portugal*, Application Nos. 62235/12 and 57725/12, CE:ECHR:2013:1008DEC006223512; ECtHR, *Da Silva Carvalho Rico v. Portugal*, Application No. 13341/14, CE:ECHR:2015:0901DEC001334114.

within the material scope of protection[73] and could thus give rise to a breach of the right of property.[74]

4.3.3 *Equality before the law and non-discrimination*

The Charter includes two separate provisions expressing the principle of equality: Article 20, which requires equality before the law, and Article 21, which generally prohibits discrimination on the basis of 'suspect' criteria, such as sex, race, colour, ethnic or social origin, genetic features, language, religion or belief, political or any other opinion, membership of a national minority, property, birth, disability, age or sexual orientation, and which specifically prohibits, but only 'within the scope of application of the Treaties', discrimination on grounds of nationality.

The existence of two separate provisions implies that each has its separate legal object. Whilst Article 21(2) Charter mainly provides a link with the fundamental freedoms in the Treaty on the Functioning of the European Union,[75] Article 21(1) has the same goal as Article 14 ECHR and Protocol 12 ECHR (a general prohibition of discrimination on grounds of inherent personal characteristics), and Article 20 Charter prohibits class justice and possibly also implies formal equality before the law, or *égalité devant les charges publics* (equality vis-à-vis public expenditure).

This Charter equality principle may possibly also cover reverse discrimination and preferential treatment of cross-border situations as compared to purely domestic ones, which until now cannot be remedied by application of the free movement rights. At any rate, it binds EU institutions to operate in conformity with the principles of equality and non-discrimination, which may influence how the EU Commission exercises its powers, including in some delicate fields, such as currently the application of the prohibition of state aids in tax matters: all comparable national fiscal aid measures should ideally be tackled by the Commission at the same time and in the same way.[76]

73 ECtHR took this position in respect of the right to fair trial in *Janosevic v. Sweden* (Application No. 34619/97, CE:ECHR:2002:0723JUD003461997, and, after the *Ferrazzini* judgment, in various other cases starting from *Jussila*, Application No. 73053/01, CE:ECHR:2006:1123JUD007305301, point 45.

74 As the ECtHR already held in the *Capital Bank AD v Bulgaria Case*, Application No. 49429/99, CE:ECHR:2005:1124JUD004942999, point 134, "any interference with the peaceful enjoyment of possessions must be accompanied by procedural guarantees affording to the individual or entity concerned a reasonable opportunity of presenting their case to the responsible authorities for the purpose of effectively challenging the measures interfering with the rights guaranteed by this provision".

75 Therefore, also considering the implications of Article 6 TEU, this provision may not introduce additional constraints on the exercise of taxing powers by EU Member States that would broaden the scope of this principle as applicable under the provisions contained in the TFEU. See further on the scope of the non-discrimination principle under Section 3.

76 This conclusion could in our view be justified in the light of the convergence between non-discrimination and the prohibition of state aids in tax matters, on which see further Wattel, P. J., in Richelle, I., Schön, W., Traversa, E. (eds.), State Aid Law and Business Taxation, Springer Verlag, 2016, pp. 65-67.

4.3.4 Freedom of movement and residence

Article 45 Charter protects freedom of movement and residence within the territory of the European Union for citizens of the Union in a way that reiterates the right of residence and free movement enshrined in Article 21 (1) TFEU.

Furthermore, it covers the possible extension of such rights to third country nationals legally resident in the territory of a Member State, subject to the conditions contained in the EU Treaties.

4.3.5 Right to an effective remedy and fair trial

Title VI (Articles 47-50) of the Charter secures the right to judicial review and access to justice within the European legal order with a view to protecting the rule of law.[77]

Settled case law of the CJEU confirms that the right to fair trial includes the application of the *audita altera parte* principle, thus obliging tax authorities throughout the entire administrative procedure to allow taxpayers to express their views before adopting any measure that may affect their personal sphere. In this sense, taking into account the strict links between the administrative and judicial part of tax procedures, there may be no right to fair trial without a right to a fair administrative procedure.[78] CJEU settled case law recognizes this right without any exception.

This general principle of EU law protects a free and effective exercise of the right to defence under Article 47 of the Charter, but also has implications under Article 48 of the Charter in respect of penalties,[79] and Article 41 of the Charter for acts issued by the EU institutions.[80]

Therefore, in principle in every case in which national tax authorities intend to take an administrative decision, such as an (additional) tax assessment, which is not to the benefit of the taxpayer (and which is within the scope of application of EU law), the taxpayer must be given an opportunity to make known his view and to access the documents underlying that intended decision before it is taken (also known as *habeas data*),[81] unless there is a justification for immediate imposition and enforcement[82] or if a prior hearing could not have produced a different outcome.[83]

77 In this sense see Kokott, J., Pistone, P., Taxpayers in international law, Hart Publishing, 2022, p. 206.
78 See Pistone, P., General Report, in Pistone, P. (ed.), Tax Procedures, IBFD Publications, 2020, p. 5.
79 See further under 4.3.6.
80 See Case C-349/07, *Sopropé*, EU:C:2008:746, point 37; Joined Cases C-129/13 and 130/13, *Kamino International and Datema*, EU:C:2014:2041, points 29-30.
81 See also Case C-419/14, *WebMindLicences*, EU:C:2015:832, point 84. In both Case C-349/07, *Sopropé*, EU:C:2008:746, and Case C-276/12, *Sabou*, EU:C:2013:678, point 38, the Court explained that this right of prior hearing binds tax authorities of the Member States when they take decisions within the scope of EU law, even if the EU law concerned does not expressly provide for such a procedural requirement.
82 See, e.g., Case C-28/05, Dokter, EU:C:2006:408 concerning the necessity for immediate action to stop a cattle plague from spreading and which could therefore be put into place without giving the farmer involved a prior say in the matter.
83 See CJEU, Joined Cases 129/13 and 130/13, *Kamino and Datema Hellman*, EU:C:2014:2041.

In general terms, the relevant provisions of the EU Charter entirely absorb the contents of both Article 6 (fair hearing) and Article 13 (effective remedy) ECHR, and it secures higher standards of protection than those applicable under the ECHR.

This has four important implications in tax matters.

First, the right to a fair trial under Article 6 (1) ECHR is subject to the condition of a link with 'the determination of civil rights and obligations' or of 'any criminal charge against the person'. No such limitation exists for the right to access justice and an effective remedy under the provisions contained in Title VI of the Charter. This means that within the EU, all tax litigation is also covered, provided a link with EU law exists.

Second, in line with the principle *ubi ius, ibi remedium*, the CJEU has always protected the effectiveness of EU rights, by giving each person entitled to such rights effective legal remedies in respect of EU law provisions with direct effect. In line with such concept, every substantive or procedural obstacle for the effective exercise of an EU right may be held incompatible with the EU standards of protection. It is therefore no surprise that Article 47, which is the core provision of Title VI of the Charter, bundles the right to a fair trial together with that to an effective remedy. In the *Berlioz* case the CJEU has held that Article 47 Charter requires a right to an effective judicial review, thus such that the (national) court must dispose of all relevant information to carry out the legality of the review.[84]

Third, since the CJEU has held the obligation to pay taxes before the income is available to be a potential restriction on the exercise of EU fundamental freedoms,[85] we believe that rules requiring provisional payment of tax[86] without immediate access to justice or without effective suspension of tax collection until a final assessment opens access to justice, may be in contravention of the effective remedy requirement.[87]

Fourth, unlike the ECHR, the Charter does not require all national legal remedies to have been used and exhausted. Immediately at first instance, a national tax court may already refer to the CJEU the question of whether EU law opposes application of the national tax rule at issue by way of a request for a preliminary ruling.

The Charter contains four blocks of procedural rights, namely (i) a general right to an effective remedy and a fair trial within the scope of application of EU law (Article 47 of the Charter), (ii) a presumption of innocence and a right of defence in criminal matters (Article 48 of the Charter), (iii) procedural rights concerning EU institutions (Articles 41-43 of the Charter), (iv) *ne bis in idem*: the right not to be tried or punished twice in criminal proceedings for the same offence (Article 50 of the Charter). Below, we will separately address these blocks.

84 See Case C-682/15, *Berlioz*, point 84. Surprisingly, after the latter judgment recognized this right in respect of penalties applicable to the third party holder of information, the CJEU denied in C-245/19 and 246/19, *État luxembourgeois*, EU:C:2020:795 the Court that such right could be activated also by the affected taxpayer.

85 See for instance Case C-9/02, de Lasteyrie, EU:C:2004:138, which is discussed in Chapter 20.

86 This type of mechanism is also known in various legal systems as *solve et repete*, i.e. first pay and then request repayment.

87 Interim suspensions should be granted by the judiciary when the application for them clearly states the circumstances of an urgent intervention and the pleas of fact and law establish a *prima facie* case for granting such suspension. This matter raises critical issues that arise in cases of suspension of national taxes, but which could also present similar features in connection with the immediate effects of a decision on state aids.

As indicated by tax literature[88] and ECtHR case law,[89] due to the close connection between administrative and judicial procedures, the effective protection of fundamental rights within tax procedures would be meaningless if it did not stretch from initial tax audits to the final judicial decision. This line of reasoning is settled case law of CJEU too.

The dimension of the two rights bundled in Article 47 of the Charter consists of four clauses, which are contained in Article 47 (1) (effective remedy), the first sentence of Article 47 (2) (fair hearing), the second sentence of Article 47 (2) (legal representation) and Article 47 (3) (legal assistance) of the Charter.[90]

All of these clauses are generally applicable, and therefore also apply where no criminal charge or civil right is at issue, provided that there is a link with a right or freedom of EU law. This means that in all cases involving EU harmonized taxation, notably VAT, customs duties and excise duties, as well as in those direct tax cases which involve either EU integration measures (e.g. the EU Parent-Subsidiary Directive, the EU ATAD, the EU DAC and the EU Dispute Settlement Directive) or EU law prohibitions (e.g. the free movement rights or the State aid prohibition), the Charter requires an effective legal remedy and a fair and public hearing.

The fair hearing requirement contains three clauses, which entirely match those of Article 6 (1) first sentence, ECHR:

First, it acknowledges the right to a fair and public hearing. In our view, the fairness argument should at least imply the right of the person to be heard in open Court before any decision is taken, as well as – if besides taxation also a punitive tax surcharge is at issue – the privilege against self-incrimination. However, considering the strongly documentary nature of administrative and judicial tax procedures, the right to present written arguments may be equivalent to that of being heard during a public session. The ECtHR has held, in the *Jussila* case, that even if in a tax case also a punitive surcharge has been imposed, not in all cases a public hearing is necessary.[91]

Second, the right to fair trial also means the right to be tried within a reasonable time. This aspect has already been the object of interpretation in CJEU tax case law, which handed down a judgment surely leading to the quashing, by the referring Italian court, of a tax audit on the grounds of the excessive duration of litigation without addressing the merits of the case.[92]

Third, it reaffirms the right of everyone to have their case judged by an impartial and independent tribunal established by law, which issues binding and effectively enforceable decisions.[93] The review of legality of the tax assessment should be effective. Therefore, the court should have all relevant powers and competences to exercise its judicial function, also

88 Maisto, G., The Impact of the European Convention on Human Rights on Tax Procedures and Sanctions with Special Reference to Tax Treaties and the EU Arbitration Convention, in Kofler, G. et al. (eds.), IBFD Publications, 2010, p. 376; Baker, P., Pistone, P., General Report on the Practical Protection of Taxpayers' Rights, IFA 2015 Congress, Basel, p. 36.

89 See *ex multis* ECtHR, *Imbrioscia*, Application No. 13972/88, CE:ECHR:1993:1124JUD001397288, *Janosevic*, Application No. 34619/97, CE:ECHR:2002:0723JUD003461997; *Ravon*, Application No. 18497/03, CE:ECHR:2008:0221JUD001849703.

90 As indicated by CJEU, Case C-682/15, *Berlioz*, EU:C:2017:373, point 54, Article 47 of the Charter corresponds to both Article 6 (1) and Article 13 ECHR.

91 ECtHR, *Jussila v. Finland*, Application No. 73053/01, CE:ECHR:2006:1123JUD007305301.

92 CJEU, Case C-500/10, *Belvedere Costruzioni*, EU:C:2012:186.

93 This conclusion is in line with the position of the Court in CJEU, *Berlioz*, point 55.

where the taxpayer challenges the legality or the results of international administrative cooperation between tax authorities.[94] However, the principle of equality of arms does not imply in such circumstances that also persons required to provide information to be exchanged and having been fined for not cooperating have immediate access to the foreign request for information.[95]

Fourth, in line with the minimum standard of Article 6 (3) (c) ECHR, Article 47 (2) second sentence established the right of access to justice through legal advice, defence and representation. Article 47 (3) secures the effectiveness of this system by means of legal aid also for persons who lack sufficient financial resources to exercise it.

Furthermore, just like under Article 6 ECHR, the right to fair trial under Article 47 Charter also entails the right to non-self-incrimination in respect of all matters that have a potential or actual criminal relevance.[96] However, this right does not prevent tax authorities from requesting the taxpayers and private parties to supply information connected to the assessment of taxes and required by law.[97]

4.3.6 *Presumption of innocence and right of defence*

Article 48 of the Charter contains two important procedural guarantees, which correspond to Article 6 (2) and Article 6 (3) ECHR.

The presumption of innocence requires in tax matters that tax authorities give evidence of the conditions established by law for requiring the criminal liability of the private person beyond any reasonable doubt.[98] Such guarantees apply also to tax cases in so far as these involve not only taxation (if they involve only taxation, Article 48 is not applicable, as it only extends to 'criminal charges'), but also punitive measures (e.g. such as criminal sanctions and administrative fines that are equivalent under the so-called Engel criteria)[99] for not complying with tax obligations (*and* in so far as these cases are within the scope of application of EU law).

The 'criminal' right of defence envisaged in Article 48 of the Charter is not to be mixed up with the much wider *administrative* principle of 'observance of the rights of the defence', which is a general administrative principle of EU law recognized by the Court, and therefore also applicable in pure tax cases. The 'right of defence' of Article 48 of the Charter only concerns cases in which a 'criminal charge' is at issue, including all administrative and judicial procedures involving punitive administrative sanctions such as, most notably, surcharges and fines for not complying with the tax law.

---

94 See CJEU, *Berlioz*, point 84.

95 See CJEU, *Berlioz*, point 101.

96 Nevertheless, as indicated by Baker, P. and Pistone, P., General Report: The Practical Protection of Taxpayers' Rights, IFA 2015 Basel Congress, 2015, p. 39, taxpayers may not invoke the right of non-self-incrimination in order to escape their obligation to cooperate with the tax authorities, in particular when the tax system relies on them to keep documents, such as accounting books.

97 Kokott, J., Pistone, P., Taxpayers in international law, cit., p. 269 differentiate between will-dependent information (covered by the privilege against self-incrimination) and will-independent information, which exists independently of the taxpayer's will and may thus be requested by tax authorities.

98 In this sense see Kokott, J., Pistone, P., Taxpayers in international law, cit., p. 343.

99 ECtHR, *Engel and others v the Netherlands (Plenary)*, nos 5100/71, 5102/71, 5354/72 and 5370/72, (8 June 1976). See further for the actual content of the criteria under 4.3.9.

In particular, Article 48 (1) of the Charter presumes innocence of the person charged until proved guilty according to law. This requires prior completion of judicial appeals. Therefore, when the taxpayer contests the view of tax authorities before a Court, any other tax procedure operating in parallel may not regard such person as guilty of the first violation until all judicial instances have been completed.[100]

Article 48 (2) Charter adds a general clause aimed at securing the respect for the right of defence.

The content of the latter right is to be determined in line with the specific provisions contained in Article 6 (3) ECHR. In particular, the person has the rights (a) to be informed promptly of the nature and cause of the accusation; (b) to have time and facilities for the defence; (c) to defend oneself in person or through (free) legal assistance; (d) to examine witnesses *à charge* and to present witnesses *à décharge*; and (e) to free assistance of an interpreter.

In connection with the application of Article 47 of the Charter, the person charged should be able to exercise the right of defence based on access to the complete file (*habeas data*),[101] have the freedom to give evidence and to refuse to provide self-incriminating evidence.[102] Furthermore, its application in tax matters may imply the emasculation of irrefutable presumptions of fact which may be permissible to determine the tax base, but which are incompatible with the presumption of innocence in so far as (also) a punitive measure is at issue, whether or not characterized as 'criminal' or as 'administrative' by national law.[103]

---

100 In this sense, see for the Court of Justice: Case C-203/21, *Delta Story 2003*, EU:C:2022:865; Case C-336/24, *Sinhren Invest*, EU:C:2024:982: and for the European Court of Human Rights, *Kangers v. Latvia*, Application No. 35726/10.

101 In Case C-682/15, *Berlioz*, cit., the Court acknowledged the right of the interested person to judicial review as to the compliance with legal requirement, but excluded the direct access of the taxpayer to relevant documents connected with cross-border exchange of information, allowing instead for a screening by judicial authorities. By contrast, in *Chambaz v Switzerland*, Application No. 11663/04, CE:ECHR:2012:0405JUD001166304, concerning a purely domestic case, the ECtHR concluded that the denied access to documents held by tax authorities and concerning the taxpayer had deprived him of the right to fair trial under Article 6 ECHR.

102 In the case *Saunders vs United Kingdom*, Application no. 19187/91, CE:ECHR:1996:1217JUD001918791, the ECtHR held that the right not to self-incriminate implies first of all that to remain silent during the trial. In *Murray v United Kingdom*, Application No. 18731/91, CE:ECHR:1996:0208JUD001873191, the ECtHR concluded that the privilege against self-incrimination protects against any reversal in the burden of proof. In *Chambaz*, cit., and in *J.B. v Switzerland*, Application no. 31827/96, CE:ECHR:2001:0503JUD003182796, the ECtHR extended this protection to the refusal by the taxpayer of exhibiting documents. However, as indicated in Baker, P., Pistone, P., General Report, cit., p. 39, we think that "the essence of the right not to self-incriminate is that the taxpayer should not be under pressure to answer questions, whether orally or in writing, which might lead to self-incrimination. There is no such danger in the case of pre-existing books and records and we see no reason why the taxpayer should not supply those. The position, of course, is different where the taxpayer, in the audit process, is asked to answer questions in writing, which is exactly the same as giving oral answers, and the right against self-incrimination therefore applies." Since most tax systems allow the taxpayer to keep official documents, the conclusions reached by the ECtHR can in our view undermine the correct and effective functioning of tax audits. See further on this Baker, P., Pistone, P., General Report, cit., p. 39.

103 See ECtHR, *Engel*, cit.

4.3.7 *Provisions geared solely at the EU institutions*

Articles 41, 42, 43 and 44 of the Charter only apply to the EU institutions. They state the rights to good administration, of access to documents, of complaining to the EU Ombudsman and to petition the European Parliament.

Article 41 of the Charter protects the right of everyone to good administration by the EU institutions.[104] This implies the right to impartial and fair treatment within a reasonable time, as well as three specific rights: (i) the right of being heard before any individual measure negatively affects the the person concerned (as part of the *administrative* rights of the defence), (ii) the right to access files related to the person concerned (another part of the *administrative* rights of the defence), and (iii) the right to have proper reasoning for all decisions issued by EU institutions.

This provision could be relevant in tax matters where the European Commission has wide discretionary powers, as in the field of infringement actions, and especially where such powers are capable of directly affecting individual taxpayers, such as in the case of state aid decisions.

In essence, Article 41(1) and (2) of the Charter codify the general *administrative* principle of observance of the rights of the defence as laid down in the case law for the EU institutions.[105] This does not at all mean that such principle would not apply any more to the member States in so far as they take administrative (tax) decisions which have a link with EU law; on the contrary: it is a *general* principle of EU law. The third paragraph of Article 41 of the Charter recognizes the non-contractual liability of the EU for damages caused by its institutions or servants.

Article 42 of the Charter confirms the right to access documents of the EU institutions, also known as *habeas data*, and is presupposed for an effective exercise of the right to defence under Article 48 of the Charter. In line with the general interpretative attitude by the CJEU, the protection of this right is not unconditional, but subject to the limits of preserving confidentiality and business secrecy.

Article 43 of the Charter establishes the European Ombudsman in order to secure the compliance of EU institutions (except the CJEU) with the standards of good administration. This provision does not contain any additional legal remedy, but rather aims to secure the effective functioning of EU institutions without the need to bring the case before the judiciary. The involvement of the European Ombudsman in tax matters has been limited so far, which makes sense, as there are no taxes at EU level (except for the payroll tax for the Eurocrats), nor is there a tax administration at EU level.

Finally, Article 44 of the Charter admits the right of petition for all EU citizens and persons residing, or established, in the European Union to the European Parliament. We believe that this right of impulse may have important direct and indirect repercussions on the activity of the European Parliament in tax matters, especially in connection with the relevant tax scandals that have drawn considerable attention in the public opinion.

---

104 See Case C-419/14, *WebMindLicences*, point 83.

105 See Case C-349/07, *Sopropé*, EU:C:2008:746, point 37; Joined Cases C-129/13 and 130/13, *Kamino International and Datema*, EU:C:2014:2041, points 29-30.

4.3.8 Principles of legality and proportionality of criminal offences and penalties

Article 49 of the Charter confirms the applicability of the principles of legality and proportionality as regards penalties for criminal offences (including punitive administrative measures).

This provision secures that a prior law identifies criminal offences and the applicable penalties, it reserves criminal prosecution to more serious violations of the law[106] and it requires that punitive measures are suitable to achieve their goal and do not exceed what is necessary to protect the legal interest offended.[107]

This does not prohibit deterrence by penalties, but avoids overkill in line with a well-established principle of proportionality of European Union law. Interestingly, the CJEU has until now repeatedly applied the principles of legality and proportionality in its tax case law without any specific reference to Article 49 of the Charter.[108]

4.3.9 Prohibition of double jeopardy

Article 50 of the Charter corresponds to Article 4 of Protocol 7 ECHR, which has not been ratified by all EU Member States. It extends the right not to be tried or punished twice in criminal proceedings for the same offence, also known as the prohibition of double jeopardy. This provision codifies the *ne bis in idem* principle, which is intrinsic in the right to a fair trial under Article 6 ECHR as regards procedures concerning a criminal charge. Accordingly, it secures that for one criminal act there will only be one criminal proceeding (*ne bis vexari*) and, if the charged person is proved guilty, only one punishment (*ne bis puniri*).[109]

The CJEU determines whether or not an offence is 'criminal' in nature according to the so-called *Engel*-criteria of the ECtHR,[110] *i.e.* on the basis of (i) the legal characterization of the offence under national law,[111] (ii) the very nature of the offence and (iii) the degree of severity of the penalty liable to be incurred.[112] The latter two criteria are alternative,

106 In tax matters, the CJEU has suggested the use of criminal penalties in respect of cases of VAT fraud. See Case C-105/14, *Taricco*, point 39.

107 Also the ECtHR recognises the principles of legality and proportionality as intrinsic in the protection of rights. Accordingly, in the *Khodorkovskiy and Lebedev vs. Russia* [Yukos] case, Application Nos. 11082/06 and 13772/05, CE:ECHR:2013:0725JUD001108206, points 873-885 it held that the interference of tax penalties in the possession was contrary to Article 1 of Protocol No. 1 to the ECHR.

108 The CJEU generally applies proportionality in tax matters as the expression of the general principle of EU law, thus without specifically referring to Article 49 Charter even when it addresses reactions to breaches of legal requirements and the levying of penalties. See, in the field of VAT, Case C-259/12, *Rodopi*, EU:C:2013:414; Case C-24/15, *Plöckl*, EU:C:2016:791, point 58; Case C-576/15, *Maya Marinova*, EU:C:2016:740, point 47.

109 See, for an in-depth analysis: van Bockel, B., Groussot, X., Nazzini, R., Sarmiento, D. and Wattel, P. J.: *Ne Bis in Idem in EU Law*, Cambridge University Press, 2016.

110 See See ECtHR, *Engel v Netherlands*, Application Nos. 5100/71, 5101/71, 5102/71, 53454/72 and 5370/72, CE:ECHR:1976:1123JUD000510071.

111 In itself, that characterization is not decisive, otherwise States could manipulate the reach of the right by simply transferring an offence from their criminal code to, e.g., their tax procedure Act or general administrative law Act.

112 Case C-617/10, *Åkerberg Fransson*, EU:C:2013:105, point 35.

not necessarily cumulative.[113] It is settled ECtHR case law after the Grand Chamber judgment in *Jussila v. Finland*[114] (2006), concerning a tax fine of a mere € 309 for poor VAT-bookkeeping, that all tax penalties, also minor ones, are 'criminal charges' within the meaning of Article 6 ECHR and with that, also within the meaning of Article 4 Protocol 7 ECHR, as the ECtHR interprets the term 'criminal charge' homogeneously.[115]

The *ne bis in idem* principle is of great importance in tax matters, as in some Member States administrative tax surcharges may be imposed for the failure to (timely) pay taxes, or to comply with information and bookkeeping requirements, and on top of that, criminal sanctions may be imposed if the non-payment or non-compliance was intentional or the case concerns serious tax fraud.

The application of this simple criterion is in fact extremely problematic and potentially raising issues of different standards of legal interpretation between ECtHR and CJEU.

Following the *Zolotukhin* judgment of the ECtHR, the CJEU held that the 'same' offence means the same factual behaviour, irrespective of whether national law qualifies that behaviour as two offences, an administrative one and a criminal one, and that in principle, no criminal proceedings may be initiated – or must be discontinued – when a punitive administrative measure has become final.[116] However, in the tax case A. *and B.v. Norway*,[117] the ECtHR apparently yielded to the criticism of CoE Member States and allowed two punitive proceedings in respect of the same tax offence, one imposing a tax surcharge and one involving criminal indictment, provided (i) that these 'dual' proceedings could be considered as sufficiently parallel and interconnected as regards, inter alia, simultaneity and use of evidence, and (ii) that the criminal court takes account of the administrative penalty in order to reach overall a proportionate sanction in respect of the tax fraud committed.

The position held by the Court of Justice is more complex and far from constituting settled case law. On the one hand, in *Di Puma and Zecca*,[118] the CJEU applied this second requirement to the levying of an administrative fine of a criminal nature after a final criminal judgment of acquittal, acknowledging the different aspects of the same unlawful conduct. On the other hand, in *Åkerberg Fransson* it prohibited the duplication in tax matters when administrative penalties are in fact akin to criminal sanctions.[119] The view held in *Åkerberg Fransson* is not overruled by the more recent judgments, which reflect

113 See, a.o., ECtHR, *Jussila v. Finland*, Application No 73053/01), CE:ECHR:2006:1123JUD007305301.
114 ECtHR, *Jussila v. Finland*, Application No. 73053/01, cit.
115 See ECtHR, *Sergey Zolotukhin v. Russia*, Application No. 14939/03), CE:ECHR:2009:0210JUD001493903.
116 Case C-617/10, *Åkerberg Fransson*, cit., point 37; Case C-105/14, *Taricco*, cit., point 39.
117 ECtHR, *A. and B. v. Norway*, Application Nos. 24130/11 and 29758/11, CE:ECHR:2016:1115JUD002413011.
118 See joined cases C-596/16 and C-597/16, *Di Puma and Zecca*, ECLI:EU:C:2018:192, para. 42.
119 Case C-617/10, *Åkerberg Fransson*, cit.

the caution used by CJEU to admit exceptions to the prohibition of bis in idem,[120] thus taking a substantially different view from the one held by the ECtHR in *A and B v. Norway*.[121]

Article 50 of the Charter does not prohibit the imposition of two tax penalties on two different persons (both a legal person and its effective director) as a consequence of the same act or omission.[122]

120 The exceptions are justified by CJEU when the different sanctions and procedures pursue an objective of general interest, have a complementary function and are coordinated in a way that limits their impact to what is strictly necessary for reacting to the violation. This cautious attitude shows that in fact, also when interpreting the different requirements of Article 52 (1) of the EU Charter, the CJEU bundles them together in its reasoning. See, in this sense, cases C-524/15, *Menci*, ECLI:EU:C:2018:197; C-537/16, *Garlsson Real Estate SA*, ECLI:EU:2018:193; C-117/20, *Bpost*, ECLI:EU:C:2022:202, para. 46; C-151/20, *Nordzucker*, ECLI:EU:C:2022:203.

121 ECtHR, *A. and B. v. Norway*, Application No. 24130/11 and 29758/11, CE:ECHR:2016:-1115JUD002413011.

122 Joined Cases C-217/15 and 350/15, *Orsi and Baldetti*, point 27.

CHAPTER 5

Third States and External Tax Relations

Ana Paula Dourado[1] *and Peter Wattel*[2]

Update and elaboration by Daniel Smit[3] and Philip Baker[4]

5.1 Overview

This chapter covers topics relating to the EU's external tax relations, especially (i) free movement of capital and payments to and from non-Member States (third States), (ii) tax implications of the special status of overseas countries and territories (OCTs) of Member States, (iii) tax implications of international agreements between the EU and non-Member States, especially the European Economic Area Agreement (EEAA) and EU-association agreements, (iv) (external) tax treaty making powers, and (v) 'exportation' to third States of EU tax good governance rules (the EU blacklist of non-cooperative tax jurisdictions).

5.2 Third State Capital Movement[5]

5.2.1 Introduction; Differences Between Intra-EU and Third State Capital Movement

Art. 63(1) TFEU prohibits all restrictions on the movement of capital between Member States *and* between Member States and third States. Paragraph 2 prohibits all restrictions on payments between Member States and between Member States and third countries. This one-sided liberalization *erga omnes* is exceptional in international investment law and the implementation of the *erga omnes* principle in Article 63(1) TFEU was a controversial point during the Maastricht Treaty negotiations.[6] It was not until the final

1 Professor of Tax Law, International and European Tax Law, University of Lisbon; General Editor, Intertax.

2 Professor of EU Tax Law, ACTL, University of Amsterdam; Advocate-General, Supreme Court of the Netherlands; State Councillor extraordinary, Netherlands Council of State.

3 Professor (by special appointment) of Taxation of the Digital Economy, ACTL, University of Amsterdam; Head of the Scientific Tax Department of EY, Amsterdam.

4 King's Counsel, Field Court Tax Chambers, Gray's Inn, London; Visiting Professor, Faculty of Law, Oxford University.

5 See for in-depth analysis, Daniël Smit, 'Freedom of Investment between EU and non-EU Member States and its Impact on Corporate Income Tax Systems within the European Union,' CentER dissertations series, December 2011, University of Tilburg, the Netherlands.

6 See in more detail: A.F.P. Bakker, *The liberalization of capital movements in Europe. The Monetary Committee and Financial Integration* (Dordrecht: Kluwer Academic Publishers), 1996, p. 230 and p. 233.

stage of negotiations in the early 1990s (under the Netherlands Presidency) that it was agreed to include the *erga omnes* principle in the Treaty, although subject to a number of derogations. It can therefore be said that the introduction of the *erga omnes* principle, although revolutionary, was a thought-out decision.[7] However, in order to meet the concerns raised by several Member States, a number of derogations to the *erga omnes* liberalization were inserted.[8] Third State capital movement is therefore in principle as free as intra-EU capital movement, but it is not *quite* as free.

First, the *erga omnes* scope of Art. 63 TFEU may be limited in case of concurrence of capital movement and establishment, or of concurrence of capital movement and service provision, as establishment and services provision have *not* been liberalized in third State relations and the concurrence with other movements than capital movement may result in the freedom of capital movement not being applicable to avoid that indirectly, establishment and service provision would in fact be liberalised in third State relations. See Section 5.2.4.

Second, Art. 64 TFEU contains a standstill or grandfather clause saving restrictions on four categories of capital movement. Member States may retain measures as regards third States which existed on 31 December 1993 and which restrict capital movement involving (i) direct investment (including real estate), (ii) establishment, (iii) provision of financial services and (iv) admission of securities to capital markets. Many restrictive tax measures as regards third States are thus still permitted. See Section 5.2.3.

Third, Art. 64(3) empowers the Council to approve restrictive measures (Union law measures) as regards third States (a 'step backwards'). These restrictive measures are not specifically or necessarily related to taxes and do not need to be justified, as long as the special procedure and unanimity are observed; Moreover, Art. 65(4) was added in the TFEU by the Treaty of Lisbon, effective as of 1 December 2009: under conditions the European Commission or, the Member States by unanimous agreement, may "bless" new restrictive *tax* measures of a *Member State* (tax and national restrictions) as regards one or more third States. The preparatory work suggests that this provision was introduced to address the concerns of some Member States in respect of free movement of capital.[9] Probably, some Member States realized that unilateral total liberalization of capital movement with third States may be hazardous, especially in tax matters, as third States may not be inclined, *e.g.*, to extend tax benefits to EU residents if the EU has already unilaterally given away, in Art. 63 TFEU, its negotiation position. Remarkably, and despite these concerns, this new procedure, which raises many questions notably with respect to the Court's competence,

7 D. Servais, *Een Europese financiële ruimte* (Luxembourg: Bureau voor officiële publikaties der Europese Gemeenschappen, 1995), p. 66.

8 A.F.P. Bakker, *The liberalization of capital movements in Europe. The Monetary Committee and Financial Integration* (Dordrecht: Kluwer Academic Publishers), 1996, p. 233.

9 Conference of the Representatives of the Governments of the Member States, Brussels, 29 April 2004, PRESID 16, CIG 73/04, Meeting of Focal Points (Dublin, 4 May 2004) working document, 121.

has – to our knowledge – never been used yet by the Member States and has almost not been examined in detail in the scholarly tax literature until now.[10]

Fourth, Art. 66 allows temporary safeguarding measures in exceptional circumstances seriously impeding the functioning of the economic and monetary union. The impact on direct taxes is limited and this provision is therefore not discussed in more detail.

Last, the Court recognizes (see Section 5.2.2) that third State capital movement takes place in a 'different legal context' from intra-Union capital movement, as third States are not bound by EU rules such as, in particular, the duty to cooperate sincerely (Art. 4(3) TEU), the Directive on Administrative Cooperation (DAC; see Chapter 28) and the Recovery Assistance Directive (see Chapter 30). Hence, Member States justifications for restrictive tax measures, especially those aimed at effective fiscal supervision and recovery of tax, stand a better chance of being accepted in third State situations than in intra-EU situations.

In general terms one can conclude that, as a rule of thumb, the larger the threshold of the third State investment is (e.g. 100% shareholding), the lower the taxpayer protection under the free movement of capital typically tends to be. By contrast, the smaller the threshold of the third State investment is (e.g. portfolio investment), the higher the taxpayer protection under the free movement of capital tends to be.[11] As far as the impact of the free movement provisions under the Association Agreements and comparable other international agreements concluded by the EU with (groups of) third countries (see section 5.2.2) is concerned, the conclusion is precisely the opposite (subject to the preliminary question whether these provisions can be directly relied on by a taxpayer): small portfolio investments are typically left out of scope whereas large investments are typically in scope under at least a large number of these Agreements. On balance, the free movement of capital under Article 63 TFEU and the free movement provisions under the said Agreements can therefore be seen as supplementary. Despite the above rules of thumb, the level of protection eventually needs to be determined on a case-by-case basis.

5.2.2 In Principle the Same Substance as Intra-EU, but: 'a Different Legal Context'

In principle, free movement of capital has the same meaning in a third State context as it has in an intra-EU-context, and the concept of a restriction is the same as it is in an intra-EU context. The *Bordessa* case[12] and the *Sanz de Lera* case[13] offered a unique chance to compare the scopes of the free capital movement intra-Union and extra-Union, as both cases concerned the exact same national currency restrictions, *Bordessa* in an intra-EU situation and *Sanz de Lera* in relation to a non-member State (Switzerland). The Court's

10 This provision has deserved some attention in non-tax literature; see *e.g.* F.L. Fraga, Review of *The Free Movement of Capital and Foreign Direct Investment. The Scope of Protection in EU Law*, by S. Hindelang, *European Journal of International Law*, 21 (2010), p. 499; O'Brien, 'Canada, Capital Movements and the European Union', *Canadian Tax Journal* 2 (2009), 290; L. Flynn, Review of *The Free Movement of Capital and Foreign Direct Investment: The Scope of Protection in EU Law* by S. Hindelang, *European Law Review* 6 (2010), p. 892-895; C. Barnard, *The Substantive Law of the EU*, 3rd ed. (Oxford: Oxford University Press, 2010), 565. See also, lastly, Snell, 'Evolution as a non-linear process', p. 553.

11 See more elaborately: D.S. Smit, 'EU Freedoms, Non-EU Countries and Company Taxation', Alphen aan den Rijn: Kluwer Law International, 2012.

12 Joined cases C-358/93 and C-416/93, *Bordessa*, EU:C:1995:54.

13 Joined cases C-163, 164 and 250/94, *Sanz de Lera*, EU:C:1995:451.

analysis showed no differences of principle or approach. In both cases, the requirement of prior authorization for the export of currency was considered disproportional, but in both cases the requirement of prior declaration was considered proportional in relation to the justified goal of prevention of money-laundering, drugs trafficking and the financing of terrorism. The Member States have tried to convince the Court otherwise in *Skatteverket v A.*,[14] arguing (i) that unlike the liberalisation of intra-EU movement of capital, which is intended to complete the internal market, the extension of free movement of capital to third countries is linked to the completion of the economic and monetary union, (ii) that in relations with third countries, compliance with the prohibition in Art. (now) 63(1) TFEU would lead to unilateral liberalisation without the EU securing a guarantee of equivalent liberalisation by the third countries concerned and without, in the relations with those countries, harmonisation of, in particular, rules on direct taxation, (iii) that if free movement of capital were interpreted in an identical manner in relations with third countries and intra-EU relations, the latter would be deprived of the means of negotiating liberalisation with third countries, since such liberalisation would have already automatically and unilaterally opened up the EU market to those countries, and (iv) that free movement of capital in EU association agreements with third countries often have a more limited scope than that of Art. 63 EU, which would be meaningless if Art. 63 were as rigorously applicable in relations with third countries as in Union relations.[15] In vain, however; the Court answered:

> "31. (...), even if the liberalisation of the movement of capital with third countries may pursue objectives other than that of establishing the internal market, such as, in particular, that of ensuring the credibility of the single Community currency on world financial markets and maintaining financial centres with a world-wide dimension within the Member States, it is clear that, when the principle of free movement of capital was extended, (...), to movement of capital between third countries and the Member States, the latter chose to enshrine that principle in that Article and in the same terms for movements of capital taking place within the Community and those relating to relations with third countries."

So, if the Member States did not want to unilaterally liberalize third State capital movement, they should not have done so. But they did. Therefore, the Member States should use the grandfather clause (Art. 64 TFEU) to distinguish third State capital movement from intra-EU capital movement. Likewise, in the subsequent cases *Haribo* and *Salinen*,[16] the Court explicitly rejected the lack-of-reciprocity argument. However, the Court did not leave the Member States entirely in the cold. Taxation of third State capital movement is not always comparable to taxation of intra-EU capital movement, and wider justification for restrictions is possible in third State situations, because of the 'different legal context' of third State movement. As the Court considered in *Skatteverket v A*:[17]

> '36. (...) the extent to which the Member States are (...) authorised to apply certain restrictive measures on the movement of capital cannot be determined without taking account of

14 Case C-101/05, *Skatteverket v. A*, EU:C:2007:804.
15 Case C-101/05, *Skatteverket v. A*, EU:C:2007:804, points 29-30.
16 Joined Cases C-436/08 and C-437/08, *Haribo and Österreichische Salinen*, EU:C:2011:61.
17 Case C-101/05, *Skatteverket v. A*, EU:C:2007:804.

the fact (...) that movement of capital to or from third countries takes place in a different legal context from that which occurs within the Community.
37. Accordingly, because of the degree of legal integration that exists between Member States (...), in particular by reason of the presence of Community legislation which seeks to ensure cooperation between national tax authorities, such as [the Directive on Administrative Cooperation; *authors*], the taxation by a Member State of economic activities having cross-border aspects which take place within the Community is not always comparable to that of economic activities involving relations between Member States and third countries (....). (...), it may also be that a Member State will be able to demonstrate that a restriction on the movement of capital to or from third countries is justified for a particular reason in circumstances where that reason would not constitute a valid justification for a restriction on capital movements between Member States (...).'

In *Haribo* and *Salinen*, this 'effective fiscal supervision' justification for restrictive measures was relied on by Austria to refuse a credit for corporation tax levied in third States with which Austria had not concluded a tax treaty providing for (sufficient) exchange of tax information to verify the amount of corporation tax levied in the third State:

'129. The Austrian Government contends (...) that its tax regime is justified by the need to guarantee the effectiveness of fiscal supervision since the relevant double taxation conventions with non-member States do not guarantee the same level of exchange of information with the competent authorities of the States concerned as that provided for, by Directive 77/799, between the authorities of the Member States.
130. It is to be remembered that the framework established by Directive 77/799 for co-operation (...) does not exist between those authorities and the competent authorities of a non-member State where that State has not entered into any undertaking of mutual assistance (...).
131. It follows that, where legislation of a Member State makes the grant of a tax advantage dependent on satisfying conditions compliance with which can be verified only by obtaining information from the competent authorities of a nonmember State other than a State party to the EEA Agreement, it is in principle legitimate for the Member State to refuse to grant that advantage if – in particular, because that non-member State is not bound under an agreement to provide information – it proves impossible to obtain the requisite information from it (...).'

The Court accepted that where legislation of a Member State makes the grant of a tax advantage dependent on conditions, compliance with which can be verified only by obtaining information from a non-EU, non-EEA State, it is in principle legitimate for that Member State to refuse to grant that advantage if, in particular because the third State is not bound under an agreement to provide information, it proves impossible to obtain the requisite information from it. The (objective) absence or deficiency of exchange of tax information with the third State involved may therefore function as a safe harbor for Member States wishing to apply restrictive tax measures in respect of third State investors, even where the taxpayer would (subjectively) be fully transparent and cooperative, provided however that there is a real need to obtain information from the third State involved[18] and that the Member State involved pursues the objective to

18 Case C-377/07, *STEKO Industriemontage*, EU:C:2009:29, point 55.

ensure effective fiscal supervision in a consistent and systematic manner.[19] A similar decision was taken in *Rimbaud*,[20] in which France had made equal treatment of French real estate entities controlled by non-EU residents conditional on the existence of either sufficient exchange of tax information with the non-EU State concerned (in this case Liechtenstein) or a nondiscrimination provision in the tax treaty with that non-EU State. Although Liechtenstein is an EEA Member and Art. 40 of the EEA Agreement (see Section 5.4) provides for an equivalent right of establishment as Art. 49 TFEU, France could refuse an exemption from real estate tax because Liechtenstein – at that time – did not provide information as to the beneficial owners of the shares in the entity.[21]

In *Emerging Markets Series*,[22] the CJEU held that it is for the national court to decide whether or not there is equivalence between the EU legal framework and the international regulatory framework on mutual assistance. The case concerned a US investment fund requesting from the Polish tax authority the refund of a 15% corporation tax applied to dividends paid to it by Polish companies. Had the fund been resident in Poland, it would have been granted such refund. Its request was rejected on the ground that, as an investment fund established in the USA, it did not satisfy the exemption conditions set out in Art. 6(1)(10) of the Polish law on corporation tax. The Court considered this to be a restriction on the free movement of capital which was in principle prohibited by Art. 63 TFEU (points 42-43). On the need for effectiveness of fiscal supervision as a justification, it acknowledged the existence of a regulatory framework for exchange of information established between Poland and the USA under the applicable bilateral tax treaty as well as under Art. 4 of the OECD and the Council of Europe Convention, on mutual administrative assistance in tax matters (points 85-87). However, it did not rule itself on the question of whether that was sufficient to produce a comparable legal context as within the EU:

> "88. It is none the less for the referring court to examine whether the obligations under agreements, are in fact capable of enabling the Polish tax authorities to verify, where it may be necessary, the information provided by investment funds established in the United States of America on the conditions for their formation and operation, in order to determine that they operate within a regulatory framework equivalent to that of the European Union."

The *SECIL* case[23] confirms previous case law, adding that Member States may not rely on the need for effective fiscal supervision to categorically refuse equal treatment in third State relations if a legal framework for the exchange of information is present which enables the EU Member State involved to obtain the information necessary to check whether the conditions for the benefit claimed by the taxpayer are met. Such framework could be a bilateral tax treaty or a TIEA[24] concluded with the third State concerned, but possibly also an association agreement between the EU and the third State involved if

19 Joined Cases C-436/08 and C-437/08, *Haribo and Österreichische Salinen*, EU:C:2011:61, point 122.
20 Case C-72/09, *Établissements Rimbaud*, EU:C:2010:645.
21 See also Case C-521/07, *Commission v the Netherlands*, EU:C:2009:360, and, again, Case C-540/07, *Commission v Italy*, EU:C:2009:717.
22 Case C-190/12, *Emerging Markets Series*, EU:C:2014:249.
23 Case C-464/14, *SECIL v Fazenda Pública*, EU:C:2016:896.
24 Tax Information Exchange Agreement.

that agreement provides for exchange of tax information. Similarly to *Emerging Markets*, in SECIL the CJEU asked the referring court to

> "examine whether the obligations arising under the Portugal-Tunisia Convention are such as to enable the Portuguese tax authorities to obtain from the Republic of Tunisia the information which would allow them to verify satisfaction of the condition that the distributing company be subject to tax. If so, the restriction resulting from the refusal to grant full or partial deductions, provided for in Article 46(1) and (8), respectively, of the CIRC, cannot be justified by the need to ensure the effectiveness of fiscal supervision".[25]

In any event, as indicated above, there must be a real need for the information which is said to be unattainable: in *STEKO*,[26] the Court held the argument that effective fiscal supervision instruments were not available to be irrelevant because the value drop of the holdings in non-resident companies was caused by a bear stock market, which was publicly available information.

The "different legal context" criterion may be an important factor in relation to the UK post-Brexit. At the time of the departure of the UK from the EU (31st January 2020 for the formal departure, but 1st January 2021 in practical terms following the transitional implementation period – see 5.6 below) the legal context of the UK and rest of the Member States was identical. Relatively little changed in the realm of direct taxation immediately after that date. In respect of exchange of information and cooperation to combat tax avoidance and evasion, the UK undertook in the Trade and Cooperation Agreement[27] to maintain the existing international standards at the time of Brexit. Thus, Article 186 (International Standards) of the Trade and Cooperation Agreement provides as follows:

> The Parties shall make their best endeavours to ensure that internationally agreed standards in the ... fight against tax evasion and avoidance, are implemented and applied in their territory. Such internationally agreed standards are, inter alia, those adopted by: ... the Global Forum on Transparency and Exchange of Information for Tax Purposes of the Organisation for Economic Cooperation and Development.

At the time of Brexit, the Directive on Administrative Cooperation[28] ceased to apply as between the UK and other Member States. However, provisions for exchange of information and administrative cooperation contained in the bilateral tax treaties between the UK and other Member States or in the OECD/Council of Europe MCAA[29] provided for equivalent arrangements. Additionally, Art 100 of the Withdrawal Agreement[30] made provision for mutual administrative assistance in the collection of tax debts to continue to apply for

25 Case C-464/14, *SECIL v Fazenda Pública*, EU:C:2016:896, point 68.

26 Case C-377/07, *STEKO Industriemontage*, EU:C:2009:29, point 55.

27 *Trade and Cooperation Agreement between the European Union and the European Atomic Energy Community, of the one part, and the United Kingdom of Great Britain and Northern Ireland, of the other part (OJ L 149, 30.4.2021, p. 10–2539).*

28 *Council Directive 2011/16/EU of 15 February 2011 on administrative cooperation in the field of taxation and repealing Directive 77/799/EEC* (OJ L 64, 11.3.2011, p. 1–12).

29 *The Multilateral Convention on Mutual Administrative Assistance in Tax Matters.*

30 *Agreement on the withdrawal of the United Kingdom of Great Britain and Northern Ireland from the European Union and the European Atomic Energy Community* (OJ C 384I, 12.11.2019, p. 1–177).

five years after Brexit; after that date, bilateral or multilateral arrangements are expected to be put in place. Thus, in terms of exchange of information, mutual assistance in the collection of taxes and other forms of cooperation to combat tax avoidance and evasion, the legal context of the UK remains essentially the same after Brexit as before. This may, of course, change over time.

5.2.3 *The Grandfather Clause (Article 64(1) TFEU)*

Although the *erga omnes* applicability of free capital movement was a thought-out decision, it appeared undesirable to treat third State capital movement identical to intra-EU capital movement in every respect. Therefore, the 'standstill' clause of Art. 64 TFEU protects ('grandfathers') national restrictions in respect of the movement of capital to or from third countries involving (i) direct investment, including real estate[31], (ii) establishment, (iii) provision of financial services and (iv) admission of securities to capital markets, provided these restrictions of free movement already 'existed' on 31 December 1993.

The Brexit effectively renders the United Kingdom a third country in the meaning of Article 64(1) TFEU as per 31 January 2021 whereas before that date the United Kingdom qualified as a Member State back to 1973. To apply the benchmark date of 31 December 1993 for restrictions vis-à-vis the United Kingdom therefore seems a bit odd in that case. Yet, in the context of the accession to the EU of the 10 new Member States in 2004, this benchmark date was specifically modified for a couple of accessing countries.[32] This implies that Member States believe that a specific provision would be required if they want to deviate from the 31 December 1993 benchmark. This view is supported in *e.g.* the Court cases Optimus[33] and Holböck.[34] Advocate General Kokott in her Opinion in the Bouanich case, by contrast, suggests that for accession countries (in the case at hand: Sweden) the date could be set at the date of accession.[35] Based on the rationale of the standstill clause, it would make sense to adopt this approach (from the perspective of the Member States) vis-à-vis the United Kingdom as well. One should not dig up old bones. In addition, accession is not the same as departure. Since the free movement of capital was already fully liberalized between Member States (including vis-à-vis the United Kingdom) before 31 December 1993, there should actually not have any existing restrictions vis-à-vis the United Kingdom been left, as such restrictions would be contrary to the free movement of capital as applicable between Member States and, hence, forbidden. By analogy to the cases *Ospelt*[36] and *SECIL*[37], we submit that Member States could therefore not justify restrictions imposed vis-à-vis the United Kingdom after Brexit on the basis of the standstill clause under Article 64(1) TFEU.

---

31 Real estate that does not form part of a direct investment is excluded from the grandfathering effect of Article 64 TFEU; see Case C-181/12, *Welte*, ECLI:EU:C:2013:662.

32 In respect of restrictions existing under national law in Bulgaria, Estonia and Hungary, the relevant date is 31 December 1999.

33 Case C-366/05, Optimus - Telecomunicações SA v Fazenda Pública, ECLI:EU:C:2007:366.

34 Case C-157/05, *Winfried Holböck*, EU:C:2007:297 vis-à-vis Austria (date of accession: 1995).

35 Opinion of Advocate General Kokott in Case C-265/04, Margaretha Bouanich v Skatteverket, ECLI:EU:C:2005:479, footnote 29.

36 Case C-452/01, Margarethe Ospelt and Schlössle Weissenberg Familienstiftung, ECLI:EU:C:2003:493.

37 Case C-464/14, *SECIL v Fazenda Pública*, EU:C:2016:896.

The question arises what 'existing' means. The Court has explained that even if a restrictive measure has been amended subsequent to 31 December 1993, it will still be considered as 'existing' on 31 December 1993 (and can thus be saved) if its basic idea ('underlying logic') and procedures remained unchanged or if the change only *reduced* restrictions to free movement. It held in *Test Claimants in the FII GLO I*:[38]

> '192. As the Court stated in *Konle*,[39] any national measure adopted after a date laid down in that way is not, by that fact alone, automatically excluded from the derogation laid down in the Community measure in question. If the provision is, in substance, identical to the previous legislation or is limited to reducing or eliminating an obstacle to the exercise of Community rights and freedoms in the earlier legislation, it will be covered by the derogation. By contrast, legislation based on an approach which is different from that of the previous law and establishes new procedures cannot be regarded as legislation existing at the date set down by the Community measure in question (see Konle, paragraphs 52 and 53).'

Art. 64 has grandfathered, a.o., an Austrian measure denying the Austrian half rate applicable to domestic and EU dividends to residents receiving third State (Swiss) dividends.[40] By contrast, it did not save a German switch from its (existing) imputation system to a new exemption system for foreign participation dividends.[41] It might have saved a restrictive Portuguese measure which was already in force in 1993 (a denial of exemption of dividends received from subsidiaries in Tunisia and Lebanon), were it not for the fact that although Portugal itself had not changed its restrictive legislation, the EU-Tunisia and EU-Lebanon association agreements had come into force *after* 1993, which altered the 'underlying logic' of the applicable legal framework, as these agreements liberalised 'direct investment' between the EU and Tunisia and between the EU and Lebanon. As the Court held, in *SECIL*,[42] even if a Member State does not formally repeal its restrictive measure, it nevertheless waives its power under Art. 64(1) TFEU by concluding an international agreement such as an association agreement, which liberalizes, with direct effect, a category of capital mentioned in Art. 64(1) (in that case: 'direct investment'). Such a change in the legal frame-work amounts to the introduction of new legislation since it is based on a logic different from that of the existing legislation. Also, such liberalisation of capital movement would be meaningless if a Member State could continue to apply restrictive legislation which the association agreement precisely prohibits. Thus, the standstill clause of Art. 64 TFEU may be overruled by free movement of capital provisions in an association agreement. If Member States would not have envisaged this result, they should have included a specific standstill clause in the Agreement as well. Eventually, Portugal seemed to be saved, not by the grandfather clause, but (partly) by the fact that no effective legal framework for exchange of tax information with Tunisia and Lebanon was provided for, making it impossible for Portugal to check whether the Tunisian subsidiary was effectively subject to corporation tax in Tunisia (a condition for the exemption). The national Court still needed to check, however, whether Portugal could obtain the necessary

38 Case C-446/04, *Test Claimants in the FII Group Litigation I*, EU:C:2006:774.
39 Case C-302/97, *Konle*, EU:C:1999:271.
40 Case C-157/05, *Winfried Holböck*, EU:C:2007:297.
41 Case C-685/16, EV v Finanzamt Lippstadt, ECLI:EU:C:2018:743, point 82.
42 Case C-464/14, *SECIL v Fazenda Pública*, EU:C:2016:896.

information from Tunisia on the basis of the Portugal-Tunisia tax treaty (with Lebanon, no tax treaty had been concluded). If that was the case, then Portugal could not rely on the need for effective fiscal supervision to refuse the exemption.

Since the standstill-clause was originally not designed with the aim to protect existing restrictive tax measures (it primarily aimed at respecting existing (non-tax) reservations in the context of the OECD Code of Liberalisation of Capital Movements), its application in the field of direct taxation raises numerous and often rather complex questions, sometimes leading to rather complex answers. For example, in Case C-135/17, *X GmbH v Finanzamt Stuttgart*, one of the questions referred was whether a measure is still substantially the same as on 31 December 1993 if, even though it has substantially been changed after 31 December 1993 and the new regime has formally been in force for a short time, the new regime has never in practice been applied because the law shortly after changed again into a regime which *is* substantially similar to the pre-1994 regime. Earlier, we thought we knew the (easy) answer, given point 87 of *SECIL*:

> "Article 64(1) TFEU does not cover provisions which, whilst in substance identical to legislation which existed on 31 December 1993, have reintroduced an obstacle to the free movement of capital which, following the repeal of the earlier legislation, no longer existed (...)."

Eventually, the Court ruled differently. If we understand the Court correctly, one has to look at the legislative technique used. Once the temporary tax measure has actually entered into force, there is no longer an existing measure. Neither the subsequent revocation nor the fact that the measure has not actually been applied changes that conclusion. If, by contrast, the entry into force of the temporary scheme has been postponed and the tax measure subsequently repealed, the new scheme has never actually existed and the standstill clause continues to apply in full.[43]

It should be noted that by grandfathering capital movement which 'involves' establishment or (financial) services, Art. 64 TFEU acknowledges that Art. 63 also covers movements which would also be covered, in intra-EU cases, by other fundamental freedoms, especially the freedom of establishment and the free provision of services, otherwise it would be superfluous to grandfather them. Art. 64 thus explicitly recognizes overlap between Capital on the one hand and Establishment and Services on the other. This is important for the determination of the scope of free capital movement in third State relations (see Section 5.2.4).

As Art. 64 TFEU is a derogation from the main rule of free movement of capital and payments (Art. 63), it must be interpreted strictly, as all derogations from the goals of the EU, so that the practical effect of the main rule of Art. 63 is preserved.[44] This narrows the scope of the grandfather clause, but on the other hand, for Art. 64(1) to apply, it is not necessary that the restrictive national measure has the *aim* to restrict capital movement in respect of the four categories it enumerates. To be grandfathered, it is sufficient that the national measure has a restrictive *effect* on capital movement in one of the four categories mentioned. This was confirmed in *X v Staatssecretaris*,[45] concerning a Netherlands

43 Case C-135/17, X-GmbH v Finanzamt Stuttgart, ECLI:EU:C:2019:136, points 48 *et seq.*

44 Case C-560/13, *Wagner-Raith*, EU:C:2015:347, point 43.

45 Case C-317/15, *X v Staatssecretaris*, EU:C:2017:119.

measure permitting an extended assessment period (12 years) in case of hidden foreign (in the case at hand: Swiss) bank account(s) as compared to the assessment period in domestic cases (5 years). Obviously, that measure did not seek to regulate any of the four categories of capital movement mentioned in Art. 64(1); it applied (also) to situations wholly alien to direct investment, establishment, the provision of financial services or the admission of securities to capital markets. However, that did not preclude applicability of the grandfather clause.

The Court held that the scope of Art. 64(1) TFEU does not depend on the specific purpose of a national restriction, but on its effect on the movements of capital referred to in that provision; if Art. 64(1) TFEU would apply only where the national legislation at issue relates solely to the movements of capital referred to in that article, that would undermine the practical effectiveness of that provision.

> "21 (...), the applicability of Article 64(1) TFEU depends, not on the purpose of the national legislation containing such restrictions, but on its effect. That provision applies to the extent to which that national legislation imposes a restriction on movements of capital involving direct investment, establishment, the provision of financial services or the admission of securities to capital markets. Accordingly, the fact that that legislation may also apply to other situations is not such as to preclude Article 64(1) TFEU from being applicable in the circumstances which it covers.
> 22. (...), that interpretation is confirmed by the Court's case-law. (...). It is clear from those judgments [*authors*: *SECIL*, C-464/14, EU:C:2016:896, paragraph 78, and *Orange European Smallcap Fund*, C-194/06, EU:C:2008:289, paragraph 102], (...), that the scope of Article 64(1) TFEU does not depend on the specific purpose of a national restriction, but on its effect on the movements of capital referred to in that provision.
> 24. (...) an interpretation according to which Article 64(1) TFEU applies only where the national legislation at issue relates solely to the movements of capital referred to in that Article would undermine the practical effectiveness of that provision. As the Netherlands Government has noted (...), such an interpretation would have had the consequence of compelling all the Member States, in order to be able to apply the restrictions set out in Article 64(1) TFEU, to revise their national legislation and adapt it very precisely to the scope of that provision before the deadline of 1 January 1994."

Nevertheless, for the grandfather clause to apply, there should be a sufficient causal link between the capital movement concerned (in *X v Staatssecretaris*: the opening of a bank account in the third country) and the provision of financial services, but the Court was satisfied that the capital movements resulting from the opening of a securities account with a bank involve 'the provision of financial services' and that there is a causal link between those capital movements and the provision of financial services, given that the holder places his capital in a securities account in return for management services from the bank:

> "28. (...), in order to be capable of being covered by the derogation provided for in Article 64(1) TFEU, the national measure must relate to capital movements that have a sufficiently close link with the provision of financial services, which requires that there be a causal link between the movement of capital and the provision of financial services (...).
> 29. (...) the capital movements resulting from the opening of a securities account with a banking institution involve the provision of financial services. (...).

> 30. (…), there is a causal link between the capital movements concerned and the provision of financial services given that the holder places his capital in a securities account by reason of the fact that, in return, he benefits from the management services which he receives from the banking institution. Accordingly, in a situation such as that at issue in the main proceedings, there is a sufficiently close link between the capital movements and the provision of financial services."

Subsequently, in *College Pension Plan of British Columbia* the question was before the Court whether a discriminatory (German) withholding tax levied from a non-EU pension fund sufficiently links-up with the provision of financial services (by the pension fund) and thus may be grandfathered under Art. 64 TFEU.[46] An affirmative answer would imply that also third State portfolio (i.e. passive) investors would be caught by the standstill clause of Art. 64 TFEU and hence be denied the protection of Art. 63 TFEU. However, the Court answered this question – in the absence of a sufficient link – in the negative:

> "108. As the Advocate General observed in point 100 of his Opinion, the acquisition of shareholdings by a pension fund and the dividends which it receives as a result serve the purpose, first and foremost, of preserving its assets and of guaranteeing the provisions constituted by the fund, through increased diversification and better spreading of risk, in order to ensure that it can meet its pension commitments to its insured persons. Those acquisitions of shareholdings and those dividends thus constitute, in the first place, a means by which a pension fund can honour its pension commitments and not a service that it provides to those insured persons."

Although we agree with the outcome in this case, we find it a bit difficult to understand why honouring pension commitments would not be considered a service towards the insured persons; isn't this precisely what customers expect a pension fund to do? Yet, in our view, the discriminatory withholding tax indeed affects the provision of services by the Canadian pension fund indirectly and in any case does not sufficiently relate to the provision of financial services by the pension fund to its customers. This is simply because such a tax does leave the provision of services by the pension fund towards its customers completely free, or at most affects those services only indirectly. An important difference with the case of *X v Staatssecretaris* is that that case involved only two parties (the Dutch taxpayer and the Swiss bank) between which the capital transaction and the concomitant financial service took place. In the case of *College Pension Plan of British Columbia* this is different; there were three parties involved. The capital transaction took place between the Canadian pension fund and the German dividend-paying company whereas the financial services took place between the Canadian pension fund and its (presumably mainly Canadian) beneficiaries. The levy of German withholding tax at the expense of the Canadian pension fund has in our view nothing to do with these third party beneficiaries.[47] The intra-EU case of *Fidelity Funds* seems to confirm our view.[48] In any case, it is observed that the Court's case law seems difficult to grasp in this respect.

46 Case C-641/17, *College Pension Plan of British Columbia*, ECLI:EU:C:2019:960.

47 Assume the beneficiaries would be resident of an EU Member State, we do not believe that they could successfully invoke the free movement of services in order to reduce the withholding tax levied at the expense of the pension fund.

48 Case C-480/16, Fidelity Funds and Others v Skatteministeriet, ECLI:EU:C:2018:480, point 37.

In its recent decision in the case *European Commission v Kingdom of Spain*[49], an intra-EU case which for the rest is comparable to the case of *X v Staatssecretaris*, the Court all of the sudden held the free movement of services inapplicable since this freedom would appear to be secondary in relation to the free movement of capital. This would imply that also the provision of financial services in the meaning of Article 64(1) TFEU would not be affected. The question is how this decision relates the Court's earlier case law, as cited above. To sum up, in each individual case, an analysis of the possible applicability of the grandfather clause is essential to determine the scope of protection of third State investors under the free movement of capital. In any case, as time goes by, the impact of the standstill clause is expected to gradually decrease. After all, tax measures as they stand today (2025) will typically tend to no longer correspond with the legal *status quo* more than 30 years ago (1993).

5.2.4 *Mutual Exclusion or Overlap? How to Distinguish Capital Movement From Establishment and Service Provision*

As the other Treaty Freedoms do not extend to third-State situations, it is essential to distinguish between capital operations on the one hand (liberalized) and all other operations, especially establishment of undertakings and service provision (not liberalized as regards third States, but to be negotiated within the World Trade Organization (WTO) rounds). That is not always easy,[50] as the TFEU does not contain any hierarchy of free movement rights, nor conflict rules the Court cares for. As for the most important distinction, between Capital and Establishment, the Court used to apply a 'definite influence' test (see Chapter 3.2.5(iii), especially the *Baars* case cited there), afterwards complemented by the purpose of the legislation (*Franked Investment Income GLO I*[51]) and recently by the market access test (*Franked Investment Income GLO II*[52]). It further observed, a.o. in *SEVIC*,[53] that establishment requires the pursuit of an activity on a stable and continuous basis, whereas capital movement does not require such indefinite presence.[54] As regards the distinction between Capital and Services, the Court has observed that capital movement may be an indirect consequence of services (see, *e.g. Bachmann*[55] and *Fidium Finanz*[56]) and further rather vaguely considered, in *Wagner-Raith*,[57] that:

> "it is appropriate, first of all, to recall the demarcation between the Treaty provisions relating to the freedom to provide services and those governing the free movement of capital. The Court has already held that it is apparent from the wording of Article 56 TFEU

49 Case C-788/19, European Commission v Kingdom of Spain, ECLI:EU:C:2022:55.

50 See: Ana Paula Dourado, 'The EU Free Movement of Capital and Third Countries: Recent Developments", 45 *Intertax* 3 (2017), pp. 40-60.

51 Case C-446/04, *Test Claimants in the FII Group Litigation I*, EU:C:2006:774.

52 Case C-35/11, *Test Claimants in the FII GLO 2*, EU:C:2012:707.

53 Case C-411/03, *SEVIC Systems*, EU:C:2005:762, point 18.

54 See Case C-112/14, *Commission v. UK*, EU:C:2014:2369, point 20. *See also SEVIC systems*, point 18. For elaboration, *see* W. Schön, *Europaïsche Kapitallverkehrsfreiheit und nationales Steuerrecht*, in *Gedächtnisschrift für Brigitte Knobbe-Keuk*, at 747 (W. Schön ed., Verlag Dr. Otto Schmidt 1997.

55 Case C-204/90, *Bachmann*, EU:C:1992:35.

56 Case C-452/04, *Fidium Finanz*, EU:C:2006:631.

57 Case C-560/13, *Wagner-Raith*, EU:C:2015:347, point 29-30.

> and Article 63 TFEU, and the position which they occupy in two different chapters of Title IV of the Treaty, that, although closely linked, those provisions were designed to regulate different situations and they each have their own field of application (see, (...) Fidium Finanz, C-452/04, EU:C:2006:631, paragraph 28)."

The CJ's case law on the concurrence of Services, Establishment and Capital has long been somewhat enigmatic.[58] That mysteriousness is probably caused by the fact that the Court was worried that Services and Establishment, which have not been liberalized in third State context, would nevertheless apply through the back door by riding piggy-back on the free movement of capital.

Both the establishment of an undertaking and the provision of financial services (e.g. money lending) usually also entail capital movement, as obviously, money is needed to set up an establishment of an undertaking or to extend loans, but that capital movement is only incidental to the greater intention (the 'predominant consideration') of *establishment* or financial *service* provision. If that kind of ancillary capital movement were to be brought under the free movement protection, it would mean that indirectly, the freedoms of establishment and of services would in fact be unilaterally extended to third State relations. That was manifestly not the intention of the Treaty drafters, and it would produce undesirable and implausible results, such as, in particular, a serious weakening of the EU's negotiation position within the WTO rounds. Access of undertakings and service providers into the internal market would come free for third State parties, i.e. without reciprocal access to *their* markets for secondary establishment and service provision by EU undertakings. As the Court considered in the 2012 *FII GLO 2*:[59]

> "100. Since the Treaty does not extend freedom of establishment to third countries, it is important to ensure that the interpretation of Article 63(1) TFEU as regards relations with third countries does not enable economic operators who do not fall within the limits of the territorial scope of freedom of establishment to profit from that freedom. (...)."

Until this *FII GLO 2* case, the Court usually distinguished Capital from Establishment by using tie-breaker rules: *only* Establishment or *only* Capital would be considered; these would not overlap. The Court used the following tie-breakers to exclude one of the two possibly applicable freedoms: (i) the principal purpose of the national measure at issue (is it aimed at controlling interests or at portfolio investments? Is it aimed at service providers or at capital movement?), and (ii) the facts of the case (does the case *in fact* concern a controlling interest or a mere portfolio investment?).

The Court often precluded application of the free movement of capital in third State relations by holding that the main purpose of the national measure at issue was not related to (passive) capital investment, but to either Establishment or Service provision, which are both not liberalized in relation to third States.[60] In *FII GLO 2*, however, the

58 See Case C-452/04, *Fidium Finanz*, EU:C:2006:631, Case C-492/04, *Lasertec*, EU:C:2007:273, Case C-157/05, *Holböck*, EU:C:2007:297, Case C-196/04, *Cadbury Schweppes*, EU:C:2006:544, Case C-524/04, *Test Claimants in the Thin Cap GLO*, EU:C:2007:161, Case C-101/05, *Skatteverket v. A*, EU:C:2007:804, Case C-298/05, *Columbus Container Services*, EU:C:2007:754.

59 Case C-35/11, *Test Claimants in the FII GLO 2*, EU:C:2012:707.

60 *See also* Smit, *supra*, at 238-239.

Court's Grand Chamber changed direction and introduced a new criterion for determining whether free movement of capital applies in a third State situation, not visibly caring much anymore for an exclusive choice (*either* Establishment *or* Capital). It introduced the *market access criterion*. It held that if in third State relations both Establishment and Capital may be at issue, then the freedom of capital movement can in principle be relied on by the economic operator involved, *unless* the restrictive national rule at issue affects the conditions of access to the EU internal market for third State economic operators. Since direct tax measures will typically not restrict *market access* (taxation will come into play only *after* access to the market was granted), one may wonder whether the market access criterion serves a meaningful purpose in the field of direct taxation.

The'old' approach is represented by cases such as *Fidium Finanz*,[61] *Thin Cap*,[62] *Lasertec*,[63] *Skatteverket v. A and B*,[64] and *Holböck*:[65] in order to ascertain whether national legislation, in third State situations, must be judged under one or the other Treaty freedom, the purpose of the legislation at issue is decisive. National provisions aimed at holdings in companies giving the holder effective control of the company (allowing him to determine its activities), come under the freedom of establishment. By contrast, national measures targeting portfolio investors (not seeking definite influence) come under the freedom of capital. Where an establishment or a service provision also brings along capital movement, the Court in principle examined the national measure only under one single freedom if it appeared that, *e.g.*, the capital aspect of the operation was entirely subordinate to the establishment or service provision character of the operation.

Thus, in *Thin Cap* and *Lasertec* – both concerning refusal of deduction of interest payments to third States under national thin capitalization rules – the Court considered Establishment to be preponderant, which pushed out possible application of the rules on capital movement, because thin cap rules by their nature address *groups* of companies, *i.e.* controlling interests. In both cases, capital movement was considered entirely subordinate to Establishment: a possible restrictive effect of this type of legislation on the free movement of capital 'must be seen as an unavoidable consequence of the restriction on freedom of establishment.' The result was that for the taxpayers concerned there was no free movement right to rely on in third State relations: free establishment does not exist in third State relations, and the capital movement involved was too subordinate to Establishment to make the rules on free capital movement applicable. Likewise, in *Skatteverket v. A and B*, the Court considered a restrictive Swedish shareholder taxation measure in relation to a company with two Russian branches as mainly concerning Establishment and therefore not to be covered by the free movement of capital.

Where, however, the national measure is generic, potentially affecting both capital *and* establishment or both capital *and* services (not specifically aimed at effective control situations, nor at portfolio investment, nor at service provision), then the facts of the case are decisive: does the case at issue concern in fact a 'definite influence' situation, then only Establishment is at issue, even though also ancillary capital movement may be involved. Does the case in fact concern the provision of (financial) services, then the

61 Case C-452/04, *Fidium Finanz*, EU:C:2006:631.
62 Case C-524/04, *Test Claimants in the Thin Cap GLO*, EU:C:2007:161.
63 Case C-492/04, *Lasertec*, EU:C:2007:273.
64 Case C-102/05 (order), *Skatteverket v. A and B*, EU:C:2007:275.
65 Case C-157/05, *Holböck*, EU:C:2007:297.

measure will only be tested under the freedom to provide services, much as though also ancillary capital movement may be involved. Does the case at issue in fact concern portfolio investment, having neither 'definite influence' nor (mainly) service provision as its principal aspect, then the free movement of capital applies.

The Court caused some confusion in *Holböck*, concerning an Austrian low income tax rate for dividends which was not available for third State (Swiss) sourced dividends. The measure applied to all sizes of shareholdings, therefore. The Court seemed to examine it under the free movement of capital even though Mr Holböck in fact owned two thirds of the shares in the Swiss company and therefore a controlling interest (which is Establishment), but we understand that case as merely saying that *even if* the freedom of capital would have applied (*quod non*, as Mr Holböck had definite influence), that would not have helped him, because the Austrian measure was grandfathered by Art. 64(1) TFEU as it already existed on 31 December 1993.

Until the 2010 *FII GLO 2* case, the Court's system of choosing between Establishment and Capital in third State situations thus appeared to be the following. It distinguished three types of national measures:

i. legislation whose principal purpose relates to majority interests in companies, or at least to situations of definite influence in the management of the company, especially measures concerning groups of companies (fiscal examples: thin cap legislation, CFC legislation, transfer pricing legislation, earnings stripping legislation, group loss relief rules, group taxation and consolidation rules, etc.);
ii. legislation whose principal purpose relates to portfolio (passive) investment, even though situations of definite influence may sometimes also be affected but that is only coincidental (fiscal example: anti dividend stripping legislation[66]); and
iii. generic legislation, whose principal purpose relates to all shareholders or participants, however small or big, in companies or firms, thus affecting any interest, whether portfolio or controlling (fiscal example: dividend withholding tax).

National measures type (i) were scrutinized in principle only under the right of establishment.[67] That means that in third State relations, the TFEU Freedoms do not apply. Thus, Member States' legislation on thin capitalization, CFCs, transfer pricing, earnings stripping, group loss relief, tax consolidation, etc. are generally safe from being struck down under the Treaty freedoms in third State cases: Establishment and Services do not extend to third State situations, and Capital is in general effectively switched off. This must have relieved the member States.

National measures type (ii) were judged in principle only in the light of the freedom of capital.[68] This means that in third State situations, the economic operator involved can rely on the free movement of capital and that if the national measure distinguishes between domestic situations and third State situations, it may be incompatible with that freedom in the same manner as it would be in intra-EU cross-border situations. As

66 Case C-182/08, *Glaxo Wellcome*, EU:C:2009:559.

67 See, a.o. Case C-464/14, *SECIL v Fazenda Pública*, EU:C:2016:896, point 32, and Case C-35/11, *FII GLO 2*, point 91, EU:C:2012:707.

68 *See*, a.o. Case C-464/14, *SECIL v Fazenda Pública*, EU:C:2016:896, point 33, Case C-35/11, *FII GLO 2*, point 92, Case C-190/12, *Emerging Markets*, EU:C:2014:249, point 29, and Case C-628/15, *The Trustees of BT Pension Scheme* EU:C:2017:687, points 30-31.

observed, however, in third State situations more possibilities exist for the Member States to justify a restrictive rule, especially under the grandfather clause of Art. 64(1) TFEU and under the 'different legal context'-escape (the need for effective fiscal supervision).

A remarkable consequence of this was that portfolio investment into or from third States (indeed: capital movement) was better protected than majority investment into or from third States (as that is Establishment, which is not protected in third State relations). This rather odd result[69] may have been one of the reasons why the Court has changed direction as regards type (iii) measures in the *FII GLO 2* case, making it possible that also majority interests in third State companies are protected by the free movement of capital, provided the restrictive national measure (e.g. taxation of third State group dividends or group royalties) is not a measure on market access. See below.

An example of a type (ii) national measure was the German anti-dividend stripping legislation at issue in the *Glaxo Wellcome* case[70] (concerning an *intra*-EU case of concurrence between Capital and Establishment). The German measure sought to prevent tax avoidance by foreign shareholders through short-lived transfer of their shares in German companies into German hands, shortly before a dividend payment, to indirectly enjoy the German imputation credit through a higher sale price, although that credit was only intended for shareholders subject to tax in Germany. The ECJ applied only the freedom of capital provisions, despite the fact that the case at issue concerned a group restructuring, and the shares transferred represented full control in a German subsidiary:

> '49. It is (...) common ground that the application of that legislation does not depend on the size of the holdings acquired from the non-resident shareholder and is not limited to situations in which the shareholder can exercise definite influence on the decisions of the company concerned and determine its activities. 50 In addition, since the purpose of the legislation at issue in the main proceedings is to prevent non-resident shareholders from obtaining an undue tax advantage directly through the sale of shares with the sole objective of obtaining that advantage, and not with the objective of exercising the freedom of establishment or as a result of exercising that freedom, it must be held that the free movement of capital aspect of that legislation prevails over that of the freedom of establishment. (...) 52. It follows that the legislation at issue in the main proceedings must be examined exclusively in the light of the free movement of capital.'

National measures type (iii) (generic measures), indiscriminately affect both Establishment and Capital situations. Which of the two freedoms then applies, was, until the 2012 *FII GLO 2* Case, determined by the facts of the case, to be established by the national court, as the ECJ does not establish facts in preliminary proceedings.[71] If the facts would show definite influence on the company policy (a controlling interest), then only Establishment would be at issue and the rules on capital movement would be switched off (meaning that in third State situations, no freedom at all applies). If the facts of the case would show mere portfolio investment, then only the freedom of capital movement would

69 Which may have been intended by the Member States: big third State parties minded to take over EU industry would not be protected, whereas the more welcome small third State portfolio investors would be protected.

70 Case C-182/08, *Glaxo Wellcome*, EU:C:2009:559.

71 Except maybe in the unclear Case C-157/05, *Holböck*, EU:C:2007:297.

apply. For intra-EU situations this analysis was confirmed by *Burda*[72] (concerning a 50% holding) and *Aberdeen Property*[73] (concerning a 100% holding). For third State situations it was confirmed in the joined cases *KBC Bank and BRB NV*[74] and, later one, in *Itelcar*[75] and *Kronos.*[76] As *KBC Bank and BRB NV* concerned third State dividends, there can be no doubt that the Court's findings apply to third State situations (see point 71 quoted below). The Court decided *KBC Bank and BRB NV* by Order, implying that it saw nothing out of the ordinary, but rather an *acte clair*, probably because it felt it had already explained its system of choosing between Establishment and Capital – as explained above – in *Burda* and *Aberdeen*, albeit for intra-EU situations. *KBC Bank and BRB NV* concerned the Belgian participation exemption for subsidiary dividends, which applied to both small holdings and controlling interests. The issue was whether a dividend from a non-Member State (Switzerland) should also be exempt. The Court held:

> '68. (...) in order to determine whether national legislation falls within the scope of one or other of the freedoms of movement, it is clear from what is now well established case-law that the purpose of the legislation concerned must be taken into consideration (...).
> 69. (...) national legislation, the application of which does not depend on the extent of the holding which the company receiving the dividend has in the company paying it, may fall within the purview both of Article 43 EC on freedom of establishment and of Article 56 EC on the free movement of capital (....).
> 70. However, to the extent to which the holdings in question confer on their owner a definite influence over the decisions of the companies concerned and allow it to determine their activities, it is the provisions of the Treaty relating to freedom of establishment which apply (....).
> 71. Consequently, it is for the referring court to determine, in the light of the purpose of the national legislation and the facts of the case before it, whether Article (now 63 TFEU; *authors*) may be invoked. If so, it is for that court to determine whether that Article precludes the different treatment of dividends from subsidiaries established in a non-member State compared to dividends from subsidiaries with their seat in Belgium.'

Thus, the facts of the case (definite influence or portfolio investment?) determined whether Capital was preponderant and pushed away Establishment, or *vice versa*, and it was for the referring national court to make that assessment of facts.

As observed, in *FII GLO 2*,[77] however, the Court's Grand Chamber changed direction. It introduced a *market access criterion* for determining whether free movement of capital applies in a third State situation in which a type (iii) national measure is at issue, not visibly caring much anymore for an exclusive choice (*either* Establishment *or* Capital). It considered that if in third State relations both Establishment and Capital may be at issue (type (iii) measures), then the freedom of capital movement can in principle be relied on by the economic operator involved, *unless* the restrictive national rule at issue affects the conditions of access to the EU internal market for third State economic operators or

72 Case C-284/06, *Burda*, EU:C:2008:36.
73 Case C-303/07, *Aberdeen property Fininvest Alpha Oy*, EU:C:2009:377.
74 Joined cases C-439/07 and C-499/07, *België v KBC Bank NV* and *BRB NV v België*, EU:C:2009:339.
75 Case C282/12, Itelcar – Automóveis de Aluguer Lda v Fazenda Pública, ECLI:EU:C:2013:629.
76 Case C47/12, Kronos International Inc. v Finanzamt Leverkusen, ECLI:EU:C:2014:2200.
77 Case C-35/11, *Test Claimants in the FII GLO 2*, EU:C:2012:707.

vice versa. Since direct tax measures typically apply *after* accessing a market, one may wonder whether the market access criterion makes a difference in the field of direct taxation. This does not imply that the Court ignores Member States' concerns as regards unilateral capital liberalization vis-à-vis third States. These concerns, however, will have to be addressed on a case-by-case basis by reliance on the standstill clause (Art. 64 TFEU) or on the lack-of-administrative-cooperation justification, rather than through the 'old' either/or-approach applied in the Court's pre-*FII GLO 2* case law.

The Court's 2012 turn in *FII GLO 2* changed the assessment of national measures type (iii) (generic measures). The Court realized that the grandfather clause of Art. 64(1) TFEU refers to 'establishment', which logically implies that capital movement to and from third States may *coincide* with Establishment.[78] It also implies that the grandfather clause – which saves existing national measures restricting 'movement of capital to or from third countries involving *direct investment* (...), *establishment* (...) (and) the provision of financial *services* (...)" – would be meaningless if free movement of capital would already be switched off by the mere *fact* that the holding in a third State company in effect represents 'definite influence' in that company and with that, represents 'establishment'. It would be impossible to conceive a situation in which capital movement would 'involve establishment'. By grandfathering capital movement which involves Establishment or Services, Art. 64 TFEU acknowledges that Art. 63 also covers movements related to other fundamental freedoms, such as establishment and services, otherwise it would be superfluous to grandfather them.

Therefore, and possibly also because of (i) the odd result of the previous case law (portfolio investment was better protected than majority investment), and (ii) the consideration that making the application of the Treaty Freedoms dependent on assessments of fact by national Courts may not be very helpful to uniform application of the Treaty Freedoms, the Court held, in *FII GLO 2*, that the fact that the economic operator holds a controlling interest (and with that, an 'establishment'), does not in itself switch off the freedom of capital movement. Also an EU majority shareholder in a third State company may rely on the free movement of capital, provided (a) the restrictive national measure he opposes to is not exclusively aimed at situations of 'decisive influence' (*i.e.* is not a type (i) measure), and provided (b) the national measure does not relate to the conditions for access to the third State market or to the market in the Member State involved (market access). The Court considered, derogating from its judgment in *KBC Bank and BRB NV*, that if the national rules discriminately taxing third State dividends does not apply exclusively to 'decisive influence'-situations, the EU shareholder may rely on Art. 63 to call into question the legality of such rules, *irrespective* of the size of its shareholding in the third State company paying the dividends. However, if the impugned national rules regulate market access, then the shareholder cannot rely on the free movement of capital to invalidate them:

> "100. Since the Treaty does not extend freedom of establishment to third countries, it is important to ensure that the interpretation of Article 63(1) TFEU as regards relations with third countries does not enable economic operators who do not fall within the limits of the territorial scope of freedom of establishment to profit from that freedom. Such a risk does

78 The Court may already have realized that in Case C-157/05, *Holböck*, EU:C:2007:297.

> not exist in (...) the main proceedings. The legislation of the Member State in question does not relate to the conditions for access of a company from that Member State to the market in a third country or of a company from a third country to the market in that Member State. It concerns only the tax treatment of dividends which derive from investments which their recipient has made in a company established in a third country."

The Court explicitly repealed its previous findings that in case of generic restrictive measures (addressing all participations in undertakings irrespective of size or influence) the facts of the case would be decisive for the applicability of Art. 63 TFEU. Upon a closer look, it made only the purpose of the national measure decisive:

> "101. (...) the line of argument (...) that the freedom applicable to the tax treatment of dividends originating in third countries depends not only on the purpose of the national legislation at issue (...) but also on the particular circumstances of the case in those proceedings would produce effects incompatible with Article 64(1) TFEU.
> 102. It is apparent from that provision that Article 63 TFEU on the free movement of capital covers, in principle, capital movements involving establishment or direct investment. The latter terms relate to a form of participation in an undertaking through the holding of shares which confers the possibility of effectively participating in its management and control (...)."
> 103. (...).
> 104. (...), European Union law must be interpreted as meaning that a company that is resident in a Member State and has a shareholding in a company resident in a third country giving it definite influence over the decisions of the latter company and enabling it to determine its activities may rely upon Article 63 TFEU in order to call into question the consistency with that provision of legislation of that Member State which relates to the tax treatment of dividends originating in the third country and does not apply exclusively to situations in which the parent company exercises decisive influence over the company paying the dividends."

Thus, even if *in fact* the case concerns a controlling interest in a third State company (and with that, 'establishment'), that does not preclude the EU shareholder in that third State company to rely on the free movement of capital, except when (a) the restrictive national measure is a type (i) measure (*aimed* at controlling interests) or (b) it is a measure affecting the conditions for access of EU economic operators to third State markets or of third State economic operators to member State markets. In both cases, the purpose of the national measure is decisive, not the question whether the shareholder happens to hold a controlling interest or a very small interest. The latter type of measures (on market access) are to be negotiated in WTO rounds: the EU is not unilaterally going to give up its internal market access restrictions for establishment and service provision by third State economic operators if these third States are not going to open up *their* markets for establishment and service provision by EU economic operators. Rules on (the taxation of) dividends, however, do not regulate conditions for market access, whether or not the dividend recipient has a controlling interest.

As observed, it is difficult to think of direct tax measures which affect the conditions of establishment of undertakings or the market access of service providers. For all practical purposes, therefore, one may conclude that unless the national tax measure at issue is a type (i) rule (*aimed* at controlling interests), the free movement of capital applies in third State situations. In any event, dividend taxation seems to be covered by the free movement of capital in third State situations, unless the impugned national tax rule applies *exclusively* to group situations ('definite influence'). Only in that case, Establishment pushes aside Capital. It would seem that in general, tax measures which are not aimed at intra-group relations ('definite influence'), are not regulating market access either, so that virtually all generic tax measures seem to be covered by the free movement of capital in third State situations.

The Court's new approach was confirmed most recently in *Gallaher*[79] and earlier in *e.g. SECIL*,[80] in which a Portuguese company could rely on Art. 63 TFEU as regards dividends received from subsidiaries in Lebanon and Tunisia even though it held an influential (28,64%) and a controlling (98,72%) interest, respectively, in these subsidiaries, because the restrictive Portuguese measure (discriminatory refusal of exemption of the dividends) was not intended to apply exclusively to situations in which the recipient company has a decisive influence in the distributing company.

Therefore, and to sum up, the above classification of national measures into three categories had to be rewritten after *FII GLO 2*, as follows (the first two categories did not change):

i. legislation whose principal purpose relates to situations of definite influence on a company's decisions, determining its activities, especially measures concerning groups of companies concern Establishment and are therefore outside the scope of the free movement of capital in third State relations;
ii. legislation whose principal purpose relates to portfolio (passive) investment, even though situations of definite influence may sometimes also be affected, falls under the free movement of capital;
iii. generic legislation, whose principal purpose relates to all participants in an undertaking, whether or not capable of exerting definite influence, are also covered by the free movement of capital, unless that legislation regulates access to the internal market or to the market of third States, in which case no Treaty freedom can be relied on.

Given the somewhat stormy and unpredictable development in the Court's case law, one should perhaps be cautious in drawing too firm conclusions; the above categories are not set in stone. We do not exclude that the Court will further modify its case law.

A final question is whether a tax measure would still fall outside the scope of the free movement of capital if a Member State deliberately modified an existing generic tax measure (falling under category iii and hence under protection of Article 63 TFEU) by reducing its personal scope such that it would – going forward – only apply to situations of definite influence (falling under category i) with the only objective to "switch off" the protection under the free movement of capital, although it would make sense – seen from the rationale of the measure – to continue to apply that measure generically. Would such behavior be in breach with the loyalty principle as enshrined in Article 4(3) TEU? At least in extreme situations, we do not rule out that the Court will answer that question in the affirmative, which could imply an exception to category (i). Time will tell.

79 Case C-707/20, Gallaher, ECLI:EU:C:2023:101.
80 Case C-464/14, *SECIL v Fazenda Pública*, EU:C:2016:896.

5.2.5 No Intra-EU Cherry-Picking From Tax Treaties With Third States, nor Vice Versa

In *Riskin and Timmermans*,[81] the Court reiterated, this time in a third State situation, its findings in an intra-EU situation in *D. v Inspecteur*[82] (see section 16.3.4): Member States are not required to extend the benefits they extend in a tax treaty with (Member or third) State A to State A residents also to residents of (Member or third) State B, as tax treaties are a package deal negotiation result dependent, a.o., on the unharmonised national laws of the two treaty partners involved and they apply, therefore, by their nature only to residents of the Contracting States. A resident of Belgium cannot, therefore, cherry-pick from tax treaties Belgium has concluded with third States in order to have a Polish source tax credited against his Belgian income tax which is not creditable under the Belgian-Polish tax treaty.

5.3 Member States' Overseas, Associated and Dependent Territories: Member State, Third State, 'Second' State?[83]

A still rather murky area of free (capital) movement rights is their application to Member States' overseas, associated and dependent territories, such as the Portuguese Azores and Madeira, the Finnish Åland Islands, the French overseas DOM, ROM and COM,[84] the Danish Faeroe Islands and Greenland, the Caribbean part of the Netherlands[85] and its *status aparte* islands of Aruba, Curaçao and St. Maarten, the Spanish Canary Islands and, until Brexit, Gibraltar, the Channel Islands, and British Overseas territories such as the Virgin, Cayman and Falkland Islands. The applicability of the Treaty Freedoms, or at least of the free capital movement, depends on whether and to what extent the TFEU applies to these territories (see Arts. 52 TEU, 355 TFEU, Annex II to the TFEU, Part Four (Arts. 198-204) of the TFEU, and the Council's Decision on the association of Overseas Countries and territories (OCT),[86] based on that Part Four of the TFEU).

Depending on a Member State's Constitution, its overseas territories may be an integral part of that Member State, or OCTs (Overseas Countries and Territories) in some form of constitutional or administrative dependency. In the former case, they can either be fully

81 Case C 176/15, *Riskin and Timmermans*, EU:C:2016:488.

82 Case C-376/03, *D. v Inspecteur*, EU:C:2005:424.

83 See, a.o. Dimitry Kochenov, 'Substantive and Procedural Issues in the Application of European Law in the Overseas Possessions of European Union Member States,' 17 *Michigan State Journal of International Law* 2 (2008-2009), p. 195-289; Daniël S. Smit, 'The Position of the EU Member States' Associated and Dependent Territories under the Freedom of Establishment, the Free Movement of Capital and Secondary EU Law in the Field of Company Taxation,' 39 *Intertax* 2 (2011), p. 40-60; and Daniël Smit, 'Freedom of Investment between EU and non-EU Member States and its Impact on Corporate Income Tax Systems within the European Union,' Dissertation, December 2011, University of Tilburg, the Netherlands.

84 *Départements d'Outre-mer*, *Régions d'Outre-mer* and *Collectivités d'Outre-mer.*

85 The islands of Bonaire, St. Eustatius and Saba.

86 (Nineth) Council Decision (EU) 2021/1764 of 5 October 2021 on the association of the Overseas Countries and Territories with the European Union including relations between the European Union on the one hand, and Greenland and the Kingdom of Denmark on the other (Decision on the Overseas Association, including Greenland), *OJ L* 355 2021, p. 6 *et seq.*, Effective as of 1 January 2021.

subject to EU Law or to a special regime on the basis of Art. 349(2) TFEU. In the latter case, they can be associated territories on the basis of Art. 198 and Annex II TFEU and subject to a special regime provided for by the OCT Association Decision[87] of the Council.[88] There are also European territories for whose external relations a Member State is responsible within the meaning of Art. 355(3) TFEU, e.g. (until Brexit) Gibraltar.[89]

Art. 349(2) TFEU empowers the Council to decide on the conditions of application of the EU treaties and specific regimes, including common policies, to peripheral (remote and insular) EU regions, i.e., to Guadeloupe, French Guiana, Martinique, Mayotte (as of 1 January 2014), Réunion, Saint-Barthélemy (until 2012), Saint-Martin (French DOM; départements d'outre-mer), the Azores, Madeira (Portuguese autonomous regions) and the Canary Islands (Spanish autonomous regions), provided these conditions are not incompatible with the EU treaties.[90] These regions are constitutionally an integral part of 'their' Member States. All EU free movement rights apply to movements between these overseas parts of one Member States and *other* Member States.[91] Unless otherwise specified by the Council and to the extent compatible with the TFEU, free movement of capital then also applies to facts involving those member State regions and third countries.

Depending on the circumstances, Member States' overseas territories may therefore be (i) (parts of) Member States to which the TFEU applies, possibly with certain exceptions and limitations, (ii) third countries, possibly with certain exceptions, or (iii) *sui generis* status countries (aptly called 'second countries'), governed by specific status and association rules. If they are to be regarded as third countries, the question arises whether they are also third countries in relation to their own 'motherland' (in that case, the free capital movement rules apply) or merely an internal situation within one sovereign State (in which case the free movement rules do not apply to operations between that region and its motherland, but only to operations between that region and *other* Member States).

The case law of the CJEU in this area suggests that this question must be answered case-by-case, on the basis of a substance over form approach.[92] From that case law, one may draw the general conclusion that to the extent an associated or dependent territory is bound to apply the free movement of capital vis-à-vis EU Member States, pursuant to

87 *ibid.*

88 Denmark: Greenland; France: French overseas collectivities (Saint-Pierre and Miquilon, French Polynesia and Wallis and Futuna Islands), New Caledonia and dependencies, the French Southern Territories (including the Scattered Islands and Clipperton Islands) and Saint Barthélemy; The Netherlands: Aruba, Bonaire, Curaçao, Saba, Sint Eustatius and Sint Maarten.

89 Although the EU free movement rights applied, until Brexit, *in* Gibraltar, they did not apply between Gibraltar and the UK, as from a free movement point of view, that is an internal situation within one single Member State. See Case C-591/15, *The Gibraltar Betting and Gaming Association Limited*, EU:C:2017:449, and Case C-192/16, *Stephen Fischer et al*, ECLI:EU:C:2017:762. Likewise, in the non-tax case C-293/02, *Jersey Produce Marketing Organisation*, ECLI:EU:C:2005:664, the Court held that, for the purposes of the application of Articles 23, 25, 28 and 29 EC (old), the Channel Islands, the Isle of Man and the United Kingdom must be treated as a single Member State.

90 See, e.g., Joined cases C-363/93, 407/93, 408/93, 409/93, 410/93, and 411/93, René Lancry, EU:C:1994:315, point 32.

91 See, e.g., Case C-163/90, *Legros a.o.*, EU:C:1992:326, and Joined Cases C-363/93, 407/93, 408/93, 409/93, 410/93, and 411/93, *René Lancry*, EU:C:1994:315.

92 See, for elaboration, D.S. Smit, 'The position of the EU Member States' associated and dependent territories under the freedom of establishment, the free movement of capital and secondary EU law in the field of company taxation', *Intertax* 2 (2011), p. 40-61.

Art. 52(1) *juncto* Art. 355 TFEU, such a territory should be treated as (part of) a Member State for the territorial application of Art. 63 TFEU from the perspective of the Member States. On the other hand, to the extent an associated or dependent territory is not bound by these provisions, to apply the free movement of capital vis-à-vis the Member States, such a territory should be treated as a third State for the territorial application of Art. 63 TFEU from the perspective of the Member States. In practical terms, this means that Gibraltar (until Brexit), the Åland Islands, Ceuta and Melilla and the outermost regions[93] are to be considered as (part of) a Member State also for the application of the Anti-Tax Avoidance Directive (ATAD; see Chapter 12). Conversely, the Overseas Countries and Territories,[94] the Faeroe Islands and (until Brexit) the United Kingdom sovereign base areas of Akrotiri and Dhekelia in Cyprus and the Channel Islands and the Isle of Man would have to be considered third countries for purposes of Art. 63 TFEU (and even more so after Brexit).

However, despite the above, the situation of the OCTs under Art. 63 TFEU is complicated. Art. 198 TFEU provides the legal basis for the Member States to agree to associate, with the Union, the non-European countries and territories which have special relations with Denmark, France, the Netherlands and (until Brexit) the United Kingdom. These territories are the OCTs listed in Annex II of the TFEU: Greenland, New Caledonia and Dependencies, French Polynesia, French Southern and Antarctic Territories, Wallis and Futuna Islands, Saint Pierre and Miquelon, and Saint-Barthélemy, Netherlands Antilles (Aruba, Bonaire, Curaçao, Saba, Sint Eustatius, Sint Maarten) and (until Brexit) Anguilla, Cayman Islands, Falkland Islands, South Georgia and the South Sandwich Islands, Montserrat, Pitcairn, Saint Helena and Dependencies, British Antarctic Territory, British Indian Ocean Territory, Turks and Caicos Islands, British Virgin Islands, and Bermuda.[95] These OCTs are not part of the territory to which the TFEU applies, and are therefore not part of the internal market, but they are subject to the special association regime contained in the Council OCT Association Decision. The purpose of their association is to promote their economic and social development and to establish close economic relations between them and the Union as a whole. The *Leplat* case[96] shows that, failing express reference to them, the general provisions of the TFEU, including the treaty freedoms, do not apply to the OCTs listed in Annex II. The OCT Association Decision itself also contains free movement rights, however, but these are much more frugal and narrowly framed than the EU free movement rights. For instance,

93 France: French overseas departments and overseas regions (Guadeloupe, French Guiana, Martinique, Mayotte, and Réunion) and Saint-Martin; Portugal: Azores and Madeira; Spain: Canary Islands.

94 Denmark: Greenland; France: French overseas collectivities (Saint-Pierre and Miquilon, French Polynesia and Wallis and Futuna Islands), New Caledonia and dependencies, the French Southern Territories (including the Scattered Islands and Clipperton Islands) and Saint Barthélemy; The Netherlands: Aruba, Bonaire, Curaçao, Saba, Sint Eustatius and Sint Maarten; United Kingdom (until Brexit): Anguilla, British Antarctic Territory, British Indian Ocean Territory, British Virgin Islands, Cayman Islands, Falkland Islands, Montserrat, Pitcairn Islands, Saint-Helena, Ascension Island, Tristan da Cunha, South Georgia and the South Sandwich Islands and Turks and Caicos Islands.

95 Upon its own request, Bermuda was not part of the Overseas Countries and Territories Association Decision.

96 Case 260/90, *Leplat*, ECLI:EU:C:1992:66.

Art. 59 of the most recent Council OCT Association Decision provides in respect of free movement of capital as follows:

"1. No restrictions shall be imposed on any payments in freely convertible currency on the current account of balance of payments between residents of the Union and of the OCTs.
2. With regard to transactions on the capital account of balance of payments, the Member States and the OCTs authorities shall impose no restrictions on the free movement of capital for direct investments in companies formed in accordance with the laws of the host Member State, country or territory and shall ensure that the assets formed by such investment and any profit stemming therefrom can be realised and repatriated.
3. The Union and the OCTs shall be entitled to take the measures referred to in Articles 64, 65, 66, 75 and 215 TFEU in accordance with the conditions laid down therein mutatis mutandis.
4. The OCTs authorities, the Member State concerned or the Union shall inform one another immediately of any such measures and submit a timetable for their elimination as soon as possible."

Whatever this means, it is clearly less liberal than Art. 63 TFEU, but the Court thinks otherwise (see the *X and TBG* case below and the *SECIL* case discussed in Section 5.2.2).

The fourth recital of the (2013) OCT Association Decision (and the tenth recital of the current OCT Association Decision (2021) rather aptly catches the murky status of Member States' OCTs: they are neither Member State nor third State:

> "(4) The TFEU and its secondary legislation do not automatically apply to the OCTs, with the exception of a number of provisions which explicitly provide for the contrary. Although not third countries, the OCTs do not form part of the single market and must comply with the obligations imposed on third countries in respect of trade, particularly rules of origin, health and plant health standards and safeguard measures."

Two recent cases seem to more or less clear up in which cases the free movement of capital applies between (i) the OCT of one Member State and another Member State, and (ii) between the OCT and its own 'motherland.'

In the first place the rather confusing *Prunus* case,[97] which concerned an exemption from French real estate tax for companies. Two companies indirectly owning French real estate and established in the British Virgin Islands were not exempt, however, because neither a sufficient exchange of information clause nor a nondiscrimination clause applicable to the Virgin Islands was included in the tax treaty between France and the UK. The first question was whether these companies could rely on the free movement of capital, *i.e.* whether the Virgin Islands were a third country vis-à-vis France. Surprisingly, the Court did not apply the *specialis* (the free movement provisions in the OCT Association Decision as applicable at that time), but rather laconically held that the *generalis* (Art. 63 TFEU) was applicable:

> '20. Article 63 TFEU prohibits 'all restrictions on the movement of capital between Member States and between Member States and third countries'. In view of the unlimited territorial scope of that provision, it must be regarded as necessarily applying to movements of capital to and from OCTs.'

97 Case C-384/09, *Prunus*, EU:C:2011:276.

Thus, between a member State and the OCT of *another* member State, the free movement of capital applied as if those OCTs were third countries. We believe the Court applied Art. 63 TFEU instead of the (much) narrower free movement provision in the dedicated OCT Associations Decision, because otherwise the paradoxical result would have been that capital movement between France and, *e.g.* Panama or Bhutan would have been better protected than capital movement between the EU and its OCTs.

This judgment did not shed light on the question of whether Art. 63 TFEU also applies to movements of capital between a Member State and its *own* OCT, *i.e.* to capital movements *within* one and the same public international law entity, *e.g.* between Curaçao and the Netherlands. That question was raised in *X and TBG Ltd*,[98] concerning a discriminatory Netherlands 8.3% withholding tax on dividends paid to Curaçao which would not have been levied if they had been paid within the Netherlands. The Court took an approach different from the one in *Prunus*. Instead of applying Art. 63 TFEU and ignoring the OCT Association Decision as applicable at that time, it this time did the opposite:

> "45. The existence of [the Association Decision; *authors*] results in the general provisions of the EC Treaty (...) not referred to in Part Four of that treaty, not being applicable to OCTs in the absence of an express reference (...).
> 46. As regards Part Four of the Treaty, it should be noted that, although it contains some provisions concerning the free movement of goods, (...), and the free movement of workers, (...), as well as the freedom of establishment, (...), by contrast it does not contain any provision relating to the free movement of capital.
> 47. As regards the OCT Decision, (...), it states, in Article 47(1) [now 59, cited above; *authors*], what restrictions on payment and on movements of capital are prohibited between the European Union and OCTs.
> 48. By referring to (...), Article 47(1) [now 59; *authors*] of the OCT Decision has a particularly wide scope, close to the scope of Article 56 EC [now 63 TFEU; *authors*] in the relations between Member States and third countries (...).
> 49. Consequently, by prohibiting, inter alia, restrictions on the acquisition of shares in companies and the repatriation of profits stemming therefrom, Article 47(1)(b) [now 59] of the OCT Decision prohibits, among others, restrictions on the payment of dividends between the European Union and OCTs, along the lines of the prohibition of such measures set out in Article 56 EC [now 63 TFEU; *authors*] as regards, inter alia, relations between Member States and third countries."

We surmise the Court wanted to reach the same result as in *Prunus* (equal protection of free movement between the EU and its OCTs and between the EU and third States), however this time not by equating OCTs to third States, as in *Prunus*. Indeed, that would sit uneasily with the preamble to the OCT Association Decision, which explicitly states that the OCTs are *not* third States. Instead, the Court interpreted Art. (now) 59 of the OCT Association Decision as wide as possible, preferably as having the same width as Art. (now) 63 TFEU; see points 48 and 49 quoted above, in which the Court speaks of 'a particularly wide scope, close to the scope' of Art. (now) 63 TFEU and states that Art. (now) 59 of the OCT Decision prohibits restrictions 'along the lines' of the prohibition in Art. (now) 63 TFEU.

We conclude that the Court has come 'close to' interpreting Art. 59 of the OCT Association Decision as having the *same* substance as Art. 63 TFEU. That would be a welcome

98 Joined cases C-24/12 en C-27/12, *X and TBG Ltd*, EU:C:2014:1385.

simplification and clarification of the capital movement status of the OCTs: capital movement to and from the OCTs will be treated in principle as comparable to the treatment of third State capital movement, i.e. 'along the lines' of Art. 63 TFEU.

There are also European territories for whose external relations a Member State is responsible, within the meaning of Art. 355 (3) TFEU. According to that provision, the provisions of the EU Treaties shall apply to such European territories. That is the case of Gibraltar (until Brexit). The Court's case law shows that the freedom to provide services and the freedom of establishment and capital apply to Gibraltar.[99] That did not help *the Gibraltar Betting and Gaming Association Ltd*,[100] however, as the Court also held that it results from the Constitutional position of Gibraltar and from Art. 355(3) TFEU that transactions between service providers in Gibraltar and customers in the UK are to be considered as taking place within one single Member State. In such an internal situation, the EU free movement rights do not apply. In *Stephen Fischer et al*,[101] it reached the same conclusion in respect of the freedom of establishment and free movement of capital: those freedoms "do not apply to a situation which is confined in all respects within a single Member State".[102] Under circumstances Member States' (own) overseas, associated and dependent territories may thus be better protected if they can claim the third State status. This is a somewhat counter-intuitive conclusion.

5.4 The European Economic Area Agreement (EEAA)

The Agreement on the European Economic Area (EEAA) entered into force on 1 January 1994. It brings together in a single market, referred to as the 'Internal Market', the EU Member States and three of the EFTA[103] States: Iceland, Liechtenstein and Norway. EFTA-Member Switzerland did not accede to the EEAA but concluded its own agreements with the EU. The EEAA guarantees equal rights and obligations within the Internal Market for citizens and economic operators in the EEA. It provides for the application of the EU fundamental freedoms – the free movement of goods, services, persons and capital – throughout the 31 EEA States. When a State becomes a member of the European Union, it shall also apply to become party to the EEAA (Art. 128), thus also leading to an enlargement of the EEA.

The EEAA also covers cooperation in research and development, education, social policy, the environment, consumer protection, tourism and culture, collectively known as "flanking and horizontal" policies.

EEA partners accept almost the entire EU *acquis communautaire*. In the words of Court, the EEAA establishes "in the most complete way possible, the free movement of goods, persons, services and capital, so as to extend the internal market established in the Union to States which are parties to that agreement."[104] In principle, all of the CJEU case law on

---

99 Even though, under Article 29 of the 1972 Act of Accession, in conjunction with Annex I, Section I, point 4, thereto, Gibraltar does not form part of the EU customs territory. See Case C-591/15, The Gibraltar Betting and Gaming Association Ltd, EU:C:2017:449, point 29, and Case C-192/16, *Stephen Fischer et al*, EU:C:2017:762, points 6-8.

100 Case C-591/15, *The Gibraltar Betting and Gaming Association Limited*, EU:C:2017:449.

101 Case C-192/16, *Stephen Fischer et al*, EU:C:2017:762.

102 See also Case C-293/02, *Jersey Produce Marketing Organisation*, EU:C:2005:664.

103 European Free Trade Association.

104 Case C-464/14, *SECIL v Fazenda Pública*, point 125, EU:C:2016:896.

the EU free movement rights is therefore also relevant for movement between EU Member States and the other EEA-Members, as well as between the three non-EU EEA-States. The EFTA-part of the EEA has its own Court, the EFTA Court, which concords with the CJEU: the free movement rights in the EEAA are interpreted by the CJEU and the EFTA Court in the same manner as the CJEU interprets the free movement rights in the TFEU. The EFTA EEA-Member States also have their own 'Commission': the EFTA Surveillance Authority. One important difference is, however, that the EU Directives, such as DAC and ATAD, do not apply in the relations between EU Member States and the three other EEA-Members, nor between the three non-EU EEA-States. To that extent, there is less legal integration with the three EFTA/EEA-Members, which may be relevant when assessing whether a tax measure restricting free movement to or from an EFTA is justified, as the *Rimbaud*[105] case discussed in Section 5.2.2 showed in respect of Liechtenstein.

In respect of capital, Art. 40 EEAA provides for the same free movement of capital as within the EU, but contrary to Art. 63 TFEU, it does not extend free movement of capital to non-contracting parties (non-EEA countries); third State (non-EEA) capital free movement therefore only applies for EU Member States, not for the three other EEA Member States.

In Case C-521/07, *Commission v Netherlands*,[106] Netherlands dividends paid to another Netherlands company or to a company of another EU Member State were exempted from dividend withholding tax if the parent company held at least 5% of the capital, whereas dividends paid to a company established in Iceland or Norway were exempted only if the latter held at least 10% (Icelandic parent company) or 25% (Norwegian parent company) of the capital of the Netherlands company. The Court recalled that one of the principal aims of the EEA Agreement is to extend the EU internal market to the three EFTA States joining the EEA, and that the fundamental freedoms in the EEA Agreement, which are identical in substance to those of the Treaty, are to be interpreted uniformly within the Member States (point 32). It concluded that the Dutch regime constituted a restriction on the free movement of capital which is, in principle, prohibited by Art. 40 of the EEA Agreement (point 39).

The Netherlands pointed out that the mutual assistance Directive in force between the Member States did not apply to Iceland and Norway and that there was no binding rule enabling it to obtain information to verify whether the conditions laid down in domestic legislation were fulfilled. The Court, however, considered that verification of the conditions for the exemption to apply did not require exchange of information.

Commission v Italy (C-540/07),[107] concerned an Italian 95% exemption of profits distributed to recipient companies resident in Italy. In contrast, tax of 27% was withheld from profits distributed to taxpayers not resident in Italy. The rate of tax withheld was reduced to 12.5% for profits paid to holders of savings shares. In respect of recipient companies in EEA States, the Court held the fundamental freedoms in the EEAA, including Art. 40 on free movement of capital to be identical in substance to and having the same scope as those of the TFEU and to be interpreted accordingly.

It can be concluded, that the free movement rights contained in the EEAA are interpreted by the CJEU and the EFTA Court in the same manner as the free movement rights

105 Case C-72/09, *Établissements Rimbaud*, EU:C:2010:645.
106 Case C-521/07, *Commission v Netherlands*, EU:C:2009:360.
107 Case C-540/07, *Commission v. Italy*, EU:C:2009:717.

in the TFEU. However, the lack of effective fiscal supervision (exchange of information at a level comparable to that between EU Member States) in the relation with a non-EU EEA Member State has been accepted by the CJEU as a justification for discriminatory or restrictive tax measures, even where these would not be accepted within the EU.

5.5 External Tax Relations

5.5.1 External Tax Treaty-Making Powers

As explained in Chapter 2, Union competence is based on the principle of conferral: the Union has only the competences conferred on it by the treaties (Art. 5 TEU). The Union's competence in tax matters is shared with the Member States, except as regards the customs union, which is an exclusive Union competence (Art. 3(1)(a) TFEU). Indirect taxation other than customs duties and direct taxation are an 'internal market' matter (Art. 4(2)(a) TFEU) and therefore a shared competence with preemption: as soon as and to the extent in which the Union has exercised its competence to regulate a tax matter, the Member States have to that extent lost their individual competences to regulate that tax matter.

The Treaties confer not only internal powers on the Union, but obviously also external powers, such as those regarding the common commercial policy (Arts. 206 and 207, an *exclusive* external power), cooperation with third countries, development coordination, and humanitarian aid (Arts. 208-214), international agreements (Arts. 216-219), environment (Art. 191(4)), exchange-rate systems for the Euro (Art. 219), Research and development (Art. 186), and the common foreign and security policy (Art. 24 TEU); for the latter, a specific set of rules and procedures is provided. In areas of external competence, the TFEU also provides for treaty-making power, making the Union competent to negotiate and conclude treaties with third States and international organizations, also if internally the Union may not have as yet exercised any regulatory competence. It is important to realize that since the entry into force of the Lisbon Treaty, the Union's common commercial policy includes foreign direct investments as well.[108] Direct investment consists in investments of any kind made by natural or legal persons which serve to establish or maintain lasting and direct links between the persons providing the capital and the undertakings to which that capital is made available in order to carry out an economic activity. Acquisition of a holding in an undertaking constituted as a company limited by shares is a direct investment where the shares held by the shareholder enable him to participate effectively in the management of that company or in its control.[109] It follows that the European Union has exclusive competence to approve any commitment vis-à-vis a third State relating to investments made by natural or legal persons of that third State in the European Union and vice versa which enable effective participation in the management or control of a company carrying out an economic activity.[110] This is the reason why, for example bilateral investment agreements with third countries have come under the Union's exclusive competence. Commitments vis-à-vis a third State relating to other foreign investment,

108 This was different under ex-Article 133 EC, which excluded foreign direct investment from the common commercial policy.
109 Opinion 2/15 of the Court, 16 May 2017, ECLI:EU:C:2017:376, point 80.
110 *Ibid.*, point 82.

on the other hand, do not fall within the exclusive competence of the European Union.[111] The foregoing leads to the one-million dollar question whether Member States are still fully competent to conclude bilateral tax treaties with third countries. Our impression is that, at least until now, they *think* they are.

One should furthermore carefully distinguish from the above question of (exclusive) competence the fact that the Union is not prohibited from using the *internal powers* conferred on it in order to specify the treatment which is to be accorded to nationals of non-EU Member States.[112] In such a case, the Union is merely exercising its internal competences.[113] However, when the Union has included in its internal legislative acts such provisions relating to the treatment of nationals of third countries, it acquires exclusive external competence in the spheres covered by those acts.[114]

Except where the Union's external competence is exclusive (such as in the field of common commercial policy, including direct investments), the Member States also remain competent to conclude treaties with third States, but because of the precedence of Union law over national law, external action of the Union limits the area left for the Member States. As it appears from Arts. 3(2) and 216 TFEU, the Union is not only competent to conclude treaties with third States where the TFEU explicitly so provides (primary power), but also 'where the conclusion of an agreement is necessary in order to achieve, within the framework of the Union's policies, one of the objectives referred to in the Treaties' (implied power), where its conclusion is necessary to enable the Union to exercise its internal competence, where the conclusion of an agreement is provided for in a legally binding Union act (self-conferral of treaty-making power), or where the conclusion of the agreement is likely to affect common rules or alter their scope.[115] The preemption rule and the 'implied powers' rule in the TFEU are based on case law of the European Court, notably the *AETR* case,[116] and on several opinions on external treaty making-powers issued by the Court.[117]

These rules thus entail, a.o., that whenever EU law confers internal powers on the Union in order to achieve an objective, the Union is also competent to conclude international agreements necessary to achieve that objective, even in the absence of a specific Treaty provision conferring such competence, as well as that where the exercise by the Union of internal powers to achieve the aims of Treaties lead to adoption of common rules, the Member States no longer have the power to conclude their own agreements with third States on the subject matter covered by the common rules if such agreements with third States could jeopardize the full effectiveness of the common rules. A good example in tax matters may be the negotiation by the Union of the agreements with Switzerland, Liechtenstein, Andorra, Monaco, and San Marino as regards the exchange of information and/or

111 *Ibid.*, point 83.
112 Opinion of the Court of 28 March 1996, 2/94, ECLI:EU:C:1996:140, point 90.
113 See also G. Kofler, *Doppelbesteuerungsabkommen und Europäisches Gemeinschafsrecht* (Vienna: Linde Verlag, 2007), 322 with further references.
114 Opinion of the Court of 15 November 1994, 1/94, EU:C:1994:384, point 95.
115 T C Hartley, *The Foundations of European Union Law, An Introduction to the Constitutional and Administrative Law of the European Union*, 7th ed., 2010, pp. 186-187.
116 Case 22/70, *Commission v. Council*, EU:C:1971:32.
117 Opinions 2/91, EU:C:1993:106, 2/92, EU:C:1995:83 and 1/94, EU:C:1994:384.

withholding of source tax on savings interest, as the intra-EU Directive on Administrative Cooperation (DAC; see Chapter 13) cannot be effective without such external agreements.

The question thus arises whether the fact that the Union adopted common rules, such as the Parent-Subsidiary Directive (see Chapter 16), the Merger Directive (see Chapter 17), the Interest and Royalty Directive (see Chapter 18), the Directives on administrative cooperation (DAC; see Chapter 28), the Anti-Tax Avoidance Directive (ATAD; see Chapter 19), and the Pillar Two Directive (see Chapter 22) implies that the Union also has external powers to negotiate and conclude tax treaties with third States as regards these issues (leaving aside the potential impact of Article 207(1) TFEU since the entry into force of the Lisbon Treaty; see above).[118] It is evident that a possible competence of the Union in this respect can only be shared, not exclusive, as the Treaties do not confer any powers as regards tax treaties, not even as regards intra-EU harmonization of national tax laws, except in so far as necessary for the functioning of the *internal* market. Furthermore, tax treaties have a much wider scope than the EU direct tax directives mentioned, and these directives apply only to intra-EU situations. The *Open Skies* cases[119] illustrate that in fields which are primarily the responsibility of the Member States, such as aviation rights or direct taxation, the Union's competence to conclude treaties with third States is at the most a shared competence with preemption.

Therefore, the Union in our view has at least shared external powers in respect of the areas covered by the direct tax directives and the administrative cooperation directives, *i.e.* on the tax treatment of cross-border intragroup dividends and interest and royalties, the (automatic) exchange of tax information, and the application of measures against tax base erosion and profit shifting (BEPS) and exit taxes on companies, as well as on the tax treatment of cross-border mergers, and maybe even in fields of direct taxation where the Union itself has not yet exercised any regulatory powers, but where external use of powers is necessary for the functioning of the internal market (see Art. 4(2)(a)). The Member States are no doubt still competent to conclude individual tax treaties with third States, even if these treaties contain provisions at variance with the intra-EU system, provided this variance does not frustrate in any way the useful intra-EU effect of the EU tax directives. It is difficult to see how they could: we cannot think of a situation in which, *e.g.*, the tax treatment of dividend flows between the Czech Republic and China would frustrate the full effect of the Parent-Subsidiary Directive rules as regards a group dividend payment between the Czech Republic and Portugal. It is equally difficult to see how tax treaty-based mutual assistance in the assessment or recovery of tax claims between a Member State and a third State could jeopardize effective mutual assistance between that Member State and another Member State on the basis of the Mutual Assistance Directives.

There are, however, at least three direct-tax fields in which the EU may be on the way of preempting the external competence of the Member States. These are: (i) the tax treatment of mergers and company seat transfers in external situations involving a

118 See Hubert Hamaekers: 'Corporate Tax Policy and the Competence of the European Community: An EC Tax Convention with Non-Member States?', 1990 *European Taxation* 358; Dirk van Unnik and Maarten Boudesteijn: 'The New US-Dutch Tax Treaty and the Treaty of Rome', *EC Tax Review* 1993/2, p. 107-110; and Paul Farmer: 'EC Law and Direct Taxation – Some Thoughts on Recent Issues', 1 *The EC Tax Journal 2* (1995-1996).

119 Cases C-446-469/98, C-471-472/98, C-475-476/98 (*Commission v. UK, Denmark, Sweden, Finland, Belgium, Luxembourg, Austria and Germany*, respectively), EU:C:2002:624 – 631.

European Company (SE) or a European Cooperative Society (SCE), (ii) the fight against BEPS and for tax transparency, especially common anti-hybrid mismatch rules in relation to third States ('ATAD II'; see Chapter 12) and tax good governance rules such as the common blacklist of non-cooperative third States (see 5.5.3) and the rules on a global minimum effective tax rate under the Pillar Two Directive (see Chapter 22). The useful effect of the common EU rules on the taxation of mergers and seat transfers of SE's and SCE's are likely to be affected if every separate Member State would be free to negotiate with third States any tax treatment it pleases for an SE/SCE merger/transfer in an external cross-border situation.

In the ATAD II Directive (see Chapter 19) the EU has embarked upon a common external policy as regards hybrid mismatches, which in our view implies external competence to the extent necessary to make that common policy work. Also, tax good governance clauses in tax treaties requiring exchange of information, or requiring the adoption of the EU BEPS standards by the external tax treaty partner, or requiring a minimum level of taxation, may be expected to become exclusive competence of the Union. However, bilateral tax treaties negotiated according to the international (OECD) standard of exchange of information and OECD BEPS will probably remain under (shared) Member State competence.

Common external policy exists perhaps most obviously as far as the rules on a global minimum effective tax rate under the Pillar Two Directive are concerned. The mandatory and coordinated nature of these rules which give the individual Member States no further leeway whatsoever do not allow individual Member States to agree on deviations on these rules with third states.

Finally, the question can be raised whether the EU has obtained exclusive competence to negotiate and sign any future Multilateral Pillar-One Convention since this Convention is expected to govern *direct investments* only and hence could fall within the exclusive external competence by virtue of Article 207(1) TFEU.

5.5.2 LOB-Provisions in Tax Treaties with Third States;[120] Derivative Benefits

In their mutual relations, Member States may not conclude (tax) treaties containing provisions which violate EU law. Such provisions must be set aside, whether these treaties were concluded before or after 1958 (or the date of EU-accession of the Member State involved).[121]

As regards treaties between a Member State and a third State, concluded before 1958 or before the EU-accession of the Member State involved, Art. 351 TFEU provides that they will be respected. However, where these treaties are incompatible with EU law, the

120 See on this issue, a.o., Braedon Clark: 'The Limitation on Benefits Clause Under an Open Sky' *European Taxation* January 2003, p. 22-26; Adam Craig: 'Open Your Eyes: What the "Open Skies" Cases Could Mean for the US Tax Treaties with the EU Member States', *European Taxation*, February 2003, p. 63-74; Eric Osterweil, 'Are LOB Provisions in Double Tax Conventions Contrary to EC Treaty Freedoms?', 18 *EC Tax Review* 5 (2009), p. 241; Tom O'Shea, 'Limitation on Benefit (LoB) Clauses and the EU,' *International Tax Report*, November 2008, p. 2; Pasquale Pistone, 'Test Claimants in Class IV of the ACT Group Litigation: Limitation-on-Benefits Clauses Are Clearly Different from Most-Favoured-Nations Clauses,' 4 *British Tax Review* 2007, p. 144; and José Calejo Guerra, 'Limitation on Benefits Clauses and EU Law,' *European Taxation* February/March 2011, p. 85.

121 See, *e.g.*, Case 235/87, *Annunziata Mateucci*, EU:C:1988:460 and Case 286/86 (*Gérard Deserbais*), EU:C:1988:434.

Member State involved shall do its utmost to renegotiate the treaty in order to align its provisions with EU law, if necessary backed by a 'common attitude' of all EU Member States vis-à-vis the third State involved.

Many bilateral tax treaties with third States postdate the entry into force of (or the accession to) the predecessors of the TFEU, the EEC Treaty and the EC Treaty. It is clear that a Member State concluding a tax treaty with a third State which is incompatible with EU law fails to fulfill its EU obligations, but the consequences are less clear. Obviously, the Member State involved must undertake to eliminate the incompatibility. It is also clear, however, that in principle it is not the concern of the third State involved that its bilateral treaty partner possibly neglected its obligations under EU law, except in the unlikely case where Art. 46 of the Vienna Convention on the Law of Treaties would apply. That Article provides that a contracting State is not held to observe the treaty if the other contracting State must have been aware of the fact that it was not competent to conclude the treaty because of a fundamental rule of national law.

The problem arises most poignantly in connection with anti-treaty shopping clauses in bilateral tax treaties concluded with third States, especially those concluded with the US and Japan, but also the 2017 OECD Multilateral Convention against BEPS (MLI)[122] contains an LOB-provision.[123] Member States' tax treaties with these third States typically contain lengthy and impenetrable 'limitation on benefits' (LOB) provisions.[124] In order to qualify for the tax treaty benefits, especially the reduction of withholding taxes on dividends, interest and royalties, a taxpayer must be a resident of one of the contracting States. To ensure that only genuine residents benefit, rather than 'conduit' structures of which the ultimate beneficiaries are residents of neither contracting State – to exclude treaty shopping – LOB provisions contain various residence tests, such as the ownership and base erosion test, the publicly traded stock test, the active trade or business test and the headquarters test. Where an EU parent company receives dividends or interest from its US or Japanese subsidiary, failure of these tests in principle results in denial of the treaty reduction of US or Japanese withholding tax. If the tax treaty benefits are denied on the grounds that the shareholders of the EU parent company are resident in another Member State than the parent company itself, we are looking at a discrimination within the meaning of the ECJ's case law on free movement: domestic parent companies with EU shareholders are treated less favourably than domestic parent companies with domestic shareholders, which offends free capital movement, the right of establishment and the principle of loyal cooperation.

The (non-tax) *Gottardo* case[125] shows that the free movement of persons precludes Member States from limiting the benefits of a bilateral treaty they conclude with a third State to their own nationals exclusively. The case concerned Mrs Gottardo, of Italian origin,

122 BEPS Multilateral Instrument: the Multilateral Convention to Implement Tax Treaty Related Measures to Prevent Base Erosion and Profit Shifting, signed in Paris on 7 June 2017.

123 However, only 12 signatories have chosen to supplement the principle purpose test (PPT) for identifying abuse with a simplified Limitation on Benefits provision: Argentina, Armenia, Bulgaria, Chile, Colombia, India, Indonesia, Mexico, Russia, Senegal, Slovak Republic and Uruguay.

124 On the limitation on benefits clauses in the MLC, and the reasons on its limited adoption by the signatory States, see, B. Kuzniacki, The Limitation on the Benefits (LOB) Provision in BEPS Action 6/ MLI: Ineffective Overreaction of Mind-Numbing Complexity (Part I), 46 Intertax 1, 2018, pp. 68-79.

125 Case C-55/00, *Gottardo*, EU:C:2002:16.

but through her marriage of French nationality, who had worked in Italy, Switzerland and France, paying social security contributions in all three States, and later applying for an Italian pension. However, she did not reach the requisite number of employment years if her Swiss employment period was not taken into account. The Italian-Swiss treaty provided for such inclusion, but only for nationals. The Court held that the free movement of workers required Italy to include the Swiss employment period irrespective of Mrs Gottardo's nationality, as long as it was an EU nationality.

In the *Open Skies* cases,[126] the Court disqualified a similar nationality clause in the bilateral aviation agreements of eight Member States with the US, granting both contracting States the right to disallow the treaty benefits to airline carriers which were not substantively owned or controlled by nationals of the contracting States (but by nationals of other EU States, EEA States or third States).

Member States renegotiating their tax treaties with the US, Japan and other third States therefore usually try to include at least a 'derivative benefits' clause,[127] providing that companies also qualify as 'good' residents if they are controlled by persons resident in an EU (or EEA) State who would have been eligible for the same treaty benefits if they had derived the third State income themselves directly, *i.e.* if there is a tax treaty in force between the third State concerned and the EU or EEA State of residence of the controlling person(s) which provides for the same benefits. This gives rise to a specific issue in relation to companies of Member States controlled by UK parent companies post-Brexit. Since the UK will no longer be a Member State, these 'derivative benefit' clauses would not ensure that the treaty applied. It is likely that this issue will ultimately be resolved by amendment to the treaties to ensure that they do apply to companies controlled by UK parents.

After the *Open Skies* judgments, Member States agreeing to a restrictive LOB provision in a tax treaty with a third State may violate their EU law obligations. What are the consequences? A Member State cannot, in its relation with a third State, rely on EU law in order to withdraw from its tax treaty consent. It is not in a position to stop the third State involved from applying the tax treaty as agreed. Tax levied in breach of EU law should be refunded 'as a matter of principle' (see section 3.5.2.2), but it is not the Member State which levied the tax, and it is not the third State which is in breach of EU law. Thus, the only legal route to remedy seems to be a damages claim for State tort under the *Francovich* case law (see section 3.5.4). However, *Open Skies* and *Gottardo* may not be clear enough in their implications for LOB-clauses in tax treaties with Third States to speak of a 'manifest breach' of EU law. Moreover, the causal link between the alleged damages and the tax treaty negotiation result seems doubtful. If the EU Member State concerned had not agreed to the LOB clause insisted upon by the third State, no tax treaty, or at least no reduction of source taxation might have been concluded at all. Insisting on a third State waiver of LOB clauses would have jeopardized the very treaty negotiation result. This means that there is a justification for – reluctantly – consenting to the LOB provision, and that the Member State's tax treaty negotiation result is proportional in

126 Cases C-466-469/98, C-471-472/98 and C-475-476/98 (*Commission v. UK, Denmark, Sweden, Finland, Belgium, Luxembourg, Austria and Germany*, respectively), EU:C:2002:624 – 631.

127 In their tax treaties with the US, the following EU Members have included such a test: Belgium, Bulgaria, Denmark, Finland, Germany, Ireland, Luxembourg, the Netherlands, Sweden and the UK.

relation to the mandatory requirement of public interest that comprehensive tax treaties are concluded by EU Member States with, *e.g.*, the US and Japan which mutually reduce restrictive source taxation. Such treaties are manifestly more important for the internal market than avoiding possible but rather remote unequal treatment of EU nonresidents at the cost of not having a tax treaty or no reduction of source taxation at all. The European Commission seems to be on the same page: on 30 October 2020, the Commission closed its infringement case (No. 20144233) which concerned the LOB-provisions contained in Article 21 of the 2010 income tax treaty between the Netherlands and Japan.

Moreover, LOB-clause may possibly be seen as presumptive anti-abuse rules, which may, despite being in principle disproportionate for in principle excluding nonresident grandparents irrespective of actual abuse, be justified if sufficiently targeted against abuse and/or if they allow rebuttal, by the taxpayer, of the presumption of abuse through the LOB-tests and possibly a safety net provision calling for mutual agreement (see section 15.5). We observe however, that the Court did not accept a German (domestic) anti-abuse measure which denied the dividend withholding tax exemption of Art. 5 of the Parent-Subsidiary Directive to EU parent companies where *their* shareholders would not have been eligible for the exemption, had they received the dividend directly.[128]

We have not put forward the *Class IV ACT* case[129] as authority for Member States to justify LOB clauses in their tax treaties with third States because we believe that case addresses another issue. It concerned the Member State *applying* LOB-provisions rather than the Member State whose residents suffered from them. The Court was asked whether the UK could apply an LOB provision in its tax treaty with the Netherlands excluding residents of the Netherlands from an imputation credit if they were controlled by other persons than residents of the Netherlands, even though the UK, in other tax treaties with other Member States like Italy, had extended the same imputation credit *without* applying a similar LOB. The Court allowed it, to the surprise of some. In our view, this acceptance has little significance for LOB-provisions in tax treaties with third States, as there is an important difference between *Class IV ACT* and *Open Skies:* the latter case involved Member States discriminating against *nonresidents* as compared to *residents* (which violates the freedoms of establishment and of capital movement), whereas the former concerned a Member State (the UK) distinguishing between *two nonresidents* from different Member States (the Netherlands and Italy) with mutually different tax systems and different tax treaty negotiation stakes.[130] As in *D. v Inspecteur,*[131] the Court considered these two nonresidents not to be in the same position. That does not relate to the comparability of *residents* and *nonresidents*, which is at issue in case of LOB-provisions in tax treaties with third States. We believe, therefore, that *Class IV ACT* does not revoke *Open Skies,* and that notwithstanding *Class IV ACT*, Member States need to justify the inclusion of

128 Joined Cases C 504/16 and C 613/16, *Deister Holding AG and Juhler Holding A/S*, EU:C:2017:1009. See also Case C-6/16, *Eqiom SAS/Enka former Holcim France SAS*, EU:C:2017:641.

129 Case C-374/04, *Test Claimants in Class IV of the ACT Group Litigation v. Commissioners of Inland Revenue*, EU:C:2006:773.

130 One important difference between Italy and the Netherlands was that Italy, like the UK, applied both a credit system and an imputation system, whereas the Netherlands applied neither, but rather an exemption system and a classical system of dividend taxation.

131 Case C-376/03, *D. v Inspecteur*, EU:C:2005:424.

LOB provisions in their tax treaties with third States which distinguish between resident companies with nonresident EU shareholders and resident companies with resident shareholders. We also believe, however, that they are able to justify them, provided they undertook to have an active trade or business test, a derivative benefits test ('equivalent beneficiaries') and a safety net provision included for the benefit of EU grandparents, all to be interpreted in line with the EU abuse of law doctrine in order to avoid not only overkill but also to avoid under-inclusiveness.

5.5.3 *The EU Blacklist of Non-cooperative Third States*

On 5 December 2017, the Council approved[132] an EU blacklist of non-cooperative jurisdictions in respect of tax transparency, fair taxation and implementation of anti-BEPS measures. Seventeen jurisdictions had been listed: American Samoa, Bahrain, Barbados, Grenada, Guam, Korea (Rep.), Macao, Marshall Islands, Mongolia, Namibia, Palau, Panama, Saint Lucia, Samoa, Trinidad and Tobago, Tunisia, and the United Arab Emirates. Apparently, the operation is rather effective, as newsmedia report that Panama, South Korea, the United Arab Emirates, Barbados, Grenada, Macao, Mongolia and Tunisia have offered to change their laws and may be delisted shortly.

Another 47 jurisdictions (the 'grey' list), were expected to upgrade their 'tax good governance principles' sufficiently so as not to be blacklisted. These 47 had publicly committed to implement automatic exchange of information, to conclude a relevant network of agreements covering EU Member States, to implement minimum anti-BEPS standards, to abolish harmful tax regimes and tax regimes facilitating offshore structures that attract profits without real economic activity and/or to become a member of the OECD Global Forum on Transparency and Exchange of Information for Tax Purposes.

The blacklisting process consisted of three steps and was based on a scoreboard, screening and listing. The EU Code of Conduct Group (see Chapter 23) and the Member States applied three risk indicators to 160 third countries (these risk indicators were also used to select the 160 jurisdictions to be screened): (i) transparency and exchange of information, (ii) preferential tax regimes (including territorial regimes) and (iii) absence of corporate income tax or a zero or nearly zero tax rate.

The Council adopted defensive measures against the blacklisted jurisdictions, both non-tax countermeasures (related to the European Fund for Sustainable Development) and tax countermeasures (reinforced monitoring of certain transactions, increased audit risks for taxpayers investing or using structures or arrangements involving the black-listed jurisdictions, and several anti-BEPS measures). Reinforced monitoring and increased audit efforts are mandatory; application of the anti-BEPS measures is optional. Counter measures much be as dissuasive and effective as possible.[133] As of 1 January 2021, the Member States committed to use the EU list in the application of at least one of the following four specific countermeasures: i) non-deductibility of costs incurred in a listed

132 Council of the European Union – Council conclusions on the EU list of non-cooperative jurisdictions for tax purposes, 5 December, 2017, No. 15429/17, FISC 345 ECOFIN 1088, available at: http://www.consilium.europa.eu/media/31945/st15429en17.pdf (last visited on 16 Jan. 2018).

133 Communication from the Commission to the European Parliament and the Council on Tax Good Governance in the EU and beyond COM(2020) 313 final.

jurisdiction; ii) controlled foreign company (CFC) rules, to limit artificial deferral of tax to offshore, low-taxed entities; iii) withholding tax measures (WHT), to tackle improper exemptions or refunds; iv) limitation of the participation exemption on shareholder dividends. This number may increase in the future; *e.g.* the European Commission may consider a legislative proposal for coordinated defensive measures.[134]

As per 8 October 2024, the following 11 jurisdictions were black-listed: American Samoa, Anguilla, Fiji, Guam, Palau, Panama, Russia, Samoa, Trinidad and Tobago, US Virgin Islands and Vanuatu whereas another 9 jurisdictions are still on the grey list.[135] On 18 February 2025 the list was further revised with 11 jurisdictions in Appendix I (non-cooperative jurisdictions) and 8 jurisdictions in Appendix II (committed jurisdictions).[136] The 11 non-cooperative jurisdictions are: American Samoa, Anguilla, Fiji, Guam, Palau, Panama, the Russian Federation, Samoa, Trinidad & Tobago, US Virgin Islands, and Vanuatu. Apparently, quite a large number of Third states decided to comply with the EU's requirements and to modify their tax systems. Hence, although not politically binding, the EU black list seemed to be an effective political tool to force Third states to adopt to the EU minimum tax standards. From this perspective it does not come as a surprise that the European Commission wishes to upgrade the black list criteria, for example by proposing to introduce Pillar 2 in the criteria used for assessing third countries in the EU listing process. Also tax measures which could pose the same risk of preferential tax regimes (e.g. broad tax exemptions) could come under the scope of the listing criteria.[137] For the time being, however, the Code of Conduct Group will "continue reflections on a possible further strengthening the EU listing process".[138]

Finally, and somewhat surprisingly, the Member States nor the European Commission seem to wonder whether counter measures towards black-listed jurisdictions – which must be "dissuasive and effective as possible" – would comply with the free movement of capital under Article 63 TFEU, in particular in the light of the principle of proportionality. It is true that the Court has accepted the need to combat tax havens as a valid justification, but until now subject to strict requirements.[139] We would think that the special procedure provided for under Article 65(4) TFEU could be helpful in this respect (see 5.2.1) for the Member States in order to limit the risk that taxpayers could successfully challenge the countermeasures before the Court on the basis of Article 63 (TFEU).

134 Communication from the Commission to the European Parliament and the Council on Tax Good Governance in the EU and beyond COM(2020) 313 final.

135 It concerns Antigua and Barbuda, Belize, British Virgin Islands, Costa Rica, Curaçao, Eswatini, Turkey and Vietnam.

136 Directorate-General of Taxation and Customs Union, News Announcement, 18 February 2025.

137 Communication from the Commission to the European Parliament and the Council on Tax Good Governance in the EU and beyond COM(2020) 313 final.

138 Council of the European Union, 5 October 2023, Multiannual Work Package, No. 13649/23.

139 Case C80/12, *Felixstowe Dock and Railway Company Ltd and Others v The Commissioners for Her Majesty's Revenue & Customs*, ECLI:EU:C:2014:200, point. 32; Joined Cases C-24/12 and C-27/12, *X BV and TBG Limited*, ECLI:EU:C:2014:1385, point 51 *et seq.*

5.6 Brexit[140]

The UK ceased to be a Member State of the EU at midnight (CET) on 31st January 2020. This was followed by a transitional period during which, for practical purposes, the legal position remained unchanged. Thus, the UK fully ceased to be a Member State at midnight (CET) on 31st December 2020. The process of withdrawal was provided for in the Withdrawal Agreement.[141] The on-going relationship between the UK and the EU is governed by a Trade and Cooperation Agreement (the "TCA").[142]

The TCA contains a relatively limited number of provisions relating to taxation. Interestingly, Chapter 5 of Title XI (Level Playing Field for Open and Fair Competition and Sustainable Development) of the TCA contains relatively nebulous commitments on tax good governance and taxation standards, as follows:

> CHAPTER 5
>
> TAXATION
>
> ARTICLE 383 (Good governance)
> The Parties recognise and commit to implementing the principles of good governance in the area of taxation, in particular the global standards on tax transparency and exchange of information and fair tax competition. The Parties reiterate their support for the OECD Base Erosion and Profit Shifting (BEPS) Action Plan and affirm their commitment to implementing the OECD minimum standards against BEPS. The Parties will promote good governance in tax matters, improve international cooperation in the area of taxation and facilitate the collection of tax revenues.

---

140 There is a growing literature discussing the impact of Brexit on tax matters, though the level of interest has decidedly diminished since 2021 and the realisation of the limited impact that Brexit has had in practice. This includes the following: Alice Pirlot, *Some observations on the tax-related provisions in the EU-UK Trade and Cooperation Agreement* [2021] British Tax Review 1-14. Francesco de Lillo, Teresa Morales and Oana Popa, *Brexit: Selected Tax Implication of the Trade and Cooperation Agreement* (2021) European Taxation 165-169. Belema Obuoforibo, *Brexit and the EU Tax Directives: The Emerging UK Tax Landscape* (2021) European Taxation 307-312. J. Korving and J. van der Have, *Brexit: The Direct and Indirect Effect of the EU-UK Trade and Cooperation Agreement* (2022) 50 Intertax 28-39. Christiana Panayi, *Brexit and Corporate Taxation: New Perspectives* (2022) EC Tax Review 50-61. Judith Freedman and Glen Loutzenhiser, *Tax policy in the UK post-Brexit* (2022) 38 Oxford Review of Economic Policy, pp. 108-204. Nicola Saccardo: *Tax Implications of Brexit* (Bloomsbury Publishing, 2021).

141 *Agreement on the withdrawal of the United Kingdom of Great Britain and Northern Ireland from the European Union and the European Atomic Energy Community* (OJ C 384I, 12.11.2019, p. 1–177).

142 *Trade and Cooperation Agreement between the European Union and the European Atomic Energy Community, of the one part, and the United Kingdom of Great Britain and Northern Ireland, of the other part (OJ L 149, 30.4.2021, p. 10–2539).*

ARTICLE 384 (Taxation standards)

1. A Party shall not weaken or reduce the level of protection provided for in its legislation at the end of the transition period below the level provided for by the standards and rules which have been agreed in the OECD at the end of the transition period, in relation to:
   a) the exchange of information, whether upon request, spontaneously or automatically, concerning financial accounts, cross-border tax rulings, country-by-country reports between tax administrations, and potential cross-border tax planning arrangements;
   b) rules on interest limitation, controlled foreign companies and hybrid mismatches.
2. A Party shall not weaken or reduce the level of protection provided for in its legislation at the end of the transition period in respect of public country-by-country reporting by credit institutions and investment firms, other than small and non-interconnected investment firms.

These provisions appear to reflect a compromise between a desire on the part of the EU that the UK post-Brexit did not adopt a policy of deliberate competition on tax matters (the "Singapore on Thames" syndrome), and a UK desire to resume autonomy over all tax matters. As can be seen, the provisions largely commit the UK to maintaining the existing OECD-based standards at the time of Brexit, including those derived from the base erosion and profit shifting (BEPS) project. There is no reason to believe that the UK would not have respected these standards irrespective of the provisions of the TCA.

The TCA also replaced the EU State Aid rules with a commitment to introduce a new system of subsidy control, and those provisions of the TCA contain some quite specific, tax-related provisions on subsidies.[143] The UK has now put in place a distinctly mild form of subsidy control which is unlikely to prohibit all but the most egregious forms of tax-related subsidies.[144]

The Labour Government that was elected in July 2025 had a manifesto commitment to "resetting" the UK's relationship with the European Union. While this does not (at present) involve any plan to seek to rejoin the Union, it does involve plans to reach agreement on alignment in several areas, most notably security, trade in goods and some immigration issues. At present, however, direct tax issues are not apparently on the agenda for any such discussions.[145]

143 TCA, Art 363 et seq.

144 On this, see Philip Baker, *Fiscal subsidy control in the post-Brexit era* [2021] British Tax Review 14-23 and 361-364. See also Nicholas Crafts, *Brexit and control of subsidies* (2022) 38 Oxford Review of Economic Policy 154-164.

145 For an excellent summary on this, see Stefano Fella, *Resetting the UK's relationship with the European Union* (House of Commons Library Research Briefing, 5 March 2025).

PART 2 INTEGRATION OF DIRECT TAXATION

CHAPTER 6

Conceptual Background of the CJEU Case Law in Direct Tax Matters

Peter Wattel and Dennis Weber[1]

Update and elaboration by Dennis Weber

6.1 The Basic Clash between (International) Tax Law and Internal Market Law

6.1.1 Basics of International Tax Law; Residence and Source Taxation

International tax law is basically concerned with four issues: taxation of foreign income of residents, taxation of domestic income of nonresidents, prevention of the double taxation ensuing from the parallel exercise of taxing jurisdiction by two States as regards the same cross-border tax base, and prevention of international tax avoidance. At its basis is a distinction between residents (taxable for their worldwide income or worldwide wealth) and nonresidents (taxable only for domestically-sourced income or for domestic wealth (real estate)). The national laws of a State on taxation of nonresidents and of foreign-source income ('national international tax law' or unilateral international tax law) and the tax treaties it concluded with other States (bilateral international tax law; 'international international tax law') are aimed at (i) exclusive attribution of tax base to one State, or (ii) dividing tax base between the two (exclusive distribution of *parts* of the tax base to both States), or (iii) shared competence (both States tax the same tax base, but one of them – or both of them in part – grant a reduction of the tax calculated in order to take away the ensuing double burden).

This is fundamentally different from the concept of an internal market (one single jurisdiction), in which no 'foreign' tax base would exist, nor any difference between residents and nonresidents. But as long as there are 27 separate sovereign, unharmonized and uncoordinated taxing jurisdictions, there is a need to divide or share tax base over these separate jurisdictions, which all have a legitimate interest in taxing income resulting from economic activity carried out within their territory, as well as taking into account, for ability-to-pay purposes, the worldwide income of their residents. Within the logic of an internal market, economic operators (taxpayers) should be free to choose their (taxing) jurisdiction, but as long as no primary or secondary EU legislation on personal

1 Peter Wattel is professor of EU Tax Law, ACTL, University of Amsterdam; Advocate-General, Supreme Court of the Netherlands; State Councillor extraordinary, Netherlands Council of State; Dennis Weber is professor European Corporate Tax Law at the ACTL of the University of Amsterdam and of counsel at Loyens & Loeff.

and substantive tax jurisdiction exists, Member States must define and divide their tax jurisdictions themselves, and protect it against base erosion and mismatches (fiscal incoherence, misallocation of taxing power, and tax avoidance). In an internal market, a change of jurisdiction or a division of activities over more than one jurisdiction should not matter for the economic operator as compared to staying or operating in just one single jurisdiction, but tax-wise, there is no greater difference, neither for the taxpayer nor for the Member States involved, than between being subject to tax and *not* being subject to tax in a jurisdiction, or between being able to set off profits and losses within one jurisdiction and not being able to do so because the profit is in one jurisdiction and the loss is in another.

One basic principle of international tax law – at the basis of the OECD Model Double Taxation Convention and Commentary[2] – is the distinction between residence taxation (home State taxation; unlimited tax liability; worldwide taxation) and source taxation (source State taxation; limited tax liability; territoriality taxation). Worldwide (total income) taxation is applied to residents, the idea being that all persons resident or established in a State, benefiting from economic, social, cultural and physical infrastructure and public expenditure of that State and usually deriving most of their income from that State, should contribute according to their ability to pay, including application of the progressive rate matching their total income. A second reason for worldwide taxation of residents is that there should be no 'residual' income escaping taxation altogether because no State considers it sourced within its territory: there should be one jurisdiction which taxes 'residual' income not clearly sourced in any specific (other) jurisdiction, otherwise tax advisors and taxpayers will organize their affairs such that they avoid as much as possible the sourcing rules of all States involved. A third reason for worldwide taxation of residents is the possibility to provide residents with the opportunity to (temporarily) set off foreign losses which cannot be set off abroad yet, in order to take into account the current and actual total ability to pay of residents with negative foreign-source income. Therefore, a resident's total income and, in the case of individuals, also his personal and family circumstances, should in principle be taken into account by his home State.

Limited taxation (only for domestic-source income), by contrast, is applied to nonresidents, the idea being that the country offering the economic opportunity to earn income should have the prior right to tax that income, wherever the beneficiary may reside, and whatever his personal circumstances may be (which are to be taken into account by the Home State anyway). Historically, there are also two practical reasons for limiting taxation of nonresidents to their domestically sourced income: (i) the domestic source of income is the only object available for the source State to recover tax payable by nonresidents, as no residence State will allow extraterritorial enforcement – by attachment – on its territory of any foreign tax claims, and (ii) the source State cannot easily gather the information necessary for assessing nonresidents on their worldwide income.[3] Within the Union, however, these historical reasons for limited tax liability of nonresidents have little significance any more, due to the proliferation of international and especially EU

2 Model Double Taxation Convention on Income and on Capital, with Commentaries to the Articles, OECD, Paris, 1977, revised in 1992 and in loose-leaf format since. A condensed version is also available from the OECD.

3 See Philip Baker: 'Changing the Norm on Cross-Border Enforcement of Tax Debts,' 30 *Intertax* 6-7 (2002), p. 216-218.

instruments for mutual administrative assistance in the assessment and the recovery of tax claims (see Chapters27 to 31), providing for ever more automatic exchange of tax information and even for the presence of officials of the requesting State during tax audits in the requested State, as well as for conservatory and execution measures on behalf of the requesting State.

Residence taxation thus focuses on the person of the taxpayer and his overall ability to pay, whereas source taxation focuses on the fact that income was generated within a certain territory.[4] In both approaches the tax must be connected to a person, the taxpayer. If both approaches are applied simultaneously, then obviously foreign-source income is taxed twice in the hands of the same person (international double taxation). Established international tax law therefore distinguishes between foreign-source income and domestic-source income. In general, it allocates the prior right to tax income sourced within a jurisdiction to that jurisdiction. If the Home State of the taxpayer chooses to tax that income as well (worldwide taxation), then regular international tax law requires the home State to provide relief to eliminate double taxation on the foreign-source income, either unilaterally or on the basis of a bilateral tax treaty, either exempting the foreign-source income or crediting the foreign tax against the domestic tax on the worldwide income (see Section 8.2).

6.1.2 Opposing Points of Departure of International Tax Law and Internal Market Law

The OECD Model Double Taxation Convention, which is widely used by EU Member States and (other) OECD Member countries, although containing a provision prohibiting discrimination based on the nationality of the taxpayer or of its shareholders (Art. 24), clearly does not consider residents and nonresidents to be in the same position for tax purposes. Article 24(1) of the OECD Model reads (our italics):

> 'Nationals of a Contracting State shall not be subjected in the other Contracting State to any taxation or any requirement connected therewith, which is other or more burdensome than the taxation and connected requirements to which nationals of that other State in the same circumstances, *in particular with respect to residence*, are or may be subjected. (....)'

It follows that regular international tax law prohibits only *direct* discrimination based on nationality, not discrimination on the basis of residence; on the contrary: residents and nonresidents are explicitly viewed as not comparable.

EU law, by contrast, regards different treatment of nonresidents in principle as a prohibited discrimination (denial of national treatment) because different tax treatment of the cross-border situation as compared to the similar domestic situation is in principle incompatible with the free movement of persons.

Consequently, the basic clash is that (international) tax law regards as fundamentally different a taxpayer or (a source of) income which *stays* within the same taxing jurisdiction and a taxpayer or (a source of) income which *leaves* a taxing jurisdiction, or which

4 See, for arguments to replace the residence principle as outdated for the source principle in international tax law: Eric Kemmeren: 'Principle of Origin in Tax Conventions; A Rethinking of Models,' dissertation, University of Tilburg, the Netherlands, 2001.

divides itself *up* over two jurisdictions. By contrast, EU law regards these positions as fundamentally comparable, as within an internal market it should make no difference in (tax) treatment of the economic operator *where* in the internal market he invests, trades, accepts a job or provides services. If economic operators could be taxed differently solely because they operate in or relocate to other Member States, then the free movement rights (market access and market equality principles) would be meaningless. International tax law views cross-border positions as quite incomparable to purely domestic positions because they entail a loss or a conflict of taxing power and the risk of BEPS (base erosion and profit shifting), whereas internal market thinking views them as comparable as long as income is taxed *some*where in the internal market and expenses and losses are deductible *some*where in the internal market. In the absence of significant harmonisation of direct taxation, the result is a continuous stream of case by case negative integration in the form of hundreds of CJEU judgments arbitrating the ensuing balancing of the Union interest of free movement and the Member States' sovereign interest of protecting the integrity of their tax bases.

6.2 The Court Accepts All Tax Connecting Factors and All Methods for Double Tax Relief

As explained in section 3.2.7, EU law contains no legal basis for choosing connecting factors for defining taxing jurisdiction. Therefore, it is impossible to decide on the basis of EU law whether the source State, the residence State or the nationality State has the prior right to tax the income of a person. Because that is impossible, it is equally impossible to designate the State which is responsible for taking away any double taxation resulting from the overlap between the assumption of taxing power by two member States, such as the double taxation resulting from the exercise in parallel of the source principle by the source State and the residence principle by the residence State. From especially the *Damseaux* and *Block* cases, both quoted in Section 8.1.2, it follows clearly that the Court leaves prevention of double taxation, although a major impediment to free movement, to the Member States.

The Court therefore accepts that tax impediments to free movement which result from differences or overlap in the assertion of taxing power by two States are outside the scope of the Treaty freedoms, as they are not a result of any discrimination by one of the two States involved (they are not a one-country problem), but result from the interaction of two *different* tax systems (disparities; see section 3.2.7.2), or from the parallel application of two *identical* systems, which both, however, choose *another* connecting factor for residents (worldwide income) than for nonresidents (source) (see section 3.2.7.3: dislocations, or 'quasi-restrictions', or 'exercise in parallel of taxing power'). These phenomena are two-country problems and cannot be remedied by the Court for lack of a legal basis to choose which of the two States is the culprit. That choice is a political one, not to be made by a Court, but by chosen representatives of taxpayers. The Court is very cautious in that respect. In *Sauvage*[5] the Court reiterated that the use of different connecting factors in a tax treaty does not constitute a prohibited discrimination against the movement of workers.

5 Case C-602/17 (*Sauvage*), EU:C:2018:856.

The Court could have gone further than it did, by following the US Supreme Court's case law based on the (dormant) interstate commerce clause in the US Constitution (which represents a comparable concept as the EU free movement rights). In *Comptroller v Wynne*,[6] the US Supreme Court used that clause to require the US States to be 'internally consistent', i.e. to apply the same system as a *residence* State as in their capacity as a *source* State and *vice versa*. The US Supreme Court left the US States free to apply any tax connecting factor they might see fit, but they should apply it also in the inverse situation: if they consider source taxation to take priority over home State taxation of nonresidents' income, then they should recognise other States' source taxation taking priority over their residence taxation and should therefore credit source tax on out-of-State income of their residents. If, on the other hand, they consider residence to be the tax connecting factor taking precedence over source, then they should refrain from taxing domestic-source income of nonresidents. The CJEU, however, has a different view on nondiscrimination (see Section 3.2.7). It sees no legal basis for an 'internal consistency'-approach in the Union Treaties; it allows Member States to apply, at the same time, worldwide taxation to residents and source taxation to nonresidents, probably reasoning that (i) source taxation is not less favourable than worldwide taxation (which is not always true, given that home State income may be negative) and (ii) the Union Treaties show no clue as to how to choose for either of these (or other) direct tax connecting factors.[7]

Because of the absence of EU law guidance, all currently used connecting factors for delineating taxing jurisdiction are compatible with EU law. *Worldwide* taxation by the residence State was explicitly accepted by the Court in, *e.g.*, *CIBA*:[8]

> '37. (...), it must be recalled that the Member State in which the seat of the undertaking is located enjoys, in the absence of a double taxation convention, the right to tax that undertaking overall (see, to that effect, Case C-279/93 *Schumacker* (...), paragraph 32, and Case C-414/06 *Lidl Belgium* (...), paragraph 33).'

Source State taxation (limited liability, only for domestic-source income) was explicitly accorded in, *e.g.*, the *SGI* Case:[9]

> '60. (....) the right of a Member State to exercise its tax jurisdiction in relation to activities carried out in its territory (see, (...), *Marks & Spencer*, paragraph 46; Case C-347/04 *Rewe Zentralfinanz* (...), paragraph 42; *Oy AA*, paragraph 54; and *Aberdeen Property Fininvest Alpha*, paragraph 66).'

The Court accepted *nationality* taxation, independent of source or residence, in *Van Hilten-Van der Heijden*:[10]

6 US Supreme Court, *Comptroller (Maryland) v. Wynne*, 18 May 2015, *docket no.* 13-485.

7 See, for an early plea for internal consistency, Ruth Mason, 'Made in America for European Tax: the Internal Consistency Test', 5 Boston College law Review XLIX (November 2008), p. 1277-1326; and for a comparison of the judicial policies as regards double taxation of the USSC, the Swiss federal court and the CJEU:Anne van de Vijver, 'International Double Taxation in the European Union: Comparative Guidelines from Switzerland and the United States', EC Tax Review 2017/1, p. 10-22.

8 Case C-96/08, *CIBA*, EU:C:2010:185, [2010] ECR I-2911, point 37.

9 Case C-311/08, *Société de gestion industrielle*, EU:C:2010:26, [2010] ECR I-487.

10 Case C-513/03, *Van Hilten-van der Heijden*, EU:C:2006:131, [2006] ECR I-1957.

'45. National legislation (...), which provides that the estate of a national of a Member State who dies within 10 years of ceasing to reside in that Member State is to be taxed as if that national had continued to reside in that Member State, while providing for relief in respect of the taxes levied in the State to which the deceased transferred his residence, does not constitute a restriction on the movement of capital.'

And it accepted *territoriality* taxation – meaning that the *home* State applies the source principle also to its *residents* – in *Lidl Belgium*,[11] concerning the German tax treaty system of *base* exemption, i.e. exclusion from the German tax base of both profits and losses of foreign permanent establishments of German resident companies:

'31. (...), it should be noted that the preservation of the allocation of the power to impose taxes between Member States may make it necessary to apply to the economic activities of companies established in one of those States only the tax rules of that State in respect of both profits and losses (see Marks & Spencer, paragraph 45, and Case C-231/05 Oy AA [2007] ECR I-6373, paragraph 54).'

As EU law does not clear up which of the two States exercising overlapping taxing jurisdiction should prevent possibly ensuing double taxation, the Court also accepts all currently used methods for the elimination or mitigation of international double taxation, especially both exemption and credit, and both base exemption and tax exemption (exemption with progression), as well as both direct credit (juridical double taxation) and indirect credit (economic double taxation). Logically, it even accepts the absence of double tax relief, provided neither State discriminates between cross-border and purely internal situations. See for elaboration and authority Section 8.2, especially 8.2.5.

6.3 Territoriality Taxation or EU-Wide Taxation

At the outset, it should be observed that there may be a mix-up of 'territoriality' concepts in the Court's case law. *Futura Participations SA*[12] clearly suggests that it understands 'the fiscal principle of territoriality,' not as tax lawyers understand it (i.e. as excluding extraterritorial income: base exemption of foreign-source income of residents, i.e. as the *opposite* of worldwide or residence taxation of residents), but as the (non-tax) international public law principle of 'territoriality', i.e. as worldwide jurisdiction in respect of residents and territorial jurisdiction in respect of non-residents. Clearly, the Court's advocate-general Bobek understands the territoriality principle as applied by the Court in the latter sense: as worldwide taxation of residents and source taxation of non-residents[13] (see the quotation in Section 7.8.2). However, in other case law, the Court seems to understand 'territoriality' in the fiscal meaning of the term (territoriality taxation: source taxation), as it seems to equate the principle of territoriality with the notion that a Member State cannot be denied the right to tax economic activities carried out within its territory, i.e. with the need to safeguard a balanced allocation of taxing rights (see Section 7.8.3). We use the term 'territoriality (taxation)' only as meaning taxation of domestically sourced

11 Case C-414/06, *Lidl Belgium*, EU:C:2008:278, [2008] ECR I-3601.

12 Case C-250/95, *Futura Participations SA*, EU:C:1997:239.

13 Opinion of 14 December 2017 in Case C-382/16, *Hornbach-Baumarkt AG*, EU:C:2017:974.

income, i.e. as excluding extraterritorial income from the tax base, irrespective of whether the taxpayer is resident or nonresident.

From an EU law perspective, a very basic question arises as regards the usual worldwide taxation of residents and subsequent double taxation relief to give priority to source State taxation: why does the home State tax foreign-source income at all? What business does it have taxing income arising outside its jurisdiction? Why does it first assume extraterritorial taxing jurisdiction and subsequently step back by undoing the ensuing double taxation in favour of the source jurisdiction? Why does it not simply refrain from taxing the foreign-source income in the first place, thus eliminating the need for complex mechanisms of international double taxation relief? Although the residence State is not discriminating against its residents earning foreign-source income if it taxes their total income (as it does the same with residents not earning foreign-source income), it does dissuade them from earning foreign-source income, even if it avoids international double taxation, as it exposes its residents at least temporarily to double taxation and at any rate to administrative misery necessary to undo it. One could argue that this amounts to a restriction of the free movement of persons, requiring justification, as the same administrative burden and remaining risk of double taxation does not occur in comparable internal situations.[14] Is there such justification? The reason why a home State applies worldwide taxation (with relief) to its residents is twofold: first, if it adheres to capital export neutrality (see Section 8.2.2), it needs to ensure that (at least) the home State level of taxation is reached on the foreign-source income. Therefore, it needs to include all, also foreign-source income of its residents in its tax base, and subsequently give credit for possible foreign tax paid. Second, as observed in Section 6.1.1 above, a home State in principle wants to tax the total ability to pay of its residents. Therefore, home States first assume total, also extraterritorial jurisdiction, and subsequently eliminate from the resulting tax debt the tax attributable to foreign-source income (exemption system) or the tax paid abroad (credit system) (see Section 8.2).

Since companies do not have personal circumstances influencing their ability to pay, and corporate income tax rates tend to be flat rather than progressive, it would seem that under exemption systems this worldwide approach is pointless for companies, and strict territoriality would be more appropriate or in any case much simpler. Even for rate progression purposes in the individual income tax there is no need for worldwide taxation under an exemption system: the home State could exempt the foreign-source income (eliminate it from its tax base), but apply to the remainder of the income the tax rate which corresponds with the worldwide income. The source country could do the same, for that matter. Thus, there seems to be no justification for the cumbersome consequences of worldwide taxation, except for ensuring capital export neutrality (credit system). Then why do almost all States, including exemption States, apply worldwide taxation? The answer lies in the fact that the foreign-source income may be negative (foreign losses). As observed, worldwide taxation by the home State ensures for both individuals and undertakings that foreign losses are (temporarily) 'imported' and deducted currently from positive domestic income, thus reducing the overall tax burden to correspond to the

14 See Case C-118/96, *Jessica Safir*, EU:C:1998:170, [1998] ECR I-1897: even making the cross-border situation administratively more burdensome than the internal situation is a dissuasion requiring justification.

real overall income in that year. As shown in Sections 3.2.7.3 (ii) and 10.2, the import of foreign losses is temporary: if in subsequent years positive income arises in the foreign jurisdiction, no prevention of double taxation will be extended by the home State until the loss deducted in previous years has been recaptured. That is reasonable, as the foreign loss will be offset against the future profits in the foreign jurisdiction, thus reducing tax exposure there. Therefore, worldwide taxation provides current (but temporary) relief for foreign losses which temporarily cannot be offset in their source jurisdiction, where they belong and will be returned as soon as positive income arises there. If no positive income will ever arise there any more (disillusioned, our taxpayer closes his foreign shop), the home State must decide whether it will accept the loss deduction permanently. Some States do, and therefore do not recapture the previous loss deduction, reasoning that the taxpayer should be able to deduct his losses *some*where, if not in the correct jurisdiction, then in his home jurisdiction, where he should be taxed in accordance with his total ability to pay. Other States reinstate previously deducted foreign losses into the taxable base after five years or upon liquidation of the foreign branch, reasoning that if the foreign activities still yield no profits after so many years, or are terminated, they apparently are not viable, which is not attributable to the home State jurisdiction, but to the foreign jurisdiction where the loss was made.

The conclusion is that although worldwide taxation with relief to prevent double taxation, and certainly capital export neutrality (the credit system), at first sight looks imperialistic and burdening the cross-border position with red tape and risks of remaining double taxation, it has one very important justifying merit serving the objectives of the internal market: horizontal cross-border loss relief. Base exemption (territoriality) would rid us of double taxation and the intricate mechanics to eliminate it, but the tax base compartmentalization problems described in section 3.2.7.3(ii) would be exacerbated, and capital export neutrality (credit) would become impossible and would be replaced by capital import neutrality (exemption) (from an internal market point of view, such replacement might be applauded, however). Base exemption for both residents and nonresidents (territoriality taxation) is a simple and neutral system,[15] removing both international tax law inconsistencies and discrimination against non-residents. Precisely because it is based on territoriality, however, it is also an internal market fragmentizer. The Court has accepted the territoriality (base exemption) system for residents with foreign source income, first in *Lidl Belgium*,[16] as *justified* (by the need for of a balanced allocation of taxing rights), and subsequently, in *Timac Agro*,[17] even as *nondiscriminatory* (and therefore not even needing any justification), as under a base exemption system, foreign and domestic branches are not objectively comparable, the latter being subject to tax and the former not being subject to tax. This, in contrast to an exemption with progression system, under which foreign and domestic branches *are* considered comparable, as both are subject to tax, and under which system recapture of previously deducted foreign branch losses is *justified* to safeguard a balanced allocation of taxing rights). In *Timac Agro* both systems were at issue, as Germany had changed systems during the

15 See Peter J. Wattel. 'Corporate Tax Jurisdiction in the EU with Respect to Branches and Subsidiaries; Dislocation Distinguished from Discrimination and Disparity; A Plea for Territoriality,' *EC Tax Review* 2003/4, p. 194-202.

16 Case C-414/06, *Lidl Belgium*, EU:C:2008:278, [2008] ECR I-3601.

17 Case C-388/14, *Timac Agro Deutschland GmbH*, EU:C:2015:829.

period litigated. The Court accepted both systems, territoriality (base exemption) as *nondiscriminatory*, and worldwide taxation combined with exemption with progression as (in itself discriminatory, but) *justified* (*italics* added):

> "27. As regards comparability of the situations, it must be pointed out that, in principle, permanent establishments situated in a Member State other than the Member State concerned are not in a situation comparable to that of resident permanent establishments in relation to measures laid down by that Member State in order to prevent or mitigate the double taxation of a resident company's profits ((...) *Nordea Bank Danmark*, C-48/13, EU:C:2014:2087, paragraph 24).
> 28. However, *by permitting the deduction of losses incurred by a permanent establishment situated in Austria*, (...) Germany granted a tax advantage to the resident company to which that permanent establishment belonged, in the same way as if that permanent establishment had been situated in Germany, and, therefore, *equated* it with a resident permanent establishment so far as concerns the deduction of losses (see, to that effect, (...) *Krankenheim Ruhesitz* (...), C-157/07, EU:C:2008:588, paragraph 35, and *Nordea Bank Danmark*, C-48/13, EU:C:2014:2087, paragraph 24). In those circumstances, the situation of a resident company with a permanent establishment situated in Austria is accordingly *comparable to* that of *a resident* company with a permanent establishment situated in Germany.
> (...).
> 65. In the present case, it must be held that, since (...) Germany does *not* exercise any tax powers over the profits of such a permanent establishment, the deduction of its losses no longer being permitted in Germany, the situation of a permanent establishment situated in Austria is *not comparable* to that of a permanent establishment situated in Germany in relation to measures laid down by (...) Germany in order to prevent or mitigate the double taxation of a resident company's profits (see, to that effect, (...) *Nordea Bank Danmark*, C-48/13, EU: C:2014:2087, paragraph 24 and the case-law cited).

Thus, the Court accepts territorial compartmentalization of the tax base, both in the source State (taxing only sourced income) and in the State of residence (taxing only domestic income: base exemption). This makes sense, as the Court is clearly not competent to require Member States to extend their taxing jurisdiction outside their territory if they have symmetrically chosen not to assert any extraterritorial taxing power.[18]

However, *if* a residence State applies worldwide taxation to its residents (and exemption with progression to prevent double taxation), we believe that also non-residents may require worldwide taxation with the same prevention if that is in their interest. It is in their interest where they have a negative income at home and a positive income abroad. Source taxation abroad would not take into account the home State loss; worldwide taxation in the foreign source jurisdiction, by contrast, would enable the non-resident, like a resident in that State, to set off out-of-State losses there against positive income. Worldwide (EU-wide) taxation of non-residents would also ensure a correct division of personal tax allowances between the residence State and the source State, which would

18 Sometimes, nevertheless, the Court gets carried away and forgets it is not competent to delineate Member States' assertion of taxing power, most notably in cases such as Case C-385/00, *De Groot*, EU:C:2002:750, [2002] ECR I-11819, Case C-293/06, *Deutsche Shell*, EU:C:2008:129, Case C-446/03, *Marks & Spencer II*, EU:C:2005:763, [2005] ECR I-10837 and Case C-527/06, *Renneberg*, EU:C:2008:566.

both be responsible in proportion to the part of the income to which they extend their taxing power (see Sections 3.2.7.3(ii) and (v), and 13.4). It would also (but this would often not benefit the non-resident[19]) ensure correct rate progression also on the foreign-source part of the income (see Sections 3.2.7.3(ii) and (v) and 13.4).

Although the EU Treaties offer no legal basis for a choice between EU-wide taxation and territoriality taxation, nor any legal basis for prevention of international double taxation, they do seem to require non-residents, if they so desire, to be treated as residents. The free movement of persons indisputably confers upon employees and undertakings the right to national treatment in the source State. Therefore, we believe they can rely – if that is in their interest – on the Articles 45, 49 and 54 TFEU (and employees, moreover, on Article 7(2) of EU Regulation 492/2011 on freedom of movement for workers,[20] explicitly entitling non-national workers to the same tax benefits as nationals) to require the source State to tax them on the same footing as residents. Therefore, if a State taxes its residents on a worldwide basis, it should in our view tax non-residents on an EU-wide basis where they request it to do so. Where, by contrast, the source State applies a territoriality system also for its own residents, obviously a non-resident cannot require EU-wide taxation.

In *Renneberg*,[21] the Court came close to forcing the source State to apply EU-wide taxation to non-residents. It required the source State (the employment State) to accept a *foreign* loss from *foreign* real estate of a *non*resident employee. It did not so so, however, on any basis of EU-wide taxation of non-residents, but on the basis of an abundance of fallacies (see our discussion of the *Renneberg* case in section 3.2.7.3(iv)). *Renneberg* cannot be aligned with either (i) the Court's acceptance of Member States' divergent taxation of residents and nonresidents (the former on a worldwide basis and the latter on a source basis), and (ii) its acceptance of the territoriality principle as regards foreign losses in *Lidl Belgium* and *Timac Agro*.

Difficult to understand as well is the Court's rejection, in *Gielen*,[22] of a national system in which nonresident taxpayers are entirely free to choose between resident (worldwide) taxation and nonresident (source) taxation, whichever would be more advantageous to them. Possibly, the Court reasoned that making available such a choice cannot save the source State from disqualification of its source taxation system if that source taxation system in itself is discriminatory. The result was, however, that nonresidents could cherry-pick whatever they liked from the residence taxation system, while at the same time avoiding the parts of residence taxation they did not like, such as, notably, the rate progression residents suffered. This clearly amounts to a discrimination against residents, who could not in any way cherry-pick from any system and who could not even choose between two systems without cherry-picking from them. The Court seems to have realised and repaired its mistake in the later *Hirvonen* Case,[23] distinguishing a similar Swedish dual system from the Netherlands dual system in *Gielen*, but we fail to see the relevant difference in this respect between the two national systems.

19 Except where his home State income is negative. In that case, worldwide-based rate progression in the source State will then have a *degressive* rate effect.

20 Regulation (EU) No 492/2011 of the European Parliament and of the Council of 5 April 2011 on freedom of movement for workers within the Union, O.J. 2011 L 141, p. 1.

21 Case C-527/06, *Renneberg*, EU:C:2008:566, [2008] ECR I-7735.

22 Case C-440/08, *Gielen*, EU:C:2010:148, [2010] ECR I-2323.

23 Case C-632/13, *Hirvonen*, EU:C:2015:765.

6.4 Basic Notions in the Court's Direct Tax Case Law

6.4.1 'Discrimination', not Mere 'Restriction'; Nondiscriminatory 'Obstacles', 'Parallel Exercise' and Disparities are Outside Free Movement Scrutiny

Section 3.2.7 explained and discussed the Court's conceptual framework for approaching fiscal impediments to free movement. As explained there, the Court now seems to follow a (de facto) *discrimination*-based approach of assessing the internal market compatibility of national tax measures, rather than the traditional, much wider *obstacle*-(restriction-) based approach followed in other areas, probably because *every* tax is an obstacle to the economic activity it taxes, and the Court would have to test *every* national tax measure on suitability, reasonableness and proportionality if it were to stick to a prohibition of even nondiscriminatory obstacles to free movement also in tax matters. A restriction approach in tax matters could also make the responsibility for having to remedy tax obstacles in cross-border cases (as compared to domestic cases) dependent on which of the two States' tax systems involved would happen to be challenged first before the Court.

To apply an obstacle-based approach in taxation would, therefore, entail an unacceptable competence creep in violation of both the attribution and the subsidiarity principle, unacceptable legal uncertainty, and arbitrary budget shifts between Member States. In tax matters, the Court in general correctly looks for unjustifiable inequality, not just hindrances, before finding national tax rules to fall foul of the TFEU free movement rights[24] and therefore to require justification by a mandatory requirement of public interest.

Only in *exceptional* situations the Court applies in tax matters the obstacle case law. For example, when taxes actually restrict access to the market and thus in fact constitute a prohibition to be active in the market. An example is Berlington[25], where there was a tax that was so high that no profit could be made. Such a high tax, although not discriminatory, is a restriction of the freedoms.

For car taxation, the Court already in 2004 pointed out, in *Weigel*,[26] that for the Treaty freedoms to engage, the tax legislation of one Member State must cause some sort of disadvantage as compared to the domestic situation in that State (a discrimination therefore), and that a mere 'negative bearing' on free movement is not enough in tax matters to engage free movement rights:

> "53. A rule such as that at issue in the main proceedings [car taxation upon entering the country; authors] applies without regard to the nationality of the worker concerned to all those who register a car in Austria and, accordingly, it is applicable without distinction.
> 54. It is true that it is likely to have a negative bearing on the decision of migrant workers to exercise their right to freedom of movement.

---

24 See also, on the issue of mere obstacles (market access) and discriminatory obstacles: Gareth Davies, 'Between market access and discrimination: free movement as a right to fair conditions of competition,' in: Panos Koutrakos, Jukka Snell (ed.), *Research Handbook on the Law of the EU's Internal Market*, Edward Elgar Publishing, 2017, p. 13-28 (at 20 for tax cases).

25 Case C-98/14 (Berlington), EU:C:2015:386.

26 Case C-387/01, *Weigel*, EU:C:2004:256.

> 55. However, the Treaty offers no guarantee to a worker that transferring his activities to a Member State other than the one in which he previously resided will be neutral as regards taxation. (...), in principle, any disadvantage, by comparison with the situation in which the worker pursued his activities prior to the transfer, is not contrary to Article 39 EC if that legislation [of Austria; authors] does not place that worker at a disadvantage as compared with those who were already subject to it (...)."

Partly on the basis of this basic limitation to the question of whether there is a (one-country) *inequality* (discrimination), instead of a further-reaching scrutiny of whether there is an *obstacle*, however neutral, the Court developed three further basic notions:

(i) Double taxation ensuing from nondiscriminatory 'exercise in parallel' of taxing jurisdiction cannot be remedied by relying on free movement rights. Despite being a formidable obstacle to free movement, such double burden is outside the Court's scrutiny, provided that the exercise of taxing power by both States involved is nondiscriminatory. We observe that this finding confirms that in tax matters, the Court avoids an 'obstacle'-based approach (which, indeed, would also catch *non*discriminatory hindrances of free movement). See, a.o., the *Damseaux* Case[27] (emphasis added):

> '27. (...) the disadvantages which could arise from the parallel exercise of tax competences by different Member States, *to the extent that such an exercise is not discriminatory*, do not constitute restrictions prohibited by the EC Treaty (....).
> (...)
> 30. In the absence of any unifying or harmonising Community measures, Member States retain the power to define, by treaty or unilaterally, the criteria for allocating their powers of taxation, particularly with a view to eliminating double taxation (...). It is for the Member States to take the measures necessary to prevent situations of double taxation by applying, in particular, the criteria followed in international tax practice (...).'

(ii) The free movement rights do not guarantee that moving or investing abroad will have no disadvantageous tax effects, as these may be caused by differences or interactions between two legal systems, none of which can be held responsible on its own. In respect of undertakings, the Court pointed this out in *Krankenheim* Ruhesitz, quoted sub (iii) below, concerning the question of whether the head office State may be required to allow deduction of a foreign branch loss not eligible for set-off in the branch State. For individual income taxation, the *Schempp* Case,[28] concerning an ex-husband whose alimony payments stopped being deductible because his ex-wife moved from Germany (alimony payments deductible and taxable) to Austria (alimony payments nondeductible and exempt), contains the same message: Member States cannot be required to take away disadvantageous effects of disparities between the tax systems of the Member States:

> '45. (...) the Treaty offers no guarantee to a citizen of the Union that transferring his activities to a Member State other than that in which he previously resided will be neutral as regards taxation. Given the disparities in the tax legislation of the Member States, such

27 Case C-128/08, *Damseaux*, EU:C:2009:471, [2009] ECR I-6823.
28 Case C-403/03, *Schempp*, EU:C:2005:446, [2005] ECR I-6421.

> a transfer may be to the citizen's advantage in terms of indirect taxation or not, according to circumstances (...).'

(iii) (Therefore) Member States are under no obligation to adapt their systems so as to take away disadvantages caused by dislocations (parallel exercise; see (i) above) and disparities (see (ii) above). In the absence of secondary EU law on the issue, there is no obligation to coordinate tax systems. In *Krankenheim Ruhesitz*,[29] the Court considered:

> '49. (...) a Member State cannot be required to take account, for the purposes of applying its tax law, of the possible negative results arising from particularities of legislation of another Member State applicable to a permanent establishment situated in the territory of the said State (...).
> 50. (...) freedom of establishment cannot be understood as meaning that a Member State is required to draw up its tax rules on the basis of those in another Member State in order to ensure, in all circumstances, taxation which removes any disparities arising from national tax rules, given that the decisions made by a company as to the establishment of commercial structures abroad may be to the company's advantage or not, according to circumstances (...).'

At the end of the day, all of these findings in our view boil down to one basic notion, which deviates from general internal market law[30] in at least one important respect:

In (unharmonised) tax matters, not only (a) disparities, but also (b) nondiscriminatory parallel exercise of taxing power and (c) (all other) nondiscriminatory obstacles to free movement are in principle outside the scope of the TFEU's free movement rights and therefore outside the Court's scrutiny.

We emphasize that 'disparities' and 'parallel exercise' are not identical. The fact that Member States apply worldwide taxation to residents and territorial taxation to nonresidents is not a disparity (almost all Member States apply that same system to a certain extent), but still the double burden resulting from the parallel taxation of the cross-border income by both the residence State and the source State cannot be remedied by the free movement rights if the former does not distinguish between domestic-source and foreign-source income, and the latter does not distinguish between nonresidents and residents.

Having said all of the above, and minded to say some more below, we must warn the reader that the above (and what follows) contains our structuring and explanation of the Court's case law and of the principles we discern therein, but that the Court itself "repeats its principles rather than structuring and explaining them".[31] As one commentator observed: "not explaining the law has the advantage of maintaining the importance of the Court".[32] Advocate-general Bobek has invited the Court in the pending *Hornbach* case,[33]

29 Case C-157/07, *Krankenheim Ruhesitz am Wannsee-Seniorenheimstatt GmbH*, EU:C:2008:588.
30 See Gareth Davies, 'Between market access and discrimination: free movement as a right to fair conditions of competition,' in: Panos Koutrakos, Jukka Snell (ed.), *Research Handbook on the Law of the EU's Internal Market*, Edward Elgar Publishing, 2017, p. 13-28.
31 Davies, o.c., at 28.
32 Davies, o.c., at 27.
33 Opinion of 14 December 2017 in Case C-382/16, *Hornbach-Baumarkt AG*, EU:C:2017:974.

"to clearly articulate which is the approach to freedom of establishment in the area of direct taxation. (...), it ought to be, from my point of view, the discrimination approach."

6.4.2 *Comparability (Subject-to-Tax) and Justifiability (Tax Base Integrity); Assertion and Exercise of Taxing Power*

Taking non-discrimination (rather than non-restriction) as the point of departure, the Court's test of compatibility of national direct tax measures with EU free movement rights comes down then to the following rule of reason test (see for extensive discussion section 3.2.2):

(1a) Does the national tax measure *prima facie* or *de facto* distinguish between cross-border investment/work/establishment and comparable domestic investment/establishment/work?

(1b) Is there an *objective difference* between the cross-border and the internal case which explains the different tax treatment of the cross-border case? Are the two positions still comparable viewed in the light of object and purpose of the impugned tax measure?

(2) is there a mandatory requirement of public interest (a *legitimate aim*) justifying the discriminatory measure, *e.g.* curbing abuse, safeguarding tax base integrity, or ensuring effective fiscal supervision? If so:

(3) Are the restrictive effects of the discriminatory, but justifiable tax measure *proportionate* to its legitimate aim?

As observed in Sections 3.2.2 and 3.2.7.1, the Court wanders between test 1b and test 2,[34] sometimes presenting incomparability as a justification, possibly triggered by its 'obstacle'-reflex in non-tax matters. In an obstacle-based approach, comparability of cross-border and domestic situations is irrelevant, as in such an approach, *all* restrictions, whether discriminatory or not, are in principle prohibited unless they can be justified. Although the Court is far from clear on this issue, we observe that in the end it may not make much difference, because, as advocate-general Bobek pointed out in the pending *Hornbach* case,[35] if one embraces the restriction approach rather than the discrimination approach (therefore skipping comparibility analysis), then the same argument and the same discussion are nonetheless carried out at the justification stage instead of at the comparability stage. Indeed, the Court sometimes considers Member States' tax measures as discriminatory but nonetheless justified because in the end, the cross-border and the domestic position are ..... not comparable.[36] *De facto*, in these cases the comparibility test is carried out at the justification stage and we are therefore in reality looking at a discrimination approach in the guise of a justification analysis.

---

34 Luc de Broe and Niels Bammens point out, e.g., that in *Truck Center* the Court transposed administrative nuisance from the justification test to the comparability test: 'Truck Center (etc.): A Critical Look (etc.)' *EC Tax Review* 2009/3, at 132-133.

35 Opinion of 14 December 2017 in Case C-382/16, *Hornbach-Baumarkt AG*, EU:C:2017:974.

36 E.g. in Case C-446/03, *Marks & Spencer II*, EU:C:2005:763, [2005] ECR I-10837, Case C-231/05, *Oy AA*, EU:C:2007:439, and Case C-157/07, *Krankenheim Ruhesitz*, EU:C:2008:588.

Ostensibly, there is one major difference, however: if there is no discrimination, then in a discrimination approach the analysis stops there: no discrimination, no need for any justification of such non-existent discrimination, let alone for any proportionality assessment. By contrast, if a discrimination can be discerned or asserted, then the Member State involved is impelled to justify its measure. Even if the Court is going to accept the justification(s) advanced, it has brought itself in a position where it can assess the proportionality of the measure in the light of its aim *and* of the interests of free movement. In a discrimination approach, the finding of a discrimination is the gateway to a proportionality assessment. If a wish to keep a proportionality check on national tax measures explains the Court's confusing of comparability and justifiability, then we believe the confusion may be ended, as in our view, a proportionality test is also possible in a discrimination approach: cross-border cases may only be taxed differently *to the extent* that they are different from purely domestic cases in the light of the goals of both national tax law and the internal market.

- Comparability

First, therefore, a comparability standard is needed to decide whether the two positions are comparable from the point of view of the object and purpose of the impugned national tax measure. As observed, for that the Court first looks (test 1a) for a *prima facie* difference, which is usually present but does not need to be discriminatory because, as the Court observed itself, residents and nonresidents are not, as a rule comparable[37] (in the sense of test 1b: object and purpose). Often, in our view, the Court makes mistakes in its comparability analysis. For instance, in *X Holding*,[38] concerning a Netherlands parent company wishing to include a non-subject, non-resident subsidiary in the Netherlands group taxation scheme, the Court considered parent companies of non-subject nonresident subsidiaries comparable to parents of subject-to-tax resident subsidiaries, because they too 'seek to benefit from the advantages of the scheme.' Even *prima facie*, we do not consider this comparison to make sense. The mere wish to benefit from a tax measure obviously does not make a non-addressee of that measure comparable to the addressees of that measure. As object and purpose of the measure are considered to be decisive (test 1b; see point 22 of *X Holding*), one would expect the Court to consider that aim, but the Court did not relate what it regarded as the aim of the group taxation scheme. That aim was, clearly, taxing a group of companies as one single taxpayer *to the extent they are subject to tax in the same taxing jurisdiction*. This shows (i) how important it is to choose the correct comparator, and (ii) the fundamental difference between international-tax thinking and internal-market thinking: for taxation purposes, a nonresident subsidiary *not* subject to tax in the parent company State is manifestly and fundamentally incomparable to a subsidiary – wherever resident – which *is* subject to tax in the parent State (either for its residence or for a permanent establishment there), as the former is completely outside the taxing jurisdiction of the parent company State (meaning that no subsidiary results whatsoever are present within that jurisdiction to be consolidated there) and the latter *is* present within the parent company State's taxing jurisdiction, making profits or losses subject to tax there, which can, therefore, be consolidated there. To internal

37 Case C-279/93, *Schumacker*, EU:C:1995:31, [1994] ECR I-5535.

38 Case C-337/08, X Holding BV, EU:C:2010:89.

market lawyers, by contrast, the two positions seem comparable, as they think from the perspective of a parent company exercising its right of secondary establishment through the incorporation or acquisition of a subsidiary either at home or abroad, in the first case being able to consolidate and in the latter case not being able to consolidate: discrimination!

In general, however, especially in more recent case law, the Court seems to realize that object and purpose of the tax measure become relevant only *after* having passed the first and most important comparability test, given object and purpose of taxation itself, i.e. the extent to which a person or income is *subject to tax* within a taxing jurisdiction. If a Member State neutrally does not assert taxing power, neither in respect of nonresidents having no domestic source of income, nor in respect of (positive or negative) foreign-source income, then the Court is not competent to force it to do so (*e.g.* in respect of foreign losses of nonresident, non-subject foreign subsidiaries, as in *X Holding*). If it would, it would force the parent company State to also tax the *positive* results of foreign subsidiaries, because obviously, no-one in their right mind is going to accept deduction of losses or expenses without taxation of the corresponding profits or proceeds, respectively. That *is*, however, what the Court did in its erroneous *Bosal* and *Marks & Spencer II*[39] cases in respect of the financing cost and definitive losses, respectively, of foreign subsidiaries *not* subject to tax, and in *Renneberg* in respect of financing cost of foreign real estate *not* subject to tax.

Despite these mistakes, the main comparability criterion used by the Court seems to be the extent to which a Member State assumed taxing jurisdiction over the cross-border position (the nonresident or the foreign-source income). *If* a Member State assumes such jurisdiction, it must exercise that jurisdiction so assumed in the same manner as in domestic positions. Therefore: (the extent of) *assumption* of taxing jurisdiction is national sovereignty, but the *exercise* of the jurisdiction so assumed is subject to Court scrutiny.[40] This explains why the UK, in *Class IV ACT*,[41] did not need to extend its imputation credit to foreign shareholders which were subject neither to UK corporation tax, nor to UK dividend withholding tax in respect of outbound dividends, although the UK did extend such credit to resident (and therefore subject-to-tax) shareholders. That is also why conversely, in *Manninen*,[42] Finland had to grant its imputation credit to residents receiving foreign-source dividends: Finland taxed foreign dividends in the same manner as domestic dividends.[43] To illustrate, we quote (one of the many) *Denkavit* Case(s),[44] stating that as regards outbound dividends nonresident shareholders are not necessarily comparable to residents, but that they become comparable when they are, like residents, made liable to tax in respect of those dividends by the source State:

39 Case C-446/03, *Marks & Spencer II*, EU:C:2005:763, [2005] ECR I-10837.

40 *E.g.* Case C-307/97, *Saint-Gobain*, C:1999:438, [1999] ECR I-6163.

41 Case C-374/04, *Test Claimants in Class IV of the ACT Group Litigation*, EU:C:2006:773, [2006] ECR I-11673.

42 Case C-319/02, *Manninen*, EU:C:2004:484, [2004] ECR I-7477.

43 Similarly, in *Verkooijen*, *Commission v. France*, and *Lenz* and *Manninen*, the residence State of the taxpayer had to grant national treatment in respect of the foreign-source dividend and interest received by its residents, as it subjected the foreign source income to the same extent as domestically sourced dividends and interest.

44 Case C-170/05, *Denkavit Internationaal and Denkavit France*, EU:C:2006:783, [2006] ECR I-11949.

> '34. It is true that, (...), resident shareholders receiving dividends are not necessarily in a situation which is comparable to that of shareholders receiving dividends who are resident in another Member State (...).
> 35. However, as soon as a Member State, either unilaterally or by way of a convention, imposes a charge to tax on the income, not only of resident shareholders, but also of non-resident shareholders, from dividends which they receive from a resident company, the situation of those non-resident shareholders becomes comparable to that of resident shareholders (....).'

The taxation to which residents are subject, thus is the outer limit for subjecting non-residents, and the taxation to which domestic income is subject, is the outer limit for taxing foreign-source income. Nonresidents may be made subject to tax on a *narrower* tax base than residents, but not on a *wider* tax base than residents. Nonresidents may be exempted (EU law does not oppose 'reverse discrimination') or may be taxed only for sourced income although residents are taxed for worldwide income,[45] but nonresidents may not be taxed for items of income not included in the tax base of residents, nor less favourably for the same item of income[46] (unless such discriminatory taxation is neutralized by the home State of the nonresident; see section 6.5.4).

The *Timac Agro* case[47] (see Section 6.3 above) shows that the Court considers liability to tax as the most relevant comparator. That case concerned foreign branch losses of a German company. Germany had first applied worldwide taxation (foreign branch losses were therefore imported, but their deduction from domestic profits was later recaptured after a specified period) and had subsequently changed its system to territoriality taxation (exclusion of all foreign-source results, whether positive or negative (base exemption)). Therefore, in the first period, foreign branches were subject to tax in Germany, but after the change of system they were not subject to tax anymore. For the *first* period, the Court considered foreign and domestic branches as comparable because both were subject to profit taxation in Germany (that is an error, as in the end, foreign branch results are exempt and domestic results are not, but that is not the point here), whereas for the *second* period the Court viewed foreign and domestic branches as *not* comparable because foreign branches were *not* subject to tax anymore in Germany.

In *W AG*[48] the Court restricted this case law. In this case a German bank has maintained a branch (in the form of a permanent establishment) in the United Kingdom since 2004. This branch was subsequently closed down in 2007. The activities of the branch resulted in a net loss. The question is whether the German bank may deduct this liquidation loss – invoking the freedom of establishment pursuant to Article 49 in conjunction with Article 54 TFEU – from its German result. The Court answered this question in the negative. The reason is that Germany, as a country of residence under the tax treaty between Germany and the United Kingdom, has waived its right to levy tax on the results of the English branch due to the base exemption included in that tax treaty. For this reason, the

45 See, e.g. Case C-250/95, *Futura*, EU:C:1997:239, [1997] ECR I-2471, and Case 279/93, *Roland Schumacher*, EU:C:1995:31, [1995] ECR I-225.

46 See, *e.g.*, Case C-311/97, *Royal Bank of Scotland*, EU:C:1999:216, [1999] ECR I-2651, Case C-170/05, *Denkavit International BV and Sàrl, Denkavit France*, EU:C:2006:783, [2006] ECR I-11949, and Case C-383/05, *Talotta v. Belgium*, EU:C:2007:181, [2007] ECR I-2555.

47 Case C-388/14, *Timac Agro Deutschland GmbH*, EU:C:2015:829.

48 Case C-538/20, *W AG*, EU:C:2022:717.

English branch (not subject to tax in Germany) is not comparable to a branch established in Germany (subject to tax in Germany) and Germany does not have to take the English liquidation loss into account (see further: Section 10.1.3).

We conclude: subject-to-tax (*within* the jurisdiction sovereignly – and neutrally – defined by a Member State) is not comparable to not-subject-to-tax (*outside* a Member State's jurisdiction). Only after it has been established that the cross-border case and the domestic case are comparable in the sense that both are within the taxing power of the same Member State, object and purpose of the specific tax measure at issue become relevant. In the light of that object and purpose, the cross-border and the domestic positions may then still be found incomparable, *e.g.* because the measure at issue is aimed at preventing base erosion and profit shifting which is only conceivable in cross-border situations, not in purely domestic ones.[49]

We make one rather general final observation on comparability: the Court is no doubt reluctant to straightforwardly state that in (direct) tax matters, neutral (nondiscriminatory) measures are outside the scope of the prohibition on restriction of free movement and therefore outside Court scrutiny. It probably has mixed memories of its *Keck*-judgment. Nevertheless, even in all other areas than tax, one may discern in the Court's case law a principle of market distortion: even in the area of trade in goods, hindering neutral measures may be accepted if they do not in some way distort (access to) the market and do not change competitive positions. The neutral measures the Court strikes down, always seem to be measures which in some way cause economic substitution or other market effects.[50] That may be a wise policy, and in direct tax matters that kind of distortion may be caught by looking at (i) the extent of being subject to tax and (ii) object and purpose of the impugned tax measure. One might also argue, however, that object and purpose of the national measure should not be decisive, as otherwise one hands over one's fate to the national legislator. The comparator should be: are the economic operators in the cross-border and the internal situation in competition? And one could argue that they are not if the cross-border situation is not subject to tax and the internal situation is. Obviously, the tax connecting factor should be entirely neutral and objective, such as, most notably: territoriality (source) or residence.

– Justifiability[51] *(see also Section 7.2)*

Next – if a national tax measure is found to be discriminatory – an assessment standard is needed for deciding whether justifications offered by the Member States concerned are good enough to warrant a differential treatment of nonresidents or foreign-source income. We infer from the Court's case law that its policy of accepting or rejecting

49 This is the approach of advocate-general Bobek in his Opinion of 14 December 2017 in Case C-382/16, *Hornbach-Baumarkt AG*, EU:C:2017:974, concerning German arm's length legislation only applying to cross-border situations. See also – but less clear – Case C-3011/08, *Société de Gestion Industrielle (SGI)*, EU:C:2010:26.

50 See Gareth Davies, 'Between market access and discrimination: free movement as a right to fair conditions of competition,' in: Panos Koutrakos, Jukka Snell (ed.), *Research Handbook on the Law of the EU's Internal Market*, Edward Elgar Publishing, 2017, p. 13-28.

51 See Axel Cordewener, Georg Kofler and Servaas van Thiel, 'The Clash Between European Freedoms and National Direct Tax Law: Public Interest Defences Available to the Member States,' 46 *Common Market Law Review* 2009, p. 1951-2010.

justifications put forward by the Member States (see section 3.2.2 and Chapter 7) shows that at the end of the day, only one justification is accepted: the need to protect tax base integrity, i.e. the need to safeguard Member States' right to tax economic activity carried out within their territory and to tax value increases recorded in their jurisdiction. All of the ostensibly different mandatory requirements of public interest the Court has accepted as justifying differential tax treatment of cross-border positions (see Chapter 7: the need (i) to curb fraud and abuse and the needs for (ii) fiscal coherence, (iii) fiscal territoriality, (iv) a balanced allocation of taxing rights, (v) effective fiscal supervision and (vi) fighting the use of tax havens) effectively come down to the need to protect tax base integrity. The need for effective fiscal supervision is the procedural counterpart of the need to substantively preserve base integrity: supervision is needed to effectuate base integrity.

The scope of the need for effective fiscal supervision seemed to become smaller as administrative cooperation and recovery assistance between Member States intensified (see Chapters 24 to 27): Member States were routinely denied reliance on administrative and supervision difficulties as a justification for less favourable treatment of the cross-border situation if they could use the administrative cooperation directives, but more recent case law indicates a judicial revaluation of the effective supervision argument. In *Persche*,[52] *Haribo and Salinen*[53] and *Meilicke II*,[54] the court observed that Article 2 of the (old) Assistance Directive (since 1 January 2013 the DAC; see Chapter 25) provided that Member States 'may' request other Member States for information, but are therefore not *obliged* to use their powers under the DAC, at any rate not if the burden of proof for an advantage claimed by the taxpayer is on the taxpayer (*e.g.* the proof of the amount of underlying corporation paid in respect of foreign dividends for which an imputation credit is claimed) and that burden is not excessive or impossible. Further, in cases such as *Truck Center*[55] and *National Grid Indus*,[56] the (recovery) interest of the tax administration rather than that of the taxpayer is explicitly taken into account.

If one follows the Court's language, the overarching need for (substantive) tax base integrity includes three sub-needs (see, for elaboration, Chapter 7). First, the need to match corresponding positive and negative elements of a source of income within the same taxing jurisdiction, *e.g.*, between taxation of income and deduction of the costs incurred in earning it, between deduction of contributions to pension schemes or annuity policies and future taxation of the corresponding benefits,[57] between untaxed accrual of unrealized capital gains and future taxation upon realization,[58] between deduction and reinstatement of foreign branch losses,[59] etc. The Court calls this kind of tax base integrity 'fiscal coherence,' but sometimes also fiscal 'symmetry.'[60]

52 Case C-318/07, *Persche*, EU:C:2009:33, [2009] ECR I-359.
53 Case C-436/08 and C-437/08, *Haribo and Österreichische Salinen*, EU:C:2011:61.
54 Case C-262/09, *Meilicke II*, EU:C:2011:438.
55 Case C-282/07, *Truck Center*, EU:C:2008:762, [2008] ECR I-10767.
56 Case C-371/10, *National Grid Indus BV*, EU:C:2011:785.
57 Case C-204/90, *Bachmann*, EU:C:1992:35, [1992] ECR I-249.
58 Case C-470/04, *N. v Inspecteur*, EU:C:2006:525, [2006] ECR I-7409.
59 Case C-157/07, *Krankenheim Ruhesitz am Wannsee-Seniorenheimstatt*, EU:C:2008:588, [2008] ECR I-8061.
60 Case C-157/07, *Krankenheim Ruhesitz am Wannsee-Seniorenheimstatt*, EU:C:2008:588, [2008] ECR I-8061.

Second, the need to avoid a State having to give up tax on income sourced within its territory by having to accept deduction of foreign losses to which it has not extended its taxing power, *e.g.* losses made by a foreign subsidiary not subject to tax[61] or in an exempt foreign business operation;[62] inversely, this category includes the need to avoid EU law preventing a Member State to tax profits to which it *did* extend its taxing jurisdiction.[63] For this kind of tax base integrity the Court uses the term 'the need to preserve the (balanced) allocation of the power to impose taxes between the Member States,'[64] but also metaphors such as 'two sides of the same coin' and 'symmetrical treatment in the same tax system,'[65] which makes it difficult to distinguish from 'fiscal coherence.' Confusingly, the Court also uses the concept of fiscal territoriality, apparently (also) representing the need to ensure that Member States can tax income of value creation attributable to economic opportunity and activity within their jurisdiction. This sounds like the source principle of taxation.

Lastly, the need to prevent abuse of law, *i.e.* international tax avoidance through 'wholly artificial arrangements' which 'do not reflect economic reality'.[66] We submit that the need to fight the use of tax havens is encompassed in this category.

In his Opinion in case *Hornbach*, advocate-general Bobek[67] proposes to spring-clean the Court's junk room of justifications, firstly by not considering application of the territoriality principle as a justification, but as nondiscriminatory, obviating the need for any justification, and alternatively, by doing away with most of them and retaining only one: the preservation of the balanced allocation of the powers of taxation between Member States as an 'emanation' of the principle of tax territoriality, the latter to be determined in accordance with generally accepted international tax law, especially the arm's length principle of profit allocation:

> "129. (...). The Court's case-law clearly confirms that the Member States have the power to impose direct taxes and that they may do so in relation to profits generated within their jurisdiction, in accordance with the principle of territoriality. Moreover, the arm's-length principle is internationally recognised as a valid means of allocating profits geographically. (...).
> 133. (...). From a systemic point of view, Member States' insistence on taxing cross-border transactions in accordance with the principle of tax territoriality and recognised international principles applicable in this field cannot in my opinion be considered as anything requiring justification."

61 Case C-446/03, *Marks & Spencer II*, EU:C:2005:763, [2005] ECR I-10837.

62 Case C-414/06, *Lidl Belgium*, EU:C:2008:278, [2008] ECR I-3601, Case C-157/07, *Krankenheim Ruhesitz am Wannsee-Seniorenheimstatt*, EU:C:2008:588, [2008] ECR I-8061, Case C-337/08, *X Holding*, EU:C:2010:89, [2010] ECR I-1215.

63 Case C-231/05, *Oy AA*, EU:C:2007:439, [2007] ECR I-6373, Case C-311/08, *SGI*, EU:C:2010:26 [2010] ECR I-487, and Case C-371/10, *National Grid Indus BV*, EU:C:2011:785.

64 Case C-231/05, *Oy AA*, EU:C:2007:439, [2007] ECR I-6373, and Case C-470/04, *N. v Inspecteur*, EU:C:2006:525, [2006] ECR I-7409.

65 Case C-446/03, *Marks & Spencer II*, EU:C:2005:763, [2005] ECR I-10837.

66 *E.g.* Case C-196/04, *Cadbury Schweppes*, EU:C:2006:544, [2006] ECR I-7995.

67 Opinion of 14 December 2017 in Case C-382/16, *Hornbach-Baumarkt AG*, EU:C:2017:974.

We agree that the Court systemically mixes up comparability and justifiability, but we are not convinced this is caused (always) by its "oscillation between the discrimination approach, the hindrance approach, and the mix between the two." Indeed, the Court itself seems convinced and minded to consistently follow a discrimination approach in tax matters.

– *Proportionality*
Lastly, a standard is needed by which to judge whether the national measure tested does not restrict exercise of free movement more than necessary to attain the legitimate aim of tax base integrity. As observed in section 3.2.2, the proportionality test is often the stumbling block for national tax legislators, who mostly have good reasons for distinguishing between domestic and cross-border positions, but tend to stay on the safe side of their own financial interests and who are not prone to arrogate many good intentions to mobile taxpayers and mobile capital and their tax advisors. Tax base protective measures containing *overkill* (overinclusive measures, also affecting cases in which no international fiscal incoherence or abuse is at issue) are evidently disproportionate.

Measures affecting only ill-advised taxpayers and therefore being largely ineffective (and discriminatory against the ill-advised), are not so much disproportionate as they are unsuitable (under-inclusive), which is unacceptable as well (under the subtest of suitability), because such inadequacy demonstrates that the national legislator did not take its legitimate aim seriously (enough) itself.

For the rest, one can say either very little in general or an awful lot in particular about the proportionality of the effect of tax measures in respect of their aim of (interjurisdictional) tax base integrity; we refer to the first option, as in the following chapters, there will be ample illustration of the application of the Court's proportionality test. See, for just a few illustrative instances out of many to come, the exit tax cases in sections 12.2 and 12.3.

6.5 Departures from the Subject-to-Tax Approach or the One-Country Approach

The more recent case law of the Court seems to follow the approach explained in section 6.4 (subject-to-tax as the leading comparability criterion) more or less consistently. There are some – mostly older – cases, however, which sit uneasily with the subject-to-tax approach. That may in the first place be explained by the fact that it has taken the Court some time (see Section 3.2.7.1) to realize that an obstacle-based approach of free movement rights in direct tax matters is an impossible undertaking. The Court has developed, by trial and (quite some) error, its own concepts and policy for finding a balance between tax sovereignty and the EU free movement rights. Below, we will discuss some approaches used by the Court which seem to deviate either from the subject-to-tax comparability approach or from the distinction between (remediable) one-country-problems and (irremediable) two-country-problems (disparities and parallel exercise of taxing power).

6.5.1 The 'Always-Somewhere' or 'One-Market' Approach

The Court has explicitly accepted, in cases such as *Kerckhaert-Morres*, *Damseaux*, and *Block*, that exercise in parallel by two States of their (indiscriminately defined) taxing jurisdiction may lead to double taxation which is irremediable under the free movement rights, but it is reluctant to accept the implication that, inversely, such exercise in parallel may also lead to double non-deductibility of certain charges or losses. Thus, although the Court seems to realise it is neither competent nor equipped to eliminate international double taxation for migrant taxpayers in the Union, it is slower in acknowledging that neither does it possess the competence or instruments to ensure that all charges and losses and all personal and family circumstances will be taken into account *some*where in the internal market for tax purposes.

We list some cases that stand out as anomalous to the one-country/subject-to-tax approach, in which the Court makes too simple comparisons, apparently with a view to ensuring deduction *some*where:

- In Case C-385/00, *De Groot*[68] (see section 13.4.5) and recently confirmed in Case C-241/20, *BJ*[69], the Court required the home State of a migrant employee to grant him the tax value of 100% of its personal tax allowances, although that State exempted 66% of his income, as that 66% was subject to tax in the employment states; the home State thus did *not* in the end exercise its jurisdiction as regards that 66%. The employment States were explicitly allowed by the Court to discriminate against Mr De Groot by denying him national treatment although for the income sourced in their territories, these States had clearly exercised their taxing power in exactly the same manner as in respect of resident employees. The Court thus allocated deductions on no other basis than its own idea of reasonableness. What it should have done, is to require the employment States to grant Mr De Groot a proportion of their personal allowances equal to the proportion of his income they taxed. This case was probably an unfortunate echo of the Court's misconceived discrimination concept in the *Schumacker* case ('discrimination arises from the fact that his personal and family circumstances are taken into account neither in the State of residence nor in the State of employment'). The fact that something is not taken into account in either State, is not, however, a discrimination (it may be a disparity or a parallel non-exercise of taxing power), and is anyway not telling us *which* of the two States then is doing the alleged discriminating (see section 3.2.7.3(v)). Although in the recent cases *Kieback*[70] and *X v Staatssecretaris*[71] the Court proportionally allocated mortgage interest paid in the home State to two employment States where there was no Home State income, that does not say that it will also do so if there *is* home State income. See for elaboration Section 13.4.9. Moreover, it remains unclear why an employment State with no taxing power whatsoever in respect of the real estate in the home State, should be required in the first place to selectively extend its taxing power to the foreign expenses connected only to that foreign, not-subject real estate (see our discussion of the *Renneberg* Case in Section 3.2.7.3(iv)).

68 Case C-385/00, *De Groot v. Inspecteur van belastingen*, EU:C:2002:750, [2002] ECR I-11819.
69 Case C-241/20 (*BJ v Belgische Staat*), EU:C:2021:605.
70 Case C-9/14, Kieback, EU:C:2015:406.
71 Case C-283/15, X v Staatssecretaris, EU:C:2017:102.

- In Case C-168/01, *Bosal Holding BV*[72] (see Section 16.4.6), the Court required the parent company State to accept deduction of the cost of financing a nonresident subsidiary not subject to tax, the dividends paid by which and the capital gains on the holding in which were equally not subject to tax in the parent company State. Although the parent State thus did not assert any taxing jurisdiction in respect of the income or the value of the holding in the nonresident subsidiary, it was forced by the Court to *extend* its exertion of jurisdiction to the expenses solely attributable to the subsidiary profits it did not subject. Again, the idea seems to have been: if these charges cannot be deducted in the subsidiary State, then they must be deducted somewhere else, as charges, losses and allowances must always be deductible somewhere in the internal market;
- In Case C-446/03, *Marks & Spencer II*[73] (see section 10.5), the Court made an exception to its finding of principle that a parent company State cannot be required to provide relief for losses suffered by nonresident, non-subject subsidiaries: it required the parent company State to accept deduction of definitive foreign subsidiary losses (liquidation losses) as if they were losses of a person liable to tax. Again, the Court thus required a Member State to *extend* its assumption of taxing power selectively to one specific negative element of a foreign tax base wholly to its taxing jurisdiction;
- In Case C-470/04, *N. v Inspecteur*[74] (see Section 12.2), the Court required the former residence State of an emigrated shareholder to accept deduction of post-emigration value losses on the shares, although that State exerted no post-emigration taxing power, neither as regards the person nor as regards the shares, and therefore did not tax any post-emigration *gains* either. We believe both post-emigration losses and gains are a matter for the new tax jurisdiction. In *National Grid Indus* (see Section 12.3), the Court seems to have recognized that in respect of the assets and liabilities of an emigrating undertaking, and in C-503/14, *Commission v Portugal*[75] (see Section 12.4) it seems to have recognised that also in respect of the assets of individuals, as it stated that there should be no difference (anymore) between exit taxation of natural persons and exit taxation of legal persons.
- Case C-293/06, *Deutsche Shell*[76] (see section 10.5) is possibly the finest example of an explicit obstacle-based approach in tax matters ('constitutes an obstacle'; 'increases the economic risk'), as well as of the Court's 'always-somewhere'-reasoning. A currency loss on a German company's capital contribution to its Italian branch was qualified by the Court as a 'specific operational factor which is capable of being taken into consideration only by the German tax authorities. (...), it is unacceptable for a Member State to exclude from the basis of assessment of the principal establishment currency losses which, by their nature, can never be suffered by the permanent establishment.' This seems to say: *because* this currency loss does not exist in Italy, but needs to be deductible *some*where, it *must* be deducted in Germany – even though Germany did

72 Case C-168/01, *Bosal Holding BV*, EU:C:2003:479, [2003] ECR I-9409. See for extensive comments on the case: Dennis Weber: 'The Bosal Holding Case: Analysis and Critique,' *EC Tax Review* 2003/4, p. 220-230.
73 Case C-446/03, *Marks & Spencer II*, EU:C:2005:763, [2005] ECR I-10837.
74 Case C-470/04, *N. v Inspecteur*, EU:C:2006:525, [2006] ECR I-7409.
75 Case C-503/14, *Commission v Portugal* (exit tax), EU:C:2016:79.
76 Case C-293/06 *Deutsche Shell*, EU:C:2008:129, [2008] ECR I-1129.

not assert any taxing jurisdiction, *i.e.* not to currency *gains* either. The Court seems to have remedied this – in our view – *ultra vires* and erroneous reasoning in the subsequent Case *X AB v Skatteverket*[77] (see Section 10.8).

In all five cases, the Court obligated Member States to selectively assume taxing jurisdiction where they had symmetrically not done so. The home States were forced to welcome into their taxing jurisdiction negative items of income to which their jurisdiction did not extend because they either:

- had exempt the foreign income (*De Groot, Deutsche Shell*), or
- had not even made the person/entity liable to tax in the first place, either not from the outset (*Marks & Spencer II*), or not any more (*N. v Inspecteur*); or
- had subjected to tax neither the nonresident subsidiary for its profits nor the resident parent company for the receipt of distributions of those profits or for capital gains on the holding in that nonresident non-subject subsidiary (*Bosal*).

Given the more recent subject-to-tax approach, it is possible that these cases would not be decided in the same manner anymore today, although *Bosal* seems to have been reiterated in the recent *Groupe Stéria* Case[78] and *De Groot* is confirmed in *BJ*.

The inadequacy of the 'always-somewhere' approach, however understandable within the general idea of an internal market, and however sympathetic, is evident if one realizes that it inevitably leads to the Court having to define Member States' taxing jurisdictions and selectively allocate positive or negative parts of income to convenient jurisdictions, as it in fact did in the cases cited, disrupting tax base coherence between causally connected negative and positive items, and even requiring national taxing jurisdiction to be extended to persons entirely *not* liable to tax (*Marks & Spencer II; N. v Inspecteur*). The Court is prone to choose – without visible legal basis – the home State, as usually that is where the best chances of positive income lie, but if it is the other way around, as in the *Renneberg* case, it simply makes the source State responsible, equally without legal basis. We see the same in *Sofina*[79] and *Credit Suisse Securities*[80] in these cases the source State had to take into account (non-final) losses from the home state, contrary to the fiscal principle of territoriality (see furtherSection 7.8.2.).

6.5.2 The Mutual Recognition Approach

Mutual recognition is at the basis of the internal market in the sense that only if the Member State of destination has a good reason in the general interest (the rule of reason), it may restrict market access of products and services legally marketed in other Member States.[81] *Cassis de Dijon*[82] made clear that to the extent it is not *necessary* and *proportionate*

77 Case C-686/13, *X AB v Skatteverket*, EU:C:2015:375.
78 Case C-386/14, *Groupe Stéria SCA*, EU:C:2015:524.
79 Case C-575/17, *Sofina*, ECLI:EU:C:2018:943.
80 Case C-601/23, *Credit Suisse Securities* case, ECLI:EU:C:2024:1048.
81 See on mutual recognition in the internal market in general: Wulf-Henning Roth, 'Mutual recognition', in Panos Koutrakos, Jukka Snell (ed.), *Research Handbook on the Law of the EU's Internal Market*, Edward Elgar Publishing, 2017, p. 427-459.
82 Case 120/78, *Rewe-Zentral*, EU:C:1979:42.

in the general interest to restrict access of goods and services originating under a different regulatory system in another Member State, the Member State of destination will have to recognize the regulatory system of the production State and grant access. Later, the Court followed the same reasoning as regards diplomas, certificates and documents issued in another Member State,[83] and in C-110/05 *Commission v Italy*[84] and *Ker-Optika*[85] it actually used the term 'mutual recognition'. Mutual recognition is better than nondiscrimination, as nondiscrimination only entails national treatment, i.e. market access on the same conditions as local producers and service providers in the destination State. National treatment (nondiscrimination) is in itself neutral from the destination's State perspective, but it is not from the perspective of the economic operator from another Member State, as it still forces him to observe *two* different regulatory systems: the systems of his origin State *and* of the destination State, putting him at a disadvantage as compared to local economic operators, who only need to comply with one regulatory system.

Mutual recognition is, therefore, to a certain extent, positive discrimination of foreign producers and service providers: they get market access without having to comply with all local standards; they only need to comply with the standards of their origin State and to those (few) destination State standards which are (absolutely) necessary in the general interest. For instance, a Greek surgeon may be requested to learn the language before venturing into amputation surgery in France, as it is vital to be able to communicate with the patient and the surgery personnel, but France may not require him to go to medical school again on France.

In the absence of full harmonisation, Member States are thus not required to grant unconditional access to, e.g. lawyers or dentists educated in another Member State. However, they must take into account, when applying their national professional standards, the professional skills and qualifications already acquired in the origin State, and accept them in so far as they are equivalent to its own.

The clearest example of mutual recognition in a field very relevant for direct taxation, especially exit taxation, is recognition of foreign legal entities. Member States of destination cannot require companies to reincorporate in their jurisdiction if the original jurisdiction of incorporation allows companies to transfer their seat without losing their legal personality, and origin States cannot terminate the legal personality of their companies on the occasion of a seat transfer abroad if the jurisdiction of destination recognises their legal personality and accepts its continuation under local law (cross-border transformation), unless there are weighty reasons in the general interest for doing so.[86] See Chapter 12.3.

Most indirect taxes have been either abandoned (customs duties) or harmonised (excise duties and VAT), but mutual recognition could be of relevance as regards unharmonised indirect taxation, such as car registration tax, but until now, the Court does not require the destination State of a second-hand car to credit, when levying its registration tax, the (residual) registration tax already paid in the State where the car was first registered when new. It merely requires the destination State to limit its registration tax to the

83 See e.g. Case C-442/02, *CaixaBanque France*, EU:C:2004:586 and Case C-340/89, *Vlassopoupou*, EU:C:1991:193.

84 Case C-110/05, *Commission v Italy*, EU:C:2009:66, point 34.

85 Case C-108/09, *Ker-Optika*, EU:C:2010:725, point 48.

86 See, e.g. Case C-208/00, *Überseering*, EU:C:2002:632, [2002] ECR I-9919, and Case C-210/06, *Cartesio*, EU:C:2008:723, [2008] ECR I-9641.

residual amount of its own registration tax which may still be considered present in the second-hand price of a domestic second-hand car (see Section 3.1.0). That is national treatment, not mutual recognition.

As observed un Section 6.4.1, the free movement rights are no guarantee that border-crossing will not be disadvantageous tax-wise, and member States have no obligation to prevent double taxation as long as they provide national treatment (nondiscrimination) in respect of nonresidents and in respect of foreign-source income. The destination State is not required in any way to 'recognise' the origin State's level of taxation as 'equivalent' to its own. It may impose its own tax, without having to take account of possible taxation of the same income elsewhere, as long as it does not impose a higher tax than it would in a comparable internal case (nondiscrimination).

There is, however, a line in the CJEU case law in tax matters which has the smell of 'reverse' mutual recognition, deviating from symmetric jurisdictional allocation of tax base. In some cases, the Court seems to require the member States to recognize the taxing jurisdiction of other Member States in respect of tax base, not *entering*, but *leaving* their territory. The Court's reasoning here seems to be that the Member State of origin cannot complain of losing tax base if that tax base will be subject to tax in the jurisdiction of destination. The basic thought seems to be that as long as tax base is taxed *somewhere* within the internal market, separate jurisdictions should not bemoan the fact that it was not *their* jurisdiction to be the lucky one. This looks like inverse mutual recognition: the other State's requirements are in principle as good as yours; the other State's tax is in principle as good as yours. This approach is visible in older cases such as *Eurowings*,[87] *ICI v. Colmer*,[88] *Lankhorst-Hohorst*,[89] and *Metallgesellschaft*.[90] In the latter case, the Court observed that:

> '57. (...) as regards the risk of tax avoidance, the Court has already held that the establishment of a company outside the United Kingdom does not, of itself, necessarily entail tax avoidance, since that company will in any event be subject to the tax legislation of the State of establishment (*ICI*, paragraph 26).'

Admittedly, the UK had no case, but the reasoning suggests that national tax base protective measures are not allowed where the tax base will be normally taxed in another Member State, even at a lower rate. In *Oy AA*,[91] concerning a Finnish group contribution system, the Court explicitly did not care that foreign group companies were *not* subject to tax. The Finnish group contribution system allowed profitable group companies to contribute (and deduct) their profits to loss-making group companies subject to Finnish tax. Obviously, the loss-makers were required to report the contribution as a profit. *Oy AA*, however, wished to contribute its profits to its loss-making, non-subject UK parent. The Court saw a discrimination because it reasoned that Finnish resident subsidiaries held

87 Case C-294/97, *Eurowings Luftverkehrs AG*, EU:C:1999:524, [1999] ECR I-7447.
88 Case C-264/96, *ICI v. Colmer*, EU:C:1998:370, [1998] ECR I-4695.
89 Case C-324/00, *Lankhorst-Hohorst*, EU:C:2002:749, [2002] ECR I-11779.
90 Joined Cases C-397/98 and C-410/98, *Metallgesellschaft* and *Hoechst*, EU:C:2001:134, [2001] ECR I-1727.
91 Case C-231/05, *Oy AA*, EU:C:2007:439, [2007] ECR I-6373.

by non-subject parents were treated less favourably (no deductible profit contribution) solely because of the place of establishment of their parent:

> '38. Therefore, in relation to the aim pursued by the Finnish system of intra-group financial transfers, the mere fact that parent companies which have their corporate establishment in another Member State are not subject to tax in Finland does not differentiate the subsidiaries of those parent companies from the subsidiaries of parent companies which have their establishment in Finland, and does not render the positions of those two categories of subsidiary incomparable.
> 39. A difference in treatment between resident subsidiary companies according to the seat of their parent company constitutes an obstacle to the freedom of establishment if it makes it less attractive for companies established in other Member States to exercise that freedom and they may, in consequence, refrain from acquiring, creating or maintaining a subsidiary in the State which adopts that measure (Case C-324/00 Lankhorst-Hohorst [2002] ECR I-11779, paragraph 32, and Test Claimants in the Thin Cap Group Litigation, paragraph 61).'

Admittedly, different taxation of domestic subsidiaries solely on the basis of the seat of their parent cannot be tolerated, but that was clearly not the issue. Indeed, the decisive criterion for deductibility of the profit transfer was *not* seat, incorporation, nationality or residence of the receiving company, but solely subjection of the contribution to Finnish tax in the hands of the receiving group company. As in *Marks & Spencer II* (see section 18.4), the Court focused on the wrong legal entity. Viewed in the light of the aim of the Finnish group contribution system and of the Finnish delineation of taxing power (providing for consolidation of *Finnish* tax base within *Finnish* taxing jurisdiction), local subsidiaries of non-subject foreign parents are obviously not comparable to local subsidiaries of domestic parents, because *not* being subject to tax is quite incomparable to being subject to tax. The Court's approach in *Oy AA* is also incompatible with its case law since *Schumacker* stating that residents and nonresidents are, as a rule, not comparable. It is not surprising that the justification which the Court considered present in *Oy AA* (balanced allocation of taxing power) after having assumed a discrimination, in fact is the insight that subject-to-tax and not-subject-to-tax in the same jurisdiction are *not* comparable:

> '56. (...), to accept that an intra-group cross-border transfer, (...), may be deducted from the taxable income of the transferor would result in allowing groups of companies to choose freely the Member State in which the profits of the subsidiary are to be taxed, by removing them from the basis of assessment of the latter and, where that transfer is regarded as taxable income in the Member State of the parent company transferee, incorporating them in the basis of assessment of the parent company. That would undermine the system of the allocation of the power to tax between Member States because, according to the choice made by the group of companies, the Member State of the subsidiary would be forced to renounce its right, in its capacity as the State of residence of that subsidiary, to tax the profits of that subsidiary in favour, possibly, of the Member State in which the parent company has its establishment (see also *Test Claimants in Class IV of the ACT Group Litigation*, paragraph 59). (...).
> 63. Even if the legislation at issue in the main proceedings is not specifically designed to exclude from the tax advantage it confers purely artificial arrangements, devoid of economic reality, created with the aim of escaping the tax normally due on the profits generated by

activities carried out on national territory, such legislation may nevertheless be regarded as proportionate to the objectives pursued, taken as a whole.'

Of course it is justified and proportionate to ensure that a resident person who is subject to tax, is in fact, subject to tax, rather than, in fact, *not* subject to tax as a result of a tax base transfer abroad. It is impossible *not* to find a justification for Finland's sovereign right to tax its residents for their domestic income, which is completely outside the UK's taxing jurisdiction. This case, therefore, is a good example of the Court mixing up comparability and justifiability (see Sections 6.4.1 and 6.4.2).

Mutual recognition simply does not work in direct tax matters, as EU law does not say which jurisdiction should recognize which other jurisdiction's taxing power. This sets direct tax cases apart from cases on (mutual recognition of) legal personality of companies incorporated elsewhere, professional diploma's obtained elsewhere, foreign product safety requirements, phytosanitary checks, etc. We observe that from the *Columbus Container* case[92] it appears that the court does not require other Member States to recognize the residence State's characterization of an entity (in this case a limited partnership) as fiscally opaque (separately liable to tax) or as fiscally transparent (participants/partners being directly liable to tax for their share in the result of the entity). That is national sovereignty as long as comparable domestic and foreign entities are treated alike. In any event, mutual recognition of taxation elsewhere of income shifted abroad is clearly incompatible with the Court's principles of fiscal coherence, balanced allocation of taxing rights and foremost with its 'fiscal principle of territoriality' (see Sections 6.4.2 and 7.8).

Still, in more recent tax cases the (inverse) mutual recognition approach is again visible. In both *Eqiom* and *Deister and Juhler* (see, a.o., Sections 7.2 and 7.4), on the anti-abuse reservation of national competence in the Parent-Subsidiary Directive (PSD; see Chapter 16), the Court held that subsidiary States cannot deny the PSD-benefits on the grounds that the recipient parent company in another Member State is in its turn held by persons not eligible for those benefits had they held the subsidiary directly, a.o. because (quote from *Eqiom*):

> "35. (...) such a company [the EU parent company; authors] is, in any event, subject to the tax legislation of the Member State in which it is established (see, to that effect, judgment of 12 December 2002, *Lankhorst-Hohorst*, C-324/00, EU:C:2002:749, paragraph 37 and the case-law cited)."

This may be explained, however, by the fact that these cases concerned in principle full harmonization of intercompany dividend taxation within the EU: the exemption from source State dividend taxation in the PSD *is* in fact a recognition of the exclusive taxing power of the parent company State as regards distributions of profits by EU-subsidiaries to EU-parents. These cases concern the scope of harmonising secondary EU law rather than the confrontation between unharmonised national tax measures and primary EU law.

In the recent *Deka* case[93] the Court opened the door to mutual recognition in direct taxation. In this case the Dutch fiscal investment institution scheme in Dutch corporate income tax

92 Case C-298/05, *Columbus Container Services*, EU:C:2007:754, [2007] ECR I-10451.
93 Case C-156/17, (Deka), EU:C:2020:51.

was at issue. Under this scheme, investment funds are subject to a 0% corporate income tax and they could reclaim the Dutch dividend tax they paid. Investment funds established in the Netherlands as well as investment funds established abroad can qualify for that regime (and can therefore reclaim Dutch dividend tax). To do this, these investment funds must, among other things, meet the so-called shareholder requirements and the dividend pass-through obligation. These two requirements applied without distinction to investment funds established in the Netherlands as well as investment funds established abroad. In *Deka*, the Court first of all recalled that *de facto* discrimination is also prohibited under the treaty freedoms (para. 55):

> 'However, national legislation which applies without distinction to resident and non-resident operators may constitute a restriction on the free movement of capital. It follows from the Court's case-law that even a differentiation based on objective criteria may de facto disadvantage cross-border situations (see, to that effect, judgment of 5 February 2014, *Hervis Sport-és Divatkereskedelmi*, C-385/12, EU:C:2014:47, paragraphs 37 to 39)'

As to whether the dividend pass-through obligation is a *de facto* discrimination, the Court first noted that (para. 71):

> 'As noted in paragraph 43 of this judgment, in the absence of harmonisation at European Union level, each Member State is free to determine whether, in order to encourage the use of collective investment undertakings, to provide for a specific tax regime applicable to those undertakings and to the dividends received by them, and to define the material and formal conditions which must be complied with to benefit from such a regime. The conditions of such regimes are therefore necessarily specific to each Member State and differ between Member States'.

In addition, the Court also recalled established case law:

> 'Furthermore, the free movement of capital cannot be understood as meaning that a Member State is required to adjust its tax rules on the basis of those of another Member State in order to ensure, in all circumstances, taxation which removes any disparities arising from national tax rules'

(paragraph 72) and

> 'given that the decisions made by a taxpayer as to investment in another Member State may be to the taxpayer's advantage or not, according to circumstances'

The Court points out here that differences arising from disparities between the Member States cannot constitute an obstacle to free movement (see also Case C-403/03, Schempp).

Subsequently, however, the Court in *Deka* takes a different direction. The Court considered (paragraph. 73):

> 'However, making the possibility of obtaining a refund of withholding tax subject to strict compliance with the conditions laid down by national legislation, irrespective of the legal conditions to which non-resident investment funds are subject in their State of establishment,

would amount to reserving the possibility of benefiting from an advantageous treatment of dividends only to resident investment funds. Subject to verification by the referring court, resident investment funds would generally be likely to meet all the conditions laid down by the legislation of their State of establishment, whereas non-resident investment funds would generally be likely to meet only the conditions laid down by their Member State of establishment.'

The Court then considers in paragraph 74 and 75:

> 'In those circumstances, it cannot be excluded that a non-resident investment fund which, because of the regulatory framework in force in its State of establishment, does not meet all the conditions laid down by the Member State conferring the tax advantage in question, is nevertheless in a situation which is *essentially comparable* to that of a resident investment fund meeting such conditions. Consequently, in order to ensure that the conditions laid down by the legislation of a Member State, while applying without distinction to resident and non-resident investment funds, do not de facto disadvantage non-resident investment funds, the latter must be able to prove that they are, in particular because of the regulatory framework in force in their State of establishment, in a situation that is comparable to that of resident investment funds meeting those conditions'.

Here we see that, in order to prevent *de facto* discrimination, the Court does in fact *oblige* a Member State to take the legislation of another Member State into account, when this foreign legislation is 'essentially comparable'. The Court here opens the door to mutual recognition in tax matters to recognize special tax regimes which have comparable aims.

An unharmonised tax area where mutual recognition may work, is the procedural area, especially the mutual recognition of documentary evidence, in particular tax accounts and certificates. This is illustrated by the *Futura* case:[94] although Luxembourg was allowed to require loss calculation on the basis of Luxembourg tax accounting standards, it was required to accept that the base material for these calculations was drawn from the books of the French head office of the Futura company. It could not require the books to have been kept in Luxembourg according to Luxembourg standards. A similar decision was taken in *Meilicke II*[95] on the basis of the principle of effectiveness of EU law: requiring a (non-existent) foreign certificate of corporation tax paid identical to the domestic certificate required for crediting domestic corporation tax, may formally ensure equivalence, but is in substance discriminatory and disproportionate. Germany should accept other evidence as well.

Mutual recognition is a result of mutual trust between the Member States. In *Heavyinstall*[96] for the interpretation of the Tax Recovery Directive[97] the Court applied the principle of mutual recognition and mutual trust between the Member States and ruled that, inter alia, on the basis of these principles 'the courts of the requested Member State are, in principle, bound by the assessment made by the authorities of the applicant Member State of compliance with the conditions of application of precautionary measures'. We

94 Case C-250/95, *Futura Participations*, EU:C:1997:239, [1997] ECR I-2471.
95 Case C-262/09, *Meilicke II*, EU:C:2011:438.
96 Case C-420/19 (*Heavyinstall*), EU:C:2021:33.
97 Council Directive 2010/24/EU of 16 March 2010 concerning mutual assistance for the recovery of claims relating to taxes, duties and other measures (OJ 2010 L 84, p. 1). See also Chapter 27.

therefore see that for documentary evidence and precautionary measures in relation to the recovery of tax, the principle of mutual recognition is already being applied in tax cases.

6.5.3 The Follow-Secondary-EU-Law or the OECD Model Approach[98]

The subject-to-tax approach requires equal tax treatment of cross-border positions only to the extent they are subject to tax in the same jurisdiction. Accordingly, in the Cases C-315/02, *Lenz*, C-319/02, *Manninen*, and C-292/04, *Meilicke* (see section 11.3.1), the Court required the shareholder's home State, which taxed both domestic-source dividends and foreign-source dividends in the hands of the shareholder, to extend the same imputation credit for underlying corporation tax in respect of both foreign-source dividends and domestic dividends. By contrast, in *Test Claimants in the FII Group Litigation*,[99] and *Haribo and Salinen*,[100] the Court allowed different treatment of foreign group dividends (cumbersome credit for underlying tax) and domestic group dividends (exemption), which is a *direct* discrimination on the basis of origin: domestic group dividends were not even subject to tax at all in the hands of the parent. The explanation for this surprising departure from both national treatment and the subject-to-tax approach seems to be the Court's referral to Article 4 of the Parent-Subsidiary Directive. That provision allows Member States a choice between exemption and indirect credit for foreign-source group dividends. However, it would seem that it does not allow a *different* choice for domestic dividends, as the Court explicitly held in *Bosal*[101] in respect of the second paragraph of the same Article 4 PSD. The Court thus interpreted the Treaty Freedoms in conformity with secondary EU law, although one would expect the reverse, as the Court did in *Bosal*. Also in *Burda*,[102] the Court leaned on Article 4 PSD in respect of economic double taxation of outbound inter-company dividends.

Possibly, the Court did not want to shake up settled international tax law, which accepts such distinction between domestic and cross-border cases wholeheartedly, as the credit method is considered better suited to combat tax avoidance and unfair tax competition. As observed in section 3.1.2, taking inspiration from existing positive integration on related issues is not limited to EU law: the Court also takes leads from settled international tax law, as represented by the OECD Model Double Taxation Convention and the Official Commentary. It regularly refers to the (principles underlying the) OECD Model Tax Convention, starting cautiously, in *Gilly*,[103] by observing that it is not 'unreasonable' for Member States to 'find inspiration' in that Model, but sometimes more or less relying on an OECD Commentary, as in *Van Hilten-Van der Heijden*,[104] in which the Court accepted assertion of (tracing) tax jurisdiction on the basis of nationality because this 'complied'

98 See Servaas van Thiel, 'The Taxation of Intra-Community Dividend Flows and the Avoidance of Double Taxation; The European Court Takes the "Parent-Subsidiary Directive" Approach', in Servaas van Thiel (editor), 'The Internal Market and Direct Taxation: Is the European Court of Justice Taking a New Approach?' (thirteen contributors), *Confédération Fiscale Européenne*, 2007, p. 113-154.

99 Case C-446/04, *Test Claimants in the FII Group Litigation*, EU:C:2006:774, [2006] ECR I-11753.

100 Case C-436/08 and C-437/08, *Haribo and Österreichische Salinen*, EU:C:2011:61.

101 Case C-168/01, *Bosal Holding BV*, EU:C:2003:479, [2003] ECR I-9409.

102 Case C-284/06, *Burda*, EU:C:2008:365, [2008] ECR I-4571.

103 Case C-336/96, *Gilly*, EU:C:1998:221, [1998] ECR I-2793.

104 Case C-513/03, *Van Hilten-van der Heijden*, EU:C:2006:131, [2006] ECR I-1957.

with (the commentaries on) Articles 4, 7, 9A and 9B of the OECD Model Double Taxation Convention concerning Inheritances and Gifts (which was not a lucky strike, as there are hardly any bilateral inheritance tax treaties in force, and the one at issue dated from well before that model).

There are now indications that the Court is less likely to accept OECD commentaries or guidelines as a source of inspiration.

In the State aid case *FIAT Chrysler*[105], the Court, unlike the General Court, refused to use the OECD transfer pricing guidelines as a 'tool' for the question whether the price for certain transactions was at arms length. The Court considered that 'assuming that there is a certain consensus in the field of international taxation that transactions between economically linked companies, in particular intra-group transactions, must be assessed for tax purposes as if they had been concluded between economically independent companies, and that, therefore, many national tax authorities are guided by the OECD Guidelines in the preparation and control of transfer prices'; it is only the *national provisions* that are relevant for the purposes of analysing whether particular transactions must be examined in the light of the arm's length principle. If these national provisions do not explicitly refer to the OECD guidelines, then the guidelines are not relevant. Here we see that the Court, for determining the reference framework in state aid cases, does not simply take the OECD guidelines as 'inspiration' or as a 'tool'. The reason for this finding was in *FIAT Chrysler* the 'principle of legality of taxation', 'which forms part of the legal order of the European Union as a general principle of law, requiring that any obligation to pay a tax and all the essential elements defining the substantive features thereof must be provided for by law, the taxable person having to be in a position to foresee and calculate the amount of tax due and determine the point at which it becomes payable', according to The Court (para. 97 in FIAT).

We also see a more reserved Court in the *Keva-case*[106]. In this case Swedish resident pension funds were governed by public law exempt from the withholding tax on dividends, whereas non-resident pension institutions governed by public law do not benefit from such an exemption.

The Court considered this to be an obstacle to the free movement of capital. The Swedish government argued that the principle of non-discrimination, within the meaning of Article 24 of the OECD Model Tax Convention, does not mean that a State granting special tax advantages to its own public bodies is required to grant the same advantages to public bodies of another State, as is apparent from paragraphs 10 and 12 of the Commentary on Article 24.

The Court noted 'In that regard, it is sufficient to note that that government cannot rely on those paragraphs in the Commentary on Article 24 of the OECD Model Tax Convention for the purpose of avoiding its obligations under the Treaty' (para. 48). Here we see that,

105 Joined Cases C-885/19 P en C-898/19 P, *FIAT Chrysler Finance Europe*, ECLI:EU:C:2022:859.
106 Case C-39/23, *Keva*, ECLI:EU:C:2024:648.

in answering the question of whether there is an obstacle to free movement, the Court, unlike in *Van Hilten-Van der Heijden*, does not draw inspiration from the OECD Model tax treaty practice. This is correct because there is no Union law basis to follow the interpretation of the non-discrimination principle in the OECD Model Tax Convention.

In the *Belgian Association of Tax Lawyers*-case[107] the Court ruled with regard to the broad concepts of the DAC6 directive (see for this Directive: Chapter 29) that 'when those concepts correspond to those employed in relevant international agreements and practices, those agreements and practices may provide further guidance to the court responsible for that interpretation'.

In the *Belgian Association of Tax Lawyers*-case the Court refers to the OECD BEPS Action 12 Report for a further interpretation of a number of concepts of DAC6 Directive[108]. The fact that the Court does take OECD material into account in this case is justified because the EU legislature refers to this OECD report in recital 4 of the DAC6 Directive[109]. There is therefore a Union legal basis for taking this OECD report into account.

We thus see that in more recent case law the Court is more reluctant to follow OECD commentary/Guidelines, etc., unless there is a Union or national legal basis for this.

6.5.4 *The Overall Approach: 'Neutralisation' in the Other Jurisdiction; De Groot, Denkavit France, Amurta, Miljoen*

Another departure from the unilateral subject-to-tax approach is the notion that a Member State, although exercising its taxing power in a discriminating manner, may be forgiven if the effect of its discriminatory taxation is compensated by a counterbalancing exercise of taxing power by the other State involved. This approach was already visible in *De Groot:*[110] first, the home State of a migrant employee was made responsible for full personal tax allowances although it exempted the greater part of his income, but subsequently, the home State could be 'released' from this EU law obligation if it was discharged by the employment State extending *its* personal tax allowances. The Court at first did not care whether the employment State would do so on the basis of a tax treaty or unilaterally, as long as 'the end result' would be that the taxpayer's personal and family circumstances were 'duly' taken into account (*emphasis added*):

> '99. The Member States are of course free, in the absence of unifying or harmonising measures adopted in the Community, to alter, by way of bilateral or multilateral agreements for the avoidance of double taxation, that correlation between the total income of residents and residents' general personal and family circumstances to be taken into account by the State of residence. The State of residence *can therefore be released by way of an international*

107 Case C-623/22, *Belgian Association of Tax Lawyers*, ECLI:EU:C:2024:639.

108 Including the concept of 'arrangement' and for the 'main benefit test' (see paras. 50 and 74 of *Belgian Association of Tax Lawyers*).

109 See Case C-623/22, *Belgian Association of Tax Lawyers*, ECLI:EU:C:2024:639, para. 50.

110 Case C-385/00, *De Groot v. Inspecteur van belastingen*, EU:C:2002:750, [2002] ECR I-11819.

> *agreement from its obligation* to take into account in full the personal and family situation of taxpayers residing in its territory who work partially abroad.
> 100. The State of residence *may also be released from that obligation* if it finds that, *even in the absence of a convention*, one or more of the States of employment, with respect to the income taxed by them, grant advantages based on the personal and family circumstances of taxpayers who do not reside in the territory of those States but receive taxable income there.
> 101. However, the mechanisms used to eliminate double taxation or the national tax systems which have the effect of eliminating or alleviating double taxation must permit the taxpayers in the States concerned to be certain that, *as the end result*, all their personal and family circumstances will be duly taken into account, *irrespective of how those Member States have allocated that obligation amongst themselves*, in order not to give rise to inequality of treatment which is incompatible with the Treaty provisions on the freedom of movement for workers and in no way results from the disparities between the national tax laws'

This implies that discriminatory taxation in one jurisdiction may be canceled by a corresponding tax credit in in another jurisdiction. The same approach was visible in *Denkavit France*,[111] concerning a discriminating French withholding tax on outbound dividends, which was creditable, on the basis of the applicable tax treaty, against the corporation tax of the Netherlands parent company. The Netherlands, however, exempted participation dividends in the hands of parent companies, meaning that there was no corporation tax against which to credit the French withholding tax. Therefore, the discrimination persisted. *A contrario*, had the Netherlands been a credit country instead of an exemption country, and had it therefore credited the French tax, then France would have been forgiven, because in the end result, the taxpayer would not have been worse off. In our view, that is a reasonable and realistic approach[112], as it does not make sense to interfere, on the basis of EU law, in the division of taxing power and tax revenue agreed on by the source and the residence State if that interference does not benefit the taxpayer. If the source tax is creditable in the home State, the only effect of requiring the source State to abolish its source tax, would be a correspondingly lower credit in his home State. The only effect would be a budget shift from the source State to the residence State at variance with their bilateral division of taxing power, not benefiting the taxpayer. Only where the discriminatory source tax cannot be set off in the home State (as in the *Denkavit France* case), the source State should be thrown the book at. The overall or neutralisation approach was reiterated in Miljoen e.a. in the case of an individual resident in Belgium and receiving Netherlands dividends who was entitled to a credit for the Netherlands dividend withholding tax in Belgium which, however, did not fully absorb the Netherlands withholding tax in excess of what a comparable Netherlands resident shareholder would have paid in income tax.

We consider the 'overall approach' as the only departure from the subject-to-tax approach which makes sense and which adds a systematically sound nuance to it, albeit

111 Case C-170/05, *Denkavit International BV and Sàrl Denkavit France*, EU:C:2006:783, [2006] ECR I-11949.

112 See for a different view on this: D. Weber, In Search of a (New) Equilibrium Between Tax Sovereignty and the Freedom of Movement Within the EC, Intertax, 2006, Vo. 34-12, paragraph 2.E.3.

that its practical application may be cumbersome due to the technical intricacy of the credit method[113].

We do not understand, however, why the Court, derogating from *De Groot*, in subsequent case law required the neutralisation in the other State to be based on a tax treaty rather than on unilateral prevention of double taxation by that other State. The Court required a treaty base in *Amurta*,[114] concerning Netherlands source tax withheld on dividends paid by a Netherlands 14% subsidiary to its Portuguese parent. The tax would not have been withheld from a domestic parent because a domestic parent would have been exempt from corporation tax on the dividend and source taxation would have to be refunded. Therefore, the source tax was clearly discriminatory, as in the *Denkavit France* case. The Netherlands could nevertheless be considered to comply with its EU obligations where it ensured that its discriminatory source tax was credited in Portugal. Derogating from *De Groot*, the Court now required the shareholder State credit to be provided for in a tax treaty between the source State and the recipient State:

> '78. (...) the Netherlands cannot rely on the existence of a tax advantage granted unilaterally by another Member State in order to escape its obligations under the Treaty.
> 79. However, it cannot be excluded that a Member State may succeed in ensuring compliance with its obligations under the Treaty through the conclusion of a convention for the avoidance of double taxation with another Member State (see, to that effect, Test Claimants in Class IV of the ACT Group Litigation, paragraph 71).'

In *Miljoen e.a.*,[115] this treaty-requirement was reiterated in respect of cross-border dividends received by nonresident individuals subject to gross source tax where residents were subject to a lump sum tax on the *value* of their shares (which tax could be lower than the source tax on nonresidents), and in *Arens-Sikken*,[116] the same finding was reiterated in respect of the possibility of a neutralising credit in the residence State for a discriminatory inheritance tax.

In *Miljoen et al.* an ordinary tax credit mechanism was included in a tax treaty. An ordinary tax credit does not always offset all dividend withholding tax levied in the source state. The Court ruled that this mechanism does not always neutralize the restriction, but left it to the national court to determine whether, on balance, all dividend withholding tax was offset in the present case. With this ruling, the Court accepted that an ordinary credit mechanism included in a tax treaty can be a sufficient method of neutralisation as long as it leads to full offset of the dividend withholding tax in the specific situation (see paragraphs 86 and 87 in *Miljoen*).

In *ACC Silicones*[117], however, the Court ruled on an ordinary tax credit mechanism included in a tax treaty:

---

113 See for a different view and some practical problems: D. Weber, In Search of a (New) Equilibrium Between Tax Sovereignty and the Freedom of Movement Within the EC, Intertax, 2006, Vo. 34-12, paragraph 2.E.3.

114 Case C-379/05, *Amurta*, EU:C:2007:655, [2007] ECR I-9569.

115 Joined Cases C-10/14, C-14/14 and C-17/14, *Miljoen, X and Société Générale*, EU:C:2015:608.

116 Case C-43/07, *Arens-Sikken*, EU:C:2008:490, [2008] ECR I-6887.

117 Case C-572/20, *ACC Silicones*, ECLI:EU:C:2022:469.

> "Such a mechanism does not seem capable of guaranteeing in all cases that the difference in treatment resulting from the national legislation will be compensated for, such compensation being possible only where the amount of United Kingdom tax calculated on the dividends distributed is at least equal to the amount of the withholding tax levied by the Federal Republic of Germany'. (para. 47)

In *ACC Silicones* the Court is of the opinion that neutralisation by means of an ordinary credit mechanism is not sufficient because it is uncertain whether a compensation of all withholding tax can be obtained, while resident companies always receive reimbursement of the excess withholding tax. The *Miljoen* case and *ACC Silicones* therefore seem to contradict each other and in any case causes confusion for us.

The overall approach is not only a derogation from – or a nuance to – the subject-to-tax approach, but also an exception to the Court's settled case law implying that counterbalancing incidental advantages of being nonresident cannot justify discriminatory disadvantages of being nonresident. In *Avoir Fiscal,*[118] the Court did not accept the absence of capital duty for branches as a justification for the denial of the French imputation credit to French branches of German insurance companies. In *Commerzbank,*[119] the Court did not accept that a UK branch of a German bank was not granted interest on a tax refund, even though a UK resident bank would not have been eligible for any refund in the first place, let alone for interest on that non-existent refund. In *Asscher,*[120] the Court did not accept that nonresidents faced a higher first-bracket rate (25%) than residents (12%) even though nonresidents did not pay the extra 28% in social security contributions which residents paid in that first bracket (and therefore 40% in total). In *Deutsche Shell*[121] (see section 6.5.1 above and section 10.5), it was (incorrectly) not accepted that the exclusion from the German tax base of currency losses on an Italian branch was justified on the grounds that currency profits (and in general, *all* results on that branch) were also exempt.

Possibly for these reasons, the Court is not easy in accepting the 'overall' defense. In C-540/07, *Commission v Italy*[122] and in *Secilpar,*[123] it seems to reduce the scope of the 'overall'-escape for Member States. Still, the overall-approach seems inevitable as the source State can hardly be required to refund tax which has already been credited by the home State. Even if the tax treaty does not provide for a full credit, the source State can scarcely be obliged to refund more than the excess. Obliging it to refund creditable source tax would not make sense in any event: if the source State refunds withholding tax despite its (partial) crediting in the home State, then the source State will communicate that refund to the home State on the basis of the DAC (see Chapter 26). Obviously, the home State will subsequently undo the credit, which leaves the taxpayer none the wiser.

118 Case 270/83, *Commission v France (avoir fiscal)*, EU:C:1986:37, [1986] ECR 273.
119 Case C-330/91, *Commerzbank AG*, EU:C:1993:303, [1993] ECR I-4017.
120 Case C-107/94, *Asscher v. Staatssecretaris van Financiën*, EU:C:1996:251, [1996] ECR I-3089.
121 Case C-293/06, *Deutsche Shell*, EU:C:2008:129, [2008] ECR I-1129.
122 Case C-540/07, *Commission v Italy*, EU:C:2009:717, [2009] ECR I-10983.
123 Case C-199/10, *Secilpar Sociedade Unipessoal SL*, EU:C:2010:706.

CHAPTER 7

Free Movement and Tax Base Integrity[1]

Dennis Weber and Peter Wattel[2]

Update and elaboration by Dennis Weber

7.1 Overview of the Development of the ECJ's View on Tax Avoidance

Long before the adoption of the Anti-Tax Avoidance Directive[3] (ATAD; see Chapter 19) in 2016, the Court's acceptance of regulatory competition between the Member States affected the taxing powers of the Member States. At first, the Court was reluctant to accept

---

1 See on this issue a.o. Dennis Weber: 'Tax Avoidance and the EC Treaty Freedoms' (diss. University of Amsterdam), Eucotax series on European Taxation, Kluwer Law International, The Hague, 2005; Dennis Weber, 'Abuse of Law in European Tax Law: An Overview and Some Recent Trends in the Direct and Indirect Tax Case Law of the ECJ', 53 *European Taxation* 2013/6 pp 251-264 and 2013/7, pp. 313-328; Karsten Engsig Sørensen, 'Abuse of Rights in Community Law: A Principle of Substance or merely Rhetoric?,' 43 *Common Market law Review* 2006, p. 423-459; Frans Vanistendael, 'Halifax and Cadbury Schweppes: One Single European Theory of Abuse in Tax Law?,' *EC Tax Review* 2006/4, p. 192-195; Rita de la Feria, 'Prohibition of Abuse of Community law: The Creation of a New General Principle of EC Law through Tax,' 45 *Common Market law Review* 2008, p. 395-441; Luc de Broe, 'International Tax Planning and Prevention of Abuse' IBFD Doctoral Series, 2008; Adolfo Jimenez, 'Towards a Homogeneous Theory of Abuse of EU (direct) Tax Law', *Bulletin for International Taxation* 2012/4-5, pp.270-242; Alexandre Saydé, 'Defining the Concept of Abuse of Union Law' *Yearbook of European Law* 2014, pp. 138-162; Koen Lenaerts, The Concept of 'Abuse of Law' in the Case Law of the European Court of Justice on Direct Taxation', *Maastricht Journal of European and Comparative Law*, 2015/3, pp. 329-351; Alexandre Maitrôt de La Motte, 'Tax sovereignty, national transfers of tax losses within international groups of companies and freedom of establishment: Felixstowe Dock and Railway Company Ltd' 45 *Common Market law Review* 2015, pp. 1079-1094; Luc de Broe/Dorien Beckers, 'The General Anti-Abuse Rule of the Anti-Tax Avoidance Directive: An Analysis Against the Wider Perspective of the European Court of Justice's Case Law on Abuse of EU Law', *EC Tax Review* 2017/3, pp 133-144; Axel Cordewener, 'Anti-Abuse Measures in the Area of Direct Taxation: Towards Converging Standards under Treaty Freedoms and EU Directives?' *EC Tax Review* 2017, pp 60-66.; Ivan Lazarov, Anti-Tax Avoidance in Corporate Taxation under EU Law: The Internal Market Narrative, Vol. 62, 2022, IBFD Doctoral Series; M.J. Velthoven, 'The general anti-abuse rule of article 6 of the EU Anti-Tax Avoidance Directive', doctoral thesis, University of Amsterdam, 2024.

2 Peter Wattel is professor of EU Tax Law, ACTL, University of Amsterdam; Advocate-General, Supreme Court of the Netherlands; State Councillor extraordinary, Netherlands Council of State; Dennis Weber is professor European Corporate Tax Law at the ACTL of the University of Amsterdam and of counsel at Loyens & Loeff.

3 Council Directive (EU) 2016/1164 of 12 July 2016 laying down rules against tax avoidance practices that directly affect the functioning of the internal market (ATAD 1), O.J. L193/1 of 19 July 2016, and Council Directive (EU) 2017/952 of 29 May 2017 amending Directive (EU) 2016/1164 as regards hybrid mismatches with third countries (ATAD 2), O.J. L 144/1 of 7 July 2017.

that the use of mismatches (disparities) between Member States' (tax) systems could be an abuse of rights, as the very idea of an internal market is that economic operators may avail themselves of the regulatory system that optimizes their cost/yield ratio. In early non-tax cases, such as *Centros*,[4] on the incorporation of purely Danish economic activities in a UK Limited company by two Danes solely to circumvent Danish minimum capital requirements for companies, the Court separated the question of whether a factual situation enters the scope of application of the Treaty Freedoms, from the question of whether a Member State may apply measures to prevent attempts to circumvent its domestic legislation. Thus, (attempted) abuse (in the eyes of the Member State concerned) does not in itself bar access to the free movement rights, as their engagement is in principle dependent on objective factors rather than on subjective intent, but (intent of) abuse may justify restrictive national measures. Therefore, the Treaty also guarantees, to a certain extent, free movement of tax avoiders; they are not, by way of some *Keck*[5]-test, excluded altogether from the scope of the Treaty Freedoms for bad behavior, as tax avoidance in itself does not need to be abusive from an internal market point of view. The Court's early non-tax case law[6] showed the need for clear criteria for distinguishing between legitimate exercise of free movement rights and abusive practices.

Initially, the Court scarcely accepted the need to prevent tax avoidance (sometimes mixed up by the Court with 'tax evasion') as a mandatory requirement of public interest capable of justifying restrictions to free movement rights. The *Avoir Fiscal* case[7] concerned the French refusal to attach an imputation credit for corporation tax paid (*avoir fiscal*) to French dividends paid to French branches of non-resident companies, although such credit was extended to residents. The Court tersely and flatly rejected the French argument that extending that credit to non-residents would create the risk of tax avoidance. It mechanically applied the national treatment requirement under the right of establishment, and did not even apply its *rule of reason* test. It only looked at the text of the Treaty and observed that prevention of (fiscal) abuse was not in the list of permissible reasons for restrictions of the treaty provisions on free establishment.

The Court has come a long way from that initial judgment. In subsequent case law, the need to prevent abuse was fully accepted under its *rule of reason*, although it was at first frugal in allowing Member States to successfully rely on it. It did not accept exclusion of categories of cases from beneficial tax rules for purposes of curbing tax avoidance. Such categorical exclusions were almost automatically considered to be disproportionate (over inclusive: 'overkill') as they were not (enough) targeted at 'wholly artificial arrangements'. In principle, the Court required every cross-border case in which a taxpayer relied on free movement rights to invalidate restrictive national tax measures to be judged on its individual merits, i.e. on a case by case basis. Denial of free movement was justified only in case of an (actual) 'wholly artificial arrangement'.

Gradually, however, the Court integrated its views on tax abuse, first in the field of indirect taxes, especially VAT, and subsequently also in the field of direct taxes, into a general principle of EU law developed by the Court: a general prohibition of abuse

4 Case C-212/97, *Centros*, EU:C:1999:126, [1999] ECR I-1459.
5 Joined Cases C-267 and 268/91, *Keck* and *Mithouard*, EU:C:1993:905, [1993] ECR I-6097.
6 Case C-110/99, *Emsland-Stärke*, EU:C:2000:695; Case C-376/96, *Kefalas*, EU:C:1988:222.
7 Case 270/83, *Commission v. French Republic*, EU:1986:37, [1986] ECR 273.

of rights. The result has been that for unacceptable tax avoidance to be present, two cumulative conditions must be satisfied: (i) object and purpose of the EU rules relied on by the economic operator are not served or achieved, but defied by its (trans)actions, the result of the (trans)action being alien to that object and purpose (objective element), and (ii) intent: the economic operator has the intention of obtaining benefits not meant for it by artificially creating the conditions for obtaining them (subjective element).

More recently, the Court has also accepted more abstract and generally restrictive measures, based on presumptive criteria, apparently being satisfied that already the (real) *risk* of tax avoidance justifies exclusion of certain categories of transactions or operations, or at least a reversal of the burden of proof after the tax administration has provided *prima facie* evidence of abuse. This acceptance of certain categorical exclusions looks as if the Court changed direction, but as in its present case law it still requires anti-abuse measures to be aimed at 'wholly artificial arrangements' (see recent: *X BV* (Dutch interest deduction limitation-case[8]), we believe that what really happened is a combination of two developments:

i. it occurred to the Court that if a real *risk* of tax avoidance obtains, then at the same time the 'coherence of the tax system' (or 'a balanced allocation of taxing rights') is jeopardized, meaning that the need to prevent abuse and the needs to safeguard fiscal coherence and/or a balanced division of taxing rights may overlap or coincide, and
ii. the Court realized that by dividing the burden of proof, a balanced result could be achieved which respects the proportionality principle, duly taking into account both the free movement interests of taxpayers and the legitimate base erosion and profit shifting (BEPS)-and practicability concerns of the Member States.

Ad (i): the main difference between the abuse-defense and the fiscal-coherence/balanced-allocation defense is that the former requires two conditions to be met which do not need to be met for application of the latter: (a) abusive *intent* and (b) objective *artificiality* (which also indicates subjective intent, so the two may overlap). International tax avoidance mostly consists of *intentionally* creating, in individual cases and through artifices, jurisdictional incoherence or a shift in income allocation, especially 'mismatches' (double non-taxation, double deduction or deduction/no inclusion) and profit shifts from a high tax jurisdiction to a low tax jurisdiction. It is difficult to conceive fiscal abuse which does not also involve (artificial) fiscal incoherence or disruption of the balanced allocation of taxing rights.

Ad (ii): if no rebuttal possibility is provided for, *then* a restrictive national anti-abuse rule must be narrowly targeted at 'wholly artificial arrangements' if it is to be considered proportional, i.e. it should target actual abuse, to be assessed on a case-by-case basis and to be demonstrated by the tax administration; if, by contrast, a rebuttal possibility is provided for, *then* wider *categories* of cases may be excluded on the basis of a *presumption* of tax avoidance, provided such presumption/exclusion is based on foreseeable, objective and relevant criteria (*e.g.* departure from the OECD's arm's length pricing standards), the fulfilment of which is *prima facie* shown by the tax administration, and provided that rebuttal by the taxpayer – by showing genuine business reasons – is possible without

8 Case C-585/22, *X BV*, ECLI:EU:C:2024:822.

undue administrative or procedural difficulties. Below, we will illustrate and elaborate on both developments.

The Court summarized its present views on the permissible restriction of free movement rights for anti-abuse reasons in *Deister* and *Juhler*.[9] That case concerned German legislation denying the dividend withholding tax exemption of Article 5 of the Parent-Subsidiary Directive to EU parent companies where *their* shareholders would not have been eligible for the exemption, had they received the dividend directly. The Court considered as follows:

> '60. The Court has stated that, in order for national legislation to be regarded as seeking to prevent tax evasion and abuses, its specific objective must be to prevent conduct involving the creation of wholly artificial arrangements which do not reflect economic reality, the purpose of which is unduly to obtain a tax advantage ((…) *Eqiom and Enka*, C-6/16, EU:C:2017:641, paragraph 30 and the case-law cited).
> 61. Therefore, a general presumption of fraud and abuse cannot justify either a fiscal measure which compromises the objectives of a directive or a fiscal measure which prejudices the enjoyment of a fundamental freedom guaranteed by the treaties ((…), *Eqiom and Enka*, C-6/16, EU:C:2017:641, paragraph 31 and the case-law cited).
> 62. In order to determine whether an operation pursues an objective of fraud and abuse, the competent national authorities may not confine themselves to applying predetermined general criteria, but must carry out an individual examination of the whole operation at issue. The imposition of a general tax measure automatically excluding certain categories of taxable person from the tax advantage, without the tax authorities being required to provide even *prima facie* evidence of fraud and abuse, would go further than is necessary for preventing fraud and abuse ((…), *Eqiom and Enka*, C-6/16, EU:C:2017:641, paragraph 32 and the case-law cited).'

7.2 Abuse of rights in primary and secondary law: Correspondence?[10]

The Parent-Subsidiary Directive (PSD), the Merger Directive, and the Interest and Royalty Directive (IRD) contain anti-abuse reservations (see Sections 16.8, 17.13 and 18.7.1 respectively). The question arises how these reservations relate to the general principle of EU law which prohibits abuse of rights. The same question may be asked in respect of the Anti-Tax Avoidance Directive (ATAD: see Chapter 19).

As regards the anti-abuse reservations in the corporate tax directives, we observe that in the *Eqiom* case (concerning a French refusal to apply the withholding tax exemption of Article 5 PSD to dividends paid to an EU parent company where the ultimate beneficiary was non-EU) and the *Euro Park Service* case (on the French requirement of prior evidence of genuine business reasons for a cross-border merger where no prior approval procedure applied to domestic mergers), the Court held that the objective of preventing tax avoidance and tax evasion "has the same scope whether it is relied on under [the anti-abuse reservations in the corporate tax directives] or as justification for an exception

9 Joined Cases C-504/16 and C-613/16, *Deister Holding AG and Juhler Holding A/S*, EU:C:2017:1009.

10 See also: Luc de Broe and Dorien Beckers, 'The General Anti-Abuse Rule of the Anti-Tax Avoidance Directive: An Analysis Against the Wider Perspective of the European Court of Justice's Case Law on Abuse of EU Law', *EC Tax Review* 2017/3, p. 133-144.

to primary law".[11] The Court considers the anti-abuse provisions in the corporate tax directives as 'reservations of competence'[12] which – therefore – switch off the rights extended by the directives where abuse is present. This implies that the *exercise* of that reserved competence is not governed by the directive at issue – precisely because that competence has been reserved – but by *primary* EU law, notably the free movement rights and the *rule of reason* justifications for restricting them, amongst which the need to curb abuse. Only the *scope* of these reservations (to what *extent* are the directive rights switched off by these reservations?) is governed by the directives; that scope is narrow, according to the Court, as these reservations are exceptions to the overall goals of the directives.[13] Within that scope (to the extent the directives' rights are switched off), the Member States remain free to deny the directive's benefits, but only within the limits posed by primary EU law, notably the Treaty freedoms, i.e. only in so far as the general prohibition of abuse of rights justifies restricting those freedoms. As the Court considered in *Deister* and *Juhler*:[14]

> '55. (...), in interpreting Article 1(2) of the Parent-Subsidiary Directive, it is irrelevant that the word 'necessary' does not appear expressly in the German language version of the provision. The Member States may, in any event, exercise the option provided for in that Article only whilst observing the general principles of EU law and, more specifically, the principle of proportionality (see, by analogy, (...), *Leur-Bloem*, C-28/95, EU:C:1997:369, paragraphs 38 and 43).'

We understand this case law as meaning that no matter how a competence reservation to curb abuse in secondary EU law is framed, its scope and meaning coincides with the scope and meaning of the general principle of EU law which prohibits abuse of rights. That seems to imply that the competence reservations in secondary EU tax law are superfluous: apparently, their only effect is retaining a certain limited room for application of national (or tax treaty) law, which obviously may only be applied, however, in conformity with primary EU law (the free movement rights). That would have been the case also if there had been no such reservation.

That the abuse competence reservations are superfluous is confirmed by the Court in the *Danish BO* cases[15] in which case the Court explained extensively that in the event of abuse of an advantage arising from EU law, Member States are even obliged to refuse it on the basis of the general legal principle that EU law cannot be relied on for abusive or fraudulent ends. This obligation therefore arises from EU law itself and a competence reservation is not necessary for this and the benefits in abusive situations must therefore also be refused if national law itself does not provide a national legal basis for this.

---

11 See Case C-6/16, *Eqiom SAS/Enka*, EU:C:2017:641, point 64 (in respect of the Parent-Subsidiary Directive) and Case C-14/16, *Euro Park Service*, EU:C:2017:177, point 69 (in respect of the Merger Directive).

12 See, a.o., *Euro Park Services*, point 23, and Case C-28/95, *Leur-Bloem*, EU:C:1997:369, point 39.

13 See, a.o. *Euro Park Service*, point 49, on the Merger Directive, and *Eqiom*, point 26, on the Parent-subsidiary Directive.

14 Joined Cases C-504/16 and C-613/16, *Deister Holding AG and Juhler Holding A/S*, EU:C:2017:1009.

15 Joined Cases C-115/16, C-118/16 and C-119/16 (*N Luxembourg 1*), EU:C:2019:134.

Next to the (superfluous) abuse competence reservations there are provisions that impose the *obligation* on the Member States to combat abuse. For instance (i) the AT-AD-obligation for Member States to apply both a general anti-avoidance rule (GAAR; Article 6 ATAD) and ii) specific anti-abuse rules (SAARs: minimum harmonization of CFC-rules, anti-hybrid mismatches provisions and anti-earnings stripping rules; see Chapter 19). These provisions are not just reservations of national competence. As they *require* Member States to enact (at least) the anti-abuse measures specified in these directives, they are not exceptions to the obligation to *extend* tax facilities (such as the prevention of economic double taxation under the PSD or tax deferral under the Merger Directive), but *oblige* Member States to *deny* deduction or exemption in certain cases. They do not *allow* tax base protection, they *demand* it. Therefore, unlike the anti-abuse reservations in the PSD, the Merger Directive and the IRD, these ATAD (and PSD provisions) do not leave room for national law, but, on the contrary, require national law to conform. The question of compatibility with EU law therefore does not in the first place concern the question of whether Member States went too far in fighting abuse (disproportionally restricting free movement), but rather the question of whether they went far enough to satisfy the (minimum) abuse control standards of the amended PSD, the ATAD, i.e. the question of whether these directives have been implemented correctly.

7.3 Ancillary Soft and Hard Law

The ATAD was preceded by soft law based on the Court's case law on abuse in tax matters: in 2007, the Commission summarized and outlined the Court's case law on abuse in tax matters and drew guidelines from it for the Member States for the purpose of designing and applying their national anti-abuse measures, both intra-EU and as regards (other) EEA-Members and third countries.[16] Five years later, the Commission issued a Recommendation on aggressive tax planning urging the Member States to adopt both a subject-to-tax-requirement in their tax treaties (as a condition for granting double tax relief) and a GAAR in their domestic laws.[17]

Within the framework of EU-BEPS, not only the ATAD was adopted in 2016. Also, a specific linking rule (2014) and a general anti-abuse rule (2015) were included in the Parent-Subsidiary Directive.[18]

7.4 Abuse of Rights as a General Principle of EU Law;[19] Objective and Subjective Element

As observed, the Court initially required strict and case-by-case proportionality of anti-abuse measures (no overkill): only 'wholly artificial' structures could be outlawed. To

16 Communication from the Commission to the Council, the EP and the EcoSoC of 10 December 2007 on the application of ant-abuse measures in the area of direct taxation, COM(2007)785 final.

17 Commission Recommendation of 6 December 2012 on aggressive tax planning C (2012) 8806 final.

18 Council Directive 2014/86/EU of 8 July 2014, amending Directive 2011/96/EU, O.J. L 219/40 of 25 July 2014 (linking rule), and Council Directive 2015/121 of 27 January 2015 amending Directive 2011/96/EU, O.J. L 21/1 of 28 January 2015 (GAAR).

19 See Rita de la Feria and Stefan Vogenauer (eds.), 'Prohibition of Abuse of Law: A New General Principle of EU Law?' (37 contributors), Hart Publishing, 2011.

illustrate, *ICI v. Colmer*[20] concerned the UK 'consortium relief' which allowed *pro rata parte* loss carry-over from joint venture subsidiaries to the parent companies, but only if the majority of the joint venture's holdings were UK-resident. The Court did not accept that condition:

> '26. As regards the justification based on the risk of tax avoidance, suffice it to note that the legislation at issue in the main proceedings does not have the specific purpose of preventing wholly artificial arrangements, set up to circumvent UK tax legislation, from attracting tax benefits, but applies generally to all situations in which the majority of a group's subsidiaries are established, for whatever reason, outside the United Kingdom. However, the establishment of a company outside the United Kingdom does not, of itself, necessarily entail tax avoidance, since that company will in any event be subject to the tax legislation of the State of establishment.'

General exclusion of all or an entire category of cross-border cases for a (remote) possibility of abuse is thus disproportional or even unsuitable to attain the goal of prevention of abuse. The subsequent *Eurowings*[21] and *Cadbury Schweppes*[22] and *Lexel*[23] cases showed that the Member States may not penalize the use of low tax regimes in other jurisdictions if the economic activity in that jurisdiction is genuine. *Eurowings* concerned the German *Gewerbesteuer* (a regional tax on business yield and assets). To prevent double taxation, relief was available if assets had been leased from another undertaking which was also subject to *Gewerbesteuer*. Consequently, German companies leasing assets from a foreign lessor (not subject to *Gewerbesteuer*) were not eligible for relief. *Eurowings Luftverkehrs* leased its aircrafts from a lessor established in Ireland and subject there to a special low tax regime (10% rate). The Court saw refusal of the relief as a restriction of the freedom to provide services, as leasing from foreign providers was made less attractive. It did not see why Eurowings should not be allowed to benefit from relative differences in tax burden (regulatory competition) between Member States by choosing an Irish special-rate lessor, as that was the very idea of an internal market:

> '44. Any tax advantage resulting for providers of services from the low taxation to which they are subject in the Member State in which they are established cannot be used by another Member State to justify less favorable treatment in tax matters given to recipients of services established in the latter State [see (...) *Commission v. France*, paragraph 21, *and Asscher*, paragraph 53].
> 45. As the Commission rightly observed, such compensatory tax arrangements prejudice the very foundations of the single market.'

In *Eurowings*, the lessee and the lessor were not associated. Therefore, there could be no doubt that the lease was agreed at arm's length conditions. There was no BEPS-issue: no artificial profit shift from a high tax country (Germany) to a low tax country (Ireland). *Cadbury Schweppes*, by contrast, concerned two *controlled* group financing subsidiaries of a UK group benefiting from the Irish (then) special low-tax IFSC regime. The UK applied its

20 Case C-264/96, *ICI v. Colmer*, EU:C:1997:182, [1998] ECR I-4695.
21 Case C-294/97, *Eurowings Luftverkehrs AG*, EU:C:1999:524, [1999] ECR I-7447.
22 Case C-196/04, *Cadbury Schweppes*, EU:C:2006:544, [2006] ECR I-7995.
23 Case C-484/19, *Lexel*, EU:C:2021:34, H&I 2021/342 (comments by Wattel).

CFC legislation, taxing the subsidiaries' profits on an accrual basis in the hands of the UK parent as if they were branches (and crediting the (low) corporation tax paid in Ireland). The Court did not visibly care that the subsidiaries were benefiting from a special low tax regime which was regarded as (acceptable) State aid by the Commission. It reiterated its 'wholly artificial arrangements' test. Appreciating that the Irish subsidiaries were fully controlled and that the tax regime might be suspect, it held that if the establishment and the economic activities were genuine (no letterbox-like companies), then no restriction on grounds of prevention of abuse was acceptable. It had not been demonstrated that the financing arrangements between the UK part of the group and the Irish financing companies were not at arm's length. In *X GmbH*[24] the Grand Chamber of Court reconfirmed the *Cadbury Schweppes* line of reasoning (see more: Chapter 9).

In other areas than taxation, economic operators were being creative as well. The *Emsland-Stärke*[25] case involved a company exporting agricultural products from Germany to a third State (Switzerland) for which export restitutions were paid by Germany on the basis of EC Regulation 2730/79. However, the goods were re-imported into the EU, either in Germany or in Italy, untouched, in the same packaging and with the same means of transportation, where they entered free circulation after payment of applicable customs duties. Apparently, the export restitutions were higher than the customs duties upon importation plus the cost of having the lorries drive around in circles. At a given moment, Germany refused to pay out new export restitutions and wanted to recover previously paid restitutions as clearly, the export restitutions did not serve any of the purposes they were meant for, but all of this was completely legal. The Court held that in these circumstances, EU Regulation 2730/79 could not be relied on by *Emsland-Stärke* to resist recovery, formulating an objective and a subjective test for establishing abuse ((i) defeating object and purpose of the rule relied on, and (ii) abusive intent):

> '52. A finding of an abuse requires, first, a combination of objective circumstances in which, despite formal observance of the conditions laid down by the Community rules, the purpose of those rules has not been achieved.
> 53. It requires, second, a subjective element consisting in the intention to obtain an advantage from the Community rules by creating artificially the conditions laid down for obtaining it. The existence of that subjective element can be established, *inter alia*, by evidence of collusion between the Community exporter receiving the refunds and the importer of the goods in the non-member country.
> 54. It is for the national court to establish the existence of those two elements, evidence of which must be adduced in accordance with the rules of national law, provided that the effectiveness of Community law is not thereby undermined.'

24 Case C-135/17 (*X GmbH*), EU:C:2019:136 6.
25 Case C-110/99, *Emsland-Stärke*, EU:C:2000:695, [2000] ECR I-11569.

A long list of consistent CJEU case law in non-tax cases[26] shows that economic operators may be denied recourse to EU law where that recourse is frivolous, where the connecting factor to EU law, especially the cross-border aspect, is artificially created ('U-turns') and therefore lacks real economic substance (see, in particular, *TV10*[27] and *Factortame II*[28]), as well as where reliance on EU law serves purposes alien to object and purpose of EU law relied on (see, in particular, *Kefalas*[29]). This general EU law principle of prohibiting abusive practices obviously extends to all areas of law, *e.g.* access to professions such as those of lawyers,[30] tariff quotas for import of Chinese garlic,[31] the EU citizens' right to reside freely in the EU,[32] equal treatment between men and women in employment,[33] and even to customs duties.[34]

The same test as adopted in *Emsland-Stärke* for abuse of fully harmonized *EU law* (EU export restitutions) was applied in the field of *indirect* taxes (half EU law, half national law, VAT-proceeds feeding both the Member States' budgets and the EU's budget, and customs duties almost entirely forming an 'own resource' of the EU, collected by the Member States). The *Halifax* Case[35] concerned a legal structure set up by a UK bank (banking services are exempt from VAT; as a consequence, banks cannot deduct input-VAT) aimed at artificially avoiding the non-deductibility of input-VAT on the construction of call centers. The Court firmly curbed abusive practices, but also stressed the importance of legal certainty for economic operators and the fact that they are free to structure their business so as to limit their tax liability:

> '68. (…), Community law cannot be relied on for abusive or fraudulent ends (….).
> 69. The application of Community legislation cannot be extended to cover abusive practices by economic operators, that is to say transactions carried out not in the context of normal commercial operations, but solely for the purpose of wrongfully obtaining advantages provided for by Community law (see, to that effect, (…) *Emsland-Stärke*, paragraph 51).
> 70. That principle of prohibiting abusive practices also applies to the sphere of VAT.
> 71. Preventing possible tax evasion, avoidance and abuse is an objective recognized and encouraged by the Sixth Directive (…).
> 72. However, as the Court has held (…), Community legislation must be certain and its application foreseeable by those subject to it (…). That requirement of legal certainty must

26 See, *e.g.*, Case 33/74, *Van Binsbergen*, EU:C.1974:131, [1974] ECR 1299; Case 115/78, *Knoors*, EU:C:1979:31, [1979] ECR 399; Case 229/83, *Leclerc v. Au blé vert*, EU:C:1985:1; Case 79/85, *Segers*, EU:C:1986:308, [1986] ECR 2375; Case 39/86, *Sylvie Lair*, EU:C:1988:322, [1988] ECR 3161; Case 292/86, *Claude Gullung*, EU:C:1988:15; Case C-221/89, *Factortame II*, EU:C:1991:320, [1991] ECR I-3905; Case C-357/89, *Raulin*, EU:C:1992:87, [1992] ECR I-1027; Case C-370/90, *Surinder Singh*, EU:C:1992:296, [1992] ECR I-4265; Case C-23/93, *TV 10*, EU:C:1994:362, [1994] ECR I-4795; Case C-212/97, *Centros*, EU:C:1999:126, [1999] ECR I-1459; Case C-367/96, *Kefalas*, EU:C:1998:222, [1998] ECR I-2843.

27 Case C-23/93, *TV 10*, EU:C:1994:362, [1994] ECR I-4795.

28 Case C-221/89, *Factortame II*, EU:C:1991:320, [1991] ECR I-3905.

29 Case C-367/96, *Kefalas*, EU:C:1998:222, [1998] ECR I-2843.

30 Case C-58/13, *Torresi*, EU:C:2014:2088.

31 Case C-155/13, *SICES*, EU:C:2014:145.

32 Case C-202/13, *Mc Carthy*, EU:C:2014:2450.

33 Case C-423/15, *Kratzer*, EU:C:2016:604.

34 Case C-522/16, *A.*, EU:C:2017:778.

35 Case C-255/02, *Halifax a.o.*, EU:C:2005:200, [2006] ECR I-1751.

> be observed all the more strictly in the case of rules liable to entail financial consequences, in order that those concerned may know precisely the extent of the obligations which they impose on them (...).
> 73. Moreover, it is clear from the case-law that a trader's choice between exempt transactions and taxable transactions may be based on a range of factors, including tax considerations relating to the VAT system (...). Where the taxable person chooses one of two transactions, the Sixth Directive does not require him to choose the one which involves paying the highest amount of VAT. On the contrary, (...), taxpayers may choose to structure their business so as to limit their tax liability.
> 74. In view of the foregoing considerations, it would appear that, in the sphere of VAT, an abusive practice can be found to exist only if, first, the transactions concerned, notwithstanding formal application of the conditions laid down by the relevant provisions of the Sixth Directive and the national legislation transposing it, result in the accrual of a tax advantage the grant of which would be contrary to the purpose of those provisions.
> 75. Second, it must also be apparent from a number of objective factors that the essential aim of the transactions concerned is to obtain a tax advantage. (...), the prohibition of abuse is not relevant where the economic activity carried out may have some explanation other than the mere attainment of tax advantages.'

Thus, the objective element in *Emsland-Stärke* ('the purpose of those rules has not been achieved', as there was no genuine export from the Union) was rephrased for tax cases to (emphasis added): '*contrary* to one of more of the objectives of' the rule of EU at issue. This was reiterated in *Part Service*,[36] again a VAT case, this time concerning the splitting of a lease contract into a rental contract (taxed) and a financing contract (exempt), in which the Court also clarified that the term 'the essential aim of the transactions concerned' does not mean the *only* aim; if the 'principal aim' of the transaction(s) is tax avoidance, that may be enough for a finding of a prohibited abuse:

> '62. As regards the second criterion [the subjective element; *authors*], the national court, (...), may take account of the purely artificial nature of the transactions and the links of a legal, economic and/or personal nature between the operators involved (*Halifax and Others*, paragraph 81), those aspects being such as to demonstrate that the accrual of a tax advantage constitutes the principal aim pursued, notwithstanding the possible existence, in addition, of economic objectives arising from, for example, marketing, organization or guarantee considerations.'

An ancillary or concomitant business purpose is therefore not enough to protect a (set of) transaction(s) against a finding of abuse if the main ('essential', 'principal') goal is to (artificially) avoid tax.[37]

Subsequently, the Court followed the same approach in the field of *harmonized direct* taxation. In *Foggia*[38] and subsequent cases concerning the anti-abuse reservations in the Merger and Parent-Subsidiary Directives (see Sections 17.13 and 16.7, respectively), the Court reiterated that the anti-abuse reservations reflect a general principle of EU law

36 Case C-425/06, *Part Service Srl*, EU:C:2008:108, [2008] ECR I-897.
37 See also Case C-251/16, *Edward Cussens a.o.*, EU:C:2017:881, point 53.
38 Case C-126/10, *FOGGIA-Sociedade*, EU:C:2011:718.

prohibiting abuse of rights, and that fiscal motives are not necessarily fatal, as long as they are not 'predominant'. In, a.o., *Kofoed*[39] (point 38), *Eqiom*,[40] (point 23) and *Argenta Spaarbank II*[41] (point 60) the Court reiterated that the anti-abuse provisions in Article (now) 15 of the Merger Directive and Article 1(2) (now 1(4)) of the Parent-Subsidiary Directive 'reflect the general EU law principle that abuse of rights is prohibited (...), and that EU law therefore cannot be relied on for abusive or fraudulent ends' and in *Eqiom* explicitly considered that these anti-abuse provisions have the same scope as that general principle prohibiting abuse of rights:

> '64. (...), it must be noted that the objective of combating fraud and tax evasion, whether it is relied on under Article 1(2) of the Parent-Subsidiary Directive or as justification for an exception to primary law, has the same scope. Therefore, the findings set out in paragraphs 30 to 36 of the present judgment [on the narrow interpretation of the anti-abuse provision in Article 1(2, now 4) of the Parent-Subsidiary Directive; authors] also apply with regard to that freedom.'

The same language (except for the incomplete 'combating fraud and tax evasion' having been reframed as 'preventing tax avoidance and tax evasion') is contained in the *Euro Park Service* Case[42] concerning the anti-abuse reservation in Article (now) 15 of the Merger Directive and in the *Danish BO* cases[43] concerning the PSD and the IRD. As observed and elaborated on in Section 7.2 above, this raises the question of whether the anti-abuse reservations of competence in the corporate tax directives serve any purpose next to the autonomous and general principle of EU law that abuse of rights is prohibited.

The above does not mean that taxpayers may not choose the most tax-efficient route if there are several possibilities to attain a (mostly) non-tax aim. *Weald Leasing*,[44] again a VAT case, illustrates what the Court meant in point 73 of *Halifax* as regards a taxpayer's freedom to choose the least taxed commercial route: the significant tax timing advantage for an undertaking arising from asset leasing instead of outright purchase of assets, is not contrary to the purpose of the relevant VAT provisions and of the national legislation transposing it, provided that the contractual terms of the transactions, particularly those setting the level of rentals, 'correspond to arm's length terms' and that the involvement of an intermediate third party in the transactions is not such as to preclude the application of those VAT provisions. The fact that the undertaking does not engage in leasing transactions in its normal commercial operations is irrelevant. Likewise, the Court made clear in *WebMindLicences*[45] that the licensing of a business by a Hungarian undertaking to a third party in Madeira enjoying a lower VAT rate could not in itself be regarded as a tax advantage contrary to the objectives of the VAT Directive, unless the services were in fact supplied by the Hungarian undertaking and the economic activity in Madeira

39 Case C-321/05, *Kofoed*, EU:C:2007:408, [2007] ECR p. I-5795.
40 Case C-6/16, *Eqiom SAS/Enka former Holcim France SAS*, EU:C:2017:641.
41 Case C-39/16, *Argenta Spaarbank NV II*, EU:C:2017:813.
42 Case C-14/16, *Euro Park Service*, EU:C:2017:177, point 69.
43 Joined Cases C-115/16, C-118/16 and C-119/16 (*N Luxembourg 1*), EU:C:2019:134.
44 Case C-103/09, *HMRC v Weald Leasing Ltd*, EU:C:2010:633.
45 Case C-419/14, *WebMindLicenses*, EU:C:2015:832. See also Case C-653/11, *Newey*, EU:C:2013:409, point 46.

was therefore not genuine in terms of premises and human and technical resources (no genuine exercise of any Treaty freedom).

It is very interesting – and helpful with a view to consistency – that in *Weald Leasing*, the Court also in the context of VAT relied on 'arm's length terms' test as a criterion for distinguishing between presumable abuse and genuine business purposes, as it does in the direct tax field (see the *Thin Cap*,[46] *Itelcar*[47], *Verder LabTec*[48] and *Lexel*[49] cases).

Finally, the same language as in *Emsland-Stärke* (points 52 and 53) and in *Halifax* (points 74 and 75) was also used for *un*harmonized *direct* tax matters by the Court in *Cadbury Schweppes*, cited above, concerning, moreover, exclusively *national* tax legislation, namely the UK CFC legislation. For the scope of application of the abuse of rights doctrine, it is therefore immaterial whether the economic operator relies on EU law to frustrate *EU* law or to circumvent *national* law. The EU abuse of right doctrine applies irrespective of the field of law involved, whether exclusively governed by EU law (regulations; customs duties, export restitutions), minimally or fully harmonized law (directives; VAT; excises), or completely unharmonized (national) law (direct taxes): EU law simply cannot be relied on to circumvent the law, be it national law, bilateral treaty law, EU law, or Murphy's law. Although the Court in *Cadbury Schweppes* first reiterated its 'wholly artificial arrangement' standard, it went on to apply the *Emsland* test as an elaboration of that standard, referring to both *Emsland-Stärke* and *Halifax*:

> '64. In order to find that there is such an arrangement there must be, in addition to a subjective element consisting in the intention to obtain a tax advantage, objective circumstances showing that, despite formal observance of the conditions laid down by Community law, the objective pursued by freedom of establishment, as set out in paragraphs 54 and 55 of this judgment, has not been achieved (see, to that effect, Case C-111/99 *Emsland-Stärke* [2000] ECR I-11569, paragraphs 52 and 53, and Case C-255/02 *Halifax and Others* (...), paragraphs 74 and 75).
> 65. In those circumstances, in order for the legislation on CFCs to comply with Community law, the taxation provided for by that legislation must be excluded where, despite the existence of tax motives, the incorporation of a CFC reflects economic reality.
> 66. That incorporation must correspond with an actual establishment intended to carry on genuine economic activities in the host Member State, as is apparent from the case-law recalled in paragraphs 52 to 54 of this judgment.'

The subsequent VAT Case *Cussens*[50] and *Danish BO* cases[51] confirms that it is immaterial (i) whether EU law is relied on to frustrate EU law or national law, (ii) which substantive field of law is involved and (iii) whether and to which extent that field of law has been harmonized, coordinated or unified at EU level: EU law can simply not be relied on for abusive purposes.

46 Case C-524/05, *Test Claimants in the Thin Cap Group Litigation*, EU:C:2006:436.
47 Case C-282/12, *ITELCAR and Fazenda Publica*, EU:C:2013:629.
48 Case C-657/13, *Verder Labtec GmbH &Co KG*, EU:C:2015:331.
49 Case C-484/19, *Lexel*, EU:C:2021:34, H&I 2021/342 (comments by Wattel).
50 Case C-251/16, *Edward Cussens a.o.*, EU:C:2017:881.
51 Joint Cases C-115/16, C-118/16 and C-119/16, *N Luxembourg 1*, ECLI:EU:C:2019:134.

See the *Danish BO* cases[52]:

> '96. It is settled case-law that there is, in EU law, a general legal principle that EU law cannot be relied on for abusive or fraudulent ends (judgments of 9 March 1999, *Centros*, C-212/97, EU:C:1999:126, paragraph 24 and the case-law cited; of 21 February 2006, *Halifax and Others*, C-255/02, EU:C:2006:121, paragraph 68; of 12 September 2006, *Cadbury Schweppes and Cadbury Schweppes Overseas*, C-196/04, EU:C:2006:544, paragraph 35; of 22 November 2017, *Cussens and Others*, C-251/16, EU:C:2017:881, paragraph 27; and of 11 July 2018, *Commission* v *Belgium*, C-356/15, EU:C:2018:555, paragraph 99).
> 97. That general principle of law must be complied with by individuals. Indeed, the application of EU legislation cannot be extended to cover transactions carried out for the purpose of fraudulently or wrongfully obtaining advantages provided for by EU law (see, to that effect, judgments of 5 July 2007, *Kofoed*, C-321/05, EU:C:2007:408, paragraph 38; of 22 November 2017, *Cussens and Others*, C-251/16, EU:C:2017:881, paragraph 27; and of 11 July 2018, *Commission v Belgium*, C-356/15, EU:C:2018:555, paragraph 99).
> 98. It thus follows from that principle that a Member State must refuse to grant the benefit of the provisions of EU law where they are relied upon not with a view to achieving the objectives of those provisions but with the aim of benefiting from an advantage in EU law although the conditions for benefiting from that advantage are fulfilled only formally.
> 99. That is so, for example, where the completion of customs formalities does not fall within the context of normal commercial transactions but is purely formal and is designed solely to obtain wrongfully the grant of compensatory amounts (see, to that effect, judgments of 27 October 1981, *Schumacher and Others*, 250/80, EU:C:1981:246, paragraph 16, and of 3 March 1993, *General Milk Products*, C-8/92, EU:C:1993:82, paragraph 21) or export refunds (see, to that effect, judgment of 14 December 2000, *Emsland-Stärke*, C-110/99, EU:C:2000:695, paragraph 59).
> 100. Furthermore, the principle of prohibition of abuse of rights is applicable in fields as varied as the free movement of goods (judgment of 10 January 1985, *Association des Centres distributeurs Leclerc and Thouars Distribution*, 229/83, EU:C:1985:1, paragraph 27), freedom to provide services (judgment of 3 February 1993, *Veronica Omroep Organisatie*, C-148/91, EU:C:1993:45, paragraph 13), public service contracts (judgment of 11 December 2014, *Azienda sanitaria locale n. 5 'Spezzino' and Others*, C-113/13, EU:C:2014:2440, paragraph 62), freedom of establishment (judgment of 9 March 1999, *Centros*, C-212/97, EU:C:1999:126, paragraph 24), company law (judgment of 23 March 2000, *Diamantis*, C-373/97, EU:C:2000:150, paragraph 33), social security (judgments of 2 May 1996, *Paletta*, C-206/94, EU:C:1996:182, paragraph 24; of 6 February 2018, *Altun and Others*, C-359/16, EU:C:2018:63, paragraph 48; and of 11 July 2018, *Commission* v *Belgium*, C-356/15, EU:C:2018:555, paragraph 99), transport (judgment of 6 April 2006, *Agip Petroli*, C-456/04, EU:C:2006:241, paragraphs 19 to 25), social policy (judgment of 28 July 2016, *Kratzer*, C-423/15, EU:C:2016:604, paragraphs 37 to 41), restrictive measures (judgment of 21 December 2011, *Afrasiabi and Others*, C-72/11, EU:C:2011:874, paragraph 62) and value added tax (VAT) (judgment of 21 February 2006, *Halifax and Others*, C-255/02, EU:C:2006:121, paragraph 74).
> 101. As regards that last field, the Court has observed on a number of occasions that, whilst preventing possible tax evasion, avoidance and abuse is an objective recognised and encouraged by Sixth Council Directive 77/388/EEC of 17 May 1977 on the harmonisation of the laws of the Member States relating to turnover taxes – Common system of value added tax: uniform basis of assessment (OJ 1977 L 145, p. 1), the principle that abusive practices are prohibited nonetheless constitutes a general principle of EU law which applies

52 Joint Cases C-115/16, C-118/16 and C-119/16, *N Luxembourg 1*, EU:C:2019:134.

irrespective of whether the rights and advantages that are abused have their basis in the Treaties, in a regulation or in a directive (see, to that effect, judgment of 22 November 2017, *Cussens and Others*, C-251/16, EU:C:2017:881, paragraphs 30 and 31).'

The *Cussens* Case and *Danish BO* cases[53] also makes clear that, given the general prohibition of abuse of rights, no national legal basis for refusal of advantages is required if extending those advantages would amount to abuse of rights within the autonomous EU law meaning of that concept, as according to the Court, the occurrence of abuse 'simply' takes away the entitlement to that advantage.

See *Cussens:*[54]

'32. (...), according to the Court's case-law, refusal of a right or an advantage on account of abusive or fraudulent acts is simply the consequence of the finding that, in the event of fraud or abuse of rights, the objective conditions required in order to obtain the advantage sought are not, in fact, met, and accordingly such a refusal does not require a specific legal basis (see, to that effect (...) Emsland-Stärke, C-110/99, (...) *Halifax* (...) and (...) Pometon, C-158/08).
33. Therefore, the principle that abusive practices are prohibited may be relied on against a taxable person to refuse him, inter alia, the right to exemption from VAT, even in the absence of provisions of national law providing for such refusal (see, to that effect, (...) 'Italmoda' (...), C-131/13, C-163/13 and C-164/13 (...).'

This was confirmed in the *Danish BO* cases.

We conclude that:
- the need to prevent tax avoidance is both (i) a mandatory requirement of public interest under the Court's rule of reason, justifying restrictions on free movement which are suitable and proportional to take away the abuse, and (ii) a species of the Court's general EU law concept of a general prohibition of abuse of rights;
- the same test is used by the Court for establishing abuse of secondary EU law, whether tax (VAT; EU corporate tax directives) or non-tax (fish quota, export restitutions), and for establishing abuse of Treaty rights to circumvent legitimate national law, namely: a 'wholly artificial arrangements' test; these occur where (i) there is intent to obtain, through artifices, benefits not intended for the economic operator involved (subjective test), and (ii) granting the benefits artificially sought would defeat object and purpose of the provision of EU law relied on (objective test);
- it is not necessary for the finding of an abuse that tax avoidance is the only or the almost exclusive aim or the transaction(s) performed; it is enough that the 'principal', 'main' or 'predominant' aim is tax avoidance;
- abuse must in principle be established on a case by case basis to be capable of restricting recourse to rights conferred by EU law, but – as will be elaborated on in Section 7.5 below – it may also be curbed by generally excluding from tax benefits certain categories of cross-border cases (entailing a risk of over inclusiveness ('overkill')), provided that (i)

53 Joint Cases C-115/16, C-118/16 and C-119/16, *N Luxembourg 1*, ECLI:EU:C:2019:134.
54 Case C-251/16, *Edward Cussens a.o.*, EU:C:2017:881.

such exclusion is based on objective and relevant presumptive criteria (e.g. departure from OECD arm's length standards) and (ii) the taxpayer has a genuine opportunity to rebut the presumption of abuse (to reduce the 'overkill' scope to actual abuse cases);
- the abuse of right doctrine applies irrespective of the field of law involved, and irrespective of whether that field is governed exclusively by EU law, by (minimum) harmonization *and* national law, or in principle only by unharmonized national law (such as the bulk of direct taxation): EU law can simply not be relied on to circumvent the law in general, as was to be expected;
- the anti-abuse reservations in the PSD, the Merger Directive and the IRD are redundant, as they reserve national competence no different from national competence in restricting free movement: exercise of the reserved competence will be tested by the Court in the same manner as any other restriction of free movement;
- the Court does not easily consider abuse present where taxpayers seek to avail themselves of tax benefits by using other jurisdictions, foreign company law or other opportunities provided for by regulatory competition between Member States, or where taxpayers choose the least taxed path to a certain (mainly) non-tax goal, as long as the migration, the arrangement or the transaction 'reflects economic reality' (represents a genuine exercise of a free movement right; does not hinge on artifices). Tax jurisdiction shopping (tax policy competition) is an intrinsic part of an internal market.

7.5 Exclusion of Categories of Cross-Border Cases; Fiscal Coherence; Balanced Allocation; Fiscal Supervision; Territoriality; Overlap of Justifications for Free Movement Restrictions[55]

7.5.1 General presumptions of abuse justified by different reasons in the general interest of a Member State

In most older tax cases, the Court required a case by case assessment of whether actual abuse was present. In more recent cases, the Court also accepts general presumptions of abuse, or at least *a priori* taxation of categories of cross-border cases, sometimes even without requiring an opportunity for the taxpayer to rebut a presumption of abuse, as the justification for such exclusion is not (solely) based on prevention of abuse, but more generally on the need for tax base integrity (the right to tax economic activities carried out within a Member State's territory and unrealized capital gains recorded within a Member State's jurisdiction). The Court thus shows more understanding for both Member States' genuine concerns as regards aggressive tax planning, especially BEPS (base erosion and profit shifting) and more generally: the need for tax base integrity. It does not limit itself any more to examining what a shift of jurisdiction or of legal form means for the taxpayer, but also pays heed to what it means for the 'coherence' of the tax

55 See, for elaboration, Peter J. Wattel, 'Fiscal Cohesion, Fiscal Territoriality and Preservation of the (Balanced) Allocation of Taxing Power; What is the Difference?' in: Dennis Weber (ed.): *The Influence of European Law on Direct Taxation*, Kluwer Law International, 2007, p. 139-156; Werner Haslehner '"Consistency" and Fundamental Freedoms: The Case of Direct Taxation,' 50 *Common Market Law Review*, 2013 pp. 739-772, 766; Marcel Schaper, 'The Need to Prevent Abusive Practices and Fraud as a Composite Justification', 23 *EC Tax Review* 2014/4, pp. 220-229.

systems and for the 'balanced allocation of taxing power' of the Member States involved. Possibly inspired by the opinion of A-G. Geelhoed in Case C-524/04, *Thin Cap GLO*, the Court began to accept reasonable presumptive criteria which contribute to reasonable tax base protection against BEPS, legal certainty and practicability for both tax authorities and taxpayers. This brings the abuse justification for fiscal restrictions closer to both the fiscal coherence justification first accepted in Case C-204/90, *Bachmann*,[56] and the balanced-allocation-of-taxing-power-justification first accepted in Case C-466/03, *Marks & Spencer II*.[57]

A clear example of acceptable restrictive taxation although 'wholly artificial arrangements' are not present, is exit taxation: whether or not there is any intent of avoiding tax is irrelevant if a Member State is losing its tax connecting factor due to the emigration of the taxpayer. It may then tax the emigrant (provided it does so proportionally) irrespective of artifices or bad intentions. *Van Hilten-Van der Heijden*[58] concerned a Dutch anti-abuse measure treating as resident, for inheritance tax purposes, emigrating nationals who decease within ten years after emigration (trailing tax). Application was entirely independent of the reasons for emigration. Mrs. Van Hilten first moved abroad and died just before the ten-year period expired. As the Court found no restriction of the free movement of capital (Mrs. Van Hilten and her heirs were not taxed less favorably than if she had stayed in the Netherlands), no justification seemed necessary. Nevertheless, the Court referred to the OECD Model Double Inheritance Tax Convention and its official commentary, which endorsed this kind of extended fictitious residence for anti-abuse reasons:

> '48. (....) It is clear from the commentaries on Articles 4, 7, 9A and 9B of that model that that type of legislation is justified by the concern to prevent a form of tax evasion whereby a national of a State, in contemplation of his death, transfers his residence to another State where the tax is lower. (...).'

This is surprising, as the tax administration never even suggested any intent of tax avoidance, and as it is clear that as an abuse remedy, the measure is *quite* disproportional. Indeed, in another exit tax case, *De Lasteyrie du Saillant*,[59] in which solely an abuse-defense was put forward by France, even a five-year blind tracing rule for emigrants was considered unacceptable. The measure could impossibly be justified in terms of 'wholly artificial arrangements,' as there was absolutely nothing artificial about Mrs. Van Hilten's residence.

In subsequent cases, the permissibility of general exclusions or presumptions on the basis of mere *fear* for or *risk* of abuse or the mere fact of loss of taxing jurisdiction was crucial for upholding not very targeted national measures fragmentizing the internal market. In *Marks & Spencer II*,[60] the Court saw a restriction of the right of establishment in the fact that the UK did not provide relief for foreign losses of foreign subsidiaries not subject to UK taxing jurisdiction, but it also found a justification for such restriction in a combination of three factors, one of which was the mere *risk* of abuse:

56 Case C-204/90, *Hans Martin Bachmann v. Belgium*, EU:C:1992:35.
57 Case C-446/03, *Marks & Spencer II*, EU:C:2005:763, [2005] ECR I-10837.
58 Case C-513/03, *Van Hilten-van der Heijden*, EU:C:2006:131, [2006] ECR I-1957.
59 Case C-9/02, *Hughes de Lasteyrie de Saillant*, EU:C:2004:138, [2004] ECR I-2409.
60 Case C-446/03, *Marks & Spencer II*, EU:C:2005:763, [2005] ECR I-10837.

> '42. (...), the United Kingdom (...) put forward three factors to justify the restriction.
> 43. First, in tax matters profits and losses are two sides of the same coin and must be treated symmetrically in the same tax system in order to protect a balanced allocation of the power to impose taxes between the different Member States concerned. Second, if the losses were taken into consideration in the parent company's Member State they might well be taken into account twice. Third, and last, if the losses were not taken into account in the Member State in which the subsidiary is established there would be a risk of tax avoidance.
> (...)
> 49. As regards, last, the third justification, relating to the risk of tax avoidance, it must be accepted that the possibility of transferring the losses incurred by a nonresident company to a resident company entails the risk that within a group of companies losses will be transferred to companies established in the Member States which apply the highest rates of taxation and in which the tax value of the losses is therefore the highest.
> 50. To exclude group relief for losses incurred by non-resident subsidiaries prevents such practices, which may be inspired by the realization that the rates of taxation applied in the various Member States vary significantly.
> 51. In the light of those three justifications, taken together, it must be observed that restrictive provisions such as those at issue in the main proceedings pursue legitimate objectives which are compatible with the Treaty and constitute overriding reasons in the public interest and that they are apt to ensure the attainment of those objectives.'

Point 49 implies that the UK was allowed to prevent not only factual abuse, but also the abstract *risk* of abuse. The Court did not require the UK to assess, let alone on a 'case by case' basis, whether cross-border relief would be 'wholly artificial', nor whether the *EmslandStärke* test of abuse was satisfied. That test was clearly not met, as it was common ground that there was no artificiality or intent of abuse present in the *M&S II* case. Nevertheless, any and all cross-border loss relief was excluded categorically (except definitive subsidiary losses, as the Court (incorrectly, in our opinion) considered it disproportionate if these would not be deductible anywhere). The Court did not require the UK to provide for the possibility to rebut the presumption or for an opportunity for the taxpayer to eliminate the risk of abuse. The 'risk of tax avoidance' was one out of three justifications which were 'taken together' by the Court. The two others were the risk of double dips, and the need for a balanced allocation of taxing power. As these three were 'taken together,' it was impossible to see how they interrelated, but it is clear that the justifications (i) preventing tax avoidance, (ii) preventing double dips (= fiscal incoherence) and (iii) maintaining a balanced allocation of taxing power are overlapping. We submit that justifications (i) and (ii) were irrelevant: all that mattered, was the fact that if the UK were required to offset foreign losses of non-subject, nonresident group companies, the UK would be prevented from taxing the group profits generated *within* its territory, which clearly destroys an appropriate allocation and exercise of taxing power. As the Court regularly considers: Member States must be able to tax economic activities carried out within their territories. At any rate, the case marks a shift from 'case by case' abuse-testing on the basis of artificiality, to presumptive abuse risk management on the basis of overlapping 'coherence' and 'balanced allocation' concepts. The Court's reasoning in *M&S II* resembles application of the *Bachmann* justification: the coherence of national tax systems (and a proper exercise of taxing power) would be destroyed if company losses sourced within one jurisdiction could at will be carried over to any other jurisdiction in order to erase profits sourced there.

In *Oy AA*,[61] like *M&S II* concerning intra-group cross-border carry-over of tax base (this time profits instead of losses), the Court realized that, 'taken as a whole' (see point 63 in the quotation below) it was not any more testing individual 'wholly artificial arrangements', but generally safeguarding jurisdictional tax base integrity. It 'linked' the categories 'prevention of tax avoidance' and 'safeguarding a balanced allocation of taxing power'. In substance, it held (point 62) that preservation of a balanced allocation *encloses* the smaller category of curbing tax avoidance:

> '62. It should be noted at the outset that the objectives of safeguarding the balanced allocation of the power to impose taxes between Member States and the prevention of tax avoidance are linked. Conduct involving the creation of wholly artificial arrangements which do not reflect economic reality, with a view to escaping the tax normally due on the profits generated by activities carried out on national territory is such as to undermine the right of the Member States to exercise their tax jurisdiction in relation to those activities and jeopardise a balanced allocation between Member States of the power to impose taxes (*Cadbury Schweppes and Cadbury Schweppes Overseas*, paragraphs 55 and 56, and *Test Claimants in the Thin Cap Group Litigation*, paragraphs 74 and 75).
> 63. Even if the legislation at issue in the main proceedings is not specifically designed to exclude from the tax advantage it confers purely artificial arrangements, devoid of economic reality, created with the aim of escaping the tax normally due on the profits generated by activities carried out on national territory, such legislation may nevertheless be regarded as proportionate to the objectives pursued, taken as a whole.
> 64. In a situation in which the advantage in question consists in the possibility of making a transfer of income, (...), any extension of that advantage to cross-border situations would, (...), have the effect of allowing groups of companies to choose freely the Member State in which their profits will be taxed, to the detriment of the right of the Member State of the subsidiary to tax profits generated by activities carried out on its territory.'

From paragraph 64 of *OY AA* it becomes clear that tax regimes that have 'the effect' of allowing groups of companies to choose freely the Member State in which their profits will be taxed can be, justified by the balanced allocation, refused in cross-border situations. Following cases such as *SGI* and *X Holding*, the Court defines this more broadly in *Lexel* (para. 61):[62]

> 'The justification based on the preservation of the balanced allocation of the power to impose taxes between Member States has inter alia been allowed by the Court where a condition of residence is required in order to benefit from a particular tax scheme in order to avoid the taxable subject *having the free choice of deciding in which State a profit is taxed or a loss is taken into account and the possibility of freely moving the taxable base between Member States'* (italics authors)

This shows that a certain tax regime can be refused in cross-border situations if this leads to what tax experts call 'Base Erosion or Profit Shifting' (BEPS). This is protection

61 Case C-231/05, *Oy AA*, EU:C:2007:439, [2007] ECR I-6373.
62 Case C-484/19, *Lexel*, EU:C:2021:34, H&I 2021/342 (comments by Wattel).

of the national tax base (territoriality). That being said it also appears from *Lexel* that the Court's balanced allocation justification only applies to a limited extent to anti-BEPS rules. Interest deduction limitation rules for instance that only apply within the same group of companies (only to internal interest payments) and which try to protect the national tax base against BEPS cannot be justified by the balanced allocation of taxing rights between the Member States. The Court ruled in *Lexel* (para. 67):

> 'Within that context, it must be made clear that, according to the legislative preparatory works regarding the exception, that provision seeks expressly to prevent the erosion of the Swedish tax base which could result from tax planning linked to the deduction of interest expenses in a cross-border situation. However, such an objective cannot be confused with the need to preserve the balanced allocation of the power to impose taxes between the Member States'[63]

In *Deister* and *Juhler*,[64] it rather vaguely considered 'combating tax evasion and avoidance' and 'seeking to safeguard a balanced allocation of taxation powers' to be 'connected.'

We observe (see, for elaboration, Section 6.4.2), conceptually the justification accepted in *Oy AA*, is also very close to the need to safeguard the 'integrity' or the 'coherence' of the national tax system as postulated for the first time in *Bachmann* and reiterated in *Krankenheim Ruhesitz*[65] and *Timac Agro*,[66] both cases concerning the recapture of foreign branch losses previously deducted in the head office's jurisdiction (see Section 18.7). The only new aspect seems to be the name given to the coherence justification, now called the need for 'preservation of the (balanced) allocation of taxing power between the member States', or the need to prevent 'serious undermining of a balanced allocation of the power to impose taxes between the Member States'. In *National Grid Indus*,[67] on exit taxation upon the transfer of a company seat, the Court more or less equated 'coherence' and 'balanced allocation', considering (point 80), that

> 'the requirements of coherence of the tax system and the balanced allocation of powers of taxation coincide.'

Apparently, there is little difference between the two concepts. *SIAT*[68] confirms that finding: the Court considered 'closely linked' (this probably means: largely overlapping)

63 See also: EFTA Court 1 June 2022, E-3/21, PRA Group Europe, point 48: "However, such considerations are not capable of justifying a restriction such as that arising in circumstances in which a tax deduction has been granted in a national but not a cross-border situation. Rather, and in particular, if an EEA State grants such a benefit in a domestic situation (and renounces part of its taxation rights), that EEA State cannot argue the same taxing right is important in the cross-border situation in an attempt to limit equal treatment (compare the judgment in *Rewe Zentralfinanz*, C-347/04, EU:C:2007:194, paragraph 43). Consequently, the difference in treatment does not appear justified by the need to safeguard the balanced allocation of the power to impose taxes between EEA States".

64 Joined Cases C-504/16 and C-613/16, *Deister Holding AG and Juhler Holding A/S*, EU:C:2017:1009, point 96.

65 Case C-157/07, *Krankenheim Ruhesitz am Wannsee-Seniorenheimstatt GmbH*, EU:C:2008:588.

66 Case C-388/14, *Timac Agro Deutschland GmbH*, EU:C:2015:829.

67 Case C-371/10, *National Grid Indus BV*, EU:C:2011:785 referring to AG opinion; EU:C:2011:563.

68 Case C-318/10, *SIAT*, EU:C:2012:415.

no less than three justifications for a national tax measure restricting free movement of payments: (i) the need to curb abuse, (ii) the need for effective fiscal supervision and (ii) the need to safeguard a balanced allocation of taxing power. In that case, it found in principle justified (but not proportionate in its effects) a Belgian rule making deduction of expenses paid abroad to a recipient not seriously taxed (i.e. in a tax haven) conditional upon the taxpayer showing that its payments related to genuine transactions and did not exceed 'normal limits'. Although incompatible with the Treaty freedoms for excessive vagueness, it considered such legislation in principle:

> '48. (...) suitable for attaining the objectives of preventing tax evasion and avoidance and of preserving both the effectiveness of fiscal supervision and the balanced allocation between Member States of the power to impose taxes, all of which – as is apparent from the foregoing – are closely linked in the case before the referring court.'

If the word 'intentional' is inserted in the term 'the need to prevent serious undermining of the balanced allocation of powers of taxation' (*intentional* undermining), then the description of the balanced-allocation justification becomes identical (is reduced) to the abuse justification.

It may be concluded, therefore, that in direct tax cases, if a restrictive national measure can be justified under the fiscal-coherence justification, the balanced-allocation justification or the effective-supervision justification, there is no need for a separate anti-abuse analysis, and therefore no need for establishing 'wholly artificial arrangements.' It is immaterial whether cross-border situations causing jurisdictional imbalance or fiscal incoherence are artificial or intentionally disruptive or not; if they are objectively such as to jeopardize a balanced allocation of taxing rights or the coherence of the national tax system by resulting in (the real risk of) impeding Member States to tax economic activities carried out within their territories, then Member States may exclude them from the regime applicable to domestic situations, but (i) they should limit such exclusion to situations which objectively and verifiably present the risk of such tax imbalances or incoherencies, and (ii) depending on the circumstances, they may in some instances have to provide – for the exclusion to be proportionate – for the opportunity for the taxpayer to rebut a presumption of anti-fiscal motives.

7.5.2 *General presumptions of abuse: examination of objective and ascertainable factors in a consistent and systematic manner*

If a member State uses the regulatory technique of presuming abuse on the basis of certain listed factual circumstances, then the Court in more recent judgments requires that national legislation must rely on an examination of objective and ascertainable factors in order to determine whether a transaction represents a wholly artificial arrangement[69] and is proportionate to that objective, which means that it is suitable for securing, in a consistent and systematic manner, the attainment of the objective pursued and does not go beyond what is necessary in order to attain it[70].

69 Case C-585/22, *X BV*, ECLI:EU:C:2024:822, para. 67.
70 Case C-585/22, *X BV*, ECLI:EU:C:2024:822, para. 33.

In *Felixstowe*[71] – in which the Court also more or less of its own motion introduced a *specific* anti-abuse justification, *i.e.* combating the use of tax havens – the Court reiterated that blind overkill is disproportionate and therefore prohibited. The Case concerned a UK consortium claiming a loss transfer between two UK based group companies, one of them being held by an intermediary holding company in Luxembourg, which was itself held by a Hong-Kong based majority shareholder. It was unclear which of these controlling entities was to blame for the use of a tax haven, which would justify restricting the freedom of establishment. However, the mere fact that an EU-company is directly or indirectly controlled by third State residents is not a good indicator for abuse. Applying such an untargeted indicator is disproportionate. As the Court considered in *Eqiom:*[72]

> '32. In order to determine whether an operation pursues an objective of fraud and abuse, the competent national authorities may not confine themselves to applying predetermined general criteria, but must carry out an individual examination of the whole operation at issue. The imposition of a general tax measure automatically excluding certain categories of taxpayers from the tax advantage, without the tax authorities being obliged to provide even *prima facie* evidence of fraud and abuse, would go further than is necessary for preventing fraud and abuse (see, to that effect, judgment of 8 March 2017, *Euro Park Service*, C-14/16, EU:C:2017:177, paragraphs 55 and 56).'

The *SGI* case[73] concerned Belgian rules – which did not apply internally – against profit shifts abroad through payments to foreign associated companies not at arm's length. Although the Court explicitly established that the restrictive legislation was *not* targeting wholly artificial arrangements but rather the general *risk* of profit shifting, it nevertheless accepted the restrictive rule for tax base integrity reasons (the need to maintain a balanced allocation of taxing powers), provided the taxpayer could rebut the legal presumption of profit shifting where the tax administration provided *prima facie* reasons for believing that the payments abroad were not arm's length (see points 66 and 68; *italics* added):

> '63. (...), it must be held that to permit resident companies to transfer their profits in the form of unusual or gratuitous advantages to companies with which they have a relationship of interdependence that are established in other Member States may well undermine the balanced allocation of the power to impose taxes between the Member States. It would be liable to undermine the very system of the allocation of the power to impose taxes between Member States (....).
> 64. By providing that the resident company is to be taxed in respect of an unusual or gratuitous advantage which it has granted to a company established in another Member State, the legislation at issue (...) permits the Belgian State to exercise its tax jurisdiction in relation to activities carried out in its territory.
> 65. (...), as regards the prevention of tax avoidance, it should be recalled that a national measure restricting freedom of establishment may be justified where it specifically targets wholly artificial arrangements designed to circumvent the legislation of the Member State concerned (....).

71 Case C-80/12, *Felixstowe Dock and Railway Company Ltd et al.*, EU:C:2014:200.
72 Case C-6/16, *Eqiom SAS/Enka former Holcim France SAS*, EU:C:2017:641 points 32-34.
73 Case C-311/08, *Société de Gestion Industrielle (SGI)*, EU:C:2010:26.

> 66. In that context, *national legislation which is not specifically designed to exclude (…) such purely artificial arrangements* – devoid of economic reality, created with the aim of escaping the tax normally due on the profits generated by activities carried out on national territory – *may nevertheless be regarded as justified by the objective of preventing tax avoidance, taken together with that of preserving the balanced allocation* of the power to impose taxes between the Member States (see, to that effect, *Oy AA*, paragraph 63).
> 67. (…), to permit resident companies to grant unusual or gratuitous advantages to companies with which they have a relationship of interdependence that are established in other Member States, without making provision for any corrective tax measures, *carries the risk that*, by means of artificial arrangements, *income transfers may be organized* within companies having a relationship of interdependence towards those established in Member States applying the lowest rates of taxation or in Member States in which such income is not taxed (see, to that effect, *Oy AA*, paragraph 58).
> 68. By providing that the resident company is to be taxed in respect of an unusual or gratuitous advantage which it has granted to a company established in another Member State, the legislation at issue (…) is able to prevent such practices, liable to be encouraged by the finding of significant disparities between the bases of assessment or rates of tax applied in the various Member States and designed only to avoid the tax normally due in the Member State in which the company granting the advantage has its seat (see, to that effect, *Oy AA*, paragraph 59).'

In the seminal *Thin Cap GLO* Case,[74] the Court had already accepted an (OECD-based) arm's length test as appropriate for distinguishing genuine business financing from possibly abusive tax base erosion through interest deduction, but for proportionality reasons, it 'de-generalized' the exclusion by requiring the taxpayer to be given the opportunity to demonstrate genuine business purposes despite failure of the categorical test. That at least shifted the burden of proof: in the old days, it was the tax administration having to demonstrate 'wholly artificial arrangements'; now, it was the taxpayer having to demonstrate genuine business purpose if the tax administration could give *prima facie* that something fishy was afoot. As observed in Section 7.4, the Court later also in the field of VAT used 'arm's length terms' as a criterion for telling apart presumable abuse and genuine business purposes (in *Weald Leasing*[75]). In *SGI*, the Court added a reasonable division of the burden of proof to the proportionality test of arm's length legislation (see Section 7.6 below).

In *Lexel*[76] a Swedish interest limitation deduction provision was at issue that did not apply domestically and excluded interest from deduction in cross-border intra group situations if the debt relationship was primarily established to obtain a significant tax advantage. The Swedish provision therefore only took into account the question of whether there was i) a tax advantage and did not take ii) the artificiality of the transaction into account when answering the question of whether there was tax avoidance. In the *X BV*-case[77] the Court confirmed that the Swedish interest limitation deduction provision at issue in *Lexel* was not proportionate because it limited the deduction of interest in cases where

74 Case C-524/04, *Test Claimants in the Thin Cap Group Litigation*, EU:C:2007:161, [2007] ECR I-2107.
75 Case C-103/09, *HMRC v Weald Leasing Ltd*, EU:C:2010:804.
76 Case C-484/19, *Lexel*, EU:C:2021:34, H&I 2021/342 (comments by Wattel).
77 Case C-585/22, *X BV*, ECLI:EU:C:2024:822.

a debt was incurred 'mainly for tax reasons' (see paragraph 80) and the provision did not apply to 'fictitious arrangements' (paragraph 81), and was therefore not limited to wholly artificial arrangements (and the Swedish tax administration also admitted this during the hearing of the case).

In *X BV*, the Court (i) further elaborated on the question of when an interest limitation deduction provision is specific enough to be accepted under EU law as a proportionate anti-abuse measure and (2) when there may be an artificial arrangement in the case of intra-group interest payments. In this case, a Dutch interest deduction limitation applied (Article 10a of the Dutch Corporate Income Tax Act (CIT)). Article 10a of the CIT limited the deduction of interest in certain situations (including the case of external takeovers) unless the interest is subject to a net tax on profit or income levied on the recipient of the interest that is reasonable by Dutch standards (at least 10% of a taxable profit determined by Dutch standards) (the reasonable compensatory levy test). The Court first ruled that this 'reasonable compensatory levy test' could constitute an obstacle to free movement, because although it appears objective (applicable without distinction), it is in fact be satisfied the case of domestic intra-group interest payments and only affect cross-border situations. In practice, therefore, only cross-border situations are treated less favourably (see paragraphs 43-46 of *X BV*). The Court reiterated its case law that restrictive measures combating artificial arrangements could be justified where 'it is designed to combat wholly artificial arrangements, aimed at circumventing the legislation of the Member State concerned' (para. 56). The Court ruled that Article 10a of the CIT 'undeniably aims to combat tax fraud and avoidance and is intended to prevent equity of a group from being artificially presented as debt to a Dutch entity of that group and to prevent the interest on that loan from being deductible from the taxable result in the Netherlands' (para. 60). The Court found the Dutch provision proportionate because the provision used criteria that indicate that there may be a wholly artificial arrangement. The Court referred in particular to 'the fact that those loan debts are owed to a related entity and relate to the acquisition or extension of an interest in an entity which, following that acquisition or extension, is a related entity' (para. 70 in *X BV*), so the anti-abuse regulation only applied in intragroup situations. The Court could also have mentioned that one of the relevant criteria was the 'reasonable compensatory levy test', although this test is de facto discriminatory, is also an objective and relevant indication that there is an artificial arrangement, namely for the question of whether there is an advantage. In addition, the Dutch regulation was proportional because it provided for the possibility that the taxpayer could rebut the presumption of abuse. According to the Court, this rebuttal possibility was also such that only wholly artificial arrangements were affected (paras. 71 and 72 in *X BV*).

The Court then went into detail in *X BV* on the question of when, in the case of an anti-abuse provision that excludes interest from deduction in intra-group situations, there is a wholly artificial arrangement. It pointed out that such a regulation is permitted when 'the refusal to deduct loan interest [is limited] solely to situations in which the loan within a group of connected companies is dictated by tax reasons to such an extent that that loan is not necessary for the attainment of economically justified objectives and where it would not have been contracted at all between entities which have no special relationship' (para. 71). In *X BV*, the Court clarified the *Lexel* judgment and repeated in that context what it had already ruled in *Test Claimants in the Thin Cap Group Litigation*, namely that there is an artificial arrangement when 'a company has been granted a loan by another company on terms which do not correspond to those which would have been agreed on *an arm's length basis*' (paragraph 74 in *X BV*; italics authors).

The Court then clarified that the question of whether there is 'an arm's length basis' relates in particular to i) the amount of the loan and ii) the interest rate, but also relates to (paragraph 75):

> 'the economic sense of the loan at issue and the related legal transactions. The latter examination involves verifying the economic validity of that loan and the related legal transactions, by ensuring that such transactions could have been concluded between the companies party to the contract in the absence of a special relationship'

The Court added (paragraph 76):

> 'An examination aimed at ensuring that not only the terms of the loan at issue, but also the very fact of contracting it and the related legal transactions, correspond to what the companies would have agreed in arm's length circumstances amounts to ascertaining the economic reality of the transactions whose absence, as is apparent from the case-law referred to in paragraphs 57, 59 and 67 of the present judgment, constitutes one of the decisive factors in classifying a purely artificial arrangement transaction'.

In *X BV* we therefore see that, with regard to an interest limitation deduction regulation, the Court makes it clear that interest can only be refused deduction because there is a wholly artificial arrangement if either i) the amount of the loan, or ii) the interest rate, or iii) the loan itself, or iv) the related legal transactions, do not correspond to what companies would have agreed under normal market conditions.

As observed in Section 7.1, the upshot seems to be:

i. the abuse-defense is encompassed by the fiscal-coherence/balanced-allocation/territoriality/fiscal-supervision defense(s), the main difference being that the abuse defense adds the subjective element of abuse (intent) and the objective element of artificiality (which also indicates subjective intent); therefore, there is no need for any abuse defense if the fiscal-coherence/balanced-allocation/territoriality/fiscal-supervision defense(s) can be relied on;
ii. if no rebuttal possibility is provided for, a national anti-abuse rule must in principle be targeted at 'wholly artificial arrangements', but if a rebuttal possibility is provided for, then categories of cross-border cases may be excluded on the basis of a presumption of tax avoidance based on foreseeable, objective and relevant criteria.

7.6 Procedural Issues; Division of the Onus of Proof

From the above it transpires that although the Court allows exclusion of categories of cases from EU law benefits because of their risk of BEPS, it requires (i) these categories to be defined objectively and relevantly (in the light of the real risk of abuse or tax base disintegration), (ii) the tax administration to provide *prima facie* evidence of that real risk, and (iii) if denial of EU law benefits is based on a (proportionate) presumption of abuse, the taxpayer to be given a real opportunity to provide evidence of genuine business reasons for its artificial looking cross-border arrangement.

From the above it also follows that for a finding of abuse of (EU) rights, a subjective test (intent) and an objective test (defeat of object and purpose of the law) must be satisfied. As regards the latter: object and purpose of the (EU) law relied on by either the taxpayer or the tax administration are not susceptible to proof. The question of whether object and purpose of a rule are defeated, is a question of law, not of fact, and the answer to that question is not, therefore, dependent on the production of evidence by the tax administration or by the taxpayer. Questions of law must be answered by a court *ex officio*; that is its core business: explain the law.

Whether a measure is suitable and proportionate to curb abuse or, more generally, to safeguard tax base integrity, however, is partly a question of facts and therefore open to the production of evidence. That is why the tax administration, in case of exclusion from EU benefits of *categories* of cases, must provide *prima facie* evidence in individual cases that there are genuine tax base integrity risks, and the taxpayer must subsequently be permitted to rebut the presumption of tax avoidance by adducing evidence of genuine business purposes.

The question, finally, of whether a taxpayer had bad intentions, is entirely a question of fact, which can only, therefore, be answered on the basis of evidence lead by the parties. The proof of the subjective requirement of abusive intent for a finding of abuse of law – which has to be provided by the tax administration – may, however, be included in the proof of the presence of artifices: bad intent is inferred from suspiciously looking facts and circumstances which the taxpayer is unable to explain satisfactorily if one ignores their tax effects. Where a taxpayer does not simply admit that its main driver was tax (arguing that nevertheless no abuse obtains because object and purpose of the law relied on are not being defeated), the motive test thus operates as a rebuttal possibility: the tax administration must demonstrate the artificiality of the taxpayer's (cross-border) set up, e.g. by showing absence of economic substance, derogation from the arm's length standard, or a transaction result which is foreseeably negative but for its tax effects, after which the taxpayer may demonstrate otherwise by pointing out significant non-tax purposes.

Abuse must be prevented without discrimination: access to EU law rights may not be made more burdensome than access to similar domestic law rights. In principle, nor may a cross-border situation be regarded with more *a priori* suspicion than a similar internal situation (principle of equivalence; see Section 3.5.2.). As the *Bent Vestergaard* Case[78] first showed, in principle no heavier burden of proof can be applied in cross-border situations, given also the availability of mutual administrative assistance between the Member States (see Chapter 26), even though effective fiscal supervision is a mandatory requirement of public interest which may, in certain circumstances, justify different evidential requirements in cross-border positions as compared to purely internal positions.[79] See also the *X and X* case[80]. In this case the risk of tax avoidance was no less in a cross-border than in

78 Case C-55/98, *Skatteministeriet v. Bent Vestergaard*, EU:C:1999:533, [1999] ECR I-764.

79 See, e.g., Case 120/78, *Rewe Zentrale AG*, EU:C:1979:42, [1979] ECR 649; Case C-204/90, *Bachmann v. Belgium*, EU:C:1992:35, [1992] ECR I-249, and Case C-250/95, *Futura Participations SA*, EU:C:1997:239, [1997] ECR I-2471.

80 Joined Cases C-398/16 and C-399/16, *X and X*, EU:C:2018:110.

a domestic situation and thus the Court did not allow discrimination of a cross-border situation with a domestic situation on the basis of combating tax avoidance[81].

However, sometimes there *is* no comparable internal situation: in *Scorpio*,[82] the Court allowed Member States to require a residence certificate issued by the Member State of residence of the artist, in order for a domestic concert agency to apply a tax treaty exemption from the national obligation to withhold tax on the foreign artist's remuneration. In *SGI*, it allowed Member States to apply arm's length rules in cross-border situations which were not applied internally and which required the taxpayer to demonstrate business reasons for transactions with associated companies abroad which could be considered BEPS-suspect.

EU law is not intended to alleviate the taxpayer from its normal burden of proof. A general rule of division of the burden of proof is that a taxpayer claiming a benefit must show that it satisfies the conditions for that benefit. In *SIAT*,[83] the Court held that effective fiscal supervision presupposes the capability of Member States to require taxpayers claiming a deduction or benefit to demonstrate satisfaction of the applicable conditions. In that context, the Directive on administrative cooperation (DAC; see Chapter 13) does not serve to relieve taxpayers from their burden of demonstrating entitlement to deductions or (double) tax relief, but rather the fiscal and administrative interests of the Member States.[84] In *Haribo* and *Salinen*,[85] the Court held that the parent company State (Austria) was not required to use its powers under the DAC to assist the taxpayers in obtaining information from abroad necessary for entitlement to a credit for underlying foreign corporation tax, even though the referring Austrian tax court had indicated that Haribo and Salinen would not be able to obtain the Austrian imputation credit if Austria would not use its DAC discretion, resulting in Haribo and Salinen suffering economic double taxation which would not have occurred in the comparable domestic situation (in which a participation exemption would apply). The Court considered that clearly discriminatory state of affairs to be the problem of Haribo and Salinen. There are situations, therefore, in which Member States may require evidence (and in the absence thereof, refuse deductions, credits or benefits) in cross-border situations even though similar ('equivalent') deductions, credits or benefits are available in comparable domestic situations without any comparable evidential requirements.

As observed, in *Thin Cap GLO*, the Court accepted the (OECD's) arm's length test as a criterion for *prima facie* telling abuse from genuine business purposes, but it also required an easily accessible opportunity for the debtor to rebut the presumption of base erosion:

> '82. (...), national legislation which provides for a consideration of objective and verifiable elements in order to determine whether a transaction represents a purely artificial

81 Para 50: 'the risk that that loan does not reflect a genuine economic transaction and is intended simply to create a deductible charge artificially is no less if the parent company and the subsidiary are both resident in the same Member State and together form a single tax entity than if the subsidiary is established in another Member State and is not, therefore, permitted to form a single tax entity with the parent company'.

82 Case C-290/04, *Scorpio Konzertproduktionen*, EU:C:2006:630, [2006] I-9461.

83 Cases C-318/10, *SIAT*, EU:C:2012:415, point 44.

84 Case C-185/05, *Twoh International BV v. Staatssecretaris van Financiën*, EU:C:2007:550.

85 Joined Cases C-436/08 and C-437/08, *Haribo* and *Österreichische Salinen*, EU:C:2011:61.

> arrangement, entered into for tax reasons alone, is to be considered as not going beyond what is necessary to prevent abusive practices where, in the first place, on each occasion on which the existence of such an arrangement cannot be ruled out, the taxpayer is given an opportunity, without being subject to undue administrative constraints, to provide evidence of any commercial justification that there may have been for that arrangement.'

This is now settled case-law and is repeated by the Court in cases such as *X GmbH*[86] and *X BV*[87].

As regards 'wholly artificial arrangements' justifying application of CFC rules, the Court seemed to provide some onus division rules also in *Cadbury Schweppes*,[88] where it accepted automatic exclusion of certain categories of CFC's from tax benefits provided that the group of companies involved may demonstrate that it satisfies one or more of the tests which preclude application of the CFC rules. That would square to the starting point that the division of the onus of proof is a matter of national procedural autonomy, provided the requirements of equivalence and effectiveness (see Section 3.5.2) are observed. The evidential requirements in cross-border cases may not be more burdensome than in comparable domestic cases, and they may not be such as to make enjoyment of the free movement right excessively difficult. The evidential rule may not go further than necessary for effective fiscal supervision (proportionality). The *SGI* Case (quoted in Section 15.5) already pointed in that direction:

> '73. According to the Belgian Government, the burden of proof as to the existence of an 'unusual' or 'gratuitous' advantage (...) rests with the national tax authorities. It states that when those authorities apply that legislation, the taxpayer is given an opportunity to provide evidence of any commercial justification that there may have been for the transaction in question. (...). If, however, those authorities persist in their intention of issuing a revised assessment and do not accept the taxpayer's arguments, the latter can challenge the assessment to tax before the national courts. (...).
> 75. In those circumstances, subject to verification to be carried out by the referring court (...), it must be concluded that, in the light of the foregoing, national legislation such as that at issue in the main proceedings is proportionate to the set of objectives pursued by it.'

Similarly, in *SIAT*,[89] the Court accepted a shift to the taxpayer of the burden to prove the reasonableness of payments into a low tax jurisdiction in listed circumstances. The BEPS-presumption in this case was therefore better targeted than the presumptions of abuse in the *Eqiom* and *Deister and Juhler* Cases cited above, which were struck down by the Court for being disproportionately indiscriminate. Even though the indicators used for presuming profit shifting in the *SIAT* Case and the ensuing reversal of the burden of proof were in themselves acceptable (50: 'predicated on an assessment of objective and verifiable elements'; 53: 'the need to provide proof of the genuine and proper nature of the transactions and the normal nature of the expenses incurred does not seem, in and of itself, to go beyond what is necessary to attain the objectives pursued'), the Court still

86 Case C-135/17, *X GmbH*, EU:C:2019:136, para. 87.
87 Case C-585/22, *X BV*, ECLI:EU:C:2024:822, para. 67.
88 Case C-196/04, *Cadbury Schweppes*, EU:C:2006:544.
89 Case C-318/10, *SIAT*, EU:C:2012:415, points 42, 27 and 58.

held Belgium's denial of deduction to violate EU free movement law, but for another reason: the Belgian rule was too vague ('appreciably more advantageous than the Belgian regime') as to which jurisdictions were *prima facie* to be considered suspect; it therefore offended the general EU law principle of legal certainty. It was insufficiently clear, precise and predictable as regards its effects, in particular where it might have unfavorable consequences for individuals and undertakings.

7.7 Consequences of a Finding of Abuse: 'Redefine so as to Re-Establish'

In respect of the legal consequences of a finding of abuse of rights, the proportionality principle implies that application of anti-abuse legislation or doctrine should reinstate the situation as if the abuse had not occurred; it should not degenerate into punishment. The consequence of a finding of abuse must be the taking away of that abuse; no more; no less. In the *Halifax* case quoted above (a VAT avoidance case, the judgment was admittedly influenced by the VAT principle of neutrality), the Court held that after a finding of abuse, the situation of the attempted tax avoider must be 'redefined so as to re-establish' the situation without abuse:

> '93. (...) a finding of abusive practice must not lead to a penalty, for which a clear and unambiguous legal basis would be necessary, but rather to an obligation to repay simply as a consequence of that finding, which rendered undue all or part of the deductions of input VAT (see, to that effect, *Emsland Stärke*, paragraph 56).
> 94. It follows that transactions involved in an abusive practice must be redefined so as to re-establish the situation that would have prevailed in the absence of the transactions constituting that abusive practice.'

This finding was reiterated in *Weald Leasing*[90] summarized above. Thus, as much as possible, the situation must be reconstructed which would have prevailed, had the abusive act or transaction not taken place. We observe that this is similar to the legal mechanics applied to correct malicious transfer pricing: the conditions must be reconstructed which would have obtained if the companies involved had not been associated. The very instructive *Cussens* Case[91] (also a VAT case) added that the transactions which constitute abusive practices should be 'disregarded' and that, since a (VAT-)directive cannot of itself impose obligations on individuals (no reverse vertical direct effect; see Chapter 3), taxation of the 'redefined' transactions should have a legal basis in national law: taxation cannot be based solely on a directive if it has not been implemented into national law.

In the *Test Claimants in the Thin Cap Group Litigation* case[92], the Court considered that 'where the consideration of those elements leads to the conclusion that the transaction in question represents a purely artificial arrangement without any underlying commercial justification, the re-characterisation of interest paid as a distribution is limited to the proportion of that interest which exceeds what would have been agreed had the relationship between the parties or between those parties and a third party been one at arm's length'

90 Case C-103/09, *HMRC v Weald Leasing Ltd*, EU:C:2010:804.
91 Case C-251/16, *Edward Cussens a.o.*, EU:C:2017:881, points 45-51.
92 Case C-524/05, *Test Claimants in the Thin Cap Group Litigation*, EU:C:2006:436.

(para. 83). In *X BV*[93], the Court confirmed this judgment, and emphasized, in light of the principle of proportionality, that 'It would go beyond the objective of preventing wholly artificial arrangements to refuse all deduction of that interest' (para. 87). The Court then ruled in *X BV* that the interest may be refused deduction in its entirety if the loan itself constitutes an artificial arrangement. According to the Court, the reason for this is that the tax authorities must then 'ignore' the loan; in addition, in the case of partial interest deduction, a taxpayer could still obtain part or even the entire tax advantage sought through abuse. This would call into question the coherence of the anti-abuse regime, according to the Court in *X BV*.

7.8 Allowing General Tax Base Protection[94]

As observed in Section 6 and as appears from the above, the justification concepts of 'fiscal coherence' (or 'symmetry'), 'balanced allocation of taxing power', 'fiscal principle of territoriality', and 'prohibition of abuse of rights' in the Court's case law, as well as the Court's comparability criterion (mostly: the extent of being subject-to-tax) and the concept of 'exercise in parallel of taxing jurisdiction' seem to overlap and to converge. Below, we will compare these different concepts used in connection with tax base protection. At the outset, we observe that in our view, they may all be comprised into one justification for restricting free movement: the need to avoid situations capable of jeopardizing the right of the Member State of origin to exercise its powers of taxation in relation to activities carried on within its territory, in short: the need for tax base integrity.

7.8.1 Rise, Fall and Revival of Fiscal Cohesion[95]

The Court's fiscal cohesion concept refers to the need to match, within the same taxing jurisdiction, tax base reductions and corresponding tax base increases, such as:
- losses and profits arisen from the same source of income within the same taxing jurisdiction,
- deductions and corresponding benefits, such as annuity contributions and annuity benefits,
- income and the expenses incurred in earning it,
- accrual of unrealized capital gains and taxation of those gains upon realization, etc.

As a justification for denying, in a cross-border situation, tax deductions which would have been allowed in an internal situation, the fiscal cohesion justification first appeared in the *Bachmann* case,[96] concerning the jurisdictional link between deduction of annuity contributions and taxation of the future annuity benefits. It was accepted by the Court that:

93 Case C-585/22, *X BV*, ECLI:EU:C:2024:822.
94 See also Axel Cordewener, Georg Kofler and Servaas van Thiel, 'The Clash Between European Freedoms and National Direct Tax Law: Public Interest Defences Available to the Member States,' 46 *Common Market Law Review* 2009, p. 1951-2010.
95 See also: *P.J. Wattel*, Thirty years of fiscal (in)coherence, Intertax, 2022/50, nr. 10, p. 736.
96 Case C-204/90, *Hans Martin Bachmann v. Belgium*, EU:C:1992:35.

> '22. (...) in such a tax system the loss of revenue resulting from the deduction of life assurance contributions from total taxable income (...) is offset by the taxation of pensions, annuities or capital sums payable by the insurers. Where such contributions have not been deducted, those sums are exempt from tax.
> 23. The cohesion of such a tax system, the formulation of which is a matter for each Member State, therefore presupposes that, in the event of a State being obliged to allow the deduction of life assurance contributions paid in another Member State, it should be able to tax sums payable by insurers. (...)
> 27. It follows that, as Community law stands at present, it is not possible to ensure the cohesion of such a tax system by means of measures which are less restrictive than (...) the non-deductibility of contributions.
> 28. In the light of the foregoing, it must be recognized that, in the field of pensions and life assurance, provisions (...) are justified by the need to ensure the cohesion of the tax system of which they form part, and that such provisions are not, therefore, contrary to (...) the Treaty.'

Although the legitimacy of the fiscal cohesion defense was formally reiterated in subsequent cases like *Danner*,[97] the Court in fact never accepted it again as a justification for restriction of free movement until the 2008 *Krankenheim Ruhesitz* Case (discussed in Section 18), where it was used for establishing the truism that deduction and subsequent reinstatement of foreign branch losses is quite coherent.

In the period between *Bachmann* (1992) and *Krankenheim* (2008), the Court apparently regretted having accepted fiscal cohesion as an excuse, as it sized it down to virtual non-existence in cases such as C-80/94, *Wielockx* C-35/98 *Verkooijen*, C-168/01 *Bosal Holding* and C-319/02 *Manninen*. It did so by holding that it can only apply in one-tax, one-taxpayer, one-transaction positions (*e.g.* deduction of pension contributions and taxation of the pension benefits within the same pension contract of the same taxpayer)[98]. The Court's advocate-general Geelhoed[99] even suggested that the concept could be done away with, as the assessment of accept ability of a 'fiscal cohesion defense' was conceptually indistinct from determining whether national legislation is discriminatory. This is true if one adheres to the subject-to-tax approach posited in Section 6.4.2, which the advocate-general apparently did. We agree. In later cases, such as *K*[100] and *Papillon*,[101] however, coherence of the tax system was considered a legitimate objective. In these cases, the coherence of the tax system was assessed together with the need to prevent double dips, or to ensure symmetric treatment of profits and losses. The Court applied the same reasoning in *Timac Agro*,[102] allowing recapture of previously deducted PE-losses for "logical symmetry," not referring any more to the 'direct link' requirement in previous case law:

> '41. (...), it is sufficient to find that in so far as (...) Germany does not have the right to tax the income generated by a permanent establishment situated in Austria, the reincorporation

97 Case C-136/00, *Danner*, EU:C:2002:558, [2002] ECR, I-8147.

98 See also: D. Weber, Does the cohesion of the tax system justification still have a right to exist?, Landmark decisions of the ECJ in direct taxation, Wolters Kluwer, 2015, p. 159-180.

99 Opinion in case C-524/04, *Thin Cap GLO*, EU:C:2006:436.

100 Case C-322/11, *K.*, EU:C:2013:716.

101 Case C-418/07, *Papillon*, EU:C:2008:659.

102 Case C-388/14, *Timac Agro*, EU:C:2015:829.

of the relevant losses into the taxable profit of the resident company to which that permanent establishment belonged reflects a logical symmetry and is thus the indissociable complement of the deduction previously granted. Accordingly, a tax regime such as that at issue in the main proceedings is also justified by the need to guarantee the coherence of the German tax system.'

More recently, the Court further relaxed its 'direct link' requirement. In *Feilen*,[103] coherence did not exist within the same tax, nor as regards the same taxpayer. The case concerned a German taxpayer claiming an inheritance tax rebate because of Austrian inheritance tax having already been levied on the same object less than ten years ago. If that previous transfer of ownership and connected inheritance taxation had taken place in Germany, the rebate would have been available, as its objective was to mitigate cumulative *German* inheritance taxation where within 10 years multiple transfers of the same asset would take place between family members. The Court considered the ensuing multiple taxation to restrict free capital movement, but accepted it as justified by 'a logical symmetry', apparently referring to its concept of fiscal coherence:

'33. (...), it is apparent that, by providing that only persons receiving assets by way of an inheritance which has given rise to the imposition of such taxes in Germany can benefit from the reduction in inheritance tax, the configuration of that tax advantage reflects a logical symmetry (see (...) *Commission* v *Belgium*, C-250/08, EU:C:2011:793, paragraph 73, and (...) *Commission* v *Hungary*, C-235/09, EU:C:2011:795, paragraph 74). That logic would be disturbed if that tax advantage were also to benefit persons inheriting assets which did not give rise to the imposition of inheritance tax in that Member State.'

We see that the coherence justification is alive again in *Fidelity funds*[104] in which the Court accepted, in principle, the coherence between an exemption from withholding tax and the levy of withholding tax on a fictitious paid dividend.

In *XY*[105], an inheritance tax case, the Court accepted the coherence justification because there was a a direct link 'between the allowance on which the heir may rely and the extent of the tax jurisdiction exercised'. In that case, the AG also found that the discrimination was justified for essentially the same reason, but found that it is 'necessary to safeguard its power of taxation' and referred to the balanced allocation and the principle of territoriality. Here we also see that the coherence justification, the balanced allocation of the power to tax and the principle of territoriality seems interchangeable.

Whatever its name, there is clearly a need for jurisdictional cohesion between positive and corresponding negative items of the tax base over which a State has symmetrically asserted taxing power or has symmetrically not asserted taxing power (such as inheritance transfers abroad of profits and losses of non-subject foreign subsidiaries). Given that 'fiscal cohesion' by definition concerns cohesion between tax base reductions (or unrealized gains) and corresponding base increases (or realization, respectively) within the *same*

103 Case C-123/15, *Max-Heinz Feilen vs Finanzamt Fulda*, EU:C:2016:496.
104 Case C-480/16, Fidelity Funds, EU:C:2018:480.
105 Case C-394/20, *XY*, EU:C:2021:1044.

taxing jurisdiction, the question rises what the difference is, if any, between the fiscal cohesion principle and (i) the need for preservation of a balanced allocation of taxing powers and (ii) the 'fiscal principle of territoriality'. In *National Grid Indus*,[106] concerning exit taxation upon the seat transfer of a company, the Court referred to all three concepts, every time to the effect that a territorial cohesion – or balance – should be safeguarded between, on the one hand, profits and value increases recorded within a Member State during the period of residence of the taxpayer in that Member State, and the possibility for that Member State to tax that profit or unrealized gain sourced within its jurisdiction. It more or less equated 'coherence' and 'balanced allocation':

> '80. (...), the requirements of coherence of the tax system and the balanced allocation of powers of taxation coincide.'

Apparently, there is little difference between the concepts of 'fiscal coherence', 'balanced allocation of taxing power', and the principle of fiscal territoriality.

7.8.2 *The Fiscal Principle of Territoriality*

The fiscal principle of territoriality was first referred to in an *obiter dictum* in *Futura Participations SA*,[107] which concerned temporal loss carry-over *within* a Luxemburg branch of a French company. The judgment states rather straightforwardly that if a national tax system (its delineation of jurisdiction) accords with the fiscal territoriality principle, it cannot be found discriminatory:

> '20. (...) Luxembourg Law provides that, as regards resident taxpayers, all of their income is taxable, the basis of assessment to tax not being limited to their Luxembourg activities. Consequently, although there are exemptions under which a part or even, in certain cases, all of their income earned outside Luxembourg is not subject to tax in that country, the basis for assessment for resident taxpayers at any rate includes profits and losses arising from their Luxembourg activities.
> 21. On the other hand, for the purpose of calculating the basis of assessment for nonresident taxpayers, only profits and losses arising from their Luxembourg activities are taken into account in calculating the tax payable by them in that State.
> 22. Such a system, which is in conformity with the fiscal principle of territoriality, cannot be regarded as entailing any discrimination, overt or covert, prohibited by the Treaty.'

The fiscal territoriality principle thus had the appearance, not so much of a mandatory requirement of public interest which may justify free movement restrictions (rule of reason), but of a *Keck*[108]-like exclusion altogether from the scope of the treaty freedoms of territorially coherent taxing power exercise. That would fit with both the Court's later developed concept of 'exercise in parallel' of taxing jurisdiction, used for the first time in *Kerkhaert-Morres*,[109] and the subject-to-tax criterion for comparability in direct tax matters (see Section 14): disadvantages arising from taxation in accordance with territoriality

106 Case C-371/10, *National Grid Indus BV*, EU:C:2011:785.
107 Case C-250/95, *Futura Participations SA*, EU:C:2009:479.
108 Joined cases C-267 and 268/91, *Criminal Proceedings against Keck and Mithouard*, EU:C:1996:905.
109 Case C-513/04, *Kerckhaert-Morres*, EU:C:2006:713.

are not discriminations and therefore outside the Court's scrutiny. On the other hand, the A-G's opinion in *Futura* (point 27) explains that the requirement of an economic link between deductible losses and taxable profits is in line with the "territoriality principle, as suggested by the Commission", and more importantly, results from Article 4(2) of the then French/ Luxembourg tax treaty (which allocates taxing rights). The territoriality principle in this approach seems equivalent to the fiscal 'symmetry' (coherence) concept in the Court's later case law, but also to the notion that a Member State cannot be denied the right to tax economic activities carried out within its territory (balanced allocation of taxing power).

Both the territoriality principle *and* fiscal coherence seemed to be abandoned by the Court in *Bosal Holding*,[110] concerning a national measure denying deduction of expenses incurred by a parent company (wherever established) to finance its subsidiary (wherever established) insofar as they were not instrumental in earning subsidiary profits subject to tax in the same jurisdiction as where the parent sought to deduct those connected expenses. Despite this manifestly coherent, symmetrical and balanced, jurisdictional and territorial match between (non)deduction of expenses and (non)taxation of the profits generated by them, the Court held:

> '38. In that respect, it should be noted that the application of the territoriality principle in Futura Participations and Singer concerned the taxation of a single company which carried on business in the Member State where it had its principal establishment and in other Member States from secondary establishments.
> 39. (…). The difference in tax treatment in question concerns parent companies according to whether or not they have subsidiaries making profits taxable in the Netherlands, even though those parent companies are all established in that Member State. As regards the tax situation of the latter in relation to the profits of their subsidiaries, however, it must be noted that those profits are not taxable in the hands of those companies, whether the profits come from subsidiaries taxable in the Netherlands or from other subsidiaries.'

Like the cohesion defense, the territoriality defense was thus – without any clarification – limited to one-taxpayer, one-tax situations.

The territoriality principle reappeared, however, in *Marks & Spencer II*, clearly in a *two*-taxpayer situation. In contrast to *Bosal*, the Court this time accepted the territoriality plea: it accepted that (non-definitive) foreign losses of a (non-subjected) foreign subsidiary could not be transferred to the domestic parent company – even though losses of domestic subsidiaries could be so transferred – because of territorial 'symmetry of the tax system' ('profits and losses are two sides of the same coin and must be treated symmetrically in the same tax system'). An exception was made only where loss relief would permanently be lost: for 'definite' foreign subsidiary losses, the Court still disrupted the 'symmetry' and the 'balanced allocation', although in the 2015 'Marks & Spencer III' Case (*Commission v UK*[111]), it (correctly) also seems to regret *that* mistake, like its *Bosal*-mistake. Conceptually, this reasoning implies that fiscal territoriality is viewed as a justification for free movement restriction, rather than as a description of a territorially coherent *and therefore*

110 Case C-168/01, *Bosal Holding BV*, EU:C:2003:479, [2003] ECR I-9409.
111 Case C-172/13, *Commission v UK* ('Marks & Spencer III'), EU:C:2015:50.

nondiscriminatory assertion of taxing jurisdiction which would be, like the *Keck* modes of sale rules, outside the scope of free movement scrutiny.

The territoriality principle also reappeared in exit tax cases such as *N. v. Inspecteur*[112] and *National Grid Indus*,[113] and in cases involving (other) corporate tax issues.[114] In the same manner as the Court 'linked' (combined) balanced allocation and the need to curb abuse in *Oy AA* and *SGI*, the Court in *N. v Inspecteur* ostensibly equated the fiscal principle of territoriality with 'preserving the allocation of the power to tax between Member States:'

> '41. (...), the national court observes that, (...), the national provisions at issue (...) are designed, in particular, to allocate between Member States, on the basis of the territoriality principle, the power to tax increases of value in company holdings. (...).
> 42. This Court finds that preserving the allocation of the power to tax between Member States is a legitimate objective recognized by the Court of Justice (see, (...), *Marks & Spencer*, paragraph 45).
> (...).
> 46. (...). (...), it is in accordance with that principle of fiscal territoriality, connected with a temporal component, namely residence within the territory during the period in which the taxable profit arises, that the national provisions in question provide for the charging of tax on increases in value recorded in the Netherlands, the amount of which has been determined at the time the taxpayer concerned emigrated and payment of which has been suspended until the actual disposal of the securities.'

Thus, from a *Keck*-like safe haven for territorially consistent national tax measures addressing cross-border cases, the fiscal principle of territoriality gradually seemed to turn into the new clothes of the late fiscal cohesion concept, *and* to become integrated in the more recent justification for restrictive direct tax measures: the preservation of a balanced allocation of the power to tax. Indeed, it is not easy to see any significant difference between fiscal territoriality and fiscal cohesion (which by definition refers to coherence within the same taxing jurisdiction) or between fiscal territoriality and a balanced preservation of taxing power, especially as the Court in the exit taxation cases cited above referred to all three concepts as if they are interchangeable. However, it appears to link 'fiscal territoriality' to the *assertion* (delineation) of taxing power by the source State as regards nonresidents and emigrants on the basis of the source principle, and possibly to the assertion of worldwide taxing power of the residence State. If *that* is what the fiscal territoriality principle means, then it comes close to the concept of 'exercise in parallel' of taxing jurisdiction developed in *Kerckhaert-Morres*.[115] If a tax system that agrees with 'the fiscal principle of territoriality' and cannot, therefore, be considered to be discriminatory (*Futura*), then also the parallel exercise of two overlapping tax connecting factors (source and residence), falls outside the scope of the treaty freedoms (*first* step of the rule of reason test). However, in *N. v Inspecteur* and *National Grid Indus*, territoriality is apparently relied on as a *justification* for free movement hindrance (*second* step of the rule of reason test). The latter approach is confirmed by subsequent case law such as

112 Case C-470/04, *N v Inspecteur van de Belastingdienst*, EU:C:2006:525.
113 Case C-371/10, *National Grid Indus*, EU:C:2011:785.
114 Cases C-164/12, *DMC*, EU:C:2014:20, C-591/13 *Commission* v *Germany*, EU:C:2015:230, C-657/13, *Verder LabTec GmbH & Co. KG*, EU:C:2015:331.
115 Case C-513/04, *Kerckhaert-Morres*, EU:C:2006:713.

the *Trustees of the P Panayi* Case,[116] in which the Court stated, referring to the *DMC* Case,[117] that the 'fiscal principle of territoriality, linked to a temporal consideration' justified exit taxation of an emigrating trust:

> '52. (...), it follows from the Court's case-law that the transfer of the place of management of a trust from one Member State to another Member State cannot mean that the Member State of origin has to abandon its right to tax a capital gain which arose within the ambit of its powers of taxation before that transfer. In that regard, the Court has held that, in accordance with the principle of fiscal territoriality linked to a temporal consideration, namely the taxpayer's residence for tax purposes within national territory during the period in which the capital gains arise, a Member State is entitled to charge tax on those gains at the time when that taxpayer leaves the country. Such a measure is intended to prevent situations capable of jeopardising the right of the Member State of origin to exercise its powers of taxation in relation to activities carried on within its territory, and can therefore be justified on grounds connected with the preservation of the allocation of powers of taxation between the Member States ((...), *National Grid Indus*, C-371/10, EU:C:2011:785, paragraph 46 and the case-law cited).
> 53. However, the Court has made it clear that the objective of preserving the allocation of powers of taxation between the Member States can justify a national measure only where the Member State in whose territory income was generated is actually prevented from exercising its power of taxation in respect of such income (judgment of 23 January 2014, *DMC*, C-164/12, EU:C:2014:20, paragraph 56).'

This language again suggests that the fiscal territoriality principle and the need for preservation of the allocation of taxing powers are identical and, taken together, may be described as the need to avoid situations "capable of jeopardising the right of the Member State of origin to exercise its powers of taxation in relation to activities carried on within its territory", in short: the need for tax base integrity (especially of the source State).

The Court's advocate-general Bobek, on the other hand, clearly understands the territoriality principle as applied by the Court, not as tax lawyers understand it (as a source principle), but as the international public law principle of territoriality, i.e. as worldwide jurisdiction as regards residents and as territorial (source) jurisdiction as regards non-residents:[118]

> '20. The principle of territoriality of States' powers of taxation is well recognised internationally, including in the Court's case-law. According to that principle, Member States can tax resident companies on their worldwide profits (taxation based on residence) and non-resident companies on the profits of their activities in that state (taxation based on source).
> 21. One of the consequences of the principle of territoriality is that companies are not free to shift profits and losses between tax jurisdictions at will. That has repeatedly been recognised in the Court's case-law, in particular through application of the concept of the 'balanced allocation of the powers of taxation'. In applying that latter concept, the Court has confirmed that if a Member State were required to accept the free transfer of profits of resident companies outside its jurisdiction, it 'would be forced to renounce its right, in

116 Case C-646/15, *Trustees of the P Panayi Accumulation & Maintenance Settlements*, EU:C:2017:682.
117 Case C-164/12, *DMC*, EU:C:2014:20.
118 Opinion of 14 December 2017 in Case C-382/16, *Hornbach-Baumarkt AG*, EU:C:2017:974.

its capacity as the State of residence of that company to tax its income in favour, possibly, of the Member State in which the recipient company has its establishment'.
22. It follows naturally from that observation that Member States can legitimately adopt measures which are designed to prevent the erosion of their tax base through the shifting of profits out of the jurisdiction. They can take steps to ensure that profits are correctly allocated.'

The question is also whether the Court still has in mind that it accepted the fiscal principle of territoriality as a source principle in *Futura Participations*[119] and what the inherent consequences of that decision are. In the *Futura participations*, the Court had (as noted above) clearly ruled that the taxable base for non-resident taxpayers could be limited to domestic source income. The Court considered:

> 'Such a system, which is in conformity with the fiscal principle of territoriality, cannot be regarded as entailing any discrimination, overt or covert, prohibited by the Treaty'.

The inherent consequence of this was that in *Futura Participations*, Luxembourg, as the source State, did not have to take into account the losses incurred in France (the resident state of Futura Participations).

For dividends paid to a non-resident taxpayer, the Court has now made an exception to this in the *Credit Suisse Securities* case[120].

Credit Suisse Securities was established in the United Kingdom and received a dividend from Spain (a domestic source for Spain) on which Spain withheld 10% withholding tax (as a non-resident taxpayer). Credit Suisse Securities could not reclaim this 10% (final levy); Spain did not take into account the fact that Credit Suisse Securities had incurred losses in the United Kingdom. Credit Suisse Securities, if it had been established in Spain, could have reclaimed the withholding tax on dividends at the time that a loss was made in a tax year; *i.e.* in situations in which the dividend was offset against losses from (other) activities of the company.

The Court was of the opinion that, on the basis of the *Sofina* judgment[121] (see Section 11.5.2), there was an obstacle to the free movement of capital. Appeal to the *Futura participations-case* and the fiscal principle of territoriality was also rejected, while in *Futura participations* the same issue was at stake as in the *Credit Suisse Securities*-case. Namely the question whether for a non-resident taxpayer the tax base could be limited to domestic sources, with the result that no account had to be taken of losses that cannot be attributed to (in this case) Spanish sources. In *Credit Suisse Securities*, the Court nevertheless regarded such a system as an obstacle to the free movement, thus implicitly overruling the *Futura participations* judgment.

119 Case C-250/95, *Futura Participations SA*, EU:C:2009:479.
120 Case C-601/23, *Credit Suisse Securities* case, ECLI:EU:C:2024:1048.
121 Case C-575/17, *Sofina*, ECLI:EU:C:2018:943.

However, it seems that the Court did not understood the Spanish system properly. The Court gave its ruling on the *assumption* that a similar system as in the French *Sofina* judgment was at issue in *Credit Suisse Securities*[122]. The *Sofina*-case concerned whether deferral of taxation on dividends in the case of losses (applicable to resident taxpayers), which deferral of taxation was not applied in the case of dividends paid to a non-resident taxpayer, could be justified. This system of *deferral* of taxation could, in *Sofina*, not be justified by the balanced allocation to tax, but this is a different question from the more fundamental question at issue in *Credit Suisse Securities*. The *Credit Suisse Securities* case was not about the question whether a difference between non-resident and resident taxpayers regarding *deferral* of taxation on dividends is a restriction of free movement, but about the question whether limited (source) tax liability for non-resident taxpayers and unlimited (world-wide) tax liability for resident taxpayers is permitted. In our view, the answer to this question is still "yes" and the consequences thereof have to be accepted: For example, the fact that a non-resident taxpayer i) cannot take into account losses that are not attributed to the source state and ii) therefore cannot benefit from a cash advantage (paying less or later taxes) that such losses entail, are an *inherent* consequence of the application of the fiscal principle of territoriality which must therefore be accepted. If you do not accept the *inherent* consequences that the fiscal principle of territoriality entails then you are in effect rejecting the application of the fiscal principle of territoriality. This is what the Court did, perhaps unintentionally, in *Credit Suisse Securities* and *Sofina*. Let us hope that both cases are a slip of the pen.

7.8.3 A Balanced Allocation of Taxing Power between Member States

This most successful justification for fiscal restriction of intra-EU movement of capital and persons was introduced in points 43 of *Marks & Spencer II* (see the quotation in Section 7.5) The Court went on:

> '45. (...), as the United Kingdom rightly observes, the preservation of the allocation of the power to impose taxes between Member States might make it necessary to apply to the economic activities of companies established in one of those States only the tax rules of that State in respect of both profits and losses.
> 46. In effect, to give companies the option to have their losses taken into account in the Member State in which they are established or in another Member State would significantly jeopardise a balanced allocation of the power to impose taxes between Member States, as the taxable basis would be increased in the first State and reduced in the second to the extent of the losses transferred.'

122 See para. 75 of *Credit Suisse Securities*, whereby the Court *assumes* that in this case, as in Sofina, there is a system of deferral of taxation: 'Second, deferring the taxation of dividends received by a loss-making non-resident company would not mean that the fiscally autonomous historical territory of Biscay has to waive its right to tax income generated in its territory. The *dividends* distributed by the resident company *would be taxed once the non-resident company became profitable during a subsequent tax year*, in the same way as occurs, *subject to verification by the referring court*, in the case of a resident company experiencing a similar situation (see, by analogy, judgment of 22 November 2018, *Sofina and Others*, C-575/17, EU:C:2018:943, paragraph 59)'. (italics authors).

This was reiterated in *N. v. Inspecteur*, and there again linked to the fiscal territoriality principle. The word 'balanced' was omitted, but in all subsequent cases, it reappeared again. The Court's language since *Marks & Spencer II* seems consistent: prevention of the undermining of the balanced allocation of taxing power is a legitimate objective justifying national measures distinguishing cross-border from domestic operations, provided they are proportionate in relation to that objective of preservation of tax base integrity. This third concept resembles the source country entitlement principle underlying the Ruding Committee Report and underlying (OECD) international tax law. Indeed, in all of these cases, the concept serves to protect the source State against tax base erosion in the form of (i) 'imported' tax base reductions alien to its taxing jurisdiction, (ii) conversely, the 'exportation' of tax base, either artificially (*e.g.* excessive interest payments on artificial intra-group loans, or transfer pricing manipulation) or by having to extend group profit contribution schemes abroad (*Oy AA*), or (iii) emigration of the taxpayer and his unrealized tax base accrued in the origin State. To cite just a few examples: in *Class IV ACT*, the balanced allocation concept entailed that the source State cannot 'be obliged to abandon its right to tax a profit generated through an economic activity undertaken on its territory'. In *Rewe Zentralfinanz eG*,[123] the Court used the balanced allocation concept to curb 'courses of action which are capable of jeopardising the right of the Member States to exercise their taxing powers in relation to activities carried on in their territory and thus of undermining a balanced allocation of the power to impose taxes.' In *Oy AA* (see 7.1.3) the Court held that the system of allocation would be 'undermined' if 'the Member State of the subsidiary would be forced to renounce its right, (...), to tax the profits of that subsidiary' and in *Cadbury Schweppes*, the balanced allocation justified prevention of 'the type of conduct (...) such as to undermine the right of the Member States to exercise their tax jurisdiction in relation to the activities carried out in their territory'. In *Amurta*,[124] *Aberdeen*,[125] *Beker and Beker*,[126] *Santander*,[127] *Argenta Spaarbank I*[128] *and Imfeldt and Garcet*,[129] similar language was used in respect of withholding tax on outbound dividends, individual tax allowances, and notional interest deduction to the effect of protecting the tax base of the source State. The gist of this case law is that taxpayers should not be able to choose freely in which Member State they want income to be taxed and expenses or losses to be deducted, disconnected from the territory where the economic activity is performed which generated the income, expenses or losses (*OY AA*,[130] *Lidl Belgium*[131]).

Again, it may be inferred that the balanced allocation of taxing power and the fiscal territoriality principle are identical and, taken together with the apparently also (almost) identical concept of 'fiscal coherence', may be described as the need to avoid situations" capable of jeopardising the right of the Member State of origin to exercise its powers of

123 Case C-347/04, *Rewe Zentralfinanz eG*, EU:C:2007:194.
124 Case C-379/05, *Amurta*, EU:C:2007:655 point 58.
125 Case C-303/07, *Aberdeen Property Fininvest Alpha*, EU:C:2009:377 points 59-60.
126 Case C-168/11, *Manfred Beker & Christa Beker*, EU:C:2013:117 point 57.
127 Case C-337/11, *Santander Asset Management SGIIC SA*, EU:C:2012:286 point 47.
128 Case C-350/11, *Argenta Spaarbank NV I*, EU:C:2013:477 point 53.
129 Case C-303/12, *Imfeldt and Garcet*, EU:C:2013:822 point 75.
130 Case C-231/05, *Oy AA*, EU:C:2007:439.
131 Case C-414/06, *Lidl Belgium GmbH & Co. KG v Finanzamt Heilbronn*, EU:C:2008:278.

taxation in relation to activities carried on within its territory", in short: the need for tax base integrity (of the source State). See above Chapter 7.5.

If secondary EU law allocates taxing power, then in principle Member States cannot take the position any more that the result of that EU law allocation is not balanced, except if they can show abuse. As the Court consistently holds, if an issue has been exhaustively harmonized by secondary EU law, national (implementing) measures on that issue will not be assessed any more in the light of primary EU law, but in principle solely in the light of that secondary EU law. The Parent-Subsidiary Directive does not exhaustively harmonize anti-abuse measures but leaves Member States national competence (see Sections 16.2 and 7.2). Therefore, the Court, in *Deister* and *Juhler*,[132] did scrutinize a German measure against abuse of the dividend withholding tax exemption in Article 5 PSD also in the light of the need to curb abuse as a justification for restricting the freedom of establishment. It did *not*, however, scrutinize the German rule in the light of the balanced allocation of taxing powers as a justification for restricting the freedom of establishment, as the allocation of taxing rights as regards participation dividends had already exhaustively been regulated by the PSD:

> '98. Furthermore, about the balanced allocation of taxation powers between the Member States, by precluding Member States from imposing withholding tax on the profits distributed by a resident subsidiary to its non-resident parent company, the Parent-Subsidiary Directive governs the issue of that allocation.'

7.8.4 *Territorial Financial Cohesion and Jurisdictional Balance in Some Non-Tax Areas*

In non-tax cases, especially in the field of social security and health insurance, the need for a balanced allocation (territorial matching) of benefits and corresponding expenditure also arose. The Court recognized that need in those fields as well as an overriding reason for different treatment of cross-border and internal situations. In the *D'Hoop* case[133] the Court in principle allowed – if proportionate – national legislation ensuring the territorial fencing off a national social security scheme. In the subsequent *Collins* case,[134] concerning a UK unemployment benefit conditional upon residence and employment (search) requirements, the Court held it to be legitimate for a member State to grant an employment allowance only if a genuine link could be established between the person seeking work and the employment market of that State. Member States may thus require a genuine link between persons who claim such an allowance and its employment market. It is submitted that if such market fragmentation is allowed for financial coherence reasons, then by the same token, Member States should be able to require a genuine link between tax base reductions and the corresponding base increases. The same may be inferred from the Court's case law on territorial cohesion between contributions to national health insurance schemes and the granting of benefits, *e.g.* its judgment in *the*

132 Joined Cases C 504/16 and C 613/16, *Deister Holding AG and Juhler Holding A/S*, EU:C:2017:1009.
133 Case C-224/98, *Marie Nathalie D'Hoop*, EU:C:2002:432.
134 Case C-138/02, *Collins*, EU:C:20014:172.

Müller-Fauré case.[135] To a certain extent, the Court allowed (if proportionate) restrictive measures to ensure a territorial balance (within one jurisdiction) between the funding of the scheme from contributions and the payment for the cost of hospitalization of the insured patients.

Rather blunt in its market compartmentalization effects and different treatment of nonresidents for public budget cohesion reasons seemed the judgment in Case C-213/05, *Wendy Geven*, concerning the German refusal to grant Mrs Geven a child-raising allowance because she was not 'sufficiently close connected' with 'German society', even though she worked in Germany, but not more than 15 hours a week. Such 'social policy' was left by the Court to the 'wide discretion of the Member States.' It is difficult to see why there would not exist a similarly wide discretion in respect of individual taxation policy.

Although Union citizens have a right of residence in the territory of another Member State for three months without any conditions or formalities other than a valid identity card or passport, it is conditional upon them and their family members not becoming an unreasonable burden on the social assistance system of the host Member State.[136] If no such 'welfare tourism' is acceptable, then it is difficult to see why 'fiscal tourism' would be acceptable.

Tax base erosion and structural jurisdictional mismatches between tax base reductions and corresponding benefits could also have serious consequences for the overall level of public goods protection, entailing the risk of seriously undermining the financial balance of the public budget. If reasonable anti-base erosion measures are not allowed, then the entire EU will end up with the lowest possible effective taxation of corporate profits (zero in Estonia for undistributed profits, 10% on Cyprus, 12,5% in Ireland), which implies either huge cutbacks on public goods or over taxation of labor and sales. This dystopian scenario may have guided Member States in 2016 when they adopted the Anti-tax avoidance Directive (see Section 19).

7.9 Conclusion – A Single Concept – Tax Base Integrity as the Fiscal Manifestation of the Court's General Abuse of Rights Doctrine

It is a general principle of EU law that it cannot be relied on to circumvent the law, whether national or Union law, whether harmonized or unharmonized, and irrespective of the type or field of law involved. Abuse (in tax cases: unacceptable tax avoidance) is considered present if two cumulative conditions are satisfied: (i) object and purpose of the EU rules relied on are not served or achieved, but defied (objective element), and (ii) intent to obtain benefits not meant for the economic operator involved by artificial creation of the conditions for obtaining them (subjective element). The Court seems to allow apparent artificiality to be used as an indicator of both defiance of object and purpose of the law and of subjective abusive intent.

135 Case C-385/99, *Müller-Fauré and van Riet*, EU:C:2003:370.

136 Case C-424/10 and C-425/10, *Ziolkowski and Szeja*, EU:C:2011:866; Case C-333/13, *Dano* EU:C:2014:2358; Case C-299/14, *Vestische Arbeit Jobcenter Kreis Recklinghausen*, EU:C:2016:114.

As an independent rule of reason justification for fiscal free movement restrictions, the Court initially accepted the abuse defense only where 'wholly artificial arrangements' were present. Later, it also accepted abstract and generally restrictive measures, excluding *categories* of cross-border cases, especially where the abuse feared is typical for cross-border situations (such as BEPS), provided that (i) such exclusion is based on objective and relevant criteria justifying a presumption of abuse (to be *prima facie* demonstrated by the tax administration), and (ii) the taxpayer may, without undue administrative difficulties, rebut that presumption and *prima facie* suspiciousness by showing genuine business reasons for its contraptions.

EU law cannot be relied on to alleviate taxpayers from a normal burden of proof. Effective fiscal supervision (the procedural part of the preservation of tax base integrity) presupposes that Member States may put the burden of proof of satisfying the conditions for entitlement to a tax benefit on the taxpayer claiming such benefit, as they would in purely domestic cases, provided that that burden is not heavier in cross-border cases than it would be in a comparable domestic case.

The objective of preventing tax avoidance and tax evasion has the same scope whether it is relied on under the anti-abuse reservations in the corporate tax directives or as justification for an exception to primary law. This means that the exercise of the competence reserved by these anti-abuse provisions is governed by primary EU law: to the extent in which the directives' rights are switched off by their anti-abuse reservations, the Member States may deny the directive's benefits, but only in so far as the general prohibition of abuse of rights justifies restricting the free movement rights of taxpayers. Therefore, it does not seem to make any difference whether the abuse defense is relied on under the rule of reason for restricting free movement or under the anti-abuse reservations in the PSD, the Merger Directive or the IRD. The latter thus seem redundant.

We understand the Court's case law on the prohibition of abuse in tax matters as accepting two types of justification in tax matters for differential and therefore restrictive treatment of cross-border situations, one substantive, one procedural: (i) protection of tax base integrity, and (ii) the need for effective fiscal supervision. The latter is necessary to implement the former, and therefore they may conceptually be considered to represent one single concept:[137] the need, in the absence of harmonization, to maintain tax base integrity, especially for the State within whose territory the economic activity is being carried on giving rise to the income to be taxed.

The Court's concept of (fiscal) *cohesion* (or coherence) justifying restrictive tax measures mainly refers to the need to ensure that positive and negative elements of the same source of income (income and expenses incurred in earning it, taxation of profits and set-off of losses from the same source; deductible contributions to and subsequent taxable benefits from annuity and pensions schemes; accrual of unrealized capital gains

137 In this vein: Marcel Schaper, 'The Need to Prevent Abusive Practices and Fraud as a Composite Justification', 23 *EC Tax Review* 2014/4, pp. 220-229.

and later realization of those gains) of the same (group) of taxpayer(s) within the same taxing jurisdiction remain matched within that same taxing jurisdiction.

The need to preserve a *balanced allocation* of taxing power as a justification for restrictive tax measures mainly seems to refer to the concept of BEPS ((tax) base erosion and profit shifting): a Member State cannot be required to accept deduction of a loss made by a person, or flowing from a source of income to which that State has symmetrically *not* extended its taxing jurisdiction, nor, conversely, to relinquish its power to tax income to which it *did* symmetrically extend its taxing jurisdiction. In many cases in which the Court accepted the 'balanced allocation' justification, for that matter, there was no need for a justification, as there was – in our view – no discrimination in the first place; the 'balanced allocation' defense in those cases was no more than a description of a nondiscriminatory disparity or dislocation (a parallel *non*-exercise of taxing power).

The fiscal principle of *territoriality* more or less directly refers to the need to avoid jeopardising the right of the Member State of origin to exercise its powers to tax activities carried on within its territory. This seems to catch the overall concept encompassing all of the justifications for (perceived) fiscal restrictions of free movement: the need to avoid situations "capable of jeopardising the right of the Member State of origin to exercise its powers of taxation in relation to activities carried on within its territory," i.e. the need to preserve tax base integrity, in the first place for the source/origin State, but also for the residence State. Both States remain free, in the present state of EU law, to exercise in parallel taxing power they – symmetrically – assert on the basis of neutral criteria such as source/origin, residence, nationality, or territoriality.

In recent cases (*Credit Suisse Securities* and *Sofina*) the Court considers inherent consequences of the application of the fiscal principle of territoriality as a restriction of free movement. As a result, the Court in fact no longer accepts the fiscal principle of territoriality. We assume that both cases are a slip of the pen.

Obviously, also the need to prevent abuse, finally, refers to tax base integrity, but it has a narrower scope than coherence/balanced-allocation/territoriality/symmetry/mismatch-prevention. It only covers cases of *intentional* and *artificial* fiscal incoherencies and interjurisdictional imbalances (mismatches). The abuse-defense for free movement restrictions is therefore encompassed by the coherence/balanced-allocation/territoriality defense(s). This implies that there is no need for reliance on an abuse defense if the fiscal-coherence/balanced-allocation/territoriality defense(s) can be relied on, as in cases such as *Marks & Spencer II*.

CHAPTER 8

Division of Tax Jurisdiction; Double Tax Relief Mechanisms; Tax Treaty Issues[1]

Peter Wattel

Update by Otto Marres[2]

8.1 International Double Taxation (and why its Elimination is a Union Goal but not an Obligation for the Member States)

8.1.1 Why is there International Double Taxation in the first Place?

If all (Member) States were to confine themselves to taxation of income sourced within their territory or at least economically attributable to their jurisdiction, then apart from some tuning mismatches there would be very little (juridical) double taxation of the same income. Nonresidents are in fact taxed according to this source principle. By contrast, for residents, most member States apply worldwide income taxation, for reasons explained in section 6.1.1 (residence principle). The CJEU accepts both of these tax jurisdiction assertion principles (as well as the third taxing jurisdiction principle: the nationality principle[3]). These tax connecting factors are considered to be neutral assumption principles (or, between two States, neutral principles of division) of taxing jurisdiction, escaping the reach of the prohibitions of the Treaty Freedoms, which do not contain any indications

1 See on these issues also: Maria Hilling, *Free Movement and Tax Treaties in the Internal Market*, Iustus Förlag, Uppsala, 2005; Michael Lang, 'Double Taxation and EC Law,' Chapter 2 in Avi-Yonah, Hines and Lang, eds., *Comparative Fiscal Federalism: Comparing the European Court of Justice and the US Supreme Court's Tax Jurisprudence*, Kluwer Law International, The Netherlands, 2007, pp. 11-53; Pasquale Pistone, *The Impact of Community Law on Tax Treaties*, Kluwer Law International, 2002; Michael Lang and Sabine Dommes, 'Tax Treaty Law and EC Law: Reciprocity and the Balance of a Tax Treaty,' in Lang/Schuch/Staringer (eds.), *Tax Treaty Law and EC Law*, Linde Verlag, Austria, 2007; Juliane Kokott, 'European Court of Justice,' in Guglielmo Maisto (ed.), *Courts and Tax Treaty Law*, IBFD Amsterdam 2007, pp. 101-114; Peter J. Wattel, 'EC Treaty Freedoms, Tax Treaties and National Courts,' in Guglielmo Maisto (ed.), *Courts and Tax Treaty Law*, IBFD Amsterdam 2007, pp. 115-158; Raffaele Russo, 'Double Taxation Agreements between International and European Law, in Jutta Kruthoffer-Röwekamp (Hrsg.), *Die Rechtsprechung des EuGH in ihrer Bedeutung für das nationale und internationale Recht der direkten Steuern*, Nomos/C.H. Beck, 2010, pp. 53-60; Michael Lang, 'Double Taxation Conventions in the Case-Law of the CJEU', *Intertax* 2018/3, p. 181-193; and Ilaria Panzeri, 'Tax Treaties versus EU Law: Which Should Prevail?', *European Taxation* 2021/4.3.

2 Professor, Amsterdam Centre for Tax Law (ACTL), University of Amsterdam; tax lawyer, Lubbers, Boer & Douma, The Hague.

3 See Case C-513/03 *Van Hilten-Van der Heijden*, [2006] ECR I-1957, EU:C:2006:131 and Case C-336/96, *les époux Gilly*, [1998] ECR I-2793, EU:C:1998:221.

as to the priority of taxing jurisdiction. The *exercise* of the taxing jurisdiction so assumed or so divided, however, must answer to the nondiscrimination principle of the Treaty Freedoms (see section 6.4.2). Thus, as residence taxation and source taxation may overlap without EU law objections (as long as neither the source State nor the residence State distinguishes between the domestic and the cross-border situation), foreign-sourced income will be taxed twice, once in the source State and once in the residence State of the taxpayer deriving the income, and the need to prevent double taxation arises.

Although source and residence are in principle neutral criteria, they are not, in our view, applied indiscriminately: residence (unlimited, worldwide) taxation is usually only applied to residents (usually nationals), whereas source (limited) taxation is usually only applied to nonresidents (usually non-nationals). Whatever else this is, it is inconsistent, and at any rate a difference in treatment, for which the necessity is difficult to see, at least as regards individuals. Genuine nondiscrimination would mean either worldwide income taxation for both residents and (EU) non-residents (with prevention of double taxation as for residents), or territoriality taxation, disregarding foreign-source income and losses as regards both residents and nonresidents.

8.1.2 National Autonomy; no Obligation to Eliminate Double Taxation

Although, obviously, international double taxation and the cumbersome mechanics for its elimination or mitigation are a serious impediment for working, investing, establishing or selling abroad, primary EU law offers no remedy for it. It contains no rule on the question of which of the two States involved should prevent double taxation. EU law has no position on the choice between the source principle and the residence principle (or the nationality principle). It is even worse: there is no rule of EU law prohibiting intra-EU double taxation. Article 293(2nd indent) of the old EC Treaty, calling for bilateral negotiations between the Member States, was repealed in 2009 (see section 2.2.2.4), and anyway had no direct effect,[4] nor did it provide for the case where no such negotiations were initiated or the case where double taxation persisted. In cases such as *Kerckhaert-Morres*,[5] the Court held that the Treaty Freedoms are not capable of preventing international double taxation as a result of 'exercise in parallel by two member States of their fiscal sovereignty,' meaning the overlap of source taxation and residence taxation. In the follow-up Case *Damseaux*,[6] the Court explicitly left prevention of double taxation to the Member States:

> '30. In the absence of any unifying or harmonising Community measures, Member States retain the power to define, by treaty or unilaterally, the criteria for allocating their powers of taxation, particularly with a view to eliminating double taxation (....). It is for the Member States to take the measures necessary to prevent (...) double taxation by applying, in particular, the criteria followed in international tax practice (...).
> (...)
> 34. (...) the fact that both the Member State in which the dividends are paid and the Member State in which the shareholder resides are liable to tax those dividends does not

4 Case C-336/96, *les époux Gilly*, [1998] ECR I-2793, EU:C:1998:221.
5 Case C-513/04, *Kerckhaert en Morres*, [2006] ECR I-10967, EU:C:2006:713.
6 Case C-128/08, *Damseaux*, [2009] ECR I-6823, EU:C:2009:471.

> mean that the Member State of residence is obliged, under Community law, to prevent the disadvantages which could arise from the exercise of competence thus attributed by the two Member States.'

The *Margarete Block* Case,[7] on double inheritance taxation, was even clearer:

> '30. Community law, in the current stage of its development and in a situation such as that in the main proceedings, does not lay down any general criteria for the attribution of areas of competence between the Member States in relation to the elimination of double taxation within the European Community. Consequently, apart from [the Parent-subsidiary Directive, the Arbitration Convention and the Savings interest Directive; *authors*], no uniform or harmonisation measure designed to eliminate double taxation has as yet been adopted at Community law level (see *Kerckhaert and Morres*, paragraph 22, and *Columbus Container Services*, paragraph 45).
> 31. It follows from this that, in the current stage of the development of Community law, the Member States enjoy a certain autonomy in this area provided they comply with Community law, and are not obliged therefore to adapt their own tax systems to the different systems of tax of the other Member States in order, inter alia, to eliminate the double taxation arising from the exercise in parallel by those Member States of their fiscal sovereignty and, in consequence thereof, to allow the inheritance tax paid in a Member State other than that in which the heir is resident to be deducted in a case such as that of the main proceedings (see, to that effect, *Columbus Container Services*, paragraph 51).'

The implication of this case law is rather disenchanting: EU law has nothing to offer to a taxpayer suffering international double – but in both jurisdictions in itself indiscriminate – taxation, as there is no EU legal basis for a priority choice between source and residence taxation.[8] Therefore, within the internal market, there is an objective difference between a taxpayer staying at home and a taxpayer exposing himself to two taxing jurisdictions: unlike the first, the latter is subject to 'exercise in parallel by two Member States of their fiscal sovereignty', without this (double) subjection or its consequences being addressed by EU law. One of the strange phenomena in the Court's case law[9] is that it requires Member States to apply their double tax treaties or unilateral relief rules for residents earning foreign source income in a specific manner on some detail (*e.g.* personal allowances and tax-free amounts); that is strange because if there had not been any tax treaty or unilateral relief rule in the first place, the Court could have done nothing at all for the taxpayer, according to its own case law cited above. We fail to see how EU law could require a Member State to prevent double taxation in a certain detailed manner if EU law does not require that State to prevent double taxation in the first place. This cannot be based on a discrimination analysis by reference to the domestic situation, as in the purely domestic situation, obviously there *is* no 'exercise in parallel of fiscal sovereignty' and therefore no international double taxation to be prevented. We nevertheless agree that *if* the Court were competent to make a choice, the principle of source country entitlement should prevail, and the residence State should prevent double taxation, as it was the source State's economy which offered the economic opportunity to earn the

7 Case C-67/08, *Block*, [2009] ECR I-883, EU:C:2009:92.
8 See also Lang, l.c., paragraph 1.
9 Most notably in its Case C-385/00, *De Groot*, [2002] ECR I-11819, EU:C:2002:750.

income. Still, this does not tell us *how* the home State should do this; by exempting the foreign-source income entirely (territoriality principle; base exemption), by granting a proportionate tax reduction (exemption with progression), or by crediting the foreign tax against the attributable domestic tax (ordinary credit).

8.2 Capital Import Neutrality (CIN; Exemption) and Capital Export Neutrality (CEN; Credit)

8.2.1 *Source Taxation and Residence Taxation; Assumption and Exercise of Taxing Jurisdiction*

CIN and CEN, explained in detail below, are irreconcilable. Although both concepts aspire to international tax neutrality (prevention of international double taxation, CIN implying the method of tax exemption of foreign source income and CEN implying a credit against tax for foreign tax already paid), they start from fundamentally different neutrality concepts. Simultaneous import neutrality and export neutrality is impossible. Some commentators attribute the inconsistencies in the CJEU's case law in direct tax matters, precisely, to its brave but vain efforts to attain that unattainable goal.[10]

8.2.2 *Capital Export Neutrality (CEN); the Credit Method*

The starting point for prevention of international double taxation in established international (OECD-modeled) tax law is source country entitlement, meaning that the residence State should prevent double taxation by either exempting the foreign source income (CIN) or crediting the foreign tax (CEN). States adhering to CEN take the view that the residence State of the taxpayer should tax foreign-source income such that its residents are neither encouraged nor discouraged to invest abroad (home market neutrality). Taxation should not affect their decision as to where to invest or to work, so in either case they should pay the home State level of tax (say 30%), also if the tax level in the Source State is only 20%. A taxpayer earning foreign-source income is therefore taxed in his home country on his world-wide income, including the foreign-source income, but he may credit, against the home State tax attributable to his foreign-source income, the foreign tax already paid in the source State. The result is that the home State levies additional tax on the foreign-source income of 10 points (the difference). Credit systems thus ensure that at least the home State level of tax (30%) is levied on a resident's total income, wherever earned.

Where the source State tax is higher (say 35%) than the tax the home State would levy on the foreign-source income, consistent application of CEN would lead to the home State having to refund foreign tax (5 points). Invariably, CEN/credit States exchange the CEN principle for CIN where this effect would arise. The foreign tax credit is limited to the amount of domestic tax attributable to the foreign source income, in order to avoid having to refund domestic tax on other, domestic, income *(ordinary credit*, as opposed

10 Michael J. Graetz and Alvin C. Warren, Jr., 'Income Tax Discrimination and the Political and Economic Integration of Europe,' *The Yale law Journal*, April 2006, p. 1187-1255.

to *full credit*). Because of this limitation, home neutrality is not achieved where the source State tax is higher than the home State tax. Instead, capital *import* neutrality is the result for these cases. Usually, the excess foreign tax credit may be carried over to subsequent years, but that is of little help if the foreign tax on the foreign-source income is structurally higher than the attributable domestic tax or if there is no foreign-source income in those subsequent years.

Further complications ensue from (i) administrative complexity and the division of the burden of proof (the taxpayer must demonstrate that, and how much, tax was paid in the source country), (ii) per country application of the credit, (iii) foreign losses and (iv) an overall loss position of the taxpayer as a result of negative home State income.

In case of per country crediting, an excess foreign tax of one State (the 35% State) cannot be absorbed by unused credit space of another State (the 20% State). Where, by contrast, the credit is applied overall instead of per country, the attributable domestic tax is not calculated per country, but for all foreign-source income together, meaning that all credit space can be pooled and fully used. Groups of companies residenced in a State applying per country credit are therefore impelled to establish an intermediate holding company abroad (called a 'mixer') to hold all of their foreign holdings, for the sole purpose of mixing high taxed foreign source income with lower taxed foreign source income before remitting the resulting averagely taxed foreign-source income to the home State.

In case of negative foreign source income, usually such loss is included in the total income of the resident taxpayer, resulting in an immediate horizontal set-off of the foreign loss against domestic income, thus reducing the tax due on the *domestic* income. If in subsequent years a profit is made abroad, then first this tax lost in the previous year on the positive domestic income must be recaptured before any credits can be extended.

Where the overall income of the taxpayer is negative because of home State losses, no crediting is possible, as no tax is due. In such a case, a mechanism must be applied to carry over the unused foreign tax credit to previous or later years in which there is enough tax exposure (enough positive domestic income) to use the credit.

A characteristic of credit systems is that they are administratively cumbersome: not only must the attributable domestic tax be calculated for limitation purposes, but also the foreign tax to be credited must be determined, which implies either application of foreign tax law or imposing a separate home State system of determining the foreign tax connected to the foreign source income. The latter is especially intricate where so-called further tier credit for underlying tax is to be extended, *i.e.* where a resident parent company receives foreign subsidiary profit distributions and is granted credit for the foreign tax paid by the subsidiary on that profit, or by the sub-subsidiary in a third State, or by the sub-sub-subsidiary in a fourth State, etc.

Another characteristic of a credit system for the prevention of international double taxation is that it has built-in protection against both fair and unfair tax competition: both against the tax efficiency of other States in general, and against specific tax incentives of other States aimed at attracting specific foreign investment. If the source State lowers its rate, this will ultimately not benefit the taxpayer under a credit system, but only his home State treasury, as the less foreign tax is paid, the less credit will be granted to the taxpayer by his home State. Relative tax advantages of doing business abroad will be taxed away by the home State. Obviously, the same is true as regards specific source State tax incentives: the benefit of a tax holiday[11] or a specific tax reduction designed to attract mobile international capital will ultimately be taxed away by the home State of the investor. This pre-empting effect, outdoing any foreign tax competition is the explicit objective of the credit system; *home* market neutrality. This pre-empting effect may thus also lead to inadvertent 'reverse development aid': the tax revenue foregone by a developing country for the purpose of attracting investors from developed countries does not benefit these investors, but turns into extra tax revenue for the developed home State of the investor. So-called *tax-sparing credits*[12] are then needed to avoid this intrinsic effect of credit systems. Obviously, credit countries do not extend tax-sparing credits if they consider the source country to be a tax haven, or if they have no tax treaty with it, or if they consider the source country's tax reduction to be unfair tax competition.

8.2.3 Capital Import Neutrality (CIN); the Exemption Method

Capital import neutrality (CIN) starts from the view that a residence State should exempt the foreign-source income of its residents, as that income has already borne tax in the source State, and it is a matter for the source State to determine the level of tax that income sourced within its territory should bear. The aim of CIN is that all income sourced within a certain jurisdiction suffers only the level of taxation of that jurisdiction (source market neutrality). The neutrality thus attained is that foreign and domestic investors compete in the foreign market on the same tax conditions. In this approach, the home State of the investor should not tilt the level playing field on the foreign market by imposing additional home State taxation. States adhering to CIN therefore apply the exemption method for relief of international double taxation for their residents, entailing either (i) elimination of foreign-source income from the tax base altogether (base exemption; strict territoriality principle), or (ii) inclusion of the foreign-source income in the taxable base, but only for the purpose of calculating the tax bracket on the domestic income

11 A tax holiday is a temporary exemption from tax, designed to attract foreign investors, bringing with them jobs and know-how, typically the first five to ten years of operation of the investment, and conditional upon a minimum size of the investment, in asset value and/or in number of jobs created.

12 Tax-sparing credits are credits for foreign tax not actually paid, but which would have been paid had the tax incentive not existed. Credit is granted by the home State of the investor as if the investor were subject to the normal tax regime, without incentives.

(exemption with progression).[13] In the latter case, the taxpayer's home State tax will be calculated on his total (world-wide) income, but will subsequently be reduced by that part of the domestic tax which is attributable to the foreign-source income (as opposed to the credit method, under which the *foreign* tax is credited).

An important difference between base exemption (territoriality) and tax exemption (exemption with progression) is that in the first system both foreign profits *and* foreign losses are ignored, fragmenting the tax base into separate non-communicating national bits, whereas the latter system may include foreign losses as well as profits in the taxable base, thus automatically providing for cross-border horizontal loss relief (which will later be recaptured, once the foreign source becomes profitable again: the domestic tax forgone by allowing the foreign loss to be deducted, will be recaptured by not granting exemption for positive foreign income in subsequent years as long as these subsequent foreign profits do not exceed the foreign losses previously deducted; see section 10.2).

Under an exemption system, tax efficiency and tax incentives of the source State will automatically benefit the foreign investor rather than the Treasury of his home country, as under a credit system. Tax-sparing credits are thus not needed. If, reversely, the foreign tax is higher than the home State tax, then under CIN that is not a problem whatsoever. Indeed, there should be tax neutrality on the foreign market, so if in the foreign market a high tax level prevails, then the foreign investor in that market should pay that high tax, just as it pays only the lower tax if the foreign tax is lower than his home State tax. In an exemption system, the exemption is granted from *home* State taxation, whatever the level of the *foreign* tax.

A drawback of exemption is that it may encourage resident taxpayers to invest in foreign, relatively low-tax countries instead of investing at home. On a before-tax basis, such investments may well be sub-optimal from a capital productivity viewpoint.

8.2.4 *Differences and Similarities; Deferral; CFC Legislation*

Exemption and credit both start from neutrality, but from different neutrality concepts. Credit countries view the world from the home window (home neutrality). Exemption States, by contrast, view the world from the foreign trading post window. Consequently, credit systems allow for a home State tax reduction equal to the *foreign* tax on the foreign-source income, whereas exemptions systems allow for a reduction of home State tax equal to the *home State* tax attributable to the foreign-source income. Thus, residents of credit

13 If the tax rate is progressive, elimination of the foreign-source income from the taxable base altogether would result in placing the domestic income in the lower tax brackets and eliminating the foreign income from the highest tax bracket. If exemption with progression is applied, the division between foreign and domestic income is the same in every tax bracket. An exemption system may also invite resident taxpayers to divert domestic income to foreign tax havens (tax avoidance). Exemption systems are thus intrinsically more vulnerable to both fair and unfair tax competition, although the differences in this respect must not be exaggerated, as credit systems as well need anti-deferral legislation (such as CFC legislation) against (unfair) tax competition by tax havens.

countries compete on foreign markets on *home* State conditions, whereas residents of exemption countries compete on foreign markets on *source* State conditions.

This does not mean that CIN/exemption States are more altruistic than CEN/credit States. Although exemption respects the tax sovereignty of the source State as final, whereas the credit system levies additional tax to equalize with the home State tax level, the point of exemption is not so much to pay respect to foreign tax sovereignty, but rather to avoid home-based multinational companies suffering a higher tax burden in foreign markets than foreign-based multinationals and local undertakings on that same foreign market.

Not surprisingly, the credit system was and mostly still is applied by countries with traditionally either large or closed home markets (*e.g.* the US, the UK,[14] Japan, India, Italy,[15] Germany,[16] and Spain[17]; although many of them allow exemptions for profits from foreign permanent establishments carried on by corporate taxpayers nowadays), whereas the exemption method is traditionally used, at least in their many tax treaties, by countries with open markets and/or home markets which are too small to support significant expansion of their undertakings (*e.g* Belgium, and the Netherlands). France unilaterally exempts foreign-source business income (and losses) on the basis of a territoriality principle (base exemption), and usually uses exemption with progression under tax treaties for active income.

Even less surprisingly, the OECD Model,[18] which is widely used between EU Member States, endorses both credit and exemption (and no other method).

Exemption States are also credit States in that they usually exempt only *active* income (*e.g.* business profits, dividends from qualifying subsidiary companies, and employment

14 In 2011 an optional exemption for profits of foreign permanent establishments of UK companies was introduced (Irene Martínez Curra, United Kingdom - Corporate Taxation, IBFD publications [online; accessed 14 January 2025], at 7.2.1.1).

15 Resident companies may elect to exempt the income derived through foreign permanent establishments (Cesare Silvani, Italy - Corporate Taxation, IBFD publications [online; accessed 14 January 2025], at 7.2.1.1 and 7.2.6.1).

16 Almost all of Germany's tax treaties provide for an exemption for the income of foreign permanent establishments of resident companies for corporate income tax (Körperschaftsteuer); for the business tax (Gewerbesteurer) foreign-source income is generally disregarded (Andreas Perdelwitz, Germany - Corporate Taxation, IBFD publications [online; accessed 14 January 2025], at 7.2.1.2 and 7.2.3.1).

17 Profits derived from foreign permanent establishments by resident companies are exempt if (i) they have effectively been subject to a tax comparable to the Spanish corporate income tax, (ii) the permanent establishment is not located in a listed tax haven and (iii) the taxpayer proves that it was established in that State for sound business reasons and that it carries out business activities; these conditions are generally deemed to be met for permanent establishments in States which have concluded a tax treaty with Spain containing an exchange of information clause, or if the permanent establishment is taxed at a nominal rate of at least 10% (Álvaro de la Cueva González-Cotera and Esther Quintana Ortiz, Spain - Corporate Taxation, IBFD publications [online; accessed 14 January 2025], at 7.2.6.1).

18 See alternative Articles 23 A and 23 B of the Model Double Taxation Convention on Income and on Capital, with Commentaries to the Articles, OECD, Paris, 1977, revised in 1992 and in loose-leaf format since.

or self-employment income). For passive investment income (*e.g.* dividends, interest and royalties on passive investment), all States usually grant only a credit. This is mainly because of the mobility of portfolio investment capital and the problematic territorial sourcing of passive investment income. Exempting passive investment return would invite capital flight to tax havens and would reward unfair tax competition. Another reason for applying the credit method for passive income, is that passive investment is usually taxed at moderate rates (but on gross income!) by the State of source. Exemption of the income in the State of residence may then result in undertaxation.[19] Exemption countries may also use the credit system even for items of active income, depending on the conclusion of a tax treaty – and the content thereof – with the source State, on the status of the taxpayer (corporation or individual), or might apply a switch-over rule for foreign low-taxed income.[20] It should be observed that lately, both the traditional credit States and the traditional exemption States are reassessing the merits and drawbacks of both systems. For instance, the UK switched from an indirect credit system to an exemption system for inter-company dividends, where the Netherlands did the opposite as regards low-taxed passive foreign subsidiaries. In general, there has been a trend towards credit instead of exemption for directors' fees and artists' and athletes' income, caused by the aggressive tax planning as regards these items of income.[21]

Although the credit method may be the most widespread method worldwide, many credit countries, even the UK, use the exemption method in respect of one very important item of foreign-source income, *i.e.* dividends received by resident parent companies from their foreign subsidiaries. Within the EU, a majority of countries use some form of such participation exemption (affiliation privilege) to prevent economic international double taxation on profits distributed by foreign-based subsidiaries to resident parent companies holding a specific amount of capital and/or of voting power. With respect to these inter-company dividends, the difference between exemption and credit is not impressive anyway, since a foreign subsidiary company is a separate legal entity whose profits may be retained abroad instead of distributed to the parent company. Consequently, a parent company based in a credit State can easily avoid additional home State taxation of the foreign subsidiary's profits by simply having its foreign subsidiaries not distribute their profits. As long as the after-tax profits of the subsidiary are not remitted to the parent company, the home State of the latter in principle has no taxing jurisdiction. Thus, as long as the foreign subsidiary's profits stay abroad, credit or exemption does not make any difference. In order to curb tax avoidance by resident companies diverting passive investment income to offshore legal entities in tax havens (controlled foreign corporations; CFCs), almost all States apply some form of CFC legislation, entailing extra-territorial exercise of taxing power: the CFC is either treated as a branch of the resident parent company, allowing current taxation of the subsidiary's profits on an accrual basis in the parent company's hands (with credit for possible foreign tax paid by the CFC), or it is deemed to have distributed its profit every year to the parent company, allowing for the

19 For this reason Article 23 A (2) of the OECD and UN Model Convention switch to the credit method; see OECD Commentary on Article 23 at 47.
20 Cf. the switch-over rule in the ATAD proposal; see Section 19.2.1.
21 See the Commentary on Article 17 OECD Model Convention at 12.

same current taxation in the parent company State. Further, the OECD, in its initiative against unfair tax competition, especially against tax havens, invited the OECD States to take unilateral measures against unfair tax competition and tax havens, especially by applying credit and CFC legislation as regards these jurisdictions, and the application of CFC legislations was one of the Action Points (No. 3) of the OECD/G20 BEPS Action Plan. With effect from 1 January 2019 the implementation of CFC legislation is mandatory under the Anti-Tax Avoidance Directive (ATAD; see Chapter 19). In intra EU cases these rules need be compatible with the Cadbury Schweppes case law (see section 19.4.3.4). The CJEU narrowed the permissible reach – within the EU and the EEA – of CFC legislation under the freedom of establishment to 'wholly artificial arrangements' in Case C-196/04, *Cadbury Schweppes* (see section 7.4), as such legislation subjects parent companies holding foreign subsidiaries to less favourable tax treatment (current taxation in the hands of the parent) than parent companies of domestic subsidiaries.[22] The *SGI* Case[23] suggests, however, that necessary anti-base erosion and anti-deferral measures may distinguish between domestic and cross-border cases if it makes no sense to apply them in purely domestic situations (see section 7.5). Obviously, CFC legislation makes no sense as regards domestic subsidiaries, which are fully subject to domestic tax.

As observed, an important practical difference between credit and exemption is the intricacy of a credit system for both the taxpayer and the tax administration, and the burden of evidence for the taxpayer, especially in respect of the calculation of the indirect credit (credit for underlying tax) for corporation tax paid abroad by subsidiaries (or sub-sub-sidiaries, or sub-sub-subsidiaries in further foreign countries, or in respect of previous fiscal years), and because of the 'compartmentalization' of the credits in a *per country* system (separately for every different source State, or for groups of countries – 'baskets' – instead of overall for all foreign-source income). An exemption system, by contrast, is fairly simple to apply and to comply with, especially a base exemption system. Several credit countries therefore apply a credit system selectively (only for foreign subsidiaries in jurisdictions without a comparable tax level, or only if no treaty has been concluded

22 We do not understand this reasoning in the light of the almost simultaneous Case C-446/04, *Test Claimants in the Franked Investment Income (FII) Group Litigation*, in which the Court reasoned that credit for foreign dividends and exemption for domestic dividends was no violation of the freedom of establishment, as substantively, the foreign dividends were not taxed more heavily than the profits of a domestic subsidiary. Under CFC legislation as well, in the end the CFC's profits are not taxed more heavily than the profits of a domestic subsidiary. The only difference between the cases, is that in Cadbury Schweppes, *un*distributed foreign subsidiary profits were taxed, whereas in *FII*, distributed foreign subsidiary profits were taxed.

23 Case C-311/08, *SGI*, [2010] ECR I-487, EU:C:2010:26. See for comments: Philip Baker, 'Transfer Pricing and Community Law: The SGI Case', Editorial, *Intertax* 2010/4, p. 194-196; Adolfo Martín Jiménez, 'Transfer pricing and EU Law Following the ECJ Judgement in SGI: Some Thoughts on Controversial Issues', *Bulletin for International Taxation*, May 2010, p. 271-282; and Gerard Meussen, 'The SGI Case: ECJ Approves Belgian System of Selective Profit Corrections in Relation to Foreign Group Companies', *European Taxation* June 2010, p. 245-249. especially a base exemption system. Several credit countries therefore apply a credit system selectively (only for foreign subsidiaries in jurisdictions without a comparable tax level, or only if no tax treaty has been concluded with the subsidiary State). Indeed, if the tax burden in the source State is comparable to the tax burden at home, then there is little point in putting up with the intricacies of a credit system, since it will not yield significant additional tax revenue.

with the subsidiary State). Indeed, if the tax burden in the source State is comparable to the tax burden at home, then there is little point in putting up with the intricacies of a credit system, since it will not yield significant tax revenue.

8.2.5 Acceptance of Both Credit and Exemption in Secondary EU Law; the Court Accepts All Methods for Double Tax Relief; Remaining Inconsistencies

Despite the inherent inconsistency and the home market protective effect of the credit method, secondary EU law regards CIN and CEN with equal affection, as it is probably impossible to get any proposal adopted which does not allow for both OECD-endorsed methods. The Parent-Subsidiary Directive allows Member States a choice between the two methods (see section 16.4.1). The Arbitration Convention also embraces both methods (see Chapter 21). The same was true for the (withdrawn) proposal for a directive on the taking into account of foreign losses (see section 18.3), and for the (repealed) 2016 CCTB Proposal[24] (see Chapter 25).

The Ruding Committee Report[25] stated – admittedly in a slightly different context (of relief from double taxation of dividends distributed by an EU subsidiary to its EU parent company):

> 'The Committee does not hold any strong views concerning the relative merits of the two methods of providing relief for double taxation, believing that both methods can coexist. (....) it would be unrealistic to expect Member States to relinquish this choice. Nevertheless, the Committee considers that the exemption method would be preferable on the grounds of administrative simplicity provided it is accompanied by measures that prevent excessive tax competition among Member States.'[26]

Although the latter condition could be considered fulfilled since the application of the Code of Conduct for Business Taxation and the Commission's anti-State aid actions in the tax field, there is little chance of a fundamental choice within the EU between CIN and CEN,[27] less so as the CJEU considers them both compatible with primary EU law as well. The Court's case law on double tax relief mechanisms implies that, in conformity with settled international (OECD) tax law, all usual mechanisms are acceptable, which makes sense, as even the absence of double tax relief must be accepted as long as both States involved do not discriminate against the cross-border situation but double taxation still

24 Proposal for a Council Directive on a Common Corporate Tax Base, Strasbourg, 25 October 2016, COM(2016) 685 final, 2016/0337 (CNS). It provided for an exemption of profit distributions received, provided that the taxpayer had maintained a minimum holding of 10% in the capital or 10% of the voting rights of the distributing company for 12 consecutive months, and of income of a permanent establishment in a Member State (Art. 8(d) and (e); see Article 53 for a switch-over rule).

25 'Report of the Committee of Independent Experts on Company Taxation to the Commission of the European Communities', Office for Official Publications of the European Communities; Brussels/ Luxembourg 1992.

26 O.c. p. 204.

27 A switch-over rule was proposed in the ATAD proposal, but appeared to be too controversial; see Section 19.2.1.

persists as a result of 'exercise in parallel' of taxing power. This follows from, *e.g.* Case C-513/04, *Kerckhaert-Morres*, and Case C-67/08 *Block*. Thus, the Court has accepted (see also, for elaboration and conceptual context, sections 6.2, 7.5 and 10.5), as will be further discussed below:

- the (direct) ordinary credit method for double taxation relief in Case C-513/03, *Van Hilten*, and in Case C-298/05, *Columbus Container*, where it was allowed even in the context of national CFC-legislation overriding a tax treaty provision calling for exemption (see section 8.3.6);[28]
- the indirect credit method in Case C-446/04, *Test Claimants in the FII Group Litigation*, and the joined Cases C-436 and 437/08, *Haribo and Salinen*, even where exemption was granted in domestic situations;
- the base exemption method (excluding all foreign source profits and losses – except for final losses – from the tax base) in Case C-414/06, *Lidl Belgium* and Case C-650/16, *A/S Bevola and Jens W. Trock ApS* (see Section 18.3.2);
- exemption with progression (with recapture of deducted foreign losses in later years) in Case C-157/07, *Krankenheim Ruhesitz am Wannsee;*
- the recapture of losses of a permanent establishment (pe) situated in another Member State, in the event of transfer of the pe to a non-resident group company, where, under a tax treaty, the profits of the pe are exempt in the Member State of the company to which the pe belonged (Timac Agro)[29] and
- the refusal to deduct the losses of a pe situated in another Member State, under the abovementioned circumstances (Timac Agro).[30]

For the exemption method, the compatibility with EU law is obvious. For the credit method, the CJEU's reasoning is probably that the credit method, at the end of the day, does not – at least should not – result in a higher tax burden on foreign source income than on domestic income. Probably, the Court also considered that primary EU law does not even require the Member States to prevent international double taxation in the first place, let alone according to a specific method.

Thus, the Court accepted the direct *credit* method (prevention of international *juridical* double taxation: double taxation of the same income in the hands of the *same* person) in the Cases C-513/03, *Van Hilten-Van der Heijden*,[31] C-336/96, *Gilly*,[32] and C-298/05, *Columbus Container*.[33] In the latter case, the Court even accepted asymmetrical application of it, i.e. only in respect of disagreeable foreign tax regimes (Germany applied in principle exemption for foreign business profits, but switched to credit where the foreign profit was not taxed seriously enough according to German standards). In Case C-446/04, *Test*

28 See also the more recent Case C-403/19, *Société Générale SA*, EU:C:2021:136.

29 Case C-388/14, *Timac Agro Deutschland GmbH*, EU:C:2015:829. This is different if the credit method is applicable (Case C-48/13, *Nordea Bank Danmark A/S*, EU:C:2014:2087). See section 18.3.4.

30 Case C-388/14, *Timac Agro Deutschland GmbH*, EU:C:2015:829.

31 Case C-513/03, *Van Hilten-van der Heijden*, [2006] ECR I-1957, EU:C:2006:131.

32 Case C-336/96, *les époux Gilly*, [1998] ECR I-2793, EU:C:1998:221.

33 Case C-298/05, *Columbus Container Services*, [2007] ECR I-10451, EU:C:2007:754.

Claimants FII GLO,[34] and in the joined Cases C-436 and 437/08, *Haribo* and *Salinen*,[35] the Court accepted the *indirect* credit system (prevention of international *economic* double taxation: credit extended to domestic parent companies for underlying corporation tax paid by their foreign subsidiaries on the same distributed profits). It even accepted *asymmetric* application of the indirect credit method, *i.e.* only for foreign inter-company dividends, whereas domestic inter-company dividends were exempt. The court considered indirect credit and exemption to be 'equivalent', unless, as the Court stipulated in the *Test Claimants FII GLO II*[36] case, the effective level of taxation of company profits in the Member State concerned is generally lower than the prescribed nominal rate of tax (see section 16.4.1). In Case C-414/06, *Lidl Belgium*,[37] the base exemption method (exclusion of all foreign source profits and losses from the tax base: strict territoriality) was accepted. The Court further accepted the method of exemption with progression (with recapture of deducted foreign losses in later years) in Case C-157/07, *Krankenheim*.[38] The logical final consequence of this reasoning came with the *Damseaux* and *Block* cases, cited in section 3.2.2.7: if *no* relief from double taxation at all is available and neither of the two States involved discriminates against non-residents or against foreign-source income (if the double burden is caused by 'exercise in parallel' of taxing jurisdiction by two member States at the same time; therefore by a disparity or a dislocation rather than by a discrimination), then that is, in the present state of EU Law, irremediable. Taxpayers will have to wait for positive integration.

From an internal market point of view, however, we consider the credit method for active income as suspect. The very aim of the credit method is to take away any possible tax advantage of doing business or accepting a job abroad. It destroys the policy competition by more tax efficient Member States. From an internal market point of view relative differences in direct tax level between Member States are not different from factors such as economic opportunity, skilled labour force, distribution infrastructure, consumer purchasing power, political stability, or climate. Relative differences between the regular tax levels of States usually fairly accurately reflect relative differences in economic opportunity, public services and tax efficiency. Preempting such differences is clearly protective of the home market. In Case C-294/97, Eurowings[39] (see section 7.4), although concerning a different factual situation (unrelated traders in different Member States), the Court held that Member States may not levy a – what the Court in that case called – 'compensatory tax' to undo tax advantages of doing business abroad. The credit method is also fundamentally inconsistent, switching from CEN to CIN according to the budgetary interest of the home State, and, as especially the *Haribo* and *Salinen* case (see above) shows, administratively so burdensome for the taxpayer that he runs the real risk of not receiving the credit he is theoretically entitled to.

---

34 Case C-446/04, *Test Claimants in the FII Group Litigation*, [2006] ECR I-11753, EU:C:2006:774.

35 Joined Cases C-436/08 and 437/08, *Haribo Lakritzen Hans Riegel* and *Österreichische Salinen*, EU:C:2011:61 and EU:C:2009:17.

36 Case C-35/11 (*Test Claimants in the FII Group Litigation*), [2012], EU:C:2012:707.

37 Case C-414/06, *Lidl Belgium*, [2008] ECR I-3601, EU:C:2008:278.

38 Case C-157/07, *Krankenheim Ruhesitz am Wannsee-Seniorenheimstatt*, [2008] ECR I-8061, EU:C:2008:588.

39 Case C-294/97, *Eurowings Luftverkehr*, [1999] ECR I-7447, EU:C:1999:524.

Another problem of the credit method is that it interferes with the EU principle of national (tax) treatment of non-residents in the source State. Any tax relief extended by the source country on the basis of the EU Treaty Freedoms to nonresidents will be taxed away by the home State of those nonresidents, making it rather pointless for the taxpayer to require national treatment in the source State and for the source State to extend it: the only one benefiting from the national treatment will be the Treasury of the home State rather than the taxpayer. The interaction of the credit method with the Treaty Freedoms thus leads to arbitrary budget shift from the source State to the home State, running counter to the division of taxing power they bilaterally negotiated. To a certain extent this is acknowledged by the Court, which allows, in certain circumstances, a more burdensome taxation from non-residents if the tax is fully credited in the State of residence (the 'overall'-approach; see section 6.5.4).

As observed, as effective tax burdens for active income converge within the EU, and as unfair tax competition is phased out within the EU by the adoption of ATAD 1 and ATAD 2 (see Chapter 19), the work of the Code of Conduct Group (see Chapter 26), and the State aid investigations by the Commission, there is less budgetary reason for the Member States currently applying it, to put up with the intricacies of the credit method.

8.3 Tax Treaty Issues

8.3.1 National Autonomy; Conclusion of Bilateral Tax Treaties[40]

Primary EU law offers little guidance on the rules governing the conclusion of international agreements by the Member States. It is clear that Member States are entitled to conclude tax treaties. Art. 3(2) TFEU holds that '[t]he Union shall also have exclusive competence for the conclusion of an international agreement when its conclusion is provided for in a legislative act of the Union or is necessary to enable the Union to exercise its internal competence, or in so far as its conclusion may affect common rules or alter their scope', but there is no such legislative act or necessity. Obviously, the Member States must obey EU law when they conclude tax treaties, either amongst themselves or with third States. Treaties concluded before 1 January 1958 or, for acceding States, before the date of their accession, between one or more Member States on the one hand, and one or more third countries on the other, are not affected by the provisions of the Treaties, but to the extent that such agreements are not compatible with the Treaties, the Member State(s) concerned must take all appropriate steps to eliminate the established incompatibilities (Art. 351 TFEU).

Before 1 December 2009, Article 293(2nd indent) of the then repealed EC Treaty provided that 'Member States shall, so far as is necessary, enter into negotiations with each other with a view to securing, for the benefit of their nationals, (....) [inter alia] the abolition of double taxation within the Community, (...).' This provision did not have direct effect,[41] but

40 Parts of this subparagraph are taken from Peter J. Wattel: Taxation in the Internal Market; Chapter 15 in: Panos Koutrakos/Jukka Snell: (ed.) Research Handbook on The Law of the EU's Internal Market; Edward Elgar Publishing, 2017, paragraph 3.

41 Case C-336/96, *les époux Gilly*, [1998] ECR I-2793, EU:C:1998:221.

it showed that the abolition of international double taxation was a Community objective, which makes sense, as it is difficult to think of better ways to thwart cross-border economic activity than to double-tax it. It also showed, however, that the EC Treaty considered abolition of international double taxation as a matter to be negotiated between Member States in regular treaties, rather than as a policy matter at EC level. Article 293 EC was deleted in the Treaty of Lisbon. The accompanying documents did not explain why, so speculation on the implications has been ongoing in literature.[42] It would appear, however, that there was no substantive or political reason for its vanishing, but merely a wish to simplify the Treaties.[43] Article 293 EC was already repealed under the Constitutional Treaty of 2003, which was never ratified as it was voted down by the French and the Dutch. On the eve of the Intergovernmental Conference (IGC) on the Constitutional Treaty, the drafters wanted to simplify the Treaties then in force, and the Council's legal service suggested the preparatory Working Group IX to reduce the number of EU legal instruments – which had grown to 15 in 2002 – to the initial five instruments in the first Treaty of Rome (now art. 288 TFEU).[44] Convention-negotiating between Member States as envisaged in Article 293 was considered ineffective and superfluous in respect of the goals intended, which mostly had been or could be attained through other means; as far as the elimination of double taxation was concerned: through bilateral tax treaties. Working Group IX agreed that Article 293 EC was outdated and unnecessary,[45] the presidency of the IGC adopted the proposal to delete it and in 2003, the ICG adopted the Constitutional Treaty. Although that was never ratified, the repeal of Article 293 EC was maintained – as was 90% of the content of the Constitution – in the replacing Treaty of Lisbon in 2008. This is probably why the travaux preparatoires for the latter Treaty do not give reasons for the repeal, but it has to be inferred that the Lisbon IGC simply implemented the 2002 Working Group IX simplifications already adopted under the Constitutional IGC. In our view, therefore, the repeal of Article 293 EC does not mean anything in particular for taxation or any other area. It does not mean that elimination of double taxation is not a Union goal any more, nor, inversely, that the Court now has competence to eliminate double taxation under the Treaty Freedoms.

8.3.2 *Treaties to be Regarded as National Law; the Overall Approach*

Case C-265/04, *Bouanich*,[46] Case C-170/05, *Denkavit France*,[47] and Case C-379/05, *Amurta*,[48] show that, for purposes of examining the compatibility of national law with the EU free

42 See Eric Kemmeren, 'After Repeal of Article 293 EC Treaty under the Lisbon Treaty,' EC Tax Review 2008, p. 145 et seq.; Luc Hinnekens: 'The Uneasy Case and Fate of Article 293 Second indent EC,' 37 Intertax 2009, p. 602-609; Herwig Hofmann: 'Double Tax Agreements: Between EU Law and Public International Law', in: Alexander Rust (ed.): 'Double Taxation within the European Union,' Wolters Kluwer 2011, p. 75-86; and Ekkehart Reimer: 'The Abolition of Article 293 EC: Comments on Hofmann's Analysis,' idem, p. 87-96.

43 The following is based on research conducted by UvA-student Cecilia Dan-Thuy Le for her master's thesis in international and EU taxation.

44 Working Group IX Simplification, Working Document 06, 6 November 2002, p. 2.

45 Working Group IX Simplification, Working Document 21, 15 November 2002, p. 5 and 14-15.

46 Case C-265/04, *Bouanich*, [2006] ECR I-923, EU:C:2006:51.

47 Case C-170/05, *Denkavit International and Denkavit France*, [2006] ECR I-11949, EU:C:2006:783.

48 Case C-379/05, *Amurta*, [2007] ECR I-9569, EU:C:2007:655.

movement rights, tax treaties in principle take the same position as national law. They are to be taken into account as part of the overall legal framework to be judged in order to establish the overall (international) tax position of the taxpayer for purposes of comparing it to the domestic position. That makes sense, as from an EU law point of view, national law of a Member State and bilateral law of two Member States is fundamentally the same. What is prohibited if enacted in national law, remains prohibited if included in a bilateral tax treaty. From an EU law point of view, a tax treaty is no more than two Member States coordinating their national laws. The logical consequence of this approach is that if a tax treaty, being a part of national law in both contracting States, makes undone a freedoms restriction contained in (purely) national law, that should be acceptable under EU law: if the assertion and division of taxing power is a sovereign matter for the Member States, then EU law does not oppose that they bilaterally agree that one of them reduces its tax claim in order to compensate for a – from an EU law point of view – excessive claim of the other State. Thus, a discriminatory refusal of tax personal and family related tax benefits in one State may be compensated for by extension of similar benefits in the other Contracting State (Case C-385/00, *De Groot*), or a discriminatory withholding tax of one State may be credited in the other State (Case C-379/05, *Amurta*) (see section 6.5.4). This is a useful differentiation from the 'unconditional' approach in *Avoir Fiscal* (see section 8.3.5 below). At first, the Court did not care whether the compensating effect was due to a tax treaty or to unilateral tax measures in the other Member State, as long as 'the end result' was that the restrictive effect in one State was taken away by the other State (*De Groot*). The Court retracted this finding, however, in *Amurta*. Unilateral relief in the other Member State is not enough: the removal, in the shareholder State, of a discriminatory source tax must be provided for in a bilateral tax treaty:

> 78. (...), the Kingdom of the Netherlands cannot rely on the existence of a tax advantage granted unilaterally by another Member State in order to escape its obligations under the Treaty.
> 83. It is (...) for the national court to (...) determine whether [the] convention enables the effects of the restriction on the free movement of capital (...) to be neutralised.

For some guessing why the Court requires a tax treaty obligation, see section 6.5.4. At any rate, tax treaties are apparently looked at as extensions of national law in the sense that Member States are in principle free to comply with their TFEU obligations in the form of a tax treaty requiring their tax treaty partner to undo (to credit) taxation which on the basis of only a one-jurisdictional analysis would have been found discriminatory and prohibited. The Court requires that the tax levied by the State of source be deducted in its entirety from the tax due in the Member State of residence of the taxpayer receiving the income.[49] However, a full credit need not be agreed upon in the bilateral agreement; a credit based upon the bilateral agreement and resulting in a full credit in the case at hand suffices.[50]

The Court thus not only follows an overall approach, but also, at least in some cases (see section 6.5.1) a parallel 'always somewhere' approach, insisting that taxpayers must not

49 Joined Cases C-10/14, C-14/14 and C-17/14, *Miljoen*, EU:C:2015:608, point 80.
50 Joined Cases C-10/14, C-14/14 and C-17/14, *Miljoen*, EU:C:2015:608, points 85-86.

lose, because of their working abroad or earning foreign-source income, part of their possibilities to deduct expenses, to obtain loss relief, to obtain personal tax reductions, to deduct pension contributions, etc. In this approach, the Court does not always seem to care very much about the income allocation the tax treaty in force prescribes. Notorious in this respect is Case C-527/06, *Renneberg*, in which the Court considered:

> '70 (...) the mechanisms used to eliminate double taxation or the national tax systems which have the effect of eliminating or alleviating double taxation must, (...), permit the taxpayers in the Member States concerned to be certain that, ultimately, all their personal and family circumstances will be duly taken into account, irrespective of how those Member States have allocated that obligation amongst themselves, in order not to give rise to inequality of treatment which is incompatible with the Treaty provisions on the freedom of movement for workers and in no way results from the disparities between the national tax laws. (...), those considerations also apply with regard to the taking into account of workers' overall ability to pay tax.'

As this language ignores the question of *who* is doing the unequal treatment, the Court does not seem to care which of the two States 'duly' takes ability to pay into consideration, as long as it happens somewhere. This is odd, as (i) EU law does not require member States to take ability to pay into account at all, and Member State's systems differ widely as regards the extent in which they do, resulting in disparities which deprives the Court's term 'duly' of any meaning; (ii) Member States are not required to prevent double taxation in the first place, according to the Court (*Block; Damseaux*), so how can they be required to provide double tax relief in some detailed manner?; and (iii) the Treaty freedoms do not entail several liability of Member States for 'unequal treatment'. For unequal treatment one single culprit is needed. If the interaction of two separate national systems is to blame for the unfavourable effect, then we are looking at a regulatory disparity or at a dislocation of income (i.e. a parallel exercise or a parallel non-exercise of taxing power).

8.3.3 *Tax Treaties and their Substantive Rules*

Tax treaties between EU Member States are patterned after the OECD Model and basically consist of three categories of rules: (i) distributive rules (which State may tax what first or exclusively?), (ii) double taxation relief rules (credit or exemption method; modes of application), and (iii) general and implementing rules (scope, definitions, exchange of information, recovery assistance, mutual agreement, anti-abuse, non-discrimination, etc.). Taxing jurisdiction is divided on the basis of connecting factors such as the place of employment or of the business activity of the taxpayer, the location of real property, the place of mind and management of a company, the residence of an individual, the duration of cross-border employment, or even the nationality of the employee. These distributive rules do not usually entail exclusive allocation in the sense of exclusion from the tax base (base exemption). On the contrary: the income allocated to one State may still be included in the tax base of the other State (typically the residence State) for progression calculation purposes, for home State neutrality purposes (credit method: additional taxation on foreign-source income) and for (temporary) cross-border loss relief purposes. The home State usually taxes the worldwide income of its residents, including the income allocated to the other State (the source State), and subsequently grants a relief from the home State tax on that worldwide income, calculated either as the home State tax attributable to the foreign-source income (exemption system), or as the tax actually levied abroad on the foreign-source income (credit system) (see, for elaboration, sections 8.2.2 and 8.2.3).

Case C-336/96, *Gilly*, addressed the questions of whether (i) the connecting factors used for the division of taxing jurisdiction between Member States and (ii) their double taxation relief mechanisms, are compatible with the free movement of persons. Mrs Gilly was a teacher resident in France. She was employed in public service in Germany. The France-Germany tax treaty laid down different connecting factors for employment income, resulting in different allocations, depending on different factual circumstances. Because of her German nationality, Mrs Gilly's wages ended up being allocated non-exclusively to Germany, requiring France to provide double taxation relief. The German tax rate was higher than the French rate. Mrs Gilly complained of three things:

i. she and her husband losing part of their French personal tax benefits as a consequence of the *pro rata* calculation of the double taxation relief; this part of their complaint was not fully appreciated;
ii. her employment income being allocated to Germany on the basis of her nationality, which she considered a direct discrimination (she would rather be taxed in France); and
iii. the French relief mechanism not providing full prevention of double taxation as she was paying more tax than if she had earned the same income solely in France.

Issue (i) was implicitly and apparently inadvertently decided, which was later overturned by the *De Groot* case (see section 13.4.5).

As regards the choice of tax jurisdiction connecting factors (issue (ii)), the Court held:

> '30. Although the criterion of nationality appears as such in the second sentence of Article 14(1) [of the tax treaty; *authors*] for the purpose of allocation of fiscal jurisdiction, such differentiation cannot be regarded as constituting discrimination prohibited under Article 48 [now 45; *authors*] of the Treaty. It flows, in the absence of any unifying or harmonizing measures adopted in the Community context under, in particular, the second indent of Article 220 [now deleted; *authors*] of the Treaty, from the contracting parties' competence to define the criteria for allocating their powers of taxation as between themselves, with a view to eliminating double taxation.
> 31. Nor, in the allocation of fiscal jurisdiction, is it unreasonable for the Member States to base their agreements on international practice and the model convention drawn up by the OECD (...).
> 34. (...), whether the tax treatment of the taxpayers concerned is favourable or unfavourable is determined not, strictly speaking, by the choice of the connecting factor but by the level of taxation in the competent State, in the absence of any Community harmonization of scales of direct taxation.
> 35. The answer (...) must therefore be that, (...), Article 48 [now 45; *authors*] of the Treaty does not preclude the application of provisions such as those in Articles 13(5)(a), 14(1) and 16 of the Convention, under which the tax regime applicable to frontier workers differs depending on whether they work in the private sector or the public sector and, where they

> work in the public sector, on whether or not they have only the nationality of the State of the authority employing them, and the regime applicable to teachers differs depending on whether their residence in the State in which they are teaching is for a short period or not.'

It follows that EU law is in principle indifferent as to the criteria used for the division of taxing power between the two States involved.[51] They are free to use the usual OECD Model connecting factors. Their choice may be good luck or bad luck for the taxpayer, depending on whether he pays tax in the higher-rate State or in the lower-rate State, but that is a disparity between the national laws, which are a matter of national sovereignty. EU law does not require the Member States to apply identical tax scales, nor to prevent double taxation in such a way that the income is always taxed at the lowest level of taxation of the two States involved: the Treaty freedoms do not require the Member States to adapt their tax system to that of the other State,[52] nor do they guarantee that the relocation of a taxpayer always passes off neutrally tax-wise.[53] It only requires equal treatment (national treatment) of nonresidents and of foreign-source income within the subject-to-tax area so divided (see section 3.2.7.3).

As regards issue (iii) – the French mechanism to prevent double taxation – it should be noted that France credited the amount of tax France would have levied on Mrs Gilly's German income, had it not given relief. This mechanism therefore clearly boils down to an *exemption* system. Obviously then, if the German tax is higher than France would have levied, France is not going to refund the higher German tax. The Court held on this issue:

> '46. (...), it must be stressed, (...), that the object of a convention such as that in issue is simply to prevent the same income from being taxed in each of the two States. It is not to ensure that the tax to which the taxpayer is subject in one State is no higher than that to which he or she would be subject in the other.
> 47. However, it is common ground that any unfavourable consequences entailed in the present case by the tax credit mechanism set up by the bilateral convention, as implemented in the context of the tax system of the State of residence, are the result in the first place of the differences between the tax scales of the Member States concerned, and, in the absence of any Community legislation in the field, the determination of those scales is a matter for the Member States.
> 48. Furthermore, (...), if the State of residence were required to accord a tax credit greater than the fraction of its national tax corresponding to the income from abroad, it would have to reduce its tax in respect of the remaining income, which would entail a loss of tax revenue for it and would thus be such as to encroach on its sovereignty in matters of direct taxation.'

Thus, for lack of harmonization of the methods of double taxation relief, Member States also remain free to choose that method. As observed above (section 8.2.5) the Court therefore accepted all current methods for the prevention of double taxation, and even the absence of such prevention, provided that the double taxation is a result not of any discrimination

51 Cf. Case C-602/17, *Benoît Sauvage and Kristel Lejeune*, EU:C:2018:856, point 22.
52 Case C-298/05, *Columbus Container Services*, [2007] ECR I-10451, EU:C:2007:754.
53 Case C-403/03, *Schempp*, [2005] ECR I-6421, EU:C:2005:446, and Case C-365/02, *Lindfors*, [2004] ECR I-7183, EU:C:2004:449.

by one of the States, but ensues from disparities or dislocations (see sections 3.2.7.2 and 3.2.7.3), or, as the Court calls it, 'exercise in parallel' of taxing jurisdiction. For elaboration and conceptual context of the acceptance of all double tax relief methods, see sections 6.2 and 8.2.5. Not only negative integration leaves Member States free to choose a method, so too does positive integration: the Parent-Subsidiary Directive (see Chapter 16) and the Arbitration Convention (see Chapter 21) explicitly accept both exemption and credit.

8.3.4 *Personal Scope of Tax Treaties: Nationals versus Foreigners, Residents versus Non-Residents, Non-Residents versus Non-Residents, Limitation on Benefits*

As regards tax treaties with third States, it follows from the non-tax Case C-55/00 *Gottardo*,[54] that benefits negotiated for nationals in treaties with third States must also be extended to nationals of other Member States in otherwise equal circumstances, especially as regards residence. Normally, tax treaties satisfy this requirement, as they connect to residence. However, precisely because they connect to residence, branches of nonresident companies are excluded from the treaty benefits. Case C-307/97, *Saint-Gobain*[55] made clear that such exclusion is an unacceptable discrimination, also as regards treaty benefits contained in treaties with third States. Germany was required to extend the double tax relief for US dividends provided for in the German-US treaty also to the German branch of the French company Saint-Gobain. The German government argued that the content and application of tax treaties with third States was a Member State competence, not a Union competence, and that since double taxation treaties are based on the principle of reciprocity, the balance inherent in such treaties would be disturbed if the benefit of their provisions was to be extended to companies established in Member States which were not parties to them. The Court observed, referring to C-336/96, *Gilly*, that Member States remain competent to determine the tax bases and, by way of tax treaties, to determine the connecting factors for the purposes of allocating powers of taxation as between themselves, but:

> '57. As far as the exercise of the power of taxation so allocated is concerned, the Member States nevertheless may not disregard Community rules. According to the settled case law of the Court, although direct taxation is a matter for the Member States, they must nevertheless exercise their taxation powers consistently with Community law (...).
> 58. In the case of a double-taxation treaty concluded between a Member State and a non-member country, the national treatment principle requires the Member State which is party to the treaty to grant to permanent establishments of non-resident companies the advantages provided for by that treaty on the same conditions as those which apply to resident companies.
> 59. (...) the obligations which Community law imposes on (...) Germany do not affect in any way those resulting from its agreements with the United States of America and the Swiss Confederation. The balance and the reciprocity of the treaties concluded by (...) Germany with those two countries would not be called into question by a unilateral extension, on the part of (...) Germany of the category of recipients in Germany of the tax advantage provided for by those treaties, in this case corporation tax relief for international groups, since such

54 Case C-55/00, *Gottardo*, [2002] ECR I-413, EU:C:2002:16.
55 Case C-307/97, *Saint-Gobain ZN*, [1999] ECR I-6161, EU:C:1999:438.

an extension would not in any way affect the rights of the non-member countries which are parties to the treaties and would not impose any new obligation on them.'

No-one seems to have drawn the Court's attention to the fact that tax treaties with the US and Switzerland were also concluded by France, the Member State of establishment of Saint-Gobain, nor to the fact that also France and Germany had concluded a tax treaty, all of which results in a triangular tax treaty situation which is very difficult to oversee. That is exactly why many countries explicitly exclude triangular situations. One effect seems clear as a result of this judgment: if the State of the seat of the company (France in this case) applies the credit method for the prevention of international double taxation on the branch profit, then *Saint-Gobain* does not seem to benefit the company, but only the Treasury of its seat State, at the cost of the Treasury of the branch State. Indeed, if the branch State is required to grant exemption or credit in respect of foreign dividends received by the branch, then very little or no tax is levied in the branch State. Consequently, the seat State will hardly grant any double tax relief when taxing the company on its world-wide income. Further, in the *D. v. Inspecteur* and *Class IV ACT* cases (see below in this section), the Court rather contradictorily observed that tax treaties are by their nature limited in their scope to residents. In our view the difference can be explained by the fact that Saint-Gobain was comparable to a resident taxpayer to the extent it derived profits attributable to its permanent establishment, whereas D. (and the foreign shareholders in the *Class IV ACT* cases respectively) were not comparable to a resident of either contracting State of the relevant tax treaty.

Whereas the *Saint-Gobain* case dealt with the different treatment of resident and non-resident taxpayers, the abovementioned *D. v. Inspecteur* case dealt with the different treatment of two non-resident taxpayers. Although two persons, resident in different Member States, are in principle comparable from the perspective of a third Member State (see also the *Sopora* case[56]), this appears to be different for the purpose of a double tax treaty: a person who is not resident of a contracting State is incomparable to a resident of a contracting State (*D. v. Inspecteur* and *Class IV ACT*), unless he is treated similar as a resident in that specific contracting State (*Saint-Gobain*). The Court rejected mandatory most-favoured nation treatment as regards tax treaty benefits for EU-residents in Case C-376/03, *D. v. Inspecteur*.[57] Member State A does not need to extend benefits granted to residents of member State B (such as a tax free basic allowance) also to residents of Member State C,

56 See Case C-512/513, *C.G. Sopora*, EU:C:2015:108, point 25 (as regards the free movement of workers): '(...), having regard to the wording of Article 45(2) TFEU, which seeks to abolish all discrimination based on nationality 'between workers of the Member States', read in the light of Article 26 TFEU, the view must be taken that that freedom also prohibits discrimination between non-resident workers if such discrimination leads to nationals of certain Member States being unduly favoured in comparison with others'.

57 Case C-376/03, *D. v. Inspecteur*, [2005] ECR I-5821, EU:C:2005:424. See, for comments: Georg Kofler and Clemens Philipp Schindler, 'Dancing with Mr D. (etc.),' *European Taxation*, December 2005, pp. 530-540; Servaas van Thiel (ed.), 'The European Union's Prohibition of Discrimination, Most-Favoured-Nation Treatment and Tax Treaties: Opinions and Materials,' *Confédération Fiscale Européenne*, 2006; and Peter J. Wattel, 'EC Law Does Not Require Most-Favoured Nation Tax Treatment and a Disparity is Not a Discrimination: *D v. Inspecteur van de belastingdienst*,' *British Tax Review*, 2005, 575-583.

as residents of Member States B and C are not comparable for the purposes of tax treaty negotiation by Member State A. Tax treaties are negotiation results between two different national tax systems and, in the absence of harmonization, Member State B's system is not comparable to Member State C's tax system in its interacting with Member State A's system. Separating specific treaty benefits from the remainder of the tax treaty is not possible without disturbing the overall balance of the negotiation result. Tax treaties are by their nature limited to residents of one of the contracting States. This judgment implied that also LOB-provisions within the Union should be acceptable, as these provisions serve to ensure that the distinction made between residents of B and residents of C is maintained also if a resident of State B interposes a company in State C in order to obtain, via that intermediate company, the benefits of the tax treaty A-C not intended for residents of B. Thus, in Case C-374/04, *Test Claimants in Class IV of the ACT Group Litigation* the Court allowed the UK to ensure, by way of LOB-provisions, that the payment of its ACT credit only benefited residents of Member States with which it had agreed to pay that credit. At first sight, this does not seem to tally with Case 235/87, *Annunziata Mateucci*, para. 23, where the Court disqualified the limitation of scholarships to nationals of only the two member states concluding a bilateral agreement. However, the benefit at issue in *Annunziata Mateucci* was a benefit that would have to be extended to EU nationals anyway, because it is extended to *nationals*: it was applied domestically, whereas tax treaty benefits are extended to (certain) *non*residents. Having to extend them to everyone, would largely do away with tax sovereignty (Member States would not conclude meaningful tax treaties any more), and a balanced allocation of taxing rights. The question of whether a Member State may treat differently two nonresidents of different Member States may also be relevant as regards CFC legislation requiring a minimum level of taxation in the State of the subsidiary. In C-196/04, *Cadbury Schweppes*, point 44, the Court considered that a parent company holding foreign subsidiaries within the scope of the CFC rules of its home State is not only treated differently as compared to parents holding domestic subsidiaries, but also as compared to parents holding foreign subsidiaries not caught by the CFC rules, although being taxed at a lower rate than domestic subsidiaries.

It would seem that limitations on treaty benefits (LOB provisions) in treaties with third States, distinguishing on the basis of the place of residence of the controlling shareholders in the domestic company claiming tax treaty benefits, in principle fall foul of the Treaty Freedoms, as they affect domestic companies with EU shareholders unfavourably as compared to domestic companies with domestic shareholders (see the non-tax case *Open Skies*[58]). Indeed, the European Commission requested the Netherlands to amend the LOB provision in the Netherlands-Japanese Tax Treaty in the form of a reasoned opinion. The Commission argued, on the basis of Case C-55/00 *Gottardo* and C-466/98 *Open Skies*, that a Member State concluding a treaty with a third country cannot agree better treatment for companies held by shareholders resident in its own territory, or

58 Cases C-446-469/98, C-471-472/98, C-475-476/98, *Commission v. UK, Denmark, Sweden, Finland, Belgium, Luxembourg, Austria and Germany*, respectively), [2001] ECR I-9427 ff., EU:C:2000:691, EU:C:2000:586, EU:C:2000:663, EU:C:2001:275, EU:C:2002:628, EU:C:2002:629, EU:C:2002:630, EU:C:2002:631. Cf. CFE ECJ Task Force, Opinion Statement ECJ-TF 1/2018 on the Compatibility of Limitation-on-Benefits Clauses with the EU Fundamental Freedoms, European Taxation 9/2018, p. 4.19-425.

traded on the local stock exchange, than for comparable companies held by shareholders who are resident elsewhere in the EU/EEA, or traded on stock exchanges elsewhere in the EU/EEA, respectively, as the Netherlands allegedly did.[59] Perhaps the Netherlands' response was satisfactory, or the European Commission lost interest (and moved the case to the bottom of its priority list), because we have since heard nothing of this case. Anyway, a Member State concluding a tax treaty with a third State which insists on an LOB-provision, can in our view successfully argue – provided it did its utmost to include a derivative benefits test and a safety net provision – that there is a justification (a tax treaty is better for everyone than no tax treaty). Therefore, no 'serious' breach of EU law exists within the meaning of the State liability case law. Also, there seems to be no or insufficient causal link between the tax damages claimed by companies with EU parents and the tax treaty negotiation result (see for elaboration section 5.5.2).

8.3.5 *The Court's struggle with the meaning of bilateral tax treaties*

The Treaty Freedoms are unconditional and may therefore not be made dependent on bilateral tax treaty negotiation results. As the Court held in Case 270/83, *Commission v. France (Avoir fiscal):*

> 'the rights conferred by Article 52 [now 43; *authors*] of the Treaty are unconditional and a Member State cannot make respect for them subject to the contents of an agreement concluded with another Member State. In particular, that Article does not permit those rights to be made subject to a condition of reciprocity imposed for the purpose of obtaining corresponding advantages in other Member States'.

The Court has nuanced this finding slightly in its 'overall' or 'neutralization' approach (see sections 8.3.2 and 6.5.4).

In the first cases in which tax treaties were involved, Case 270/83, *Avoir Fiscal*, and Case C-204/90, *Bachmann*, the Court more or less ignored them for purposes of testing the national tax measures under the Treaty Freedoms, probably for three reasons:
- the fact that another Member State agrees to a tax arrangement which contravenes EU law, obviously cannot justify that contravention;
- as observed: the Treaty Freedoms are unconditional and therefore independent of the absence or presence of tax treaties, and
- as the Court suggested in *Bachmann:* tax treaties are coordinating measures, which is a form of positive integration outside the Court's competence.

However, the Court subsequently changed its mind, taking into account the effects of – and interpreting – tax treaties, probably because it realized that:
- there is little point in ignoring a well-settled, well-functioning, very effective, wide-spread and greatly standardized body of international law to which all Member States adhere in their bilateral relations;

59 See Press Release of 19 November 2015 (http://europa.eu/rapid/press-release_MEMO-15-6006_en.htm), point 7.

- the trade-off in tax treaties may have consequences for the territorial fiscal cohesion between tax reductions/latencies and the corresponding benefits (C-80/94, *Wielockx; C-436/00, X & Y v. Riksskatteverket; C-470/04 N. v. Inspecteur*);
- tax treaties may compensate for or undo unilateral restrictive measures, and the overall ('end result') tax position of the taxpayer in a cross-border situation is the economic reality to be compared with the strictly internal situation (C-58/01, *Océ-Van der Grinten*, C-385/00, *De Groot*, C-265/04, *Bouanich*, and C-379/05, *Amurta*);
- limitation of treaty benefits to only residents may well constitute a violation of the national treatment requirement, especially as regards branches of nonresidents (C-307/97, *Saint-Gobain*[60]).

The Court is in principle[61] not competent, however, to interpret bilateral tax treaties,[62] and it was not very successful at it. In *Wielockx* it made the wrong income characterization and introduced a non-existent concept of tax cohesion at interstate level created by a tax treaty. If that cohesion had really existed, then the taxpayer would have been in no need of EU law, as he could in that case have relied directly on the tax treaty. In C-436/00, *X & Y v. Riksskatteverket*, the Court considered a provision of the Swedish-Belgian tax treaty applicable which was not applicable. In *Océ-Van der Grinten* it derived from the UK-Netherlands tax treaty that a restrictive UK dividend withholding tax would be credited in the hands of the Netherlands shareholder, overlooking the fact that the shareholder was exempt for the dividend. The Court sometimes refers to the Commentaries to OECD Model treaties, but in C-513/03, *Van Hilten-Van der Heijden*, it forgot to check (i) whether the Model referred to represented settled international practice (*quod non*), (ii) whether the Model referred to conformed *verbatim* to the tax treaty to be applied (*quod non*), (iii) whether the Model even *existed* at the time of the conclusion of the tax treaty concerned (*quod non:* the Double Inheritance Tax Model and its commentary came only 31 years after the Treaty at issue), (iv) whether, if the Model already existed, the Commentaries relied on were changed after the conclusion of the tax treaty, and (v) which interpretational value, if any at all, the Commentaries relied on possessed under (a) the domestic law system in which the tax treaty had been implemented by way of a national law, and (b) the Vienna Treaty on the Law of Treaties.

In later cases such as C-265/04, *Bouanich* and C-513/04, *Kerckhaert-Morres*, the Court steered clear from tax treaty interpretation, referring issues regarding their possible effects on the tax position of the taxpayer back to the national Courts, thus showing more judicial restraint than in the cases C-336/96, *Gilly* and C-513/03, *Van Hilten-Van der Heijden*.

Case C-336/96, *Gilly*, was a landmark case, not only because the Court very extensively ventured into tax treaty interpretation, but particularly because it implied that the Member States remain free to (i) choose the connecting factors (source, residence, even

60 Case C-307/97, *Saint-Gobain ZN*, [1999] ECR I-6161, EU:C:1999:438.

61 See for an exception Case C-648/15, Austria v. Germany, EU:C:2017:664, H&I 2017/406 (with a critical comment by Jonathan Schwarz), where Austria asked the Court, pursuant to Article 273 TFEU, to rule on the dispute between Austria and Germany concerning the interpretation of Article 11(2) of the Austrian/German double tax treaty.

62 Cf. Lang, l.c., at 2.1.

nationality) for the division of their taxing jurisdiction, therefore to define, divide, share, and allocate their taxing jurisdictions ('with a view to eliminating double taxation') and (ii) to design their own double tax relief mechanisms. We discussed that case more extensively in section 8.3.3.

Case C-307/97, *Saint-Gobain*, made the very important addition that the *exercise* of the taxing powers 'so allocated' remains subject to CJEU scrutiny under the Treaty Freedoms, also if such exercise is based on a tax treaty and even if it is based on a tax treaty with a third State. In section 6.4.2, we have discussed the far-reaching implications of the distinction between assumption of taxing power and exercise of taxing power. The Court, in principle, assesses the comparability of the domestic and the cross-border situation on the basis of the question of whether the member State has asserted comparable taxing power (subject-to-tax approach). Case C-385/00, *De Groot*, further added that the home State must ensure that application of its method of double taxation relief does not lead to an individual taxpayer losing part of the benefit of his personal allowances. This view was extended to all factors determining the ability to pay of natural persons in Case C-182/06, *Lakebrink-Peters*, and Case C-527/06, *Renneberg*.[63]

Many cases, *e.g. Gilly, Saint-Gobain, Van Hilten-Van der Heijden* and C-470/04, *N. v. Inspecteur*, state that it is 'not unreasonable' for the Member States, in defining and dividing taxing jurisdiction, to 'find inspiration' in international practice, especially as embodied in the OECD Model Double Taxation Convention and its Official Commentary. These cases further suggest that such conforming to OECD practice provides a certain protection from interference in (the division of) taxing jurisdictions by the CJEU on the basis of the Treaty Freedoms, in the form of the benefit of the doubt.

8.3.6 Treaty Overrides

Case C-298/05, *Columbus Container*,[64] concerned national German CFC legislation providing for a switch-over from exemption to credit for foreign direct investment exposed to less than 30% taxation abroad, thus overriding the applicable tax treaty providing for exemption. The case shows that the Court does not consider tax treaty overrides incompatible with EU law, as long as the Member State involved does not tax, in the end, cross-border investment less favourable than comparable domestic investment. On the treaty override issue it considered:

> '46. Although the Member States have, within the framework of their powers referred to in paragraph 27 of this judgment, entered into numerous bilateral conventions designed to eliminate or to mitigate those negative effects, the fact none the less remains that the Court has no jurisdiction, under Article 234 EC, to rule on the possible infringement of the provisions of such conventions by a contracting Member State.
> 47. (...), the Court may not examine the relationship between a national measure, such as that in issue in the main proceedings, and the provisions of a double taxation convention,

63 See also Case C-174/18, *Jacob en Lennertz*, EU:C:2019:205, and Case C-241/20, *BJ*, EU:C:2021:605.
64 Case C-298/05, *Columbus Container Services*, [2007] ECR I-10451, EU:C:2007:754.

> such as the Bilateral Tax Convention, since that question does not fall within the scope of Community law (see, to that effect, Case C-141/99 *AMID* [2000] ECR I-11619, paragraph 18).'

Similarly, in Case C-128/08, *Damseaux*, the question was at issue whether Belgium had circumvented the French-Belgian tax treaty – which called for the crediting of French dividend withholding tax by Belgium in line with the Belgian domestic crediting of domestic withholding tax – by changing its domestic tax system such that its domestic *creditable* withholding tax was replaced by a *non*-creditable ('final') withholding tax, after which crediting of dividend withholding tax was abolished altogether. Again, the Court held that it was not its task adjudicate on the interaction between domestic law and tax treaty law if no issue of possible contravention of EU law was involved:

> '19. The applicant in the main proceedings considers also that the correct implementation by the Kingdom of Belgium of Article 19A of the France-Belgium Convention would have the effect of preventing the double taxation of French dividends received by a shareholder residing in Belgium. However, the Kingdom of Belgium does not implement Article 19A, in so far as the Belgian legislation no longer provides for the procedure for setting off the fixed percentage, which constitutes not only an infringement of the France-Belgium Convention, but also discrimination prohibited by Article 56 EC.
> 20. In proceedings under Article 234 EC, it is not for the Court to interpret Article 19A of the France-Belgium Convention and to establish the obligations which arise under it, as such an interpretation is within the jurisdiction of the national courts.
> 21. If, in the context of that interpretation, that national court holds that Article 19A of the France-Belgium Convention obliges the Kingdom of Belgium to prevent double taxation by means of the fixed percentage or a tax credit, it will also be for that court to draw, in compliance with its national law, the conclusions arising from the absence of implementation of that Article 19A.
> 22. It follows from the case-law that the Court does not have jurisdiction, under Article 234 EC, to rule on a possible infringement, by a contracting Member State, of provisions of bilateral conventions entered into by the Member States designed to eliminate or to mitigate the negative effects of the coexistence of national tax regimes (see, to that effect, Case C-298/05 *Columbus Container Services* [2007] ECR I-10451, paragraph 46). Nor may the Court examine the relationship between a national measure and the provisions of a double taxation convention, such as the bilateral tax convention at issue in the main proceedings, since that question does not fall within the scope of the interpretation of Community law (see, to that effect, Case C-141/99 *AMID* [2000] ECR I-11619, paragraph 18, and *Columbus Container Services*, paragraph 47).'

Thus, as Member States are free, from an EU law point of view, to enter into tax treaties and determine distribution rules and double tax relief rules, they are also free to change these rules, bilaterally or unilaterally, or to override them, or even to terminate the tax treaty, as long as they do not, in doing so, discriminate the cross-border position (non-resident or foreign-source income) as compared to the comparable domestic situation.

CHAPTER 9

Corporate Income Taxation

Peter Wattel

Update and elaboration by Hein Vermeulen[1]

9.1 Introduction

The mantra remains the same: cross-border situations must be taxed in the same manner as comparable domestic situations in so far as the Member State concerned has asserted taxing power over the cross-border situation in the same manner as over the comparable domestic situation. This implies both home state neutrality, i.e. the right not to be hindered to earn income abroad (national tax treatment of foreign-source income) and host state neutrality (equal treatment of nonresidents as regards the tax base for which they are subject to tax like residents). The rest of this chapter would thus consist of a list of more or less interesting applications of this insight to various factual and legal situations, if it were not for the fact that there is a special feature about legal persons which makes their cross-border tax position interesting: they can split themselves up in as many different legal persons in as many different jurisdictions as they want, which raises the question of which legal person to look at for the subject-to-tax comparison criterion (the parent or the subsidiary). Conversely, the Member States may put them back together again for tax purposes, either purely domestically (group taxation schemes or fiscal consolidation), which raises the questions of (i) whether it is discriminatory not to allow non-subject group companies into such group schemes, (ii) whether certain advantages arising from a domestic group taxation scheme should be limited to entities falling within that scheme; or internationally (CFC legislation), which raises the question of whether it is discriminatory to treat a CFC as a branch where a domestic subsidiary is not treated so, or conversely not to treat a non-domestic subsidiary as a branch, where in a domestic situation a domestic subsidiary would be treated as a branch of the domestic parent company.

Most of the unruly issues in company taxation have already been, or will be, discussed elsewhere: exit taxes upon corporate relocation (chapter 12), cross-border loss relief (chapter 10) and cross-border inter-company dividend taxation (chapter 11). In section 9.1 below we will elaborate on the equal treatment by the host state of branches and subsidiaries. It goes without saying that the host state should also treat equally domestic subsidiaries, as can be demonstrated by *Faurécia* (C-420/23). In this case, Portugal treated a Portuguese subsidiary with a Portuguese parent company different from a Portuguese subsidiary with a French parent company. The Court did not accept that stamp duty was

1 Director of PwC's EU Direct Tax Group.

levied in the cross-border situation where such levy was not applicable in a domestic situation. Portugal had to extend the same treatment to the Portuguese subsidiary with a French parent company.[2]

9.2 Host State: Equal Treatment of Branches and Subsidiaries[3]

Differential tax treatment of branches of nonresident companies as compared to resident (subsidiary) companies is in principle a prohibited discrimination if these branches are otherwise regularly subject to corporation tax on the same footing as resident companies (which they invariably are). Tax schemes and benefits available to resident companies must be applied on the same footing to branches of nonresident companies. Thus, branches of nonresident companies are entitled to application of the same fiscal profit determination rules as residents (*Talotta*,[4] concerning a minimum tax base only for nonresidents), to the same imputation credits as residents for dividends received (*Avoir Fiscal*[5]), to the same interest compensation on late repayments of overpaid taxes (*Commerzbank*[6]), to the same rates of taxation as residents (*Royal Bank of Scotland*[7]), even if for residents companies a split rate applies depending on distribution or retention of profits, which is hard to apply to a branch which never distributes dividends (*CLT-UFA*[8]), to the same domestic loss carry-over possibilities as residents (*Futura*[9]), to the same transfer of losses as residents (*Philips Electronics*[10]), to the same benefits which resident companies derive from tax treaties with third states, such as exemption of, or indirect credit for, third state dividends (*Saint-Gobain*[11]), and to the same exemption from an immovable property tax upon disclosing the identity of the shareholders (*Société Elisa*[12]).

---

2 Case C-420/23 (*Faurécia*), EU:C:2024:534.

3 See Wolfgang Schön, 'The Free Choice between the Right to Establish a Branch and to Set Up a Subsidiary: A Principle of European Business Law,' 2 *European Business Organization Law Review* 2001, pp. 339-364; Peter J. Wattel, 'Corporate Tax Jurisdiction in the EU with respect to Branches and Subsidiaries: Dislocation Distinguished from Discrimination and Disparity: A Plea for Territoriality,' *EC Tax Review* 2003/4, pp. 194–202; M. Lang, Has the Case Law of the ECJ on Final Losses Reached the End of the Line?, 54 Eur. Taxn. 12 (2014); CFE ECJ Task Force, Opinion Statement ECJ-TF 4/2015 on the Decision of the European Court of Justice in Groupe Steria SCA (Case C-386/14), on the French Intégration Fiscale, 56 Eur. Taxn. 5 (2016); CFE ECJ Task Force, Opinion Statement ECJ-TF 2/2015 on the Decision of the European Court of Justice in European Commission v. United Kingdom ("Final Losses") (Case C-172/13), Concerning the "Marks & Spencer Exception", 56 Eur. Taxn. 2/3 (2016); G.T.K. Meussen, Thin Capitalization Rules and Corresponding Tax Exemptions: All or Nothing, 57 Eur. Taxn. 11 (2017).

4 Case C-383/05 (*Talotta*), EU:C:2007:181.

5 Case 270/83 (*Commission v. France*), (*Avoir Fiscal*), EU:C:1986:37.

6 Case C-330/91 (*Commerzbank*), EU:C:1993:303.

7 Case C-311/97 (*Royal Bank of Scotland*), EU:C:1999:216.

8 Case C-253/03 (*CLT-UFA SA*), EU:C:2006:129.

9 Case C-250/95 (*Futura Participations SA and Singer v. Administration des contributions*), EU:C:1997:239.

10 Case C-18/11 (*Philips Electronics*), EU:C:2012:532.

11 Case C-307/97 (*Saint-Gobain*), EU:C:1999:438.

12 Case C-451/05 (*Société Elisa*), EU:C:2007:594.

Comparability of branches and subsidiaries for taxation purposes from a host state perspective was extensively at issue in *Saint-Gobain*,[13] raising the question of whether a branch in Germany of a French company was entitled to German tax reliefs (exemption or indirect tax credit) for dividends received on shares in companies established in other EU Member States (Italy and Austria) and in third states (Switzerland and the US). These tax reliefs were granted either under a bilateral tax treaty concluded between Germany and the other state concerned, or – where no treaty applied – unilaterally under German national law, but both legal instruments restricted entitlement to the tax relief to residents. Saint-Gobain was therefore denied the tax relief at issue. The Court held this to be incompatible with the freedom of establishment:

> '42. In those circumstances, the refusal to grant the tax concessions in question to the permanent establishments in Germany of non-resident companies makes it less attractive for those companies to have intercorporate holdings through German branches, since under German law and double-taxation treaties the tax concessions in question can only be granted to German subsidiaries which, as legal persons, are subject to unlimited tax liability, which thus restricts the freedom to choose the most appropriate legal form for the pursuit of activities in another Member State, which the second sentence of the first paragraph of Article 52 of the Treaty expressly confers on economic operators.
> 43. The difference in treatment to which branches of non-resident companies are subject in comparison with resident companies as well as the restriction of the freedom to choose the form of secondary establishment must be regarded as constituting a single composite infringement of Articles 52 and 58 of the Treaty.'

This consideration illustrates the compound character of the right of establishment: it comprises several distinct rights: the right to be treated as a resident in the host state (national treatment), the right not to be hindered in establishing abroad by the origin state, and the right to choose the appropriate legal form.

The Court further held that, on the basis of the relevant comparison criterion (tax liability in Germany for the dividends received from abroad), a German branch of a nonresident company and a resident company were in identical positions (as they also were in *Avoir Fiscal* for French dividends). The fact that a nonresident is subject to German tax only for its German-source (branch) profits (limited tax liability) and a German resident to worldwide (unlimited) tax liability, is irrelevant, as in both cases the dividend received is included in the German tax base. The Court observed that in the case at hand the distinction between limited and unlimited tax liability was even less relevant because of the tax relief at issue: residents, although theoretically subject to tax for their worldwide income, were in fact, due to the tax relief, not taxed for the foreign-source dividends, whereas nonresidents were denied such non-taxation.

The equal treatment of branches and subsidiaries by the host state was also at issue in *Cofidis* (C-340/22). This case does not concern corporate income tax but rather a Portuguese

13 Case C-307/97 (*Saint-Gobain*), EU:C:1999:438.

additional solidarity tax on the banking sector. The Court held that Portugal should treat the Portuguese branch of a French bank equal to a domestic subsidiary.[14]

9.3 Origin State: Are Parents of Foreign and Domestic Branches and Subsidiaries Comparable?

If the perspective is shifted from the host state to the *origin* state, things look different because a branch abroad remains part of a resident company and therefore usually remains subject to tax also in the origin state, whereas a subsidiary incorporated abroad is only subject to tax in its residence state. A foreign subsidiary is a nonresident and therefore it is not liable to tax in the origin state (the parent company state or home state). From the perspective of the parent company a subsidiary, whether domestic of foreign, is not taxed at the level of the parent company. As will be discussed in section 11.3 the Court makes a distinction between distributed and undistributed company profits. It treats what happens before distribution as one thing, and what happens after distribution as another.[15] So the Court holds that a parent with a domestic subsidiary and a parent with a non-domestic subsidiary are in a comparable situation. That is also true for a branch provided that the branch remains subject to tax also in the origin state. Again, from the perspective of the parent company or head office company the profits of the domestic branch and non-domestic branch are taxed in the hands of the parent company or head office company. Therefore, a parent with a domestic subsidiary and a parent with a non-domestic subsidiary are in a comparable situation.[16] However, if the origin state defines its taxing jurisdiction on the basis of territoriality, i.e. excluding branch results altogether from the tax base of its resident companies (base exemption; see section 10.3), a domestic subsidiary and a parent with a non-domestic subsidiary are in principle not comparable.[17] Then, from an origin state perspective, there is no reason to treat foreign branches and domestic branches alike, as they are not comparable on the basis of the relevant criterion, which is subject-to-tax (see chapter 6). In *Bevola*, the Court made clear that as regards measures laid down by a Member State in order to prevent or mitigate the double taxation of a resident company's profits, companies which have a permanent establishment in another Member State are not, in principle, in a comparable situation to that of companies possessing a resident permanent establishment.[18] However, the Court deems them comparable if it concerns final losses.[19]

In addition to the questions on comparability between domestic and foreign branches and comparability between domestic and foreign subsidiaries, there is also the question on comparability between a foreign subsidiary and a foreign branch. Are these two different

14 Case C-340/22 (Cofidis), ECLI:EU:C:2023.
15 See also Case C-347/04 (*Rewe Zentralfinanz*), EU:C:2007:194, point 48, where the Court holds that a loss on shares in a subsidiary is something different from the losses of that subsidiary itself.
16 Case C-388/14 (*Timac Agro*), EU:C:2015:829.
17 Case C-388/14 (*Timac Agro*), EU:C:2015:829.
18 Case C-650/16 (*A/S Bevola, Jens W. Trock ApS v Skateministeriet*), EU:C:2018:424, point 37.
19 Case C-650/16 (*A/S Bevola, Jens W. Trock ApS v Skateministeriet*), EU:C:2018:424, point 38. See section 10.12.

forms comparable from the state of origin perspective? The cases *Columbus Container*[20] and *X Holding*[21] made explicit that direct investment abroad (branch) and indirect investment abroad (subsidiary) are not comparable. A company investing abroad directly cannot claim the tax treatment in the home state which would have applied if it had invested indirectly abroad. *Columbus Container* concerned a German partnership with a permanent establishment in Belgium in the form of a low-taxed coordination center. Because of that low tax, Columbus was faced with a switch-over from exemption of its Belgian-source profits to the credit method for prevention of double taxation. It complained, *inter alia*, that it would not have suffered that switch-over if it had made the same investment in Belgium in the form of a subsidiary.[22] The Court replied:

> '53. In this respect, it must be recalled that the fiscal autonomy referred to in paragraphs 44 and 51 of this judgment also means that the Member States are at liberty to determine the conditions and the level of taxation for different types of establishments chosen by national companies or partnerships operating abroad, on condition that those companies or partnerships are not treated in a manner that is discriminatory in comparison with comparable national establishments.'

In *X Holding*, it added that:

> '38. Permanent establishments situated in another Member State and non-resident subsidiaries are not in a comparable situation with regard to the allocation of the power of taxation as provided for in an agreement such as the Double Taxation Agreement, and in particular in Articles 7(1) and 23(2) thereof. Whereas a subsidiary, as an independent legal person, is subject to unlimited tax liability in the State party to such an agreement in which that subsidiary is established, the same does not apply in the case of a permanent establishment situated in another Member State, which remains in principle and in part subject to the fiscal jurisdiction of the Member State of origin.
> 39. It is, admittedly, true that the Court has held in other cases that the second sentence of the first paragraph of Article 43 EC leaves traders free to choose the appropriate legal form in which to pursue their activities in another Member State and that freedom of choice must not be limited by discriminatory tax provisions (see, to that effect, *Commission v France*, paragraph 22; *Oy AA*, paragraph 40; and Case C-253/03 *CLT-UFA* [2006] ECR I-1831, paragraph 14).
> 40. However, the Member State of origin remains at liberty to determine the conditions and level of taxation for different types of establishments chosen by national companies operating abroad, on condition that those companies are not treated in a manner that is discriminatory in comparison with comparable national establishments (Case C-298/05 Columbus Container Services [2007] ECR I-10451, paragraphs 51 and 53). As permanent establishments situated in another Member State and non-resident subsidiaries are not, as has been stated in paragraph 38 of the present judgment, in a comparable situation with regard to the allocation of the power of taxation, the Member State of origin is not obliged to apply the same tax scheme to non-resident subsidiaries as that which it applies to foreign permanent establishments.'

20 Case C-298/05 (*Columbus Container Services*), EU:C:2007:754.
21 Case C-337/08 (*X Holding*), EU:C:2010:89.
22 We note that Case C-342/20 (*A SCPI*), EU:C:2022:276, concerns the mirror image of *Columbus Container Services*.

The tax treatment of foreign branches is not compared, therefore, to the tax treatment of foreign subsidiaries, but only to the tax treatment of a domestic branch.[23] This is confirmed in the case *A Oy*:[24]

> '29. As to whether the situations are comparable, it must be stated that, with reference to legislation of a Member State which seeks to tax capital gains generated within its tax jurisdiction, the situation of a company which, in the course of a transfer of assets, transfers a non-resident permanent establishment to a company that is also non-resident is, as regards the taxation of the capital gains of that permanent establishment which were generated within the tax jurisdiction of that Member State before the transfer, comparable to that of a resident company which, in the course of a transfer of assets, transfers a permanent establishment to another resident company (see, to that effect, judgment of 21 May 2015, Verder LabTec, C-657/13, EU:C:2015:331, paragraph 38 and the case-law cited). '

The Court takes the same approach when it comes to subsidiaries: it compares the tax positions of their parents, which are both residents and therefore subject to tax and therefore comparable, according to the Court. In principle, the Court requires equal treatment of parent companies holding EU subsidiaries and parent companies holding domestic subsidiaries.[25] Admittedly, this makes sense in that establishment abroad should not be hindered as compared to domestic secondary establishment, but it ignores that being (entirely) in another taxing jurisdiction is not comparable to being (entirely) in the parent state's taxing jurisdiction. As the Court held: relocation is not necessarily tax-neutral.[26] One may argue that secondary establishment through a local subsidiary is not quite a relocation (not an emigration), as something stays behind (the parent). That however, implies looking through the separate legal personality of the subsidiary, which is tantamount to fiscal consolidation of a non-subject subsidiary into the parent; to equating it with a branch, or rather: a CFC. Such assimilation of a non-subject foreign subsidiary to a branch, however, clearly contradicts point 38 of *X Holding*, quoted above: nonresident, non-subject subsidiaries are – for purposes of the justification based on the balanced allocation of taxing powers between the Member States – *not* comparable to foreign branches, as the latter remain subject to tax. Neither does it tally with the Court's rejection of CFC regimes in *Cadbury Schweppes*, to be discussed below, nor with its *not* requiring extension of a domestic consolidation scheme abroad in case C-337/08, *X Holding*, to be discussed below. As the *Bosal* Case shows (see section 9.4), equating secondary establishment in another taxing jurisdiction with secondary establishment in the parent state's taxing jurisdiction leads to destruction of the very possibility to levy tax. In *Marks & Spencer II* and *Oy AA* (see chapter 10), the Court acknowledged this, but it saw in that fact a mere justification for a discrimination, rather than the absence

23 For a different view, Sjoerd Douma, Secondary Establishment and the Right to Choose its Legal Form: An Analysis with Particular Reference to Case C-399/16 (Pending) on Foreign Exchange Losses (July 5, 2017). Available at SSRN: https://ssrn.com/abstract=2997404.

24 Case C-292/16 (*A Oy*), EU:C:2017:888, point 29.

25 Case C-386/14 (*Groupe Steria*), EU:C:2015:524, Case C-66/14 (*Finanzamt Linz*), EU:C:2015:242, Joined Cases C-39/13 to C-41/13 (*SCA, X AG MSA*), EU:C:2014:1758 and Case C-749/18 (*B and Others*), EU:C:2020:370.

26 Case C-403/03 (*Schempp*), EU:C:2005:446, and Case C-365/02 (*Lindfors*), EU:C:2004:449.

of comparability, *i.e.* the absence of a discrimination. Nevertheless, it is in line with the Court's assertion that distributed and undistributed company profits are not the same.

9.4 Group Taxation Schemes

Most Member States provide for their *resident* companies which form part of the same group of companies, a possibility to pool their results, in order to reduce tax exposure and to promote equal treatment as compared to undertakings which expand by setting up branches rather than subsidiaries. Such scheme may be limited to loss-trading (as in the *Marks & Spencer II* Case) or the inverse: profit contribution (the *Oy AA* Case), but it may also consist of total tax *consolidation*, i.e. taxation as if all group companies had collapsed into the parent, leaving only one single taxpayer (the *X Holding* Case) or *integration*, i.e. taxation of all group companies by adding the profits of the subsidiaries to the profit of the parent company (the *Société Papillon* and *Groupe Steria* Cases). Depending on the intensity of the scheme, it relieves the group of loss relief lock-up, withholding taxes on inter-company dividends, interest and royalties, intercompany arm's length pricing requirements, separate filing of tax returns, etc. Usually, non-subject group companies are not admitted to the scheme, although some Member States allow cross-border group loss relief or even a form of consolidation. A domestic branch of a nonresident group company, by contrast, may be included, as that branch is subject to tax like a resident subsidiary.

Case *X AB & Y AB v. Riksskatteverket*[27] concerned a Swedish group scheme allowing tax-free transfers of assets between group companies. Although both the transferring and the acquiring company had to be Swedish residents, the benefit was also available if a Swedish subsidiary involved in the operation was *in*directly wholly owned by the Swedish parent via one or more wholly owned intermediate group companies in *one* other Member State. This extension was based on the nondiscrimination clause in the applicable OECD Modelled tax treaties between Sweden and the Member States of the intermediate companies. The benefit was denied, however, if the Swedish subsidiary was wholly owned via intermediate group companies established in *more than one* other Member State, because Sweden feared that in that case tax treaty benefits could be accumulated. As the Swedish government had to admit during the hearing before the CJEU, this denial was a manifest breach of the right of establishment, and inexplicable in the light of the aim pursued.[28]

The *Metallgesellschaft and Hoechst* case[29] concerned a UK group income election scheme, which had the advantage of not having to prepay corporation tax upon intragroup profit distributions. It did not lower the ultimate tax debt, but it could be paid close to a year later. The scheme was not available if the parent company was nonresident. That residence requirement was held to be discriminatory.

27 Case C-200/98 (*X AB & Y AB*), EU:C:1999:566. Case C-484/19 (*Lexel AB*), EU:C:2021:34 also concerns the Swedish group scheme.

28 Case C-607/17 (*Memira Holding AB*), EU:C:2019:510, and Case C-608/17 (*Holmen AB*), EU:C:2019:511, also concern the Swedish group scheme. See Chapter 10.

29 Joined Cases C-397/98 and C-410/98 (*Metallgesellschaft and Hoechst*), EU:C:2001:134.

The *Marks & Spencer II*[30] case is also extensively discussed elsewhere (see chapters 10 and 6). It showed that domestic group loss relief schemes do not have to be extended for current losses to non-subject subsidiaries. An exception applies however in respect of definitive foreign subsidiary losses which will never be set off in the subsidiary state. The *Oy AA* Case concerned the inverse system (carry-over of profits rather than losses to other group companies). Such profit contribution schemes may be confined to group companies subject to tax in the same taxing jurisdiction. It will be discussed in chapter 10.

9.4.1 Group Taxation Schemes of Domestic Entities

A branch in the Court's case-law concerns the possibility to include domestic entities in a group taxation scheme where there is a foreign link. These cases are not about cross-border consolidation but a consolidation of domestic profits and domestic losses. Case C-418/07, *Société Papillon*,[31] concerned the French *intégration fiscale* (tax consolidation) scheme available for parent companies and their ≥ 95% subsidiaries. Société Papillon held more than 95% of the shares in several French sub-subsidiaries indirectly, through a Netherlands intermediate 100% subsidiary not subject to tax in France. The Papillon group filed a consolidated return (including the French sub-subsidiary but not the Netherlands intermediate company) in order to set off French group company losses against French group company profits, but consolidation was denied because the Netherlands intermediate company was not subject to tax in France. Had the intermediate company been resident in France, the tax consolidation would have been available. Thus, the ability to elect for the tax integration regime was dependent on whether the parent company held its indirect French subsidiaries through a direct subsidiary in France or in another Member State. We stress that in fact no cross-border consolidation was at issue, as both the parent company and the (sub) subsidiaries to be fiscally integrated with it were French residents. France argued, however, that there was a risk of double loss deduction because if the French sub-subsidiary were integrated with the French parent and made a loss, that loss would be recorded twice at parent level: once through its integration of the profits of the sub-subsidiary and once through depreciation of its holding in the intermediate Netherlands company as due to the French integration system the subsidiary remained a subsidiary. The Court agreed that such double dip should be avoided, and that exclusion of that risk was justified by the need to safeguard the coherence of the integration regime, but it considered the total exclusion of the possibility to integrate the French sub-subsidiary to be disproportional, as nothing prevented France to use the Directive on Administrative Cooperation (discussed in chapter 28) to request the Netherlands to provide the necessary information, nor to require the French companies to adduce convincing documentary evidence that there was no risk of the losses being used twice. Integration of the sub-subsidiary had to be allowed therefore, notwithstanding the presence of a non-subject intermediate company which would not be integrated. In the Joined Cases *SCA, X AG and MSA* it was confirmed that in a situation where two domestic sister

30 Case C-446/03 (*Marks & Spencer*), EU:C:2005:763.

31 Case C-418/07 (*Papillon*), EU:C:2008:659. See for comments, Pierre-Henri Durand and Yves Rutschmann, 'The Papillon Case: A First Step Toward a New Era in European Tax Treatment of Groups?' *EC Tax Review* 2009/3, p. 122-130.

companies held by the same parent company resident in another Member State access to the integration scheme must also be allowed.[32] In addition these cases reconfirmed the *Société Papillon* judgment. It addressed the compatibility of the Netherlands legislation on group taxation scheme ('fiscal unity') with the freedom of establishment and particularly, the fact that Netherlands group companies held by a foreign intermediary group company or a foreign parent company could not be included in a fiscal unity.

Two structures were examined by the Court namely: a potential fiscal unity between a Netherlands parent company and a Netherlands sub-subsidiary held by an EU intermediary and a potential fiscal unity between two Netherlands subsidiaries, which were either directly or indirectly held by an EU parent. The Court ruled that in both cases, the Netherlands legislation amounted to a restriction on the freedom of establishment since denying the possibility of forming a fiscal unity to all Netherlands companies with an EU connection, disadvantaged situations with a cross-border element in comparison to wholly domestic situations. The Court did not accept the argument brought forward by the Netherlands in the first structure that no restriction was imposed since the intermediate EU company or the EU parent company could not be included in the fiscal unity. What was significant according to the Court was the fact that Netherlands companies with an EU connection were fully excluded from the scope of the fiscal unity purely by virtue of that connection. Moreover, as pertains the second structure, the Court also rejected the argument that the fiscal unity regime allowed for consolidation of the results only at the level of the parent company, which was not possible in the event of a fiscal unity of two Netherlands subsidiaries with an EU parent. Having regard to the object of the fiscal unity, which is to treat all group companies as a single taxpayer, the Court concluded that such objective could still be achieved regardless of the residence of the parent company. The Court further rejected a justification based on the need to preserve the fiscal coherence of the Netherlands system noting that the Netherlands applies a holding exemption mechanism based on which the results of a holding in a subsidiary in another Member State can never be taken into account. Therefore, no direct link could be established between a tax advantage resulting from the fiscal unity and the offsetting of that advantage by a certain levy. Finally, the justification based on the need to prevent tax avoidance was also dismissed as the legislation on fiscal unity was not aimed at countering wholly-artificial arrangements.

In *B and Others* the Court confirmed its judgments in *Papillon* and *SCA, X AG and MSA.*[33] The case concerned the Luxembourg group taxation scheme. A French parent held various Luxembourg subsidiaries in different legal branches. Absent a common Luxembourg parent, the 'vertical' tax integration of the Luxembourg subsidiaries was not possible. The Court held that this requirement infringed the freedom of establishment which could not be justified. Luxembourg was required to allow both vertical integration (between parent and subsidiary companies) and horizontal integration (between sister companies) of the profits and losses of the Luxembourg entities.

32 Joined Cases C-39/13 to C-41/13 (*SCA, X AG MSA*), EU:C:2014:1758.
33 Case C-749/18 (*B and Others*), EU:C:2020:370.

9.4.2 *Group Taxation Schemes of Domestic Entities and Non-Domestic Entities: current losses*

Neither *Société Papillon* nor *SCA Holding* or *B and Others* were the real thing. Another branch in the Court's case-law concerns the possibility to include non-domestic entities in a group taxation scheme. These cases are about a consolidation of current domestic profits and current foreign losses. Genuine cross-border consolidation was at issue in the *X Holding* Case,[34] concerning the Netherlands group taxation scheme ('fiscal unity'), which comes down to single entity taxation as the subsidiary company collapses into the parent company. X Holding was a Netherlands company holding a Belgian subsidiary. It had applied for single entity taxation including its Belgian subsidiary. The effect of single entity taxation would have been that the subsidiary would for tax purposes have been treated as a foreign branch. This would have enabled the group, a.o., to effectuate cross-border loss relief and to ignore intercompany transactions. The Netherlands tax administration had rejected the application. The Court started as usual by judging the comparability of the domestic and the cross-border position; it considered parents of non-subject subsidiaries comparable to parents of resident subsidiaries:

> '21. The Netherlands, German and Portuguese Governments submit that those two situations are not objectively comparable, as resident subsidiaries and nonresident subsidiaries are not in comparable tax situations with regard to a tax scheme such as that at issue in the main proceedings. They argue in particular that a subsidiary which is established in another Member State is not subject to the fiscal jurisdiction of the State in which the parent company is established, with the result that it cannot be integrated into a tax entity subject to tax in the latter State.
> 22. In that context, it is settled case-law of the Court that the comparability of a Community situation with an internal situation must be examined having regard to the aim pursued by the national provisions at issue (see, to that effect, Case C-231/05 *Oy AA* [2007] ECR I-6373, paragraph 38).
> 23. In tax law, the taxpayers' residence may constitute a factor that might justify national rules involving different treatment for resident and non-resident taxpayers. However, that is not always the case. To accept that the Member State of establishment may in all cases apply different treatment solely because the registered office of a company is situated in another Member State would deprive Article 43 EC of its substance (see, to that effect, Case 270/83 *Commission v France* [1986] ECR 273, paragraph 18, and *Marks & Spencer*, paragraph 37).
> 24. However, the situation of a resident parent company wishing to form a single tax entity with a resident subsidiary and the situation of a resident parent company wishing to form a single tax entity with a non-resident subsidiary are objectively comparable with regard to the objective of a tax scheme such as that at issue in the main proceedings in so far as each seeks to benefit from the advantages of that scheme, which, in particular, allows the profits and losses of the companies constituting the single tax entity to be consolidated at the level of the parent company and the transactions carried out within the group to remain neutral for tax purposes.

34 Case C-337/08 (*X Holding*), EU:C:2010:89. See, for a very critical comment, 'Servaas van Thiel and Marius Vascega, 'X Holding: Why Ulysses Should Stop Listening to the Siren,' *European Taxation* August 2010, p. 334-349.

Point 23 seems to respond to another plea than the subject-to-tax comparability argument. The distinction made by the Netherlands legislation did not rely on incorporation or registration, but exclusively on liability to tax within the same taxing jurisdiction, the delineation of which is national sovereignty. Netherlands branches of nonresident group companies could be consolidated as well. The Court considered parents of non-subject subsidiaries comparable to parents of subjected subsidiaries, because they too 'seek to benefits from the advantages of the scheme.' We submit that the mere wish to benefit from a tax measure, does not make a non-addressee of that measure – for lack of liability to tax of its subsidiary – comparable to the addressees of that measure. As the aim pursued by the measure is decisive (point 22), one would expect the Court to refer to that aim, but it does not relate what it regards as the aim. We believe the aim to be to cancel the autonomous liability to *Netherlands* corporation tax of the subsidiary and to merge that liability into the *Netherlands* liability to tax of the parent, in order to create one single entity under the Netherlands corporation tax, which has one single consolidated object of taxation. The autonomous liability to tax of a person who is not even liable to Netherlands tax, cannot be cancelled or merged by the Netherlands. A non-subject subsidiary is autonomously liable to tax in *another* jurisdiction; the Netherlands is unable to cancel that liability to tax, which it never intended to cancel, for that matter. If it would have to include a non-subject subsidiary, its sovereign and symmetric delineation of taxing power on the basis of source and residence would be denied. A nonresident subsidiary, incorporated under foreign law, without any source of income in the Netherlands has no connecting factor whatsoever to the Netherlands taxing jurisdiction. So, in our view, as in the cases *Marks & Spencer*, *Lidl Belgium* and especially *Krankenheim*, there was no discrimination for lack of comparability (see sections 10.2 and 10.3). A justification was thus not needed. In the *Timac Agro* case the Court embarked on this route.[35] If the origin state defines its taxing jurisdiction on the basis of territoriality, i.e. excluding branch results altogether from the tax base of its resident companies (base exemption; see section 10.3), a domestic subsidiary and a parent with a non-domestic subsidiary are not comparable.[36] Then, from an origin state perspective, there is no reason to treat foreign branches and domestic branches alike, as they are not comparable on the basis of the relevant criterion, which is subject-to-tax. So in *Timac Agro* no justification was needed for the difference in treatment of the cross-border and the domestic situation simply because these were not comparable. This is true for current losses as was confirmed in *Bevola*.[37] In the latter case the Court made clear that as regards measures laid down by a Member State in order to prevent or mitigate the double taxation of a resident company's profits, companies which have a permanent establishment in another Member State are not, in principle, in a comparable situation to that of companies possessing a resident permanent establishment. Again as said, the Court holds differently when it concerns final losses as then the situations become comparable.[38]

---

35 Case C-388/14 (*Timac Agro*), EU:C:2015:829.

36 Case C-388/14 (*Timac Agro*), EU:C:2015:829.

37 Case C-650/16 (*A/S Bevola, Jens W. Trock ApS v Skateministeriet*), EU:C:2018:424, point 37.

38 Case C-650/16 (*A/S Bevola, Jens W. Trock ApS v Skateministeriet*), EU:C:2018:424, point 38. See section 10.12.

In the Court's reasoning in *X Holding*, by contrast, a justification *was* needed, which it found in the need to safeguard the allocation of taxing power: according to the Court, equating a subsidiary with a branch would create the risk of a free choice by the taxpayer of jurisdictional allocation of losses within the group. We doubt whether that is true, since three Member States apply a cross-border intercompany loss carry-over system[39] – it has also existed in the Netherlands – and since most Member States include losses of foreign branches in the tax base of the domestic principal undertaking.[40] But obviously: if one holds a measure to be discriminatory and does not want to condemn it, one needs a justification. In *Groupe Steria*, discussed below, the Court clarified that *X Holding* only pertains to current losses. A difference in treatment with respect to current losses may be justified by the need to safeguard the balanced allocation of taxing powers between the Member States. Any other advantages arising from a group taxation scheme must be assessed individually (see section 9.4.3):

> '28 As regards tax advantages other than the transfer of losses within the tax-integrated group, a separate assessment must therefore be made, as the Advocate General noted in point 34 of her Opinion, as to whether a Member State may reserve those advantages to companies belonging to a tax-integrated group and consequently exclude them in cross-border situations.'

The last step was the proportionality question. Remarkably, the Court considered the exclusion of non-subject entities to be proportionate because, unlike residents and branches, non-residents are ... not subject to tax. It would thus seem that what was still denied at the first step (subject-to-tax is not comparable to not subject-to-tax), became accurate and decisive in the third step (proportionality): at the end of the day, non-subject subsidiaries did not need to be included like subject-to-tax subsidiaries, because the former are ... not subject to tax. We observe that point 38 of the judgment (see the quotation in section 9.3), explicitly states – in the context of (not) comparing nonresident subsidiaries to foreign branches – that to remain subject-to-tax in the origin state is *not* comparable to not-remaining subject-to-tax in the origin state.[41] The very least the Court thus says, is that to be subject to tax in two states is not comparable to being subject to tax in only one state. We agree. Furthermore, the operative part of the judgement reads (emphasis added, *authors*):

> 'Articles 43 EC and 48 EC do not preclude legislation of a Member State which makes it possible for a parent company to form a single tax entity with its resident subsidiary, but which prevents the formation of such a single tax entity with a non-resident subsidiary, *in that the profits of that non-resident subsidiary are not subject to the fiscal legislation of that Member State.*'

39 See Bruno Farinha da Silva, *The impact of tax treaties and EU law on group taxation regimes*. Kluwer Law International 2016, p. 45.

40 See Reinout Kok, 'Domestic and Cross-Border Loss Relief in the European Union,' 38 *Intertax* 12 (2010), at at 668-669.

41 The Court's assumption that branches remain subject to tax in the State of origin is not necessarily correct, as the *Krankenheim Ruhesitz* case shows (see section 18.7): Germany excluded foreign branch results from its tax base.

From the perspective of the origin state (the parent company state or home state), we conclude on *current* losses, therefore that subject-to-tax and not subject-to-tax are not comparable when assessing the justification of the need to safeguard the balanced allocation of taxing powers between the Member States. Interestingly, *Sofina and Others* (C-575/17)[42] and *Credit Suisse Securities (Europe) Ltd* (C-601/23)[43] stand for the proposition that from the perspective of the host state (destination state) foreign *current* losses should be taken into account to determine the tax base over which the host state exercises its taxing rights. We refer to section 11.5.2 and 7.8.2.

9.4.3 *Group Taxation Schemes of Domestic Entities and Non-Domestic Entities: other advantages than current losses*

A final branch in the Court's case-law concerns the possibility to extend other advantages than cross-border loss consolidation. It is clear that Member States are not obliged to include not subject-to-tax entities in their group taxation schemes. It does not mean that any advantages arising from such schemes should be limited to entities falling within the group taxation scheme. This can be derived from *Groupe Steria*[44] and Joined Cases *Manitou and Bricolage*[45] regarding France, *Finanzamt Linz*[46] regarding Austria and Joined Cases *X BV* and *X NV*[47] regarding the Netherlands.

In Case *Groupe Steria*, the Court came to the conclusion that a French rule, which granted a full tax exemption on dividend income only to the extent that such income was received from a company belonging to the same tax-integrated group (i.e. established in France) but not to dividend income received from a company outside the group (i.e. outside of France), constituted an unjustifiable restriction to the freedom of establishment.[48] The French rule at stake was derived from the Parent-Subsidiary Directive, which in addition to providing for either an exemption or a credit on the amount of dividends received from a parent company by its subsidiary, also grants an option to the Member States that any charges relating to the holding and any losses resulting from the distribution of the profits of the subsidiary may not be deducted from the taxable profits of the parent company. Insofar as the management costs related to the holding are fixed at a flat rate, this rate may not exceed 5% of the profits distributed by the subsidiary (see Section 16.4). Groupe Steria was a French parent company with subsidiaries in both France and in the EU. It argued that in relation to its EU subsidiaries, essentially only 95% of the dividends received were exempt (due to France having opted for the 5% flat rate) whereas in a fully domestic situation, the parent company would be included within the same tax-integrated group rendering the dividend income received from a subsidiary within that same group fully exempt by means of a so-called add back provision. Groupe Steria claimed that the unequal treatment of dividends received by a parent company of a

42 Case C-575/17 (*Sofina and Others*), EU:C:2018:943.
43 Case C-601/23 (*Credit Suisse Securities (Europe) Ltd*), EU:C:2024:1048.
44 Case C-386/14 (*Groupe Steria*), EU:C:2015:524.
45 Joined Cases C-407/22 and C-408/22 (*Manitou and Bricolage*), EU:C:2023:392.
46 Case C-66/14 (*Finanzamt Linz*), EU:C:2015:242.
47 Joined Cases C-398/16 (*X BV*) and C-399/16 (*X NV*), EU:C:2018:110.
48 Case C-386/14 (*Groupe Steria*), EU:C:2015:524.

tax-integrated group, depending on whether the dividends originated from companies which were themselves members of that integrated group (i.e. established in France) or from subsidiaries established in other Member States constituted a restriction on its freedom of establishment. The Court ruled in favour of the taxpayer. In referring to its previous judgment in *Papillon*, *X Holding* and *SCA*, it held that the fact that only French residents could be members of a tax-integrated group meant that the advantage was only reserved to dividends of national origin, which amounted to a restriction as it could deter a company from investing in subsidiaries in other Member States. The Court rejected the argument brought forward by France, the Netherlands and the UK that the neutralization of the proportion of costs was indissociable from the tax integration scheme and clarified that not every difference in treatment between companies belonging to a tax-integrated group and companies not belonging to such a group was compatible with Article 49 TFEU. The Court advocated for the so-called "per element approach" as was cited above.

The Court argued that the objective of the tax integrated group, namely that all undertakings are treated as a single entity, can still be achieved even if that tax advantage (the full exemption of dividends) would be extended to companies not within the tax-integrated group. Furthermore, the Court also rejected the balanced allocation of taxing rights, the need to maintain the cohesion of the tax system and the fact that the 5% fixed rate was derived from an EU Directive as justification grounds. In Joined Cases *Manitou and Bricolage* the Court confirmed its ruling in *Groupe Steria.*[49] Further, the Court confirmed its "per element approach" and the need to carry out a separate assessment of particular advantages arising within a group regime in *Finanzamt Linz*[50] regarding the possibility of a parent company to amortise goodwill upon the acquisition of a domestic subsidiary and the non-possibility in case a foreign subsidiary[51] and Joined Cases *X BV* and *X NV* regarding interest deductibility, which could be taken into account within a Dutch fiscal unity but not in a cross-border situation.[52]

9.5 CFC Legislation[53]

Many Member States[54] already apply some sort of legislation targeting passive, low-taxed, controlled foreign companies (CFC legislation) in order to prevent artificial profit shifts, especially through interest deduction, from the tax jurisdiction of the home state of the group to low tax jurisdictions. Such legislation involves either (i) the disregard of the

49 Joined Cases C-407/22 and C-408/22 (*Manitou and Bricolage*), EU:C:2023:392.

50 Case C-66/14 (*Finanzamt Linz*), EU:C:2015:242.

51 In this respect, the case is the mirror image of the Spanish goodwill-cases on State aid (Joined Cases C-20/15 and C-21/15, *World Duty Free*, EU:C:2016:981), where the measure at issue involved the possibility of a parent company to amortise goodwill upon the acquisition of a foreign subsidiary and the non-possibility in case a foreign subsidiary. See Chapter 15.

52 Joined Cases C-398/16 (*X BV*) and C-399/16 (*X NV*), EU:C:2018:110.

53 See, a.o., Michael Lang e.a. (eds.), 'CFC Legislation, Tax Treaties and EC Law,' Kluwer Law International, 2004.

54 See Renata Fontana: 'The Uncertain Future of CFC Regimes in the Member States of the European Union,' Parts 1 and 2, *European Taxation*, June and July 2006; at that time: Cyprus, Denmark, Estonia, Finland, France, Germany, Hungary, Ireland, Italy, Lithuania, the Netherlands, Portugal, Spain, Sweden and the UK.

separate legal personality of the foreign subsidiary and the treating of it as if it were a branch, or (ii) a profit attribution mechanism, taxing the profits of the CFC currently in the hands of the domestic parent, or (iii) a deemed dividend paid by the subsidiary to the domestic parent.

EU law itself as well contains CFC legislation. Articles 8 and 9 of the Anti-Tax Avoidance Directive contain a provision of CFC rules in the form of a profit attribution mechanism (see Section 19.4.3). As the Anti-Tax Avoidance Directive had to be implemented by 31 December 2018, all Member States therefore now have CFC legislation applying to both subsidiaries and branches. See Chapter 19. Furthermore, the Income Inclusion Rule (IIR) laid down in the Pillar 2 Directive (EU) 2022/2523 may also be seen as a form of CFC legislation, as it operates to have a parent entity to tax low-taxed profits of a lower-tier group entity. See Chapter 22.

Case C-196/04, *Cadbury Schweppes*[55] concerned application of the UK CFC legislation to Irish low-taxed group finance subsidiaries. For UK CFC purposes, 'low tax' meant less than three quarters of the UK corporation tax level. Several escapes applied (sufficient dividend distributions; trading activities; publicly quoted; a *de minimis* exception and a 'motive test'), but none to the avail of Cadbury Schweppes' Irish subsidiaries, which were thus deemed to have distributed their profits to their UK parent. The question arising from a free movement perspective is more or less a double inverse of the question whether branches of nonresident companies must be given national treatment by the host state: does the freedom of establishment *preclude* the origin state (the parent company state) from taxing a nonresident subsidiary's profits as if it were a nonresident *branch* of a resident company? The doubtful aspect of CFC legislation, from an EU law point of view, is that it typically does not apply in domestic situations (the F stands for 'foreign'). The Court thus found a discrimination in contravention of the right of establishment because parents of domestic subsidiaries were not currently taxed for their subsidiaries' results (see point 45 quoted further below). The outcome of the case therefore depended on whether a good enough and proportionate justification was available for the different treatment (profit imputation) in the cross-border position. Obviously, the UK pleaded the need to prevent tax avoidance. The Court was not entirely convinced, however:

> '65. (...), in order for the legislation on CFCs to comply with Community law, the taxation provided for by that legislation must be excluded where, despite the existence of tax motives, the incorporation of a CFC reflects economic reality.
> 66. That incorporation must correspond with an actual establishment intended to carry on genuine economic activities in the host Member State, (...).
> 67. As suggested by the United Kingdom Government and the Commission at the hearing, that finding must be based on objective factors which are ascertainable by third parties with regard, in particular, to the extent to which the CFC physically exists in terms of premises, staff and equipment.
> 68. If checking those factors leads to the finding that the CFC is a fictitious establishment not carrying out any genuine economic activity in the territory of the host Member State, the creation of that CFC must be regarded as having the characteristics of a wholly artificial

55 Case C-196/04 (*Cadbury Schweppes*), EU:C:2006:544.

> arrangement. That could be so in particular in the case of a "letterbox" or "front" subsidiary (see Case C-341/04 Eurofood IFSC [2006] ECR I-0000, paragraphs 34 and 35).
> 69. On the other hand, (...), the fact that the activities which correspond to the profits of the CFC could just as well have been carried out by a company established in the territory of the Member State in which the resident company is established does not warrant the conclusion that there is a wholly artificial arrangement.'

From this, it may be inferred that genuine relocation of economic activity (however volatile, mobile, or passive) is no abuse of rights, but on the contrary a legitimate use of the internal market for the purposes for which it was intended. Thus, not only profits from captive financing, licensing, leasing, insurance and other easy-to-move-around group activities may be relocated to a convenient jurisdiction, but the proceeds of passive investment may also be shifted elsewhere, as long as the subsidiary, however thin, is equipped commensurately to its task, even if that is passive investment, and the day-to-day management decisions are left to a local employee or trust office, even where head office determines general (portfolio) investment policy. The same holds true for passive holding, for the exercise of which not much physical presence is required either. This might bring some states to conclude that if CFC legislation is to be meaningful, it will have to be applied domestically as well (CC legislation or compulsory fiscal consolidation above a certain holding threshold). At any rate, automatic exclusion of categories of foreign subsidiaries (low-tax, non-trading, non-quoted, non-distributing) without checking for individual artificiality seemed to be prohibited.[56]

That did not entirely knock out the UK CFC legislation, however, as the Court concluded that it was for the national court to judge whether possibly the 'motive test' (why was the CFC established in Ireland and why were the financial transactions undertaken?) could be interpreted in such a way as to conform to the requirements of EU law, meaning that the CFC rules were acceptable in so far as they would catch only 'wholly artificial arrangements.' At any rate, the Court is very stringent for the Member States. Even where a CFC is only (but 'genuinely') administering the passive (portfolio) investment of a group's cash surplus from Ireland (or Cyprus, or Luxembourg), it does not seem to be 'wholly artificial.' Indeed, a 'wholly artificial' establishment apparently means a 'letterbox' or 'front' subsidiary or a 'fictitious establishment'. Cadbury Schweppes' subsidiaries looked like more substance and presence than a letterbox.[57]

The Court rejected the UK argument that at the end of the day, a CFC was not worse off than a UK subsidiary, the latter also being taxed at the UK tax level:

> '45. That difference in treatment creates a tax disadvantage for the resident company to which the legislation on CFCs is applicable. Even taking into account, as suggested by the United Kingdom, Danish, German, French, Portuguese, Finnish, and Swedish Governments, the fact referred to by the national court that such a resident [parent; *authors*] company

56 This is confirmed by Case C-6/16 (*Eqiom*), EU:C:2017:641 and Joined Cases C-504/16 and C-613/16 (*Deister and Juhler Holding*), EU:C:2017:1009.

57 We also refer to Joined EFTA-Court Cases E-3/13 and E-20/13 (*Fred. Olsen and Others v the Norwegian State*) as well as Case C-135/17 (*X GmbH*), EU:C:2019:136 for guidance on the question whether an establishment is 'wholly artificial' or not.

> does not pay, on the profits of a CFC within the scope of application of that legislation, more tax than that which would have been payable on those profits if they had been made by a subsidiary established in the United Kingdom, the fact remains that under such legislation the resident company is taxed on profits of another legal person. That is not the case for a resident company with a subsidiary taxed in the United Kingdom or a subsidiary established outside that Member State which is not subject to a lower level of taxation.'

The same argument was raised by the same UK government in the same context (credit instead of exemption) in *Test Claimants in the FII Group Litigation*,[58] and in that case, the Court considered it valid and even decisive to base its holding on that indirect credit and exemption are 'equivalent.' That being said, we reiterate that the Court makes a distinction between distributed and undistributed company profits. In *FII Group Litigation*, the Court allowed the UK to apply indirect credit for foreign group dividends, although domestic group dividends were exempt, on the grounds that such credit would at the end of the day amount to treating foreign dividends 'in the same way' as exempt domestic dividends. We disagree, but that is not the point here. The point is that if indirect credit and exemption are considered 'equivalent' *after* distribution of the profit, one would expect current taxation of the CFC at the same time and at the same overall amount as a comparable resident company would have to pay also to be equivalent. A *domestic* subsidiary is also taxed on an accrual basis for its profits at year end, irrespective of distribution, just like the CFC. Therefore, compared to the domestic situation, apparently there was not even a timing or cash flow difference. Nevertheless, as observed in section 11.3, the Court seems to see as fundamentally distinct what happens before distribution and what happens after distribution.

In *Columbus Container Services*,[59] a measure comparable to CFC legislation was applied to a branch. Germany applied a treaty-override consisting of a switch-over from its normal exemption system for foreign branch profits to a (direct) credit in case the foreign branch was a passive investment vehicle in a low tax regime (in this case: a Belgian coordination centre). The foreign low tax burden was thus effectively replaced by the German tax level, which has the same effect as CFC legislation has in case of foreign subsidiaries instead. As was to be expected, after *FII Group Litigation*, in which *indirect* credit and exemption were considered equivalent, the Court saw no discrimination as long as foreign branches were not taxed at a higher level than domestic branches. The Court reiterated its finding in *FII Group Litigation*: the credit method (in this case the direct credit method) does not discriminate against foreign investment as compared to domestic investment. The Advocate-General Mengozzi did find a discrimination, however, as compared to participants in investment vehicles in jurisdictions with a tax level high enough not to engage the German switch-over (30% up), but still significantly lower than the German tax level. That distinction in his view amounted to a unilateral discrimination between two cross-border direct investments in different Member States. Although such a distinction between two other jurisdictions is permissible within the framework of tax treaty negotiations if it contributes to the overall balance of the respective tax treaties with these different other jurisdictions (see *D.* and *Class IV ACT* in section 11.4), there is no justification available,

58 Case C-446/04 (*Test Claimants in the FII Group Litigation*), EU:C:2006:774.
59 Case C-298/05 (*Columbus Container Services*), EU:C:2007:754.

according to the Advocate-General, for making such distinction unilaterally, as can be demonstrated by cases *Sopora*[60] and *Riskin and Timmermans*.[61] It must be admitted there is something disproportionate about the 'jump' in taxation level both in the German switch-over system and in the UK CFC legislation: if a certain tax level in the subsidiary state (UK: three quarters of the UK rate; Germany: 30%) is enough not to engage CFC legislation or not to engage the switchover, then why do the UK and Germany insist on imposing *more* than that level in case of subsidiaries in lower tax jurisdictions? Why do they not confine themselves to supplementing the tax level which they explicitly consider good enough for other cases (30% or three quarters, respectively)? On the other hand, if leveling up is not acceptable, then artificial arranging turns into a prize with every draw for the arranger: no downside risks.

The Court did not agree with the Advocate-General: it allowed different taxation of two direct foreign investments in two different other Member States, and therefore allowed the 'jump' in taxation between 30% (for 'good' foreign direct investment) and the higher German rate (for 'bad' foreign direct investment):

> '51. As stated in paragraph 44 of this judgment, in the current state of harmonisation of Community tax law, Member States enjoy a certain autonomy. It follows from that tax competence that the freedom of companies and partnerships to choose, for the purposes of establishment, between different Member States in no way means that the latter are obliged to adapt their own tax systems to the different systems of tax of the other Member States in order to guarantee that a company or partnership that has chosen to establish itself in a given Member State is taxed, at national level, in the same way as a company or partnership that has chosen to establish itself in another Member State.'

This means that Member States are at liberty to determine unilaterally which foreign regimes they (dis)like and to complement that regime's tax level so as to impose, on balance, its own level (capital export neutrality), also in the absence of any wholly artificial contraptions. It remains to be seen whether the Court still endorses this view since it held in *Sopora* that a unilateral distinction, thus made in domestic legislation, between two cross-border situations is in breach with the Treaty Freedoms.[62] In addition, if the Court is so relaxed about that – a treaty override is of no EU law concern – in the context of direct foreign investment, this may mean that it will also relax its very stringent criteria for CFC measures in respect of indirect foreign investment (possibly, therefore, the permissible scope for CFC rules is wider by now – legitimate protection of tax base integrity – than just combating 'wholly artificial' establishment), although there remains the apparently important difference to the Court between direct and indirect foreign investment: CFC legislation impacts on the foreign subsidiary's profits *before* their distribution and thus disrespects its separate legal personality. No such disrespect is present in the case of a switch-over similar to the one applied in *Columbus Container*. On the other hand: like a switch-over taxes foreign branch profits at the same level as domestic branch profits, CFC legislation seeks to tax foreign subsidiary profits at the same level as domestic subsidiary

60 Case C-512/13 (*Sopora*), EU:C:2015:108.
61 Case C-176/15 (*Riskin and Timmermans*), EU:C:2016:488.
62 Case C-512/13 (*Sopora*), EU:C:2015:108.

profits. Conceptually, it is in that respect not very relevant that in the case of a foreign branch no disrespect for separate legal personality is needed (as there *is* no separate legal personality), whereas in the case of a foreign subsidiary looking through its separate legal personality (or at least to deem it to have distributed its profit) is necessary, precisely, in order to impose the same taxation on foreign indirect investment as on domestic indirect investment.

As we derive from *Sopora* and *Riskin and Timmermans* mentioned above, we suppose the home state of the investor may not unilaterally distinguish between two branch states thus that 20% is considered enough in one source state but not enough in the other, as that difference in treatment cannot be explained by the need to retain an overall balance in a tax treaty.[63] There is case law that suggests that the court leaves more room for CFC legislation nowadays. From the *SGI* case (see section 17.6) it follows that restrictive base protective measure (arm's length corrections) may be exclusively applied to cross-border situations if they make no sense in domestic situations (like CFC rules). Also, in the *X GmbH & Co. KG* case the Court held that although the obligation to furnish fiscal documentation for cross-border group transactions and not for domestic group transactions constituted a restriction that was justified in order to ensure the preservation of the allocation of the power of taxation between Member States.[64]

X GmbH[65] concerns the compatibility of German CFC legislation with the freedom of capital as the German rule at issue already applied in case of a shareholding of 1 percent of a company established in a third country paying tax at a rate of less than 25%. X GmbH held 30% of the shares in a Swiss company. This Swiss company was low-taxed in view of the German measure. As a result, certain interest income earned by the Swiss company was (pro rata parte) taxed as current income of X GmbH. X GmbH argued that the German rule infringed the freedom of capital. The Court held – referring to Cadbury Schweppes – that the rule indeed in principle constitutes a restriction on the free movement of capital. The Court then continued to establish that the cross-border situation and internal situation are objectively comparable in light of the purpose of the legislation at issue, which was to treat the situation of resident companies which have invested capital in a company established in a third country with a low tax rate in the same way as that of resident companies which have invested their capital in another company resident in Germany, with a view to offsetting any tax advantages which the former might obtain from investing their capital in a third country. Therefore, the Court went on to determine whether the German measure could be justified by an overriding reason in the public interest. It investigated three justifications in concert, namely (i) safeguarding the balanced allocation between Member States and third countries of the power to impose taxes, (ii) preventing tax evasion and avoidance and (iii)) ensuring the effectiveness of fiscal supervision. Noting that these justifications are in this case closely linked, the Court held that the measure at issue in essence correspond to these overriding reasons in the public interest and went on to judging whether the measure was suitable

63 Case C-512/13 (*Sopora*), EU:C:2015:108.
64 Case C-431/21 (*X GmbH & Co. KG*), EU:C:2022:792. See also Case C-52/21 (*Pharmacie populaire*), EU:C:2022:127.
65 Case C-135/17 (*X GmbH*), EU:C:2019:136.

and proportionate. As the Court held that the measure is suitable, one question remained: whether that measure goes beyond what is necessary in order to attain its objective? Here the Court reiterates that the mere fact that a resident company holds shares in another company established in a third country cannot, as such, give rise to a general presumption of tax evasion and avoidance and, on that basis, justify a measure which compromises the free movement of capital. A justification is only available if the measure is designed specifically to prevent conduct that consists of creating wholly artificial arrangements. In the context of the freedom of establishment, as was the case in *Cadbury Schweppes*, this concept has the eye on establishing, based on objective factors which are ascertainable by third parties, that that company is a fictitious establishment in so far as it does not carry out any genuine economic activity in the territory of the host Member State, account being taken, in particular, of the extent to which that company physically exists in terms of premises, staff and equipment. In the context of the freedom of capital, which is the case in *X GmbH*, the Court notes that the concept of 'wholly artificial arrangement' is broader as it is also capable of covering any scheme which has as its primary objective or one of its primary objectives the artificial transfer of the profits made by way of activities carried out in the territory of a Member State to third countries with a low tax rate. The Court held however that the automatic nature of the German measure, in essence, was comparable to an irrebuttable presumption of tax evasion or avoidance, which could not be justified solely on the basis of the criteria established by that measure. The taxpayer should always be given the opportunity to provide evidence of any commercial justification that there may have been for the transaction at issue, without subjecting him to undue administrative constraints.

9.6 Thin Capitalization,[66] Profits Adjustments, and the Treaty Freedoms

The substantive rules (the arm's length principle) of the Arbitration Convention and Dispute Resolution Directive (see chapter 21), as well as the Anti-Tax Avoidance Directives (see chapter 19) have to a certain extent been unionized and made operational by the CJEU's case law on the right of establishment in direct tax cases.[67] That case law, especially the *SGI* case to be discussed below, also shows that negative integration (the prohibition of restrictions on the freedom of establishment) is not necessarily kept at bay by the existence of the Arbitration Convention in cases in which national arm's length or thin cap rules are selectively applied only to cross-border cases. But *SGI* further shows that it is not necessary for Member States to always apply their tax base protective measures indiscriminately to domestic cases as well as to cross-border cases, as such measures

66 See Linda Brosens: 'Thin Capitalization Rules and EU Law', *EC Tax Review* 2004/4, p. 188-213, and Otmar Thommes, Robert Stricof and Katja Nakhai: 'Thin Capitalization Rules and Nondiscrimination Principles', 32 *Intertax* 3 (2004), p. 126-137.

67 Although one may also argue that the CJEU case law departs from the OECD understanding of the arm's length test; see Adolfo Martín Jiménez, 'Transfer pricing and EU Law Following the ECJ Judgement in SGI: Some Thoughts on Controversial Issues', *Bulletin for International Taxation*, May 2010, at 276-277.

usually make sense only in cross-border configurations. The recent *Impresa Pizzarotti* and *X GmbH & Co. KG* confirm this.[68]

Case C-415/93, *Lankhorst-Hohorst*,[69] concerned German thin capitalization rules denying deduction of interest paid on a loan taken out by a German subsidiary with its Netherlands parent company, financing the subsidiary's German losses. This debt-financing exceeded the German statutory debt/equity ratio (3:1) for controlling shareholder loans, which applied in substance only to nonresident shareholder loans. Moreover, the subsidiary would not have been able to take out a similar loan with an independent moneylender on similar terms, as demonstrated by the fact that the parental loan replaced a bank loan carrying a much higher interest. The excess interest was treated as a covert dividend. The Court held the denial of deduction to be incompatible with the right of establishment (Art. 49-55 TFEU) because in domestic cases the interest would have been deductible. According to Germany and the intervening UK, denial of deduction was justified because the loan (terms) was (were) not at arm's length. The Court dismissed that defence:

> '39. (...), the German and United Kingdom Governments submit that [the German provisions; *authors*] are justified by the need to ensure the coherence of the applicable tax systems. More specifically, that provision is in accordance with the arm's length principle, which is internationally recognised and pursuant to which the conditions upon which loan capital is made available to a company must be compared with the conditions which the company could have obtained for such a loan from a third party. Article 9 of the Model Convention of the (...) (OECD) reflects that concern in providing for inclusion in profits for tax purposes where transactions are concluded between linked companies on conditions which do not correspond to market conditions.
> (...)
> 42. Although in *Bachmann* and *Commission v. Belgium*, since the taxpayer was one and the same person, there was a direct link between deductibility of pension and life assurance contributions and taxation of the sums received under those insurance contracts and preservation of that link was necessary to safeguard the coherence of the relevant tax system, there is no such direct link where, as in the present case, the subsidiary of a non-resident parent company suffers less favourable tax treatment and the German Government has not pointed to any tax advantage to offset such treatment (see, to that effect, *Wielockx*, paragraph 24; Case C-484/93; *Svensson and Gustavsson* [1995] ECR I-3955, paragraph 18; *Eurowings Luftverkehr*, paragraph 42; Verk*ooijen*, paragraphs 56 to 58, and *Baars*, paragraph 40).'

Interestingly, if the parent had not been resident abroad, deduction would apparently have been denied as well:

> '30. In reply to a question put by the Court, the German Government stated that the interest paid by a resident subsidiary to its, likewise resident, parent company on a loan of capital from the parent company is also treated for tax purposes as a covert dividend in

68 Case C-558/19, (*Impresa Pizzarotti & C SPA Italia Sucursala Cluj*), EU:C:2020:806 and Case C-431/21 (*X GmbH & Co. KG*), EU:C:2022:792. See also Case C-52/21 (*Pharmacie populaire*), EU:C:2022:127.

69 Case C-324/00, *Lankhorst-Hohorst GmbH*, EU:C:2002:749. See Axel Cordewener, 'Company Taxation, Cross-Border Financing and Thin Capitalization in the EU Internal Market: Some Comments on *Lankhorst-Hohorst GmbH*, *European Taxation*, April 2003, p. 102-113.

a case where the parent company has issued a *Patronatserklärung* [*i.e.* a guarantee for the creditors of the subsidiary; *authors*].'

That being so, one would expect the Court not to have objected, as the domestic position was treated in the same manner as the cross-border position (no deduction). But the Court decided otherwise:

'31. That fact is not, however, such as to affect the existence of a treatment which differs according to the seat of the parent company. The classification of an interest payment as the covert distribution of profits results, in the case of a resident company which has received a loan from a non-resident parent company, solely and directly from application of Paragraph 8a(1), Head 2, of the KStG, irrespective of whether or not a *Patronatserklärung* has been issued'.

The Court thus seemed to consider the denial of deduction in a similar domestic case to be merely coincidental, not taking away that the debt-equity ratio requirement and the reclassification of excess interest as covert dividend was only applied to cross-border positions. It should be observed, however, that in domestic positions, no debt-equity ratios are needed, as no base erosion is possible except for certain loss arbitration situations. In domestic cases, deduction and taxation fall within the same taxing jurisdiction. For taxation purposes it is unnecessary to ascertain arm's length conditions of group transactions purely within one taxing jurisdiction. That is why group companies subject to tax within the same jurisdiction in many Member States may elect to be treated as a single entity for corporation tax purposes or to pool their results, both of which eliminates results on intra-group transactions for tax purposes. A breach of territorial tax coherence will only occur if one of the associated parties to the transaction is not subject to tax in the same jurisdiction. Purely domestic cases by definition pose no problem of correct jurisdictional allocation of profits and losses. Therefore, transfer pricing rules, CFC rules, earnings stripping rules, and thin capitalization rules typically target only cross-border situations. *Lankhorst-Hohorst* forced Member States wishing to maintain anti-base erosion provisions to apply these also in domestic situations. In France, the *Conseil d'État* held, without referring questions to the CJEU, that the (old) French thin cap rules, distinguishing between domestic and cross-border situations, offended the right of establishment by restricting the creation of foreign subsidiaries through tax conditions which differ from those applied to domestic situations.[70] Thus, *Lankhorst-Hohorst* implied having either to give up CFC legislation, thin cap rules, earnings stripping rules, transfer pricing documentation requirements, etc., in cross-border situations, or to apply these ghastly rules also for domestic group relations. Many Member States did the latter because they could not afford to give them up in cross-border situations. Without them, tax advisors would have reduced the domestic corporation tax base of multinationals to naught. Denmark, Germany, Spain and the UK changed their thin cap rules and arm's length pricing rules so as to also encompass domestic group financing[71] and transfer pricing,

70 Conseil d'État, 30 December 2003 No. 249047, *SàrL Coréal Gestion*, ECLI:FR:CESEC:2003:249047.2 0031230. See Séverine Baranger: 'France: Supreme Court Rules on Thin Capitalization Provisions', *European Taxation*, June 2004, p. 287 ff. See also Cécile Brokelind, *EC Tax Review* 2004/4, p. 181-187.

71 See Linda Brosens: 'Thin Capitalization Rules and EU Law', *EC Tax Review* 2004/4, p. 202.

and the Netherlands introduced indiscriminate thin cap rules immediately after the incorrect *Bosal* judgment, which were subsequently repealed and replaced with other rules. On the same footing, the Anti-Tax Avoidance Directive contains an earnings stripping provision that applies equally to domestic and cross-border situations (see Chapter 19.) Sure enough, domestic businesses were not at all amused by these blessings of European integration falling down upon them, although exceptions from the cumbersome antibase erosion rules were often provided for small and medium-sized enterprises. The opposite happened as well, though: Spain, for instance, after *Lankhorst-Hohorst* at first excluded EU associated enterprises from its thin cap and CFC legislation in the same manner as domestic associated enterprises.[72]

Possibly, the *Lankhorst-Hohorst* judgment was based on mutual recognition reasoning, transplanted from the area of product requirements and free circulation of goods and services to the area of taxation of persons. The Court's reasoning may have been that the interest payment deducted in Germany did not escape taxation, as it would be taxed in the hands of the parent company in the Netherlands; Germany should not impose its own taxation on top of the Netherlands taxation, causing a double burden; Germany should 'recognize' the Netherlands taxation. Point 37 of the judgment seems to indicate such reasoning: the Court did not accept that deduction denial was justified to curb tax avoidance.

> '... since such a company [the foreign creditor company; *authors*] will in any event be subject to the tax legislation of the State in which it is established.'

As explained in section6.5.2., however, mutual recognition is not suitable for dealing with tax jurisdiction mismatches. Mutual recognition presupposes the existence of a 'natural' priority of the rules of one jurisdiction over the other. In taxation, however, there is no 'consumer' or 'target' state, and EU law provides no indications on whether source taxation or residence taxation takes priority, nor as to which of the states involved the results of an associated transaction should be allocated for tax purposes. Especially the interjurisdictional division of taxing power as regards income from capital investment is highly arbitrary (roughly: equity remuneration is for the investment state to tax; debt-finance remuneration is for the investor state to tax), making the correct characterization of the income of the utmost importance. In circumstances such as those of *Lankhorst-Hokorst*, one cannot tell – at least not on the basis of EU law – whether the German characterization of the cross-border payment (constructive dividend or repayment of capital; non-deductible) is better or worse than the Netherlands characterization (interest; taxable). The Court nevertheless did make such choices in cases such as *De Groot, Bosal, Marks & Spencer II*, and *N. v. Inspecteur* (see section 3.2.7.3.(v)), which it may regret.

In the UK, *Lankhorst-Hohorst* led to claims for restitution of tax and/or damages by taxpayers for alleged violation of the right of establishment by the UK's thin cap rules. These claims prompted preliminary questions which were answered by the CJEU in Case

72 See Adolfo Martín Jiménez, 'Transfer Pricing and EU Law Following the ECJ Judgement in SGI: Some Thoughts on Controversial Issues', *Bulletin for International Taxation*, May 2010, at 273.

C-524/04, *Test Claimants in the Thin Cap Group Litigation*[73]. As under the German thin cap rules, also under the UK thin cap rules a domestic group company's risk of being denied interest deduction – obviously – depended on the place of residence of its group creditor. The UK argued that there was no real restriction, because at the end of the day, the overall position of the group was neutral, as the UK's reclassification of the interest into a nondeductible profit distribution would be followed, pursuant to the applicable tax treaty (*cf.* Art. 9 of the OECD Model), by a corresponding adjustment in the creditor company state. The Court was not convinced. Indeed, the other state may not see why the source state's unilateral reclassification of income would be any better than its own classification.[74] We observe that it is unclear and controversial whether Article 9 of the OECD Model covers not only price (interest rate) adjustments, but also thin cap rules and reclassifications of debt into equity. Especially controversial is the question of whether Article 9 requires national thin cap rules to conform to arm's length standards (whether Article 9 merely endows adjustment *competence* upon the Contracting states or also imposes an *obligation* on them to refrain from mechanical thin cap rules which ignore the arm's length question). At any rate, tax treaties do not require one Contracting state to unquestioningly follow the other Contracting state's unilateral thin cap rules or reclassification of loans or interest income. We observe that the EFTA Court decision in the *Seabrokers* Case[75] demonstrates that it may be contrary to the right of establishment to mechanically attribute costs to a permanent establishment which are not causally connected to the business of that establishment.

A restriction of the freedom of establishment being established, the question was whether the UK thin cap legislation could be justified by the need to prevent tax base erosion in the UK. The Court reiterated that anti-avoidance measures, in order to be acceptable, must be targeted to catch only 'wholly artificial arrangements which do not reflect economic reality'. The Court was satisfied that the UK thin cap legislation was suitable for curbing abusive base erosion, and proceeded to examine whether it was proportionate to that end. The most important aspect of the *Thin Cap* case in our view is that the Court – different from *Lankhorst-Hohorst* – accepted the arm's length test as an objective and verifiable test of absence of artifice, the failing of which may give rise to a presumption that the loan arrangement is artificial, and stipulated two conditions to ensure proportionality of the tax administration's response:

i. the taxpayer must be given an opportunity, without being subject to undue administrative constraints, to demonstrate commercial justification for the arrangement. Indeed, even though the loan arrangement in *Lankhorst-Hohorst* did not pass the arm's length test, it served commercial purposes (debt restructure in order to keep the shop open) and there was no question of artificial base erosion; and
ii. even where the conclusion must be that the loan or the interest arrangement is artificial (lacking underlying commercial justification), the response of the tax administration may not go beyond what is necessary to re-characterize the transaction such that it

73 Case C-524/04, *(Test Claimants in the Thin Cap Group Litigation)*, EU:C:2007:161.

74 *Cf.* Case C-298/05 (*Columbus Container Services*), EU:C:2007:754.

75 EFTA-Court 7 May 2008, Case E-7/07 (*Seabrokers*), EFTA Court Report 2008, p. 172.

corresponds to what would have been agreed between unrelated parties; only the *excess* interest may be excluded from deduction.

This is a much more rational and practicable result than *Lankhorst-Hohorst*, and it means that the arm's length test has become part of the Court's assessment, under its rule of reason (see sections 3.2.1 and 3.2.2), of whether restrictive tax measures can be justified by mandatory requirements of public interest, such as the need to prevent tax avoidance and the need to preserve the allocation of taxing power between the Member States. *Thin Cap* was firstly reiterated in *Lammers & Van Cleeff*,[76] in which the Court condemned a Belgian measure mechanically excluding from deduction the payment of interest by a Belgian subsidiary to its nonresident parent company/director where in otherwise identical circumstances interest payments to a domestic parent/director would have been deductible, as a mechanical 1/1 thin cap ratio was clearly disproportional to combat possible abuse. Secondly, *Thin Cap* was confirmed in the recent *Lexel AB*.[77] There the Court condemned a Swedish measure that disallowed the deduction of interest paid by a Swedish group company to another EU group company, whereas deduction within Sweden was always allowed. The Court held that the Swedish measure was not limited to countering purely artificial arrangements only. As a result, a wider range of arrangements was caught by the Swedish measure. The Court reiterated that arm's length interest should be deductible in Sweden; only the *excess* interest may be excluded from deduction.[78] The Court was called to explain its *Lexel AB* judgment in the *X BV* case (C-585/22). It confirmed that in cases where the loan and the related transaction make economic sense in a way that such transactions could have been concluded between the companies party to the contract in the absence of a special relationship, the principle of proportionality requires that that arm's length interest should be deductible.[79] *Viva Telecom Bulgaria* (C-257/20) further stands for the proposition that a tax provision that automatically excludes the deduction of interest on a non-arm's length intercompany loan without the possibility to demonstrate commercial justification for that loan constitutes a restriction, which requires justification.[80]

This means that Member States' transfer pricing rules, including their documentation and disclosure requirements, are under suitability and proportionality supervision of the CJEU, unless they apply them in exactly the same manner in both purely internal and cross-border situations. It means that an EU group of companies facing double taxation as a result of a discriminatory transfer price adjustment in one Member State, not followed by a corresponding adjustment in the other Member State, may rely on the TFEU Freedoms to have the adjustment tested by a national court for its necessity and proportionality in combating base erosion. It may further rely on the proportionality requirement in order to challenge onerous documentation requirements and onerous reversal of the burden of proof where its tax administration is not satisfied by the evidence provided

76 Case C-105/07 (*Lammers & Van Cleeff*), EU:C:2008:24.

77 Case C-484/19 (*Lexel AB*), EU:C:2021:34, points 50 and 51.

78 The EFTA Court followed this reasoning in its judgment of 1 June 2022, Case E-(E-3/21), *PRA Holding SA*. In that case the interest limitation rule at issue is an earnings stripping rule.

79 Case C-585/22 (*X BV*), EU:C:2024:822, point 75.

80 Case C-257/20 (*Viva Telecom Bulgaria*), EU:C:2022:125. This case is also discussed in chapter 11.

if less cumbersome rules of documentation and evidence apply in comparable internal situations. It may even argue that mechanical thin cap rules, ignoring the arm's length standard, are disproportional if they do not provide for the possibility, without undue administrative constraints, to rebut the presumption of base erosion by demonstrating the business purpose of the excessive debt/equity ratio.

Unlike some hoped, in *Thin Cap* the Court did not require the Member State wishing to make a transfer price adjustment causing double taxation, either to convince the other state that it should make a corresponding adjustment or, where that other state does not oblige, to refrain from making the adjustment altogether. The Commission and the Advocate-General in *Thin Cap* had suggested such a ruling, but the Court did not read in the TFEU Freedoms an obligation for the adjusting state to ensure that the other state conforms to the adjusting state's views, failure of which would rob the adjusting state of its competence to adjust. We agree, as Member States must be granted the possibility to (proportionally) protect their tax base, as the definition of their tax base (the assertion of taxing power) is national sovereignty, not dependent on the mode of sovereign assertion of tax jurisdiction by another Member State. As the Court held in, a.o., *Columbus Container Services*[81], *A SCPI*[82] and *Margarete Block*:[83]

> '31. It follows (...) that, in the current stage of (...) Community law, the Member States enjoy a certain autonomy (...) provided they comply with Community law, and are not obliged therefore to adapt their own tax systems to the different systems of tax of the other Member States in order, *inter alia*, to eliminate the double taxation arising from the exercise in parallel (...) of their fiscal sovereignty (...).'

As observed, neither the TFEU nor an OECD-modelled Double Tax Convention provide for a priority rule by which to determine which state's debt/equity and interest/dividend characterizations are better and which state should oblige.

As also observed, it does not seem to enhance the internal market to force the Member States to apply their anti-base erosion measures also in purely internal cases, where these measures serve no meaningful purpose whatsoever. The Court's Advocate-General Geelhoed commented on the undesirable effects of *Lankhorst-Hohorst* in that respect in his opinion in the *Thin Cap* case:[84]

> '68. Nor am I of the view that, in order to conform with Article 43 EC [now 49 TFEU; *authors*], Member States should necessarily be obliged to extend thin cap legislation to purely domestic situations where no possible risk of abuse exists. I find it extremely regrettable that the lack of clarity as to the scope of the Article 43 EC justification on abuse grounds has led to a situation where Member States, unclear of the extent to which they may enact *prima facie* 'discriminatory' anti-abuse laws, have felt obliged to 'play safe' by extending the scope of their rules to purely domestic situations where no possible risk of abuse exists [reference to *Lankhorst-Hohorst*; *authors*]. Such an extension of legislation

81 Case C-298/05 (*Columbus Container Services*), EU:C:2007:754.
82 Case C-342/20 (A SCPI), EU:C:2022:276.
83 Case C-67/08 (*Block*), EU:C:2009:92.
84 Case C-524/04 (*Test Claimants in the Thin Cap Group Litigation*), EU:C:2007:161.

to situations falling wholly out with its rationale, for purely formalistic ends and causing considerable extra administrative burden for domestic companies and tax authorities, is quite pointless and indeed counter-productive for economic efficiency. As such, it is anathema to the internal market.'

This opinion resounded in the *SGI* case,[85] concerning a Belgian company which had (i) granted an interest-free loan to its French 65%-subsidiary and (ii) paid € 8000 per month as management fee to its Luxembourg 34%-parent for management services which were not in fact performed by that Luxembourg parent. The Belgian tax administration taxed SGI for a notional interest on the loan and denied deduction of the management fee, as neither transaction was at arm's length. The Court considered explicitly that the Belgian arm's length legislation did not apply in comparable purely domestic cases. It therefore found a *prima vista* discrimination in contravention of the right of Establishment. The question was whether this distinction between domestic and cross-border cases, which seemed fatal in *Lankhorst-Hohorst*, could be justified, and whether the Belgian measure was proportional in serving that justification. To the relief of both the Member States and domestic industry, the Court accepted that applying arm's length profit adjustment rules only in cross-border cases could be justified by the need to combat tax avoidance and the need to preserve the balanced allocation of the power to impose taxes, as accepting SGI's profit shifts would allow companies to organize income transfers to the lowest possible rate jurisdiction, and thus jeopardize a Member States' right to exercise its tax jurisdiction in relation to activities carried out in its territory. *Impresa Pizzarotti* and *X GmbH & Co. KG* confirm this.[86]

This judgment implies that the Court does not force the Member States (any more) to apply, also in purely domestic positions, necessary tax base protective measures which make no sense in purely domestic positions. It would seem, therefore, that the Member States may repeal their extension of thin cap, earnings stripping and transfer pricing rules to domestic cases. Also, the case suggests that the Court would be inclined to relax its very tight limits on the acceptability of CFC rules (only if aimed at 'wholly artificial contraptions'), which are obviously not applied at home, although *Eqiom, Deister and Juhler Holding* and *Lexel AB*[87] seem to suggest otherwise.[88] Although anti-base erosion measures only affecting cross-border positions may thus be justified, in order for them to be proportional, the Court reiterated its finding in *Thin Cap* that (i) the national legislation should proceed on the basis of objective and verifiable facts, (ii) the taxpayer should have the opportunity to demonstrate, without undue administrative constraints,

---

85 Case C-311/08 (*Société de gestion industrielle*), EU:C:2010:26. See for comments: Philip Baker, 'Transfer Pricing and Community Law: The SGI Case,' Editorial, *Intertax* 2010/4, p. 194-196; Adolfo Martín Jiménez, 'Transfer pricing and EU Law Following the ECJ Judgement in SGI: Some Thoughts on Controversial Issues,' *Bulletin for International Taxation*, May 2010, p. 271-282; and Gerard Meussen, 'The SGI Case: ECJ Approves Belgian System of Selective Profit Corrections in Relation to Foreign Group Companies,' *European Taxation* June 2010, p. 245-249.

86 Case C-558/19, (*Impresa Pizzarotti & C SPA Italia Sucursala Cluj*), EU:C:2020:806 and Case C-431/21 (*X GmbH & Co. KG*), EU:C:2022:792. See also Case C-52/21 (*Pharmacie populaire*), EU:C:2022:127.

87 Case C-484/19 (*Lexel AB*), EU:C:2021:34.

88 C-6/16 (*Eqiom*), EU:C:2017:641 and Joined Cases C-504/16 and C-613/16 (*Deister and Juhler Holding*), EU:C:2017:1009.

valid commercial reasons for the derogation from arm's length consideration, and (iii) if the taxpayer would not succeed in so demonstrating, the corrective assessment should be confined to restoring arm's length conditions, and should not go beyond that (*e.g.* interest deduction should not be denied altogether on a loan larger than arm's length would permit if a smaller loan could have been obtained with an independent finance company). In *Lexel AB* and *X BV* the Court confirmed this.[89]

The *SGI* case is important for three more reasons. The first one is that Court added a reasonable division of the burden of proof to the proportionality test of arm's length legislation, which is further discussed in Chapter 7. Second, the existence of the Arbitration Convention and Dispute Resolution Directive (see Chapter 21), which might eventually remedy double taxation caused by arm's length profit adjustments, is no justification for causing double taxation which would not occur in purely domestic situations. Belgium argued, as the UK did in *Thin Cap*, that overall SGI was not treated less favourably than in comparable domestic circumstances, as the other states involved were required to make corresponding adjustments. As compared to the argument in *Thin Cap*, Belgium added that if the other states would not make such adjustment, SGI could rely on the Arbitration Convention to have the resulting double taxation eliminated. As in *Thin Cap*, the Court was not convinced; to the argument concerning the possibility of arbitration it replied as follows:

> '54. As regards the possibility of applying the Arbitration Convention, it should be pointed out, as observed by the Advocate General at point 48 of her Opinion, that where the tax authorities in question endeavour to resolve a matter by mutual agreement, as provided for by Article 6 in Section 3 of the Convention, an additional administrative and financial burden is imposed on the company which has submitted its case to such a procedure. Moreover, a procedure aimed at resolution by mutual agreement, followed, if necessary, by an arbitration procedure, may extend over several years. During that period, the company in question must bear the burden of double taxation. Furthermore, it is apparent, in particular in the light of the matters set out at paragraph 29 above, that the legislation at issue in the main proceedings is applicable in certain situations falling outside the scope of the Convention.'

The Court thus does not seem awfully impressed by the measure in which the Arbitration Convention meets its goals. In any case, the possibility of a time-consuming mutual agreement procedure, possibly followed by arbitration, with uncertain result that may deviate from equal treatment as compared to domestic cases, cannot justify discrimination against cross-border grouped companies. It remains to be seen whether the Court is impressed by Dispute Resolution Directive (discussed in chapter 21).

Third, *SGI* says something on the division of the burden of proof required for arm's length rules to be proportionate:

> '73. According to the Belgian Government, the burden of proof as to the existence of an 'unusual' or 'gratuitous' advantage within the meaning of the legislation at issue in the main

89 Case C-484/19 (*Lexel AB*), EU:C:2021:34, points 50 and 51 and Case C-585/22 (*X BV*), EU:C:2024:822, point 86.

> proceeding rests with the national tax authorities. It states that when those authorities apply that legislation, the taxpayer is given an opportunity to provide evidence of any commercial justification that there may have been for the transaction in question. The taxpayer has a month, a period which may be extended, within which to establish that no unusual or gratuitous advantage is involved, having regard to the circumstances in which the transaction was effected. If, however, those authorities persist in their intention of issuing a revised assessment and do not accept the taxpayer's arguments, the latter can challenge the assessment to tax before the national courts.
> (...)
> 75. In those circumstances, subject to verification to be carried out by the referring court (...), it must be concluded that, in the light of the foregoing, national legislation such as that at issue in the main proceedings is proportionate to the set of objectives pursued by it.'

The Court accepts the Belgian legislation because the initial burden of proof (of the unusualness and the gratuitousness of the advantages conferred on associated enterprises) is on the tax authorities. Apparently, it would be disproportionate to require the taxpayer to prove the usualness of all transactions the tax administration wishes to challenge. We submit that given *Eqiom* and *Deister and Juhler Holding* this does imply that in all transfer pricing cases in which the restrictive legislation does not apply to domestic cases, the initial burden of proof is always on the tax administration.[90] If the tax administration argues there is an artificial profit shift or another abuse, it initially falls on the tax administration to prove this position. If in an intercompany pricing case no CUP and no comparables are available, it may well fall on the taxpayer to come up with the information and documentation as to how the transfer price was determined.[91] The Advocate-General Cruz Villalón, in the Case C-318/10, *SIAT SA v État belge*, opined that it could be acceptable to shift the burden of proof of the reasonableness of outbound payments into a lower tax jurisdiction to the taxpayer in specific circumstances, such as the intra-group transactions at issue in the SGI case. *SIAT* concerned Belgian rules providing that professional expenses paid to an (unrelated) service provider in a low or no tax jurisdiction are not deductible unless the taxpayer demonstrates that the payments have real economic foundation and do not surpass what is normal. The Court found the rule to restrict the freedom to provide services, which could be justified. The Court however referred to *SGI* when it stated that the corrective tax measure must, in order not to be considered disproportionate, be confined to the non-arm's length part of the professional expenses.[92]

Lastly, we observe that Article 4 of the Anti-Tax Avoidance Directive contains an earnings stripping provision to curb excessive interest deduction in a generic manners (see Chapter 19).

Case C-282/12 *Itelcar*[93] concerned the Portuguese thin capitalization rules, which denied deductibility of excessive interest, which was paid to a company in a non-EU Member

90 C-6/16 (*Eqiom*), EU:C:2017:641 and Joined Cases C-504/16 and C-613/16 (*Deister and Juhler Holding*), EU:C:2017:1009.
91 See Meussen, l.c., p. 247-248.
92 Case C-318/10 (*SIAT*), EU:C:2012:415.
93 Case C-282/12 (*Itelcar*), EU:C:2013:629.

State, with which the borrowing company had special relations. However, deductibility of the excess interest was allowed if the interest was paid to a resident or an EU lending company. The question was whether this treatment could be regarded as contrary to the free movement of capital. The Court ruled that this was indeed the case since the rules had the potential to deter a Portuguese resident company from entering into credit arrangements in a manner considered as excessive with a non-EU resident company, with which it has special relations. When it came to the justifications, the Court accepted the Portuguese Government's argument of the necessity of the rule to prevent tax evasion and avoidance. However, the rule was found to be disproportionate due to the fact that the term "special relations" involved situations where the lending company of a non-EU member country did not *per se* have a shareholding in the resident borrowing company. Where no such shareholding was present, the consequence of the method of calculating the excess, under the Portuguese thin capitalization rules, was that any credit arrangement between those two companies would be considered as excessive. There was therefore a presumption that any credit scheme between a Portuguese company and a company from a non-EU member country, which are considered to have "special relations" not based on shareholding, forms part of an arrangement designed to avoid tax. According to the Court, such presumption went beyond what was necessary to achieve the objective of combatting tax avoidance.

Thin capitalization rules were also at stake in Case C-593/14 *Masco Denmark and Damixa*.[94] The case concerned multiple loans granted by a Danish company to its German subsidiary, which was in a loss making position. The interest payable on the loan was considered to be non-deductible under the German rules limiting deduction in cases of thin capitalization. In Denmark, the recipient of the interest was nonetheless taxed on the interest received when the interest originated in another EU Member State regardless of the fact that the interest had not been deducted in Germany. However, if the interest had originated from a Danish subsidiary, it would have been tax exempt at the level of the Danish parent in so far as that subsidiary could not deduct the interest due to the application of thin capitalization rules. The question at hand was whether the Danish legislation was contrary to the freedom of establishment. The Court highlighted that the interest paid was liable to be subject to economic double taxation, which is what the Danish legislation seeks to avoid. This amounted to a restriction as it was liable to render less attractive the exercise by a Danish parent company of its freedom of establishment by deterring it from setting up subsidiaries in other Member States as opposed to setting up Danish subsidiaries. Although the Court accepted the justification set forth by Denmark on the need to ensure the balanced allocation of taxing rights, the Danish rule was considered to be disproportionate. The Court recognized that:

> '40. It is true that freedom of establishment cannot be understood as meaning that a Member State is required to draw up its tax rules on the basis of those in another Member State in order to ensure, in all circumstances, taxation which removes any disparities arising from national tax rules, given that the decisions taken by a company as to the establishment of

94 Case C-593/14 (*Masco Denmark*), EU:C:2016:984.

> commercial structures abroad may be to the company's advantage or not, depending on the circumstances (...)'

However, it then went on to reiterate that its established case law on economic double taxation:

> '42. (...) where a Member State has a system for preventing or mitigating a series of charges to tax or economic double taxation for dividends paid to residents by resident companies, it must treat dividends paid to residents by non-resident companies in the same way (...)'

Finally, the Court also rejected the justification based on the need to prevent tax avoidance by reiterating that in order for such a justification to succeed, the measure at hand needs to be limited to wholly artificial arrangements, which was not the case with the Danish rule. The result is that the Danish parent also has to exempt interest income paid by it non-domestic subsidiary in so far that interest was nondeductible in Germany and would also not be deductible under Finnish thin capitalization rules.

It seems therefore that the concept of a 'wholly artificial arrangement' as part of the justification analysis takes different forms. In the context of freedom of establishment, it has the eye on letter box companies when the legislation of the Member State at issue seeks to tax profits that are generated on its territory (cfc-legislation; *Cadbury Schweppes*). A broader concept applies in the context of the freedom of capital (cfc-legislation; *X GmbH*). In the field of legislation that seeks to target erosion of the Member State at issue (intra-group payments; *Thin cap, SIAT, Lexel AB and X BV*), the concept of a 'wholly artificial arrangement' takes the forms of addressing non arm's length transactions in cases where such transactions make economic sense meaning that such transactions could have been concluded between the companies party to the contract in the absence of a special relationship, the principle of proportionality requires that that arm's length interest should be deductible.[95] However, where the loan is, in itself, devoid of economic justification and, but for the relationship between the companies and the tax advantage sought, would never have been contracted, it is consistent with the principle of proportionality to refuse the deduction of the interest wholly, since such a wholly artificial arrangement must be ignored by the tax authorities when calculating the corporate tax due.[96]

95 Case C-585/22 (*X BV*), EU:C:2024:822.
96 Case C-585/22 (*X BV*), EU:C:2024:822, point 88.

CHAPTER 10

Cross-Border Loss Relief

Georg Kofler

10.1 Introduction and Overview

10.1.1 Background and Issues

Generally, profits and losses of a taxpayer within a single tax jurisdiction are automatically aggregated to align taxation with a taxpayer's ability to pay. This is true, for example, for profits and losses made by different domestic branches of an undertaking or where a taxpayer derives positive and negative income from different sources within one taxing jurisdiction (e.g., positive employment income and negative rental income). When losses exceed profits in a given year, their value is not refunded by the tax administration, but rather, under certain conditions, the losses can typically be offset against profits in future years (carry-forward), sometimes even in prior years (carry-back).

Losses are also a focus point when it comes to corporate groups, where some group members are profitable while others are loss-making. Economically, a loss of a subsidiary may be reflected (at least) on two levels: First, each subsidiary is a separate taxpayer that can typically carry-back or carry-forward its own losses. Second, the subsidiary's losses may lead to a decrease in value of the shareholding in the subsidiary, which may trigger the need to write-down the book value of the holding at the level of the parent company. However, such indirect utilization of losses through write-downs does not always directly correspond to a subsidiary's actual losses, and quite often they are not tax effective (reflecting, e.g., a participation exemption[1]). To prevent disadvantages for corporate groups, Member States have made different policy choices how to deal with losses of group entities, and most of them provide for some form of group taxation that permits the *current* netting of profits and losses of the various group entities (while, correspondingly, neutralizing write-downs of holdings in group entities[2]). For example, intra-group loss transfer systems allow for a definitive transfer between group members, either by surrendering losses from a loss-making to profitable group member (so-called "group relief") or by transferring profits from a profitable to a loss-making group member (so-called "group contribution"). Intra-group loss utilization can also be achieved through the "pooling" of profits and losses of the group members at the level of the parent company,

---

1 See, e.g., Cases C-39/13 to C-41/13, *SCA Group Holding BV*, EU:C:2014:1758, paras 37-38. However, if a Member State permits tax-effective write-downs of holdings in domestic subsidiaries, it must extend that treatment to holdings in EU subsidiaries in comparable situations (Case C-347/04, *Rewe Zentralfinanz*, EU:C:2007:194).

2 See, e.g., Case C-418/07, *Société Papillon*, EU:C:2008:659, paras 42-51.

or by a "full tax consolidation" ("tax integration scheme"), where, for tax purposes, the legal personality of the group members and any intra-group transactions are disregarded, so that results of the group are determined on the basis of a single profit and loss account.

Both, the automatic aggregation of the profits and losses of different branches of an under-taking within one single tax jurisdiction as well as a domestic group taxation regime offer two advantages:[3] First, there is a cash flow advantage because losses can be immediately netted with profits of the same enterprise or within the group, so that (ideally) tax will be paid later (e.g., once the group member returns to profits but has, of course, no loss carry-forward available).[4] Second, there can be a permanent advantage where the branch or group member never returns to profit but rather incurs a "total loss" (or could, for other reasons, not use its own losses, e.g., because of time-limitations of the loss carry-forward).

The picture drawn above changes dramatically once profits and losses arise in different Member States, i.e., in cross-border situations where (at least) two States are involved. Typically, cross-border business activities are either exercised through a permanent establishment (e.g., branches, agencies etc; Article 5 OECD MC) or through a subsidiary in another State (the "source" or "host" State). The main difference between these two forms of establishment, both of which are covered by the freedom of establishment under Article 49 TFEU ("agencies, branches or subsidiaries") within the EU, is that a subsidiary is a separate legal entity and hence a corporate taxpayer in its residence State (oftentimes wholly-owned by a parent company in another State), whereas a permanent establishment does not have legal personality, but is rather a mere part of the non-resident taxpayer's enterprise ("head office").[5] Hence, the non-resident taxpayer will typically be taxed, in the source State, on the profits attributable to a permanent establishment, which is also customary in tax treaties (Articles 5, 7 OECD MC). If, conversely, losses are incurred in a permanent establishment in another State, the permanent establishment must, in principle, be granted the same treatment under national law as resident entities under EU law (e.g., loss carry-forward, carry-back). Likewise, the subsidiary in the source State, which is a taxpayer there, will benefit from the loss carry-forward or carry-back regime available there. So, in the best case, losses incurred in permanent establishments or by subsidiaries will be offset against future or past profits in the *host* State.

Switching to the perspective of the residence State ("home State") of the taxpayer operating the foreign permanent establishment or the parent company owning the foreign subsidiary, profits earned by the foreign permanent establishment are often exempt from taxation

3 Opinion AG Kokott, 23 October 2014, Case C-172/13, *Commission v UK (Marks & Spencer II)*, EU:C:2014:2321, paras 20-21.

4 See Case C-446/03, *Marks & Spencer*, EU:C:2005:763, para. 32, and Case C-80/12, *Felixstowe Dock and Railway Company*, EU:C:2014:200, para. 19.

5 It might be noted that the Court, in the past, has described a permanent establishment "as an autonomous fiscal entity" (Case C-414/06, *Lidl Belgium*, EU:C:2008:278, para. 22) and has frequently used the notion of "residence" when referring to permanent establishments (e.g., Case C-650/16, *Bevola*, EU:C:2018:424, para. 30). However, permanent establishments are neither taxpayers nor persons nor residents in the traditional meaning of international tax law and tax treaty law. It therefore seems that this terminology is not used in a technical sense.

(either under domestic law or under tax treaty law, e.g., based in Article 23A OECD MC) and (undistributed) profits of a foreign subsidiary are, in any event, outside the home State's taxing jurisdiction (Article 7 OECD MC).[6] However, where the *home* State does not tax the profits earned in a foreign subsidiary or by a foreign permanent establishment ("non-resident establishment"[7]), a "symmetrical" exclusion of losses seems to be a sensible policy choice in light of fiscal sovereignty. From the perspective of taxpayers and the Internal Market, however, the exclusion of cross-border loss utilization can lead to cash-flow disadvantages (because the losses can only be carried forward or back in the State of the permanent establishment or the subsidiary, awaiting better times for setting off) and "overtaxation" (because a "total" foreign loss cannot be utilized in any State) and may therefore deter cross-border economic engagement. It is hence unsurprising that the issue of cross-border loss utilization has been in the focus of the Commission's tax policy work as well as the Court's case-law on the freedom of establishment and the so-called "final loss exception", starting nearly 20 years ago with *Marks & Spencer*[8] (for foreign subsidiaries) and *Lidl Belgium*[9] (for treaty-exempt foreign permanent establishments) and resulting in a complex body of decisions and continuing uncertainty in legal practice.[10]

Conversely, taxpayers may find themselves disadvantaged also in the reverse cross-border situation, i.e., if losses arise in the *home* State and profits are earned in the *source* State. Where profits and losses are distributed over several Member States so that, e.g., negative rental income in the home State cannot be deducted from employment income earned in another State, this will result in a (semi-)permanent higher tax burden compared with purely domestic activities. Obviously, this fragmentation of the loss relief market along national borders disadvantages cross-border economic activities as compared to activities in just one single tax jurisdiction. Some of these issues have been addressed by the Court through an application of the *Schumacker*-doctrine[11] to, specifically, negative rental income.[12] It is not entirely clear, however, if the fundamental freedoms require that a taxpayer's losses in its residence State are to be taken into account by the source State (e.g., when it taxes outbound dividends paid to that taxpayer), although recent case law[13] points in that direction.

10.1.2 Lack of Positive Integration: From the Commission's 1990 Proposal to "BEFIT"

The Commission's work has not yet resulted in binding EU legislation on cross-border loss relief. Already in its April 1990 "Guidelines on company taxation",[14] the Commission had identified the lack of cross-border loss relief for permanent establishments and subsidiaries as a "factor penalizing transfrontier activities", and soon thereafter, in December 1990,

6 Unless covered by so-called CFC rules (see Chapters 8.2.4. and 9.5).
7 See for that terminology, e.g., Case C-388/14, *Timac Agro*, EU:C:2015:829, para. 53.
8 Case C-446/03, *Marks & Spencer*, EU:C:2005:763.
9 Case C-414/06, *Lidl Belgium*, EU:C:2008:278.
10 See *infra* Chapters 10.2 and 10.3.
11 Case C-279/93, *Schumacker*, EU:C:1995:31.
12 Case C-527/06, *Renneberg*, EU:C:2008:566; Case C-283/15, *X*, EU:C:2017:102.
13 Case C-575/17, *Sofina*, EU:C:2018:943; Case C-601/23, *Credit Suisse Securities*, EU:C:2024:1048.
14 SEC(90)60 (20 April 1990), 5.

tabled a proposal for a "directive concerning arrangements for the taking into account by enterprises of the losses of their permanent establishments and subsidiaries situated in other Member States".[15] Interestingly, this 1990 Proposal was not limited to corporations but rather covered all "enterprises" irrespective of their legal form (Art 2), so long as the "enterprise" was considered a tax resident in the home State and subject to a domestic income or corporate tax (Art 3).

As for foreign permanent establishments of an enterprise (Article 5), the goal of avoiding excessive taxation could either be achieved through the application of the credit method (Article 6) or, if a country has chosen the exemption method, a system where foreign losses are *currently* deductible at the enterprise level in the home State, but that subsequent profits of the permanent establishment are included in the enterprise's income in the home State to the extent of a prior loss deduction ("deduction/reincorporation method", Article 7). This "deduction/reincorporation method" was also foreseen for (at least) 75%-owned subsidiaries of foreign enterprises (Article 9). In both cases, however, an automatic recapture was triggered where reincorporation has not occurred within five years after the loss deduction, where the permanent establishment or subsidiary has been sold, wound up, transformed into a subsidiary or permanent establishment, respectively, or, in the case of a subsidiary, the ownership level has fallen below the minimum level (Articles 8 and 10).

The latter rules show that the 1990 Proposal was aimed at preventing a cash-flow disadvantage and hence providing (merely) a *temporary* loss transfer, but that it did not address the "total loss" situation (which, in effect, is the opposite approach to the subsequent "final loss" doctrine of the Court in *Marks & Spencer*[16]). Moreover, the 1990 Proposal also addressed the (hard) question, which State's law should be decisive for determining the existence and amount of a loss, and deferred to the laws of the State where the permanent establishment or subsidiary is situated (Articles 7(2) and 9(2)) (again, arguably the opposite of what the Court later held in *A Oy*[17]). Finally, the 1990 Proposal clearly saw the relationship between direct loss relief and the write down of a holding (i.e., the "indirect" utilization of losses) and clarified that the "deduction/reincorporation method" "shall be incompatible with any correction of the value of the holding of that enterprise in a subsidiary" (Article 11); indeed, if Member States permit (tax effective) write-downs, it shall "be avoided that an enterprise applies at the same time both the method provided by this directive and the method of writing down the book value, because otherwise the same loss would be taken into account twice".[18]

15 Proposal for a Council directive concerning arrangements for the taking into account by enterprises of the losses of their permanent establishments and subsidiaries situated in other Member States, COM(90)595 (24 January 1991), [1991] OJ C 53, p. 30 (28 February 1991) (the "1990 Proposal").

16 See *infra* Chapter 10.2.

17 See *infra* Chapter 10.2.3.

18 See para. 29 of the Explanatory Memorandum of the 1990 Proposal, COM(90)595 final (24 January 1991), [1991] OJ C 53, p. 30.

While, e.g., the Ruding Committee[19] had supported the Commission's 1990 Proposal, it never became EU law and has eventually been withdrawn in 2001 as "obsolete".[20] The Commission nevertheless announced further work on cross-border relief in October 2001[21] and again stressed, in November 2003, that offsetting losses cross-border "remains very important for businesses" and contemplated a system of "EU group taxation" along the lines of the Danish "joint taxation" system of cross-border loss relief with recapture.[22] It was only in 2006 that the Commission, under the impression of the Court's *Marks & Spencer* judgment, reacted with a detailed policy analysis in its Communication on the "Tax Treatment of Losses in Cross-border Situations",[23] where it addressed various options of cross-border loss relief within one enterprise (i.e., losses incurred by a branch or "permanent establishment" of the company situated in another Member State) and within a group of companies (i.e. losses incurred by a group member in another Member State).

The Commission later focused on the Common (Consolidated) Corporate Tax Base (C(C) CTB), by putting forward a first proposal in 2011,[24] subsequently re-launching the project under a two-step approach (that envisaged tax base harmonization in a first step and consolidation and formulary apportionment in a second step) in 2016[25] and finally, after announcing it in 2021,[26] replacing the C(C)CTB in 2023 by a new proposed framework for corporate taxation in the EU, the so-called "BEFIT" ("Business in Europe: Framework for Income Taxation").[27] The contemplated consolidation of corporate profits under BEFIT (and, previously, the CCCTB) would lead to an automatic cross-border loss relief for covered companies (Chapter 22).

10.1.3 Negative Integration: The Court's Case Law on Loss Utilization

One core issue in the Court's case law concerns the cross-border utilization of losses incurred by foreign subsidiaries and exempt permanent establishments from the perspective of the *home* State in light of the freedom of establishment under Article 49 TFEU (or Article

19 See the "Conclusions and Recommendations of the Committee of Independent Experts on Company Taxation" (1992), p. 12.

20 See the withdrawal of Commission proposals which are no longer topical, COM(2001)763 final/2 (21 December 2001), p. 24, [2004] OJ C 5, p. 2 (9 January 2004).

21 See the Commission's Communication "Towards an Internal Market without tax obstacles", COM(2001)582 (23 October 2001), p. 12-13.

22 See the Commission's Communication "An Internal Market without company tax obstacles – achievements, ongoing initiatives and remaining challenges", COM(2003)726 (24 November 2003).

23 COM(2006)824 final (19 December 2006).

24 Proposal for a Council Directive on a Common Consolidated Corporate Tax Base (CCCTB), COM(2011)121/4 (16 March 2011).

25 See the Proposal for a Council Directive on a Common Corporate Tax Base, COM(2016)685 (25 October 2016), and the Proposal for a Council Directive on a Common Consolidated Corporate Tax Base (CCCTB), COM(2016)683 (25 October 2016). The former proposal provides for *temporary* cross-border utilization of a subsidiary's losses through the "deduction/reincorporation method" (Art 42), the latter for a *permanent* cross-border utilization of a subsidiary's losses, as cross-border loss relief would be an automatic outcome of consolidation.

26 See Pt. 4. in the Communication on "Business Taxation for the 21st Century", COM(2021)251.

27 Proposal for a Council Directive on Business in Europe: Framework for Income Taxation (BEFIT), COM(2023)532 (12 September 2023).

31 EEA Agreement).[28] Starting with the Grand Chamber's decision in *Marks & Spencer* in 2005 for cross-border group relief and *Lidl Belgium* in 2008 for losses of foreign exempt permanent establishments, the Court has consistently held that a *current* cross-border utilization of losses and hence a treatment in the same way as domestic losses is not required by the freedom of establishment. Also, the "deduction/reincorporation method" (which was proposed by the Commission as a general measure in 1990[29] and as a part of the CCTB in 2016[30] as well as favored by several Advocates General[31]) could not be derived from the fundamental freedoms but would "in any event require harmonization rules adopted by the Community legislature".[32] However, the principle of proportionality requires that the Member State of the parent company or the head office, respectively, takes into account so-called "final" or "definitive" foreign losses. This line of case law, and specifically the "final loss exception", has since permeated the case law for systems of group relief,[33] group contributions[34] and tax consolidation[35] (Chapter 10.2.2.). It is also the decisive criterion when it comes to loss-utilization in the case of cross-border mergers;[36] however, it requires a *temporal* link between a taxing jurisdiction and the creation of losses[37] (Chapter 10.2.3.). More generally, the logic of this case law, including the "final loss exception", seems to be relevant for all base-exempt income, e.g., the sale of immovable property by an individual taxpayer.[38]

The "final loss" doctrine and the underlying reasoning with regard to comparability, justification, and proportionality has also been transplanted to permanent establishments

28 E.g., Case C-231/05, *Oy AA*, EU:C:2007:439, para. 20-24; Case C-414/06, *Lidl Belgium*, EU:C:2008:278, paras 15-16; Case C-48/13, *Nordea Bank Danmark*, EU:C:2014:2087, para. 18; EFTA Court, 24 May 2024, Case E-7/23, *ExxonMobil*, para. 20. And not under the free movement of capital under Art. 63 TFEU, which would extend to third-country situations. See, e.g., for the exclusion of third-country situations involving permanent establishments Case C-415/06, *Stahlwerk Ergste Westig*, EU:C:2007:651, and concerning group taxation regimes Case C-231/05, *Oy AA*, EU:C:2007:439, para. 24.

29 See Art. 5-10 of the Commission's 1990 Proposal, COM(90)595 (24 January 1991), [1991] OJ C 53, p. 30 (28 February 1991).

30 See Art. 42 of the Commission's Proposal for a Council Directive on a Common Corporate Tax Base, COM(2016)685 (25 October 2016), on "Loss relief and recapture".

31 Opinion of AG Sharpston, 14 February 2008, C-414/06, *Lidl Belgium*, EU:C:2008:88, para. 25; see also the detailed discussion by Opinion AG Kokott, 23 October 2014, Case C-172/13, *Commission v UK (Marks & Spencer II)*, EU:C:2014:2321, paras 49-53.

32 Case C-446/03, *Marks & Spencer*, EU:C:2005:763, para. 58.

33 Case C-446/03, *Marks & Spencer*, EU:C:2005:763; Case C-172/13, *Commission v UK (Marks & Spencer II)*, EU:C:2015:50.

34 Case C-608/17, *Holmen*, EU:C:2019:511; EFTA Court, 13 September 2017, Case E-15/16, *Yara International*, [2017] EFTA Ct. Rep. 434; EFTA Court, 24 May 2024, Case E-7/23, *ExxonMobil*. It should be noted that *Oy AA* (Case C-231/05, *Oy AA*, EU:C:2007:439) on the Finnish group contribution system followed a similar reasoning with regard to comparability and justification, but did not concern losses.

35 See Case C-337/08, *X Holding*, EU:C:2010:89, which did not concern "final" losses and where the Court found the limitation of the Netherlands' fiscal unity regime to domestic entities justified.

36 Case C-123/11, *A Oy*, EU:C:2013:84; Case C-607/17, *Memira*, EU:C:2019:510.

37 Case C-405/18, *AURES*, EU:C:2020:127.

38 Case C-322/11, *K*, EU:C:2013:716.

that are either symmetrically base-exempt (either under a tax treaty[39] or under domestic law[40]), where an asymmetrical "deduction/reincorporation system" applies,[41] or where losses are recaptured despite the application of the credit method[42] (Chapter 10.3.) However, the Court's recent judgment in *W AG*[43] on cross-border loss utilization has revealed some deep cracks in the consistency of the direct tax case law. Almost two decades ago, the landmark decisions in *Marks & Spencer*[44] and *Lidl Belgium*[45] had assumed comparability between domestic and cross-border situations and embraced the "final loss exception" for foreign subsidiaries and treaty-exempt exempt permanent establishments. After some uncertainty following *Timac Agro*[46] and *Bevola*,[47] in *W AG* the Court clearly turned its back on *Lidl Belgium* and found that domestic and treaty-exempt branches are not comparable in the first place (but confirmed comparability and the continuing relevance of the "final loss doctrine" for situations outside an exemption under a tax treaty, e.g., for domestic exemptions, the "deduction/reincorporation method", or recaptures under the credit method). However, by declaring domestic and treaty-exempt foreign losses to be categorically incomparable, the Court in *W AG* has not only "overruled" *Lidl Belgium* in substance (indeed, *Lidl Belgium* was not even mentioned, let alone explicitly distinguished),[48] but has also created uncertainty not only as to the initial premise of *Marks & Spencer* but

39 Case C-414/06, *Lidl Belgium*, EU:C:2008:278.

40 Case C-650/16, *Bevola*, EU:C:2018:424.

41 See Case C-388/14, *Timac Agro*, EU:C:2015:829; see also Case C-157/07, *Krankenheim Ruhesitz am Wannsee*, EU:C:2008:588.

42 Case C-48/13, *Nordea Bank Danmark*, EU:C:2014:2087.

43 Case C-538/20, *W AG*, EU:C:2022:717.

44 Case C-446/03, *Marks & Spencer*, EU:C:2005:763.

45 Case C-414/06, *Lidl Belgium*, EU:C:2008:278.

46 Case C-388/14, *Timac Agro*, EU:C:2015:829.

47 Case C-650/16, *Bevola*, EU:C:2018:424.

48 Indeed, *W AG* has sparked a passionate discourse on the transparency, certainty, and clarity regarding the Court's (substantive) "overruling" of its precedents: The Court's transition from *Lidl Belgium* to *W AG* is puzzling, highly unsatisfactory, and has been labelled as "the clearest case of an 'overruling' (in substance, but not with respect to visibility) that can be identified". See Axel Cordewener, "We Need to Know When Previous Case-Law Has Been 'Overruled'! – A Plea for More Legal Certainty in EU Tax Law", 32 EC Tax Rev. 2023, 144 (147); for further discussion see also Georg Kofler, *Cross-border losses and W AG: The beginning of the end of the "final loss exception"?*, 2 Cahiers de fiscalité luxembourgeoise et européenne 73 (90-91) (2023); Rita Szudoczky, *Foreign Permanent Establishment Losses Under the Fundamental Freedoms: Does W AG Bring an End to a Rollercoaster Ride?*, 51 Intertax 432-443 (2023); see also Savvas Kostikidis and Florian Striefler, *Cross-Border Loss Relief in the European Union Following* W AG *(Case C-538/20)*, 64 European Taxation 210-218 (2024).

also as to the viability of other leading cases.[49] Moreover, one might say: If *Lidl Belgium* fell, so should *Marks & Spencer* – which would be a step back for the Internal Market's negative integration and should put renewed pressure on positive harmonization. This will be addressed again in Chapter 10.2.2. and Chapter 10.3.2.A quite different issue, which should be mentioned briefly, concerns "straightforward" prohibited discriminations where the territoriality of a tax system is not at issue, i.e., where a *home* State, under domestic law, taxes domestic and foreign profits of its residents alike, but treats domestic and foreign losses differently. This was the case in *Busley and Cibrian*,[50] where Germany included income from foreign real estate in the worldwide tax base of resident individuals as if it were domestic income, but it allowed deduction of losses from foreign real estate only against subsequent positive income from foreign real estate, although losses from domestic real estate were currently deductible from other income.

While much of the Court's case law was concerned with cross-border loss utilization from the perspective of the taxpayer's *home* State, it has also dealt with the – perhaps subtler – question of whether non-resident taxpayers are entitled, under the fundamental freedoms, to set off losses that they have incurred in their home State against (unrelated) positive income that they derive in the *source* State. Generally, a source State that only takes into account profits and losses arising from activities in its own territory is not only consistent with the international principle of territoriality but also with the fundamental freedoms.[51] However, in expanding the *Schumacker*-doctrine,[52] the Court has held that source Member States must take into account foreign losses (e.g., negative rental income) of individuals if the taxpayer's home Member State is not in a position to grant that benefit, both with regard to progressivity[53] and to the tax base.[54] The scope of this line of case law is not entirely clear, and indeed the Court has recently held that a corporate taxpayer's losses in its residence State need to be taken into account by the source State when it taxes outbound dividends paid to that taxpayer.[55] This topic will be explored in Chapter 10.4.

49 See *infra* Chapter 10.3.2. For detailed discussions of *W AG* and its implications see, with further references, e.g., CFE ECJ Task Force, *Opinion Statement ECJ-TF 4/2022 on the CJEU decision of 22 September 2022 in Case C-538/20,* W AG, *on the deductibility of foreign final losses*, 63 European Taxation 105-110 (2023); Georg Kofler, *Cross-border losses and* W AG*: The beginning of the end of the "final loss exception"?*, 2 Cahiers de fiscalité luxembourgeoise et européenne 73-97 (2023); Rita Szudoczky, *Foreign Permanent Establishment Losses Under the Fundamental Freedoms: Does W AG Bring an End to a Rollercoaster Ride?*, 51 Intertax 432-443 (2023); Savvas Kostikidis and Florian Striefler, *Cross-Border Loss Relief in the European Union Following* W AG *(Case C-538/20)*, 64 European Taxation 210-218 (2024). For a discussion of the Opinion of AG Collins see Georg Kofler, *Should We Cut "Final" Losses?*, 31 EC Tax Review 108-114 (2022), and for analysis of the German Bundesfinanzhof's follow-up decisions see Georg Kofler, *Curia Locuta, Causa Finita*: Some Further Conclusions from *W AG*, 32 EC Tax Review 190-194 (2023).

50 Case C-35/08, *Busley/Cibrian*, EU:C:2009:625.

51 Case C-250/95, *Futura Participations*, EU:C:1997:239; Case C-345/04, *Centro Equestre da Lezíria Grande*, EU:C:2007:96, para. 22.

52 Case C-279/93, *Schumacker*, EU:C:1995:31.

53 Case C-152/03, *Ritter-Coulais*, EU:C:2006:123; Case C-182/06, *Lakebrink*, EU:C:2007:452.

54 Case C-527/06, *Renneberg*, EU:C:2008:566; Case C-283/15, *X*, EU:C:2017:102.

55 Case C-575/17, *Sofina*, EU:C:2018:943; Case C-601/23, *Credit Suisse Securities*, EU:C:2024:1048.

Apart from these issues of straightforward cross-border losses, the Court's case law has also addressed numerous situations involving ***domestic*** losses in the Court's case law. Early judgments were, for example, concerned with the reduction of a domestic loss carry-forward because of treaty-exempt foreign income (Chapter 10.5).[56] Much of the more recent case law dealt with various restrictions of loss relief in group situations that were based not on the territoriality of the losses, but rather on the fact that a taxpayer also had foreign holdings[57] or because a domestic group member[58] or a domestic permanent establishment[59] was held via a non-resident group member (Chapter 10.6). Finally, the case law has also dealt with currency losses, i.e., losses which are generally only "visible" from the perspective of one State (Chapter 10.7).[60]

10.1.4 Existence and Amount of a "Tax Loss"

A final preliminary issue needs to be highlighted: A "tax loss" is not a natural phenomenon. Its existence and amount depend on domestic tax law. It might therefore be the rule rather than the exception that if two Member States look at the same facts, the amount of profit or loss would diverge depending on their respective domestic tax rules. One State may, e.g., allow accelerated depreciation, deferral, or the deduction of even private expenses, while the other might have a much broader definition of the tax base. That said, it could even be the case that one State "sees" a loss, the other a profit. It is therefore quite important, also from an EU law perspective, under which State's rules a relevant "loss" is determined. This is relevant not only when it comes to cross-border loss relief from the perspective of the *home* State, but also where it is for the *source* State to take into account foreign losses.[61]

The Court's case law is not entirely clear on that point. In *Marks & Spencer* it had tacitly accepted the prerogative of the home State when it comes to the determination of foreign losses.[62] In *A Oy* it has explicitly stressed that such "calculation must not lead to unequal treatment compared with the calculation which would have been made in a similar case for the taking over of the losses of a resident subsidiary",[63] i.e., in principle under the rules of the home State,[64] but that this "question cannot, however, be addressed in an abstract and hypothetical manner, but must be analysed where necessary on a case-by-case basis".[65] The detailed dogmatic and technical problems surrounding that question are exemplified by the long-lasting UK litigation following the Court's 2005 *Marks & Spencer* judgment,

56 Case C-141/99, *AMID*, EU:C:2000:696; Case C-431/01, *Mertens*, EU:C:2002:492.
57 Case C-264/96, *ICI*, EU:C:1998:370.
58 Case C-418/07, *Société Papillon*, EU:C:2008:659; Case C-80/12, *Felixstowe Dock and Railway Company*, EU:C:2014:200; Cases C-39/13 to C-41/13, *SCA Group Holding*, EU:C:2014:1758.
59 Case C-18/11, *Philips Electronics*, EU:C:2012:532; Case C-28/17, *NN*, EU:C:2018:526.
60 Case C-293/06, *Deutsche Shell*, EU:C:2008:129; Case C-686/13, *X AB*, EU:C:2015:375.
61 See *infra* Chapter 10.4.
62 Case C-446/03, *Marks & Spencer*, EU:C:2005:763, para. 22, noting that the parties agreed "that the losses must be computed on a United Kingdom tax basis".
63 Case C-123/11, *A Oy*, EU:C:2013:84, para. 59.
64 See also specifically Opinion AG Kokott, 19 July 2012, Case C-123/11, *A Oy*, EU:C:2012:488, paras, paras 70-76.
65 Case C-123/11, *A Oy*, EU:C:2013:84, para. 60.

where the UK Supreme Court eventually favored an approach whereby the unutilized losses as determined under source State rules are converted to home State rules.[66]

More generally, it is still unclear whether the amount of the foreign losses (as determined under the rules of the *source* State) is an *upper* limit for loss-relief in the *home* State, so that only the lower amount of the loss, as determined under home State rules as well as under source State rules, has to be taken into account.[67] The answer is not obvious: Equal treatment with domestic situations would arguably require determination solely under *home* State rules. The logic of "final" losses, however, would likewise suggest that the home State does not need to take more losses into account than could have been used in the source State under that State's rules (because if the losses had been used there, they would never have become "final" in the first place). It is not the home State's obligation to equalize tax base differences. Indeed, AG A. Collins in his Opinion in *W AG* advocated for such a "dual limit" that is determined as the lower amount of loss as determined both under *home* State and *host* State rules.[68] This interpretation would also provide a link to the Court's decision in *K*, where losses were not considered "final" because under source State rules the loss at issue could not be used at all,[69] which resembles the extreme situation that the foreign loss exists only under *home* State rules, whereas the *source* State would "see" a profit.

10.2 Losses of Foreign Subsidiaries

10.2.1 Technical Background

Nearly all Member States provide for some form of *current* profit-loss-matching in domestic groups. As noted before, this can take the form of surrendering losses from a loss-making to a profitable group member (so-called "group relief" or "loss surrender", e.g., in the former Member State UK), of transferring profits from one group member to another group member, often from a profitable to a loss-making entity (so-called "group contributions", e.g., Finland's "konserniavustuksesta verotuksessa", Sweden's "koncernbidrag", and, extending the picture to the EEA, Norway's "konsernbidrag"), of "pooling" of profits and losses of the group members at the level of the parent company (e.g., Austria's "Gruppenbesteuerung" and Germany's "Organschaft"), or of a "full tax consolidation" of the group (e.g., the Netherlands' "fiscale eenheid"). However, only few Member States extend these regimes to cross-border situations (e.g., Austria, Denmark, and Italy), although the Commission had called on Member States to introduce measures

66 See paras. 49-53 of UK Supreme Court, 19 February 2014, *Commissioners for Her Majesty's Revenue and Customs v Marks and Spencer plc*, [2014] UKSC 11.

67 Indeed, the UK legislation at issue in *Commission v. UK* (Case C-172/13) required that "final" losses need to be recomputed in accordance with UK rules but also provided a further limitation, i.e., that only the lower of the two amounts (foreign computed loss v. domestic computed loss) is to be taken into account at the UK level. Unfortunately, the Court did not (have to) address this issue.

68 See Opinion AG Collins, 10 March 2022, Case C-538/20, *W AG*, EU:C:2022:184, paras 72-75. As the Court (Case C-538/20, *W AG*, EU:C:2022:717) has found the situations of a domestic and foreign treaty-exempt permanent establishment incomparable (Chapter 10.3.2), it did not have to address this issue.

69 Case C-322/11, *K*, EU:C:2013:716, para. 77.

addressing cross-border loss relief to "ensure that corporate groups doing business in several Member States are treated as far as possible in the same way as groups doing business with a single Member State" and that, in particular, losses can be "set off from the tax base for the year in which they are incurred".[70]

As the lack of cross-border loss relief for groups of companies, however, can distort business decisions as regards both the legal form and the location of investment, it was quite foreseeable that taxpayers would bring challenges under the fundamental freedoms. The first such case arriving at the Court was *Marks & Spencer* on the UK group relief system, in which the Court essentially could not derive, from the freedom of establishment, an obligation for *current* cross-border loss relief (e.g., a "deduction/reincorporation method") but rather held that (only) so-called *"final"* ("definitive", "terminal") losses of foreign subsidiaries need to be taken into account in the home State as *ultima ratio* (the "final loss exception", "*Marks & Spencer* exception", or "no possibilities test"). The Court therefore accepts a significant difference in timing of intra-group loss relief and therefore in cash-flow position: A non-resident subsidiary in a loss position will have to wait for better years in order to offset its losses against its own future profits, whereas a resident subsidiary may carry over its losses immediately within the same tax year to profitable resident group companies to limit tax exposure there.

10.2.2 Cross-Border Loss Relief and Group Taxation Regimes (Marks & Spencer, X Holding, Commission v. UK, Yara, Holmen, ExxonMobil)

The 2005 *Marks & Spencer* judgment by the Grand Chamber is certainly one of the landmarks in the Court's direct tax jurisprudence[71] and its legacy perhaps one of the

70 See the Commission's Communication on the "Tax Treatment of Losses in Cross-border Situations", COM(2006)824 final (19 December 2006), p. 8.

71 It was preceded and succeeded by lengthy, sophisticated litigation in the UK up to the Supreme Court; see United Kingdom Supreme Court, 22 May 2013, *Revenue and Customs v Marks and Spencer plc* [2013] UKSC 30, and UK Supreme Court, 19 February 2014, *Commissioners for Her Majesty's Revenue and Customs v Marks and Spencer plc*, [2014] UKSC 11.

most discussed aspects of EU direct taxation.[72] It concerned losses incurred by the French, German, and Belgian subsidiaries of the UK-based Marks & Spencer group. In 2001, Marks & Spencer announced its intention to divest itself of its Continental European activity; the French subsidiary was sold (to Galeries Lafayette) and the German and Belgian subsidiaries ceased trading. Marks & Spencer's claim for group relief, i.e., for a transfer of the subsidiaries' losses of the taxable years ending in 1998, 1999, 2000, and 2001 to its UK parent, was rejected on the ground that group relief could only be granted for losses recorded in the UK. In hindsight, the challenge under the freedom of establishment was obvious: First, under an argument based on the neutrality of the legal form (i.e., a *horizontal* comparison between two cross-border situations), the UK should allow the cross-border loss transfer because it also allowed the deduction of losses of foreign branches (under the credit method). Second, from the perspective of a vertical comparison between domestic and cross-border situations, the UK should allow cross-border loss-relief because such relief is available for losses of UK resident subsidiaries ("group relief"). The Court did not even engage with the first argument,[73] but AG Maduro's Opinion[74] and subsequent case

72 See, for many, Michael Lang, *The* Marks & Spencer *Case – The Open Issues Following the ECJ's Final Word*, 46 *European Taxation* 54-67 (2006); CFE ECJ Task Force, *Opinion Statement of the CFE Task Force on ECJ Cases on the Judgment in the Case of* Marks & Spencer plc v. Halsey *(Case C-446/03)*", 47 European Taxation 51-54 (2007); Maarten de Wilde, *On* X Holding *and the ECJ's Ambiguous Approach Towards the Proportionality Test*, 19 EC Tax Review 170-182 (2010); Otto Marres, *The Principle of Territoriality and Cross-Border Loss Compensation*, 39 Intertax 112-125 (2011); Bruno da Silva, *From* Marks & Spencer *to* X Holding: *The Future of Cross-Border Group Taxation in the European Union*, 39 Intertax 257-265 (2011); Michael Lang, *Has the Case Law of the ECJ on Final Losses Reached the End of the Line?*, 54 European Taxation 530-540 (2014); Erik Pinetz & Karoline Spies, *'Final Losses' after the Decision in Commission v. UK ('Marks & Spencer II')*, 24 EC Tax Review 309-319 (2015); Yariv Brauner, Ana Paula Dourado and Edoardo Traversa, *Ten Years of* Marks & Spencer, 43 *Intertax* 306-314 (2015); Axel Cordewener, *Cross-Border Compensation of 'Final Losses" for Tax Purposes – The Drama Continues ...*, 22 Maastricht Journal of European and Comparative Law 417-431 (2015); Luca Cerioni, *The Never-Ending Issue of Cross-Border Loss Compensation within the EU: Reconciling Balanced Allocation of Taxing Rights and Cross-Border Ability-to-Pay*, 24 EC Tax Review 268-280 (2015); CFE ECJ Task Force, *Opinion Statement ECJ-TF 2/2015 on the Decision of the European Court of Justice in* European Commission v. United Kingdom *("Final Losses") (Case C-172/13), Concerning the* 'Marks & Spencer *Exception'*, 56 European Taxation 87-93 (2016); Axel Cordewener, *Cross-Border Loss Compensation and EU Fundamental Freedoms: The 'Final Losses' Doctrine Is Still Alive!*, 27 EC Tax Review 230-236 (2018); Johanna Hey, "Taxation of business in the EU: Special problems of crossborder losses and exit taxation", in: Christiana HJI Panayi, Werner Haslehner and Edoardo Traversa (eds.), *Research Handbook on European Union Taxation Law* (Edward Elgar Publishing 2020), 194 (194-211).

73 Case C-446/03, *Marks & Spencer*, EU:C:2005:763, para. 52 (merely noting that the analysis "is not affected by the indications, set out in the second part of the first question, relating to the arrangements applicable in the United Kingdom [...] to the profits and losses of a foreign subsidiary of a company established in that Member State"). See in this respect also A. Cordewener and I. Dörr, "*Case C-446/03,* Marks & Spencer plc. v. David Halsey (HM Inspector of Taxes), *Judgment of the Court of Justice (Grand Chamber) of 13 December 2005*", 43 Common Market Law Review 855 (861 et seq., 873 et seq.) (2006).

74 Opinion of A.G. *Poiares Maduro*, 7 April 2005, Case C-446/03, *Marks & Spencer*, EU:C:2005:201, paras. 42 et seq.

law[75] made it clear that these situations are not to be regarded as comparable from the perspective of the *home* State.[76]

What remained to be decided by the Court in *Marks & Spencer* was the *vertical* comparison between domestic and cross-border situations: Does the freedom of establishment require a Member State to take into account losses of foreign subsidiaries (over whose undistributed profits it does not exercise taxing jurisdiction) if it does so for domestic subsidiaries (whose profits are taxable in that Member State)? Considering loss-relief mainly as a "cash advantage" (through the "speeding up of relief of losses of the loss-making entities"[77]) that was denied in cross-border situations, the Court quickly concluded the existence of a restriction on freedom of establishment. It also rejected the argument that the situations of foreign and domestic subsidiaries are not comparable: While the Court obviously accepted that the UK's regime complies with the Union-recognized principle of territoriality,[78] it nevertheless held that "the fact that it does not tax the profits of the non-resident subsidiaries of a parent company established on its territory does not in itself justify restricting group relief to losses incurred by resident companies".[79] This rather superficial assumption of comparability in case of a fragmentation of the tax base over multiple jurisdictions – dubbed as the "original sin"[80] – has been heavily criticized,[81] and intensely debated before the Court specifically in cases involving exempt permanent establishments.[82] Indeed, after the Court has quietly overruled *Lidl Belgium* (2008)[83] in *Timac Agro* (2015)[84] and in *W AG* (2022),[85] holding in those latter two cases that domestic and foreign treaty-exempt permanent establishments are not even comparable in the first place (so that not even "final losses" need to be taken into account), it remains to be seen if *Marks & Spencer* will be upheld by the Court in the future (Chapter 10.3.2.). Indeed, the German government has already – albeit unsuccessfully – argued before the EFTA Court that, in light of *W AG*, the "final loss exception" should flatly be rejected

---

75 See, e.g., Case C-298/05, *Columbus Container Services*, EU:C:2007:754, paras. 51 and 53; Cases C-439/07 and C-499/07, *KBC Bank*, EU:C:2009:339, para. 80; Case C-337/08, *X Holding*, EU:C:2010:89, paras 37-41.

76 For analysis see, e.g., G. Kofler, "'Horizontal Discrimination' in European Tax Law", in: Heike Jochum et al. (eds.), *Practical Problems in European and International Tax Law, Essays in honour of Manfred Mössner* (IBFD Amsterdam 2016), 187 (191-197).

77 Case C-446/03, *Marks & Spencer*, EU:C:2005:763, para. 32.

78 Case C-446/03, *Marks & Spencer*, EU:C:2005:763, para. 39, referring to Case C-250/95, *Futura Participations*, EU:C:1997:239, para. 22.

79 Case C-446/03, *Marks & Spencer*, EU:C:2005:763, para. 40.

80 See Yariv Brauner, Ana Paula Dourado and Edoardo Traversa, *Ten Years of* Marks & Spencer, 43 *Intertax* 306-314 (308).

81 Also, e.g., in the Opinion AG Kokott, 23 October 2014, Case C-172/13, *Commission v UK (Marks & Spencer II)*, EU:C:2014:2321, paras 23-29.

82 See *infra* Chapter 10.3.2 and 10.3.3.

83 Case C-414/06, *Lidl Belgium*, EU:C:2008:278.

84 Case C-388/14, *Timac Agro*, EU:C:2015:829.

85 Case C-538/20, W AG, EU:C:2022:717.

also in the context of a group contribution regime.[86] To date, however, both the Court and the EFTA-Court, have not yet wavered and explicitly or implicitly upheld that line of comparison also in subsequent cases (some of which decided after *Timac Agro* and *W AG*) involving group relief (*Commission v. UK*[87]), group contributions (*Oy AA*,[88] *Yara*,[89] *Holmen*,[90] *ExxonMobil*[91]), and tax consolidation (*X Holding*[92]).

Finding a discrimination in *Marks & Spencer* required the UK to defend its legislation by bringing forward acceptable grounds of justification. The UK and other Member States brought forward three such grounds, which the Court accepted "taken together"[93]:

First, it was argued that "in tax matters profits and losses are two sides of the same coin and must be treated symmetrically in the same tax system in order to protect a balanced allocation of the power to impose taxes between the different Member States concerned".[94] The Court acknowledged the need to "safeguard the symmetry between the right to tax profits and the right to deduct losses",[95] also because optionality for taxpayers where to utilize losses "would significantly jeopardise a balanced allocation of the power to impose taxes between Member States".[96] This argument of a balanced allocation of taxing powers was further accepted and developed in subsequent case law, and, e.g., also accepted with regard to domestic group contribution systems[97] and tax consolidation regimes,[98] as well as cross-border mergers.[99]

Second, "if the losses were taken into consideration in the parent company's Member State they might well be taken into account twice" ("douple dip"). Again, the Court accepted this argument as is because "Member States must be able to prevent that from occurring",[100] and subsequent case law has confirmed this argument.[101]

---

86 See the written submission by Germany of 29 September 2023, EA6-81 2041007#007, in Case E-7/23, *ExxonMobil*. The EFTA Court has not addressed that argument, but rather merely answered the referring Norwegian court's questions regarding the "finality" of losses. See for analysis Adam Zalasiński, The Final Loss Saga under the EEA Agreement – Comments on the EFTA Court's Judgment in E-7/23 *ExxonMobil Holding Norway*, 31 International Transfer Pricing Journal 269 (2024).

87 Case C-172/13, *Commission v UK (Marks & Spencer II)*, EU:C:2015:50, paras 22-23.

88 Case C-231/05, *Oy AA*, EU:C:2007:439, paras 31-38.

89 EFTA Court, 13 September 2017, Case E-15/16, *Yara International ASA*, [2017] EFTA Ct. Rep. 434.

90 Case C-608/17, *Holmen*, EU:C:2019:511.

91 EFTA Court, 24 May 2024, Case E-7/23, *ExxonMobil*.

92 Case C-337/08, *X Holding*, EU:C:2010:89, paras 17-24.

93 Case C-446/03, *Marks & Spencer*, EU:C:2005:763, para. 51; see also Case C-172/13, *Commission v UK (Marks & Spencer II)*, EU:C:2015:50, para. 24.

94 Case C-446/03, *Marks & Spencer*, EU:C:2005:763, para. 43.

95 Case C-322/11, *K*, EU:C:2013:716, para. 51.

96 Case C-446/03, *Marks & Spencer*, EU:C:2005:763, para. 46.

97 Case C-231/05, *Oy AA*, EU:C:2007:439, paras 53-56; EFTA Court, 13 September 2017, Case E-15/16, *Yara International ASA*, [2017] EFTA Ct. Rep. 434, paras 35-36.

98 Case C-337/08, *X Holding*, EU:C:2010:89, paras 27-32.

99 Case C-123/11, *A Oy*, EU:C:2013:84, paras 41-44.

100 Case C-446/03, *Marks & Spencer*, EU:C:2005:763, paras 47-48.

101 See, e.g., Case C-123/11, *A Oy*, EU:C:2013:84, para. 44.

Third, and finally, "if the losses were not taken into account in the Member State in which the subsidiary is established there would be a risk of tax avoidance".[102] The Court accepted that "loss-trafficking", i.e., the vertical or horizontal transfer of losses to the group member in the highest-taxing Member State (where the losses are most valuable), is a relevant risk that justifies its prevention.[103] This reasoning was not only accepted in the context of group relief[104] and group contributions,[105] but also with regard to a cross-border merger in light of the risk that a reorganization could be structured in a way that the losses end up where they are most valuable.[106] Arguably, however, the risk of tax avoidance is less pronounced where the domestic rules permit a loss transfer only "upwards" to the parent company (e.g., in pooling regimes). Indeed, it was not even brought forward in cases involving losses of foreign branches.[107]

The Court in *Marks & Spencer* accepted "those three justifications, taken together",[108] but then went on to introduce the concept of "final" losses on the level of proportionality. The relevant paragraph in *Marks & Spencer* – number 55 – is certainly among the most notorious in EU tax case law history and reads as follows:

> "55 In that regard, the Court considers that the restrictive measure at issue in the main proceedings goes beyond what is necessary to attain the essential part of the objectives pursued where:
>
> – the non-resident subsidiary has exhausted the possibilities available in its State of residence of having the losses taken into account for the accounting period concerned by the claim for relief and also for previous accounting periods, if necessary by transferring those losses to a third party or by offsetting the losses against the profits made by the subsidiary in previous periods, and
> – there is no possibility for the foreign subsidiary's losses to be taken into account in its State of residence for future periods either by the subsidiary itself or by a third party, in particular where the subsidiary has been sold to that third party."

If those conditions for a "final" loss are met, the denial of cross-border loss relief would violate the freedom of establishment under Article 49 TFEU.[109] This "final loss exception" has become an overarching theme for cross-border loss relief concerning foreign subsidiaries

102 Case C-446/03, *Marks & Spencer*, EU:C:2005:763, para. 43.
103 Case C-446/03, *Marks & Spencer*, EU:C:2005:763, para. 49.
104 Case C-172/13, *Commission v UK (Marks & Spencer II)*, EU:C:2015:50, para. 24.
105 EFTA Court, 13 September 2017, Case E-15/16, *Yara International ASA*, [2017] EFTA Ct. Rep. 434, para. 38.
106 Case C-123/11, *A Oy*, EU:C:2013:84, para. 45.
107 See *infra* Chapter 10.3.2.
108 Case C-446/03, *Marks & Spencer*, EU:C:2005:763, para. 51.
109 See, e.g., Case C-446/03, *Marks & Spencer*, EU:C:2005:763, para. 56; Case C-172/13, *Commission v UK (Marks & Spencer II)*, EU:C:2015:50, para. 27.

(e.g., group relief[110] and group contributions[111]) and foreign permanent establishments. It will be explored in more detail in Chapters 10.2 and 10.3.

In principle, the logical link between justification and proportionality established by the Court in *Marks & Spencer* is quite sensible. Especially the need to prevent "double dips" and tax avoidance directly connects to the Court's proportionality test and the category of "final losses": Where losses can no longer be used anywhere, "the risk of double deduction of losses no longer exists",[112] and neither does the risk that those losses are transferred to the jurisdiction where they are most valuable.[113] Corresponding to this logic, the Court has subsequently clarified that domestic tax rules may not only be justified by "three justifications, taken together",[114] but also by a combination of two of them, e.g., the need to safeguard the allocation of the power to tax between the Member States either together with the need to prevent tax avoidance[115] or together with the need to prevent the danger that the same losses will be taken into account twice.[116] Surprisingly, in *X Holding*, a case not involving "final" losses, the Court has accepted the balanced allocation as a standalone ground of justification.[117] This has raised additional doubts if the Court has essentially abandoned the "*Marks & Spencer* exception" altogether by severing the conceptual link between the grounds of justification and the finality of losses.[118] However, the Court has since upheld the full *Marks & Spencer* reasoning in, e.g., *A Oy*.[119]

A final issue relates to multi-tier structures and especially the question which group entity, e.g., the intermediate or the ultimate parent company, may be entitled to take "final" losses of sub-subsidiaries into account. That situation was already on the table in *Marks & Spencer*, where the loss-making continental European subsidiaries were held by a Netherlands holding company, which in turn was wholly owned by a UK holding company that was wholly owned by Marks & Spencer plc, a UK resident.[120] It was, however, neither asked[121] nor answered if such multi-tier structure would have any impact on the potential loss utilization at the parent level in the UK. It was only in *Holmen* that the Court had to address a situation where the loss-making subsidiary was not directly owned

110 See Case C-446/03, *Marks & Spencer*, EU:C:2005:763; Case C-172/13, *Commission v UK (Marks & Spencer II)*, EU:C:2015:50.
111 EFTA Court, 13 September 2017, Case E-15/16, *Yara International ASA*, [2017] EFTA Ct. Rep. 434; Case C-608/17, *Holmen*, EU:C:2019:511.
112 Case C-650/16, *Bevola*, EU:C:2018:424, para. 58; see also Opinion AG Kokott, 19 July 2012, Case C-123/11, *A Oy*, EU:C:2012:488, para. 48.
113 However, the justifying symmetry argument that profits and losses are "two sides of the same coin" does not directly relate to the category of "final" losses.
114 Case C-446/03, *Marks & Spencer*, EU:C:2005:763, para. 51.
115 See Case C-231/05, *Oy AA*, EU:C:2007:439, para. 60.
116 Case C-414/06, *Lidl Belgium*, EU:C:2008:278, para. 42.
117 Case C-337/08, *X Holding*, EU:C:2010:89, paras 27-33; see also Opinion AG Kokott, 19 July 2012, Case C-123/11, *A Oy*, EU:C:2012:488, para. 50.
118 See also Opinion AG Kokott, 19 July 2012, Case C-123/11, *A Oy*, EU:C:2012:488, paras 47-54.
119 See *infra* Chapter 10.2.3.
120 See the explanation of Marks & Spencer's group structure in England and Wales High Court, 2 May 2003, *Marks & Spencer Plc v Halsey (HM Inspector of Taxes)* [2003] EWHC 1945 (Ch).
121 See also UK Special Commissioners, 25 and 26 November 2002, *Marks and Spencer, Plc v. David Hasley (HM Inspector of Taxes)*, SPC00352, para. 3.

by the parent company. Focusing potential planning strategies for the optimization of the group tax rate (by choosing in which Member State the "final" losses are used), the Court held that the "final" loss exception does not apply to a sub-subsidiary unless all the intermediate companies between the parent company applying for group relief and the sub-subsidiary sustaining "final" losses are established in the same Member State.[122] Hence, if the loss-making sub-subsidiary and the intermediate subsidiary are resident in different Member States, only the Member State of the intermediate subsidiary directly owning the sub-subsidiary could be the subject of a claim for relief for the "final" losses of that sub-subsidiary (such claim would, of course, require that the Member State of the intermediate subsidiary also operates some form of group taxation).

10.2.3 *Cross-Border Loss Relief in Mergers (A Oy, Memira) and Transfers of Residence (AURES)*

Issues regarding cross-border losses can obviously also arise in cases of transnational "movements" in the broadest sense. Indeed, the Court was already concerned with loss relief in cases of cross-border mergers (A *Oy*,[123] *Memira*[124]) and a company's transfer of its place of effective management to another Member State (*AURES*[125]). Both situations involve the freedom of establishment under Article 49 TFEU.[126]

As for cross-border mergers, the obvious question is if the freedom of establishment requires that losses that were incurred by the merging (and hence dissolving) subsidiary in the source State can be "imported" to the parent's home State, where the latter State would allow such loss carry-over in domestic merger but does not grant it in cross-border situations. In *A Oy* and *Memira*, the Court basically engaged the same reasoning as in its decisions on cross-border loss relief:[127] After affirming the comparability of domestic and cross-border mergers and the consequential discriminatory restriction exercised by the parent's home State, it accepted various grounds of justification along the lines set by *Marks & Spencer*, i.e., the balanced allocation of taxing powers, the need to prevent "double dips", and the risk of tax avoidance.[128] Denial of a loss carry-over by the parent's home State would, however, not be proportionate in the case of "final losses" of the subsidiary. Such "finality" is not present, e.g., so long as that subsidiary continues to be in receipt of even minimal income[129] or where those losses could "be used by a third party, in particular after a sale for a price including the tax value of the losses".[130] Issues of a

---

122 Case C-608/17, *Holmen*, EU:C:2019:511, paras 26-32.
123 Case C-123/11, *A Oy*, EU:C:2013:84.
124 Case C-607/17, *Memira*, EU:C:2019:510.
125 Case C-405/18, *AURES Holdings*, EU:C:2020:127.
126 Case C-123/11, *A Oy*, EU:C:2013:84, paras 21-28; Case C-405/18, *AURES Holdings*, EU:C:2020:127, paras 23-28.
127 For analysis, see, e.g., Harm van den Broek, *Final Losses in Respect of Cross-Border Mergers:* Memira *(Case C-607/17) and* Holmen *(Case C-608/17)*, 60 European Taxation 53-61 (2020).
128 See *supra* Chapter 10.2.3.
129 Case C-123/11, *A Oy*, EU:C:2013:84, paras. 53-54; see also Case C-172/13, *Commission v UK (Marks & Spencer II)*, EU:C:2015:50, para. 36; Case C-388/14, *Timac Agro*, EU:C:2015:829, para. 55.
130 Case C-607/17, *Memira*, EU:C:2019:510, para. 30-31.

loss carry-over in cross-border mergers therefore seem to fall in the overarching theme of "final" losses, which will be explored in detail in Chapter 10.2.4.

All cases discussed so far have an implicit common aspect: There was at least a *temporal* connection between the home State and the losses incurred in the source State, i.e., the parent company in the home State was connected to the foreign subsidiary or branch during the loss-making times, and, if there were no border between them, the losses could have *currently* been used in the home State. What then, one may ask, if there is neither a *territorial* nor a *temporal* connection between losses and a Member State? This issue was raised in *AURES*,[131] where a Netherlands' company, which had incurred losses in the Netherlands, had transferred its tax residence to the Czech Republic and wished to "import" its Netherlands' losses to its new residence State. Unsurprisingly, the Czech authorities declined such loss carry-over, and eventually the question was raised whether the freedom of establishment requires the Czech Republic to accept the claim of a tax loss incurred in another Member State *before* relocation. The Court in *AURES* appreciated a difference in treatment, but upheld the Czech Republic's denial of the claim on various grounds, essentially (and correctly) because of a lack of comparability in light of the objective of preserving the allocation of taxing powers and preventing "double dips":

> "[W]here the host Member State has no tax jurisdiction over the tax year during which the loss at issue arose, the situation of a company, which has transferred its tax residency to that Member State and subsequently claims a loss there previously incurred in another Member State, is not comparable to that of a company the turnover of which was subject to the tax powers of the previous Member State on the basis of the tax year during which that company incurred that loss [...]."[132]

In light of this non-comparability, it was thus not decisive whether or not the losses incurred in the Netherlands were "final". Quite correctly, the Court distinguished *AURES* from its *Marks & Spencer* line of case law by noting that the latter is characterised "by the fact that, during the same tax year, the company which seeks to deduct a loss of its non-resident permanent establishment from its tax base and that permanent establishment are situated in two different Member States". Hence, there is no "free movement" of ("final") losses in the EU. This result chimes with the Court's more recent case law on exit taxation following *National Grid Indus*,[133] which "shows that a company's profits generated prior to an exit (and also, in accordance with the principle of symmetry, the company's losses) fall within the competence of the exit State (here: the Netherlands) and not of the host State (here the Czech Republic)".[134]

131 Case C-405/18, *AURES Holdings*, EU:C:2020:127. For analysis see, e.g., Markus Mittendorfer and Mario Riedl, *The Comparability Analysis of the Court of Justice of the European Union in the Light of the* Aures *Case*, 30 EC Tax Review 166-176 (2021); Eva M. Goetz, AURES Holdings a.s. *(C-405/18) at the Intersection of Cross-Border Loss Relief, Corporate Exit Taxation and Dual Residency Mismatches*, 49 Intertax 166-185 (2021).

132 Case C-405/18, *AURES Holdings*, EU:C:2020:127, para. 42.

133 Case C-371/10, *National Grid Indus*, EU:C:2011:785; Case C-657/13, *Verder LabTec*, EU:C:2015:331; Case C-164/12, *DMC*, EU:C:2014:20. For detailed analysis see *supra* Chapter 12.

134 See Opinion AG Kokott, 17 October 2019, Case C-405/18, *AURES Holdings*, EU:C:2019:879, paras 72-74, and agreeing Case C-405/18, *AURES Holdings*, EU:C:2020:127, paras 50-52.

10.2.4 The "Finality" of Losses

After *Marks & Spencer*, the "elephant in the room" was and is the meaning and scope of "final" losses. As pointed out before, this is the decisive concept not only for cross-border loss relief within corporate groups[135] and in cross-border mergers,[136] but also for losses of foreign permanent establishments.[137] Over the years that concept has been explained and operationalized by the Court,[138] but the precise scope is (still) ambiguous,[139] intensely debated[140] and awaiting further clarification;[141] it is not even clear that the concept has the same meaning in all situations.[142] In that regard, *Marks & Spencer* has not "brought about *quieta*, as it has consistently remained unclear with regard to its effects",[143] and frequent calls for its extremely restrictive application[144] or even complete abandonment[145] are made.

That said, at least the following characterizing criteria for a "final" loss can be derived from the Court's case law since *Marks & Spencer*:[146]

First, "losses sustained by a non-resident subsidiary cannot be characterised as definitive [...] by dint of the fact that the Member State in which the subsidiary is resident precludes all possibility of losses being carried forward".[147] More generally, in cases of mere *legal* restrictions to loss-utilization in the subsidiary's State ("legal finality", such as, e.g., lack

135 See, e.g., Case C-172/13, *Commission v UK (Marks & Spencer II)*, EU:C:2015:50; EFTA Court, 13 September 2017, Case E-15/16, *Yara International ASA*, [2017] EFTA Ct. Rep. 434, paras 40-46; Case C-608/17, *Holmen*, EU:C:2019:511; EFTA Court, 24 May 2024, Case E-7/23, *ExxonMobil*.

136 Case C-123/11, *A Oy*, EU:C:2013:84; Case C-607/17, *Memira*, EU:C:2019:510.

137 See on that and the question of comparability *infra* Chapter 10.3.

138 Most notably in Case C-123/11, *A Oy*, EU:C:2013:84, paras 49-55; Case C-322/11, *K*, EU:C:2013:716, para. 74-82; Case C-172/13, *Commission v UK (Marks & Spencer II)*, EU:C:2015:50; Case C-608/17, *Holmen*, EU:C:2019:511; see also EFTA Court, 24 May 2024, Case E-7/23, *ExxonMobil*.

139 See, in this regard, Opinion AG Geelhoed, 23 February 2006, Case C-374/04, *ACT Group Litigation*, EU:C:2006:139, para. 65; Opinion AG Kokott, 19 July 2012, Case C-123/11, *A Oy*, EU:C:2012:488, paras 47-54; Opinion AG Kokott, 23 October 2014, Case C-172/13, *Commission v UK (Marks & Spencer II)*, EU:C:2014:2321, paras 42-53; Opinion AG Mengozzi, 21 March 2013, Case C-322/11, *K*, EU:C:2013:183, paras 63-89.

140 See the references *supra* in footnote 64.

141 See, e.g., the questions raised by the German Bundesfinanzhof, 6 November 2019, I R 32/18, pending before the Court as Case C-538/20, *W*.

142 See Erik Pinetz & Karoline Spies, *'Final Losses' after the Decision in Commission v. UK ('Marks & Spencer II')*, 24 EC Tax Review 309 (314-318) (2015).

143 Opinion AG Kokott, 23 October 2014, Case C-172/13, *Commission v UK (Marks & Spencer II)*, EU:C:2014:2321, para. 42.

144 See Opinion AG Geelhoed, 23 February 2006, Case C-374/04, *ACT Group Litigation*, EU:C:2006:139, para. 65, pointing out that the "final loss exception" "has introduced an additional disparity in the interrelation between national tax systems, thereby further distorting the exercise of the freedom of establishment and free movement of capital within the Community".

145 See for that call the Opinion AG Kokott, 23 October 2014, Case C-172/13, *Commission v UK (Marks & Spencer II)*, EU:C:2014:2321, paras 42-53, which would, however, imply that the home State would not be required to take into account even foreign "final" losses.

146 For further details with regard to permanent establishments see *infra* Chapters 10.3.2. and 10.3.3.

147 Case C-172/13, *Commission v UK (Marks & Spencer II)*, EU:C:2015:50, para. 33; Case C-322/11, *K*, EU:C:2013:716, paras. 75-79; see also Case C-388/14, *Timac Agro*, EU:C:2015:829, para. 54; Case C-608/17, *Holmen*, EU:C:2019:511, para. 44.

or expiration of a loss carry-forward or carry-backward, anti-abuse provisions, legal non-transferability etc) "the Member State in which the parent company is resident may not allow cross-border group relief without thereby infringing Article 49 TFEU".[148] Although such losses cannot be used anywhere in the Internal Market (so that, e.g., no risk of a "double dip" exists), the Court attempts to strike a balance between the needs of the Internal Market and the existence of non-harmonized tax systems: The freedoms do not require that one Member State adjusts its legislation to the "particularities of legislation of another Member State" or to remove "any disparities arising from national tax rules, given that the decisions made by a taxpayer as to investment abroad may be to the taxpayer's advantage or not, according to circumstances".[149] Consequently, a "final" loss would also require a "total" loss with regard to the establishment's activities. Indeed, AG Kokott has argued that "[t]he only case where a loss remains" – and could become "final" – "despite the possibility of carrying forward or back losses without restriction would be the case of an undertaking which is loss-making on the whole and which has never made sufficient profit, even after all economic assets have been sold".[150]

Second, losses may only be considered "final" if the subsidiary no longer has any income in its Member State of residence. More concretely, "[s]o long as that subsidiary continues to be in receipt of even minimal income, there is a possibility that the losses sustained may yet be offset by future profits made in the Member State in which it is resident",[151] which may include (very small) income from assigning existing leases and capital gains made on the assets and liabilities[152] or passive loan interest from a cash pool.[153] Hence, ceasing trading or being put into liquidation alone is not sufficient in itself to satisfy the *Marks & Spencer* exception if some income is still being generated (e.g., when the company's assets are liquidated).[154] The amount of the (potential) reduction of the loss by subsequent (minimal) income in the subsidiary's residence State is not significant.[155] However, if losses cease to exist following a liquidation of the subsidiary, they may only be considered "final", if it was "impossible for those losses to be used by a third party, in

148 Case C-172/13, *Commission v UK (Marks & Spencer II)*, EU:C:2015:50, para. 33; see also EFTA Court, 24 May 2024, Case E-7/23, *ExxonMobil*, paras 29-32.

149 Case C-322/11, *K*, EU:C:2013:716, paras 79-80, referring to Case C-293/06, *Deutsche Shell*, EU:C:2008:129, paras 42-43, and Case C-157/07, *Krankenheim Ruhesitz am Wannsee*, EU:C:2008:588, paras 49-50.

150 Opinion AG Kokott, 10 January 2019, Case C-608/17, *Holmen*, EU:C:2019:9, para. 59.

151 Case C-172/13, *Commission v UK (Marks & Spencer II)*, EU:C:2015:50, para. 36; see also, e.g., Case C-123/11, *A Oy*, EU:C:2013:84, para. 53-54; Case C-388/14, *Timac Agro*, EU:C:2015:829, para. 55; EFTA Court, 24 May 2024, Case E-7/23, *ExxonMobil*, paras 25-26.

152 Case C-123/11, *A Oy*, EU:C:2013:84, para. 53.

153 See for that situation the discussion EFTA Court, 13 September 2017, Case E-15/16, *Yara International ASA*, [2017] EFTA Ct. Rep. 434, para. 44.

154 See Case C-123/11, *A Oy*, EU:C:2013:84, paras 51 and 54, EFTA Court, 24 May 2024, Case E-7/23, *ExxonMobil*, paras 25-26; see also Opinion AG Kokott, 23 October 2014, Case C-172/13, *Commission v UK (Marks & Spencer II)*, EU:C:2014:2321, para. 40.

155 EFTA Court, 24 May 2024, Case E-7/23, *ExxonMobil*, para. 35 (finding it unnecessary to answer that precise question of the referring Norwegian court). For the question whether a provisional determination of the impossibility of loss utilization or a distinction between "real" and "theoretical" possibilities is feasible, see also Opinion AG Kokott, 23 October 2014, Case C-172/13, *Commission v UK (Marks & Spencer II)*, EU:C:2014:2321, para. 45.

particular after a sale for a price including the tax value of the losses".[156] It seems, however, that the "finality" of losses might be flatly excluded in situations where the transfer of a losses to a buyer is legally excluded by the subsidiary's State.[157]

Third, losses are not "final" "if there is a possibility of deducting those losses economically by transferring them to a third party before the completion of the liquidation".[158] Such "economic" deduction would, for example, be implied if the subsidiary could be sold (instead of being liquidated) and the buyer takes "into account for tax purposes the losses of the subsidiary in that subsidiary's State of establishment, for example following a sale of that subsidiary for a price including the tax advantage represented by the deductibility of losses for the future".[159] Taken to the extreme, this would mean that even a (theoretical) possibility of a transfer of losses to a third party would exclude their "finality". The Court, however, seems to accept that "finality" is possible if such sale of losses is *legally* not permitted by the source State (and hence no one would pay for them).[160]

Fourth, the Court has accepted that the assessment of "finality" of losses, i.e., the determination that there is no possibility for the losses being taken into account, is to be made "immediately after the accounting period".[161] While this does not necessarily require that the subsidiary is (completely) wound up by then,[162] it would at least require that "immediately after the end of the accounting period in which the losses have been sustained, that subsidiary ceased trading and sold or disposed of all its income producing assets".[163] In assessing, at the end of the accounting period in which the losses were sustained, whether losses are "final", "[e]vidence of an intention to wind up a loss-making subsidiary and initiation of the liquidation process soon after the end of the accounting period would be factors to be taken into account".[164] On this view, "finality" of losses needs to be determined immediately after the period in which the losses were incurred, and not – as, e.g., the UK Supreme Court[165] and other domestic courts[166] have thought – at any later time even if it is clear by then that the loss would not be used in any period after it arose. Hence, if (immediately after the end of the accounting period) there is still some hope of using a subsidiary's losses (e.g., through future profits), no relief in the parent's

156 Case C-608/17, *Holmen*, EU:C:2019:511, paras 42-43; see also Case C-607/17, *Memira*, EU:C:2019:510, paras 30-31; EFTA Court, 24 May 2024, Case E-7/23, *ExxonMobil*, para. 27.
157 See EFTA Court, 24 May 2024, Case E-7/23, *ExxonMobil*, paras 30-31.
158 Case C-608/17, *Holmen*, EU:C:2019:511, para. 37; Case C-607/17, *Memira*, EU:C:2019:510, para. 25.
159 See Case C-608/17, *Holmen*, EU:C:2019:511, para. 38; Case C-607/17, *Memira*, EU:C:2019:510, para. 26.
160 Case C-608/17, *Holmen*, EU:C:2019:511, paras 42-43; see also Case C-607/17, *Memira*, EU:C:2019:510, paras 30-31.
161 Case C-172/13, *Commission v UK (Marks & Spencer II)*, EU:C:2015:50, paras. 34-24.
162 Case C-172/13, *Commission v UK (Marks & Spencer II)*, EU:C:2015:50, para. 35.
163 See the UK's position as restated in Case C-172/13, *Commission v UK (Marks & Spencer II)*, EU:C:2015:50, para. 37.
164 See for that understanding of UK legislation Case C-172/13, *Commission v UK (Marks & Spencer II)*, EU:C:2015:50, para. 18.
165 UK Supreme Court, 22 May 2013, *Commissioners for Her Majesty's Revenue and Customs v Marks and Spencer plc*, [2013] UKSC 30.
166 See, e.g., German Bundesfinanzhof, 9 June 2010, I R 107/09; German Bundesfinanzhof, 9 November 2010, I R 16/10.

State need be granted, even if it subsequently becomes clear that no such future profits materialised (and, e.g., the subsidiary was later liquidated). It is therefore in line with the freedom of establishment for a State "to require, in order to demonstrate that a loss is final, that a liquidation process be formally decided upon immediately after the end of the fiscal year for which a deduction is claimed".[167]

Fifth, and closely related, the Court might have further accepted that the determination of the finality of a loss should be made at the end of each year, and once a loss is not "final" then, it can never become "final" again.[168] This would essentially mean that only losses arising in the last year (and, perhaps, the one incurred in the accounting period that immediately follows[169]) can be regarded as the "final" loss, whereas losses which are regarded as non-final in one year (because they can be carried forward or setting off the losses was precluded under national law) cannot subsequently become "final". This rather narrow understanding was strongly supported by AG Juliane Kokott[170] and most recently by AG Anthony Collins,[171] arguing that regarding accumulated (carried forward) losses as "final losses" would upset the appropriate allocation of the power to impose taxes, as "the initially successful activity of the subsidiary (or of the permanent establishment) would be taxed solely in the State in which it is situated, while the subsequently loss-making activity would be financed by the tax revenue of the State of residence of the parent company".[172] Excluding "carried forward" losses from the potential to become "final", however, would certainly come as a surprise for those domestic courts that have applied the "final loss exception" to accumulated foreign losses.[173] Moreover, the "final loss exception" would clearly lose much of its practical relevance (because at

167 EFTA Court, 24 May 2024, Case E-7/23, *ExxonMobil*, paras 36-39.

168 See Case C-172/13, *Commission v UK (Marks & Spencer II)*, EU:C:2015:50, para. 37.

169 According to the UK's legislative implementation of *Marks & Spencer*, "final losses" can also exist "where, immediately after the end of the accounting period in which the losses have been sustained, that subsidiary ceased trading and sold or disposed of all its income producing assets" (see the UK's position as restated in Case C-172/13, *Commission v UK (Marks & Spencer II)*, EU:C:2015:50, para. 37). This implies that loss relief is possible not only in "respect of a single accounting period" (as the Commission had claimed) but rather for losses from *two* accounting periods, i.e., *(1)* for the losses incurred in the accounting period *before* the subsidiary ceased trading and sold or disposed of all its income producing assets, and *(2)* for the losses incurred *in* the accounting period in which the subsidiary ceased trading and sold or disposed of all its income producing assets. One might then pose the question if the losses of even more accounting periods may be eligible for relief, e.g., because disposing of assets takes more than one accounting period.

170 See Opinion AG Kokott, 10 January 2019, Case C-608/17, *Holmen*, EU:C:2019:9, paras 50-55, and Opinion AG Kokott, 10 January 2019, Case C-607/17, *Memira*, EU:C:2019:8, paras 57-60.

171 Opinion AG Collins, 10 March 2022, Case C-538/20, *W AG*, EU:C:2022:184, paras 70-71. As the Court (Case C-538/20, *W AG*, EU:C:2022:717) has found the situations of a domestic and foreign treaty-exempt permanent establishment incomparable (Chapter 10.3.2), it did not have to address this issue.

172 Opinion AG Collins, 10 March 2022, Case C-538/20, *W AG*, EU:C:2022:184, paras 70, referring to Opinion AG Kokott, 10 January 2019, Case C-608/17, *Holmen*, EU:C:2019:9, para. 54-55, Opinion AG Kokott, 10 January 2019, Case C-607/17, *Memira*, EU:C:2019:8, para. 58-59, and Opinion AG Kokott, 17 October 2019, Case C-405/18, *AURES Holdings*, EU:C:2019:879, paras 61 to 65.

173 See concerning "final" permanent establishment losses, e.g., German Bundesfinanzhof, 9 June 2010, I R 107/09 (taxable years 2000-2001), and German Bundesfinanzhof, 5 February 2014, I R 48/11 (taxable years 1997-1998).

most the loss incurred in the final taxable year would be considered "final"). It should be noted, however, that the Court has not addressed the issue in subsequent cases where accumulated losses of several years were at issue,[174] which could either imply that the Court has not intended to fully settle that question yet or that it tacitly applies a different standard of "finality" depending on the tax regime and context at issue.[175]

Sixth, and finally, the EFTA-Court in *Yara* has recalled a further limit to tax planning with regard to the artificial creation of losses' "finality" by holding that, "[i]n assessing the fulfilment of the conditions for the application of the final loss exception, the national court must equally take account of [the principle of prohibition of abuse of rights], in order to preclude arrangements designed merely to secure a tax advantage and to avoid taxation in an EEA State".[176]

All these clarifications have made the "final loss exception" so narrow that, as AG Kokott has succinctly pointed out, it is indeed "very difficult to identify any cases in which it might apply".[177] The "final loss exception" is also hard to justify conceptionally, not only because the initial link to the Court's accepted justifications based on the prevention of "double dips" and "loss shifting" has been severed over time,[178] but also because it leads to arbitrary outcomes. From an Internal Market perspective, it is too narrow as it ignores cash-flow disadvantages (and therefore treats cross-border investments less favorably), whereas from a Member States' perspective it might even be overshooting: Assume, for example, that a foreign subsidiary has a profitable phase (with the profits not taxable in the parent's home State) and turns into a loss-making phase that ends with its liquidation, and that the subsidiary's profits and losses are equal over its period of existence (i.e., the subsidiary had an "overall" profit or loss of zero). It seems that there might still be a "final" loss under *Marks & Spencer* (e.g., the liquidation loss), even though there is no "overall" ("total") loss of the foreign subsidiary, and its utilization in the parent's State might lead to better treatment of the cross-border situation than of a purely domestic situation. In the past two decades, the Court might well have realized that *Marks & Spencer*'s "final loss exception" is hard to apply in practice, conceptually vague, or even a dead-end street altogether. This would then put additional pressure on legislative solutions for cross-border loss utilization, such as the recently proposed "BEFIT" ("Business in Europe: Framework for Income Taxation").[179]

174 See, in particular, Case C-608/17, *Holmen*, EU:C:2019:511, and Case C-607/17, *Memira*, EU:C:2019:510.

175 For such a differentiated approach see Erik Pinetz & Karoline Spies, *'Final Losses' after the Decision in Commission v. UK ('Marks & Spencer II')*, 24 EC Tax Review 309 (314-318) (2015).

176 EFTA Court, 13 September 2017, Case E-15/16, *Yara International ASA*, [2017] EFTA Ct. Rep. 434, para. 50.

177 Opinion AG Kokott, 23 October 2014, Case C-172/13, *Commission v UK (Marks & Spencer II)*, EU:C:2014:2321, paras 38-41.

178 See *supra* Chapter 10.2.2.

179 Proposal for a Council Directive on Business in Europe: Framework for Income Taxation (BEFIT), COM(2023)532 (12 September 2023).

10.3 Losses of Foreign Permanent Establishments

10.3.1 Technical Background

A permanent establishment is not a separate taxpayer, but rather part of the non-resident's enterprise. Under international tax rules, therefore, the profits attributable to permanent establishments ("branches") of non-resident taxpayers are subject to so-called limited tax liability in the *source* State. Conversely, the *home* State will generally tax a taxpayer's worldwide income, including the enterprise's profits attributable to foreign permanent establishments. Double taxation is then typically prevented through a direct tax credit or exemption: The fundamental difference between those two methods is that, under the exemption method, the State that gives up the taxing right for certain income "leaves out that income in determining taxable income", while, under the credit method, the State that gives the relief "allows a deduction of tax relevant to the income that is taxed in the other State",[180] i.e. "the exemption method looks at income, while the credit method looks at tax".[181]

This different focus becomes obvious in the case of foreign losses and their impact on the home State's tax base. While the *source* State will typically allow the non-discriminatory offset of the permanent establishment's losses against profits in past or future years (i.e., a loss carry-back and/or a carry-forward), the treatment in *home* State depends on the domestic and tax-treaty framework, which also informs the Court's decisions:[182]

Where the taxpayer's residence Member State taxes worldwide income and the relevant domestic law or the tax treaty foresees the credit method (Article 23B OECD MC), the loss incurred in the permanent establishment will automatically be taken into account when determining worldwide income. It is hence a natural consequence of the credit method that losses are taken into account in two Member States,[183] but that, conversely, this loss utilization in the home State is automatically recaptured once the permanent establishment becomes profitable (because the home State will not grant any credit relief in respect of subsequent untaxed foreign profits, and no foreign tax will be paid on the subsequent branch profits as long as previous losses in the branch State are offset against them). That said, a State may nevertheless provide a special mechanism to guarantee that this automatic recapture is not avoided, e.g., by converting the permanent establishment into a subsidiary before the former becomes profitable (at issue in *Nordea Bank Danmark*[184]).

180 FC/WP15(59), supra n. 11, Part I, p. 5-6.

181 Art. 23 no. 17 OECD MC Comm. (2017).

182 For recent and detailed analyses on the Court's case law on losses of foreign permanent establishments see, e.g., CFE ECJ Task Force, *Opinion Statement ECJ-TF 3/2018 on the ECJ Decision of 12 June 2018 in* Bevola *(Case C-650/16), Concerning the Utilization of "Definitive Losses" Attributable to a Foreign Permanent Establishment*, 59 European Taxation 113-119 (2019); Roland Ismer & Harald Kandel, *A Finale* Incomparabile *to the Saga of Definitive Losses? Deduction of Foreign Losses and Fundamental Freedoms After* Bevola *and* Sofina, 47 *Intertax* 573-589 (2019).

183 In the permanent establishment's State through, e.g., a loss carry-forward, and in the taxpayer's residence State as part of worldwide income.

184 Case C-48/13, *Nordea Bank Danmark*, EU:C:2014:2087.

The treatment of foreign losses under the exemption method, either under a territorial system under domestic law or based on a tax treaty (Article 23A OECD MC) depends on the concrete application of the exemption method.[185] Some States apply the exemption "symmetrically" to profits and losses and hence exempt losses as "negative profits",[186] i.e., a foreign loss is never included in the taxable base in the home State; this can either be based on a so-called "base exemption" under a tax treaty (at issue in *Lidl Belgium*,[187] *Timac Agro*,[188] and *W AG*,[189] as well as in *K*[190] for the sale of real estate by an individual taxpayer) or on domestic law (at issue in *Bevola*[191]). This method not only disregards a "total loss" of the foreign permanent establishment, but also deprives cross-border situations of the cash flow advantage of netting *current* profits (of the head office) with *current* losses (of the permanent establishment) on the level of the tax base. In such a system, foreign losses would (at most)[192] have an impact with regard to the calculation of the tax *rate* on the non-exempt income in the home State (so-called "negative" progressivity).[193] Other States apply the treaty exemption method only *after* a worldwide tax base has been calculated ("tax exemption"), so that foreign profits are exempt but – asymmetrically – foreign losses reduce the *current* tax base in the home State (rather than being treated as "exempt" negative income).[194] Conversely, subsequent profits of the permanent establishment will be "reinstated" in the home State until the loss previously deducted has been recaptured (at issue in *Krankenheim Ruhesitz am Wannsee*,[195] and *Timac Agro*[196]). This so-called "deduction/reincorporation method" can take various forms: Just as in the Commission's

---

185 See also, e.g., Art 23 no. 44 OECD MC Comm. (2017).

186 See for such long-standing "symmetry theory" ("Symmetriethese") in German case law, e.g., German Reichsfinanzhof, 26 June 1935, VI A 414/35; German Bundesfinanzhof, 28 March 1973, I R 59/71; German Bundesfinanzhof, 29 November 2006, I R 45/05; German Bundesfinanzhof, 11 March 2008, I R 116/04. Until 2001, this position was also held by Austrian case law; see, e.g., Austrian Verwaltungsgerichtshof, 6 March 1984, 83/14/0107; Austrian Verwaltungsgerichtshof, 21 May 1985, 85/14/0001.

187 Case C-414/06, *Lidl Belgium*, EU:C:2008:278.

188 Case C-388/14, *Timac Agro*, EU:C:2015:829.

189 Case C-538/20, *W AG*, EU:C:2022:717.

190 Case C-322/11, *K*, EU:C:2013:716, paras 44-45.

191 Case C-650/16, *Bevola*, EU:C:2018:424.

192 It might be noted that the Court obviously reads tax treaty provisions similar to Article 23A(3) OECD MC as implying not only "positive", but also "negative" progressivity; see Case C-322/11, *K*, EU:C:2013:716, paras 44-45.

193 I.e., the negative foreign income is taken into account to determine the tax rate ("bracket") on worldwide income, which is then applied to the non-exempt income. However, this "negative progressivity" would only have an effect if either the home State's rate structure progressive (which is often not the case for the corporate income tax, which typically has a proportionate rate) or if the foreign losses exceed the non-exempt income. See for progressivity clauses in tax treaties, e.g., F. Pötgens, "Article 23" in: *Global Tax Treaty Commentaries (GTTC)* (IBFD Amsterdam, Feb. 2020), Chapter 2.11.3.3.; A. Rust in E. Reimer and A. Rust (eds.), *Klaus Vogel on Double Taxation Conventions*, 5th edn. (Kluwer, 2022), Art. 23 m.no. 91, with further references.

194 See, e.g., the Austrian Verwaltungsgerichtshof, 25 September 2001, 99/14/0217, and, implementing this case law, the explicit provision in § 2(8) of the Austrian Income Tax Act. For the same perspective in case law in Luxembourg, the Netherlands, France, and Spain, as well as for sporadic tax treaty provisions to that effect see A. Rust in E. Reimer and A. Rust (eds.), *Klaus Vogel on Double Taxation Conventions*, 5th edn. (Kluwer, 2022), Art. 23 m.no. 24.

195 Case C-157/07, *Krankenheim Ruhesitz am Wannsee*, EU:C:2008:588.

196 Case C-388/14, *Timac Agro*, EU:C:2015:829.

1990 Proposal, the focus may be (merely) on temporary loss relief. In that case, the home State would take into account foreign losses and reinstate them when the permanent establishment can offset its losses against its own subsequent profits in the source State. The focus on a merely temporal relief would also imply, just as in the Commission's 1990 Proposal, that an automatic reinstatement takes place for certain non-temporary losses, irrespective of whether sufficient branch profits were generated (e.g., after a certain number of years or if the permanent establishment is sold or converted into a subsidiary, such as in *Timac Agro*). However, the "deduction/ reincorporation method" could also address both temporary and non-temporary loss situations (without an automatic reinstatement of losses), which would effectively provide for relief also in respect of a *total* loss of the foreign branch.[197]

It is noteworthy for the following discussion that many of the leading CJEU cases on losses of foreign permanent establishments dealt with the German system: *Lidl Belgium*,[198] *Krankenheim Ruhesitz am Wannsee*,[199] *Timac Agro*,[200] and *W AG*[201] all concerned the German interpretation of the treaty-exemption method: Since tax treaties themselves are generally "silent" on how the exemption method should apply to losses,[202] this remains a question for domestic law or of treaty interpretation. Germany, for example, used the "deduction/ reincorporation method" based on domestic law from 1969 until 1998,[203] but reverted to the "symmetry theory" based on its traditional judicial interpretation of the exemption method in tax treaties[204] from 1999 onwards.[205] Both periods have been scrutinized by the CJEU: *Lidl Belgium* and *W AG* dealt with Germany's treaty-based "symmetric

197 Opinion AG Kokott, 23 October 2014, Case C-172/13, *Commission v UK (Marks & Spencer II)*, EU:C:2014:2321, para. 49.

198 Case C-414/06, *Lidl Belgium*, EU:C:2008:278.

199 Case C-157/07, *Krankenheim Ruhesitz am Wannsee*, EU:C:2008:588.

200 Case C-388/14, *Timac Agro*, EU:C:2015:829.

201 Case C-538/20, *W AG*, EU:C:2022:717.

202 And so is Art 23 no. 44 OECD MC Comm. (2017).

203 Introduced in §(2) 2 of the "Gesetz über steuerliche Maßnahmen bei Auslandsinvestitionen der deutschen Wirtschaft", German Federal Gazette (BGBl) I 1969, p. 1214, as a measure to mitigate the traditional German judicial interpretation that treaty-exempt losses are not taken into account on the level of the tax base (see for this background also German Bundesfinanzhof, 5 June 1986, IV R 268/82, BFHE 146, 447, BStBl II 1986, 659), and later transferred to § 2a(3) of the German Income Tax Act.

204 See for such long-standing "symmetry theory" ("Symmetriethese") in German case law, e.g., German Reichsfinanzhof, 26 June 1935, VI A 414/35; German Bundesfinanzhof, 28 April 1983 IV R 122/79, BFHE 138, 366, BStBl II 1983, 566; German Bundesfinanzhof, 28 March 1973, I R 59/71; German Bundesfinanzhof, 29 November 2006, I R 45/05; German Bundesfinanzhof, 11 March 2008, I R 116/04. It might be noted that, until 2001, this position was also held by Austrian case law; see, e.g., Austrian Verwaltungsgerichtshof, 6 March 1984, 83/14/0107; Austrian Verwaltungsgerichtshof, 21 May 1985, 85/14/0001.

205 This legislative change (i.e., the deletion of former § 2a(3) of the German Income Tax Act by the "Steuerentlastungsgesetz 1999/2000/2002", German Federal Gazette I 1999, 402) was motivated by three reasons: That the deduction/reincorporation method was "contrary to the system" (of symmetrically exempting profits and losses), that it was difficult to handle for the tax administration, and that consideration of foreign losses through "negative progressivity" was a sufficient consideration of foreign losses (see the legislative materials Bundestag-Drucksache 14/23, 167 [9 November 1998]).

exemption", *Krankenheim Ruhesitz am Wannsee*[206] with the "deduction/reincorporation method", and *Timac Agro*[207] with both, i.e., periods before and after 1999. It is also clear from the Court's case law that it accepts a State's treaty interpretation (e.g., the German "symmetry theory" with regard to the symmetrical exemption of foreign positive and negative income) without engaging in such interpretation itself.[208]

10.3.2 Symmetrical Base Exemption (Lidl Belgium, Timac Agro, Bevola, W AG)

The Court's first decision on foreign branch losses, *Lidl Belgium*,[209] dealt with Germany's symmetrical base exemption of profits and losses of a Luxembourg branch. Lidl Belgium, a German (and not a Belgian) partnership, had a loss-making permanent establishment in Luxembourg and asked for *current* relief of those losses against its German profits (in 1999), which was denied based on an understanding of the treaty exemption method as a "symmetrical" base exemption (since 1999). As Germany, of course, did *not* exclude losses of *domestic* business activities from its tax base, the question of a potential infringement of the freedom of establishment was brought to the Court. From an EU law perspective, the Court in *Lidl Belgium* equated a permanent establishment with an "autonomous entity"[210] and decided the case along the path charted by *Marks & Spencer*.[211] It qualified the current loss relief as a tax advantage,[212] which was not available because of the cross-border situation of the Luxembourg branch, and nearly automatically concluded that the treatment "is less favorable than it would be if the latter were to be established in Germany".[213] This implicitly reaffirms the principle that comparability needs to be assessed having regard to the aim pursued by the national provision.[214] Given the Court's line of argumentation, *Lidl Belgium* was generally understood as an extension of *Marks & Spencer* to treaty-exempt permanent establishments within the EU, hence requiring that the *home* State takes into account "final losses". For example, the German Bundesfinanzhof had accepted that *Lidl Belgium* required that a "final loss" of a treaty-exempt permanent

206 Case C-157/07, *Krankenheim Ruhesitz am Wannsee*, EU:C:2008:588.

207 Case C-388/14, *Timac Agro*, EU:C:2015:829.

208 Case C-538/20, *W AG*, EU:C:2022:717, para. 10.

209 Case C-414/06, *Lidl Belgium*, EU:C:2008:278.

210 Case C-414/06, *Lidl Belgium*, EU:C:2008:278, paras 21-22.

211 Indeed, conceptually, the denial of cross-border group relief or group contributions and the exemption of a permanent establishment's losses raise the same issues, since the main difference between those cases was merely that, e.g., in *Marks & Spencer* the entire foreign legal entity was outside the UK taxing jurisdiction, whereas in *Lidl Belgium* only foreign branch income was outside the German taxing jurisdiction.

212 Case C-414/06, *Lidl Belgium*, EU:C:2008:278, para. 23; Case C-650/16, *Bevola*, EU:C:2018:424, para. 18.

213 Case C-414/06, *Lidl Belgium*, EU:C:2008:278, para. 25.

214 Case C-650/16, *Bevola*, EU:C:2018:424, para. 32; see also, e.g., Case C-337/08, *X Holding*, EU:C:2010:89, para. 22; Cases C-39/13 to C-41/13, *SCA Group Holding*, EU:C:2014:1758, para. 28.

establishment must be taken into account in the German head office,[215] and this view was also broadly adopted in legal scholarship.[216]

It hence had no bearing on the Court's discrimination analysis in *Lidl Belgium* that Germany's tax system was, from an international tax perspective, a consistent, entirely neutral territorial system, as it neither taxed the profits of the Luxembourg branch nor took its losses into account. Many have therefore argued that such a symmetrical, territorial system does not even entail any discrimination or urged the Court to reconsider its traditional approach to comparability in such cases.[217] Indeed, in *Nordea Bank Danmark* and specifically in *Timac Agro*[218] the Court seems to have wavered with respect to comparability of taxed domestic ("resident") and exempt foreign ("non-resident") permanent establishments. It noted that "companies which have a permanent establishment in another Member State are not, in principle, in a comparable situation to that of companies possessing a resident permanent establishment" with respect to measures concerned with the prevention of double taxation,[219] and followed in *Timac Agro* on the post-1999 German "symmetry theory" with a seemingly absolute statement regarding the non-discriminatory nature of Germany's treaty-based exemption:

> "In the present case, it must be held that, since the Federal Republic of Germany does not exercise any tax powers over the profits of such a permanent establishment, the deduction of its losses no longer being permitted in Germany, the situation of a permanent establishment situated in Austria is not comparable to that of a permanent establishment situated in Germany in relation to measures laid down by the Federal Republic of Germany in order to prevent or mitigate the double taxation of a resident company's profits [...].[220]

This statement of the Court in *Timac Agro* was broadly understood as a departure from the comparability standard under *Lidl Belgium*,[221] rejecting the existence of an unequal treatment and therefore not only the need for justification but also the obligation of the home State to take into account even "final" losses on the level of proportionality. Others

215 See, e.g., German Bundesfinanzhof, 17 July 2008, I R 84/04, BFHE 222, 398, BStBl II 2009, 630; German Bundesfinanzhof, 9. June 2010, I R 107/09, BFHE 230, 35; German Bundesfinanzhof, 5 February 2014, I R 48/11, BFHE 244, 371; German Bundesfinanzhof, 22. September 2015, I B 83/14, BFH/NV 2016, 375.

216 For a detailed analysis and further references see, e.g., Daniela Hohenwarter, *Verlustverwertung im Konzern* (Vienna, LexisNexis, 2009); Axel Cordewener, *Cross-Border Loss Compensation and EU Fundamental Freedoms: The 'Final Losses' Doctrine Is Still Alive!*, 27 EC Tax Review 230-236 (2018).

217 See Opinion AG Kokott, 19 July 2012, Case C-123/11, *A Oy*, EU:C:2012:488, para. 50; Opinion AG Mengozzi, 21 March 2013, Case C-322/11, *K*, EU:C:2013:183, para. 88; Opinion AG Kokott, 13 March 2014, Case C-48/13, *Nordea Bank Danmark*, EU:C:2014:153, para. 21-28; Opinion AG Kokott, 23 October 2014, Case C-172/13, *Commission v UK (Marks & Spencer II)*, EU:C:2014:2321, paras 49-53.

218 Case C-388/14, *Timac Agro*, EU:C:2015:829.

219 Case C-48/13, *Nordea Bank Danmark*, EU:C:2014:2087, para. 24; Case C-388/14, *Timac Agro*, EU:C:2015:829, para. 27; Case C-650/16, *Bevola*, EU:C:2018:424, para. 37.

220 Case C-388/14, *Timac Agro*, EU:C:2015:829, para. 65.

221 See the submissions by Denmark, Germany, Austria and the Commission in *Bevola* (Case C-650/16, *Bevola*, EU:C:2018:424, paras. 30-31), and for such reading of *Timac Agro* by several national supreme courts in Europe, e.g., German Bundesfinanzhof, 22 February 2017, IR 2/15, and Austrian Verwaltungsgerichtsof, 29. March 2017, Ro 2015/15/0004. See also, e.g., Opinion AG Kokott, 23 October 2014, Case C-172/13, *Commission v UK (Marks & Spencer II)*, EU:C:2014:2321, para. 26.

have, however, pointed out that the Court's statement should be understood in light of the fact that *Timac Agro* did not concern "final" losses at all.[222] This confusion was (seemingly) addressed by the Court's Grand Chamber in 2018 in *Bevola*, where foreign losses could be taken into account based on the tax-treaty credit method but were "exempt" under domestic law. The Grand Chamber attempted to clarify that it had not abandoned its approach to comparability of domestic and foreign situations[223] and to reconcile its decisions in *Nordea Bank* and *Timac Agro* with its previous case law, by resorting to link the question of comparability to the existence of "final" losses (and thereby establishing a difference in comparability between "current" and "final" losses, and blurring the line between comparability and proportionality as regards the latter):[224]

> "[A]s regards losses attributable to a non-resident permanent establishment which has ceased activity and whose losses could not, and no longer can, be deducted from its taxable profits in the Member State in which it carried on its activity, the situation of a resident company possessing such an establishment is not different from that of a resident company possessing a resident permanent establishment, from the point of view of the objective of preventing double deduction of the losses."[225]

This question of comparability between domestic and cross-border situations, which was at the core of *Timac Agro* and *Bevola*, is this metaphorical second "elephant in the room": Some have argued that after *Bevola* – and in line with *Lidl Belgium* – comparability with taxable domestic situations must be taken to exist (at least where losses are somewhat "final") even if a tax system symmetrically "exempts" foreign profits and losses.[226] Others, however, have tried to reconcile the different outcomes in the Court's case law by distinguishing between base exemption under domestic law (*Bevola*) and under a tax treaty (*Timac Agro*),[227] and that in the latter situation domestic and cross-border situations would not be comparable at all. It was only in 2022 that the Court in *W AG* has resolved this issue by finding that a treaty-exempt permanent establishment is not in a comparable situation (so that not even "final losses" need to be taken into account

222 As indeed argued by AG Campos Sánchez-Bordona in his Opinion, 17 January 2018, Case C-650/16, *Bevola*, EU:C:2018:424, EU:C:2018:15, para. 57, and also pointed out by in the Opinion AG Wathelet, 3 September 2015, Case C-388/14, *Timac Agro*, EU:C:2015:533, para. 67.

223 Case C-650/16, *Bevola*, EU:C:2018:424, para. 33.

224 Case C-650/16, *Bevola*, EU:C:2018:424, para. 38; see also Case C-28/17, *NN*, EU:C:2018:526, para. 35.

225 Case C-650/16, *Bevola*, EU:C:2018:424, para. 38.

226 See for that general conclusion for all cases concerning the lack of symmetry between taxation of profits and use of losses also Opinion AG Kokott, 10 January 2019, Case C-608/17, *Holmen*, EU:C:2019:9, para. 39, and Opinion AG Kokott, 10 January 2019, Case C-607/17, *Memira Holding*, EU:C:2019:8, para. 47.

227 See Roland Ismer & Harald Kandel, *A Finale* Incomparabile *to the Saga of Definitive Losses? Deduction of Foreign Losses and Fundamental Freedoms After* Bevola *and* Sofina, 47 *Intertax* 573 (581-584) (2019), who indeed assume that comparability would not exist in the case of an exemption under a tax treaty.

by the home State).[228] Methodologically, *W AG* concerns the same German treaty-based base exemption of foreign permanent establishments at issue already in *Lidl Belgium* and *Timac Agro*. Faced with the uncertainty after the Court's recent case law, the referring German Bundesfinanzhof inquired, *inter alia*, if "final losses" of treaty-exempt foreign branches (in the UK in 2004-2007) need to be taken into account in the home State (in Germany).[229] Largely following along the lines set by AG Collins,[230] the Fourth Chamber in *W AG* indeed found that domestic and treaty-exempt foreign permanent establishments are treated differently, but that they are not in an objectively comparable situation to begin with (so that not even a restriction on the freedom of establishment guaranteed by Articles 49 and 54 TFEU could be established, let alone the need to justify it or take into account "final losses" on the level of proportionality). Four steps of reasoning in *W AG* are decisive: First, "comparability of an internal situation with a cross-border situation must be examined having regard to the aim pursued by the national provisions at issue".[231] Under that standard, taxed domestic and exempt foreign branches are, in principle, not comparable: Citing *Bevola*,[232] the Court found that with regard to "measures laid down by a Member State in order to prevent or mitigate the double taxation of a resident company's profits, companies which have a permanent establishment in another Member State are not, in principle, in a comparable situation to that of companies possessing a resident permanent establishment".[233]

Second, however, they may become comparable based on domestic or treaty rules: Referring to *Nordea Bank Danmark*[234] (concerning the Danish credit method, both under treaty and domestic law) and *Timac Agro*[235] (concerning the pre-1999 German "deduction/ reincorporation method"), the Court held that "[t]he situation is different where national tax legislation itself treats those two categories of establishment in the same way for the purposes of taking into account the losses and profits made by them".[236]

---

228 Case C-538/20, *W AG*, EU:C:2022:717. For detailed discussions of *W AG* and its implications see, with further references, e.g., CFE ECJ Task Force, *Opinion Statement ECJ-TF 4/2022 on the CJEU decision of 22 September 2022 in Case C-538/20,* W AG, *on the deductibility of foreign final losses*, 63 European Taxation 105-110 (2023); Georg Kofler, *Cross-border losses and* W AG*: The beginning of the end of the "final loss exception"?*, 2 Cahiers de fiscalité luxembourgeoise et européenne 73-97 (2023); Rita Szudoczky, *Foreign Permanent Establishment Losses Under the Fundamental Freedoms: Does W AG Bring an End to a Rollercoaster Ride?*, 51 Intertax 432-443 (2023); Savvas Kostikidis and Florian Striefler, *Cross-Border Loss Relief in the European Union Following* W AG *(Case C-538/20)*, 64 European Taxation 210-218 (2024). For a discussion of the Opinion of AG Collins see Georg Kofler, *Should We Cut "Final" Losses?*, 31 EC Tax Review 108-114 (2022), and for analysis of the German Bundesfinanzhof's follow-up decisions see Georg Kofler, *Curia Locuta, Causa Finita*: Some Further Conclusions from *W AG*, 32 EC Tax Review 190-194 (2023).

229 See German Bundesfinanzhof, 6 November 2019, I R 32/18, BFHE 269, 205, BStBl II 2021, 68.

230 Opinion AG Collins, 10 March 2022, Case C-538/20, *W AG*, EU:C:2022:184, paras 21-50.

231 Case C-538/20, *W AG*, EU:C:2022:717, para. 19, referring to Case C-650/16, *Bevola*, EU:C:2018:424, para. 32; see also, e.g., Case C-337/08, *X Holding*, EU:C:2010:89, para. 22.

232 Case C-650/16, *Bevola*, EU:C:2018:424, para. 37.

233 Case C-538/20, *W AG*, EU:C:2022:717, para. 20.

234 Case C-48/13, *Nordea Bank Danmark A*, EU:C:2014:2087, para. 24.

235 Case C-388/14, *Timac Agro*, EU:C:2015:829, para. 28.

236 Case C-538/20, *W AG*, EU:C:2022:717, para. 21.

Third, the Court again refers to *Timac Agro*[237] (this time concerning the post-1999 German "symmetry theory") and addresses the question of an exemption based on a tax treaty:

> "However, where the Member State in which a company is resident has waived, pursuant to a double taxation convention, the exercise of its power to tax the profits of the non-resident permanent establishment of that company, situated in another Member State, the situation of a resident company possessing such a permanent establishment is not comparable to that of a resident company possessing a resident permanent establishment in the light of the measures taken by the first Member State in order to prevent or mitigate the double taxation of profits and, symmetrically, the double deduction of resident companies' losses".[238]

As Germany has "waived its power to tax the profits made and losses incurred" by a foreign permanent establishment "under a double taxation convention",

> "a resident company which has such an establishment is not in a situation comparable to that of a resident company which has a permanent establishment situated in Germany in the light of the objective of preventing or mitigating the double taxation of profits and, symmetrically, the double taking into account of losses".[239]

Fourth, the Court had to address the obvious tension between its comparability analysis in *W AG* and the Grand Chamber decision in *Bevola*, where the Court had accepted comparability (at least regarding "final" losses) in a situation where Denmark could have taxed foreign branches under the tax treaty[240] but exempted under domestic law. Here, the Court drew a (unfortunate and largely unmotivated) distinction between exemption under domestic law and exemption under tax treaty law: "It is true", the Court stated, that in *Bevola*

> "the Court held, as regards losses attributable to a non-resident permanent establishment which had ceased activity and whose losses could not, and no longer could have been deducted from its taxable profits in the Member State in which it carried on its activity, that the situation of a resident company possessing such an establishment did not differ from that of a resident company possessing a resident permanent establishment, from the point of view of the objective of preventing double deduction of the losses. It added that the ability to pay tax of a company possessing a non-resident permanent establishment which has definitively incurred losses is affected in the same way as that of a company whose resident permanent establishment has incurred losses, with the result that the two situations are comparable in that regard.[241] [...] However, in that case, the Member State of residence of the company which requested that the final losses incurred by its non-resident permanent establishment be taken into account had not, by means of a double taxation convention, waived its power to tax that establishment's profits. It had decided unilaterally, except in the event of the option, by the company in question, for an international joint taxation scheme, not to take into account the profits made and losses

237 Case C-388/14, *Timac Agro*, EU:C:2015:829, para. 65.
238 Case C-538/20, *W AG*, EU:C:2022:717, para. 22.
239 Case C-538/20, *W AG*, EU:C:2022:717, para. 27.
240 I.e., under the credit method in the Nordic Convention.
241 Case C-538/20, *W AG*, EU:C:2022:717, para. 24, referring to Case C-650/16, *Bevola*, EU:C:2018:424, paras 38 and 39.

> incurred by non-resident permanent establishments of resident companies, even though that Member State would have been competent to do so, which is different."[242]

After *W AG*, comparability seems to depend on the legal basis for the exemption: The comparability analysis in *Bevola* is confirmed for unilateral exemption (where the applicable tax treaty would permit taxation based on the credit method), whereas *Timac Agro* and its finding of non-comparability is confirmed for treaty-based exemption (where domestic law would otherwise tax the income based on the principle of worldwide taxation).[243] However, the "final loss doctrine" has not been fully abandoned in the context of foreign permanent establishments, as the Court has approvingly referred to its previous decisions where comparability was indeed established by the Member State's applicable legal framework, i.e., the credit method (*Nordea Bank Danmark*) or the asymmetrical "deduction/reincorporation method" (*Timac Agro*). Expanding on *Bevola*, one might also assume that comparability – at least with regard to "final losses"[244] – is not excluded if no tax treaty is applicable at all.

That said, *W AG*, which has in the meantime been followed by German domestic case law,[245] raises a host of issues and inconsistencies. A few might be mentioned:

- The Court in *Bevola* has linked comparability to a (cross-border) ability-to-pay principle, noting that base exemption aims at ensuring taxation in line with the taxpayer's ability to pay, which requires the prevention of both double taxation and a double deduction of losses, but that a taxpayer is "affected in the same way" whether its domestic establishment has incurred losses or a foreign permanent establishment

242 Case C-538/20, *W AG*, EU:C:2022:717, para. 25.

243 The underlying reasoning for that rather arbitrary sovereignty-based distinction between domestic and treaty-based exemption may be found in AG Collins' Opinion, who – referring to AG Wathelet's Opinion in *Timac Agro* (Opinion AG Wathelet, 3 September 2015, Case C-388/14, *Timac Agro*, EU:C:2015:533, paras 31 and 32) – related comparability to the question "of whether or not the Member State [...] of residence of the principal company seeking to deduct the losses of its permanent establishment established in another Member State [...] has taxation powers over the income at issue" (Opinion AG Collins, 10 March 2022, Case C-538/20, *W AG*, EU:C:2022:184, para. 36). Or, in AG Wathelet's words, "there can be no tax advantage if there is no power of taxation" (Opinion AG Wathelet, 3 September 2015, Case C-388/14, *Timac Agro*, EU:C:2015:533, para. 74). The German Bundesfinanzhof has rationalized this distinction by arguing that *W AG* aims to distinguish between unilateral, uncoordinated rules on the one hand and agreements between States about the allocation of taxing powers on the other – but likewise fails to explain why this distinction should be relevant for purposes of the EU fundamental freedoms. For critical analyses of this quite mislead distinction see, e.g., Georg Kofler, *Cross-border losses and* W AG*: The beginning of the end of the "final loss exception"?*, 2 Cahiers de fiscalité luxembourgeoise et européenne 73 (88-90) (2023); Savvas Kostikidis and Florian Striefler, *Cross-Border Loss Relief in the European Union Following* W AG *(Case C-538/20)*, 64 European Taxation 210-218 (2024); for further criticism see, e.g., CFE ECJ Task Force, *Opinion Statement ECJ-TF 4/2022 on the CJEU decision of 22 September 2022 in Case C-538/20,* W AG, *on the deductibility of foreign final losses*, 63 European Taxation 105-110 (2023).

244 See Case C-538/20, *W AG*, EU:C:2022:717, paras 20 and 22 versus para. 24.

245 German Bundesfinanzhof, 22 February 2023, I R 35/22 (ex I R 32/18) (this case was subject of the reference in *W AG*), and German Bundesfinanzhof, 12 April 2023, I R 44/22 (ex I R 49/19, I R 17/16) (this case has initially been paused until *Bevola* and then again until *W AG*).

has "definitively incurred losses".[246] This argument was not taken up by the Court in *W AG*. However, AG Collins had straightforwardly rejected the relevance of the ability-to-pay principle for treaty-exempt permanent establishments, finding it not appropriate "to add to the exemption method under the Convention a purpose that is not already expressed in the specific objectives of avoiding double taxation and avoiding double deduction of losses".[247]

- The Court's transition from *Lidl Belgium* to *Timac Agro* and eventually *W AG* is even more puzzling and unsatisfactory as *Lidl Belgium* was not even mentioned, let alone explicitly distinguished.[248] This quiet "overruling" of the line of reasoning of a rather clear precedent is quite unsettling because prior decisions of the Court not only have broad *practical* impact, but also *legal* impact well beyond the actual case decided.[249] Another tension remains unresolved, as *W AG* does not mention or distinguish *K*:[250] That case concerned a loss arising from the sale of immovable property in France by a Finnish individual taxpayer, and the Court affirmed comparability because the treaty exemption was – as usual (Article 23A(3) OECD MC) – with progression and the taxpayer's residence State (Finland) was not precluded "from taking into account of income related to an asset situated in France in the calculation of the tax of a taxpayer

246 Case C-650/16, *Bevola*, EU:C:2018:424, para. 39; see also, in more detail, Opinion AG Campos Sánchez-Bordona, 17 January 2018, Case C-650/16, *Bevola*, EU:C:2018:15, para. 37-39.

247 Opinion AG Collins, 10 March 2022, Case C-538/20, *W AG*, EU:C:2022:184, para. 48. This effective irrelevance of the ability-to-pay principle for the issue at hand was recently supported by the German Bundesfinanzhof in light of the right to equal treatment under Germany's constitution (Article 3 of the German Basic Law, "Grundgesetz"); see German Bundesfinanzhof, 12 April 2023, I R 44/22 (ex I R 49/19, I R 17/16), para. 34. For further discussion in light of Article 20 of the Charter of Fundamental Rights of the European Union ([2012] OJ C 326, p. 391 [26 October 2012]) see Jens Schönfeld and Thomas Sendke, *Finale Verluste – ein Fall für die (EU-)Grundrechte?*, 32 Internationales Steuerrecht 333 (336-341) (2023).

248 One might, of course, argue that the Court in *Lidl Belgium* did not find that cross-border loss utilization was required by the freedom of establishment (because the losses in that case were not "final", as they could be taken into account in Luxembourg in future taxable periods) so that it was not technically "overruled". However, the Court's reasoning in *Lidl Belgium* clearly implied that Germany would have had to take into account the foreign loss had it been final. This understanding was, e.g., also adopted by German Bundesfinanzhof, 17 July 2008, I R 84/04, BFHE 222, 398, BStBl II 2009, 630; German Bundesfinanzhof, 9. June 2010, I R 107/09, BFHE 230, 35; German Bundesfinanzhof, 5 February 2014, I *R 48/11, BFHE 244, 371; German Bundesfinanzhof, 22. September 2015, I B 83/14, BFH/NV 2016, 375. See also, e.g., CFE ECJ Task Force, Opinion Statement ECJ-TF 4/2022 on the CJEU decision of 22 September 2022 in Case C-538/20,* W AG, *on the deductibility of foreign final losses, 63 European Taxation 105-110 (2023).*

249 Indeed, *W AG* has sparked a passionate discourse on the transparency, certainty, and clarity regarding the Court's (substantive) "overruling" of its precedents: The Court's transition from *Lidl Belgium* to *W AG* is puzzling, highly unsatisfactory, and has been labelled as "the clearest case of an 'overruling' (in substance, but not with respect to visibility) that can be identified". See Axel Cordewener, "We Need to Know When Previous Case-Law Has Been 'Overruled'! – A Plea for More Legal Certainty in EU Tax Law", 32 EC Tax Rev. 2023, 144 (147); for further discussion see also Georg Kofler, *Cross-border losses and* W AG*: The beginning of the end of the "final loss exception"?*, 2 Cahiers de fiscalité luxembourgeoise et européenne 73 (90-91) (2023); Rita Szudoczky, *Foreign Permanent Establishment Losses Under the Fundamental Freedoms: Does W AG Bring an End to a Rollercoaster Ride?*, 51 Intertax 432-443 (2023).

250 Case C-322/11, *K*, EU:C:2013:716.

residing in Finland".[251] It did not even matter for the Court, that, in fact, Finland did not exercise this progressivity as it taxed income from capital assets at a fixed rate.[252] This taxing right *in abstracto* in terms of the tax rate was sufficient for the Court to assume comparability, even if it was not exercised *in concreto* (because of the non-progressive rate on the gain in Finland) and despite the fact that the exempt foreign income did not increase Finland's tax base (because of the treaty-based exemption). Unconvincing as this connection between comparability and progressivity is, its use in *K* still rests uneasy with *Timac Agro* and *W AG*, as the respective tax treaties in the latter two cases likewise provided for exemption with progression.[253] It seems that the only potentially relevant difference between those cases is that *K* concerned an individual taxpayer (subject to a flat rate in his home State, though) and *Timac Agro* and *W AG* concerned corporate taxpayers. However, it would seem incoherent to apply two different standards of comparability regarding cross-border loss utilization depending on the nature of the taxpayer.

- Of course, *W AG* also raises a number of technical questions.[254] For example, how would the Court treat a situation where a foreign permanent establishment is exempt both under domestic law and tax treaty law? This situation was indeed raised in *W AG* with regard to the structurally territorial German trade tax ("Gewerbesteuer"), under which "income, whether positive or negative, of non-resident permanent establishments is excluded from the basis of assessment to trade tax, irrespective of whether the applicable convention for the avoidance of double taxation has recourse to the exemption method or to the credit method or that no such convention applies".[255] The German Bundesfinanzhof, however, had only asked about the "final loss" doctrine with regard to the trade tax in case that the first question regarding "final losses" in the corporate tax framework was answered in the affirmative (which it was not), and the Court

251 Case C-322/11, *K*, EU:C:2013:716, para. 45.

252 Case C-322/11, *K*, EU:C:2013:716, paras 44-45.

253 See Article 15(3) of the Austria-Germany DTC (1954) in *Timac Agro* and Article XVIII(2) of the Germany-UK DTC (1966, as amended in 1971) in *W AG*.

254 For example, one issue highlighted in German literature is that the exemption method in tax treaties might be subject to various conditions (e.g., activity clauses, subject-to-tax provisions etc). Is this still the treaty-based exemption that the Court has focused on in *Timac Agro* and *W AG*? In its post-*W AG* case law, the German Bundesfinanzhof has already dealt with a special clause in the tax treaty between Germany and Italy, according to which Germany only exempts income from permanent establishments that is "effectively taxed" in Italy in accordance with the tax treaty (Para. 16(d) of the Protocol to the DTC Germany/Italy 1989) (German Bundesfinanzhof, 12 April 2023, I R 44/22 (ex I R 49/19, I R 17/16), paras 15-26). What about the "effective taxation" of losses? The Bundesfinanzhof argued that – symmetrically to profits – it was sufficient that the losses of the permanent establishment are included in the Italian tax base (and can be carried forward in Italy) to be treated as "effectively taxed", so that in the case at issue the taxing right did not revert to Germany. In other words, the mere existence of such qualified fallback clause ("qualifizierte Rückfallklausel") does not make the treaty-based exemption *per se* "incomplete" (so that the application of *W AG* would be excluded), but rather requires a case-by-case analysis regarding the applicability of the treaty-based exemption in light of the fallback clause (see also Roland Ismer, "Kein Abzug von Verlusten einer Freistellungsbetriebsstätte – *FA B/W AG*", 60 Deutsches Steuerrecht 1996 (1996-1997) (2022)). That said, it should nevertheless be noted that, of course, a "final loss" is per definition not "effectively taxed" in the other State. However, this was not decisive for the Bundesfinanzhof from the point of view of the fundamental freedoms.

255 See Opinion AG Collins, 10 March 2022, C-538/20, *Finanzamt B v W AG*, EU:C:2022:184, para. 53.

therefore refrained from providing an answer.[256] In its subsequent decision, however, the Bundesfinanzhof has now solved that issue based on the technical structure of the German trade tax: It reasoned that positive and negative income that is exempt from corporation tax under a tax treaty in the first place does not enter the tax base for the trade tax (§ 7 of the Trade Tax Act), so that the explicit domestic deductions relating to income of foreign permanent establishments (§ 9 of the Trade Tax Act) run "idle".[257] Therefore, according to the Bundesfinanzhof, the non-consideration of "final" losses also for trade tax purposes does not violate the freedom of establishment.[258]

- Finally, the discussion in Germany has also raised the question if the non-utilization of foreign "final" losses could infringe on the Charter of Fundamental Rights of the European Union,[259] in particular on the right to "equality before the law" under its Article 20.[260] Interestingly, the Bundesfinanzhof seems to accept – at least for the sake of the argument – that the freedom of establishment at issue in this cross-border loss situation (Articles 49, 54 TFEU) likewise opens the applicability of the Charter, which binds Member States "only when they are implementing Union law" (Article 51(1) of the Charter).[261] However, with regard to the freedom of establishment the Bundesfinanzhof pointed out that *W AG* had shown that there were no comparable circumstances between taxpayers who maintain a permanent establishment in another EU Member State, whose (positive and negative) income is exempt from taxation by the State of residence due to a tax treaty, and purely domestic cases. From this, it concludes that

256 It might be noted that AG Collins had suggested that "an affirmative answer to the first question should also lead to an affirmative answer to the second question", i.e., that "final losses" would have to be taken into account not only for corporate tax but also for trade tax purposes (Opinion AG Collins, 10 March 2022, C-538/20, *Finanzamt B v W AG*, EU:C:2022:184, para. 55). AG Collins has argued that with regard to the German trade tax "the solution adopted by the Court in paragraph 38 of the judgment in Bevola and Jens W. Trock as regards the objective comparability of the respective situations of non-residents and residents in relation to the deductibility of final losses should equally apply to the assessment to trade tax" (Opinion AG Collins, 10 March 2022, Case C-538/20, *W AG*, EU:C:2022:184, para. 57, referring to Case C-650/16, *Bevola*, EU:C:2018:424, para. 38), which might have implied that "final" losses would indeed have to be taken into account in the home State if the exemption of the foreign permanent establishment is based on both domestic and tax treaty law.

257 German Bundesfinanzhof, 22 February 2023, I R 35/22 (ex I R 32/18), para. 17, referring to German Bundesfinanzhof, 9 June 2010, I R 107/09, BFHE 230, 35.

258 German Bundesfinanzhof, 22 February 2023, I R 35/22 (ex I R 32/18), paras 18 and 22.

259 See [2012] OJ C 326, p. 391 (26 October 2012).

260 See especially Jens Schönfeld and Thomas Sendke, *Finale Verluste – ein Fall für die (EU-)Grundrechte?*, 32 Internationales Steuerrecht 333-341 (2023).

261 German Bundesfinanzhof, 12 April 2023, I R 44/22 (ex I R 49/19, I R 17/16), para. 30. This is surprising. Indeed, it is established case-law of the CJEU that the Charter rights are relevant in cases where a Member State attempts to justify the restriction of a fundamental freedom (see, e.g., Case C-390/12, *Pfleger*, EU:C:2014:281, paras 35-36; Case C-235/14, *Safe Interenvios v Liberbank*, EU:C:2016:154, para. 103; Case C-201/15, *AGET Iraklis*, EU:C:2016:972, paras 63-64), but it was disputed if the mere exercise of a fundamental freedom likewise triggers the applicability of the Charter. The Court has recently held that in such case the applicability of the Charter is not triggered (Case C-257/20, *Viva Telecom Bulgaria*, EU:2022:125, paras 126 to 128; Case C-380/23, *Monmorieux*, EU:C:2024:500, paras 29-30). It might also be noted that previously the Bundesfinanzhof has flatly rejected the applicability of the Charter in a case of cross-border double taxation of an inheritance (see German Bundesfinanzhof, 19 June 2013, II R 10/12, BFHE 241, 402, BStBl II 2013, 746).

> it seems impossible that there are different standards for the comparability test in the context of the general principle of equality (Article 20 of the Charter) on the one hand and those established by the CJEU for the discrimination analysis under the freedom of establishment (Articles 49, 54 TFEU) on the other.[262]

That all said, the "final loss" exception for foreign treaty-exempt branches that was initially acknowledged in *Lidl Belgium* has now been fully abandoned by *W AG*. This puts the whole body of *Marks & Spencer* case law in doubt, even though the Court has upheld the final loss exception in *Commission v. UK*, *Holmen*, and *Memira*,[263] all of which were handed down after *Timac Agro*; likewise, and despite calls from Germany to find incomparability between domestic and foreign subsidiaries, the EFTA Court recently confirmed that reasoning in *ExxonMobil*.[264] However, *Lidl Belgium* was decided based on the blueprint of *Marks & Spencer*: If comparability is now clearly rejected by the Court in *W AG* where a State could tax the profits and losses of a *foreign branch* under domestic law (but agreed in a tax treaty to exempt), how could comparability be assumed to exist in cases of *foreign subsidiaries*, which are outside the parent's State's taxing jurisdiction altogether? Moreover, the foreign subsidiary is not only outside the parent's State's taxing jurisdiction for reasons of domestic law (and perhaps customary international law), the exemption also typically follows from an applicable tax treaty: Under Article 7(1) first sentence OECD MC, "[p]rofits of an enterprise of a Contracting State shall be taxable only in that State unless the enterprise carries on business in the other Contracting State through a permanent establishment situated therein". This means that, unless the subsidiary has a permanent establishment in the parent's State, the subsidiary's State of residence has the exclusive taxing right and the parent's State is generally barred from taxing the subsidiary's profits.[265] It is hard to see how the logic of *Marks & Spencer* can be upheld in light of *W AG*.[266] Does the Court view the "exemption" of the profits of a foreign subsidiary as a purely unilateral one? Did it, for example, matter for the Court in *Marks & Spencer* that the UK operated an indirect credit system for the taxation of dividends?[267] It remains to be seen how the CJEU will eventually tie up all those loose ends.

After *W AG*, for the time being, *Bevola* still stands: For those situations where the Court still assumes comparability (i.e., in the case of a domestic exemption as in *Bevola*) and hence the existence of a discriminatory restriction, the "final loss" doctrine is still "alive". Indeed, the Court in *Lidl Belgium* and *Bevola* has taken the symmetry argument and its

262 German Bundesfinanzhof, 12 April 2023, I R 44/22 (ex I R 49/19, I R 17/16), para. 31.

263 See *supra* Chapter 10.2.

264 See *supra* Chapter 10.2.2.

265 Of course, there might be applicable CFC rules (e.g., based on Articles 7 and 8 of Council Directive (EU) 2016/1164 of 12 July 2016 laying down rules against tax avoidance practices that directly affect the functioning of the internal market, [2016] OJ L 193/1) or similar provisions under which the parent's State may exercise taxing jurisdiction over (some of) the subsidiary's profits.

266 See also, e.g., CFE ECJ Task Force, *Opinion Statement ECJ-TF 4/2022 on the CJEU decision of 22 September 2022 in Case C-538/20,* W AG, *on the deductibility of foreign final losses*, 63 European Taxation 105-110 (2023); Georg Kofler, *Cross-border losses and* W AG*: The beginning of the end of the "final loss exception"?*, 2 Cahiers de fiscalité luxembourgeoise et européenne 73 (93-95) (2023).

267 See in that direction, e.g., Roland Ismer, "Kein Abzug von Verlusten einer Freistellungsbetriebsstätte – *FA B/W AG*", 60 Deutsches Steuerrecht 1996 (1996) (2022).

implications into consideration at the level of justifications (in line with the reasons given in *Marks & Spencer*) and also clarified that each of the grounds of justification is sufficient by itself (and that no cumulation of reasons of justification, as implied in *Marks & Spencer*,[268] is required):[269]

First, the Court accepted the "need to preserve the allocation of the power to impose taxes between the Member States" (i.e., a "balanced allocation of powers of taxation between Member States"[270]). It recognized that "the objective of preserving the allocation of the power to impose taxes between the two Member States concerned", which is reflected in the provisions of the applicable tax treaty, "is capable of justifying the tax regime at issue in the main proceedings, since it safeguards symmetry between the right to tax profits and the right to deduct losses".[271] Indeed, the Court assumes that – *ceteris paribus* – "to accept that the losses of a non-resident permanent establishment might be deducted from the taxable income of the principal company would result in allowing that company to choose freely the Member State in which those losses could be deducted". Moreover, the symmetrical treatment of profits and losses is also justified based on the coherence of the tax system since disadvantage (taxation of profits) and advantage (use of losses) are directly linked.[272] Such direct link is moreover in line with the aim to tax according with the company's ability to pay, because a "company's ability to pay tax would be systematically underestimated" if such "company possessing a permanent establishment in another Member State were allowed to set off against its results the losses incurred by that establishment without being taxed on the profits made by it".[273] Indeed, in these situations the "the requirements of the balanced allocation of powers of taxation and coherence of the tax system coincide".[274]

Second, the Court acknowledged "the need to prevent the danger that losses may be taken into account twice" ("double dips"):[275] By offsetting them in the home State and then, again, by way of a loss carry-forward in the source State "when that establishment generates profits", thereby preventing – *ceteris paribus* – "the Member State in which the principal company has its seat from taxing that profit."[276] The prevention of "double dips" directly connects to the Court's proportionality test and the category of "final losses". Indeed, "[w]here there is no longer any possibility of deducting the losses of the non-resident permanent establishment in the Member State in which it is situated, the risk of double deduction of losses no longer exists".[277]

268 See *supra* Chapter 10.2.2.
269 Case C-414/06, *Lidl Belgium*, EU:C:2008:278, paras 37-42; see also Case C-322/11, *K*, EU:C:2013:716, paras 50-70.
270 Case C-650/16, *Bevola*, EU:C:2018:424, para. 43.
271 See Case C-414/06, *Lidl Belgium*, EU:C:2008:278, para. 33.
272 Case C-650/16, *Bevola*, EU:C:2018:424, paras 45-51; see also Case C-322/11, *K*, EU:C:2013:716, paras 64-70.
273 Case C-650/16, *Bevola*, EU:C:2018:424, paras 49-50.
274 C-371/10, *National Grid Indus*, EU:C:2011:785, para. 80; CJEUCase C-388/14, *Timac Agro*, EU:C:2015:829, para. 47.
275 Case C-650/16, *Bevola*, EU:C:2018:424, para. 52.
276 Case C-414/06, *Lidl Belgium*, EU:C:2008:278, para. 36.
277 Case C-650/16, *Bevola*, EU:C:2018:424, para. 58.

Finally, however, in situations involving permanent establishments, losses can only move "up" to the head office, but not sidewards or downwards, as may be the case with group relief or group contributions, so that "[t]he risk of tax avoidance is very limited for the losses incurred by a permanent establishment".[278] This might also explain why *Lidl Belgium* did not deal with the additional justification brought forward in *Marks & Spencer*, i.e., to the need to prevent jurisdiction shopping through the transfer of losses to the jurisdiction with the highest tax rates (and hence to where the losses are most valuable).

Of course, these grounds of justification would lose force if a Member State operated a "deduction/reincorporation method" (as, e.g., Germany did before 1999,[279] and as other Member States still do). That method would indeed be a less restrictive system for safe-guarding symmetry, as the Commission,[280] Lidl Belgium[281] and AG Sharpston[282] had pointed out, but the Court – following again *Marks & Spencer*[283] – did not accept that argument.[284] Obviously, the Court (rightly) did not feel competent to order Germany to make that particular choice of defining and exercising its taxing jurisdiction (worldwide taxation with double tax relief).[285] Rather, it merely referred to the *Marks & Spencer* exception for "final" losses, which were clearly not present in *Lidl Belgium*, as the relevant losses had indeed been carried forward in Luxembourg and used against profits subsequently.[286]

This was different in *Bevola*, also a case on base exemption (albeit not under a tax treaty, but rather under domestic law), where Bevola's Finnish permanent establishment was closed and the losses incurred there "were not and cannot be deducted in Finland following the closure".[287] In such a case, proportionality required that "final" losses be taken into account in the taxpayer's home State, which would also align the overall tax burden with the taxpayer's ability-to-pay.[288] Referring to the criteria established in *Marks & Spencer*,[289] the Court concluded that

> "the losses attributable to a non-resident permanent establishment become definitive when, first, the company possessing the establishment has exhausted all the possibilities of deducting those losses available under the law of the Member State in which the establishment is situated and, second, it has ceased to receive any income from that

278 See also, e.g., See the Commission's Communication on the "Tax Treatment of Losses in Cross-border Situations", COM(2006)824 final (19 December 2006), p. 6.
279 See *infra* Chapter 10.3.3.
280 Case C-414/06, *Lidl Belgium*, EU:C:2008:278, para. 45.
281 Case C-414/06, *Lidl Belgium*, EU:C:2008:278, para. 45.
282 Opinion AG Sharpston, 14 February 2008, C-414/06, *Lidl Belgium*, EU:C:2008:88, para. 25.
283 Case C-446/03, *Marks & Spencer*, EU:C:2005:763, para. 54.
284 Case C-388/14, *Timac Agro*, EU:C:2015:829, paras 45-46. It is unclear if the Court assumed that the "reincorporation method" would undermine the balance of taxing power (see Case C-414/06, *Lidl Belgium*, EU:C:2008:278, para. 52), which it arguably does not, just as it does *not* produce any significant risk of double dips and is *not* inviting abuse.
285 See also Opinion AG Kokott, 23 October 2014, Case C-172/13, *Commission v UK (Marks & Spencer II)*, EU:C:2014:2321, para. 49.
286 Case C-414/06, *Lidl Belgium*, EU:C:2008:278, paras. 49-51.
287 Case C-650/16, *Bevola*, EU:C:2018:424, para. 8.
288 Case C-650/16, *Bevola*, EU:C:2018:424, para. 59.
289 See *supra* Chapter 10.2.4.

establishment, so that there is no longer any possibility of the losses being taken into account in that Member State."[290]

While the Court in *Bevola* did not give much additional clarification to the concept of "final" losses (and left it for the national court to assess whether those conditions are satisfied in the case of Bevola's Finnish establishment), it might implicitly have added a nuance for situations involving permanent establishments: While a subsidiary is a separate taxpayer and its losses "disappear" once liquidated, in some national tax systems a permanent establishment's loss "stick" to the non-resident taxpayer ("head office") even after the branch is closed, and might indeed be used at a later point in time if the non-resident taxpayer resumed a business in the source State. Taken to the extreme, such losses could therefore never become "final" (also when the re-opening of a branch is a purely hypothetical option) – a result indeed accepted by AG Wathelet in *Timac Agro*,[291] but rejected by AG Collins in *W AG*.[292] The Court in *Bevola* seems to have provided a first hint on that issue by referring to a situation where the taxpayer has ceased to receive any income from "that" establishment,[293] which could imply that (future) positive income from other activities of the non-resident taxpayer in the source State is irrelevant, i.e., that the Court equates a permanent establishment effectively with a separate entity also in that regard.

10.3.3 *Asymmetrical Deduction/Reincorporation (Krankenheim Ruhesitz am Wannsee, Timac Agro)*

In contrast to "symmetrical" base exemption (of profits and losses), some Member States apply the "asymmetrical" deduction/reincorporation method with regard to treaty-exempt permanent establishments, where profits remain exempt but *current* losses are first deducted and later recaptured (e.g., once the branch returns to profits). Interestingly, Germany used this method until 1998, but reverted to base exemption from 1999 onwards.[294] Both periods have been scrutinized by the Court: *Lidl Belgium* dealt with Germany's base

290 Case C-650/16, *Bevola*, EU:C:2018:424, paras 61-64, with reference to Case C-446/03, *Marks & Spencer*, EU:C:2005:763, para. 55.

291 Opinion AG Wathelet, 3 September 2015, Case C-388/14, *Timac Agro*, EU:C:2015:533, para. 67 with note 45. See also the short remark by the Court that "the Republic of Austria has indicated that not all the possibilities for taking those losses into account have been exhausted in Austria" (Case C-388/14, *Timac Agro*, EU:C:2015:829, para. 56).

292 Opinion AG Collins, 10 March 2022, Case C-538/20, *W AG*, EU:C:2022:184, paras 60-67. The case is currently pending before the Court and was referred by the German Bundesfinanzhof, 6 November 2019, I R 32/18.

293 Case C-650/16, *Bevola*, EU:C:2018:424, para. 64; see also with regard to the "recapture" of losses Case C-388/14, *Timac Agro*, EU:C:2015:829, para. 55.

294 This legislative change (i.e., the deletion of former § 2a(3) of the German Income Tax Act by the "Steuerentlastungsgesetz 1999/2000/2002", Federal Gazette I 1999, 402) was motivated by three reasons: That the deduction/reincorporation method was been "contrary to the system" (of symmetrically exempting profits and losses), that it was difficult to handle for the tax administration, and that consideration of foreign losses through "negative progressivity" was a sufficient consideration of foreign losses (see the legislative materials BT-Drs. 14/23, 167 [9 November 1998]).

exemption,[295] *Krankenheim Ruhesitz am Wannsee*[296] with the "deduction/reincorporation method", and *Timac Agro*[297] with both, i.e., periods before and after 1999.

Krankenheim Ruhesitz am Wannsee concerned a German company with a permanent establishment in Austria. This branch had made losses (from 1982 to 1990) but subsequently returned to profitability (from 1991 to 1994). When Germany recaptured parts of the previously deducted losses upon disposal of the branch (but not exceeding the amount of the profits made), the taxpayer challenged that recapture based on the freedom of establishment. The crux of the case was, of course, that in effect some of the branch loss remained unrelieved because Germany recaptured it and Austria had – arguably in violation of the freedom of establishment[298] – not granted a loss carry-forward at that time. The Court viewed the reintegration of the losses in Germany as a withdrawal of "the benefit of the tax advantage" and hence – in comparison to domestic branches – as "less favourable" treatment"[299] of comparable situations. Comparability was assumed by the Court because Germany had "equated" domestic and foreign permanent establishments "so far as concerns the deduction of losses".[300] While this analysis is certainly questionable (because also subsequent profits of a German permanent establishment would automatically be taxed, so that the reintegration just effectuates equal treatment and not a discrimination), the Court at least fully endorsed the "deduction/reincorporation method" on the level of justification: Reintegration of losses in the "case of a company with a permanent establishment in another State in relation to which that company's State of residence has no power of taxation, as the referring court indicates, reflects a logical symmetry", it is "the logical complement of the deduction previously granted" and hence "justified by the need to guarantee the coherence of the German tax system".[301] Any blame for an overall unrelieved loss would be imputable not to Germany but rather to Austria.[302]

The Court, however, made a small remark in *Krankenheim Ruhesitz am Wannsee* that became highly relevant in *Timac Agro*: It noted that the restriction effectuated by reintegration "is entirely proportionate to the objective pursued, since the reintegrated losses are reintegrated only up to the amount of the profits made".[303] What then, one might ask, would happen if reintegration were to exceed subsequent profits (e.g., because the branch is sold or incorporated before returning to profitability), a result that the Commission's

295 See *supra* Chapter 10.3.2.
296 Case C-157/07, *Krankenheim Ruhesitz am Wannsee*, EU:C:2008:588.
297 Case C-388/14, *Timac Agro*, EU:C:2015:829.
298 See Case C-157/07, *Krankenheim Ruhesitz am Wannsee*, EU:C:2008:588, paras 51-53.
299 Case C-157/07, *Krankenheim Ruhesitz am Wannsee*, EU:C:2008:588, para. 37; see also CJEU, 17 December 2015, Case C-388/14, *Timac Agro*, EU:C:2015:829, para. 28.
300 See Case C-388/14, *Timac Agro*, EU:C:2015:829, para. 28, and Case C-157/07, *Krankenheim Ruhesitz am Wannsee*, EU:C:2008:588, para. 35; see also Case C-48/13, *Nordea Bank Danmark*, EU:C:2014:2087, para. 24.
301 Case C-157/07, *Krankenheim Ruhesitz am Wannsee*, EU:C:2008:588, paras 42-44.
302 Case C-157/07, *Krankenheim Ruhesitz am Wannsee*, EU:C:2008:588, paras 51-53. It might be noted that the administrative practice in Austria now indeed grants a loss carry-for-ward to branches based on EU law (see Para. 8059 of the Austrian Income Tax Guidelines, GZ 06 0104/9-IV/6/00, as last amended by GZ 2021-0.103.726).
303 Case C-157/07, *Krankenheim Ruhesitz am Wannsee*, EU:C:2008:588, para. 45.

1990 Proposal had indeed promoted.[304] That issue came before the Court in *Timac Agro*, where the reincorporation of losses (for the years 1997 and 1998) was not linked to profits of that establishment but rather triggered by the transfer of the foreign permanent establishment (in 2005). Again, the Court saw this reincorporation as discriminatory, but accepted a number of justifications:[305] First, the "need to safeguard a balanced allocation of the power to impose taxes between the Member States" is intended "to safeguard the symmetry between the right to tax profits and the right to deduct losses", which is indeed effectuated by the reintegration. Second, as before in *Krankenheim Ruhesitz am Wannsee*, reintegration of previously deducted losses is justified by the need to guarantee the coherence of the tax system, as it reflects a logical symmetry and is the indissociable complement of the deduction previously granted. Finally, the Court got to the core of the issue regarding the reintegration of losses irrespective of any profits of the permanent establishment. Germany argued that such reintegration is necessary to prevent tax avoidance, and the Court accepted this argument:

> "As to the relevance of that justification in the light of circumstances such as those at issue in the main proceedings, it must be acknowledged that there is a risk that a group of companies might organise its business in such a way that it deducts from its taxable income in Germany the losses incurred by a loss-making permanent establishment situated in Austria, and then, once that establishment has become profitable, transfers the establishment's business to another company of the same group which is liable to tax in another Member State."[306]

Moreover, the reincorporation of such losses into the taxable profit of the transferring company is also proportionate to the intended aims, namely the safeguarding of a balanced allocation of the power to impose taxes, the need to ensure fiscal coherence and the prevention of tax avoidance.[307] There is, however, a limit to reintegration: It would be disproportionate to reincorporate "final" losses. *Timac Agro* did, however, not add much to clarify the concept of "final" losses (discussed in Chapter 10.3.2). It merely recalled that a loss will not become "final" merely because "the Member State in which the permanent establishment is situated precludes all possibility of losses being carried forward",[308] and confirmed that a loss will not be "final" so long as the permanent establishment "continues to be in receipt of even minimal income".[309]

10.3.4 Credit Method and "Recapture" (Nordea Bank Danmark)

In a credit system (Article 23B OECD MC), profits and losses of a foreign permanent establishment are automatically and symmetrically taken into account in the home State when determining worldwide income. Also, losses will be automatically "recaptured"

304 See *supra* Chapter 10.1.2.
305 Case C-388/14, *Timac Agro*, EU:C:2015:829, paras 34-45.
306 Case C-388/14, *Timac Agro*, EU:C:2015:829, para. 43.
307 Case C-388/14, *Timac Agro*, EU:C:2015:829, paras 46-52.
308 Case C-388/14, *Timac Agro*, EU:C:2015:829, para. 54, referring to Case C-172/13, *Commission v UK (Marks & Spencer II)*, EU:C:2015:50, para. 33.
309 Case C-388/14, *Timac Agro*, EU:C:2015:829, para. 55, referring to Case C-172/13, *Commission v UK (Marks & Spencer II)*, EU:C:2015:50, para. 36.

when the foreign permanent establishment returns to profitability: This automatic recapture takes place because the branch's losses will typically be carried forward and offset future profits in the source State. These future profits will also be fully taxed in the home State – without the need to grant a credit insofar as the profits have been soaked up by the loss carry-forward in the source State and hence are not taxed there. Domestic and foreign branches are treated equally on the level of the tax base and no discrimination arises. Indeed, the Commission's 1990 Proposal advocated the credit method as a possible approach to deal with cross-border losses of enterprises.[310]

However, also in a credit system a Member State may have the concern that a taxpayer first gains relief for losses of a foreign permanent establishment on an ongoing basis and, as soon as the branch becomes profit-making, sells it to an affiliated foreign company outside the home State's taxing jurisdiction in order to "prevent" having to pay tax on the branch's (future) profits (a concern also present in "reintregration systems", as exemplified by *Timac Agro*). While the Commission's 1990 Proposal did not contain a recapture provision for Member States with a credit system, the Danish system at issue in *Nordea Bank Danmark*[311] did: Nordea Bank Danmark had loss-making branches in Sweden, Finland, and Norway, and those foreign losses were currently deducted from Nordea's tax base. Subsequently, the loss-making branches were closed (and about half of the employees and certainly were taken over by Swedish, Finnish, or Norwegian companies forming part of the Nordea Group and customers could seamlessly retain their accounts). This transaction was treated as a partial sale and triggered, under Danish rules, a recapture of the sum of the losses for which relief had been claimed in previous year. Nordea argued that this recapture infringes both EU law and the EEA Agreement.

The Court in *Nordea Bank Danmark* was quick in identifying a discriminatory restriction: As a recapture would not take place if a Danish company sold a domestic branch to a foreign affiliate, it was clear that the operation of a branch in another Member State was treated less favorably for tax purposes.[312] The situations are also comparable: By using the credit method and "making the profits of permanent establishments situated in Finland, Sweden and Norway subject to Danish tax, the Kingdom of Denmark has equated those establishments with resident permanent establishments so far as concerns the deduction of losses".[313] As for justification, the Court, in principle, accepted the need to preserve the balanced allocation of taxing rights and the need to prevent tax avoidance: If Denmark were denied the power to reincorporate the relevant losses when it has lost the power to tax any future profits, this "would artificially erode its tax base and, therefore, affect the allocation of the power to impose taxes resulting from the Nordic Convention."[314] However, the Danish recapture rule was not proportionate in light of the symmetry of the credit method and therefore violated the freedom of establishment: Reincorporation of the losses previously deducted in respect of the establishment transferred "goes beyond

310 See Art. 6 of the Commission's 1990 Proposal, COM(90)595 (24 January 1991), [1991] OJ C 53, p. 30 (28 February 1991).
311 Case C-48/13, *Nordea Bank Danmark*, EU:C:2014:2087.
312 Case C-48/13, *Nordea Bank Danmark*, EU:C:2014:2087, paras. 20-22.
313 Case C-48/13, *Nordea Bank Danmark*, EU:C:2014:2087, para. 24.
314 Case C-48/13, *Nordea Bank Danmark*, EU:C:2014:2087, paras 25-30.

what is necessary to attain the objective relating to the need to safeguard the balanced allocation of the power to impose taxes if the first Member State taxes the profits made in respect of that establishment before its transfer, including those resulting from the gain made upon the transfer".[315] Therefore, and unlike in *Timac Agro*, the Court did not have to deal with Nordea's additional proportionality argument that the losses in the foreign branches were "final" (because the acquiring affiliates could no longer claim relief against their own taxation for the losses previously made by the permanent establishments).[316]

A comparison between *Timac Agro* on the "deduction/reincorporation method" and *Nordea Bank Danmark* on the credit method demonstrates that the difference in systems matters: The "taxation of a foreign permanent establishment by way of the credit method cannot be regarded as being the same as its non-taxation under the exemption method".[317] If a Member State operates an "asymmetrical" deduction/reincorporation system, the Court allows the recapture of loss relief (up to the limit of "final" losses), whereas in a "symmetrical" credit system the recapture of loss relief is barred (irrespective of whether those losses are "final" or not) because the home State "*did* wish to exercise its power of taxation in respect of foreign permanent establishments and there was at least a possibility that some of their profits would also be taxed".[318] It did therefore not matter for the Court that in *Nordea Bank Danmark* the home State will not be able to "benefit" from the credit method's symmetry regarding the taxation of future profits, a situation that would likely never arise in a comparable domestic setting: If a domestic loss-making branch was sold to a foreign affiliate, there would generally be no need to provide for a similar recapture rule as the branch (and its future profits) would stay within Denmark's taxing jurisdiction (as a permanent establishment of the non-resident affiliate).

10.4 Impact of Residence State Losses on Taxation in the Source State (Ritter-Coulais, Renneberg, Lakebrink, X, Sofina, Credit Suisse Securities)

There is also the – perhaps subtler – EU law question of whether non-resident taxpayers are entitled, under the fundamental freedoms, to set off losses that they have incurred in their *home* State against (unrelated) positive income that they derive in the *source* State. Generally, a source State that only takes into account profits and losses arising from activities in its own territory is not only consistent with the international principle of territoriality but also with the fundamental freedoms. This was confirmed in *Futura*: While residents were subject to worldwide taxation, the Luxembourgian law at issue in *Futura* provided that non-residents were only liable to tax in relation to their domestic source income earned by their permanent establishment and, conversely, limited loss utilization and carry-forward to losses arising from the non-resident taxpayer's activity in Luxembourg. "Such a system", the Court found, "which is in conformity with the fiscal

315 Case C-48/13, *Nordea Bank Danmark*, EU:C:2014:2087, paras 31-36.
316 Opinion AG Kokott, 13 March 2014, Case C-48/13, *Nordea Bank Danmark*, EU:C:2014:153, para. 66.
317 Opinion AG Kokott, 13 March 2014, Case C-48/13, *Nordea Bank Danmark*, EU:C:2014:153, para. 54.
318 Opinion AG Kokott, 13 March 2014, Case C-48/13, *Nordea Bank Danmark*, EU:C:2014:153, para. 54.

principle of territoriality, cannot be regarded as entailing any discrimination, overt or covert, prohibited by the Treaty".[319]

However, in expanding the *Schumacker*-doctrine with regard to "personal and family circumstances" (such as, e.g., spousal income-splitting, zero-rate bracket, deduction of childcare costs),[320] the Court has held that source Member States must extend its domestic benefits to non-residents also with regard to foreign losses of individuals (i.e., negative rental income) if the taxpayer's home Member State is not in a position to grant that benefit. This applies both with regard to "negative" progressivity on the level of the tax *rate* (*Ritter-Coulais, Lakebrink*)[321] and with regard to a reduction of the tax *base* (*Renneberg, X*).[322] All these cases involved negative rental income from the taxpayer's owner-occupied dwelling in the home State, i.e., negative imputed income, where the respective national rules of the source States were structured so as to essentially grant an inherently *subjective* benefit to homeowners. It is not clear, if this line of case law is limited to such situations relating to taxpayer's *subjective* ability-to-pay, or if it expands to all aspect of a taxpayer's overall ability to pay, including ("real") losses from an economic activity if the taxpayer's home Member State is not in a position to take them into account.[323] If that were the case, a home State loss of an individual would *always* be transferred to the source State because, by definition, that home State loss also brings him in a *Schumacker*-position in the source State.[324] Indeed, an extension of *Schumacker* to all losses would be incompatible with the Court's case law with regard to income-related expenses ("expenditure linked directly to the income of a person"[325]), i.e. expenses relating to a taxpayer's *objective* ability to pay, where comparability of non-resident and resident taxpayers is not in doubt when the source State exercises its taxing right over the respective income. Indeed, applying *Schumacker* to those income-related expenses as well (because expenses exceeding revenues lead to losses) would allow Member States to deny such deductions unless

319 Case C-250/95, *Futura Participations*, EU:C:1997:239, para. 22; see also Case C-345/04, *Centro Equestre da Lezíria Grande Lda*, EU:C:2007:96, para. 22. For a comprehensive analysis of that principle in light of the broader case law of the Court see W. Schön, *Neutrality and Territoriality – Competing or Converging Concepts in European Tax Law?*, 69 BIT 2015, p. 271 (p. 271-293).

320 Case C-279/93, *Schumacker*, EU:C:1995:31.

321 Case C-152/03, *Ritter-Coulais*, EU:C:2006:123 (where the taxpayers had already opted, under § 1(3) of the German Income Tax Act, to be treated as residents in line with *Schumacker*); Case C-182/06, *Lakebrink*, EU:C:2007:452.

322 Case C-527/06, *Renneberg*, EU:C:2008:566; CJEU, 9 February 2017, Case C-283/15, *X*, EU:C:2017:102.

323 See in that direction, e.g., Case C-182/06, *Lakebrink*, EU:C:2007:452, para. 34, and quite clearly so Opinion AG Mengozzi, 29 March 2007, C-182/06, *Lakebrink*, EU:C:2007:203, paras 35-36. For critical analysis see, e.g., Eric C.C.M. Kemmeren, *Renneberg Endangers the Double Tax Convention System or Can a Second Round Bring Recovery?*, 18 EC Tax Review 4-15 (2009); CFE ECJ Task Force, *Opinion Statement ECJ-TF 4/2017 on the Decision of the Court of Justice of the European Union of 9 February 2017 in X (Case C-283/15) ("Pro-Rata Personal Deductions"), Concerning Personal and Family Tax Benefits in Multi-State Situations*, 58 European Taxation 163-169 (2018).

324 Moreover, of course, it would challenge the domestic tax law of the source State regarding a potential recapture of that benefit should the loss be usable in the taxpayer's home State in a future taxable year, while the Court was much more protective of Member State's interests concerning the double deduction of losses from the home State's perspective in, e.g., *Marks & Spencer*.

325 *See*, for this terminology, e.g., Case C-346/04, *Conijn*, EU:C:2006:445, para. 20.

the non-resident taxpayer's home State is not in a position to take those expenses into account – a position that is clearly rejected by the Court.[326]

In any event, it was generally accepted[327] that the Court's judgments in *Renneberg* and *X* cannot be relevant for corporate taxpayers, which, per definition, do not have a personal sphere ("personal and family circumstances") and hence do not raise issues of *subjective* ability to pay. This perspective was (implicitly) confirmed in cases such as *Futura* and *Centro Equestre*,[328] but was recently challenged (and, arguably, overturned) in *Sofina*[329] and *Credit Suisse Securities*,[330] both of which concerned the withholding taxation of outbound dividends by the source State. The facts of *Sofina* are straightforward and can be simplified: Sofina, a Belgian company, received portfolio dividends from various French companies. French tax law differentiated between domestic and cross-border portfolio dividends. In the case of non-resident corporate shareholders, such as Sofina, France levied a (treaty reduced) 15% final withholding tax. In contrast, resident corporate shareholders had to include dividends in their taxable income, which also meant, e.g., that if losses exceeded the dividend income in a given year, the dividends received decreased those general losses, but effectively remained untaxed in that year. That effect is typically *temporary* (as future profits of the shareholder will be taxed earlier because the loss-carry-forward has been reduced by the dividends),[331] but could, of course, also become *permanent* (if the shareholder never returns to a profit). As Sofina was in a loss-position in Belgium (with those losses being completely unrelated to France), it sought reimbursement of the withholding tax levied in France based on its freedom of capital movement under Articles 63 and 65 TFEU.

Indeed, that French system of dividend taxation was already subject to an investigation by the Commission,[332] and the French Conseil d'État eventually decided to refer *Sofina* to the Court,[333] asking, essentially, whether the (temporary or permanent) cash disadvantage suffered by loss-making non-resident dividend recipients because of the withholding taxation constitutes an unjustified restriction. The Court identified such prohibited

326 See, e.g., Case C-234/01, *Gerritse*, EU:C:2003:340; Case C-290/04, *Scorpio*, EU:C:2006:630.
327 See, e.g., J. Monsenego, *Taxation of Foreign Business Income within the European Internal Market* (IBFD Amsterdam, 2012), Chapter 5.
328 Case C-250/95, *Futura Participations*, EU:C:1997:239; Case C-345/04, *Centro Equestre da Lezíria Grande Lda*, EU:C:2007:96. *Centro Equestre*, concerned a Portuguese company, where the ECJ considered that a source Member State cannot be required to accept any foreign expenses or costs for deduction from its tax base. As losses are the consequence of costs or expenses exceeding revenues, *Centro Equestre* clearly follows a territorial approach to both costs and losses of non-individuals.
329 Case C-575/17, *Sofina*, EU:C:2018:943.
330 Case C-601/23, *Credit Suisse Securities*, EU:C:2024:1048.
331 That effect of a diminished loss-carry forward had already been appreciated in Case C-138/07, *Cobelfret*, EU:C:2009:82, paras 37-41, and Cases C-439/07 and C-499/07, *KBC Bank*, EU:C:2009:339, paras 45-54.
332 See the Commission's information on the reasoned opinion concerning "Free movement of capital: Commission requests France to abolish withholding tax imposed on non-resident companies in deficit", MEMO/17/1280 (17 May 2017).
333 See French Conseil d'État, 20 September 2017, *Sofina, Rebelco, Sidro*, Nos. 398662, 398663, 398666, 398672, 398674 and 398675.

restriction in a seemingly traditional, but substantively revolutionary analysis. It first focused on the losses that a resident and a non-resident corporate shareholder might have and noted that "the dividends paid to a non-resident company are subject to immediate and definitive taxation", while "the tax imposed on dividends paid to a resident company depends on whether the latter's financial year is net loss-making or net profit-making". In case of losses, the taxation of those dividends is not only deferred to a subsequent profit-making year (procuring a cash-flow advantage), but is also thereby uncertain, since that tax will not be levied if the resident company never becomes profitable.[334] This, in the Court's view (and without even acknowledging *Futura* or a potential tension with the principle of territoriality), leads to three relevant restrictions:[335]

> "First, the exclusion of a cash-flow advantage in a cross-border situation when it is granted in an equivalent situation on national territory constitutes a restriction on the free movement of capital". "Secondly, the assessment of whether there exists a potentially less favourable treatment of the dividends paid to non-resident companies must be undertaken for each tax year, taken individually". Relevant is therefore the financial year in which the distribution of those dividends occurs, and in that year "there is no such tax burden when the resident company is loss-making at the end of such a financial year". "Thirdly, such a deferral of taxation will be a definitive exemption of the dividends paid to a resident company if the latter does not become profitable before it ceases trading".

Accordingly, French tax law was liable to procure an advantage for loss-making resident companies, "since it gives rise, at the very least, to a cash-flow advantage, or even an exemption in the event of that company ceasing trading, whereas non-resident companies are subject to immediate and definitive taxation irrespective of their results".[336] This restriction could moreover not be justified based on either the argument that the positions of resident and non-resident companies are objectively different or on the balanced allocation of powers of taxation between the Member States or the need for the effective collection of tax.[337] Hence, the French system violated the free movement of capital. Recently, *Credit Suisse Securities* confirmed that holding for the Spanish system, which likewise does not reimburse to non-residents the dividend withholding tax levied (whereas residents who likewise suffer losses during the financial year are reimbursed that tax in full).[338] To remedy this infringement, the Court in *Sofina* effectively proposed a deferral of taxation that is combined with a domestic regime that leads to a subsequent recapture if (and only if) the non-resident taxpayer becomes profitable during a subsequent tax year.[339] Needless to say that such an approach raises numerous technical and policy issues. Moreover, it needs to be determined which State's rules are decisive for determining the existence and amount of the relevant loss. This issue was not raised in *Sofina* (presumably because the taxpayer had a loss under both States' rules). However, it would seem consistent (albeit burdensome) to apply the *source* State's rules to avoid

---

334 Case C-575/17, *Sofina*, EU:C:2018:943, para. 28.
335 Case C-575/17, *Sofina*, EU:C:2018:943 para. 29-33.
336 Case C-575/17, *Sofina*, EU:C:2018:943, para 34.
337 Case C-575/17, *Sofina*, EU:C:2018:943, paras 43-79.
338 Case C-601/23, *Credit Suisse Securities*, EU:C:2024:1048.
339 Case C-575/17, *Sofina*, EU:C:2018:943 para. 59.

unequal treatment,[340] whereas the French Conseil d'État in *Sofina* has taken a different position and referred to the *home* State's rules,[341] and the Court in *Credit Suisse Securities* seems to have accepted that perspective.[342]

The Court's analysis in *Sofina* and *Credit Suisse Securities* is misguided.[343] The fallacy lies in the chosen comparison, i.e., that for comparing the tax treatment of domestic and outbound dividends the non-dividend income of the recipient is taken into consideration. This has strange effects: Indeed, after *Sofina* and *Credit Suisse Securities*, the source State's rules on taxation of outbound dividends are discriminatory if the non-dividend income of the domestic and foreign shareholder is negative so that both are in an overall loss position; conversely, if the recipient only had dividend income or positive non-dividend income, the source State's rules would, in principle, be non-restrictive.[344] It is hard to see that the *legal* question of whether the source State discriminates should depend on the rather arbitrary *factual* criterion of the taxpayer's worldwide (positive or negative) income (and even, more arbitrarily, the taxpayer's subsequent discretionary decision to liquidate or not before becoming profitable). Moreover, *Sofina* and *Credit Suisse Securities* clearly upset the principle of territoriality previously upheld in *Futura* and *Centro Equestre*. While one might argue that, in the reverse situation, the *Marks & Spencer* line of case law has also undermined the international tax law concept of territoriality, those cases nevertheless took a very cautious approach by limiting cross-border loss transfers to "final" or "definitive" losses,[345] whereas *Sofina* and *Credit Suisse Securities* require an annual analysis and rejects an approach akin to a "reverse final loss exception".[346]

Finally, if the Court chooses to follow along the lines of *Sofina* and *Credit Suisse Securities* in future cases and more generally, this could unsettle established principles of international taxation. Taken to the extreme, the Court's reasoning in those judgments would not only concern dividends but rather attach a "no-loss condition" to all source State taxing rights. It is indeed hard to see why the Court's logic in *Sofina* and *Credit Suisse Securities* would not likewise prevent *source* State taxation where, for example, a profit-making permanent establishment belongs to a loss-making foreign head office. Concluding so, however, would not only overthrow the allocation of taxing rights under Article 7 OECD MC, but also create an additional distortion in comparison to the taxation of profits of resident

340 See for the reverse situation from the residence State's perspective *supra* Chapter 10.1.4.
341 See French Conseil d'État, 27 February 2019, *Sofina*, No. 398662.
342 Case C-601/23, *Credit Suisse Securities*, EU:C:2024:1048, para. 26.
343 For analyses see, e.g., Georg Kofler, "Foreign Losses and Territoriality: Did *Sofina* Revolutionize Source State Taxation?", in: Servatius van Thiel, Piergiorgio Valente and Stella Raventós-Calvo (eds.), *CFE Tax Advisers Europe – 60th Anniversary Liber Amicorum* (IBFD Amsterdam 2019), 147-168; CFE ECJ Task Force, *Opinion Statement ECJ-TF 3/2019 on the ECJ Decision of 22 November 2018 in* Sofina *(Case C-575/17) on Withholding Taxes, Losses and Territoriality*, 60 European Taxation 91-97 (2020).
344 What is disregarded here is, of course, the issue of the tax base, i.e., the deductibility of dividend-related costs in a subsequent refund procedure.
345 See *supra* Chapter 10.2.
346 Case C-575/17, *Sofina*, EU:C:2018:943, para. 30; Case C-601/23, *Credit Suisse Securities*, EU:C:2024:1048, para. 38; see also Cases C-10/14, C-14/14 and C-17/14, *Miljoen*, EU:C:2015:608, para. 51; Case C-252/14, *Pensioenfonds Metaal en Techniek*, EU:C:2016:402, paras 64-65.

corporations (which are certainly not required to take into account the losses of their shareholders). Carried to its logical conclusion, after *Sofina* and *Credit Suisse Securities* on the one hand and *W AG* on the other, the friction would be even more extreme: The residence State can ignore treaty-exempt source State losses of its residents (*W AG*), whereas the source State might have to take unrelated residence State losses into account (*Sofina* and *Credit Suisse Securities*). This would be a truly odd result, not only from the perspective of international tax law, but also from the perspective of the Internal Market.

10.5 Impact of Profits in the Source State on Losses in the Residence State (AMID, Mertens)

In two decisions from the early 2000s, *AMID*[347] and *Mertens*,[348] the Court had to deal with an intriguing issue: The so-called "Velasquez doctrine"[349] had the effect that losses incurred by a resident taxpayer in Belgium were reduced by treaty-exempt foreign income (i.e., profits attributable to a permanent establishment in Luxembourg in *AMID* and employment income in Germany in *Mertens*). This, of course, leads to a reduction of the loss carry-forward that could have been used against future profits in Belgium.[350] Finding the right comparison in that situation, however, is not an easy task: If the taxpayers were to exercise profitable and loss-making activities only in Belgium, those results would also be netted, and if losses exceeded profits, only the excess amount could be carried forward. Hence, at first glance, the "Velasquez doctrine" does not discriminate between cross-border and domestic situations, as in both cases the carry-forward is reduced. However, for the Court the decisive criterion for the identification of a discrimination by the Belgian system was the exemption method under the applicable tax treaty, as

> "[a] Belgian company which, having no establishments outside Belgium, incurs a loss during a given tax year finds itself, for tax purposes, in a comparable situation with that of a Belgian company which, having an establishment in Luxembourg, incurs a loss in Belgium and makes a profit in Luxembourg during that same tax year. [...] Since an objective difference in the companies' respective positions has not been established, a difference in treatment as regards the deduction of losses when calculating the companies' taxable income cannot be accepted."[351]

The Court's analysis hence requires that the treaty-exempt Luxembourg profits are completely ignored in the comparability analysis. Treating exempt foreign and taxable domestic branch profits equally is, under that perspective, equal treatment of different

347 Case C-141/99, *AMID*, EU:C:2000:696.

348 Case C-431/01, *Mertens*, EU:C:2002:492.

349 Developed by the Belgian Cour de Cassation, 29 June 1984, *N.V. Sigarenfabriek Velasquez*; see also the discussion by A. Rust in E. Reimer and A. Rust (eds.), *Klaus Vogel on Double Taxation Conventions*, 5th edn. (Kluwer, 2022), Art. 23 m.no. 22.

350 That effect of a diminished loss-carry forward has also been appreciated in Case C-138/07, *Cobelfret*, EU:C:2009:82, paras 37-41, and Cases C-439/07 and C-499/07, *KBC Bank*, EU:C:2009:339, paras 45-54.

351 Case C-141/99, *AMID*, EU:C:2000:696, para. 29-30.

situations and therefore a prohibited discrimination[352] (which could also not be justified by Belgium).

Again, *AMID* and *Mertens* demonstrate that the *legal* (tax treaty) context – exemption or credit – matters, not the *economic* effects. Indeed, under the ordinary credit method (e.g., based on Article 23B OECD MC), foreign profits also reduce home State losses (so that those losses are not available to offset future profits of the enterprise in the home State); moreover, under the typical "credit limitation" the home State will not (be able to) grant a credit for the source State tax, since the taxpayer is in an overall loss position without any *current* home State tax burden on the source State income. Economically, this outcome resembles the result under the "Velasquez doctrine" at issue in *AMID* and *Mertens*. It could, for example, be remedied through a so-called credit carry-forward, where the foreign tax not currently creditable would be carried-forward to future years to avoid intertemporal double taxation. However, such credit carry-forward is neither required by the OECD MC,[353] nor by the fundamental freedoms.[354] Moreover, the legal context is again different where a Member State does *not* foresee any relief from juridical double taxation, neither through a tax treaty nor under domestic law. In that situation, double taxation and the ensuing disadvantage for cross-border economic activities would persist, but it would – as the Court has held, e.g., in *Kerckhaert and Morres*[355] – not be prohibited under the fundamental freedoms, but rather be the result of the parallel exercise of fiscal sovereignty by two Member States.[356] In other words, (only) once a Member State has chosen a method of relief, the Court will hold it to that method (and not accept, as a justification, that the taxpayer would be even worse off had it instead chosen a different method or no relief at all).[357] Implicit in the case law is the overriding relevance of the Court's specific understanding of the particular method chosen by a Member State (perhaps oddly so, as the Court is not competent to interpret domestic law or tax treaties[358]). In *AMID*, e.g., for the Court "exemption" meant "exemption", and not – as for the Belgian Cour de Cassation[359] – "exemption so far as the foreign profits exceed the taxpayer's domestic losses".

---

352 Case C-431/01, *Mertens*, EU:C:2002:492, paras 32-33; see also Case C-141/99, *AMID*, EU:C:2000:696, para. 27.

353 See, e.g., G. Kofler, "Article 23" in: *Global Tax Treaty Commentaries (GTTC)* (IBFD Amsterdam, Feb. 2020), Chapter 3.2.2.3.5.

354 See Cases C-436/08 and C-437/08, *Haribo and Salinen*, EU:C:2011:61, paras 166-172.

355 Case C-513/04, *Kerckhaert and Morres*, EU:C:2006:713; see also, e.g., EFTA-Court, 7 May 2008, Case E-7/07, *Seabrokers AS*, [2008] EFTA Court Report 172, paras 49 et seq.; Case C-67/08, *Block*, EU:C:2009:92, paras 28 et seq.; Case C-128/08, *Damseaux*, EU:C:2009:471, paras 27 et seq.; Case C-540/11, *Levy and Sebbag*, EU:C:2012:581, paras 18 et seq.; Case C-194/15, *Baudinet*, EU:C:2016:81, paras 30 et seq.; Case C-403/19, *Société Générale*, EU:C:2021:136, para. 29.

356 For extensive discussion see *supra* Chapter 8.2.1.

357 See also, by analogy, Case C-138/07, *Cobelfret*, EU:C:2009:82, paras 48 and 50, and Cases C-439/07 and C-499/07, *KBC Bank*, EU:C:2009:339, para. 43.

358 See, e.g., Case C-141/99, *AMID*, EU:C:2000:696, para. 18; Case C-298/05, *Columbus Container Services*, EU:C:2007:754, para. 47; Case C-128/08, *Damseaux*, EU:C:2009:471, para. 22.

359 See again Belgian Cour de Cassation, 29 June 1984, N.V. *Sigarenfabriek Velasquez*.

10.6 Domestic Losses and "Sandwich Situations" (*Société Papillon, Philips Electronics, Felixstowe Dock and Railway Company, SCA Group Holding, NN, B*)

Much of the more recent case law dealt with various restrictions of loss relief in group situations that were based not on the territoriality of the losses, but rather on the fact that a taxpayer also had foreign holdings (*ICI*[360]) or because a domestic group member (*Société Papillon*,[361] *Felixstowe Dock and Railway Company*,[362] *SCA Group Holding*,[363] *B*[364]) or a domestic permanent establishment (*Philips Electronics*,[365] *NN*[366]) was held by a non-resident group member. The latter issues – so-called "sandwich situations" – relate to situations where a transfer of losses under a domestic group taxation regime between two domestic group entities (subsidiaries or permanent establishments) has not been granted by a Member State because the "linking" entity was non-resident. Here, the Court has developed a consistent line of case law on the various types of group taxation regimes and irrespective of how many tiers of intermediate non-resident EU-companies are "sandwiched" between resident group entities, as each of the intermediate companies exercises its freedom of establishment and each lower-tier company can also derive rights from that freedom.[367]

Briefly, the Court generally assumed comparability in these "sandwich situations" and, in essence, required that benefits of a group taxation regime are not denied merely because of a foreign "link":[368] In *Société Papillon*, the Court objected to the exclusion of a domestic sub-subsidiary from the French "tax integration" regime where the intermediate subsidiary was established in another Member State. In *Philips Electronics*, the Court held that UK national legislation excluding the transfer of domestic losses incurred by a branch of a non-resident company to a resident company of the same group violates the freedom of establishment. In *Felixstowe Dock and Railway Company*, the Court found it to be an infringement on the freedom of establishment where UK legislation required the "link company" to be a resident in order to facilitate a loss transfer between a company belonging to a consortium and a company that is a member of a group. In *SCA Group Holding BV*, the Netherland's refusal to permit a loss transfer under the rules of "fiscal unity" ("fiscale eenheid") between domestic companies in cases where one or more intermediate companies are residents of another Member State or the common parent

360 Case C-264/96, ICI, EU:C:1998:370.
361 Case C-418/07, *Société Papillon*, EU:C:2008:659.
362 Case C-80/12, *Felixstowe Dock and Railway Company*, EU:C:2014:200.
363 Cases C-39/13 to C-41/13, *SCA Group Holding*, EU:C:2014:1758.
364 Case C-749/18, B, EU:C:2020:370.
365 Case C-18/11, *Philips Electronics*, EU:C:2012:532.
366 Case C-28/17, *NN*, EU:C:2018:526.
367 See also Chapter 9.4. The Court has explicitly held that a company may, for tax purposes, rely on a restriction of the freedom of establishment of another company which is linked to it in so far as such a restriction affects its own taxation; see, e.g., Case C-18/11, *Philips Electronics*, EU:C:2012:532, para. 39; Case C-80/12, *Felixstowe Dock and Railway Company*, EU:C:2014:200, para. 23.
368 See on this line of case law, e.g., CFE ECJ Task Force, *Opinion Statement ECJ-TF 4/2014 of the CFE on the decision of the European Court of Justice in* SCA Group Holding BV et al. *(Joined Cases C-39/13, C-40/13 and C-41/13), on the requirements to form a 'fiscal unity'*, 55 European Taxation 116-121 (2015).

company of two domestic sister companies is resident in another Member State infringed upon the freedom of establishment. In *B*, the Court found the Luxembourg rules to infringe on the freedom of establishment, as they allowed the tax consolidation of Luxembourg sister companies (i.e., horizontal tax consolidation) only insofar as the non-resident controlling entity maintained a permanent establishment in Luxembourg, through which the share-holdings in the controlled companies were held. The Court, however, did not deal with the technical issues, e.g., how consolidation (which, e.g., in the Dutch "fiscal unity" regime, is effectuated at the level of the parent company) should take place if the common parent of two resident sister companies is resident in another Member State. Those issues were merely "of secondary importance"[369] and left for domestic law to resolve.[370]

This line of case law is a good example for the operation of the Internal Market. Also, enabling loss relief in these "sandwich structures" does not threaten the balanced allocation of taxing powers between the Member States, since both the loss-transferring and the loss-receiving entity are resident in the same Member State.[371] However, those cases have also addressed the risk of double loss utilization, albeit in two completely different contexts, i.e., double *economic* loss utilization on the one hand and double *cross-border* loss utilization on the other hand:

In *Société Papillon*, the Court was faced with the risk of a double *economic* loss utilization in one Member State: Within the French "tax integration" regime write-downs of group entities are neutralized through the complete chain of holdings, so that one and the same loss originating at the level of the sub-subsidiary cannot be used multiple times, once *directly* through integration and again *indirectly* through write-downs of the holding in the sub-subsidiary and other intermediate entities. This coherence would be distorted where the intermediate subsidiary is a non-resident, because then the French sub-subsidiary's loss would be relieved *once* in the tax integration regime and *again* through a non-neutralized write-down of the French parent's holding in the non-resident subsidiary (which is not subject to the tax integration regime). In these circumstances the Court accepted that the French regime was, in principle, justified based on its coherence,[372] but it failed on the level of proportionality because it prevented resident companies from proving that there is no risk of losses being used twice under the tax integration regime (by showing, e.g., that decreases in share values in the subsidiary do not indirectly relate to a loss of the sub-subsidiary).

369 See Opinion AG Kokott, 27 February 2014, Cases C-39/13 to C-41/13, *SCA Group Holding*, EU:C:2014:104, para. 77.

370 For the judicial resolution of that issue with regard to Austria's group taxation regime see Austrian Verwaltungsgerichtshof, 27 March 2024, Ro 2023/13/0018 (in essence treating two Austrian sister companies of a German parent company as permanent establishments).

371 Case C-18/11, *Philips Electronics*, EU:C:2012:532, paras 25-26; Case C-80/12, *Felixstowe Dock and Railway Company*, EU:C:2014:200, para. 30; Case C-28/17, *NN*, EU:C:2018:526, para. 40.

372 Case C-418/07, *Société Papillon*, EU:C:2008:659, paras 41-51. It might be noted that the Court did not accept a similar argument by the Netherlands in *SCA Group Holding BV*, as the Netherland's neutralization of write-downs was a consequence of the general holding exemption and not directly linked to the tax integration regime (see Cases C-39/13 to C-41/13, *SCA Group Holding*, EU:C:2014:1758, paras. 36-40).

Philips Electronics[373] and *NN*[374] raised the quite different issue of double *cross-border* loss utilization. *Philips Electronics* concerned a situation where, within the UK group relief system, losses of a UK branch of a foreign "linking" group entity could only then be surrendered to another UK subsidiary "where it is clear that at the time of the claim there can never be any deduction or allowance in any State outside the UK". This categorical prevention of a "double dip" by the *host* State was not accepted by the Court: The risk of double utilization of losses, the Court argued, "has no effect on the power of the Member State where the permanent establishment is situated to impose taxes" and, moreover, "[t]hat power is not at all impaired by the fact that the losses transferred might also, in appropriate circumstances, be used in the Netherlands".[375] Consequently.

> "the objective of preventing the risk of double use of losses cannot, as such, allow the Member State in which the permanent establishment is situated to exclude the use of losses on the ground that those losses may also be used in the Member State in which the non-resident company has its seat".[376]

In light of *Philips Electronics* one might conclude that the risk of double loss utilization might justify restrictions imposed by the *home* State (as in *Marks & Spencer*), but does not allow the *source* State to do so.

That clear conclusion might have been called into question by the Court's subsequent judgment in *NN.*[377] NN was the group parent company of a Danish group which included, *inter alia*, a Swedish subsidiary with a loss-making branch in Denmark. In contrast to *Philips Electronics*, Denmark was both the *home* State of the ultimate parent company and the *host* State of the Swedish subsidiary's branch. Denmark's group taxation regime, in principle, permits setting off the branch's loss against group income, but only under the condition that "the rules in the foreign State [...] in which the company is resident provide that a loss cannot be set off in the calculation of the company's income in the foreign State". Based on this, the Danish authorities denied relief for the branch's losses, "since those losses could be set off against the taxable income in Sweden of the Swedish company which owned the branch". This was obviously the case because the tax treaty applicable between Denmark and Sweden provided for the credit method. Conversely, if the Danish permanent establishment had been owned by one of NN's Danish subsidiaries, its losses could, in any event, be set off against the group's profits.

The Court's response was, with all due respect, strange and confusing, as the Court – unlike AG Sánchez-Bordona[378] – seems to have focused on Denmark's role not as the *host* State of the branch but rather as the *home* State of the group.[379] From that *home* State's

373 Case C-18/11, *Philips Electronics*, EU:C:2012:532.
374 Case C-28/17, *NN*, EU:C:2018:526.
375 Case C-18/11, *Philips Electronics*, EU:C:2012:532, paras 30-31.
376 Case C-18/11, *Philips Electronics*, EU:C:2012:532, paras 32.
377 Case C-28/17, *NN*, EU:C:2018:526.
378 See Opinion AG Sánchez-Bordona, 21 February 2018, Case C-28/17, *NN*, EU:C:2018:86, para. 75.
379 This becomes not only obvious in the comparator chosen in Case C-28/17, *NN*, EU:C:2018:526, para. 34, but also in the Court's broad reference to *Bevola*, which concerned the perspective of the *home* State regarding the cross-border utilization of ("final") losses of a base-exempt *foreign* branch.

perspective, the Court saw the cross-border and the domestic situation as comparable, in light of the objective of the Danish provision to prevent the double deduction of losses, only if "there is no other possibility of deducting the losses of the non-resident subsidiary attributable to the permanent establishment which is resident in the Member State in which the subsidiary is established".[380] Second, the Court – surprisingly[381] – fully endorsed the Danish justification based on the need to prevent the double deduction of losses in two States. Proportionality only sets a limit where utilization of the branch's losses against the subsidiary's profits is actually – i.e., "in practice" (e.g., because the loss-creating transaction is tax neutral in the subsidiary's State)[382] – impossible in the other Member State (either currently or, e.g., through a carry-forward[383]).

The different perspectives taken by the Court in *Philips Electronics* and *NN* may explain the different outcomes. Moreover, the Court did not further entertain AG Sánchez-Bordona's argument that the EU legislature has paid special attention to the "fight against double deduction" since *Philips Electronics* was decided.[384] And even if the Court had intended to limit *Philips Electronics*, it would certainly go too far to argue, based on *NN*, that it might generally be permissible for a *source* State to make the – otherwise generally available – carry-forward of a branch's losses dependent on whether or not the loss can be used in the taxpayer's *home* State, as this would clearly lead to a "restriction [...] imputable" to the source State.[385]

380 Case C-28/17, *NN*, EU:C:2018:526, para. 35.

381 As mentioned, under the Nordic Convention the credit method applies, i.e., both Sweden and Denmark may *currently* tax the branch's profit, with Sweden eliminating double taxation through a credit for the Danish tax. Symmetrically, losses would be *currently* deducted in both States and automatically recaptured once the branch returns to profit (see also *supra* Chapter 10.3.2.): This automatic recapture takes place because the branch's losses will typically be carried forward and offset future Danish profits. These future profits will also be fully taxed in Sweden – without the need to grant a credit insofar as the profits have been soaked up by the loss carry-forward in Denmark and hence not been taxed there. In that framework the double deduction of losses in the first period makes complete sense because of the automatic recapture in a future period. Indeed, the Court has acknowledged this from the home State's perspective already in *Nordea Bank Danmark* (Case C-48/13, EU:C:2014:2087). However, in *NN* the Court seems to have a different understanding: Based on Sweden's obligation to grant a tax credit for Danish tax under the Nordic Convention, the Court concluded that "the parallel exercise of the powers of taxation of the Kingdom of Denmark and the Kingdom of Sweden does not entail an obligation for the Swedish company which has a permanent establishment in Denmark to pay income tax twice. In those circumstances, the ability, claimed by the Danish group to which the Swedish company belongs, to deduct the losses of such an establishment twice, that is to say, in one and the other national tax systems, does not appear to be justified" (Case C-28/17, *NN*, EU:C:2018:526, paras 46-47). While it is not clear from the stated facts in *NN* if a specificity of Danish or Swedish law indeed led the Court to that conclusion, under the general credit method (as, e.g., foreseen in Article 23B OECD MC) the double deduction would clearly "appear to be justified" because of the automatic recapture in future periods.

382 Case C-28/17, *NN*, EU:C:2018:526, paras 53-54.

383 See Opinion AG Sánchez-Bordona, 21 February 2018, Case C-28/17, *NN*, EU:C:2018:86, para. 82.

384 See Opinion AG Sánchez-Bordona, 21 February 2018, Case C-28/17, *NN*, EU:C:2018:86, paras 64-70.

385 Case C-157/07, *Krankenheim Ruhesitz am Wannsee*, EU:C:2008:588, para. 51.

10.7 Excursus: Currency Losses (Deutsche Shell, X AB, X BV and X NV)

Finally, the Court has also dealt with currency losses, i.e., losses which are generally only "visible" from the perspective of one State. Indeed, cross-border business is often conducted in foreign currency, which may result in a currency gain or loss from the home State's perspective. From an EU law perspective, it is precisely the exercise of a fundamental freedom that increases a taxpayer's risk of a currency loss, e.g., if a cross-border investment in a permanent establishment or in a foreign holding is denominated in a different currency. How to deal with that specific type of losses was addressed by the Court in two cases, *Deutsche Shell*[386] and *X AB*[387] (and, in the context of a group consolidation regime, in *X BV and X NV*[388])

Deutsche Shell concerned the investment of start-up capital by Deutsche Shell GmbH, a German company, in its permanent establishment in Italy. The injection of the start-up capital ("Dotationskapital") in Italian Lira (LIT) between 1974 and 1991 was, for purposes of Deutsche Shell's tax accounting in Germany, translated into German Deutsche Mark (DM). After a series of transactions, in 1992 that start-up capital was repatriated to Germany and translated, at that time, back into DM. Due to the change in currency value between 1973 and 1992, the comparison between the amount of the original injection of the start-up capital (in DM) and the repatriated start-up capital (again, in DM) resulted, from the home State's perspective, in a currency loss. Naturally, the Italian permanent establishment did not even "see" that currency loss, as its operative currency was LIT. Germany considered that currency loss to be part of the income attributable to the Italian permanent establishment and "exempted" it under the applicable tax treaty ("base exemption").[389] Deutsche Shell challenged the respective assessment, and the Court eventually sided with it.

The core issue in *Deutsche Shell* was to identify the relevant restriction, as no comparable currency devaluation could take place regarding the start-up capital injected in a *domestic* permanent establishment: The referring German court argued a discrimination by equating the injection of start-up capital in a foreign permanent establishment with the "normal" acquisition of, e.g., foreign fixed assets, which, if settled in a foreign currency, could also lead to a currency loss at the German head office (that would then be tax deductible under domestic law).[390] However, for lack of true *internal* comparators, AG Sharpston[391] and the Court phrased the issue in *Deutsche Shell* as (one of the few, if not the only) case of a true non-discriminatory restriction ("obstacle-based approach")[392] in EU direct tax case law: "It must be observed", the Court said, that because Deutsche Shell exercised its freedom

386 Case C-293/06, *Deutsche Shell*, EU:C:2008:129.

387 Case C-686/13, *X AB*, EU:C:2015:375.

388 Cases C-398/16 and C-399/16, *X BV and X NV*, EU:C:2018:110.

389 See for that understanding of the exemption method already *supra* Chapter 10.3.2.

390 See German Finanzgericht Hamburg, 8 June 2006, 6 K 274/03.

391 Opinion AG Sharpston, 8 November 2007, Case C-293/06, *Deutsche Shell*, EU:C:2007:660, paras 29-36.

392 See also Sjoerd Douma, *Non-discriminatory Tax Obstacles*, 21 EC Tax Review 2 (2012), p. 67 (p. 81-82).

of establishment it "suffered financial loss which was not taken into account either by the national tax authorities for the purposes of calculating the basis of assessment for corporation tax in Germany or with respect to the assessment for tax of its permanent establishment in Italy", which "constitutes an obstacle to the freedom of establishment".[393] The Court also rejected a justification based both on the coherence of the German tax system (for lack of a direct link between the treatment of currency losses, on one hand, and currency gains, on the other)[394] and the treaty-based allocation of tax competence between the two Member States. As for the latter, Germany had argued that under the tax treaty profits (including currency gains) and losses (including currency losses) of foreign permanent establishments are symmetrically exempt, and the Court acknowledged that

> "a Member State cannot be required to take account, for the purposes of applying its tax law, of the negative results of a permanent establishment situated in another Member State which belongs to a company with a registered office in the first State solely because those negative results are not capable of being taken into account for tax purposes in the Member State where the permanent establishment is situated. [...] Freedom of establishment cannot be understood as meaning that a Member State is required to draw up its tax rules on the basis of those in another Member State in order to ensure, in all circumstances, taxation which removes any disparities arising from national tax rules, given that the decisions made by a company as to the establishment of commercial structures abroad may be to the company's advantage or not, according to circumstances [...]."[395]

However, an outcome where such currency losses could not be taken into account anywhere was obviously unsatisfactory for the Court at that time. Although Germany's system was not inconsistent, the Court in *Deutsche Shell* nevertheless adopted a restriction-based "always somewhere approach" and identified Germany as the only State in the Internal Market that could take such loss into account:

> "As far as concerns the main proceedings, it must be noted that the tax disadvantage concerned relates to a specific operational factor which is capable of being taken into consideration only by the German tax authorities. Although it is true that any Member State which has concluded a double taxation convention must implement it by applying its own tax law and thereby calculate the income attributable to a permanent establishment, it is unacceptable for a Member State to exclude from the basis of assessment of the principal establishment currency losses which, by their nature, can never be suffered by the permanent establishment."[396]

It is not immediately obvious how to link the restriction-based reasoning in *Deutsche Shell* on *currency losses*, which existed *only* in the taxpayer's *home* State, to the Court's discrimination-based case law on base-exempt *foreign* economic losses, e.g., in *Lidl Belgium* and *Bevola*.[397] Moreover, in light of *K*, the currency loss in *Deutsche Shell* would also not be considered a "final" loss under a traditional discrimination-based approach: As Italy

393 Case C-293/06, *Deutsche Shell*, EU:C:2008:129, paras 31-32.
394 Case C-293/06, *Deutsche Shell*, EU:C:2008:129, paras 37-40.
395 Case C-293/06, *Deutsche Shell*, EU:C:2008:129, paras 42-43.
396 Case C-293/06, *Deutsche Shell*, EU:C:2008:129, paras 44.
397 See for that case law *supra* Chapter 10.3.2.

did not even "see" the currency loss, *K* implies that Deutsche Shell has "not exhausted the possibilities" of loss-utilization in Italy because "such a possibility has never existed".[398]

In any event, the Court's subsequent judgment in *X AB* has put the "always somewhere approach" into context. *X AB* required the Court to analyze if and to what extent the findings in *Deutsche Shell* on a (treaty-exempt) currency loss relating to a foreign permanent establishment may be transposed to a (domestic law-exempt) currency loss incurred in connection with an investment in a subsidiary. Over a number of years, X AB, a Swedish company, purchased shares in a subsidiary in the UK, which were issued in US dollars.

X AB, wishing to put an end to the UK subsidiary's activities, planned to transfer those shares. This transaction, however, presented a risk of currency loss because the exchange rate at the time of the investments was more favorable than that existing at the time of the transfer. Since the shares in the UK subsidiary were so-called "holdings for business purposes", under Swedish rules all gains and profits (including currency gains and losses) from transferring such shares, whether in a domestic or a foreign subsidiary, were exempt from taxation. X AB, referring to *Deutsche Shell*, argued that this "exemption" of currency losses would violate, *inter alia*, its freedom of capital movement. The Court disagreed, finding neither a discriminatory nor a non-discriminatory restriction:

> „[C]apital losses on the transfer of 'holdings for business purposes' having their origin in a currency loss cannot be deducted either in the situation in which, as in the case in the main proceedings, the shares are held in a company established in another Member State or in that in which they are held in a company established in Sweden– whether the capital of the latter be denominated in Swedish Krona or in any other currency permitted by the national legislation." Hence, cross-border investments are not "treated more unfavourably than similar investments effected in Sweden". Moreover, "even assuming that such non-deductibility might be likely to disadvantage a company having invested in 'holdings for business purposes' in a company established in another Member State by the fact of its exposure to currency losses when, as in the case in the main proceedings, that investment is made in shares denominated in a currency other than that of the host Member State, it follows from the Member States' competence in tax matters that the freedom of companies to choose between different Member States of establishment by no means implies that the latter are required to adapt their own tax systems to the different taxation systems of other Member States so as to ensure that a company that has chosen to establish itself in one Member State is taxed at national level in the same way as a company having chosen to establish itself in another Member State, it being the case that that choice can, in the circumstances, be more or less advantageous or disadvantageous for that company [...]."[399]

The Court distinguished *X AB* from *Deutsche Shell* based on the different legal context: It argued that the German legislation at issue in *Deutsche Shell* "provided that, as a general rule, currency gains were taxed and, at the same time, currency losses were deductible unless a convention to prevent double taxation stipulated otherwise",[400] which was indeed the case based on the exemption method under the applicable 1925 tax treaty between

398 Case C-322/11, *K*, EU:C:2013:716, paras 76-77.
399 Case C-686/13, *X AB*, EU:C:2015:375, paras 31-33.
400 Case C-686/13, *X AB*, EU:C:2015:375, para. 38.

Germany and Italy. In contrast, the Swedish legislation at issue in *X AB* "is, in principle, indifferent to the results of capital transactions on 'holdings for business purposes', in respect of which the Kingdom of Sweden has chosen, as a general rule, not to exercise its powers of taxation".[401] The decisive difference between those cases is that EU law does not require Sweden "to exercise – asymmetrically, moreover – its taxation powers so as to permit the deduction of losses from operations whose results, if they were positive, would not in any event be taxed".[402] As the Court confirmed in *X BV and X NV*,[403] this cross-border symmetry argument would even hold in the quite exceptional[404] case that currency losses and gains were to arise in respect of domestic shareholdings and could be taken into account at the parent level in a domestic group consolidation regime. That is a subtle nuance. Perhaps the Court viewed the currency loss in *Deutsche Shell* as "more" of a cross-border problem because the exemption was based on a tax treaty, which, by definition, only applies to cross-border activities. However, it is hard to see the significant difference between a situation where a Member State would tax under domestic law but exempts under a tax treaty (*Deutsche Shell*) and a situation where a Member State could tax under the tax treaty[405] but exempts under domestic law (*X AB*) (and perhaps even a situation where a Member State exempts both under domestic law and under treaty law). Moreover, the Court's reasoning stands in an odd relationship to its case law on the cross-border utilization of losses of foreign permanent establishments.[406]

401 Case C-686/13, *X AB*, EU:C:2015:375, para. 39.

402 Case C-686/13, *X AB*, EU:C:2015:375, para. 40; see also Cases C-398/16 and C-399/16, *X BV and X NV*, EU:C:2018:110, para. 58.

403 Cases C-398/16 and C-399/16, *X BV and X NV*, EU:C:2018:110, paras 52-60.

404 Indeed, a domestic parent company does "not sustain currency losses on its shareholding in a resident subsidiary, except in the very special case where that shareholding is denominated in a currency other than that in which the company's profits are expressed" (see Cases C-398/16 and C-399/16, *X BV and X NV*, EU:C:2018:110, para. 56).

405 Under both, the 1983 and the 2015 tax treaties between Sweden and the UK, the residence State, i.e., Sweden in *X AB*, has the exclusive right to tax gains from the alienation of shares (other than those in a real estate company).

406 Indeed, regarding exempt foreign losses of permanent establishments the Court in *Bevola* clearly accepted comparability of domestic and cross-border situations where the foreign losses could be taken into account under treaty law (i.e., under the credit method in the Nordic Convention) but were exempt under *domestic law*, while *Timac Agro* might imply non-comparability where the foreign losses could be taken into account under domestic law but were exempt under *tax treaty law* (see supra Chapter 10.3.2.).

CHAPTER 11

Cross-Border Dividend Taxation

Peter Wattel

Update and elaboration by Hein Vermeulen[1]

11.1 Taxation of Distributed Company Profits

A serious disparity between Member States' tax systems concerns the question of whether, and if so, how to eliminate domestic economic double taxation of distributed company profits. The case law of the Court has almost done away with this disparity, as imputation systems of taxation of distributed company profits, which integrate the domestic corporation tax on the profits out of which the dividend is paid into the individual income tax of the shareholder, proved to discriminate against foreign dividends, and were therefore held to be incompatible with the internal market.

Economists generally consider economic double taxation of distributed company profits as harmful discrimination against equity financing of companies (as compared to debt financing). Since interest is deductible from the company's taxable profit, the remuneration for debt-financing is taxed only once, in the hands of the owner of the debt-claim. If, by contrast, the remuneration for equity financing (dividend) is taxed twice because dividend is not deductible, once at company level (corporation tax) and once at shareholder level (income tax), then obviously, companies are encouraged to 'gear' themselves with debt financing instead of equity financing. Excessive debt financing, however, makes that even a slight increase in interest rates may cause serious cash-flow problems, and possibly bankruptcy, for the company. Therefore, most national tax systems provide for mitigation or elimination of economic double taxation of equity remuneration in order to create a level playing field between equity financing and debt financing.

Not all of these systems are internationally neutral: not all of them treat domestic and cross-border dividends alike. This section looks at different systems of distributed company profits taxation, and at their domestic and cross-border effects. The main distinction is between on the one hand classical systems, under which corporation tax and individual income tax ignore each other's existence (leading to economic double taxation of distributed profits), and on the other hand integration systems, which, by contrast, impute (credit) the corporation tax paid by the distributing company to (against) the individual income tax of the shareholders receiving the distribution (taking away the economic

1 Director of PwC's EU Direct Tax Group.

double taxation). Schedular (semi-classical) systems are somewhere in between classical and imputation systems.

In 2003, the Commission published a Communication 'Dividend taxation of individuals in the internal market'[2] (see section 2.2.5.1), concluding that Member States must both tax inbound EU dividends in the same manner as domestic dividends, and treat foreign shareholders (outbound dividends) in the same manner as domestic shareholders. The subsequent *Lenz* and *Manninen* judgments of the CJEU (see section 11.4.1) underpinned that conclusion. For practical purposes, this means that imputation systems have become too expensive to maintain. Schedular (semi-classical) systems prove to be much better suited for the internal market.

11.1.1 Classical Systems

In a classical system, company profits are taxed with corporate income tax, irrespective of whether and to what extent they are retained or distributed. If they are distributed, the dividend is subject to income tax in the hands of the individual shareholder. The result is economic double taxation of company profits. Usually, by virtue of some type of participation exemption (affiliation privilege), a *corporate* shareholder of any significance (holding, *e.g.*, at least 5% or 10% of the shares or votes in the subsidiary) does not (again) pay corporate income tax on dividends received. Further, a dividend withholding tax is normally applied at a flat rate on the gross dividend, to be withheld by the company upon distribution. The individual shareholder may credit such withholding tax against the income tax due on the (net) dividends received, but he may not credit the corporation tax levied at the company level. A *corporate* shareholder is usually not subject to such withholding tax, as it is pointless to levy a withholding tax to the account of a shareholder which is exempt from taxation on the dividend received: the withholding tax would have to be reimbursed to corporate shareholders which qualify for the participation exemption.

Classical systems are by far the simplest systems to apply in practice. A company profit of 100 is first taxed at corporate level (say 25% = 25). If the after-tax profit (75) is distributed, it is taxed with income tax in the hands of the individual shareholder (say 50% = 37.5). Possibly, a dividend withholding tax is levied at, say, 25% (= 18.75), which is creditable against the 37.5 income tax due. In total, 25 corporation tax, plus 37.5 income tax is levied: 62.5 of the profit of 100 goes to the Treasury.

11.1.2 Schedular (Semi-Classical) Systems: Half-Rate, Partial-Base, or Final With-holding

There are not many 'pure' classical systems in practice. In order to avoid (most of) the economic double taxation connected to classical systems, states applying them usually distinguish between dividend income and other income of individual shareholders, and tax the dividend income at a flat rate lower than the general progressive rate of the

2 Communication from the Commission to the Council, the EP and the EcoSoC of 19 December 2003, COM(2003)810 final.

income tax. The aim is to calculate a total (corporate plus individual income tax) burden close to the regular (progressive) income tax rate. Austria, *e.g.*, used to tax dividends in the individual income tax at half the rate for other income (*Halbsatzverfahren;* half-rate system). By now, however, Austria applies a final withholding tax at a 27.5% rate, which is much easier to implement (see below).

Obviously, the same effect of reducing the economic double taxation on distributed company profits may be obtained by reducing, not the tax rate, but the tax base ("half-base system").

An example of a *half-base system* (half base):

- company profit:	100		
- corporate income tax 25%	25		
- available for distribution	75		
- dividend distribution		75	
- dividend withholding tax 25%		18.75	
- net receipt by shareholder:		56.25	
- income tax 50% on *half* of 75			18.75
- credit for the withholding tax			18.75
- remains payable			0.00

The result is that, of a company profit of 100, a total tax is levied of 43.75 (25 corporation tax and 18.75 additional income tax). Thus, the total tax burden is 43.75%, leaving 56.25% after tax. That is (i) close to the normal (marginal) 50% rate of the income tax, *i.e.* close to the result to which full imputation of the corporate tax on the income tax would have lead, (ii) better than the 62.5% overall tax burden which would have ensued from a pure classical system, and (iii) close to neutral from a debt/equity financing point of view, as loan financing would have led to a tax burden of 50% (100 would have been paid out as interest by the company, deductible for the company, and would have been taxed at the 50% rate in the hands of the individual lender and at the 25% rate in the hands of a corporate lender).

Another possibility, which is very attractive from a bureaucratic point of view, is to refrain from individual income taxation altogether, and instead levy a final withholding tax at the level of the distributing company. The after-tax distribution is exempted at shareholder level. This system is very simple but effective. It integrates the two taxation levels into one level, approximating the income tax level of the shareholder, without, however, having to levy and administrate (and credit) tax on two levels. Only the company pays tax: 25% upon making the profit, and an additional gross 17.5% (25% of the net distribution) upon distributing it. Neither the tax administration, nor the shareholder needs to bother with taxation and crediting in the hands of the shareholder. As observed, Austria applies such a system. Belgium applies a final withholding tax of 30% for domestic dividends, and a 30% rate in the individual income tax for foreign dividends.

An example of a *final withholding tax* system with a rate of 25%:

- company profit:	100	
- corporate income tax 25%	25	
- available for distribution	75	
- dividend distribution		75
- final withholding tax 25%		18.75
- net receipt by shareholder:		56.25

11.1.3 *Either/Or Systems*

The simplest way of providing full relief from double economic taxation at shareholder level is to exempt dividend income from individual income taxation altogether. Greece has applied this system since 1992. Such a system makes sense if the marginal income tax rate is not much higher than the corporate tax rate. It has the same effect as a schedular income tax system with a zero rate for dividend income.

The simplest way of providing full relief from economic double taxation at the company level is to tax only retained profits, either by allowing profit distributions to be deducted from the taxable profit, or by allowing a corporation tax refund upon distribution of the profits. This last system amounts to replacing the corporate income tax for the individual income tax at the moment the profit is distributed. Greece applied such a system before 1992, under which it was essential to apply a high withholding tax on profit distributions, both for domestic purposes (preventing tax evasion by domestic shareholders not declaring the dividends received on their tax returns) and for international purposes (if the recipient is not subject to Greek tax, then Greece would have had no tax revenue whatsoever).

Estonia goes even further: it levies no corporate income tax until the profit is distributed. This corporation tax upon distribution is final: shareholders do not need to include the dividend received in their income tax base. Evidently, under such a system, there is no economic double taxation. On retained profits, there is not even single taxation.

11.1.4 *Imputation*

The most sophisticated (and therefore the most intricate) integration systems are imputation systems. They provide for full or partial imputation of the corporate income tax into the income tax payable by the shareholder. The shareholder may credit against his income tax all or part of the corporation tax attributable to the profits out of which the dividend was paid. In effect, in an imputation system, the corporation tax functions as a withholding tax creditable against the individual income tax. The credit available is called an imputation credit *(avoir fiscal, Anrechnung, credito d'imposto)*. It may be expressed as a percentage of the net dividend received by the shareholder (this may amount to either partial or full imputation, depending on the percentage chosen), or as a percentage of the underlying corporate income tax (partial imputation), or it may be equal to the underlying corporate income tax (full imputation).

The imputation credit may be regarded as a cheque with which the shareholder can pay (part of) his income tax due on the dividend received. It is, therefore, taxable income. An example to show how imputation works:

(a) Company profit before tax	100	
(b) Less: corporate income tax at 36%	36	
(c) Net distribution (a minus b)	64	
(d) Add: *imputation credit* (56.25% of (c))	36	
(e) Shareholder income (c + d; 'gross-up')	100	
(f) Individual income tax, say 45%, of (e)	45	
(g) Less: *imputation credit* (d)	36	
(h Income tax still payable (f minus g)	9	
(i) Total tax burden (b + h)	45	(= 45% of 100)
(j) Net after tax dividend (a minus i)	55	

In this example, the imputation is full: the entire corporate income tax (36) is credited against the individual income tax. This is a result of the fact that 36% of the gross profit of 100 (= 36) equals 56.25% of the net distribution of 64 (= also 36). Full imputation was applied, *e.g.*, by Finland[3] and Italy[4] before these states changed to semi-classical systems under pressure of the CJEU case law (see section 11.1.5). If the corporation tax rate is increased in excess of 36%, while at the same time the imputation credit remains at 56.25% of the net dividend, then the corporation tax is only partially credited and some economic double taxation remains.

11.1.5 International Neutrality; Negative Integration; CJEU and EFTA Case Law; Exit Imputation

A classical system is internationally neutral. Foreign profits, foreign dividends and foreign shareholders are treated in the same manner as domestic profits, domestic dividends and domestic shareholders. There are no distortions caused by the border-crossing of dividends. However, from a company financing point of view, a classical system is far from neutral. It is biased against equity financing of companies. Dividend income is discriminated against as compared to income from other sources, such as non-securitized capital and employment. By contrast, (full) imputation systems have the same effect as deductibility of dividends and thus treat debt-financing (interest) and equity financing (dividends) alike. From an international tax point of view, however, imputation systems are not neutral at all, as neither inbound nor outbound dividends are taxed in the same manner as domestic dividends:

3 Case C-319/02 (*Manninen*), EU:C:2004:484.
4 Case C-540/07 (*Commission v. Italy*), EU:C:2009:717.

(i) Discrimination of Inbound Dividends (Home Member State Perspective); the Manninen, Lenz and Meilicke Cases

Imputation credits were granted only in respect of domestic dividends, as foreign dividends have not borne domestic corporation tax: there was no double economic taxation within one jurisdiction to be relieved. The home state of the shareholder was not prepared to credit, against its domestic income tax, a foreign corporation tax not contributing to its Treasury. However, this meant different treatment of cross-border dividends as compared to domestic dividends, making it less attractive for domestic investors to invest in foreign shares. Therefore, the CJEU held this effect of imputation systems to be incompatible with the freedom of establishment. The imputation states could not convince the Court that from the viewpoint of the rationale of imputation (corporation tax as a creditable withholding tax/advance payment on the income tax) foreign and domestic dividends were not in a comparable position, as foreign dividends were paid out of profits which were not taxed in the shareholder jurisdiction, but had benefited another jurisdiction's Treasury. In the Cases C-315/02, *Lenz*, C-319/02, *Manninen*, and C-292/04, *Meilicke* (see section 11.4.1), the Court held that the granting of imputation credits cannot be limited to domestically sourced dividends without falling foul of the free movement of capital.

These judgments, Case C-334/02, *Commission v. France (fixed levy)* and Case C-416/17, *Commission v. France*, implied that, whatever the mechanism applied to reduce economic double taxation in the home state of the shareholder (imputation, half rate, half base or final withholding), exactly the same mechanism must be applied for foreign dividends. This meant that maintaining full imputation became very unattractive from a budgetary point of view: the credit must also be extended to shareholders receiving dividends from other Member States, even if these were no imputation states and (thus) would not return the favour. Since prevention of economic double taxation may also, and without budgetary damage, be reached in a nondiscriminatory manner by way of a schedular system described above – choosing the rates at the right level – most imputation states changed their systems to schedular.

(ii) The Mirror Image: (No) Discrimination of Outbound Cross-Border Dividend (Host Member State Perspective); The Fokus Bank, Class IV ACT and Miljoen, X and Société Générale Cases; Priority to Source Country Entitlement

Imputation credits are not granted for outbound dividends (to non-resident shareholders), for the same reason as such credits are not given in respect of incoming foreign dividends. Again, the logic is that it is difficult to see why one state (this time the state of the distributing company) should relinquish tax revenue (this time the corporation tax) for the benefit of someone (the shareholder) who is not paying tax in the company state, but only in his home state. Again, the reasoning is that there is no economic double taxation within the same jurisdiction. In practice, sometimes the company state *does* extend its imputation credit to foreign shareholders under bilateral tax treaties, at least as regards individual shareholders. Article 10(3) of the former UK-Netherlands tax treaty, *e.g.*, provides for the payment, by the UK Treasury, of the UK imputation credit to Netherlands resident individual shareholders (subject to UK withholding tax, as the payment of the credit is regarded as income). Netherlands corporate shareholders are granted half of the UK imputation credit (subject to UK withholding tax).

On this issue, the imputation countries (the UK) succeeded in convincing the Court, in Case C-374/04, *Test Claimants in Class IV of the ACT Group* (see section 11.5.1), that outbound dividends are not comparable to domestic dividends. This required some slightly different reasoning, as the reasoning in the *Lenz, Manninen* and *Meilicke* cases (a shareholder receiving cross-border dividends suffers just as much from economic double taxation as a shareholder receiving domestic dividends and must therefore be treated equal) leads to the exact same result for the company state as it does for the shareholder state: if the *shareholder* state may not, in order to justify imputation denial, point out that the distributing company was not subject to tax within its jurisdiction, then by the same token the *company* state may not, in order to justify *its* imputation denial, point out that the foreign shareholder is not subject to tax within its jurisdiction. The Court this time reasoned from a different angle: a nonresident shareholder was not considered comparable to a domestic shareholder if the former is not subject to tax in the source state in respect of the profit distribution.[5] The Court thus in this case seemed to reason (only) from the viewpoint of the individual income tax: in *Lenz, Manninen* and *Meilicke*, the shareholder was subject to income tax for both domestic and foreign dividends, which were, therefore, comparable. In *Class IV ACT*, by contrast, outbound dividend was not subject to shareholder taxation, and therefore not comparable to domestic dividend, which indeed was taxed in the hands of the resident shareholder.[6] This reading of the case law is confirmed by the fact that if the source state *does* subject outbound dividend to tax (*e.g.* a dividend withholding tax), then the Court requires it to extend its imputation credit also to nonresident shareholders in so far as they are subject to that source state tax on the dividend. The Court thus converted to a subject-to-tax criterion for comparability assessment (see section 6.4.2). The Court further observed that if the company state were required to extend its credit in respect of outbound dividends not subject to tax within its jurisdiction, it would have to refund its corporate tax revenue abroad and would thus receive less or no tax revenue on profits sourced within its jurisdiction. The latter argument would seem particularly unconvincing in the light of the Court's observation that nothing prevented the UK (the source state) from levying income tax from foreign shareholders as if they were resident: that would recapture the credit and safeguard the UK's corporate tax revenue, just as in the case of domestic shareholders.

---

5 In other words, in case the home Member State subjects the nonresident shareholder to taxation, then the nonresident shareholder becomes comparable to a domestic shareholder.

6 Based on the same-suffering-from-double-tax-criterion used in *Lenz, Manninen*, and *Meilicke*, however, *Class IV ACT* seems inconsistent; indeed, in the first three cases, the fact that the foreign distributing *company* was not subject to tax in the shareholder State, was no excuse for the *shareholder* State to refuse imputation of the corporation tax, paid to another jurisdiction, by that non-subject and nonresident company. From the viewpoint of *that* criterion, it is then difficult to see why the exact same argument in the mirror image position of *Class IV ACT* (the foreign *shareholder* is *not* subject to tax in the *company* State) is a valid excuse for the *source* State *not* to extend its credit. The Court explained that if the source State were required to extend its credit, it would lose its corporation tax revenue. That is true, but loss of revenue has never been accepted as an excuse.

The Court thus made a quite reasonable, but also political choice for source country entitlement. *Legally* however, either *both* states were at fault, or *neither* of them, as – according to the Court itself (see Chapter 6) – there is no EU legal basis priority to source taxation over residence taxation or the other way around.

Be this as it may, the rather fortunate result of this case law is that the internal market has virtually been – almost – rid of the intricate and internationally distorting imputation system of taxation of distributed corporate profits.

The EFTA[7] Court had already decided a similar case, at first sight in the opposite sense. In a Norwegian preliminary Case E-1/04, *Fokus Bank*,[8] the EFTA Court held that the (TFEU-like) free movement rights in the EEA[9] Treaty required Norway to extend its imputation credit to foreign (UK and German) shareholders of a Norwegian company as if they were domestic shareholders. This looks at odds with *Class IV ACT*, as the UK and German shareholders were not subject to Norwegian income tax like Norwegian residents. However, the UK and German shareholders *were* subject to Norwegian dividend withholding tax at a rate of 15%. Apparently (the judgment is not very clear on this), resident taxpayers were subject to a withholding tax as well (at a rate of 28%), which was, however, immediately undone – apparently still at company level – by an imputation credit of also 28%. At any rate, the result was that for domestic shareholders, the dividend was tax-free (the dividend bore only corporation tax), whereas for foreign taxpayers 15% dividend tax was withheld. *To that extent* (15%), the foreign shareholders were thus subject to Norwegian income tax and therefore in a comparable position as residents. This being so, also the CJEU would, according to its reasoning in *Class IV ACT*, have required Norway to extend its imputation credit to the foreign shareholders to the extent necessary to extinguish the withholding tax of 15%. Although the EFTA Court was not clear on this point, we suppose it required Norway to extend its imputation credit to EU shareholders only to the extent necessary to undo the 15% withholding tax[10] (making the dividend tax-free as in purely domestic situations), and that it did not mean to go so far as to require Norway to actually *pay out* the excess above 15% up to the level of a domestic imputation credit (28%). Therefore, in this respect, the two Courts seem to agree after all.[11] The *Fokus Bank* case ignited claims filed by non-resident investments funds for refund of dividend withholding tax levied on dividends in cases where a Member State operates a certain mechanism to promote

7 EFTA = European Free Trade Association: Norway, Liechtenstein, Iceland and Switzerland.

8 Case E-1/04, *Fokus Bank ASA v The Norwegian State*, EFTA Court Report 2004, p. 11; O.J. C 45 of 23 February 2006, p. 10.

9 EEA = European Economic Area, that is: the EU Members plus three EFTA Members (Norway, Iceland and Liechtenstein).

10 For an analysis of Norway's inventive ways of avoiding having to refund the withholding tax to foreign shareholders, see Andreas Bullen: 'The Norwegian Response to the EFTA Court Judgment in the Fokus Bank Case,' *European Taxation*, June 2007, p. 273-280.

11 However, in another respect there seems to remain an inconsistency between the CJEU case law and the EFTA Court case law: the latter explicitly denied the relevance of whether the foreign shareholder could credit the Norwegian withholding tax against the income tax in his home State, whereas the CJEU held, in *Denkavit France* and *Amurta* that discriminatory withholding tax in the source State may be pardoned if it is 'neutralized' by a credit in the home State of the shareholder (see Chapter 14.5.4 and section 11.5.2).

fiscal neutrality between individual and collective investments by mitigating the tax burden of resident investments funds when investing in domestic shares: *Santander Asset Management*[12], *Fidelity Funds*,[13] *Deka*[14], *A SCPI*[15] and *AllianzGI-Fonds*.[16] Also, it led to non-resident pension funds filing for a refund of dividend withholding tax levied on dividends in cases where a Member State exempts resident pension funds when investing in domestic shares: *College Pension Plan of British Columbia*[17], *PMT*[18] and *Keva*.[19] The gist of these cases is that a Member State should extend the favourable tax regime for resident investments funds to non-resident investments funds, insofar as these non-resident investments funds are objectively comparable to resident investments funds. A case to be mentioned in this respect is *UBS Real Estate*, which deals with transfer taxes.[20] The Court held that a tax benefit granted to resident investments funds should be extended to non-resident investments funds. In *L Fund* (C-537/20), the Court held that Germany should extend its favourable treatment for German real estate investment funds to a Luxembourg fund.[21] This means that what holds for investment in shares also holds for investment in real estate. In the same vein, in *XX* (C-782/22) the Court used a similar reasoning for 'unit-linked' insurance companies investing in shares.[22] The favourable treatment afforded to Dutch insurance companies should also be available to foreign insurance companies.

11.1.6 Preliminary conclusion

A system of taxation of distributed company profits should meet three requirements:
- Internal neutrality: Similar tax treatment of equity and debt-financing;
- External neutrality: Equal treatment of domestic and foreign dividends and of foreign and domestic shareholders;
- Administrative practicability.

Classical systems are biased against equity financing, but they are internationally neutral and relatively easy to apply and to comply with. Imputation systems are neutral as regards equity or debt financing, but disadvantaging cross-border investment, and cumbersome in their application. After the *Lenz, Manninen* and *Meilicke* judgments of the CJEU, and the *Fokus Bank* judgment of the EFTA Court, imputation systems have become budgetary unattractive for the Member States. Semi-classical (schedular) systems unite the best of all worlds: they avoid the bias against equity financing; they are internationally neutral, provided the taxation of domestic dividends (half rate, half base or final withholding) is applied indiscriminately to foreign dividends, and such indiscriminate application does

12 Case C-338/11 (*Santander Asset Management*), EU:C:2012:286.
13 Case C-480/16 (*Fidelity Funds*), EU:C:2018:480.
14 Case C-156/17 (*Deka*), EU:C:2020:51.
15 Case C-342/20 (*A SCPI*), EU:C:2022:276.
16 Case C-545/19 (*AllianzGI-Fonds*). EU:C:2022:193.
17 Case C-641/17 (*College Pension Plan of British Columbia*), EU:C:2019:960.
18 Case C-252/14 (*Pensioenfonds Metaal en Techniek v Skatteverket*), EU:C:2016:402.
19 Case C-39/23 (*Keva*), EU:C:2024:648.
20 Joint Cases C-478/19 and C-479/19 (*UBS Real Estate*), EU:C:2021:1015.
21 Case C-537/20 (*L Fund*), EU:C:2023:339.
22 Case C-782/22 (*XX*), EU:C:2024:932.

not lead to budgetary distress; schedular systems are also much more practicable than imputation systems and even more practicable – because of the flat rate, or even better: a final withholding tax – than purely classical systems.

A majority of the Ruding Committee[23] therefore favoured a final withholding tax system, as applied in (at that time) Belgium, Austria and Italy, as (i) only the company would be involved in the taxation process, (ii) both international and internal neutrality would be achieved (provided the aggregate of the corporation tax and the final withholding tax would approximate the average income tax rate against which interest income is taxed).

It would seem that, due to the case law of the CJEU (and the EFTA Court), the need for positive harmonization has been drastically reduced: for practical purposes, imputation systems have become obsolete, and Member State have little choice but to apply some variation on a semi-classical (schedular) system or a final withholding tax system.

11.2 Possible Unequal Treatment of Cross-Border Dividends

Outbound cross-border dividends may be fiscally treated different from internal dividends basically in two ways (discrimination of foreign parents/shareholders by the host state):

- Juridical double taxation (same person, same object of taxation) where this would not occur internally: Taxation in the source state which would not be levied, or levied effectively lower in case of distribution to a domestic shareholder; this is the issue in *Bouanich,*[24] *Denkavit,*[25] *Amurta,*[26] *Aberdeen Property,*[27] *Secilpar,*[28] *Santander Asset Management,*[29] *Miljoen, X and Société Générale*[30], *PMT,*[31] *Fidelity Funds*[32], *College Pension Plan of British Columbia*[33], *Deka*[34], *A SCPI*[35], *AllianzGI-Fonds,*[36] *ACC Silicones*[37] and *Keva.*[38] It is also the issue in numerous infringements proceedings the Commission initiated against individual Member States, such as *Commission v Germany,*[39] as well as (in

23 *Report of the Committee of Independent Experts on Company Taxation*, Commission of the European Communities, March 1992, Office for Official Publications of the European Communities, Luxembourg, 1992, 210 pages text plus 240 pages annexes.
24 Case C-265/04 (*Bouanich*), EU:C:2006:51.
25 Case C-170/05 (*Denkavit Internationaal*), EU:C:2006:783.
26 Case C-379/05 (*Amurta*), EU:C:2007:655.
27 Case C-303/07 (*Aberdeen Property Fininvest Alpha Oy*), EU:C:2009:377.
28 Case C-199/10 (*Secilpar Sociedade Unipessoal SL v Fazenda Pública*), EU:C:2010:706.
29 Case C-338/11 (*Santander Asset Management*), EU:C:2012:286.
30 Joined cases C-10/14, C-14/14 and C-17/14 (*Miljoen, X, Société Générale SA*), EU:C:2015:608.
31 Case C-252/14 (*Pensioenfonds Metaal en Techniek v Skatteverket*), EU:C:2016:402.
32 Case C-480/16 (*Fidelity Funds*), EU:C:2018:480.
33 Case C-641/17 (*College Pension Plan of British Columbia*), EU:C:2019:960.
34 Case C-156/17 (Deka), EU:C:2020:51.
35 Case C-342/20 (*A SCPI*), EU:C:2022:276.
36 Case C-545/19 (*AllianzGI-Fonds*). EU:C:2022:193.
37 Case C-572/20 (*ACC Silicones*), EU:C:2022:469.
38 Case C-39/23 (*Keva*), EU:C:2024:648.
39 Case C-284/09 (*Commission v. Germany*), EU:C:2011:670.

respect of outbound inter-company interest payments) in *Truck Center*;[40] *Brisal*[41] and *Viva Telecom*;[42]
- Economic double taxation (same object of taxation, different person) where this would not occur internally: Denial, by the source state, of an imputation credit or other relief which would have been extended upon distribution to a domestic shareholder; *Avoir Fiscal*,[43] *Class IV ACT*,[44] *Burda*[45] and the EFTA Court case *Fokus Bank*[46] address this position.

Inbound cross-border dividends may be fiscally treated different from internal dividends basically in four ways (discrimination of foreign-source income by the home state):
- Juridical double taxation: Refusal, by the shareholder state, to credit foreign with-holding tax although domestic withholding tax is credited. This is not considered to be a discrimination, but an 'exercise in parallel' of taxing power (a dislocation). It is at issue in *Kerckhaert-Morres*,[47] *Damseaux*,[48] and *Orange European Smallcap*,[49] *Riskin and Timmermans*,[50] *Stanleyparma and Stanleybet*[51] and *Société Générale*.[52]
- Economical double taxation: Refusal, by the shareholder state, of an imputation credit for the elimination of the previous tier (foreign) corporation tax on the company profits out of which the dividends are paid, although such credit is granted in respect of domestic-source dividends paid out of domestically taxed company profits. This is the position in *Lenz*[53] and *Manninen*,[54] and the *Meilicke* cases,[55] as well as the refusal by the home state of an exemption for inter-company interest income, although such exemption is granted in respect of domestic interest income paid out of domestically taxed company profit (*Damixa*);[56]
- Asymmetrical prevention of economical double taxation: The shareholder state discriminates foreign dividends in that it allows the recipient of foreign-source dividends only a credit for underlying tax, whereas domestic-source dividends are exempt in

40 Case C-282/07 (*Truck Center*), EU:C:2008:762.
41 Case C-18/15 (*Brisal and KBC Finance Ireland*), EU:C:2016:549.
42 Case C-257/20 (*Viva Telecom*), EU:C:2022:125.
43 Case 270/83 (*Commission v. French Republic*), EU:C:1986:37.
44 Case C-374/04 (*Test Claimants in Class IV of the ACT Group Litigation*), EU:C:2006:773.
45 Case C-284/06 (*Burda*), [2008] ECR I-4571.
46 EFTA Court 23 November 2004, Case E1-04, *Fokus Bank ASA*, EFTA Court Report 2004, 11.
47 Case C-513/04 (*Kerckhaert and Morres*), EU:C:2006:713.
48 Case C-128/08 (*Damseaux*), EU:C:2009:471.
49 Case C-194/06 (*Orange European Smallcap Fund*), EU:C:2008:289.
50 Case C-176/15 (*Riskin and Timmermans*), EU:C:2016:488.
51 Case C-788/18 (*Stanleyparma and Stanleybet*), EU:C:2020:110.
52 Case C-403/19 (*Société Générale*), EU:C:2021:136.
53 Case C-315/02 (*Lenz*), EU:C:2004:446.
54 Case C-319/02 (*Manninen*), EU:C:2004:484.
55 Case C-292/04 (*Meilicke a.o.*), EU:C:2007:132, and Case C-262/09 (*Meilicke II*), EU:C:2011:438.
56 Case C-593/14 (*Masco Denmark ApS and Damixa ApS tegen Skatteministeriet*), EU:C:2016:984.

the hands of the shareholder. *Test Claimants in the FII Group Litigation*,[57] *Haribo and Salinen*,[58] *Accor*,[59] *FII II*[60] and *Wagner Raith*[61] address this position);
- Refusal of tax incentives for portfolio investment in foreign shares where these would be granted for portfolio investment in shares in domestic companies. The cases that address this are *Verkooijen*,[62] *Weidert-Paulus*[63] *Real Vida Seguros*[64] and *E* or *Veronsaajien oikeudenvalvontayksikkö*[65]. We will not separately discuss such measures here, but refer to section 13.7. Another case that may be mentioned in this respect is *H Lebensversicherung* (C-258/22), where the Court held that Germany did not treat foreign dividends worse than domestic dividends.[66]

11.3 The CJEU's basic Notions: Juridical and Economic Double Taxation, and Exertion of Taxing Power

The Court regards economic and juridical double taxation of distributed company profits (see section 11.4.1) as fundamentally different, although both occur both domestically and in cross-border positions. Juridical double taxation in this respect is withholding taxation at source (to be withheld by the company distributing its profits) followed by final income taxation by assessment in the hands of the shareholder. Within one jurisdiction such juridical double taxation is taken away by crediting the withholding tax against the final income tax levied by assessment from the shareholder (a refund is given in case of an excess credit). The Court apparently sees this as one single (income) taxation of the same dividend in the hands of the same person, and the Member States are free to apply such system in any configuration they consider expedient. They may choose to have two taxes (a withholding tax plus a final income tax) and integrate these two by crediting one against the other, but they may also choose to have only one of these two, *i.e.* either have no withholding tax but only taxation by assessment in the income tax, or have only a withholding tax ('final withholding tax', meaning that the dividend is exempt in the assessment income tax).

Economic double taxation, on the other hand, consists first of taxation of the company profits in the corporation tax to which the company is subject, and subsequently, after distribution of that profit, income taxation in respect of the profit after distribution to which the shareholder is subject. In order not to discriminate against equity financing as compared to debt financing, Member States may choose to undo this accumulation of corporation tax at company level and income tax at shareholder level, by crediting the corporation tax underlying the dividend against the income tax of the shareholder (imputation credit; see section 11.4.1). For intra-group dividends, it is common to prevent

57 Case C-446/04 (*Test Claimants in the FII Group Litigation*), EU:C:2006:774.
58 Joined Cases C-436/08 and C-437/08 (*Haribo and Österreichische Salinen*), EU:C:2011:61.
59 Case C-310/09 (*Accor*), EU:C:2011:581.
60 Case C-35/11 (*FII 2*), EU:C:2012:707.
61 Case C-560/13 (*Wagner-Raith*), EU:C:2015:347.
62 Case C-35/98 (*Verkooijen*), EU:C:2000:294.
63 C-242/03 (*Weidert and Paulus*), EU:C:2004:465.
64 Case C-449/20 (*Real Vida Seguros*), EU:C:2021:721.
65 Case C-480/19 (*E* or *Veronsaajien oikeudenvalvontayksikkö*), EU:C:2020:94.
66 Case C-258/22 (*H Lebensversicherung*), EU:C:2023:506.

economic double taxation by either exempting subsidiary dividends in the hands of the parent company or to grant the parent an indirect credit for the corporation tax already levied at subsidiary level (this could also be called 'imputation credit' as it is basically the same thing, but usually this credit is called 'indirect' if applied in inter-company relations). Unlike the integration of withholding tax and shareholder income tax by way of credit – which the Court sees as one single integrated tax to the account of one single taxpayer – the Court sees the integration of corporation tax at the level of the distributing company and the income tax at shareholder level as an interaction of two separate independent taxes to the account of two separate independent taxpayers, even though economically, one may view the corporation tax, just as a withholding tax, as a prepayment on the final shareholder income tax. This is perfectly illustrated by the Estonian tax system, in which effectively no corporation tax is levied on the company's profit as long as it does not distribute them. If it does distribute, then 'corporation tax' is levied, but since the shareholders are exempt from income tax for dividends and there is no withholding tax (why should there be, if the shareholder is exempt anyway?), this 'corporation tax' might just as well be called a 'final withholding tax' or an 'income tax' to the account of the shareholder levied by withholding at source. In the *Accor* case,[67] the French imputation credit (*avoir fiscal*) was a credit for the French *précompte* levied upon profit (re)distribution, which might just as well be called a dividend withholding tax as a corporation tax. Remarkably, under Article 7(1) of the Parent-Subsidiary Directive, the term 'withholding tax' does not cover an advance payment or prepayment (précompte) of corporation tax to the Member State of the subsidiary which is made in connection with a distribution of profits to its parent company. As previously mentioned, Member States were apparently trying to say, through Article 7(1), that the Court should not interfere with imputation systems of taxation of distributed company profits. That did not stop the Court from destroying imputation systems, however from the perspective of the treaty freedoms (primary law). In case C-556/20, the compatibility of the French system with the Parent-Subsidiary Directive is addressed.[68]

It is vital, in order to understand the case law to see that the Court regards a *dividend* withholding tax as the same thing as an assessment income tax on *dividends*,[69] and the corporation tax on the *profits* of the company as quite another. It treats what happens *before* distribution as one thing, and what happens *after* distribution as another.

We do not know why it does so, but its case law makes sense if one starts from that separation. Especially the puzzling difference between on the one hand *Manninen*, *Lenz*, *Meilicke* and *Damixa* (Member States must prevent economic double taxation if they do so internally) and on the other hand *Class IV ACT*, *Kerckhaert-Morres*, *Damseaux*, *Riskin and Timmermans* and *Truck Center* (Member States are not required to prevent juridical double taxation even though they do so internally) can be explained easily on the basis of this insight. Two states taxing the *same* cross-border income (the dividend; the income *after*

67 Case C-310/09 (*Accor SA*), EU:C:2011:581.

68 Case C-556/20 (*Schneider Electric SA a.o.*), EU:C:2022:378. See also Chapter 16 in this respect.

69 The same goes for purposes of the Parent Subsidiary Directive. In case C-294/99 (*Athinaïki Zythopoiia*), EU:C:2001:505, the Court held that art. 5 also forbids levying tax in another form than a withholding tax at source, i.e. an income tax assessment on the dividend recipient.

distribution) of the *same* taxpayer (whether in a comprehensive assessment income tax or under a withholding tax) is viewed by the Court as an irremediable 'exercise in parallel' of two sovereign powers delineating the object of taxation in respect of their residents and nonresidents, respectively, being in this case the same person, who has the bad luck of being exposed to two separate taxing jurisdictions for the same income at the same time (resulting in a disparity or a dislocation; see sections 3.2.7.2 and 3.2.7.3). Especially *Damseaux* and *Kerckhaert-Morres* and *Riskin and Timmermans* show this reasoning: the Court has no competence to decide which of the two state's claims on the same income of the same taxpayer is better and has priority over the other (*Damseaux*, points 32 and 34). By contrast, two states of which *one* taxes the *profit* of a company within its jurisdiction under its *corporation* tax, and the *other* taxes a *dividend* received by a *shareholder* within its jurisdiction under its individual or corporate *income* tax, are in principle two separate worlds (different object of taxation, different tax, different taxpayer), and – and this is crucial – these are different worlds also *within* one and the same jurisdiction: taxation of the company and taxation of the shareholders are also separate worlds if the company and the shareholders reside in the same taxing jurisdiction. Therefore: if a state decides to *internally* integrate these two separate worlds by crediting the company profits tax against the shareholder dividend tax in order to alleviate the economic double burden, it must do so as well in the cross-border situation (see, especially, the Grand Chamber decision *Manninen*). By contrast, if a state decides to levy both a withholding tax on a dividend to the account of the shareholder *and* a final assessment income tax on the same dividend of the same taxpayer, then these are just two manifestations of essentially the same single income taxation to the account the same person, irrespective of whether they cumulate or get credited the one against the other (see, especially *Kerckhaert-Morres*, *Truck Center* and *Haribo and Salinen*). Even if the dividend withholding tax is not credited against the final assessment income tax, it is still a (prepaid) part of that same income tax, comparable to an advance payment (estimated assessment) during the income tax year. In point 49 of *Truck Center* the Court explicitly points at this likeness of withholding taxes to advance payments of final income tax by the same taxpayer. We believe that the relevance of *Truck Center* is limited by the Court in later case-law. From *Cartrans Preda* (C-461/21) it follows that the only distinguishing factor in *Truck Center* was the tax collection technique. If there is any other advantage in the domestic situation which is not afforded to the cross-border situation, such as a timing difference, then *Truck Center* cannot be relied upon and a restriction exists which requires justification.[70]

Also, the ostensible contradiction between the *FII GLO* and *FII II* cases and the *Cadbury Schweppes* case[71] disappears if the point of departure is that the world before distribution is separate from the world after distribution. Indeed, *Cadbury Schweppes* concerned taxation of nonresident subsidiary profits in the hands of the parent *before* distribution, whereas the *FII GLO* case concerned taxation of nonresident subsidiary profits in the hands of the parent company *after* distribution. See section 9.5. Also, the ostensible contradiction disappears between *Cadbury Schweppes* (the parent company state is not at liberty to include nonresident subsidiaries' positive tax base in the parent's tax base) and *Marks*

70 Case C-461/21 (*Cartrans Preda*), EU:C:2023:632.
71 Case C-196/04 (*Cadbury Schweppes*), EU:C:2006:544.

& Spencer II (the parent company state is required to include nonresident subsidiaries' negative tax base in the parent's tax base in so far that negative tax base represents final losses; see section 10.2).

The conclusion must be that the Court sees the persistence or alleviation of economic double taxation as a single Member State's policy choice, whereas it sees the persistence or alleviation of juridical double taxation as an interaction of two separate sovereign jurisdictions, neither of which can be held responsible on its own. We do not understand this distinction (in our view, in both cases a single state policy choice is at the basis of the double taxation), but if one wants to understand the Court's case law, one must start from this distinction made by the Court.

A second basic notion – which, as explained in section 6.4.2, in principle underlies all the Court's (recent) direct tax decisions – is the liable-to-tax criterion for establishing whether a cross-border dividend flow is or is not comparable to an internal dividend flow: if a state decides to assume taxing jurisdiction in respect of a certain cross-border profit distribution, whether inbound or outbound, then it will have to treat that cross-border distribution in the same manner as a comparable purely internal profit distribution.

The third basic notion to see in order to understand the CJEU's case law on cross-border distributed company profits is the distinction between worldwide taxation (residence taxation) and source taxation. The court starts from the assumption that the company state taxes a *resident* shareholder on his worldwide income, at any rate in its comprehensive assessment income tax, but does not tax a *nonresident* shareholder other than by way of a dividend withholding tax. This means that in respect of a purely internal dividend, the Member State concerned is acting in two capacities at the same time (both source *and* residence jurisdiction), and in respect of an outbound or inbound dividend only in one capacity: either as source state (outbound) *or* as residence state (inbound). The best illustration of this notion in the Court's case law is point 42 of the *Truck Center* case (concerning outbound inter-company interest).

As regards cross-border dividends, usually a tax treaty provides for a reduction of the withholding tax in the company state and for an ordinary credit in the home state of the shareholder, 'ordinary' meaning that the credit is capped: no more will be credited than the home state levies itself on the dividend itself (no refund of foreign withholding tax). Tax treaties do not prevent international economic double taxation, except as regards inter-company dividends, but for these, the EU Parent-Subsidiary Directive already goes further in preventing double economic taxation.

11.4 Inbound Dividends (Residence Taxation); National Treatment; Exit Imputation Systems

11.4.1 Economic Double Taxation of Inbound Dividends

As follows from the above, if a Member State chooses to prevent economic double taxation of internal dividends, it must do so as well in case of inbound (or outbound; see 11.5) dividends. Member States providing various forms of such economic double tax relief (exemption, half rate, half base, imputation credit, final withholding tax), must provide the same relief for dividends paid by companies of other Member States, because they exercise their taxing jurisdiction, as residence state, to the same extent to both domestic and foreign dividends received by their residents. This first appeared from the *Lenz*[72] and *Manninen*[73] cases. Mrs Lenz, a resident of Austria, was denied the choice of having her foreign-source dividends taxed, not under the normal progressive tax system, but under either a 25% final withholding tax, or a 'half rate' scheme (*Halbsatzverfahren*) available for domestic dividend income, meaning that although the net dividends are included in the taxable base of the shareholder, they would be taxed at only half the normal rate, the dividend tax withheld being creditable/refundable. This measure discourages both domestic investors to invest in foreign companies and foreign companies to raise capital in Austria. Since foreign profits out of which foreign dividends are paid have not borne Austrian corporation tax, Austria did not see why it should credit such foreign corporation tax. In itself, there is some merit to this reasoning. However, the Austrian system was inconsistent in that it did not bother whether there was any (and if so, how much) corporation tax levied on *domestic* dividend sources either: both the final withholding tax and the *Halbsatzverfahren* were available for domestic dividends even if no or low corporation tax was levied. The Court considered foreign dividend and domestic dividend to be in a comparable position in view of the rationale of an imputation system, as they both suffer economic double taxation. It dismissed the Austrian argument that it is impossible to levy a final withholding tax on foreign dividends, the distributing company being outside the Austrian taxing jurisdiction. Although this argument in itself makes sense, it does not prevent Austria from achieving the same effect as a final withholding tax by allowing shareholders to be taxed in the assessment income tax at 25% of the gross amount of the foreign dividends. Four months earlier, the Court had already held, in infringement proceedings brought by the Commission against France,[74] that the advantage of a (low) final withholding tax could not be restricted to proceeds from debt-claims paid by debtors resident in France. Although obviously it is impossible for France to levy a withholding tax on proceeds paid by foreign debtors, that does not preclude France from extending similar benefits to beneficiaries to such proceeds. As the Court laconically held: 'disadvantages of a purely administrative nature' cannot justify refusal of national treatment.

In *Manninen*, the Court went even further and for all practical purposes did away with imputation systems for taxation of distributed company profits. A Finnish resident received dividends from a Swedish company. Under the Finnish imputation system a 29% tax credit was granted to the shareholder in the income tax in order to impute Finnish corporation tax of 29% on profits out of which dividends are paid. The credit was not granted for foreign dividends. It should be noted that if less than 29% Finnish corporation tax had been levied at company level, an additional tax was levied from the company in order to match the credit at shareholder level. Therefore, unlike the Austrian *Halbsatzverfahren*

72 Case C-315/02 (*Lenz*), EU:C:2004:446.

73 Case C-319/02 (*Manninen*), EU:C:2004:484.

74 Case C-334/02 (*Commission v. France (fixed levy)*), EU:C:2004:129.

in *the Lenz* case, the Finnish system was consistent: it ensured that not a penny more was credited against shareholder income tax than had in fact been levied at company level. That difference in consistency made no difference to the Court, as the rationale of imputation still was prevention of economic double taxation and residents receiving foreign dividends still suffered the same double economic taxation as residents receiving domestic dividends. Therefore, in the light of the identical subjection to tax of foreign and domestic dividends and of that rationale, foreign dividends and domestic dividends were comparable, the need for fiscal cohesion between corporate and shareholder taxation being the same in both cases. We observe that if one limits one's view to merely the resident shareholder, this reasoning may make sense, but if one looks at the liability to tax of the combination of the profit source (the company) and the profit receiver (the shareholder), then there is no comparability from the point of view of liability to tax, as a nonresident, non-subject company paying foreign corporation tax to a foreign treasury is not comparable to a domestic company paying domestic corporation tax to the domestic treasury out of which the imputation credit is paid to the shareholder.

In *Damixa*, the Court extended the prevention of double taxation to interest income.[75] A Danish resident company, Damixa ApS, received interest income from its German subsidiary. In the case at hand, the Danish system links the tax treatment of the taxpayer, the domestic parent company, to the tax treatment of the domestic subsidiary. Insofar as interest paid by the domestic subsidiary to its domestic parent company is not deductible because of a (Danish) thin-capitalization interest limitation rule, the interest received by the domestic parent company is not taxed. This is an example of a consistent approach. Where the interest paid leads to a deduction at the level of the subsidiary, it is taxed in the hands of the parent company. However, if the interest paid does not lead to a deduction at the level of the subsidiary, it is not taxed in the hands of the parent company. Here, the parent company, Damixa ApS, exercised the freedom of establishment through a wholly-owned German subsidiary, Damixa Armaturen GmbH. This non-domestic subsidiary paid interest to its Danish parent company. In Germany, the deduction of interest was denied due to a German thin-capitalization interest limitation rule. Damixa ApS argued that it should not be required to include these non-deductible interest payments in its Danish taxable income, as it would not have been required to include Danish-sourced non-deductible intragroup interest either. The question of whether a domestic parent company holding a nonresident subsidiary (cross-border situation) is comparable to a domestic parent company holding a domestic subsidiary (internal situation) must be examined having regard to the aim of the national provisions at issue. The aim here is to avoid economic double taxation. It is, therefore, not surprising that the CJEU considers the cross-border and internal situations to be objectively comparable, given, *e.g.*, its Grand Chamber decision on economic double taxation of dividends in *Manninen*.

The *Manninen* case law effectively almost wiped out imputation systems throughout the Union. Having to refund foreign corporation tax is budgetarily intolerable. Also, as the imputation system was held to fall foul of the free movement of *capital*, the Member States applying imputation were facing the unappealing prospect of having to credit US,

75 Case C-593/14 (*Masco Denmark ApS and Damixa ApS tegen Skatteministeriet*), EU:C:2016:984.

Japanese and Chinese corporation tax underlying inbound dividends. This issue was raised by the UK in the *Manninen* case, and Advocate-General Kokott touched on it, suggesting that third state situations are not equal to intra-EU situations, but the Court laconically observed that third state relations were not the issue in the case at hand. The Court later recognized, however, that third state positions may be less equal than intra-EU positions (see section 3.2.6).

We do not regret the virtual disappearance of the impracticable and distorting imputation systems, although we are not sure the Court was competent to do away with them. Imputation systems have been replaced by, mostly, schedular systems of taxation of distributed company profits).

The (first) *Meilicke* case[76] was a reiteration of *Manninen* in respect of the former German imputation system. The Court rejected Germany's request to limit the effects of the judgment in time in order to limit the otherwise considerable budgetary consequences for Germany, as the Member States could have known better since Case C-35/98 *Verkooijen*,[77] the effects of which had not been limited in time, and anyway *Lenz* and *Manninen* were not limited in time either.[78]

The imputation states were not required to refund an excess credit if the corporation tax in the source state was higher than the domestic corporation (or individual income) tax.

The court held, in *Test Claimants in the FII Group Litigation*:[79]

> '52. Where, (…), those profits are subject in the Member State of the company making the distribution to a higher level of tax than the tax levied by the Member State of the company receiving them, the latter Member State is obliged to grant a tax credit only up to the limit of the amount of corporation tax for which the company receiving the dividends is liable. It is not required to repay the difference, that is to say, the amount paid in the Member State of the company making the distribution which is greater than the amount of tax payable in the Member State of the company receiving it.'

We understand from this judgment that an ordinary tax credit is in line with EU law.

The free movement of capital prevents a Member State from exempting domestic subsidiary dividends in the hands of the domestic parent company and at the same time fully tax foreign subsidiary dividends in the hands of a domestic parent company, as the UK did in respect of smaller than 10%-holdings in the *Test Claimants in the FII Group Litigation* case. The same follows from *Commission v. Greece*.[80] Similarly, the Court held in the *Groupe Steria* case that the free movement of establishment prevents a Member State from effectively exempting under a group taxation system the domestic parent

76 Case C-292/04 (*Meilicke*), EU:C:2007:132.
77 Case C-35/98 (*Verkooijen*), [2000] EU:C:2000:294.
78 See Michael Lang, 'Limitation of the Temporal Effects of Judgments of the ECJ,' *Intertax*, April 2007, p. 230-245.
79 Case C-446/04 (*Test Claimants in the FII Group Litigation*), EU:C:2006:774.
80 Case C-406/07 (*Commission v. Greece*), EU:C:2009:251.

company from domestic subsidiary dividends when it does not do so for EU and EEA subsidiaries.[81] See section 9.4.3.

11.4.2 Juridical Double Taxation of Inbound Dividends

By contrast, the home state of the shareholder is not obliged to undo juridical double taxation even though it credits its domestic withholding tax against the income tax of the shareholder. Although an obligation to also undo this type of double taxation would seem to follow from the *Manninen* reasoning (if double taxation is removed internally, than it must also be removed for cross-border dividends), foreign withholding tax does not need to be credited in the same manner as domestic withholding tax, as the Court apparently sees the domestic withholding tax and the domestic assessment income tax as one single tax levied on one single tax object (the dividend) from one single taxpayer, unlike the domestic corporation tax and the domestic income tax, which tax two different objects in the hands of two different taxpayers. See section 11.3. If the source state levies a withholding tax, then it is asserting tax jurisdiction in respect of the *same* object as the shareholder state does (the dividend), and there is no way of telling – at least not on the basis of the Treaty freedoms – which of the two states has priority. Therefore, the home state cannot be required under EU law to credit any source state tax on the same object (see *Damseaux*, paras. 32 and 34), irrespective of how the home state chooses to tax internal dividends: under a final withholding tax, an assessment income tax or both, whether or not imputed on each other (see section 11.5.1).

This appeared for the first time in the *Kerckhaert-Morres* case,[82] concerning a Belgian couple receiving French-source dividends subject to a French withholding tax of 15%. Belgium taxed both domestic and foreign-source dividends at a flat income tax rate of 25%, without credits, and therefore also without crediting the 15% French withholding tax. Belgium charged its 25% income tax on *domestic* source dividends in the form of a final (uncreditable) withholding tax, meaning that Belgium did not credit its own withholding tax. The 25% charge on *foreign*-source dividends was levied by way of the comprehensive assessment income tax. As the French withholding tax was not credited, juridical international double taxation ensued. The Court saw no discrimination, as Belgium exercised its taxing jurisdiction over resident shareholders in the same extent and at the same rate for both domestic and foreign dividends. The fact that France also taxed the French-source dividends, was not Belgium's responsibility. Belgium did not discriminate within its area of exercise of taxing jurisdiction. Assuming that France did not discriminate either (that it withheld the same source tax on French internal dividend payments), what we were looking at was a disparity or a dislocation, an 'exercise in parallel' of taxing power by two jurisdictions (indiscriminately) subjecting the same item of income of the same taxpayer. The double tax effect was thus a consequence of the 'coexistence' of two in themselves nondiscriminatory – but unharmonized and uncoordinated – national tax systems:

81 Case C-386/14 (*Groupe Steria*), EU:C:2015:524.
82 Case C-513/04 (*Kerckhaert and Morres*), EU:C:2006:713.

'20. In circumstances such as those of the present case, the adverse consequences which might arise from the application of an income tax system such as the Belgian system (...) result from the exercise in parallel by two Member States of their fiscal sovereignty.
21. It must be recalled, in that regard, that conventions preventing double taxation such as those envisaged in Article 293 EC are designed to eliminate or mitigate the negative effects on the functioning of the internal market resulting from the coexistence of national tax systems referred to in the preceding paragraph.
22. Community law, in its current state and in a situation such as that in the main proceedings, does not lay down any general criteria for the attribution of areas of competence between the Member States in relation to the elimination of double taxation within the Community. (...)
23. Consequently, it is for the Member States to take the measures necessary to prevent situations such as that at issue in the main proceedings by applying, in particular, the apportionment criteria followed in international tax practice. (...).'

In the subsequent *Damseaux* case,[83] it was pointed out to the Court that the tax treaty between France and Belgium provided for the mutual crediting of withholding taxes, but that Belgium had changed its national system as described, involving a final withholding tax, with the result that under national law there was no crediting of withholding taxes available any more. That had the looks of tax treaty obligation avoidance,[84] causing juridical double taxation which would have been prevented if Belgium had charged a *creditable* withholding tax, as it previously had done. That did not change the Court's analysis, however, as the Court is not competent to adjudicate on the interpretation of bilateral tax treaties, nor on the possible overriding of them.

This case did not yet ensure that foreign dividend withholding tax did not need to be credited, as Belgium did not levy a creditable withholding tax, but a final withholding tax, meaning that technically, it was not discriminating, since it did not credit its own withholding tax either.[85] The question remained what would happen in a national system featuring a creditable withholding tax. That question was presented in the *Orange European Smallcap* case,[86] but remained obscure because the Court interpreted the Netherlands portfolio investment vehicle regime at issue in that case as an *exemption* both from final assessment income tax and from the prepayment of it in the form of withholding tax (which was refunded in respect of domestic dividends). Since in this interpretation domestic dividend withholding tax was not credited against anything (but refunded because it was incorrectly levied), one could still think that if it had been creditable,

83 Case C-128/08 (*Damseaux*), EU:C:2009:471.

84 Marc Dassesse, 'Double Taxation of Foreign Dividends: The Damseaux Case Aiming at the Wrong Target! Criticism Should Be Directed towards France and Not Belgium,' *EC Tax Review* 2010/3, p. 117-122, argues that France (as well) was rather relaxed about its tax treaty and especially its Union loyalty obligations.

85 In the meantime the Belgium Supreme Court has held that the Belgium Tax Authorities must grant a credit for the French withholding tax based on the Belgium – France income tax treaty because of the supremacy of the international treaties concluded by Belgium over Belgian domestic legislation. See Hof van Cassatie 16 June 2017, case F.15.0102.N.

86 Case C-194/06 (*Orange European Smallcap Fund*), EU:C:2008:289. See for a comment: Thomas Spaas and An Weyn, 'The Lessons of *Orange European Smallcap Fund*,' *EC Tax Review* 2009/2, p. 53-66.

foreign withholding tax would have to be credited as well. The *Haribo and Salinen*[87] case, however, showed that the Court's analysis did not pivot around the question of whether or not domestic withholding tax was credited, but around the insights explained in section 11.3: it is immaterial which mechanics the home state applies to tax domestic dividends in the hands of residents; as long as it does not tax foreign dividends more heavily – by whatever levying mechanism – it cannot be held to discriminate, as the fact that the source state taxes the inbound dividend as well, is not the shareholder's state responsibility. *Haribo and Salinen* concerned foreign portfolio dividends received by Austrian corporate shareholders from which dividend tax was withheld abroad. Unlike Belgium, Austria *did* credit its domestic withholding tax against the (corporate) income tax of the shareholder, so it might have been viewed as discriminating if it would not also credit foreign withholding tax. The Court, however, still saw no discrimination, *and* it referred to *Kerckhaert-Morres*, which implies that the difference between the Belgian and the Austrian system (a creditable or an uncreditable domestic withholding tax) was not relevant for its analysis (as explained in more detail in section 11.2):

> '169. (...) the disadvantages which may arise from the parallel exercise of powers of taxation by different Member States, in so far as such an exercise is not discriminatory, do not constitute restrictions prohibited by the Treaty (....).
> (...)
> 171. Accordingly, Article 63 cannot be interpreted as obliging a Member State to provide, in its tax legislation, that a credit is to be granted for the withholding tax levied on dividends in another Member State in order to prevent the juridical double taxation – resulting from the parallel exercise by the Member States concerned of their respective powers of taxation – of the dividends received by a company established in the first Member State (see, to this effect, Case C-513/04 *Kerckhaert and Morres* [2006] ECR I-10967, paragraphs 22 to 24).
> 172. The same finding is called for a fortiori where the juridical double taxation results from the parallel exercise by a Member State and a non-member State of their respective powers of taxation, as follows from paragraphs 119 and 120 of the present judgment.'

The same conceptual approach is revealed by *Truck Center* (see section 11.5), concerning the inverse situation; the *source* state applying different mechanics to domestic and outbound capital investment proceeds (in that case; intercompany interest) as long as there is no other benefit afforded to the domestic situation.[88] A different collection mechanism which is otherwise neutral, is acceptable. Further, *Riskin and Timmermans*[89] seems to confirm *Kerckhaert-Morres* and *Damseaux*.

Although we (think we) understand the conceptual approach behind the Court's judgments, we are not sure *why* the Court follows it, as it leads to unexplained opposite treatment of international economic double taxation and international juridical double taxation, although (i) for the Treaty freedoms addressee (the shareholder), it is utterly irrelevant whether the double taxation he suffers is called 'economic' or 'juridical', and (ii) it is difficult to see why the Court holds the shareholder state responsible for the source

87 Joined Cases C-436/08 and C-437/08 (*Haribo and Österreichische Salinen*), EU:C:2011:61.
88 Case C-461/21 (*Cartrans Preda*), EU:C:2023:632.
89 Case C-176/15 (*Riskin and Timmermans*), EU:C:2016:488.

state's *corporation* tax where it does not hold the shareholder state responsible for the source state's *withholding* tax. As observed above (section 11.3), the distinction between the two is just mechanics: in the *Accor* case,[90] the French imputation credit (*avoir fiscal*) was a credit for the French *précompte* levied upon profit (re)distribution, which might just as well be called a dividend withholding tax as a corporation tax.

Both within the Court's logic of subject-to-tax and within its logic of exercise-in-parallel, the difference in treatment between economic and juridical double taxation is puzzling. We submit that either *both* economic double taxation and juridical taxation result 'from the exercise in parallel by two Member States of their fiscal sovereignty,' or both economic double taxation and juridical double taxation are discriminatory since both foreign dividends and domestic dividends are subjected to tax by the shareholder state in the hands of the shareholder and should therefore be treated alike.

Within the exercise-in-parallel reasoning of *Kerckhaert*, *Damseaux*, *Haribo* and *Salinen* and *Riskin and Timmermans*, we have difficulty avoiding the conclusion that in *both* cases exercise in parallel of jurisdiction is afoot. In the case of *economic* double taxation, the two states exercise in parallel their jurisdiction to charge (corporate) income tax: the *source* state on the profit before distribution; the *shareholder* state on the profit after distribution. In the case of *juridical* double taxation, they also exercise in parallel their competence to charge (corporate) income tax; both on the profit after distribution. Therefore, within the exercise-in-parallel approach, in both cases the double burden results from the interaction of two separate taxing jurisdictions.

Within the subjection-to-tax reasoning of *Manninen* and *Class IV ACT*, we have difficulty avoiding the conclusion that in *both* cases a discrimination arises: the shareholder state subjects both foreign and domestic dividends to tax on the same footing in the hands of the shareholder, but in both cases it takes away the ensuing double burden (in one case economic, in the other juridical) only for domestic dividends. That would seem to be a discrimination against foreign dividends in both cases, not just in the case of economic double taxation. If the Treaty freedoms require the shareholder state which internally prevents *economic* double burdens to also prevent such burdens in case of foreign dividends, then those same Treaty freedoms logically also require that same Member State which internally prevents *juridical* double burdens to also prevent such burdens in case of foreign dividends.

Therefore, in our view either *both* economic and juridical double taxation of distributed company profits are prohibited under the TFEU freedoms if they are prevented domestically, or *neither* of them are remediable under the TFEU free movement rights.

We thus do not see why economic and juridical international double taxation should be treated fundamentally different. Although we can intellectually follow the Court's conceptual approach reproduced in section 11.3, we are not convinced by it, especially given (i) its abstractness (as observed, the taxpayer could not care less about the label

90 Case C-310/09 (*Accor SA*), EU:C:2011:581.

of the double burden), (ii) the fact that – as far as we know – it has no basis in general national or international tax theory, nor in EU law, and (iii) the fact that the Court *does* require the source state to take away juridical double taxation of *outbound* dividends in cases such as *Commission v. Germany* and *Miljoen, X and Société Générale cases*.[91] It escapes us why the *residence* state is *not* required to prevent juridical double taxation of inbound dividends although it prevents such double taxation of internal dividends, while at the same time the *source* state *is* required to prevent juridical double taxation of outbound dividends if it prevents such double taxation internally.

11.4.3 Asymmetric Undoing of Economic Double Taxation of Inbound Dividends

In *FII GLO*,[92] *Haribo and Salinen*,[93] *Accor*,[94] *FII II*,[95] and *Commission v France*[96] the Court accepted that for inbound foreign intercompany dividends only indirect credit was extended, although internal intercompany dividends were exempted, as it views these two systems for avoiding economic double taxation as 'equivalent'. It also accepted that the entire – onerous – burden of proof of the precise amount of corporate tax levied abroad was put on the taxpayer. However, in the *FII II* case the Court in a Grand Chamber session clarified that the exemption and imputation methods cease to be equivalent in case the effective level of taxation usually is lower than the nominal rate of tax.[97] In section 11.4.1 we have already showed our surprise and explained the reasons why exemption and indirect credit cannot be considered 'equivalent', neither substantively (exemption is clearly better in terms of how much tax is in the end effectively payable) nor in terms of administrative burden and burden of proof (exemption is clearly better, as there is no procedural or evidentiary obstacle whatsoever).

Especially *Haribo and Salinen* seems to reveal a preference for OECD Fiscal Committee logic over internal market logic. According to the Court, if it would require the shareholder state to apply the exemption system it applied to domestic dividends also to foreign dividends, this would lead to an absence of additional tax on foreign dividends which equalizes the total tax burden on foreign dividends to the domestic tax burden on domestic dividends, and this would give investors in foreign holdings 'an advantage'. That may be so if the overall tax burden in the subsidiary state is lower, but was benefiting from advantages of investing in other EU Member States not the very essence of the EU internal market? Is that 'advantage' any different from advantages such as lower wages, cheaper premises, more consumers, less competitors or better weather in the subsidiary state? Are we going to tax away the difference in wages level as well? Taking away this 'advantage', may be viewed as rewarding tax-inefficient states for their tax-inefficiency and punishing tax-efficient states. It is clearly protective of the home market as it annihilates (fair) policy competition.

---

91 Case C-284/09 (*Commission v Germany*), EU:C:2011:670 and Joined Cases C-10/14, C-14/14 and C-17/14 (*Miljoen, X and Société Générale*), EU:C:2015:608.
92 Case C-446/04 (*Test Claimants in the FII Group Litigation*), EU:C:2006:774.
93 Joined Cases C-436/08 and C-437/08 (*Haribo and Österreichische Salinen*), EU:C:2011:61.
94 Case C-310/09 (*Accor*), EU:C:2011:581.
95 Case C-35/11 (*FII II*), EU:C:2012:707.
96 Case C-416/17 (*Commission v France*), EU:C:2018:811.
97 Case C-35/11 (*FII II*), EU:C:2012:707.

Indeed, usually, the overall effective tax burden in a state fairly accurately reflects the level of economic opportunity, infrastructure, political stability, availability of skilled labour, purchasing power of consumers, and social security. Forcing the cross-border investor to always pay his home state level of taxation no matter whether he invests in a country with comparable or incomparable infrastructure and public expenditure, is a policy choice for capital export neutrality (CEN) for which there is no legal basis in the Treaties. This may be acceptable under the Treaty freedoms if it is certain that effectively, the credit system for foreign dividends does not lead to a greater burden than exemption does for domestic dividends. We consider it evident, however, that this is not the case (see section 11.4.1). Indeed, why would a Member State apply credit selectively only to foreign dividends? Obviously because it does not want to hinder domestic industry with its huge administrative disadvantages as compared to exemption, especially in minority multi-tier foreign holding cases.

Fortunately, the Court clarified in the *FII II* case that the exemption and imputation methods cease to be equivalent in case the effective level of taxation in the subsidiary state is usually lower than the nominal rate of tax e.g. if the commercial and taxable profits differ. The Court required that for the calculation of the imputation credit, the nominal instead of the lower effective rate on the profits underlying the dividends in the subsidiary state is taken into account.[98]

11.5 Outbound Dividends (Source Taxation): National Treatment of Nonresident Shareholders and the gross/net Dilemma

The state of residence of the company distributing a dividend is not to treat nonresident shareholders less favourably than domestic shareholders in respect of the same dividends. This has the following consequences:

11.5.1 Economic Double Taxation

First, just as the shareholder state is required to undo economic double taxation if it does so internally, the source state is also required to extend its imputation credit to nonresident shareholders to the extent in which it subjects those nonresident shareholders to its dividend withholding or (corporate) income tax in respect of dividends distributed by resident companies. This implies, first, that if the shares pertain to a domestic branch of the nonresident shareholder and the dividends are thus attributable to that branch, that branch is entitled to the exact same tax benefits in respect of the dividends received as a domestic corporate shareholder (assuming it is subject to the same profits taxation regime as resident companies), especially the same participation exemption (if the source state is an exemption state) or the same credit for underlying tax/imputation credit (if the source state is a credit state). This was clear already from the first direct tax case ever before the Court: *Avoir Fiscal*.[99]

98 Case C-35/11 (*FII II*), EU:C:2012:707, point 62.
99 Case 270/83 (*Commission v. French Republic*), EU:C:1986:37.

In *Class IV ACT*[100] the Court considered that to the extent nonresidents are taxed for the dividends like residents, they become comparable to resident shareholders and must therefore be granted an imputation credit corresponding to the credit a resident shareholder enjoys. See also section 11.4.1 above.

The effect of the combination of *Class IV ACT* and its inverse *Manninen* (see section 11.4.1) is that the residence state of a company paying dividend abroad can levy (i) the corporation tax on the company profit and (ii) a withholding tax if such a tax is levied internally as well, minus a possible imputation which is granted internally; and that the home state of the shareholder receiving inbound dividend is entitled to (corporate) income tax on the profit after distribution minus a possible domestic imputation credit.

11.5.2 Juridical Double taxation or Denial of Exemption

Second, although a nonresident shareholder may be taxed differently (*e.g.* on a narrower tax base than residents), he may not be taxed *less* favourably in respect of the same tax base than residents; this follows from *Gerritse*,[101] discussed below, and from *Bouanich*,[102] the latter case concerning a share repurchase which was characterized as a dividend for nonresident shareholders, taxed at a flat rate of 15% with a deduction of the nominal value of the repurchased shares., and as a capital gain for resident shareholders, taxed at a rate of 30%, also with deduction of necessary expenses. This differential tax treatment is permissible in so far as it does not lead to higher effective taxation for nonresident shareholders. This means that a foreign shareholder has a choice and that it has to be calculated in each individual case which of the two systems is more advantageous. This rather eliminates the point of having a low flat tax for outbound dividends, as that point is not having to calculate each individual case. In *Brisal* it was held that in respect of loans generating interest income the same principles apply: the nonresident lender may not be taxed *less* favourably in respect of the same tax base than resident lenders.[103] This is confirmed in *Viva Telecom* where the Court held that where a Member State chose to exercise its tax jurisdiction over loans concluded between resident borrowing companies and non-resident lending companies, the consequence must be that non-resident companies must be considered to be in a situation comparable to that of resident companies as regards the expenses directly related to those loans.[104] *Lexel AB*[105] and *X BV*[106] are mere confirmations of this determination: from the perspective of the creditor it does not matter whether the debtor is a resident or a non-resident: these situation are comparable.[107]

Third, neither may a nonresident parent company be subject to a withholding tax which is not charged in respect of resident parent companies; this follows from *Denkavit*

100 Case C-374/04 (*Test Claimants in Class IV of the ACT Group Litigation*), EU:C:2006:773.
101 Case C-234/01 (*Gerritse*), EU:C:2003:340.
102 Case C-265/04 (*Bouanich*), EU:C:2006:51.
103 Case C-18/15 (*Brisal and KBC Finance Ireland*), EU:C:2016:549.
104 Case C-257/20 (*Viva Telecom*), EU:C:2022:125.
105 Case C-484/19 (*Lexel AB*), EU:C:2021:34.
106 Case C-585/22 (*X BV*), EU:C:2024:822.
107 This is also held in Case C-420/23 (*Faurécia*), EU:C:2024:534.

Internationaal/France,[108] *Amurta*,[109] *Aberdeen Property*[110] and *Secilpar*.[111] Also, the Advocate General made this point in *GVC Services* but the Court did not address this.[112] Nor may outbound dividends be taxed at a higher rate of withholding tax or otherwise be taxed unfavourably as compared to internal dividends, as the Commission had the Court establish in a series of infringement proceedings against Member States.[113]

The recurring basic notion is clear: the effective (gross) source tax on dividends paid to nonresident shareholders should not be higher than the eventual effective net tax burden which a domestic shareholder carries as a result of the combination of corporate or individual income taxation and (creditable or refundable) dividend withholding tax on dividends.

Thus the *modes* of taxation of resident and nonresident recipients in respect of the same domestic-sourced investment income may differ. The source state is in principle free to subject nonresidents to a tax withheld at source, and residents to a comprehensive assessment income tax, as the *Truck Center* Case[114] shows, provided that (i) the withholding tax is not effectively higher than the assessment income tax, and (ii) the timing difference is negligible because residents must make advance payments (must pay estimated (self-assessments) of income tax during the tax year. The latter was explained in *Viva Telecom*.[115] The Court considers that in *Truck Center* the different taxation arrangements did not necessarily procure an advantage for resident recipient. In a situation where there is an advantage, such as a cash-flow advantage which stems from the different point in time at which the expenses directly related to the income may be deducted, then there is a difference in treatment. *Truck Center* is the mirror image of *Kerckhaert-Morres* and *Damseaux* (see section 11.4.2): in the latter two cases, the Court accepted that domestic dividends were subject to a (final) withholding tax, and inbound dividends to the assessment income tax, provided the latter were not taxed more heavily than the former. In *Truck Center*, the Court, conversely, accepted that nonresidents were liable to a withholding tax, and residents to an assessment income tax, provided the latter were not better off than the first. In all three cases, there was no discrimination, because only the mechanics (the mode of levying the otherwise indiscriminate tax) differed, not the tax burden itself. In *Truck Center*, the Court used the additional argument that residents and nonresidents are not in a comparable position as regards recovery of the tax due. It is true that this could *justify* a different mode of taxation, but surprisingly, the Court seemed to use it to establish incomparability.[116] We observe, however, that it did not make any difference,

108 Case C-170/05 (*Denkavit International BV*), EU:C:2006:783.

109 Case C-379/05 (*Amurta*), EU:C:2007:655.

110 Case C-303/07 (*Aberdeen Property Fininvest Alpha Oy*), EU:C:2009:377.

111 Case C-199/10 (*Secilpar Sociedade Unipessoal SL v Fazenda Pública*), EU:C:2010:706.

112 Opinion in Case C-458/18 (*GVC Services*), EU:C:2019:897.

113 Case C-521/07 (*Commission v. the Netherlands*), EU:C:2009:360 (concerning outbound dividend to the EEA Members Norway and Iceland), Case C-540/07 (*Commission v. Italy*), EU:C:2009:717, and Case C-487/08 (*Commission v. Spain*), EU:C:2010:310.

114 Case C-282/07 (*Truck Center*), EU:C:2008:762. See for a comment Luc de Broe and Niels Bammens, 'Truck Center (etc.): A Critical Look (etc.),' *EC Tax Review* 2009/3, p. 131-137.

115 Case C-257/20 (*Viva Telecom*), EU:C:2022:125.

116 See Luc de Broe and Niels Bammens, o.c., at 132-133.

as the Court had already established the absence of a discrimination. It should also be noted, however, that the argument has more weight in respect of outbound interest than in respect of outbound dividends, as interest is deductible from the profit of the debtor and dividend is not. In respect of interest, a withholding tax is therefore essential if the source state is to get any tax at all on the profit out of which the interest is paid. As noted above, the *Brisal* case shows that a nonresident lender in that case may not be taxed *less* favourably in respect of the same tax base than resident lenders.[117] The nonresident lender in that case was subject to a withholding tax on gross interest, whereas resident lenders were subject to a comprehensive assessment income tax on net interest income. The Court reiterated that the modes of taxation of resident and nonresident recipients in respect of the same domestic-sourced income may differ as long as they entail the same tax burden. In our view *Viva Telecom* confirms this as the Court held that the expenses directly related to loans should be taken into account.[118]

There is one exception to the rule that the source state may not tax outbound dividends (nonresident shareholders) less favourably than internal dividends: discriminatory source taxation may be 'neutralized' (considered undone) to the extent that the tax treaty in force between the source state and the home state of the shareholder provides for the crediting of the discriminatory source state tax in the shareholder state. This follows from the 'overall' approach adopted by the Court in *Denkavit Internationaal/France, Amurta, Commission v. Italy, Secilpar* and *Miljoen, X and Société Générale* (discussed in section 6.5.4).

As regards source taxation of outbound dividends (and interest and royalties) one very important issue has been resolved in the *Brisal* case, which follows the case law in cases like *Bouanich* (see above), *Gerritse*[119] and *Turpeinen.*[120] It is the issue of *gross* withholding taxation and *net* assessment taxation: outbound dividends and interest (and often also outbound remunerations of only temporary visiting sportsmen and artists; see *Gerritse, Scorpio*[121] and *Centro Equestre da Lezíria Grande*[122] and *X NV;*[123] but sometimes also non-resident pensioners[124]) are subject to gross taxation at a moderate flat rate in order to avoid having to assess and supervise nonresidents. The flat rate is usually moderate in order to take account of the fact that taxation is effectuated on a gross basis, *i.e.* without deduction of any expenses incurred, let alone personal and family circumstances of the nonresident. The Court did not accept this kind of practical flat taxation of nonresidents, at least not without giving them the possibility to be taxed on a net basis like residents. On the basis of cases such as *Bouanich, Gerritse, Miljoen, X and Société* Générale, *Brisal, Viva Telecom* and *Cartrans Preda* it follows that if a nonresident shareholder – or bond-holder – has incurred high costs in earning the sourced investment income, and gross

117 Case C-18/15 (*Brisal and KBC Finance Ireland*), EU:C:2016:549.
118 Case C-257/20 (*Viva Telecom*), EU:C:2022:125.
119 Case C-234/01 (*Gerritse*), EU:C:2003:340.
120 See, *e.g.*, Case C-520/04 (*Turpeinen*), EU:C:2006:703.
121 Case C-290/04 (*FKP Scorpio Konzertproduktionen*), EU:C:2006:630.
122 Case C-345/04 (*Centro Equestre da Lezíria Grande*), EU:C:2007:96.
123 Case C-498/10 (*X NV*), EU:C:2012:635.
124 See, *e.g.*, Case C-520/04 (*Turpeinen*), EU:C:2006:703.

withholding would therefore lead to a higher tax debt than net taxation for residents would, the Treaty freedoms oppose collection of the excess.

The *PMT* case is somewhat difficult to understand in this respect.[125] It deals with the comparability of a foreign private pension fund and a domestic private pension fund. *Commission v Finland* suggests that based on the aim pursued by the national provision at issue (taxing capital income), a difference in taxation technique does not create an objective difference between the foreign and the domestic pension fund.[126] *Truck Center*, mentioned above suggests the same. In *PMT*, the question was whether a Netherlands private pension fund is comparable to a Swedish private pension fund as regards the taxation of Swedish-sourced capital income (dividends). Foreign private pension funds were subject to a 15% gross withholding tax; domestic private pension funds to a 15% tax on a deemed yield on their total net capital equal to the yield on state bonds the year before. The Court apparently viewed resident and nonresidents pension funds *prima facie* as comparable as it explicitly examined the cross-border situation and the internal situation in the light of the aim pursued by the national provisions at issue. Unlike the Finnish legislation in *Commission v Finland*, the aim of the Swedish legislation was not to exempt Swedish private pension funds from Swedish income tax, but to subject domestic private pension funds to a notional capital yield tax, replacing the regular Swedish corporate income tax, to achieve neutral taxation independent of the economic climate surrounding various kinds of assets. Given this system of taxation of resident private pension funds (taking the total capital of the fund into account), the Court considered PMT (only taxable for sources in Sweden) not to be comparable to a Swedish resident private pension fund having regard to the aim pursued by the national provision at issue, which was to tax, over time, a yield corresponding to the normal taxation of all yields on capital under the general law regime. The taxes on resident private pension funds and nonresident private pension funds were levied in different ways and calculated on different tax bases and therefore, according to the Court, the aim of the Swedish domestic system could not be achieved in the case of a non-resident private pension fund that was only subject for sourced income in Sweden. Sweden could therefore tax the Netherlands private pension fund on a gross basis for the dividends actually received without having to calculate whether such gross withholding tax would be higher than the tax on the notional yield of a domestic private pension fund. This is very difficult to understand, as the Court decided the exact opposite in a conceptually identical case in *Miljoen a.o.*: the Netherlands 'box 3'-system at issue in that case is conceptually identical to the Swedish notional income tax system for domestic private pension funds. It has exactly the same aim ('introduce neutral taxation independent of the economic climate surrounding various kinds of assets (…) which presupposes that pensions funds are taxed on the whole of the assets') on exactly the same tax base (net wealth). The only difference is the rate: the Netherlands notional income tax presupposed a fixed 4% yield (on the total net wealth of individuals) rather than the state bonds yield in the previous year, but like the Swedish notional yield, that 4% is intended to approximate in the long run the normal yield on passive capital investment. Nonresident shareholders, by contrast, were – like PMT in Sweden – subject

125 Case C-252/14 (*Pensioenfonds Metaal en Techniek v Skatteverket*), EU:C:2016:402.
126 Case C-342/10 (*Commission v Finland*), EU:C:2012:688.

to a 15% gross withholding tax on the actual dividends received. Therefore, the difference between the domestic and the cross-border position in *Miljoen a.o.* was conceptually identical to the difference between the domestic and the nonresident private pension fund in *PMT*. Nevertheless, in *Miljoen a.o.* the Court considered the Belgian resident Mr. Miljoen to be comparable to a Netherlands resident, and it required the Netherlands to calculate whether Mr. Miljoen was taxed unfavourably compared to a resident receiving the same Netherlands dividends. This means that either *PMT* or *Miljoen a.o.* is wrong. It is clear, therefore, that these two identical cases with opposite outcomes cannot be both correct at the same time; they squarely contradict each other. To us, it is also clear which case is incorrect: *PMT*. Even if *Miljoen a.o.* did not exist, PMT is clearly incompatible with consistent previous case law, e.g. *Gerritse*, *Bouanich* and *Truck Center*: although Member States may apply different bases and different rates for residents and nonresidents for the same income, they should always make sure that the nonresident does not pay more tax on that same income than residents. PMT opens the possibility to ignore that simply by introducing different systems for residents and nonresidents. At the end of the day, *PMT* says: Member States may tax nonresidents less favourably for the same income by making them look incomparable through different engineering.

Where *PMT* concerns a foreign *private* pension fund claiming equal treatment in Sweden, *Keva* concerns a foreign *public* pension fund claiming equal treatment in Sweden. Ignoring *PMT*, the Court laconically held that Finnish public pension fund should receive the same treatment as Swedish public pension fund.[127] This can be explained by the fact that Swedish *public* pension funds were fully exempt from tax and not subject to an alternative yield tax.

Another puzzling issue in *PMT* is the following: despite having decided that resident and nonresident pension funds were not objectively comparable, the Court considered that in respect of professional expenses directly linked to generating a yield on capital, residents and non-residents *are* comparable. From the perspective of the source of income, nonresidents and residents are in an objectively comparable situation, according to the Court. Therefore, they are also in an objectively comparable situation in respect of the expenses made directly for generating that income. PMT was therefore allowed to deduct from the Swedish gross dividends received the expenses directly linked to its investment in Swedish securities. We understand this part of the judgment as saying that no matter how the tax base (the yield on capital) is calculated, there are always expenses connected to large scale passive capital investment (such as overhead[128] but possibly also other expenses, such as financing cost[129]), and these should be deductible for both residents and nonresidents, irrespective of the fact that the systems of taxation for these two groups

127 Case C-39/23 (*Keva*), EU:C:2024:648.

128 See Advocate General in Case C-461/21 (*Cartrans Preda*), EU:C:2023:35, point 67: "Moreover, it is for the referring court, before which the dispute in the main proceedings has been brought and which must assume responsibility for the subsequent judicial decision, to determine in those proceedings, first, which of the expenses claimed may be regarded as business expenses directly related to the activity in question for the purposes of national legislation, and second, what is the portion of the general expenses which may be regarded as directly related to that activity."

129 See especially point 34. This is in line with the Court's reasoning in Case C-18/15 (*Brisal and KBC Finance Ireland*), EU:C:2016:549.

differ. We submit, however, that it does not make sense to require Sweden to extend an identical deduction from the gross tax bases of residents and nonresidents if Sweden can have a totally different tax base for nonresidents in the first place. Insisting on identical deductions only makes sense if one first insists on the same gross tax base. We believe that *Sofina and Others* (C-575/17), *College Pension Plan of British Columbia* (C-641/17) and *Viva Telecom* (C-257/20) and *XX* (C-782/22) provided clarity in this respect.

Sofina and Others[130] is in a way the mirror image of *Marks & Spencer II*[131], where the latter case concerns the import of foreign losses in the Residence State (where the shareholder is located) and the former concerns the import of foreign losses in the Source State (where the subsidiary is located). France levied a withholding tax on gross dividend received by non-resident shareholders. In a domestic situation, the resident shareholder was taxed on a net basis, which basis included losses at shareholder level. In case the resident shareholder was in a loss making position, there was effectively no French tax on the dividend. The tax foregone would however become due in a later year if the resident shareholder would become profit making (resulting in a temporary advantage), but in a case where the resident shareholder would cease to exist the tax foregone would be permanent. The Court held that this system resulted in a difference in treatment which could not be justified. As a result, France has to take into account foreign losses at the level of the non-resident shareholder in the same way as it does with the resident shareholder. Interestingly, *Sofina and Others* (C-575/17)[132] and *Credit Suisse Securities (Europe) Ltd* (C-601/23)[133] stand for the proposition that from the perspective of the host state (destination state) foreign *current* losses should be taken into account to determine the tax base over which the host state exercises its taxings rights. We refer to section 11.5.2.

College Pension Plan of British Columbia[134] concerns a case where a Canadian pension fund invests in German shares. In a domestic situation, a German pension fund is taxed with corporate income tax on a net basis, which bases includes provisions for future liabilities that lower the tax base. Conversely, non-resident pension funds are taxed on a gross basis. College Pension Plan of British Columbia claims to be taxed on a net basis as well. The Court, i.a. referring to Sofina and Others, held that there is a restriction on the movement of capital which cannot be justified by the difference in the situation of resident and non-resident pension funds. Also, there is no justification. The Courts held that non-resident pension funds should also be able to take into account provisions when calculating the net taxation since there is a causal link between the receipt of the dividends and these provisions, where these provisions are made voluntarily or statutorily. In *XX* (C-782/22) the Court used a similar reasoning for 'unit-linked' insurance companies.[135] This concerns a case where a UK 'unit-linked' insurance company invests in Dutch shares. Similar to the German rules for pension funds in *College Pension Plan of British Columbia* in a domestic situation, a Dutch 'unit-linked' insurance company is taxed with corporate

130 Case C-575/17 (*Sofina and Others*), EU:C:2018:943.
131 Case C-446/03 (*Marks & Spencer II*), EU:C:2005:763.
132 Case C-575/17 (*Sofina and Others*), EU:C:2018:943.
133 Case C-601/23 (*Credit Suisse Securities (Europe) Ltd*), EU:C:2024:1048.
134 Case C-641/17 (*College Pension Plan of British Columbia*), EU:C:2019:960.
135 Case C-782/22 (*XX*), EU:C:2024:932.

income tax on a net basis, which basis includes provisions for future liabilities that lower the tax base. The Court held that such national treatment should also be afforded to foreign 'unit-linked' insurance companies.

A different view may be taken from *AllianzGI-Fonds*[136] which shows similarities with *PMT*. Portuguese investments funds were held to be objectively comparable with non-resident investment funds, although resident Portuguese investments funds were exempt from Portuguese corporate income tax and subject to a stamp duty and a particular tax. Non-resident investment funds were taxed with 15% on gross dividends. The Court considered that the stamp duty and particular tax could be circumvented by resident Portuguese investments funds by distributing its income in full. Therefore, in the Court's view the stamp duty and particular tax could not be considered to replace the Portuguese corporate income tax. In this view, *PMT* should be understood to be limited to situations where domestic corporate income tax is actually replaced by another tax, such as the Swedish yield tax. This is confirmed by *Keva* (C-39/23). Where *PMT* concerns a foreign *private* pension fund claiming equal treatment in Sweden, *Keva* concerns a foreign *public* pension fund claiming equal treatment in Sweden. Swedish public pension funds were fully exempt from tax. Ignoring *PMT*, the Court laconically held that Finnish public pension fund should receive the same treatment as Swedish public pension fund.[137]

136 Case C-545/19 (*AllianzGI-Fonds*), EU:C:2022:193.
137 Case C-39/23 (*Keva*), EU:C:2024:648.

CHAPTER 12

Exit Taxes

Servaas van Thiel[1]

12.1 Exit Taxation on Accrued Income

12.1.1 Discriminatory exit taxes

Protectionism is traditionally understood as covering all measures by which States try to provide a competitive advantage to their domestic producers (e.g. to protect domestic jobs) for instance by restricting or burdening inbound economic activity (access restrictions) or by promoting outbound economic activity (exit subsidies).[2] This is probably why the EU Treaty focuses on market access restrictions imposed by a host Member State on inbound economic activity,[3] while also prohibiting subsidies that affect competition and trade (State aid).[4] In an internal market, however, exit restrictions can be as distortive as access restrictions, and unsurprisingly therefore the Court has traditionally interpreted the Treaty Articles on the free movement as prohibiting not only market access restrictions on inbound economic activity by the host or destination Member State, but also exit restrictions on outbound economic activity by the home, origin or departure Member State.[5]

---

1 Prof van Thiel is Emeritus Professor in International and European Tax Law at the Free University Brussels and teaches as a guest Professor at the WU (Vienna University of Economics and Business). He occasionally acts as a Deputy Judge at the Regional Court of Appeal in Den Bosch, the Netherlands. In November 2021, he retired from the European Union, where he worked since 1988, including as Head of the Tax Division of the Council of Ministers. The observations in this contribution are personal and cannot be attributed to the organizations mentioned above. Comments are welcome at: servaasvanthiel@hotmail.com.

2 For an indication of protective measures see: Report to the Trade Policy Review Body from the Director General on trade-related developments, WTO Document WT/TPR/OV/W/10 of 4 July 2016, available at: https://www.wto.org/english/news_e/news16_e/trdev_22jul16_e.htm.

3 The Treaty articles on the free movement of workers, for instance, essentially provide workers with the right of access to a host Member State in order to seek or accept employment there. See Article 45 TFEU.

4 Article 107 TFEU provides that any aid granted by a Member State or through State resources in any form whatsoever which distorts or threatens to distort competition by favoring certain undertakings or the production of certain goods, shall, in so far as it affects trade between member States, be incompatible with the internal market. See Chapter 15.

5 For early case law on free movement of workers, see for instance Case 48/75 *Royer* EU:C:1976:57 point 28 and Case 8/77 *Sagulo* EU:C:1977:131 point 4; Case 157/79 Pieck [1980] ECR 2171 (point 4); Case 249/86 Commission v. Germany [1989] ECR 1263 (at 1289 point 9); Case C-376/89 Giagounidis [1991] ECR I-1069 (at I-1091 point 12). For professionals and companies, see Case 81/87 Daily Mail [1988] ECR 5483 (at 5510 point 16).

Discriminatory exit taxes can be defined as exit restrictions caused by a higher tax burden on the outbound than on the similar domestic economic activity. They were already mentioned by the 1962 General Program for the abolition of restrictions on establishment,[6] and they were first considered contrary to the freedom of establishment of companies in the 1988 *Daily Mail* decision.[7] Even though the Court seemed initially hesitant to live up to its own doctrine (see *Biehl*,[8] *Werner*,[9] *Bachmann*,[10] and other early tax decisions of the Court),[11] the turning point came with the 1998 *ICI* decision, which concerned a UK rule that excluded corporate groups from the benefits of consolidation between domestic companies if the majority of group members were not established in the UK. The Court explicitly repeated its *Daily Mail* formula[12] and would apply it consistently in subsequent case law.[13]

The *ICI* decision opened the way for a large number of tax cases which are all based on the principle that any higher tax burden imposed by the home state on an outbound economic activity as compared to a similar domestic activity constitutes a prohibited

6 See also Title III of the General Programme for the abolition of restrictions on establishment, OJEC 36 of 15 January 1962 at 62, Special Edition Second Series IX at 7 (which mentions among the restrictions to be abolished any measures that make taking up a cross-border economic activity more expensive, such as higher taxes).

7 Case 81/87 *Daily Mail* EU:C:1988:456 point 16. See also Title III of the General Programme for the abolition of restrictions on establishment, OJEC 36 of 15 January 1962 at 62, Special Edition Second Series IX at 7, which mentions among the restrictions to be abolished any measures that make taking up a cross-border economic activity more expensive, such as higher taxes.

8 A German worker left his job in Luxembourg in the middle of the fiscal year to return to Germany, but, unlike permanent residents, he could not reclaim the excessively withheld wage tax. Though this was clearly an exit restriction the Court did not repeat its explicit *Daily Mail* formula. Case C-175/88 *Biehl* EU:C:1990:186.

9 Germany refused to allow a worker who worked in Germany but lived in the Netherlands the deduction of personal and family expenses, but rather than qualifying this as an exit restriction on the German worker, the Court considered the case purely internal to Germany. Case C-112/91 *Hans Werner v Finanzamt Aachen-Innenstadt*, EU:C:1993:27 point *17 ('Accordingly, it must be stated in reply to the national court that Article 52 of the EEC Treaty does not preclude a Member State from imposing on its nationals who carry on their professional activities within its territory and who earn all or almost all of their income there or possess all or almost all of their assets there a heavier tax burden if they do not reside in that State than if they do.')*.

10 The Court considered the refusal of Belgium to allow an immigrant German worker a deduction of annuity contributions paid to a German insurer, in terms of an access restriction on the German worker, rather than in terms of a possible exit restriction on Belgian insurers. Case C-204/90 *Hans Martin Bachmann v. Belgium* EU:C:1992:35. See also Case C-300/90 *Commission v. Belgium* EU:C:1992:37.

11 See van Thiel (2002): 'Free movement of persons and income tax law: the European Court in search of principles', IBFD Doctoral Series 3, at 241–269.

12 Case C-264/96 *ICI* EU:C:1998:370 point 21. *('It should also be pointed out that, even though, according to their wording, the provisions concerning freedom of establishment are directed mainly to ensuring that foreign nationals and companies are treated in the host Member State in the same way as nationals of that State, they also prohibit the Member State of origin from hindering the establishment in another Member State of one of its nationals or of a company incorporated under its legislation which comes within the definition contained in Article 58* (reference to *Case 81/87 Daily Mail and General Trust [1988] ECR 5483*, 81/87, EU:C:1988:456 *paragraph 16)).'*

13 For recent decisions see for instance Case C-646/15 *Panayi* EU:C:2017:682 points 27 and 42 and Case C-292/16 *A Oy* EU:C:2017:888 point 24 and case law cited there.

discriminatory exit tax. It is irrelevant what specific aspect of the tax system leads to the higher burden on outbound activity, and a prohibited exit tax may result from tax rate differentiation (such as the higher tax rate on outbound compared to similar domestic investment income flows as in *Denkavit*,[14] or the lower tax rate on domestic as compared to inbound investment income flows as in *Lenz*[15] and *Commission v. France II*[16]), tax base differentiation as a result of different tax exemptions (as in *Verkooijen*)[17] or tax deductions (as in *Eurowings*),[18] and even from a different definition of the taxable person in domestic and cross border situations (such as joint assessment of spouses as in *Zurstrassen*[19] or group taxation of legal persons as in *ICI*).

Even if there is no higher tax burden on cross-border as compared to domestic situations, the procedural obligation to pay tax at an earlier moment can be qualified as a prohibited discriminatory exit tax. Taxpayers who permanently leave their tax jurisdiction are for instance routinely required to settle their tax position before departure and for that purpose to file an emigration tax return and to pay the tax due on all income earned up to that moment. However, in *Case* C-269/09, *Commission v Spain*,[20] the Commission argued that immediate recovery on exit constituted an EU incompatible restriction, and the Court agreed that this constituted a cash-flow disadvantage and thus a restriction on the freedom of establishment (points 51 to 59).[21] The Court held that the determination of the tax debt at the moment of exit was justified by the 'need to ensure the effective recovery of the tax debt', but considered immediate recovery disproportional, because Spain could ask the host Member State to help with the post emigration recovery of the tax

14 In Case C-170/05 *Denkavit Internationaal BV* EU:C:2006:783, a higher withholding tax rate on outbound compared to domestic dividend flows was treated by the Court as a discrimination of inward investment/establishment by the foreign parent company (point 30), but would, in the case of a non-substantial holding be treated as a restriction of the outbound movement of capital.

15 Case C-315/02 *Lenz* EU:C:2004:446 points 20 and 21 (the Austrian option to be subject to a fixed or a half income tax rate on domestic but not foreign source investment income, discriminated both against outbound investment by Austrian residents and against foreign companies seeking to raise capital in Austria).

16 Case C-334/02 *Commission v. France* EU:C:2004:129 points 10, 12, 23 and 24 (the French option for a mostly lower fixed income tax rate on domestic but not foreign source investment income, discriminated both against foreign financial and insurance service providers and against domestic investors' outbound investment).

17 Case C-35/98 *Staatssecretaris van Financiën v B.G.M. Verkooijen* EU:C:2000:294 points 34 and 35 (the Dutch tax exemption for dividends received from domestic but not from foreign companies discriminated both against domestic investors investing in non-resident companies and against foreign companies seeking to raise capital in the Netherlands).

18 Case C-294/97 *Eurowings* EU:C:1999:524.

19 In Case C-87/99 *Zurstrassen* EU:C:2000:251, a resident of Luxembourg was refused the advantage of joint assessment because his spouse lived in Belgium.

20 Case C-269/09 *Commission v Spain*, EU:C:2012:439.

21 The Court recalls previous case law that even minor restrictions are prohibited (point 55 citing Case 270/83 *Commission* v *France* EU:C:1986:37 point 21; Case C-34/98 *Commission* v *France* EU:C:2000:84 point 49; Case *de Lasteyrie du Saillant* EU:C:2004:138 point 43) including cash flow disadvantages (point 59 citing Joined Cases C-397/98 and C-410/98 *Metallgesellschaft* EU:C:2001:134 points 44, 54 and 76; Case C-436/00 *X and Y* EU:C:2002:704 points 36 to 38; Case C-446/03 *Marks & Spencer* EU:C:2005:763 point 32; and Case C-347/04 *Rewe Zentralfinanz* EU:C:2007:194 point 29).

debt under existing EU mutual assistance Directives (points 64 to 75). The Court rejected other justifications such as the balanced allocation of taxing powers between the Member States (points 76 to 82) and the coherence of the national tax system (points 83 to 90).[22]

12.1.2 *Exit taxes on accrued but unrealized gains*

In the literature, however, exit taxation is often understood in a stricter sense as referring to the inclusion in taxable income of accrued but not yet realized income or capital gains when assets or asset-owners leave their tax jurisdiction (tax on unrealized gains), but not when they stay at home (tax deferral until income is realized).[23] The reason for such an exit tax is that departing taxpayers may seek to benefit from a tax base mismatch between the accrual jurisdiction and the realization jurisdiction, by moving to a destination jurisdiction which does not tax the realization at all or which extends a *step up*, meaning that only gains accrued after immigration will be taxed. In these cases, the taxpayer may actually partly avoid taxation or avoid it altogether.

In international tax law, therefore, a broad understanding developed that the state in which gains on business assets accrued, has the right to tax these gains and may exercise that tax jurisdiction when taxpayers or assets leave the accrual jurisdiction.[24] Exit taxes thus seek to ensure the correct allocation of tax jurisdiction and to prevent tax avoidance. They may take different forms. A state may for instance try to recapture previously enjoyed deductions or deferrals (claw back), or it may extend the tax liability of the departing taxpayer for a certain period of time after emigration (residence fiction, trailing tax), or it may simply impose a tax on accrued value at the moment of exit (exit tax). In practice, not all accrued income is treated in the same way upon exit. Unrealized capital gains locked up in assets of an undertaking (fiscal reserves, goodwill, value increases of assets or value decreases of liabilities) are typically subject to an exit tax, whether or not under security and without the exit state waiving the claim after a certain period of time. On the other hand, unrealized capital gains that are locked up in shareholdings, movable assets or pension reserves in the hands of private individuals often remain taxable under an extended residence fiction or a recovery deferral until realization abroad, with the home state often crediting similar destination state taxes and relinquishing the claim after five to ten years.[25]

Even though exit taxes are not unreasonable from an international tax law point of view, their application causes a dilemma for EU Member States, because taxing domestic tax-payers on realized gains (tax deferral until realization) while taxing departing taxpayers on accrued gains (no tax deferral) may constitute a discriminatory exit restriction under

22 Immediate recovery was not considered contrary to the EEA agreement with Norway, Iceland and Liechtenstein, because the Commission had not shown that exchange of information equivalent to that provided by the EU Directive, existed between Spain and those countries (points 94 to 100).

23 See for instance Terra and Wattel *European Tax Law*, 6th edition 2012, Chapter 20 Exit Taxes.

24 See for instance IFA, Cahiers de droit fiscal international, The *tax treatment of transfer of residence by individuals*, Volume 2002b. See also: Rijkele Betten, *Income Tax Aspects of Emigration and Immigration of Individuals*, IBFD Publications, Amsterdam, 1998.

25 See for instance Terra and Wattel *European Tax Law*, 6th edition 2012 Chapter 20 Exit Taxes.

EU law (discriminatory because the emigration of a person or of an asset is not the same as the realization of that asset). Exit taxes may also constitute a serious hindrance to the exercise of free movement rights for the simple reason that they tax something which is not there yet and they require a payment for which the cash may not be available. It is this dilemma that has been referred by the national courts of the EU Member States to the European Court and that has given rise to different lines of case law on the different categories of unrealized gains distinguished above.

Subsequent sections of this chapter will therefore discuss exit taxes on accrued gains locked into privately held assets, whereby a distinction is made between shares and pension rights (Section 12.2), and exit taxes on accrued gains locked into business assets (Section 12.3). Section 12.4 will conclude on the state of play on both categories.

As a preliminary remark, it should be noted that this chapter focuses in principle on the taxation of unrealized capital gains, but it is useful to mention that there also is case law of the Court concerning the different treatment of realized capital gains in domestic and cross border situations (e.g. realized gains on shares[26] and on residences[27]).

12.2 Exit taxes on accrued gains locked into privately held assets

12.2.1 Exit taxation on the accrued value of shares

Exit taxation on the accrued value of shares first came up in 2002 in *X & Y v. Riksskatteverket*[28] in which Sweden taxed capital gains upon the transfer of shares in a closely held Swedish company to a Belgian company controlled by the same individual shareholders. Had they transferred their shares to their own Swedish company, no tax would have been payable (tax deferral). The Court considered the Swedish measure disproportionate because it

26 In Case C-268/03 De Baeck EU:C:2004:342, the Court considered it contrary to the free movement of capital for Belgium to tax capital gains on the outbound sale of shares in a Belgian company, whereas a domestic sale would be exempt. In Case C-436/06 Gronfeldt EU:C:2007:820, the Court considered it contrary to the free movement of capital for Germany to tax capital gains on the sale of shares in a company established in another Member State where the seller had held, either directly or indirectly, a share of at least 1% of the company's capital within the previous five years, whereas the profits from the sale of shares in a German company were subject to tax only in the case of a substantial shareholding of at least 10%. In Case C-370/11 Commission v. Belgium EU:C:2012:287, the Court considered it incompatible with the EU and EEA rules on free movement of capital for Belgium to tax capital gains obtained on the repurchase of shares in certain collective investment undertakings only if established in Norway and Iceland, but not if established in Belgium.

27 In Case C-345/05 *Commission v. Portugal* EU:C:2006:685 and in Case C-104/06 *Commission v. Sweden* EU:C:2007:40, for instance, the Court considered it incompatible with the EU and EEA provisions of the free movement of persons for Portugal/Sweden to defer capital gains tax on the sale of a private residence only if the proceeds were re-invested in the acquisition of a new residence situated in Portugal/Sweden and not if invested in a new residence in another Member State. In a slight variation, in Case C-443/06 *Erika Waltraud Ilse Hollmann v Fazenda Publica*, EU:C:2007:600, the Court considered it incompatible with the EU provisions on the free movement of capital for Portugal to tax only half the capital gains realized on the sale of real property by a resident of Portugal whereas a resident of another Member State was taxed on the entire capital gains.

28 Case C-436/00 *X & Y v. Riksskatteverket* EU:C:2002:704.

taxed holders of foreign shares too early: both prior to emigration and prior to (eventual) alienation of their shares.[29] Moreover, nothing prevented Sweden from applying a trailing tax to emigrants holding foreign shares (as it did in a domestic situation).

The 2004 *De Lasteyrie de Saillant*[30] case concerned a French resident moving to Belgium, taking along a substantial share-holding in a French company. He was taxed on the accrued gains but could avoid immediate payment (collection deferral) if he provided a bank guarantee and appointed a fiscal representative. Upon subsequent realization of the gains, France would take account of post emigration losses and would credit possible taxes imposed by the destination state (point 29). If he held on to his shares, however, the tax and security would be cancelled after five years. The Court considered the exit tax discriminatory because:

> '46. A taxpayer wishing to transfer his tax residence outside French territory, in exercise of the right guaranteed to him by Article 52 of the Treaty, is subjected to disadvantageous treatment in comparison with a person who maintains his residence in France. That taxpayer becomes liable, simply by reason of such a transfer, to tax on income which has not yet been realised and which he therefore does not have, whereas, if he remained in France, increases in value would become taxable only when, and to the extent that, they were actually realised. That difference in treatment concerning the taxation of increases in value, which is capable of having considerable repercussions on the assets of a taxpayer wishing to transfer his tax residence outside France, is likely to discourage a taxpayer from carrying out such a transfer.
> 47. An examination of the rules for applying that measure confirms that conclusion. Although it is possible to benefit from suspension of payment, that is not automatic and it is subject to strict conditions (...), in particular, conditions as to the setting up of guarantees. Those guarantees in themselves constitute a restrictive effect, in that they deprive the taxpayer of the enjoyment of the assets given as a guarantee.'

The Court rejected several justifications for the measure, including the need to prevent tax avoidance (the exit tax was not targeted at tax avoiders – points 50-58), the need to maintain fiscal coherence (France itself gave up coherence by crediting possible similar foreign taxes and by cancelling the claim after five years[31] – points 61 to 67), and the need to ensure the balanced allocation of the power to tax 'the case did not concern the allocation of tax jurisdiction' (point 68).

The 2006 *Van Hilten-Van der Heijden* case[32] concerned a Dutch national who emigrated via Belgium to Switzerland, but died within 10 years of emigration. Under a Dutch 10-year residence fiction for Dutch nationals her heirs were taxed on the estate as if she had been a Dutch resident at the moment of death, but they could credit similar taxes

29 Peter J. Wattel: 'Red Herrings in Direct Tax Cases Before the ECJ', 2 *Legal Issues of Economic Integration* 2004 (Vol. 31), p. 81-95.
30 Case C-9/02, *Hughes de Lasteyrie de Saillant* EU:C:2004:138.
31 The drawback to this type of reasoning is that emigration States could consider *not* to give double tax credits, and *not* to give up tax claims after 5 years, which would be worse for the emigrating taxpayer.
32 Case C-513/03, *Van Hilten-van der Heijden v. Inspecteur* EU:C:2006:131.

imposed by Switzerland (points 12, 13, 19, 27 and 51). The Court accepted this 10 year trailing tax in the form of a post exit residence fiction, because, for both non-resident taxpayers with Dutch nationality and resident taxpayers with Dutch nationality, tax was assessed and collected only at the moment of death (so that Dutch nationals were treated equally irrespective their residence and post emigration decreases in value were automatically taken into account), and because there was protection against double taxation (point 51). It held that:

> 45. National legislation such as that in question in the main proceedings, which provides that the estate of a national of a Member State who dies within 10 years of ceasing to reside in that Member State is to be taxed as if that national had continued to reside in that Member State, while providing for relief in respect of the taxes levied in the State to which the deceased transferred his residence, does not constitute a restriction on the movement of capital.
> 46. By enacting identical taxation provisions for the estates of nationals who have transferred their residence abroad and of those who have remained in the Member State concerned, such legislation cannot discourage the former from making investments in that Member State from another State nor the latter from doing so in another Member State from the Member State concerned, and, regardless of the place where the assets in question are situated, nor can it diminish the value of the estate of a national who has transferred his residence abroad. (....).
> 51. The reply to the questions referred must therefore be that Article 73b of the Treaty is to be interpreted as meaning that it does not preclude legislation of a Member State, such as that in question in the main proceedings, by which the estate of a national of that Member State who dies within 10 years of ceasing to reside in that Member State is to be taxed as if that national had continued to reside in that State, while enjoying relief in respect of inheritance taxes levied by other States.

In the same year the Court decided the important *N. v. Inspecteur* case,[33] concerning a Dutchman emigrating to the UK, taking along all shares in two closely held companies whose seats were transferred at the same moment to the Netherlands Antilles. He was issued a conservatory assessment for the unrealized capital gains in those holdings (i.e. tax was assessed but recovery was deferred) and had to provide security for payment upon realization. Subsequent to the *De Lasteyrie* judgment, the Dutch government had already canceled the security requirement and had released the collateral provided by Mr N.

The Court first essentially repeated *De Lasteyrie*, holding that the exit tax was discriminatory and that the bank guarantee constituted a restriction (points 35 and 36). It also noted that post emigration decreases in value were not taken into account (point 37) and that the exit tax declaration was an additional formality likely further to hinder the departure (point 38), and concluded that such a tax system is likely to hinder the exercise of the freedom of establishment (point 39).

Subsequently, however, the Court accepted as a justification that the contested provisions were 'designed, in particular, to allocate between Member States, on the basis of the territoriality principle, the power to tax increases of value in company holdings' and 'to

33 Case C-470/04, *N. v. Inspecteur* EU:C:2006:525.

prevent double taxation' (point 41), and thus pursued an objective in the public interest, and were appropriate for ensuring the attainment of that objective' (point 47). When considering the proportionality of the contested measure, the Court allowed the requirement to file an exit tax declaration, but not the requirement to provide a bank guarantee which it considered disproportionate because the Netherlands could make use of the mutual assistance Directives (see Chapter 13) to request assistance from other Member States with the recovery of its tax debts (points 49 to 53). Finally, the Court held that for the measure to be proportional the Netherlands should take account of post emigration reductions in value unless already taken into account in the host Member State (point 54).

In 2019, the Court came to a similar conclusion when it was asked to consider a German exit tax imposed on unrealized gains locked into shares held by a German self-employed national (in the Swiss company of which he was the managing director and a 50% share-holder) at the moment he moved his residence to Switzerland.[34] The Court noted a different treatment (because residents were taxed only on realized gains) resulting in a cash flow disadvantage (points 56 and 57) that constituted discrimination contrary to the 1999 EU-Swiss agreement on the free movement of persons. In the interest of preserving the allocation of tax jurisdiction between Germany and Switzerland, Germany could, on exit, determine the amount of tax due, but it had to defer the collection of the tax until the moment of realization (point 64). Immediate collection was disproportional and could not be justified by the effectiveness of fiscal supervision, because the German-Swiss tax treaty provided for the exchange of information (point 65). A bank guarantee, to ensure effective collection and to prevent tax revenue loss, was allowed only where there was a risk of non-recovery of the tax payable, particularly in the absence of a recovery assistance mechanism (66, reference to *National Grid Indus*, paragraphs 73 and 74, and *DMC*, paragraphs 65 to 67).

12.2.2 Exit taxes on accrued pension rights

In a separate line of cases the Court also considered that the Treaty precluded exit taxes on accrued pension rights. Apart from the traditional international tax law question which Member State has the right to tax the income resulting from a pension or life insurance contract (allocation of tax jurisdiction addressed in Double Tax Treaties), several questions arise from an EU law point of view. A first question is to what extent EU law prescribes the tax deductibility of cross border pension premiums or contributions on the same footing as domestically paid premiums or contributions. In *Bachmann*, the CJEU held that the Belgian refusal to allow the deduction of annuity contributions paid to insurers established outside Belgium was justified by the need to preserve the coherence of the Belgian tax system (coherence between deduction of contributions and taxability of the future benefits).[35] A surprising position that was unsurprisingly reversed in a stream of

34 Case C-581/17 (*Martin Wächtler v. Finanzamt Konstanz*), EU:C:2019:138.

35 Case C-204/90 *Bachmann* [1992] EU:C:1992:35 and Case C-300/90 *Commission v. Belgium* EU:C:1992:37.

subsequent cases in which the Court, following the position of the European Commission,[36] essentially held that Member States which allow the deduction of pension contributions and insurance premiums paid at home, should also allow the deduction of outbound pension contributions or premiums, irrespective of whether paid by the beneficiary[37] or his employer.[38] This became a general line of case law[39] which was explicitly re-confirmed in *Case C-296/12 Commission v. Belgium*, in which the Court also rejected Belgium's repeated claim that the discrimination was justified by the need to preserve the coherence of the tax system (points 34 to 40), the need for effective fiscal supervision (points 41 to 45) or the need to protect consumers or taxpayers (points 46 to 49).[40]

The second question concerns the EU compatibility of the taxation of accrued pension reserves once taxpayers and/or their pension reserves leave the accrual/deduction jurisdiction. Departure causes a problem in particular for Member States applying a so called 'EET' system (they **e**xempt contributions as these are deductible, **e**xempt the investment income of the pension fund as it is exempt from corporation tax, but **t**ax the pension benefits), which, upon departure of the taxpayer or the reserve, may no longer be able to tax the pension benefits. In fact, the taxpayer may benefit from double non-taxation if he moves to a TTE system (contributions not deductible, income of pension funds taxed, but pension benefits exempt) or a TEE system (contributions not deductible, income of pension funds and pension benefits exempt). EET states therefore routinely exit tax the reserve when the beneficiary or the pension reserve leaves their jurisdiction, which under EU law may constitute a discriminatory exit restriction because it is only applied in cross-border situations.

Indeed, in Case *C-522/04 Commission v. Belgium* the Court considered that EU law precluded a Belgian rule under which 'capital or surrender values which are transferred to a pension fund or insurance undertaking established abroad are taxed, while no such taxation is provided for where transfers are made to a pension fund or to an insurance undertaking established in Belgium'. The Belgian rule hindered not only the inbound supply of insurance services (point 40) but also the outbound movement of workers and professionals 'by preventing them from forwarding their savings' (point 68 to 73). The Court first considered the Belgian measure contrary to the freedom to provide services because that 'measure is liable to further impede the activities of a provider of insurance services established in a Member State other than the Kingdom of Belgium where it lawfully provides such services' (point 40). Second, the Court also considered the Belgian measure contrary to the right to free movement of employed persons, the freedom of

36 Communication from the Commission to the Council, the European Parliament and the Economic and Social Committee: The elimination of tax obstacles to the cross-border provision of occupational pensions, COM(2001) 214 final".

37 Case C-80/94 *Wielockx* EU:C:1995:271; Case C-118/96 *Safir* EU:C:1998:170; Case C-136/00, *Rolf Dieter Danner* EU:C:2002:558; Case C-436/05 *De Graaf en Daniels* EU:C:2006:656; Case C-544/07 *Uwe Rüffler* EU:C:2009:258.

38 Case C-422/01 *Försäkringsaktiebolaget Skandia, Ola Ramstedt v. Riksskatteverket* EU:C:2003:380.

39 Case C-150/04 *Commission v. Denmark*, EU:C:2007:69; Case *C-522/04 Commission v. Belgium* EU:C:2007:405.

40 Case C-296/12 *Commission v. Belgium* EU:C:2014:24.

establishment of self-employed persons and the general right to free movement, because it allowed taxation by reason of them crossing a border (points 68 to 72). The Court adds:

> '73. Third by levying tax on transfers of capital or surrender values where the transfer is made by the pension fund or insurance institution with which the capital or surrender values have been built up in favour of the beneficiary or persons entitled through him, to another insurance institution established outside Belgium, Article 364b of the CIR 1992 dissuades employed and self-employed persons from establishing themselves in another Member State by preventing them from forwarding their savings'.

Likewise, in Case C-269/07 *Commission v. Germany*,[41] the Court held that EU law precluded several discriminatory German pension rules, including first, the rule that reserved a savings-pension bonus to resident workers only (points 51 to 59), second the rule that the subsidised capital can be used for the acquisition or construction of an owner-occupied dwelling only if that dwelling is situated in Germany (points 70 to 85), and third, the rule that 'a beneficiary of the bonus who leaves his domicile or habitual residence in Germany, and who is therefore no longer fully liable to tax, must reimburse the savings-pension bonuses obtained and, as the case may be, the deductions of special expenses under Paragraph 10a of the EStG' (points 86 to 112).

The Court confirmed its earlier line in two decisions of November 2023 concerning Dutch conditions for the tax-free outbound transfer of pension reserves, imposed respectively on workers taking up employment abroad and on foreign pension funds to which Dutch pension reserves were being transferred. In Case C-360/22 *Commission v. Netherlands*[42] it considered a Dutch rule incompatible with the free movement of workers (EU and EEA), because a worker changing jobs domestically could transfer his pension reserves to another Dutch pension fund without being taxed, whereas a worker accepting employment in another Member State could transfer his pension reserves to a pension fund in the other Member State without being taxed, only if the possibilities of redeeming the pension as a capital sum were the same as, or more limited than, in the Netherlands. In Case C-459/22 it considered a Dutch rule incompatible with the free movement of workers (EU and EEA), because it required foreign as well as domestic pension funds to which Dutch workers transferred their pension reserves to either provide security for the ultimate collection of Dutch taxes or to accept themselves liability to pay those taxes. Even though that condition applied in the same way in domestic and cross border situations, it disadvantaged in particular the cross-border situation because it required foreign pension funds to have a detailed knowledge of applicable Dutch tax law, which could dissuade them from accepting the tax free transfer of Dutch pension reserves, a risk which did not occur in the case of domestic transfers.[43]

A third EU law question concerns the taxation of investment income of pension funds and in particular the question to what extent withholding taxes on investment income flows (dividends, interest) received by pension funds are the same for domestic flows

41 Case C-269/07 *Commission v Germany* EU:C:2009:527.
42 Case C-360/22 European Commission v Kingdom of the Netherlands ECLI:EU:C:2023:875.
43 Case C-459/22 European Commission v Kingdom of the Netherlands ECLI:EU:C:2023:878.

to resident funds and outbound flows to non-resident funds, and the case law on this question is discussed in other chapters of this book, especially Chapter 11.[44]

12.2.3 Conclusions on exit taxes on privately held assets

From these two lines of case law on exit taxes on accrued gains locked into privately held assets in the case of emigrating natural persons, a number of conclusions can be drawn. A first conclusion is that EU law precludes exit taxation of pension reserves and, unlike in other cases it seems that Member States cannot rely on the need to ensure a balanced allocation of tax jurisdiction to justify such restrictions. This would be in line with the rather strict approach which the Court generally takes towards restrictions on the free movement of workers and self-employed natural persons.

A second conclusion is that an exit tax on other accrued gains is also considered a discriminatory exit restriction, which can, however, be justified by the need to preserve the balanced allocation of the power to tax between Member States. Because Member States have the right, on the basis of the territoriality principle, to tax value increases that accrue while the taxpayer was resident in their territory, they are allowed to assess the size of the unrealised gain upon exit and, so to say, establish a provisional tax claim. Although the departure Member State may require the taxpayer to file an exit tax declaration, the actual recovery of the exit tax must be deferred until realization of the gains, as in domestic situations, and in such cases no posting of security or appointment of a fiscal representative may be required from the taxpayer to ensure the future payment of the tax, unless there is a real risk of non-recovery. Moreover, the exit Member State is obliged to take account of post-emigration decreases in value, but it is not clear whether that state is also obliged to credit similar taxes which the destination state might impose when the capital gains are ultimately realized. In *De Lasteyrie* the Court noted explicitly that the exit state did provide such a foreign tax credit (point 29), but it stopped short of actually requiring the exit Member State to prevent double taxation, which is in line with its broader stance that double taxation is not prohibited by directly applicable Treaty Articles, because it results from disparities between the tax systems of the Member States (see Chapters 6.4.1 and 8.1).[45]

A third conclusion is that a trailing tax in the form of a residence fiction for nationals in the exit State is also compatible with free movement because it defers taxation to the moment of realization, like in domestic situations.[46] To be noted that in the case of trailing taxes the Court may require the exit state to prevent double taxation, because in

44 Subsequent to Case C-170/05 *Denkavit Internationaal BV* EU:C:2006:783 and Case C-379/05 *Amurta* EU:C:2007:655, the Commission initiated proceedings against 14 Member States which levied withholding taxes on outbound dividend and interest payments to pension funds, while exempting similar payments to domestic funds (Spain, the Netherlands, Portugal, Germany, Italy, Austria, Denmark, Sweden, Finland, Estonia, Lithuania, Slovenia, the Czech Republic and Poland). See also Case C-252/14 *Pensioenfonds Metaal en Techniek* EU:C:2016:402.

45 Consistent case law since Case C-513/04 Kerckhaert Morres EU:C:2006:713.

46 The Court sometimes notes that the home state provides a credit for a similar tax of the destination state, but does not seem to require this for the exit tax to be EU compatible.

Van Hilten-Van der Heijden, it made it explicit that the trailing tax was allowed and tax could be imposed 'as if that national had continued to reside in that State, while enjoying relief in respect of inheritance taxes levied by other States.' On the other hand, it may also drop that requirement in future cases in view of the fact that its case law on double taxation largely developed after the decision in *Van Hilten-Van der Heijden*.

12.3 Exit taxes on accrued gains locked into business assets

12.3.1 Preliminary on corporate mobility rights

Since 1988, a line of cases developed in which the Court decided on the mobility rights of companies in the EU,[47] but the tax consequences of corporate mobility would only become clear in the 2011 *National Grid Indus* Case.[48]

The first relevant case is *Daily Mail*,[49] which concerned a UK investment company that wanted to avoid UK capital gains taxation (which was imposed on residents only) by transferring its central management/tax residence to the Netherlands, where it would benefit from a step up (i.e. its holdings would enter the books at current market value). If the holdings were sold shortly afterwards, the capital gains would be taxed neither in the Netherlands nor in the UK. However, UK law required Treasury consent for a transfer of central management which usually triggered an exit capital gains tax.

The Court confirmed that the Treaty not only prohibited access restrictions by the host or destination state but also exit restrictions by the home or *origin* State, but it did not rule on the substantive question whether the UK consent requirement constituted an EU incompatible exit restriction. In fact, the Court held that corporate exit, especially retention or loss of legal personality upon a real seat transfer, was not covered by primary EU law, because, under the Treaty, Member States should have negotiated an agreement on exiting companies maintaining their legal personality, but neither an agreement nor any harmonized rules were in place. In a somewhat confusing way, the Court concluded that the right of establishment does not confer on companies the right to transfer their seat to another Member State while retaining their status as companies incorporated under the law of the Member State of origin. It stressed that companies, unlike individuals, are creatures of law, existing only by virtue of varying national legislation.

47 In particular Case 81/87 *Daily Mail* EU:C:1988:456; Case C-212/97 *Centros* EU:C:1999:126; Case C-208/00 *Überseering* EU:C:2002:632; Case C-167/01 *Inspire Art* EU:C:2003:512; Case C-411/03 *SEVIC Systems* EU:C:2005:762; Case C-210/06 *Cartesio* EU:C:2008:723; Case C-378/10 *VALE* EU:C:2012:440 and Case C-106/16 *Polbud* EU:C:2017:804. See also Directive 2005/56/EC of 26 October 2005 on mergers of limited liability companies (OJ 2005 L 310, p. 1) and Regulation No 2157/2001 of 8 October 2001 on the Statute for a European Company (SE) (OJ 2001 L 294, p. 1).

48 Case C-371/10 *National Grid Indus* EU:C:2011:785. See, a.o. Reinout Kok, 'Compatibility of Exit taxes and Community Law,' *EC Tax Review* 2011/2, p. 62-74, and Jos van Daele, 'Tax Residence and the Mobility of companies: Borderline Cases under Private International Law and Tax Law,' *European Taxation* May 2011, p. 190-200.

49 Case 81/87, *Daily Mail*, EU:C:1988:456.

This was a puzzling answer, not only because it looked like a substantive decision (even though corporate exit was not covered by EU law), but also because both the UK and the Netherlands applied an incorporation system of company law (rather than a real seat system), meaning that Daily Mail could transfer its real seat (central management) without any repercussions in either State as regards the retention and recognition of its legal personality and company law Statute, and without any other company law consequences. That is why the question referred did not concern company law, but tax law. The Court therefore answered a question which was not asked, without answering the question that was asked.[50]

The line of cases on corporate mobility continued with *Überseering*,[51] which concerned a seat transfer from an incorporation jurisdiction (the Netherlands) to a real seat jurisdiction (Germany). Germany refused to recognize the Netherlands company's legal existence and procedural *locus standi*, as it was not (re)incorporated under German law when it moved its seat to Germany. The Court, however, held that Member States are required to grant national treatment to companies of other Member States which allow seat transfer without loss of legal personality (incorporation systems), so that real seat Member States could no longer restrict *immigration* of companies of such other Member States. *Überseering* also explained *Daily Mail* as follows:

> '70 (...), the Court confined itself to holding that the question whether a company formed in accordance with the legislation of one Member State could transfer its registered office or its actual center of administration to another Member State without losing its legal personality under the law of the Member State of incorporation and, in certain circumstances, the rules relating to that transfer were determined by the national law in accordance with which the company had been incorporated. It concluded that a Member State was able, in the case of a company incorporated under its law, to make the company's right to retain its legal personality under the law of that State subject to restrictions on the transfer of the company's actual center of administration to a foreign country.'

In *Centros*,[52] a Danish businessman wanted to incorporate his Danish business without complying with Danish minimum requirements for paid up capital. He thus set up a company in the UK (no minimum paid up capital requirements) and turned his Danish business into a branch of that UK company (outbound establishment in the form of a company). While conceding that certain anti-fraud measures could be applied (point 38), the Court held that the freedom of establishment precluded Denmark from refusing to register the branch, even though it only had business in Denmark and not in the UK and even though the structure was set up to avoid more restrictive Danish company law. The Court held:

---

50 Servaas van Thiel, "Daily mail case: tax planning and the European right of establishment - a setback", 28 *European Taxation* 11 of November 1988 at 357 ff.; Dennis Weber, 'Exit Taxes on the Transfer of Seat and the Applicability of the Freedom of Establishment after Überseering,' *European Taxation* 2003, at 351, suggested that the Court should have examined the proportionality of the Treasury consent requirement and the possible sanctions on a transfer of seat without consent.

51 Case C-208/00 *Überseering* EU:C:2002:632.

52 Case C-212/97 *Centros* EU:C:1999:126.

> 27. That being so, the fact that a national of a Member State who wishes to set up a company chooses to form it in the Member State whose rules of company law seem to him the least restrictive and to set up branches in other Member States cannot, in itself, constitute an abuse of the right of establishment. The right to form a company in accordance with the law of a Member State and to set up branches in other Member States is inherent in the exercise, in a single market, of the freedom of establishment guaranteed by the Treaty.

The Court would decide along the same lines in the Cases *Inspire Art* (inbound establishment in the form of a branch)[53] and *Vale* (inbound conversion)[54] and thus consistently allowed companies to exercise their right to freedom of establishment in order to benefit from the least restrictive corporate regime in the EU (and the least burdensome tax regime, as confirmed in *Cadbury Schweppes*).[55]

In *Cartesio*[56] the Court held that a 'real seat' jurisdiction (in this case Hungary, as regards a limited partnership) may terminate an entity's legal existence upon the transfer abroad of its real seat, except if the immigration State's legal system recognizes the immigrating foreign entity and provides it with a host state legal personality (cross-border *transformation* or *conversion*). Thus, the departure State may require emigrating companies to give up their legal status as a company under their laws, but they may not require liquidation if the immigration State seamlessly puts new life into them and continues their legal existence in a legal form of the immigration State (inbound transformation).

In *Polbud*,[57] concerning a Polish company that wanted to convert into a Luxembourg company by transferring its registered office (but not its economic activity) to Luxembourg, Polish law allowed the transfer without loss of legal personality, but the subsequent removal of the company from the commercial register triggered a liquidation requirement which Polbud considered to be an exit restriction. The Court confirmed that Polbud could rely on EU law to convert itself into a Luxembourg company, irrespective of whether it conducted any business in the host state Luxembourg. The liquidation requirement constituted a restriction that could be justified neither by the need to protect the interests

53 In Case C-167/01 *Inspire Art* EU:C:2003: 512, the Court held that EU law precluded national legislation that imposed, in connection with an inbound secondary establishment in the form of a branch, domestic law conditions relating to minimum capital and directors' liability, on the company exercising its freedom of establishment. '.the fact that a national of a Member State who wishes to set up a company can choose to do so in the Member State the company-law rules of which seem to him the least restrictive and then set up branches in other Member States is inherent in the exercise, in a single market, of the freedom of establishment guaranteed by the Treaty. In addition, the fact that a company does not conduct any business in the Member State in which it has its registered office and pursues its activities only or principally in the Member State where its branch is established is not sufficient to prove the existence of abuse or fraudulent conduct which would entitle the latter Member State to deny that company the benefit of the provisions of Community law relating to the right of establishment.' (Points 105, 136-139, 143, operative part 2).

54 In Case C-378/10 *VALE* EU:C:2012:440 the Court held that EU law precluded national legislation which enables domestic companies to convert but which does not allow inbound conversion (by a company of another Member State into a domestic company).

55 Case C-196/04 *Cadbury Schweppes* EU:C:2006:544.

56 Case C-210/06, *Cartesio* EU:C:2008:723, point 47.

57 Case C-106/16 *Polbud* EU:C:2017:804.

of creditors, minority shareholders or employees (because the liquidation was mandatory in any event and therefore without specific regard to any of those or any other public interests, points 52 to 59), nor by the need to prevent abuse (because establishing in a Member State with more favorable legislation does not in itself constitute abuse and a mere transfer of registered office cannot be the basis for a general presumption of fraud - points 40, 60 to 64).

Other cases in which the court confirmed the right of corporate mobility include *Aures*,[58] which confirmed that a Dutch company with a Czech branch could transfer its effective management and thus its tax residence to the Czech branch, and *VP Capital*,[59] which confirmed that a Luxembourg company was allowed to transfer its registered office to Belgium and become a Belgian company.

In conclusion, companies or firms formed in accordance with the legislation of a Member State and having their registered office, their central administration or principal place of business within the European Union have an extensive right to transfer their registered office, central administration or principal place of business to another Member State, without either the home state or the host state being able to hinder such a transfer.

12.3.2 Exit taxes on businesses or business assets

From this line of case law on the company law aspects of corporate mobility, however, the status under EU law of exit taxes on corporate assets initially remained unclear, and different views developed after *Daily Mail*. A traditional international law reasoning was that if Member States can grant corporate legal existence and withdraw it if the real seat is transferred abroad, they should *a fortiori* be allowed to impose the lesser evil of an exit tax.[60] Another, more European, reasoning was that Member States should always impose exit taxes in accordance with EU law (i.e. no immediate recovery, no interest, no bank guarantee, and take account of post emigration losses cf. *De Lasteyrie* and *N. v. Inspecteur*). A nuanced combination of these views suggested a staggered recovery of the exit tax over several years, observing that usually the immigration State would grant a *step up* to current value of the corporate assets and liabilities upon immigration, which would subsequently be depreciated in the immigration State in roughly the same number of years as the number in which the exit tax installments in the exit State had to be paid. In this manner, (i) the tax paid in the exit State would be offset by a comparable tax saving (deductible depreciation) in the immigration State, and (ii) the taxpayer would be relieved of an immediate recovery burden and of the administrative difficulty of a recovery deferral until realization, which requires the ongoing tracing of many tangible

58 Case C-405/18 *Aures Holdings* EU:C:2020:127, points 25 and 26.

59 Case C-414/21 *VP Capital NV v Belgische Staat*, EU:C:2022:871.

60 However, a similar reasoning had already been rejected by the Court in Case C-204/90 *Bachmann* EU:C:1992:35 points 15 and 16 (Germany had argued that, since Member States were not obliged to authorize insurance contracts with foreign insurers, they could a fortiori not be obliged to grant tax advantages in relation to such contracts, but the Court did not agree).

and intangible assets and liabilities that have different realization moments and that may have been depreciated for tax accounting purposes in the exit State.[61]

In its 2006 Communication on exit taxes[62] the Commission took the European view and transposed the Court's findings in *N. v Inspecteur* on natural persons to the transfer of seats of undertakings and of single business assets: taxation should not occur *sooner* and not be *less favorable* than in domestic situations; collection should be automatically deferred until realization without security requirements; post-emigration value decreases should be taken into account; the departure State should use the Directive on Administrative Cooperation Directive (DAC; see Chapter 25) to acquire the necessary information; and the immigration State should either grant a *step up* in value, or, if not, it should share the tax upon the realization of the capital gains with the departure State proportionally in time. Along those lines, the Commission started infringement proceedings against Member States not complying with its Communication.[63]

Two years later, however, the Council took the international law view when it adopted a Resolution[64] that essentially safeguarded the exit State's tax claim and called upon the immigration State to provide for a step up, while requiring the immigrating taxpayer to provide proof that the departure State had in fact exercised its exit taxing right. By contrast, the resolution said nothing on the timing of the payment of the exit tax.

In 2011, the Court decided *National Grid Indus*,[65] which concerned the transfer of the effective management of a Netherlands company to the UK (both incorporation jurisdictions so a transfer was possible without loss of legal personality). There were enough legitimate non-tax reasons for relocation to grant *National Grid Indus* treaty standing and the only asset of the emigrating company was a receivable of £ 38 million which contained an unrealized currency gain of Dfl. 22 million. As the Netherlands lost its tax jurisdiction under the applicable tax treaty it taxed the unrealized currency gain.

The Court first rejected the international law view defended by seven Member States and noted that since the exit state applied the incorporation theory and allowed companies to transfer their real seat (place of effective management) without losing their legal personality, those companies could rely on their freedom of establishment to test the EU compatibility of the exit tax (points 22 to 33).

Secondly, the Court confirmed that the contested exit tax caused a cash flow disadvantage, because departing taxpayers were taxed at the moment of exit rather than at the

61 Terra and Wattel *European Tax Law* 6th Edition 2012, Chapter 20.
62 Commission Communication of 19 December 2006, COM (2006) 825.
63 Case C-269/09 *Commission v Spain* (individuals) EU:C:2012:439; Case C-38/10 *Commission v Portugal* (companies *and* their shareholders) EU:C:2012:521; Case C-64/11 *Commission v Spain* (companies and asset relocation) EU:C:2013:264; Case C-301/11 *Commission v the Netherlands* (companies and unincorporated businesses) EU:C:2013:47; and Case C-261/11 *Commission v Denmark* (transfer of assets) EU:C:2013:480.
64 Council Resolution of 2 December 2008, O.J. C 323, p. 1.
65 Case C-371/10 *National Grid Indus* EU:C:2011:785.

moment of realization of the gains, which constituted a restriction on their outbound establishment which was, in principle, contrary to the Treaty provisions on the freedom of establishment (points 34 to 41).

Thirdly, the Court examined to what extent the contested measure could be justified. As regards the need to preserve the balanced allocation of taxing powers between Member States (points 43 to 78) the Court reiterated established case law that this was a legitimate objective and that a Member State was entitled to tax the gains that had accrued while the departing taxpayer was resident in its jurisdiction (points 45 to 49). It also held that the definitive establishment, at the moment of exit, of the amount of tax due, was proportional, thus rejecting the Commission's reliance on *N v Inspecteur* that the origin Member State had to take account of post emigration decreases in value. The Court distinguished *N. v Inspecteur*, which concerned a private individual, and noted that corporate profits are partly influenced by the valuation of corporate assets, and that, after exit, those profits would be taxed in the host Member State, so that it was also for that Member State 'to take account in its tax system of fluctuations in the value of the assets of that company which occur after the date on which the Member State of origin loses all fiscal connection with the company'.[66] A possible 'omission by the host state to take account of decreases in value does not impose any obligation on the Member State of origin to revalue, at the time of realization of the asset concerned, a tax debt which was definitively determined' at the moment of exit, and a restrictive effect of that situation was due to the disparities between the tax systems of the Member States (points 52 to 64 and in particular 61 and 62). Finally, as regards proportionality of the method of recovery of the tax, the Court weighed the cash flow disadvantage of immediate recovery for the taxpayer against the administrative burden related to the post emigration tracing of the assets in case of a deferred recovery, and noted that: 'the asset situation of a company may appear so complex that an accurate cross-border tracing of the destiny of all the items making up the company's fixed and current assets until the unrealized capital gains incorporated into those assets are realized is almost impossible, and that such tracing will entail efforts representing a considerable or even excessive burden for the company in question.' It then decided that it would be proportional for national legislation to offer a choice to the taxpayer between immediate payment of the tax, or deferred payment[67] 'possibly together with interest' and, depending on the risk of non-recovery of the tax, additional measures such as the provision of a bank guarantee (points 65 to 78).

66 Point 57 notes that the assets of a company are assigned directly to economic activities intended to produce a profit, the amount of which is influenced by the depreciation of the assets, and point 58 notes that since the profits of the company are, after the transfer, taxed exclusively in the destination State, which agrees with the principle of fiscal territoriality, it is also for that Member State, in view of the need for symmetry between the right to tax profits and the deduction of corresponding losses (the depreciation), to take account in its tax system of fluctuations in the value of the assets after the origin State's loss of all fiscal connection with the company.

67 The Court rejected the argument of several Member States that deferral would impose an excessive administrative burden on the Member State of origin amongst others with the argument that that state could rely on European Directives providing for mutual assistance in the recovery of taxes. Points 75 to 78.

The Court also examined the need to maintain the coherence of the tax system and the need to prevent tax avoidance as a justification for the immediate recovery of the exit tax, but rejected both, respectively because deferred recovery would not call into question the direct link between the tax advantage (of tax deferral as long as the company obtains profits in the Netherlands) and the offsetting charge (the tax due assessed at the moment of exit), and because the mere transfer of corporate seat cannot 'set up a general presumption of tax evasion' (points 79 to 84).

In short, for legal persons and business assets, the Court departed from *N. v Inspecteur* in several ways: (i) the origin Member State does not have to take into account post-emigration decreases in value; (ii) a security for later payment of the tax may be required if there is a risk of non-recovery of the exit tax 'which increases with the passage of time'; (iii) the company itself may choose between immediate payment or an interest-bearing trailing tax (in *N. v Inspecteur*, the possible charging of interest was not discussed, as the Netherlands did not charge any). At first sight, this choice seems an elegant and creative solution, but one may ask whether there is real value to the right to opt for tax deferral, if the deferred exit tax debt bears interest, requires provision of security and comes with the ongoing burden of filing tax returns in the exit state. Under these circumstances, a company which can afford it, will probably prefer paying immediately, possibly depending on whether the interest on the deferred tax and the cost of security are deductible.

Subsequently the Court further nuanced *National Grid Indus*, by allowing exit tax recovery in five-(*DMC*, point 64)[68] respectively ten annual instalments (*Verder Lab Tec*).[69] This latter system (recovery of the exit tax in instalments or staggered recovery), combined with an obligation for the immigration State to provide a step up in value (producing deductible depreciation cost in the immigration State), has been incorporated in the recent Anti-Tax Avoidance Directive (ATAD: see Chapter 19) as the EU standard for emigrating companies and cross-border transfer of business assets. The ATAD also seems to end the difference between incorporation systems or real seat system of company law. Member States must accept emigration and immigration of EU companies.

The Court followed its *National Grid Indus* precedent in several subsequent decisions on the tax aspects of corporate mobility so that it can now be considered established case law. Both Case C-38/10 *Commission v Portugal*,[70] and Case C-64/11 *Commission v Spain*,[71]

68 Case C-164/12 *DMC* EU:C:2014:20. The case concerned the contribution of the assets of a limited partnership to the capital of a domestic company and the Court allowed the departing partners to be taxed on the value of those assets as part of a going concern, and thus on the capital gains relating to those assets generated in that territory before they were actually realized. The Court allowed the exit tax to the extent 'it will in fact be impossible for that Member State to exercise its powers of taxation in relation to those gains when they are in fact realised' (a decision which was left to the national court).

69 Case C-657/13 *Verder Lab Tec* EU:C:2015:331. The case concerned a German limited partnership which was taxed on unrealized gains when it transferred its own patent, trademark and model rights to its Dutch permanent establishment. The tax was not collected immediately but spread over 10 years.

70 Case C-38/10, *Commission v Portugal* EU:C:2012:521.

71 Case C-64/11 *Commission v Spain* EU:C:2013:264.

concerned national tax rules under which unrealized corporate capital gains were taxed immediately in the case of transfer of the company or of corporate assets to another Member State. The Court considered the immediate recovery of that tax a restriction (points 27 to 29 in both cases), and reiterated that the company should have a choice between immediate or deferred payment 'possibly together with interest' (points 31 and 32 in both cases). In *Commission v. Spain* the Court, moreover, reiterated that determining the amount of tax due at the moment of exit is proportionate and that the exit state therefore does not have to take into account possible future losses (point 31). In Case C-301/11, *Commission v the Netherlands*, which concerned the same Netherlands exit tax rule as in *National Grid Indus*, the Court simply recalled that previous judgment (point 16).[72]

In Case C-261/11 *Commission v Denmark*, the Court considered that the Danish exit tax on the outbound transfer of corporate assets constituted an exit restriction (points 27 to 31) which could be justified by the need to preserve a balanced allocation of tax jurisdiction, but it considered the immediate recovery of the tax disproportionate.[73] In a slight variation on the theme, the Court held in *Commission v. Germany*,[74] that Germany could not defer capital gains tax on the sale of assets of a permanent establishment only if the gains were re-invested in replacement assets of a permanent establishment in Germany, and not if they were invested in replacement assets of a permanent establishment in another EU/EEA Member State. Though Germany was entitled to tax the capital gains in the cross-border situation (balanced allocation of the power to tax between the Member States) the immediate recovery of the tax would be disproportional and the taxpayer should have the option of either bearing the administrative burden relating to a tax deferral or the immediate recovery of that tax (points 72 and 73).

In Case C-503/14, *Commission v. Portugal*, the Fourth Chamber of the Court brought the exit tax case law for natural persons holding business assets, in line with the exit tax case law for legal persons.[75] The case concerned a Portuguese tax, upon shareholder emigration, on the unrealised gains locked in the value of shares that had been exchanged for other shares (termination of deferral), and on the transfer to a foreign company of business assets connected with the exercise by a natural person of an economic or professional activity (whereas for a shareholder staying in Portugal the unrealised gain would be taxable only when the new shares are sold and a domestic asset transfer would not be taxable). As in previous cases the Court first notes that the exit tax causes a cash flow disadvantage that constitutes a restriction on free movement which may be justified by the need to preserve the balanced allocation of taxing powers between the Member States. The Court continues that the Member State of origin is *not* obliged to take into account post emigration decreases in value and that the taxpayer should be given a choice of deferred payment 'possibly together with interest' and with additional measures, such as a bank guarantee, in case of risk of non-recovery of the tax (points 51 to 61). The Court explicitly notes that 'there is no objective reason for distinguishing ..., between

72 Case C-301/11 *Commission v the Netherlands* EU:C:2013:47.
73 Case C-261/11 *Commission v Denmark* EU:C:2013:480.
74 Case C-591/13 *Commission v Germany* EU:C:2015:23.
75 Case C-503/14 *Commission v. Portugal* EU:C:2016:979.

the exit taxation of natural persons and that of legal persons in respect of unrealised capital gains' (point 56). The Court follows the same reasoning for the transfer of business assets to a non-resident company (points 74 to 91). This decision is thus more in the line of *National Grid Indus* than *De Lasteyrie* and *N. v. Inspecteur*, and extends the case law on corporate emigration to all *undertakings*, whether incorporated or not, considering that it concerned an exchange of shares and a transfer of assets connected with the exercise of a professional activity or a business (rather than privately held assets.

In its September 2017 *Panayi* decision on UK Trusts, the Court confirmed that the freedom of establishment applied to UK trusts, and repeated that the exit tax on the holdings of a UK trust when the majority of the trustees cease to be UK resident (which triggers a transfer of central management), constituted a discriminatory exit restriction (points 42 to 47), which could, however, be justified by the need to preserve the balanced allocation of tax jurisdiction provided that the taxpayer 'may choose between immediate payment of the tax due on those capital gains or deferred payment of that tax, together with, if appropriate, interest.' (points 50 to 60).[76] In November 2017, the Court decided Case C-292/16 *A Oy* which concerned capital gains tax on the transfer by a Finnish company of its non-resident permanent establishment to a non-resident company. Again the Court considered this a discriminatory exit restriction (points 24 to 29), which could be justified by the need to preserve the balanced allocation of tax jurisdiction provided if the taxpayer has a choice of deferred payment, possibly together with interest (points 30 to 37).[77] Finally, in 2023, the Court confirmed in *Gallaher*, that the UK could impose a capital gains tax when a UK company sold its shares in an Isle of Man company, to a related Dutch company (even though a sale to another UK company was untaxed).[78] The tax constituted an exit restriction which could be justified by the need to maintain the balanced allocation of the power to impose taxes between the Member States, and in this particular case, the tax could also be collected immediately (*i.e.* without the deferral option), because the UK company obtained, by way of consideration for the disposal of the shares, an amount equal to their full market value (i.e. the capital gains were realised).

Though not the subject of this chapter, it is probably useful to note that, in the case of corporate transfers within the EU, the Court not only developed a line of case law on the tax consequences of such transfers in the home state or state of exit (as discussed in this sub-chapter), but also on the tax consequences of such transfers in the host state or state of access In *Aures*,[79] for instance, the Court confirmed that a Dutch company with a Czech branch could transfer its effective management and thus its tax residence to the Czech branch, but it clarified that host state Czechia was not obliged to allow the deduction of losses that had accrued in the Netherlands prior to the transfer. In *VP Capital*,[80] the Court confirmed that a Luxembourg company was allowed to transfer its registered office to Belgium and become a Belgian company, but it clarified that host state Belgium could

76 Case C-646/15 *Panayi* EU:C:2017:682.
77 Case C-292/16 *A Oy* EU:C:2017:888.
78 Case C-707/20 *Gallaher Limited v The Commissioners for Her Majesty's Revenue and Customs*, EU:C:2023:101.
79 Case C-405/18 *Aures Holdings* EU:C:2020:127.
80 Case C-414/21 *VP Capital NV v Belgische Staat*, EU:C:2022:871.

treat value increases of shareholdings held by VP capital as non-realized capital gains, without being obliged to take into account write-downs by that company prior to the transfer, i.e. when it was a taxable resident of Luxembourg.

12.3.3 Conclusions on exit taxes on business assets

Therefore, in the case of business assets held by emigrating legal or natural persons, the Court accepted that Member States assess exit tax on unrealized gains at the moment the person ceases to be subject to the exit country's tax jurisdiction because this helps preserve the balanced allocation of tax jurisdiction between Member States. It is for the host Member State to take account of subsequent decreases in value, and the restrictive effect of host Member States not doing this is considered to be due to disparities between the tax systems of the Member States.[81] Moreover, immediate recovery of the exit tax by the home state is disproportional, unless collection is staggered over a number of years (e. g. five or ten), or the departing company is given the choice between immediate and deferred payment, the latter option possibly accompanied by the need to pay interest (if appropriate and if in similar domestic cases interest is charged as well) and of providing a bank guarantee if there is a risk of non-recovery.

In the mean-time, the Council intervened for a second time, by adopting the 2016 ATAD I Directive (see Chapter 19), under which exit Member States are, from 1 January 2020 onwards, obliged to tax the difference between the market-and tax value of assets, when EU corporate income taxpayers (including EU permanent establishments of third country

81 See points 61 and 62 of Case C-371/10 *National Grid Indus* EU:C:2011:785. In exceptional cases, however, discrimination may still arise, as illustrated by Advocate General Wathelet in points 90 to 94 of his Opinion on Joined Cases C-327/16 and C-421/16 *Jacob and Lassus* (pending). He distinguishes, from *National Grid Indus* (where the Member State of origin had fully exercised its right to tax the unrealised capital gains generated in its territory pertaining to the assets transferred outside its territory *at the time of that transfer*), the situation of *Lassus* in which the Member State of origin (France) had established a mechanism to defer taxation of the capital gain arising out of the exchange of securities until their subsequent transfer, in which case, according to the Advocate General, it: 'should not refuse to grant a taxpayer who has exercised his freedom of establishment in another Member State a tax credit derived from capital losses sustained under its national law if such an advantage would be granted to a resident taxpayer.'

entities) transfer assets[82] or residence[83] to another Member State (or a third country), and destination Member States must provide a step up. The taxpayer must be given the right to pay the exit tax in instalments over five years, if the transfer is to another Member State or an EEA country that has a bilateral agreement with the exit Member State providing for mutual recovery assistance equivalent to EU mutual recovery assistance.[84] If a taxpayer defers the payment, interest may be charged, and if there is a demonstrable and actual risk of non-recovery, taxpayers may also be required to provide a guarantee.

12.4 Exit taxes on privately held assets versus exit taxes on business assets

From the previous sections it may be clear that the Court developed two different lines of exit tax case law respectively for emigrating individuals and privately held assets and for emigrating businesses (natural or legal persons) and business assets.

As regards privately held assets, the Court sometimes does not allow an exit tax at all (pension reserves). Sometimes it considers the requirement of filing of a tax return upon exit and establishing the tax liability on that basis, an exit restriction, which is, however, justified by the need to ensure a balanced allocation of the power to tax between Member States. Collection of the tax upon exit is, however, disproportional, and must be postponed until the actual realization of the gains. In that case, the deferral may not be accompanied by requirements that the taxpayer provides security, pays interest or appoints a fiscal representative.

The case law on business assets is leaving Member States more leeway to collect exit tax on accrued gains upon exit. In fact, in general terms, the tax debt can be established upon exit without the need to take account of post emigration losses, the tax may be collected in yearly installments in which case interest may be charged, and a bank guarantee may be required from the taxpayer depending on the actual risk of non-recovery. More specifically, as regards assets held as part of a business undertaking subject to corporate income tax, the Court is likely to accept the obligation of Member States to impose exit taxes in line with the rules of the ATAD I Directive, as set out above.

82 Including a transfer of assets from a head office to a permanent establishment (or from a permanent establishment to its head office or another permanent establishment) in another Member State or in a third country, or a transfer of the business carried on by a permanent establishment from a Member State to another Member State or to a third country in so far as the Member State of the permanent establishment no longer has the right to tax the transferred assets due to the transfer. See also Chapter 19.

83 If a taxpayer transfers its tax residence to another Member State or to a third country, except for those assets which remain effectively connected with a permanent establishment in the first Member State. Article 2 paras 6,7 and 8 define: 'transfer of assets' as an operation whereby a Member State loses the right to tax the transferred assets, whilst the assets remain under the legal or economic ownership of the same taxpayer; transfer of tax residence' as an operation whereby a taxpayer ceases to be resident for tax purposes in a Member State, whilst acquiring tax residence in another Member State or third country; 'transfer of tax residence' means an operation whereby a taxpayer ceases to be resident for tax purposes in a Member State, whilst acquiring tax residence in another Member State or third country. See also Chapter 19.

84 As provided for in Council Directive 2010/24/EU (See Chapter 27).

CHAPTER 13

Individual Income Taxation

Peter Wattel

Update and elaboration by Hein Vermeulen[1]

13.1 Introduction[2]

The mantra may become boring by now: cross-border situations must be taxed in the same manner as comparable domestic situations in so far as the Member State concerned has asserted taxing power over the cross-border situation in the same manner as over the comparable domestic situation. This implies national tax treatment of foreign-source income and equal treatment of nonresidents as regards the tax base for which they are subject to tax like residents. It implies, for instance, that tuition fees, paid to a university in another Member State must be deductible if such payment would have been deductible, had the fee been paid to a domestic university;[3] that gifts to non-resident charities or institutions of general public interest must in principle be deductible on the same footing as gifts to comparable domestic entities,[4] albeit that exceptions are possible; that mandatory sickness insurance contributions withheld in another Member State must be deductible on the same footing as payment of comparable domestic contributions;[5] that real estate held in another Member State must be taxed in the same manner as locally held real estate;[6] that a capital gain realised on a sale of foreign shares must be taxed in a similar

1 Director of PwC's EU Direct Tax Group.

2 See a.o., See also, P.J. Wattel, Non-Discrimination à la Cour: The ECJ's (Lack of) Comparability Analysis in Direct Tax Cases, 55 Eur. Taxn. 12 (2015); N. Mattsson, Does the European Court of Justice understand the policy behind tax benefits based on personal and family circumstances? European Taxation, 2003 (Volume 43), No 6; B. Peeters, Kieback: When Schumacker emigrates ..., 25 EC Tax Rev. 2, p. 66 (2016); H. Niesten, Growing Impetus for Harmonisation of Personal and Family Allowances: Current State of Affairs of the Schumacker-Doctrine after Imfeld and Garcet, 24 EC Tax Rev. 4, pp. 185-201 (2015); CFE ECJ Task Force, Opinion Statement ECJ-TF 1/2016 on the Decision of the European Court of Justice in Joined Cases Miljoen (Case C-10/14), X (Case C-14/14) and Société Générale (Case C-17/14) on the Netherlands Dividend Withholding Tax, 56 Eur. Taxn. 6 (2016); CFE ECJ Task Force, Opinion Statement ECJ-TF 2/2016 on the Decision of the Court of Justice of the European Union of 13 July 2016 in Brisal and KBC Finance Ireland (Case C-18/15), on the Admissibility of Gross Withholding Tax of Interest, 57 Eur. Taxn. 1 (2017); H.M.L. Niesten, Pro Rata Deduction of Negative Income from Income Received in Each Member State, 58 Eur. Taxn. 2/3 (2018).

3 Case C-56/09 (*Zanotti*), [2010], EU:C:2010:288.

4 Case C-318/07 (*Persche*), EU:C:2009:33.

5 Case C-544/07 (*Rüffler*), EU:C:2009:258.

6 Case C-110/17 (*Commission v. Belgium*), EU:C:2018:250.

way as a capital gain realised on a sale of domestic shares[7] and that interest received from a foreign bank must be taxed at the same rate as interest received from a domestic bank.[8] The rest of this chapter could consist of a further list of more or less interesting applications of this insight to various factual and legal situations, if it were not for the fact that there is a special feature about natural persons which makes their cross-border income tax position difficult to tackle under the Treaty freedoms and in international tax law in general: unlike companies, they have personal and family circumstances, and many Member States take account of these circumstances in that their personal ability to pay is to a certain extent co-decisive for the tax burden to which they are subjected. The trouble with these person-related tax allowances is that they are by their nature not attributable to any specific source or item of income. They connect to the person, not to any particular part of the tax base. It is therefore impossible to say in which jurisdiction they belong. The Court has taken a rather unfortunate course in this respect in its *Schumacker* line of case law, based on erroneous understanding of the double tax relief mechanisms, and has even exacerbated the resulting *im*balanced allocation of taxing power by proliferating its *Schumacker* line to *all* aspects which determine personal ability to pay, including losses and any other negative part of the tax base allocated to the other jurisdiction. In *X*,[9] however, the Court elaborated on the application of the Schumacker doctrine for cases involving three states (see section 13.4.9). That is what most of this chapter will be about, but there are also some other issues to cover, such as the compatibility with the free movement of persons of a tax regime for non-resident natural persons which derogates from the regime for residents, but with an option for them to be treated as a resident (the *Gielen* case, *Hirvonen* case and *MK* case). What does not need to be covered here is individual income taxation in respect of emigration, of cross-border dividends and of inheritances. For these issues, we refer to Chapters 11, 12 and 14, respectively.

13.2 Tax Scales; Correction of Overpaid Withholding Tax by Assessment

The *Asscher* case[10] shows that non-resident individuals are not to be subjected to a higher tax scale than residents, not even to compensate for the fact that nonresidents are not liable for social security contributions. From the *Biehl*[11] and '*Biehl II*'[12] cases it appears that nonresidents must have the same opportunity as residents for correction at the end of the fiscal year by way of an assessment, *e.g.* to obtain repayment of payroll tax exceeding the final income tax liability.[13] The *Gerritse* case[14] shows that although in itself it is permitted to subject non-resident artists and sportsmen, etc. to a special nonresidents' regime such as a flat tax (25%) without basic tax-free allowance (nor deduction of necessary expenses),

7 Case C-472/22 (*NO*), EU:C:2023:880.
8 Case C-312/22 (*FL*), EU:C:2023:771.
9 Case C-283/15 (*X*), EU:C:2017:102, involving Spain as the Residence Member State and the Netherlands (Member State) and Switzerland (third state) as work states.
10 Case C-107/94 (*Asscher*), EU:C:1996:251.
11 Case C-175/88 (*Biehl*), EU:C:1990:186.
12 Case C-151/94 (*Commission v. Luxembourg*), EU:C:1995:357.
13 Case C-575/17 (*Sofina and Others*), EU:C:2018:943, shows that this also holds true in the sphere of corporate income taxation.
14 Case C-234/01 (*Gerritse*), EU:C:2003:340. For comments, see Dick Molenaar and Harald Grams, 'The *Arnoud Gerritse* Case of the *ECJ*,' 31 *Intertax* 5 (2003), p. 198-204.

the tax burden ensuing may not exceed the tax which would have been levied on the income if the non-resident had been taxed as a resident, *i.e.* not higher than the amount which would have been payable if the normal progressive table and tax-free allowance (and cost deductions) had been applied. To a similar finding the Court came in *Turpeinen*,[15] concerning a retired Finnish civil servant who after retirement moved to Belgium and subsequently to Spain (better weather), finding herself subject to a flat 35% Finnish withholding tax on her pension, whereas a Finnish-resident retired civil servant would be subject to the normal progressive scales and basic allowance. In Mrs Turpeinen's case the latter would have resulted in taxation at an average rate of 28.5%. We submit that this implies that flat rate withholding for non-resident artists, sportsmen and pensioners may make little sense any more, as they are not capable of meeting their objective of administrative simplicity, at least not in many intra-EU situations. Since they may only be applied one way (only if they benefit the non-resident), the entire calculation of normal progressive taxation must be carried out to find out whether or not it is beneficial, which was precisely what flat rate withholding served to avoid. In any event, flat rate withholding for nonresidents should not lead to an overall tax burden which is greater than that placed on residents. This was confirmed in *Hirvonen*[16] (see section 13.5 for the optional aspect of resident-or nonresident-taxation), in which the Court held that the (optional) taxation-at-source regime for non-residents which ignores personal and family circumstances, is permissible where nonresidents can also opt for resident taxation (in which case their personal and family circumstances would have been considered, but they would also pay the progressive rate).

The simplest manner to cope with this finding probably is to grant nonresidents the opportunity of correction by assessment upon request, or even better, to avoid all trouble, to provide the opportunity to be taxed for worldwide income, with double tax relief, as if they were resident. This last option seems to have been condemned by the Court though, in the *Gielen*[17] and *X*[18] cases, on which we will comment in section 13.5, also in the light of the *Hirvonen* case.

Although residents and non-residents are not as a rule comparable for tax purposes (nonresidents maybe taxed on a source basis where residents are taxed on a worldwide basis), this does not mean that nonresidents may be subjected to less favourable rate progression than residents as a consequence of such limited liability to tax: from two Cases, *Ritter-Coulais*[19] and *Lakebrink-Peters*,[20] it follows that the employment state, for tax *rate* determination purposes, must take into account negative home state income from real estate if negative income from real estate is also taken into account for residents. The subsequent *Renneberg* case[21] showed that – at least for nonresidents in a so-called *Schumacker* position (see section 13.4.6) – negative home state income must not only be

15 Case C-520/04 (*Turpeinen*), EU:C:2006:703.
16 Case C-632/13 (*Hirvonen*), EU:C:2015:765.
17 Case C-440/08 (*Gielen*), EU:C:2010:148.
18 Case C-283/15 (*X*), EU:C:2017:102.
19 Cases C-152/03 (*Ritter-Coulais*), EU:C:2006:123.
20 Case C-182/06 (*Lakebrink-Peters*), EU:C:2007:452.
21 Case C-527/06 (*Renneberg*), EU:C:2008:566.

taken into account by the employment state for determining the tax rate on the sourced employment income, but must even be deducted from the employment income (from the tax base) if for residents such negative foreign-source income is (temporarily) deductible because of their worldwide taxation. We consider it to be unfortunate, as, for that matter, the entire *Schumacker* line of case law.

13.3 Income-Related Deductions

Where an individual taxpayer earns income abroad, the question arises in which state he should be granted (i) person-related deductions or credits and (ii) deduction of necessary expenses incurred in earning that income ("income-related deductions"). The case law of the Court draws a distinction between income-related deductions (such as business expenses, refunds of overpaid wage withholding tax, payment of imputation credits attaching to dividends, tax-free amounts not relating to personal status, e.g. to the holding of capital assets etc.) and person-related deductions (such as tax-free basic amounts relating to personal status, splitting of income between spouses, deduction of sickness expenses or alimony payments, etc.). The *Biehl,*[22] *Schumacker,*[23] *Gerritse,*[24] *Scorpio*[25] and *AB*[26] cases show that the source state must grant national tax treatment to nonresidents as regards income-related deductions, and therefore allow them (at least) the same income-related deductions as it allows residents in respect of the same income. These deductions connect to the activity generating the income in the source Member State, which is objectively comparable for both residents and nonresidents.

Biehl[27] concerned a German national who, after living and working in Luxembourg for ten years, moved back to Germany in the course of 1983. Payroll tax withheld by his Luxembourg employer exceeded the Luxembourg income tax due for that year. Luxembourg law stipulated, however, that refund of overpaid payroll tax was available only for taxpayers resident in Luxembourg during the entire taxable year. The Court held this exclusion to be disadvantageous for border-crossers. Luxembourg put forward two justifications: (i) the need to protect the progression in the tax rate, and (ii) a non-contentious refund procedure existed for taxpayers demonstrating unfair consequences. The Court rejected both: *ad* (i): the limitation to year-round residents was disproportionate for rate progression purposes; *ad* (ii): respect for the free movement rights cannot be made dependent on the discretion of the tax administration. Although Luxembourg subsequently deleted the year-round requirement, it needed to be corrected once more by the Court in an infringement procedure brought by the Commission[28] for (still) making refund of overpaid payroll tax conditional upon the employee having been resident in Luxembourg for at

22 Case C-175/88 (*Biehl*), EU:C:1990:186.
23 Case 279/93 (*Schumacher*), of 14 February 1995, EU:C:1995:31.
24 Case C-234/01 (*Arnoud Gerritse*), EU:C:2003:340.
25 Case C-290/04 (*Scorpio Konzertproduktionen GmbH*), EU:C:2006:630. See, for comments: Dick Molenaar and Harald Grams, 'Scorpio and the Netherlands: Major Changes in Artiste and Sportsman Taxation in the European Union,' *European Taxation*, February 2007, p. 63-68.
26 Case C-627/22 (*AB*), EU:C:2024:431.
27 Case C-175/88 (*Biehl*), EU:C:1990:186.
28 Case C-151/94 (*Commission v. Luxembourg*), [1995] ('*Biehl II*'), EU:C:1995:357.

least *nine months* of the taxable year. The *Biehl* case was reiterated, as regards the right of refund of overpaid wage withholding tax, in *Schumacker*.[29]

Gerritse, concerned deduction of necessary expenses of a Netherlands drummer performing in Germany:

> '27. It is to be noted (...) that the business expenses in question are directly linked to the activity that generated the taxable income in Germany, so that residents and non-residents are placed in a comparable situation in that respect.
> 28. In those circumstances, a national provision which, in matters of taxation, refuses to allow non-residents to deduct business expenses, whereas residents are allowed to do so, risks operating mainly to the detriment of nationals of other Member States and therefore constitutes indirect discrimination on grounds of nationality, contrary in principle to (...) the Treaty.'

Scorpio[30] required the Member States to allow deduction of necessary expenses from the contract remuneration of foreign artists for the purposes of calculating the withholding tax to be retained by the impresario paying the remuneration. However, 'expenses that are not directly linked to' the concert itself (indirect expenses, overhead), do not need to be deducted at the time of payment (probably because the impresario cannot be required to have knowledge of them). For such indirect expense, a subsequent refund procedure may be applied. The *Centro Equestre*[31] case suggests that Member States may entirely exclude operating expenses of foreign service providers which are not 'inextricably linked' to the service performed on their territory for which the remuneration is paid, apparently because the Court presumes these indirect expenses will be deducted in the home state of the service provider.

In *AB* (C-627/22) the Court held that Germany should take into account income related deductions under the Agreement on the free movement of persons between the European Union and the Swiss Confederation for a Swiss resident that worked in Germany where both German residents and EU/EEA residents were also allowed to deduct these expenses.[32]

The Court clarified the concept of income-related deductions in the *Miljoen* and *Brisal* cases. In *Miljoen*[33] the Court ruled that only expenses of nonresidents which are directly linked to the actual payment of outbound domestic dividends must be deductible in the source Member State on the same footing as for residents.[34] In that regard, financing costs incurred for the acquisition of a shareholding lack that direct link, according to the Court in *Miljoen*, as they concern only the ownership *per se* and are thus not linked

29 Case C-279/93 (*Schumacher*), EU:C:1995:31.
30 Case C-290/04 (*Scorpio Konzertproduktionen GmbH*), EU:C:2006:630. See, for comments: Dick Molenaar and Harald Grams, 'Scorpio and the Netherlands: Major Changes in Artiste and Sportsman Taxation in the European Union,' *European Taxation*, February 2007, p. 63-68.
31 Case C-345/04 (*Centro Equestre da Lezíria Grande Lda*), EU:C:2007:96.
32 Case C-627/22 (*AB*), EU:C:2024:431. See also Case C-581/17 (*Wächtler*), EU:C:2019:138.
33 Joined Cases C-10/14, C-14/14 and C-17/14 (*Miljoen, X, Société Générale SA*), EU:C:2015:608.
34 Joined Cases C-10/14, C-14/14 and C-17/14 (*Miljoen, X, Société Générale SA*), EU:C:2015:608, point 58.

to the actual payment of dividends arising from the shares.[35] By contrast, in *Brisal*, the Court considered that business expenses directly related to interest income arising from a loan, also financing cost and overhead, should be deductible in the source state on the same footing as for residents.[36], [37] Remarkably, the Court provided in *Brisal* much wider examples of these expenses, contrary to its previous case law, especially *Miljoen*, in which it only looked at the direct cost of collecting the dividends, and also contrary to its policy of leaving the determination of these direct expenses to the national court:

> '47. With regard to the service at issue in the main proceedings, that is to say, the granting of a loan, it must be noted that the performance of that service necessarily gives rise to business expenses such as, for example, travel and accommodation expenses, and legal or tax advice, for which it is relatively easy both to establish the direct link with the loan in question and to prove the actual amount involved. Since taxpayers with limited liability must be able to enjoy the same treatment as taxpayers with unlimited liability, they must be granted, as regards those expenses, the same opportunities to make deductions, whilst being subject to the same requirements as regards, in particular, the burden of proof.'

Furthermore, in computing business expenses, only real costs can be considered if also for residents only real costs are taken into account. Therefore, the Court explicitly refused deduction of costs calculated on a notional basis.[38]

It is clear that the Court in *Brisal* adopted a more generous approach towards deductibility of business expenses than in *Miljoen*. A possible explanation may be that in the view of the Court, the mere holding of shares is not the same as carrying out the activity that produces the profits out of which the dividends are paid: in *Brisal*, both financing costs and overhead costs were regarded as directly linked to the loan income. It is difficult to understand why the costs of providing equity financing (holding shares) are not deductible on the same footing as for residents where the costs of providing loan financing are. The fact that *Miljoen* concerned the free movement of capital while *Brisal* concerned the freedom to provide services can hardly explain the difference. Unfortunately, *Sofina and Others*[39], *College Pension Plan of British Columbia*[40], and *Société Générale*[41] and did provide not more clarity in this respect. On the contrary, the Court reaffirms in *XX* (C-782/22) that the financing costs concern the ownership per se of the shares giving rise to the dividends and that these financing costs cannot be regarded as expenses of nonresidents

35 Id., point 60.
36 Case C-18/15 (*Brisal*), EU:C:2016:549.
37 *Brisal* refers to the same legislation as in case C-105/08(*Commission v. Portugal*), EU:C:2010:345. However, the latter case was an infringement procedure in which the CJEU considered that the Commission had failed to show how the withholding method would lead to a less favourable position for non-resident financial institutions (as according to the Court, it had merely raised hypothetical examples instead of relying on actual data). However, in *Brisal* there was a specific nonresident taxpayer who could demonstrate its disadvantageous position as compared to resident banks.
38 Case C-18/15 (*Brisal*), EU:C:2016:549, point 53.
39 Case C-575/17 (*Sofina and Others*), EU:C:2018:943.
40 Case C-641/17 (*College Pension Plan of British Columbia*), EU:C:2019:960.
41 Case C-403/19 (*Société Générale*), EU:C:2021:136.

which are directly linked to the actual receipt of the dividends.[42] In other words, in view of the Court it is not for the host state but rather for the home state to take into account these financing costs when investing in shares.[43] We refer to section 11.1.5 in this respect.

13.4 Personal Ability to Pay; the Schumacker Case Law

13.4.1 Home State Responsibility; No National Treatment in the Source State

In contrast with income-related tax deductions, which connect to specific (sources of) income and can therefore be territorially allocated, personal and family-related tax benefits are not attributable to any specific item or source of income, because the expenses for which they seek to compensate are not instrumental in earning any specific income, but burden the taxpayer's total personal ability to pay tax. Therefore, they cannot be attributed to home state or source state income other than arbitrary. Reasonable would be attribution in proportion to the division of the total income between the home state and the source state. Regular international tax law starts from worldwide taxation in the home state (with relief for the ensuing double taxation) and limited taxation (only for sourced income) in the source state, as the home state wants to tax its residents for their total ability to pay, where the source state limits itself to objective taxation of the income for which its economy provided the opportunity, leaving the total ability to pay to the home state to assess. Regular international practice is, therefore, that the source state does not bother with personal benefits for nonresidents, as it in principle does not know his personal and family circumstances. Indeed, he lives elsewhere. Unfortunately, the facts of the first case on personal tax allowances to reach the Court (*Schumacker*)[44] were too simple to see the effects of double tax relief mechanisms on the attribution of personal allowances to home state and source state. The case involved two Member States, Belgium and Germany. Mr Schumacker, a Belgian resident, earned his *entire* income in Germany, which was entirely *exempt* in Belgium. He therefore paid no tax in Belgium and the Belgian personal allowances, although granted to him, were of no use to him. For that reason, Mr Schumacker instead wanted the *German* personal allowances, notably the income splitting benefit for married couples. Surprisingly, given the explicit EU law requirement of national treatment, the CJEU considered residents and nonresidents not, as a rule, to be in the same objective circumstances, at least in this case not as regards personal tax allowances. In principle therefore, it surprisingly did *not* require the source state to grant national treatment to non-resident employees. Thus, it allowed a direct discrimination against nonresidents (usually non-nationals) by the employment state, in contravention, not only of the free movement of workers, but also of Article 7of EC Regulation 1612/68 on the free movement of workers (now Article 7(2) of EU Regulation 492/2011), which explicitly entitles non-national workers to the same *social and tax* benefits as nationals. The Court considered:

> '(...) In relation to direct taxes, the situations of residents and of non-residents are not, as a rule, comparable. (...) The situation of a resident is different in so far as the major

42 Case C-782/22 (*XX*), EU:C:2024:932.
43 This is in line with Case C-168/01 (*Bosal*), EU:C:2003:479.
44 Case 279/93 (*Schumacker*), EU:C:1995:31.

> part of his income is normally concentrated in the State of residence. Moreover, that State generally has available all the information needed to assess the taxpayer's overall ability to pay, taking account of his personal and family circumstances. Consequently, the fact that a Member State does not grant to a non-resident certain tax benefits which it grants to a resident is not, as a rule, discriminatory since those two categories of taxpayers are not in a comparable position.'

This departure from the EU law imperative of national treatment is probably explained by the Court's tacit assumption that normally a non-resident receives personal allowances at home and therefore does not *need* any in the source state. Requiring also the source state to extend allowances, might even lead to unjust enrichment (double allowances). Presumably, the Court assumed that it was only for the absence of any taxation at home that Mr Schumacker had no access to (full) home state allowances. That, however, was a misunderstanding. Whatever the division of income between home state and job state, the taxpayer always receives only a part of the home state allowances, in proportion to the income allocated to the home state, leaving the other part to be granted by the source state, which is, after all, also taxing that part of the income. We will dwell on this point in section 13.4.3.

The distinction of principle between residents and nonresidents seemed to open a wide field for fiscal discrimination of non-resident workers and self-employed persons. Fortunately, in *Asscher*,[45] the Court pointed out that any such distinction between the two needs to be explained by a relevant difference in factual circumstances. In *Schumacker*, the Court apparently believed such relevant difference to be that nonresidents enjoy full personal benefits in the home state and therefore do not *need* national treatment in the source state. This misunderstanding did not, however, influence the correct outcome of the specific case of Mr Schumacker because of the peculiarity that he had no taxed income at all in his home state. In the eyes of the Court, that put him in virtually the same position as a German resident. Consequently, and by chance correctly (national treatment), the Court, *in this particular case*, required the job state (Germany) to extend *its* personal tax allowances, but on the basis of rather astonishing reasoning:

> '38. In the case of a non-resident who receives the major part of his income and almost all his family income in a Member State other than that of his residence, discrimination arises from the fact that his personal and family circumstances are taken into account neither in the State of residence nor in the State of employment.'

As observed in section 3.2.7.3, this is untenable: one cannot define discrimination by reference to something *another* state is *not* doing. *Who* is doing the discriminating here? Discrimination only arises if the difference in treatment is caused by the rules of one single jurisdiction. The question is, therefore, which of the two states is the culprit. In our view, it is quite obvious that it is the employment state which clearly offends Article 45 TFEU by refusing national treatment to non-resident employees. Germany was flatly denying national treatment where it should have extended – in proportion to the income allocated to it – its personal tax allowances as if Mr Schumacker had been a resident.

45 Case C-107/94 (*Asscher*), EU:C:1996:251.

Although the Court in this specific case eventually arrived at this correct finding, it regrettably did so only exceptionally, probably because it assumed that in other cases, a non-resident employee would receive (full) allowances at home. Consequently, as a matter of principle, the Court unfortunately limited the source state's obligation to respect the Treaty freedoms to situations in which the employee earns 'entirely or almost all' of his income in the source state:

> 'Article 48 [now 45; *authors*] (...) (precludes) the application of rules of a Member State under which a worker who is a national of, and resides in, another Member State and is employed in the first State is taxed more heavily than a worker who resides in the first State and performs the same work there when (...) the national of the second State obtains his income entirely or almost exclusively from the work performed in the first State and does not receive in the second State sufficient income to be subject to taxation there in a manner enabling his personal and family circumstances to be taken into account.'

Germany had argued that the source state is unable to ascertain the worldwide income and the personal circumstances of nonresidents, but the Court referred Germany to the Directive on Administrative Cooperation (see Chapter 28), which, according to the Court, provides for ways of obtaining foreign information comparable to those existing in respect of domestic information (it should be observed that the Court seems to have retracted from this position in cases such as *Persche, Haribo and Salinen* and *Accor*; see section 11.4.3).

The subsequent *Wielockx* case[46] shows that the *Schumacker* rule applies not only to workers, but also to non-resident self-employed persons (right of establishment), which makes sense: they are natural persons with personal circumstances as well. The *Gschwind* case[47] provided some quantitative elaboration. After *Schumacker*, Germany had introduced a rule granting national treatment to nonresidents earning 90% or more of their income in Germany (denying it below that threshold). The Court considered that sufficient implementation of its *Schumacker* judgment. The puzzling *Wallentin* case[48] added that if the non-resident employee *does* have some income at home – which could absorb his home state personal reductions – but this home state income is 'income which, by its nature, is not subject to tax', such non-taxable income is to be ignored when assessing whether the employee is capable of benefiting from his home state allowances. Mr Wallentin, a German student performing a three-week holiday job in Sweden, enjoyed in his home state a monthly subsistence allowance from his parents and a student's grant paid by the German state, both not subject to tax under German tax law. *Wallentin* implies that if a non-resident has only exempt home state income, the source state is still required to extend its allowances. We fear that *Wallentin*, like *Schumacker*, was a mistake: there are no items of income which 'by their nature' are not subject to tax. Subsistence allowances and grants could just as well constitute taxable income (and could be deductible just as

46 Case C-80/94 (*Wielockx*), EU:C:1995:271.

47 Case C-391/97 (*Gschwind*), EU:C:1999:409. See for a comment Robert Newey, '*Gschwind* Decision; German Tax Law Not Discriminatory for Non-Resident Married Couples', 40 *European Taxation* 3 (2000), p. 114.

48 Case C-169/03 (*Wallentin*), [EU:C:2004:403.

well for the payer) as employee's wages. Whether or not an increase in wealth is taxed is sovereign national policy, not nature, and at any rate completely outside the Court's competence or assessment. The *Meindl* case[49] was a sort of combination of *Schumacker, Gschwind* and *Wallentin:* the Court held that Germany could not deny a married couple the benefit of marital splitting of the husband's income on the grounds that although the husband was living and working in Germany, his wife, from whom he was not separated, was living in Austria and received there more than 10% of the marital income and more than DM 24.000, but exempt from Austrian tax (confinement allowance and maternity and family allowances).

In *Gerritse* (see section 13.3) the Court ruled that Mr Gerritse's German-source income should be proportionately increased by the amount of personal tax-free allowances (which Germany grants to residents) to arrive at comparable situations, although the tax-free allowance in *Gerritse* was considered a person-related deduction[50] and Mr Gerritse did not by far earn almost his entire income in Germany.[51] We applaud that finding but we doubt whether it was intentional. Similarly, in *Miljoen*, the Court held that the Netherlands had to take into account the tax-free capital allowance – which was considered an income-related deduction – when comparing the final tax burdens of resident taxpayers and non-resident taxpayers.[52]

Obviously, the distinction made between income-related reductions (national treatment in the source state taxing the income, irrespective of how much of his income the non-resident earns in the source state) and person-related deductions (no national treatment in the source state; sole responsibility of the home state, except where the non-resident earns so little in his home state that he cannot benefit from home state allowances) incites discussions on the boundary between the two categories. For instance, the *Conijn* Case[53] raised the question of whether the costs of a tax consultant to file a tax return (deductible for residents in Germany) follow the *Schumacher* rule (person-related: allocation to the home state) or the *Biehl/Gerritse* rule (necessary expenses: allocation to the source state). As Mr Conijn, a Netherlands resident earning business income in Germany, was required to file a return because of the German source of his business income, and as he was in a comparable position as German residents in respect of the complexity of the German tax legislation, the Court held that the costs were directly linked to the income taxed in Germany and were therefore to be deductible in Germany. The same holds true with regards other business expenses such as travel and accommodation expenses, legal or tax advice, for which it is relatively easy both to establish the direct link with the activity in the source Member State and to prove the actual amount involved (*Brisal*[54] and *Cartrans Preda*).[55]

49 Case C-329/05 (*Meindl*), EU:C:2007:57.
50 Id., point 48.
51 Case C-234/01 (*Gerritse*), EU:C:2003:340, point 54.
52 Joined cases C-10/14, C-14/14 and C-17/14 (*Miljoen, X, Société Générale SA*), EU:C:2015:608, point 53.
53 Case C-346/04 (*Conijn*), EU:C:2006:445.
54 Case C-18/15 (*Brisal*), EU:C:2016:549, point 53.
55 Case C-461/21 (*Cartrans Preda*), EU:C:2023:632.

In *BJ* (C-241/20) the Court held that Belgium as the residence state must make sure that a resident with Belgian and Luxembourg income is able to take into account personal and family-related tax benefits. These benefits may not be impacted by the way Belgium grants relief for double taxation under its tax treaty with Luxembourg.[56]

13.4.2 But: Residents and Nonresidents Are Not in a Different Position[57]

The *Schumacker* judgment left difficult technical questions unanswered, especially where the home state applies a credit system for international double taxation relief (see section 13.4.3), but the main problem with the *Schumacker* approach is that it is at odds with EU law (national treatment) and exacerbates inconsistencies of international tax law instead of doing away with them. This becomes immediately clear if one considers the position of a taxpayer who earns his entire income abroad, but not in *one*, but in *two* other Member States, *e.g.* a resident of Luxembourg earning half of his income in France and half of it in Belgium. When applying the *Schumacker* test, this non-resident is left entirely in the cold: in neither of the source states does he pass the *Schumacker* test ('almost his entire income'), meaning that his personal circumstances are taken into account nowhere. That would be a manifest discrimination, also according to the Court (see point 38 of *Schumacker*, quoted above). Probably for that reason, twelve years after *Schumacker*, the Court held in *X*[58] that in three-country situations, if no income is earned in the residence state, the source states should grant their person-related deductions proportionately to the share of the nonresident's income they tax. We applaud this judgment, but it is not clear whether the Court will extend this reasoning to three state situations in which sufficient income is earned in the residence state to fully deduct that Member State's person-related deductions. In such a case, the Court may still stick to its – in our view erroneous – Schumacker doctrine (see section 13.4.5 on the *De Groot* case).[59] In our view, it is *im*balanced and disproportionate to require the home state to accord 100% of its allowances even though it taxes only 15% of the income, and to allow the job state to refuse all of its personal allowances although it taxes 85% of the income.

As observed, the Court probably embarked upon the erroneous Schumacker course because it incorrectly thought that allowances are deducted from allocated income instead of total income in the home state (see section 13.4.3 below for the mechanics). In *Schumacker*, it gave two justifications for denial of national treatment to nonresidents as regards person-related reductions (points 32 and 33):

i. residents usually derive only part of their income abroad, which is concentrated in their home state;
ii. the home state is in a better position than the job state to take into account the total ability to pay and the personal circumstances of the taxpayer because it is more likely to have the necessary information.

---

56 Case C-241/20 (*BJ*), EU:C:2021:605.

57 See Peter J. Wattel, 'Red Herrings in Direct Tax Cases before the ECJ,' 2 *Legal Issues of Economic Integration* 2004 (Vol. 31), pp. 81-95.

58 Case C-283/15 (*X*), EU:C:2017:102.

59 Case C-283/15 (*X*), EU:C:2017:102, involving Spain as the Residence Member State and the Netherlands (Member State) and Switzerland (third state) as work states, seems to confirm this.

Neither of these arguments can explain, however, why nonresidents should be refused national treatment. Argument (i) even lacks factual basis as regards the persons most concerned: Mr Schumacker, Mr Gschwind and Mrs Gilly all earned their *entire* personal income abroad; Mr De Groot (see below) earned more than 60% of his income in three other Member States. But even if that were otherwise, we fail to see a justification for discrimination against nonresidents in the percentage division of their total income between the states concerned. As the Court regularly reiterates, the Treaty Freedoms prohibit all discriminations, including minor ones.[60] Unequal treatment can only be explained in proportion to the objective difference in situation. This means that the host state must extend its personal allowances in proportion to the part of the total income over which it asserts taxing power. For that, the job state needs to know the total income and the personal circumstances of the non-resident. The Court's argument (ii) relies on the source state not having such information. However, in all of the many cases in which Member States argued exactly that point as a justification for different treatment of nonresidents or of foreign-source income, the Court has always firmly rejected it.[61] The Court even rejected that argument in the very same judgment in which it relied on it![62] Administrative difficulties are not accepted by the Court as a justification for discrimination, because (i) the Member States may use the Directive on Administrative Cooperation (see Chapter 26), which, according to the Court, offers comparable possibilities for gathering tax information in cross-border situations as in internal situations, and (ii) even if that were otherwise, nothing prevents the host state from requiring the taxpayer to provide convincing evidence (*e.g.* the tax return submitted in the home state and the subsequent home state tax assessment). In *Terhoeve*,[63] the CJEU explicitly rejected administrative (im)practicability as a reason for distinguishing between residents and nonresidents. 'Disadvantages of a purely administrative nature' were explicitly rejected also in *Commission v. France (fixed levy)*[64] and *Société Papillon*.[65] It is rather difficult to see how the same argument which the Court itself consistently considers invalid if relied on by a Member State, could be persuasive if relied on by the Court.

In *Schumacker*, the Court further noted that the OECD Model Double Taxation Convention distinguishes between resident and non-resident taxpayers. We submit, however, that the Treaty Freedoms are not subordinate to the *soft law* opinions of the OECD Fiscal Committee, as was also argued by Advocate General Kokott in her opinion in *N Luxembourg 1* (omitting footnotes):[66]

60 For instance in Case 270/83 (*Commission v. France (Avoir Fiscal)*), EU:C:1986:37, point 21, and in Case C-212/06 (*Gouvernement de la Communauté française et Gouvernement wallon*), EU:C:2008:178.

61 Case 204/90 (*Bachmann*), EU:C:1992:35, points 18 and 20; Case C-279/93 (*Schumacker*), EU:C:1995:31, point 45; Case C-55/98 (*Vestergaard*), EU:C:1999:533, points 26 and 28; Case C-1/93 (*Halliburton*), EU:C:1994:127, point 22; Case C-136/00 (*Danner*), EU:C:2002:558, points 49-52; Case C-334/02 (*Commission v. France (fixed levy)*), EU:C:2004:129, point 31; etc., etc.

62 See points 43-45 of the *Schumacker* judgment.

63 Case C-18/95 (*Terhoeve*), EU:C:1999:22.

64 Case C-334/02 (*Commission v. France (fixed levy)*), EU:C:2004:129, point 31.

65 Case C-418/07 (*Papillon*), EU:C:2008:659.

66 Case C-115/16 (), EU:C:2018:143.

> 'OECD MTCs are not legally binding, multilateral conventions under international law; they are the unilateral acts of an international organisation in the form of recommendations to its member countries. Even the OECD does not consider these recommendations to be binding; rather, under the OECD Rules of Procedure, the member countries must consider whether their implementation is opportune. This applies a fortiori to the commentaries published by the OECD, which ultimately only contain legal opinions.'

Obviously, tax treaties between Member States based on the OECD Model in principle are binding upon these states, but, if incompatible, they are simply overruled by EU law.[67] If a *Member State* relies on a bilateral treaty as a justification for denial of national treatment, the Court always points out that Member States are required to organize their treaties, like their national laws, such that they respect EU law, *e.g.*, in *Avoir Fiscal*[68] and *Saint-Gobain*[69], and *Sauvage*.[70] The Court even rejected discriminatory provisions in treaties between Member States and third states in the *Open Skies* cases.[71] If the Court, by referring to the incomparability of residents and nonresidents, alludes to the difference in subjection to tax (worldwide or restricted) in tax treaties, then it must be observed that in this respect non-resident employees – after 183 days[72] – are subject to tax in the source state in the same manner and to the same extent for employment income as residents, *except* for personal allowances. Therefore, according to its subject-to-tax approach (see Chapter 6), the Court should require national treatment of the employee in the employment state.

13.4.3 *Exacerbating Disparities; the Mechanics of Double Tax Relief; Rate Progression; Two Inconsistencies of International Tax Law*

One might be inclined not to care too much in which jurisdiction tax-free amounts, extraordinary expenses, marital splitting of income, and other personal tax allowances are taken into account, as long as they are taken into account somewhere. That approach, however, leads to a result opposite to the desired result, as there are significant differences between the Member States as regards the taking into account of personal deductions. The only manner in which a balanced and fair result can be achieved, is by proportional allocation to home state and source state; in proportion to the part of the total income they tax. A fallacy underlying the *Schumacker* case law is the tacit assumption that all Member States have more or less the same tax system as regards the taking into account of personal ability to pay. It presupposes that all Member States' tax system have (the same) tax-free basic amounts, (the same) marital splitting, (the same) deduction of alimony payments, etc., etc., etc. That is not the case at all however, as tax base and tax rate are interchangeable, and some Member States may prefer precision and individual tax justice on the postage stamp (leading to an abundance of personal deductions and credits, but also to a high and progressive income tax rate), whereas other states may

67 See, *e.g.*, Case 235/87 (*Annunziata Mateucci*), EU:C:1988:460; and Case 286/86 (*Gérard Deserbais*), EU:C:1988:434.

68 Case 270/83 (*Avoir Fiscal*), EU:C:1986:37, point 26.

69 Case C-307/97 (*Saint-Gobain*), EU:C:1999:438.

70 Case C-602/17 (*Sauvage*), EU:C:2018:856.

71 Cases C-466-469/98, C-471-472/98, C-475-476/98 (*Commission v. UK, Denmark, Sweden, Finland, Belgium, Luxembourg, Austria and Germany*, respectively), EU:C:2002:627.

72 See Article 15(2) of the OECD Model Double Taxation Convention.

prefer simplicity and robust practicability (no opportunity for abuse of deductions) and therefore apply a flat tax, entailing a moderate flat rate and no deductions or allowances. The tax rate and the tax base are two sides of the same coin and should not be disorganized over two different sovereign tax systems, as that is contrary to a balanced allocation of taxing power. As shown in section 3.2.7.3. in our discussion of the *Renneberg* case, the question to which jurisdiction mortgage interest is allocated, is very material if such interest is deductible in one state and nondeductible in the other.

In *Schumacker*, however, the Court apparently assumed (i) that it does not matter very much which of the two state's personal allowances' system is applied, and (ii) that nonresidents earning 10% or more of their income at home can (fully) benefit from their home state allowances, because 10% at home should in general be enough to absorb those allowances, and are therefore in a position different from source state residents. The example below will show both assumptions to be incorrect. Every taxpayer earning foreign-source income, regardless of its proportion to his total income, loses part of the benefit of his home state personal tax allowances, due to the proportional calculation of double tax relief. Both exemption states and credit states calculate the reduction of the home state tax to prevent double taxation of the foreign-source part of the total income *pro rata parte, i.e.* by way of a fraction, the numerator of which is the foreign-source income and the denominator of which is the total income.

Let us calculate: suppose that Mr Schumacker had earned € 10 000 in Germany and € 30 000 in his home state Belgium, then Belgium would have calculated the Belgian income tax due as follows. First, total income is calculated (€ 40 000), followed by a reduction to take into account personal and family circumstances (say € 5 000). On the remaining € 35 000 the Belgian tax scales are applied (say 50%), resulting in tax of € 17 500. Finally, a reduction to prevent double taxation is granted in the amount of 10 000/40 000 * 17 500 = € 4 375. Remains payable: € 17 500 minus € 4 375 is € 13 125. Let us suppose the German rate is 50% as well, so that € 5 000 tax is charged in Germany on the € 10 000 German-source income, without taking into account any personal circumstances, as the taxpayer does not pass the *Schumacker* 90% test. In total, our taxpayer thus pays € 18 125.

By contrast, if Mr Schumacker had earned his entire income at home, he would in this example have paid 50% of € 35 000 or € 17 500, which is € 1 250 less. That is exactly one quarter (10000/40000) of his personal allowances of € 5 000. Because 25% of the income is earned abroad and therefore exempted in the home state, also 25% of the home state allowances are exempt in the home state: that quarter of his personal and family allowances is attributed to the exempted quarter of the total income, which is entirely appropriate and (literally) proportionate, as the other state taxes that quarter. That source state should therefore grant one quarter of *its* personal allowances.

Combining the *pro rata* double taxation relief mechanism and the Court's *Schumacker* regime would be very unsatisfactory for individual taxpayers: a taxpayer earning 75% of his income abroad would lose 75% of his home state personal allowances without getting any source state allowances in return, since he fails the *Schumacker* test. By contrast, a taxpayer earning 95% of his income in (one single) other Member State obtains 100% of the source state allowances while also retaining 5% of his home state allowances (105% result). The Court was faced with this unreasonable result in the *De Groot* case.

Before discussing that case, we observe that the division of the tax base over two jurisdictions also has (advantageous) progression effects for the taxpayer working abroad. Earning foreign-source income may provide a taxpayer with a significant tax benefit as compared to taxpayers earning their entire income in one single state: source states usually calculate the progression in their tax rate on the basis of the source state income alone. Unlike the home state, they do not take into account the worldwide income for determining their tax bracket.[73] Therefore, a taxpayer earning foreign-source income may enjoy a marked progression benefit: if the home state is an exemption country (CIN), the foreign-source income escapes progression in both states. All kinds of salary split contracts for internationally mobile executive officers of multinational companies are based on this fact.

Thus, regular international tax law is inconsistent in two respects:[74]

i. in general, home states correctly attribute a part of the personal tax benefits of their residents to the source jurisdiction, in proportion to that foreign-source income for which they grant relief, but in the inverse situation (in their capacity of source states) they incorrectly do not proportionally extend their personal allowances to nonresidents earning income sourced and taxed within their territory;
ii. in general, states calculate progression of tax brackets on the basis of worldwide income if they are the home state, but only on the basis of sourced income if they are the source state.

13.4.4 Trying to Get It Right

The Asscher,[75] *Gilly*[76] and *Gschwind*[77] cases showed that the Court did not see the *pro rata* effect of double tax relief described, nor the progression reduction effect described. It assumed that personal allowances are deducted from (only) domestic income rather than from total income. Consequently, it incorrectly presumed that:

- a taxpayer is able to use his full home state allowances as long as his domestic income is higher than those allowances;
- a disparity was present where in fact a discrimination by the source state was present; and
- the source state income is taxed at the same progressive rate as the home state income.

73 We observe, however, that the Court requires the source state to take into account negative home state income of nonresidents as if they were residents for calculating the progression in its tax rate applied to the source state income: Cases C-152/03, *Ritter-Coulais*, EU:C:2006:123, and C-182/06, *Lakebrink-Peters*, EU:C:2007:452.

74 See Peter J. Wattel, 'ProgressiveTaxation of Non-Residents and Intra-EC Allocation of Personal Tax Allowances; Why Schumacker, Asscher, Gilly and Gschwind Do Not Suffice,' 40 *European Taxation* 6 (June 2000), p. 210.

75 Case C-107/94 (*Asscher*), EU:C:1996:251.

76 Case C-336/96 (*Gilly*), EU:C:1998:221.

77 Case C-391/97 (*Gschwind*), EU:C:1999:409.

The *Gilly* case shows the first three misunderstandings. It concerned Mrs Gilly, of both German and French nationality, earning her entire employment income in Germany, but living in France with her husband, who earned 45% of the total family income in France. In France, spouses were jointly assessed for the total family income. The Gilly couple complained of the disadvantageous tax effects of Mrs Gilly being employed abroad as compared to being employed in France. The Court considered (emphasis added):

> '49 As regards the effect on the amount of the tax credit [the French double taxation relief; *authors*] of the fact that the taxpayer's personal and family circumstances are taken into account in the state of residence but not in the state of employment, it must be pointed out that the *disparity* derives from the fact that, in relation to direct taxes, the situations of residents and of non-residents are not, as a rule, comparable, since income received in the territory of a state by a non-resident is in most cases only a part of his total income, which is concentrated at his place of residence (...).
> 50. Nor is that observation inapplicable to a situation such as that of Mrs Gilly; although her individual income from employment is received in Germany, it is none the less aggregated within the basis for assessing the personal income tax payable by her tax household in France, *where she is therefore entitled to the tax advantages, rebates and deductions provided for in the French legislation.* The German tax authorities, however, were not obliged to take account of her personal and family circumstances in such a situation.'

This shows that the Court reasons, simply, that the source state is not required to do anything because the non-resident Mrs Gilly already receives personal allowances in France as spouse of Mr Gilly in respect of their aggregate family income. In reality, however, the Gilly couple lost 55% of their French family allowances (55% of the family income being earned abroad and exempted at home), without receiving any German allowances in return.[78] This is not a disparity, as this effect would not disappear if the French and German tax systems were made identical. The Gillys should have received 55% of the German splitting benefit. Nonetheless, the result of the *Gilly* case is correct, since, unlike Mr Schumacker, the Gillys litigated against their *home* state (France), which cannot be required to grant 100% of its family allowances if it exempts 55% of the family income. However, the Court tacitly overturned the *Gilly* outcome again in its later *De Groot* case (see below), probably because it realized that *Schumacker* and *Gilly* were incompatible. The factual outcome in the *Gilly* case was that France effectively granted only 45% of its family allowances, rightly so, as it also taxed only 45% of the family income. The Court however, mistakenly thought that France extended 100% of its family allowances.

The *Asscher* case[79] demonstrates the Court's misunderstanding of the progression effect, which works in the opposite direction (to the benefit of the non-resident taxpayer). It concerned a self-employed Netherlands national, resident in Belgium and doing business in both the Netherlands and Belgium. The Netherlands justified a higher first-bracket rate for nonresidents than for residents, a.o., on the grounds that nonresidents escape progression on their foreign-source income. That is true, as explained above. The Court nonetheless

78 For elaboration, see Wattel, 'Progressive Taxation of Non-Residents and Intra-EC Allocation of Personal Tax Allowances' 40 *European Taxation* 6 (June 2000), paragraphs 5.17-5.33.

79 For a comment, see David Williams, 'Asscher: The European Court and the Power to Destroy', *EC Tax Review* 1997-1, p. 4.

dismissed this plea, considering that a non-resident does not escape progression, as his home state calculates the tax bracket on the basis of his worldwide income. That is true as well, but it fails to take into account that foreign-source income was exempt in the home state: it was *not* taxed by the home state, let alone progressively. The home state rate progression was *calculated* on the basis of worldwide income, but it was *applied* only to the allocated *domestic* part of the income, leaving taxation of the foreign-source income to the source state. As explained in Chapter 8 and 10, home states include foreign-source income in the tax base in order to (i) calculate the progression in the rate applied to the part of the total income allocated to the home states and (ii) to provide for temporary loss relief in respect of foreign losses. (Nonetheless, in *Asscher*, the Court correctly rejected the Netherlands' higher rate for nonresidents, but for other reasons: it was an unsuitable and at any rate disproportionate measure in view of the objective of ensuring progressive taxation of the Netherlands-source income.)

The Court still missed the *pro rata* and progression effects of double tax relief and income allocation in the *Gschwind* case. That case concerned a taxpayer resident with his family in the Netherlands, earning his entire personal employment income (58% of the family income) in Germany, his wife earning the other 42% in the Netherlands. Like Schumacker (who got it), the Gschwinds wanted the German splitting benefit, or at least 58% of it. They did not get it, however, because 42% of the family income was earned at home, and the Court thought that for that reason 'sufficient tax base' was available to offset the Netherlands deductions (emphasis added):

> 'In the present case, given that nearly 42% of the total income of the Gschwinds is received in their state of residence, that state is in a position to take into account Mr Gschwind's personal and family circumstances according to the rules laid down by the legislation of that State, *since the tax base is sufficient there to enable them to be taken into account.*'

It is true that the home state tax base was high enough to absorb the Netherlands personal and family allowances, but as explained above, the double taxation relief mechanism – correctly – allocated 58% of the Gschwinds' personal and family circumstances to the German part of the family income, without the Gschwinds receiving 58% of the German benefits in return, although Germany taxed that 58% of their income.

13.4.5 The De Groot Case: A Chance Missed

In case C-385/00, *De Groot*,[80] the Court was faced with the undesirable effects of its *Schumacker* line of case law and the fallacies in *Gilly*, *Asscher* and *Gschwind*. The case was a perfect chance to elegantly integrate EU law and international tax law and improve them both to the benefit of taxpayers, tax administrations and the internal market. It was a unique chance to get it right both on the principle (national treatment), *and* on the three unbalanced inconsistencies of international tax law for individuals in one sweep: (i) correct interjurisdictional allocation and division of the obligation to take into account personal circumstances, (ii) correct progression on the total income, and (iii) full

80 Case C-385/00 (*De Groot*), EU:C:2002:750.

horizontal cross-border loss relief for individuals. The only thing the Court needed to do was to require national treatment in the source state. It did not do so.

Mr De Groot, resident of the Netherlands, earned his income partly in Germany, partly in France, partly in the UK and partly at home in the Netherlands. More than 60% of his total income was foreign-source. Thus, in none of the source states did he come close to the *Schumacker* threshold of 'almost all' of his income. Consequently, he did not get any personal benefits in France, Germany or the UK. In the tax year concerned, he paid a Hfl. 180 000 lump sum alimony termination to his ex-wife. Such payments were deductible personal expenses in the Netherlands. The Netherlands calculated double tax relief at 60/100 of the Netherlands tax otherwise due on the total income (which was first reduced by the alimony payment). Consequently (see the mechanics in section 13.4.3), 60% of the alimony deduction was – correctly – allocated to the foreign-source income. That 60% should have reappeared in the three source states, in each of them proportionately, because Article 45 TFEU and Article 7(2) of EU Regulation 492/2011 on the free movement of workers explicitly require the host states to grant national treatment to non-resident workers, which means, in this respect, to entitle them to the source state personal benefits in proportion to the part of total income taxed in that state. If so desired, that state may tax him progressively on that part of the income on the basis of the rate connected to the level of the worldwide income. By such simple requiring of national treatment, everything would have turned out correctly: (i) every state getting a slice of the tax base, would also grant the exact same slice of its personal allowances, (ii) the correct progression could have been calculated on every part of the total income, wherever sourced, instead of three parts (totalling more than 60%) escaping such progression, and (iii) losses in the home state and profits in the source state would have extinguished each other currently, reducing the taxpayer's tax exposure in the same manner as for residents in a purely domestic situation.

The Court, however, tried to adapt reality to its initial misunderstanding of it. Without legal basis, and in contravention of the free movement of workers, it prohibited the Netherlands to correctly calculate double tax relief *pro rata parte* and allowed France, Germany and the UK to discriminate against non-resident employees. Tacitly overturning *Gilly* in this respect, it required the Netherlands to ensure that Mr De Groot would enjoy 100% of the benefit of the Netherlands tax allowances, although the Netherlands taxed less than 40% of his income:

> '110. The answer (...) must therefore be that Article 48 [now 45; *authors*] of the Treaty precludes rules such as those at issue in the main proceedings – irrespective of whether or not they are laid down in a convention for the avoidance of double taxation – whereby a taxpayer forfeits, in the calculation of the income tax payable by him in his State of residence, part of the tax-free amount of that income and of his personal tax advantages because, during the year in question, he also received income in another Member State which was taxed in that State without his personal and family circumstances being taken into account.'

Technically, this means that the home state must attribute its personal allowances not to total income, but entirely to the domestic-sourced part of the total income. It must deduct the personal allowances from the denominator of the double taxation relief fraction (in the example above resulting in a denominator of 35 000 instead of 40 000, yielding a higher amount of double taxation relief).

If the domestic part of the income is high enough to absorb the home state personal deductions, the taxpayer will thus receive 100% of the home state allowances. Apparently, the Court failed to see that 100% of nothing is nothing. This system will significantly *dis*advantage the taxpayer if his home state is a flat tax jurisdiction and his job state is a high deductions/high rate jurisdiction: in that case, the taxpayer gets the worst of both worlds: he gets no allowances whatsoever, because his home state does not apply any, and the source state may refuse to extend national treatment, and he does not get the matching low tax rate at home either, as his income is allocated to the source state. On the contrary: he must suffer the high rate in the source state which accompanies the high deductions in that state which he, however, does not enjoy because the Court has decided otherwise. Conversely, if the job state is the flat tax jurisdiction and the home state is the high tax/ high deductions jurisdiction, the taxpayer will be unjustly enriched. Only if both states, or, in Mr De Groot's case, all four States extend more or less *identical* personal allowances, will this imbalanced system yield a balanced result; and in *Schumacker* cases, because only in such cases the taxpayer gets his fundamental right to national treatment in the source state.

The Court added that if the source state, in non-*Schumacker* situations, *voluntarily* provides national treatment (takes account of the non-resident's personal circumstances), then the home state is at liberty to refuse its allowances to the extent they are effected in the source state (the 'overall'-approach; see section 6.5.4). As observed, there was no need for such approach, as the Court should have *required* the source state to provide national treatment.

Thus, in *De Groot*, the Court assumed competence to (i) allocate to a particular taxing jurisdiction, chosen by the Court, certain tax debt determining factors, moreover separated from linked opposite tax debt determining factors, and (ii) force the home state to provide double tax relief in a particular technical manner (exemption with progression and attribution of home state allowances exclusively to home state source income). We believe such competence not to exist. This follows directly from the fact that the Treaties do not require the Member States to prevent double taxation in the first place. If there had been no tax treaty or unilateral prevention of double taxation (or a treaty which did not cover his case), the Court could have done nothing for Mr De Groot. That is clearly demonstrated by cases such as *Damseaux* and *Block*:[81] double taxation as a result of 'exercise in parallel' of taxing power is insoluble under the treaty freedoms. In the reasoning of the Court, Mr De Groot did not lose part of the benefit of his personal allowances because he went abroad, but because his home state gave him proportionate double tax relief! In reality, however, Mr De Groot lost part of his personal allowances benefit because

81 Case C-128/08 (*Damseaux*), EU:C:2009:471, and Case C-67/08 (*Block*), EU:C:2009:92.

the source states refused national treatment without justification. Unfortunately, the Court repeated, in *Renneberg*, its legislative prescription that Member States must apply their double tax relief mechanisms in a particular way, which presupposes that they are obliged to apply such mechanisms at all (which however, according to *Damseaux* and *Block*, is not the case):

> '70 (...), it should be noted that, in paragraph 101 of the judgment in *de Groot*, the Court held that the mechanisms used to eliminate double taxation or the national tax systems which have the effect of eliminating or alleviating double taxation must, however, permit the taxpayers in the Member States concerned to be certain that, ultimately, all their personal and family circumstances will be duly taken into account, irrespective of how those Member States have allocated that obligation amongst themselves, in order not to give rise to inequality of treatment which is incompatible with the Treaty provisions on the freedom of movement for workers and in no way results from the disparities between the national tax laws. Having regard to the guidance given in *Lakebrink and Peters-Lakebrink*, referred to in paragraph 63 of this judgment, those considerations also apply with regard to the taking into account of workers' overall ability to pay tax.'

It should be noted that again, the Court fails to specify *who* is doing the discriminating, and that it wrongly presupposes that all ability to pay factors are 'duly' taken into in account in both states *and* in the same way (that disparities do not exist). We fully agree, however, that there is no disparity: there is a discrimination in the *source* state.

It is regrettable that because of this case law, national treatment in the host state remains unattainable for nonresidents earning income in their home Member State, resulting in (i) an incomplete and unfair set of rules, especially where the allowances and accompanying rates of the two states differ substantially, (ii) a persisting progression unfairness, and (iii) no structural solution for the base fragmentation problem described in section 3.2.7.3. Only in *Schumacker* and *X* cases (almost the entire income earned abroad) a balanced result ('fractional taxation' of nonresidents[82]) may be achieved. (see 13.4.9).

13.4.6 *Renneberg: Schumacker Applies Also to Home State Losses*

The *Schumacker* line of case law is based on the points of departure that (i) all Member States take account, in their taxation of income of natural persons, in a more or less comparable manner, of personal ability to pay, and that (therefore) (ii) the exercise of the Treaty freedoms by a natural person may not have the effect of depriving that person of any of the factors taking that ability into account (the Court's 'always somewhere'– or 'one market'– principle; see Chapter 6). It was to be expected, therefore, that the *Schumacker* case law would be extended to other factors determining that ability to pay, such as negative income from a personal dwelling or other losses in the home state which cannot be deducted in the employment state (see the calculation example in section 3.2.7.3). This is what happened in *Lakebrink*,[83] although that case only concerned *rate* calculation. In

82 The term was coined by Kees van Raad, 'Fractionele belastingheffing van EU buitenlands belastingplichtigen,' in *Liberalte Gifte* (*Festschrift* Ferdinand Grapperhaus), Kluwer Deventer 1999.

83 Case C-182/06 (*Lakebrink and Peters-Lakebrink*), EU:C:2007:452.

Renneberg,[84] the Court applied its ability-to-pay-approach also to the tax *base*. The case concerned a resident of Belgium paying mortgage interest in Belgium which he could not entirely deduct from the positive income from his personal Belgium dwelling. He wanted to deduct the remainder from his Netherlands employment income. Belgium did not allow deduction of losses from real estate from other income than positive income from that real estate. Obviously, the Netherlands did not allow deduction of interest paid on a Belgian loan financing Belgian real estate of a resident of Belgium, the income from which was exclusively allocated to Belgium.

The Court, however, simply did not accept that losses of a natural person in his home state are not deductible anywhere. It required the Netherlands to selectively and asymmetrically extend its taxing jurisdiction to a specific negative item of income not allocated to it and flowing from a foreign source of income in respect of which the Netherlands had not asserted any taxing power.[85] As was observed in Chapter 10, given this case law, the Court will probably not accept either that in the opposite position (source state loss, home state positive income), the home state applies a base exemption system, although in *Lidl Belgium* and *Timac Agro* it has inconsistently accepted base exemption (territoriality taxation) for *company* taxation.[86]

The Court thus extended its *Schumacker* case law to home state losses: it required the Netherlands, as employment income source state (NB: the Netherlands was *not* the source state of the negative income from real estate), to allow deduction of the negative income from Belgian real estate on the basis of the simple reasoning that Mr Renneberg earned all of his *positive* income in the Netherlands (the Court *in this respect* ignored the substantial negative Belgian income) and was therefore in a *Schumacker*-like position. If one ignores the negative home state income in applying the *Schumacker* test ('almost his entire income'), then a non-resident with – on balance – a loss in his home state is *always*, by definition, in a *Schumacker* position. The Court further reasoned that for residents with a *second* (holiday) house abroad, such interest was (temporarily) deductible, and that therefore it should also be deductible for Mr Renneberg. It did not consider relevant that (i) mortgage interest was not deductible in the home state, meaning that if Mr Renneberg had worked in his home state, he would not have been able to deduct it either, which is a disparity for which the employment state cannot be made responsible; (ii) for residents, deduction was only temporary, whereas for nonresidents, it would be permanent, as nonresidents are not comparable for tax treaty application purposes.

In section 3.2.7.3 we have commented extensively on the *Renneberg* case. From that discussion, as well as from the observations above on *De Groot*, it may be inferred that it is our conviction that the *Schumacker* line of case law leads to imbalances, arbitrary and unfair results and new discriminations, as well as into an ever more detailed legislative

84 Case C-527/06 (*Renneberg*), EU:C:2008:566.

85 This contrary to the Court's own findings on the basis of the principle of territoriality in many other cases. See for elaboration, Otto Marres, 'The Principle of Territoriality and Cross-Border Loss Compensation', 39 *Intertax* 3 (2011), p. 112-125.

86 Case C-388/14 (*Timac Agro*), EU:C:2015:829.

role for the Court, which it is not equipped for. In *X*[87] the Court took the opportunity to elaborate on its Schumacker doctrine in in a three-states situation where no income was earned in the residence state. It decided that a pro-rata deduction should be granted in the two source states (see section 13.4.9).

13.4.7 Imfeld: Two Situations in which the Residence State is not Obliged to Take Account of Personal and Family Circumstances

In *Imfeld* the Court clarified in which situations the Member State of the taxpayer's residence is not obliged to grant the person-related deductions. Mr Imfeld, a German national and Mrs Garcet, a Belgian national, were married and had two children. They were both residing in Belgium. Mr Imfeld worked as a lawyer in Germany and earned all of his income there. His German-sourced income was tax-exempt in Belgium under the Belgium – Germany tax treaty. The Belgian tax authorities issued a correction notice, stating that the couple should be taxed jointly (despite the fact that Mr Imfeld was earning only tax-exempt income in Belgium). Under Belgian law, however, a specific allowance, the extra allowance for dependent children, was allocated to the spouse with the higher income, i.e. to Mr Imfeld. As he had no taxable income in Belgium, he could not actually benefit from the allowance. In addition, Mr Imfeld qualified for an advantage for dependent children in the form of a tax-free income allowance in Germany (since he was meeting the Schumacker test therein).

The Court decided – citing the *De Groot* and *Beker* judgments – that the residence state can be released from having to take into account personal and family circumstance if (i) there is an international agreement which obliges the source Member State to do so or (ii) in the absence of such an agreement, the source state voluntarily does so:

> '69. However, the Court has already held that such a justification cannot be invoked by a taxpayer's State of residence in order to evade its responsibility in principle to grant to the taxpayer the personal and family allowances to which he is entitled, unless that State is released by way of an international agreement from its obligation to take full account of the personal and family circumstances of taxpayers residing in its territory who work partially in another Member State or it finds that, even in the absence of such an agreement, one or more of the States of employment, with respect to the income taxed by them, grant advantages based on the personal and family circumstances of taxpayers who do not reside in the territory of those States but earn taxable income there (see, to that effect, De Groot, paragraphs 99 and 100, and Beker, paragraph 56).'

In *Imfeld*, however, the Belgian – Germany tax treaty does not impose on the source state any obligation to take into account the personal and family circumstances of taxpayers living in the other Contracting state. Furthermore, the Belgian legislation did not establish a link between the tax-free income allowance for dependent children and the equivalent German allowance. Therefore, Belgium had to grant the tax-free income allowance for dependent children to the Belgian couple. We observe, however, that since Mr Imfeld was in a Schumacker situation in Germany (as he was earning his entire income there),

87 Case C-283/15 (*X*), EU:C:2017:102.

the couple was effectively receiving two similar tax benefits in two different Member States. For the Court this is apparently not an issue.

13.4.8 Schumacker Test for the Whole Tax Year

In *Kieback*,[88] the Court clarified that the *Schumacker* test must be met for the whole tax year. Mr Kieback was a German resident who worked in the Netherlands from 1 January to 31 March 2005, after which he moved to work in the US. During the time he worked in the Netherlands, he owned, and lived in, a dwelling in Germany. He sought to deduct his German interest on the German mortgage attached to his German dwelling against his Netherlands employment income. However, the Netherlands tax authorities denied deduction because he did not earn at least 90% of his 2005 worldwide income in the Netherlands. In fact, Mr Kieback was earning the majority of his 2005 income in the US.

The Court decided that the *Schumacker* test ('almost all of his income') should be applied on a year basis. In the Court's view, the Netherlands was not in a better position to assess Mr Kieback's personal and family-related circumstances and the tax advantages linked thereto than the United States was for the year 2005. One may surmise, however, that the US was not minded to allow deduction of the German mortgage interest for the first three months of 2005.

13.4.9 Case C-283/15, X:[89] Proportional Extension of Personal Deductions by Multiple Source States in the Absence of Home State Income

If a taxpayer earns, like Mr Schumacker, his entire income abroad, but unlike Mr Schumacker, not in one source state, but in two or more source states, then which of these two or more source states is take into account his personal and family circumstances? If he does not pass the *Schumacker* test in these states, his personal and family circumstances are not taken into account anywhere, as the residence state cannot take them into account for lack of taxed income and in the two or more source states he did not earn "all or almost his entire income".

In case C-283/15, *X*, the Court therefore modified its *Schumacker* doctrine. Notwithstanding the fact that in neither source state 'all or almost his entire income' was earned, both source states should extend their personal deductions in proportion to the part of the total income they tax. Mr X, a Netherlands national resident in Spain paid mortgage interest on a loan taken out to finance his Spanish dwelling. In 2007, Mr X received income from two closely held companies, one in the Netherlands and the other in Switzerland. From the Netherlands company he received 60% of his income and from the Swiss company 40%. He could deduct the interest from his Netherlands income only if he would opt to be taxed as a resident, which he declined because of the connected disadvantages he did not care for (see section 13.5) and *Schumacker* did not help him, as he was not in any Schumacker position.

88 Case C-9/14 (*Kieback*), EU:C:2015:406.
89 Case C-283/15 (*X*), EU:C:2017:102.

The Court held that the Netherlands should extend 60% of its personal and family deductions and (rather implicitly) that Switzerland should extend 40% of its personal tax allowances (the fact that Mr X received 40% of his taxable income in a non-Member State was of no relevance).

We believe that unfortunately, the *X* Case does not correct the erroneous *Schumacker* doctrine. It does not say that the *pro rata parte* approach also obtains if in absolute terms there is sufficient home state income to absorb the personal deductions of the home state. It does not say that Mr. De Groot would now get 40% of his home state deductions and the remaining 60% proportionally to taxing rights assumptions in Germany, France and the UK. It only says that if there is no or insufficient home state taxable income to absorb the home state deductions *and* there are two or more source states in which income is earned (instead of one, as in *Schumacker*), then both source states should take responsibility. We doubt, therefore, that the *X* case fundamentally changes the erroneous *Schumacker* case law.

13.4.10 *The Zyla case: Schumacker doctrine not applied for social security contributions*

The *Zyla* case demonstrates that the Court makes a distinction between direct taxation on the one hand and the social security system on the other hand.[90] Ms. Zyla lives and works in the Netherlands between 1 January 2013 and 21 June 2013. Then she returns to Poland to live there. In the Netherland, income tax and social security contributions are collected by means of a combined tax. The total amount of the combined tax is calculated by adding the amount of tax on income from employment and from other sources such as residential property and savings, to the amount of social security contributions. The rate is the sum of the tax rate for the first band of income and the rates of the applicable contributions. However, the amount of the combined tax is be reduced by a certain tax credit. The question was whether Ms Zyla was entitled to the tax credit, either in whole (as would be the case if she had stayed in the Netherlands) or in part (*pro rata parte* calculated for the period she lived and worked in the Netherlands). The Court noted that income tax and social security contributions are not the same.

> '31 In those circumstances, the principles derived from the case-law concerning the conditions governing liability for payment of tax on income from employment, in particular from the judgments of 14 February 1995, Schumacker (C 279/93, EU:C:1995:31) and of 16 October 2008, Renneberg (C 527/06, EU:C:2008:566), relied on by Ms Zyla in her observations, are not applicable in a situation such as that in the main proceedings.'

Nevertheless, the Court went on to hold that the Netherlands should allow for a partial credit so to achieve the same position for Ms. Zyla for the period she lived and worked in the Netherlands. For the period that she lived in Poland, the Court holds that she is not in an objectively similar position as a Dutch resident.

90 Case C-272/17, (*Zyla*), EU:C:2019:49.

13.5 Option to Be Taxed as a Resident

A very interesting but puzzling case is the *Gielen* Case,[91] on the question of whether it is compatible with the free movement of persons to operate a tax regime for non-resident self-employed persons which derogates from the regime for residents, but which gives them the option to be taxed as a resident. Under Netherlands law a reduction of taxable profit was available for self-employed persons who had worked more than 1225 hours in the tax year in their undertaking. Mr Gielen lived in Germany and operated with two others a horticultural business there. He also had a permanent establishment in the Netherlands. The major part (around € 73.300) of his income was attributable to the German part of his business and therefore exempt in the Netherlands. He had worked more than 1225 hours in his undertaking(s), but less than 1225 hours in his Netherlands branch. The Netherlands, as a source state, taxed him exclusively for the modest profit attributable to the Netherlands branch, meaning that his Netherlands-source income was not taxed at the progressive rate which would have been applicable had he been resident. That resulted in a very significant advantage for him, as he was taxed at a rate of 2.95%, whereas if he would have been resident in otherwise exactly the same circumstances, the rate on the Netherlands-source part of his business profit would have been, on average, around 35% (exemption with progression; see for the mechanics section 13.4.3). On the other hand, if he had been resident and thus had been taxed for his worldwide income (with double tax relief), the hours in his German business would have been taken into account for the 1225 hours threshold. Netherlands tax law provided for an option for nonresidents like Mr Gielen to be taxed as a resident. Mr Gielen had not exercised that option, obviously not, as that would have cost him a lot of money: the disadvantage caused by the rate difference would have exceeded by far the advantage of being entitled to the self-employed persons reduction. The Court first looked at the self-employed person reduction scheme in itself, disregarding the opportunity to opt for resident's taxation. It found a discrimination to be present, as residents in otherwise identical circumstances could count their German hours. Apparently, the Court did not consider it relevant that a comparable resident with the same German/Netherlands undertaking and the same income, would pay considerably more tax on the Netherlands part of the profit than Mr Gielen did. It thus applied a selective detailed-rule-comparison rather than a regime comparison. Next, the Court examined whether that discrimination was taken away by the opportunity to opt for resident's taxation. It was not, for the following reasons:

> '50. It should be noted, at the outset, that the option to be treated as a resident taxable person provides non-resident taxable persons, such as Mr Gielen, with a choice between a discriminatory tax regime and one which is ostensibly not discriminatory.
> 51. It has, however, to be pointed out in that regard that such a choice is not, in the present case, capable of remedying the discriminatory effects of the first of those two tax regimes.
> 52. (...), if such a choice were to be recognised as having the effect described, the consequence would be to validate a tax regime which, in itself, remains contrary to Article 49 TFEU by reason of its discriminatory nature.
> 53. In addition, as the Court has already had the opportunity to clarify, the fact that a national scheme which restricts the freedom of establishment is optional does not mean

91 Case C-440/08 (*Gielen*), EU:C:2010:148.

that it is not incompatible with European Union law (see, to that effect, Case C-446/04 *Test Claimants in the FII Group Litigation* [2006] ECR I-11753, paragraph 162).
54. Consequently, the choice offered, in the dispute in the main proceedings, to non-resident taxable persons by means of the option to be treated as resident taxable persons does not serve to neutralise the discrimination established in paragraph 48 above.'

We infer that either (i) the Court fears that Member States might introduce all kinds of discriminatory rules, referring complaining nonresidents routinely to the option of being taxed as a resident, or (ii) the Court does not consider resident taxation nondiscriminatory.

It should be pointed out, first, that as long as a choice for the resident's regime is unattractive, apparently the non-resident is treated *more* favourably than a resident in otherwise identical circumstances. Second, we do not understand the reference to the *FII* Case, as *FII* concerned the opposite question: does a restrictive national rule remain incompatible with free movement rights if its application is optional? Thus, in *FII*, the choice was not between discriminatory taxation and nondiscriminatory taxation of the same factual situation, but between not opting for a certain regime and opting for a discriminatory regime. The opting and non-opting regimes were both disadvantageous. That was not the case in the *Gielen* case, in which the optional regime was by definition completely *non*discriminatory as it was the resident's regime. National treatment by definition has no 'discriminatory nature.' *Not* allowing nonresidents a choice – taxing them mandatory as residents – is not contrary to EU law, as the Court held in *Van Hilten-Van der Heijden*.[92] That being so, we do not see how the conclusion can be avoided that it is even less contrary to EU law to grant them a choice between two regimes, whichever is most advantageous to them; a choice which is *not* granted to residents, who only get the resident's regime with the high tax rate. The only way we see to avoid that conclusion is to regard national treatment of nonresidents as discriminatory. That would be a novel approach, and it would require overturning *Van Hilten-Van der Heijden*, as well as the case law holding that the assertion of taxing power and the choice of connecting criteria (worldwide, nationality, territoriality, source, asset location) is outside the scope of EU law and therefore outside Court scrutiny.[93] Besides, as argued above (section 13.4), the Court would do free movement of persons a favour by requiring national tax treatment of nonresidents.

The word 'ostensibly' (in French 'pretendument') in point 50 does in fact suggest that the Court considers that *actually*, national tax treatment of nonresidents – which the Court itself virtually *forced* upon the source state in *Renneberg* – is discriminatory in the sense that the same rules are applied to persons who are not in a comparable position. It is true that the Court routinely considers, since *Schumacker*, that residents and nonresidents are not, as a rule, comparable. And it is true that it may be *disproportionate* to require a non-resident like Mr Wallentin, who worked only three weeks in the host state, to file as a resident in order to be eligible for some small reduction. But that is not the reasoning the Court applies. And at any rate, it does not seem very balanced either that nonresidents

92 Case C-513/03 (*Van Hilten-van der Heijden*), EU:C:2006:131.
93 Case C-513/04 (*Kerckhaert and Morres*), EU:C:2006:713, Case C-67/08, (*Block*), EU:C:2009:92, Case C-128/08 (*Damseaux*), EU:C:2009:471.

like Mr Gielen can cherry-pick from the resident's regime. As the Court only looks at the particular detailed tax scheme at issue and ignores the (disadvantageous) rest of the tax position of a resident self-employed person in otherwise identical circumstances, non-residents like Mr Gielen can collect separate advantages in detailed rules while avoiding the connected disadvantages in other detailed rules and especially while avoiding the much higher tax rate for residents. The question arises what the Court would decide of the national measure were inverted: all nonresidents earning active income (employment, business) in the source state are compulsory taxed as residents, with either (i) no option or (ii) an option to choose for the nonresidents regime if that is more favourable for them. Would such national treatment be discriminatory? If so, would it still be discriminatory if the rule were supplemented with a temporal threshold: all nonresidents working in the source state for more than 6 months (compare the 183 days rule in the OECD Model tax treaty) are taxed as residents?

The Court could have provided the Member States with more guidance on the extent in which they are expected *not* to provide or impose national treatment or *not* to give nonresidents a choice. The present case law says on the one hand that national treatment of nonresidents is required and on the other hand that it is discriminatory and prohibited. We observe that if the Netherlands had taxed nonresidents in the exact same manner as residents (for worldwide income with relief from double taxation), *without* any choice, then the Court could have done nothing for Mr. Gielen, as he would have enjoyed full national treatment. We fail to see why giving him an extra option – unavailable for residents – which may be more beneficial than national treatment or not, depending on his circumstances, produces a discrimination. The counter-productive but obvious result of this judgment was that the Netherlands deleted the choice and introduced a compulsory single system for nonresidents.

The *Hirvonen* Case[94] may provide that guidance, as it seems to overturn the puzzling *Gielen* Case. Sweden taxed employment income of non-residents under a taxation-at-source-regime. Their *gross* income earned in Sweden was taxed at a flat tax rate of 25% without any deductions. Alternatively, non-residents could opt for the ordinary (residents) tax regime, under which their *net* income earned in Sweden was taxed at the normal progressive income tax rates and they were entitled to deductions relating to personal and family circumstances. Mrs Hirvonen, resident in Finland, received a pension, an annuity and sickness benefit from Sweden. She was taxed under the taxation-at-source regime. She could therefore not deduct mortgage interest which she was not able to deduct in her state of residence (Finland) either. Like Mr. Gielen, who only wanted one single beneficial element from the resident's regime, not the disadvantages, she declined to be taxed under the normal resident's regime, as that was not beneficial to her, not even after the interest deduction she would be entitled to under that regime. Like Mr. Gielen, she only wanted one single beneficial element of the resident's regime, in her case: mortgage interest deduction.

94 Case C-632/13 (*Hirvonen*), EU:C:2015:765.

The Court observed that the taxation-at-source regime was overall more favourable to Mrs. Hirvonen than the ordinary tax regime, even if it did not include mortgage interest deduction and personal allowances, and that it required less administrative effort. From this, the Court concluded that Sweden was not discriminating against Mrs Hirvonen. Allowing taxation-at-source *and* interest and personal deductions would have resulted in a lower tax burden than under national treatment (the resident's regime) and would enable nonresidents to cherry-pick the low rate from the taxation-at-source regime and the deductions desired from the ordinary tax regime. The Court decided that Sweden had done nothing wrong, and it made an effort to distinguish *Hirvonen* from *Gielen* by considering that the latter case concerned a nonresidents regime that turned out to be discriminatory in Mr. Gielen's case and that this could not be taken away by the option to choose for national treatment (which we do not understand, as it would seem very obvious that national treatment by definition *does* take away discrimination), whereas *Hirvonen* concerned a nonresidents regime which was usually more favourable than the residents regime. That may be so, but it does not take away that (i) as long as national treatment is freely available, there simply is no discrimination, (ii) also the Swedish source system could in certain circumstances be less favourable than the residents regime and (iii) the Court discriminated against residents in *Gielen*.

In the case *MK* a French resident owned a property (house) in Portugal which he sold with a profit.[95] The capital gain was taxed in Portugal with income taxation at a special flat rate of 28% for non-residents. There was an option to be taxed as a resident, meaning access to progressive tax rates and a reduction of the tax base with 50%. The French resident did not choose to be taxed as a resident. Consequently, a tax assessment was issued taxing the whole capital gain at 28%. The French resident appealed to the domestic court claiming that his tax burden may not exceed the tax which would have been levied on the income if he had been taxed as a resident. The domestic court had doubt on the Portuguese system and referred the matter to Luxembourg. The Court notes that the Portuguese system allows residents to benefit systematically from a tax burden which is lower than for non-residents. Referring to *Holmen*[96] the Court reiterates that the tax base reduction for residents of 50% constitutes a restriction on the movement of capital. The option to be taxed as a resident cannot mend this, as according to the Court non-residents are systemically subject to a tax burden greater than that applied to residents where capital gains are realised on the sale of property. This in contrast to *Hirvonen*, where Sweden had demonstrated that the regime for non-residents was overall more favourable to non-residents than the ordinary tax regime applicable to residents.

13.6 Pensions and Annuities

Contributions paid by residents to foreign pension funds or on annuity policies taken out with foreign life insurance companies must be deductible on the same footing as domestic contributions, at least in so far these contributions are compulsory.[97] In *Commission v.*

95 Case C-388/19 (*MK*), EU:C:2021:212.
96 Case C-443/06 (*Holmen*), EU:C:2007:600.
97 Case C-480/17 (*Montag*), EU:C:2018:987.

Denmark,[98] the Court overturned *Bachmann* in this respect: a refusal of equal deduction cannot be based on the need to preserve the cohesion of the national tax system in respect of tax base reductions and corresponding base increases, not even if it is impossible for the contribution state to tax the future benefits as a consequence of the relocation of the taxpayer, *after* having contributed and *before* starting benefiting. This is (also) a consequence of the fact that Member States adhere to Article 18 of the OECD Model Double Taxation Treaty, which allocates private pension benefits to the residence state.[99] Nor can the contribution state successfully plead that effective fiscal supervision is impossible in case of payments abroad, as nothing prevents it to either use the Directive on Administrative Cooperation (see Chapter 26) in order to obtain the necessary information, or to require the taxpayer to submit convincing documentary evidence, and anyway denial of deduction is not an appropriate means of ensuring effective fiscal supervision (*Bachmann, Commission v. Denmark*). However, the applicable tax treaty allowing, and given the Court's ruling in *Lasteyrie du Saillant*,[100] *N. v. Inspecteur*,[101] *Commission vs Portugal*[102] and *Picart*[103] it would seem the contribution state may recapture the deductions (or tax the entire value built up tax-free within its residence) upon emigration of the taxpayer, provided it requires no immediate payment and extends unconditional extension of payment until the benefits start flowing or the policy is redeemed for lump sum. The *Danner* Case[104] shows that if a national system is inconsistent in itself, the Member State involved cannot plead the need for consistency. *Commission v. Belgium*,[105] concerned not only discriminatory denial of deduction of contributions paid abroad, but also other free movement incompatible measures implying that:

- deductibility of employer contributions to long-term employee savings were dependent on whether they were paid to an insurance undertaking or welfare fund established in Belgium;
- payments of capital or redemption values to a non-resident previously resident, were fictitiously deemed to have taken place prior to emigration and the pension fund or insurer was required to withhold and transfer to the tax administration the Belgian income tax on such payments in so far as the capital had been built up in the Belgian residency period;
- Belgian income tax was levied upon the transfer to another pension fund or insurer of the capital or surrender values built up by means of employers' or personal contributions for supplementary retirement benefits, if that other fund was established outside Belgium.

The *Safir*[106] case concerns the inverse life insurance policy taxation system: no deduction of contributions, and no taxation of the later benefit either. If a Member State applies

98 Case C-150/04 (*Commission v. Denmark*), (*supported by Sweden*), EU:C:2007:69.
99 See, apart from *Commission v. Denmark*, also Case C-80/94 (*Wielockx*), EU:C:1995:271.
100 Case C-9/12 (*Lasteyrie du Saillant*), EU:C:2004:138.
101 Case C-470/04 (*N.*), EU:C:2006:525.
102 Case C-503/14 (*Commission v. Portugal*), EU:C:2016:979.
103 Case C-355/16 (*Picart*), EU:C:2018:184.
104 Case C-136/00 (*Danner*), EU:C:2002:558.
105 Case C-522/04 (*Commission v. Belgium*), EU:C:2007:405.
106 See Case C-118/96 (*Jessica Safir*), EU:C:1998:170.

such system, it must do so uniformly for both domestic and cross-border contracts. If it wishes to tax the investment proceeds, then that is all right, but it cannot do so by taxing the insurance company for domestic contracts and taxing the policyholder (on the contributions paid) for foreign contracts. Although this may promote fairer competition between domestic and foreign insurance companies, it hinders taxpayers contracting with a foreign insurer, and hinders foreign insurers to provide insurance services, where a less restrictive measure is available: a uniform levy on both domestic and cross-border contracts. Similarly, a national system providing for deduction of employer contributions for domestic contracts at the time of contributing and for foreign contracts only at the (much later) time of the (ex-) employee receiving the benefits, offends the Treaty Freedoms, as the *Skandia and Ramstedt* Case shows.[107]

The *Montag* case makes clear that the Court makes a distinction between voluntary contributions and compulsory contributions.[108] Mr. Montag lived and worked as a lawyer in Belgium and generated business income in Belgium and Germany. He paid compulsory and voluntary contributions to the German lawyers' provident institution as he was admitted to the bar in Germany. The Court held that only the compulsory contributions must be deductible in the source state Germany on the same footing as domestic contributions following the *Gerritse*-doctrine, whereas the voluntary contributions should be deducted in the residence state Belgium following the *Schumacker*-doctrine.

See also Chapter 12.2 on exit taxation as regards pension reserves.

13.7 Private Investment Incentives also for Cross-Border Investments

Tax advantages aimed at encouraging residents to invest in a particular manner, must also be extended to residents investing abroad or borrowing abroad. Thus, a tax incentive for mortgaged loan financing of a personal dwelling must also be extended to residents taking out their mortgaged loans not with a domestic bank but with an EU bank (*Svensson*[109]); a tax incentive for investing in company shares must also be extended if the taxpayer concerned buys shares in companies from other Member States (*Verkooijen*[110], *Weidert-Paulus*[111] and *Real Vida Seguros*[112]); a tax benefit connected to buying a personal dwelling must also be extended to residents buying a home across the border (*Eigenheimzulage*[113]); a tax benefit for savings at a domestic bank must also be extended to savings at a foreign bank (*Van der Weegen-Pot*)[114]; and a tax benefit connected with a dividend from a domestic investment fund must also be extended to a dividend from a foreign investment fund (*E* or *Veronsaajien oikeudenvalvontayksikkö*).[115]

107 Case C-422/01 (*Skandia and Ola Ramstedt v. Riksskatteverket*), EU:C:2003:380.
108 Case C-480/17 (*Montag*), EU:C:2018:987.
109 Case C-484/93 (*Svensson and Gustavsson*), EU:C:1995:379.
110 Case C-35/98 (*Verkooijen*), EU:C:2000:294.
111 Case C-242/03 (*Jean-Claude Weidert, Élisabeth Paulus*), EU:C:2004:465.
112 Case C-C-449/20 (*Real Vida Seguros SA*), EU:C:2021:721.
113 Case C-152/05 (*Commission v. Germany*), (*Eigenheimzulage*), EU:C:2008:17.
114 Case C-580/15 (*Van der Weegen-Pot*), EU:C:2017:429).
115 Case C-480/19 (*E* or *Veronsaajien oikeudenvalvontayksikkö*), EU:C:2020:942.

Similarly, the Member States may not make a deferral of or exemption from capital gains tax on the sale of a private dwelling conditional upon the taxpayer reinvesting the proceeds within their territory (*e.g. Commission v. Sweden*,[116] and *Commission v. Portugal*[117]).

A slight variation on the theme was at issue in *Nord Vest Pro Sani Pro* with respect to a Romanian measure.[118] In an attempt to keep workers in the construction sector in Romania and stop them from working abroad, Romania introduced a rule exempting a Romanian employer in the construction sector who employs construction workers working on Romanian territory from withholding wage tax. At the same time, the construction worker was exempted from income tax with the idea that such worker would receive a larger net income. These rules did not apply to a Romanian employer employing construction workers working on German or Austrian territory. According to the Court this constituted an indirect discrimination which could be justified not only to combat abuse but also to protect the social security of employees of the construction sector and to ensure fair working conditions. The latter were viewed as legitimate objectives of social policy. However, the Court was not convinced whether the measure observed the principle of proportionality. It left it to the referring court to ascertain whether the measure was appropriate for the purpose of ensuring, in a consistent and systematic manner, the social security protection of employees in the construction sector by reducing the pay gap existing at EU level, by ensuring, in particular, that undertakings pass on, in practice, the tax and social security advantages received to the salaries paid to employees leading to an increase in those salaries.

116 Case C-104/06 (*Commission v. Sweden*), EU:C:2007:40.
117 Case C-345/05 (*Commission v. Portugal*), EU:C:2006:685.
118 Case C-387/22 (*Nord Vest Pro Sani Pro*), EU:C:2024:786.

CHAPTER 14

EU inheritance and gift taxation

Vassilis Dafnomilis[1]

14.1 Introduction

The first judgment on the compatibility of an EU Member State's inheritance tax laws with EU law was delivered by the Court on 11 December 2003 in the *Barbier* case (C-364/01). In this ruling, the Court held that Dutch inheritance tax legislation violated the free movement of capital by allowing certain liabilities connected to inherited property to be deductible only if the deceased was a resident of the Netherlands, while denying such deductions if the deceased was a non-resident. By ruling in favor of Mr. Barbier's heirs, the Court not only upheld their claims but also set a precedent for subsequent judgments on inheritance and gift taxation—an area previously unexplored in terms of EU law compatibility. Over the following years, the Court issued 24 judgments on EU inheritance and/or gift taxation, scrutinizing the legislation of five Member States: Germany, Belgium, the Netherlands, Spain, and Greece.[2] In the majority of the cases, the Court found that the national inheritance and gift tax laws were contrary to EU law, with the free movement of capital being the most frequently invoked freedom.[3][4]

Since 2003, the Court has ruled on various facets of EU Member States' inheritance and gift tax laws, specifically addressing issues in:

a) Subjective tax exemptions, as seen in *Mattner* (C-510/08), *Welte* (C-181/12), *Commission v Germany* (C-211/13), *Hünnebeck* (C-479/14), and *XY* (C-394/20);
b) Objective tax exemptions, in cases such as *Commission v Spain* (C-127/12), *Q (Bean House)* (C-133/13), *Commission v Greece* (C-244/15), *Huijbrechts* (C-679/17) and *BA v Finanzamt X* (C-670/21);
c) Special tax deductions related to specific liabilities and debts, including obligations to transfer title (*Barbier* (C-364/01)), mortgage debts (*Eckelkamp* (C-11/07)), over-endowment debts (*Arens-Sikken* (C-43/07)), and liabilities tied to reserved portions (*XY* (C-394/20));

---

1 Assistant Professor at the University of Amsterdam and Academic Coordinator of the Adv. LLM in International Tax Law. Senior Manager Tax at PwC the Netherlands Knowledge Centre.

2 The representation of only five EU Member States takes on a different perspective when considering that not all EU Member States impose inheritance and gift taxes, unlike personal income taxes.

3 The Court addressed the inheritance laws of Belgium and Germany, respectively, in light of the freedom of establishment only in *Geurts* (C-464/05, EU:C:2007:631) and *Scheunemann* (C-31/11, EU:C:2012:481).

4 In six cases, the Court determined that EU law did not preclude the EU Member States' inheritance and/or gift tax laws.

d) Valuation rules, as in *Jäger* (C-256/06), *Halley* (C-132/10), *Scheunemann* (C-31/11) and *BA* (C-670/21);
e) Reduced tax rates for domestic non-profit organisations, illustrated by *Missionswerk Werner* (C-25/10) and *Commission v Greece* (C-98/16);
f) Tax treatment of family businesses, examined in *Geurts* (C-464/05), and family foundations, to be examined in *Familienstiftung* (C-142/24, pending);
g) Extended residence rules, as in *Van Hilten* (C-513/03);
h) Double taxation of inheritances, discussed in *Block* (C-67/08); and
i) Reductions for previously paid inheritance taxes, seen in *Feilen* (C-123/15).

These 24 judgments have undoubtedly established certain foundational principles for assessing the compatibility of EU Member States' inheritance and gift tax laws with EU law. In 2011, the European Commission (EC) consolidated these principles in its Working Paper titled *Non-discriminatory inheritance tax systems: principles drawn from EU case-law*.[5] The EC acknowledged that the Court judgments on EU inheritance and gift taxation had enhanced clarity and predictability regarding the principle of non-discrimination in this area of tax law. Nevertheless, the EC noted some ambiguity regarding the extent to which a judgment concerning the legislation of one EU Member State should influence legislation in another.[6] Although the Working Paper predates many subsequent judgments and has been issued more than ten years ago, its principles remain relevant and largely affirmed by more recent Court judgments.

Before discussing these principles, it is essential to understand the application of inheritance and gift taxes, which differ in nature, structure, and elements from personal income taxes.

14.2 Technical background on inheritance and gift taxes

Inheritance taxes are classified as "death taxes", a category encompassing taxes imposed on property transfers occurring upon a person's death. Originating in ancient civilizations such as Egypt, Greece, and Mesopotamia, death taxes persist today in various forms, including inheritance tax, estate tax, generation-skipping tax, *mortis causa* property transfer tax, substitute inheritance tax, and transfer tax. Notably, not all EU Member States impose death taxes. Those that do generally employ an *inheritance tax*, an acquisition-based tax levied on each beneficiary's share of inherited property. The taxable event here is the beneficiary's financial enrichment at the deceased's death, with each beneficiary taxed individually on their received inheritance.[7] Typically, tax rates vary according to both the inherited property's size and the degree of kinship with the deceased: generally, the

5 EU, European Commission Staff Working Paper, "Non-discriminatory Inheritance Tax Systems: Principles Drawn from EU Case law", SEC 1488, 2011.
6 *Idem*, p. 4.
7 Guglielmo Maisto, "General Report: Death as a Taxable Event and its International Ramifications," in Cahier de droit fiscal international 95b, ed. IFA (The Hague: Sdu Uitgevers, 2010), 29.

higher the inherited amount, the higher the tax rate; conversely, closer kinship usually results in a lower rate.[8]

For establishing tax jurisdiction, states rely primarily on a personal nexus (residence, domicile, or nationality[9]) of the deceased or, less commonly, the beneficiary to the state's territory and therefore apply an *ad personam* taxing principle. With this nexus, the state can exercise worldwide tax jurisdiction,[10] subjecting each beneficiary's share—including domestic and foreign property—to taxation.[11] In the absence of a personal nexus, a state may still impose inheritance taxes based on an objective nexus and therefore apply an *in rem* principle, limiting jurisdiction to specified domestic assets.

Most states with inheritance taxes provide subjective and objective exemptions or tax-free allowances. Subjective tax exemptions – rooted in the so-called "windfall justification" – are intended to enable closely related family members to retain a larger portion of their inheritance.[12] Conversely, objective exemptions are designed to serve broader policy objectives, such as promoting social, environmental, cultural, or historical goals. These exemptions are generally territorial in nature, applying to inheritances involving domestic assets irrespective of the familial relationship.[13]

Property valuation for inheritance tax purposes often follows the principle of market value, though exceptions exist, such as using cadastral values or market values adjusted post-death.[14] Similarly, many states allow deductions for tax debts of the deceased and *post-mortem* expenses, like funeral and probate or notary fees related to inheritance proceedings. Some states apportion liabilities and costs between taxable and non-taxable shares when certain assets are excluded from the taxable base due to objective exemptions or limitations in tax jurisdiction.[15]

8 Frans Sonneveldt, "General Report: Avoidance of Multiple Inheritance Taxation within Europe," EC Tax Review 10, no. 2 (2001): 89. See also V. Dafnomilis, Taxation of cross-border inheritances and donations: suggestions for improvement. Deventer: Wolters Kluwer, 2021, section 2.1.

9 More on the personal nexus links, Jan Karol Szczepanski, 'Personal Genuine Links under Domestic Inheritance Tax Rules in the Light of International and European Standards', (2015), 43, Intertax, Issue 10, section 2.

10 Guglielmo Maisto, "General Report: Death as a Taxable Event and its International Ramifications," in Cahier de droit fiscal international 95b, ed. IFA (The Hague: Sdu Uitgevers, 2010), 29.

11 Some states, however, limit their worldwide tax jurisdiction even when a personal nexus is established, likely to prevent potential double or multiple taxation of the deceased's assets. For example, they may exempt foreign-located immovable and/or movable property under specific conditions.

12 The granting of subjective tax exemptions primarily rests on the windfall justification, regarded as the most convincing, comprehensive, and unique rationale for death taxation. This justification elucidates why states consider it fair to tax incidental and unexpected wealth receipts ("why to tax") while simultaneously protecting family property when it is acquired by family members ("how to tax"). See V. Dafnomilis, *Taxation of Cross-Border Inheritances and Donations: Suggestions for Improvement*, Deventer: Wolters Kluwer, 2021, section 2.4.2.

13 See also V. Dafnomilis, Taxation of cross-border inheritances and donations: suggestions for improvement. Deventer: Wolters Kluwer, 2021, section 2.1.

14 Guglielmo Maisto, "General Report: Death as a Taxable Event and its International Ramifications," in *Cahier de droit fiscal international 95b*, ed. IFA, (The Hague: Sdu Uitgevers, 2010), 31.

15 *Idem*, p. 31-32.

Beyond death taxes, states may also impose taxes on gifts, which often mirror inheritance tax principles in terms of jurisdictional nexus, tax base, rates, and available exemptions.[16] In many jurisdictions, gift taxes complement inheritance taxes[17] and may take the form of a gift tax or an income tax on gifts. For instance, in the *Welte* case, the Court applied reasoning from *Mattner*, a gift tax case, to interpret inheritance taxes, illustrating how inheritance tax judgments can inform gift tax interpretations by analogy.

14.3 Principles drawn from Court case law on EU inheritance and gift taxation

14.3.1 *Applicable freedom*

According to the EC's Working Paper, "*[t]he free movement of capital, as enshrined in Article 63 TFEU, is the most essential freedom in the area of inheritance taxation, as Court decisions in the inheritance tax area have been mainly based on this freedom. The Court has repeatedly confirmed that an inheritance involving a transfer to one or more persons of assets left by the deceased is a movement of capital within the meaning of Article 63 TFEU, except in cases where its constituent elements are confined within a single [EU] Member State.*"[18] These core elements are, in our view, the inherited asset(s), the deceased, and the heir(s). If any one of these elements is located outside the territory of the EU Member State concerned, the inheritance in question falls within the free movement of capital. Similar analysis applies to the consideration of a donation in light of the free movement of capital.

The Court's early case law reflected this analysis, referencing heading XI of Annex I to the (former) EU Directive 88/361, entitled "Personal Capital Movements", to support the view that an inheritance is a capital movement.[19] Indeed, gifts and endowments (B) as well as inheritances and legacies (D) appear, among other types of capital, under heading XI of Annex I to the EU Directive 88/361.[20]

Examining national inheritance and gift tax laws in the context of the free movement of capital is essential, as this freedom extends to situations involving third countries, thereby encompassing inheritances and gifts with components located outside the EU. For instance, in *Welte* (C-181/12), both the deceased and the heir were residents of Switzerland, and the inherited assets included immovable property located in Germany. Similarly, in *BA* (C-670/21), both the deceased and the beneficiary were residents of Germany, whereas

16 Frans Sonneveldt, "Application of death taxes in the emigration and immigration countries," in *Inheritance and wealth tax aspects of emigration and immigration of individuals*, ed. IFA (The Hague, London, New York: Kluwer Law International, 2003), 8.

17 In most countries, taxes on *inter vivos* gifts are primarily seen as a mechanism to prevent the erosion of the inheritance tax base, rather than as a tool for raising revenue or redistributing wealth. See Wolfe D. Goodman, "General Report: International Double Taxation of Inheritances and Gifts," in *Cahiers de Droit Fiscal International* 70b (London: IBFD, 1985), 55.

18 EU, European Commission Staff Working Paper, "Non-discriminatory Inheritance Tax Systems: Principles Drawn from EU Case law", SEC 1488, 2011, p. 3.

19 Despite arguments from EU Member States to the contrary in efforts to exclude inheritance from the scope of the free movement of capital.

20 See, for instance, Case *Van Hilten* (C-513/03), par. 39, Case *Jäger* (C-256/06), par. 25, EU:C:2008:20 and Case *Welte* (C-181/12), par. 20, EU:C:2013:662.

the bequeathed property was located in Canada. In both cases, the German legislation was examined in the context of the free movement of capital.

Before moving to the next section, it is useful to note that the Court ruled in *Welte* that such personal capital movement could not be legitimized under the standstill provision of Article 64(1) TFEU as a "direct investment – including in real estate". The Court held that real estate investments of a "patrimonial" nature for private, non-economic purposes[21] do not fall within the scope of the standstill provision. Moreover, inheritances fall under heading XI, distinct from "direct investments" (I) and "investments in real estate" (II) in Annex I of the EU Directive 88/361.[22]

Finally, we observe that in *Geurts* and *Scheunemann*—cases involving inheritance of company shares—the Court assessed the Belgian[23] and German laws[24], respectively, under the freedom of establishment. Applying reasoning from *Baars* (C-251/98), the Court examined the objective of the legislations in question,[25] concluding that both sets of rules were meant to apply to control situations or those with definite influence. Notably, in all other cases, the Court did not seem to address the objective of the inheritance or gift laws. Instead, it focused on whether the elements of the inheritance or donation were confined within a single EU Member State (with[26] or without[27] reference to the EU Directive 88/361) to establish the application of the free movement of capital.

14.3.2 Restriction – difference in treatment

The Court consistently holds that EU Member State legislation granting inheritance or gift tax advantages (such as tax exemptions, favorable valuations, or reduced rates) based on either (a) the residence of the deceased or the heir, or (b) the location of inherited or donated assets, constitutes a restriction on the free movement of capital.[28] This restriction subjects cross-border inheritances or donations to potentially higher tax liabilities than domestic ones, diminishing their monetary value.[29] When an EU Member State levies taxes as the EU Member State of situs (i.e., as the "host State" with limited tax jurisdiction based on objective nexus), the foreign residence of the deceased or heir often prompts the difference in treatment.[30] Conversely, when an EU Member State taxes

21 Case *Welte* (C-181/12), par. 35, EU:C:2013:662.
22 *Idem*, par. 31.
23 And more specifically, the Flemish inheritance tax legislation in *Geurts* (C-464/05), EU:C:2007:631.
24 *Scheunemann* (C-31/11), EU:C:2012:481.
25 In *Geurts*, an inheritance tax exemption was granted to family companies, defined as those in which at least 50% of the share capital was held by the deceased, possibly together with close family members, during the three years preceding the death. This shareholding provided these individuals with influence over the company's decisions and allowed them to determine its activities (par. 13, EU:C:2007:631). In *Scheunemann*, the tax-free amount and reduced-rate valuation depended on a direct holding in the nominal capital, requiring a shareholding exceeding 25% by the testator or donor (paras. 25 and 27, EU:C:2012:481).
26 Case *Jäger* (C-256/06), par. 25, EU:C:2008:20.
27 Case *Feilen* (C-123/15), par. 16, EU:C:2016:496, and Case *XY* (C-394/20), par. 29, EU:C:2021:1044.
28 See Case *Feilen* (C-123/15), par. 19, EU:C:2016:496.
29 *Idem*.
30 See, for instance, Case *Welte* (C-181/12), EU:C:2013:662 and Case *XY* (C-394/20), EU:C:2021:1044.

as the EU Member State of personal nexus (i.e., as the "home State" with worldwide tax jurisdiction), it is typically the asset location that causes a difference in treatment.[31] In both scenarios, however, the Court considers that the mere reduction in the value of cross-border inheritances or donations, compared to domestic ones, is the decisive factor in determining a restriction on the free movement of capital.

Interestingly, in *Halley*, the Court found that inheritance tax law of Belgium, as the EU Member State of personal nexus, restricted the free movement of capital by imposing a ten-year valuation period on shares in companies with their management centre in another EU Member State, compared to a two-year period for companies based in Belgium. This extended period of uncertainty for heirs inheriting shares in foreign companies (regarding potential tax adjustments) was sufficient for the Court to deem Belgium's legislation restrictive on the free movement of capital.[32] Notably, however, a longer valuation period for foreign company shares does not necessarily result in a higher tax liability.

14.3.3 Objectively comparable situations

For a difference in treatment to be compatible with EU law, it must involve situations that are not objectively comparable or be justified by an overriding reason in the general interest. In addition, the national provision should not be more restrictive than necessary to achieve its purpose, as it must therefore also be proportionate.[33]

As regards objectively comparable situations, the EC stated in its 2011 Working Paper that '[a]s a starting point, it may be noted that while, as a rule, residents and non-residents may be treated differently in relation to direct taxes where this is warranted by a difference in circumstances, the Court has found in most of its rulings in inheritance tax cases that residents and non-residents should be treated equally.'[34] This has been affirmed in later Court decisions, though with one exception in the Q case.

Situations to be Compared

Typically, the comparability test in the Court's case law on inheritance and gift taxes is based on comparing the cross-border inheritance or donation in question with a hypothetical inheritance or donation. This hypothetical inheritance or donation may either be a domestic one or another cross-border situation involving some domestic elements. In this hypothetical situation, the element that created the difference in treatment is notionally transferred to the territory of the EU Member State whose legislation gives rise to a difference in treatment. This element could be the property location (leadings

31 See, for instance, Case *Q (Bean House)* (C-133/13, EU:C:2014:2255) and Case *Huijbrechts* (C-679/17), EU:C:2018:940.

32 Case *Halley and others* (C-132/10), par. 24, EU:C:2011:586.

33 EU, European Commission Staff Working Paper, "Non-discriminatory Inheritance Tax Systems: Principles Drawn from EU Case law", SEC 1488, 2011, p. 4.

34 *Idem.*

to a comparison *ratio materiae*) or the residence of the deceased or the heirs (leading to comparison *ratio personae*), or both.[35]

For instance, in *Jäger*, the location of agricultural and forestry *land* caused a difference in treatment under German inheritance tax laws (with Germany as the EU Member State of personal nexus). To perform its comparability test, the Court notionally "moved" the land from France to Germany to create a hypothetical domestic situation (comparison *ratio materiae*).[36] Similarly, in *Eckelkamp*, the residence of the deceased created a difference in treatment under Belgian inheritance tax law (with Belgium as the EU Member State of objective nexus). Here, the Court compared the cross-border scenario (domestic property and non-resident deceased) to a hypothetical domestic scenario (domestic property and resident deceased) by "moving" the deceased's residence from Germany to Belgium, a comparison based on *ratio personae*.[37] In *Missionswerk Werner*, where Belgium was the EU Member State of personal nexus, the Court used a comparison *ratio personae* based on the heir's residence by "moving" the non-profit's residence from Germany to Belgium, comparing a cross-border scenario (a Belgian resident donating to a German non-profit) to a hypothetical domestic one (a Belgian resident donating to a Belgian non-profit).[38] Lastly, in cases such as *Mattner*,[39] *Welte*,[40] *Hünnebeck*,[41] *Feilen*,[42] and *XY*,[43] the Court performed a *ratio personae* comparison based on the residence of both the deceased and the heirs. This is because Germany asserts worldwide inheritance tax jurisdiction based on either the deceased's or the heir's residence. Accordingly, the Court compared the scenario of a non-resident beneficiary with limited tax liability in Germany to two alternative scenarios: (a) a non-resident beneficiary inheriting from a resident and (b) a resident inheriting from a non-resident, both of whom have worldwide tax liability in Germany.

Criteria for Comparison

To determine whether a difference in treatment involves objectively comparable situations, the Court frequently examines the object and purpose of the national provisions in question. However, in several cases, the Court has also employed a subject-to-tax criterion alongside the rules governing tax liability and the calculation of inheritance or gift taxes.[44] This subject-to-tax criterion appears, in our view, to be distinct from the object and purpose of national provisions typically considered by the Court when assessing the objectives of national legislation, thereby warranting independent analysis.

---

35 See also J.K. Szczepański, Foreign-Located Immovable Property Protected against Discriminatory Taxation of Cross-Border Inheritance: Comments on the Huijbrechts Decision (Case C-679/17), 59 Eur. Taxn. 7 (2019), Journal Articles & Opinion Pieces IBFD, par. 4.1.

36 Case *Jäger* (C-256/06), par. 44, EU:C:2008:20.

37 Case *Eckelkamp* (C-11/07), par. 58, EU:C:2008:489.

38 Case *Missionswerk Werner Heukelbach* (C-25/10), paras. 33-34, EU:C:2011:65.

39 Case *Mattner* (C-510/08), par. 38, EU:C:2010:216.

40 Case *Welte* (C-181/12), par. 51, EU:C:2013:662.

41 Case *Hünnebeck* (C-479/14), par. 53, EU:C:2016:412.

42 Case *Feilen* (C-123/15), par. 27, EU:C:2016:496.

43 Case *XY* (C-394/20), par. 39, EU:C:2021:1044.

44 See also V.I. Dafnomilis, A Comprehensive Analysis of ECJ Case Law on Discriminatory Treatment of Cross-Border Inheritances – Part 1, 55 Eur. Taxn. 11 (2015), Journal Articles & Opinion Pieces IBFD, par. 6.3.2.

Objective Pursued by National Legislation
The comparability test primarily relies on the objective of the national provision that creates a difference in treatment. The application of this test is evident in cases involving objective tax exemptions, such as in Q and *Huijbrechts*. In Q, the Court found that the cross-border donation of foreign property with historic buildings was not comparable to a hypothetical domestic situation involving domestic property with historic buildings (a Dutch "*landgoed*"), as the Dutch legislation was designed to protect the Netherlands' cultural and historical heritage.[45] Conversely, in *Huijbrechts*, where the Belgian (Flemish) legislation pursued an environmental aim, the Court considered that the cross-border scenario at hand (a sustainably managed foreign forest) was objectively comparable to the hypothetical domestic scenario (a sustainably managed domestic forest in the Flemish region of Belgium).[46] Therefore, the Court ruled in *Huijbrechts* that an heir inheriting a sustainably managed forest area located in an EU Member State bordering the Flemish region was in an objectively comparable situation with an heir inheriting a sustainably managed forest area located in the Flemish region of Belgium.

Subject-to-Tax Criterion in Conjunction with Tax Liability Determination
The subject-to-tax criterion has been widely applied by the Court in cases involving subjective tax exemptions.[47, 48] In *Mattner*, for instance, the Court ruled that the cross-border situation (domestic property, non-resident deceased, and non-resident heir) was comparable to a hypothetical cross-border situation with (i) domestic property, resident deceased, and non-resident heir, and (ii) domestic property, non-resident deceased, and resident heir. The Court deemed them comparable because, in all cases, the heirs were taxable persons in Germany. According to the Court,

> "[...] the amount of the tax on gifts of immovable property in Germany is calculated pursuant to the [German inheritance and gift legislation] on the basis both of the value of the property and of the family relationship, if any, between the donor and the donee. Neither of those criteria depends on the place of residence of the donor or the donee."[49]

This reasoning has been reaffirmed consistently in *Welte*, *Hünnebeck*, *Commission v Germany*, and, more recently, in *XY*. The subject-to-tax criterion has also been employed in cases other than those dealing with subjective tax exemptions, such as *Feilen*, *Jäger*,[50] *Eckelkamp*,[51] *Arens-Sikken*,[52] *Commission vs Greece* (C-244/15), and *Commission vs Greece*

45 Case Q *(Bean House)* (C-133/13), par. 27 EU:C:2014:2255.
46 Case *Huijbrechts* (C-679/17), par. 28, EU:C:2018:940.
47 The subject to tax criterion is what Szczepański calls "features of tax liability". See Foreign-Located Immovable Property Protected against Discriminatory Taxation of Cross-Border Inheritance: Comments on the Huijbrechts Decision (Case C-679/17), 59 Eur. Taxn. 7 (2019), Journal Articles & Opinion Pieces IBFD, par. 4.2.2.
48 A subject to tax criterion, however, is not new in Court case law. See for instance, Case *Timac Agro* (C-388/14).
49 Case *Mattner* (C-510/08), par. 36 EU:C:2010:216. See also Case Welte (C-181/12), par. 49, EU:C:2013:662.
50 Case *Jäger* (C-256/06), par. 44, EU:C:2008:20.
51 Case *Eckelkamp* (C-11/07), par. 63, EU:C:2008:489.
52 Case *Arens-Sikken* (C-43/07), par. 57, EU:C:2008:490.

(C-98/16). However, the use of the subject-to-tax criterion is not entirely new, as it has also been applied in cases involving corporate taxes. See also chapter 9.

The subject-to-tax criterion should, in our view, be applied cautiously in inheritance and gift tax cases, and in any case, not when, following the assessment of the objective of the national provision, the situations are not objectively comparable. For example, had the Court applied the subject-to-tax criterion in case *Q*, it might have concluded that an heir in the Netherlands inheriting foreign property with historic buildings was comparable to an heir inheriting a Dutch *landgoed*. In both cases, the heirs would be taxable persons for gift tax purposes in the Netherlands, with their tax liability determined under the same rules. However, in *Q*, it was the objective of the Dutch legislation that made these situations objectively incomparable.

This means that the assessment of the objective shall take precedence over the subject-to-tax criterion (despite the fact that, in some cases, the Court does not even examine the objective of the legislative provision in question). While this may be more evident in cases involving objective tax exemptions, it should be the starting point in all EU inheritance and gift tax cases.

14.3.4 Justifications

Once the Court determines that a national provision imposes a restriction on an EU freedom in an objectively comparable situation, it examines the justifications put forward by the EU Member States to defend the difference in treatment. In the context of inheritance and gift taxation within the EU, the most commonly invoked justifications are the coherence of the tax system and the effectiveness of fiscal supervision.

In most cases reviewed, except for *Feilen* and *XY*, the Court rejected the coherence justification. This was because the EU Member State at hand could not establish a direct link between the tax advantage granted and the corresponding tax that offsets this advantage, in the light of the objective of the relevant national provision. Conversely, in *Feilen*, the Court identified a direct link between the tax advantage—manifested as a reduction in inheritance tax—and the tax liability imposed on an *earlier* acquisition of the same estate. This reduction was specifically aimed at alleviating the tax burden in situations where multiple transfers of the same asset occurred within a ten-year period between individuals in tax class one, allowing for a reduction of up to 50% of the inheritance tax linked to that asset. Notably, the Court acknowledged this direct link despite the absence of the "same taxpayer", which is typically a prerequisite for establishing such a connection. This was rooted in the fact that the individual who had paid (or was expected to have paid) inheritance tax at the time of the earlier transfer (representing the tax disadvantage) was deceased, and thus the reduction in German inheritance tax (representing the tax advantage) was enjoyed by that individual's heir.[53]

53 Case *Feilen* (C-123/15), par. 36, EU:C:2016:496.

Furthermore, in *XY*, the Court appeared to recognize a direct link between the basic tax-free allowance (a tax advantage) granted under circumstances where Germany exercised worldwide tax jurisdiction and the scope of the tax jurisdiction asserted by Germany (which seemed to have been viewed by the Court as a tax disadvantage).[54] Specifically, in *XY*, a beneficiary with unlimited tax liability in Germany, identified as the EU Member State of personal nexus, qualifies for the basic allowance, as the taxable base in such cases is broader than for a beneficiary with limited liability in Germany (who receives a pro-rata allowance), in which case Germany is the state of the objective nexus.[55] Nevertheless, we observe that the basic allowance does not correspondingly offset a disadvantage in the form of a particular tax, as typically understood within the framework of coherence justification. The only viable interpretation of the Court's reasoning in relation to coherence justification may be to contextualize it within the justification of the balanced allocation of taxing powers and territoriality.

In the pending case *Familienstiftung*, the Court will again assess the coherence justification that Germany will present to justify the reduced taxation provided to German family foundations (C-142/24). The main argument will be that the more favourable taxation is offset in a domestic situation by the imposition of a substitute inheritance tax on the German foundation. On the contrary, Germany has no jurisdiction to apply a substitute inheritance tax to foundations registered abroad. In this context, the referring German court has raised doubts as to whether the German legislation establishes a direct, personal, and material link between the more favourable taxation and the substitute inheritance tax, as required by Court to assume coherence.

Regarding the justification of the effectiveness of fiscal supervision, the Court has consistently rejected this rationale in all pertinent cases, including *Geurts, Halley,* and *Welte*. Given the applicability of the EU Directive on Administrative Cooperation (2011/16/EU) to inheritance and gift taxes,[56] this justification appears nowadays insufficient to legitimize restrictive inheritance and gift tax legislation, at least in EU situations.[57] See chapter 29.

14.3.5 *Proportionality*

In most inheritance and gift tax cases, national restrictive provisions could not be justified by an overriding reason in the public interest, eliminating the need for the Court to assess their proportionality. However, in the *BA* case (C-670/21), the Court examined the proportionality of a German inheritance tax rule which allowed a tax reduction for inherited rental properties located in Germany, the EU, or the EEA but excluded properties in third countries. As a result, Mr. A's beneficiary faced a higher tax liability for inheriting a property in Canada than if the property had been within the EU or EEA. Germany justified this rule as a means to ease the financial burden on heirs who might otherwise

54 Case *XY* (C-394/20), par. 50, EU:C:2021:1044.
55 *Idem*, par. 49.
56 See Article 2, par. 1 and 2 of the Directive.
57 See also V.I. Dafnomilis, A Comprehensive Analysis of ECJ Case Law on Discriminatory Treatment of Cross-Border Inheritances – Part 2, 55 Eur. Taxn. 12 (2015), Journal Articles & Opinion Pieces IBFD, par. 9.1.

be forced to sell rental properties to meet their tax obligations, a problem institutional investors do not face as they are not subject to inheritance tax. The Court acknowledged that promoting affordable rented accommodation within the EU and EEA could be an overriding reason in the public interest, potentially justifying a restriction on the free movement of capital. However, it found that the German rule to be inconsistent with this objective, as it applied uniformly (regardless of whether the area was urban or rural)and to all types of properties (from the most basic to the most luxurious). As a result, the Court ruled the rule disproportionate and incompatible with EU law.[58] See also section 14.4.4.

14.4 Elements of inheritance and gift tax legislation that can be contrary to EU law

14.4.1 Subjective tax exemptions

Subjective tax exemptions are tax-free allowances or deductions granted to certain beneficiaries or donees due to their kinship with the deceased or the donor. The amount of such exemptions often depends on the proximity of kinship between the parties involved. For instance, children of the deceased are typically entitled to a greater amount of a subjective tax exemption than siblings. The windfall justification, rooted in the protection of family property, primarily justifies the granting of these exemptions.

In the context of EU law, tensions can arise when an EU Member State's inheritance or gift tax legislation grants a higher subjective tax exemption under worldwide tax jurisdiction (as the state of personal nexus) than under limited tax jurisdiction (as the state of situs). The Court has addressed the compatibility of such legislation with EU law in cases including *Mattner*, *Welte*, *Hünnebeck*, and *XY*.

Following *Mattner* and *Welte*, it was established that the EU Member State of situs cannot apply a lower *fixed* subjective tax exemption (as a tax-free allowance) for purposes of gift and inheritance tax than it would if it were the EU Member State of personal nexus, in which case it provides a higher basic tax-free allowance.. In both judgments, the Court held that a beneficiary with limited tax liability in the EU Member State of situs is objectively comparable to one with unlimited liability, as both are subject to the same rules for gift or inheritance tax, which hinge on the value of the transferred property and the kinship degree between the parties (a *ratio materiae* comparison and a "subject to tax" criterion). The Court rejected justifications based on the coherence of the tax system (*Mattner*, *Welte*), avoidance of double tax benefits (*Mattner*), prevention of tax avoidance (*Mattner*), and effectiveness of fiscal supervision (*Mattner*). Notably, the Court found no

58 See also Dafnomilis, BA (C-670/21). *EU law precludes German rules on calculation of inheritance tax on property in a third country*, Highlights & Insights on European Taxation no. 2 (2024).

direct link between the higher basic tax-free allowance granted to beneficiaries with unlimited liability and any offsetting tax levy applied in Germany.[59]

Germany resisted, finding it hard to "believe" it should grant the basic tax-free allowance in cases where it had only limited tax jurisdiction. This led to *Hünnebeck*, where the Court ruled that offering non-resident beneficiaries the option to be taxed as residents to benefit from the higher basic tax-free allowance did not remedy the discriminatory effects of German gift tax legislation, which, as a baseline, continued to deny non-resident beneficiaries with limited tax liability the subjective tax exemptions granted to residents.[60]

Germany continued to resist, believing that persistence might eventually succeed. The *XY* case represents Germany's latest attempt to interpret *Welte* without automatically granting non-resident beneficiaries with limited tax liability in Germany the fixed high basic tax-free allowance. Following *Hünnebeck*, German inheritance and gift tax laws were revised so that the basic tax allowance (in this case, €400,000) would apply *pro rata*. The pro-rata allowance reflects the proportion of domestic assets subject to limited tax liability in Germany relative to the total assets inherited or received as a gift. Consequently, if a non-resident beneficiary inherits property located solely in Germany, they receive the full basic allowance. However, if the inheritance includes assets in Germany and elsewhere, the allowance is reduced according to the ratio of non-German property to the total worldwide property.

In *XY*, a non-resident beneficiary, an Austrian resident and national, inherited immovable property in Germany from a non-resident deceased. Germany, holding limited jurisdiction over the German property, applied the basic allowance pro-rata: since the German property constituted 43% of the total inheritance, the beneficiary received €172,000 (i.e., €400,000 x 43%) as a tax-free allowance. The case raised the question of whether this proportionate allowance aligned with EU law in light of *Welte*.

The Court found that German inheritance tax legislation restricts the free movement of capital by imposing a higher tax burden on inheritances between non-residents compared to those involving at least one resident, thereby diminishing the estate's value. The Court also determined that a non-resident beneficiary inheriting from a non-resident deceased

59 What is also important to note is that in *Welte*, the Court rejected the application of the Schumacker doctrine in the context of EU inheritance taxation. The starting point of this doctrine is the State of residence, which is, in principle, required to assess the taxpayer's overall ability to pay and to grant tax-free allowances, if necessary, in view of their personal situation. See also chapter 13. The Belgian and German Governments argued that a similar approach should apply to EU inheritance and gift taxation, asserting that it should be the state with the personal nexus of the deceased that provides the subjective tax exemptions to the beneficiaries. However, the Court dismissed this argument, reasoning that a beneficiary with limited tax liability in the EU Member State of situs is objectively comparable to one with unlimited liability, irrespective of the proportion of inherited property located in the EU Member State of source relative to the total inherited property. See V. Dafnomilis, Taxation of cross-border inheritances and donations: suggestions for improvement. Deventer: Wolters Kluwer, 2021, section 7.3.3.1., p. 183-184.

60 See also M. Weiss, The Influence of ECJ Case Law on the German Inheritance and Gift Tax Act, 56 Eur. Taxn. 10 (2016), Journal Articles & Opinion Pieces IBFD, par. 3.1.

(with Germany exercising limited tax jurisdiction) is objectively comparable to cases where either the beneficiary or the deceased is a resident (with Germany exercising worldwide tax jurisdiction). In all these cases, the inheritance tax liability is based on the size of the estate and the kinship between beneficiary and deceased, regardless of the beneficiary's residence.[61] Furthermore, a beneficiary with unlimited liability in Germany is objectively comparable to a beneficiary with limited liability in Germany, as they are both taxable persons there.[62] This approach aligns with the Court's comparability analysis in *Mattner*, *Welte*, and *Hünnebeck* (comparison *ratio materiae*, subject to tax criterium).

Nevertheless, the Court considered that the restriction posed by a proportionate tax allowance could be justified by the need to ensure coherence within the German tax system. More specifically, it recognized a direct link between the basic allowance (a tax advantage) and the extent of tax jurisdiction exercised in relation to the enrichment the heir gains from the inheritance (a tax disadvantage).[63] In other words, a beneficiary with unlimited tax liability in Germany is entitled to the basic allowance because the taxable base in such cases is broader than for a beneficiary with limited liability. According to the Court, this direct link is suitable for achieving the legislative objective. Firstly, for an inheritance of equal overall value, the allowance represents a proportional share of the estate subject to taxation, regardless of whether unlimited or limited tax liability applies.[64] Secondly, if the immovable property taxed by Germany constitutes the entire estate, the heir with limited liability, like an heir with unlimited liability, can fully benefit from the allowance based on their family relationship with the deceased.[65] Consequently, the Court found that German legislation aligns with EU law on this point.

Although the Court's judgment may seem reasonable, the coherence justification raises questions. The Court appeared to find it sufficient that a tax advantage (i.e., the basic allowance of €400,000) is counterbalanced by a tax disadvantage in the form of a broader taxable base when Germany exercises worldwide tax jurisdiction. However, a broader taxable base does not necessarily imply a "specific tax" (considered a disadvantage that offsets the advantage, a requirement for coherence justification). Additionally, as the Court noted, "the amount of the allowance on the taxable value [...] does not vary according to the amount of the taxable value within German tax jurisdiction."[66] Thus, in cases where Germany exercises worldwide tax jurisdiction, the basic allowance is not directly tied to any specific taxable value; it remains a lump sum of €400,000, regardless of the extent of German tax jurisdiction. Consequently, someone could argue that there is no direct link between that allowance and any specific tax levy.

---

61 Case *XY* (C-394/20), par. 38, EU:C:2021:1044.
62 *Idem*. 42.
63 *Idem*, par. 50.
64 *Idem*, par. 51.
65 *Idem*, par. 53.
66 *Idem*, par. 41.

The only way to interpret the Court's reasoning on coherence justification may be through the lens of balanced allocation of taxing powers and the principle of territoriality.[67] See also section 7.8.1. Advocate General J. Richard de la Tour argued that Germany has demonstrated that the difference in treatment was necessary for Germany to safeguard its power of taxation and is proportionate to the objective pursued in so far as it takes account of the difference in the tax base.[68] Additionally, German laws appear proportionate to prevent double non-taxation of inherited property,[69] which might occur if the non-resident beneficiary were to receive the full subjective tax exemptions across multiple EU Member States.

14.4.2 Objective tax exemptions

As noted in Section 14.2, inheritance and gift tax laws provide certain objective tax exemptions, which are varied and rooted in policy objectives related to social, environmental, cultural, and historical concerns. These exemptions are often territorial, extending beyond cases where there is a kinship between the deceased and beneficiaries.

Under EU law, tensions may arise when an EU Member State serving as the personal nexus does not extend an objective tax exemption if the inheritance or donation includes foreign assets, whereas the exemption would apply if only domestic assets were involved. The underlying purpose of a given objective tax exemption is central to determining whether its denial in a cross-border inheritance or donation context aligns with EU law.

The Q Case: Cultural/Historical Background of Objective Tax Exemptions
In Q, the Netherlands applied preferential tax treatment to estates classified as "landgoeden", typical of the Dutch landscape and protected under Dutch nature conservation laws. This legislation allowed for a reduction (or even zero valuation) of the estate's value for tax purposes, based on specific qualifying characteristics. However, only estates situated in the Netherlands could qualify as "landgoeden". Consequently, Q, a Dutch resident, could not apply this preferential treatment to the Bean House, a historic property listed under UK conservation laws.

The Court found that Dutch legislation restricted the free movement of capital, observing that donations of property located outside the Netherlands incurred a higher tax burden than domestic properties qualifying as "landgoeden". Referring to *Jäger*, the Court concluded that this differential treatment could be justified if the situations were not objectively comparable or if there were an overriding reason in the public interest. According to the Court, the Dutch law's objective of preserving cultural and historical heritage rendered domestic donations of "landgoeden" not objectively comparable to foreign properties with historic significance.[70] However, the Court, referencing *X* (C-87/12), noted that if a

67 See also, Dafnomilis, *XY. Inheritance tax. EU law precludes non-deductibility of debt arising from reserved portions in case of limited tax liability*. Highlights & Insights on European Taxation no. 15 (2022).
68 AG's Opinion in *XY* (C-394/20), par. 86, EU:C:2021:749.
69 AG's Opinion in *XY* (C-394/20), par. 86, EU:C:2021:749.
70 Case Q *(Bean House)* (C-133/13), paras. 24 and 27, EU:C:2014:2255.

foreign estate formed part of Dutch heritage and met the criteria for protection under Dutch nature conservation laws, then domestic and cross-border donations would indeed be objectively comparable. This could apply, for example, to estates in Belgium, Germany, or even Greece, provided they form part of Dutch cultural and historical heritage.

Commission v Greece (C-244/15): Social Background of Objective Tax Exemptions
In *Commission v Greece*, Greece offered an inheritance tax exemption for primary residences inherited by Greek nationals and nationals of other EU Member States who were permanent residents of Greece. However, if the recipient was not a Greek tax resident – such as the author – they were ineligible for the exemption. The purpose of the exemption was to address housing needs by allowing family members to inherit the family home with tax relief. Eligibility was contingent on the beneficiaries' connection to Greek society and their level of integration within it.

The Court ruled that Greek legislation restricted the free movement of capital by reducing the estate's value for heirs who fulfilled all conditions except permanent residence in Greece.[71] Furthermore, the Court held that Greek nationals and EU citizens residing in Greece were objectively comparable to non-residents, as they were subject to identical inheritance tax rules when the property was located in Greece (*comparison ratio personae*, subject to tax criterium). Greece's justification that the tax relief was based on a social aim was rejected, as the exemption did not require the heir to establish the inherited property as his primary residence or to occupy the property at all.[72] Additionally, the Court found the residency requirement overly restrictive, noting that a non-resident could still have close ties to Greek society and may intend to use the property as a primary residence.[73]

Huijbrechts: Environmental Background of Objective Tax Exemptions
In *Huijbrechts*, Belgium provided an inheritance tax exemption for forest areas managed sustainably under national law, but only for forests within Flanders. Mr. Huijbrechts questioned the compatibility of this exemption with EU law after Belgian authorities denied him an inheritance tax exemption for a sustainably managed forest located in the Netherlands, which he inherited from a Belgian-resident testator.

The Court concluded that the Belgian rule restricted the free movement of capital and the restriction concerned situations that were objectively comparable in light of the objective pursued (comparison *ratio materiae* and objective pursued). The environmental goal of Belgium's legislation was not considered by the Court to be limited to national territory, as effective sustainable forest management involves cross-border environmental responsibilities for EU Member States.[74]

In response to Belgium's argument that verifying sustainable management of foreign forests was difficult (for fiscal supervision purposes), the Court ruled that Belgian authorities could use mutual assistance with the authorities of other EU Member States to verify that

71 Case *Commission vs Greece* (C-244/15), par. 32, EU:C:2016:359.
72 *Idem*, par. 40.
73 *Idem*, par. 41.
74 Case *Huijbrechts* (C-679/17), par. 35, EU:C:2018:940.

foreign forests met comparable sustainability standards.[75] In our view, the comparison should not take place on a one-by-one basis as this would lead to a *de facto* exclusion of forest areas that are sustainably managed abroad.

Comparing Q and Huijbrechts
Huijbrechts shares similarities with the Q case, as in both instances, the EU Member State acting as the personal nexus (Belgium and the Netherlands, respectively) offered tax advantages exclusively to domestic inheritances and donations. While the Court found that both the Dutch and Belgian rules restricted the free movement of capital, the distinct objectives behind each rule led to different conclusions on objective comparability. In *Huijbrechts*, the Court concluded that environmental protection was a cross-border, intra-EU concern, rendering domestic and cross-border inheritances objectively comparable. Conversely, in Q, the Court held that the goal of preserving Dutch cultural and historical heritage made domestic and cross-border donations incomparable. Thus, in cases involving objective tax exemptions, the specific purpose of the exemption is crucial in determining comparability, even if the subject-to-tax criterion may indicate that these situations are objectively comparable.

14.4.3 Deductions of liabilities/debts

According to the EC's Working Paper, EU Member States' inheritance tax laws may not align with EU law when they restrict the deductibility of debts and liabilities tied to assets inherited by a non-resident heir but do not impose similar restrictions on assets inherited by resident heirs.[76] Four cases – *Barbier*, *Eckelkamp*, *Arens-Sikken*, and *XY* – shaped the Court's position on such restrictions, finding in each case an unjustified restriction on the free movement of capital.

Before discussing these cases, a general observation is necessary: when an EU Member State of situs denies the deduction of liabilities or debts, a direct link between the debt and the taxable property is typically required to establish a restriction. In *Eckelkamp* and *Arens-Sikken*, the Court referenced case law on income-related deductions, which are consistently deductible in the EU Member State of source due to their direct connection with income-generating activities.[77] In *Eckelkamp*, the Court ruled that the Belgian court should examine the nature of the mortgage mandate and its connection to the inherited Belgian property.[78] Conversely, in *Arens-Sikken*, the Court concluded that assessing a direct link was unnecessary; the debt in question, an overendowment, was associated with the property simply because it arose from inheritance. Importantly, it was not the debt itself that led to a difference in treatment but rather its apportionment: in cross-border cases, the debt was not apportioned between the family members, resulting in a higher taxable

75 *Idem*, par. 40.
76 EU, European Commission Staff Working Paper, "Non-discriminatory Inheritance Tax Systems: Principles Drawn from EU Case law", SEC 1488, 2011, p. 11.
77 Case *Eckelkamp* (C-11/07), par. 50, EU:C:2008:489 and Case *Arens-Sikken* (C-43/07), par. 44, EU:C:2008:490.
78 Case *Eckelkamp* (C-11/07), par. 61, EU:C:2008:489.

base, whereas in domestic cases, apportionment led to a lower taxable base.[79] Thus, in *Arens-Sikken*, the difference in treatment stemmed from the debt's apportionment.

A similar reasoning was applied in *XY*. The Court found that liabilities under the reserved portions were linked, at least partially, to the inherited immovable property in Germany (the Member State of situs), over which Germany exercised limited tax jurisdiction, regardless of classification under German law.[80] The Court thus recognized a direct link between the reserved portions and the taxable immovable property in Germany. However, we argue that a case-by-case analysis is crucial to properly assess the direct link between liabilities, debts, and taxable property—an assessment that the national referring court should undertake where relevant.

Barbier: Deduction of the Obligation to Transfer Legal Title

The first inheritance tax case. *Barbier*, involved a Dutch national who had moved to Belgium while maintaining legal ownership of properties in the Netherlands and transferring their financial/economic ownership to private Dutch companies he controlled. This arrangement was intended to avoid a 6% Dutch real estate transfer tax in the Netherlands. In addition, he undertook the obligation to transfer the legal title to those properties and waived any rights relating to them in the meantime. Upon Mr. Barbier's death, inheritance tax was due. However, as Mr. Barbier was not a Dutch resident, his obligation to transfer legal title was not deductible. Had he been a resident, this obligation would have been deductible, thus eliminating the inheritance tax liability for his heirs.

The Court held that restricting the deduction of the obligation to transfer legal title to cases where the deceased was a resident was incompatible with the free movement of capital. Furthermore, the restriction imposed by Dutch legislation could not be justified by Mr. Barbier's tax benefit from avoiding the registration duty in the Netherlands as a result of the transfer of the financial and economic ownership of the property. As per the Court, "[...] a Community national cannot be deprived of the right to rely on the provisions of the Treaty on the ground that he is profiting from tax advantages which are legally provided by the rules in force in a Member State other than his State of residence."[81]

Eckelkamp: Deduction of Mortgage Debt

In *Eckelkamp*, the Flemish Code of Succession Duties denied the deduction of a mortgage debt secured on immovable property subject to inheritance tax when the testator was residing abroad, like Ms. Eckelkamp at the time of her death. Had she been a resident of Belgium, this mortgage debt would have been deductible, thus reducing the value of the immovable property subject to inheritance tax.

The Court held that denying the deduction constituted a restriction on the free movement of capital. This restriction could not be justified, as resident and non-resident heirs were deemed objectively comparable, with no overriding public interest justifying the difference

79 Case *Arens-Sikken* (C-43/07), par. 46, EU:C:2008:490.
80 Case *XY* (C-394/20), par. 64, EU:C:2021:1044.
81 Case *Barbier* (C-364/01), par. 71, EU:C:2003:665.

in treatment. First, the Court determined that under Belgian legislation, non-resident and resident heirs are objectively comparable. Belgium, as the EU Member State of situs, treats both groups similarly in terms of tax liability, linking it directly to the value of the immovable property, except for debt deductions (comparison *ratio personae*, subject to tax criterion). Second, the justification of avoiding double deduction was dismissed: the potential deductibility of the mortgage debt in Germany (the deceased's country of residence) could not prevent Ms. Eckelkamp's heirs from claiming the deduction in Belgium. Furthermore, Belgium, in the absence of an inheritance and gift tax treaty with Germany, could not rely on a credit by Germany that could rectify the discriminatory Belgian inheritance tax. By this way, the Court applied the concept of neutralization of discriminatory taxation (that has initially applied to cases involving income taxes such as *Amurta*), also to cases involving inheritance taxes. See also section 6.5.4 in this respect.

Arens-Sikken: Deduction of Overendowment Debt
An overendowment debt refers to a financial obligation arising from an unequal distribution of inheritance. When a deceased parent leaves the family estate, part of the estate is distributed to one heir (often a surviving spouse) with a larger share than others. This created a "debt" or financial obligation to the other heirs, known as an overendowment debt, which had to be repaid or adjusted in favor of the less-endowed heirs.[82] In *Arens-Sikken*, the Netherlands, acting as the EU Member State of situs, denied the deduction of an overendowment debt on property in the Netherlands inherited by the widow of Mr. Arens-Sikken, an Italian resident. Consequently, Mrs. Arens-Sikken paid inheritance tax on the full value of the inherited property in the Netherlands. Had Mr. Arens-Sikken been a resident of the Netherlands, the overendowment debt would have been factored into the inheritance tax base.

Arens-Sikken shares such strong similarities with *Eckelkamp* and both cases were decided on the same day, a decision that was no coincidence. As in *Eckelkamp*, the Court ruled in *Arens-Sikken* that Dutch legislation restricting the deduction of overendowment debts restricted the free movement of capital. This differential treatment between resident and non-resident deceased persons could lead to a higher tax burden on cross-border inheritances due to the progressive tax rates determined based on the size of the inherited property. The Court deemed the situations objectively comparable, applying the comparison *ratio personae* and the subject-to-tax criterion. Moreover, the Netherlands could not justify denying the deduction based on the potential deductibility of the overendowment debt in Italy, the deceased's country of residence. First, there was no inheritance tax treaty between the Netherlands and Italy to determine in which state the debt will be deductible. More importantly, the Court ruled that an EU Member State cannot evade its EU law obligations by relying on advantages granted by other EU Member States.

82 Under Dutch inheritance tax laws, the testamentary parental partition *inter vivos* provided that all assets and liabilities of the estate were transferred to Mrs. Arens-Sikken. Consequently, she received assets and liabilities that exceeded the value of her legal share of the estate and was required to pay her children the value of their inheritance share in cash (overendowment debt).

XY: Deduction of Liabilities Under Reserved Portions
Reserved portions in inheritance law refer to the legally protected shares of an estate that certain close family members (typically spouses, children, or parents) are entitled to receive, regardless of the deceased's wishes in a will. This concept, often rooted in civil law traditions, aims to prevent disinheritance of close relatives and to provide them with financial security. In *XY*, Germany, as the EU Member State of situs, denied the deduction of liabilities related to the reserved portions, claiming no economic link between these portions and the inherited German assets. XY, an Austrian national and resident, was the sole heir of her Austrian father, who designated XY as the sole heir while entitling his wife and son to reserved portions. The inherited assets included German property representing 43% of the total inheritance. XY sought to deduct 43% of the liabilities under the reserved portions from the value of the German estate, which was subject to inheritance tax. However, the German tax authorities rejected this deduction. Conversely, had Germany applied worldwide tax jurisdiction (in the case of a resident testator or heir), the liabilities under the reserved portions would have been fully deductible. The Court ruled, consistent with its previous case law on deductions, that Germany's denial of the deduction of liabilities under the reserved portions violated the free movement of capital.[83]

14.4.4 Valuation rules

According to the European Commission's Working Paper, EU Member States' inheritance tax provisions are in breach of the provisions on free movement of capital if they provide for different tax treatment for assets that are part of the inheritance, depending on whether these assets have a given link to the national territory, notably whether they are located there. .[84] The cases of *Jäger* and *Halley* illustrate this principle, as the valuation rules of Germany and Belgium, respectively, were found incompatible with EU law within an intra-EU context. The *BA* case further explores the compatibility of valuation rules under EU law in a third-country context.

Jäger: Favorable Valuation Rules for Domestic Assets
In *Jäger*, Germany, as the EU Member State of the personal nexus, applied a preferential valuation method to domestic agricultural and forestry land, typically valuing it at only 10% of its market value. Additionally, some cases received a special tax-free allowance, and the remaining value was taxed at 60%. However, these valuation rules did not apply to foreign agricultural and forestry land, such as the land inherited by Mr. Jäger, which was located in France. Consequently, Mr. Jäger incurred a higher inheritance tax liability than he would have had the property been located in Germany.

---

83 Paternotte and the Netherlands Advocate General Wattel have already proposed that the EU Member State with the objective nexus should provide a proportionate tax-free allowance or exemption when taxing cross-border inheritances and donations. See Rens Paternotte, "Welte, German Inheritance Tax: Different Treatment of Residents and Non-Residents Violates Free Movement of Capital," *Highlights & Insights on European Taxation* no. 1 (2014): 33-34; Opinion of Netherlands AG Wattel in 14/00521 (Netherlands Supreme Court, NL:PHR:2014:585).

84 EU, European Commission Staff Working Paper, "Non-discriminatory Inheritance Tax Systems: Principles Drawn from EU Case law", SEC 1488, 2011, p. 10.

The Court held that limiting the favorable valuation method to domestic land constituted a restriction on the free movement of capital. The timing of the property's acquisition, even if it occurred before 1 June 1990 (the deadline for implementing EU Directive 88/361/EEC), was deemed irrelevant to the case.[85] The Court also considered the cross-border and domestic inheritance to be objectively comparable and that there was no justification in the public interest justifying the difference in treatment. More specifically, the Court noted that Germany, as the State of the personal nexus, applied uniform rules to domestic and cross-border inheritances, except for the special valuation method, which was exclusive to domestic assets (comparison *ratio materiae*, subject to tax criterion). This finding sufficed for the Court to deem Mr Jäger objectively comparable to any other beneficiary whose inheritance consists only of agricultural land and forestry situated in Germany. Furthermore, regarding the justification grounds presented by Germany, the Court found that Germany's social objectives, such as supporting agriculture and forestry, preserving jobs, and addressing administrative challenges with foreign assets, were insufficient to justify the restriction on the free movement of capital.

Halley: Extended Valuation Period for Foreign Shares

In *Halley*, Belgium, as the EU Member State of the personal nexus, enforced a ten-year limitation period for imposing additional inheritance tax on foreign assets, compared to a two-year period for domestic assets. This limitation period began with the filing of the inheritance tax return, during which authorities could reassess the declared value of shares. The issue was whether applying the longer limitation period to registered shares held in companies based in another EU Member State (specifically, France in *Halley*) aligned with the free movement of capital and freedom of establishment.

The Court found that the Belgian provision restricted the free movement of capital, as it subjected taxpayers to a prolonged period of uncertainty regarding potential tax adjustments. Belgium put forward two justifications: ensuring the effectiveness of fiscal supervision and preventing tax evasion. However, referring to *X* and *Passenheim-van Schoot*, the Court held that the extended period for shares *already declared* in the inheritance tax return was disproportionate, as it was not based on the time necessary for recourse to mutual assistance or other investigative measures. Although the previous Mutual Assistance Directive (EU Directive 77/799/EEC) did not cover inheritance taxes, Belgium could have sought assistance under its inheritance and gift tax treaty with France to ascertain the value of shares. This approach is similar to the Court's reasoning in income tax cases, where it considers treaty-based information exchange to be as effective as EU Directive mechanisms.[86]

In our view, *Halley* implies that EU Member States may apply a longer limitation period for valuing foreign assets compared to domestic assets, provided this period corresponds to the time genuinely needed for tax authorities to use mutual assistance or other methods to verify asset values.

85 Case *Jäger* (C-256/06), paras. 29 and 33, EU:C:2008:20.
86 See, for instance, Case *Emerging Markets* (C-190/12), EU:C:2014:249. See also section 5.2.4.

BA: More Favourable Valuation Method for Property Located in the EU Member State, EU/EEA but Not in a Third Country

In the *BA* case, a dispute arose over the compatibility of a specific valuation rule—the "10% rule" in German inheritance tax law—with EU law. This rule allowed a 10% reduction in the taxable value of inherited immovable property rented for residential purposes, but only for properties located in Germany, the EU, or EEA countries. Properties in third countries were excluded from this reduction, resulting in a higher inheritance tax liability in Germany for the beneficiary of Mr. A, who inherited a property in Canada. If the property had been located within Germany, the EU, or the EEA, a lower tax liability would have applied. Germany justified the 10% rule as a means to reduce the tax burden on residential rental properties, which might otherwise force heirs to sell the property to meet tax obligations – an issue that institutional investors, not subject to inheritance tax, would avoid.

The *BA* case mirrors *Jäger*: in both cases, Germany, as the personal nexus state, applied different valuation rules depending on asset location. In *Jäger*, the Court found Germany's rule incompatible with EU law, holding that favorable valuation should extend to inheritances of agricultural and forestry land in any EU Member State. However, the German tax authority in *BA*, while acknowledging the *Jäger* decision, argued that its findings did not apply to property situated in third countries, like Canada. The Court found that the 10% rule imposed a restriction on capital movement by discouraging cross-border investments and limiting beneficiaries' ability to retain foreign property. Using both the subject-to-tax criterion and an analysis of the rule's objective, the Court ruled that inheriting property in Germany, the EU, or EEA was objectively comparable to inheriting property in Canada.

Furthermore, the Court acknowledged that an objective relating to social policy – such as promoting affordable rented accommodation within the EU and EEA – could constitute an overriding reason in the public interest justifying restrictions on the free movement of capital, which might explain a distinction between EU/EEA and third countries like Canada. However, when testing the proportionality of the measure, the Court deemed Germany's public housing policy inconsistent with this objective, as the 10% rule applied uniformly to all properties, regardless of location (failing to address specific areas of housing need) or type (from the most basic to the most luxurious). Consequently, the Court ruled that the 10% rule was incompatible with EU law.

In our view, this does not imply that Germany is prohibited from distinguishing between properties located in the EU/EEA and those in third countries. If Germany refines the scope and criteria of the 10% rule to target only cases that address genuine housing policy needs, the exclusion of properties in third countries would align with EU law.[87] Germany decided to extend the 10% rule to properties located in a third country and an exchange of information with this third country is ensured with regard to inheritance tax.

87 Dafnomilis, BA (C-670/21). *EU law precludes German rules on calculation of inheritance tax on property in a third country*, Highlights & Insights on European Taxation no. 2 (2024).

14.4.5 *Taxation of non-profit organisations and family foundations*

The tax treatment of non-profit organisations regarding inheritance and gift tax can lead to discriminatory outcomes in cross-border situations. According to the EC's Working Paper, EU Member States' inheritance tax laws cannot impose less favorable inheritance tax treatment on legacies left to charities solely because the charity is based in another EU Member State rather than in the taxing state. The cases of *Missionswerk Werner* and *Commission v Greece* provide insights into how the Court has evaluated national inheritance laws relating to non-profit organisations.[88]

Missionswerk Werner: Reduced Rates for Domestic Non-Profits

In *Missionswerk Werner*, Belgium reserved a reduced inheritance tax rate for non-profit organisations operating within Belgium or within the EU Member State where the deceased either resided or worked at the time of death or previously had done so. Since Missionswerk Werner, a religious organisation, was based in Germany (where the deceased had never lived or worked), it was subject to Belgium's high marginal inheritance tax rate of 80%. If, however, Missionswerk Werner had been established in Belgium, it would have benefited from a substantially reduced tax rate of 7%, as Belgium intended the lower rate to benefit the broader Belgian community.

The Court determined that Belgium's inheritance tax legislation restricted the free movement of capital by making bequests to foreign non-profit organisations less favorable than those to domestic ones. Referring to *Persche* (Case C-318/07), the Court extended non-discrimination principles from prior rulings regarding personal income tax to inheritance tax legislation.[89] In line with *Persche*, the Court ruled that a body established in one EU Member State, but meeting the conditions for tax advantages in another EU Member State, is in a comparable position to bodies established in the latter EU Member State that are recognized as having charitable purposes.[90] Although it is legitimate for the taxing EU Member State to require a close link between the non-profit's activities and benefits to that state, it cannot categorically exclude foreign non-profits, as their activities may still provide benefits to the taxing state, either directly (*stricto sensu*) or more broadly (*lato sensu*). The Court, however, did not provide guidance on how the activities should benefit the taxing EU Member State. Nonetheless, we believe the decisive factor should be the specific conditions imposed by the taxing EU Member State for granting tax advantages: if a foreign non-profit organisation fulfils these conditions (aside from residence), it should be eligible for the relevant tax benefits.[91]

Commission v Greece (C-98/16): Reduced Rate for Foreign Non-Profit Organisations Based on Reciprocity

In *Commission v Greece*, Greece applied a reduced inheritance tax rate of 0.5% to legacies left to foreign non-profits that served a national, religious, philanthropic, educational, or

88 EU, European Commission Staff Working Paper, "Non-discriminatory Inheritance Tax Systems: Principles Drawn from EU Case law", SEC 1488, 2011, p. 11.

89 *Idem*, par. 9.

90 Case *Missionswerk Werner* (C-25/10), par. 33, EU:C:2011:65.

91 *Idem*, par. 76.

artistic purpose, provided reciprocity conditions were met. Without reciprocity, inheritance tax rates rose to 20% or 40%. Greek non-profit organisations, by contrast, automatically qualified for the reduced 0.5% tax rate. The Court found that Greek inheritance tax laws were incompatible with the free movement of capital. Although the judgment did not explicitly address reciprocity, the Court held that compliance with EU law by an EU Member State should not be conditional on reciprocity. Furthermore, and in line with settled case law, domestic and foreign non-profits were deemed objectively comparable, as both were subject to tax in Greece (comparison *ratio personae* and subject to tax criterion) and fulfilled the same activities.[92]

Familienstiftung: Higher Tax Rates for Foreign Family Foundations
In the pending case *Familienstiftung* (C-142/24), the Court will assess the compatibility with EU law[93] of a German inheritance and gift tax provision that grants more favorable tax treatment to donations made to domestic family foundations than to those made to foreign family foundations. In Germany, a family foundation is defined as a foundation established primarily for the benefit of a particular family or families. For donations to German family foundations, the tax rate and tax-free allowance are based on the rates and amounts applicable to acquisitions between relatives in tax brackets I or II. However, for donations to family foundations registered abroad, the tax rates and exemptions are determined according to tax bracket III, even if the foundation primarily serves the interests of a specific family or families. Tax bracket III rates are higher than those for brackets I or II, and the tax-free allowance in bracket III is lower than the allowances in brackets I or II. According to the Advocate General Campos Sánchez-Bordona, Germany can justify the more favorable taxation of German foundations based on the coherence of the tax system, as this favorable taxation is counterbalanced by the imposition of a substitute inheritance tax on these foundations. In contrast, foreign foundations are not liable for this tax because Germany has no jurisdiction over them.

14.4.6 *Tax treatment of family businesses*

The compatibility of EU Member States' legislation regarding the tax treatment of family businesses has also been examined by the Court. In *Geurts*, the Court reviewed Belgian inheritance tax legislation[94], which exempted shares in closely held family businesses from inheritance tax, provided these companies continuously employed at least five full-time employees in the Flemish region for three years preceding the owner's death. Conversely, shares in a family business established in the Netherlands, with employees based in the Netherlands, did not qualify for the exemption from inheritance tax in Belgium.

92 See also, V.I. Dafnomilis, European Commission v. Hellenic Republic (Case C-98/16): The Third Act of the Greek Tax Tragedy in Europe, 57 Eur. Taxn. 9 (2017), Journal Articles & Opinion Pieces IBFD (accessed 14 Jan. 2022).

93 To be more specific, the Court will evaluate the compatibility of the German legislation with EEA law, particularly focusing on Article 40 of the EEA Agreement, which prohibits restrictions on the movement of capital and aims to prevent discrimination in relations between the States party to the EEA Agreement. In the present case, the foreign foundation is established in the Principality of Liechtenstein, an EEA member state.

94 And more specifically, the Flemish inheritance tax legislation.

The Court assessed the Belgian exemption in light of the freedom of establishment, as it applied to family companies where owners exercise a degree of control indicative of "definite influence".[95] The Court considered that Belgian legislation imposed indirect discrimination, as the requirement for companies to employ at least five full-time employees in the Flemish region was more easily met by companies established within that region.[96]

14.4.7 *Extended residence rules*

To counteract potential abuse, certain EU Member States, such as Germany and the Netherlands, have implemented extended residence rules, typically based on the nationality of the deceased or beneficiary. These rules reflect concerns that the residence criterion is vulnerable to manipulation. Under these rules, states exercise worldwide tax jurisdiction when their nationals relocate to another state within a specified period before death. This taxing right is generally retained for a limited period after the deceased has moved abroad, often for five or ten years.

In *Van Hilten*, the Court examined the compatibility of the Dutch inheritance tax's extended residence rule. This rule deems Dutch nationals who emigrate to remain residents of the Netherlands for ten years post-emigration. Accordingly, the Netherlands imposes inheritance tax as if it were the state of residence, despite the lack of an actual personal nexus with the deceased and allows a tax credit for taxes levied by the state of the deceased's actual residence. This rule is intended as an anti-abuse measure; however, it does not apply to foreign nationals who have resided in the Netherlands and subsequently emigrate. The issue before the Court was whether this rule aligned with the free movement of capital.

The Court concluded that the Dutch rule did not restrict the free movement of capital, basing its decision on two distinctions:

1. Domestic vs. Cross-Border Situation: The Court compared the case of a Dutch national who remains in the Netherlands until death (domestic situation) with that of a Dutch national who emigrates but dies abroad within ten years of emigration (cross-border situation). In both cases, the inheritance is subject to the same tax treatment.[97] According to the Court:

> "Since [authors: the rule at hand] applies only to nationals of the Member State concerned, it cannot constitute a restriction on the movement of capital of nationals of the other Member States."

It seems that the Court considers the cross-border situation in question (a Dutch national who emigrates but dies abroad within ten years of emigration) to be a domestic one due to the deceased's Dutch nationality.

95 A family company was defined as a company in which at least 50% of the share capital was held by the deceased and/or their spouse during the three years preceding the death. This shareholding granted them influence over the company's decisions and enabled them to determine its activities.
96 Case *Geurts* (C-464/05), par. 22, EU:C:2007:631.
97 Case *Van Hilten* (C-513/03), paras. 44-46, EU:C:2006:131.

2. Dutch National vs. Foreign National in Cross-Border Situation: The Court also compared a Dutch national and a foreign national who both emigrate and die abroad within ten years. The extended residence rule applies only to the Dutch national.[98] The Court found that:

> "47. [...] such distinctions, for the purposes of allocating powers of taxation, cannot be regarded as constituting discrimination prohibited by Article 73b of the Treaty. They flow, in the absence of any unifying or harmonising measures adopted in the Community context, from the Member States' power to define, by treaty or unilaterally, the criteria for allocating their powers of taxation (see to that effect, as regards Article 48 of the EC Treaty (now, after amendment, Article 39 EC), Case C-336/96 *Gilly* [1998] ECR I-2793, paragraph 30, and, as regards Article 52 of the EC Treaty (now, after amendment, Article 43 EC) and Article 58 of the EC Treaty (now Article 48 EC), Case C-307/97 *Saint-Gobain ZN* [1999] ECR I-6161, paragraph 57)."

The Court reasoned that the less favorable treatment of the Dutch national emigrating situation results from the lack of positive harmonization in the EU in this area of law. Thus, EU Member States retain the right to define their taxing rights, whether unilaterally or through tax treaties. The Court also acknowledged that such allocation may align with international standards, notably the OECD Model Convention on the avoidance of double taxation for inheritance and gift tax (OECD IHTMTC). Here, the Court referenced the OECD IHTMTC's commentary, which allows states to preserve subsidiary taxing rights based on the donor's or deceased's nationality for up to ten years post-emigration.[99]

Based on these two comparisons, the Court concluded that the Dutch rule did not result in a difference in treatment and, therefore, did not restrict the free movement of capital. By integrating the reasoning from these comparisons, the Court introduced the concept of "reverse discrimination" under EU fundamental freedoms. This concept establishes that when legislation disadvantages a domestic situation relative to a cross-border one, it does not infringe upon EU fundamental freedoms, as these freedoms are designed to ensure that cross-border situations are treated at least as favorably as domestic ones. Consequently, if an EU Member State opts to treat a domestic situation less favorably than a cross-border one, such a choice falls outside the scope of EU fundamental freedoms. See also Chapter 6 for further discussion.

14.4.8 Double taxation of inheritances

Block: Double Taxation of the Same Inheritance by two EU Member States
Despite the negative impact of double taxation on the smooth functioning of the internal market, it is established case law that EU fundamental freedoms do not protect taxpayers

98 *Idem*, paras. 47-50.
99 Articles 4, 7, 9A and 9B of the OECD Model Convention on the avoidance of double taxation with respect to inheritance and gift tax (IHTMTC).

against juridical double taxation.[100, 101] Although the Van Hilten ruling emphasized the importance of a unilateral credit from the state of the deceased's extended residence,[102] Block (C-67/08) clarified that EU Member States are not required to align their tax systems with those of other EU Member States to address possible double taxation.[103]

In Block, Ms. Block, a German resident, was the sole heir of a deceased person who had also resided in Germany. The inheritance included capital claims against Spanish financial institutions. Germany, acting as the state of the personal nexus, taxed these claims, as both the deceased (the creditor of the capital claims) and the heir were German tax residents. Spain also taxed the claims, applying its objective nexus, as the claims were considered to be "located" within its jurisdiction under its situs rules and the debtor (i.e., the financial institution) was a resident in Spain. As a result, Ms. Block paid inheritance tax in both countries and later requested a credit against the German tax to avoid double taxation. However, the German authorities denied her request, as the claims did not qualify as "foreign assets" eligible for a foreign tax credit under German law, which only permitted credits if the assets were deemed foreign under German situs rules. This was not the case here, as Germany would not have taxed the claims if it were merely the state of the objective nexus.[104, 105] The result was juridical double taxation due to a residence versus source conflict.

Nevertheless, the Court held that:

> "30. Community law, in the current stage of its development and in a situation such as that in the main proceedings, does not lay down any general criteria for the attribution of areas of competence between the Member States in relation to the elimination of double taxation within the European Community. Consequently, [...] no uniform or harmonisation measure designed to eliminate double taxation has as yet been adopted at Community law level (see Kerckhaert and Morres, paragraph 22, and Columbus Container Services, paragraph 45).
> 31. It follows from this that, in the current stage of the development of Community law, the Member States enjoy a certain autonomy in this area provided they comply with Community law, and are not obliged therefore to adapt their own tax systems to the different systems of tax of the other Member States in order, inter alia, to eliminate the double taxation arising

100 Case *Kerckhaert and Morres* (C-513/04), EU:C:2006:713, Case *Jacques Damseaux v Belgian State* (C-128/08), EU:C:2009:471.

101 More on the three types of conflicts that can give rise to (juridical) double taxation of inheritances, see Hedwig F. van der Weerd-van Joolingen, Inge J.F.A. van Vijfeijken, 'Double Taxation of Inheritances and the Recommendations of the European Commission', (2012), 21, EC Tax Review, Issue 6, section 2.1., p. 310-311. See also Edouard-Jean Navez, 'The Influence of EU Law on Inheritance Taxation: Is the Intensification of Negative Integration Enough to Eliminate Obstacles Preventing EU Citizens from Crossing Borders within the Single Market?', (2012), 21, EC Tax Review, Issue 2, section 2.2.1, p. 89–90.

102 Vassilis Dafnomilis, 'Double Taxation of Inheritances: Does the Ineffectiveness of EU Law Lead to an Effective EC Recommendation?', (2015), 24, EC Tax Review, Issue 6, section 1.2.1.2., p. 323-324.

103 CJEU, *Block* (C-67/08), para. 31, EU:C:2009:92.

104 This is because some states offer unilateral double taxation relief only for assets they would have taxed if they were acting as the state of objective nexus.

105 Ms Block was only allowed to deduct the Spanish tax from the German inheritance tax base as a debt of the estate.

from the exercise in parallel by those Member States of their fiscal sovereignty and, in consequence thereof, to allow the inheritance tax paid in a Member State other than that in which the heir is resident to be deducted in a case such as that of the main proceedings (see, to that effect, Columbus Container Services, paragraph 51)."[106]

The Block judgment, consistent with prior Court judgments on juridical double taxation,[107] positions double taxation as an outcome of disparities in tax systems across EU Member States.[108] This issue falls outside the scope of EU fundamental freedoms, which address discrimination within a single EU Member State. In the Court's view, double taxation arises from the parallel application of distinct inheritance tax laws by two EU Member States. Addressing this issue, the Court highlighted, would require a harmonized approach within the EU. Notably, no such measure has been introduced to date, and cross-border inheritance and donation taxation is currently "advised" to be addressed through the EC's 2011 recommendation on relief for double taxation of inheritances.[109]

Feilen: Reduction for Previously Paid Tax to Avoid Double Taxation in a Single Member State
In Feilen, Germany provided a reduction in inheritance tax when inheritances included assets already taxed in an earlier German inheritance.[110] However, Germany did not grant a reduction when the earlier tax was levied by a foreign country. The German legislation aimed to partially reduce the burden of repeatedly taxing the same assets within a short timeframe. Since Mr. Feilen's previous acquisition involved an asset subject to tax in Austria, Germany denied him a reduction on his German inheritance tax liability.

The Court found that this German legislation restricted the free movement of capital, and treated objectively comparable situations differently, based on a *comparison ratio personae* and a subject-to-tax criterion. However, the restriction could be justified based on the need to maintain the coherence of the German tax system. In that regard, the Court viewed the German system as symmetrical: only those inheriting assets previously taxed in Germany could benefit from a reduction. And although the "initial" taxpayer in *Feilen* was deceased (Mr. Feilen's mother), and the reduction in Germany would have benefited Mr. Feilen (the heir),[111] the Court acknowledged a direct link between the tax advantage and disadvantage in purely German situations. The Court relied on the German law's objective – to mitigate double taxation of assets within the same tax class – to affirm the link. Due to the specific context of Feilen, we believe that in other inheritance and, by analogy, gift tax cases, a direct link should still be assessed at the level of the same person.[112]

---

106 *Idem.*, paras. 30, 31.
107 CJEU, Case *Kerckhaert and Morres* (C-513/04), CJEU, Case *Jacques Damseaux v Belgian State* (C-128/08). See also Chapter 11.
108 On the concept of disparities, see also CJEU, *Egon Schempp v Finanzamt München V* (C-403/03) and Sjoerd Douma, "*Optimization of tax sovereignty and free movement*" (Amsterdam, IBFD, 2011), 135-142.
109 Commission Recommendation 2011/856/EU of 15 December 2011 regarding relief for double taxation of inheritances.
110 In addition, the assets must have already been acquired, through inheritance, by individuals within that tax class within the 10 years preceding the acquisition.
111 CJEU, Case *Feilen* (C-123/15), par. 36, EU:C:2016:496.
112 See also CJEU, Case *XY* (C-394/20).

Feilen differs from Block in that, while both cases concern legislation aimed at mitigating double taxation, Feilen addresses the tax treatment of an inheritance within a single EU Member State. Specifically, it deals with whether assets already subject to tax in a previous inheritance within that EU Member State qualify for tax relief in subsequent inheritances. In contrast, *Block* involves the tax treatment of an inheritance across two EU Member States, where the taxation by each EU Member State on the same asset results in juridical double taxation.

Commission Recommendation of 15 December 2011 on Relief for Double Taxation of Inheritances

Part of the 2011 EC's Inheritance Tax package, this recommendation seeks to "resolve cases of double taxation so that the overall inheritance tax does not exceed what would apply if only the Member State with the highest tax level exercised jurisdiction over the entire inheritance."[113] Aware that full harmonization would exceed the scope needed to address double or multiple taxation, the EC opted for a coordination-based approach to align national laws rather than harmonize them. By adopting this recommendation, the EC anticipated that EU Member States could collectively address double taxation.

The recommendation contains three primary relief provisions. Under Article 4.1, an EU Member State should grant tax relief for inheritance tax levied by another EU Member State on immovable property located in that other EU Member State (Article 4.1(a)) and on movable property which is the business property of a permanent establishment situated in that other EU Member State (Article 4.1(b)). These rules align with Articles 5 and 6 of the OECD IHTMTC, respecting the recommended allocation of taxing rights. Article 4.2 states that, for movable property not associated with a permanent establishment, an EU Member State without a personal link to either the deceased or heir should refrain from applying inheritance tax if another EU Member State is already taxing this property due to personal links with the deceased or heir. This Article seeks to limit the expansive situs rules used by some EU Member States,[114] which might otherwise tax such movable property.

Article 4.3 states that when an inheritance is taxable in multiple EU Member States due to personal links with both the deceased and the heir, the state with the deceased's personal link should take precedence. This approach prioritizes the deceased's habitual residence, recognizing that inheritances often reflect a lifetime's accumulation within the deceased's country of residence. Moreover, the assets contained in an inheritance are more likely to be located in the EU Member State to which the deceased has personal links than in the EU Member State to which the beneficiary has personal links. Given

113 Article 3 of Commission Recommendation 2011/856/EU of 15 December 2011 regarding relief for double taxation of inheritances.

114 See also, Frans Sonneveldt, "Voldoet Nederland aan de aanbeveling van de Europese Commissie op het gebied van grensoverschrijdende erfbelasting?," *WPNR Weekblad voor Privaatrecht Notariaat en Registratie* 6334 (2012): 444.

that most EU Member States apply worldwide inheritance tax based on the deceased's personal nexus, Article 4.3 underscores the importance of this principle.[115]

However, according to the 2015 inheritance tax report discussed next, the recommendation has not led to significant action or fundamental shifts in EU Member States' approaches to double taxation of inheritances, though it has seen some recognition. For example, it was discussed in Poland in 2011, and the Netherlands' finance minister has since stated that the Netherlands would apply its unilateral relief more liberally.[116]

The 2015 Inheritance Tax Report: "One Inheritance – One Inheritance Tax"
In 2014, the EC formed an expert group to explore practical ways of addressing tax issues facing EU residents who move across borders. The group's tasks included assessing EU Member States' progress in implementing the 2011 Recommendation and identifying solutions for cross-border inheritance issues, including double taxation. Ultimately, the group endorsed a novel solution called "one inheritance – one inheritance tax," as outlined in its report Ways to Tackle Inheritance Cross-Border Tax Obstacles Facing Individuals within the EU.[117] The proposed approach would allow only one EU Member State – the deceased's habitual residence –to impose inheritance tax on cross-border inheritances, effectively precluding any other EU Member State from taxing the same inheritance. To date, the EC has not officially commented on the report nor taken further action to address inheritance double taxation within the EU.

---

115 Preamble p. 17 of the recommendation and Frans Sonneveldt, "Voldoet Nederland aan de aanbeveling van de Europese Commissie op het gebied van grensoverschrijdende erfbelasting?," *WPNR Weekblad voor Privaatrecht Notariaat en Registratie* 6334 (2012), 444.

116 EU, "Ways to Tackle Inheritance Cross-Border Tax Obstacles Facing Individuals within the EU", report prepared by the European Commission Expert Group, p. 18.

117 EU, "Ways to Tackle Inheritance Cross-Border Tax Obstacles Facing Individuals within the EU", report prepared by the European Commission Expert Group.

CHAPTER 15

State Aid and Direct Taxation

Sjoerd Douma[1]

15.1 Introduction

EU State aid law has become increasingly important for the design of direct tax measures and administrative practices of the Member States. Although the first tax related case dates back to 1974,[2] followed by a wave of cases around the turn of the century as a result of political agreement on a Code of Conduct for direct business taxation,[3] many companies and Member States had chosen to neglect the impact of EU State aid law on their tax practices. The absence of retrospective recovery of State aid in many of these cases, due to an 'existing aid' qualification of the tax measure or to the application of general principles of EU law by the Commission, has contributed to this lack of urgency. In 2014, this changed dramatically when the Commission opened under State aid rules formal investigations in three cases, respectively: Apple in Ireland, Starbucks in the Netherlands and Fiat in Luxembourg.[4] Since then, the Commission, as guardian of the treaties (see section 15.4 below), has been opening new cases regularly, with vast amounts of retrospective recovery of aid, supplemented with compound interest, as a consequence.[5] It is clear that a firm grasp of EU State aid law has become essential for anyone who deals with direct taxation in the European Union and the European Economic Area. In this light, section 15.2 discusses the notion of State aid, followed by a review of the Commission competence to declare State aid compatible with the internal market in section 15.3. In section 15.4, an overview of procedural law in the area of State aid is provided. Section 15.5 contains concluding remarks.

1 Professor of International and European Procedural Tax Law, ACTL, University of Amsterdam; Partner, Lubbers, Boer & Douma, The Hague.

2 Case 173/73, *Italy v. Commission ('Italian textiles')*, EU:C:1974:71.

3 Resolution, annexed to the ECOFIN Council conclusions of 1 December 1997, O. J. No. C 2 of 6 January 1998, p. 1, quickly followed by Commission Notice 98/C384/03 of 11 November 1998 on the application of State aid rules to measures relating to direct business taxation. This Notice formed the basis of a number of new State aid cases opened by the Commission.

4 Commission Decisions of 11 June 2014, Case numbers SA.38373, SA.38374 and SA.38375.

5 An updated overview of the Commission's activity in the area of State aid and tax planning is provided on the following webpage: http://ec.europa.eu/competition/state_aid/tax_rulings/index_en.html.

15.2 The notion of State aid

15.2.1 Introduction

In 2016, the Commission published a new Notice on the notion of State aid.[6] This notice contains a helpful summary and systemisation of Commission practice and case law in this area. The notion of State aid is defined in Article 107(1) TFEU: "any aid granted by a Member State or through State resources in any form whatsoever which distorts or threatens to distort competition by favouring certain undertakings or the production of certain goods shall, in so far as it affects trade between Member States, be incompatible with the internal market." It is possible to discern a number of criteria from the definition which should be met before a tax measure can be qualified as State aid within the meaning of this provision. Firstly, only 'undertakings' are subject to State aid control. Secondly, Article 107(1) TFEU requires that there is an intervention by the State or through State resources. Thirdly, the measure at issue must confer an advantage (an 'aid') on the recipient. Fourthly, that advantage should be selective in that it favours certain companies or the production of certain goods. Fifthly, the intervention must be liable to affect trade between the Member States and distort or threaten to distort competition. All of those criteria will be discussed below. Finally, a number of selected topics which are especially relevant for direct taxation will be reviewed.

15.2.2 Undertaking

According to settled case-law, in the field of competition law, the concept of 'undertaking' covers any entity insofar it is engaged in an economic activity, regardless of its legal status and the way in which it is financed.[7] For instance, the public or private status of the entity engaged in the activity in question has no bearing on the question as to whether or not that entity is an 'undertaking'.[8] With regard to the notion of 'economic activity, it suffices that goods or services are offered on a given market.[9] It is irrelevant in this regard whether the offer of goods or services is made on a not-for-profit basis, since that offer exists in competition with that of other operators which do seek to make a profit. Therefore, services or goods normally provided for remuneration may be classified as 'economic activities'.[10] Usually the economic activity is carried on directly on the market, but – in case of a group of companies – it can also be carried out on the market indirectly. An entity which owns controlling shareholdings in a company actually exercises that control by involving itself directly or indirectly in the management thereof, must be regarded as taking part in the economic activity carried on by the controlled undertaking. In such

6 Commission Notice on the notion of State aid as referred to in Article 107(1) of the Treaty on the Functioning of the European Union (2016/C 262/01). This Notice was preceded by a draft notice in 2014 and by Commission Notice 98/C384/03 of 11 November 1998 on the application of State aid rules to measures relating to direct business taxation.

7 Case C-222/04, *Cassa di Risparmio di Firenze*, EU:C:2006:8, point 107. An entity that carries out both economic and non-economic activities is to be regarded as an undertaking only with regard to the former; T-128/98, *Aéroports de Paris v Commission*, EU:T:2000:290, point 108.

8 Case C-74/16, *Congregación de Escuelas Pías Provincia Betania*, EU:C:2017:496, point 42.

9 Case C-222/04, *Cassa di Risparmio di Firenze*, EU:C:2006:8, point 108.

10 Case C-74/16, *Congregación de Escuelas Pías Provincia Betania*, EU:C:2017:496, points 46-47.

a case, the controlling entity itself must be regarded as an undertaking. On the other hand, the mere fact of holding shares, even controlling shareholdings, is insufficient to characterise as economic an activity of the entity holding those shares, when it gives rise only to the exercise of the rights attached to the status of shareholder or member, as well as, if appropriate, the receipt of dividends, which are merely the fruits of the ownership of an asset.[11] By contrast, the provision of intra-group loans does seem to be an economic activity.[12] Finally, it should be noted that an advantage granted directly to certain natural or legal persons who are not necessarily undertakings may constitute an indirect advantage, hence State aid, for other natural or legal persons who are undertakings.[13]

15.2.3 State resources and imputability

Article 107(1) TFEU requires that the measure at issue is granted out of State resources and is imputable to a Member State before it can be classified as State aid.[14] The present section discusses both requirements.

Imputability
In direct tax cases, the requirement that the measure is imputable to a Member State is especially relevant for two reasons. In the first place, it follows from this requirement that advantages which result from disparities between the direct taxation systems of one or more States are outside the scope of State aid control.[15] After all, these advantages are not imputable to a single Member State. Rather, they are the result of the interaction between those tax systems, which may result in double taxation or double non-taxation, as the case may be.[16] In the second place, the requirement of imputability stresses that measures which Member States are required to take under Union law, for instance by implementation of a directive, cannot give rise to State aid.[17] However, where Union law simply allows for certain national measures and the Member State enjoys discretion as to whether or how to adopt the measures in question, the national measure is imputable to the Member State.[18]

State resources
Classification as 'State aid' within the meaning of Article 107(1) TFEU also requires that there is an intervention by the State or through State resources. Favourable tax treatment which, although not involving the transfer of State resources, places the recipients in a financial position more favourable than that of other taxpayers can also come under

11 Case C-222/04, *Cassa di Risparmio di Firenze*, EU:C:2006:8, point 109 et seq.
12 Case C-77/01, *EDM*, EU:C:2004:243, point 65 et seq.
13 Case C-403/10, *Mediaset*, EU:C:2011:533, point 81 (benefit to consumers); Case T-445/05, Fineco, EU:T:2009:50, point 127 et seq (benefit to investment funds).
14 C-482/99, *France v Commission (Stardust)*, EU:C:2002:294, point 24.
15 Compare P.J. Wattel, 'Stateless Income, State Aid and the (Which?) Arm's Length Principle, Intertax 2016, p. 791-801.
16 Commission Decision of 8 July 2009, *Groepsrentebox*, C(2009) 4511 final, at 125.
17 C-460/07, *Puffer*, EU:C:2009:254, point 70 (deduction of input VAT); T-351/02, *Deutsche Bahn*, EU:T:2006:104, point 102 (exemption from excise taxes).
18 C-189/15, *IRCCS - Fondazione Santa Lucia*, EU:C:2017:17, point 51; Commission Notice on the notion of State aid (2016/C 262/01), at 45.

Article 107(1) TFEU.[19] This satisfies the requirement that State resources be transferred. A positive transfer of funds does not have to occur; foregoing State revenue is sufficient.[20] This means that the criterion largely coincides with the criterion of 'advantage', discussed in the next section.

15.2.4 Advantage

General observations

The definition of aid is more general than that of a subsidy because it includes not only positive benefits, such as subsidies themselves, but also measures which, in various forms, mitigate the charges which are normally included in the budget of an undertaking and which thus, without being subsidies in the strict sense of the word, are similar in character and have the same effect.[21] This means that, in direct taxation cases, an advantage exists in relation to a certain benchmark rule. Indeed, the very existence of an advantage may be established only when compared with 'normal' taxation or a 'system of reference'.[22] The level of this 'normal' taxation should be derived from the national tax system at issue. After all, as European Union law currently stands, direct taxation largely falls within the competence of the Member States. Thus it is solely the latter that have competence to devise systems of (corporate) income taxation which they consider the best suited to the needs of their economies. Furthermore, application of the Union rules on State aid is without prejudice to the power of the Member States to decide on their economic policy and, therefore, on the tax system – and the common or 'normal' regime under it – which they consider the most appropriate and, in particular, to spread the tax burden as they see fit across the different factors of production and economic sectors.[23] Sometimes, it may be contentious to identify the normal rule with which a certain more favourable rule should be compared. As the Court held in *World Duty Free Group*, where the tax measure in question is inseparable from the general tax system of the Member State concerned, reference must be made to that system. On the other hand, where it appears that such a measure is clearly severable from that general system, it cannot be ruled out that the reference framework to be taken into account may be more limited than that general system, or even that it may equate to the measure itself, where the latter appears as a rule having its own legal logic and it is not possible to identify a consistent body of rules external to that measure.[24]

The case of *Heitkamp BauHolding* provides an example. This case centred around the German change-of-control rules which state that a company loses the right to carry-forward its

19 Joined Cases C-106/09 and C-107/09, *Commission and Spain v Gibraltar and UK*, EU:C:2011:732, point 72.

20 Commission Notice on the notion of State aid (2016/C 262/01), at 51.

21 Case C-143/99, *Adria-Wien Pipeline*, EU:C:2001:598, point 38.

22 Case C-88/03, *Portugal v Commission ('Azores')*, EU:C:2006:511, point 56.

23 Case T-211/04, *Gibraltar v Commission*, EU:T:2008:595, point 146, upheld in Joined Cases C-106/09 and C-107/09, *Commission and Spain v Gibraltar and UK*, EU:C:2011:732, point 97. See also Opinion AG Kokott in Joined Cases C-236/16 and C-237/16, *ANGED*, EU:C:2017:854, point 47 and 93, Case C-417/10, *3M Italia*, EU:C:2012:184, point 25, and Joined Cases C-51/19 and C-64/19, *World Duty Free Group*, EU:C:2021:793, point 64.

24 Joined Cases C-51/19 and C-64/19, *World Duty Free Group*, EU:C:2021:793, point 63.

tax losses when a new shareholder has taken control over the company. This measure is aimed at preventing the trade in loss companies; it is an anti-abuse measure. The change-of-control rule did not apply if the company finds itself in financial difficulty and the new shareholder decides to restructure it (the '*Sanierungsklausel*'). In such a case, the question arises what the 'normal' rule is: i) the rule that a company can normally carry-forward its losses, or ii) the rule that a company cannot carry-forward its losses in case of a change-of-ownership. In the first situation, the *Sanierungsklausel* does not create any advantage, in the second situation it does lead to a benefit. The General Court decided that the benchmark rule should be the change-of-control rule itself, as a result of which the exception to that rule should be regarded as an 'advantage'.[25] It is irrelevant in this regard whether the change-of-control rule itself may be regarded as unconstitutional or in breach of EU free movement law, because the rule produces effects as long as it is applied.[26] When one accepts that the objective of the measure which potentially gives rise to an advantage should be decisive for the answer to the question whether that measure deviates from the 'normal' situation, the General Court is obviously correct: the objective of the *Sanierungsklausel* was to provide an advantage to companies in difficulty. Indeed, such an approach would make a lot of sense, because it takes the Member State's design of its own tax system as a starting point. On appeal, however, the Court of Justice decided that the General Court had defined the relevant reference framework too narrowly by excluding from it the general rule of loss carry-forward.[27] As a consequence, it annulled the Commission's decision for a lack of reasoning. In our view, this does not mean that the General Court's decision was wrong in substance. It should have arrived at the same conclusion had it reviewed the object and purpose of all relevant rules on loss-carry-forward as a whole. It is important to note in this regard that the Member State in question obliged to provide, in good faith pursuant to Article 4(3) TEU, the Commission with all relevant information requested by it concerning the interpretation of the provisions of national law that are relevant for the purpose of determining the reference framework, as derived from national case-law or administrative practice. If the Member States perform this duty sincerely, the Commission must respect it unless it proves that the interpretation advocated by the Member State is inconsistent with the wording of the relevant national legislation. In a case concerning the British CFC-regime the Commission had not provided such proof. In particular it had not shown that the British rules which allowed an exemption for non-trade finance profits arising from UK significant people functions were designed as a favourable deviation from the normally applicable system.[28]

The objective of a measure can be established through normal rules of interpretation (e.g. by having recourse to legislative history, the system of the law, principles underlying the law and the effects produced by the measure). Taking the objective of the measure at issue as a starting point also makes it possible to distinguish 'advantages' from 'disadvantages' which are not covered by Article 107 (1) TFEU: an exceptional burden cannot

25 Case T-287/11, *Heitkamp BauHolding*, EU:T:2016:60, point 106.
26 Case T-287/11, *Heitkamp BauHolding*, EU:T:2016:60, point 108; Case C-164/15, *Aer Lingus*, C:2016:990, points 68 et seq and 119 et seq.
27 Case C-203/16, *Andres (faillite Heitkamp BauHolding) v Commission*, EU:C:2018:505, point 103.
28 Joined Cases C-555/22 P, C-556/22 P and C-564/22 P, *United Kingdom United Kingdom v Commission and Others*, EU:C:2024:763, point 97 et seq.

be regarded as the grant of aid in favour of the market participants coming under the 'normal' measure.[29] For instance, the specific non-deductibility of bribes in a corporate income tax system deviates from the normal rule that business expenses are deductible, in order to discourage the practice of bribing. The objective of this rule is to implement a disadvantage, as a result of which it is outside of the scope of State aid law. However, if the objective of a measure which implements a specific burden is to create an advantage for undertakings which are in direct competition with the disadvantaged group of undertakings, State aid may be involved. In such a case, the aid measure is the tax itself, that tax and the aid constituting two elements of one and the same fiscal measure which are inseparable. In such circumstance, a disadvantaged undertaking may plead the illegality of the tax.[30] In conclusion, it is decisive to examine the objective of the measure at issue, from which it should be derived whether it deviates from another measure in order to create an advantage or disadvantage, as the case may be.

Tax rulings

Applying the just-discussed approach to tax rulings, the objective of the system through which rulings are provided is decisive for the existence of an 'advantage' relative to a 'normal' situation. As the Commission has stated, the function of a tax ruling is to establish in advance, for reasons of legal certainty, the application of the ordinary tax system to a particular case in view of its specific facts and circumstances.[31] As such, a tax ruling regime is not aimed at proving an advantage relative to another benchmark. However, if a tax ruling establishes a favourable application of the ordinary tax system in a situation where no legal uncertainty exists, it deviates from the normal tax ruling regime. In such a case, the ruling gives rise to an advantage. However, in situations where objective uncertainty exists about the correct application of the ordinary tax system, a tax ruling does not seem to provide any advantage because there is, in such a case, no deviation from the normal regime.[32] The following three examples provided by the Commission should be interpreted against this background:

a) the ruling misapplies national tax law and this results in a lower amount of tax;
b) the ruling is not available to undertakings in a similar legal and factual situation; or
c) the administration applies a more 'favourable' tax treatment compared with other taxpayers in a similar factual and legal situation.[33]

29 Opinion AG Geelhoed in Case C-308/01, *GIL Insurance*, EU:C:2003:481, point 77.

30 Case C-449/14, *DTS*, EU:C:2016:848, point 75; Case C-526/04, *Laboratoires Boiron*, EU:C:2006:528, point 30 et seq. An undertaking may also plead illegality of a tax if that tax is an integral part of an unlawful aid measure. For that to be so, it must be hypothecated to the aid measure (e.g. an exemption) under the relevant national rules, in the sense that the revenue from the tax is necessarily allocated for the financing of the aid (e.g. an exemption) and has a direct impact on the amount thereof and, consequently, on the assessment of the compatibility of that aid with the internal market; see Case C-174/02, *Streekgewest*, EU:C:2005:10, point 26.

31 Commission Notice on the notion of State aid (2016/C 262/01), at 169.

32 In practice, the Commission does not easily accept that objective uncertainty existed at the time of the ruling; see for instance Commission Decision of 03.12.2015, No. SA.38945 (Luxembourg - Alleged aid to McDonald's) on a sophisticated tax treaty analysis in the light of the OECD Commentary.

33 Commission Notice on the notion of State aid (2016/C 262/01), at 174.

Settlements

A tax settlement may occur in the context of a dispute between a taxpayer and the tax authorities concerning the amount of tax owed. As the Commission acknowledges, the conclusion of such tax settlements allows tax authorities to avoid long-standing legal disputes and to ensure quick recovery of the tax due. According to the Commission, State aid may be involved in the conclusion of a tax settlement, in particular where it appears that the amount of tax due has been reduced without clear justification (such as optimising the recovery of debt) or in a disproportionate manner to the benefit of the taxpayer.[34] This is not surprising, because in these circumstances there is a favourable deviation from the normal settlement regime. The Commission has noted that a transaction between the tax administration and a taxpayer may in particular entail an advantage where:

a) in making disproportionate concessions to a taxpayer, the administration applies a more 'favourable' discretionary tax treatment compared to other taxpayers in a similar factual and legal situation;
b) the settlement is contrary to the applicable tax provisions and has resulted in a lower amount of tax, outside a reasonable range.[35]

It is interesting to compare these examples with the case of *Frucona*. In this case, the question arose whether the tax collector had made disproportionate concessions to Frucona when collecting taxes due. The Court, applying the private creditor test, held that it is decisive whether the recipient undertaking would manifestly not have obtained comparable facilities from a private creditor in a situation as close as possible to that of the public creditor that sought to recover sums due to it.[36] The words used by the Commission and the Court – 'outside a reasonable range' and 'manifestly' favourable – indicate that the Member States enjoy a certain amount of leeway when concluding tax settlements with the applicable national settlement regime. This confirms the competence of the Member States to operate such a system as part of their 'normal' regime.

Indirect advantages

An advantage can be conferred on undertakings other than those to which State resources are directly transferred.[37] As the Commission states, an indirect advantage is present if the measure is designed in such a way as to channel its secondary effects towards identifiable undertakings or groups of undertakings. This is the case, for example, if the aid is, *de facto* or *de jure*, made conditional on the purchase of goods or services produced by certain undertakings only.[38] In direct tax cases, this may be relevant where a Member State implements tax incentives for consumers with the aim of providing an indirect advantage to undertakings or where a Member State awards certain benefits to an undertaking with the aim of indirectly creating an advantage for other undertakings.[39]

34 Commission Notice on the notion of State aid (2016/C 262/01), at 175.
35 Commission Notice on the notion of State aid (2016/C 262/01), at 176.
36 Case C-300/16, *Frucona*, EU:C:2017:706, point 28.
37 Commission Notice on the notion of State aid (2016/C 262/01), at 115.
38 Commission Notice on the notion of State aid (2016/C 262/01), at 116.
39 Compare Case C-403/10, *Mediaset*, EU:C:2011:533, point 81 (benefit to consumers); Case T-445/05, Fineco, EU:T:2009:50, point 127 et seq (benefit to investment funds).

In such a situation, the companies which have received a benefit indirectly may be faced with a State aid probe.

15.2.5 Selectivity

General observations

The notion of 'advantage', discussed in the preceding section, is closely connected to the requirement of selectivity: according to Article 107(1) TFEU the advantage should favour certain undertakings or the production of certain goods. This close connection exists, because the presence of an 'advantage' presupposes that the tax measure at issue deviates from a 'normal' rule and, therefore, almost automatically favours a certain group of undertakings. Indeed, as the Court has held in *British Aggregates*, measures which differentiate between undertakings are *prima facie* selective, unless that differentiation arises from the nature or the overall structure of the system of which they form part.[40] This approach is understandable when one acknowledges that the selectivity test is essentially a discrimination test or an application of the principle of equality which very much resembles the analysis under EU free movement law.[41] This means that the fact that the number of undertakings able to claim entitlement under a national measure is very large, or that those undertakings belong to various economic sectors, is not sufficient to call into question the selective nature of that measure and, therefore, to rule out its classification as State aid.[42] All that matters is whether any advantage granted by the tax measure at issue may be selective by demonstrating that the measure granting the advantage differentiates between economic operators who, in light of the legitimate objective assigned to the tax system of the Member State concerned – the system of reference –, are in a comparable factual and legal situation.[43] This means that the objective of the measure determines which characteristics of undertakings are relevant in the discrimination analysis; characteristics of undertakings outside of this reference framework are irrelevant.[44] Similarly, the fact that only taxpayers satisfying the conditions for the application of a measure can benefit from the measure cannot, in itself, make it a selective measure; the distinction may very well be justified by the objective pursued by the measure.[45] The objective pursued by the tax system is only capable of objectively distinguishing the advantaged undertaking from another if the tax measure at issue pursues a legitimate goal related to the nature or the overall structure of the system of which it forms part. Indeed, a measure which creates an exception to the application of the general tax system may be justified by the nature and overall structure of the tax system if the Member State concerned can show that that measure results directly from

40 Case C-487/06, *British Aggregates*, EU:C:2008:757, point 83.

41 Joined Cases C-20/15 and C-21/15, *World Duty Free*, EU:C:2016:981, points 54, 86 and 93-94; Opinion AG Kokott in Case C-169/08, *Presidente del Consiglio dei Ministri v Regione autonoma della Sardegna*, EU:C:2009:420, point 134. See also Peter Wattel, 'Comparing Criteria: State Aid, Free Movement, Harmful Tax Competition and Market Distorting Disparities', in: I. Richelle, W. Schön, & E. Traversa (Eds.), *State Aid Law and Business Taxation*, MPI Studies in Tax Law and Public Finance, Vol. 6), Berlin: Springer 2016, p. 59-71.

42 Case C-172/03, *Heiser*, EU:C:2005:130, point 42.

43 Joined Cases C-78/08 to C-80/08, *Paint Graphos*, EU:C:2011:550, point 49.

44 Joined Cases C-20/15 and C-21/15, *World Duty Free*, EU:C:2016:981, point 78.

45 Case C-417/10, *3M Italia*, EU:C:2012:184, point 42.

the basic or guiding principles of its tax system. In that connection, a distinction must be made between, on the one hand, the objectives attributed to a particular tax scheme which are extrinsic to it and, on the other, the mechanisms inherent in the tax system itself which are necessary for the achievement of such objectives.[46] In other words, the measure at issue should pursue a *legitimate* aim in that it is not aimed at stimulating certain (economic) behaviour through the tax system, much in a way a direct subsidy would do.[47] It is sufficient that one of the objectives pursued by the measure is legitimate.[48] For State aid purposes an objective of a direct tax measure cannot be regarded as legitimate if it goes directly against Article 107(1) TFEU (i.e. if the aim is to provide aid).[49] All other aims should be regarded as being inherent in the tax system itself. Examples include goals such as setting the rate of taxation, depreciation rules and rules on loss carry-overs, the need to take into account specific accounting requirements, administrative manageability, the principle of tax neutrality, the progressive nature of income tax and its redistributive purpose, provisions to prevent double taxation or tax avoidance and evasion, and the objective of optimising the recovery of fiscal debts.[50] Once it has been established that any *prima facie* selective treatment can be justified by objectives inherent in the tax system, it is still necessary to ensure that tax measure at issue is consistent with the principle of proportionality and does not go beyond what is necessary, in that the legitimate objective being pursued could not be attained by less far-reaching measures.[51] When performing this proportionality analysis, the effects of the measure are of particular importance. They serve as a 'check' on the 'real' objective of the measure and as a way to make sure the measure is not overinclusive in relation to its stated objective.[52] Here, as AG Kokott has explained, the Court respects the discretion enjoyed by the Member States in laying down general laws. In particular, political, economic and social choices with complex assessments are entailed on the part of the national legislature when drafting tax legislation. Therefore, when performing proportionality analysis, the criterion should be whether the drafting of the tax measure at issue is not manifestly inappropriate having regard to the objective. The national legislature is not required to prove empirically how it fixed a certain threshold and it also does not matter whether the threshold is credible or even 'right', as long as it is not manifestly erroneous. This test has to be performed *ex ante*, not *ex post*.[53] We will now discuss a number of specific features related to the selectivity test.

46 Case C-88/03, *Portugal v Commission ('Azores')*, EU:C:2006:511, point 81.
47 Joined Cases C-78/08 to C-80/08, *Paint Graphos*, EU:C:2011:550, point 75.
48 Opinion AG Kokott in Joined Cases C-236/16 and C-237/16, *ANGED*, EU:C:2017:854, point 94.
49 A possible exception applies where the objective of the measure, applying generally to all undertakings, is in conformity with other fundamental objectives of the Union, e.g. the promotion of research and development (Article 179(1) TFEU; compare, in a fundamental freedoms context, Case C-39/04, *Laboratoires Fournier*, EU:C:2005:161.
50 Commission Notice 98/C384/03 of 11 November 1998 on the application of State aid rules to measures relating to direct business taxation, at 13; Commission Notice on the notion of State aid as referred to in Article 107(1) of the Treaty on the Functioning of the European Union (2016/C 262/01), at 139.
51 Joined Cases C-78/08 to C-80/08, *Paint Graphos*, EU:C:2011:550, point 75.
52 Joined Cases C-20/15 and C-21/15, *World Duty Free*, EU:C:2016:981, point 67.
53 Opinion AG Kokott in Joined Cases C-236/16 and C-237/16, *ANGED*, EU:C:2017:854, points 47, 55 and 93.

General measures

It is settled case-law that a tax advantage resulting from a general measure applicable without distinction to all economic operators does not constitute State aid.[54] This is due to the fact that, in such a case, proportionality analysis cannot be performed; general measures have no 'deeper purpose' which is suitable for such an analysis under the principle of equality or, in other words, the selectivity test. An example is provided by the case of *Gibraltar*. This case centred around the question whether selectivity is involved if i) a payroll tax and a business property occupation tax (BPOT) are payable only where the taxable person makes a profit and ii) the amount of tax is capped in respect of both those bases of assessment at 15% of the profits. The Court held that the requirement to make a profit and the capping of taxation of profits are *per se* general measures applicable without distinction to all economic operators and are therefore not liable to confer selective advantages. Admittedly, the requirement to make a profit would benefit unprofitable operators, and the capping of tax benefit very profitable operators. However, the Court stated, those effects are not such that they favour 'certain undertakings' or 'the production of certain goods' within the meaning of Article 107(1) TFEU, but are merely the consequence of the random event that the undertaking in question is unprofitable or very profitable during the period of assessment.[55] Another decision by the Court would have disregarded the tax system – which was also a profits tax – *as such*. Under the division of competences between the Member States and the Union, this would not have been possible. In other words, selectivity and proportionality analysis are possible only within the reference framework provided by the tax legislation of the Member State concerned. The rules which make up this reference framework should be regarded as 'general measures'.[56] The (now abolished) 1998 Notice on direct business taxation also identified another group of tax measures as being general, provided that they apply without distinction to all firms and to the production of all goods: measures pursuing general economic policy objectives through a reduction of the tax burden related to certain production costs (research and development (R&D), the environment, training, employment).[57] It is difficult to interpret this statement in conformity with the Court's case law on objectives inherent in the tax system itself and objectives which are extrinsic to the tax system (see the preceding paragraph). The 2016 Notice of the notion of State aid no longer contains such a statement.[58] Having said this, the Court does not seem to exclude *per se* that a measure can be general even if it pursues objectives external to the tax system.[59]

54 Joined Cases C-20/15 and C-21/15, *World Duty Free*, EU:C:2016:981, point.

55 Joined Cases C-106/09 and C-107/09, *Commission and Spain v Gibraltar and UK*, EU:C:2011:732, points 80 and 83.

56 For example, accelerated and early depreciation rules for leased assets may be seen as general measures if the lease contracts in question are really accessible to companies of all sectors and sizes. These rules – assuming that they do not pursue an extrinsic objective – are not suitable for proportionality analysis; Commission Decision of 20 November 2012 on SA.34736 on the early depreciation of certain assets acquired through a financial leasing (OJ C 384, 13.12.2012, p. 1).

57 Commission Notice 98/C384/03 of 11 November 1998 on the application of State aid rules to measures relating to direct business taxation, at 13.

58 Commission Notice on the notion of State aid as referred to in Article 107(1) of the Treaty on the Functioning of the European Union (2016/C 262/01).

59 Case C-453/23, Prezydent Miasta Mielca, points 50, 58 and 71-72.

Aid schemes and individual aid

It appears from the case-law that a distinction should be made between aid schemes and individual aid for the purposes of the selectivity test. The case of *P Oy* concerned a potential aid scheme on the basis of which the Finnish tax authorities could grant prior authorisation rulings for the carry-forward of losses in case of a change-of-control. The Court held that the application of an authorisation system which enables losses to be carried forward to later tax years cannot, in principle, be considered to be selective if the competent authorities have, when deciding on an application for authorisation, only a degree of latitude limited by objective criteria which are not unrelated to the tax system established by the legislation in question, such as the objective of avoiding trade in losses. On the other hand, if the competent authorities have a broad discretion to determine the beneficiaries or the conditions under which the financial assistance is provided on the basis of criteria unrelated to the tax system, such as maintaining employment, the exercise of that discretion must then be regarded as selective.[60] It is easy to recognise in the words of the Court the above-discussed difference between objectives inherent in the tax system, which constitute a legitimate aim which is capable of objectively distinguishing one undertaking from another, and objectives which are extrinsic to the tax system, which cannot lead to such an objective difference. If rulings are not issued on the basis of a scheme but rather on an individual basis, this distinction is less relevant. In the case of *MOL*, the Court noted that the selectivity requirement differs depending on whether the measure in question is envisaged as a general scheme of aid or as individual aid. In the latter case, the identification of the economic advantage is, in principle, sufficient to support the presumption that it is selective. By contrast, when examining a general scheme of aid, it is necessary to identify whether the measure in question, notwithstanding the finding that it confers an advantage of general application, does so to the exclusive benefit of certain undertakings or certain sectors of activity.[61] This means that an individual tax ruling which favourably deviates from the national reference framework satisfies, in principle, the criterion of selectivity. In case of individual tax rulings which are granted on the basis of a systematic policy leaving no or very limited discretion to the tax authorities, the question which needs to be answered is whether this policy deviates favourably from the national reference framework without proportionate justification.[62] Once such a deviation has been established, all tax rulings granted under that policy will be caught be a recovery procedure.

Discretionary administrative powers

It follows from the above-discussed case of *P Oy* that tax measures which confer upon the tax administration a discretionary power to grant or not to grant an advantage to individual undertakings, without being confined by objective criteria which are not unrelated to the tax system, are selective in nature. It is not necessary in this regard to determine whether the conduct of the tax authority is arbitrary. It suffices to establish that the authority has a discretionary power, because such a power is liable to place

60 Case C-6/12, *P Oy*, EU:C:2013:525, points 26-27.

61 Case C-15/14, *Commission v MOL*, EU:C:2015:362, point 60.

62 Case C-337/19, *Commission v Belgium and Magnetrol International*, EU:C:2021:741 (Belgian excess profits rulings).

certain undertakings in a more favourable situation than others.[63] In the case of *Smits and Peerbooms*, a fundamental freedoms case, the Court added that a scheme of prior authorisation cannot legitimise discretionary decisions taken by the national authorities which are liable to negate the effectiveness of provisions of Union law. Therefore, in order for a prior administrative authorisation scheme to be justified even though it derogates from a fundamental freedom, it must, in any event, be based on objective, non-discriminatory criteria which are known in advance, in such a way as to circumscribe the exercise of the national authorities' discretion, so that it is not used arbitrarily. Finally, the Court held that such a prior administrative authorisation scheme must be based on a procedural system which is easily accessible and capable of ensuring that a request for authorisation will be dealt with objectively and impartially within a reasonable time and refusals to grant authorisation must also be capable of being challenged in judicial or quasi-judicial proceedings.[64] There does not seem to be a good reason not to follow this approach for State aid law as well.[65] Indeed, in a tax context, the Commission has stated that it would be best practice if administrative ruling practices are transparent and the rulings are published.[66] Already in 1998, the Commission held that the opacity of decisions taken by the tax authorities and the room for manoeuvre which they sometimes enjoy support the presumption of State aid.[67] In 2014, the Commission stated that the tax ruling practice in *Gibraltar* constituted an aid scheme on grounds of a discretionary exercise of powers.[68]

Regional aid

In *Denkavit italiana*, the Court held that Article 107(1) TFEU refers to the decisions of Member States by which they, in pursuit of their own economic and social objectives, give, by *unilateral and autonomous* decisions, undertakings or other persons resources or procure for them advantages intended to encourage the attainment of the economic or social objectives sought.[69] This reference to unilateral and autonomous decisions makes sense, because the existence of an advantage or a disadvantage for a taxpayer should be assessed within a certain framework of reference, i.e. a certain jurisdiction. The case of *Porto Antico di Genova* provides another example. This case concerned the Italian tax on the income of legal persons (IRPEG) and the Italian regional tax on production (IRAP). These taxes included grants paid by the Community Structural Funds in the assessment of taxable income. The taxpayer argued, *inter alia*, that the differences which existed between the beneficiaries of the Structural Funds, by reason of the different rates of taxation imposed

63 Joined Cases T-227/01 to T-229/01, T-265/01, T-266/01 and T-270/01, *Diputación Foral de Álava and Gobierno Vasco v Commission*, point 171; Case C-241/94, *France v. Commission ('Kimberly Clark')*, EU:C:1996:353, points 23-24; Joined Cases C-649/20 P, C-658/20 P and C-662/20 P, Spain v Commission, EU:C:2023:60, points 57 et seq.

64 Case C-157/99, *Smits and Peerbooms*, EU:C:2001:404, point 90.

65 Commission Notice on the notion of State aid as referred to in Article 107(1) of the Treaty on the Functioning of the European Union (2016/C 262/01), at 125.

66 Commission Notice on the notion of State aid as referred to in Article 107(1) of the Treaty on the Functioning of the European Union (2016/C 262/01), at 169.

67 Commission Notice 98/C384/03 of 11 November 1998 on the application of State aid rules to measures relating to direct business taxation, at 22.

68 Commission Decision to open the formal investigation procedure of 01.10.2014, C(2014) 6851 final, at 50-52.

69 Case 61/79, *Denkavit italiana*, EU:C:1980:100.

in the Member States on amounts received by way of Community assistance, should be considered as being liable to breach the principle of equal treatment, which precludes comparable situations from being treated in a different manner unless the difference in treatment is objectively justified. The Court rejected this argument:

> "For that to be the position, it would be necessary for the situations of the beneficiaries of Community aid to be comparable. That cannot be the case since those beneficiaries receive that aid in a socio-economic context specific to each Member State and, in the absence of Community harmonisation on the assessment of taxable income, objective disparities between the rules in Member States still exist in that field, thereby inevitably creating such differences between those beneficiaries."[70]

Again, advantages or disadvantages as a result of the fact that other rules apply in other tax jurisdictions are outside the scope of the principle of equality and, therefore, also outside of the scope of selectivity analysis. It is important to note that it is possible that a separate tax jurisdiction may also exist and occur within one Member State. Where this is the case, this separate tax jurisdiction necessarily serves as the framework of reference to determine whether a tax measure gives rise to a selective advantage. As the Court stated in *Azores*, the very existence of an advantage may be established only when compared with 'normal' taxation. The 'normal' tax rate is the rate in force in the geographical area constituting the reference framework.[71] Since the reference framework need not necessarily be defined within the limits of the Member State concerned, a measure conferring an advantage in only one part of the national territory is not selective on that ground alone for the purposes of Article 107(1) TFEU. It is possible that, in a situation of asymmetrical devolution of tax powers, an infra-State body enjoys a legal and factual status which makes it sufficiently autonomous in relation to the central government of a Member State to accept the jurisdiction exercised by that body as the reference framework.[72] Sufficiently autonomous powers exist where i) a regional or local authority has, from a constitutional point of view, a political and administrative status separate from that of the central government, ii) the tax measure at issue has been adopted without the central government being able to directly intervene as regards its content, and iii) the financial consequences of a reduction of the national tax rate for undertakings in the region are not offset by aid or subsidies from other regions or central government. In other words, the political and fiscal independence of central government presupposes that the infra-State body not only has powers in the territory within its competence to adopt tax measures, regardless of any considerations related to the conduct of the central State, but that in addition it assumes the political and financial consequences of such a measure.[73] If these conditions are not met, any more advantageous regional tax measures in comparison with the measures applying centrally are *prima facie* selective.

---

70 Case C-427/05, *Porto Antico di Genova*, EU:C:2007:630, point 20.
71 Case C-88/03, *Portugal v Commission ('Azores')*, EU:C:2006:511, point 56.
72 Case C-88/03, *Portugal v Commission ('Azores')*, EU:C:2006:511, points 57-58.
73 Case C-88/03, *Portugal v Commission ('Azores')*, EU:C:2006:511, points 67-68.

15.2.6 *Effect on trade and competition*

Public support to undertakings only constitutes State aid under Article 107(1) TFEU if it 'distorts or threatens to distort competition by favouring certain undertakings or the production of certain goods' and only insofar as it 'affects trade between Member States'. This is a very low threshold, but it remains a threshold. It is up for the Commission to prove that it has been met.[74] In respect of the requirement regarding distortion of competition, the Court has consistently held that an aid in principle distorts the conditions of competition existing within the EU internal market if it is intended to relieve a company in a liberalised sector where there is, or could be, competition, of the expenses, which it would normally have had to bear in its day-to-day management or its usual activities.[75] It is not necessary to establish that competition is actually being distorted; it is sufficient that the aid is liable to distort competition.[76] Finally, it is not required that the distortion of competition is significant or material. The fact that the amount of aid is low or the recipient undertaking is small will not in itself rule out a distortion of competition or the threat thereof, provided however that the likelihood of such a distortion is not merely hypothetical.[77] This means that, in direct taxation cases, the condition that completion is distorted, or threatened to be distorted, is normally met in case a selective advantage has been provided to an undertaking, except for cases of *de minimis* aid.[78] In respect of the requirement that the measure should affect trade between Member States, again, it is necessary not to establish that the aid has a real effect on trade between Member States; it is sufficient that the aid is liable to affect such trade. As regards aid schemes, it should also be borne in mind that the Commission may merely make a general assessment of the scheme at issue and is not required to carry out an analysis of the aid granted in individual cases under the scheme.[79] The just-mentioned considerations mean, as the General Court has stated, that the grant of aid by a Member State in the form of a tax advantage to certain of its taxable persons must be regarded as liable to have an effect on trade and, consequently, as meeting that condition, where those taxable persons exercise an economic activity in the field of such trade or it is conceivable that they are in competition with operators established in other Member States.[80]

74 Joined Cases T-515/13 and T-719/13, *Lico Leasing*, EU:T:2015:1004, points 181-208.

75 Case C-172/03, *Heiser*, EU:C:2005:130, point 55; Commission Notice on the notion of State aid as referred to in Article 107(1) of the Treaty on the Functioning of the European Union (2016/C 262/01), at 187.

76 Case C-222/04, *Cassa di Risparmio di Firenze*, EU:C:2006:8, point 140.

77 Commission Notice on the notion of State aid as referred to in Article 107(1) of the Treaty on the Functioning of the European Union (2016/C 262/01), at 189.

78 Commission Regulation (EU) No 1407/2013 of 18 December 2013 on the application of Articles 107 and 108 TFEU to de minimis aid maintains as a general rule a ceiling of € 200.000 as an amount of *de minimis* aid that a single undertaking may receive per Member State over any period of three years; in such a case the measure is deemed not to have any effect on trade between Member States and not to distort or threaten to distort competition.

79 Joined Cases T-515/13 and T-719/13, *Lico Leasing*, EU:T:2015:1004, point 189-190.

80 Joined Cases T-515/13 and T-719/13, *Lico Leasing*, EU:T:2015:1004, point 191.

15.2.7 Selected topics

The present section discusses a number of selected topics which are of specific significance for taxation in relation to State aid law: transfer pricing, tax treatment of cooperative societies, undertakings for collective investment, tax amnesties, depreciation and amortisation rules, fixed basis tax regimes for specific activities, anti-abuse rules, IP regimes, and rules on avoidance of double taxation.[81] Tax rulings and tax settlements have already been dealt with in sections 15.2.4 and 15.2.5.

Transfer pricing[82]

The issue of transfer pricing deserves special attention in the field of selectivity, because the European Commission has been focusing on this issue in a number of high profile cases such as Apple, Starbucks, Fiat, Amazon, IKEA, Nike, and the Belgian Excess Profits exemption.[83] In a common approach of these cases, the Commission considers the reference system to be the general corporate income tax system which has as its objective the taxation of profits of all companies subject to tax in the Member State concerned, irrespective of whether they are non-integrated companies (i.e. not belonging to a corporate group and thus 'standalone') or integrated companies (i.e. those belonging to a corporate group). According to the Commission, this difference has no bearing on the objective of a corporate income tax system which aims to tax profits of all companies subject to tax in the Member State, whether non-integrated or integrated. After all, according to the Commission, under a corporate income tax system, the profits of all companies are taxed in the same manner without any distinction as to group and uncontrolled companies, both types of companies should be considered to be in a similar factual and legal situation in light of the intrinsic objective of that system. On these grounds, it is the general corporate income tax system that constitutes the reference system against which it should be examined whether a 'correct' transfer pricing between group companies has taken place.[84] The Commission has invoked the case of *Forum 187* in support of its reasoning. This case involved the special Belgian tax regimes regarding so-called 'coordination centres' which were subject to a different tax regime than 'normal' companies. The Court considered with respect to a certain aspect of this regime:

---

81 Commission Notice on the notion of State aid as referred to in Article 107(1) of the Treaty on the Functioning of the European Union (2016/C 262/01), section 5.4.

82 Literature includes Richard Lyal, 'Transfer Pricing Rules and State Aid', 38 FORDHAM INT'L L.J. 1017, 1022–23 (2015); P.J. Wattel, 'Stateless Income, State Aid and the (Which?) Arm's Length Principle, Intertax 2016, p. 791–801; Werner Haslehner, 'Transfer pricing rules and State aid law', in: *Research Handbook on European Union Taxation Law* (Panayi/Haslehner/Traversa, eds.), Elgar 2020; Stefano Castagna, 'On the European Commission's Understanding of the Arm's Length Principle in International Taxation versus State Aid Matters' World Tax Journal 2021, 13(3).

83 Commission Decisions of 04.10.2017 (Amazon – Luxembourg), No. SA.38944; 30.08.2016 (Apple, Ireland), No. SA.38373; 11.01.2016 (Excess Profit exemption – Belgium), No. SA.37667; 21.10.2015 (Starbucks – Netherlands), No. SA.38374; 21.10.2015 (Fiat – Luxembourg), No. SA.38375; 18.12.2017, No. SA.46470 (IKEA – Netherlands); 10.1.2019 (Nike – Netherlands), No. SA.51284.

84 See for instance Commission Decision of 21.10.2015 (Starbucks – Netherlands), No. SA.38374, at 232 et seq.

"95. In order to decide whether a method of assessment of taxable income such as that laid down under the regime for coordination centres confers an advantage on them, it is necessary (...) to compare that regime with the ordinary tax system, based on the difference between profits and outgoings of an undertaking carrying on its activities in conditions of free competition.
96. In that regard, the staff costs and the financial costs incurred in cash-flow management and financing are factors which make a major contribution to enabling the coordination centres to earn revenue, inasmuch as those centres provide services, particularly of a financial nature. Accordingly, the effect of the exclusion of those costs from the expenditure which serves to determine the taxable income of the centres is that the transfer prices do not resemble those which would be charged in conditions of free competition.
97. It follows that such an exclusion confers an economic advantage on the centres."[85]

These considerations have been handed down in the context of the special Belgian regime for coordination centres. Nevertheless, the Commission attaches great importance to it in support of its transfer pricing approach in the above-mentioned cases in which it says:

"The arm's length principle therefore necessarily forms part of the Commission's assessment under Article 107(1) of the Treaty of tax measures granted to group companies, independently of whether a Member State has incorporated this principle into its national legal system and in what form. It is used to establish whether the taxable profit of a group company for corporate income tax purposes has been determined on the basis of a methodology that approximates market conditions, so that that company is not treated favourably under the ordinary corporate income tax system as compared to standalone companies whose taxable profit is determined by the market. Thus, for any avoidance of doubt, the arm's length principle that the Commission applies in its State aid assessment is not that derived from Article 9 of the OECD Model Tax Convention and the OECD TP Guidelines, which are non-binding instruments, but a general principle of equal treatment in taxation falling within the application of Article 107(1) of the Treaty, which binds the Member States and from whose scope the national tax rules are not excluded".[86]

The Court of Justice has rejected this line of reasoning. In its landmark judgment *Fiat Chrysler Finance Europe*, the Court reiterated that only the national law applicable in the Member State concerned must be taken into account in order to identify the reference system for direct taxation.[87] It went on to say that:

"95. (...) without harmonisation in that regard, any fixing of the methods and criteria for determining an 'arm's length' outcome falls within the discretion of the Member States. Although the member States of the OECD recognise the merits of using the arm's length principle in order to establish the correct allocation of company profits between different

85 Joined Cases C-182/03 and C-217/03, *Forum 187*, EU:C:2006:416.
86 Commission Decision of 11.01.2016 (Excess Profit exemption – Belgium), No. SA.37667, at 150. Compare also the Commission Notice on the notion of State aid as referred to in Article 107(1) of the Treaty on the Functioning of the European Union (2016/C 262/01), at 172.
87 Joined Cases C-885/19 P and C-898/19 P, *Fiat Chrysler Finance Europe v Commission*, EU:C:2022:859, point 74.

countries, there are significant differences between those States in the detailed application of transfer pricing methods. (...)
96. (...) it is only the national provisions that are relevant for the purposes of analysing whether particular transactions must be examined in the light of the arm's length principle and, if so, whether or not transfer prices, which form the basis of a taxpayer's taxable income and its allocation among the States concerned, deviate from an arm's length outcome. Parameters and rules external to the national tax system at issue cannot therefore be taken into account in the examination of the existence of a selective tax advantage within the meaning of Article 107(1) TFEU and for the purposes of establishing the tax burden that should normally be borne by an undertaking, unless that national tax system makes explicit reference to them.
97. This finding is an expression of the principle of legality of taxation, which forms part of the legal order of the European Union as a general principle of law, requiring that any obligation to pay a tax and all the essential elements defining the substantive features thereof must be provided for by law, the taxable person having to be in a position to foresee and calculate the amount of tax due and determine the point at which it becomes payable (...)."

The Court took a similar decision in *Amazon.*[88] We fully agree with this decision, because another approach would ultimately have led to a judicial harmonisation of transfer pricing systems in the European Union, in contravention of the procedures prescribed by Articles 114(2) and 115 TFEU.[89] The importance of the national reference framework cannot be overestimated, which was also shown by the case of *Commission v Ireland and Others (Apple)*. This case pivoted around the application of the Irish branch allocation provision, which – in view of the EU courts relying on the text of the law and on explanations by the Irish government – aimed at dividing the profits of a company between its head office and its permanent establishment.[90] Since this provision did not concern the allocation of profits between group companies, but only the allocation of profits within one company, the Court held that the Commission was right in taking the profits reported in the Apple group companies concerned as a starting point. It was also right in subsequently allocating those profits to either the Irish branches of those companies or to their foreign head offices, without requiring any account to be taken of the role played by other group companies. This approach resulted in a disproportionate allocation of profits to Ireland, when one looks at the assets, functions and risks of those companies. It was however the result of the application of the national reference framework as understood by the Court of Justice. Returning to transfer pricing rules applicable between group companies, once the appropriate national reference framework has been determined, the question remains how one should assess whether the transfer prices which were used by the tax administration are acceptable. In the case of *Frucona*, discussed in section 15.2.4 above, the question arose whether the tax collector had made disproportionate concessions to Frucona when collecting taxes due. The Court, applying the private creditor test, held that it is decisive whether the recipient undertaking would manifestly not have obtained comparable facilities from a private creditor in a situation as close as possible to that of

88 Case C-457/21 P, *Commission v Amazon.com and Others*, EU:C:2023:985, points 53-54.
89 Joined Cases C-885/19 P and C-898/19 P, *Fiat Chrysler Finance Europe v Commission*, EU:C:2022:859, point 115.
90 Case C-465/20 P, *Commission v Ireland and Others*, EU:C:2024:724, point 203.

the public creditor that sought to recover sums due to it.[91] This language, which allows a range of possible economic outcomes at the discretion of the domestic (tax) authorities, is echoed in the working paper which was published by the Commission services in 2016. This paper states that some transfer pricing arrangements do not seem to reflect the arm's length principle when the outcome *manifestly* deviates from a reliable approximation of a market based outcome; the Commission's focus is, therefore, on cases where there is a manifest breach of the arm's length principle.[92] Such an approach shows appropriate respect for the sovereignty of the Member States in the area of direct taxation and for the domestic tax administrations as the authorities primarily responsible for the application of domestic transfer pricing rules.

Cooperative societies

With respect to cooperative societies, the 2016 Notice builds on the Court's judgment in *Paint Graphos*.[93] In this judgment, the Court indicated that cooperative societies cannot be regarded as being in a comparable factual and legal situation to that of commercial companies, provided that they act in the economic interest of their members and their relations with their members are not purely commercial but personal and individual, the members being actively involved in the running of the business and entitled to equitable distribution of the results of economic performance.[94] However, if they in fact behave like a commercial company – e.g. by being used in an international tax structure – they must be taxed like a normal company. In addition, it may be possible to rely on the nature or general scheme of the national tax system as a justification for the fact that cooperative societies which distribute all their profits to their members are not taxed themselves as cooperatives, provided that tax is levied on the individual members. Appropriate control and monitoring procedures must be applied by the Member State concerned.[95]

Investment funds[96]

Regarding *undertakings for collective investment*, the 2016 Notice accepts as an objective intrinsic to a tax system that Member States may seek to reduce adverse taxation effects on investments through investment funds or companies compared to direct investments by individual investors and, as far as possible, to ensure that the overall final tax burden on the basket of various types of investments is about the same, irrespective of the vehicle used for the investment (tax neutrality): taxpayers are treated the same whether they invest in assets directly or indirectly through investment funds.[97] However, a State aid issue may arise if an investment fund regime discriminates between certain types of

91 Case C-300/16, *Frucona*, EU:C:2017:706, point 28.

92 DG Competition, Working Paper on State Aid and Tax Rulings, Background to the High Level Forum on State Aid of 3 June 2016, at 14 and 23.

93 Joined Cases C-78/08 to C-80/08, *Paint Graphos*, EU:C:2011:550.

94 Summary in the Commission Notice on the notion of State aid as referred to in Article 107(1) of the Treaty on the Functioning of the European Union (2016/C 262/01), at 157 et seq.

95 Joined Cases C-78/08 to C-80/08, *Paint Graphos*, EU:C:2011:550, points 71 and 74-75.

96 See also Sjoerd Douma, 'The tax treatment of CIVs and REITs from a State aid perspective: limits on national tax policy', in: Hein Vermeulen (Ed.), *The tax treatment of CIVs and REITS*, Amsterdam: IBFD 2014, p. 169-182.

97 Commission Notice on the notion of State aid as referred to in Article 107(1) of the Treaty on the Functioning of the European Union (2016/C 262/01), at 161-162.

investment. In *Fineco*, for example, investment funds which invested in SMEs were treated – within the investment fund regime – more favourably than other investment funds. If is difficult to see how such a differential treatment could be based on objectives inherent in the tax system itself, rather than on extrinsic policy objectives.[98] It is also necessary that an investment fund regime respects the principle of proportionality, in that the measure is suitable to achieve (enhanced) tax neutrality and does not go beyond what is necessary to achieve this. One relevant example from the practice of the Commission concerns the *Finnish REIT* case. In this case, the Commission went at length to ensure that the investment fund would receive no corporate tax exemption if it would not be ensured that the resident and non-resident participants in the fund would be taxed in its place; as a consequence, the fund was forced to distribute its proceeds to the participants.[99] Indeed, a more beneficial tax treatment of a collective investment than of an individual investment would be disproportionate and would go beyond what is necessary to achieve the objective of tax neutrality, as a result of which it would constitute a selective measure.[100]

Tax amnesties

Member States may choose to introduce a tax amnesty for a variety of reasons. They are at liberty to do this under the fiscal sovereignty retained by them. A tax amnesty may for instance include the possibility to report, in a limited period of time, undeclared assets or incomes without a risk of criminal penalties or fines. The 2016 Notice recognises that a tax amnesty may pursue a legitimate objective (e.g. to give taxpayers the possibility to leave the past behind them and to start with a clean sheet of paper).[101] According to the Notice, the measure should effectively be open to any undertaking of any sector or size that has outstanding tax liabilities due at the date set by the measure, without favouring any pre-defined group of undertakings. Second, it should not entail any de facto selectivity in favour of certain undertakings or sectors. Third, the tax administration's action should be limited to administering the implementation of the tax amnesty without any discretionary power to intervene in the granting or intensity of the measure. Finally, the measure should not entail a waiver from verification.[102]

Depreciation and amortization rules

In a tax system, depreciation and amortisation rules are normally introduced in order to spread deduction expenses related to an asset over time, corresponding with the expected economic lifetime of the asset. In this way, those expenses are matched with the income which the asset is expected to produce in the future. This reflects a legitimate objective

98 Case T-445/05, *Fineco*, EU:T:2009:50.

99 Commission Decision of 12 May 2010, C (2010) 2974 final (State Aid No. N131/2009 – Finland. Residential Real Estate Investment Trust (REIT) Scheme).

100 Commission Notice on the notion of State aid as referred to in Article 107(1) of the Treaty on the Functioning of the European Union (2016/C 262/01), at 163. See also H. Vermeulen, 'Fiscal state aid and real estate collective investment vehicles (CIVs)', *EC Tax Review* 2011, p. 155-158.

101 Another legitimate objective may be to provide legal certainty to taxpayers which have been litigating in the court system against a tax assessment for an unreasonable period of time; see Case C-417/10, *3M Italia*, EU:C:2012:184.

102 Commission Notice on the notion of State aid as referred to in Article 107(1) of the Treaty on the Functioning of the European Union (2016/C 262/01), at 166.

which is inherent in a tax system.[103] State aid issues, however, arise when the objectives underlying a system depreciation or amortisation are extrinsic to the tax system.[104] This may, for instance, be the case when a Member State introduces a straight line depreciation for the assets for wind power plants over five years, in order to promote the production of renewable energy and a more environmentally friendly and diversified electricity sector. Such a rule differentiates between assets on the basis of objectives which are extrinsic to the tax system. As a result, the rule grants a selective advantage to undertakings which invest in such assets.[105]

Fixed basis tax regimes for specific activities
According to the 2016 Notice, it may be justified by the nature and general scheme of the system to determine income tax on a fixed basis, provided that the following conditions are fulfilled: (a) the fixed basis regime is justified by the concern to avoid disproportionate administrative burden on certain types of undertakings because of their small size or sector of activity (for example in the agriculture or fisheries sectors); (b) on average, the fixed basis regime does not have the effect of implying a lower tax burden for those undertakings as compared to other undertakings excluded from its scope and does not entail advantages for a sub-category of beneficiaries of the regime.[106] An example is the Belgian alternative income tax regime for the wholesale diamond sector. The calculation of a trader's gross profit is based on a fixed percentage of turnover. The Commission decided that this alternative income tax does not constitute State aid since i) the vast majority of diamond traders will pay more taxes than under the ordinary rules of income taxation, ii) it also saves the most cumbersome audit verifications (in particular, the valuation and follow-up of the diamond inventories, as well as iii) the uncertainty linked to taxpayers challenging the tax bill. These objectives are legitimate and inherent to the tax system: they are in no way intended to grant a benefit to the diamond sector.[107] It should be noted that tonnage tax regimes should, in principle, be considered as State aid, because the objectives of those regimes is to enhance to competitiveness of the shipping sector (compare the remarks in section 22.3 below).

Anti-abuse rules
According to the Commission, anti-abuse rules may be justified as measures to prevent tax avoidance by taxpayers. However, such rules might be selective if they provide for a derogation (non-application of the anti-abuse rules) to specific undertakings or transactions, which would not be consistent with the logic underlying the anti-abuse rules in question.[108] In *Luxembourg v Commission (Engie)*, the Court of Justice dealt with

103 Compare Case C-100/15, *Netherlands Maritime Technology Association*, EU:C:2016:254, with respect to a system of depreciation of certain assets acquired through financial leasing.
104 Commission Notice on the notion of State aid as referred to in Article 107(1) of the Treaty on the Functioning of the European Union (2016/C 262/01), at 179.
105 Decision EFTA Surveillance Authority of 06.07.2016, No: 150/16/COL.
106 Commission Notice on the notion of State aid as referred to in Article 107(1) of the Treaty on the Functioning of the European Union (2016/C 262/01), at 181-182.
107 Commission Decision of 29.7.2016, C(2016) 4809 final, at 55.
108 Commission Notice on the notion of State aid as referred to in Article 107(1) of the Treaty on the Functioning of the European Union (2016/C 262/01), at 183.

the question whether a failure by the tax administration to apply its GAAR in a concrete situation could result in State aid. The Court held that the non-application of such a provision by the tax authorities in order to refuse the tax treatment sought by a taxpayer in a tax ruling request does not lead to the grant of a selective advantage unless that non-application departs from the national case-law or administrative practice relating to that provision. Another approach would be incompatible with the fiscal autonomy of the Member States.[109] Indeed, the Court of Justice has been very careful in the area of anti-abuse measures to sufficiently respect the autonomy of the Member States in their design of such systems. Only in case of a clear deviation from the national reference system, State aid may occur.[110]

IP regimes

The question arises whether an IP regime of general application may give rise to selective advantages. This question is difficult to answer, because, on the one hand, the advantage granted by the regime is based objectives which are extrinsic to the tax system, but, on the other hand, the advantage is in conformity with another fundamental objective of the Union, namely the promotion of research and development (Article 179(1) TFEU).[111] In any case, the Commission has in the past accepted that IP regimes which are applied generally do not give rise to State aid.[112] In 2014, the Code of Conduct Group reached a compromise on the so-called 'modified nexus approach' for IP regimes.[113] According to the Group, this is the appropriate method to ensure that patent boxes require sufficient substance.[114] If EU Member States fail to fully implement the modified nexus approach agreed in the Code of Conduct Group, the European Commission has a powerful weapon at its disposal to whip them in the right direction: Article 107 TFEU. Indeed, in 2014 the Commission criticised IP regimes as follows:

> "Over the last ten years, several Member States have also introduced special tax regimes for IP rights that are supposed to stimulate innovation and investments in new technologies. Such regimes include "patent boxes", which provide for tax reductions on income from patents. In 2008, the Commission reviewed such a regime in Spain and concluded that the scheme did not constitute aid (see IP/08/216). Since then, however, the Commission has received indications that special tax regimes seem to mainly benefit highly mobile businesses and do not trigger significant additional research and development activity. The Commission is therefore gathering information to assess whether the regimes grant a selective advantage to a particular group of companies, in breach of EU state aid rules."[115]

109 Joined Cases C-451/21 P and C-454/21 P, Luxembourg v Commission (Engie), EU:C:2023:948, point 155.
110 See for instance Joined Cases C-555/22 P, C-556/22 P and C-564/22 P, *United Kingdom United Kingdom v Commission and Others*, EU:C:2024:763, point 97 et seq.
111 Compare, in a fundamental freedoms context, Case C-39/04, *Laboratoires Fournier*, EU:C:2005:161.
112 E.g. Commission Decision of 13.02.2008, No. N480/2007 (Spain - reduction of tax from intangible assets).
113 Report of the Code of Conduct Group (Business Taxation) of 11 December 2014, 16553/1/14 REV 1 LIMITE, FISC 225 ECOFIN 1166 (Annex 1).
114 Code of Conduct Group (Business Taxation), Report to the Council of 28 November 2016, 14750/16, FISC 202 ECOFIN 1092, para. 12 et seq.
115 European Commission, press release of 24 March 2014, IP/14/309.

Specifically with regard to the Luxembourg regime the Commission noted that the Luxembourg regime that was introduced allows for tax exemption of 80% of profits derived from the use or licensing of IP rights such as patents, trademarks, designs, models, internet domain names and software copyrights. The European Commission has not brought this action further, because of the agreement reached in the Code of Conduct Group. However, the issue of patent box regimes has not disappeared from the Commission's agenda. This is evident from a policy paper, which states that "R&D&I support granted to larger firms is often less attractive than that granted to smaller firms" and that "[t]he specific design of the tax incentives should also be carefully considered.[...] Effects of multinationals' cross-border tax planning strategies should also be looked at".[116] So, if Member States do not contribute to solve this issue, the Commission may easily argue that State aid has been granted through the following argumentation: i) the IP box is a favourable deviation from the normal tax regime, ii) this gives rise to a *prima facie* selective advantage unless it can be justified by legitimate objectives pursued by the tax system in a proportionate manner, iii) the objective of the IP box is to foster research & development in line with international consensus on the modified nexus approach, iv) the IP regime at issue goes beyond what is necessary to achieve this objective because it deviates from this consensus.[117] In any case, the General Court has held that an exemption of passive interest and royalty payments from corporate income tax may amount to State aid to companies receiving such income.[118]

Prevention of double taxation

As stated in section 15.2.5 above, the prevention of economic double taxation represents an objective inherent to a tax system. The question arises whether a rule which implements this objective, such as a participation exemption, may give rise to State aid if it is applied in situations whether no double taxation exists. The simple example of a hybrid loan may illustrate the issue. A hybrid loan is a loan agreement between a parent company and a subsidiary, which is qualified as debt in the State of the subsidiary (the debtor) and as equity in the State of the parent (the creditor). The international mismatch which is achieved relates to deductible interest at the level of the subsidiary and non-taxable income at the level of the parent (participation exemption). The question arises as to whether application of participation exemption may constitute State aid. The argument would be that the participation exemption provides an advantage to an undertaking in comparison with a company not entitled to it which is, in the light of the object and purpose of the tax system, in a comparable situation. This advantage may be justified by the wish to avoid economic double taxation – an objective which is intrinsic to the tax system – but may be disproportionate in a situation where no such double taxation exists (i.e. where the payment was deductible at the level of the subsidiary). In *Luxembourg v Commission (Engie)*, the Court of Justice clarified that this conclusion should not be

116 EC, How evaluation can help: The case of financial support to business R&D&I, Competition policy brief, 2016-03, May 2016.

117 Let alone that the objective of promoting research & development does not seem to be an objective which is itself intrinsic to the tax system.

118 Case T-508/19, *Mead Johnson*, EU:T:2022:217.

reached too quickly. For such a conclusion, a positive policy intention to prevent double non-taxation is required.[119]

Finally, it should be noted that the exemption of foreign income in the context of a tax treaty does not constitute aid, because the issue of international juridical double taxation or international juridical double non-taxation is outside the scope of free movement or State aid law.[120]

15.3 Compatibility of State aid with the internal market

15.3.1 Introduction

If an envisaged tax measure constitutes State aid, it should be notified to the Commission under Article 108(3) TFEU. The Commission should then assess whether the aid is compatible with the internal market. According to Article 107 (2) TFEU, the following shall be compatible with the internal market:
a) aid having a social character, granted to individual consumers, provided that such aid is granted without discrimination related to the origin of the products concerned;
b) aid to make good the damage caused by natural disasters or exceptional occurrences;
c) aid granted to the economy of certain areas of the Federal Republic of Germany affected by the division of Germany, in so far as such aid is required in order to compensate for the economic disadvantages caused by that division. Five years after the entry into force of the Treaty of Lisbon, the Council, acting on a proposal from the Commission, may adopt a decision repealing this point.

Once the Commission has found that the notified measure falls within the scope of this provision, it has no further discretion than to approve it. Such discretion does exist, however, under Article 107(3) TFEU which states that the following may be considered to be compatible with the internal market:
a) aid to promote the economic development of areas where the standard of living is abnormally low or where there is serious underemployment, and of the regions referred to in Article 349, in view of their structural, economic and social situation;
b) aid to promote the execution of an important project of common European interest or to remedy a serious disturbance in the economy of a Member State;
c) aid to facilitate the development of certain economic activities or of certain economic areas, where such aid does not adversely affect trading conditions to an extent contrary to the common interest;
d) aid to promote culture and heritage conservation where such aid does not affect trading conditions and competition in the Union to an extent that is contrary to the common interest;
e) such other categories of aid as may be specified by decision of the Council on a proposal from the Commission.

119 Joined Cases C-451/21 P and C-454/21 P, Luxembourg v Commission (Engie), EU:C:2023:948, point 128 et seq.
120 Case C-513/04, *Kerckhaert and Morres*, EU:C:2006:713; Commission Decision of 8 July 2009, *Groepsrentebox*, C(2009) 4511 final.

This provision confers on the Commission a wide discretion to declare certain aid compatible with the internal market by way of derogation from the general prohibition laid down in Article 107(1) TFEU. The final determination whether an aid measure is compatible with the internal market is the exclusive responsibility of the Commission, subject to review by the Court of Justice of the European Union.[121] The present section will discuss how the Commission exercises this discretion, with a focus on tax cases, and how this discretion is limited in certain situations.

15.3.2 Limitations on the Commission's discretion

The Commission may declare an aid measure compatible with the internal market under Article 107(3) TFEU. Where a tax specifically intended to finance aid proves to be contrary to other provisions of the Treaty, the Commission cannot declare the aid scheme of which the charge forms part to be compatible with the internal market.[122] This is also true more generally: State aid, certain conditions of which contravene other provisions of the Treaty – for instance free movement provisions, the Charter of Fundamental Rights of the European Union, or general principles of Union law –, cannot be declared by the Commission to be compatible with the internal market.[123] At the same time, aspects of aid which contravene specific provisions of the Treaty other than Articles 107 and 108 TFEU may be so indissolubly linked to the object of the aid that it is impossible to evaluate them separately so that their effect on the compatibility or incompatibility of the aid viewed as a whole must therefore of necessity be determined in the light of the procedure prescribed in Article 108 TFEU. The position is different if it is possible when a system of aid is being analysed to separate those conditions or factors which, even though they form part of this system, may be regarded as not being necessary for the attainment of its object or for its proper functioning. In the latter case, there are no reasons based on the division of powers under Articles 107 and 108 TFEU which permit the conclusion to be drawn that, if other provisions of the Treaty which have direct effect are infringed, those provisions may not be invoked before national courts simply because the factor in question is an aspect of aid. Indeed, the fact that the inevitable consequence of the aid itself is often protection and therefore some partitioning of the market in question, as far as concerns the production of undertakings which do not derive any benefit from it, cannot imply that the aid produces restrictive free movement effects which exceed what is necessary to enable it to attain the objectives permitted by the Treaty.[124] The case of *Germany v Commission* provides an interesting example. This case evolved around paragraph 6b of the German Income Tax Act ('the EStG') which had been amended in view of the reunification of Germany. Under the amendment, up to 100% of a taxable gain on the sale of assets gain could be set off against the costs of purchasing new shares in capital companies, provided that the purchase is connected to an increase in capital, or the setting-up of new capital companies, and provided that such companies have both their registered office and their central administration in one of the new *Länder* or in

121 Case C-143/99, *Adria-Wien Pipeline*, EU:C:2001:598, point 29-30.
122 Joined cases C-261/01 and C-262/01, *Van Calster*, EU:C:2003:571, paragraphs 47-48.
123 Case C-156/98, *Germany v Commission*, EU:C:2000:467, paragraph 78 et seq.
124 Case 74/76, *Ianelli v Meroni*, EU:C:1977:51, paragraph 14 et seq; Case C-225/91, *Matra*, EU:C:1993:239, points 41-42.

Berlin. According to the Commission, this latter requirement breached Articles 49 and 54 TFEU (freedom of establishment), as a result of which it could not approve the measure to this extent. This finding was upheld by the Court.[125]

15.3.3 *The Commission's State aid policy*

The vast majority of aid measures in the Union is implemented without prior authorisation by the Commission. The General Block Exemption Regulation (GBER) makes this possible.[126] With this regulation, the Commission has declared specific categories of State aid compatible with the Treaty if they fulfil certain conditions, thus exempting them from the requirement of prior notification and Commission approval. The GBER contains detailed rules for regional aid, aid to SMEs, aid for research and development and innovation, training aid, aid for disadvantaged workers and for workers with disabilities, aid for environmental protection and the green and digital transition, aid to make good the damage caused by certain natural disasters, social aid for transport for residents of remote regions, aid for broadband infrastructures, aid for culture and heritage conservation, aid for sport and multifunctional recreational infrastructures, and aid for local infrastructures (including port and airport infrastructure). In addition, many other rules and guidelines have been adopted, for instance on rescue and restructuring aid, sectoral aid (e.g. agriculture, energy and transport), State aid in the context of the financial crisis, and transparency.[127] Obviously, Member States still need to notify State aid measures in advance if they have not been relieved of the obligation of Article 108(3) TFEU. A good example is provided by the notification by Sweden of a tax regime designed to enable young and small companies to recruit and retain the key employees they need to achieve their growth potential. The aid would be granted in the form of a reduction in the taxes which are due when employees exercise their stock options. The Commission's decision provides insight into the assessment framework used in such cases. According to Article 107(3) (c) TFEU, aid may be compatible with the internal market if it facilitates the development of certain economic activities or of certain economic areas, where such aid does not adversely affect trading conditions to an extent contrary to the common interest. In order to determine the compatibility of a measure under Article 107(3)(c) TFEU, the Commission performs a balancing test, weighing positive effects in terms of a contribution to the achievement of well-defined objectives of common interest and negative effects on trade and competition in the common market. In this regard, the Commission considers the following principles:

125 Case C-156/98, *Germany v Commission*, EU:C:2000:467, points 78 et seq.

126 Council Regulation (EC) No 1588/2015 of 13 July 2015 on the application of Articles 107 and 108 of the Treaty on the Functioning of the European Union to certain categories of horizontal State aid enables the Commission to adopt so-called Block Exemption Regulations for State aid (this regulation has replaced as of 14.10.2015 Council Regulation (EC) No 994/98 of 7 May 1998). The GBER has been implemented through Commission Regulation (EU) N°651/2014 of 17 June 2014 declaring certain categories of aid compatible with the internal market in application of Articles 107 and 108 of the Treaty, as subsequently amended multiple times.

127 The reader is referred to the following website with extensive references to relevant materials: http://ec.europa.eu/competition/state_aid/legislation/legislation.html.

"a) contribution to a well-defined objective of common interest: a State aid measure must aim at an objective of common interest in accordance with Article 107(3) TFEU;
b) need for State intervention: a State aid measure must be targeted towards a situation where aid can bring about a material improvement that the market cannot deliver itself, for example by remedying a market failure or addressing an equity or cohesion concern;
c) appropriateness of the aid measure: the proposed aid measure must be an appropriate policy instrument to address the objective of common interest;
d) incentive effect: the aid must change the behaviour of the undertaking(s) concerned in such a way that it engages in additional activity, which it would not carry out without the aid or would carry out in a restricted or different manner or location;
e) proportionality of the aid: the amount and intensity of the aid must be limited to the minimum needed to induce the additional investment or activity by the undertaking(s) concerned;
f) avoidance of undue negative effects on competition and trade between Member States: the negative effects of aid must be sufficiently limited, so that the overall balance of the measure is positive;
g) transparency of aid: Member States, the Commission, economic operators, and the public, must have easy access to all relevant acts and to pertinent information about the aid awarded thereunder."[128]

In the light of these criteria, the Commission decided not to raise objections to the aid measure on the grounds that it is compatible with the internal market pursuant to Article 107(3)(c) TFEU. Indeed, the criteria above are instructive for the Commission's approach when assessing the compatibility of aid through a tax measure.[129]

15.4 State aid procedure and enforcement

15.4.1 Introduction

The enforcement of State aid law is an essential part of a successful competition policy. The present section will discuss how the Commission monitors existing aid, how it deals with the notification of new aid and how unlawful aid may be recovered. In addition, the process of judicial appeal will be reviewed.

128 Commission Decision of 26.6.2017, C(2017) 4237 final (Sweden – Tax reduction of employee share options).

129 For a comprehensive overview, reference is made to Conor Quigley's excellent *European State Aid Law and Policy*, Oxford: Hart Publishing 2015, Part II.

15.4.2 Monitoring of existing aid

According to Article 108(1) TFEU, the Commission shall, in cooperation with Member States, keep under constant review all systems of aid existing in those States.[130] On the basis of Article 109 TFEU, the Council has adopted Regulation 2015/1589/EU of 13 July 2015 laying down detailed rules for the application of Article 108 TFEU (the 'procedural regulation'). Under Article 1(b) of this Regulation, 'existing aid' means:

i. all aid which existed prior to the entry into force of the TFEU in the respective Member States, that is to say, aid schemes and individual aid which were put into effect before, and are still applicable after, the entry into force of the TFEU in the respective Member States;[131]
ii. authorised aid, that is to say, aid schemes and individual aid which have been authorised by the Commission or by the Council;
iii. aid which is deemed to have been authorised by the Commission for a lack of response within the prescribed time limit of two months after notification of an aid measure (Article 4(6) of the Regulation);
iv. aid which is deemed to be existing aid because the recovery period of ten years for unlawful aid has expired (Article 17 of the Regulation);
v. aid which is deemed to be an existing aid because it can be established that at the time it was put into effect it did not constitute an aid, and subsequently became an aid due to the evolution of the internal market and without having been altered by the Member State.[132] Where certain measures become aid following the liberalisation of an activity by Union law, such measures shall not be considered as existing aid after the date fixed for liberalisation.

According to Article 21 of the procedural regulation, the Commission shall obtain from the Member State concerned all necessary information for the review of existing aid schemes pursuant to Article 108(1) TFEU. Where the Commission considers that an existing aid scheme is not, or is no longer, compatible with the internal market, it shall inform the Member State concerned of its preliminary view and give the Member State concerned the opportunity to submit its comments. Article 22 of the procedural regulation states that where the Commission, in the light of this information, concludes that the existing aid scheme is not, or is no longer, compatible with the internal market, it shall issue a recommendation proposing appropriate measures to the Member State concerned. The recommendation may propose, in particular:
a) substantive amendment of the aid scheme; or

130 According to Article 26 of Regulation 2015/1589/EU of 13 July 2015 (the procedural regulation), the Member States shall submit to the Commission annual reports on all existing aid schemes with regard to which no specific reporting obligations have been imposed.

131 This is without prejudice to different agreements in Articles 144 and 172 of the Act of Accession of Austria, Finland and Sweden, to point 3 and the Appendix of Annex IV to the Act of Accession of the Czech Republic, Estonia, Cyprus, Latvia, Lithuania, Hungary, Malta, Poland, Slovenia and Slovakia, to points 2 and 3(b) and the Appendix of Annex V to the Act of Accession of Bulgaria and Romania, and to points 2 and 3(b) and the Appendix of Annex IV to the Act of Accession of Croatia.

132 This may, for instance, be the case where trade between Member States has evolved where it was, at first, non-existent (compare the conditions of Article 107(1) TFEU).

b) introduction of procedural requirements; or
c) abolition of the aid scheme.

Where the Member State accepts the proposed measures, it shall be bound by its acceptance to implement the appropriate measures (Article 23 of the procedural regulation). However, where the Member State concerned does not accept the proposed measures and the Commission still considers that those measures are necessary, it shall take a decision to initiate the formal investigation procedure. As Article 6 of the procedural regulation stipulates, this decision shall summarise the relevant issues of fact and law, shall include a preliminary assessment of the Commission as to the aid character of the proposed measure and shall set out the doubts as to its compatibility with the internal market. The decision shall call upon the Member State concerned and upon other interested parties to submit comments within one month. For that purpose, it is sufficient for them to be aware of the reasoning which led the Commission provisionally to conclude that the measure at issue might constitute new aid incompatible with the internal market.[133] In this context, 'interested party' means any Member State and any person, undertaking or association of undertakings whose interests might be affected by the granting of aid, in particular the beneficiary of the aid, competing undertakings and trade associations (Article 1(h) of the procedural regulation). According to Article 9 of the procedural regulation, the formal investigation procedure shall be closed by means of one of the following decisions:

i. a 'no aid' decision, where the Commission finds that, where appropriate following modification by the Member State concerned, the notified measure does not constitute aid;
ii. a 'positive decision', where the Commission finds that, where appropriate following modification by the Member State concerned, the doubts as to the compatibility of the notified measure with the internal market have been removed;
iii. a 'conditional decision', where the Commission attaches to a positive decision conditions subject to which aid may be considered compatible with the internal market and may lay down obligations to enable compliance with the decision to be monitored;
iv. a 'negative decision', where the Commission finds that the notified aid is not compatible with the internal market.

Those decisions shall be taken as soon as the doubts referred to in the decision to open the formal investigation procedure have been removed.[134] The Commission shall as far as possible endeavour to adopt a decision within a period of 18 months from the opening of the procedure (Article 9(6) of the procedural regulation). Once this time limit has expired, and should the Member State concerned so request, the Commission shall, within 2 months, take a decision on the basis of the information available to it. If appropriate, where the information provided is not sufficient to establish compatibility, the Commission shall take a negative decision (Article 9(7) of the procedural regulation).

133 Case T-648/19, *Nike*, EU:T:2021:428, point 74.
134 Note that the Commission may revoke its decision, after having given the Member State concerned the opportunity to submit its comments, where the decision was based on incorrect information provided during the procedure which was a determining factor for the decision. Before revoking a decision and taking a new decision, the Commission shall open the formal investigation procedure; see Article 11 of the procedural regulation.

An interesting example of the procedure regarding existing aid in the area of direct taxation is provided by the Commission Decision of 21 January 2016 on aid measure SA.25338 implemented by the Netherlands (corporate tax exemption for public undertakings).[135]

15.4.3 Notification of new aid

Article 2 of the procedural regulation states that aAny plans to grant new aid shall be notified to the Commission.[136] In this context, 'new aid' means all aid, that is to say, aid schemes and individual aid, which is not existing aid, including alterations to existing aid (Article 1(c) of the procedural regulation). In practice, the question under which circumstances an existing aid scheme is altered such that it has become new aid, is very relevant. After all, existing aid may, in accordance with Article 108(1) TFEU, be lawfully implemented so long as the Commission has made no finding of incompatibility. In respect of new aid, Article 108(3) TFEU provides that plans to grant new aid or alter existing aid must be notified, in due time, to the Commission and may not be put into effect until the procedure has resulted in a final decision.[137] After notification of the measure, the Commission shall decide, if necessary after having opened the formal investigation procedure, whether the notified measure constitutes State aid and, if so, to what extent it can be regarded as compatible with the internal market. The standstill obligation of Article 108(3) has direct effect.[138] This means that national authorities, including the judicial authorities, are obliged to disapply domestic tax law measures which have been put into effect in contravention of this provision.[139] In Article 4(1) of Regulation No 794/2004, the Commission has indicated that it considers an alteration to existing aid to mean 'any change, save modifications of a purely formal or administrative nature which cannot affect the evaluation of the compatibility of the aid measure with the common market'. In *Namur-Les assurances du crédit*, the Court held that 'the emergence of new aid or the alteration of existing aid cannot be assessed according to the scale of the aid or, in particular, its amount in financial terms at any moment in the life of the undertaking if the aid is provided under earlier statutory provisions which remain unaltered'. The Court went on to state that 'whether aid may be classified as new aid or as alteration of existing aid must be determined by reference to the provisions providing for it'.[140] As AG Wahl has noted, whether a given measure constitutes an 'alteration to existing aid' depends on the answer to three questions. First, what is the national measure conferring the existing aid? Second, has that national measure been amended? Third, if so, is that alteration

135 Groningen Seaports and Others have lodged an appeal against this decision; see case T-160/16.

136 Note that the Commission has declared specific categories of State aid compatible with the Treaty if they fulfil certain conditions, thus exempting them from the requirement of prior notification and Commission approval; see the General block exemption Regulation 1588/2015 of 13 July 2015, discussed in section 22.3.3 above.

137 Case C-74/16, *Congregación de Escuelas Pías Provincia Betania*, EU:C:2017:496, point 86.

138 Case C-143/99, *Adria-Wien Pipeline*, EU:C:2001:598, paragraph 26; Case C-368/04, *Transalpine Ölleitung*, EU:C:2006:644, paragraph 41.

139 Compare Joined Cases C-78/08 to C-80/08, *Paint Graphos*, EU:C:2011:550, point 25; Case C-6/12, *P Oy*, EU:C:2013:525; Case C-172/03, *Heiser*, ECLI:EU:C:2005:130, point 18. See generally R. Luja, 'Defining the Scope of State Aid: How Tax Cases Affect the State Aid Framework' (July 2014), SSRN: https://ssrn.com/abstract=2470462.

140 Case C-44/93, *Namur-Les assurances du crédit*, EU:C:1994:311, points 28-31.

purely formal or administrative?[141] In a notification of new aid, the Member State shall provide all necessary information in order to enable the Commission to take a decision ('complete notification'). The Member State may withdraw the notification in due time before the Commission has taken a decision; in cases where the Commission initiated the formal investigation procedure, the Commission shall close that procedure (Article 10 of the procedural regulation). In the meantime, Article 3 determines that notifiable aid shall not be put into effect before the Commission has taken, or is deemed to have taken, a decision authorising such aid. Under Article 4 of the procedural regulation, the Commission shall examine the notification as soon as it is received. Subsequently, it shall take one of the following decisions:

i. a 'no aid' decision, where the notified measure does not constitute aid;
ii. a 'decision not to raise objections', where the Commission, after a preliminary examination, finds that no doubts are raised as to the compatibility with the internal market of a notified measure, in so far as it falls within the scope of Article 107(1) TFEU;
iii. a 'decision to initiate the formal investigation procedure', where the Commission, after a preliminary examination, finds that doubts are raised as to the compatibility with the internal market of a notified measure.

Those decisions shall be taken within 2 months after the notification has been considered complete. Where the Commission has not taken a decision in time, the aid shall be deemed to have been authorised by the Commission. The Member State may thereupon implement the measures in question after giving the Commission prior notice thereof, unless the Commission takes a decision within a period of 15 working days following receipt of the notice (Article 4(6) of the procedural regulation). If the Commission decides to open the formal investigation procedure, that decision contains a summary of the relevant issues of fact and law, a preliminary assessment as to the aid character of the proposed measure and a summary of the doubts as to its compatibility with the internal market (Article 6 of the procedural regulation). The decision shall call upon the Member State concerned and upon other interested parties to submit comments within one month. During the formal investigation, the Commission may request any other Member State, an undertaking or an association of undertakings to provide all market information necessary to enable the Commission to complete its assessment of the measure at stake taking due account of the principle of proportionality, in particular for small and medium-sized enterprises (Article 7). The Commission may request information only: (a) if it is limited to formal investigation procedures that have been identified by the Commission as being ineffective to date; and (b) in so far as aid beneficiaries are concerned, if the Member State concerned agrees to the request. The undertakings or associations of undertakings providing information following a Commission's request for market information shall submit their answer simultaneously to the Commission and to the Member State concerned, to the extent that the documents provided do not include information that is confidential vis-à-vis that Member State. They are obliged to cooperate and subject to penalties if they fail

141 Opinion AG Wahl in Case C-510/16, *Carrefour Hypermarchés*, EU:C:2017:929, at 53. A parallel may be drawn here with Article 64 TFEU where it speaks of measures which 'existed' on 31 December 1993.

to submit complete and accurate information (Article 8). According to Article 9 of the procedural regulation, the formal investigation procedure shall be closed by means of one of the following decisions:

i. a 'no aid' decision, where the Commission finds that, where appropriate following modification by the Member State concerned, the notified measure does not constitute aid;
ii. a 'positive decision', where the Commission finds that, where appropriate following modification by the Member State concerned, the doubts as to the compatibility of the notified measure with the internal market have been removed;
iii. a 'conditional decision', where the Commission attaches to a positive decision conditions subject to which aid may be considered compatible with the internal market and may lay down obligations to enable compliance with the decision to be monitored;
iv. a 'negative decision', where the Commission finds that the notified aid is not compatible with the internal market.

Those decisions shall be taken as soon as the doubts referred to in the decision to open the formal investigation procedure have been removed.[142] The Commission shall as far as possible endeavour to adopt a decision within a period of 18 months from the opening of the procedure (Article 9(6) of the procedural regulation). Once this time limit has expired, and should the Member State concerned so request, the Commission shall, within 2 months, take a decision on the basis of the information available to it. If appropriate, where the information provided is not sufficient to establish compatibility, the Commission shall take a negative decision (Article 9(7) of the procedural regulation).

15.4.4 *Recovery of unlawful aid*

New aid put into effect in contravention of Article 108(3) TFEU is 'unlawful aid' (Article 1(f) of the procedural regulation). According to Article 12, the Commission may on its own initiative examine information regarding alleged unlawful aid from whatever source.[143] The Commission may also act on the basis of a complaint submitted by any interested party in accordance with Article 24(2). The Commission shall examine such a complaint without undue delay and shall ensure that the Member State concerned is kept fully and regularly informed of the progress and outcome of the examination. In the course of the examination, the Commission has wide powers to request for information as described above. Indeed, after the initiation of the formal investigation procedure, the Commission may request information from the Member State concerned, any other Member State, from an undertaking, or association of undertakings. Where the Member State concerned does not provide the information requested within the period prescribed by the Commission, or where it provides incomplete information, the Commission shall by decision require

142 Note that the Commission may revoke its decision, after having given the Member State concerned the opportunity to submit its comments, where the decision was based on incorrect information provided during the procedure which was a determining factor for the decision. Before revoking a decision and taking a new decision, the Commission shall open the formal investigation procedure; see Article 11 of the procedural regulation.

143 Article 25 of the procedural regulation provides the Commission, more generally, with investigative powers into sectors of the economy and into aid instruments.

the information to be provided ('information injunction' pursuant to Article 12(3) of the regulation). The decision shall specify what information is required and prescribe an appropriate period within which it is to be supplied. Under Article 13 of the procedural regulation, the Commission may also adopt a decision requiring the Member State to suspend any unlawful aid until the Commission has taken a decision on the compatibility of the aid with the internal market ('suspension injunction'). In addition, it may adopt a decision requiring the Member State provisionally to recover any unlawful aid until the Commission has taken a decision on the compatibility of the aid with the internal market ('recovery injunction'), if all the following criteria are fulfilled:

a) according to an established practice there are no doubts about the aid character of the measure concerned;
b) there is an urgency to act;
c) there is a serious risk of substantial and irreparable damage to a competitor.

If the Member State fails to comply with a suspension injunction or a recovery injunction, Article 14 of the procedural regulation authorises the Commission, while carrying out the examination on the substance of the matter on the basis of the information available, to refer the matter to the Court of Justice directly and apply for a declaration that the failure to comply constitutes an infringement of the TFEU. The examination of possible unlawful aid shall result in a decision pursuant to Article 4, described in section 22.4.3 above. In the case of decisions to initiate the formal investigation procedure, proceedings shall be closed by means of a decision pursuant to Article 9, also described in section 22.4.3 above. Importantly, in cases of possible unlawful aid and without prejudice to Article 13(2), the Commission shall not be bound by any time-limits (Article 15(2) of the procedural regulation).[144] Under Article 16(1) of the procedural regulation, where negative decisions are taken in cases of unlawful aid, the Commission shall decide that the Member State concerned shall take all necessary measures to recover the aid from the beneficiary ('recovery decision'). The Commission shall however not require recovery of the aid if this would be contrary to a general principle of Union law (see below). Pursuant to Article 16(2) of the Procedural Regulation, the aid to be recovered shall include interest at an appropriate rate fixed by the Commission. Interest shall be payable from the date on which the unlawful aid was at the disposal of the beneficiary until the date of its recovery. Interest rate shall be applied on a compound basis until the date of the recovery of the aid.[145] According to Article 17 of the procedural regulation, the powers of the Commission to recover aid shall be subject to a limitation period of 10 years. This period shall begin on the day on which the unlawful aid is awarded to the beneficiary either as individual aid or as aid under an aid scheme. Any action taken by the Commission or by a Member State, acting at the request of the Commission, with regard to the unlawful aid shall interrupt the limitation period. Each interruption shall start time running afresh. The limitation period shall be suspended for as long as the decision of the Commission is the subject of proceedings pending before the Court of Justice. According to Article 29

144 The Commission is however bound to decide within a 'reasonable time' within the meaning of Article 47 of the Charter of Fundamental Rights of the European Union.
145 Article 11 of Commission Regulation (EC) No 794/2004 of 21 April 2004.

of the procedural regulation, if the Member State concerned does not comply with the obligation to recover unlawful aid, the Commission may refer the matter to the Court of Justice directly in accordance with Article 108(2) TFEU. If the Commission considers that the Member State concerned has not complied with a judgment of the Court, the Commission may pursue the matter in accordance with Article 260 TFEU (which means that penalties may be imposed).

Background of recovery
As the Court has explained, the obligation on the Member State concerned to abolish, through recovery, aid considered by the Commission to be incompatible with the single market has as its purpose, according to the Court's established case-law, to restore the situation as it was before the aid was granted. That objective is attained once the aid in question, together, where appropriate, with default interest, has been repaid by the recipient, or, in other words, by the undertakings which actually enjoyed the benefit of it. By repaying the aid, the recipient forfeits the advantage which it had enjoyed over its competitors on the market, and the situation prior to payment of the aid is restored.[146]

General principles of Union law
As a general rule of State aid law, the Commission shall order the recovery of unlawful aid, unless such recovery would be contrary to a general principle of Union law,[147] such as the principle of legal certainty, the principle of equality and the principle of legitimate expectations. The Commission applies the principle of legal certainty such that in case of a really 'novel' application of State aid law which no diligent business operator could have expected, no recovery should take place.[148] The threshold for acceptance of such 'novelty' is very high, although the Commission has accepted it occasionally.[149] The principle of equality has been at issue in the case of *FrieslandCampina*.[150] In this case, the Court reiterated that a breach of the general principle of equal treatment arises through the application of different rules to comparable situations or the application of the same rule to different situations. It recognised that the principle of equal treatment, if violated by the Commission, may prevent the recovery of aid. A great deal of similarity between an approved system of a Member State and a system of another Member State which was adopted after that approval, may create legitimate expectations as well, according to the Commission.[151] Indeed, the principle of legitimate expectations also forms part of the EU legal order as a general principle of law; in practice, this is the most important principle. Only the Commission, as the competent authority on State aid, may create legitimate

146 Case C-164/15, *Aer Lingus*, C:2016:990, points 89-90.
147 Art. 16(1) of the procedural regulation.
148 See for instance Commission Decision 2006/621/EC of 2 August 2004 on State aid implemented by France in favour of France Télécom, at 263.
149 E.g. Commission Decision of 30.03.2006, No. 2005/77/EC (UK - United Kingdom in favour of Gibraltar Qualifying Companies), at 45-48.
150 Case C-519/07, *Koninklijke FrieslandCampina*, EU:C:2009:556, point 100 et seq.
151 *E.g.* Decision 2003/512/EC (OJ 2003 L177/17); Decision 2003/438/EC (OJ 2003 L 153/40); Decision 2003/755/EC (OJ 2003, L 282/25); Decision 2003/515/EC.

expectations in that area.[152] Any hopes wrongly raised by the national authorities cannot under any circumstances affect the lawfulness of a Commission decision on recovery of State aid.[153] With regard to statements made by a member of the Commission, an individual may rely on the principle of protection of legitimate expectations only in so far as the administration has led him to entertain justified hopes by giving him consistent, unconditional, specific and precise assurances.[154] In addition, a reasonable expectation can only arise "in the mind of a reasonably prudent economic agent".[155] In the law of State aid, it is of crucial importance whether the procedure of Article 108(3) TFEU has been followed or not. In principle, legitimate expectations can only be invoked successfully if the aid is granted in compliance with the procedure laid down in Article 108 TFEU. A 'diligent businessman' should normally be able to determine whether that procedure has been followed. Only in "exceptional circumstances" the protection of legitimate expectations could refrain the Commission from ordering the recovery of aid.[156] It is settled case-law that if the beneficiary of the aid considers that exceptional circumstances exist on which it was entitled to base a legitimate expectation that the aid was lawful, and such a case is brought before a national court, it is for that court to assess the aid, if necessary after obtaining a preliminary ruling on interpretation from the Court.[157] Accordingly, exceptional circumstances can only be relied upon in proceedings before the national court.[158] This does not mean, however, that the Union courts always refuse to examine the question as to exceptional circumstances.[159] In *Spain v Commission* the Court held that a Member State whose authorities have granted aid contrary to the procedural rules laid down in Article 108(3) TFEU may not itself rely on the legitimate expectations of the recipient undertaking in order to justify a failure to comply with the obligation to take the steps necessary to implement a Commission decision instructing it to recover the aid. If it could do so, Articles 107 and 108 TFEU would be set at naught, since national authorities would thus be able to rely on their own unlawful conduct in order to deprive of their effectiveness decisions taken by the Commission under provisions of the Treaty. The fact that the Commission initially decided not to raise any objections to the aid in issue cannot be regarded as capable of having caused the recipient undertaking to entertain any legitimate expectation since that decision may be challenged in due time before the Court.[160] Decisions of the Commission stating that aid is compatible with the internal market where it should have decided to open the formal investigation procedure cannot,

152 In addition, according to Article 108(2) TFEU, the Council may, on application by a Member State, acting unanimously and in exceptional circumstances, decide that aid shall be considered to be compatible with the internal market; in such a situation the Council may also give rise to legitimate expectations.

153 For example Case 5/89, *Commission v Germany*, EU:C:1990:320; Case C-169/95, *Spain v Commission*, EU:C:1997:10; Case T-109/01, *Fleuren Compost*, EU:T:2004:4.

154 Case T-129/96, *Preussag Stahl*, EU:T:1998:69, point 89.

155 Joined Cases C-181-183/04, *Elmeka*, EU:C:2006:563, point 32.

156 Case C-148/04, *Unicredito Italiano*, EU:C:2005:774, point 104.

157 Case C-310/99, *Italy v Commission*, EU:C:2002:143, point 103; Case T-109/01, *Fleuren Compost*, EU:T:2004:4, point 136. Opinion AG Cosmas in Case C-83/98, *Ladbroke Racing*, EU:C:1999:577, at 96.

158 Case T-459/93, *Siemens v Commission*, EU:T:1995:100, point 104-105.

159 For example Case T-55/99, *CETM*, EU:T:2000:223, point 123.

160 Case C-169/95, *Spain v Commission*, EU:C:1997:10.

therefore, give rise to legitimate expectations if that decision has been appealed by a competitor and subsequently annulled by the Court.[161] It is difficult to see why similar findings which are not laid down in a formal decision – no appeal possible – would give rise to legitimate expectations. After all, this would render the formal procedure of Article 108 TFEU meaningless and would violate interests of competitors.

Once it is established that economic operators have legitimate expectations that a certain measure does not constitute State aid, they may legitimately expect that for transactions irrevocably undertaken by them a reasonable transitional period will be adopted.[162]

Implementation of recovery in the domestic legal order

Article 16(3) of the Procedural Regulation states that recovery shall be effected without delay and in accordance with the procedures under the national law of the Member State concerned, provided that they allow the immediate and effective execution of the Commission's decision. To this effect and in the event of a procedure before national courts, the Member States concerned shall take all necessary steps which are available in their respective legal systems, including provisional measures, without prejudice to Union law. An appeal to the General Court shall not suspend any recovery. Indeed, Article 278 TFEU states that actions brought before the Court of Justice of the European Union shall not have suspensory effect. The Court may, however, if it considers that circumstances so require, order that application of the contested act be suspended. In this respect, the Commission has published a Notice 'Towards an effective implementation of Commission decisions ordering Member States to recover unlawful and incompatible State aid' which should give Member States the necessary guidance.[163]

Who may enforce the recovery of unlawful aid?

As discussed above, any person, undertaking or association of undertakings whose interests might be affected by the granting of aid, in particular competing undertakings and trade associations, may submit a complaint to inform the Commission of any alleged unlawful aid or any alleged misuse of aid. To that effect, the interested party shall use a compulsory complaint form. If, according to the Commission, the facts and points of law put forward by the interested party do not provide sufficient grounds to show, on the basis of a *prima facie* examination, the existence of unlawful aid or misuse of aid, it shall inform the interested party thereof and call upon it to submit comments within one month. If the interested party fails to make known its views within the prescribed period, the complaint shall be deemed to have been withdrawn. The Commission shall send a copy of the decision on a case concerning the subject matter of the complaint to the complainant. In addition to filing a complaint with the Commission, proceedings may be brought before the domestic courts, for instance by a competitor of the undertaking receiving unlawful aid. In such a procedure, the courts of the Member States may ask the

161 See Opinion AG Tizzano in Joined Cases C-442/03 and C-471/03, *P&O European Ferries*.

162 Commission Decision of 19 July 2006 on the Luxembourg 1929 holding regime, 2006/940/EC, at 109 et seq.

163 Notice from the Commission – Towards an effective implementation of Commission decisions ordering Member States to recover unlawful and incompatible State aid, OJ C 272, 15.11.2007, p. 4-17.

Commission to transmit to them information in its possession or its opinion on questions concerning the application of State aid rules (Article 29 of the procedural regulation). More generally, where the coherent application of Article 107(1) or Article 108 TFEU so requires, the Commission, acting on its own initiative, may submit written observations to the courts of the Member States that are responsible for applying the State aid rules.[164] It may, with the permission of the court in question, also make oral observations. As the Court held in *Transalpine Ölleitung*, the implementation of the system for supervision of State aid, resulting from Article 108 TFEU, is a matter, on the one hand, for the Commission and, on the other, for national courts.[165] The national courts and the Commission fulfil complementary and separate roles: whilst assessment of the compatibility of aid measures with the common market falls within the exclusive competence of the Commission, subject to review by the Union Courts, it is for the national courts to ensure that the rights of individuals are safeguarded where the obligation to give prior notification of State aid to the Commission pursuant to Article 108(3) TFEU is infringed. A national court may, therefore, have cause to interpret the concept of aid contained in Article 107(1) of the Treaty in order to determine whether a State measure has been introduced in disregard of Article 108(3) (TFEU. Thus, it is for that court to verify, inter alia, whether the measure at issue constitutes an advantage and whether it is selective, that is to say whether it favours certain undertakings or certain producers within the meaning of Article 107(1) TFEU. If the national court concludes that unlawful aid has been granted, it may be called upon, depending on what is possible under national law and the remedies available thereunder, to order recovery of unlawful aid from its recipients. In the same way, a national court may be required to rule on an application for compensation for the damage caused by reason of the unlawful nature of the aid.[166] However, a national court is not bound to order the recovery of unlawful aid if the Commission has subsequently adopted a final decision declaring that aid to be compatible with the common market, within the meaning of Article 107 TFEU. In such a case, the national court must order the aid recipient to pay interest in respect of the period of unlawfulness. Within the framework of its domestic law, it may, if appropriate, also order the recovery of the unlawful aid, without prejudice to the Member State's right to re-implement it, subsequently. It may also be required to uphold claims for compensation for damage caused by reason of the unlawful nature of the aid.[167]

Quantification

With regard to unlawful aid granted in the form of a tax advantage, recovery of aid means that the transactions actually carried out by the recipients of the aid in question must be subject to the tax treatment which the recipients would have received in the absence of the unlawful aid. It is irrelevant in this regard that the taxpayer would have carried out different transactions if it would have realised that it benefitted from unlawful State aid.[168] The advantage which should be recovered from the beneficiary is equal to the tax benefit;

164 E.g. Case C-429/07, *X BV*, EU:C:2009:359.

165 Case C-368/04, *Transalpine Ölleitung*, EU:C:2006:644, points 36 et seq.

166 Case C-368/04, *Transalpine Ölleitung*, EU:C:2006:644, point 56.

167 Case C-199/06, *CELF*, EU:C:2008:79.

168 Case C-148/04, *Unicredito Italiano*, EU:C:2005:774, point 119; Case C-164/15, *Aer Lingus*, C:2016:990, point 93.

no further economic analysis has to be performed.[169] With regard to the recovery of indirect aid, it should be noted that Regulation 2015/1589/EU does not draw a distinction, for the purposes of the recovery to be carried out by the Member State concerned, according to whether a party is a direct or an indirect beneficiary of the unlawful aid in question. In direct taxation cases, it seems that, as a main rule, the recovery should concern the difference between the standard tax and the reduced tax resulting from the measure at issue at the level of the direct beneficiary, even though an indirect beneficiary may have the option of subsequently effecting recovery in turn from others under applicable provisions of national law.[170]

Economic passing on of the benefit

A beneficiary of aid cannot, in principle, argue successfully that the benefit concerned has been passed on to third parties, such as consumers. An example is the case or *Aer Lingus* in which the airline argued that it had passed on the benefit of a lower air travel tax rate to its customers, as a result of which it had not actually enjoyed any economic advantage. The Court rejected this argument: the recovery of aid entails the restitution of the advantage procured by the aid for the beneficiary, not the restitution of the economic benefit that may have been conferred by the aid as a result of the exploitation of the advantage. The recovery of the aid necessarily entails the repayment of the difference between the two travel tax rates applicable.[171] This is the case even where the recipients of the aid have derived no benefit from the advantage in question, either because they have passed that advantage on to their customers, or for some other reason.[172]

Absolute impossibility to recover

Recovery of unlawful aid is the logical consequence of the finding that it is unlawful. That that consequence does not depend on the form in which the aid was granted, for instance through the tax regime or through other means. If a Member State wishes to oppose this consequence, it may file a direct action with the General Court and/or plead that it is absolutely impossible for it to implement the decision properly. It may not plead this lightly. Article 4(3) TEU requires that a Member State contacts the Commission if, in giving effect to a Commission decision on State aid, encounters unforeseen and unforeseeable difficulties or becomes aware of consequences overlooked by the Commission. In such a case, the Member State should submit those problems to the Commission for consideration, together with proposals for suitable amendments to the decision in question. In any event, the condition that it be absolutely impossible to implement a decision is not fulfilled where the Member State merely informs the Commission of the legal, political or practical difficulties involved in implementing the decision, without taking any real step to recover the aid from the undertakings concerned, and without proposing to the Commission any alternative arrangements for implementing the decision which could have enabled the difficulties to be overcome.[173] Even if the recipient of aid has ceased its

169 Case C-164/15, *Aer Lingus*, C:2016:990, point 92.
170 Case T-445/05, *Fineco*, EU:T:2009:50, point 196 et seq.
171 Case C-164/15, *Aer Lingus*, C:2016:990, point 100.
172 Case C-164/15, *Aer Lingus*, C:2016:990, point 115.
173 Case C-404/00, *Commission v Spain*, EU:C:2003:373, points 44-47.

activities, the buyer of its assets may be subject to recovery proceedings, in particular in circumstances where the transactions have not taken place under market conditions.[174]

15.4.5 *Judicial appeal*

General

According to Article 263 TFEU, the Court of Justice of the European Union shall review, inter alia, the legality of acts of the Commission. It shall for this purpose have jurisdiction in actions brought by, inter alia, a Member State, on grounds of lack of competence, infringement of an essential procedural requirement, infringement of the Treaties or of any rule of law relating to their application, or misuse of powers. Any natural or legal person may institute proceedings against an act addressed to that person or which is of direct and individual concern to them, and against a regulatory act which is of direct concern to them and does not entail implementing measures. The proceedings provided for in Article 263 TFEU shall be instituted within two months of the publication of the measure, or of its notification to the plaintiff, or, in the absence thereof, of the day on which it came to the knowledge of the latter, as the case may be. According to Article 256 TFEU, the General Court shall have jurisdiction to hear and determine at first instance actions or proceedings referred to in Article 263 TFEU. Decisions given by the General Court may be subject to a right of appeal to the Court of Justice on points of law only, under the conditions and within the limits laid down by the Statute of the Court of Justice of the European Union. Whereas it is clear that the Member States have legal standing in the Court, it is less clear under what circumstances a company may have standing. After all, a State aid decision is addressed to the Member State, as a result of which a company may only lodge an appeal against a decision which is of direct and individual concern to it. For a person to be directly concerned by a Commission decision, that decision must directly affect the legal situation of the company and leave no discretion to its addressees who are entrusted with the task of implementing it, such implementation being purely automatic and resulting from Union rules without the application of other intermediate rules.[175] Persons other than those to whom a decision is addressed may claim to be individually concerned only if that decision affects them by reason of certain attributes which are peculiar to them or by reason of circumstances in which they are differentiated from all other persons and by virtue of those factors distinguishes them individually just as in the case of the person addressed by such a decision.[176]

Beneficiaries of unlawful aid

A beneficiary of unlawful aid which is confronted with the recovery thereof, meets both of the just-mentioned tests.[177] Indeed, where a contested measure affects a group of persons who were identified or identifiable when that measure was adopted by reason of criteria specific to the members of the group, those persons might be individually concerned by that measure inasmuch as they form part of a limited class of traders.[178]

174 Case C-214/07, *Commission v France*, EU:C:2008:619, point 55 et seq.
175 Case C-519/07, *Koninklijke FrieslandCampina*, EU:C:2009:556, point 48.
176 Case 25/62, *Plaumann v Commission*, EU:C:1963:17.
177 Joined Cases C-15/98 and C-105/99, *Sardegna Lines*, EU:C:2000:570, point 34-35.
178 Case C-519/07, *Koninklijke FrieslandCampina*, EU:C:2009:556, point 54.

Competitors of undertakings in case of a 'positive decision'
Competing undertakings have been recognised as individually concerned by a Commission decision terminating the formal investigation procedure where they have played an active role in that procedure, provided that their position on the market is substantially affected by the aid measure which is the subject of the contested decision.[179] This must be proven by the competing undertakings. If an effect of that kind is established, the fact that an undefined number of other competitors may, in appropriate circumstances, allege that they have suffered similar harm does not constitute an obstacle to the admissibility of the action brought by the appellant undertaking, especially if a tax measure is specifically designed to have an effect on the structure of the market in question and is specifically intended to affect the competitive position of undertakings active on the market.[180]

Competitors of undertakings in case of a 'no aid' or 'no recovery' decision
Under the third limb of the fourth paragraph of Article 263 TFEU, an appeal may be lodged by a person against a regulatory act which is of direct concern to it. In *Scuola Elementare Maria Montessori*, the Court held that a competitor may lodge an appeal on this basis against a Commission decision finding that no aid has been provided through a national tax measure or that 'no recovery' shall be ordered, if it is shown that this finding is of direct concern to the competitor. After all, such a decision does not entail any implementing measures. It is, therefore, sufficient that the competitor shows that the decision is liable to place him in an unfavourable competitive position and thus to produce effects on his legal situation.[181]

A refusal to approve a notified measure
If a Member State has notified an aid scheme which the Commission has subsequently not approved, potential beneficiaries of that aid and competitors of those potential beneficiaries will normally not be directly and individually concerned by that decision if that scheme does not apply to a predefined closed group of undertakings. Even if the company argues that it belongs to a closed group of undertakings, the fact that it is possible to determine more or less precisely the number, or even the identity, of the persons to whom a measure applies by no means implies that it must be regarded as being of individual concern to them, as long as it is established that application takes effect by virtue of an objective legal or factual situation defined by the measure in question.[182] This will normally preclude admissibility in case of a tax measure aiming at implementing an aid scheme.

A refusal to initiate the formal investigation procedure
Where the Commission adopts, after notification of a measure, a decision not to raise objections, it declares not only that the measure is compatible with the internal market, but also – by implication –it refuses to initiate the formal investigation procedure laid down in Article 108(2) TFEU. In order to safeguard the rights of 'interested parties' within the meaning of Article 1(h) of the procedural regulation, any such interested party is *insofar*

179 Case 169/84, *Cofaz*, EU:C:1986:42, points 22 to 25; Case C-260/05, *Sniace*, EU:C:2007:700, point 55.
180 Case C-487/06, *British Aggregates*, EU:C:2008:757, point 56.
181 Joined Cases C-622/16 to C-624/16, *Scuola Elementare Maria Montessori*, EU:C:2018:873.
182 Case C-451/98, *Antillean Rice Mills v Council*, EU:C:2001:622, point 52.

directly and individually concerned by such a decision, but only in respect of the formal issue.[183] The same should apply to a 'no aid' decision after notification of an aid measure.

The position of business associations
A professional association which is responsible for protecting the collective interests of its members is entitled to bring an action for the annulment of a final decision of the Commission on State aid if the undertakings which it represents or some of those undertakings themselves have locus standi.[184]

Challenging a Commission decision before the national courts
The question arises whether a company may challenge a Commission decision before the national courts if it has failed to do so before the Union courts.[185] In this respect, a company cannot make such a challenge if it would have had legal standing within the meaning of Article 263 TFEU before the Union courts.[186] Such a company must accept the definitive nature of the decision. However, this is true only if the company could undoubtedly have instituted an action for annulment in the Union Courts.[187] If objective uncertainty exists, a company may seek to challenge the decision in the national courts.

15.5 Concluding remarks

The present chapter has discussed the impact of EU State aid law on the design of direct tax measures and administrative practices of the Member States, both from a substantive and procedural perspective. It has become clear that this impact is quite substantial. It should be expected that the influence of EU State aid law on the direct business taxation systems in the Union will continue to increase in the future, which makes it a fascinating and indispensable area of law to follow. The present chapter has aimed to introduce the reader to the most fundamental issues thereof.

183 Case C-83/09, *Kronoply and Kronotex*, EU:C:2011:341.

184 Case C-487/06, *British Aggregates*, EU:C:2008:757, point 33. In addition, a business association may be directly in individually concerned if it can prove an interest of its own, but that seems difficult in direct taxation cases.

185 See the Opinion of AG Kokott in Case C-333/07, *Régie Networks*, EU:C:2008:371, at 33 et seq.

186 Case C-188/92, *TWD Textilwerke Deggendorf*, point 17.

187 Case C-188/92, *TWD Textilwerke Deggendorf*, point 24.

PART 3 POSITIVE INTEGRATION OF CORPORATE TAXES

CHAPTER 16

The Parent-Subsidiary Directive

Peter Wattel

Update and elaboration by Otto Marres[1]

16.1 Introduction

Two tax problems may arise where a subsidiary company in one State distributes its profits to its parent company in another State:

i. the State of establishment of the subsidiary may levy a withholding tax on outbound dividends; and
ii. the State of establishment of the parent company may include the incoming dividend in the taxable profit of the parent company, leading to economic double taxation of the profits out of which the dividends were paid, once in the hands of the subsidiary and once in the hands of the parent.

Council Directive 2011/96/EU of 30 November 2011 on the common system of taxation applicable in the case of parent companies and subsidiaries of different Member States (recast) (the Parent-Subsidiary Directive, or PSD),[2] seeks to abolish both tax impediments to cross-border payment of dividends within groups of companies, thus improving the functioning of the internal market, especially the free movement of capital and the freedom of establishment. The preamble to the Directive states that it is aimed at eliminating the disadvantages of cooperation between companies of different Member States in comparison to cooperation between companies within one Member State, and at facilitating the cross-border grouping together of companies at Union level. The Directive applies solely to cross-border situations (Art. 1(1)). Parent-subsidiary relations within the same Member State are not addressed. Neither are EEA-or third State parent-subsidiary relations.

Directive 2011/96/EU is a recast of Council Directive 90/435/EEC of 23 July 1990.[3] It took the Council over 20 years to adopt Directive 90/435/EEC. The Commission tabled its first proposal on 16 January 1969. The adopted Directive was more modest in scope than the Commission's proposals; it thus differed from earlier versions in several respects. In the first place, the adopted version provided for some transitional exceptions to the ban on dividend withholding tax in favour of three Member States (see Section 16.6.2.). All of these

1 Professor, Amsterdam Centre for Tax Law (ACTL), University of Amsterdam; tax lawyer, Lubbers, Boer & Douma, The Hague.
2 O.J. No. L 345 of 29 December 2011, p. 8.
3 O.J. No. L 225 of 20 August 1990, p. 6.

exceptions expired and have since 2004 been deleted from the Directive. A new exception was introduced for Estonia on the occasion of the accession of ten new Member States in 2004. This exception expired as well, on 31 December 2008 (see Section 16.6.2.). Secondly, the adopted Directive did not make a choice between capital import neutrality (CIN) and capital export neutrality (CEN) (see Sections 8.2 and 16.4.1). The original proposal – which was submitted when the European Community counted only six Member States – was based on CIN, requiring the State of the parent company to exempt incoming subsidiary dividends. The adopted version (adopted after the accession of credit countries like the UK[4] and Ireland) left Member States a choice between exemption and credit for underlying corporation tax. Unlike the original proposal, the adopted Directive did not contain an option for parent companies to fiscally consolidate foreign subsidiaries in which they held a majority interest. Consolidation would make controlled foreign subsidiaries part of the parent company for tax purposes in the State of the parent company, comparable to a foreign branch. The tax treatment of subsidiary profits in the parent company State would thus approximate the tax treatment of foreign branch profits:

- immediate taxation and relief for double taxation instead of taxation and relief only on remittance basis; and
- immediate cross-border set off of subsidiary losses against the parent company's profits (to be recaptured in later years when the subsidiary makes a profit again against which it may itself offset its losses).

But the Member States were not ready for such assimilation of controlled subsidiaries to branches (except in the case of portfolio subsidiaries in tax havens: CFC legislation; see Section 9.5). In 2011, the Commission submitted a proposal for a common consolidated corporate tax base, and in 2016 it relaunched that proposal.[5] Such CCCTB would go even further than fiscal consolidation of individual subsidiaries: it would imply unitary taxation and formula apportionment of the unitary business' aggregate EU result among the Member States in which the unitary business operates. The CCCTB proposal is replaced by the proposal for a BEFIT ('Business in Europe: Framework for Income Taxation'), based on formulary apportionment and a common tax base (see Chapter 25).

It should be observed that although the Parent-Subsidiary Directive does not provide for equal treatment of branches and subsidiaries, primary EU law (the Treaty Freedoms, especially the freedom of establishment; Article 49) may in certain circumstances require Member States to treat wholly owned foreign subsidiaries for tax purposes as if they were domestic subsidiaries eligible for domestic group taxation schemes: in Case C-446/03, *Marks & Spencer II*[6] (see Section 10.2.2), the Court required the UK to offset continental subsidiary losses which could not be offset any more by the subsidiary itself in its Member State of establishment, against the UK parent company's domestic profits, as if they were domestic subsidiary losses (*group relief*).[7]

4 The UK introduced a participation exemption only as per 1 July 2009.
5 In fact it is a split proposal, one for a Common Corporate Tax Base (CCTB) and one for a Common Consolidated Corporate Tax Base (CCCTB); see Chapter 11.
6 Case C-446/03, *Marks & Spencer*, ECR 2005 p. I-10837, EU:C:2005:763.
7 However, the impact of this requirement is drastically reduced by subsequent case-law; see Section 10.2.4.

Finally, in the 1969 proposal a 20% holding was sufficient for the parent-subsidiary status, whereas the adopted version was in keeping with the 25% threshold contained in Article 10 (dividends) of the widely used OECD Model Double Taxation Convention. Since 1 January 2009, however, a 10% holding already suffices for application of Directive 90/435/EEC and the current Parent-Subsidiary Directive (see below).

By Directive of 22 December 2003,[8] Directive 90/435/EEC was amended substantially. Its scope was widened to include more legal forms as eligible, amongst which the European Company (SE). The minimum holding requirement was reduced from 25% to 20% in 2005, 15% in 2007 and finally 10% in 2009 (see Section 16.3.2.). For Member States applying indirect credit instead of exemption, a *multi*-tier credit for underlying corporation tax became obligatory (see Section 16.4.3.3.). Further, the position of branches 'receiving' cross-border dividends was clarified (see Section 16.3.1.). Finally, a provision for hybrid entities was included (see Section 16.5.2.). The amending Directive came in force in February 2004 and had to be transformed into national law by 1 January 2005.[9] As per the accession date of ten new Member States (1 May 2004), their corporation taxes were added to the list in Article 2(1)(c) of the Directive, and their legal company forms were added in the Annex to the Directive.[10] The Parent-Subsidiary Directive was again amended[11] upon the accession of Bulgaria and Romania in order to include their corporation taxes in Article 2 and their legal forms in the Annex to the Directive.

On 30 November 2011, the Council adopted Directive 2011/96/EU, and repealed Directive 90/435/EEC, for a consolidated ('recast') text of the Parent-Subsidiary Directive, as the numerous amendments to the original 1992 text hampered consultation of the version in force. The Recast Directive (i) codified the text as amended and accordingly slightly changed the paragraph numbers within some of the Articles, (ii) moved the list of national corporation taxes from Article 2 to a separate second Annex to the Directive, and (iii) introduced one new procedural rule: it specified in Article 4(5) that 'the Council, acting unanimously in accordance with a special legislative procedure and after consulting the European Parliament and the Economic and Social Committee, shall at the appropriate time adopt the rules to apply after the entry into force of a common system of company taxation.'[12] That time would – originally – be the adoption of the CCCTB; however, since the Communication on Business Taxation for the 21st century, this would now be the BEFIT (see Chapter 22).

8 Directive 2003/123/EC of 22 December 2003, amending Directive 90/435/EEC, O.J. No. L 7, 2004, p. 41.

9 For extensive and detailed comments on the 2003 amendments, see Guglielmo Maisto: 'The 2003 Amendments to the EC Parent-Subsidiary Directive: What's Next?', 13 *EC Tax Review* 4 (2004), p. 164–181.

10 See Part 9 (Taxation), paragraph 8, of Annex II (list referred to in Article 20) to the Act of Accession, O.J. No. L 236 of 23 September 2003.

11 Council Directive 2006/98/EC of 20 November 2006 adapting certain Directives in the field of taxation, by reason of the accession of Bulgaria and Romania, O.J. No. L 363 of 20 December 2006, p. 129–136.

12 This provision was prompted by the judgment of the Court of Justice in Case C-133/06 (*Parliament v Council*), [2008] ECR I-03189, EU:C:2008:257.

Directive 2011/96/EU has been amended twice, by Council Directive 2014/86/EU of 8 July 2014[13] and by Council Directive (EU) 2015/121 of 27 January 2015.[14] Directive 2014/86/EU introduced a provision requiring the Member State of the parent company to tax profit distributions by its subsidiaries to the extent these distributions are deductible by the subsidiary, to avoid double non-taxation. This directive also updated Part A of Annex I to Directive 2011/96/EU to include some companies established under the law of Poland and Romania. Directive (EU) 2015/121, finally, introduced a common minimum anti-abuse rule, the present Article 1(2) and (3).

16.2 Main Features

The gist of the Directive is that cross-border profit distributions paid out of after-tax profits by an EU subsidiary to its EU parent company (or a branch of such company) must be exempt from dividend withholding tax in the Member State of source, and free of double corporate income taxation in the Member State of the parent company. To that end, the Directive stipulates that:

a) intragroup cross-border payments of dividends must be exempted from withholding tax by the Member State of the subsidiary (Art. 5); and
b) the Member State of the recipient parent company must either refrain from taxing the incoming dividend altogether, unless the profit is deducted by the subsidiary (exemption method), or tax it, but in that case credit, against the parent's corporation tax, the corporation tax already paid by the subsidiary in its Member State, and by the subsidiary of that subsidiary in a third Member State, etc. (multi-tier indirect credit; credit for underlying corporation tax) (Art. 4).

There are several conditions to be satisfied for entitlement to the Directive benefits (see Section 16.3 below). There are some exceptions to, or mitigations of, the Member States' obligations under the Directive to abolish withholding taxes on qualifying distributions (see Section 16.6).

The Directive does not address the issue of unrealized capital gains and losses (value increases or reductions) or gains or losses upon the alienation (sale) of (part of) the shareholding in the subsidiary, as it only addresses *distributions* of profit (see Section 16.5). In our view, this is an omission, as dividends and capital gains upon alienation are economically to a large extent interchangeable.

16.3 Qualifying Companies (Arts. 2 and 3)

16.3.1 'Company of a Member State' and 'Permanent Establishment' (Art. 2)

To be eligible for the Directive benefits, a taxpayer must be both a company of a Member State and either a parent company or a subsidiary. Article 2 defines the term 'company of a

13 Council Directive 2014/86/EU of 8 July 2014, amending Directive 2011/96/EU, O.J. No. L 219 of 25 July 2014, p. 40.
14 Council Directive (EU) 2015/121 of 27 January 2015, amending Directive 2011/96/EU, O.J. No. L 21 of 28 January 2015, p. 1.

Member State', and since the 2003 amendment also the term 'permanent establishment'. Article 3 lists the 'parent' and 'subsidiary' requirements. In order to qualify as a 'company of a Member State', three conditions must be met cumulatively (Art. 2(a)):

(i) Legal Form
The company must be incorporated in one of the legal forms listed in Part A of Annex I to the Directive. If it is neither expressly indicated nor caught under a residual category (*e.g.* paragraph (f) of the Annex: '(....) and other companies constituted under German law subject to German corporate tax'), it does not qualify, not even if it did not yet exist when the Directive was adopted (1992) and was, after its subsequent introduction into national law, yet included on the list at the first possible opportunity (the 2005 amendment to the Directive). According to the Court, the Directive does not seek to introduce a common system for all companies of the Member States nor for all types of holdings, and there is no possibility of extending its scope by analogy.[15] Therefore, the Court held, in Case C-247/08, *Gaz de France*,[16] that although the French *Société par actions simplifiée* was introduced in French law only after the adoption of the Directive and was listed by the 2005 amendment, it could not be accepted as a qualifying parent company of a member State before the 2005 amendment took effect.

Not being on the list does not need to be fatal, however. Sometimes, a non-qualifying entity may instead rely on the TFEU Freedoms, especially the right of establishment, and be exempt on the basis of nondiscrimination.[17] In *Aberdeen Property*,[18] a Finnish subsidiary paid dividends to its Luxembourg parent company, an open-ended investment company (*société d'investissement à capital variable, SICAV*), which did not pay tax in Luxembourg, and which is not on the list of eligible entities. All the same, the subsidiary successfully claimed exemption from Finnish withholding tax on the grounds that Finland charged neither withholding tax nor corporation tax on similar dividend receipts by similar Finnish parent companies (even though an identical legal form did not exist in Finland).

Part A of Annex I lists the common public limited companies (plc) and limited liability companies (Ltd) for each Member State, *e.g.* the French *société anonyme* (SA) and *société à responsabilité limitée* (Sàrl), and the German *Aktiengesellschaft (KG)* and *Gesellschaft mit beschränkter Haftung* (GmbH), but many other legal forms also qualify, among which (see entry (a) on Part A of Annex I to the Directive) the European legal forms of the *Societas Europaea* (SE) and the *Societas Cooperativa Europaea* (SCE[19]), as well as many national legal forms other than plcs and Ltds, especially cooperative companies of the Member States.

15 Case C 458/18, GVC Services (Bulgaria) EOOD, EU:C:2020:266, points 34-35.

16 Case C-247/08, *Gaz de France – Berliner Investissement*, [2009] ECR I-9225, EU:C:2009:600. See for a comment: G.F. Boulogne and W.W. Geursen: *Gaz de France*; Dividends to Companies Not Listed in the Parent-Subsidiary Directive Are Not Exempt; *European Taxation* 4/2010, p. 129-140.

17 Cf. Case C 458/18, GVC Services (Bulgaria) EOOD, EU:C:2020:266, point 41.

18 Case C-303/07, *Aberdeen Property Fininvest Alpha Oy*, [2009] ECR I-5145, EU:C:2009:377.

19 However, the Community legal form of the SCE is only available as of 18 August 2006 (the entry date of application of the SCE Regulation).

Following up on one of the recommendations of the Ruding Report,[20] in 1993 the Commission proposed, *inter alia*, to amend both the (initial) Parent-Subsidiary Directive and the Merger Directive (see Chapter 17) to include any undertaking subject to corporation tax, irrespective of its legal form.[21] The European Parliament approved the amendment under the consultation procedure on 19 April 1994.[22] However, asymmetries in the commercial law governing the legal forms and the different tax arrangements applicable to them caused considerable problems, and the proposal was withdrawn when in 2003 the Commission tabled a new amendment proposal. The latter proposal was adopted by the Council in December 2003[23] and entered into force in the beginning of 2004 (implementation 1 January 2005). Although that amendment considerably broadened the scope of the (initial) Directive as regards qualifying legal forms, not all legal forms subject to a national corporation tax qualify. The list approach – instead of designating all entities subject to national corporate income tax – means having to adapt the (Annex to) the Directive every time a new Member States accedes (as in May 2004: ten new Member States, causing a huge extension of the list; and in 2006: two new Member States), and every time new national or EU legal forms come into being (such as the French *Société par actions simplifiées*, which did not exist in 1990; see also the extension by Directive 2014/86/EU with the Polish companies made subject to corporation tax and the companies which had been introduced in the company law of Romania). Ireland and Lithuania (and former Member State the UK), instead of listing legal forms, designated all companies incorporated under their laws. Denmark designated all companies under Danish law subject to Danish corporation tax on the same basis as *aktieselskaber* (share companies). Some countries, like the Netherlands, provide both a list of qualifying legal forms *and* a residual clause 'and other companies constituted under Dutch law subject to Dutch corporation tax.' These references to the laws of a Member State (i.e. incorporation under the law of a Member State, and being subject to corporation tax in a Member State) must be interpreted in accordance with the national law designated as applicable.[24]

We submit that 'subject to tax' in these lists must be read as 'subject to tax according to national law', as the wording of Article 2 does not support the view that all three requirements (legal form, fiscal residence and subjection to tax) be met in the same Member State. In our view, a company incorporated under Danish law, which has operations and management only in Sweden and is therefore considered resident and subject to tax in Sweden according to the Swedish-Danish tax treaty, qualifies all the same. There is no reason whatsoever to exclude such a company.

---

20 'Report of the Committee of Independent Experts on Company Taxation to the Commission of the European Communities', Office for Official Publications of the European Communities; Brussels/ Luxembourg 1992.

21 Proposal COM (93) 293 final to amend Directive 90/435/EEC, of 23 July 1990, submitted to the Council on 26 July 1993, O.J. No. C 225/5 of 20 August 1993, withdrawn and replaced in 2003.

22 EP 1994-1995, minutes of the sitting of 19 April 1995, p. 69-71, O.J. No. C 128 of 9 May 1994, p. 91.

23 Directive 2003/123/EC of 22 December 2003, amending Directive 90/435/EEC, O.J. No. L 7, 2004, p. 41.

24 Case C 458/18, GVC Services (Bulgaria) EOOD, EU:C:2020:266, points 36-37. The CJEU held that the expressions 'companies incorporated under the law of the United Kingdom' and 'corporation tax in the United Kingdom', do not include companies incorporated in Gibraltar and subject to corporation tax there.

(ii) Fiscal Residence

The company must be resident for tax purposes in a Member State on the basis of the national tax law of that State. Moreover, the company may not, according to a tax treaty with a non-Member State, be resident for tax purposes outside the Union. This last provision disqualifies dual resident companies which are incorporated under the law of a Member State applying an incorporation or statutory seat criterion for tax subjection, and which are consequently resident for tax purposes in that Member State, but which are also resident in a non-Member State according to that State's tax law on the basis of the place of effective management, the resulting tie being broken by a tax treaty in favour of the non-Member State, either on the basis of the traditional (OECD, pre 2017 update[25]) tie-breaker rule of the place of effective management of the company, or on the basis of the new standard rule of breaking the tie by mutual agreement (OECD 2017 version). Such third-State dual resident companies were probably excluded because they may be used in tax planning and avoidance schemes, as they are not fully liable to tax within a Member State and as they may enjoy tax facilities, especially access to tax treaties, in *both* States in which they are resident for tax purposes.[26]

However, as already observed under (i) above, dual residence does not necessarily exclude a company from the Directive benefits: dual resident companies having both of their fiscal residences *within* the EU, in different Member States, are not excluded. Even if one of its tax residences lies outside the EU, a company may still qualify: a company incorporated under the laws of Member State A and therefore fully subject to tax in State A (incorporation criterion), but managed in non-Member State X and therefore fully subject to tax in State X (effective management criterion), is not excluded from the Directive benefits if there is no tax treaty between A and X. Although such a company clearly has one of its residences outside the EU, it is not considered to be a State X resident 'under the terms of a double taxation agreement concluded with a third State', as Article 2(b) requires, but only on the basis of State X's national law. There is no reason to disqualify such a dual resident company, since in the absence of a tax treaty with State X, there is nothing to prevent Member State A from fully subjecting the company to State A corporation tax. The same is true if there *is* a tax treaty between A and X, but this treaty does not break the tie, e.g. because no agreement on residency is reached under a tie-breaker rule identical to the rule contained in Article 4(3) OECD Model Convention, or where the treaty contains a tie breaker allocating the company's residence for tax treaty purposes to State A. In such cases as well, Member State A still has full corporate tax jurisdiction

25 As per the 2017 update of the OECD Model Convention, Article 4(3) provides that '[w]here ... a person other than an individual is a resident of both Contracting States, the competent authorities of the Contracting States shall endeavour to determine by mutual agreement of the Contracting State of which such person shall be deemed to be a resident for the purposes of the Convention, having regard to its place of effective management, the place where it is incorporated or otherwise constituted and any other relevant factors', and that in absence of such agreement, such person is generally not entitled to treaty benefits.

26 For a discussion of whether this condition may unlawfully restrict the freedom of establishment, see Thomas Kollruss: 'EU Companies with Third State Dual Residency and the Freedom of Establishment: Unlawful Restriction by Secondary Legislation and Corresponding National Tax Law, *European Taxation*, September 2015, p. 432-437.

over the company, notwithstanding that State X also assumes residency taxation power as regards that company.

(iii) Subject to Corporation Tax

In order to qualify, a company must also be subject to one of the national corporation taxes listed in Annex I, Part B, to the Directive or to any other tax which may substitute for any of these taxes,[27] without being exempt and without the possibility of an option. Exempted companies presumably do not qualify because there is little reason to require Member States to prevent double taxation if there can be no double taxation because of the exemption, although economic double taxation may still occur.[28] Excluded as well are entities which have a qualifying legal form, but which may opt either for corporate taxation or for fiscal transparency – in that case, it is not the entity but its participants which are directly liable to tax on the entity's profits, for their respective shares. They have probably been excluded because they pose too many implementation problems and tax-planning possibilities. If an entity does not have an option, but is mandatorily considered transparent for tax purposes, then it does not qualify, since compulsory transparency amounts to an exemption – or rather to non-existence for corporation tax purposes – and its participants should be assessed on eligibility.

Less clear was the position of entities that are neither exempted nor transparent, but that pay no tax provided they distribute their profits to their shareholders promptly after the close of the taxable year (after which the shareholders can be taxed for their share in the profit), such as the Netherlands *fiscale beleggingsinstelling*, which is taxed at a zero rate. For practical purposes, such entities are effectively more or less transparent (as the Court observed in *Orange European Smallcap*[29]), though legally they are not, nor are they exempted. Technically, therefore, they would seem to qualify. As to the *beleggingsinstelling*, the Netherlands had a proviso included in the minutes of the Council meeting in which the Parent-Subsidiary Directive was adopted, but from the judgments of the CJEU in the *Denkavit, VITIC and Voormeer* case[30] (see Section 16.3.2.(v)) and the *Epson Europe* case[31] (see Section 16.6.3.) it follows that such reservations in (non-public) Council minutes have no legal status or interpretative value whatsoever. In the *Wereldhave* case[32] the Court pointed out that Article 2(c) (currently: 2(a)(iii)) lays down a positive criterion (being

27 In its proposal COM (93) 293 final, to amend the Parent-Subsidiary Directive, submitted to the Council on 26 July 1993 (later withdrawn and replaced), the Commission proposed to change the last phrase of Article 2(b) to: 'or to any identical or substantially similar tax which is imposed later in addition to or in place of this tax'. This amendment was intended to align the designation of the taxes covered with the designation used in Article 2 of the OECD Model Double Taxation Convention.

28 See also Paolo Arginelli: The Subject-to-Tax-Requirement in the EU Parent-Subsidiary Directive (2011/96), European Taxation, August 2017, p. 334-341 (in particular paragraph 3.2.1).

29 Case C-194/06, *Orange European Smallcap Fund*, ECLI:EU:C:2008:289, [2008] ECR I-3747.

30 Joined Cases C-283/94, C-291/94 and C-292/94, *Denkavit Internationaal BV, VITIC Amsterdam BV and Voormeer BV v. Bundesamt für Finanzen*, [1996] ECR I-5063, EU:C:1996:387.

31 Case C-375/98, *Ministério Público, Fazenda Pública v. Epson Europe BV*, [2000] ECR I-4243, EU:C:2000:302.

32 Case C-448/15, *Belgische Staat v. Wereldhave Belgium Comm. VA, Wereldhave International NV and Wereldhave NV*, EU:C:2017:180.

subject to the tax in question) and a negative criterion (not being exempt from that tax and not having the possibility of an option) and that therefore the directive seeks to exclude situations involving the possibility that, despite being subject to that tax, the company is not actually liable to pay that tax, as in the case of a zero rate. This interpretation is – according to the Court – consistent with the broad logic and the objective pursued by the directive (the elimination of double taxation), since there is no risk of double taxation if the parent is taxed at a zero rate. We are not convinced by this argument, since the purpose of the PSD is to facilitate the cross-border grouping together of companies by avoiding economic double taxation (see Section 6.1). Obviously, economic double taxation still occurs if the subsidiary State taxes both the dividends (in the hands of the parent) and the profits out of which the dividends are paid,[33] to say nothing of the subsequent taxation of the shareholders in the effectively transparent *beleggingsinstelling*.

The wording of Article 2 of the Directive does not require the above three conditions to be satisfied within one tax jurisdiction. Therefore, there is no reason to assume that, for example, a Danish incorporated *Aktieselskab* X *AS* (a qualifying legal form), which has its place of effective management in Portugal (and is therefore tax resident in Portugal), and which is (also) subject to Spanish corporation tax because it derives its profits mainly from a permanent establishment in Spain, would not qualify as a 'company of a Member State'. One may even argue that X *AS* is a company of all three Member States involved. This does raise some questions, however.[34] For instance, must Portugal exempt (or grant indirect credit for) profit distributions obtained by X *AS* from a Portuguese subsidiary Y *Lda?* From a Portuguese perspective, this distribution is not covered by the Directive, because both X *AS* and its subsidiary Y *Lda* are Portuguese. Consequently, Portugal would not be prevented by the Directive from levying a dividend withholding tax from Y *Lda* and taxing X *AS* for the dividend received (unless the shareholding is effectively connected to the permanent establishment in Spain; see below). From a Danish perspective, however, the Directive *is* applicable, because X *AS* is a company of Denmark and its subsidiary *Lda* is a company of Portugal. Consequently, from a Danish perspective Portugal may neither levy a withholding tax, nor tax X *AS* for the dividends received (at least not without credit for underlying tax), and Denmark may not tax X *AS* either (at least not without credit for underlying tax). If an (OECD-Modelled tax treaty is in force between Portugal and Denmark, one might be inclined to consider X *AS* resident for tax purposes in the State in favour of which that treaty breaks the tie (place of effective management; therefore Portugal). One would then conclude that the dividend payment by Y *Lda* to X *AS* is a purely internal transaction, to be taxed according to Portugal's discretion. However, a bilateral tax treaty cannot trump an EU Directive (even though that tax treaty may take priority over national tax law), so if autonomous interpretation of the Directive concept 'company of a Member State' would lead to the finding that X *AS* is a company of both Denmark and Portugal for Directive purposes, then Portugal should grant credit or exemption to X *AS* and refrain from withholding tax at the subsidiary level, irrespective of what a possible bilateral tax treaty with Denmark may provide. A similar question arises when

33 See also Paolo Arginelli, l.c.

34 See also Peter H. Schonewille, 'Some Questions on the Parent-Subsidiary Directive and the Merger Directive', *Intertax*, January 1992, p. 13.

X *AS* receives profit distributions from a Danish subsidiary: now Denmark may in turn see this as a purely internal matter (and therefore tax the dividend without regard to the Directive), whereas Portugal sees a qualifying cross-border distribution. Another question is whether Denmark must refrain from dividend withholding tax if X *AS* in turn has an EU parent company to which it in turn pays dividends, for instance in Poland. We would submit that the levying of a withholding tax by Denmark in this situation would be at odds with object and purpose, if not with the wording of the Directive. If there is a bilateral tax treaty between Denmark and Portugal, and this treaty is framed according to the OECD Model, then the situation would in our view be covered by Art. 10(5) of that Model, which, according to the official OECD Commentary, contains a general prohibition of extra-territorial taxation of dividends.[35]

Qualifying Permanent Establishments in Another Member State of Qualifying Companies (Art. 2(b))

An initially unresolved question was addressed by the 2003 amendment to the Directive (implementation 1 January 2005). It is the problem of branches (permanent establishments) of qualifying companies in another Member State. The initial Directive ignored branches, which gave rise to questions. Where a holding in a Member State A company was effectively connected with a Member State B branch of a Member State A parent company, it was unclear whether State A was precluded from withholding tax on dividends paid by the subsidiary to the State B branch of its parent. Indeed, State A might argue this would be a mere domestic transaction between two companies of the same Member State. Equally unclear was whether the branch State B should refrain from taxing the dividends received, since State B would not be the Member State of the parent company – that would be State A. Before the 2003 amendment, Article 4 only addressed the State of the parent company, not branch State B, since branches were not taken into account. It is evident, however, that both a withholding tax in State A and corporate taxation of the dividend received in the branch State B would offend against object and purpose of the Directive. The same question as to corporate taxation in the parent company State would arise if the parent company would be resident in a third Member State C. Moreover, the case law of the Court, e.g. the cases *Avoir Fiscal*[36] and *Saint Gobain*,[37] showed that the right of establishment (Art. 49 *juncto* 54 TFEU) requires Member States to treat branches of non-resident EU companies in the same manner as resident companies. Therefore, since the 2003 amendment Article 4(1) explicitly provides that both the parent company State *and* the branch State must either refrain from taxing the dividend received or credit the corporation tax already paid by the subsidiary in its Member State (or by the subsidiary of that subsidiary in a third Member State, etc), and Article 1(1) specifies that the Directive also applies to dividends received by a State B branch of a State C company paid by a State A (or C) company (paragraph c), and dividends paid to a State B branch of a State A company by a State A subsidiary (paragraph d). Thus, (foreign subsidiaries of) domestic branches of foreign parents are treated as if they were (subsidiaries of) domestic

35 Commentary on Article 10 OECD Model Convention, at 34. To that effect: *Hoge Raad* (Netherlands Supreme Court) 2 September 1992, nr. 27 252, *BNB* 1992/379.

36 Case 270/83, *Commission v. France (Avoir Fiscal)*, [1986], ECR 273, EU:C:1986:37.

37 Case C-307/97, *Compagnie de Saint-Gobain*, [1999] ECR I-6161, EU:C:1999:438.

companies. Even if these amendments had not been included in the Directive, the Court would probably have effected the same result on the basis of primary EU law (freedom of establishment or free movement of capital).

In order to make these amendments operational, a definition of a branch was needed, which was provided for in a new paragraph (b) to Article 2. The definition substantially follows the 'permanent establishment' definition in Article 5 (1) of the OECD Model Double Taxation Convention, but adds two – logical – specifications and a subject-to-tax requirement:

> 'a fixed place of business [*Directive*: situated in a Member State] through which the business of [*OECD*: an enterprise] [*Directive*: a company of another Member State] is wholly or partly carried on [*Directive*: in so far as the profits of that place of business are subject to tax in the Member State in which it is situated by virtue of the relevant bilateral tax treaty[38] or, in the absence of such a treaty, by virtue of national law].'

The extra subject-to-tax clause ensures that the receiving branch is in a tax position comparable to a local parent company for Directive purposes. The definition of 'permanent establishment' in Article 3(c) of the Interest and Royalty Directive ('I&R Directive) is identical, except for the subject-to-tax clause, which lacks in the I&R Directive (see Section 18.3.3).

The term 'permanent establishment' has thus become a Union law concept. We expect the Court of Justice of the EU to interpret the term in the same manner for other EU corporate tax Directives, in particular the Merger Directive, even though the Merger Directive does not contain a definition of the term 'permanent establishment' as such, but only of a 'branch of activity' (see Section 7.4.2). We further expect the Court to seek inspiration in the specifications contained in Article 5 of the OECD Model Double Tax Convention, and in the Official Commentary to that Model, since the EU definition closely resembles the OECD definition and all Member States use the authoritative OECD Model and Commentary for their bilateral tax treaties, which makes it part of the common legal tradition of the Member States.

16.3.2 *Parent and Subsidiary Status (Art. 3)*

Once a company or its branch qualifies as a company of a Member State or as a permanent establishment of a company in another Member State, Article 3 still requires two conditions to be satisfied in order to qualify as a parent or a subsidiary:

(iv) Minimum Holding Requirement (Art. 3(1)(a))
Article 3(1)(a) provides that Member States must attribute parent and subsidiary status at least to all (otherwise qualifying) companies of which one company (the parent) holds

38 Addition by the authors: a tax treaty in principle does not subject to tax, but divides tax base already subjected by national tax law between the two Contracting States. What is probably meant is: '*allocated* to the Member State in which it is situated by virtue of the relevant bilateral tax treaty'.

at least 10% of the capital of the other company (the subsidiary).[39] Whereas Article 3(b) of the I&R Directive require direct holdings (only first-tier associations qualify), the PSD simply refers to 'a holding', therefore including, in our view, indirect holdings.[40] This is in accordance with the reference in Article 4(1)(b) PSD to 'any lower-tier subsidiary' meeting the requirements provided for in Article 3 (implying that also indirect shareholdings qualify). The Member States remain free to grant parent and subsidiary status also to companies affiliated by smaller shareholdings than specified in Article 3(1)(a). Some Member States thus consider 5% enough or require no minimum at all. They are not allowed, however, to do so asymmetrically: they cannot apply a 10% threshold for EU (or EEA) subsidiaries (inbound dividends) and/or EU-(or EEA-)parent companies (outbound dividends), and at the same time apply a lower (e.g. 5% or nil) threshold for internal dividends (domestic subsidiaries and/or domestic parent companies), as that would be a violation of the free movement of capital (Art. 63 TFEU and Art. 40 EEA).[41] Thus, negative integration (the TFEU Freedoms) takes over from positive integration (the Directive) where a Member State exempts domestic intercompany dividend payments on holdings below 10% at subsidiary level (no withholding tax) or parent level (exemption) or both: if it does, it will also have to exempt EU-outbound intercompany dividends from withholding tax and/or provide exemption or indirect credit for inbound intercompany EU dividends.[42]

Pursuant to Article 3(2)(a), Member States may bilaterally agree to replace the minimum shareholding requirement by a corresponding voting rights requirement. This provision accommodates Member States using a voting rights criterion rather than a capital participation criterion in their national law and in their tax treaties with other Member States. The term 'replace' in our view implies that the Member States may not require both a 10% holding and a 10% voting right simultaneously.

Surprisingly, the I&R Directive (prohibiting source State withholding taxation of cross-border interest and royalty payments between group companies; see Chapter 18) sticks to a 25% minimum affiliation requirement (Article 3(b)), without provision for gradual reduction of that threshold.

The term 'holding (...) in the capital of a company' in Article 3(1)(a) does not include the holding of shares in usufruct or another derivative legal capacity. Parent and subsidiary status are connected only to full legal ownership of the shares, as only a legal owner with full title receives the distributed profits 'by virtue of its association with its subsidiary,'

39 The 2003 amendment (implementation 1 January 2005) reduced the original 25% holding requirement to 20% as per 1 January 2005, 15% as per 1 January 2007, and finally 10% as per 1 January 2009. The 2003 amendment further ensured that parent status is also attributed to a company holding shares in a subsidiary in the same Member State through a branch in another Member State.

40 Cf. Commission proposal COM (2011) 714 final of 11 November 2011, p. 8.

41 See Case 521/07, *Commission v the Netherlands*, [2009] ECR I-4873, EU:C:2009:360, Case C-540/07, *Commission v Italy*, [2009] ECR I-10983, EU:C:2009:717, and Case C-487/08, *Commission v Spain*, EU:C:2010:310.

42 See Case C-284/09, *Commission v Germany*, EU:C:2011:670, concerning Germany's differential tax treatment of domestic (exempt) and outbound (subject to withholding tax) dividend payments on holdings smaller than 10%. See Section 24.4 for conceptual background.

and only legal ownership corresponds to the purpose of the Directive to facilitate the cross-border grouping together of companies. As the Court held in *Les Vergiers du Vieux Tauves*,[43] the legal position of a usufructuary vis-à-vis the subsidiary is not such as to endow it with the status of shareholder, as that position solely results from the transfer to it, by the full owner of the shares, of a right to the distributed profits of the subsidiary; it has no voting rights, nor is it entitled to the undistributed profits. The Court observed, however, that even if the Subsidiary does not apply to the usufructuary, primary EU law (the freedom of establishment or the free movement of capital) may lead to the same result: if a Member State exempts domestic dividends in the hands of a usufructuary, then it is required to also exempt dividends from EU Member States in the hands of a usufructuary.

(v) Minimum Holding Period (Art. 3(2)(b))
Member States may deny parent or subsidiary status to companies which are not affiliated by a qualifying shareholding for an uninterrupted period of at least two years. This is an anti-abuse provision, aimed at preventing short-lived concentrations of non-qualifying small holdings in one hand, in order to temporarily surmount the participation threshold, with a view to an expected profit distribution, after which the – on stand-alone basis non-qualifying – small participations would be transferred back to their original non-qualifying owners. Since the minimum holding requirement has been reduced to 10% of the shares/ votes, on 1 January 2009, the scope of this kind of abuse has become smaller. A similar provision is included in Article 1(10) of the I&R Directive (see Chapter 18).[44]

Article 3(2)(b) 'does not establish a general exception to the application of Directive 90/435, but merely provides an option for Member States'.[45] If a Member State does not opt, it cannot – in situations where two years have not yet expired – dodge its obligations under the Directive by referring to the minimum holding period of Article 3(2)(b).[46]

The language of Article 3(2)(b) suggests that Member States may not content themselves with a minimum holding period of less than two years. The fact, however, that they may opt to have no minimum period at all indicates that they are also at liberty to set any minimum holding period between naught and two years. Several Member States require only one year. Moreover, Member States remain free to set separate minimum holding periods for the application of Article 4 (inbound dividends) and Article 5 (outbound dividends), or to require such period only for application of just one of these provisions.

The wording of Article 3(2) leaves unresolved the question of whether the holding period must be assessed in retrospect or in prospect. Article 3(2)(b) could mean that the required time span should be completed before the companies involved are entitled to the Directive benefits. Most Member States took this view in their initial implementation of the Directive, denying the Directive benefits altogether as long as the qualifying holding had not existed for at least the time span required in national implementation law. On the other hand,

43 Case C-48/07, *Les Vergers du Vieux Tauves SA*, [2008] ECR I-10627, EU:C:2008:758.
44 Cf. the minimum holding period of 365 days in Article 10(2)(a) OECD Model Convention.
45 Case C-39/16, *Argenta Spaarbank II*, EU:C:2017:813, point 30.
46 Case C-39/16 (*Argenta Spaarbank II*), EU:C:2017:813, points 30-40.

Article 3(2) could also mean that any distribution between qualifying companies should be exempted immediately, even if the holding in the subsidiary was acquired only one day before the dividend distribution, provided that the parent company undertakes to retain – and in fact does retain – its qualifying interest until the required time span has elapsed. The Netherlands took this last view in respect of outbound dividends, exempting them immediately, but requiring the domestic distributing subsidiary to provide security for the withholding tax for the remainder of the one-year holding period in case that period would not be completed. Austria's implementation was more or less in between these two modes of implementation: although it required the holding period to be completed before an exemption was extended to the subsidiary, the subsidiary (or its EU parent) could apply for a refund of the withholding tax after completion.

Preliminary questions on the matter were referred to the Court in three cases opposing the German tax administration and three Netherlands companies (*Denkavit, VITIC* and *Voormeer*) which had acquired German subsidiaries. The German subsidiaries paid or planned to pay dividends to their Netherlands parents within a year after their acquisition, *i.e.* before the German one-year minimum holding period had elapsed. The parent companies were denied a reduction of German withholding tax altogether. Not even a refund after completion of the minimum period was available. The Court held:[47]

> 'It follows from the wording of (Art. 3(2)) and in particular from the use of the present tense ("maintain") in all language versions except the Danish, that, in order to receive the tax advantage, the parent company must have a holding in the subsidiary during a certain period of time, without it being necessary that this period should have come to an end at the time when the tax advantage is granted.
> (...) That interpretation is confirmed by the purpose of the Directive, which is to facilitate tax arrangements governing cross-border operation. Member States cannot therefore, in this regard, unilaterally introduce restrictive measures such as the requirement, as in this instance, that a minimum holding period must already have been completed when the profits in respect of which the tax advantage is sought are distributed. Likewise, the Member States' option to lay down a minimum period (...) is to be interpreted strictly, since it constitutes a derogation from the principle of exemption from withholding tax provided for in Article 5(1) of the Directive.'

Several Member States intervening in the procedure argued that the Council, when adopting the Directive in 1990, agreed to use vague language in order to enable different Member States to use different interpretations according to the needs of the national legal order. The Court flatly rejected that argument. Intentions expressed by Member States within the Council have no legal significance if they have not been laid down in statutory provisions, accessible to the public. The argument did have some weight, however, in the assessment whether Germany was liable for damages (see below).

47 Joined Cases C-283/94, C-291/94 and C-292/94, *Denkavit Internationaal BV, VITIC Amsterdam BV and Voormeer BV v. Bundesamt für Finanzen*, [1996] ECR I- 5063, EU:C:1996:387. For comments, see Dirk Schelpe, 'The *Denkavit-Vitic- Voormeer* Case,' *EC Tax Review* 1997-1, p. 17, and Dennis M. Weber, 'The First Steps of the CJEU Concerning an Anti-Abuse Doctrine in the Field of Harmonized Direct Taxes,' *EC Tax Review* 1997–1, p. 22.

Apparently, the Court approved of both the Austrian implementation (provisional with-holding of dividend tax; refund after completion of the period) and of the Netherlands implementation (provisional exemption on condition of provision of security for repayment if the holding period is not completed):

> 'It is for the Member States to draw up rules for ensuring compliance with the minimum period, in accordance with the procedures laid down in their domestic law. On no view are those States obliged under the Directive to grant the advantage immediately on the basis of an undertaking by the parent company involved to observe the minimum holding period.'

In its 2009 report on the functioning of the I&R Directive (see Chapter 18), the Commission submitted that after the coming into force of Directive 2001/44/EC on the mutual assistance in the recovery of tax claims, the Member States should grant exemption immediately and should not be permitted any more to require security for payment during the remainder of the holding period.[48]

The Court did not rule on the question – because it was not posed – whether Member States should pay interest on a refund of provisionally withheld dividend tax after completion of the minimum period (in the Austrian system), or whether the cost of security should be reimbursed (in the Netherlands system). Advocate-General Jacobs considered that interest should at any rate be payable on refunds ensuing from the Austrian system on the same terms as those applicable to refunds of tax under domestic rules. Indeed, although Member States enjoy national procedural autonomy if no EU rules are in force, they should observe the principle of non-discrimination, and therefore treat tax refunds on the basis of EU law not less favourable than tax refunds on the basis of national law.

The Court did rule on the question of whether Article 5 of the Directive (prohibition of dividend withholding tax in the subsidiary State) has direct effect (whether it can be relied on by individual taxpayers before national tax courts; see Section 3.5.1). There were doubts because Article 3(2) grants Member States discretion as regards the length and nature of the minimum holding period, and Article 1(2) confers on them the right to deny the Directive benefits for transactions their domestic law identify as abuse. The Court, however, held that Article 5 was clear and unconditional enough to have direct effect, as the discretionary powers conferred in Article 3(2):

> 'do not make it impossible to determine minimum rights on the basis of the principle contained in Article 5.'

The three parent companies could therefore claim a refund or a reduction, respectively, of the German withholding tax. They were not entitled, however, to compensation for (additional) damages ensuing from Germany's initial incorrect implementation of the Directive, because (i) Germany's understanding of the discretionary powers of the Member States under Article 3(2) was common among all Member States except Austria and the Netherlands, (ii) there was no case law of the Court on the issue yet, (iii) the Directive expressly refers to the prevention of abuse, and (iv) the wording of Article 3(2) was kept

48 See paragraph 3.3.3 of the Commission report on the functioning of the Directive, COM(2009) 179.

vague. Therefore, Germany's breach of EU Law could not be regarded as 'sufficiently serious' to warrant State liability on the basis of the Court's judgments in the *Brasserie du Pêcheur, Factortame* and *British Telecom* cases (see Sections 3.5.4.2 and 7.14).

16.3.3 No Other Requirements

The Directive does not allow Member States to require other conditions to be met than the ones set out above, except in specific cases of abuse, under the anti-abuse provisions of Article 1. In particular, the Directive does not allow Member States to require that the 10% or larger holding of the parent company in the subsidiary must serve substantive entrepreneurial purposes rather than passive investment purposes. The simple passing of the 10% threshold suffices, irrespective of the entrepreneurial activities (or lack thereof) of the subsidiary. Neither may Member States require there to be an entrepreneurial link between the activities (if any) of the parent company and the activities (if any) of the subsidiary.

Unlike the I&R Directive, the PSD does not contain a beneficial ownership clause. However, in the Danish cases there are various indications that the Court holds the view that beneficial ownership is required.[49] If this is indeed so,[50] we believe that this would not mean that an additional condition is introduced (since the Court does not allow the imposition of additional conditions for granting the benefits of the PSD[51]), but rather that the terms 'distributions of profits received by' and 'distributions of profits ... to' in Articles 4, 5 and 6 PSD must be considered as attribution rules, to be interpreted as referring to cases where the parent company is the beneficial owner of the dividend. This would mean that the direct recipient of the income is not required to be the 'beneficial owner', but that there should be a 'beneficial owner' that fulfils all the applicable conditions.[52]

On 22 December 2021 the European Commission presented a proposal for a Directive laying down rules to prevent the misuse of shell entities (also referred to as 'Unshell Directive').[53] Under this Directive, Member States would be obliged to disregard Articles 4, 5 and 6 of the PSD where undertakings would be presumed to lack 'minimum substance' and these entities could not rebut this presumption (see also Sections 18.8 and 25.3.3).

The anti-abuse provisions are discussed in more detail in Section 16.8. below.

---

49 See in particular Joined Cases C-116/16 and C-117/16, *T Danmark and Y Denmark Aps*, EU:C:2019:135, points 111 and 113.

50 Dennis Weber: EU Beneficial Ownership Further Developed: A View from a Different Angle, WTJ 2022 (Volume 14), No 1., at 3.2.4., contends that the CJEU does not read an implicit beneficial ownership requirement in the PSD.

51 Case C-6/16, *Eqiom SAS, formerly Holcim France SAS/Enka*, EU:C:2017:641, point 24 with further case law references and Joined Cases C-504/16 and C-613/16, *Deister Holding AG and Juhler Holding A/S*, EU:C:2017:1009, point 72.

52 Otto Marres and Isabella de Groot: Combatting Abuse by Conduit Companies. The Doctrine of Abuse under EU Law and Its Influence on Tax Treaties, European Taxation, (Volume 61), No. 8, at 2.5.3.

53 Proposal for a Council Directive laying down rules to prevent the misuse of shell entities for tax purposes and amending Directive 2011/16/EU, COM(2021) 565 final.

16.4 Inbound Dividends: Exemption or Indirect Credit (Art. 4)

16.4.1 The General Rule: Choice of Exemption or Indirect Credit; Even Asymmetrical

Distributed subsidiary profits already properly taxed in the Member State of the subsidiary, and received by a (branch of a) qualifying parent company in another Member State, should not suffer repetitive taxation in the Member State of that (branch of the) parent company. To that end, Article 4(1) provides that the Member State of the (branch of the) parent company receiving the dividend income must either:

- refrain from taxing the dividend income, to the extent the distributions are not deductible by the subsidiary (exemption method);[54] or
- tax the dividend income, but allow the (branch of the) parent company to deduct, from its corporation tax due, the amount of tax paid by the subsidiary in its State of residence on the profits out of which the dividend was paid (indirect credit; credit for underlying tax).

The Directive leaves the Member States a choice between exemption and indirect credit because if both methods for the prevention of international economic double taxation had not been recognized, it would not have been adopted. Both methods were and still are used by Member States. States exempting foreign-source income adhere to the principle of investment neutrality in the *foreign* market (capital import neutrality, CIN; see Section 8.2.3). They believe their (subsidiary) companies should be able to compete in the foreign market on local conditions, including local tax conditions, and therefore should pay only the local level of tax on their local profits. States adhering to the credit method start from the idea of investment neutrality in the *home* market. They believe companies investing abroad should pay the same level of tax as companies staying at home (home neutrality, or capital export neutrality, CEN; see Section 8.2). Therefore, in an indirect credit system the parent company is first taxed for the full (grossed-up) dividends received from its foreign subsidiaries, after which the foreign corporation tax attributable to the foreign (sub) subsidiary profits out of which the dividend was paid is credited against the corporation tax due by the parent company on that gross dividend.

Although Article 4(1) thus leaves the Member States a choice between exemption and indirect credit, the Court considers it to have direct effect (it can be relied on in Court by taxpayers), because the parent company's rights can be determined with sufficient precision on the basis of this provision.[55]

If a Member State has chosen for one of the systems, but has not implemented it correctly (as Belgium had not implemented the exemption system correctly in the *Cobelfret* case;

54 For Member States for whom this was not yet clear, the CJEU spelled out, in Case C-138/07, *Belgische Staat v Cobelfret NV*, [2009] ECR I-731, EU:C:2009:82, that the term 'refrain from taxing' means 'exempt from tax'.

55 Case C-138/07 (*Belgische Staat v Cobelfret NV*), [2009] ECR I-731, EU:C:2009:82. Nevertheless, the Court of First Instance of Liège wanted to hear from the Court whether Article 4 of Directive 2011/96/EU has direct effect. Unsurprisingly, the answer was affirmative (Case C-135/24, *John Cockerill SA*, EU:C:2025:176, para. 53).

see below in this section), it cannot justify its deficient implementation by arguing that it could also have chosen for indirect credit and that this would have been (even) less favourable for the taxpayer.[56]

The wording of Article 4 does not prevent Member States from applying both methods, depending on the circumstances, for example on whether a tax treaty is in force with the State of the subsidiary, or whether the level of effective taxation in the subsidiary State is comparable with the level of effective taxation in the parent company State. However, one would expect such distinction between domestic dividend and inward cross-border dividend, or between different foreign subsidiary States to fall foul of the free movement of capital and the right of establishment, as the indirect credit method is clearly less favourable than the exemption method. It was surprising, therefore, that the Court accepted, in the *Test Claimants FII GLO*,[57] and in the joined Cases *Haribo* and *Salinen*,[58] an *asymmetrical* choice by the parent company State, exempting domestic dividends and providing only indirect credit for cross-border dividends. According to the Court, neither the Directive nor the TFEU Freedoms require the parent company State to apply the *same* system of prevention of economic double taxation to cross-border and domestic intercompany dividends, as exemption and indirect credit are 'equivalent'. That is surprising, as serious discrimination against parents of foreign subsidiaries, both substantively and administratively, is thus accepted in respect of the following aspects:

i. administration, compliance, and burden of proof: a multi-tier indirect credit system is depressingly complex and administratively cumbersome for the parent company, which must demonstrate the amount of the eventual foreign corporation tax attributable to the (re)(re)distributed eventual profit of the foreign (sub)(sub)subsidiary, so complex and cumbersome that it may in practice be impossible for the parent company to actually effectuate its theoretical entitlement to indirect credit. The UK itself argued (in the very same *FII* case!) that multi-tier indirect credit is simply too complex to apply to holdings below 10%; the UK has abandoned it by now for that reason. The *Haribo and Salinen* case clearly shows that foreign dividends thus may well continue suffering unfettered economic double taxation, whereas the exemption of domestic dividends fully protects a parent of domestic subsidiaries against these procedural and administrative obstacles and risks of double taxation. Unlike exemption, indirect credit procedurally thus jeopardizes the substantive rights: sophisticated accountancy and hard-to-get evidence from abroad are required, whereas no proof whatsoever is required under an exemption system, except in cases of suspected abuse. *FII GLO* and *Haribo & Salinen* are not clear on this, but we hope they imply that if a national court finds that the burden of proof is unsustainable for a parent company receiving foreign intercompany dividends, then the indirect credit method will not be considered equivalent to the domestic exemption method and a switch-over (back) to exemption must apply to take away the effective discrimination against cross-border dividends. Much as EU law is not intended to take away the normal burden of proof on taxpayers

56 Case C-138/07, *Belgische Staat v Cobelfret NV*, [2009] ECR I-731, EU:C:2009:82.
57 Case C-446/04, *Test Claimants in the FII Group Litigation*, [2006] ECR I-11753, EU:C:2006:774.
58 Joined Cases C-436 and 437/08, *Haribo Lakritzen Hans Riegel* and *Österreichische Salinen*, EU:C:2011:61 and EU:C:2009:17.

claiming a deduction or a tax benefit (see Section 15.6), it *is* supposed to prohibit a flagrant evidential discrimination against foreign indirect investment. The Accor[59] case (para. 102) seems promising in that respect;

ii. (non)conservation of tax reliefs extended at the subsidiary level: for many reasons (*e.g.* loss relief, foreign tax credit, tax incentives, etc.) taxation at the level of the domestic subsidiary may be lower than at the level of the parent. Such advantages at domestic subsidiary level stay entirely intact at parent company level under an exemption system. By contrast, similar *foreign* reliefs and incentives extended to the foreign subsidiary are completely taxed away at parent company level under an indirect credit system; that is the very essence of a credit system for active income: taxing away the relative advantage of investing abroad, thus protecting the home State market against the tax efficiency of other States. Accepting such destruction of the competition of other States would seem at odds with the very idea of an internal market. The Court failed to explain why, if the parent State so much adheres to tax level equalization at the *parent* company level, that State is not required to apply the same cumbersome and relief-annulling indirect credit method indiscriminately also to domestic dividends. In *FII GLO II*,[60] the Court appreciated its mistake in this respect and at least required the parent company State to credit the subsidiary State corporation tax at the nominal rate, not at the effective rate (see below);

iii. (this is going to be a bit technical, but there is a lot of money involved:) in an indirect credit system, no more *foreign* corporation tax will be credited than the amount of the *domestic* tax attributable to the foreign dividend. The attributable domestic tax is reduced commensurately with the parent's expenses attributable to the holding ('net' credit): if the parent loan-financed its foreign holding, the deduction of the interest will have the effect of leaving very little attributable domestic tax, resulting in a very low credit. Thus, foreign dividends are not at all treated 'in the same way' as under an exemption system, as indeed, exemption is usually extended on a *gross* basis. The Court should therefore have required the UK to apply its *Bosal*[61] rule (see Section 16.4.4): either the indirect credit must also be granted on a gross basis (which significantly reduces the point of the indirect credit method), or also the exemption for domestic dividends must be granted *net* of expenses, resulting in a very low exemption if the holding in the domestic subsidiary is loan-financed (which significantly reduces the point of exemption).

FII and *Haribo and Salinen* were also surprising because before, the Court consistently held that the Treaty freedoms prohibit *all* discriminations, including minor ones[62] and administrative ones.[63]

59 Case C-310/09, *Accor*, EU:C:2011:581.

60 Case C-35/11, *Test Claimants in the FII Group Litigation II*, EU:C:2012:707.

61 Case C-168/01, *Bosal Holding BV*, [2003] ECR I- 9409, EU:C:2003:479.

62 A.o. Case 270/83, *Commission v. France*, [1986] ECR 273, EU:C:1986:37, and Case C-212/06, *Gouvernement de la Communauté française et Gouvernement wallon*, [2008] ECR I-1683, EU:C:2008:178.

63 A.o. Case C-118/96, *Jessica Safir*, [1998] ECR I-1897, EU:C:1998:170.

The judgments in *FII* and *Haribo & Salinen* were all the more surprising since in the previous case of *Bosal Holding*,[64] the Court prohibited an almost identical asymmetrical choice made on the basis of the very same Article 4 (see Section 16.4.4), considering such asymmetric choice incompatible with the Treaty Freedoms. Possibly, *FII* and *Haribo & Salinen* may be explained by the fact that the Court – rightly – does not feel competent to deny the parent company State the right to tax its companies holding foreign subsidiaries at the same corporate tax level as its companies holding domestic subsidiaries, as that would be a political choice for the source principle over the residence principle for which there is no legal basis. We observe, however, that no political choice is at issue, as there is a clear and imperative *legal* basis (Arts. 49 and 63 TFEU) for requiring the parent company State to apply the *same* system or at least a no less favourable system to foreign and domestic intercompany dividends. The Court does not rob the parent company State of any taxing rights by requiring such equal treatment: indeed, nothing prevents the parent company State from applying the unfavourable indirect credit system to foreign dividends, as long as it applies that same unfavourable indirect credit system also to domestic dividends. It is true, however, that *not* allowing an asymmetrical choice for exemption for domestic dividends and imputation credit for foreign dividends would not support the EU's anti-BEPS efforts.

The issue reached the Court again in *FII GLO II*,[65] in which the Court acknowledged the issue under (ii) above. It reiterated that the exemption method and the imputation method are in fact equivalent, provided that the tax rate applied to foreign-sourced dividends is not higher than the rate applied to nationally-sourced dividends and that the tax credit is at least equal to the amount paid in the State of the company making the distribution, up to the limit of the tax charged in the Member State of the company receiving the dividends. It specified, however, that Articles 49 TFEU and 63 TFEU preclude legislation of a Member State which applies the exemption method to nationally-sourced dividends and the imputation method to foreign-sourced dividends if it is established that the tax credit is equivalent to the corporation tax actually paid by the subsidiary but this effective level of taxation of company profits in the subsidiary State is generally lower than the nominal rate of tax.

A mirror-image question was referred to the Court in Case C-138/07, *Cobelfret*:[66] may taxation of foreign qualifying dividends at variance with Article 4 PSD be pardoned if similar domestic dividends are treated in exactly the same manner, thus securing international neutrality? Belgium had not implemented Article 4(1)(a) PSD correctly: under the Belgian system, qualifying dividends were first included in the taxable income of the parent company; after some other corrections, subsequently a deduction of (95% of) the dividends was allowed, but only if and insofar as the taxable income was positive. The main effect of this system was that parent companies which had suffered losses from

64 Case C-168/01, *Bosal Holding BV v Staatssecretaris van Financiën*, [2003] ECR I- 9409, EU:C:2003:479.

65 Case C-35/11, *Test Claimants in the FII Group Litigation*, EU:C:2012:707.

66 Case C-138/07, *Belgische Staat v Cobelfret NV*, [2009] ECR I-731, EU:C:2009:82. See for comments: Frank Dierckx: 'The Belgian Participation Exemption and the CJEU Decision in *Cobelfret*,' *European Taxation*, June 2009, p. 301–304.

other activities lost their exemption rights up to the amount of those losses, without the possibility to carry over any 'excess exemption': the parent company in fact paid tax in year *n* + 1 on qualifying dividends received in year *n*, contrary to Article 4(1)(a). Belgium tried to justify this effective lack of exemption of qualifying dividends, *inter alia*, by pointing out (i) that it applied the same untoward system to domestic dividends and thus safeguarded neutrality between domestic and foreign dividends, and (ii) that this system was not less favourable than indirect credit, as Article 4(1)(b) did not require the Member States to carry excess credits forward. The Court held, however, that equal treatment of domestic and inbound dividends was not the only goal of Article 4 of the Directive and that equal (equally bad) treatment of domestic and inbound dividends cannot justify incorrect implementation of the exemption system as regards foreign dividends. The fact that the system of indirect credit could also have been chosen, was not considered relevant, as Belgium had opted for the exemption system.[67] Admittedly, that answer leads to EU-dividends being treated more favourably than domestic dividends, but nothing prevents Belgium from (i) adapting its system such as to restore equal (equally favourable) treatment of domestic dividends, or (ii) to opt for an asymmetrical system such as the one accepted by the Court in *FII, Haribo & Salinen* and *FII II* (exemption for domestic dividends and indirect credit with onerous evidence requirements for foreign dividends), or (iii) to apply the indirect credit system overall. Belgium also tried to curtail PSD-rights of parent companies by denying deduction of interest payments by the parent company up to the amount of qualifying dividends received, but in *Argenta Spaarbank II*,[68] the Court rejected such a system as incompatible with the Directive (see Section 16.4.4 below).

16.4.2 The Exemption Method

16.4.2.1 'Refrain from taxing such profits'

Article 4(1)(a) PSD requires the parent company State to 'refrain from tax', which means: exempt from tax.[69] In combination with Article 4(3) PSD, which allows for the option to fix the non-deductible management costs relating to the holding at 5% of the distributed profits (see Section 16.4.4), this results in the rule that taxation is precluded to the extent the taxable amount of the dividends exceeds 5% of the distributed profits.[70] Indirect taxation is equally prohibited. We are greatly indebted to the Belgian legislator and the Belgian referring courts, who have enabled the Court to provide us with deeper and more detailed insights into this doctrine. Belgium had a system that provided 'that dividends received by the parent company were added to its tax base and that an amount corresponding to 95% of those dividends was deducted from that base, but only to the extent that the parent company continued to have taxable profits, there being no possibility of

67 Cf. Case C-556/20, *Schneider Electric SE a.o.*, EU:C:2022:378, point 39.
68 Case C-39/16, *Argenta Spaarbank NV v Belgium II*, EU:C:2017:81.
69 Case C-138/07, *Belgische Staat v Cobelfret NV*, [2009] ECR I-731, EU:C:2009:82, para. 43.
70 Case C-556/20, *Schneider Electric SE a.o.*, EU:C:2022:378. See Sections 16.4.4 and 16.6.5. See also Thomas Kollruss, Transnational Grouping of Companies and Unresolved Questions Regarding the EU Parent-Subsidiary Directive: Implications for Companies, Member States and Non-EU Member States, *European Taxation* 12/2022, p. 537-543.

carrying forward to subsequent tax years the part of the DTI which was not deducted'.[71] Parent companies that had suffered losses from other activities lost their exemption rights up to the amount of those losses, without the possibility to carry over any 'excess exemption', and as a consequence they paid tax on qualifying dividends in subsequent years when their results were positive.[72] This is incompatible with Article 4(1)(a) PSD, according to the Cobelfret judgment.[73] Following this judgment, Belgium amended its system to the effect that the part of the qualifying dividends which could not be deducted during the tax year concerned due to insufficient profits could be carried forward to subsequent tax years indefinitely.[74] A problem remained. Qualifying dividends carried forward were deducted as a priority from taxable profits in subsequent years, with the result that other deductible items that could be carried forward for a limited time only (such as the deduction for risk capital and losses) could not be used and might expire in future years. This effect was considered incompatible with the PSD in the *Brussels Securities SA* case.[75] We can infer from this decision that the relevant test is whether the parent company is being taxed more heavily than would have been the case if it had not received dividends from its non-resident subsidiary or if, as the referring court states, the dividends had simply been excluded from the parent company's tax base.[76] This test was passed in a following case, *Allianz Benelux SA (C-295/21)*, in a merger situation, where the taxpayer, a surviving company, complained that not all qualifying dividends received by the dissolved companies and carried forward, could be transferred to it. However, if Belgium had applied a full exemption system, this would have resulted in more losses being carried forward, with the same transfer limitations, so this mechanism was not precluded by the PSD.[77] However, the test was not passed in yet another similar case (*John Cockerill SA*; Case C-135/24), regarding the effect of the Belgian tax consolidation rules (the intra-group profit transfer) on the deduction of qualifying dividends. The taxpayer (having received an intra-group transfer) complained that these rules do not allow qualifying dividends, received in the current year, to be deducted from the intra-group transfer received, resulting in a higher amount of current tax than would have been payable if there had been a full exemption of qualifying dividends.[78] If the combination of the tax treatment of qualifying dividends with the intra-group transfer scheme, has the effect that the receipt of qualifying dividends is liable to result in the parent company being taxed more heavily than it would have been had it not received such dividends, or if those dividends had simply been excluded from its tax base (which is for the referring court to ascertain), this is precluded by Article 4(1) PSD.[79]

71 Case C-295/21, *Allianz Benelux SA*, EU:C:2022:812, para. 33.
72 Case C-138/07, *Belgische Staat v Cobelfret NV*, [2009] ECR I-731, EU:C:2009:82, para. 40.
73 Case C-138/07, *Belgische Staat v Cobelfret NV*, [2009] ECR I-731, EU:C:2009:82.
74 Case C-295/21, *Allianz Benelux SA*, EU:C:2022:812, para. 34.
75 Case C-389/18, Brussels Securities SA, EU:C:2019:1132. See Pieter-Jan Wouters, Does a Partial Transfer of the Dividend-Received Deduction upon a Tax-Neutral Merger Violate the EU Parent-Subsidiary Directive?, *European Taxation* 1/2023, p. 3-11 (at 2.4).
76 Brussels Securities, para. 45. See also Case C-135/24, *John Cockerill SA*, EU:C:2025:176, para. 41-42.
77 See for a more elaborate discussion: Wouters, l.c.
78 See for an analysis of the impact of the group consolidation rules on the deduction of qualifying dividends: Wouters, lc., at 9-10.
79 Case C-135/24, *John Cockerill SA*, EU:C:2025:176, para. 41-42.

Although the personal scope of the PSD is limited to companies subject to corporation tax (more in particular one of the taxes listed in Annex I, Part B), Article 4 of the PSD is not limited to these taxes. Also additional taxes (such as the Belgian fairness tax, the French 3% surtax and the former French précompte) are covered by Article 4(1), and if Member States opt for the exemption system of Article 4(1)(a) PSD, these taxes are precluded (at least if the taxable amount of these dividends exceeds the 5% ceiling provided for in Article 4(3); see Section 16.4.4).[80] If not, the goal of Article 4, prevention of economic double taxation of the profit distributions covered by the PSD, would not be achieved. In three pending cases, the IRAP cases (Banca Mediolanum a.o.; C-92/24, C-93/24 and C-94/24), the issue is whether the levy of IRAP (regional tax on productive activities) on 50% of dividend income is compatible with Article 4 PSD.[81] A-G Kokott argues that the Court did not decide that Article 4 PSD prohibits Member States from subjecting more than 5% of qualifying dividend amounts to any form of taxation. Instead, the prohibition to tax is confined solely to corporation tax or a comparable tax. Based on the purpose of Article 4 of the PSD, as clarified in recital 3 (to eliminate double taxation at the level of the parent company), and on Article 2(a)(iii) PSD, that refers to the taxes listed in Annex I, Part B, and to 'any other tax which may be substituted for any of those taxes', she argues that the question is whether such other tax (in the present case, IRAP) substitutes for, or supplements, the respective corporation tax by virtue of the fact that it is comparable to that corporation tax. This was the case for the Belgian 'fairness tax' and the French 3% surtax which amount to an additional tax to corporation tax. The question as to when a tax substitutes for one of the taxes listed in Annex I, Part B, should in her view not be answered strictly and formally. Rather, the object of taxation and the legal nature or character of the other tax should be decisive. If IRAP were to constitute an additional corporation tax that – like corporation tax – is linked to income, and thus taxes the dividends again in a comparable manner, which would be for the national court to conclude, then that tax would be covered by the prohibition of Article 4(1)(a) PSD.[82]

16.4.2.2 Linking Rule: No Exemption for Deductible Payments[83]

'It is undesirable that in the EU Internal Market a taxpayer is subject to double non-taxation on his/her cross-border activity as this gives the taxpayer a competitive advantage compared

80 See Case C-68/15, *X v Ministerraad*, EU:C:2017:379 (Belgian fairness tax), Case C-365/16, *Association française des entreprises privées (AFEP) a.o.*, EU:C:2017:378 (French 3% surcharge), and Case C-556/20, *Schneider Electric SE* a.o., EU:C:2022:378 (précompte).

81 See for a discussion of Italian case law on this issue: Valerio Forestieri and Raffaele Villa, New Trend of Italian Tax Courts to Overrule IRAP Taxation of Dividends Received by Banks, Insurance Companies and Financial Holding Companies, European Taxation, November 2022, p. 506-509.

82 Opinion of Advocate General Kokott delivered on 27 March 2025, in Joined Cases C-92/24 to C-94/24, *Banca Mediolanum a.o.*, 556/20, ECLI:EU:C:2025:223.

83 See also Christoph Marchgraber, Cross-Border Tax Arbitrage, the Parent- Subsidiary Directive (2011/96) and Double Tax Treaty Law, *Bulletin for International Taxation*, March 2016, p. 123-132.

to other taxpayers who are subject to ordinary taxation.'[84] For that reason, the European Commission started a 'fact-finding public consultation in order to establish evidence concerning double non-taxation within the EU and in relation with Third Countries'[85] in February 2012. One of the issues was international mismatches in the characterization of financial instruments (debt or equity), resulting in a deduction of payments (characterized as interest) in one jurisdiction, and an exemption of these payments (characterized as dividend income) in the other jurisdiction. Already in 2010, the EU Code of Conduct Group on Business Taxation (see Chapter 26) advised that participation exemptions should not extend to payments treated as deductible in the source State.[86] In December 2012, the Commission announced a revision of the Parent Subsidiary directive to ensure that it does not inadvertently prevent effective action against double non-taxation in the area of hybrid loan structures.[87] In November 2013, the Commission proposed to amend the PSD such that (i) Article 4(1)(a) would provide that Member States should not exempt deductible profit distributions (linking rule), and (ii) the PSD would include a mandatory common anti-abuse provision (the general anti-abuse rule; see Section 16.8).[88] Since the general anti-abuse rule proved to be far more controversial than the linking rule, the amending Proposal was split in two in April 2014.[89] Council Directive 2014/86/EU amending Article 4(1) (a) (linking rule) was adopted on 8 July 2014.[90]

Article 4(1)(a) provides that, if the Member State of the parent company or the Member State of the permanent establishment opts for the exemption method, it on the one hand must refrain from taxation to the extent that the distributed profits are not deductible, and on the other hand must tax these profits to the extent such profits are deductible by the subsidiary. The preamble of the amending Directive 2014/86/EU states that the benefits of the Parent Subsidiary directive should not lead to situations of double non-taxation and that for the purpose of avoiding double non-taxation deriving from mismatches in the tax treatment of profit distributions, the Member State of the parent company and the Member State of the permanent establishment should not allow an exemption to the extent profit distributions are deductible by the subsidiary. Obviously, if the parent company State does not exempt participation dividends, but provides only an imputation credit for the underlying subsidiary State corporation tax, there is no need for a linking

84 European Commission, The internal market: factual examples of double non- taxation cases, Consultation document, TAXUD D1 D(2012), p. 4. The consultation period started 29 February 2012 and ended 30 May 2012. See also European Commission, Summary Report of the Responses Received on the Public Consultation on Factual and Possible Ways to Tackle Double Non-Taxation Cases (5 Jul. 2012), TAXUD D1 D(2012).

85 L.c., p. 4.

86 Code of Conduct Group Progress Report of 25 May 2010, doc. 10033/10, para. 31.

87 European Commission, An Action Plan to strengthen the fight against tax fraud and tax evasion, COM(2012) 722 final (6 Dec. 2012), paragraph 4.1.1, point 14.

88 Proposal for a Council Directive amending Directive 2011/96/EU on the common system of taxation applicable in the case of parent companies and subsidiaries of different Member States, Brussels 25 November 2013, COM(2013) 814 final.

89 Note from the Presidency of 30 April 2014 to the Council, doc. 9397/14 (see in particular paragraph 4. See also Note from the Presidency of 3 June 2014 to the Council, doc. 104197/14.

90 Council Directive 2014/86/EU of 8 July 2014, amending Directive 2011/96/EU, O.J. No. L 219 of 25 July 2014, p. 40. The implementation period expired on 1 January 2016.

rule: if the distributed subsidiary profits are deductible in the subsidiary State, then obviously there is no underlying corporation tax to be credited.

In the meantime, the OECD took the lead in the international debate on aggressive tax planning. Within days of the launch of the public consultation by the European Commission it published its report on hybrid mismatch arrangements,[91] and early 2013 it coined the BEPS acronym (for Base Erosion and Profit Shifting).[92] In its 2013 BEPS Action Plan,[93] it announced its action on hybrid mismatch arrangements, resulting in a 2014 interim report[94] and a 2015 final report[95] on Action 2. Although Council Directive 2014/86/EU amending Article 4(1)(a) PSD was adopted even before the interim report on Action 2 was published, we believe that the work on BEPS Action 2 is part of the context of Council Directive 2014/86/EU, since the work was done in parallel, the EU was represented in the OECD work on BEPS,[96] and the EU's hybrid mismatch approach is in conformity with the BEPS Action 2 interim report[97] and final report.[98]

How to interpret the term 'deductible distributed profit'? A typical example would be a hybrid loan, which is characterized as debt under the law of the subsidiary jurisdiction, but as equity under the law of the parent company jurisdiction. But the provision would in our view also apply to a system where dividend distributions are deductible, e.g. for Real Estate Investment Trusts (REITs).[99] In our view, only hybrid mismatches are covered which result in an actual deduction in the subsidiary jurisdiction. If the payment would normally be deductible in the subsidiary State, but is caught by interest deduction

---

91 OECD (2012), Hybrid Mismatch Arrangements, Tax Policy and Compliance Issues, OECD Publishing, Paris.

92 OECD (2013), Addressing Base Erosion and Profit Shifting, OECD Publishing, Paris.

93 OECD (2013), Action Plan on Base Erosion and Profit Shifting, OECD Publishing, Paris.

94 OECD (2014), Neutralising the Effects of Hybrid Mismatch Arrangements, OECD Publishing, Paris.

95 OECD (2015), Neutralising the Effects of Hybrid Mismatch Arrangements, Action 2 - 2015 Final Report, OECD Publishing, Paris.

96 See also the original proposal (Proposal for a Council Directive amending Directive 2011/96/EU on the common system of taxation applicable in the case of parent companies and subsidiaries of different Member States, COM/2013/0814 final) that included an explanatory memorandum with the following reference to the BEPS work (in paragraph 1 – context of the proposal; footnotes excluded): 'The issue of corporate base erosion is very high in the political agenda of many EU and non-EU countries and has been on the agenda of recent G20 and G8 meetings; the OECD is currently undertaking work on base erosion and profit shifting ('BEPS') which is widely welcomed.'

97 OECD (2014), Neutralising the Effects of Hybrid Mismatch Arrangements, OECD Publishing, Paris, paragraph 71. Note that this amendment must be considered as implementation of the specific recommendation (recommendation 2.1) and not of the hybrid mismatch rule, see also Reinout de Boer and Otto Marres, BEPS Action 2: Neutralizing the Effects on Hybrid Mismatch Arrangements, Intertax volume 43 (2015), issue 1, p. 14-41 at 2.3, 3.1.1 and 5.3.

98 OECD (2015), Neutralising the Effects of Hybrid Mismatch Arrangements, Action 2 - 2015 Final Report, OECD Publishing, Paris, paragraphs 106-111.

99 See example 1.10 as discussed in OECD (2015), Neutralising the Effects of Hybrid Mismatch Arrangements, Action 2 - 2015 Final Report, OECD Publishing, Paris, p. 203-204 at 6: a system of deductible dividends does not give rise to a hybrid mismatch under the hybrid mismatch rule, but it would be covered by Recommendation 2.1.

limitation rules in that State, then the payment is not deductible and the linking rule should not prevent exemption in the parent company State.[100]

16.4.3 *The Credit Method*

16.4.3.1 Deduction of the Attributable Corporation Tax

Member States opting for Article 4(1)(b) PSD may tax the profit distributions but must allow for a credit (i.e. a deduction from the amount of tax due) of the corporation tax related to those profits and paid by the direct subsidiary and by lower-tier subsidiaries (see Section 16.4.3.3). An ordinary credit suffices (See Section 16.4.2).

Under the now deleted original paragraphs (2)–(4) of Article 5, three Member States were transitionally allowed to carry on levying a withholding tax on distributions of profits after 1 January 1992 (see Section 16.6.2.). Parent company States using the indirect credit method were required to grant (ordinary) credit also for any such temporarily surviving withholding tax. Those provisions have become obsolete and have therefore been omitted on the occasion of the 2003 amendment. Although Estonia upon its accession in 2003 was allowed until 2009 to levy a withholding tax on outbound dividends as long as it did not charge corporation tax on retained company profits, the accession treaty did not require the other Member States to credit this Estonian distribution tax, probably because that was not considered necessary. Indeed, such profit taxation only upon distribution of the corporate income is not, in fact, a dividend withholding tax, but a belated corporate income tax, which must be credited under Article 4 anyway (if the parent State does not exempt the net distribution), like any other corporation tax levied on the subsidiary profits out of which the dividends are paid (see Section 16.4.3.2).

16.4.3.2 Ordinary Credit; Excess Foreign Corporation Tax

Credit States do not carry their capital export neutrality principle to the point of refunding domestic tax on other income if the foreign tax on the foreign subsidiary's profit exceeds the domestic tax at parent level on the dividend received out of the subsidiary's profit. Only a so-called ordinary indirect credit is granted (as opposed to full credit): the credit for underlying foreign corporation tax cannot exceed the amount of domestic corporation tax the parent company State levies itself on the grossed-up dividend. Credit is only required 'up to the limit of the amount of the corresponding tax due' (see Art. 4(1)). Refunding domestic tax due on other income cannot reasonably be required of a Member State, as also the Court considered – in a different context – in Case C-336/96, Gilly,[101] (see Sections 16.3.3 and 13.4.4). On the other hand, if the foreign tax is lower than the home State tax, a credit State does levy (unlike an exemption State) additional home State tax until the

100 OECD (2015), Neutralising the Effects of Hybrid Mismatch Arrangements, Action 2 - 2015 Final Report, OECD Publishing, Paris, is not entirely clear in this respect. According to the analysis in Example 9.2 (p. 432-432), the hybrid financial instrument rule is applicable also if the taxpayer is subject to a general interest limitation. However, it is unclear how Recommendation 2.1 (denial of dividend exemption for deductible payments) must be applied.

101 Case C-336/96, *Les époux Gilly*, [1998] ECR I-2793, EU:C:1998:221.

level of home State taxation is reached (home neutrality). The Court judgments in the Cases C-513/03, Van Hilten-Van der Heijden,[102] C-446/04, Test Claimants FII GLO,[103] C-436 and 437/08, Haribo and Salinen[104] and FII GLO II[105] show that the Court in principle accepts this asymmetrical and protective system because, although it is designed to take away all tax competitive advantages of investing abroad instead of at home, it does not – in principle and eventually – tax foreign source income more heavily than domestic source income and thus does not seem to offend the TFEU Freedoms. As the credit granted is 'ordinary', the parent company may find itself in an excess foreign tax credit position. Groups of companies of which the top holding company is based in a credit country may therefore use an EU intermediate holding company (a so-called 'mixer') to mix profits from moderate tax-level countries with profits from excess tax-level countries, so as to minimize excess foreign tax credit positions. Excess foreign tax credit may occur not only where the subsidiary State tax is higher than the parent company State tax, but also, e.g., where the parent company is in a loss position and is therefore not paying any domestic tax against which to offset the credit.

Usually, credit States allow excess foreign tax credit to be carried over to other fiscal years. The Directive does not contain any provisions on that matter. Case C-437/08, Salinen, shows, however, that a Member State which exempts domestic subsidiary profits and gives indirect credit for foreign subsidiary profits, may rely on the posited 'equivalence' of exemption and indirect credit only if it provides for a roll-over of unused credit rights to subsequent years. We further believe that the joined Cases C-439/07 and C-499/07, KBC and BRB,[106] and Case C-138/07, Cobelfret (see Section 16.4.1) imply that under the Directive, a Member State choosing the indirect credit method must allow the carry-over to other tax years of indirect credits in respect of qualifying subsidiary dividends which could not be used by the parent company in the year of payment of those dividends because the parent was in a loss position in that year.

16.4.3.3 Multi-Tier Credit

Since the 2003 amendment (implementation 1 January 2005), the Directive requires credit States to grant credit not only for corporation tax paid by a direct subsidiary in another Member State, but also for the corporation tax levied on the profits of sub-sub-sidiaries or sub-sub-subsidiaries in other Member States. Until 2005, the Directive only covered dividends paid out of first-tier subsidiary profits. This limitation of scope could easily result in double taxation, as the following example illustrates. Parent company P in Member State P holds shares in subsidiary company S in Member State S. In its turn, company S holds shares in company SubS in Member State FT (Further tier). Company

102 Case C-513/03, *Heirs of Mrs. Van Hilten-Van der Heijden*, [2006] ECR I-1957, EU:C:2006:131.

103 Case C-446/04, *Test Claimants in the Franked Investment Income Group*, [2006] ECR I-11753, EU:C:2006:774.

104 Joined Cases C-436 and 437/08, *Haribo Lakritzen Hans Riegel* and *Österreichische Salinen*, EU:C:2011:61 and EU:C:2009:17.

105 Case C-35/11, *Test Claimants in the FII Group Litigation II*, EU:C:2012:707.

106 Joined Cases C-439/07 and C-499/07, *KBC Bank Beleggen, Risicokapitaal, Beheer* and *Beleggen, Risicokapitaal, Beheer*, [2009] ECR I-4409, EU:C:2009:339.

SubS pays corporation tax on its profits in State FT and distributes its after-tax profits to the intermediary company S. S's State of residence uses either the exemption method, i.e. refrains from taxing the dividend income altogether, or the credit method, i.e. credits the corporation tax paid by SubS in State FT against the corporation tax due by company S. If the corporation tax rates in State S and State FT are equal, than no additional corporation tax is payable in State S. Company S then redistributes the SubS dividend to its parent company P. P's State of residence applies the credit method. Therefore, company P may credit the corporation tax paid by its subsidiary S on the profit out of which the dividend was paid. Company S did not pay any such tax, however, as it benefited from an exemption or credit in State S. Therefore, if State P were to apply only a first-tier credit for underlying tax, then company P would receive no relief from economic double taxation of company SubS's distributed profits. This undesirable effect is avoided if credit is granted for any underlying corporation tax paid within the EU by any (sub-)subsidiary. As early as July 1993, the Commission submitted an amendment proposal[107] to that effect, which was approved by the European Parliament on 19 April 1994 under the consultation procedure,[108] but which was bogged down until 2003, when it was withdrawn and replaced by a proposal resulting in the adopted amendment Directive 2003/123/EC. The amended Article 4(1)(b)[109] requires credit Member States as of 1 January 2005 to credit any lower-tier EU corporation tax as well, provided that at each tier, a parent company and its lower-tier subsidiary qualify under Articles 2 and 3 as, respectively, parent and subsidiary company of a member State.

The Directive does not specifically address the case of a parent company A in Member State A with a subsidiary B in Member State B, which has a subsidiary C in Member State C, which has a permanent establishment D in State D. The profit made within the State D permanent establishment is taxed in State D. If States C and B are exemption States, no additional corporation tax is levied in these States. Should State A credit the profits tax paid by D in State D if the D-profit is eventually distributed by C via B to A? We would answer in the affirmative, as company C was the legal person which paid the profits tax, albeit not in State C, but in State D. That, however, does not prevent application of Article 4(1) (b), as the corporation tax paid in State D is 'related to those profits' and was 'paid by the subsidiary and any lower-tier subsidiary' within the meaning of that provision.

16.4.4 *(Non-)Deductibility of Charges 'Related' to the Holding (Art. 4(3)); Bosal Holding, Keller Holding and Argenta Spaarbank II*

Article 4(3) of the Directive permits Member States to deny deduction, from the taxable profit of the parent company, of any charges related to the holding in the subsidiary, e.g. management charges and interest paid on the financing of the holding. Indeed, there is little reason to allow deduction of charges incurred to obtain exempted income. Those charges must be attributed to the exempted income and must therefore also be 'exempted', otherwise the parent company State would be required to refund domestic tax on taxable

107 Proposal COM (93) 293 final to amend Directive 90/435/EEC of 23 July 1990, submitted to the Council on 26 July 1993, withdrawn and replaced in 2003.

108 EP 1994-1995, minutes of the session of 19 April 1995, p. 69-71.

109 Under Council Directive 90/435/EEC: Article 4(1)(2nd indent).

income from other sources, and would become a depot of the cost of financing foreign investment, eroding the tax base of the parent company State. Obviously this reasoning only applies to charges that are indeed 'related to' the holding in the subsidiary. A system that disallows the deduction of expenses up to the amount of income from qualifying holdings, irrespective of whether the expenses are actually connected to the income, would effectively frustrate the exemption (*Argenta Spaarbank II*).[110]

Under an indirect credit system, charges related to the holding in the subsidiary are also attributed to (*i.e.* deducted from) the grossed-up dividends for which credit is granted, thus reducing the maximum credit (*i.e.* the amount of tax the parent company State would levy itself on the dividend received), which has the same effect as non-deductibility under an exemption system.

The same provision furthermore allows parent company States to deny deduction of any decreases in value of the holding in the subsidiary as a consequence of the profit distribution by that subsidiary. If the subsidiary pays a dividend out of retained profits of previous years, this will be reflected in a lower value of its shares. The Directive does not require the parent company State to permit deduction of such book losses on the parent's participation in the subsidiary. This is especially important in case national tax law requires the parent company to value its holding in subsidiaries at fair market value (mark-to-market), as the Directive does not call for exemption of (or credit for) unrealized capital gains or gains made upon the alienation of (part of) the holding, but only for exemption of (or credit for) *distributions* of profit (see Section 16.5.1).

Some Member States fix non-deductible management charges in respect of foreign share-holdings on a percentage of the dividends paid by the foreign subsidiaries. This practice is compatible with the Directive, provided the percentage is fixed at an amount not higher than 5% of the dividends received (Art. 4(3)). The result is that only 95% of the dividends received are exempt or given credit for.[111] If additional taxes are levied from the parent company (such as the Belgian fairness tax, the French 3% surtax and the former French précompte), and the basis of assessment of such taxes includes dividend income from qualifying subsidiaries, the result will be that the taxable amount of these dividends exceeds the 5% ceiling provided for in Article 4(3); to that extent the levy is precluded by that provision.[112]

Another question is whether Member States may choose to deny deduction, from the taxable profit of the parent company, of any charges related to the holding in subsidiaries

110 Case C-39/16, *Argenta Spaarbank NV v Belgium II*, EU:C:2017:81, points 44-57.

111 Credits for possibly remaining dividend withholding tax levied in the subsidiary state (some Member States were temporarily allowed to maintain source taxation on outbound dividends; see 6.6.2. *infra*) may be included in the amount of the 'profits distributed by the subsidiary' to which the flat rate of 5% is applied, as such inclusion agrees with the fact that the credit has the effect that in total, the parent receives the gross amount of the distributed profit; see Case C-27/07 (*Banque Fédérative du Crédit Mutuel*), [2008] ECR I-2067, EU:C:2008:195.

112 See Case C-68/15, *X v Ministerraad*, EU:C:2017:379 (Belgian fairness tax), Case C-365/16, *Association française des entreprises privées (AFEP) a.o.*, EU:C:2017:378 (French 3% surcharge), and Case C-556/20, *Schneider Electric SE a.o.*, EU:C:2022:378 (précompte).

resident in other Member States (the profits of which are exempt in the Member State of the parent) and at the same time allow the deduction of any charges related to the holding in domestic subsidiaries (the profits of which are taxed in the Member State of the parent). This question was raised in the *Bosal* case. The Netherlands measure concerned provided that expenses incurred by a parent company (wherever established) to finance or manage its subsidiary (wherever established) were deductible only insofar as they were instrumental in earning profits subject to tax in the jurisdiction where the parent company sought to deduct those expenses. As Bosal's nonresident subsidiaries were not subject to tax in the Netherlands, neither before nor after distribution (capital gains on the holdings were not taxable either), deduction was denied from the Netherlands tax base of parent company expenses instrumental in earning those exempt capital gains on, and exempted income from non-subjected subsidiaries. Surprisingly, however, the Court required the parent company State to allow deduction. Although the Directive leaves the Member States the choice to disregard these expenses, the Court required the Member States to make *the same choice* whether or not the subsidiary was subject to tax in the parent company State and whether or not the parent company was taxed on capital gains on its subsidiaries. The Court did not accept the discretion granted by Article 4(2) to be exercised differently depending on whether a domestic parent company holds subsidiaries subject to tax or subsidiaries not subject to tax. The Netherlands system was therefore found to be contrary to the freedom of establishment (Articles 49 and 54 TFEU). We believe this judgment to be incorrect (the measure was perfectly balanced coherent and symmetrical; subsidiary profits subject to tax are simply not comparable to subsidiary profits not subject to tax) and a major driver for base erosion and profit shifting. See also Section 14.5.1).

A case similar to *Bosal* was *Groupe Steria*, where the add-back to taxable profit of a pro-portion of costs, fixed at 5% of the net amount of the dividends, could be neutralized in domestic situations (if the domestic group would apply for consolidation (*intégration fiscale*)) whereas such neutralization was not available for foreign dividends (since foreign subsidiaries could not be included in a tax integration); the Court found such rules to be in violation of Article 49 TFEU.[113]

16.4.5 Hybrid Entities (Art. 4(2)); Fiscal Transparency[114]

Article 4(2)[115] provides for the case where the parent company State considers the foreign subsidiary to be fiscally transparent. In such a case, the parent company State does not wait distribution, but taxes the parent company for its share of the subsidiary's undistributed profit as and when that profit arises, as if the parent were a partner in a partnership rather than a shareholder in a separate legal entity. Obviously this leads to double taxation, as the subsidiary will be taxed in its State of residence as a legally independent subsidiary company. Paragraph 2 permits the parent State to assess the

113 Case C-386/14, *Groupe Steria SCA*, EU:C:2015:524.

114 See Raffaele Russo: 'Partnerships and Other Hybrid Entities and the EC Corporate Direct Tax Directives,' *European Taxation*, October 2006, p. 478-486.

115 This paragraph (originally paragraph 1a) is inserted by the 2003 amendment (implementation 1 January 2005).

legal characteristics of the foreign subsidiary on the basis of its own national (civil) law in order to assess its transparency for domestic tax purposes. If it chooses to look through the subsidiary for tax purposes, thus taxing the subsidiary's profits in the hands of the parent, then it must obviously refrain from taxing the profits again upon later factual distribution to the parent. Further, the parent State must either exempt the amount of the subsidiary's undistributed profits it includes in the parent company's taxable base, or credit the corporation tax payable by the subsidiary in its Member State of residence.

Application of Article 4(2) to CFC legislation (taxing foreign tax haven subsidiary profits currently in the hands of the domestic parent company) is carefully avoided Article 4 (2) refers to the parent company State's 'assessment of the *legal* characteristics of that company *arising from the law under which it is constituted*'. This wording excludes fiscal transparency on the basis of parent State CFC legislation, as such transparency arises from the assessment of the *tax* characteristics of the subsidiary on the basis of *the parent* company State's *tax* law.

16.5 'Distributions of Profits'

16.5.1 Distributions of Profits (Art. 1)

The Directive applies to 'distributions of profits' (Art. 1). This term is not defined, but it is clear that it does not encompass capital gains upon the alienation of the holding, nor unrealized gains. Many Member States applying the exemption method exempt capital gains as well all the same (and, correspondingly, probably disallow deduction of capital losses). Since subsidiary dividends and capital gains upon the alienation of a holding in a subsidiary are to a large extent interchangeable, the Directive is, in this regard, incomplete.[116] In our opinion, the term 'distributions of profits' should be interpreted substantively, covering any shift of value to the parent company at the expense of the economic potential of the subsidiary in connection with the parent's provision of equity to the subsidiary. In our view, 'distributions' also encompass disguised or constructive dividends, *e.g.* gratuitous shifts of wealth from the subsidiary to the parent for which there is no other explanation – especially no arm's length explanation – than the affiliation between the subsidiary and the parent (or the shareholder of the parent). An example is the amount of excessive interest or royalties that is excluded from the scope of the I&R Directive by Article 4(2) of that Directive (see Section 18.2.4.2).[117] In our view the PSD also applies to situations where a subsidiary charges its parent a consideration below the fair market price, and where a notional dividend is recognized for tax purposes. However, we have some doubts whether the Court shares our view. In the Viva Telecom case the Court held that 'notional interest set by the tax authorities of a resident company in connection with an interest-free loan concluded between that company and its non-resident parent company cannot be regarded as distributed profits'.[118] This makes sense because interest-free loans

116 In 2002, Maisto published a draft text for a Directive on a common system of taxation on capital gains on subsidiary holdings: Guglielmo Maisto: 'Proposal for an EC Exemption of Capital Gains Realized by Parent Companies of Member States,' *European Taxation*, January 2002, p. 28-39.

117 Cf. Case C-257/20, 'Viva Telecom Bulgaria' EOOD, EU:C:2022:125, point 62.

118 *'Viva Telecom Bulgaria' EOOD*, point 63.

that are provided by a parent company obviously benefit the subsidiary, not the parent. However, the reason for this decision seems to be that 'in such a case, no actual payment of interest takes place between those companies'.[119] Also taking into consideration that, according to the same decision, notional interest on an interest-free loan is not covered by the I&R Directive,[120] this decision seems to suggest that the Court is of the opinion that the PSD does not apply to notional income. For example, in case of an interest-free loan by a subsidiary to its shareholder, where according to the tax laws of the Member States notional interest to the subsidiary and a constructive dividend to the parent company would be taken into account, the Court appears to hold the view that the notional interest and the constructive dividend would not be covered by the I&R Directive or the PSD.

16.5.2 Autonomous meaning

Unlike Article 10 (dividends) of the OECD Model Double Taxation Convention, the PSD does not refer to 'income from other corporate rights which is subjected to the same taxation treatment as income from shares by the laws of the State of which the company making the distribution is a resident' (Art. 10(3) OECD Model). Possibly, the drafters of the Directive did not want the meaning of the term 'distribution of profits' to be dependent on national tax law of the Member States. That would not be harmonization. We therefore submit that the terms 'distribution of profits' and 'distributed profits', like the term 'withholding tax' in Article 5 (see 16.6.3 *infra*), is an EU law expression, to be interpreted autonomously by the Court and by national tax courts in the light of the object and purpose of the Directive (and in the light of the object and purpose of the TFEU Freedoms, notably the right of establishment and the free movement of capital). It would be especially desirable if a cross-border distribution of profits were to be regarded as such by the tax authorities on *both* sides of the border. We observe, however, that even the official commentary to Article 10 (dividends) of the OECD Model Double Taxation Convention concludes that, notwithstanding a thorough study, 'it did not appear to be possible to work out a definition of the concept of dividends that would be independent of domestic laws' (§ 23). However, there are teleological arguments for the view that a Member State which (under its domestic tax law) requalifies payments that, under private law, are interest or royalties and treats them as dividends, should be consistent and treat such payments as 'distribution of profits' under the PSD (See Section 18.2.4.3).

16.5.3 Hybrid loans

In our view the term 'distributions of profits' also includes payments labelled 'interest' on funding which is formally designated as a 'loan' provided by the parent, through which the parent in fact fully participates in the entrepreneurial risks of its subsidiary, and which should be reclassified as equity for tax purposes. In its case law on the meaning of 'withholding tax' in Article 5, the Court refers to 'any income from shares' (see 16.6.3 below). A mismatch may occur where the subsidiary State denies – whether or not

119 Cf. Savvas Kostikidis and Florian Striefler, Fictitious Interest and Dividends Under Tax Treaties and the EU Directives, EC Tax Review, Vol. 31 (2022), issue 5, p. 251-259 (at 3.2).

120 *'Viva Telecom Bulgaria' EOOD*, point 54.

on the basis of national thin capitalization rules – deduction of an outbound interest payment by a subsidiary, whereas the parent company State taxes it as interest received, outside the scope of the Parent-Subsidiary Directive. The Directive does not address such mismatch issues. The I&R Directive (see Chapter 18) does not resolve the matter either, as it only addresses source taxation in the debtor company State, not taxation in the recipient company State. The issue was brought up by Advocate-General Mischo in his opinion in *Lankhorst-Hohorst*,[121] concerning the German denial, based on the German thin capitalization rules, of deduction of interest payments made by a German subsidiary to its Netherlands parent. Referring to *Athinaïki Zythopiia*[122] (see Section 16.6.3), the Advocate-General suggested that the corporate income tax burden in *Lankhorst-Hohorst* resulting from the non-deductibility of the interest should be regarded as a prohibited dividend withholding tax within the meaning of the Directive. The Court did not venture into this issue, but simply held the German denial to be a violation of the freedom of establishment (Arts. 49 and 54 TFEU), as the denial was based on the foreign residence of the parent company/creditor. From *Scheuten Solar Technology*[123] (see Section 18.6.1.2), it may be inferred that A.-G. Mischo was wrong: a denial of interest deduction at the subsidiary level, for whatever reason, is in itself not tantamount to a reclassification as dividend, and the denial of deduction at *subsidiary* level is in itself not the same thing as a prohibited withholding tax to the account of the *parent* (recipient) company; it impacts only on the determination of the *corporation* tax base of the *paying* (subsidiary) company; such tax base determination at payer company level is, in principle, national sovereignty; at any rate, it is not addressed by either the I&R Directive or the PSD. However, if the source State denies interest deduction on the basis of its *reclassification* of the interest payment as a (covert) *dividend*, and therefore takes the view itself that an (albeit covert) 'distribution of profit' is present, it would make sense that that State is required to be consistent and to treat such payment as a dividend under the PSD. The Commission takes the view that any amount reclassified as dividend and for that reason excluded from the benefits of the I&R Directive (see Art. 4 of that Directive), should be granted the benefits of the PSD.[124] Indeed, there are good teleological arguments for the view that reclassified dividend-like payments excluded from the benefits of the I&R Directive, (should) fall within the scope of the PSD.[125] That, however, does not yet answer the question whether the Directive opposes different income classifications in the subsidiary and the parent State. Obviously, in an ideal world, which answers to object and purpose of the Directive, both classifications concur so as to avoid double taxation, but the Directive does not contain a provision which actually says that the recipient State must follow the classification of the source State (or vice versa).[126]

121 Case C-324/00 *Lankhorst-Hohorst*, [2002] ECR I-11779, EU:C:2002:749.
122 Case C-294/99, *Athinaiki Zythopoiia*, [2001] ECR I-6797, EU:C:2001:505.
123 Case C-397/09, *Scheuten Solar Technology*, EU:C:2011:499.
124 See paragraph 3.3.8. of the Commission report on the functioning of the Directive, COM(2009) 179.
125 See Jakob Bundgaard: 'Classification and Treatment of Hybrid Financial Instruments and Income Derived Therefrom under EU Corporate Tax Directives,' Parts 1 and 2, *European Taxation*, October and November 2010.
126 See for a discussion of this issue: Jakob Bundgaard, l.c.

16.5.4 Imputation credits

From Case C-58/01, *Océ van der Grinten*[127] (see 16.6.3 below) it appears that the payment of an imputation credit by the subsidiary State to the parent company in another Member State in connection with dividends paid by the subsidiary to that parent (as called for in some bilateral tax treaties), does not qualify as a 'distribution of profits'. The Court considered:

> '56. The tax credit is a fiscal instrument designed to avoid double taxation, in economic terms, first in the hands of the subsidiary and then in the hands of the parent company in receipt of the dividends, of the profits distributed as dividends. Thus it does not constitute income from shares.'

The same characterization (no income from shares) was made by the Court[128] as regards the refund, by the subsidiary State, to the foreign parent, of imputation taxes (equalization taxes, such as the Italian *maggiorazione di conguaglio*, the French *précompte* and the German *Auschüttungsbelastung*) levied from the subsidiary upon profit distributions in case the profit has not borne (full) corporation tax (see Section 16.6.5). For Directive purposes, therefore, imputation credit payments and imputation tax refunds pursuant to a tax treaty, although economically possibly eventually financed out of the subsidiary's profits, are not to be regarded as profit distributions, but as (partial) refunds of corporation tax paid by the subsidiary, and as paid by the subsidiary State rather than by the subsidiary.

16.5.5 Liquidation

Distributions upon the liquidation of the subsidiary are expressly not covered *at the parent level* (Art. 4(1)). The reason for this exclusion is probably that it is difficult to see how the shutting down of foreign subsidiary activity is helpful in achieving the aims of the internal market and of the Directive, such as facilitating cross-border cooperation, investment and grouping together of companies. However, the Directive *does* seem to grant an exemption of withholding tax *at the subsidiary level* for distributions upon liquidation (Art. 5). We do not see the reason for this discrepancy between the parent level and the subsidiary level in the tax treatment of liquidation distributions. In Belgium, and maybe in other Member States as well, a merger by absorption (a subsidiary collapsing into its parent) is (or was) treated as a liquidation of the subsidiary and taxed accordingly in the hands of the parent company. In the *Punch Graphix* case[129] the question was whether Article 4 of the Directive permits such taxation of fictitious liquidation proceeds where in reality no liquidation, but a merger is afoot. More in particular, the question was whether the dissolution of a company in the context of a merger by acquisition could be considered to be such a liquidation. The answer is negative. The Court argued that whereas the (former) Parent Subsidary directive (Directive 90/435) does not define the concept of 'liquidation', the Merger directive (see Chapter 17), did in fact define a 'merger' as being an 'operation

127 Case C-58/01, *Océ van der Grinten*, [2003] ECR I-9809, EU:C:2003:495.

128 Joined Cases C-338/08 and C-339/08 P. *Ferrero e C.* and *General Beverage Europe BV*, [2010] ECR I-5743, EU:C:2010:364.

129 Case C-371/11, *Punch Graphix Prepress Belgium N.V. v. Belgische Staat*, EU:C:2012:647.

whereby a company, on being dissolved *without going into liquidation*, transfers all its assets and liabilities to the company holding all the securities representing its capital' (italics added).[130] The Court further argued that the fact that that definition appeared in another directive did not prevent that definition from being taken into account for the purposes of the interpretation of the concept of 'liquidation' within the meaning of Article 4(1) of Directive 90/435, because (i) the proposals for both Directives were submitted by the European Commission on the same day, (ii) both directives were adopted on the same day by the Council of the European Union and were also expected to be transposed simultaneously, and (iii) as appeared from the first recital of these directives, materially those directives have the same objective to abolish restrictions, disadvantages or distortions arising in particular from the tax provisions of the Member States for the operations covered by those directives. Accordingly, those directives constitute a whole, in that they complement each other.

16.6 Outbound Dividends: Abolition of Withholding Tax (Art. 5)

16.6.1 The General Rule

Article 5 of the Directive clearly states the main rule: the Member State of the subsidiary shall exempt qualifying dividends from withholding tax. Article 5 has direct effect; it can therefore be relied upon by individual taxpayers before national tax courts with priority over derogating national tax law (see the *Denkavit, VITIC and Voormeer* case; Section 16.3.2.(v)).

The word 'exempt' implies that exemption at source is mandatory: Member States cannot provisionally levy a withholding tax at the time of the distribution and refund it to the parent company only after the latter has applied for such refund and has demonstrated that it is a qualifying parent company. This is not to say that the source country may not require certain formalities to be satisfied in order to ensure that only qualifying dividends are exempt. Such formalities may not, however, be more burdensome than formalities in comparable domestic situations, unless the fact that a nonresident parent company is involved makes this unavoidable. Only during a possible minimum holding period on the basis of Article 3(2) (see Section 16.3.2.(v)), are Member States at liberty to levy tax provisionally (to be refunded after that period has been completed) or to set conditions such as a security for the withholding tax provisionally foregone in anticipation of the minimum holding period to be completed.

16.6.2 Transitional and Deleted Derogations

Before the 2003 amendment (implementation 1 January 2005), the Directive contained three transitional exceptions to the abolition of dividend withholding tax to accommodate three Member States, all of which are obsolete by now, and have therefore been deleted from Article 5 since 2004. These exceptions concerned Greece, which at that time did not charge corporation tax on distributed profits but only on retained profits. The distributed

130 Third indent of Article 2(a) of Directive 90/434.

profits were taxed only in the hands of the shareholder. Obviously, under such system, a dividend withholding tax on outbound dividends was needed at the rate of the corporation tax on retained profits, otherwise Greece would not collect any tax on corporate profits distributed to non-subject foreign shareholders. Greece changed (reversed) this system, now taxing the company profit, whether retained or distributed, and exempting dividends in the hands of the recipient. Germany was initially allowed to withhold tax on outbound qualifying dividends until 1 July 1996 because at that time it had a split-rate system of corporation tax[131] with separate rates for retained and distributed profits. On 1 January 2001, Germany abandoned its split-rate system, replacing it for a semi-classical system, taxing the total company profit at a single rate and exempting half of the dividend in the hands of the individual shareholder (half inclusion system; *Halbeinkommenverfahren*). In 2008, it changed to a flat rate system (25%) for dividends received by individuals. Portugal was originally allowed to withhold tax until 1 January 2000, for budgetary reasons, Portugal being a capital importing country.

Although these *ab initio* derogations no longer apply, one new exception to the withholding tax exemption was introduced upon the accession of ten new Member States in May 2004: Estonia applied a system comparable to the former Greek system, not taxing corporate profits until they are distributed, therefore only taxing distributed profits, in the hands of the shareholder. Again, in such a system, a high withholding tax is needed on outbound dividends. Estonia was therefore allowed to levy a withholding tax on qualifying dividend distributions until 31 December 2008.[132] It maintained its distribution tax also after that date, but now the taxpayer is not the shareholder, but the distributing company itself. In economic terms, this system amounts to the charging of corporate income tax and a final withholding tax at one stroke upon distribution. As will be seen below (16.6.3), Estonia probably does not run the risk of falling foul of the withholding tax prohibition under the Directive, as under its system, the taxable person is not the taxpayer, but the company, and the Court seems to have corrected its mistake in the *Athinaïki Zythopoiia* case, in which it objected to a similar Greek tax.

16.6.3 'Withholding Tax'; *Epson Europe, Athinaïki Zythopoiia, Océ van der Grinten, FII GLO, Burda,* and *Ferrero*

The term 'withholding tax' is not defined in the Directive. The case law of the Court to be discussed below shows that the Court views the expression as an EU law expression, to be interpreted autonomously and substantively, independent of national law. It even provides a definition.

131 See Section 16.6.3.

132 See part 7 (Taxation), paragraph 2, of Annex VI (list referred to in Article 24 for Estonia) to the Act of Accession: 'By way of derogation from Article 5(1) of Directive 90/435/EEC, Estonia may, for as long as it charges income tax on distributed profits without taxing undistributed profits, and at the latest until 31 December 2008, continue to apply that tax to profits distributed by Estonian subsidiaries to their parent companies established in other Member States'.

Case C375/98, *Epson Europe*,[133] concerned the Portuguese *Imposto sobre as Sucessies e Doaçies* (succession and donation tax; ISD), which was levied on the occasion of profit distributions by companies at a rate of 5% of the distribution, in parallel with the regular dividend withholding tax, which was incorporated in the corporation tax *(Imposto sobre o Rendimento das Pessoas Colectivas;* IRC). Although it was intended to substitute for an inheritance and gift tax on *assets* such as shares, the ISD was levied on the *income* from shares because, according to the Portuguese government, historically, a regular inheritance tax on the succession of shares could not be recovered. In the case under the Court's scrutiny, ISD was levied on a qualifying dividend paid by Epson Portugal *SA* to its Netherlands parent company Epson Europe *BV.* The Portuguese government argued that the ISD constituted a special regime, separate from the regular IRC, that the ISD reflected the extent to which dividends are capitalized, that it was levied not on income but on the value of the securities on the basis of a capitalization factor, and that it was not equivalent to a tax on the income from securities. The fact that it was calculated on the basis of income did not mean that it was not a genuine succession and donation tax on the transfer of assets. The Court was not convinced. It held:

> '22. In order to determine whether the levying of ISD on distributed profits falls within the scope of Article 5(1) of the Directive, reference must be made, in particular, to the wording of that provision. The term "withholding tax" contained in it is not limited to certain specific types of national taxation. (...)
> 23. It is clear (...) that ISD is a withholding tax for which the chargeable event is the payment of dividends or of any other income from shares, that the taxable amount is the income from the shares and that the taxable person is the holder of the shares. ISD thus has the same effect as a tax on income. It is immaterial in that respect that it is called "succession and donation tax" and that it is levied in parallel with IRC.
> 24. In those circumstances, the objective of the Directive, which (...) is to encourage co-operation between companies in several Member States, would be undermined if the Member States were permitted deliberately to deprive companies in other Member States of the benefit of the Directive by subjecting them to taxes having the same effect as a tax on income, even if the name given to the latter places them in the category of tax on assets.
> 25. Consequently, ISD, in so far as it involves the taxation of dividends distributed by subsidiaries established in Portugal to parent companies in other Member States, falls within the scope of the Directive. (...).'

The Portuguese government further argued that the Council, when adopting the Directive, had accepted a Portuguese reservation on the ISD, which was recorded in a Council Declaration. The Court firmly dismissed this argument in a similar way as it dismissed a similar German reliance on non-public Council minutes in the *Denkavit, VITIC* and *Voormeer* case (see Section 16.3.2.(v)).

133 Case C-375/98 (*Ministério Público, Fazenda Pública v. Epson Europe BV*), [2000] ECR I-4243, EU:C:2000:302. For a comment, see Francisco de Souza da Câmara, 'Parent- Subsidiary Directive: The Epson Case' 41 *European Taxation* 9 (September 2001), p. 307.

Case C-294/99, *Athinaïki Zythopiia*,[134] seems to have been decided incorrectly. It concerned a Greek tax levied from companies (therefore, the person subject to tax apparently was not the shareholder, but the distributing company) upon the distribution of profits that had not – or preferentially – been taxed under the Greek corporation tax. The Greek government argued that, substantively, this was a profits tax: an equalization tax designed to ensure that all corporate profits carried the same corporation tax burden at the latest upon distribution, in view of the fact that the shareholder was exempt from income tax on dividends received. The Court was not convinced, however, apparently mainly because losses from previous tax years could not be offset against the tax base, which suggested that the tax base was not profit, but dividend. It considered:

> '27. (...), it is settled case-law that the nature of a tax, duty or charge must be determined by the Court, under Community law, according to the objective characteristics by which it is levied, irrespective of its classification under national law (see, in particular, Joined Cases C-197/94 and C-252/94 *Bautiaa and Société française maritime* [1996] ECR I-5 05, paragraph 39).
> 28. It is apparent from the order for reference and the observations submitted (...) that the chargeable event for the taxation at issue (...), is the payment of dividends. In addition, the amount of tax is directly related to the size of the distribution.
> 29. Contrary to the submissions of the Greek Government, the taxation cannot be treated like an advance payment or prepayment (précompte) of corporation tax to the Member State of the subsidiary which is made in connection with a distribution of profits to its parent company, within the meaning of Article 7(1) of the Directive. The taxation relates to income which is taxed only in the event of a distribution of dividends and up to the limit of the dividends paid. That is shown by the fact *(inter alia)* that, (...), the increase in the basic taxable amount generated, (...), by the distribution of profits cannot be offset by the subsidiary using negative income from previous tax years, contrary to the fiscal principle enabling losses to be carried forward which is nevertheless laid down in Greek law.'

It arrests the attention that the Court reiterated only two of the three criteria it used in *Epson Europe* to assess the character of the tax: (i) the chargeable event is distribution of profit, and (ii) the basis of taxation is the amount of the distribution. It was silent on its third criterion, (iii) the taxable person should be the shareholder, which was not met in *Athinaïki Zythopiia*.

Case C-58/01, *Océ van der Grinten*[135] (see Section 16.5.1), concerned a withholding tax on the payment, pursuant to a tax treaty, of an imputation credit by the subsidiary State to the foreign parent company in connection with a dividend payment by that subsidiary. A withholding tax on the payment of such imputation credit is not a prohibited withholding tax within the meaning of the Directive, because, according to the Court, the payment of the credit is not a profit distribution but a tax refund (see Section 16.5.1 above). It considered:

134 Case C-294/99 (*Athinaiki Zythopoiia AE v. Elliniko Dimosio*), [2001] ECR I- 6797, EU:C:2001:505. See for comments on the case: Patrick Tardivy and others: 'Parent-Subsidiary Directive: The Long Reach of Athinaiki'; *International Tax Review*, March 2002, p. 11-18.

135 Case C-58/01 *Océ van der Grinten*, [2003] ECR I-9809, EU:C:2003:495.

'55. The part of the (...) charge applying to the tax credit to which distribution of the dividend confers entitlement, does not possess the characteristics of a withholding tax on distributed profits, in principle prohibited by Article 5(1) of the Directive, because it is not imposed on the profits distributed by the subsidiary.'

In Case C-446/04, *FII GLO*, the Court provided a definition of a 'withholding tax' for Directive purposes, returning to *three* conditions, thus tacitly correcting its earlier *Athinaiki Zythopoiia* case. The case concerned the British (then) advance corporation tax (ACT), charged upon the redistribution, by a British parent company, of dividends it had received from its foreign subsidiaries. The British parent argued that the ACT amounted to a secondary withholding tax at parent company level, prohibited by Article 6 of the Directive. The Court did not agree, because the chargeable event for the ACT was not the distribution of profit by the foreign subsidiary, nor the receipt of those dividends by the parent, but the parent's own payment of dividends to its shareholders. The Court gave the following definition of 'withholding tax' (numbers between brackets added by the authors):

'109. The expression "withholding tax" must be given a similar interpretation for the purposes of Article 6 of Directive 90/435 [as for the purposes of Article 5; authors]. There is thus a "withholding tax" for the purposes of that Article in the case of every tax on income received by a parent company from a subsidiary established in another Member State, (i) the chargeable event being the payment of dividends or of any other income from shares, (ii) where the taxable amount is the income from those shares and (iii) the taxable person is the holder of those shares.'

In Case C-284/06, *Burda*, the Court in guarded terms admitted having made a mistake in *Athinaïki Zythopiia*. The case concerned a German equalization tax at company level on profit distributions, similar to the Greek profits distribution tax in *Athinaïki Zythopiia*. Obviously, the taxpayer in *Burda* relied on *Athinaïki Zythopiia*, arguing that a prohibited withholding tax was afoot because the *two* conditions set in *Athinaïki Zythopiia* were met. The Court, however, did not consider a withholding tax present because the third condition set in *Océ* and *FII GLO* was not met: the taxable person was not the parent company, but the distributing subsidiary. It did not, as it did in *Athinaïki Zythopiia*, investigate whether losses from other years could be offset against the basis of the German tax. It simply held that the three conditions must be cumulatively fulfilled and that this finding could not be called into question by pointing at *Athinaïki Zythopiia*, because (italics added):

'61. It (...) is clear from the case-law ***subsequent*** to Athinaïki Zithopoiïa, (that) the Court maintains, as a condition for the existence of a withholding tax within the meaning of Article 5(1) of Directive 90/435, that the taxable person must be the holder of the shares (see *Océ Van der Grinten*, paragraph 47, and *Test Claimants in the FII Group Litigation*, paragraph 108).'

Joined Cases C-338/08 and C-339/08, *Ferrero* and *General Beverage*,[136] concerned the refund, pursuant to the applicable tax treaty, of the Italian *maggiorazione di conguaglio*

136 Joined Cases C-338/08 and C-339/08 P. *Ferrero e C.* and *General Beverage Europe*, [2010] ECR I-5743, EU:C:2010:364 and EU:C:2008:509.

(adjustment surtax)[137] on profit distributions to Netherlands corporate shareholders. Italy withheld a 5% tax on such refund. That withholding was challenged by the Italian distributing subsidiaries under Article 5 of the Directive, which, *inter alia*, pointed out that the tax treaty explicitly called the refund a 'dividend'. According to the Court, however, the characterization in the tax treaty was not decisive, as the nature of the tax must be determined by the Court on the basis of EU law, according to the objective characteristics by which it is levied. In this case, the second condition (the tax base must be the income from shares) was decisive: could the refund of the *maggiorazione di conguaglio* be regarded as a distribution of profits? The *maggiorazione* itself was comparable to the Greek distribution tax in *Athinaïki Zythopiia* and the German 30% tax in *Burda*, aimed at ensuring that all distributed profits carried sufficient corporation tax. The refund of it, therefore, was a refund of corporation tax, rather than income from shares (a distribution of profit). A tax withheld on that refund was thus not a dividend withholding tax as referred to in Article 5 of the Directive. Finally, in Case C-68/15, *X v Ministerraad*,[138] on the Belgian 'fairness tax', the Court clearly stated:

> '63. The settled case-law of the Court holds that, in order for a tax to be classified as a withholding tax within the meaning of Article 5 of the Parent-Subsidiary Directive, three cumulative criteria must be satisfied. Thus, first, the tax must be levied in the State in which the dividends are distributed and its chargeable event must be the payment of dividends or of any other income from shares; second, the taxable amount is the income from those shares; and third, the taxable person is the holder of the shares (see, by analogy, judgment of 24 June 2010, P. Ferrero e C. and General Beverage Europe, C-338/08 and C-339/08, EU:C:2010:364, paragraph 26 and the case-law cited).'

We conclude that the Court adheres to a substantive and independent Union law interpretation of the 'withholding tax' prohibited by Article 5 and that such withholding tax is any tax (i) for which the chargeable event is the distribution by a company to its shareholder(s) of any benefit to be regarded as income from shares, and (ii) the taxable base of which is the amount of that distribution and (iii) the taxable person for which is the holder of the shares.[139] Immaterial is the name or classification of the tax according to national law or a bilateral tax treaty. *Athinaïki Zythopiia* was a mistake.

16.6.4 Article 6; (No) Précompte Mobilier

Article 6 of the Directive addresses the situation in which a Member State levies a with-holding tax (like in Belgium the *précompte mobilier; roerende voorheffing*) from banks which handle dividend transfers from subsidiaries to parent companies. Such parent State

137 That surtax (equalization tax) was levied in order to undo the imputation credit shareholders were entitled to in cases where the distributed profit had not carried full Italian corporation tax. The surtax was to prevent that a credit was given to the shareholder for corporation tax not paid by the distributing company. Such equalization tax is superfluous after the abolition of national imputation systems of taxation of distributed company profits under the influence of EU Law.

138 Case C-68/15, *X. v Ministerraad*, EU:C:2017:379.

139 As regards condition (iii), see also the Opinion of Advocate General Kokott delivered on 14 October 2021, in Case C-556/20, *Schneider a.o.*, EU:C:2021:857, point 52.

withholding tax on the *receipt* of the dividend by the parent company is prohibited by Article 6 where it burdens qualifying dividends under the Directive.

16.6.5 Imputation Systems; Imputation Taxes; Outbound Payment of Imputation Credits (Art. 7)

One tax impediment which the Directive does not address, but which by now has been done away with as a result of the case law of the Court of Justice (see below), is the internationally distortive effect of imputation systems designed to prevent economic double taxation of distributed company profits. These systems integrate taxation at company level in the taxation at shareholder level by taking into account the corporation tax levied at the level of the distributing (subsidiary) company when taxing the shareholder for the dividends received out of those profits already taxed, usually by crediting the corporation tax paid by the distributing company against the shareholder's income tax (see Section 11.1.4). Typically, such imputation credit (*avoir fiscal; credito d'imposto; Anrechnung*) was not granted for incoming foreign dividends (bearing, after all, only foreign corporation tax), nor for outbound dividends to foreign shareholders (paying, after all, only foreign income tax).[140] Consequently, both foreign dividends and non-resident shareholders were treated less favourably than domestic dividends and domestic shareholders, respectively (see Sections 11.1.5, 11.2 and 11.4).

The message of Article 7 of the Directive is that the Directive does not affect imputation systems: neither does it affect the payment of imputation credits (paragraph 2), nor does it regard an imputation tax[141] (*précompte; maggiorazione di conguaglio; Auschüttungsbelastung*) as a prohibited withholding tax (paragraph 1). The Directive does not, therefore, prohibit the subsidiary State to levy, upon distribution. an advance payment of corporation tax (*e.g* the (then) British advance corporation tax) or prepayment (the (then) French *précompte*).[142] Such imputation tax, the aim of which is to undo the imputation credit in case of non-eligible profit distributions, should be regarded as a corporate income tax rather than as a (prohibited) withholding tax.

With Article 7 the Member States were apparently trying to tell the Court that it should not interfere with imputation systems.[143] The Court, however, did interfere, both on the basis of Article 4 PSD, and on the basis of the TFEU Freedoms (which trump secondary EU law such as a Directive).

140 Under bilateral treaties, the credit – or a half credit – was sometimes also paid to foreign (individual) shareholders (subject to the withholding tax which also applies to the dividend itself).

141 An imputation tax is a tax levied from the company upon distribution in order to neutralize the imputation credit at shareholder level in cases where the distributed profit has not been taxed (sufficiently) with corporation tax at company level, so that the credit is too generous and should be neutralized. See Section 11.1.4.

142 See also the Opinion of Advocate General Kokott delivered on 14 October 2021, in Case C-556/20, Schneider a.o., EU:C:2021:857, points 64-75.

143 Cf. the argument put forward by the French government in Case C-556/20, Schneider Electric SE a.o., EU:C:2022:378, point 68.

In the Schneider Electric SA and Others case (C-556/20), the Court held that the advance payment of tax ('précompte mobilier') due by French *parent* companies that redistributed dividends (received from their foreign subsidiaries) to their shareholders, resulted in an infringement of Article 4(1) of the PSD to the extent that it exceeded the 5% ceiling provided for in Article 4(3), and that such system was not in scope of Article 7(2) PSD.[144] According to the Court, a system where the profit distributed by the subsidiary is taxed again in the hands of the parent company, is inconsistent with the objective of the PSD.[145]

More important still was the – considerably older – case law on the TFEU freedoms. In the paradigm Case C-319/02, *Manninen*, the Court required Member States applying an imputation system to grant their residents an imputation credit for EU-dividends on the same footing as for domestic dividends. The Court thus effectively required mutual recognition of the subsidiary State's corporation tax as if it were domestic corporation tax. Because of this case law, imputation systems have virtually disappeared within the Union. Already after Case C-35/98, *Verkooijen*, was decided, most Member States wisely decided to replace them for semi-classical (schedular) systems (see Section 11.4.1). Thus, imputation systems have been abolished, *e.g.*, in Italy, Ireland (1999), Germany (2001), France (2005) and Finland (2005). Certainly after the *Manninen* judgment, no Member State in its right budgetary mind would continue to apply a system that requires it to fully credit foreign corporation tax against its domestic income tax as if it were a domestic corporation tax. Therefore, Article 7 is probably (largely) obsolete by now.[146] For *corporate* shareholders within groups of companies, by contrast, the indirect credit system (which is conceptually the same as full imputation), is still widely applied, as appeared from the above, although the exemption system seems to be on top for intragroup cross-border dividends, probably because of its practicability and of the fact it does not make much sense to put up with the cumbersome intricacies of indirect credit for further tiers if the effective corporate income tax rates within the EU do not diverge substantially any more.

16.7 No Temporal Compartmentalization of Dividends; (No) Write-Down of the Holding Subsequent to Distribution

Directive 90/435/EEC[147] and Directive 2011/96/EU did not contain any transitional provisions. A Member State could therefore take the view that distributions out of profits accrued before that State's implementation or accession date are not covered by the Directive, and hence need not be facilitated at either parent or subsidiary level. Such temporal 'compartmentalization' of dividends seems at odds, however, with the wording of Articles 1, 4 and 5 of the Directive. There is nothing in these provisions to suggest that other moments than the moment of distribution are relevant. We therefore believe that any otherwise qualifying dividend payment is within the scope of the Directive provisions, irrespective of the tax year in which the profit accrued out of which it is paid. To our

144 Case C-556/20, Schneider Electric SE a.o., EU:C:2022:378.

145 Cf. Case C-556/20, Schneider Electric SE a.o., EU:C:2022:378, points 82-87.

146 Malta still entertains a full imputation system, according to Paul Pace Ross and Noeleen Bonnici, Malta - Individual Taxation, IBFD publications [online – accessed 14 January 2025], at 1.1.3 and 1.5.1.

147 Except for the Estonian distribution tax (see Section 16.6.2.).

knowledge, no OECD Member State takes the view that dividends, paid immediately after the entry into force of a bilateral tax treaty between the parent company State and the subsidiary State, but stemming from profits predating the treaty, are outside the scope of Article 10 (dividends) of the OECD Model Double Tax Convention. We take the same position as regards dividends paid (immediately) after the acquisition of a 10% or larger holding, but out of profits derived before such acquisition. From the joined cases *Denkavit, VITIC* and *Voormeer* (see Section 6.3.2.(v)), it may be inferred that the Court takes the same position. All three cases concerned substantial dividend payments shortly after the acquisition of the qualifying holding by the parent company.

We take this position not only for withholding tax purposes at the subsidiary level, but also for corporation tax purposes at the parent company level. The language of Articles 1 and 4 of the Directive does not permit temporal allocation at the parent company level either. However, Article 4(3) retains the right for the Member States to deny a write-down, at the parent company level, of any reduction in value of the holding in the subsidiary as a result of distributions out of profit reserves of previous tax years, which has a similar effect as temporal compartmentalization of the dividends.

16.8 Anti-Abuse Reservation (Art. 1(2)-1(4))[148]

16.8.1 Introduction; Context

Initially, Article 1(2) PSD simply stated that the directive 'shall not preclude the application of domestic or agreement-based provisions required for the prevention of fraud or abuse'. According to the Court, this provision reflected the general EU law principle that abuse of rights is prohibited, and that EU law therefore cannot be relied on for abusive or fraudulent ends, but it must – insofar as it constituted a derogation from the tax rules established by that directive, be interpreted strictly (see Section 16.8.7). For the same reasons we expect that the same goes for the amended Article 1(2), the main difference being that the rule is now a minimum rule (there is no discretion but a requirement to tackle abuse). Article 1(4), which embodies the same rule as the former 1(2), seems to have little relevance, if at all (see Section 16.8.7).

The current wording of Article 1(2) through 1(4) stems from the amending Council Directive (EU) 2015/121 of 27 January 2015.[149] As discussed in Section 16.4.2.2, this Directive was a split-off of a proposal of November 2013 that also contained the amendment of Article

148 See also Dennis Weber, The New Common Minimum Anti-Abuse Rule in the EU Parent-Subsidiary Directive: Background, Impact, Applicability, Purpose and Effect, *Intertax*, Volume 44, Issue 2, p. 98-129, Filip Debelva and Joris Luts, The General Anti-Abuse Rule of the Parent-Subsidiary Directive, European Taxation, June 2015, p. 223-234, Romero J.S. Tavares & Bret N. Bogenschneider, The New *De Minimis* Anti-abuse Rule in the Parent-Subsidiary Directive: Validating EU Tax Competition and Corporate Tax Avoidance?, *Intertax* Vol. 43, Issue 8 & 9, p. 484- 494 and Otto Marres and Isabella de Groot, The General Anti-Abuse Clause in the EU Parent-Subsidiary Directive, in: D. Weber (ed), *EU Law and the Building of Global Supranational Tax Law: EU BEPS and State Aid*, IBFD, Amsterdam 2017 (Chapter 10), pp. 225-247.

149 Council Directive (EU) 2015/121 of 27 January 2015, amending Directive 2011/96/EU, O.J. No. L 21 of 28 January 2015, p. 1.

4(1)(a) (the linking rule preventing the exemption of deductible profit distributions and the introduction of a mandatory common anti-abuse provision).[150] According to the Commission, a common anti-abuse provision was needed to provide more legal certainty and to prevent "directive shopping".[151] The adoption of both the linking rule to fight hybrid loan structures and the review of the anti-abuse provision in the PSD were announced in the same action plan of December 2012.[152] Since it proved impossible to reach agreement on both issues (the change of the anti-abuse provision from a competence reservation into a minimum harmonization (an obligation, therefore) was far more controversial than the linking rule against hybrid payments), the Council settled for an amendment on the linking rule only (Directive 2014/86 of July 2014). During 2014, the Italian Presidency of the EU Council launched various proposals for the introduction of a common minimum anti-abuse rule in the PSD, resulting in a final proposal on 4 November 2014.[153] Political agreement was reached during the ECOFIN meeting of 9 December 2014,[154] resulting in Directive 2015/121 of 27 January 2015. The relevance of this amendment is significantly reduced by the Danish cases, where the Court held that an obligation already exists under primary EU law (i.e. the general principle of EU law that EU law cannot be relied on for abusive or fraudulent ends), whereby the national authorities and courts are to refuse a taxpayer the benefits under EU directives, such as the PSD.[155] The case-law on the former Article 1(2) is still relevant for purposes of interpreting the new anti-abuse provision.[156]

16.8.2 In a Nutshell

Article 1(2) of the PSD provides that Member States 'shall not grant the benefits of this Directive' in case of abuse. The wording 'shall not grant' makes explicit that the new Article 1(2) is not, like the old Article 1(2) (now Article 1(4)), a *reservation* of national competence to be used or abstained from at the Member States' will, but contains an *obligation* to refuse the Directive benefits (which they already have under primary EU law, see Section 16.8.1). Abuse is described as 'an arrangement or a series of arrangements which, having been put into place for the main purpose or one of the main purposes of obtaining a tax advantage that defeats the object or purpose of this Directive, are not genuine having regard to all relevant facts and circumstances.' This shows that, in keeping with the Court's case law on the general principle of EU law that abuse of rights is prohibited (see Section 17.4), both a subjective test (tax avoidance by an artificial arrangement is intended)

150 Proposal for a Council Directive amending Directive 2011/96/EU on the common system of taxation applicable in the case of parent companies and subsidiaries of different Member States, Brussels 25 November 2013, COM(2013) 814 final.

151 Explanatory Memorandum on the proposal of 25 November 2013, *supra*, at p. 4-5.

152 European Commission, An Action Plan to strengthen the fight against tax fraud and tax evasion, COM(2012) 722 final (6 Dec. 2012), paragraph 4.1.1, points 14 and 15, respectively.

153 Proposal for a Council Directive amending Directive 2011/96/EU on the common system of taxation applicable in the case of parent companies and subsidiaries of different Member States, 4 November 2014, doc. 14531/1/14.

154 See the proposal of 5 December 2014, doc. 16435/14; and the press release on the meeting of 9 December 2014, doc. 16603/14, p. 20.

155 Joined Cases C-116/16 and C-117/16, *T Danmark and Y Denmark Aps*, EU:C:2019:135, point 95.

156 Case C-228/24, *'Nordcurrent group' UAB*, EU:C:2025:239, point 24.

and an objective test (object and purpose of the PSD are defeated) must be met.[157] The subjective element of abuse (intention of tax avoidance by an artificial arrangement) is split: artificiality is mentioned as a separate element ('are not genuine'). In addition, Article 1(3) provides that 'an arrangement or series of arrangements shall be regarded as not genuine to the extent that they are not put into place for valid commercial reasons which reflect economic reality'. The term 'arrangement' is not defined; the final sentence of Article 1(2) only explains that an arrangement may comprise more than one step or part.

Article 1(4) is the old Article 1(2), providing in addition to the common minimum anti-abuse rule of Article 1(2), that Member States may apply 'domestic or agreement-based provisions required for the prevention of tax evasion, tax fraud or abuse'. The only difference with the old reservation of competence is that the terms 'fraud or abuse' have been replaced by the terms 'tax evasion, tax fraud or abuse'. This change does not seem very relevant, given that tax evasion is a form of fraud.

16.8.3 Main Purpose or one of the Main Purposes of Obtaining a Tax Advantage

The subjective test is met if obtaining a tax advantage is the main purpose or one of the main purposes. The term tax advantage is undefined. The requirement that the tax advantage defeats the object or purpose of the PSD (see Section 16.8.4) seems to indicate that the tax advantage must be linked to the benefits of the PSD.[158] The wording of Article 1(2) PSD suggests that it is possible for an arrangement to have more than one 'main purpose' and that the subjective test is met if at least one of these main purposes is tax avoidance. This test appears to have been met if the tax avoidance motive adequately explains the arrangement, notwithstanding commercial considerations that, in and of themselves, could also explain that arrangement. The subjective test is comparable to the subjective test in the Merger Directive (see Section 17.13: tax evasion or tax avoidance is the principal objective or one of the principal objectives).[159] In *Kofoed*[160] and *Foggia*,[161] the Court ruled that the anti-abuse provision in the Merger Directive is a 'reflection' of the general principle of EU law that abuse of law is prohibited and can only be applied if the avoidance motive was 'predominant'.[162] The Court will probably interpret the subjective test in the anti-abuse rule of Article 1(2) in the same manner, as that rule is also an expression

157 In Case C-228/24, *'Nordcurrent group' UAB*, EU:C:2025:239, points 45-49, the Court emphasised that the subjective element of the intention to obtain a tax advantage is a separate factor that must be present in order to conclude that abuse has occurred.

158 Cf. Case C-228/24, 'Nordcurrent group' UAB, EU:C:2025:239, point 53, where the Court refers to 'another justification ... inasmuch as that arrangement might seek to achieve a reduction in the tax burden rather than a benefit under that directive.'

159 Art. 15(1)(a) Merger Directive (*see also* art. 11(a) Council Directive 90/434/EEC of 23 July 1990).

160 Case C-321/05, *Hans Markus Kofoed v. Skatteministeriet*, [2007] ECR I-5795, EU:C:2007:408, point 38.

161 Case C-126/10, *Foggia – Sociedade Gestora de Participações Sociais SA v. Secretário de Estado dos Assuntos Fiscais*, [2011] ECR I-10923, EU:C:2011:718, point 50.

162 See Foggia, point 35. Apparently, no sufficient commercial reasons seem to exist where 'having regard to the magnitude of the anticipated tax benefit', the commercial benefits is 'quite marginal'. (see point 47).

of the general prohibition of abuse of rights.[163] The reservation of competence in the old Article 1(2) has been maintained in Article 1(4), but its relevance would seem to be very limited, as it does not seem to add anything to the reach of the mandatory anti-abuse rule of Article 1(2). Even before the introduction of the mandatory anti-abuse rule of Article 1(2), the old Article 1(2) did not seem to add anything to the general principle of EU law that abuse is prohibited (see Sections 7.2 and 7.4 and Section 16.8.7 below; see also the – still relevant[164] – case law on the former Article 1(2) in Section 16.8.7).

16.8.4 *Defeating Object or Purpose*

Not every tax motive is per se contrary to the object and purpose of the PSD. Should an EU parent prefer to establish a subsidiary in another Member State rather than in a third State in view of the system for avoiding double taxation as created by the PSD, this preference would be perfectly aligned with the objectives of the PSD. This is different where, for example, a letterbox or conduit company is established within a Member State in order to extend the PSD benefits to holdings in or by companies resident in third countries ('Directive shopping'). This could be the case where a non-EU based enterprise makes an investment in Member State A, and would establish an intermediate holding company in Member State B for the main purpose of avoiding Member State A dividend withholding taxation. If the investment structure (in particular the intermediate holding company) would be artificial ('not genuine'; see Section 16.8.5), this arrangement would be abusive. Another type of Directive shopping is the use of an artificial intermediate holding company in order to realize a tax-free inbound (into the EU) profit transfer. This type of Directive shopping typically makes use of a more generous participation exemption in another Member State. For example, Company A, resident in Member State A, might want to invest in Company X, resident in a third country. If the participation exemption in Member State A does not apply to dividends from Company X, but the participation exemption in Member State B would, Company A might consider structuring the investment through an intermediate holding company in Member State B. If this is done for the main purpose of being able to benefit from an exemption in Member State A based on Article 4(1)(a) of the PSD, this arrangement could be abusive, i.e. if the investment structure (in particular the intermediate holding company) would be artificial. The *Nordcurrent group* case[165] seems to suggest that the application of the participation exemption in the parent jurisdiction might also defeat object or purpose of the PSD in other cases. The *Nordcurrent group* case dealt with the application of Article 4 PSD to dividend distributions by a UK subsidiary that lacked human and material resources and actual economic activities to its Lithuanian parent. According to the Court it was for the referring Court to establish whether in that case the constituent elements of abuse were present.[166] Since the UK

163 According to the Court, in Case C-228/24, *'Nordcurrent group' UAB*, EU:C:2025:239, point 24, the clarifications provided by the Court in respect of the general principle of the prohibition of abuse in its case-law relating to Directive 90/435, are also relevant for the purpose of interpreting the anti-abuse provision. Cf. Filip Debelva and Joris Luts, l.c., at 2.3, Weber, l.c., at 6.2.3, and Marres and De Groot, l.c., at 10.4.1.

164 Cf. Case C-228/24, *'Nordcurrent group' UAB*, EU:C:2025:239, point 24.

165 Case C-228/24, *'Nordcurrent group' UAB*, EU:C:2025:239.

166 See point 30.

subsidiary appeared to pay more in the UK than it would have paid if it were resident in Lithuania,[167] the structure does not appear to be abusive. However, the question arises whether cases where profits are shifted to low-taxed CFCs might be abusive under the PSD. A counterargument might be that the main purpose of these structures is not the application of any benefits of the PSD (this is merely instrumental for achieving the end goal of the arrangement) but the reduction of tax on the operational activities of the CFC.[168]

Dividend stripping arrangements without a genuine underlying investment probably also defeat object or purpose of the PSD. This might be the case where the shares are transferred to an EU parent for a short period, only to enjoy the benefits of the PSD. It must be stressed that the PSD allows, but does not require a certain holding period to be met. Member States *can* refuse the benefits of the PSD if a participation has not been held for an uninterrupted period of at least two years, but are not required to so (see Article 3(2)(b) of the PSD).[169] As the issue of a minimum holding period has been addressed but did not result in a mandatory minimum holding period, granting the benefits of the PSD in the case of a short-term shareholding does not by definition seem to be contrary to the purpose of the PSD. The mere fact that a holding is short-term, does not constitute abuse. We submit that it should be decisive whether the short-term shareholding is artificial (for stripping purposes) or a genuine investment (see also Section 16.8.5).

16.8.5 Artificiality

In order for the anti-abuse rule to apply, the arrangement or series of arrangements must be 'not genuine'. This is the case to the extent that they are 'not put in place for valid commercial reasons which reflect economic reality' (Article 1(3) PSD). The term 'commercial reasons' appears to be used in order to exclude other tax motives (such as a beneficial tax system in the Member State where a holding company is resident). The original proposal contained a list of examples that the Member States needed to take into account when assessing artificiality (such as where 'the arrangement is carried out in a manner which would not ordinarily be used in a reasonable business conduct', and where 'the transactions concluded are circular in nature').[170] The only guidance provided by the adopted provision is that one must have regard to 'all relevant facts and circumstances' when assessing whether an arrangement is put into place for 'valid commercial reasons which reflect economic reality'. However, some guidance may be inferred from the preamble. Point 8 of the preamble, discussing the 'to the extent' approach of Article 1(3),

167 See point 54.

168 Cf. point 53: 'It cannot be ruled out that there might be another justification for putting into place an arrangement in another Member State, inasmuch as that arrangement might seek to achieve a reduction in the tax burden rather than a benefit under that directive.'

169 In the Explanatory Notes to the original proposal for the PSD of 16 January 1969, COM 69/DEF, the Commission noted that the legislation of the different Member States differed markedly on the required holding period, and it therefore proposed not to include an obligatory rule on this point, but to allow Member States to require a minimum holding period. See Marres and De Groot, l.c., at 10.4.2.

170 Proposal for a Council Directive amending Directive 2011/96/EU on the common system of taxation applicable in the case of parent companies and subsidiaries of different Member States, Brussels 25 November 2013, COM(2013) 814 final.

illustrates this approach with an example where entities concerned are 'as such' genuine, but where shares producing the dividend are not genuinely attributed to a taxpayer that is established in a Member State: this might be the case where the arrangement that transfers the ownership do not reflect economic reality. A holding structure is therefore not per se 'genuine' if the parent company has a certain level of 'substance'. The relevant question is whether the parent company performs a relevant function in respect of the shareholding.[171]

In the Danish cases the Court specified indicia that can be used as guidance for the assessment of abuse.[172] An artificial arrangement is – inter alia[173] – present where tax on dividends is avoided on account of a conduit entity interposed in the structure. This may be the case where the sole activity of the entity is the receipt of dividends and their transmission to the beneficial owner or to other conduit companies. The absence of actual economic activity must be inferred from an analysis of all the relevant factors relating, in particular, to the management of the company, to its balance sheet, to the structure of its costs and to expenditure actually incurred, to the staff that it employs and its premises and equipment. The Court refers to situations where all or almost all of the dividends are, very soon after their receipt, passed on by the recipient company to entities which do not fulfil the conditions for the application of the PSD. Other indications of an artificial arrangement may be 'the various contracts existing between the companies involved in the financial transactions at issue, giving rise to intragroup flows of funds, by the way in which the transactions are financed, by the valuation of the intermediary companies' equity and by the conduit companies' inability to have economic use of the dividends received.' It is important to note that not only contractual or legal obligations of the parent company must be taken into account but also the fact that, 'in substance', the parent company does not have the right to use and enjoy those dividends.

Although the decisions in the Danish cases seem difficult to reconcile with the decision in Deister and Juhler, they are not contradictory. It can be deduced from the latter decision that the absence of economic or other substantial reasons justifying the interposition of the non-resident company do not imply abuse (see Section 16.8.7 below), which may seem difficult to reconcile with the indicia for abuse in the decisions in the Danish cases. However one should keep in mind that these are only indications. The most important conclusion from the Danish cases and Deister and Juhler is that whether or not there is abuse must be assessed on a case-by-case basis. General presumptions of abuse and safe harbours are not acceptable.[174] In the *Nordcurrent group* case the Court further clarified that, although non-abusive arrangements might turn into abusive arrangements from a certain point (since maintaining a structure after a change in circumstances might not be justified by valid commercial reasons), one should not disregard the previous

171 See also Marres and De Groot, l.c., at 10.4.3. Cf. Weber, l.c., at 7.2.

172 Joined Cases C-116/16 and C-117/16, T Danmark and Y Denmark Aps, EU:C:2019:135, points 99-114.

173 A conduit structure is merely an example of an abusive structure; see Case C-228/24, 'Nordcurrent group' UAB, EU:C:2025:239, point 28.

174 See also Otto Marres and Isabella de Groot: Combatting Abuse by Conduit Companies. The Doctrine of Abuse under EU Law and Its Influence on Tax Treaties, *European Taxation*, (Volume 61), No. 8, at 3.

circumstances that did justify the structure: these circumstances may still be relevant to justify an arrangement and therefore also these circumstances must be taken into account.[175]

16.8.6 Refusing 'the benefits of the Directive'

Article 1(2) clearly states that in case of abuse 'Member States shall not grant the benefits of the Directive'. These benefits include the double tax relief granted by the parent State (Article 4) and the absence of withholding taxes on the distribution in both the State of the subsidiary (Article 5) and the parent company (Article 6). The Commission, however, gave the following statement to be entered in the Minutes of the Session at which the amending Directive was to be adopted:

> 'The Commission confirms that the proposed amendments to Article 1, paragraph 2 of the Parent Subsidiary directive are not intended to affect national participation exemption systems in so far as these are compatible with the Treaty provisions'.[176]

This might be understood to mean that the Commission views the mandatory anti-abuse rule as intended to curb only abuse of the exemption from source taxation. According to the settled case law of the Court, however, statements included in the minutes of Council meetings have no legal significance and cannot be used in the interpretation of a directive.[177] Since the text of Article 1(2) is clear, and as confirmed by the Court,[178] the conclusion must be that the PSD requires that also the benefit of Article 4(1)(a) must be disallowed in case of abuse of this provision. A different view was taken by the Dutch government, which argued in Parliament that Article 1(2) of the PSD does not cover the benefit of Article 4(1)(a) of the PSD, with reference to the Commission's statement.[179]

Still, in the majority of cases the mandatory anti-abuse rule will not affect the participation exemptions of the Member States. Directive shopping typically consists of avoidance of withholding tax through the use of an intermediate holding company in a Member State for a tax-free profit distribution to an ultimate shareholder not eligible to the benefits of the PSD (e.g. a parent in a third country: 'outbound profit transfers'). If such a scheme is artificial and, hence, abusive, the benefit of Article 5 PSD should not be granted. It would be quite disproportionate to also disallow the participation exemption in the Member State of the parent (the intermediate holding company) in such cases.

However, as discussed in Section 16.8.4, another type of Directive shopping is the use of an artificial intermediate holding company for a tax-free *in*bound profit transfer (into the

175 Case C-228/24, 'Nordcurrent group' UAB, EU:C:2025:239, points 36-43.

176 Annex to Council of the European Union Brussels, 16 December 2014 (OR. en), 16914/14, 2013/0400 (CNS), FISC 235 ECOFIN 1199.

177 *See* Case C-375/98, *Ministério Público and Fazenda Pública v. Epson Europe BV*, [2008] ECR I-4243, EU:C:2000:302, Cases C-197/94 and C-252/94, *Bautiaa en Société française maritime/Directeurs des services fiscaux des Landes en du Finistère* and *Société française maritime*, [1996] ECR I-505, EU:C:1996:47, point 51; and Case C- 247/08, *Gaz de France – Berliner Investissement*, [2009] ECR I-9225, EU:C:2009:600, point 39.

178 Case C-228/24, 'Nordcurrent group' UAB, EU:C:2025:239, point 31.

179 See Second Chamber, 2015-2016, 34 306, file no. 3, p. 4.

EU). This type of Directive shopping abuses the participation exemption in the Member State of the artificial intermediate holding company, and therefore the adequate response would be the denial of that exemption in the Member State of the parent company (notwithstanding the Commission's statement), rather than withholding source tax in the Member State of the artificial intermediate holding company when it redistributes the third State dividend received.

In our view, Article 1(2) PSD also requires Member States to deny tax treaty benefits equivalent to the PSD benefits which must be denied.[180] Obviously, Article 1(2) PSD would be utterly useless as a *mandatory* minimum anti-abuse rule if Member States could simply ignore it by concluding tax treaties providing the exact same benefits the PSD requires them *not* to provide. Granting the PSD benefits in case of abuse as defined by the PSD on whatever legal basis would violate the Member States' obligations to implement the mandatory anti-abuse rule and would undermine both the precedence of EU law and the principle of Union loyalty (Article 4(3) TEU). There is no relevant difference between domestic law and tax treaty law from an EU perspective (see also Section 8.3.2). Directives may be implemented through tax treaties just as well as through unilateral law, as the means of implementation are a matter for the Member States and only the result counts (Article 288 TFEU). Directives must be implemented in a binding and sufficiently clear legal framework,[181] and self-executing provisions of tax treaties meet those requirements, at least in Member States with a monistic constitutional system (thus not requiring transposition of directly effective treaty provisions into domestic law). If Member States may not grant the Directive benefits in case of abuse, then logically, they may not provide them regardless of the means of implementation they choose.

Therefore, we submit that Member States must amend their tax treaties with other Member States to prevent taxpayers from relying on those treaties to still access Directive-equivalent benefits in case of abuse as defined by the PSD.[182] Amending tax treaties is unnecessary, however, if they can be interpreted such that their equivalent benefits would not apply in cases of abuse as defined by the PSD. National courts must interpret national law, including bilateral treaties concluded by their Member State, 'as far as possible, in the light of the wording and the purpose of the directive in order to achieve the result pursued by the latter' (duty of consistent interpretation).[183] The condition 'as far as possible' refers to the limits set by general principles of law (such as legal certainty); courts are not required to interpret national law *contra legem*.[184] We submit that the principal purpose test included

180 Cf. T.M. Vergouwen, The Effect of Directives within the Area of Direct Taxation on the Interpretation and Application of Tax Treaties (Series on International Taxation, no. 84), Alphen aan den Rijn: Kluwer Law International 2023, p. 222-224.

181 See for example, Case C-296/01, *Commission of the European Communities v. French Republic*, [2003] I-13901, EU:C:2003:626, point 55; and Case C-29/14, *European Commission v. Republic of Poland*, EU:C:2015:379, point 38.

182 See also Weber, l.c., at 5.2. and Marres and De Groot, l.c., at 10.5.3. For another view see Debelva & Luts, l.c., at 3.3.2.

183 Case C-106/89, *Marleasing SA v. La Comercial Internacional de Alimentacion SA*, [1990] ECR I-4135, EU:C:1990:395, point 8.

184 Case C-212/04, *Konstantinos Adeneler and Others v. Ellinikos Organismos Galaktos (ELOG)*, [2006] ECR I-6057, EU:C:2006:443, point 110.

in Article 29(9) of the OECD Model Convention and in Article 7(1) of the OECD multilateral instrument (MLI)[185] to which all Member States have acceded, resembles the general anti-abuse rule of Article 1(2) PSD to such an extent, both in wording and in object and purpose, that it can be applied in conformity with the latter provision.[186] Even if these treaties do not contain provisions that may be interpreted in accordance with Article 1(2) PSD, there is still an obligation for the Member States to disallow treaty benefits that are equivalent to the benefits of the PSD, in cases that are in scope of the PSD and that constitute abuse within the meaning of CJEU case law.[187] Although a national tax administration cannot rely directly (without proper implementation) on Article 1(2) PSD to deny directive benefits, as a directive cannot of itself impose obligations on economic operators (no inverse vertical direct effect; see Section 3.5.1), this is irrelevant in cases of abuse. The refusal of an advantage under the PSD in these cases is merely the consequence of the finding that the conditions of the PSD have not been met (since EU law cannot be relied upon in cases of abuse).[188]

16.8.7 Article 1(4): Reservation of Competence (any Autonomy Left?)

Article 1(4) of the Directive affords Member States a certain discretionary power to apply domestic or treaty-based anti-abuse provisions in derogation of the substantive rules of the Directive. It does not define abuse, but merely specifies that Member States may rely, even if the Directive requirements are satisfied, on national and bilateral anti-abuse provisions to deny or limit the Directive benefits. The provision is almost identical to the former Article 1(2); it is renumbered and slightly changed by Directive (EU) 2015/121, the only difference being that the terms 'fraud or abuse' are replaced by the terms 'tax evasion, tax fraud or abuse' (see Sections 16.1 en 16.8.2). As the Court held in the *Argenta II*,[189] *Eqiom*[190] and Danish[191] cases, this provision reflects the general principle of EU law that no one may benefit from the rights stemming from the legal system of the European Union for abusive or fraudulent ends.

From the *Kofoed* case,[192] concerning the anti-abuse provision in the Merger Directive (see Section 17.5), we infer that the use of the term 'provisions' does not imply that the

185 Multilateral Convention to Implement Tax Treaty Related Measures to Prevent Base Erosion and Profit Shifting, Paris, 24 November 2016. See for a discussion of the compliance of the PPT with EU Law: Ana Paula Dourado, Aggressive Tax Planning in EU Law and in the Light of BEPS: The EC Recommendation on Aggressive Tax Planning and BEPS Actions 2 and 6, *Intertax*, Vol. 43, Issue 1, p. 42- 57; Frans Vanistendael, Is Tax Avoidance the Same Thing under the OECD Base Erosion and Profit Shifting Action Plan, National Tax Law and EU Law?, *Bulletin for International Taxation*, March 2016, p. 163-172 and Oleksandr Koriak, The Principal Purpose Test under BEPS Action 6: Is the OECD Proposal Compliant with EU Law?, *European Taxation*, December 2016, p. 552-559.

186 See also Otto Marres and Isabella de Groot: Combatting Abuse by Conduit Companies. The Doctrine of Abuse under EU Law and Its Influence on Tax Treaties, *European Taxation*, (Volume 61), No. 8, at 3.

187 Joined Cases C-116/16 and C-117/16, T *Danmark and Y Denmark Aps*, EU:C:2019:135, point 95.

188 Joined Cases C-116/16 and C-117/16, T *Danmark and Y Denmark Aps*, EU:C:2019:135, point 91.

189 Case C-39/16, *Argenta Spaarbank II*, EU:C:2017:813, point 60.

190 Case C-6/16, *Eqiom SAS, formerly Holcim France SAS/Enka*, EU:C:2017:641, point 26.

191 Joined Cases C-116/16 and C-117/16, T *Danmark and Y Denmark Aps*, EU:C:2019:135, point 90.

192 Case C-321/05, *Kofoed*, [2007] ECR I-5795, EU:C:2007:408.

national legal basis for denying Directive benefits needs to be Statute Law. If applied in a targeted and proportional manner, a general, unwritten, judge-made anti-abuse doctrine, such as a 'substance over form' or a *fraus legis* doctrine, should suffice, given that (i) the Court itself relies on an unwritten, Court-made prohibition of abuse of rights as a general principle of EU law (see also Chapter 7), (ii) the choice of form and method of implementing a Directive is national sovereignty (Art. 288 TFEU), and (iii) the Directive explicitly refers to *national* anti-abuse law, form and method of which obviously differs from Member State to Member State.

Relying on Article 1(4), many Member States introduced or maintained national provisions to ensure that only what they consider *bona fide* business structures benefit from the Directive. As regards *inbound* dividend, these provisions may, *e.g.*, require the foreign subsidiary not to be located in a low-tax jurisdiction and not to benefit from a special (favourable) tax regime in its country of residence (anti-tax haven rules); they may deny benefits to parent companies receiving dividends from intermediate holding companies redistributing income that would not have been exempt if it had been distributed directly to the parent (anti-conduit company rules). The question arises whether the Directive allows parent company States to make application of Article 4 conditional on the level of taxation in the subsidiary State. Since the Directive allows the indirect credit method as well as the exemption method, it seems logical that exemption States may require a minimum level of taxation in the subsidiary State. They may not, however, refuse relief altogether if the foreign level is considered too low, as that would clearly be disproportionate: they should at least provide for a switch-over to indirect credit in order to achieve the prescribed result: prevention of double taxation. Less clear is whether the parent State may consider abusive the use of a foreign special low tax regime, derogating from the normal corporation tax in the subsidiary State. We submit that even if that special regime of another Member State is prohibited State aid or is considered harmful tax competition, which should be rolled back by the Code of Conduct (see Chapter 26), the parent State cannot refuse relief altogether, as that would lead to some double taxation: it should at least provide for an indirect credit (and may be allowed to apply anti-deferral measures such as CFC legislation as well if the use of the foreign special regime is 'wholly artificial'): it should take away the yield of the abuse, but should not 'punish' the abusers by taxing them double. Tax arbitrage in itself, however, is not abusive.[193]

As regards *outbound* dividends, national legislation and tax treaties of the Member States show a wide variety of measures aimed at ensuring that the exemption from withholding tax benefits only 'good' ultimate shareholders: beneficial ownership requirements, LOB provisions[194] in tax treaties, automatic exclusion if the parent company is held by third State residents unless absence of abuse is demonstrated (reversal of the burden of proof), targeted anti-dividend stripping rules, subjection of the EU parent company to a gross income test and/or a substance test and/or a motive test and/or a management or business

193 See for a discussion of this issue, especially in connection with the use of hybrid financial instruments, Jakob Bundgaard: Classification and Treatment of hybrid Financial Instruments and Income Derived Therefrom under EU Corporate Tax Directives, parts 1 and 2, *European Taxation*, October and November 2010.

194 LOB = limitation on benefits.

connection test, or application of general anti-abuse rules (GAARs) or unwritten *fraus legis* doctrines.[195] If, for instance, Member State A concluded a tax treaty with a third State providing for a 10% withholding tax on outbound participation dividends, then State A will not be pleased with a State A company distributing its profits to an intermediate company interposed in another EU Member State free of withholding tax under the Directive, if that EU intermediate is a mere conduit subsidiary of a third State company, and between that other Member State and the third State involved a tax treaty is in force reducing withholding tax to 5% or to zero. State A will probably regard this as Directive (and treaty) shopping, resulting in State A losing 10 points, the EU intermediate State gaining 0 to 5 points and a conduit fee, and the ultimate third State shareholder avoiding 5 to 10 points. In such circumstances, State A may decide, notwithstanding the Directive, to levy a withholding tax of 10% as if the dividend were paid directly by the State A subsidiary to the ultimate third State shareholder.[196] However, the mere fact that the EU-intermediate company is held by a third country resident does not of itself constitute abuse. In the *Eqiom* case,[197] as confirmed by the joined cases *Deister and Juhler*,[198] the Court held that

> '30 [...], in order for national legislation to be regarded as seeking to prevent tax evasion and abuses, its specific objective must be to prevent conduct involving the creation of wholly artificial arrangements which do not reflect economic reality, the purpose of which is unduly to obtain a tax advantage [...].'

The competent national authorities may not confine themselves to applying predetermined general criteria, but must carry out an individual examination. A general tax measure automatically excluding certain categories of taxpayers from the tax advantage, without the tax authorities being obliged to provide even *prima facie* evidence of fraud and abuse, would go further than is necessary for preventing fraud and abuse.[199] As a result, anti-Directive shopping rules that automatically apply where the EU parent company is controlled by residents of third States cannot be applied, even if the parent company may show that the principal purpose or one of the principal purposes of the chain of interests is not to take advantage of the exemption, because such a general presumption of fraud and abuse would undermine the objective of the Parent-Subsidiary Directive (prevention

195 See, a.o. Maikel Evers and Arnoud de Graaf, 'limiting Benefit Shopping: Use and Abuse of EC Law,' *EC Tax Review* 2009/6, p. 279-298; Maikel Evers and Arnoud de Graaf, 'Limiting Benefit Shopping: Measures of Four Large EU Member States to Counter Erosion of Their Dividend Tax,' *EC Tax Review* 2010/5, p. 188- 198; and Emmanuel Picq: Abuse of EU Holding Companies: Fundamental Freedoms, EC Parent-Subsidiary Directive and the French Constitution, parts 1 and 2, *European Taxation*, October 2009, p. 471-478 and November 2009, p. 534-541, respectively, which provides an overview of anti-abuse measures as regards outbound dividends in France, the Netherlands, Germany, Spain and Austria, as well as in the US and in Canada.

196 If a tax treaty exists between State A and the EC intermediate State, which provides for a withholding tax rate lower than 10%, and which does not contain an LOB-provision (limitation on benefits: an anti-treaty shopping clause), we believe State A should apply that lower rate.

197 Case C-6/16, *Eqiom SAS, formerly Holcim France SAS/Enka*, EU:C:2017:641.

198 Joined Cases C-504/16 and C-613/16, *Deister Holding AG and Juhler Holding A/S*, EU:C:2017:1009, point 60.

199 Case C-6/16, *Eqiom SAS, formerly Holcim France SAS/Enka*, EU:C:2017:641, points 30-32. See also Joined Cases C-504/16 and C-613/16, *Deister Holding AG and Juhler Holding A/S*, EU:C:2017:1009, points 61-62.

of double taxation).[200] Anti-abuse legislation predicated on an assessment of objective and verifiable elements for the purposes of determining whether a transaction represents a wholly artificial arrangement entered into solely for tax reasons is in principle allowed, but there should be at least *prima facie* evidence of fraud and abuse, and the taxpayer should have the opportunity to rebut that *prima facie* evidence by showing commercial justification.[201] The mere fact that an EU parent company is controlled by residents of third States is not *prima facie* evidence of abuse. The joined cases *Deister and Juhler* concern the question whether Article 5(1) in conjunction with Article (now) 1(4) preclude national legislation which denies relief from source tax on dividends paid to a non-resident parent company to the extent that the shareholders of that parent company are not entitled to such relief if they earned the income directly *and* (i) there are no economic or other substantial reasons for the involvement of the foreign company, *or* (ii) the foreign company does not earn more than 10% of its entire gross earnings for the financial year in question from its own economic activity, *or* (iii) the foreign company does not take part in general economic commerce with a business establishment suitably equipped for its business purpose.[202] The Court followed its reasoning in the Eqiom case, and noted that the German legislation is not specifically designed to target wholly artificial arrangements:

> '65 [...] [T]he mere fact that such persons have such holdings does not in itself indicate the existence of a wholly artificial arrangement which does not reflect economic reality and whose purpose is unduly to obtain a tax advantage.
> 66. In that context, it cannot be inferred from any provision of the Parent-Subsidiary Directive that the tax treatment of persons with holdings in parent companies resident in the European Union or the origin of such persons affects in any way the right of those companies to rely on tax advantages provided for by that directive.
> 67. Moreover, it should be noted that the non-resident parent company is in any event subject to the tax legislation of the Member State in which it is established (judgment of 7 September 2017, Eqiom and Enka, C 6/16, EU:C:2017:641, paragraph 35 and the case-law cited).'

Furthermore, it held that the German legislation subjects the grant of the exemption from withholding tax provided for by Article 5(1) PSD to the requirement that none of the three conditions (i), (ii) and (iii) mentioned above, is satisfied, without the tax authorities being required to provide prima facie evidence of the absence of economic reasons or of fraud or abuse, and without allowing the parent company to provide evidence demonstrating the existence of economic reasons. It therefore broke both the rule that a general presumption of fraud or abuse is disallowed, and the rule that a presumption of fraud or abuse must be rebuttable. Also, the Court noted that the PSD does not contain any requirement as to the nature of the economic activity of companies falling within its scope or the amount of turnover resulting from those companies' own economic activity, and that the fact that the economic activity of a non-resident parent company consists in the management of its subsidiaries' assets or that the income of that company results

200 Case C-6/16, *Eqiom SAS, formerly Holcim France SAS/Enka*, EU:C:2017:641, points 33-36.

201 See also Case C-318/10, *Société d'investissement pour l'agriculture tropicale SA (SIAT)*, EU:C:2012:415, points 50-56.

202 Joined Cases C-504/16 and C-613/16, *Deister Holding AG and Juhler Holding A/S*, EU:C:2017:1009, point 14.

only from such management cannot per se indicate the existence of a wholly artificial arrangement which does not reflect economic reality.[203]

From the Court's judgments in the joined cases *Denkavit, VITIC* and *Voormeer* (see Section 16.3.2.(v)), point 31, and the *Argenta Spaarbank II* Case,[204] it may be inferred that a *general* anti-abuse reservation such as Article (now) 1(4) PSD cannot be relied on by Member States in cases of perceived abuse that the Directive already addresses in a *specific* anti-abuse provision (*lex specialis derogat lex generalis*). Indeed, in *Denkavit a.o.*, Germany could not rely on Article (now) 1(4) to widen the scope of the specific anti-abuse provision of Article 3(2) (minimum holding period requirement) to other cases than short-term concentration of non-qualifying interests solely for taking advantage of the Directive. In *Argenta Spaarbank II*, the Court considered that Article (now 1(4)) PSD is, in its turn, 'a provision of principle' [a GAAR, therefore], 'the content of which is explained in detail in other provisions of that directive, inter alia in Article 4(2), in that it seeks in particular to counteract abuse by parent companies resulting from a double tax deduction'.

Anti-abuse provisions, like all restrictions to EU rights, must be applied narrowly,[205] and (therefore) in accordance with the proportionality principle. The measure taken must be appropriate for combating the abuse identified, it may not be more restrictive than necessary to attain that goal, the abuse must be real (concrete), and the companies involved must at least have an opportunity to rebut, under judicial review, any legal presumption of abuse, by demonstrating that their transactions, although possibly entering the scope of a national or treaty-based anti-abuse provision and possibly not appearing to be at arm's length, nevertheless served *bona fide* business purposes.

The Directive clearly extends *some* discretion to the Member States in combating abuse, since under different national tax systems and different bilateral treaties, different kinds of abuse are possible. Therefore, in our view, *Francovich* liability of a Member State for damages (see Section 3.5.4), caused by the over stepping of its discretionary powers in countering abuse, will not easily ensue. State liability only arises where the national anti-abuse measure taken was clearly disproportionate (*overkill*) and the State concerned could not reasonably have assumed to have remained within the limits of its discretion.

---

203 Joined Cases C-504/16 and C-613/16, *Deister Holding AG and Juhler Holding A/S*, EU:C:2017:1009, points 68-74.

204 Case C-39/16, *Argenta Spaarbank NV II*, EU:C:2017: 323.

205 Case C-6/16, *Eqiom SAS, formerly Holcim France SAS/Enka*, EU:C:2017:641, point 26: '[...] although Article 1(2) of the Parent-Subsidiary Directive reflects the general principle of EU law that no one may benefit from the rights stemming from the legal system of the European Union for abusive or fraudulent ends, it must nevertheless, in so far as it constitutes a derogation from the tax rules established by that directive, be interpreted strictly (see, to that effect, judgment of 25 September 2003, Océ van der Grinten, C 58/01, EU:C:2003:495, paragraph 86)'. Cf. Joined Cases C-504/16 and C-613/16, *Deister Holding AG and Juhler Holding A/S*, EU:C:2017:1009, point 59.

From the case law of the Court as regards effectiveness of EU law, as handed down in judgments such as *Rewe*,[206] *San Giorgio*[207] and *Van Schijndel*[208] (See Sections 3.4 and 3.5.2), it follows that it should not be more difficult for companies to avail themselves of their rights under the PSD than it is for them to avail themselves of similar rights of a strictly domestic nature in situations of possible abuse (principle of non-discrimination), and that in any case it should not be excessively difficult or practically impossible to enjoy the Directive benefits (principle of effectiveness of EU law). There is one marked and remarkable exception: as discussed in Section 16.4.1, the Court surprisingly accepted, in *Test Claimants FII GLO*,[209] and in *Haribo* and *Salinen*,[210] an in our view discriminatory and protective *asymmetrical* choice of the parent company State to exempt domestic dividends without any evidential requirements, but to provide a mere indirect credit under ominous evidential requirements for cross-border dividends, irrespective of the presence or absence of any artificiality or abuse, and irrespective of whether the corporation tax the subsidiary was subject to, was the normal regime in the subsidiary State or a harmful special low-tax scheme. This clearly procedurally discriminates against foreign indirect investment and protects the parent company State against the tax efficiency of other Member States.

For further discussion of the Court's concept of abuse of law, we refer to Chapter 7. Given the Court's general 'abuse of rights' doctrine and its case law explaining that the anti-abuse reservations of competence in the corporate tax directives are expressions of that general principle of EU law and have the same scope, we do not see much added value in Article 1(4) in the Parent-Subsidiary Directive, Article 15(1)(a) in the Merger Directive, and Article 5 of the I&R Directive. We believe they are redundant (see Sections 7.2 and 7.3.17). Article 1(2) of the PSD (the mandatory anti-abuse provision) and the linking rule in Article 4(1)(a) PSD are equally redundant next to the abuse of rights doctrine: although these provisions contain EU *obligations* to fight abuse, they do not add value since, as is made clear in the Danish cases, the general principle of EU law that EU law cannot be relied on for abusive or fraudulent ends, already requires national authorities and courts to refuse a taxpayer the benefits under the PSD in cases of abuse.

16.9 Implementation; Direct Effect; Private Enforcement

Where national implementation measures do not fully comply with the Directive requirements, or where implementation has wrongly been omitted, the question arises as to whether taxpayers may rely directly on the Directive provisions before their national courts in order to invalidate incompatible national law.[211] In the *Denkavit*, *VITIC* and *Voormeer*

206 Case 33/76, *Rewe*, [1976] ECR 1989, EU:C:1976:188.

207 Case 199/82, San Giorgio, [1983] ECR 3595, EU:C:1983:318.

208 Joined Cases C-430/93 and C-431/93, Van Schijndel/Stichting Pensioenfonds voor Fysiotherapeuten and van Veen, [1995] ECR I-4705, EU:C:1995:441.

209 Case C-446/04, *Test Claimants in the FII Group Litigation*, [2006] ECR I- 11753, EU:C:2006:774.

210 Joined Cases C-436/08 and 437/08, *Haribo Lakritzen Hans Riegel* and *Österreichische Salinen*, EU:C:2011:61 and EU:C:2009:17.

211 A different question is whether the PSD applies to taxation of a Member State over a period preceeding the date of accession of that Member State to the EU. The answer is, unsurprisingly: No (Case C-113/20, *Slovenský plynárenský priemysel a.s.*, EU:C:2020:772).

cases (see Section 16.3.2.(v)), the Court considered Article 5, abolishing withholding taxes, to be sufficiently clear, precise, and unconditional to have such direct effect.

Article 4, providing for the prevention of double taxation at parent company level, clearly grants the Member States an option – and therefore a discretionary power – to choose between exemption and indirect credit. However, once a Member State has made its choice, it would appear that no discretionary power remains. In Case *Cobelfret* (see Section 16.4.1), the Court therefore ascribed direct effect also to Article 4. If the rights to which the company is entitled can be determined with sufficient precision from the Directive provision alone, it may rely directly on that provision before a national court.[212] As the Court held in *Denkavit, VITIC* and *Voormeer*, the discretionary powers conferred in Article 3(2) of the Directive as regards the possibility of requiring a minimum holding period:

> '(...) do not make it impossible to determine minimum rights on the basis of the principle contained in Article 5.'

From Case C-72/95, *Kraaijeveld*,[213] it follows that discretionary powers do not preclude a Directive provision from having direct effect if that discretion is limited by the Directive in a precise enough manner, which is the case with Article 4 of the Parent-Subsidiary Directive. As the Court held in *Cobelfret:*[214]

> '61. (...), it is consistent case-law of the Court that the right given to Member States to choose among several possible means of achieving the result required by a directive does not preclude the possibility for individuals to enforce before the national courts rights the content of which can be determined with sufficient precision on the basis of the provisions of the directive alone (see, inter alia, *Francovich and Others*, paragraph 17, and Case C-226/07 *Flughafen Köln/Bonn* [2008] ECR I-0000, paragraph 30).
> 62. In the present case, however, it is not necessary to consider whether, notwithstanding the choice left to the Member States by Article 4(1) of Directive 90/435, it is possible to identify the minimum rights accorded to individuals under that provision.
> 63. In so far as it appears from the file that (...) Belgium opted for the system set out in the first indent of Article 4(1) of Directive 90/435, it is sufficient to establish whether that provision is unconditional and sufficiently precise to be capable of being relied on before national courts.
> 64. The obligation to refrain from taxing profits which a subsidiary distributes to its parent company, set out in the first indent of Article 4(1), is worded in unequivocal terms and is not subject to any condition. Likewise, its implementation or effects are not subject to the intervention of any other act on the part of the Community institutions or the Member States.
> 65. It follows that the first indent of Article 4(1) of Directive 90/435 is unconditional and sufficiently precise to be capable of being relied on before national courts.'

If Belgium had chosen for indirect credit, then it might not have been so easy to postulate direct effect of Article 4, as indirect credits are notoriously difficult to apply: the

212 See, for instance, Case C-271/91 *Marshall/Southampton and South West Hampshire Area Health Authority*, [1992] ECR I-4367, EU:C:1993:335.
213 Case C-72/95 *Kraaijeveld a.o.*, of 24 October 1996, [1996] ECR I-5403, EU:C:1996:404.
214 Case C-138/07 *Cobelfret*, [2009] ECR I-731, EU:C:2009:82.

corporation tax must be traced which was eventually paid by the furthest tier (sub)(sub) subsidiary. Direct effect *per force* stops where a trial judge is *de facto* unable to apply, in the case brought before him, the EU rule invoked, for lack of implementation guidance. However, if Belgium had chosen for indirect credit, there would no doubt also have been some implementation mechanics which a trial judge could apply analogously.

But even if Article 4 would have no direct effect, a company suffering damages from incorrect or incomplete implementation may, under certain conditions (see Section 3.5.4), rely on the *Francovich*[215] case law of the Court in order to claim damages from a defaulting Member State, provided the incorrect or non-implementation is sufficiently 'serious' within the meaning of the *Brasserie du Pécheur II, Factortame III* and *British Telecom* case law of the Court.[216] This is the case where a Member State has apparently and seriously misjudged the limits of its discretion when transposing the Directive into national law. Again, however, it may be difficult for a trial judge to establish the exact damages, as he does not know what the defaulting Member State would have done, had it not been defaulting, and again the minimum damage is the amount of the indirect credit withheld, which may be difficult to calculate.

Suing a defaulting Member State for damages is possible on top of relying on the direct effect of Article 4: although the *tax* damage does not need to be compensated if direct effect is available (indeed, in that case, a parent company may claim the exemption or the credit directly before its national tax administration and national tax court), there may be additional damages, such as interest charges and cost of legal counsel, which may possibly be claimed under the *Francovich* case law, provided the *Brasserie* conditions are met.

Since the *Köbler* judgment[217] of the Court, under exceptional circumstances Member States may also be liable for damages in case of a 'manifest' incorrect application of the Directive (or EU law in general) by a national highest court (a court adjudicating in last instance). In case of a manifest misapplication of EU law by a lower Court, the taxpayer should appeal the judgment, otherwise the Court will consider the claimant to have failed to take requisite measures to limit his damages.

For an example of incorrect implementation of the Parent-Subsidiary Directive *not* leading to *Francovich* liability, see Section 16.3.2.(v) above.

For a more detailed discussion of the direct effect of Directives and of the *Francovich* liability of Member States, see Sections 3.5.1 and 3.5.4.

215 Joined Cases C-6/90 and C-9/90 Francovich and Bonifaci/Italy and Bonifaci, [1991] ECR I-5403, EU:C:1991:428, [1993] 2 CMLR 66, p. 107.

216 Joined Cases C-46/93 and C-48/93 *Brasserie du pêcheur/Bundesrepublik Deutschland en The Queen/ Secretary of State for Transport, ex parte Factortame e.a.* and *Factortame*, of 5 March 1996, [1996] ECR I-1029, EU:C:1996:79 and EU:C:1996:79, and Case C-392/93 *The Queen/H.M. Treasury, ex parte British Telecommunications*, [1996] ECR I-1631, EU:C:1996:131.

217 Case C-224/01 (*Köbler v. Austria*), [2003] ECR I-10239, EU:C:2003:513.

16.10 Consequences

Implementation of the Directive and of the 2003 amendment widening its scope brought into being an exempt EU intercorporate dividend circuit, through which qualifying dividends can flow freely cross-border, unhampered by withholding taxes and international economic double taxation. Especially the reduction of the minimum holding requirement from 25% before 2005 to 10% in 2009, and the extension of the indirect credit to multi-tier subsidiary situations enhanced access to the benefits of the internal market for undertakings.

The implementation of the (amendment to the) Directive reduced the head start of Member States providing a liberal participation exemption and source tax reduction. Treaty shopping and routing of profits within the EU has become less necessary for minimizing taxes on cross-border dividend payments within groups of companies. Tax competition increases between Member States soliciting the locating of holding companies of multinational groups. Many Member States revamped their tax legislation on holding companies in order to keep up with the Joneses. A remarkable 'spontaneous' harmonization occurred in holding company regimes and corporation tax rates.

For groups of companies with a top holding company outside the EU, it has become easier, withholding taxes reduced to nil, to accumulate European profits in one regional EU headquarters company serving as a reinvestment point or an EU exit point. The most attractive Member State from a tax point of view for a European holding location is probably the State whereto intragroup dividends can flow at the least possible cost, where both incoming dividends and capital gains on 10%-plus holdings (or lower) are exempt from tax, and where no withholding tax on outbound dividends to third states exists, or at least a bilateral tax treaty with the home State of the group applies, enabling it to transfer the profits home at the lowest possible tax cost.

It is not all good news for taxpayers, though. For a parent company in a Member State applying the indirect credit method for the prevention of international double taxation, the abolition of withholding tax in the subsidiary State may have little consequence. The benefit of no longer having to pay withholding tax in the subsidiary State benefits only the Treasury of the parent company State, which will no longer need to credit any foreign withholding tax. Although the group pays less source tax in the subsidiary State, it pays the same amount extra in the parent State as corporation tax is not reduced any more by a foreign tax credit. From this point of view, it is rather surprising that in 1990 the PSD was adopted at all: there is very little reason for source states, less so where they themselves exempt incoming dividends, to waive their source tax claim if such waiver is not benefiting the foreign investor in any way, but instead effectively subsidizes the Treasury of the parent company State.

Directive 2014/86/EU introduced a specific anti-abuse rule (a linking rule), avoiding double non-taxation by requiring the parent company jurisdiction to disallow an exemption for deductible payments. Furthermore, Directive (EU) 2015/121 introduced a common, mandatory *minimum* anti-abuse rule in Directive 2011/96/EU. Until this amending

Directive, the anti-abuse provision in the Directive was probably superfluous. According to established CJEU case law, Member States already may counter abuse of rights and therefore deny EU law benefits to economic operators artificially arranging eligibility for benefits not intended for them by relying on EU law for purposes wholly alien to object and purpose of EU rule relied on. However, the new provision appeared to be superfluous as well, since the Danish cases clarified that, under the general principle of EU law that EU law cannot be relied on for abusive or fraudulent ends, Member States are already required to refuse a taxpayer the benefits under the PSD in abusive cases. It is expected that Directive shopping will be reduced significantly; even more so if the proposal for the Unshell Directive goes ahead.

In conclusion, one may say the Parent-Subsidiary Directive was a success. It was even too successful, as anti-abuse rules had to be included. It provides (much) easier access to the favourable features of other Member States' tax systems, including their tax treaties with third states, which promotes free movement of investment capital and the freedoms of (secondary) establishment and of capital, thus impelling Member States to be more tax-efficient and to compete with each other on tax policy as regards holding companies and head offices. The Court dealt a serious blow to tax efficiency competition by allowing parent company states an asymmetric choice under Article 4 of the Directive: the really simple exemption method for domestic subsidiary dividends and the cumbersome indirect credit method with onerous evidence requirements for cross-border dividends.

CHAPTER 17

The Tax Merger Directive

Peter Wattel

Update and elaboration by Frederik Boulogne[1]

17.1 Introduction; Objective; History

Cross-border restructuring operations, such as mergers and divisions, tend to trigger taxation of the unrealized capital gains and tax-free reserves among the assets transferred or the shares exchanged, and evaporation of the possibility to carry forward losses from previous tax years connected to the transferred business. For domestic mergers and divisions, Member States typically provide for a tax deferral: the carry-over – to the acquiring company or to the new shares – of the capital gains tax on the transferred assets and the tax-free reserves, or on the shares exchanged. Often also losses not yet exhausted may be carried over in the course of a domestic merger or division. Obviously, unfavourable tax treatment of cross-border mergers and divisions in comparison to domestic mergers and divisions is an impediment to the cross-border (re)grouping of (groups of) companies, and, therefore, to the proper functioning of the internal market.

In order to provide for equivalent tax deferral and carry-over rules for cross-border operations as for domestic operations, the Council adopted, on 23 July 1990, Directive 90/434/EEC 'on the common system of taxation applicable to mergers, divisions, transfers of assets and exchanges of shares concerning companies of different Member States' (the Tax Merger Directive).[2] The main objectives of the Directive were to take away the tax problems arising from the cross-border restructuring of companies from two or more Member States, while at the same time safeguarding the taxing rights of the Member States. After an amendment agreed upon in 2005 (see below), the Directive also addresses the tax problems arising from the cross-border migration of a European Company (SE) and a European Cooperative Society (SCE).[3] In 2009, the Directive was codified, *i.e.* the original text and the subsequent amendments were integrated into one single continuous text, the title of which now reads: 'Council Directive 2009/133/EC on the common system of taxation applicable to mergers, divisions, partial divisions, transfers of assets and exchanges of shares concerning companies of different Member States and to the transfer of the registered office of an SE or SCE between Member States (codified version).'[4]

1 International Tax Partner, BDO; Lecturer, University of Amsterdam.
2 O.J. No. L 225 of 20 August 1990, p. 1.
3 Implementation of the amendment as regards the SE and SCE was required by 1 January 2006. The SCE Statute did not apply, however, before 18 August 2006.
4 O.J. 2009, No. L 310 of 25 November 2009, p. 34-46.

To avoid confusion, it should be noted there are two other Directives which are sometimes also referred to as 'the' Merger Directive. These are the codified Third company law Directive on the protection of stakeholders in *domestic* mergers,[5] which contains no tax provisions and does not address cross-border operations, and the Tenth company law Directive 2005/56/EC on *cross-border* mergers of limited liability companies of different Member States,[6] which does not contain any tax provisions either (because they are in the Tax Merger Directive). It is noted that cross-border mergers are also covered by Directive (EU) 2019/2121 on cross-border conversions, mergers and divisions.[7]

The Tax Merger Directive has a limited scope, even after the 2005 amendment. It only deals with the immediate (*ad hoc*) tax problems of mergers and divisions of companies of different Member States, *i.e.* the tax liability arising at the moment of the merger proper (see Section 17.2).[8] Long-term (recurrent) tax problems of the intra-EU (re)grouping of companies are not addressed, because tackling these would necessarily involve a certain measure of harmonization of Member States' systems of taxation of distributed company profits. Furthermore, the chosen route of minimum harmonisation will never fully lead to the envisaged common tax system for cross-border restructuring. In that regard, it does not help that certain tax aspects of cross-border restructuring, such as cross-border transfers of assets and of corporate residence, are also covered by the Anti-Tax Avoidance Directive (exit taxation, Article 5), see Section 12.4.2. A single cross-border restructuring tax directive would have been preferable.

The Directive provides for a common system of deferral of taxation of capital gains and tax-free reserves on the occasion of a cross-border merger, division, transfer of assets, or exchange of shares, and since the 2005 amendment, also of a cross-border seat transfer of an SE or SCE. The EU legislator did not just impose an obligation on Member States to extend national tax facilities for domestic mergers to cross-border operations, because, as the Preamble to the Directive states: 'differences between the systems presently in force in the Member States tend to produce distortions.' A simple extension of national deferral systems to cross-border operations would thus not achieve the result desired,

5 Directive 2011/35/EU of the European Parliament and of the Council of 5 April 2011 concerning mergers of public limited liability companies, O.J. No. L 110/1 of 29 April 2011 (codification of the original Directive of 9 October 1978, O.J. No. L 295 of 20 October 1978, and subsequent amendments).

6 Directive 2005/56/EC of the European Parliament and of the Council of 26 October 2005 on cross-border mergers of limited liability companies, O.J. L 310 of 25 November 2005, p. 1-9.

7 Directive (EU) 2019/2121 of the European Parliament and of the Council of 27 November 2019 amending Directive (EU) 2017/1132 as regards cross-border conversions, mergers and divisions, O.J. No. L 321/1 of 12 December 2019, p. 1-44.

8 This limited scope was clarified once more in Case C-438/18 (*Galeria Parque Nascente-Exploração de Espaços Comerciais SA*), [2019] EU:C:2019:619, in which the CJEU only needed an Order to rule that the Tax Merger Directive does not preclude national legislation, such as that at issue in the main proceedings, which leads to a situation whereby costs which were considered tax deductible for the acquired company before the merger of the companies concerned, and which would have been tax deductible if that merger had not taken place, are not considered tax deductible for the acquiring company. Similar Case C-751/18 (Totalmédia), [2019] EU:C:2019:748, was also decided by an Order.

and as the CJEU's case law has shown, such extension would already be achieved under the EU fundamental freedoms. A common system at EU level was needed.

The Directive concerns itself only with cross-border operations (Art. 1). Transactions and seat transfers within one Member State are not covered, not even if transnational elements such as a foreign branch or foreign shareholders are involved (see Section 17.11).

It took more than 20 years for the Directive proposal to be adopted. The Commission submitted its first proposal to the Council in 1969. The adopted version was toned down considerably in comparison to the initial far-reaching proposal.[9] It should be noted in particular that the Directive does not grant relief or deferral for transfer taxes upon the transfer of immovable property from one company to another in exchange for shares in that other company, not even if the immovable property is part of an entire undertaking being transferred (see the discussion of the *Zwijnenburg* case in Section 17.12.1).

The accession of ten new Member States in May 2004, two new Member States in January 2007 and Croatia's accession in July 2013 brought no changes, except the addition of their corporate taxes on the list in Annex I, Part B, and the addition of their designated legal forms on the list in Annex I, Part A. No transitional provisions were included for the new Member States.

The amending Directive 2005/19/EC of February 2005[10] substantially widened the personal scope of the Directive and clarified several other issues. The most important substantive changes in 2005 were the following:
- the SE and the SCE were included on the list of eligible entities (Art. 3(a) and Annex I, Part A, to the Directive; implementation by 1 January 2006);
- many national legal forms previously not qualifying were included on the list of eligible entities, especially cooperative, mutual and non capital-based companies, savings banks and commercial funds and associations (Art. 3(a) and Annex I, Part B, to the Directive; implementation by 1 January 2007);
- addition of two new operations: the partial division of a company (split-off; implementation 1 January 2007) and the cross-border transfer of the seat of an SE or SCE (implementation 1 January 2006);
- provisions were included addressing the case where a Member State considers a non-resident company or a shareholder involved in a qualifying operation as transparent for tax purposes (Arts. 4(3), 8(3) and 11; implementation 1 January 2007); and
- clarification that the incorporation of a foreign branch into a local subsidiary qualifies under the Directive (Art. 10(1)(last sentence); implementation 1 January 2007).

9 See Servaas van Thiel, Christine Ratträ and Michael Meër, 'Corporate Income Taxation and the Internal Market without Frontiers: Adoption of the Merger and Parent-Subsidiary Directives,' 30 *European Taxation* 11 (1990), p. 326; and Barry Larking, 'The Merger Directive: Will it Work?', 30 *European Taxation* 12 (1990), p. 362.

10 Council Directive 2005/19/EC of 17 February 2005 amending Directive 90/434/EEC 1990 on the common system of taxation applicable to mergers, divisions, transfers of assets and exchanges of shares concerning companies of different Member States, O.J. L 58 of 4 March 2005, p. 19-27.

The amendment did not address tax consequences of the migration of other companies than SEs or SCEs. It does not address tax residence of companies either, not even for the SE and SCE. As the preamble to the 2005 amendment matter-of-factly states:

> '6. (...) The tax residence of the SE or SCE continues to be determined by national legislation and tax treaties.
> 7. (....) Having regard to the obligation on Member States under the EC Treaty to take all necessary measures to abolish double taxation, it is not necessary at this stage to establish common rules governing the tax residence of the SE or SCE.'

We observe that the 'obligation under the EC Treaty to (...) abolish double taxation' referred to (apparently Article 293 of the former EC Treaty) had no direct effect,[11] and that Article 293 of the former EC Treaty was deleted from the TFEU (see Section 8.3).

Although the Directive applies only to intra-EU operations, the question rises whether the Right of Establishment laid down in Article 31 of the EEA Agreement implies that also comparable operations involving comparable companies from Norway, Liechtenstein or Iceland should receive similar tax treatment. In the case *Veronsaajien oikeudenvalvontayksikkö v A Oy*[12] the Finnish-resident company A Oy exchanged its shares in another Finnish-resident company, C Oy, for shares in a Norwegian-resident company B. A Oy was not entitled to carry-over relief under the Finnish implementation of the Tax Merger Directive as the requirement that 'companies from two or more Member States' are involved, was not met. The CJEU held that the Finnish legislation violated the right of establishment in Article 31 of the EEA Agreement as a purely Finnish exchange of shares would have qualified. The CJEU held that A Oy should receive equal treatment under the right of establishment, but observed that this "does not lead to an extension of the scope of Directive 2009/133 to companies established in a third country that is party to the EEA Agreement".[13]

It remains to be seen whether the Commission's BEFIT framework,[14] which was presented in 2023 and replaces the proposal for a CCCTB (see Chapter 25), entails comprehensive provisions that make the Tax Merger Directive provisions superfluous for certain operations within a group of companies within the scope of BEFIT and/or their shareholders.

17.2 Ad Hoc Tax Problems of Mergers and Divisions

One of the immediate (one-off) tax problems dealt with by the Directive is the realization – for taxation purposes – of capital gains, although in economic reality, there is no cash realization yet, but just substitution of assets or shares for (other) shares. To illustrate this for, *e.g.*, a transfer of assets (contribution of assets): where company A transfers a branch

11 See Case C-336/96 (*Gilly*), [1998] ECR I-02793, EU:C:1998:221.
12 Case C-48/11 (*Veronsaajien oikeudenvalvontayksikkö v A Oy*), [2012] EU:C:2012:485. See for a comment: Marjaana Helminen: Must EU Merger Directive Benefits Be Made Available where EEA States Are Involved?', *European Taxation*, May 2011, p. 179-183.
13 Case C-48/11 (*Veronsaajien oikeudenvalvontayksikkö v A Oy*), [2012] EU:C:2012:485 (para. 28).
14 See the Proposal for a COUNCIL DIRECTIVE on Business in Europe: Framework for Income Taxation (BEFIT), Strasbourg, 12 September 2023, COM(2023) 532 final 2023/0321(CNS).

of activity (*e.g.* a factory) to a company B, resident in another Member State, in exchange for shares in company B, company A must in principle pay tax on the difference between the market value and the book value of the factory transferred. Company A may not be able to pay such tax, as in return for the factory it only received shares in company B, not cash. Furthermore, upon alienating its factory assets (which of course remain in Member State A), company A will have to wind up any tax-exempt reserves it carried in respect of those assets. This means having yet to pay corporation tax on them. In her Opinion in Case C-292/16, *A Oy* (which is discussed in Section 17.10), A-G Kokott wrote that "the transfer in consideration of the grant of company shares is precisely not a genuine realisation of the value of the permanent establishment by way of sale but merely a restructuring measure" (para. 40). Finally, possible losses from previous years connected to the factory activity and not yet exhausted, cannot be carried over to the acquiring foreign company, and therefore cannot be used any more to set off against future profits.

For a shareholder involved in an exchange of shares, merger or division, similar immediate tax problems arise: for taxation purposes, a shareholder exchanging his shares in company X for newly issued shares in a foreign company Y which acquires the shares in company X (or legally absorbs company X), realizes a capital gain on his shares in company X. He may not be able to pay the capital gains tax due, since he did not receive any cash in return, but only shares in company Y.

17.3 Operations Covered and Definitions (Art. 2)

17.3.1 Operations Covered (Art. 2(a-e) and (k))

(a) Merger

One or more companies transfer all of their assets and liabilities to another company. The transferring companies are dissolved without entering into liquidation. They legally 'disappear'. The receiving company is the legal successor of the disappearing companies, issuing shares to the (former) shareholders in the disappearing companies, in exchange for their shares in the disappearing companies (paper for paper). There are three subtypes of a merger:

i. one or more existing companies merge into another existing company;
ii. two or more existing companies merge into a company newly formed by them especially for that purpose;[15] or
iii. a wholly owned subsidiary collapses into its parent company.

(b) Division

An existing company transfers all of its assets and liabilities to two or more newly incorporated or existing companies, which become its legal successors. The transferring company ceases to exist. It is dissolved without going into liquidation. In return for the assets and liabilities received, the receiving companies issue shares to the (former) shareholders in the disappearing company (paper for paper). Although Article 2(a) and (b) require an 'issue' of shares by the receiving company in order for a merger and a division to qualify

15 This kind of merger is envisaged as a vehicle for the formation of an SE (European Company). See below in this Section, and Sections 9.4. and 9.5.

under the Directive, thereby suggesting that the issuing of *new* shares is required, a transfer of assets and liabilities would also seem to qualify if the receiving company (or its parent company) transfers *existing* shares it holds in itself to the shareholders of the transferring company. Curiously the definition of 'transfer of assets' in Article 2(c) (see below) requires the 'transfer' rather than the 'issue' of shares. The 'issue' requirement seems unnecessarily restrictive in situations in which, for instance, the shareholders of the transferring company already hold all shares in the receiving company (in same proportion) or if a transferring company transfers a branch of activity to its wholly owned subsidiary.

(c) Partial Division[16]

An existing company, without being dissolved, transfers (splits off) one or more branches of its activity to one or more other new or existing companies in exchange for shares to be issued by the receiving companies to the *shareholders* of the transferring companies (*not* to the transferring company itself; that would be a drop-down division, which is not covered by this provision, but by category (d): transfer of assets).

(d) Transfer of Assets

An existing company (A) transfers one or more branches of its activity to another existing or newly incorporated company (B), in consideration for which B issues shares to A. As a result, B partially becomes a subsidiary of A.

The term 'transfer of assets' is somewhat misleading, since a transfer of unrelated assets does not qualify: the transfer of one or more 'branches of activity' is required. 'Transfer of branch(es)' would have been a more apt term.

Case C-43/00, *Andersen og Jensen*,[17] (see Section 17.3.2) shows that a branch transfer does not qualify if the transfer is structured in such a way that essentially, the transfer is not against shares, but against cash. The case concerned a transferring company taking out a very significant loan, and transferring to the receiving company not only its business, but also the obligations arising from that loan, while the proceeds of the loan (the principal) remained with the transferring company. What in economic reality thus happened, was that the receiving company took out the loan and bought with the money borrowed the business of the transferring company. The capital gains and the tax-free reserves in the business are in fact realized for cash. Allowing the Directive benefits would be inappropriate, therefore.

(e) Exchange of Shares

A company (A) acquires a holding in another existing company (B; the target/acquired company) such that it obtains a voting majority in company B (takeover). The acquiring company A 'pays' for the acquired shares B by issuing securities (shares) representing its own capital to the (former) B shareholders (paper for paper). As a result, the target/acquired company becomes a subsidiary of the acquiring company. The tax deferral provided for does not only apply to the one share exchanged which tips the balance from

16 Added by the 2005 amendment; implementation 1 January 2007.

17 Case C-43/00 (*Andersen og Jensen ApS v. Skatteministeriet*), [2002] ECR I-379, EU:C:2002:15.

a minority holding (49.999%) to a voting control (50.001%), but to the entire exchange, provided it results in a voting majority in the target company. A series of connected B share acquisitions from different shareholders (*e.g.* acquisition through a public takeover bid) also qualifies, as well as the increase of a 51% holding to a 75% or a 100% holding. The 2005 amendment confirmed this by adding '... or, holding such a majority, acquires a further holding, ...' to the text of Article 2(e).

(f) Transfer of the Registered Office of an SE or SCE[18]
This one is the odd one out, as it has no relation with merging or dividing, but only with corporate migration: an SE or an SCE, without winding up or creating a new legal person, transfers its registered office from one Member State to another. Such transfer is provided for by Article 8 of the SE Regulation[19] and by Article 7 of the SCE Regulation.[20] Since the SE and SCE Regulations require the effective management ('head office') of an SE or SCE to be located in the Member State of its registered office,[21] the transfer of the registered office necessarily also entails the transfer of the SE's or SCE's residence for tax purposes to the other Member State. It should be noted that the transfer of the registered office of an SE or SCE is not a transaction at all, but means the physical moving of the central management of the company to another Member State, and therefore in principle implies the SE/SCE turning from a resident taxpayer into a non-resident taxpayer or even a person no longer subject to tax in its State of departure.

17.3.2 'Branch of Activity' (Art. 2(j)); Independent Functioning

Operations (c) and (d) – partial divisions and transfers of assets – involve the transfer of one or more of a company's 'branches of activity.' It is unclear what the relevant distinction is between those operations and, for instance, mergers (covered by Article 2(a)), which do not have a 'branch of activity' requirement.

Article 2(j) defines a 'branch of activity' as:

> 'all the assets and liabilities of a division of a company which from an organisational point of view constitute an independent business, that is to say an entity capable of functioning by its own means.'

This autonomous definition does not ensure that a 'branch of activity' coincides completely with a 'permanent establishment' referred to in Article 4(1)(b) of the Directive, requiring a permanent establishment to remain in the State of the transferring company. As will be seen in Section 17.7.4., probably every 'branch of activity' is a 'permanent establishment', but not every permanent establishment is necessarily also a 'branch of activity' within the meaning of the Directive. The relationship between the 'branch of activity' requirement

18 Added by the 2005 amendment; implementation 1 January 2006.

19 Council Regulation 2157/2001/EC of 8 October 2001 on the Statute for a European company (SE), O.J. No. L 294, of 10/November 2001, p. 1-21, applicable as of 8 October 2004.

20 Council Regulation 1435/2003/EC of 22 July 2003 on the Statute for a European Cooperative Society (SCE). O.J. No. L 207, of 18 August 2003, p. 1-24, applicable as of 18 August 2006.

21 Article 7 of the SE Statute and Article 6 of the SCE Statute.

and the 'permanent establishment' requirement is ambiguous: if the objective is to differentiate between sustained restructuring operations and disguised disposals of assets, the 'permanent establishment' requirement would already be capable of doing that, obviating the 'branch of activity' requirement.

The definition does not clarify whether a 'branch' must be carrying on an active business (*e.g.* a production division or an automation department of a company), or may also be of a more passive nature (*e.g.* holding and control, portfolio investment). The term 'transfer of a branch of activity' also occurs in Directive 2008/7/EC on indirect taxes on the raising of capital.[22] In its judgment in Case C-164/90, *Muwi*,[23] the CJEU held that the mere 100% holding in another company does not qualify as a 'branch of activity' for capital duty purposes, but it is uncertain whether this judgment has any significance for transfers of assets under the Tax Merger Directive, which concerns corporate income tax. The CJEU's judgment in Case C-28/95, *Leur-Bloem* (see Section 17.12.2. ff), did not shed much light on the issue either. That case concerned the (limited) scope of the anti-abuse provision of Article 15 of the Directive (see Section 17.12.2. ff) and addressed the question of whether Member States may automatically disallow the Directive benefits to exchanges of shares involving a passive or 'empty' acquiring holding company. The answer was in the negative. The Court held (in respect of the acquiring company in an exchange of assets):

> '23 (...) A merger or a restructuring carried out in the form of an exchange of shares involving a newly created holding company which does not therefore have any business may be regarded as having been carried out for valid commercial reasons.'

Although, in our view, it follows from this judgment that in a transfer of assets or a partial division, the *receiving* company does not need to carry on an active business (it may be a newly incorporated – 'empty' – company), it does not answer the question whether the 'branch' which is transferred by the *transferring* company in a transfer of assets should be carrying on an active business itself.

Whatever the active or passive investment character of a 'branch of activity', it must be capable of functioning independently ('by its own means'). Case C-43/00, *Andersen og Jensen*,[24] shows that the capability of independent functioning of the transferred branch must be assessed primarily from a functional (organizational) point of view and only secondarily from a financial point of view:

> '(35) (...) the assets transferred must be able to operate as an independent undertaking without needing to have recourse, for that purpose, to additional investments or transfers of assets (...).'

22 Council Directive 2008/7/EC of 12 February 2008 concerning indirect taxes on the raising of capital, O.J. L 46, 21.2.2008, p. 11–22.

23 Case C-164/91 *(Muwi Bouwgroep BV v. Kingdom of The Netherlands)*, [1991] ECR I-6049, EU:C:1991:480.

24 Case C-43/00 *(Andersen og Jensen ApS v. Skatteministeriet)*, [2002] ECR I-379, EU:C:2002:15. See for a comment on the aspect of independence: Nikolaj Vinther and Erik Werlauff: 'Community Law and the Independent Business as Interpreted by the CJEU in *Andersen & Jensen ApS*', *European Taxation* October 2002, p. 441-445.

The case concerned a receiving company which for its future cash-flow needs took out a loan from a financial institution which required the shareholders of the receiving company to provide security for that loan by way of a lien on the entire share capital of the receiving company. Therefore, the receiving company, including the branch transferred to it, was entirely under the financial institution's control, at least financially. The Danish government argued that in these circumstances, the branch was unable to function independently. The Court, however, found that these circumstances were not, in themselves ('under normal market conditions') prohibitive, but that the situation might be different where the financial situation of the receiving company made it very probable that it would not be able to survive by its own means. Arguably, the functionally and financially independent functioning of the 'branch of activity' has to be judged autonomously, that is, regardless of the situation of the transferring or receiving company.[25]

17.3.3 *Coverage after the SEVIC, Cartesio and VALE Cases, the Implementation of the Amendment,[26] and the Company Law Directive on Cross-Border Mergers of Limited Liability Companies[27]*

Until 2006, not all the operations in Article 2 under (a) and (b) (mergers and divisions) were possible between companies of different Member States for lack of a company law framework. In most Member States, national company law did not provide for such operations, or even outright prohibited them. In that respect the Tax Merger Directive provided tax solutions for which there were no problems yet. Before 2005, the Tax Merger Directive virtually covered only four operations:

- the takeover of a State A company by a State B company issuing shares to the shareholders in A Company who exchange their shares in A for shares in B;
- the transfer of a domestic branch of activity (or of all activities) of a State A company to a State B company, the former A activities becoming a State A branch of the State B company, in exchange for shares B issued to company A;
- the transfer of a State B branch of a State A company to become a domestic branch of activity of a State B company, in exchange for shares B; and
- the transfer of a State B branch of a State A company to become a State B branch of a State C company, in exchange for shares C.

25 On the 'branch of activity' requirement, see Frederik Boulogne and Jan Gooijer, 'Merger Directive: Conceptual Clarity of the Term "Branch of Activity" Needed', *European Taxation*, 2013-5, p. 243-248.

26 See for comments on the 2005 amendments, a.o., Eva van den Brande: 'The Merger Directive Amended: the Final Version,' *EC Tax Review*, 2005-3, p. 119-127; Andreas Benecke and Arne Schnitger, 'Final Amendments to the Merger Directive: Avoidance of Economic Double Taxation and Application to Hybrid Entities, Two Conflicting Goals,' *Intertax*, 2005/4, P. 170-178; Raffaele Russo and René Offermanns, 'The 2005 Amendments to the EC Merger Directive,' *European Taxation*, June 2006, p. 250-257; and Massimiano Aurelio, 'An Analysis of the 2005 Amendments to the Merger Directive,' *Intertax*, 2006/6/7, P. 333-352.

27 Directive 2005/56/EC of the European Parliament and of the Council of 26 October 2005 on cross-border mergers of limited liability companies, O.J. L 310, 25.11.2005, p. 1-9.

Since then, Case law of the CJEU (especially Case C-411/03, *SEVIC System AG*[28] and Case C-210/06, *Cartesio*[29] and Case C-378/10, *VALE*[30]) and two pieces of secondary EU law also made cross-border mergers and divisions possible under company law.

Firstly, the *SEVIC* Case made clear that (i) a cross-border merger operation must be viewed as a mode of exercising the right of establishment of companies under Article 54 TFEU, (ii) refusing to register the merging of a foreign company into a domestic company in the national commercial register of companies on the same footing as the merging of two domestic companies is a restriction of that right of establishment, as such refusal impels foreign acquired companies – unlike domestic acquired companies – to be liquidated and re-incorporated under domestic company law despite the fact that their foreign law of incorporation permits them to merge into a domestic company, and (iii) such refusal to recognize a cross-border merger cannot be justified by relying on the needs to protect creditors, minority shareholders and employees, and to preserve the effectiveness of fiscal supervision and fairness of commercial transactions, as these in themselves legitimate interests can be served by less restrictive measures than categorical refusal (disproportionality). Several governments making observations pointed out to the Court that it was difficult to see what the, at the time, pending Tenth company law Directive on cross-border mergers was needed for if companies of different Member States could already effectuate cross-border mergers directly on the basis of the Treaty Right of establishment. The Court's reply implies that positive integration was overtaken by negative integration:

> '26 It should be noted (...) that, whilst Community harmonisation rules are useful for facilitating cross-border mergers, the existence of such harmonisation rules cannot be made a precondition for the implementation of the freedom of establishment laid down by Articles 43 EC and 48 EC (...).'

The *SEVIC* Case addressed the Member State of the absorbing company (in this case: Germany), not the State of the absorbed company (in this case, Luxembourg). Luxembourg company law allowed the merging of Luxembourg companies into a foreign legal form without liquidation and transfer of assets. Although the *SEVIC* Case implies that the State of the absorbing company must treat inbound cross-border mergers on the same footing as domestic mergers (supposing the law of incorporation of the acquired company permits absorption without liquidation), there is other case law implying that outbound mergers may still in many cases be restricted by the State of the company to be acquired. The Cases 81/87, *Daily Mail*,[31] C-208/00, *Überseering*,[32] and C-210/06, *Cartesio*, show that a Member State may, in certain circumstances, prohibit companies incorporated under its law to leave its jurisdiction: companies are creations of national law (except the SE and the SCE), and therefore, in the absence of any harmonisation at EU level, national law may also take away their legal existence if they cease to have their real seat within the

28 Case C-411/03 (*SEVIC Systems Aktiengesellschaft*), [2005] ECR I-10805, EU:C:2005:762.
29 Case C-210/06 (*Cartesio*), [2008] ECR I-9641, EU:C:2008:723.
30 Case C-378/10 (*VALE Építési kft*), [2012] EU:C:2012:440.
31 Case 81/87 *(Daily Mail and General Trust plc)*, [1988] ECR 5505, EU:C:1988:456.
32 Case C-208/00 *(Überseering)*, [2002] ECR I-9919, EU:C:2002:632.

jurisdiction which gave birth to them. On the basis of this reasoning, in *Daily Mail*, exit taxation upon corporate emigration was not considered incompatible with the freedom of establishment, as the UK might also have liquidated Daily Mail upon the transfer abroad of its seat. In *Cartesio*, the cessation of the legal existence of a legal person incorporated under Hungarian law (real seat system[33]) upon its emigration to Italy was accepted by the Court. The Court observed, however, that the freedom of establishment precluded Hungary from requiring Cartesio to dissolve and go into liquidation if Italian company law would allow it to transmute into a company under Italian law *without* dissolving and going into liquidation first.

In *VALE*,[34] an Italian-incorporated company sought to transfer its seat and business from Italy to Hungary and subsequently be governed by Hungarian law. The CJEU held that if Italian company law allowed VALE to leave its jurisdiction without being dissolved, Hungary could not, in principle, prevent that company from converting into an Hungarian company if it would meet all the requirements that would apply to a conversion of a domestic (Hungarian) company under Hungarian company law.[35] See Section 12.3 for further discussion of this issue in the context of exit taxation.

The *SEVIC*, *Cartesio* and *VALE* cases considerably increased possibilities for European business to effectuate cross-border mergers – and presumably also cross-border divisions – without having to wait for a specific EU legal framework. *Daily Mail*, *Überseering* and *Cartesio* imply, however, that the State of incorporation and seat of the company to be acquired, divided or split up may still, in many cases, prevent such operation to the extent that State is losing company law jurisdiction over its company.

Secondly, on 8 October 2004, the Statute for a European Company (*Societas Europaea;* SE) became applicable (see Chapter 20). This Statute, which consists of an SE Regulation[36] and an accompanying Directive on employee participation,[37] provides for the incorporation of an SE, *inter alia*, by way of a merger of two or more companies of different Member States. Therefore, since October 2004, the operation described in Article 2(a) is actually possible under company law throughout the EU. Thus, the Tax Merger Directive gained importance for cross-border corporate restructuring after the 2005 amendment including the SE and SCE.

Thirdly, 15 December 2007 was the last day of the period for implementation of the long-awaited Tenth company law Directive 2005/56/EC on the cross-border merger of

33 At least for partnerships endowed with legal personality, such as Cartesio.

34 Case C-378/10 (*VALE Építési kft*), [2012] EU:C:2012:440.

35 For an analysis of *VALE* and the related CJEU case law, see Zoe Adams and Simon Deakin, 'Freedom of Establishment and Regulatory Competition' in: Anthony Arnull and Damian Chalmers (eds.), *The Oxford Handbook of European Union Law*, Oxford University Press, Oxford, United Kingdom, 2015, p. 537-561.

36 Council Regulation 2157/2001/EC of 8 October 2001 on the Statute for a European company (SE), O.J. No. L 294, of 10 November 2001, p. 1-21.

37 Council Directive 2001/86/EC of 8 October 2001 supplementing the Statute for a European company with regard to the involvement of employees, O.J. No. L 294 of 10 November 2001, p. 22.

two or more national limited liability companies of different Member States.[38] Since then, a German *Aktiengesellschaft* and a British Limited Company can merge without having to resort to the legal form of an SE. Even a merger of a company of Member State A and a company of Member State B into a company of Member State C is possible if national law in State C allows. The scope of this company law Directive is limited, however, to limited liability companies, which makes its personal scope much narrower than the scope of the Tax Merger Directive, certainly after its 2005 amendment, when all kinds of other national legal forms were included.

On 1 January 2020, Directive (EU) 2019/2121 of the European Parliament and of the Council of 27 November 2019 amending Directive (EU) 2017/1132 entered into force,[39] which provides a legal framework for cross-border mergers, divisions and conversions of limited liability companies that should be implemented by the Member States.

We are still awaiting the adoption of the 14th company law Directive on the cross-border transfer of the registered office of limited companies. The last step in that process we are aware of, was a public consultation that ended in April 2013.[40]

The conclusion may be that at long last, company law more or less caught up with tax law.

For operations (still) not covered, see Section 17.11.

17.4 10% Additional Cash Pay-Out (Art. 2(a)-(c) and (e))

The value of a share in the transferring/acquired company will rarely precisely match the value of a share in the receiving/acquiring company. Moreover, it may prove difficult to agree on the exact terms of exchange in a merger, division, or exchange of shares, or to establish the correct amount of shares to be allotted in a split-off (partial division). Article 2(a)–(c) and (e) of the Directive therefore allows an additional cash payment to the (former) shareholders in the transferring, acquired or split off company, provided the payment does not exceed 10% of the nominal value (which is typically quite low compared to the real value) of the shares in the receiving/acquiring/split off company issued to these (former) shareholders. Thus, remaining differences in value can be compensated for in cash. Additional cash payments are allowed in a merger, a division, a share exchange, and a split-off, but not in a transfer of assets. For a contribution of assets to qualify under the Directive, the consideration for the transferred branch(es) of activity may solely consist of 'securities representing the capital of the receiving company' as no shareholders of the companies involved are affected (a transfer of assets is an operation between two companies). Therefore, there is no exchange ratio between 'old' and 'new' shares at issue.

38 Directive 2005/56/EC of the European Parliament and of the Council of 26 October 2005 on cross-border mergers of limited liability companies, O.J. L 310 of 25 November 2005, p. 1-9.

39 Directive (EU) 2019/2121 of the European Parliament and of the Council of 27 November 2019 amending Directive (EU) 2017/1132 as regards cross-border conversions, mergers and divisions (Text with EEA relevance), O.J. L 321/1 of 27 November 2019, p. 1-44.

40 http://ec.europa.eu/internal_market/consultations/2013/seat-transfer/index_en.htm.

Unlike the consideration in the form of shares, the additional cash payment may be taxed immediately (see Section 17.9), as there is no need for deferral. The cash has been received, and can therefore be used to pay the tax on it.

The Directive does not specify whether the additional cash must be divided proportionally among the shareholders.[41] If an unequal distribution is allowed (provided the total amount of cash remains below 10% of the nominal value of the shares issued), the cash could be used to buy out an unwelcome minority shareholder of the transferring/acquired company.[42]

In Case C-321/05, *Kofoed*[43] (see also Section 17.12.1 below), the CJEU explained that 'cash payment' in Article 2(e) – and therefore, we submit, also in Article 2(b), (c) and (e) – covers:

> 'monetary payments having the characteristics of genuine consideration for the acquisition, namely payments agreed upon in a binding manner in addition to the allotment of securities representing the share capital of the acquiring company, irrespective of any reasons underlying the acquisition.'

The case concerned a Danish company *Cosmopolit*, wholly-owned by two individuals, Kofoed and Toft, who acquired the shares in an Irish company *Dooralong* for 1 Irish pound (IEP) per person, and subsequently exchanged all their shares in *Cosmopolit* for newly issued shares in *Dooralong*. Finally, they made *Cosmopolit* declare and pay a dividend of 2.7 million IEP to *Dooralong* and made *Dooralong* two days later declare and pay to them the same amount of dividend. The Danish tax administration took the view that this was an abusive operation to avoid income tax on what in substance was either a capital gain by Kofoed and Toft on their *Cosmopolit* shares, or a profit distribution by *Cosmopolit* to Kofoed and Toft. According to the Danish tax administration, the shares in *Cosmopolit* were in economic reality not exchanged for shares in *Dooralong*, but for cash. Kofoed and Toft were therefore denied the tax deferral provided for in the Directive. The CJEU held, however, that the dividend payment did have the character of binding consideration and was, therefore, not an excessive 'cash payment' within the meaning of Article 2(e):

> '31. (...), a monetary payment made by an acquiring company to the shareholders of the acquired company cannot be classified as a "cash payment" for the purposes of Article 2(d) [now 2(e); *authors*] of Directive 90/434 merely because of a certain temporal or other type of link to the acquisition, or possible fraudulent intent. On the contrary, it is necessary to ascertain in each case, having regard to the circumstances as a whole, whether the payment in question has the characteristics of binding consideration for the acquisition.
> 32. That interpretation is supported by the purpose behind Directive 90/434, which is to eliminate fiscal barriers to cross-border restructuring of undertakings, by ensuring that any increases in the value of shares are not taxed before they are actually realised and by preventing operations involving high levels of capital gains realised on exchanges of shares from being exempt from income tax simply because they are part of a restructuring operation.

41 See Peter H. Schonewille, 'Some Questions on the Parent-Subsidiary Directive and the Merger Directive', *Intertax* 1992/1, p. 18-19.

42 This could trigger legal objections, e.g. that instead a squeeze-out procedure must be used to achieve this.

43 Case C-321/05 *(Hans Markus Kofoed v. Skatteministeriet)*, [2007] ECR I-5795, EU:C:2007:408.

> 33. The Court finds that, (...), there is nothing in the case-file demonstrating that the dividend in question formed an integral part of the necessary consideration to be paid by Dooralong for the acquisition of Cosmopolit, which is the necessary condition for it to qualify as a "cash payment" within the terms of Article 2(d) [now 2(e); *authors*] of Directive 90/434. On the contrary, according to the national court, it is common ground that at no time was there any agreement between Mr Kofoed and Mr Toft, on the one hand, and Dooralong, on the other, by which the latter was bound to distribute that dividend.
> 34. In those circumstances, the dividend in question in the main proceedings cannot be included in the calculation of the "cash payment" provided for in Article 2(d) [now 2(e); *authors*] of Directive 90/434.'

This did not mean, however, that the Danish tax administration was precluded from pleading abuse of law. The Court referred to the national Court in order to establish whether Danish national rules on abuse of (tax) law could be interpreted in accordance with the anti-abuse provision of Article 15 of the Directive such that the Directive benefits could be denied to Kofoed. See Section 17.12.1 below.

17.5 Gist and System of the Directive

The essence of the Tax Merger Directive is deferral of tax liability at the time of the operation to a moment of actual realization, by way of a carry-over of the tax value of (i) the assets and liabilities transferred, and (ii) the shares exchanged. The Directive requires Member States to refrain from taxing any gains arising on the occasion of a qualifying cross-border operation, or an SE or SCE migration or creation. Forbearance is no acquittance, so the deferral is made dependent on the securing of later taxation of the unrealized gains. Therefore, in a merger, a division and a transfer of assets, the assets and liabilities transferred must enter the (tax) accounts of the receiving company at the same tax value assigned to them in the transferring company's accounts immediately prior to the transfer. Where the receiving company later disposes of the assets transferred, tax will be levied on that occasion on the difference between the disposition price and the pre-merger book value.[44] Similarly, a person exchanging his shares in a company for shares in another company, in the course of a merger, (partial) division or transfer of assets, will not be taxed on the capital gain at the time of the exchange, provided the same tax value is attributed to the substituting shares as to the substituted shares immediately prior to the substitution.

In the *Marc Jacob* and *Marc Lassus* cases (C-327/16 and C-421/16) the CJEU approved the French 'technique' of establishing a capital gain at the time of an exchange of shares, while deferring the chargeable event for the taxation of that capital gain until the year in which an event putting an end to the deferral of taxation occurs (e.g. the shareholder subsequently sells the shares received).[45] The CJEU held that the purpose of fiscal neutrality

44 We note that, despite a carried-over tax value, a Member State which deferred taxation may not always be able to tax the gain at either company or shareholder level post-restructuring (for instance, the applicable tax treaty may change). This phenomenon does not seem to be appreciated in the Tax Merger Directive, although Article 8(6) suggests that a Member State may, in some situations, continue to invoke the previously applicable regime.

45 Cases C-327/16 and C-421/16 *(Marc Jacob and Marc Lassus)*, [2018] ECLI:EU:C:2018:210.

of an exchange of shares, expressed in Article 8 of the Tax Merger Directive, is not 'to avoid (...) a capital gain being taxed by the Member States with fiscal competence in respect of that gain, but only to prohibit them from considering that exchange as the chargeable event for the purposes of taxation.' (para. 40). Such a 'defer and pay' mechanism is similar to the mechanism the CJEU allowed in its individual exit tax case-law (notably the *N* Case (C-470/04); see Chapter 12).[46] In a certain way the CJEU thus seems to depart from the system envisaged under the Tax Merger Directive, which involves the carrying over of tax values and eventual taxation of the difference between the real values at the time of subsequent alienation and the carried-over balance-sheet values of the shareholding (if positive).[47]

The 2005 amendment added similar tax deferral and book value retention rules for the case of a transfer of the registered office of an SE/SCE from one Member State to another and for merger operations involving SEs or SCEs.

In a merger, a division, and a transfer of assets, the tax claim on the capital gain is connected to the *assets*, but is carried over to another *person* (the receiving company), whereas in an exchange of shares the tax claim on the capital gain remains with the same *person* (the shareholder), but is rolled over to other *shares* (the shares received in exchange). In the case of an SE or SCE transferring its effective management abroad, no assets are transferred, nor shares, but a resident taxpayer becomes a non-resident taxpayer in the departure State, from then on only subject to tax there for income sourced in the departure State (branch income), at the same time becoming resident and thus subject to unlimited tax liability in the State of entry.

It should be noted that the 'transfer' of assets and liabilities in a merger, a division, or an assets transfer entails only a transfer of ownership. It does not imply the physical moving of things. On the contrary: in principle, the assets and liabilities must remain where they are: in the Member State of the transferring company, constituting there a branch of the receiving company in the State of the transferring company (see Art. 4(1)(b) and Section 17.7). Otherwise the State of the transferring company would lose its jurisdiction for later taxation of the unrealized capital gains and tax-free reserves transferred together with the assets.

It should also be observed that an exchange of shares is a transaction between one company and the shareholders of the other company, whereas a transfer of assets (contribution of assets) is a transaction between two companies. Therefore, a transfer of assets does not have any shareholder income tax consequences (only Arts. 4, 5 and 6 of the Directive will apply, *via* Art. 9), whereas an exchange of shares may well involve individual shareholders, and therefore have consequences for individual income taxation (activating Art. 8).

46 Gutmann rightfully notes that the CJEU thus seems to read an implicit territoriality rule in Article 8 of the Tax Merger Directive (D. Gutmann, France: CJEU Recent Cases in: M. Lang et al (eds.) – Recent Developments in Direct Taxation 2018, Schriftenreihe IStR Band 114, Linde Verlag: Vienna, p. 69).

47 This point was re-confirmed by the CJEU in Cases C-662/18 and C-672/18 (*AQ and DN*), [2019] EU:C:2019:750.

The Directive, at least in its original framing, was drawn up very text-efficient, which did not add to easy readability. The system of substantive rules of the Directive is as follows:

Chapter II (Arts. 4–9) first sets the rules for deferral of tax and carry-over of unrealized gains, tax-free reserves and unused losses in case of a merger, a (partial) division and a transfer of assets, Articles 4–7 dealing with the companies involved and Article 8 with the shareholders involved. Article 9 subsequently provides that the rules for deferral and carry-over for the companies involved (Arts. 4–7) also apply to transfers of assets.

Chapter III contains just one Article (10), providing for the special case in which the assets transferred include a branch in a Member State other than the State of the transferring company, and calls for similar tax deferral and carry-over of tax values and tax-free reserves (but not necessarily of unused losses; see 7.8.2 below).

Chapter IV, also containing just one Article (11), deals with so-called hybrid entities: it provides for the special case in which a company involved is considered fiscally transparent by the State of which it is not a resident.

Chapter V (Arts. 12–14) is the odd one out: it does not deal with any subject related to (de)merging, but addresses the cross-border transfer of the registered office of an SE or an SCE. The only reasons why it ended up in the Tax Merger Directive is that it lays down similar deferral and carry-over rules for both company taxation purposes (Arts. 12–13) and shareholder taxation purposes (Art. 14) as in the case of a merger operation.

Chapter VI contains an anti-abuse reservation in Art. 15.

The Directive's rules for mergers, (partial) divisions, transfers of assets and exchanges of shares apply to all companies listed in Annex I, Part A, including both national legal forms and the SE and the SCE, whereas the rules for the cross-border transfer of the registered office only apply to SEs and SCEs, not to companies incorporated under national law. We believe this to be a discrimination against national legal forms in comparison to the EU legal forms of the SE and the SCE. Probably, however, also the national legal forms may benefit from comparable deferral and carry-over rules, and even more radical (not just for a permanent establishment staying behind, but also for assets leaving the Member State's tax jurisdiction) on the basis of the freedom of establishment (Arts. 49 and 54 TFEU), as the requirement to pay tax upon the cross-border transfer of the seat of an undertaking (at which moment no gains are realized nor any income is derived) is an obvious impediment to such cross-border establishment in comparison to a domestic relocation of the seat of a company. In the case *National Grid Indus*,[48] the Court gave relocating companies a choice between (i) immediate payment of the amount of tax, which creates a cash-flow disadvantage for the company but frees it from the subsequent administrative burden of having to trace the transferred assets for years after emigration and to keep filing returns in the exit state, and (ii) deferred payment of the amount of tax, with interest in accordance with national legislation (which necessarily involves

48 Case C-371/10 (*National Grid Indus BV*), [2011] EU:C:2011:785.

an administrative burden for the company in connection with tracing the transferred assets), and the provision of security for payment (see Section 12.3 on exit taxation of companies). This case, as well as the subsequent *DMC* case[49] also seems to imply that if a national legal form transfers its seat to another Member State, it may not be taxed in respect of a branch remaining in the departure State as it retains its taxing rights.

The *Pelati* case[50] concerned a Slovenian rule providing that carry-over relief would only be granted if a request for authorization had been submitted at least 30 days before the envisaged date of the restructuring operation. The CJEU held that such formal procedural rules (which the Tax Merger Directive does not call for) are acceptable, provided they comply with the principles of *equivalence* (they are imposed for domestic and cross-border restructuring operations alike) and *effectiveness* (they do not make it 'excessively difficult' to exercise rights derived from the Tax Merger Directive (see Section 3.1.3).

17.6 Qualifying Companies (Art. 3)

For entitlement to the Directive benefits, Article 1(a) of the Tax Merger Directive requires 'companies from two or more Member States' to be involved. Article 3 of the Tax Merger Directive contains the same requirements for the status of 'company from a Member State' as those listed in Article 2 of the Parent-Subsidiary Directive. These requirements are:[51]

– *Legal Form*
The company must have one of the legal forms listed in Annex I, Part A, to the Directive. The 2005 amendment considerably broadened the personal scope and therefore considerably lengthened the list of entities in the Annex by including many new national legal forms, especially cooperative and mutual societies, savings banks and commercial funds and associations, and, of course, the SE and the SCE. The list requirement is applied strictly by the CJEU, as case C-247/08, *Gaz de France*,[52] shows as regards the (then still) unlisted French *Société par actions simplifiée* (see Section 6.3.1).

– *Fiscal Residence*
The company must, according to the tax law of a Member State, be a resident for tax purposes in that Member State. Moreover, the company may not, pursuant to a tax treaty with a non-Member State, be resident for tax purposes outside the Union. Dual-resident companies having both of their fiscal residences *within* the EU (in two different Member States) are not excluded, and neither are dual-resident companies having one tax residence within and one tax residence outside the EU if there is no tax treaty with the

49 Case C-164/12, (*DMC Beteiligungsgesellschaft mbH v Finanzamt Hamburg-Mitte*), [2014] EU:C:2014:20 (para. 57).

50 Case C-603/10 (*Pelati d.o.o. v Republika Slovenija*), [2012] EU:C:2012:639. In the *Euro Park Service* case, C-14/16 (*Euro Park Service v Ministre des finances et des comptes publics*) [2017] EU:C:2017:177, the CJEU held that a procedural requirement aimed at preventing tax abuse would still have to meet the proportionality requirements developed in the CJEU's case-law on Article 15 of the Tax Merger Directive, such as *Leur-Bloem* and *Foggia*. See Section 17.12.6.

51 See Section 6.3 for a more detailed discussion of the same requirements in the Parent-Subsidiary Directive.

52 Case C-247/08 (*Gaz de France - Berliner Investissement*), [2009] ECR I-9225, EU:C:2009:600.

third State involved, or if an applicable tax treaty with that third State does not consider the company resident outside the EU. In all of those cases, there is no need to exclude a dual resident, as it is fully taxable in its Member State of EU residence. If – in line with Article 4(3) of the OECD Model Convention 2017 – a tax treaty with a third country contains a MAP (mutual agreement procedure) as a corporate residence tie-breaker, the dual resident company involved should be considered to meet the 'fiscal residence' test in the Tax Merger Directive until it would be mutually agreed that its fiscal residence is in the third country.

– *Subject to a National Corporation Tax*
The company must be subject to one of the national corporation taxes listed in Annex I, Part B, to the Directive, without being exempt and without the possibility of an option: it must be regularly subject to tax. The consequence of transparency in the eyes of the other Member State involved are addressed separately in Articles 4(3), 8(3) and 11.

The Directive does not require these three conditions of Article 3 to be met within one and the same national tax jurisdiction.

No particular requirements apply to the shareholders exchanging their shares in an exchange of shares or a merger/division operation. They may be individuals, partnerships, corporations or non-taxable entities. They may be resident outside the EU or dual resident.

The *Wereldhave Belgium* case,[53] specifically concerned the interpretation of the 'subject to tax' requirement. The CJEU held that its wording excludes companies which, despite being subject to tax, are not in fact liable to pay tax. A zero percent corporate income tax rate for Dutch 'fiscal investment institutions' is tantamount to not subjecting those companies to tax, according to the CJEU. We believe this reasoning would also apply to the 'subject to tax' requirement in the Tax Merger Directive, although its objective is different; granting benefits to a company that is *de facto* not paying taxes is not logical in light of the objective of a directive that seeks to avoid economic double taxation (the Parent-Subsidiary Directive), but could make sense in light of a directive with a broader purport (the Tax Merger Directive). We observe, for that matter, that the *Wereldhave* judgment may be criticized for ignoring the fact (which *was* recognized by the Court in the *Orange European Smallcap* Case[54]) that the Netherlands 'fiscal investment institution' is only subject to a nil percent rate in order to achieve the same effect as fiscal transparency (it must redistribute its income within eight months or it will lose its status and therefore its nil rate). The Court did not look at the tax position of the shareholders of the investment institution, who will be taxed on the redistribution received from the investment institution. Therefore, the effect of the *Wereldhave* judgment is that the economic double taxation which the Parent-Subsidiary Directive seeks to prevent or the immediate taxation as a result of restructuring operation (in the case of the Tax Merger Directive) persists.

53 Case C-448/15 (*Belgische Staat v Wereldhave Belgium Comm. VA and Others*), [2017] EU:C:2017:180.
54 Case C-194/06 (*Orange European Smallcap*), [2008] ECR I-03747, EU:C:2008:289.

17.7 Taxation of the Companies Involved

17.7.1 Deferral of Capital Gains Tax and Carry-Over of Tax Values (Arts. 4, 9 and 11)

Article 4 (for cross-border mergers and (partial) divisions) and Article 9 (for cross-border transfers of assets) provide that these operations shall not give rise to any taxation of capital gains if, and to the extent that, the assets and liabilities transferred remain effectively connected with a permanent establishment (p.e.) in the State of their fiscal location before the operation. The p.e. requirement ensures that the State within whose jurisdiction the unrealized gains have accrued, retains jurisdiction over the assets to which the unrealized gains attach (see Section 17.7.4 below). Likewise, Article 12 provides that the cross-border seat transfer of an SE or an SCE shall not give rise to taxation of profits, income or capital gains derived from the assets and liabilities which remain effectively connected with a branch (p.e.) of the SE/SCE in the jurisdiction of departure. Articles 4(4) and 12(2) make the tax deferral conditional upon the receiving/migrating company retaining the previous tax values and the previous depreciation method for the assets and liabilities involved. If, under national tax law, the receiving/migrating company may opt for a step-up in tax value (current value, 'mark-to-market') and exercises that option, then the deferral obviously does not apply to the assets and liabilities for which such option is exercised (Art. 4(5) *juncto* Art. 9, and Art. 12(3)). This implies that if domestic legislation permits, a company involved in a qualifying transfrontier operation may elect not to defer taxation of the capital gains ensuing from the operation (for instance, when it has unexhausted losses), but to pay the tax claim currently, and, consequently, entitle the receiving company to a correspondingly higher tax value and depreciation basis for the assets involved.

In the *3D I Srl* case, the CJEU held that the Directive allows Member States to make deferral of taxation conditional upon the transferring company carrying over in its own balance sheet a special reserve fund equal to the unrealized capital gain on the shares exchanged, as this would only lead to *future* taxation of that capital gain (outside the Tax Merger Directive's scope) instead of *current/immediate* taxation of it (within the Tax Merger Directive's scope).[55]

17.7.2 Carry-Over of Losses Connected to the Remaining Branch (Arts. 6 and 13(2))[56]

If for domestic mergers, divisions and assets transfers national law allows unused losses connected to the transferred branch(es) of activity to be carried over to the receiving company to be offset there, such carry-over must also be available for the equivalent cross-border operation covered by the Directive (Art. 6 *juncto* Art. 9). Similarly, Article 13(2) requires the departure State of a migrating SE or SCE to allow the remaining branch in its jurisdiction to offset the unused losses of the SE/SCE if it would allow such offset in a comparable domestic operation. We observe that if the receiving or migrating

55 Case C-207/11 (*3D I srl v Agenzia delle Entrate – Ufficio di Cremona*), EU:C:2012:818.

56 See Frederik Boulogne, 'A Proposal to Expand and Improve Art. 6 of the EU Merger Directive', *Intertax*, February (2014), pp. 70-91 and I. Vande Velde, "How Does the CJEU's Case Law on Cross-Border Loss Relief Apply to Cross-Border Mergers and Divisions?", *EC Tax Review* 3 (2016), p. 132-145.

company is (or is becoming, respectively) a resident of a State applying the credit method for the prevention of international double taxation, this loss carry-over may not benefit the receiving/migrating company, since although the loss carry-over will reduce future taxable profits of the remaining permanent establishment in the State of the transferring company/ State of departure, and will therefore reduce tax exposure in that State. The effect of such reduction is a corresponding reduction of the foreign tax credit of the receiving/migrating company in the other State.[57] However, the loss carry-over may help to prevent an excess foreign tax credit position in that other State.

Outside the framework and the scope of the directive (as no branch remained behind in the Member State of the transferring company), the CJEU decided in the *A Oy* case that the freedom of establishment requires that a resident receiving company must be allowed to use not yet exhausted foreign losses of a nonresident transferring company if such use would be allowed in the case of a domestic merger, especially where the receiving company will *not* have, after the merger, a permanent establishment in the (former) State of residence of the transferring (former) company (in other words, those losses have become 'final' in the State of the transferring company: they will never be used there).[58] In the subsequent *Memira* case (Case C-607/17), which concerned a cross-border merger, the CJEU gave some more clarity on the application of the *Marks & Spencer* 'final' losses criteria in this context.[59] The *AURES* case suggests that the 'final losses' doctrine applicable to cross-border mergers in *A Oy* and *Memira* does not extend to an SE or SCE that transfers its registered office to another Member State: in such a case the Member State of arrival is not held to accept 'final' losses incurred in the Member State of departure.[60] See Section 18.7.

17.7.3 Carry-Over of Tax-free Provisions and Reserves (Arts. 5 and 13(1))

The State of the transferring company and the departure State of a migrating SE/SCE, must refrain from recapturing (winding up and taxing) tax-free provisions or reserves formed by the transferring/migrating company in respect of assets or liabilities transferred to the receiving company, or – for migrating SEs and SCEs – in respect of the remaining branch in the State of departure. The State of the transferring company must allow a carry-over of these tax-free provisions or reserves to the (permanent establishment of the) receiving company, which may continue carrying them on the same footing (Art. 5 *juncto* Art. 9). Likewise, the State of departure of a migrating SE/SCE must allow the remaining branch in its territory to continue carrying the tax-free reserves in connection with that branch (Art. 13(1)).

57 Barry Larking, 'The Merger Directive: Will It Work?', 30 *European Taxation* 12 (1990), p. 366.

58 Case C-123/11 (*A Oy*), [2013] EU:C:2013:84.

59 For a discussion, see J.J. van den Broek, "Final Losses in Respect of Cross-Border Mergers: Memira (Case C-607/17) and Holmen (Case 608/17)", *European Taxation* 2/3 (2020), p. 53-61.

60 Case C-405/18 (*AURES Holdings a.s.*), [2020] EU:C:2020:127. For a discussion of this case and possible differences with *A Oy*/*Memira*, see M. Mittendorfer and M. Riedl, "The Comparability Analysis of the Court of Justice of the European Union in the Light of the Aures Case", *EC Tax Review* 4 [2021], p. 166-176.

An exception is made for provisions or reserves formed by the transferring/migrating company in connection with assets and liabilities of a foreign branch. As a result of the transfer, that foreign branch becomes a foreign branch of the receiving company, which is not a resident of the Member State of the transferring/migrating company and which thus cannot be subject to tax in that State if the assets of that foreign branch are later sold. For that reason, the State of the transferring company is allowed to recapture (wind up and tax) the tax-free reserves connected to the foreign branch at the moment immediately prior to losing its taxing power over that foreign branch, that is at the time of the merger operation, or of the migration of an SE/SCE to another jurisdiction, respectively.

17.7.4 Branch Requirement (Arts. 4(2)(b), 10(1), and 12(1)(b))

A collateral aim of the Directive is 'at the same time safeguarding the financial interests of the Member State of the transferring or acquired company.'[61] It is the condition under which the Directive benefits are made available. Hence Articles 4(2)(b) and 12(1)(b). The first provision makes the tax deferral and carry-over of tax values in a merger or (partial) division operation (and, via Article 9, also in a transfer of assets) conditional upon the transferred assets and liabilities remaining 'effectively connected with a permanent establishment of the receiving company in the Member State of the transferring company', and playing 'a part in generating the profits or losses taken into account for tax purposes.' Thus, the Directive benefits are available only to the extent the assets transferred amount to a permanent establishment (we use as identical the term 'branch') of the receiving company in the State of the transferring company. Similarly, Article 12 (1)(b) grants deferral and carry-over only in so far as the assets of a migrating SE or SCE remain effectively connected with a branch of the SE/SCE in the State of departure. The branch requirement ensures both jurisdiction for the source State and prevention of double taxation in the home State, as the presence of a branch is the connecting factor for source State taxing jurisdiction and for the home State obligation to prevent double taxation. Under international tax (treaty) law,[62] a State may only tax profits derived by non-residents if they are derived from carrying on a business through a permanent establishment (a branch) in that State. If the assets and liabilities transferred in a cross-border merger operation or owned by a migrating SE/SCE were not (part of) a branch in the State of the transferring company/the departure State, then that State would lose tax jurisdiction over them and would not be able to effectuate its taxing rights as regards the capital gains and fiscal reserves in the future.

Articles 4(2)(b) and 12(1)(b), therefore, are intended as claim savers, ensuring that future realization of the deferred capital gains/reserves will be part of the tax base allocated to the State of the transferring/acquired company, or the State of departure of the SE/SCE, respectively.

---

61 Recital 4 of the 1990 Preamble; recital 5 of the 2009 Preamble.

62 That is, until Pillar One becomes law, which would change the current distribution of profits and taxing rights under tax treaties for the largest companies.

The condition of a remaining branch makes it all the more clear, as does the 'branch of activity' requirement for a qualifying transfer of assets, that the mere transfer of single assets, disconnected from a business entity, is outside the scope of the Directive.

The Articles 4(2)(b), 10(1), and 12(1)(b) do not define the term 'permanent establishment,' nor do they refer for that purpose to national law, to the tax treaty in force between the Member States involved, or to the Parent-Subsidiary Directive or the Interest and Royalty Directive, which both do define the term 'permanent establishment' (see Sections 16.3.1(last heading) and Section 18.2.2.3). We submit that a 'branch of activity' as defined in Article 2(j) of the Directive should typically qualify as a permanent establishment within the meaning of Articles 4(2)(b) and 12(1). A 'branch of activity' is a business entity, from an organizational point of view independent and capable of functioning by its own means. This, in our view, amounts to a 'permanent establishment' as understood in the usual international tax law meaning, especially in view of the recent expansions of that definitions within the context of the OECD's BEPS Project. However, the exact relationship between the concepts of a 'branch of activity' and a 'permanent establishment' is nebulous. What qualifies as 'branch of activity' does not necessarily constitute a 'permanent establishment' and conversely, not every 'permanent establishment' qualifies as a 'branch of activity'. The CJEU, when called to interpret the term 'permanent establishment' in the Tax Merger Directive, will probably seek inspiration in the definition of that term in Article 1(2) of the Parent-Subsidiary Directive (see Section 16.3.1) and in Article 3(c) of the Interest & Royalty Directive (see Section 18.3.3), in the definition in Article 5 of the OECD Model Double Taxation Convention, and in the Official Commentary to that OECD Model, since all Member States use the authoritative OECD Model in their bilateral tax treaty negotiations.[63]

Articles 4(2)(b) and 12(1) do not specify for how long the assets/liabilities should remain effectively connected with the resulting permanent establishment, because once it has become part of the branch's assets for tax purposes, any asset can be taxed upon being withdrawn from the branch's balance sheet or the closing down of the branch. Likewise, the Directive does not preclude the State of the transferring company or the departure State from taxing a (deferred) capital gain on an asset if that asset leaves the jurisdiction of that State, for example to become part of a sub branch (a branch of a branch) in a third State (under certain conditions, Article 10 of the Tax Merger Directive explicitly allows such taxation).

As observed in Section 17.5, in *National Grid Indus*[64] and subsequent case-law the Court gave relocating companies (all companies, not just SEs and SCEs) a choice between first, immediate payment of the amount of tax, which creates a cash-flow disadvantage for the company but frees it from the subsequent administrative burden of having to trace the transferred assets for years after emigration and to keep filing returns in the exit

63 It is conceivable that similar to the "Danish" cases (a.o. Joined Cases C-115/16, C-118/16, C-119/16 and C-299/17 (*N Luxembourg 1 et al.*), [2019] EU:C:2019:134, par. 90-93, the CJEU will find a basis to resort for interpretation purposes to the definition of 'permanent establishment' in the OECD Model Convention and Commentary.

64 Case C-371/10 (*National Grid Indus BV*), [2011] ECR I-12273, EU:C:2011:785.

state, and, secondly, deferred payment of the amount of tax (with interest in accordance with national legislation), which necessarily involves an administrative burden for the company in connection with tracing the transferred assets (see Sections 19.4.2 and 12.3 on exit taxation). This means that for departure State taxation purposes, the emigrating company must maintain the balance sheet values it carried prior to its transfer of seat, and file a return every year in the departure State, and must pay tax to that State upon the later realization of the capital gains on the assets it owned in the departure State before emigration, in so far as attributable to the pre-emigration period, unless it opts for payment in installments (see Section 19.4.2).

On 23 May 2024 the Commission decided to refer Spain to the CJEU for failing to implement the Merger Directive. The Commission's complaint is that Spanish law sets restrictive conditions for total divisions of companies that are not provided for in the Merger Directive.[65]

17.7.5 Valuation of Shares Received

The Directive contains no rules on the question of which value the transferring company in a *transfer of assets* should assign to the shares issued to it by the receiving company. If the transferring company is required to enter the shares received in its tax accounts at the value the assets transferred had before their transfer (if it is not allowed to enter them in the books at their market value), then economic double taxation may occur. Indeed, both the receiving and transferring companies may later be taxed for effectively the same capital gain, the receiving company when disposing of the assets transferred, and the transferring company when disposing of the shares in the receiving company obtained in exchange for the assets transferred. The 1969 draft of the Directive included a provision addressing this problem of economic double taxation, but it was deleted in the final 1992 version, due to fear of the Member States it might be used for tax avoidance. Given the general anti-abuse clause of Article 15 of the Directive and the CJEU's general case law on abuse of rights, such fear does not seem justified. The Commission tried again in the proposal for the 2005 amendment, which added a new paragraph (2) to Article 9 providing that the transferring company would attribute to the shares received the market value of the assets transferred to the receiving company. On that part of the proposal, however, again no agreement was reached.

Likewise, the Directive does not lay down which value the acquiring company in an *exchange of shares* should attribute to the shares in the acquired company it obtained from the (former) shareholders in the acquired company. If it is not allowed to enter them at market value, then again economic double taxation may ensue, as the same capital gain may be taxed once in the hands of the former shareholders of the acquired company (at the moment they dispose of the shares they obtained in the acquiring company), and

65 According to the press release on https://ec.europa.eu/commission/presscorner/detail/en/ip_24_2667, Spanish law requires that after the total division of a company, shareholders of the divided company maintain the same proportion of shares in each of the companies which received the assets from the divided company, that they formerly had in the divided company. If this condition is not met, the Spanish rules require that the assets and liabilities transferred are branches of activity and therefore do not benefit from the tax regime.

again in the hands of the acquiring company (at the moment it disposes of its shares in the acquired company). The Commission tried to settle this issue as well in its proposal for the 2005 amendment, by adding a paragraph 10 to Article 8 providing that the acquiring company should attribute to the shares obtained the market value of the shares it issued in return. However, on that part of the proposal, no agreement was reached either.

The Court seems to have settled the issue in Case C-285/07, *A.T. AG*,[66] concerning the German company A.T. *AG*, which exchanged its 89.5% holding in the limited company C *GmbH* for a 1.47% shareholding in the acquiring French company G *SA*. German tax law made the benefit of Article 8 (tax deferral by preservation of tax value) for A.T. conditional upon the acquiring company G valuing the holding in C at the same value that holding had in the books of A.T. (the so-called double book value carry-over; *doppelte Buchwertverknüpfung*: the disposing shareholder could only preserve the old tax value – thus avoiding capital gains tax – if the acquiring company would also value the acquired holding at that old tax value). Germany argued that (i) as the Directive was silent on the issue, the matter was not harmonized and therefore national sovereignty, and (ii) such a measure was necessary to prevent circumvention of later taxation through the transfer of shares abroad, where the disposal of them would ultimately not be taxed at all. The Court rejected these arguments. The clear wording of Article 8 left no discretion for the Member States to make the required tax neutrality subject to additional unilateral conditions. That would also be contrary to the very objective of the directive (providing for a *common* system), and to its purpose (ensuring deferral of taxation until the moment the shares are eventually sold). As for the circumvention argument: referring to *Leur-Bloem* and *Kofoed*, the CJEU held that Article 15 does not allow predetermined general criteria for the prevention of abuse, but requires examination of each particular case. The mere fact that the acquiring company values the shares acquired at market value, is no evidence of any abuse, and at any rate, in the case at hand Germany had not demonstrated any abuse. Even if the German measure were (also) aimed at filling a gap in the taxation system left by the Union legislator, the Member States are not at liberty to unilaterally fill perceived gaps in a common system, as that would undermine the very idea of a common system, and anyway the Directive provides enough possibilities to secure taxation in individual cases, supposing that such gaps really exist. The Court even had difficulty in seeing any real interest for Germany in the *doppelte Buchwertverknüpfung* requirement, as Germany had to admit that (i) only the *French* treasury would benefit if the German measure would be applied, and (ii) the measure had already been repealed in the beginning of 2007.

Although *A.T. AG* concerned an exchange of shares, we submit the Court's findings also apply, *mutatis mutandis*, to transfers of assets: the national shareholding valuation rules may not be such as to cause current taxation of operations for which the Directive aims, precisely, to provide deferral, unless clear and present abuse is afoot.

66 Case C-285/07 (*A.T. AG v Finanzamt Stuttgart-Körperschaften*), [2008] ECR I-9329, EU:C:2008:705. See for a comment: C. Daiber: The ECJ's Decision in *A.T.* (etc.); *European Taxation* 7/2009, p. 364-368.

17.7.6 *Hybrid (Transparent) Entities*[67]

The 2005 amendment considerably extended the list of eligible national legal entities. Some of these entities, especially certain partnerships, although corporate taxpayers in their State of residence, may be considered as transparent for tax purposes by the Member State(s) of the participant/shareholder (hybrid entities). The amendment required the residence States of the participants to apply the Directive benefits to such hybrid entities. A new paragraph (3) was inserted in Article 4 (implementation 1 January 2007), providing that a Member State which considers a nonresident *transferring* company transparent for tax purposes and which therefore taxes the participants directly on their share in the hybrid's profits as they arise, must in principle refrain from taxing any unrealized capital gains on the assets transferred. However, these Member States retain the right to deny the Directive benefits to the direct or indirect shareholders in a non-resident hybrid: Article 11(1) allows Member States which consider a non-resident *transferring* company – or *acquired* company, in case of an exchange of shares – as fiscally transparent, to tax the participants within its jurisdiction directly for their share of the unrealized capital gains. In other words: the residence State of participants in a hybrid may opt out of the Directive. However, if it does, it must, according to Article 11(2), grant the participants relief (a tax credit) in the same amount as it would have done if the gains had actually been realized and tax had actually been paid on them in the residence State of the hybrid entity We understand the combination of Articles 4(3) and 11(1) and (2) as meaning that the residence State of the participants in a hybrid entity transferring its assets, or being acquired in an exchange of shares, is allowed to levy tax in the amount of the difference between the tax it would levy itself on the capital gain becoming visible in the operation, and the tax the hybrid's State would levy on that gain if the latter were not precluded from levying tax by the Directive.

If the *shareholder* exchanging its shareholding in a merger, (partial) division or exchange of shares is considered fiscally transparent by the residence State of its participants/ shareholders, then Article 8(3) prohibits that residence State to tax the unrealized capital gain on the exchange in the hands of the participants (the difference between the market value of the shares obtained by the hybrid and the book value of the shares it handed in).

Where the hybrid entity is not the *transferring* or *acquired* company, but the *receiving* company (in a merger or a (partial) division) or the *acquiring* company (in a share exchange), Article 11(3)-(4) provides that the residence State of its participants has the right to disapply Article 8(1)-(3), therefore to tax the allotment of shares to its participants. However, if it opts to do so, it must treat the nonresident hybrid as if it were a resident company; it may therefore not tax the allotment of shares to the participants more heavily than it would do if the operation were a domestic one. We believe that the Right of establishment and the Freedom of capital movement would already require equal treatment of cross-border and domestic operations unless an objective difference

67 See Gijs Fibbe and Ton Stevens, *Hybrid Entities and the EU Tax Directives*, Wolters Kluwer, Alphen aan den Rijn, the Netherlands, 2016.

in facts or a mandatory requirement of public interest warrants unfavourable treatment of the cross-border operation.

As the characterization of a foreign company as 'fiscally transparent' by the Member State taxing its shareholders/participants must be based on an 'assessment of the legal characteristics of that company arising from the law under which it is constituted,' fiscal criteria for such characterization appear to be irrelevant. The analysis must be based on civil (company and partnership) law. Thus, the *tax* regime applicable to the hybrid entity in its home State would not affect characterization as transparent or opaque by the residence State of the participant/shareholder. From the Explanatory Memorandum to the Commission proposal for the 2005 amendment it appears that the reference to the '*legal* characteristics' of the company was chosen purposely to avoid CFC[68] legislation issues. Under CFC legislation, the profits of a controlled foreign passive corporation are taxed in the hands of the domestic parent company as if that foreign corporation were not a legally separate entity, or as if it had distributed all of its profits, on the grounds that the parent company State considers the subsidiary's local tax regime low-tax and its activities devoid of substance (see Sections 19.4.3, 7.1 and 9.5).

17.8 Cancellation of Shares (Art. 7)

Article 7(2) aligns the Tax Merger Directive with the Parent-Subsidiary Directive. It is the only direct connection between the two Directives.[69] The receiving company in a merger may already hold shares in the transferring company prior to the merger, possibly even all of the shares (subsidiary collapsing into its parent). Upon merging, the shareholding already existing is cancelled, as the transferring company in a merger ceases to exist, and there is little point in the receiving company issuing new shares in itself to itself. Cancellation of shares entails a capital gain for tax purposes if the shareholding appeared on the parent company's balance sheet for a value below market of the assets and liabilities substituting for the cancelled shares. Article 7(1) of the Directive prohibits taxation of such gain triggered by the cancellation of a shareholding in the transferring already existing prior to the merger. However, the second paragraph of Article 7 revokes this prohibition if the receiving company's holding in the disappearing company's capital was below 10%.[70] The reason for this exception is the 10% minimum holding requirement in Article 3 of the Parent-Subsidiary Directive. A parent company may receive subsidiary profits through the distribution of subsidiary profits, but just as well through merging the subsidiary into the parent. If, as the Parent-Subsidiary Directive requires, Member States must exempt (or give indirect credit for) distributions of subsidiary profits at the parent company level, then they must also refrain from taxing the capital gain on the cancellation of the

68 CFC = controlled foreign corporation.

69 In the *Punch Graphix* case (Case C-371/11 (*Punch Graphix Prepress Belgium NV*), [2012] EU:C:2012:647, par. 30-37) the CJEU found sufficient links between the Parent-Subsidiary Directive and the Tax Merger Directive to consider the interpretation of the definition of 'merger' in the Tax Merger Directive relevant for interpretation of the term 'liquidation' in the Parent-Subsidiary Directive.

70 Until 1 January 2006 the percentage was 25%; between 1 January 2006 and 1 January 2007 it was 20%; between 1 January 2007 and 1 January 2009 it was 15%.

shareholding as a result of the merging of the subsidiary into the parent: that capital gain represents the profits which the subsidiary might just as well have distributed to the parent company.[71] However, Article 3 of the Parent-Subsidiary Directive allows the parent company State to tax profit distributions if the parent's holding in the subsidiary is smaller than 10%. This being so, it makes no sense to prevent the parent company State from taxing the capital gain in the course of the merging of a subsidiary, the holding in which was below that percentage prior to the merger, since that gain represents profits which would not have been exempted, had they been distributed.

It should be noted that in its attempt to achieve neutrality between taxation of distributed profits and taxation of capital gains, Article 7 seems to go further than the Parent-Subsidiary Directive by requiring an exemption from taxation of the capital gain on the cancellation of a holding larger than 10%, where Article 4 of the Parent-Subsidiary Directive allows the Member State of the parent company to tax distributed gains, provided it credits the underlying tax.

17.9 Taxation of the Shareholders Involved (Arts. 8, 11 and 14)

Article 8(1) of the Tax Merger Directive defers taxation in respect of capital gains on the shares handed in by shareholders, whether corporate or individual, in a cross-border merger, division, or exchange of shares. Since 1 January 2007, Article 8(2) also defers taxation on the allotment of shares issued in a cross-border partial division. Article 14 ensures, since 1 January 2006, that the cross-border transfer of the seat of an SE or SCE will not, of itself, lead to any taxation of the shareholders. Therefore, no corporate or individual income tax is due on the unrealized capital gain on the substituted shares or on the allotment of shares, nor on the unrealized capital gain on the shares in an SE or SCE transferring its registered office. Such gains will be taxed later, when the (substituting) shares in the acquiring/receiving, split off or migrating company are alienated by the shareholder (Articles 8(6) and 14(2)).

As mentioned above in paragraph 7.6, in the *Marc Jacob* and *Marc Lassus* cases (C-327/16 and C-421/16) the CJEU approved the French 'technique' of establishing a capital gain at the time of an exchange of shares, while deferring the chargeable event for the taxation of that capital gain until the year in which an event putting an end to the deferral of taxation occurs (e.g. the shareholder subsequently sells the shares received).[72] This technique is strictly speaking different from the carry-over technique under the Tax Merger Directive and more similar to the mechanism the CJEU allowed in its individual

71 In our view, this line of reasoning leads to the conclusion that capital gains on the alienation of the holding should be exempted from tax as well. The drafters of the Parent-Subsidiary Directive did not accept that consequence, however.

72 Cases C-327/16 and C-421/16 *(Marc Jacob and Marc Lassus)*, [2018] ECLI:EU:C:2018:210. This point was re-confirmed by the CJEU in Cases C-662/18 and C-672/18 (*AQ and DN*), [2019] EU:C:2019:750. The CJEU added that this even held true when France no longer had the fiscal competence to tax the subsequent gain (under the then applicable treaty). As in a purely domestic situation a value decrease could be taken into account, this was also required in this cross-border situation.

exit tax case-law (notably the *N* Case (C-470/04); see Chapter 20).[73] In the subsequent AQ and DN cases the CJEU held that a new (favourable) rule applying to the taxation of capital gains that was introduced later, could be applied to the deferred capital gain by essentially 'pretending' that the sale of shares in the acquiring company was a sale of shares in the acquired company.[74]

Article 8(4)-(5) contains similar tax value retention conditions for the tax deferral benefiting the shareholders as Article 4(4) contains for the tax deferral benefiting the companies involved in a merger/division or asset transfer: tax deferral is conditional upon the share-holder assigning to his new shares the same value for tax purposes as the old shares had for tax purposes, as such value carry-over enables the residence State of the shareholder to tax the capital gain in the future, upon the disposal of the substituting shares.

Apparently, some States made the benefits of Article 8 for transferring shareholders conditional upon the acquiring company assigning to the shares transferred to it the tax value these shares had in the hands of the transferring shareholders. As observed in Section 17.7.5, the Directive contains no rules on that valuation, which may lead to economic double taxation. As also observed, however, the CJEU decided, in Case C-285/07, *A.T. AG*, that object and purpose of the Directive do not allow of such a general condition, as it would jeopardize the goal of the Directive (deferral until realization).

The purpose of Article 14(1) is to prevent the Member State from which an SE or SCE emigrates, to tax its shareholders upon the emigration of the company. The emigration of a company does not involve any substitution, allotment or acquisition of shares – the shares remain the same in the same hands, and their value for tax purposes as well – but some Member States, such as Portugal, consider the emigration of a resident company as the realization of the capital gain in the shares, and tax both the company *and* the shareholders. In an infringement proceeding brought by the European Commission against Portugal, the CJEU found such taxation to be in breach of the fundamental freedoms.[75]

If national tax law allows the shareholder to opt for a step-up in the tax value of the shares received, and the shareholder so opts (the shareholder then pays tax on the unrealized capital gain currently), then obviously there is no deferral (Art. 8(8)).

For obvious reasons, taxation is not deferred on any additional cash payment (of up to 10% of the nominal value of the new shares) in the course of a merger or split-off (see Section 17.4). Article 8(9) expressly provides that the cash part of the transaction may be taxed immediately, the money needed to pay the tax being available.

73 Gutmann rightfully notes that the CJEU thus seems to read an implicit territoriality rule in Article 8 of the Merger Directive (D. Gutmann, France: CJEU Recent Cases in: M. Lang et al (eds.) – Recent Developments in Direct Taxation 2018, Schriftenreihe IStR Band 114, Linde Verlag: Vienna, p. 69).

74 For a critical analysis of this case, see the case-note by G.F. Boulogne in *Highlights & Insights on European Taxation* 2019/357.

75 Case C-503/14 (*European Commission v Portuguese Republic*), [2016] EU:C:2016:979.

The 2005 amendment provided for the case in which domestic tax law considers as fiscally transparent a shareholder handing in shares in another company in a qualifying operation (hybrid entity): the participants in that hybrid shareholder, although generally being taxed by their residence State as and when the profits and gains of the hybrid entity arise, are in principle entitled to tax deferral (Art. 8(3)), but their residence State has the right, under the enigmatic Article 11(3)-(4), to disapply Articles 8(1)-(3) and to choose to treat the operation in the same manner as it would have done, had the hybrid shareholder been a domestic entity. See Section 17.7.6.

17.10 Transfer or Incorporation of a Foreign Branch (Art. 10)

Article 10 of the Directive addresses a triangular situation, in which a branch in Member State 3 is among the assets transferred by company A in Member State 1 (in a merger, division, or transfer of assets) to a receiving company B in Member State 2. The question arises how to treat the unrealized capital gains, tax-free reserves and possible loss relief rights connected to the business of the State 3 branch.

Article 10(1) provides that State 1 may not levy any tax on the transfer of the State 3 branch to company B. This makes sense, as State 3 is entitled to tax the profits and capital gains connected with the branch in that State. This special rule was needed, because Article 4(2)(b) provides that the assets transferred must become part of a branch of the receiving company *in State 1*, which is not the case as regards the branch assets in State 3. Although State 1 thus may not tax the unrealized gains among the assets of the State 3 branch, it *is* entitled to recapture any loss deductions granted in the past to company A in respect of losses incurred by its State 3 branch. This makes sense as well, because after the transfer of assets, State 1 will no longer be able to tax any future profits of the State 3 branch against which those losses may be offset. Indeed, after the merger, the State 3 branch has become a branch of a company resident and subject to tax in State 2, not in State 1.

The Member State of the branch (State 3) is required to pretend it is the State of the transferring company. This means that State 3 may not tax any capital gains on the assets and liabilities pertaining to the branch, and must allow tax-free provisions and reserves in respect of those assets and liabilities to be preserved, provided of course that in the branch accounts the 'old' book values and depreciation system for tax purposes are preserved as well.

The 2005 amendment added a new last sentence to Article 10(1) which addresses branch incorporation and confirms what most commentators already inferred from object and purpose of the Directive, but which could not clearly be read in its original provisions (especially Art. 4(2)(b) cast doubts): the same deferral rules apply if State 2 and State 3 happen to be the same State. If the transferring company in State 1 already has a branch in State 2, the same deferral and carry-over rules apply as in the case in which the branch is in State 3 instead of State 2 (the State of the receiving company). This means that if a State 1 company with a branch in State 2 decides to incorporate that branch into a local State 2 subsidiary, such branch incorporation is covered by the Directive. Rightly so: it is one of the most natural cross-border operations, and there is no danger of State 2 losing any tax claim. On the contrary, the incorporation of the branch strengthens its claim on the business capital of the branch, as a branch (a nonresident) is converted into a domestic legal entity, resident and fully liable for tax purposes.

Article 10(2) accommodates Member States applying the direct credit method for the prevention of international double taxation of foreign branch profits. Like Article 11(2), it ventures into an imaginary world. By way of derogation from paragraph (1), State 1 is allowed, if it applies the credit method, to include the capital gain on the foreign branch's assets/liabilities in the taxable income of the transferring company, but it must then credit the tax which the branch State would have levied on those gains, had it not been required to defer taxation: it must credit the deferred tax, in order to prevent the deferral granted by the source State from being eaten by the State of the transferring/migrating company as a result of its credit system.

The 'Finnish exit tax' case concerned a Finnish resident company that transferred an Austrian permanent establishment to an Austrian-resident company (incorporation of branch).[76] Finland taxed the hidden reserves in the foreign permanent establishment currently while granting a fictitious credit for the tax in the Member State where the permanent establishment was situated. A domestic transfer of a permanent establishment would not have triggered any immediate taxation in Finland. Although Article 10(2) of the Tax Merger Directive allows Finland to tax the hidden reserves in the transferred permanent establishment, the CJEU decided that it is in breach of the freedom of establishment in Article 49 TFEU if Finland does not allow the taxpayer a deferred collection of the tax.

17.11 Operations and Migrations Not Covered

Given the requirement of Article 1(a) (two companies of different Member States must be involved), several operations are not covered.[77] For instance, a Spanish company carrying on a business through a branch in France wishing to transfer that branch to another Spanish company in exchange for securities in that other company (transfer of assets), cannot rely on the Directive provisions, because only Spanish companies are involved. The Directive does not prevent France from taxing the unrealized capital gains on the assets of the branch when the ownership changes, although there is little reason for France to require payment of tax, as the branch and the unrealized gains remain in France. The same is true where, *e.g.*, two Danish companies legally merge under domestic law, both of them maintaining a permanent establishment in Germany. The result is one Danish company with two German branches. The Directive does not prevent Germany from taxing the 'merging' of one permanent establishment into the other, as only Danish companies are involved. Only a very broad interpretation of the term 'company from a Member State' can make these operations qualify. One could argue that the Danish companies in the

76 Case C-292/16 (*A Oy*), [2017] EU:C:2017:888.

77 In our view, the coverage of the current operations is rather the result of piecemeal harmonization, rather than that the operations currently cover differ fundamentally from those not covered. That latter was the suggestion by A-G Saugmandsgaard Øe in his Opinion of 19 September 2018 in the State aid case *A-Brauerei* (C-374/17), EU:C:2018:741, paras. 168-171.

example are also German companies, because through their branches they are subject to German corporation tax (see Section 17.6). Taxation in these cases will probably be prevented, however, by the Freedom of establishment, as probably, Spain and Germany would not tax such operations if they happened entirely within their territory.

From the above, it is apparent that the creation of a holding SE *(Societas Europaea)* under the Statute of the European Company may in certain circumstances not be covered either. Such creation may be achieved (i) through the incorporation of an SE by two companies from different Member States becoming subsidiaries of the SE (in that case the Directive will apply), but also (ii) through the incorporation of an SE by two companies from the same Member State, providing that at least one of them had a branch for at least two years in another Member State (see Section 20.4). In the latter case, a very broad interpretation of the term 'company from a Member State' in Article 3 would be needed to cover the exchange of shares in the subsidiaries for shares in the holding SE.

Also outside the scope of the Directive lie transfers of non-EU branches of EU companies to other EU companies, and transfers of EU branches of non-EU companies to EU companies or to other non-EU companies. The same is true for transfers of assets not forming a 'branch of activity' within the meaning of Article 2(j).

There are other situations which are not covered by the Directive,[78] although its scope has been widened considerably on 1 January 2006 (inclusion of the SE and SCE) and again on 1 January 2007 (inclusion of many national legal entities previously not included).

For the transfer to another Member State of the registered office and the effective management of companies incorporated under national law (non SEs and non SCEs), the Tax Merger Directive does not contain any provision. As observed, we consider this to be a discrimination against national legal forms as compared to the SE and SCE, but the *National Grid Indus* case (see Section 12.3) seems to have taken that discrimination away.

17.12 The Anti-Abuse Reservation (Art. 15)

17.12.1 Evasion and Avoidance; Objective and Subjective Elements; Scope and National Implementation of the Anti-Abuse Provision

Like the Parent-Subsidiary Directive (Art. 1(2)-(4) and 4(1)(a)) and the Interest and Royalty Directive (Art. 5), the Tax Merger Directive includes a general anti-abuse clause (Art. 15). The 2005 amendment extended its scope so as to include the two new operations covered: the split-off of a company and the transfer abroad of the registered office of an SE or SCE. The anti-abuse clause in the Tax Merger Directive differs from the one in the Parent-Subsidiary Directive in that it also addresses a perceived non-fiscal abuse (see Section 17.12.8),. It is very unlikely that the difference in framing between the two Directives will lead to material differences in application by the CJEU, or that it will lead to other results than under the Court's general abuse doctrine, as it considers

78 See Barry Larking, *l.c.*, p. 364.

both provisions as an expression of the general principle of EU law that abuse of rights is prohibited. According to the Court, the objective of preventing tax avoidance and tax evasion "has the same scope whether it is relied on under [the anti-abuse reservations in the corporate tax directives] or as justification for an exception to primary law".[79] See Chapter 7 especially Section 7.2, and *infra*).

Pursuant to Article 15(1)(a), Member States may deny the Directive benefits:

> '(...) where it appears that the merger, division, transfer of assets or exchange of shares: (a) has as its principal or as one of its principal objectives tax evasion or tax avoidance; (...).'

Such appearance may be presumed if the operation:

> '(...) is not carried out for valid commercial reasons, such as the restructuring or rationalization of the activities of the companies participating (...).'

In the Cases *Leur-Bloem* (see Sections 7.13.2. ff) and C-352/08, *Zwijnenburg*,[80] the Court explained the mode of application of this provision: the Directive applies without distinction to all mergers, divisions, transfers of assets or exchanges of shares irrespective of the reasons, whether financial, economic or simply fiscal, for those operations. This has its limits where a restructuring operation is primarily driven by tax reasons and has little to none economic rationale and substance as a result of which the requirements of the Tax Merger Directive are only formally met. In such a case, the taxpayer may be considered to engage in tax avoidance, in which case it cannot avail itself of the benefits of the Tax Merger Directive.[81] This is also codified in Article 15 of the Tax Merger Directive: transactions which in principle objectively qualify are in the end carved out by Article 15 if and because they represent abuse of the directive rights. National competence thus revives, but the exercise thereof with a view to curb abuse is limited by primary EU law, especially the free movement rights and the recognized *rule of reason* justifications for restricting these rights, e.g. the prohibition of abuse of rights.

The Directive does not define evasion and avoidance and treats them alike, although the term 'evasion' would seem to refer to a criminal offence (tax fraud), whereas tax 'avoidance' is not illegal, but at most morally or socially improper. We believe a specific provision against tax fraud was unnecessary, as tax fraud is prohibited throughout the

79 See Case C-6/16, *Eqiom SAS/Enka*, EU:C:2017:641, point 64 (in respect of the Parent-Subsidiary Directive) and Case C-14/16, *Euro Park Service*, ECLI:EU:C:2017:177, point 69 (in respect of the Tax Merger Directive).

80 Case C-352/08 (*Modehuis A. Zwijnenburg*), [2010] EU:C:2010:282.

81 See Joined Cases C-116/16 and C-117/16 (T Danmark and Y Danmark), [2019] EU:C:2019:135, par. 91.

internal market.[82] Given the Court's general case law on abuse of rights, we even believe that Article 15 is redundant altogether, also as regards (legal) tax avoidance. See Section 17.12.7 *infra* and Chapter 7 and 16.

In Case C-352/08, *Zwijnenburg*, cited above, the question arose as to whether a Member State may withhold the Directive benefits from the taxpayer if it seeks to circumvent, through a merger or division, real estate transfer taxes, although transfer taxes are not covered by the Tax Merger Directive. The Court first reiterated that the Directive applies without distinction to all mergers, divisions, transfers of assets or exchanges of shares irrespective of the reasons, whether financial, economic or simply fiscal, for those operations. Therefore, bad intentions do not affect the eligibility of the transaction. By contrast, the reasons for the transaction *are* important in the implementation of the anti-abuse reservation. The Court furthermore considered that Article 15, being an exception to the Directive rules, must be subject to strict interpretation, and concluded that the Directive benefits, which concern corporate and individual income taxation, cannot be withheld in order to compensate for the circumvention of a tax which is not addressed by the Directive. In other words: denying corporate or individual income tax benefits granted by the Directive is not the appropriate reaction to avoidance, albeit through a merger, of taxes of another character, object, and base.

Case C-43/00, *Andersen og Jensen*[83] (see Section 17.3.1.(d)), shows that an anti-abuse rule is not always needed to dispose of legal maneuvers by taxpayers intending to enjoy Directive benefits not intended for them. Sometimes rational interpretation of Directive terms suffices. What in economic terms amounted to a leveraged buy-out, was in *Andersen og Jensen* made to look like a transfer of assets for Directive purposes, by artificially dissociating the borrowings and the debt arising from a loan to finance the buy-out (the debt in one legal entity; the proceeds in another). The Court held that the transaction did not qualify because the requirement 'in exchange for securities' was not met, as in economic reality, the remuneration was not shares, but cash.

In general, we would infer from the case law discussed that the anti-abuse reservation is aimed at reserving the right to counteract the artificial cloaking of transactions as mergers or divisions which in economic reality amount to a realization of capital gains (an alienation instead of a merging or dividing) or to a distribution of dividend, but also that that reservation seems redundant, as it does not seem to change the limited competence the Member States have anyway to – proportionally – fight abusive practices under the general principle of EU law that abuse of rights is prohibited. In light of the

82 See Case 50/80 (*Horvath*), [1981] ECR 385, EU:C:1981:34; Case 221/81 (*Wolf*), [1982] ECR 3681, EU:C:1982:363; Case 240/81 (*Einberger*), [1982] ECR 3699, EU:C:1982:364; Case 294/82 (*Einberger II*), [1984] ECR 1177, EU:C:1984:81; Case 269/86 (*Mol*), [1988] ECR 3627, EU:C:1988:359; Case 289/86 (*Vereniging Happy Family Rustenburgerstraat*), [1988] ECR 3655, EU:C:1988:360, Case C-343/89 (*Witzemann*), [1990] ECR I-4477, EU:C:1990:445, Case C-158/98 (*Coffeeshop'Siberië'*), [1999] ECR I-3971, EU:C:1999:334, and Case C-137/09 (*Josemans v Maastricht*), [2010] ECR I-13019, EU:C:2010:774.

83 Case C-43/00 (*Andersen og Jensen ApS v. Skatteministeriet*), [2002] ECR I-379, EU:C:2002:15.

Argenta Spaar-bank Case,[84] it is especially doubtful whether an anti-abuse reservation may be relied on by a Member State when its taxing rights as regards unrealized gains are safeguarded by the specific 'claim savers' in Articles 4 and 8 (book value retention rules); see Section 7.2.

17.12.2 The Leur-Bloem Case; Facts

Case C-28/95, *Leur-Bloem*,[85] is an important case on interpretation of Article 15(1)(a) of the Directive. It concerned a sole director/shareholder in two Netherlands limited liability companies (*besloten vennootschappen*: BVs 1 and 2). Mrs Leur-Bloem wished to incorporate a third BV (3), which was to become the holding company for her shareholdings in BVs 1 and 2, through an exchange of shares in BV's 1 and 2 for newly issued shares in the holding-BV 3. Indirectly, through BV 3, Mrs Leur-Bloem would still fully control BVs 1 and 2. This operation would qualify as two exchanges of shares under Article 2(e) of the Directive, entitling Mrs Leur-Bloem to tax deferral under Article 8. The Holding-BV 3 and BVs 1 and 2 (becoming 100% subsidiaries of BV 3), would subsequently be consolidated in a fiscal unity *(fiscale eenheid;* full tax consolidation), allowing the horizontal offsetting of current profits and losses between the BVs 1 and 2, thus reducing their tax exposure. Mrs Leur-Bloem would become the sole director/shareholder in BV 3, which would have no activities other than holding the shares in BVs 1 and 2. Therefore, in practice nothing would change, except for the creation of horizontal offsetting of losses. As BV 3 was just holding shares, it did not meet the – then – Netherlands' requirement of carrying on an active business which is enduringly united both financially and economically with the businesses of its two subsidiaries. Deferral of tax was therefore denied by the Netherlands' tax administration. Mrs Leur-Bloem went to Court, which referred the case to the CJEU, although it concerned a purely domestic situation.

17.12.3 Admissibility: Domestic Situation, but National Law Refers to EU Law

All three companies involved were companies from the Netherlands. Therefore, the situation was purely internal, not covered by Union law (see Art. 1 of the Directive).

The national Court nevertheless asked the CJEU for a preliminary ruling, considering that the Netherlands legislator had stated that domestic mergers were to be treated in the same manner as cross-border mergers covered by the Directive. This legislative technique was rather new at the time, but is seen often nowadays in Member States: in order to avoid discrimination or reverse discrimination, the national legislator makes national law implementing EU Directives indiscriminately applicable to both cross-border activity covered by the Directive and comparable domestic activity not covered by the Directive. The Court held that it could be called upon to interpret a Directive term if a national court found that (i) such term (in this case the term 'merger by exchange of shares'), taken in its EU context, needed to be interpreted in order to resolve the dispute before it, and (ii)

84 Case C-39/16 (*Argenta Spaarbank NV*), EU:C:2017:323.
85 Case C-28/95 (*Leur-Bloem v. Inspecteur*), [1997] ECR I-4161, EU:C:1997:369.

this term had been incorporated into the domestic law transposing the Directive and had been made applicable to comparable purely domestic situations:

> '65. In those circumstances, where in regulating internal situations, domestic legislation adopts the same solutions as those adopted in Community law so as to provide for one single procedure in comparable situations, it is clearly in the Community interest that, in order to forestall future differences of interpretation, provisions or concepts taken from Community law should be interpreted uniformly, irrespective of the circumstances in which they are to apply (...). 66. In such a case, (...), it is for the national court alone to assess the precise scope of that reference to Community law, the jurisdiction of the Court being confined to considering provisions of Community law only (...). Consideration of the limits which the national legislature may have placed on the application of Community law to purely internal situations is a matter for domestic law and consequently falls within the exclusive jurisdiction of the courts of the Member State (...).'

The Court therefore assumed jurisdiction and the same approach was followed in numerous cases afterwards. In case C-827/21, *Banca A*, referred by a Romanian Court on 30 December 2021, the CJEU held that EU law does not require a national Court to interpret the rules governing a purely domestic merger in accordance with the Tax Merger Directive, as that merger does not come in the scope of the directive.[86] In addition the CJEU held that it does not have jurisdiction to answer the questions referred regarding the interpretation of the Tax Merger Directive as the facts of the dispute are not within its scope and Romanian domestic law has not made it applicable directly and unconditionally.

In case C-318/22, *GE Infrastructure*, three Hungarian entities belonging to the *GE* group entered into a division agreement with a merger by acquisition.[87] The CJEU reiterated that it has jurisdiction to interpret provisions of the Tax Merger Directive where the situation at issue is of a purely domestic nature, when the national legislature has chosen to apply the same treatment to situations governed by that directive and to purely domestic situations. Substantively, the CJEU held that Article 8(2) of the Tax Merger Directive precludes that domestic law makes the benefit of that provision subject to conditions relating to a reduction in the shareholding of the shareholder of the transferring company in that company or to a reduction in the share capital of that company, which are not provided for in the Tax Merger Directive.

17.12.4 The Substantive Questions; The Character of the Anti-Abuse Clause: a 'Reservation of Competence'

As observed (in Section 17.3.1), according to the Court the Tax Merger Directive applies 'irrespective of the reasons' for the operation. Consequently, as a rule it is immaterial whether the acquiring company itself carries on a business, whether the same individual holds all shares in both the acquiring and the acquired companies, and whether a factual merging of the businesses of the companies involved is envisaged. Article 15(1)(a) makes

86 Case C-827/21 (*Banca A v Agenția Națională de Administrare Fiscală (ANAF), Președintele ANAF*), [2023] EU:C:2023:355.

87 Case C-318/22 (*GE Infrastructure Hungary Holding Kft. v Nemzeti Adó – és Vámhivatal Fellebbviteli Igazgatósága*), [2023] EU:C:2023:890.

an exception to this main rule, characterized by the Court as a 'reservation of competence' of the Member States, and to be applied narrowly: only if the operation has tax evasion or avoidance as one of its objectives. This has to be assessed on a case by case basis. Blind exclusion of entire categories of cases, without individual assessment, are not compatible with Article 15. For elaboration of this doctrine, see Chapter 7.

17.12.5 *Division of the Onus of Proof*

Although the judgment thus clearly prohibits *overkill* in national anti-abuse legislation – as *overkill* is clearly disproportionate – it is not so easy to implement it: the Directive allows Member States to presume that absence of valid commercial reasons implies abuse, but at the same time the Court precludes them from excluding categories of cases which look suspect at first sight. Neither may they enact general exclusions subject to the discretionary granting of derogations by the tax administration. On the other hand, Article 15 of the Tax Merger Directive allows denial of the Directive benefits already if the transaction has as *one* of its principal objectives tax evasion or tax avoidance. Evidence, produced by the taxpayer of one or more valid commercial reasons thus does not yet safeguard the taxpayer against application of Article 15, as the tax administration may subsequently show that in addition to business reasons, also tax avoidance was a principal reason for the transaction. As it is impossible to demonstrate that something does *not* exist, one cannot require the tax administration to prove that *no* valid commercial reasons were present. Within the context of abuse of TFEU rights, the CJEU describes abuse as 'wholly artificial arrangements which do not reflect economic reality and whose only purpose is to obtain a tax advantage.'[88] It would therefore seem reasonable to require the tax administration to point at a discrepancy between economic reality and the transaction carried out, after which it is for the taxpayer to show valid commercial reasons. As observed, however, Article 15 allows denial of the Directive benefits already if the transaction has as *one* of its principal objectives tax evasion or tax avoidance, which implies that even if valid commercial reasons can be shown, the tax administration may still prevail where it succeeds in demonstrating that in addition to these possible business reasons, tax avoidance was a 'principal reason' for the transaction as well. The wording of Article 15 thus might make one wonder whether the Council wished to encroach upon the freedom of businesses to arrange their affairs in such a way as to attract as little taxation as possible: it is not enough that valid commercial reasons are *present*; principal tax avoidance reasons must be *absent*. Unavoidably, the assessment of whether a particular operation has tax avoidance as one of its principal objectives is, to a certain extent, discretionary. Consequently, the national tax authorities cannot be denied a certain discretion, provided that their discretion is subject to full judicial review. Therefore, we believe that Member States remain competent to require the companies

88 See, *e.g.*, Case C-182/08, *Glaxo Wellcome* [2009] ECR I-8591, EU:C:2009:559: '89. With regard, c and to combat artificial arrangements designed to circumvent the German tax system, it must be held that a national measure restricting the free movement of capital can be justified where it specifically targets wholly artificial arrangements which do not reflect economic reality and whose only purpose is to obtain a tax advantage (see, to that effect, *Cad-bury Schweppes and Cadbury Schweppes Overseas*, paragraphs 51 and 55; *Test Claimants in the Thin Cap Group Litigation*, paragraphs 72 and 74; and Case C-330/07 *Jobra* [2008] ECR I-09099, EU:C:2008:685, par. 35).'

involved to state their commercial (non-fiscal) reasons for the operation if these at first sight appear absent or weak, provided that (i) every such statement and every operation is assessed on its individual merits by the tax authorities, who should at least offer *prima facie* evidence of abuse,[89] (ii) the tax administration does not ask for more information or documentation than necessary for such assessment (principle of proportionality), (iii) the tax administration does not require more information or documentation, nor does it apply less favorable procedures than it would require in a comparable domestic case (principle of equivalence), (iv) the procedural rules implementing Article 15 are sufficiently precise, clear and foreseeable, and their application not discretionary (principle of legal certainty), and (v) the procedure before the tax authorities, and its outcome, are subject to full review by an independent court. This view is supported especially by the *Euro Park Services* Case,[90] but also by case law in the field of abuse of free movement rights, e.g. Case C-196/04, *Cadbury Schweppes* (see Section 7.4).

This seems to imply that the onus of having to prove genuine business reasons may be put on the taxpayer if the tax administration challenges the existence of economic substance and genuine business reasons and at least provides *prima facie* evidence of artifice, e.g. by showing that the operation commercially seems to be disadvantageous without the envisaged tax effect. Established CJEU case law in matters of general EU law, especially the TFEU Freedoms, shows that Member States may not make it more difficult for companies involved in a cross-border merger to show valid commercial reasons than they do in a similar domestic case of possible abuse (equivalence principle), and that they may not make it excessively difficult or practically impossible to enjoy the Directive benefits (principle of effectiveness of EU law). We refer to cases such as *Rewe*,[91] *San Giorgio*[92] and *Van Schijndel*[93] (see Section 3.5.2). The *Euro Park Service* Case cited above seems to apply this case law to national implementation of Article 15 of the Tax Merger Directive. We further draw attention to Case C-129/00, *Commission v. Italy*,[94] in which the Court condemned an Italian judicial practice which made it excessively difficult for VAT-entrepreneurs to demonstrate that VAT incorrectly levied had not been passed on to customers. From Case C-524/04, *Test Claimants in the Thin Cap Group Litigation*,[95] and Case C-311/08, *SGI*,[96] it appears that in case of associated parties, the presence of conditions not at arm's length may give rise to a presumption of an artificial arrangement being present (in those cases: tax base erosion by designer loans and interest rates, and unusual or gratuitous advantages granted abroad, respectively), but that (i) the taxpayer must be given an opportunity, without being subject to undue administrative constraints, to

89 See Case C-14/16, *Euro Park Service*, EU:C:2017:177, paras. 55-56.
90 Case C-14/16, *Euro Park Service*, EU:C:2017:177.
91 Case 33/76 *(Rewe)*, [1976] ECR 1989, EU:C:1976:188.
92 Case 199/82 *(San Giorgio)*, [1983] ECR 3595, EU:C:1983:318.
93 Joined Cases C-430/93 (*Van Schijndel*) and C-431/93 *(Van Veen)*, [1995] ECR I-4705, EU:C:2012:485.
94 Case C-129/00 *(Commission v. Italy)*, [2003] ECR I-14637, EU:C:2003:656.
95 Case C-524/04 *(Test Claimants in the Thin Cap Group Litigation)*, [2007] ECR I-2107, EU:C:2007:161.
96 Case C-311/08 (*SGI*), ECLI:EU:C:2010:26, 2010 [ECR] I-487.

demonstrate commercial justification for that arrangement,[97] and that (ii) even where the conclusion must be that the transaction is an artificial arrangement (without underlying commercial justification), the response of the tax administration may not go beyond what is necessary to re-characterize the transaction such that it corresponds to what would have been agreed between independent parties. The latter conclusion (anti-abuse measures may not go beyond what is necessary to undo the abuse) may also be drawn from the indirect tax Case C-255/02 *(Halifax)*.[98]

Probably, the best way for Member States to implement Article 15(1)(a) of the Directive is to copy it more or less verbally into their national laws. However, in our view they do not need to implement it at all, as the Court sees it as a reservation of competence, the scope of exercise of which coincides with the scope of the general principle of EU law that abuse of rights is prohibited (see Section 7.2).[99]

17.12.6 Purely Fiscal Advantages Are Not 'Valid Commercial Reasons'

The last question referred by the national Court in *Leur-Bloem* was whether the aim of horizontal clearance of profits and losses for tax purposes between BVs 1 and 2 was a valid commercial reason within the meaning of Article 15. The CJEU answered:

> '47. It is clear from the wording and aims of Article 11 [now 15; *authors*], as it is from those of the Directive, that "valid commercial reasons" is a concept involving more than the attainment of a purely fiscal advantage. A merger by way of exchange of shares having only such an aim cannot therefore constitute a valid commercial reason within the meaning of that article.'

We infer that there must be a non-incidental non-fiscal reason for the operation, but also that if such genuine business reason exists, the taxpayer cannot be prevented from structuring the operation so as to attract the least possible taxation. This also follows from the Court's general case law on abuse of TFEU rights in tax matters. Case C-295/97, *Eurowings*,[100] shows that tax planning aimed at using relative differences in tax burdens between Member States is not an abuse, not even if the company in the other Member

97 The requirement to provide evidence of commercial justifications for a non-arm's length looking arrangement does not appear to be too stringent. See Otto Marres, 'Interest Deduction Limitations: When To Apply Articles 9 and 24(4) of the OECD Model', 56 *European Taxation* 1 (2016), para 4.4. In his Opinion in the *Hornbach-Baumarkt* Case (C-382/16), A-G Bobek argues that recognition of the arm's length principle, if applied correctly, implies that a taxpayer *cannot* counter a profit adjustment on the basis of that principle by providing evidence of commercial justifications (such as: "it was necessary to provide 'free' guarantees to my subsidiary to guarantee its success") as otherwise 'arm's length' would be something other than 'commercial' and "the notion of arm's length transaction would be emptied of any meaning" (point 113).

98 Case C-255/02 (*Halifax plc a.o. v. Commissioners of Customs & Excise*), [2006] ECR I-1609, EU:C:2006:121 (par. 93).

99 See also Joined Cases C-116/16 and C-117/16 (T Danmark and Y Danmark) [2019] EU:C:2019:135, par. 70-95, in which the CJEU clearly held that the benefits provided under an EU Directive may be denied in case of abusive or fraudulent acts, in which case the objective conditions required for obtaining those advantages are met only formally.

100 Case C-294/97 *(Eurowings Luftverkehrs AG)*, [1999] ECR I-7447, EU:C:1999:524.

State enjoys a special low-tax regime (it should be noted that the two (German and Irish) companies involved were not associated; see below).

The *Foggia* Case[101] concerned a merger operation between two companies of the same group where the acquired company did not carry out any activity, did not have any financial holdings, and transferred to the acquiring company only substantial tax losses of undetermined origin. The Portuguese tax administration took the view that the mere objective of transferring losses for tax purposes is no serious commercial reason for the acquiring company. The Court reiterated that (i) the anti-abuse reservation reflects the general principle of EU law that abuse of rights is prohibited, and (ii) purely fiscal motives are not valid commercial reasons. Fiscal motives are not necessarily fatal, as long as they are not 'predominant.' It held that even though the operation would have a positive effect in terms of cost structure savings for the group, the facts as presented may constitute a presumption that the operation had not been carried out for 'valid commercial reasons' within the meaning of (now) Article 15(1)(a). It was incumbent on the national court to decide on that in the light of all the circumstances of the dispute.

While the CJEU clarified in the 'Danish' cases[102] its case-law on the inability of taxpayers to avail themselves of provisions of Union law in case of abuse, the practical effect of the guidance given by the CJEU therein on cases covered by the Tax Merger Directive is limited. The 'Danish' cases concerned taxpayers who (potentially) artificially availed themselves of the benefits of the Interest-Royalty Directive and Parent-Subsidiary through interposing EU companies. The guidance on identifying whether these companies could be seen as 'beneficial owners' under these two directives and whether the indications of abuse are met seems less relevant for the Tax Merger Directive, with a fully different object and purpose and it being hard conceive interposing additional EU companies could make cross-border restructuring more advantageous for a taxpayer.[103] Yet, the most important message of the 'Danish' cases, that Member States *must* refuse to grant the advantages of an EU Directive in cases of abuse, would apply certainly to the Tax Merger Directive as well.

17.12.7 Is the Anti-Abuse Reservation Redundant?

As observed, we believe the anti-abuse provisions in the corporate tax Directives are superfluous. In the first place, tax frauds may fall outside the scope of EU law benefits altogether (see Section 17.3.1 above). Secondly, as regards (legal) tax avoidance, a long

101 Case C-126/10 (*FOGGIA-Sociedade*), [2011] ECR I-10923, EU:C:2011:718.

102 A.o. Joined Cases C-115/16, C-118/16, C-119/16 and C-299/16 (*N Luxembourg 1*), [2019] EU:C:2019:134.

103 Implicitly, this is recognised in the proposal for an ATAD3 Directive (Proposal for a COUNCIL DIRECTIVE laying down rules to prevent the misuse of shell entities for tax purposes and amending Directive 2011/16/EU, Brussels, 22 December 2021, COM(2021) 565 final 2021/0434 (CNS)) which only results denial in the benefits of the Parent-Subsidiary Directive and Interest-Royalty Directive, but not the Tax Merger Directive in cases of – essentially – a lack of minimum substance (see Article 11).

list of consistent case law of the CJEU[104] (discussed in Chapter 15) shows that economic operators may be denied recourse to EU law where that recourse is frivolous, where the connecting factor to EU law (especially the cross-border aspect) is construed by artifice and lacks economic substance, where EU law is relied on to serve purposes wholly alien to object and purpose of the EU rules invoked, and where the arrangement set up does not reflect economic reality but is aimed at artificially obtaining a tax advantage. It follows from these cases that Member States must refuse to apply EU law provisions (i) where they can show that the economic operator relying on them intends to obtain by artifice a benefit which was clearly not intended for his case (subjective element), and (ii) the result of application of the EU law provision relied on would be contrary or alien to object and purpose of that provision (objective element).

Comparing the established case law discussed in Chapter 15 to the *Leur-Bloem/Andersen og Jensen/Kofoed* case law of the Court, we do not discern any value added in Article 15(1)(a) of the Tax Merger Directive, Article 1(2)-1(4) of the Parent-Subsidiary Directive, and Article 5 of the Interest and Royalty Directive.

17.12.8 Employees' Representation

Article 15(1)(b) was included at the request of Germany, which wanted the competence to deny the Tax Merger Directive benefits where a cross-border merger (like) transaction would result in reduction or cancellation of employees' representation on the company's board (*Mitbestimmung*). We submit this provision landed in the wrong Directive. It should have been included in a company law Merger Directive (see Section 17.3.3) and maybe in the Statute for a European Company (see Section 20.4). It seems awkward and arbitrary rather than appropriate to deny a tax deferral to penalize frustration of national workers' co-determination legislation which has nothing whatsoever to do with taxation.[105]

Article 15(2) stipulates – rather superfluously, it would seem – that the Member States' competence to deny the Directive benefits for reasons of reduction of employee's representation ceases to exist if and to the extent that adequate workers' co-determination rules become applicable at Union level. The Statute on a European Company (*Societas*

104 *E.g.* Case 33/74 (*Van Binsbergen*), [1974] ECR 1299, EU:C:1974:131, Case 115/78 (*Knoors*), [1979] ECR 399, EU:C:1979:31, Case 229/83 (*Leclerc v. Au blé veri*), [1985] ECR 1, EU:C:1985:1, Case 79/85 (*Segers*), [1986] ECR 2375, EU:C:1986:308, Case 39/86 (*Sylvie Lair*), [1988] ECR 3161, EU:C:1988:322, Case 292/86 (*Claude Gullung*), [1988] ECR 111, EU:C:1988:15, Case C-221/89 (*Factortame II*), [1991] ECR I-3905, EU:C:1991:320, Case C-357/89 (*Raulin*), [1992] ECR I-1027, EU:C:1992:87, Case C-370/90 (*Surinder Singh*), [1992] ECR I-4265, EU:C:1992:296, Case C-23/93 (*TV 10*), [1994] ECR I-4795, EU:C:1994:362, Case C-212/97 (*Centros*), [1999] ECR I-1459, EU:C:1999:126 Case C-367/96 (*Kefalas*), [1998] ECR I-2843, EU:C:1998:222, Case C-110/99 (*Emsland-Stärke*), [2000] ECR I-11569, EU:C:2000:695, Case C-255/02 (*Halifax plc a.o. v. Commissioners of Customs & Excise*), [2006] ECR I-1609, EU:C:2006:121, Case C-196/04 (*Cadbury Schweppes*), [2006] ECR I-7995, EU:C:2006:544, and Case C-524/04 (*Test Claimants in the Thin Cap Group Litigation*), [2007] ECR I-2107, EU:C:2007:161.

105 Apparently, Germany eventually felt so too, since it did not implement the workers' co-determination clause into national tax law. See Richard L. Engle, in *The Merger Directive; Practical Tax Issues*, IBFD Publications BV/Editions Francis Lefebvre, Amsterdam/Paris 1993, p. 83.

Europaea, SE) consists of an SE Regulation[106] and an accompanying Directive on employee participation,[107] in force since 8 October 2004. Further, Directive (EU) 2019/2121 as regards cross-border conversions, mergers and divisions (see Section 17.3.3) also contains provisions on employee representation.[108] It would seem, therefore, that Article 15(2) of the Tax Merger Directive serves little purpose any more.

17.13 Implementation

Member States were required to bring into force their implementation measures before 1 January 1992 (Annex II, Part B). Portugal was granted a year extra. No transitional measures were provided for on the occasion of the accession of ten new Member States in May 2004, the two new member States in January 2007 and Croatia's accession in July 2013; only their corporate taxes were included in the list of taxes in Annex I, Part B, and their legal forms on the list in Annex I, Part A, to the Directive. The 2005 amendment had to be implemented before 1 January 2006 as regards the provisions on the seat transfer of an SE or SCE, and before 1 January 2007 for the remainder.

Where national legislation does not comply fully with the Directive requirements, or where implementation measures have wrongly been omitted, the question arises whether taxpayers may rely directly on the Directive provisions. The deferral and carry-over provisions of the Directive are sufficiently clear and unconditional to have direct effect. Some discretionary power is left to the Member States, but only as regards specific issues such as abuse, and even there, given the *Leur-Bloem* case, not much discretion is left. In our view, the remaining discretionary powers 'do not make it impossible to determine minimum rights on the basis of the principle contained in [the Directive provision]', as the CJEU put it in *Denkavit, VITIC and Voormeer*[109] on the direct effect of Article 5 of the Parent-Subsidiary Directive (see Section 16.6.1), and in wording to the same effect in *Cobelfret*[110] on the direct effect of Article 4 of that Directive (see Section 16.4.1).

Even if no direct effect were available in a specific case, a taxpayer who suffers damages as a consequence of incorrect or incomplete implementation may, under certain conditions (see Section 3.5.4), rely on the *Francovich* case law of the CJEU[111] in order to claim damages

106 Council Regulation (EC) No. 2157/2001 of 8 October 2001 on the Statute for a European Company (SE), O.J. No. L 294, of 10 November 2001, p. 1-21.

107 Council Directive 2001/86/EC of 8 October 2001 supplementing the Statute for a European company with regard to the involvement of employees, O.J. No. L 294 of 10 November 2001, p. 22.

108 Directive (EU) 2019/2121 of the European Parliament and of the Council of 27 November 2019 amending Directive (EU) 2017/1132 as regards cross-border conversions, mergers and divisions, O.J. No. L 321/1 of 12 December 2019, p. 1-44.

109 Joined Cases C-283/94, C-291/94 and C-292/94 (*Denkavit Internationaal BV, VITIC Amsterdam BV and Voormeer BV v. Bundesamt für Finanzen*) [1996] ECR I-5063, EU:C:1996:387. For comments, see Dirk Schelpe, 'The Denkavit-Vitic-Voormeer Case', *EC Tax Review* 1997-1, p. 17, and Dennis M. Weber, 'The First Steps of the ECJ Concerning an Anti-abuse Doctrine in the Field of Harmonized Direct Taxes', *EC Tax Review 1997-1*, p. 22.

110 Case C-138/07 (*Cobelfret*), [2009] ECR I-731, EU:C:2009:82.

111 Joined Cases C-6/90 and C-9/90 (*Francovich and Bonifaci v. Italy*), [1991] ECR I-5403, EU:C:1991:428.

from a defaulting Member State, provided the breach of EU law is 'sufficiently serious' within the meaning of the *Brasserie du Pêcheur II, Factortame III* and *British Telecom* cases.[112] A breach is sufficiently serious if the Member State involved has apparently and seriously misjudged its powers of discretion, or if an infringement has been established by the CJEU and still no measures are taken at national level. If a directive accords little or no discretionary power to a Member State, then that State is in principle liable for damages of individuals and companies ensuing from a breach of their rights contained in the directive. As Article 288 TFEU provides that directives are binding upon Member States as to the result to be achieved, we believe that failure to implement a directive altogether will invariably lead to liability for damages of the defaulting Member State. This is not necessarily the case, on the other hand, where the Directive *was* implemented, but incorrectly. Indeed, a Directive obligation may be ambiguous, enigmatic or obscure, for instance because it was a heavily negotiated compromise within the Council, and was deliberately kept rather vague. Also, if a directive clearly extends discretion to the Member States, as is the case with the anti-abuse provisions in the corporate tax Directives, liability for incorrect interpretation of the limits of that discretion will not easily ensue, unless the national anti-abuse measures taken are manifestly disproportionate (deliberate *overkill*), overstepping the limits set by Article 15 and its interpretation in *Leur-Bloem*. We observe that since the *Köbler* judgment[113] of the CJEU, Member States may also be liable for damages in case of a 'manifest' incorrect application of EU law by a national highest court (a court adjudicating in last instance).

For an example of incorrect implementation of the Parent-Subsidiary Directive not leading to *Francovich* liability, see the *Denkavit-VITIC-Voormeer* case, discussed in Section 16.3.2. For a more detailed discussion of direct effect of directives and of *Francovich* liability of Member States, see Section 3.5.4.

17.14 Consequences

The Tax Merger Directive takes away many impediments to the concentration or restructuring of groups of companies from different Member States, but it is limited in scope even though the 2005 amendment has extended its personal scope to many more legal forms, including the SE and the SCE, and has extended its substantive scope to partial divisions and to seat transfers of SEs and SCEs. It does not cover all cross-border operations it might be expected to cover, given its objective. Further, the entities list-approach has not been replaced by an approach encompassing all entities subject to corporation tax. Neither does the Directive address the long-term tax problems of cross-border merger operations; it only addresses the *ad hoc* problems. It fails to fully deal with cases in which hybrid entities are involved and it contains no provisions on the value appraisal of the shares received by the transferring company in a transfer of assets or by the acquiring company in an exchange of shares, thus still leaving a considerable risk of double economic taxation, which risk, fortunately, seems to have been averted by the CJEU on the basis of

112 Joined Cases C-46/93 and C-48/93 (*Brasserie du Pêcheur SA v. Germany* and *The Queen v. Secretary of State for Transport*, ex parte: *Factortame Ltd and others*) [1996] ECR I-1029, ECLI:EU:C:1996:79, and Case C-392/93 (*British Telecommunications*), [1996] ECR I-1631, EU:C:1996:131.

113 Case C-224/01 (*Köbler v. Austria*), [2003] ECR I-10239, EU:C:2003:513.

teleological interpretation. One might not expect provisions on corporate emigration in a Directive on mergers and demergers, but *since* tax deferral has been provided for the transfer of the registered offices of SEs and SCEs, one would expect similar deferral to be included also for the seat transfer of national legal entities. In our view, the absence of such provisions is a discrimination against national legal forms. This distortion as well seems to be done away with by the Court, this time on the basis of the freedom of establishment, which opposes exit taxation: the Case C-371/10, *National Grid Indus BV*, provides for a choice between immediate payment and tax deferral upon corporate emigration (see Section 20.3).

Nonetheless, especially where an expanding group of companies has an excellent cash position, it will usually prefer to simply take over a target company by purchasing its shares. If not enough cash is available, then there is always the possibility of the classical exchange of shares (paper for paper) which also avoids the forming of branches. This picture does not seem to have changed after the coming into force, in October 2004, of the Statute for a European Company (SE) and the implementation, on 1 January 2006, of the 2005 amendment to the Tax Merger Directive, although the combination provides for a truly cross-border and tax-deferred merger of two or more companies from different Member States into an SE, resulting in one or more branches of the SE in Member State(s) in which the SE does not have its registered office. Possibly, the employee participation provisions make it unattractive to use an employer SE. 1 January 2023 was the ultimate implementation date for Directive (EU) 2019/2121 as regards cross-border conversions, mergers and divisions, which also contains employee participation provisions.

Judging from the cases which reached the CJEU, the Directive is used more often by individual large shareholders in closely held limited companies than by international groups of companies, and often in purely domestic configurations rather than in cross-border operations.

CHAPTER 18

The Interest and Royalties Directive

Peter Wattel

Update by Axel Cordewener[1]

18.1 Introduction

One of the key requirements for a smoothly functioning internal market is the elimination of double taxation of cross-border income flows. The first EU measure to that effect was the abolition of both juridical and economic double taxation of intra-group cross-border dividend payments through the Parent-Subsidiary Directive (see Chapter 16). Two other types of cross-border flows of intra-group income were also hindered by juridical double taxation (caused, in particular, by withholding taxes) and cumbersome administrative procedures: interest and royalty payments. These hindrances are addressed by Directive 2003/49/EC 'on a common system of taxation applicable to interest and royalty payments made between associated companies of different Member States'[2] (the 'I&R Directive').

18.1.1 Background

Withholding taxes on cross-border interest and royalty payments between companies pose less of a double taxation problem than withholding taxes on dividends, because (i) interest and royalty payments are generally deductible from the taxable profits of the debtor company (disregarding here for a moment the possible existence of thin capitalization and earnings stripping rules[3] or similar limitations on interest deduction[4]; see also Section 18.6.1.2 below), (ii) many Member States do not levy any withholding tax on outbound interest and/or royalty payments under their domestic legislation, and (iii) bilateral double tax treaties usually reduce[5] or even waive[6] domestic withholding taxes, and at any rate provide for a credit of the remaining withholding tax against the corporation tax in the recipient company's State of residence.[7]

---

1 Professor of Tax Law, Katholieke Universiteit Leuven; Of Counsel, Flick Gocke Schaumburg.

2 O.J. 2003 L 157/49.

3 On the 'interest barrier' under Article 4 of the ATAD, see Section 19.4.1.

4 Countries may even decide to introduce a 'royalty barrier'. This is the case, for example, in Germany where (since 2018) royalty payments are no longer tax deductible if they are made to related parties profiting from a preferential tax regime (such as IP, patent or license 'boxes') that is not in line with the 'nexus approach' outlined in Action 5 of the OECD/G20 BEPS project.

5 See for interest payments Article 11(2) OECD MC.

6 See for royalty payments Article 12(1) OECD MC.

7 See Article 23B OECD MC.

However, withholding taxes may still cause double taxation and considerable administrative formalities. In the first place, even though the international tax treaty network is constantly developing, still not all bilateral relations between Member States are covered by a tax treaty, so that a tax reduction at source will not be available and a tax credit in the recipient's home State solely depend on that State's domestic law. Secondly, a bilateral treaty cannot provide solutions for 'triangular situations' (see Sections 18.3.3 and 18.4.1 below). Thirdly, a reduction or waiver at source under tax treaties is often not granted immediately upon payment but must be applied for by the recipient with the tax authorities of the payer's State after initial full withholding. The refunding of withholding tax is often a time-consuming procedural matter, causing cash-flow and interest losses, opportunity cost and administrative headaches.[8] Fourthly, the crediting of any remaining source tax against the corporation tax of the recipient company in its home State also takes time and red tape. Finally, and most importantly, under tax treaties the credit in the recipient's State is generally limited to the amount of corporation tax which that State would levy itself on the interest or royalty income ('ordinary credit').[9] If that limit undercuts the remaining tax withheld at source on the gross payment, juridical double taxation persists ('excess foreign tax credit'). This is a very frequent phenomenon, as the withholding tax at source is usually levied on a *gross* basis (without deduction of any costs incurred in earning the interest or royalty income[10]), whereas the credit granted by the recipient's home State is calculated on a *net* basis (*after* cost deduction).

Because of these drawbacks, nonresident loan capital providers were forced to demand a higher interest return on their loans than domestic providers in order to compensate for the extra cost. Obviously, such effects distorted international financing neutrality.

8 See in this respect also Commission Recommendation 'on withholding tax relief procedures', C(2009)7924 final of 19 October 2009; Commission Report on 'Accelerating the capital markets union: addressing national barriers to capital flows', COM(2017) 147 final of 24 March 2017, paragraph 4.2; 'Code of Conduct on Withholding Tax' proposed by the Commission on 11 December 2017. As of 2020, the Commission started preparing a common and standardized EU-wide system for withholding tax relief at source, see Commission Communication on 'An Action Plan for fair and simple taxation supporting the recovery strategy', COM(2020) 312 final of 15 July 2020, paragraph 3.3 (Action 8), and Commission Communication on 'A Capital Markets Union for people and businesses – new action plan', COM(2020) 559 final of 24 September 2020, paragraph II.3 (Action 10). This has led to the adoption of the FASTER Directive (see Chapter 24) in December 2024. However, this initiative focuses on portfolio investments and carves out situations covered by the Parent-Subsidiary Directive and, in particular, the I&R Directive (which has its own rules regarding the relief procedure, see Sections 18.6.2 and 18.7.3 below).

9 See Article 23B(1)(b) OECD MC. Only very exceptionally, tax treaties between EU Member States contain 'tax sparing provisions' or provide 'matching credits'. See on this issue Alexander Rust, in: Klaus Vogel on Double Taxation Conventions, 5th ed. (2022), Art. 23 paragraphs 62 et seq.

10 On the potential relevance of the EU fundamental freedoms in this context, see CJEU Case C-18/15, *Brisal and KBC Finance Ireland*, EU:C:2016:549, and Case C-257/20, *'Viva Telecom Bulgaria' EOOD*, EU:C:2022:125, point 76 et seq. (both on interest), and furthermore the infringement procedure INFR(2021)4042 opened by the Commission against Spain with a letter of formal notice on 12 November 2021, INF/21/5342, and continued by a reasoned opinion on 12 March 2025, INF/2025/503 (on royalties).

18.1.2 History and Aim

Only a few months after the adoption of the Parent-Subsidiary Directive in July 1990, the Commission submitted a proposal for a Directive aimed at the abolition of withholding taxes on interest and royalty payments within groups of companies.[11] The group of independent experts supporting the Commission (Ruding Committee),[12] the Economic and Social Committee[13] and the European Parliament[14] urged the Council to adopt it, and the Commission even proposed a slight amendment.[15] However, during the Council negotiations Member States disagreed about the very feasibility of a Directive and about issues of a more technical nature. In 1994, therefore, the Commission withdrew its original proposal.[16]

The 'High-Level Group' installed by the Member States in the framework of the harmful tax competition discussion then asked the Commission to resubmit a new Directive proposal, which the Commission did in March 1998.[17] The main differences with the original proposal were an extension to 'associated companies' (beyond mere parent-subsidiary relationships), the possibility of excluding payments into low-tax regimes, and the inclusion of several anti-abuse provisions. On 3 June 2003 the Council finally adopted the I&R Directive 2003/49/EC as part of the 'package of three' to tackle harmful tax competition, which also comprised the Code of Conduct for company taxation (see Chapter 26) and the Interest Savings Directive (2003/48/EC), which has meanwhile been repealed as redundant after the inclusion of automatic exchange of savings interest information in the revamped Directive on Administrative Cooperation (DAC; see Chapter 28 and in particular Section 28.3.2.2 on DAC2).

The purpose of the I&R Directive is to be understood against the background described above (Section 18.1.1). As set out in its Preamble, the main aim is to eliminate remaining juridical double taxation and administrative and cash-flow disadvantages of cross-border intra-group interest and royalty payments as compared to similar purely domestic payments (see recital 2). A collateral aim is to ensure that interest and royalty payments are taxed at least once in a Member State (see recital 3). The core rule is a prohibition of taxation in the source State (see recital 4), which implies a choice in favour of taxation in the State of the recipient where the related expenditure (the cost of raising capital and the cost of research and development, respectively) will usually have been deducted. Remarkably, however, no general objective subject-to-tax clause was included, so that – apart from the special situation of a permanent establishment (PE) as beneficial owner (Article 1(5)

11 COM(90) 571 final of 28 November 1990, O.J. 1991 C 53/26. See also the Commission's Communication 'Guidelines on company taxation', SEC(90) 601 final of 20 April 1990, paragraphs 15, 26.
12 Conclusions and Recommendations of the Committee of Independent Experts on Company Taxation (1992), p. 12 and p. 30.
13 Opinion ECO/144 A of 20 March 1991.
14 Legislative Resolution C3-0054/91 of 14 February 1992, O.J. 1992 C 67/194.
15 See COM(93) 196 final of 10 June 1993, O.J. 1993 C 178/18.
16 EC Commission press release IP/94/1023 of 8 November 1994.
17 COM(1998) 67 final of 4 March 1998, O.J. 1998 C 123/9.

(b); see Section 18.3.3 below) – the current I&R Directive does not ensure that the interest and royalty payments are effectively taxed once in the EU (see also Section 18.8 below).

The general implementation deadline was 1 January 2004 (see Section 18.5.1 below), but some Member States were temporarily allowed to maintain a withholding tax for budgetary reasons (see Section 18.5.2 below). The Directive was then extended step by step according to the subsequent accessions of new Member States to the EU (see Sections 18.4.2 and 18.5.1 below), and certain further transitional derogations were accepted (see Section 18.5.2 below).

18.2 Objective (Substantive) Scope of Application

The first issue to be determined as regards the I&R Directive's scope of application is the type of transactions that are covered. In this respect, Article 1(1) refers to 'interest or royalty payments', and Article 2 contains explicit definitions for both types of payments.

18.2.1 'Interest' Income (Article 2(a))

The definition of the term 'interest' in Article 2(b) I&R Directive is basically identical to the definition in Article 11(3) of the OECD MC, the only substantive difference being the deletion of the word 'government' before the word 'securities' in the text of the Directive:

> 'income from debt-claims of every kind, whether or not secured by mortgage and whether or not carrying a right to participate in the debtor's profits, and in particular, income from securities and income from bonds or debentures, including premiums and prizes attaching to such securities, bonds or debentures; penalty charges for late payment shall not be regarded as interest.'

The original 1990 Commission proposal had been shorter, since it had not yet included the specific examples ('in particular') and the final clause about 'penalty charges'.

A difficult issue is whether also fictitious interest based on legal fictions contained in a Member State´s domestic legislation is covered by the I&R Directive.[18] While the definition of 'royalties' in Article 2(b) explicitly refers to 'payments' (see Section 18.2.2 below), the aforementioned definition of 'interest' in Article 2(a) generally refers to 'income', which would not categorically exclude fictitious interest income. The English wording of Article 1(1) I&R Directive, which mentions 'interest or royalty payments', is somewhat ambiguous, and other language versions are not very clear in this respect, either.[19] In *'Viva Telecom Bulgaria'* the CJEU took a somewhat surprising route and excluded fictitious interest from the scope of the I&R Directive by stressing the 'beneficial owner'

18 This issue likewise presents itself in a broader context under double tax treaties. For a discussion, see Peter Wattel and Otto Marres, 'Characterization of Fictitious Income under OECD-Patterned Tax Treaties', *European Taxation*, March 2003, p. 66–79.

19 For example, while the French and the Dutch version ('paiements d'intérêts et de redevances échus', 'uitkeringen van interest or royalty´s') seems to underline the requirement of an actual 'payment', the German version ('Einkünfte in Form von Zinsen oder Lizenzgebühren') seems to take a broader view on the existence of 'income'.

concept (see Sections 18.2.3 and 18.3.4 below) and the fact that the optional exclusion for perpetuals in Article 4(1)(d) I&R Directive (see Section 18.2.4.1 below) refers to 'payments'.[20] It is submitted that this reasoning is not very convincing,[21] in particular if one takes into consideration that the Court, in the same judgment, indicated that a requalification of actual interest payments into (fictitious) dividends may be covered by the Parent-Subsidiary Directive (see Section 18.2.4.3 below).

18.2.2 'Royalties' Income (Article 2(b))

The definition of the term 'royalties' in Article 2(b) I&R Directive is a modified version of the definition in Article 12(2) of the OECD MC:

> 'payments of any kind received as a consideration for the use of, or the right to use, any copyright of literary, artistic of scientific work, including cinematograph films and software, any patent, trade mark, design or model, plan, secret formula or process, or for information concerning industrial, commercial or scientific experience; payments for the use of, or the right to use, industrial, commercial or scientific equipment shall be regarded as royalties.'

This definition under the I&R Directive is broader than the OECD definition. It explicitly mentions payments related to *software*, which even goes beyond the 1998 Commission proposal (which had excluded payments for the transfer of ownership of, *e.g.*, software copyrights). Moreover, it explicitly includes payments related to industrial, commercial or scientific *equipment*, which were deleted from the OECD definition already in 1992.

18.2.3 Role of the OECD Model Commentary

Notwithstanding these minor differences, Article 2 of the I&R Directive bears close resemblance to the OECD MC. This raises the question of whether the interpretation of Articles 11(3) and 12(2) of that Model Convention as provided by the official OECD Commentary can, or even must, be taken into account for the interpretation of the Directive. In principle, it should be assumed that the definitions employed by the Directive are autonomous terms of EU law which the CJEU will interpret on the basis of their wording, their context and the purpose of the rules of which they form part.[22] This interpretation is not dependent upon the meaning of identical or similar terms under domestic law, and the same should apply *a fortiori* to the Commentary of an international organization on a mere Model Convention as the latter is not a legal act or contract with binding force, not even for the OECD Member States.[23]

---

20 CJEU Case C-257/20, *'Viva Telecom Bulgaria' EOOD*, *l.c.*, points 49 et seq. and 56.

21 For a critical discussion, see also Savvas Kostikidis and Florian Striefler, 'Fictitious Interest and Dividends Under Tax Treaties and the EU Directives', *EC Tax Review* 2022/5, p. 251–259, at p. 255 et seq.

22 See, *e.g.*, for the area of VAT: CJEU Case C-224/11, *BGŻ Leasing*, EU:C:2013:15, point 56. For customs duties: CJEU Case C-59/16, *The Shirtmakers*, EU:C:2017:362, point 22 et seq. For other areas beyond taxation: CJEU Case C-306/16, *Marques da Rosa*, EU:C:2017:844, point 38 with further references.

23 On the debate of the importance of the OECD MC and its Commentary for OECD Member States, see Werner Haslehner, in: Klaus Vogel, *l.c.*, Introduction, paragraph 116 et seq.

Yet, the large congruence between the wording of Article 2 I&R Directive and Articles 11(3) and 12(2) OECD MC is, of course, not a coincidence. Already the 1990 Commission proposal looked for guidance in the (1977) OECD MC,[24] and the 1998 Explanatory Memorandum likewise explicitly refers to the (1995) OECD MC,[25] so that the official OECD Commentary to that Model may indeed be of some interpretative authority. The few derogations from the text of the OECD MC are probably due to the difference in purpose of the two instruments: while the Directive aims at the abolition of source taxation of intra-EU cross-border transactions specifically within groups of companies, bilateral tax treaties aim in a wider sense at a division of the tax base and of taxing powers between two States as regards interest and royalty income of any kind beyond mere groups of companies.

But while the OECD Commentary may provide *useful guidance* for the interpretation of Articles 2(a) and 2(b) I&R Directive, it is quite a different question whether the contents of that Commentary must be considered to be *binding* in this respect. The EU is not a member of the OECD, and while the situation was still different when the I&R Directive was adopted, today not even all EU Member States are OECD members.[26] Moreover, the OECD Commentary is subject to constant changes at increasingly short intervals, so that the acceptance of a binding effect for the I&R Directive leads to the question of whether only the Commentary as it stood when the I&R Directive was adopted should be relevant ('static' approach),[27] or whether also subsequent amendments must be taken into account ('dynamic' or 'ambulatory' approach). While it was hard to imagine that the CJEU would feel tempted to venture into these realms,[28] the Grand Chamber of the Court nevertheless very deliberately, and contrary to the warning of Advocate General Kokott,[29] took that step in its judgment of 26 February 2019 in the so-called 'Danish cases' which concerned, *inter alia*, the interpretation of the term 'beneficial owner' in Article 1(4) I&R Directive: by way of a historical, systematic and teleological interpretation (see Section 18.3.4) the CJEU declared not only the OECD MC, but also 'the successive amendments of that model and

24 See 1990 Commission proposal, *l.c.*, Explanatory Memorandum under 'I. General', point 7 and, in particular, under 'II. Commentary', Article 2(a) and Article 2(b).

25 *Idem*, Explanatory Memorandum under 'II. Commentary', Article 2(1)(a) and Article 2(1)(b), and also Article 5.

26 Currently (per 9 June 2025) the OECD has 38 Member States, including 22 of the 27 EU Member States, but not Bulgaria, Croatia, Cyprus, Malta, and Romania.

27 When the Directive was adopted on 3 June 2003, the 2003 update of the OECD MC and its Commentary had already been published (28 January 2003).

28 For a critical view in particular with respect to Article 2(b), but also regarding the 'beneficial owner' criterion under Article 1(4), see Cécile Brokelind, 'Royalty Payments: Unresolved Issues in the Interest and Royalties Directive', *European Taxation*, May 2004, p. 252–258, at p. 253 et seq. and p. 256 et seq. Concerning the latter criterion, see also Luc Hinnekens, 'European Commission introduces beneficial ownership in latest directives proposals adding to the confusion with regard to its meaning', *EC Tax Review* 2000/1, p. 43–44.

29 See Advocate General Juliane Kokott, Case C-115/16, *N Luxembourg 1*, EU:C:2018:143, points 51-55, Case C-118/16, *X Denmark A/S*, EU:C:2018:146, points 51-55, Case C-119/16, *C Danmark I*, EU:C:2018:147, points 51-55, and Case C-299/16, *Z Denmark ApS*, EU:C:2018:148, points 51-55.

of the commentaries relating thereto ... relevant when interpreting Directive 2003/49', strongly rejecting any potential lack of democratic legitimacy.[30]

This approach regarding the beneficial ownership concept under Article 1(4) I&R Directive is in stark contrast to the Grand Chamber judgment of 12 September 2017 in Case C-648/15 where the CJEU was asked to rule, in its function as special arbitration court under Article 273 TFEU in conjunction with Article 25(5) of the 2000 Double Tax Convention between Austria and Germany, on the interpretation of the 'interest' Article of that bilateral treaty, and more specifically of the term 'debt-claims with participation in profits' mentioned therein. While Advocate General Mengozzi had relied extensively on the similar phrasing of Article 11(3) OECD MC and of the OECD Commentary thereon,[31] the CJEU did not mention either of the two in its legal reasoning, despite the fact that a provision in the Protocol to the tax treaty even linked that treaty with the OECD Commentary.[32]

18.2.4 Exclusion of Certain Payments (Article 4)

18.2.4.1 Optional Exclusion of Dividend-Like Payments (Art. 4(1))

Article 4(1) contains an option for the source State to disallow the benefits of the I&R Directive (*i.e.* the exemption under Article 1(1); see Section 18.6.1 below) for certain types of interest or royalty payments. A first category concerns payments treated as profit distributions or as repayment of subscribed capital under the source State's domestic law (Article 4(1)(a)). A second group of situations comprises different types of 'hybrid financing', namely payments from debt-claims which entitle the creditor either 'to participate in the debtor's profits' (such as silent partnerships or profit-participating loans; Article 4(1)(b)) or to exchange his loan against 'a right to participate in the debtor's profits' (such as convertible loans; Article 4(1)(c)), or which exclude repayment of the principal amount for more than 50 years[33] or even altogether[34] (Article 4(1)(d)).

---

30 CJEU Joined Cases C-115/16, *N Luxembourg 1*, C-118/16, *X Denmark A/S*, C-119/16, *C Danmark I* and C-299/16, *Z Denmark ApS*, EU:C:2019:134, points 84-92. For a critical discussion of this (dynamic) relevance of always the most recent version of the OECD MC and its Commentary for the interpretation of the I&R Directive, see CFE ECJ Task Force, 'Opinion Statement ECJ-TF 2/2019 on the ECJ Decisions of 26 February 2019 in *N Luxembourg I et al.* (Joined Cases C-115/16, C-118/16, C-119/16 and C-299/16) and *T Danmark et al.* (Joined Cases C-116/16 and C-117/16), Concerning the "Beneficial Ownership" Requirement and the Anti-Abuse Principle in the Company Tax Directives', *European Taxation*, October 2019, p. 487-502, at p. 497 et seq., and Joachim Englisch, 'The Danish tax avoidance cases: New milestones in the Court's anti-abuse doctrine', *Common Market Law Review*, March/April 2020, p. 503-538, at p. 524 et seq.

31 Advocate General Paolo Mengozzi, Case C-648/15, *Austria v. Germany*, EU:C:2017:311, point 68 et seq.

32 CJEU Case C-648/15, *Austria v. Germany*, EU:C:2017:664.

33 See in this respect CJEU, Case C-257/20, *'Viva Telecom Bulgaria' EOOD*, *l.c.*, points 19, 56, on a convertible loan scheduled to mature after 60 years.

34 On such 'perpetual loans', see Jakob Bundgaard, 'Perpetual and Super-Maturity Debt Instruments in International Tax Law', *Derivatives & Financial Instruments*, July/August 2008, p. 126-142, at p. 137 et seq.

While the 1998 Commission proposal had exclusively referred to 'interest' payments in this context, Article 4(1) of the adopted Directive mentions 'payments' without any further distinction, and the title of Article 4 covers both 'payments as interest or royalties'. Undoubtedly the most important type of payments addressed by Article 4(1) are interest payments, but also royalties may fall into its scope. This is particularly true for profit-based royalty agreements, which might be covered by Article 4(1)(b).

18.2.4.2 *Compulsory Exclusion of Non-Arm's Length Payments (Art. 4(2))*

Article 4(2) restricts the benefits of the I&R Directive to interest and royalty payments that are 'at arm's length'. Although the provision does not explicitly mention the latter standard (or a specific method for determining it), an independent party test is inherent to it. In this respect the provision must be understood against the background that, as the Explanatory Memorandum to the 1998 Commission proposal shows, it is based on the principles laid down in Articles 11(6) and 12(4) OECD MC, which complement Article 9 OECD MC and by some are even regarded as *leges speciales* to the latter.[35] Consequently, Article 4(2) of the Directive focuses on situations where, due to 'a special relationship between the payer and the beneficial owner' (or between one of them and a third party), the amount of interest or royalties paid 'exceeds the amount which would have been agreed by the payer and the beneficial owner in the absence of such a relationship'. In these cases, the exemption from source taxation (Article 1(1)) does not apply *in so far as* the payments would not have been negotiated between unrelated parties, *i.e.* to the extent they are not 'at arm's length'. Only the excessive amount is excluded under Article 4(2), and this on a compulsory basis.

In its core, Article 4(2) is a transfer pricing provision. To take an example, if the general ('arm's length') interest rate on the market is 5% but the parties to a loan of EUR 100,000 fix an interest rate of 8% in a situation that would otherwise fulfill all conditions for the I&R Directive to apply, the interest amount corresponding to the 3% excess (*i.e.* EUR 3,000) is excluded from the Directive.

Specifically as regards interest payments, the Commission takes the view that Article 4(2) is also intended as a thin capitalization provision.[36] If this view were correct, even loans with a market-compliant interest rate could fall foul of the Directive as far as the principal amount as such is too high from an 'arm's length' perspective. For example, if parties agree on a loan of EUR 100,000 at a market rate of 5% but an independent creditor would only have granted a loan of EUR 60,000, the interest amount corresponding to the difference of EUR 40,000 (*i.e.* EUR 2,000) would be excluded from the Directive. An explicit clause to that effect had in fact been included in Article 5 of the 1998 Commission proposal but was not taken over into Article 4(2) of the final 2003 version of the Directive. While this could speak against the view that the provision can also serve as a thin cap rule,

35 On the discussion, see Georg Kofler and Jens Wittendorf, in: Klaus Vogel, *l.c.*, Art. 9, paragraph 51 et seq.; Werner Haslehner, *ibid.*, Art. 11, paragraph 141; Matthias Valta, *ibid.*, Art. 12, paragraphs 19, 213.

36 See Commission Report on the functioning of the I&R Directive, COM(2009) 179 final of 17 April 2009, *Highlights & Insights* 2009.6/4, paragraph 3.3.8.

its wording nevertheless appears broad enough to include also indirect effects on the amount of the interest payments through the extent of the underlying principal amount.

18.2.4.3 Potential Link to the Parent-Subsidiary Directive

Depending on the circumstances of the individual case, however, neither the optional exclusion of interest and royalty payments under Article 4(1) of the I&R Directive nor the compulsory exclusion under Article 4(2) must necessarily mean that such payments remain without protection under EU law. Apart from the fact that the fundamental freedoms of the TFEU become relevant where a certain economic activity is not dealt with by a Directive,[37] the question rises as to whether such payments, if flowing upstream from a subsidiary to its parent, are then covered by Article 5 of the Parent-Subsidiary Directive (see Section 16.6.1) so that taxation in the source State would still be prohibited.

The wording of Article 4 I&R Directive is not very helpful in this respect. If a Member State exercises the option under Article 4(1) to exclude the payments mentioned therein, it may be that these payments are already in substance treated as a 'distribution of profits' or at least explicitly requalified into deemed dividends under that State's domestic law. However, unlike the 1998 Commission proposal, the adopted text of the I&R Directive does not mention a possible application of the Parent-Subsidiary Directive in this respect. Nevertheless, Article 4(1)(a) refers to a 'distribution of profits', which is the same term as the one used by the Parent-Subsidiary Directive (see Section 16.5.1).

Under Article 4(2) the situation is similar. While Article 5 of the 1998 Commission proposal had not explicitly mentioned the Parent-Subsidiary Directive, the Commission, in its 2009 report on the functioning of the I&R Directive (see Section 18.8 below), extended its own explanations concerning Article 4 of the 1998 proposal also to what became Article 4(2) of the Directive and argued that any amount reclassified as dividend should be granted the benefits of the Parent-Subsidiary Directive.[38] In this respect, the Commission relied on the view of Advocate General Mischo in Case C-324/00 *Lankhorst-Hohorst* that the requalification of interest payments into deemed dividends, on the basis of a domestic thin cap provision, leads to profit distributions covered by Article 5 of the Parent-Subsidiary Directive.[39]

Unfortunately the CJEU did not rule on this issue in *Lankhorst-Hohorst*, and of course the I&R Directive had not even been adopted yet at that time. The more recent *'Viva Telecom Bulgaria'* decision of 24 February 2022 did not concern a requalification of (actual)

37 See, *e.g.*, CJEU Case C-14/16, *Euro Park Service*, EU:C:2017:177, point 19 et seq.; Case C-6/16, *Eqiom and Enka*, EU:C:2017:641, point 15 et seq.; Joined Cases C-504/16 and C-613/16, *Deister Holding and Juhler Holding*, EU:C:2017:1009, point 45 et seq.; Case C-440/17, *GS*, EU:C:2018:437, point 31 et seq.

38 See 2009 Commission Report, *l.c.*, paragraph 3.3.8. In the same sense also Economic and Social Committee, opinion of 1 July 1998, O.J. 1998 C 285/50, paragraphs 6.2 and 7.4.

39 See Advocate General Jean Mischo, Case C-324/00, *Lankhorst-Hohorst*, EU:C:2002:177, point 100 et seq.

interest payments,[40] but nevertheless indicated that a requalification of such payments into (deemed) dividends may lead to an applicability of the Parent-Subsidiary Directive.[41] We submit that a Member State which (under its domestic tax law) requalifies payments that, under private law, are interest or royalties and treats them as dividends, should be consistent and treat such payments as 'distribution of profits' under the Parent-Subsidiary Directive. There are indeed good teleological arguments for the view that such reclassified dividend-like payments fall within the scope of the latter Directive.[42]

18.3 Subjective (Personal) Scope of Application

It follows from Article 1(1) I&R Directive that, in order for the tax exemption in the source State to apply, the recipient ('beneficial owner'; see Section 18.3.4 below) must either be a 'company of another Member State' or a 'permanent establishment' (more precisely: a PE 'situated in another Member State of a company of a Member State'). From the various other paragraphs of Article 1 it can be derived that the payer, too, must either be a 'company of a Member State' or a PE in the aforementioned sense of such a company. In addition, Article 1(7) stipulates that the company making the payment (or whose PE is treated as the payer) must be 'associated' with the company which is the receiving beneficial owner (or whose PE is treated as such). All these requirements are further worked out in Article 3.

18.3.1 'Company of a Member State' (Article 3(a))

The current version of the I&R Directive follows the 1998 Commission proposal, which had ignored the Ruding Committee's recommendation to extend the scope of the initial 1990 proposal to all enterprises, irrespective of their legal form.[43] Instead, the same approach was chosen as in the Parent-Subsidiary and Merger Directives. For the purposes of the I&R Directive, a company is a 'company of a Member State' (Article 3(a)) if it is:

- (*(i) legal form*) incorporated as a legal entity listed in the Annex to the Directive (which does not yet include the SE and SCE nor the national legal forms which have been added to the Parent-Subsidiary and Merger Directives Annexes, as a 2011 Commission proposal for a similar extension has not yet been adopted; see Section 18.8 below);

---

40 CJEU Case C-257/20, *'Viva Telecom Bulgaria' EOOD*, *l.c.*, point 63, concerning interest income based on a legal fiction in a situation addressed by Article 4(1)(d) of the Directive where no actual interest payments had been made on an interest-free convertible loan (see Sections 18.2.1 and 18.2.4.1 above).

41 *Idem*, point 61 et seq., although the judgment referred to there (Case C-524/04, *Test Claimants in the Thin Cap Group Litigation*, EU:C:2007:161, points 87-89) did not concern the Parent-Subsidiary Directive.

42 For further discussion see, *e.g.*, Eva Eberhartinger and Martin Six, 'Taxation of Cross-Border Hybrid Finance: A Legal Analysis', *Intertax*, January 2009, p. 4-18, at p. 15 et seq.; Jakob Bundgaard, 'Classification and Treatment of Hybrid Financial Instruments and Income Derived Therefrom under EU Corporate Tax Directives', Parts 1 and 2, *European Taxation*, October and November 2010, p. 442-456 and p. 490-500, at p. 450 et seq.

43 See Ruding Committee, *l.c.*, p. 12 and p. 30.

- (*(ii) tax residency*) resident for tax purposes in a Member State without at the same time being considered a non-EU resident under the tie-breaker provision of a tax treaty with a third State; and
- (*(iii) subject to tax*) subject, without being exempt, to one of the Member States' corporation taxes listed in Article 3(a)(iii).

As regards the last-mentioned subject-to-tax criterion, the wording of Article 3(a) implies that it is the 'company' as such that must be subject to tax (subjective requirement), but not necessarily (all of) its income, such as the interest or royalty payments received (objective requirement). While both the 2003 and the 2011 Commission proposals to amend the Directive (see Section 18.8 below) suggested to add in Article 1(1) the explicit condition that the relevant income itself must be 'effectively subject to tax', some Member States have already run ahead and require the interest or royalty payment to be effectively taxed or even to be subject to a corporation tax comparable to that in the payer State.[44] Relying on a systematic interpretation taking into consideration the objective approach under the subject-to-tax clause for PEs in Article 1(5)(b) I&R Directive (see Section 18.3.3 below), and on a teleological interpretation paying heed to the intention of the Directive that the relevant income should be subject to tax (only, but a least) 'once in a Member State', the CJEU favoured the latter (objective) approach.[45] In this way the additional fact that not all Member States have been respecting the circumstance that Article 3(a) I&R Directive does not contain the explicit requirement (of a company being 'subject to tax') 'without the possibility of an option', which is included in both Article 2(a)(iii) of the Parent-Subsidiary Directive and Article 3(c) of the Merger Directive,[46] has lost its relevance.

Article 3(a) does not expressly require the above three conditions to be met within one and the same national jurisdiction, so that companies with dual tax residency in two Member States are not excluded. Some Member States nevertheless appear to require eligible companies to be subject to tax in the State of their effective management, although there is no legal basis for that requirement in the I&R Directive.[47]

Unlike the Parent-Subsidiary and Merger Directives, the I&R Directive does not contain a provision addressing hybrid entities, probably because the list of eligible national legal forms in its Annex is (still) limited to the usual plc- and Ltd-like companies, whereas the lists annexed to the two other directives were extended to cover many more less regular national legal entities or even all entities subject to local corporation tax. The Commission infers from the absence of a look-through provision in the I&R Directive that Member States cannot refuse the Directive benefits to a qualifying company of another Member

44 See 2009 Commission Report, *l.c.*, paragraph 3.3.5.4.
45 CJEU Joined Cases C-115/16 et al., *N Luxembourg 1 et al.*, *l.c.*, point 150 et seq., deviating in this respect from Advocate General Juliane Kokott, Case C-118/16, *X Denmark A/S*, *l.c.*, points 93-97.
46 See 2009 Commission Report, *l.c.*, paragraph 3.3.5.4. See in the context of the Parent-Subsidiary Directive also CJEU Case C-448/15, *Wereldhave Belgium Comm.VA et al.*, EU:C:2017:180, point 29 et seq.
47 *Id.*, paragraph 3.3.5.3.

State on the ground that they consider it as fiscally transparent, and even if they could, they would then be required to extend the Directive benefits to the partners/shareholders.[48]

18.3.2 Association Requirement (Article 1(7))

In order to qualify for the tax exemption in the source State, Article 1(7) I&R Directive requires a 'company of a Member State' to be 'associated' with another 'company of a Member State' at the other end of the payment, even if that payment involves a PE of one of the two companies as payer or as recipient (beneficial owner) or is exclusively made between two PEs. The Ruding Committee's recommendation to extend the scope of the (initial) 1990 proposal to encompass all interest and royalty payments between enterprises, irrespective of any affiliation,[49] has not been followed by the EU institutions. In its 1998 proposal the Commission decided to apply a gradual approach, *i.e.* to postpone a further extension to an undetermined moment in the future.[50]

18.3.2.1 'Associated' Companies (Article 3(b))

The I&R Directive does not only cover 'upstream' payments (from a subsidiary to its parent), but also 'downstream' payments from parents to subsidiaries, as well as 'sidestream' payments between sister companies. The range of possibilities is even enlarged due to the fact that also PEs of the aforementioned companies can be involved, both on the paying and the receiving side. The key criterion to be met is that the companies at both ends of the payment must, in addition to both being a 'company of a Member State' (see Section 18.3.1 above), be 'associated'. Pursuant to Article 3(b), first clause, this means that either (i)/(ii) one of the two companies involved holds directly at least 25% of the capital in the other (vertical affiliation, whichever direction), or (iii) both of them are directly held for at least 25% by the same third company (horizontal affiliation). A prospective inclusion of 'indirect holdings' is still under discussion (see Section 18.8 below).

Unlike under the Parent-Subsidiary Directive, however, only first-tier associations qualify ('direct holding'). Payments between, *e.g.*, grandparent companies and sub-subsidiaries, or between 'cousins,' or between 'aunts and nieces', even if they are eventually wholly-owned by the same common shareholder, remain as yet outside the scope of the I&R Directive. This is a derogation from the Commission proposals.[51] The recitals to the 2003 Directive

48 *Id.*, paragraph 3.3.5.2.
49 See Ruding Committee, *l.c.*, p. 12 and p. 30.
50 See 1998 Commission proposal, *l.c.*, Explanatory Memorandum under 'I. General', paragraphs 14 and 15.
51 The 1990 proposal had included all minimum holdings of 25% without further distinction between 'direct' or 'indirect' holdings. The 1998 proposal had even explicitly included 'directly or indirectly' held minimum participations of 25%.

do not explain this restriction in scope to 'direct holdings',[52] and it has been suggested[53] that the reason was purely budgetary.

The holdings must 'involve' only companies resident in the EU (Article 3(b), second clause). Since this requirement does not seem to address the common parent of two EU-resident sister companies, sidestream payments between these sister companies would seem to qualify even if both are held by a common *non*-EU parent. Interpreted in this manner, however, this requirement appears pointless next to the other qualification requirements, which leads some to the conclusion that the common parent must reside in Union territory as well.[54] That is also the position of the Commission and of almost all Member States.[55]

In its third clause, Article 3(b) grants Member States 'the option of replacing' the criterion of a 25% minimum holding in capital by a 25% minimum holding of voting rights. The term 'replace' in our view implies that Member States may only require a minimum holding either in capital or of voting rights, but not both simultaneously.

Unlike the Parent-Subsidiary Directive did as of 2005 (see Section 16.3.2), the I&R Directive does not provide for a gradual reduction of the minimum (direct) association requirement of 25%. This may lead to odd results: an interest or royalty payment by a 20% subsidiary is not exempt under the I&R Directive but may be exempt under the Parent-Subsidiary Directive if it is reclassified as a 'profit distribution' (see Section 18.2.4.3 above).

18.3.2.2 Potential Limitation: Minimum Association Period (Article 1(10))

Art. 1(10) of the I&R Directive grants Member States the option to refuse the Directive benefits if the qualifying association between the relevant companies (see Section 18.3.2.1 above) has 'not been maintained for an uninterrupted period of at least two years'. This option accommodates States wishing to ensure that the group association is genuine and not contrived just for the occasional enjoyment of the Directive benefits. In 2009, eleven of the 20 Member States surveyed by the Commission had implemented a minimum association period requirement in their domestic laws.[56]

A similar reservation is contained in Article 3(2) of the Parent-Subsidiary Directive, but the phrasing of the latter provision ('do not maintain') differs from the wording of Article 1(10) of the I&R Directive ('have not been maintained'). This textual difference may lead to a difference in substance, since in the *Denkavit* case of 1996 the CJEU explicitly

---

52 For specific problems related to the inclusion of partnerships in the holding chain, see Raffaele Russo, 'Partnerships and Other Hybrid Entities and the EC Corporate Direct Tax Directives', *European Taxation*, October 2006, p. 478-486, at p. 480 et seq.; Sandra Martinho Fernandes, Roberto Bernales, Suat Goeydeniz, Bob Michel, Oana Popa, and Emanuela Santoro, 'A Comprehensive Analysis of Proposals To Amend the Interest and Royalties Directive', Parts 1 and 2, *European Taxation*, September/October and November 2011, p. 396-417 and p. 445-464, at p. 400 et seq.

53 See Marcello Distaso and Raffaele Russo, 'The EC Interest and Royalties Directive – Comment', *European Taxation*, April 2004, p. 143-154, at p. 146.

54 *Id.*, at p. 146.

55 See 2009 Commission Report, *l.c.*, paragraph 3.3.6.2.

56 *Id.*, paragraph 3.3.3.

relied on the use of the present tense in most language versions of Article 3(2) of the Parent-Subsidiary Directive to hold that the option towards a minimum holding period under that Directive does not entitle Member States to refuse the benefits of that Directive (*in casu*: the tax exemption in the source State under Article 5; see Sections 16.3.2 and 16.6.1) if the period has not yet been completed at the time of payment, but is in fact duly completed after the payment.[57] As regards Article 1(10) of the I&R Directive, however, already the 1998 Commission proposal had used the same wording ('have not been maintained') and stated explicitly in its Explanatory Memorandum that Member States were not allowed 'to make the granting of the tax advantage provided for by the Directive subject to the condition that, at the moment of the payment of the interest and royalties, this holding period has already been completed, so long as it is subsequently observed'.[58] So despite the fact that no present tense is used, the intention was to establish the same rule like Article 3(2) of the Parent-Subsidiary Directive as interpreted by the CJEU. In its 2009 report (see Section 18.8 below), the Commission even indicated that, after the coming into force of Directive 2001/44/EC on the mutual assistance in the recovery of tax claims (now Directive 2010/24/EU; see Chapter 27), Member States should grant the tax exemption under Article 1(1) immediately without being permitted any longer to require security for payment during the remainder of the association period.[59]

We submit that the option of setting a minimum period requirement in principle precludes Member States from relying on the general anti-abuse clauses (see Section 18.7.1 below) as regards the period of association if they do not exercise that option, or if they do but are still not satisfied after that period or not satisfied with their own option (*lex specialis derogat legi generali*).

Moreover, in our view the association period is not 'interrupted' if a sister company is becoming a subsidiary of its former sister or *vice versa*, or if one of the companies involved is merged into another company (*e.g.* into the common parent) or is divided and ceases to exist, except where the resulting company after such merger or division does not fulfill the (other) requirements for eligibility, for instance because it is tax resident outside the Union. Given the object and purpose of the Directive and the CJEU's narrow interpretation of the anti-abuse clause in the Merger Directive (see Section 17.12), we see no reason for a restart of the two-year waiting period, except where the other criteria are no longer met.

18.3.3 'Permanent Establishment' (Article 3(c))

The tax exemption in the source State under Article 1(1) I&R Directive also extends to cross-border intra-EU payments made or received by PEs of 'associated' EU companies, so that 'triangular' and even 'quadrangular' situations may arise (see Section 18.4.1 below).

57 Joined Cases C-283/94, C-291/94 and C-292/94, *Denkavit Internationaal BV, VITIC BV and Voormeer BV*, EU:C:1996:387, point 22 et seq.

58 See 1998 Commission proposal, *l.c.*, Explanatory Memorandum under 'II. General', Article 3(2), second clause.

59 See 2009 Commission Report, *l.c.*, paragraph 3.3.3.

Under private law, a PE (which under company law is often, but not necessarily, a branch) is not a legal entity and cannot, therefore, 'make' or 'receive' payments in legal terms; rather, the payment is made or received by the company to whom the PE belongs. International tax law nonetheless applies a separate entity fiction and an arm's length profit calculation principle as regards PEs for the purpose of correct territorial allocation of profits and losses: for international tax base division purposes, a foreign PE is deemed to be an independent third party, dealing at arm's length with the company of which it is a PE (Article 7(2) OECD MC).[60]

For the purposes of the I&R Directive, a number of provisions determine the circumstances under which a PE is treated as a separate payer or recipient, respectively:

- For a PE to be considered as the *creditor* (beneficial owner) of an interest or royalty payment, Article 1(5) requires (a) the title for that payment (*i.e.* the underlying debt-claim or right) to be 'effectively connected' with the PE, and (b) the PE to be subject to a qualifying corporation tax on the payment received in its State of location. This subject-to-tax clause ensures that no double non-taxation occurs. Oddly, the definition of beneficial ownership thus differs depending on whether the recipient is a company or a PE of a company.
- For a PE to be considered as the *debtor* of an interest or royalty payment, that payment must be tax deductible in the State where the PE is located (Article 1(3)). Thus, the tax exemption under Article 1(1) is frustrated where the source State considers a payment made by a PE within its territory as non-deductible. This may be relevant for 'internal' payments (from the PE to its foreign head office), and in case of thin capitalization legislation in the source State.

In order to avoid possible duplication, Article 1(6) stipulates that if a PE is considered to be the payer or the beneficial owner, no other part of the company (*i.e.* the head office or another PE) can be treated as payer or beneficial owner, respectively, at the same time.

The definition of 'permanent establishment' in Article 3(c) I&R Directive as

> 'a fixed place of business situated in a Member State through which the business of a company of another Member State is wholly or partly carried on'

follows Article 5(1) OECD MC, except for the replacement of the words 'of an enterprise' by 'of a company of another Member State', and the addition of the words 'situated in a Member State'. Already based on the OECD MC definition, a 'permanent establishment' is *per se* a cross-border concept in the sense that the PE must be located in another State than its head office. For the purposes of the I&R Directive, Article 3(c) adds the double requirement that both the State of the head office and the State of the PE must be (different) Member States.

60 See in this respect, in particular, the treatment of a PE as a 'functionally separate entity' under the 'authorized OECD approach' (AOA), developed in the OECD report on 'The attribution of profits to permanent establishments' of 17 July 2008, paragraph 9 et seq., and introduced in Article 7(2) OECD MC during the 2010 amendment.

Moreover, Article 3(c) is identical to Article 2(b) of the Parent-Subsidiary Directive, except for the subject-to-tax clause which was added in the latter definition as from 2005.The term 'permanent establishment' has thus become an EU law concept, and we expect the CJEU to interpret it in the same manner for the Merger Directive, even though the latter does not contain a definition of the term as such, but only of a 'branch of activity' (see Section 17.7.4). Due to the close resemblance between the EU definition and its OECD counterpart, we further expect the Court to seek inspiration in the specifications contained in Article 5(2) to (7) OECD MC and in the official OECD Commentary to that Model (see generally also Section 18.2.3 above). This also goes for the interpretation of the term 'effectively connected' in Article 1(5)(a) I&R Directive, which finds its origin in Article 11(4) and Article 12(3) OECD MC.[61]

18.3.4 Recipient as 'Beneficial Owner' (Article 1(4), (5))

In order to qualify as 'beneficial owner', the recipient company or PE (Article 1(5)) must receive the payments for 'its own benefit', *i.e.* not as a mere 'intermediary' (such as an 'agent, trustee, or authorised signatory') for 'some other person' (Article 1(4)). This provision seeks to exclude 'conduit' companies, artificially interposed by non-qualifying (*e.g.* third State) creditors in an expedient Member State in order to become eligible for Directive (and/or tax treaty) benefits for which they would otherwise not qualify if the payments were made directly to them.

The term 'beneficial owner', too, has thus become an EU law concept,[62] and in its judgment in the famous 'Danish cases' the CJEU clarified its meaning for the purposes of the I&R Directive.[63] These cases are particularly interesting because the Court was explicitly asked to rule on the influence of the OECD Commentary in this respect, given that the concept has its roots in Articles 10 to 12 of the OECD MC. Basing itself on the aims of the I&R Directive, as well as the systematic context and various language versions of Article 1(4), the CJEU put a strong emphasis on the 'economic reality': according to the Court, the relevant 'beneficial owner' is not a recipient who is formally identified, but rather 'the entity which benefits economically' from an interest or royalty payment received and accordingly has 'the power freely to determine the use to which it is put'.[64] Taking into consideration the relevance of the OECD MC and the OECD Commentary thereon (see Section 18.2.3 above) during the historical development of Article 1(4) I&R Directive, the CJEU decided that the beneficial ownership criterion 'excludes conduit companies and must be understood not in a narrow technical sense but as having a meaning that enables double taxation to be avoided and tax evasion and avoidance to be prevented'.[65]

61 See also the OECD report on 'The attribution of profits to permanent establishments' of 22 July 2010, paragraph 72 et seq.

62 For an in-depth analysis, see Juan Rodriguez and Georg Kofler, 'Beneficial Ownership and EU Law', in: Michael Lang et al., Beneficial Ownership: Recent Trends, IBFD Amsterdam (2013), p. 215-248.

63 The issue was also addressed by the questions referred to the CJEU in Case C-682/16, *BEI ApS*, EU:C:2019:987, but after the decision in the other cases the domestic Danish court withdrew its reference for a preliminary ruling.

64 CJEU Joined Cases C-115/16 et al., *N Luxembourg 1 et al.*, *l.c.*, points 85-89.

65 *Idem*, points 90-92.

Still, where this test leads to the result that the recipient of an interest or royalty payment is not the 'beneficial owner', this does not render the I&R Directive *per se* inapplicable. It can still be applied if the relevant 'beneficial owner' is positively identified and all further requirements of the Directive's scope of application are fulfilled[66] – in particular, the beneficial owner's qualification as a 'company of a Member State' (see Section 18.3.1 above) and its association with the payer (see Section 18.3.2 above).

It remains to be seen how this interpretation of the beneficial ownership criterion under the I&R Directive in line with OECD principles will develop in practice.[67] One should not overlook the fact that under the OECD MC the scope of the term 'beneficial owner' is far from clear.[68] There are those who wished that, for the legal uncertainty it creates, the term had never been included in the OECD MC, and who argue that it should not be used for anti-abuse purposes (for which targeted LOB-provisions should be included) but only to look through dependent representatives (agents etc.). The need for a beneficial ownership requirement would possibly never have been felt if another term than 'paid' had been used to make the connection between the source and the recipient of a certain item of income, such as 'derived' or 'income from', which offer the possibility to tax the ultimate beneficiary of the payment.

18.4 Territorial Scope of Application

The regional sphere within which protection is granted under the I&R Directive is determined, in the first place, by general EU law rules. According to its Article 11, the Directive is 'addressed to the Member States' and therefore binding upon them (Article 288 TFEU). Just like the TEU and TFEU, also EU secondary law is binding in the territory of each Member State (Article 52 TEU) with certain modifications for, in particular, overseas

66 *Idem*, point 94.

67 For a first application to interest payments, see Corte Suprema di Cassazione of 10 July 2020, no. 14756, point 1.11 et seq., on a Luxembourg subholding which, contrary to the view of the Italian tax authority, was not considered to be a mere 'conduit' company. See more recently also First Instance Court of Leuven of 27 October 2023, no. 21/942/A, point 6 et seq., interpreting the term 'beneficial owner' under the 2001 Double Tax Treaty Belgium-Netherlands along the lines of CJEU Joined Cases C-115//16 et al., *N Luxembourg et al.*, *l.c.* It should be mentioned, however, that even though the CJEU's parallel judgment in Joined Cases C-116/16, *T Danmark* and C-117/16, *Y Denmark ApS*, EU:C:2019:135, points 93-94, on the taxation of dividends under the Parent-Subsidiary Directive (which does not contain an explicit beneficial ownership criterion) did not address the beneficial ownership issue, it is exactly within the framework of the latter Directive that the fight of domestic tax authorities against 'conduit' companies has now strongly increased.

68 See, *inter alia*, the OECD public discussion draft 'Clarification of the meaning of "beneficial owner" in the OECD Model Tax Convention' of 29 April 2011 and the revised public discussion draft 'Revised proposals concerning the meaning of "beneficial owner" in Articles 10, 11 and 12 of the OECD Model Tax Convention' of 19 October 2012, which led to significant amendments of the OECD Commentary on Articles 10, 11 and 12 during the 2014 Update. See also Eric Kemmeren, in: Klaus Vogel, *l.c.*, Pre Arts 10-12, paragraph 19 et seq.

territories connected with certain Member States (Article 355 TFEU).[69] In addition, it follows from different provisions of the Directive that only *cross-border* interest or royalty payments are covered.

18.4.1 Cross-border Payments between EU Member States

While Article 1(1) I&R Directive does not explicitly require a 'cross-border' payment of interest or royalties between two EU Member States, its wording makes sufficiently clear that this condition must be fulfilled: on the one hand, the payment must be 'arising in a Member State', and on the other hand the recipient (beneficial owner) must either be 'a company of another Member State' or a PE 'situated in another Member State' (of a 'company of a Member State'). It is, in particular, the inclusion of PEs both on the paying and the receiving side which leads to the effect that the structures covered by the Directive may be rather complex. Already 'triangular cases' involving only one PE either as payer or as recipient (beneficial owner) of an interest or royalty payment create difficulties, and this is even more true when it comes to 'quadrangular cases' of payments between two PEs within the EU.[70]

The requirement that the payment must be 'arising in a Member State' is further elaborated in Article 1(2), which states that payments made by a company of a Member State or by a PE located in a Member State 'shall be deemed to arise in that Member State' (labeled as the 'source State'). Hence, if the payer is (the head office of) the company, the conditions of Article 3(a) must be fulfilled, including the criterion under (ii) in case of dual residency (see Section 18.3.1 above). If the payer is a PE, it follows from the definition under Article 3(c) that this PE must belong to 'a company of another Member State' (see Section 18.3.3 above).

Taking the perspective of the source State as starting point, the requirement of a *cross-border* payment can be inferred from the fact that the recipient (beneficial owner) must either be 'a company of another Member State' or a PE 'situated in another Member State'. This excludes certain exceptional situations which do not, in their economic essence, represent cross-border payments, such as payments that are factually made by company 1 of Member State A to company 2 of Member State B, but on the basis of a debt-claim

69 It should be added that Article 15(2) of the bilateral EU-Switzerland Agreement of 26 October 2004 accompanying the Interest Savings Directive 2003/48/EC, O.J. 2004 L 385/30, contained a 'mini version' of the I&R Directive. For details, see Klaus Eicker and Ralph Obser, 'The impact of the Swiss-EC Agreement on intra-group dividend, interest and royalty payments', *EC Tax Review* 2006/3, p. 134-146, at p. 142 et seq.; Marcel Jung, 'Art. 15 of the Switzerland-EC Savings Tax Agreement: Measures Equivalent to Those in the EC Parent-Subsidiary and the Interest and Royalties Directives – A Swiss Perspective?', *European Taxation*, March 2006, p. 112-126, at p. 121 et seq. After the repeal of Directive 2003/48/EC, the relevant provision became Article 9(2); see Council Decision 2015/2400 (EU) of 8 December 2015 on the Amending Protocol, O.J. 2015 L 333/10.

70 See Klaus Eicker and Fabio Aramini, 'Overview on the recent developments of the EC Directive on Withholding Taxes on Royalty and Interest Payments', *EC Tax Review* 2004/3, p. 134-145, at p. 140 et seq., and for a detailed analysis Michele Gusmeroli, 'Triangular Cases and the Interest and Royalties Directive: Untying the Gordian Knot?', Parts 1, 2 and 3, *European Taxation*, January, February and March 2005, p. 2-13, p. 39-51 and p. 87-96.

that is effectively connected to a PE of the latter company in Member State A.[71] Included, however, would be a 'meander' structure with company 1 and company 2 both being resident in Member State A and company 1 effecting a payment to company 2, but on the basis of a debt-claim that is effectively connected to a PE of the latter company in Member State B.[72]

Last but not least, Article 1(8) excludes payments by or to a PE in a third State of a company of a Member State, while Article 1(1) and Article 3(c) also exclude payments by a company of a Member State (or of its PE in the EU) to a PE in the EU of a company of a third State even if that PE is the beneficial owner of the underlying debt-claim.

18.4.2 Accession of new Member States and 'Brexit'

When the I&R Directive was adopted in June 2003, it was addressed to the existing group of (then) 15 Member States. With each accession of a new Member State, the territorial scope of the Directive has been enlarged to that State (hand in hand with an extension of the subjective scope regarding the lists of national corporation taxes in Article 3(a)(iii) and of qualifying legal forms of eligible companies in the Annex to the Directive; see Section 18.3.1 above). Three enlargements have taken place until now. The first concerned the accession of ten new Member States per 1 May 2004, and the relevant amendments of the I&R Directive were mainly (but see Section 18.5.2 below) dealt with by Council Directive 2004/66/EC.[73] The same amendment procedure was followed with Council Directive 2006/98/EC[74] when Bulgaria and Romania acceded on 1 January 2007, and then with Directive 2013/13/EU[75] upon the accession of Croatia as from 1 July 2013.

Due to the withdrawal of the United Kingdom from the EU ('Brexit') under Article 50 TEU per 31 January 2020, the territorial scope of the I&R Directive no longer includes the UK. Based on the Withdrawal Agreement between the EU and the UK,[76] this exclusion became effective with the end of the transition period (31 December 2020).

18.5 Temporal Scope of Application

A final issue concerns the date until which Member States have to transpose the I&R Directive into domestic law. Closely connected with this transformation date is also the general question as to from when onwards taxpayers may rely on a direct effect of rules contained in the Directive.

71 See 1998 Commission proposal, *l.c.*, Explanatory Memorandum under 'II. General', Article 1(2)(a).
72 *Id.*, Explanatory Memorandum under 'II. General', Article 1(2)(b).
73 Council Directive 2004/66/EC of 26 April 2004, O.J. 2004 L 168/35, concerning the accession of the Czech Republic, Estonia, Cyprus, Latvia, Lithuania, Hungary, Malta, Poland, Slovenia, and Slovakia.
74 Council Directive 2006/98/EC of 20 November 2006, O.J. 2006 L 363/129.
75 Council Directive 2013/13/EU of 13 May 2013, O.J. 2013 L 141/30.
76 Agreement on the withdrawal of the United Kingdom of Great Britain and Northern Ireland from the European Union and the European Atomic Energy Community of 17 October 2019, O.J. 2019 CI 384/1.

18.5.1 General Deadlines for Implementation

The original implementation period of the I&R Directive was only slightly more than half a year: national law of the (then) 15 Member States had to be adapted by 1 January 2004 (Article 7(1)), which not all Member States managed to do on time.[77] Greece, Spain and Portugal were granted temporary derogations (see Section 18.5.2 below). The Directive was subsequently amended to include further States which had acceded to the EU: as of 1 May 2004 a group of ten new Member States joined, before Bulgaria and Romania followed per 1 January 2007 and Croatia per 1 July 2013 (see Section 18.4.2 above). In each case the date of accession was also the relevant deadline for the implementation of the amended Directive. In some cases, however, new temporary derogations were allowed.

18.5.2 Transitional Derogations for Some Source States; Ordinary Credit for Residual Source Tax in Home State (Article 6)

In its original 2003 version, the I&R Directive had authorized Greece, Portugal and Spain 'not to apply the provisions of Article 1' (*i.e.* the prohibition of source State taxation) for a certain period (Article 6(1)). Regarding Greece and Portugal this concerned both interest and royalty payments, whereas for Spain it concerned royalties only. These exceptions were motivated by 'budgetary reasons' (see recitals 7 and 8) and must be understood against the background that these three countries are net importers of know-how and loan capital.[78] Until 1 July 2005[79] they fully retained their taxing rights as source State, and after that date a transitional period of eight years for Greece and Portugal and six years for Spain started in which the derogations to their benefit were gradually phased out (via a 10% tax rate to a 5% tax rate and finally to a zero rate, *i.e.* full exemption).

Subsequently, such transitional derogations were also granted to certain new Member States when joining the EU. First, this was the case for some of the Member States which joined on 1 May 2004: Latvia and Poland were granted the same exception as Greece and Portugal, while Lithuania was only granted a six years period to phase out its source taxes on interest and royalty payments; the Czech Republic, on the other hand, joined the six years exception for Spain limited to royalty payments, while Slovakia was granted a two years exception in this respect.[80] During the next enlargement step per 1 January 2007, Bulgaria was granted a derogation (with phasing out) until 31 December 2014, while Romania was entitled to keep a 10% tax rate until 31 December 2010.[81] All these transitional rules have expired now, and no new exceptions were introduced for Croatia upon its accession per 1 July 2013. No use has been made of the possibility to extend a transitional

77 See IBFD, Survey on the Implementation of the EC Interest and Royalty Directive (2005), p. 5.

78 See also 1998 Commission proposal, *l.c.*, Explanatory Memorandum under 'II. General', Article 8(1).

79 This date coincided with the first application of the (now repealed) Interest Savings Directive 2003/48/EC of 3 June 2003, O.J. 2003 L 157/38. See the Council Decision of 19 July 2004 on the date of application of that Directive, O.J. 2004 L 257/7.

80 See Article 1 of Council Directive 2004/76/EC of 29 April 2004, O.J. 2004 L 157/106.

81 See Article 20 and Annexes VI.6.3 and VII.7.3 of the Protocol to the Accession Treaty of Bulgaria and Romania, O.J. 2005 L 157/20. With respect to Bulgaria, see also CJEU Case C-257/20, *'Viva Telecom Bulgaria' EOOD*, *l.c.*, point 3 et seq.

period (Article 6(1) *in fine*), which would have required a Commission proposal and a unanimous Council decision prior to the expiration of the above-mentioned deadlines.

During the transitional periods, the Member States enjoying an exception under Article 6(1) I&R Directive were nevertheless obliged to apply lower withholding tax rates if such rates had been agreed upon in a bilateral tax treaty with one of the other Member States. Moreover, the Member State of the company/PE receiving a qualifying interest or royalty payment subject to the transitional tax regime in one of the source States mentioned above was required to credit such source tax against the corporation tax of the recipient company (Article 6(2)), up to the amount of the recipient State's corporation tax attributable to the interest or royalty income ('ordinary credit'; Article 6(3)). If that attributable tax (calculated on a *net* basis with cost deduction) was lower than the withholding tax levied on a *gross* basis in the source State, double taxation persisted with respect to an amount of income equal to related costs (see also Section 18.1.1 above).

18.6 Relief Rule: Tax Exemption in the Source State

If all requirements concerning the scope of application of the I&R Directive are fulfilled, the Member State of the paying company (or of the paying PE of a qualifying company) must 'exempt' the interest and royalty payments made to a beneficial owner in another Member State (Article 1(7)) from 'any taxes', whether levied 'by deduction at source or by assessment' (Article 1(1)).

18.6.1 Exemption from 'Any Taxes' (Art. 1(1))

Since Article 1(1) I&R Directive requires an 'exemption', the usual tax treaty mechanism of an initial withholding obligation imposed on the payer by the source State, supplemented by a later tax refund upon request of the recipient, does not suffice. In principle, the source State may not tax the outbound payment at all, as not only double taxation must be removed but also cash-flow disadvantages and administrative hindrances as compared to purely domestic intra-group payments. A withholding tax can only be applied if the procedural requirements for immediate exemption at source have not been met. Moreover, the source State may not replace a withholding tax on qualifying interest or royalty payments by an assessment procedure.

18.6.1.1 Taxation 'by Deduction at Source' or 'by Assessment'

The prohibition of taxation 'by deduction at source' aims at classical withholding tax mechanisms that are triggered at the moment when interest and royalty payments are made, and that oblige the payer to act as withholding agent for the State. However, Article 1(1) likewise prevents the source State from taxing the interest and royalty payments 'by assessment', *i.e.* by way of procedures kicking in after a given payment has been made and formally subjecting the recipient to a tax liability, either through a specific notice of assessment only for that type of income or on the basis of a more generic (typically annual) assessment notice.

By explicitly including such tax assessments, the wording of Article 1(1) I&R Directive goes beyond that of Article 5 of the Parent-Subsidiary Directive, which only exempts profit distributions from 'withholding tax'. It appears that the EU legislator, when adopting the I&R Directive in June 2003, had already learned a lesson from the way the CJEU had stretched the narrow term 'withholding tax' under the Parent-Subsidiary Directive.[82] Still, already the Commission's 1998 proposal had expressly included taxation 'by assessment' even before the Court had started to rule on Article 5 of the Parent-Subsidiary Directive.

As Article 1(1) I&R Directive exempts 'payments', without temporal specification as to their accrual period, the Directive does not seem to allow temporal compartmentalization of payments. We therefore submit that the exemption from source State tax applies irrespective of the accrual period (see on temporal compartmentalization also Section 16.7 on dividend payments under the Parent-Subsidiary Directive).

18.6.1.2 Relief (only) from Juridical Double Taxation

Article 1(1) I&R Directive does not clearly say whether (only) the recipient or (also) the payer is the beneficiary of the tax exemption. In all language versions the rule leaves it rather cloudy whether the Directive only addresses *juridical* double taxation (in that case, only the recipient is entitled to the exemption) or also *economic* double taxation (so that the payer would likewise be protected against tax burdens on its cross-border interest and royalty payments in the source State, *e.g.* through denial of tax deductibility). The answer to this question is decisive for the acceptability of national anti-base erosion measures, such as thin capitalization rules and earnings stripping rules.

The importance of tax base protection for the Member States is shown by the fact that, next to Germany, eight other Member States submitted observations in Case C-397/09, *Scheuten Solar Technology*.[83] This case concerned the determination of the tax base of the German business tax (*Gewerbesteuer*), a municipal tax on undertakings (levied by applying the municipal tax rate to a tax base calculated on the basis of federal legislation), and more specifically a rule providing that half of the interest deduction accepted for federal corporation tax purposes with respect to long-term loans was added back to the tax base for the purposes of the municipal business tax. The plaintiff, a German company which had paid interest to its Netherlands parent, argued that denial of (half of the) deduction was in fact equal to taxing (half of) the interest in the source State and, therefore, in violation of the exemption prescribed by Article 1(1) I&R Directive.

In its judgment of 21 July 2011 the CJEU, however, held that Article 1(1) exclusively concerns the tax position of the *creditor* company and seeks to remove *juridical* double taxation only. The Court based its view on the terms 'beneficial owner' in Article 1(1) and 'income' in Article 2(a), both pointing at the *creditor*, on recitals 2 to 4 of the Directive, likewise pointing at the tax position of the foreign *creditor*, and on the fact that the option

82 See, at that time, CJEU Case C-375/98, *Epson Europe BV*, EU:C:2000:302, point 22 et seq., and Case C-294/99, *Athinaïki Zithopoiia AE*, EU:C:2001:505, point 25 et seq.

83 CJEU Case C-397/09, *Scheuten Solar Technology GmbH*, EU:C:2011:499.

for a minimum association period in Article 1(10) (see Section 18.3.2.2 above) can clearly only be applied to the *creditor* (the company in the *other* Member State than the one of the payer). Under the German rule, the adding back of half of the interest to the *debtor*'s tax base did not have the effect of reducing the interest income received by the foreign creditor, and thus did not in any way trigger a tax burden on the interest payment in the hands of its recipient (beneficial owner). The Directive does not, therefore, oppose such interest deduction limitation at the level of the payer. The calculation of the tax base of the payer is not an object of the I&R Directive, but of national fiscal sovereignty.[84]

We infer from this judgment that national interest deduction limitations on the basis of rules against thin capitalization or earnings stripping are not affected by the I&R Directive.[85] There is, therefore, no conflict with the interest limitation rule in Article 4 of the Anti-Tax Avoidance Directive (ATAD) which obliges Member States to disallow the deductibility of 'exceeding borrowing costs' if a certain threshold is surpassed (for details, see Section 19.4.1); the same goes for the even stricter interest limitation rule in Article 6 of the proposed DEBRA Directive (see Section 25.3.5). While Article 1(1) of the I&R Directive is, therefore, limited to a mitigation of the tax burden of a foreign recipient (company or PE as beneficial owner) in the source State, Article 1(9) concerns the tax position of a recipient company in the Member State where it is resident (or in the case of a PE, where it is 'situated'). The rule provides that the Directive does not prevent the Member State asserting tax jurisdiction over the recipient company or PE from taxing that recipient for the takings. This may lead to double taxation if the payment is beneficially owned by a PE in Member State A of a company resident in Member State B: both State A and State B may tax the receipt, and if the residence State A does not prevent double taxation by exempting the PE profit (or by granting a credit for the State B corporation tax on the PE profit), then the receipt will be taxed in both the residence State and the PE State.

18.6.2 Relief Procedure

If certain formal requirements are fulfilled, the procedural rules of the I&R Directive ensure that the tax exemption under Article 1(1) can already be enjoyed at the time when the interest or royalty payment is made (*ex ante*), so that no withholding tax will be due in the source State. If the relevant requirements are not (yet) fulfilled at that time and a withholding tax has been withheld, that tax may nevertheless be refunded (*ex post*). While these procedural rules focus on the exemption from taxation 'by deduction at source', no explicit rule deals with the prohibition of taxation 'by assessment' which is likewise contained in Article 1(1) (see Section 18.6.1.1 above). We submit that the rules contained in Article 1(11) to (16) should be applied by analogy in that respect.

---

84 *Id.*, point 24 et seq. Note that CJEU Case C-257/20, *'Viva Telecom Bulgaria' EOOD, l.c.*, did not concern the plaintiff's own corporate income tax burden but its withholding obligation with respect to (fictitious) interest income attributed to its Luxembourg parent company as the relevant (non-resident) taxpayer.

85 The same goes for domestic provisions limiting the deductibility of royalty payments, such as the 'royalty barrier' introduced in Germany as of 2018.

18.6.2.1 Immediate Exemption from Withholding Tax (Article 1(11) to (14))

The source State may require the recipient company (or PE) to demonstrate 'at the time of payment' that it is entitled to the tax exemption under Article 1(1) by way of an attestation certifying that the conditions for exemption are met (Article 1(11), first clause), and it may make application of the exemption conditional upon a preceding decision by its administration granting that exemption; such decision must be issued within three months after the submission of the attestation (and of any additional information the source State may reasonably require) and be valid for at least one year (Article 1(12)). The source State may require the attestation – which must likewise be valid for at least one year but for not more than three years – to contain (Article 1(13), first clause): (a) evidence of the fiscal residence of the recipient company or of the existence of the recipient PE, and information on (b) the beneficial ownership, (c) the fulfilment of the requirements under Article 3(a)(iii), (d) the fulfilment of the minimum holding requirement under Article 3(b), and (e) the period for which such holding has existed.

Apart from the first-mentioned evidence (which is to be certified by the tax authorities of the Member State of the recipient), the Directive does not specify who is to make these statements: the paying company or PE, the recipient company or PE, or the tax authorities of the recipient's State or of the payer's State. The source State may further require inspection of the legal title for the payment(s), such as the loan agreement or the licensing contract (Article 1(13), second clause). The receiving company or PE is required to immediately inform the paying company or PE if the conditions for exemption are no longer fulfilled, and the source State may also require that its competent authority be informed (Article 1(14)). Where the fulfilment of the conditions for exemption has not been attested timely (*i.e.*, before the payments are made), the source State is permitted to oblige the payer to withhold tax upon payment (Article 1(11), second clause).[86]

18.6.2.2 Right to Refund if Immediate Exemption Failed (Article 1(15) and (16))

If the procedural requirements legitimately imposed by the source State are not satisfied at the time when the interest or royalty payment is made and therefore tax has been withheld by the payer, the beneficial owner may, in order to obtain a refund of that withholding tax from the source State, still demonstrate that the interest or royalty payment qualified for exemption; the period for submitting this claim may be determined by the source State, but must run for at least two years after the payment was made (Article 1(15)). The source State is required to repay the tax withheld within a year after the beneficial owner has sufficiently proven its claim. If it repays later, it must pay interest on the amount overdue at a rate which would be applicable in comparable domestic cases of late repayment (Article 1(16)). Quite obviously this *ex post* relief cannot be made dependent on the existence of all relevant attestations already 'at the time of payment' (Article 1(11);

86 Questions concerning practical details of the exemption procedure have been referred to the CJEU by the Czech Supreme Administrative Court in pending Case C-828/24, *Erdrich Umformtechnik GmbH*.

see Section 18.6.2.1 above), as this would lead to a systematic frustration of the refund procedure and the purpose of the Directive.[87]

18.7 Special Issues

18.7.1 Prevention of Fraud and Abuse (Article 5)

The I&R Directive is crammed with anti-avoidance rules, which is not surprising given the tax planning opportunities it basically offers (see Section 18.8 below).

A number of provisions of the Directive address specific situations which may comprise elements of tax avoidance or abusive behaviour. Article 1(1) itself excludes payments which, in essence, are not of a cross-border nature (see Section 18.4.1 above) from the scope of the Directive, and together with Article 1(4) and (5)(a) it requires beneficial ownership of the recipient (see Sections 18.3.3 and 18.3.4 above). Article 1(5)(b) contains a subject-to-tax clause where a PE is the potential beneficial owner of a payment (see Section 18.3.3 above and also Section 18.8 below), and Article 1(6) avoids duplication of beneficial ownership (see Section 18.3.3 above). Article 1(8) excludes payments by or to a PE in a non-EU Member State (see Section 18.4.1 above), and Article 1(10) allows Member States to deny the Directive benefits to companies not maintaining a qualifying association for an uninterrupted period of two years (see Section 18.3.2.2 above). Article 4(1) permits the source State to disallow application of the Directive to considerations paid on hybrid and equity-like debt-claims (see Section 18.2.4.1 above), and Article 4(2) limits the Directive benefits to arm's length payments (see Section 18.2.4.2 above).

In addition to the aforementioned *leges speciales*, Article 5 is a *general* anti-abuse reservation: it provides that the Directive does not preclude the 'application of domestic or agreement-based provisions required for the prevention of fraud or abuse' (Article 5(1)), and that Member States may withdraw the benefits of the Directive or refuse to apply them 'in the case of transactions for which the principal motive or one of the principal motives is tax evasion, tax avoidance or abuse' (Article 5(2)). It escapes us which other 'abuse' than 'tax evasion' or 'tax avoidance' could be conceived, but it appears that Member States wanted to be prepared for all eventualities.[88]

Article 5(1) I&R Directive is a literal rendition of the original Article 1(2) (now with slight changes Article 1(4)) of the Parent-Subsidiary Directive, and we therefore expect the CJEU to apply it in the same manner (see Section 16.8.7). The phrasing of Article 5(2) I&R Directive does not appear in the Parent-Subsidiary Directive but is almost identical to the first clause of Article 15(1)(a) (originally Article 11(1)(a)) of the Merger Directive (see Section 17.12). We expect the Court to take little notice of the differences between

87 Against this background, the different view taken by the Court of Appeal Ghent of 18 March 2014, no. 2010/AR/2449, is difficult to comprehend. See Frank Mortier, 'Interest and Royalties Directive (2003/49): Court of Appeal Denies Withholding Tax Refund on Interest Due to Lack of Attestation at Time of Payment', *European Taxation*, September 2014, p. 404-407.

88 The 1998 Commission proposal, *l.c.*, had only mentioned 'tax evasion' and 'tax avoidance' in its Article 6(2), and the term 'abuse' was later added in the Council.

the various general anti-abuse provisions in the different corporate tax Directives, and to apply them all in the same restrictive manner in which it also applies its general 'abuse of rights' doctrine (see Sections 7.2 and 7.4). The Court concentrates on the object and purpose of the Directive, and on the appropriateness and proportionality of the national (or bilateral) anti-abuse measure at issue. It tends to prohibit the automatic exclusion of certain categories of suspect cases, requiring instead an individual assessment of both the intent of the economic operator and the objective effect of the transaction in the light of the object and purpose of the Directive. A critical issue is how far Member States may go in reversing the burden of proof as regards the presence or absence of valid commercial reasons for transactions (see Section 7.6).

We believe that the general anti-abuse clauses in the three aforementioned corporate tax Directives do not add much to the discretion the Member States already have under the Court's general 'abuse of rights' doctrine. This is confirmed by the parallel Grand Chamber judgments in the 'Danish cases' where the CJEU ruled that national tax authorities are entitled (and even obliged), under the general principle of EU law that abusive practices are prohibited, to refuse to grant tax benefits under the I&R Directive (and likewise, the Parent-Subsidiary Directive) in situations of fraudulent or abusive behaviour on the part of the taxpayer even in 'the absence of domestic or agreement-based anti-abuse provisions'.[89] Despite the CJEU's attempt to distinguish the aforementioned cases from another Danish case likewise concerning the question of whether, in order to be able to rely on an anti-abuse clause contained in a Directive, a Member State must have a proper legal basis for that purpose within its domestic legal order (in that case, within the framework of the Merger Directive and with an affirmative answer by the Court[90]),[91] this forms a major turning point in the Court's case law.[92]

Moreover, Article 5 I&R Directive is unnecessary to safeguard the application of national anti-base erosion rules, such as thin capitalization or earnings stripping provisions, which concern the payer who is not an addressee of the Directive benefits anyway (see Section 18.6.1.2 above). Still, Article 5 might provide a legal basis for 'limitation on benefits' (LOB) measures aimed at ensuring that the ultimate recipient of the interest or royalty payment is an EU resident. Such provisions must be proportionate, though, *i.e.* they must be carefully targeted at abusive schemes (see Section 7.4). The mere fact that a recipient company is controlled by a third country resident does not seem to warrant a categorical

89 See CJEU Joined Cases C-115/16 et al., *N Luxembourg 1 et al.*, *l.c.*, points 95-111 (I&R Directive), and Joined Cases C-116/16, *T Danmark* and C-117/16, *Y Denmark ApS*, *l.c.*, points 69-83 (Parent-Subsidiary Directive).

90 See CJEU Case C-321/05, *Kofoed*, EU:C:2007:408, point 40 et seq.

91 See CJEU Joined Cases C-115/16 et al., *N Luxembourg 1 et al.*, *l.c.*, points 112-120 (I&R Directive), and Joined Cases C-116/16, *T Danmark* and C-117/16, *Y Denmark ApS*, *l.c.*, points 84-93 (Parent-Subsidiary Directive).

92 For a critical discussion see CFE ECJ Task Force, *l.c.*, at p. 497 et seq., and, contrasting the CJEU's approach with that taken by Advocate General Juliane Kokott, also Englisch, *l.c.*, at p. 518 et seq. and p. 527 et seq. For previous CJEU case law pointing into the above direction see, however, Paolo Arginelli, '*Open Issues in the Application of the Interest and Royalty Directive to Royalty Payments*', in: Guglielmo Maisto, Taxation of Intellectual Property under Domestic Law, EU Law and Tax Treaties, IBFD Amsterdam (2018), p. 51-94, at p. 74 et seq.

presumption of abuse. The Commission, therefore, doubts whether a company that passes the 'beneficial owner' test (see Section 18.3.4 above) can nevertheless be considered an artificial conduit company within the framework of Article 5.[93]

The 1998 Commission proposal had even comprised an anti-tax haven and anti-excessive tax competition provision. This initially proposed Article 7 was the only visible connection between the I&R Directive and the harmful tax competition debate, and therefore the only apparent reason for the Directive to be part of the 'package to tackle harmful tax competition' (see Section 26.1). As the tax competition debate ended in an agreement on phasing out blacklisted national measures considered unfair and harmful (see Section 26.2.1), there was no political need for such a provision anymore.

18.7.2 *Direct Effect of Beneficial Rules*

Notwithstanding the many anti-abuse clauses and procedural requirements contained in the I&R Directive, we believe the tax exemption under Article 1(1) to have direct effect if all requirements regarding its scope of application are fulfilled, and therefore to be capable of being relied on in national courts where a Member State has not correctly transposed the Directive into national law or misapplies it. The fact that such Member State would have been allowed – had it implemented correctly – to apply procedural requirements or anti-abuse provisions, does not take away the Directive rights conferred on taxpayers as per the ultimate implementation date, as the fact that such restrictive measures were not enacted timely and correctly is entirely the responsibility of the negligent Member State concerned.[94]

In addition, the entitlement of the receiving company or PE under Article 1(16) to interest in case of a delayed tax refund by the source State (see Section 18.6.2.2 above) is, as such, sufficiently clear and precise. It is only the rate of the interest which depends on the domestic rate of the Member State concerned for 'comparable cases'.[95]

93 See 2009 Commission Report, *l.c.*, paragraph 3.3.9. For a more critical view, however, see Martinho Fernandes et al., *l.c.*, p. 402 et seq.

94 See, *e.g.*, the case of Germany which had implemented the original Directive with considerable delay by federal law of 2 December 2004. Meanwhile, however, the Federal Ministry of Finance had issued a decree (of 26 April 2004, IV B 4 – S 1316-8/04, *Bundessteuerblatt* 2004, part I, p. 479) in which it accepted the direct effect of Article 1(1) of the I&R Directive as from 1 January 2004. The same happened when Croatia acceded to the EU per 1 July 2013 and Directive 2013/13/EU was not implemented on time; see *id.*, decree of 20 January 2014, IV B 3 – S 1316/07/10025, *Bundessteuerblatt* 2014, part I, p. 110.

95 Direct effect has been accepted by the Tribunal de première instance Arlon of 8 January 2014, SA NWB v. Etat belge, *Tijdschrift voor Fiscaal Recht*, June 2014, p. 553-556, but in the context of a refund claim brought by the *debtor*, whereas according to the wording of Article 1(16) 'the receiving company or permanent establishment shall be entitled' to the interest claim (which is only logical, as the interest is supposed to compensate that company or PE for the cash-flow disadvantage caused by the withholding tax).

18.7.3 *Relation to Relief Provisions under Domestic Law or Double Tax Treaties (Article 9)*

Article 9 of the I&R Directive is titled 'Delimitation clause' and ensures that the Directive cannot be relied on by Member States to limit taxpayers' rights under national law or under existing tax treaties as regards prevention or limitation of double taxation of interest and royalty payments. If a unilateral provision of a Member State or a provision in a tax treaty between Member States is more beneficial to the taxpayer than the rules of the I&R Directive, the Directive does not bar the application of the more favourable provision.

18.8 Some Comments on the Current Status of the Directive and Proposals for Further Amendments

Within the framework of the 'package to tackle harmful tax competition', the I&R Directive was always the odd element. Rather than curbing harmful tax competition, it encourages such competition. Abolishing withholding taxes on deductible outbound payments means that the source State receives no tax revenue whatsoever, which provides tax-planning opportunities: captive finance and licensing companies will be set up in EU Member States offering low general corporate tax rates (or partial/total exemptions of interest and royalty income from the tax base), in order to grant loans or licenses etc. to group companies financed with a minimum of equity in high-tax EU jurisdictions (see also Section 26.3.1).

On the other hand, there is a certain coherence in granting the creditor State, where the expenditure for raising debt capital or for research and development was made and deducted, the right to tax the proceeds of the capital or the patent, software, know-how, etc., that was created within its jurisdiction.[96] Nevertheless, abolition of source taxation on deductible payments implies a rather arbitrary division of tax revenue: income from equity investment is taxed in the investment State (as outbound dividends are not deductible there), whereas income from loan investment is taxed in the investor's State because interest is deductible.

Against this background it is no coincidence that the last decades have seen (i) a proliferation and tightening of anti-base erosion measures throughout the EU, such as thin capitalization rules, LOB provisions, anti-conduit provisions, earnings stripping rules, etc., aimed at ensuring substance, economic reality and beneficial ownership within the EU, as well as (ii) spontaneous (or peer pressure-driven) harmonization within the Code of Conduct group (see Chapter 26) of both the corporation tax base (broadening of the base; termination of harmfully competitive special regimes) and the tax rate (at a lower level).

Some commentators[97] feel that for reasons of interjurisdictional equity and abuse prevention, withholding taxes on deductible payments should not be abolished at all but

96 This is also recognized by the Commission in its 2009 Report, *l.c.*, paragraph 3.1.

97 See Alex Easson, 'Fiscal degradation and the inter-nation allocation of tax jurisdiction', *EC Tax Review* 1996/3, p. 112-113, and Sijbren Cnossen, 'Reform and Coordination of Corporation Taxes in the EU: An Alternative Agenda', *Bulletin for International Fiscal Documentation*, April 2004, p. 134-150.

should, on the contrary, be increased to the level of the corporate income tax of which they erode the base. Another option would be to make interest non-deductible, like dividends. But the EU has chosen otherwise: source taxation is to be abolished; the investor State prevails over the source State as regards taxation of intra-group interest and royalties.

18.8.1 Commission 2003 Proposal and 2009 Report

The Commission is fully aware of the fact that the I&R Directive has several shortcomings. Already at the end of 2003 it tabled a first proposal for amendments[98] and suggested to extend the personal scope of the Directive to the *Societas Europaea* (SE) and the *Societas Cooperativa Europaea* (SCE) and beyond that to all national legal forms subject to corporation tax. Furthermore, the Commission proposed to introduce yet another anti-abuse measure: the tax exemption in the source State under Article 1(1) should be made conditional on the recipient company (or PE) being 'effectively subject to tax on the interest and royalty payments' in its own Member State, in order to ensure that the payments are actually taxed at least once within the Union (see Section 18.3.1 above).

While the 2003 proposal was still pending, the Commission in early 2009 issued a report on the functioning of the Directive (as required by Article 8) which addressed the aforementioned issues, but also several others. *Inter alia*, the Commission analyzed further possibilities to enlarge the scope and made some important observations. First of all, it stated that the Directive covered only cross-border payments between separate legal entities but not within one and the same company (*i.e.* from a PE to its head office in another Member State, or between two PEs in different Member States of the same company).[99] This may indeed become an issue to be tackled with the I&R Directive, since the OECD has adopted an approach on profit attribution which treats a PE as a separate legal entity also for intra-company interest and royalty payments,[100] and some EU/OECD Member States indicated that they would be minded to introduce a withholding tax on such (under civil law nonexistent) 'payments' to compensate for their deductibility.

A second important observation in the 2009 report concerns the 'association' requirement (see Section 18.3.2.1 above). In this respect the Commission not only suggested an alignment with the Parent-Subsidiary Directive (*i.e.* lowering the holding threshold to 10% and also including 'indirect' holdings) but also to consider dropping that requirement altogether. It observed that Articles 11 (Interest) and 12 (Royalties) of the OECD MC do not distinguish between related and unrelated parties, and that unrelated parties suffer as much as related parties from juridical double taxation, red tape, and cash-flow disadvantages.[101] We add that unrelated parties might also rely on the general nondiscrimination principle contained in (Article 6 TEU *juncto*) Article 21 of the EU Charter of Fundamental Rights, as we do not see how, in the light of the goal of the I&R Directive (same treatment

---

98 Commission proposal COM(2003) 841 final of 30 December 2003. For a detailed analysis, see Martinho Fernandes et al., *l.c.*

99 See 2009 Commission Report, *l.c.*, paragraph 3.4.1.

100 *Id.*, paragraph 3.4.1. See also Section 18.3.3 above.

101 On the potential relevance of the 'functionally separate entity' approach, or authorized OECD approach (AOA), in the present context see Martinho Fernandes et al., *l.c.*, at p. 445 et seq.

for cross-border transactions as for domestic transactions; see Section 18.1.2 above), discrimination against unrelated parties could be justified by the simple fact that they are unrelated. On the contrary: between unrelated parties there is clearly less risk of abuse of the tax exemption. The objectives and reasons stated in recitals 1 and 2 of the Directive do not support limitation of the tax exemption to related parties, and it is only in recital 4 that the EU legislator announces that 'it is particularly necessary to abolish such taxes in respect of such payments made between associated companies (...)'. This implies that it is just as necessary in respect of all other entrepreneurial cross-border interest and royalty payments as well, albeit possibly not *particularly* necessary.

18.8.2 Commission 2011 Proposal and Subsequent Discussions

After its 2009 report the Commission withdrew the 2003 proposal[102] and, following a public consultation, submitted a new proposal for a recast version of the Directive in November 2011.[103] Apart from consolidating the text in order to make it more accessible, this proposal pursues the goals of the 2003 proposal and aims at aligning the scope of the I&R Directive with that of the Parent-Subsidiary Directive and guaranteeing taxation of intra-group interest and royalties at least once in the EU. To that end, the Commission suggested to extend the list of qualifying companies to cover at least the same list as annexed to the Parent-Subsidiary Directive, to lower the minimum holding requirement for being 'associated' from 25% to 10% (including 'indirect' holdings)[104] and, last but not least, to make the tax exemption in the source State conditional upon the recipient company (or PE) being effectively subject to tax on the interest and royalty payments in the Member State where it is resident (or, in the case of a PE, where it is 'situated'[105]).

While the Commission had proposed 1 January 2013 as implementation deadline for the amendments, again no agreement could be reached in the Council. In December 2012 the Commission announced that it would review the anti-abuse provisions of, *inter alia*, the I&R Directive in the light of its recommendation on aggressive tax planning that was published at the same time.[106] From there on, debates in the Council started to drift into the direction of the broader discussion of the OECD's BEPS project (see Section 19.1), and Member States could not agree on whether to focus in a first step on a revision of the

102 See O.J. 2010 C 252/11.

103 Commission proposal COM (2011) 714 final of 11 November 2011.

104 This alignment with the Parent-Subsidiary Directive is also supported by the Economic and Social Committee, Opinion of 22 February 2012 (ECO/305), paragraph 1.1. See, however, the European Parliament's Legislative Resolution P7_TA (2012)0318 of 11 September 2012, which is in favour of keeping the 25% threshold (but accepts its extension to 'indirect' holdings).

105 We note that for PEs there is already a subject-to-tax requirement in Article 1(5)(b) (see Sections 18.1.2 and 18.3.3 above), so that the main purpose of this amendment is to establish such requirement for the (head office of the) company. Due to the interpretation of Article 3(a)(iii) in recent CJEU case law (see Section 18.3.1 above), however, this amendment would now have a mere declaratory function.

106 Commission Communication 'An Action Plan to strengthen the fight against tax fraud and tax evasion', COM(2012) 722 final of 6 December 2012, paragraph 4.1.1 with reference to the Commission Recommendation of 6 December 2012 'on aggressive tax planning', 2012/772/EU, O.J. 2012 L 338/41.

general anti-abuse clause (see Section 18.7.1 above) or to also include a rule guaranteeing effective taxation. In June 2015, at the same time when the Latvian Council Presidency presented a compromise text with a new common anti-abuse rule drawn along the lines of the new Article 1(2) and (3) of the Parent-Subsidiary Directive (see Section 16.8), the Commission emphasized the importance of only granting tax relief under the I&R Directive if there was effective taxation elsewhere in the EU.[107] Subsequent discussions in the Council then shifted towards the question of how to guarantee such effective taxation through the design of a 'minimum effective taxation' (MET) clause,[108] before at the end of 2016 the idea of introducing a so-called 'ownership/base erosion test'[109] as an additional measure entered the debate.

In April and May 2017 the Maltese Presidency proposed new compromise texts which left out most of these controversial issues and (only) comprised the inclusion of a subject-to-tax clause in Article 1(1), an amendment to Article 4(1) allowing the source State to refuse the Directive benefits to payments going into preferential tax measures in another Member State, the insertion of a so-called 'targeted anti-abuse rule' (TAAR) into Article 5, and the other amendments already contained in the 2011 Commission proposal (in particular, the alignment with the Parent-Subsidiary Directive as regards the extension of the list of companies in the Annex and the reduction of the 'association' requirements). However, still no agreement could be reached in the Council,[110] and the same is true for a compromise proposed by the Estonian Presidency towards the end of 2017 (including a 'subject-to-tax' requirement and a TAAR).[111]

It appears that some of the aforementioned discussion points may actually meanwhile have been resolved by the CJEU through mere interpretation of the existing text of the I&R Directive (see Section 18.3.1 above on the 'subject-to-tax' requirement and Section

107 Commission Communication 'A Fair and Efficient Corporate Tax System in the European Union: 5 Key Areas for Action', COM(2015) 302 final of 17 June 2015, paragraph 2.1.1. See also European Parliament Resolution PA_TA(2015)0457 of 16 December 2015 with recommendations to the Commission on 'Bringing transparency, coordination and convergence to corporate tax policies in the Union', 2015/2010(INL), recommendation C8.

108 For details, see Jan Vleggeert and Henk Vording, 'Conditional Withholding Tax: A Tax on Tax Planning', *European Taxation*, August 2017, p. 452-464, at p. 456 et seq. See also the 2012 European Parliament Legislative Resolution, *l.c.*, which had suggested to amend Article 1(1) in the sense that an interest or royalty payment must be subject to tax in the Member State of the recipient 'at a rate not lower than 70% of the average statutory corporate tax rate applicable in the Member States, without there being the possibility of exemption or a substitution or replacement by payment of another tax', and that, in addition, exemption was not to be granted by the source State 'if the payment is not taxable according to the national tax law to which the beneficial owner is subject due to a different qualification of the payment (hybrid instruments) or a different qualification of the payer and recipient (hybrid entities)'.

109 See OECD, 'Preventing the Granting of Treaty Benefits in Inappropriate Circumstances – Action 6: Final Report' (2015) and the new LOB-clause introduced in Article 29(1) to (7) OECD MC by the 2017 Update to the OECD MC of 21 November 2017.

110 ECOFIN Report of 16 June 2017 to the European Council on tax matters, 10397/17, paragraph 34 et seq.

111 ECOFIN Report of 24 November 2017 to the European Council on tax matters, 14790/17, paragraph 38 et seq. See also ECOFIN Report of 27 June 2018 to the European Council on tax matters, 10322/18, paragraph 30.

18.3.4 above on the 'beneficial owner' criterion), as well as the strengthening of the role of the general EU law anti-abuse principle in tax matters (see Section 18.7.1 above). On the other hand, however, the European Parliament added another facet to the MET debate with its call for a harmonized withholding tax framework in relation to third countries in order to ensure that a 'minimum effective withholding tax rate' is being applied by all Member States to all interest and royalty (and also dividend or even other types of) payments flowing out of the EU.[112] This broad anti-BEPS measure, which echoes previous proposals by economists,[113] would tackle a serious weakness of the EU internal market with respect to international tax planning schemes, but would require the renegotiation of a considerable number of tax treaties concluded by Member States with non-EU countries. It would reach far beyond the scope of the current I&R Directive with its limitation to 'associated' companies (see Section 18.3.2 above) and bear some similarity to the Common Customs Tariff for incoming goods from third countries, only that it would work in the opposite direction (*i.e.* hitting outbound payments towards third countries) and that the actual withholding tax rate applied by each Member State could exceed a uniform minimum rate. The Commission´s immediate reaction was rather reserved, however, and focused on further discussions of a potential introduction of an MET clause in the I&R Directive.[114]

18.8.3 *Recent Harmonization Initiatives Beyond the I&R Directive*

18.8.3.1 *'Pillar 2 Directive' and Commission Proposal for an 'Unshell Directive'*

In recent years, the discussion around the necessity of potential amendments of the I&R Directive received a new impetus from another angle when on 22 December 2021 the Commission tabled two proposals for further directives in the area of direct business taxation.

The first proposal[115] concerned a 'Pillar 2 Directive' intended to implement the global agreement on a 'two-pillar solution' reached by the OECD/G20 Inclusive Framework om BEPS on 8 October 2021,[116] and more specifically the Global Anti-Base Erosion (GloBE)

112 See European Parliament Resolution of 10 March 2022 'on a European Withholding Tax framework', 2021/2197(INI), P9_TA(2022)0075, OJ 2022 C 347/172, paragraph 6 et seq. and paragraph 10 et seq., reiterating a claim already brought forward by European Parliament Resolution of 6 July 2016 on 'Tax rulings and other measures similar in nature or effect (TAXE 2)', 2016/2038(INI), P8_TA(2016)0310, OJ 2016 C 101/79.

113 See, *e.g.*, Arjan Lejour and Maarten van ´t Riet, 'A Common Withholding Tax on Dividend, Interest and Royalties in the European Union', *FEPS Policy Brief*, September 2020, who even suggest that the minimum tax could become an own resource for the EU budget.

114 On the Commission´s response (SP(2022)254), see Elodie Lamer, 'European Commission Wants Minimum Tax on Interest and Royalties', *Tax Notes International*, Vol. 107, 26 September 2022, p. 1555-1556.

115 Commission proposal for a 'Council Directive on ensuring a global minimum level of taxation for multinational groups in the Union', COM(2021) 823 final of 22 December 2021.

116 OECD/G20 Inclusive Framework on BEPS, 'Statement on a Two-Pillar Solution to Address the Tax Challenges Arising from the Digitalisation of the Economy' of 8 October 2021.

Model Rules covering 'Pillar 2' published on 20 December 2021,[117] within the EU Internal Market in a way that is compatible with EU primary law requirements (in particular, the Treaty freedoms). This Directive was passed on 14 December 2022[118] and was, with certain exceptions, to be transposed until 31 December 2023. It requires Member States to ensure that large groups of enterprises (combined turnover of at least EUR 750 million) pay a minimum Effective Tax Rate (ETR) of 15% on their taxable income in each jurisdiction where the group has activities (for details, see Chapter 22). This could in fact induce Member States to also agree on the insertion of an MET clause (see Section 18.8.2 above) in the I&R Directive, and the Commission expressed it hope that the transposition of the 'Pillar 2 Directive' would pave the way for an agreement on the Commission´s 2011 proposal.[119] Only recently, however, the Commission rather vaguely announced that its 2011 proposal had become 'obsolete' as its scope had been 'partly taken over' by the latter Directive; therefore, the Commission withdrew the 2011 proposal and indicated that the remaining issues this proposal had intended to tackle would be 'addressed by an upcoming Omnibus act'.[120]

The second of the two new proposals[121] concerns a so-called 'Unshell Directive' aimed at preventing the 'misuse of shell entities for tax purposes' and is a response to a request by the European Parliament to come forward with an initiative against 'letterbox companies'.[122] The proposed Directive is intended to apply to all 'undertakings' (regardless of their legal form) which are 'tax resident' in a Member State, and to subject them to scrutiny as to whether they have 'minimum substance for tax purposes' (for details, see Section 25.3.3). If, after a somewhat complex filtering process, an undertaking is presumed to lack such 'minimum substance' for a given tax year and cannot rebut this presumption, the Member State concerned would be obliged to either refuse the issuance of a tax residence certificate to that undertaking for the relevant tax year, or to state in such a certificate that the undertaking cannot benefit from double taxation conventions and the relief provisions under the Parent-Subsidiary Directive and the I&R Directive; other Member States would likewise have to disregard tax conventions and relief provisions under the

117 *Idem*, 'Tax Challenges Arising from the Digitalisation of the Economy – Global Anti-Base Erosion Model Rules' of 20 December 2021.

118 Council Directive (EU) 2022/2523 of 14 December 2022 on ensuring a global minimum level of taxation for multinational enterprise groups and large-scale domestic groups in the Union, O.J. 2022 L 328/1.

119 See Commission Communication 'Business Taxation for the 21st Century', COM(2021) 251 of 18 May 2021, paragraph 2.2 in 'Box 2'.

120 See Commission Communication 'Commission work programme 2025 – Moving forward together: A Bolder, Simpler, Faster Union', COM(2025) 45 of 11 February 2025, paragraph 4 and Annex IV, no. 1. This step seems to have puzzled the European Parliament; see Elodie Lamer, 'MEPs Seel Clarification on Withdrawal of Proposed IRD Revision', *Tax Notes International*, Vol. 118, 14 April 2025, p. 262-263.

121 Commission proposal for a 'Council Directive laying down rules to prevent the misuse of shell entities for tax purposes and amending Directive 2011/16/EU', COM(2021) 565 final of 22 December 2021.

122 See European Parliament Resolution of 26 March 2019 'on financial crimes, tax evasion and tax avoidance', 2018/2121(INI), Report on financial crimes, tax evasion and tax avoidance, P8_TA(2019)0240, OJ 2021 C 108/8, paragraph 2.7 (in particular, point 133 et seq.).

aforementioned Directives, and the Member State(s) of the undertaking's shareholder(s) would have to treat the relevant income as if it had directly accrued to the latter.

Hence, in order to tackle such abusive structures it would not even be necessary to amend the I&R Directive as such. However, while the 'Unshell Directive' proposal received strong support by the European Parliament,[123] Member States could not reach an agreement during their discussions in the Council. Some Member States have been pleading in favour of a 'two-stage approach', starting with an automatic exchange of information based on certain hallmarks, followed by an exchange of best practices regarding the application of domestic tax consequences on the basis of that information.[124] The Council is still looking for a compromise solution,[125] so that the initial link with the I&R Directive may disappear.

18.8.3.2 Commission Proposal for a 'BEFIT Directive'

Finally, the Commission´s proposal of 12 September 2023 for a 'BEFIT Directive'[126] (see Section 25.3.6) must be mentioned in the present context. As successor to the failed attempt to introduce a Common Consolidated Corporate Tax Base (CCCTB; see Section 10.1.2 and Section 25.3.6), this new and encompassing project aims at harmonizing the corporate income tax base for large groups of enterprises with activities within the EU. A key element of this proposed Directive is that the 'preliminary tax results of all BEFIT group members', determined according to the rules in Chapter II of the proposal (Articles 4 to 41), will be 'aggregated to obtain a BEFIT tax base' (Article 42(1)) for the group before being reallocated to the individual group members (Articles 45 to 49).

As the Commission points out in its Explanatory Memorandum, there is basically no need to tax intra-group interest and royalty payments individually within the BEFIT group as such transactions will be included in the aggregated BEFIT tax base. Therefore, Article 43(1) of the proposed Directive prohibits Member States to 'impose withholding taxes or any other source taxation on intra-BEFIT group transactions unless the beneficial owner of the payment is not a BEFIT group member'. Where this prohibition of 'source taxation' applies, an exemption under Article 1(1) I&R Directive (see Section 18.6.1 above) will not be necessary. Article 43(2) of the proposed Directive, however, addresses situations where a Member State applies a withholding tax 'in accordance with the applicable rules of national law and double taxation conventions' to an interest or royalty payment made by a BEFIT group member because that payment goes to a recipient who is either 'not a member of the same BEFIT group' or who indeed belongs to the same BEFIT group, but is not the 'beneficial owner' (see Article 43(1) *in fine*); in such cases, the withholding tax is supposed

123 See European Parliament Resolution of 17 January 2023 'Rules to prevent the misuse of shell entities for tax purposes', P9_TA(2023)0004.

124 See ECOFIN Report of 30 November 2023 to the European Council on tax issues, 16100/23, paragraph 18 et seq.

125 See ECOFIN Report of 24 June 2024 to the European Council on tax issues, 11287/24, paragraph 21 et seq.; ECOFIN Report of 10 December 2024 to the Council on tax issues, 16673/24, paragraph 10 et seq.

126 Commission proposal for a 'Council Directive on Business in Europe: Framework for Income Taxation (BEFIT)', COM(2023) 532 final of 12 September 2023.

to be shared, for the fiscal year in which it is charged, amongst Member States using the allocation method referred to in Article 45' of the proposed Directive. It is unclear why neither the Explanatory Memorandum nor the text of Article 43(2) of the proposal take the I&R Directive into account in this context. In our view, the application of a domestic withholding tax (or of a tax levied via an assessment procedure), and likewise its sharing between Member States, will not be possible where all conditions for the application of Article 1(1) I&R Directive are fulfilled and, therefore, a tax exemption is required.

CHAPTER 19

The Anti-Tax-Avoidance Directive (ATAD)

Daniël Smit[1]

19.1 Introduction and Background: an Ambitious EU Agenda Beyond BEPS

In the wake of the financial crisis between mid 2007 and early 2009 and the consequent pressure on government's budgets, there has been an increasing awareness in society over the past decade that international tax planning practices can be problematic. Especially large multinational enterprises, such as Google, Starbucks and Apple, were perceived to deliberately seek and not rarely even aggressively exploit mismatches between national tax rules. As a result, multinationals have repeatedly been accused of not paying their fair share in repairing the costs of the financial crisis. Whether these claims are always well-founded or not – "One man's 'tax avoidance' is another man's tax efficiency!" – the increasing public attention for business taxation of multinationals has created mounting pressure on government's international tax policies. It is for that reason that in February 2013, the OECD, with the political support of the countries of the G20, has launched its ambitious project on Base Erosion and Profit Shifting.[2] Base erosion and profit shifting (in brief: BEPS) refers to "tax avoidance strategies that exploit gaps and mismatches in tax rules to artificially shift profits to low or no-tax locations."[3] With the BEPS project, the OECD and G20 seek to create one single set of consensus-based, international tax rules to protect tax bases of countries. The first stage of the BEPS project was finalized in October 2015 by releasing the so-called BEPS-package. This package contains 15 Actions that should provide governments the domestic and international tools that are needed to tackle BEPS. Subsequently, the OECD started to focus on supporting and monitoring the implementation of the BEPS package in both OECD and non-OECD countries. In the light of the recovery of the costs of the massive government aids following from the worldwide COVID-19 pandemic, the OECD has started focusing on the development and subsequent implementation of a two-pillar tax system that should address the tax challenges of the digitalizing economy (sometimes referred to as BEPS 2.0). This two-pillar system focusses on the taxation of residual profits earned by multinationals and should ensure that the largest enterprises worldwide (both digital and non-digital) not only pay their "fair share", but also pay it in the "right place" (on Pillar 2, see more elaborately Chapter 22).

---

1 Professor (by special appointment) of Taxation of the Digital Economy, ACTL, University of Amsterdam; Head of the Scientific Tax Department of EY, Amsterdam.

2 OECD (2013), *Action Plan on Base Erosion and Profit Shifting*, OECD Publishing.

3 See <https://www.oecd.org/tax/beps/about/>, retrieved 22 May 2025.

Already prior to the launch of the BEPS-project early 2013, the European Commission released an Action Plan to strengthen the fight against tax fraud and tax evasion, in December 2012.[4] It therefore does not come as a surprise that the European Commission has strongly reaffirmed the OECD's work on BEPS. In fact, it has taken the role of front-runner when it comes to the implementation of the BEPS package within the Union. Shortly after the release of the BEPS-package late 2015, the European Commission released its so-called Anti-tax avoidance package on 28 January 2016. This package contains two Directive proposals that seek to implement, on a harmonized basis, parts of the BEPS-package throughout the Union. The first proposal requires large multinationals doing business in the Union to increase their transparency with respect to their overall corporate tax liability. This means, for example, that multinationals need to report information about their global allocation of business income, economic activity and taxes paid among countries. This information is subsequently shared between the tax administrations of other Member States that have an interest. By revealing the "bigger picture", countries should thus be able to discover more easily where a multinational is performing profit generating activities. This proposal was formally adopted on 25 May 2016 (followed by several further proposals on tax transparencey afterwards).[5] Tax transparency, however, does not create taxation powers to combat tax avoidance. The second Directive proposal – an Anti-Tax-Avoidance Directive (ATAD) – therefore creates and extends Member States' corporate taxation powers by introducing one general and four specific mandatory anti avoidance rules throughout the Union. The ATAD was formally adopted on 12 July 2016.[6]

On top of this, the Commission went one step further. In October 2016 it relaunched two proposals for the phased introduction of a harmonized European corporate income tax regime, the so-called Common Corporate Tax Base (CCTB) and the Common Consolidated Corporate Tax Base (CCCTB) while repealing its earlier CCCTB-proposal from 2011. This regime would introduce one single "European corporate tax language" spoken in all EU Member States.[7] In the view of the European Commission, this should do away with many international mismatches in a more comprehensive way while this regime would at the same time be good for business by providing a harmonized set of rules, including a number of business-friendly tax incentives ("Pro Business, Anti-Avoidance"). The introduction of the ATAD would thus constitute only a first step within a broader three-step approach (ATAD, CCTB, CCCTB...) towards harmonization in the field of corporate taxation within the Union. In 2021, however, the European Commission announced that its (C)CCTB proposals will be replaced by a proposal for a so-called Framework for Income Taxation for Business in Europe (BEFIT or "CCCTB 3.0"). A proposal to that end was launched on 12 September 2023. The fate of this proposal is, however, uncertain.

4 Communication from the Commission to the European Parliament and the Council – An Action Plan to strengthen the fight against tax fraud and tax evasion, Brussels, 6 December 2012, COM(2012) 722 final.

5 Council Directive (EU) 2016/881 of 25 May 2016 amending Directive 2011/16/EU as regards mandatory automatic exchange of information in the field of taxation. More elaborately: Chapter 13.

6 Council Directive (EU) 2016/1164 of 12 July 2016 laying down rules against tax avoidance practices that directly affect the functioning of the internal market, *OJ L* 193, 19.7.2016, p. 1-14 (ATAD 1).

7 More elaborately: Chapter 12.

Finally, the Member States, together with the European Commission, have been busy to "export" at least some of the basic principles of the newly developed EU minimum standards to non-EU countries in order to ensure a minimum global level playing field. Non-EU countries that are not willing to sufficiently accept these basic principles,[8] may be put on a so-called "black-list". Once on that list, they seriously risk countermeasures by the Member States.[9]

The current chapter provides a general overview of the ATAD's provisions.

19.2 History, Objective, Scope and Main Features of the ATAD

19.2.1 Adoption of the ATAD: Politically Controversial, but Eventually Feasible

The Commission submitted its ATAD proposal to the Member States on 28 January 2016 under the Dutch EU Presidency.[10] By doing so, the Commission met the request from several EU Ministers of Finance, who had already drafted and published a text proposal for what was at that time called an "anti-BEPS Directive".[11] The Commission was specifically asked to release a Directive proposal on the basis of this draft. Both the draft text and the final ATAD proposal (that was to a large extent, but not entirely similar to the EU Council's draft) essentially "borrowed" a number of anti-tax avoidance measures that were already included in the controversial and politically sensitive CCCTB-proposal from 2011. Although the Member States had failed to reach political agreement on this proposal as an entire piece, the sense was that the BEPS-project had created the right political momentum which should make political agreement on the international, anti-tax avoidance elements of the CCCTB-proposal feasible. Harmonization of corporate tax avoidance rules "was in the air". Surfing on the waves of the BEPS-project, the adoption of the ATAD could then even serve as a first step towards the further phased harmonization of corporate taxes within the Union through the subsequent phased introduction of a CCTB and CCCTB as a more comprehensive tool to combat BEPS. To sum up, although revolutionary, the ATAD proposal did not come out of the blue.

The ATAD proposal was subsequently adopted surprisingly quickly (if not overhasty), albeit with some substantial changes; unanimous political agreement was reached on 20 June 2016 and the proposal was formally adopted on 12 July 2016.[12] For comparison: both the adoption of the Parent-subsidiary and Merger Directives took more than 20

8 In brief: compliance with standards relating to international tax transparency, harmful tax competition and anti-BEPS measures. More elaborately: Chapter 23.

9 See Council of the European Union - Council conclusions on the EU list of non-cooperative jurisdictions for tax purposes 5 December, 2017, No. 15429/17. The list currently consists of 11 non-EU countries (benchmark date: 8 October 2024).

10 Proposal for a Council Directive laying down rules against tax avoidance practices that directly affect the functioning of the internal market, 28 January 2016, COM/2016/026 final - 2016/011 (ATAD 1-proposal). The Directive proposal is based on Article 115 TFEU.

11 See Council of the European Union (2015) - Proposal for a Council Directive on a Common Consolidated Corporate Tax Base (CCCTB), 2 December 2015, No. 14544/15.

12 Council Directive (EU) 2016/1164 of 12 July 2016 laying down rules against tax avoidance practices that directly affect the functioning of the internal market, *OJ L* 193, 19.7.2016, p. 1-14 (ATAD 1).

years! That said, the quick approval does not mean that the adoption of the ATAD was a mere formality. The text of the original proposal was discussed intensively during various (technical) meetings between the EU Ministers of Finance and the European Commission and has (sometimes significantly) been revised more than fifteen times or so. The finally adopted Directive thus contains substantial differences and exceptions compared to the original proposal.

Eventually, the ATAD contains three specific anti-tax avoidance rules that form part of the BEPS-package (none of which qualify as minimum standard under the BEPS-package): an earnings stripping rule (interest limitation rule), a CFC-rule and an anti-hybrid mismatch rule. In addition, the ATAD contains two non-BEPS-items: an exit tax duty combined with a (quasi) tax base step-up right in four specific cross-border corporate mobility scenario's and a final back-stop in the form of a general anti-avoidance rule (GAAR).[13] With the adoption of the ATAD, the EU has thus clearly gone one step further than the BEPS-package would require. On the other hand, a proposed switch-over clause for income from shareholdings in companies in low-tax jurisdictions appeared to be one bridge too far, even after its proposed scope was heavily reduced.[14] Also, the ATAD measures are only concerned with the determination of the corporate tax base of the Member States; the question which (minimum) corporate tax rate subsequently has to be applied by each Member State remained a political taboo at that time and was therefore left untouched.

Shortly after its adoption, the ATAD was already revised. Upon approval of the ATAD, some Member States feared that the scope of the specific anti-hybrid mismatch rule would be too narrow in the light of the BEPS-package. In order not to delay the adoption of the ATAD, however, all Member States nonetheless agreed with the final draft proposal. Upon adoption, however, the European Commission was requested to release a second Directive proposal by the end of October 2016 at the latest which should expand the scope of the anti-hybrid mismatch rule. Indeed, a follow-up Directive proposal (often referred to as "ATAD 2") was released on 25 October 2016 which would expand the scope of the said rule both *ratione loci* and *ratione materiae*.[15] Political agreement on an amended version of the proposal was reached on 21 February 2017 and the Directive was formally adopted on 29 May 2017.[16] The agreed anti-hybrid mismatch rule under the ATAD 2 fully replaced the anti-hybrid mismatch rule as accepted under the ATAD 1.

13 It is noted that the ATAD does not explicitly address the question of uni-, bi-, or multilateral concurrence between the various measures.

14 *I.e.* reduced to shareholdings in passive, statutory low-taxed companies located in non-tax treaty countries.

15 Proposal for a Council Directive amending Directive (EU) 2016/1164 as regards hybrid mismatches with third countries, 25 October 2016, COM(2016) 687 final (ATAD 2-proposal).

16 Council Directive (EU) 2017/952 of 29 May 2017 amending Directive (EU) 2016/1164 as regards hybrid mismatches with third countries, *OJ L* 144, 7.6.2017, p. 1-11 (ATAD 2).

19.2.2 De Minimis-Standard and "Menu of Options"; Intra-EU Fragmentation Risk Not Solved

According to its preamble, the ATAD should provide for a common framework in order to prevent a fragmentation of the market. Put differently, the objective is to ensure a uniform implementation of the BEPS-package within the Union. In contrast with this objective, however, Article 3 ATAD stipulates that the ATAD provides for a "*de minimis*"-standard. This means that the ATAD does not exclude the application of domestic or agreement-based provisions aimed at safeguarding a higher level of protection for domestic corporate tax bases. Member States therefore must at least implement this minimum standard to combat tax avoidance, but may go beyond that standard.[17]

Furthermore, and again in contrast with its non-fragmentation objective, the ATAD gives Member States numerous choices in the way they wish to implement the ATAD provisions. Essentially, the ATAD has the characteristics of a "menu of options". The minimum standard (the menu) consist of a starter, a main course and a dessert, but the composition of these courses depends on the Member States' own appetite and preferences. This holds, for example, for the CFC-rule (choice between a normal and a "light" version), the interest limitation rule (choice between robust and refined) and some optional defensive anti-hybrid rules (which thus may be left out if a Member State doesn't like them).

In the light of the above, the practical effect of the ATAD will thus depend on how each individual Member State will, based on its preferences, implement the ATAD provisions in its own domestic corporate tax law. It could therefore legitimately be doubted whether the non-fragmentation objective will be really achieved in the end.[18]

19.2.3 Creation of Taxpayer Duties Instead of Taxpayer Rights; A Clash Between EU And Tax Treaty Norms; Conforming Interpretation

Unlike the other existing Directives in the field of corporate taxation, the ATAD creates duties instead of rights for taxpayers once implemented. This raises the delicate question: what does this mean for the application of tax treaties? Where the ATAD requires a Member State to levy corporate tax, while at the same time the tax treaty prohibits the same Member State to do so, which norm prevails? The ATAD is silent on this matter. In so far as tax treaties with non-EU Member States are concerned, however, an analogous application of Article 351 TFEU is conceivable. On the basis of this provision, treaties with third countries a Member State had concluded prior to its accession to the EU (or its processor E(E)C), are grandfathered. To the extent that such a treaty is not compatible with the EU

17 While respecting their obligations stemming from the TFEU freedoms and the EU state aid provisions.

18 One could even wonder whether minimum harmonization only, while at the same time pursuing the prevention of fragmentation, actually meets the requirement of suitability following from Article 115 TFEU; to this extent: W. Haslehner, The Commission Proposal for an Anti-BEPS Directive: Some Preliminary Comments, 5 February 2016, Kluwer International Blog, <http://kluwertaxblog.com/2016/02/05/the-commission-proposal-for-an-anti-beps-directive-some-preliminary-comments>, retrieved 22 May 2025.

Treaties, the Member State concerned must take all appropriate steps to eliminate that incompatibility, i.e. try to renegotiate the treaty. From the case *Generalstaatsanwaltschaft München v. HF* it can be inferred, however, that the CJ has rejected such an analogous application to the extent it would grandfather conflicting treaties concluded prior to the date of adoption of the ATAD rather than prior to the date of accession to the EU.[19] As far as treaties between Member States are concerned, the assumption probably is that in case of incompatibility, the ATAD provisions prevail over tax treaty provisions It is true that Member States cannot escape their Directive obligations by hiding behind bilateral tax treaties; EU law takes precedence. See Sections 3.5.1 and 8.3.2. Clearly, Member States cannot object against their fellow Member States limiting bilateral tax treaty rights to honour their EU Directive obligations.[20] On the other hand, Directive provisions cannot of themselves impose obligations on individuals and companies: they have no "inverse vertical direct effect" (see Section 3.5.1).[21] As against their citizens, Member States cannot therefore rely on a Directive they themselves failed to implement (*Estoppel* principle). In a Member State with a monistic constitutional tradition, taxpayers may rely directly on 'self-executing' treaty provisions (such as the distributive and relief provisions of tax treaties). If the ATAD has not been (correctly) implemented, then taxpayers may rely on tax treaties (still) protecting them in the same manner as they may rely on protective national law as long as adverse Directive provisions have not been implemented. In a Member State with a dualist constitutional tradition, tax treaties need to be transposed into national law; supposing this transposition has taken place, taxpayers can rely on the transposition law as long as it has not been changed to implement adverse ATAD provisions.

It should be noted, however, that national Courts are required, on the basis of the Union loyalty principle, to do their utmost to apply their national law (we submit: including bilateral treaties between EU States) consistently with EU Directives, also where these have incorrectly not (yet) been implemented.[22] This obligation arises after the implementation period of the Directive has expired but even before such expiration, *i.e.*, between the adoption date and the implementation date, national Courts must avoid an interpretation of national law (or bilateral treaty law between Member States) which could seriously undermine the result the adopted Directive is aimed at.[23] It should be noted that Directive consistent interpretation of national law may have far-reaching consequences: in the VAT Case *Italmoda*,[24] the Court denied restitution, deduction and exemption rights to a company on the basis of a combination of the general prohibition on abuse of rights and the fact that one of the objectives of the VAT Directive is to curb fraud and evasion, even though according to national law, all conditions for such restitution, deduction or exemption were met. A couple of years later, the Court confirmed its approach in the direct tax cases *T Danmark* and *N Luxembourg* in the context of the Parent-subsidiary

19 Case C-435/22 PPU, Generalstaatsanwaltschaft München, ECLI:EU:C:2022:852.
20 This is also consistent with the maxim lex posterior derogat legi priori as reflected in Article 33, paragraph 3 of the Vienna Convention on the Law of Treaties, United Nations, Treaty Series, vol. 1155, p. 33 *et seq.*
21 Case 80/86, Kolpinghuis Nijmegen, EU:C:1987:431.
22 Case C-106/89, Marleasing, EU:C:1990:395.
23 Case C-212/04, Adeneler, EU:C:2006:443.
24 Joined Cases C-131/13, C-163/16 and C-164/16, Italmoda a.o., EU:C:2014:2455.

and Interest and royalty Directives.[25] It even went one step further in the context of VAT fraud by creating room for Member States to overrule domestic limitation periods of criminal offences.[26] This does smell like inverse vertical direct effect (to the detriment of the citizen). See for elaboration, Chapter Section 3.5.1. The Court seems to have realized this and has taken the edge off in more recent case law by emphasizing that the principle of conforming interpretation cannot serve as the basis for an interpretation of national law *contra legem*, which is ultimately for the national court to decide.[27]

19.2.4 Personal Scope; Corporate Tax Liability as the Gateway

The personal scope of the ATAD is defined broadly. Pursuant to Article 1 ATAD, the Directive applies to all taxpayers that are subject to corporate tax in one or more Member States, including permanent establishments in one or more Member States of entities resident for tax purposes in a third country. Different from other Directives in the field of corporate taxation, no further requirements, for example with respect to the legal form of the corporate taxpayer, are imposed. Corporate tax liability in a Member State thus functions as the gateway of the ATAD although it remains within the Member States' sphere of competence to decide whether to levy corporate income taxes in the first place. Under some provisions the personal scope may be restricted specifically to associated enterprises and/or structured arrangements, as defined.

The draftsmen of the ATAD thought it not desirable to extend the scope of the ATAD to types of entities which are not subject to corporate tax in a Member State.[28] This raises the question how the subject to tax requirement must be interpreted. For example, do companies that are effectively or *de facto* not subject to tax still fall under the scope of the ATAD? In the context of the subject to tax requirement included in the Parent-subsidiary Directive, the CJ held in *Wereldhave* that, in the light of this Directive's objective to avoid double taxation, a company that is subject to a special zero rate of taxation, under the condition that all of the fund's profits are distributed to the shareholders, does not satisfy this Directive's subject to tax test. A taxation at a 0% rate is, according to the CJ, tantamount to not subjecting such a company to tax at all.[29]

Since the ATAD provisions do not aim at avoiding double taxation, but rather at creating and extending objective tax liability – either by requiring taxation or by denying a deduction – the decision in *Wereldhave* is not necessarily leading in the context of the ATAD's subject to tax condition. In our view, it seems safe to assume that the taxpayer must at least, as a subject, fall within the scope of the corporate tax act of a Member State. To put it – perhaps a bit roughly – in traditional tax treaty terms: the company should be "liable to tax". This is because creating objective tax liability for a company that is not,

25 Joined cases C116/16 and C117/16, T Danmark & Y Denmark, ECLI:EU:C:2019:135; Joined Cases C 115/16, C 118/16, C 119/16 and C 299/16, N Luxembourg 1 et al., ECLI:EU:C:2019:134.
26 Case C 105/14, Ivo Taricco, ECLI:EU:C:2015:555.
27 For example Case C-665/20 PPU (X.), ECLI:EU:C:2021:339, point 63; Case C-42/17 (M.A.S., M.B.), ECLI:EU:C:2017:936, point 59 and Case C 310/16, Petar Dzivev et al., ECLI:EU:C:2019:30.
28 Recital 4 of the preamble of Council Directive (EU) 2016/1164.
29 Case C-448/15, Wereldhave Belgium and others, EU:C:2017:180.

as a subject, liable to tax would not serve any meaningful purpose and thus would thus be contrary to the *rationale legis* (it is difficult to detect a tax avoidance risk with respect to companies that are not liable to tax in the first place). This implies in our view that, for example, subjectively tax-exempt entities, such as tax-exempt pension funds, would not fall under the personal scope of the ATAD.[30] On the other hand, the subject to tax requirement should, in our view, not be interpreted as requiring the taxpayer to actually pay corporate income tax. For example, if the taxpayer's objective tax liability results in a taxable income of nil, for example as a result of losses, the ATAD provisions will still apply, potentially reducing the amount of losses available for carry-back/carry-forward purposes. Also, and different to the CJ's approach in *Wereldhave*, a special zero rate of taxation for an investment fund that is available under the condition that all of the fund's profits are distributed to its shareholders, would in our view qualify, potentially increasing the amount of profits to be distributed.

Unlike the other Directives in the field of corporate taxation, the ATAD does not explicitly deal with the situation of dual resident companies in triangular cases, that is to say, companies that qualify as a tax resident of a Member State based on the national law of that state, but that qualify as a tax resident of a third country based on the dual-residence tie-breaker rule of a tax treaty concluded between both states. In such a case, the former Member State may lose its residence status for tax treaty purposes and would typically only be allowed to subject the taxpayer to a limited corporate tax liability, *i.e.*, only to the extent the taxpayer receives income sourced in that Member State. Following the OECD, such a company may no longer qualify as fully liable to tax in the meaning of Article 4 of the OECD Model Tax Convention.[31] Although it could be argued by analogy, and based on the *rationale legis* of the ATAD, that such a company should indeed no longer fall under the scope of the ATAD in the case there is no longer any income sourced in that Member State, the literal wording of Article 1 ATAD does not support such an interpretation. Since the residence provisions in the other Directives in the field of corporate taxation do exclude explicitly such dual resident companies from their scope, it is safe to conclude that, in the absence of such an exclusion, dual resident companies do fall *ratione personae* within the scope of the ATAD.

Partnerships that are treated as tax transparent in their state of residence cannot be considered to be subject to tax and hence fall outside the personal scope. However, one explicit exception is made for purposes of the specific hybrid mismatch rule aiming at neutralizing the use of so-called reverse hybrid entities included in Article 9a ATAD. Article 1, paragraph 2 read in conjunction with Article 9a, paragraph 1, ATAD ensure that these types of hybrid entities fall under the scope of this specific hybrid mismatch rule, despite of being not subject to tax.

Finally, companies resident outside the EU with a permanent establishment in a Member State do fall under the scope of the ATAD. As corporate tax liability rather than corporate

30 Differently, although in the context of tax treaties: OECD Commentary on the Model Tax Convention (2017), at 4/8.11.
31 OECD Commentary on the Model Tax Convention (2017), at 4/8.2.

tax residency functions as the gateway, the question is why there is a need to bring non-EU companies with a permanent establishment in a Member State explicitly within the personal scope of the ATAD. After all, also without explicit reference, non-EU companies would already fall under the ATAD's personal scope. The reference must perhaps be understood as a limitation on (rather than a mere confirmation of) the ATAD's personal scope meaning that non-EU companies would *only* fall under the personal scope of the ATAD to the extent they have a permanent establishment in a Member State. We do not see, however, a good reason for such a limitation. Be it as it may, Member States may still decide to ignore this (potential) limitation and to extent the scope of the ATAD's provision to all non-resident companies subject to (limited) tax liability in that Member State given the *de minimis* nature of the ATAD.

Without prejudice to the above observation, the question furthermore is according to which law(s) the presence of a permanent establishment should be determined. In some countries, for example, income from real estate is deemed to constitute a permanent establishment in that state based on domestic law. Should such a Member State apply *e.g.* the interest limitation rule to income derived from such a (fictitious) permanent establishment? Unfortunately, the ATAD is silent on this matter, so the answer will probably depend on the way each Member State has implemented the ATAD provisions in its domestic law.

19.2.5 Substantive and Territorial Scope: Distinction Between Member States and Third Countries not Always Clear

Under the ATAD, it is not required that the taxpayer carries on a cross-border activity. Hence, also taxpayers doing business solely within one single Member States are *prima facie* caught by the ATAD provisions. However, the scope of the CFC-rule, the exit-tax rule and the hybrid mismatch rule is subsequently specifically restricted, *ratione materiae*, to cross-border situations only. Hence, purely domestic operating businesses would effectively not be caught by these rules. On the other hand, the interest limitation rule and the GAAR do not contain a similar limitation. This means in practical terms that these provisions can be applicable *ratione materiae* in purely domestic situations as well.

In addition to the above, some ATAD provisions make a distinction *ratione materiae* between intra-EU situations and situations involving third countries. Under the CFC-rule, for example, a safe harbour rule is available that is not mandatory, however, vis-à-vis non-EU CFCs. Hence, the ATAD provisions may be more rigorous (i.e., more taxpayer unfriendly) in situations involving third countries compared to intra-EU situations. This distinction between Member States and third countries can particularly become relevant with respect to the Member State's associated territories. Do these territories qualify as third countries (ATAD may be more rigorous) or as (part of) a Member State (ATAD may be less rigorous) for purposes of the territorial scope of the ATAD?[32] Case law of the CJ in

32 See also Chapter 5. See also in-depth: D.S. Smit, 'The position of the EU Member States' associated and dependent territories under the freedom of establishment, the free movement of capital and secondary EU law in the field of company taxation', *Intertax* 2 (2011), p. 40-61.

this area indicates that this question must be answered case-by-case, on the basis of a substance over form approach.[33] That is to say, to the extent any associated and dependent territory is bound, pursuant to Article 52(1) TEU read in conjunction with Article 355 TFEU, to apply the TFEU freedoms, in particular the free movement of services, capital and establishment, and consequently to apply the ATAD provisions as being *inextricably tied* to these freedoms,[34] such a territory should – *ratione loci* – be treated as (part of) a Member State for purposes of the ATAD provisions. On the other hand, to the extent any associated and dependent territory is not bound, pursuant to Article 52(1) TEU read in conjunction with Article 355 TFEU, to apply the TFEU freedoms, in particular the free movement of services, capital and establishment, and consequently not required to apply the ATAD provisions,[35] such a territory should – *ratione loci* – be treated as third country for purposes of the ATAD provisions. In practical terms, this means that the outermost regions,[36] the Åland Islands, Ceuta, Melilla and (until Brexit) Gibraltar have to be considered (part of) a Member State *ratione loci* for purposes of the ATAD provisions. Conversely, the Overseas Countries and Territories,[37] the Faeroe Islands and (until Brexit) the United Kingdom sovereign base areas of Akrotiri and Dhekelia in Cyprus, the Channel Islands and the Isle of Man have to be considered third countries *ratione loci* for purposes of applying the ATAD provisions.

19.3 Assessment of the ATAD in the Light of the TFEU Freedoms: a Rather Complex Exercise

A question that is expected to gain significant attention in the future, is how the ATAD minimum standard provisions relate to the TFEU freedoms to the extent these provisions are discriminatory. This question may easily come up if one is to realize that at least some of the ATAD minimum standards, e.g. the anti-hybrid mismatch and interest limitation provisions, apply rather mechanically, without giving the taxpayer the opportunity to prove any business reasons for the underlying transactions. Put differently, also good and honest taxpayers may be caught by the ATAD provisions. In that respect, the ATAD at first blush seems to violate the requirement of proportionality as embedded in the Court's case law on the TFEU freedoms in tax matters (see Chapter 7). The technical analysis is, however, a bit more complex. A number of steps must be taken.

33 *ibid.*

34 *Cf.* by analogy Case C-349/03, *Commission v. United Kingdom*, EU:C:2005:488, paras 42 *et seq.*; Case C-30/01, *Commission v. United Kingdom*, EU:C:2003:489, paras 59-62.

35 *ibid.*

36 France: French overseas departments and overseas regions (French Guiana, Guadeloupe, Martinique, Mayotte and Réunion) and Saint-Martin; Portugal: Azores and Madeira; Spain: Canary Islands.

37 Denmark: Greenland; France: French overseas collectivities (Saint-Pierre and Miquilon, French Polynesia and Wallis and Futuna Islands), New Caledonia and dependencies, the French Southern Territories (including the Scattered Islands and Clipperton Islands) and Saint Barthélemy; The Netherlands: Aruba, Bonaire, Curaçao, Saba, Sint Eustatius and Sint Maarten; United Kingdom (until Brexit): Anguilla, British Antarctic Territory, British Indian Ocean Territory, British Virgin Islands, Cayman Islands, Falkland Islands, Montserrat, Pitcairn Islands, Saint-Helena, Ascension Island, Tristan da Cunha, South Georgia and the South Sandwich Islands and Turks and Caicos Islands.

First of all, the question is whether the implementation of the ATAD can be assessed in the light of the TFEU freedoms in the first place. From, for example, *Euro Park Services* it follows that a national measure in an area which has been exhaustively harmonised at the level of the European Union must be assessed in the light of the provisions of that harmonising measure, rather than in the light of the provisions of primary law.[38] Exhaustive harmonization in principle switches off primary law (see Section 7.2).[39] However, given the express *de minimis* nature of the ATAD (see Article 3 ATAD) and the fact that it leaves Member States ample room to make diverging choices when implementing its provisions, the ATAD does not represent exhaustive harmonization, just as little as the anti-avoidance reservation of competence in the Merger Directive at issue in *Euro Park Service* represented exhaustive harmonization. It is clear, however, that the *minimum* standard is (meant to be) *common* and therefore does not leave any room for national lenience. Therefore, national implementation law conforming to that minimum will in principle only be assessed by the Court in the light of that minimum (for example if the Commission would start an infringement action against a member State for not fighting abuse at least at the required minimum level). We do not expect the Court to strike down as disproportionately restrictive national law conforming to the ATAD minimum standard, as that would mean holding that the ATAD itself violates primary EU law, and that is a very unlikely scenario (see Section 7.2), especially in case of such a hard-fought political compromise. The EU legislature is allowed broad discretion by the Court in areas which entail political, economic and social choices and which involve complex assessments, and only if a Directive or Regulation is manifestly erroneous having regard to the objective pursued, will its legality be affected.[40] It is in the area *beyond* the ATAD minimum, *i.e.*, the area where Member States use their reservation of competence to apply *stricter* anti-abuse rules (Article 3 ATAD; 'overimplementation') or decide to make use of one of the options provided for by the ATAD, where primary EU law, especially the free movement rights are relevant. In that area, however, it is not the ATAD which is being assessed in the light of primary EU law, but national law outside the scope of (implementation of) the ATAD. That national law should simply conform to the Court's regular case law on free movement rights,[41] especially the *rule of reason* (see Sections 3.2.1.2 and 3.2.2) and the general principle of EU law that abuse of rights is prohibited, in the field of direct taxation. See, for elaboration, Section 15.2.

Since the ATAD covers both intra-EU and third country situations, a further distinction must be made in this respect. In intra-EU situations, one will normally easily fall within the protective scope of the TFEU freedoms, even in case of (potential) abusive situations.[42] On the other hand, the TFEU freedoms do not apply, in principle, in the relations with

38 Case C-14/16, Euro Park Services, EU:C:2017:177; Case C-6/16, Eqiom, EU:C:2017:641; Case C-198/14, Visnapuu, C-198/14, EU:C:2015:751.

39 Dissenting, however, Advocate General Kokott in her Opinion in Case C-556/20, Schneider Electric SA, ECLI:EU:C:2021:857, point 37.

40 See e.g. Case C-390/15, Rzecznik Praw Obywatelskich (RPO), EU:C:2017:174, points 54 *et seq.* and Case C-623/22, Belgian Association of Tax Lawyers, ECLI:EU:C:2024:639, point 26.

41 See, for instance, Case C-168/01, Bosal, EU:C:2003:479, point 26.

42 For example Case C-212/97, Centros, EU:C:1999:126; Case C-196/04, Cadbury Schweppes and Cadbury Schweppes Overseas, EU:C:2006:544.

third countries. But there is one exception: the free movement of capital (Article 63 TFEU) also applies to capital movements (for example portfolio and direct investments) to or from third countries. The CJEU has held, however, that the free movement of capital is not applicable to, and hence does not protect, third country investments or investors, when the contested tax measure is exclusively confined to situations involving an investment that confers on the investor definite influence over corporate decisions.[43] This roughly implies that corporate tax measures that are solely designed for groups of companies (e.g. multinational enterprises) typically fall outside the scope of the free movement of capital.[44] On the other hand, since the CJ's ruling in *FII GLO II*, it is beyond doubt that a national rule not confined to definite influence cases, can be assessed under the free movement of capital, unless the contested rule is designed to regulate market access (which will probably never be the case as far as corporate tax measures are concerned).[45] This means that such broader rules can be scrutinized under the free movement of capital, not only in case of minority investments, but also if – in fact – an investor happens to have a definite influence over its third-country investment. In the context of 'overimplementation of the ATAD, this means that the scope of the anti-avoidance measures (are they restricted to groups of companies or not?) is probably decisive when answering the question whether or not third-country situations are protected by the free movement of capital.[46]

As regards justification grounds for 'overimplementation' (on the basis of Article 3 ATAD) which restricts free movement rights, a final distinction must be made in the relations with third countries. In *FII GLO I*, the CJ recognized that a Member State may be able to demonstrate that a restriction on capital movements to or from non-Member States is justified for a particular reason in circumstances in which that same reason would not constitute a valid justification for a restriction on capital movements between Member States.[47] Although the CJ's case law continues to develop on this point, there may be more room, for example, to accept justifications relating to the need for effective fiscal supervision.[48]

43 Case C-47/12, Kronos International, EU:C:2014:2200; Case 35/11, Test Claimants in the FII Group Litigation 2, EU:C:2012:707.

44 For example Case C-446/04, Test Claimants in the FII Group Litigation 1, EU:C:2006:774, point 118; Case C-524/04, Test Claimants in the Thin Cap Group Litigation, EU:C:2007:161, point 32.

45 Case 35/11, Test Claimants in the FII Group Litigation, EU:C:2012:707.

46 Case C-492/04, Lasertec, EU:C:2007:273; Case C-415/06, Stahlwerk Ergste Westig, EU:C:2007:651; Case C-101/05, A, EU:C:2007:804.

47 Case C-446/04, Test Claimants in the FII Group Litigation, EU:C:2006:774, point 171.

48 See, for example, Case C-72/09, Établissements Rimbaud, EU:C:2010:645. For a more detailed discussion D.S. Smit, *EU Freedoms, Non-EU Countries and Company Taxation* (Kluwer Law International, 2012), p. 507 *et seq.*

19.4 The Four Specific Anti-Tax Avoidance Rules (SAARs)

19.4.1 The Earnings Stripping Rule

19.4.1.1 Introduction and Background

Companies belonging to the same multinational group can finance their activities in two ways: through debt or through equity. In a perfect world, that is to say, in the absence of agency costs, bankruptcy costs, taxes, capital market (in)efficiency, asymmetric information, etcetera, a firm should, economically speaking, be indifferent in its choice of financing: either through issuing of stocks (equity) or issuing of a loan (debt). In reality, however, tax systems tend to favour debt over equity as interest payments on debts are typically deductible for corporate income tax purposes whereas equity returns (dividends) typically are not, although both interest and the normal return on equity are usual forms of remuneration for supplying the funds to finance a company's capital.[49] It follows that in this imperfect world, a firm's financing decision is influenced by debt bias and may consequently lead to excessive leverage.[50]

Consequently, taxable income arising in the territory of a (high-tax) Member State and generated by a company forming part of a multinational enterprise could be eroded either by allocating third party debts to that company, or by creating and allocating inter-company debts to that company in excess of the group's actual third party debts. By providing group-financing services from a low or no-tax jurisdiction, corresponding taxation of the interest receivables could subsequently be avoided as well.[51] Lastly, third party or intragroup financing could be used to fund the generation of foreign tax-exempt income. In this latter respect, the CJ decided in *Bosal*, rather unfortunately,[52] that the territoriality principle could not justify a (Dutch) tax rule that tried to fix such a mismatch by making the deduction of interest expenses dependent on the question whether these expenses are directly or indirectly instrumental in making profits which are taxable in the Netherlands. As a result, Member States may be required to accept the deduction

49 See, for instance, M. P. Devereux & R.A de Mooij, *Alternative Systems of Business Tax in Europe: An applied analysis of ACE and CBIT reforms*, EC Taxation Papers, Working Paper 17 (2009), p. 7.

50 See, for instance, C. Spengel et al., Addressing the Debt-Equity Bias within a Common Consolidated Corporate Tax Base (CCCTB) - Possibilities, Impact on Effective Tax Rates and Revenue Neutrality, *World Tax Journal* 10, No. 2 (2018); H.P. Huizinga, L. Laeven & G.J.A. Nicodème, Capital structure and international debt shifting, Journal of Financial Economics, 88 No. 1 (2008), p. 80-118; M.A. Desai, C.F. Foley & J.R. Hines, *A Multinational Perspective on Capital Structure Choice and Internal Capital Markets*, Journal of Finance 59, No. 6 (2004), p. 2451-2487.

51 See, for example, M. J. Graetz, *A Multilateral Solution for the Income Tax Treatment of Interest Expenses*, Bulletin for International Taxation 11/2008, p. 487 *et seq.*

52 Also critical, for example, Advocate General Geelhoed in his Opinion in Case C-374/04, Test Claimants in Class IV of the ACT Group Litigation, EU:C:2006:773, point 63; D.M. Weber, 'The Bosal Holding Case: Analysis and Critique', *EC Tax Review* 4 (2003), p. 225; P.J. Wattel, 'Corporate tax jurisdiction in the EU with respect to branches and subsidiaries; dislocation distinguished from discrimination and disparity; a plea for territoriality', *EC Tax Review* 4 (2003), p. 200 and, by the same author, 'Fiscal Cohesion, Fiscal Territoriality and Preservation of the (Balanced) Allocation of Taxing Power; What is the Difference?', in *The Influence of European Law on Direct Taxation*, ed. D.M. Weber (Kluwer Law International, 2007), p. 145.

of interest payments even where they exempt from taxation (foreign) corresponding profits, i.e. foreign profits to which the interest payments can economically be linked. The Bosal decision thus leads to asymmetry – a perfect territorial "mismatch" – between tax deductible expenses and tax-exempt profits and thus facilitates BEPS blatantly.

In the OECD BEPS-4 report, the OECD presents its recommended approach to address the above risks. This approach is based on a fixed ratio rule (a so-called "earnings stripping rule") which limits an entity's net deductions for interest, and payments economically equivalent to interest, to a percentage of that entity's earnings before interest, taxes, depreciation and amortisation (EBITDA).[53] An entity's net interest deductions thus become directly linked to the taxable income generated by its economic activities.[54] By excluding the two major non-cash costs in a typical income statement (*i.e.* depreciation of fixed assets and amortisation of intangible assets), EBITDA is said to be a guide to the ability of an entity to meet its obligations to pay interest and therefore a standard which is said to be often used by lenders in deciding how much interest expense an entity can reasonably afford to bear.[55] The OECD recommends that this earnings stripping rule shall at least apply to entities in multinational groups.

The BEPS-4 recommendation has been endorsed within the Union through the inclusion of a specific interest limitation rule in the ATAD. Based on Article 4 ATAD, exceeding borrowing costs shall be deductible in the tax period in which they are incurred only up to 30% of the taxpayer's EBITDA. The 30%-threshold may be set at a lower rate to ensure a higher level of protection, but cannot be set higher. The wording of Article 4 ATAD ('shall be deductible") might suggest that Member States should always allow deduction of net interest expenses to the extent they do not exceed the 30%-threshold, but such an interpretation would clearly go beyond the ATAD's objective of setting a minimum standard in combatting BEPS. Hence, allowable interest under Article 4 ATAD could still be restricted based on other limitation rules, including those included in the ATAD itself, particularly the GAAR and anti-hybrid rule.[56]

Its robust simplicity and its alignment with a taxpayer's economic activities in a Member State could be seen as advantages of an interest limitation rule based on an entity's EBITDA. However, there are also a number of disadvantages. It may raise legal certainty concerns given that a taxpayer's EBITDA will usually fluctuate as time goes by. It therefore may be difficult to predict in advance how much of an entity's excess borrowing costs will be deductible in the future. The rule may also lead to overkill and may thus be felt as disproportionate under circumstances. This is because the interest limitation rule applies, at least as a general rule, to both intra-group and third party loans, to both associated and stand-alone companies and in both domestic and cross-border situations. The underlying

53 OECD (2015), *Limiting Base Erosion Involving Interest Deductions and Other Financial Payments, Action 4 - 2015 Final Report*, OECD Publishing, Paris (OECD BEPS-4 Report), p. 11.

54 *ibid.*

55 OECD BEPS-4 Report, p. 44.

56 This is also confirmed in recital 6 of the preamble of Council Directive (EU) 2016/1164, which states that Member States could in addition to the interest limitation rule provided by the ATAD also use targeted rules against intra-group debt financing, in particular thin capitalisation rules.

motives of a taxpayer and the purpose of the loan are not taken into consideration and double taxation may arise if non-deductible interest is nonetheless taxed in the hands of the (domestic or foreign) creditor. It is true that the preamble suggests that double taxation should be avoided, the ATAD fails to provide further guidance in this respect.[57] In addition, interest limitation based on an entity's EBITDA has a procyclical effect in that the interest deduction possibilities decrease in case an entity's profits decrease. In case of a negative EBITDA, no interest deduction is, in principle, available at all and taxpayers depend on the choices made by the Member States whether or not to provide for carry-forward or carry-back possibilities in such a case. This effect may particularly hit ailing companies. Finally, restricting the deduction up to 30% of an entity's EBITDA implies that a taxpayer may no longer be taxed on a net-income basis (balance of revenues and expenses). This could raise concerns in the light of the ability to pay tax principle.

19.4.1.2 Scope of the Rule: Exceeding Borrowing Costs minus 30% EBITDA = Non Deductible

Article 4 ATAD includes two main proxies for determining the amount of interest that falls under the interest limitation rule: i) exceeding borrowing costs and ii) EBITDA. In principle, both proxies apply to each single taxpayer on a standalone basis. However, in case an entity forms part of a group according to national tax law (be it on a tax-consolidation basis or otherwise) Member States may require the exceeding borrowing costs and the EBITDA to be calculated at the level of the (domestic) group, comprising the results of all its members.[58] This is one of the few examples where the ATAD deviates from its single entity approach and allows for an overall group approach. The question then comes up whether such a group approach could infringe the TFEU freedoms where a (domestic) group taxation regime (*e.g.* group contribution) is restricted to purely domestic situations and where such a regime has the effect that interest limitation rule is partly or fully switched-off (*e.g.* by making a domestic intra-group profit transfer leading to an increased EBITDA-basis). In the case *PRA Group Europe SA* the EFTA Court gave– in in a non-ATAD context – a positive answer to this delicate question under the EEA-Agreement. We submit that in an ATAD-context this question should be answered negatively since, from the perspective of the rationale of the Earnings Stripping rule in combination with any group taxation regime, domestic and cross-border situations are not comparable in this respect; one would compare apples (domestic *taxable* EBITDA) with peaches (foreign *non-taxable* EBITDA). Tax liability in our view thus functions, or at least should function, as a legitimate benchmark to distinguish foreign (non-taxable) EBITDA from domestic (taxable) EBITDA.[59] Alternatively, we submit that the limitation of the group approach to domestic situations would be justified under reference to the territoriality principle and the need to safeguard the balanced allocation of taxation powers between Member States, leaving aside the fact that the Earnings Stripping rule forms part of the minimum standards of a Directive as a result of which the Court's competence is limited to assess whether this limitation constitutes a manifest error.[60]

57 Recital 5 of Council Directive (EU) 2016/1164.

58 Article 4, paragraph 1, ATAD.

59 See also, *e.g.*, O.C.R. Marres, Waarom de earningsstrippingmaatregel niet in strijd met het primaire Unierecht is, NTFR 2019/3022.

60 Case C-390/15, Rzecznik Praw Obywatelskich (RPO), EU:C:2017:174, points 54 *et seq.*

The first proxy implies that the taxpayer must incur more interest expenses, as defined, than it receives. In calculating the taxpayer's possible exceeding borrowing costs position, only costs that are tax deductible and interest revenues that are taxable under the national law of the Member State concerned are taken into account. From this perspective, the interest limitation rule effectively functions as a back-stop; only if interest deduction is not already denied on the basis of another limitation rule, it may start falling under the scope of the EBITDA rule.

If there is no excess of interest expenses, as defined, then the interest limitation rule does not come into play. This means that financial undertakings, such as banks and insurance companies, would typically fall outside the scope of the rule. The Member States are even allowed to exclude financial undertakings from the scope of the rule from the outset in anticipation to a more customised approach at international and Union level.[61] Also conduit companies may fall outside the scope of the rule, provided that they are considered for tax purposes to be the recipient of the interest receivables.

The definition of borrowing costs is deliberately formulated very broad. It includes not only interest expenses on all forms of debt, but also other costs that economically are equivalent to interest and expenses incurred in connection with the raising of finance as defined in national law. Although it follows that the definition eventually depends on the national law of the Member State concerned, the ATAD nonetheless gives a number of non-exhaustive and (presumably[62]) autonomous examples of borrowing costs. These examples include payments under profit participating loans, imputed interest on instruments (such as convertible bonds and zero coupon bonds), amounts under alternative financing arrangements and the finance cost element of finance lease payments. Also included are notional interest amounts under derivative instruments or hedging arrangements related to an entity's borrowings, certain foreign exchange gains and losses on borrowings and instruments connected with the raising of finance, guarantee fees for financing arrangements and arrangement fees and similar costs related to the borrowing of funds. Finally, capitalised interest included in the balance sheet value of a related asset, or the amortisation of capitalised interest and amounts measured by reference to a funding return under transfer pricing rules are included as well.

In order to calculate the borrowing costs surplus, the total amount of borrowing costs, as defined, must be deducted from the total amount of taxable interest revenues and other economically equivalent taxable revenues that the taxpayer receives according to national law. It is assumed that the subject to tax condition must be understood in a qualitative rather than in a quantitative fashion meaning that it should be sufficient that interest is included in the taxable base of the taxpayer. At the same time, the reference to domestic law implies that foreign withholding taxes levied on interest receivables shall not be taken into account under this test. Contrary to the definition of borrowing costs, the ATAD does not provide for a list of examples of interest revenues, but solely refers to

61 Recital 7 of Council Directive (EU) 2016/1164.

62 More cautious: R. Snoeij & J.H.A.M. van Helvoirt, 'Een uiteenzetting van de Europese renteaftrek-bepaling uit de ATA-richtlijn (art. 4)', *Fiscaal Tijdschrift FED* 2016/108.

the domestic law definition. Assuming that the list of examples is of a declaratory nature, this might give rise to definition mismatches between interest received and interest paid leading to an increase of the amount of borrowing costs surplus.

The proxy of EBITDA must be determined, according to Article 4, paragraph 2, ATAD, by adding back to the income subject to corporate tax in the Member State of the taxpayer the tax-adjusted amounts for exceeding borrowing costs as well as the tax-adjusted amounts for depreciation and amortisation. It follows that the EBITDA must be calculated in accordance with the tax accounting rules applicable in the Member State concerned, and not on the basis of commercial accounting standards. In case the taxpayer's EBITDA is negative, the basis for deduction is nil. Tax exempt income, for example foreign tax-exempt branch income, shall be excluded from the taxpayer's EBITDA. The latter implies that holding companies receiving only tax-exempt income from their subsidiaries would have an EBITDA of zero and would thus *prima facie* fully fall within the scope of the interest limitation. Credits for foreign taxes, by contrast, seem not to reduce the taxpayer's EBITDA.[63] Tax planning strategies reducing the taxpayer's taxable income in a Member State may also reduce the taxpayer's EBITDA and therefore have an adverse effect on the taxpayer's interest deduction possibilities.[64] Finally, Member States may adopt an alternative measure referring to a taxpayer's earnings before interest and tax (EBIT) and fixed in a way that it is equivalent to the EBITDA-based ratio.[65]

In principle, the interest limitation rule of Article 4 ATAD is absolute in the sense that non-deductible exceeding borrowing costs (unrelieved borrowing costs) in a current tax period vaporize and can no longer be deducted in previous or future tax periods. However, Member States have the option to provide for carry-forward and carry-back possibilities. More in particular, they may provide for rules to carry forward, without time limitation, unrelieved borrowing costs while i) fully denying carry-back or, alternatively, ii) allowing carry-back of unrelieved borrowing costs for a maximum of three years.[66] Alternatively, Member States may provide for rules to carry forward, without time limitation, unrelieved borrowing costs while allowing, for a maximum of five years, carry forward of unused interest capacity.[67] Member States thus must limit their choice between the three alternatives. While doing so, it is assumed that Member States may restrict the carry-forward and carry-back periods, and thus may be stricter, based on the *de minimis* rule. It is observed in this respect that the ATAD does not address the possible interaction with temporal limitations on general loss carry forward and carry back rules in Member States. Also, the ATAD does not address the phenomenon of "trade" in companies with unrelieved borrowing costs or unused interest capacity. Without specific measures, for example, the shares in a (cash-box) company with previously built-up unused interest capacity

63 R. Snoeij & J.H.A.M. van Helvoirt, 'Een uiteenzetting van de Europese renteaftrekbepaling uit de ATA-richtlijn (art. 4)', *Fiscaal Tijdschrift FED* 2016/108, with further references. On the contrary, OECD BEPS-4 Report, p. 44.

64 O.C.R. Marres, as cited by R. Gielen & C. Huisman, 'Verslag van het tweede grote NOB Anti-BEPS-richtlijn congres van 3 april 2017, *Weekblad Fiscaal Recht* 2017/7199.

65 Recital 6 of the preamble of Council Directive (EU) 2016/1164.

66 Article 4, paragraph 6, sub a and sub b, ATAD.

67 Article 4, paragraph 6, sub c, ATAD.

could be sold to another party that could subsequently "channel" substantial amounts of intra-group interest expenses through the freshly acquired entity, thus potentially benefitting from the acquired interest deduction capacity for years.[68] To the extent such practices would not be governed by the GAAR under Article 6 ATAD, we assume that it is up to each individual Member State to take appropriate countermeasures against such practices.

19.4.1.3 Exceptions to the Interest Limitation Rule

Article 4 ATAD provides for a number of exceptions on the interest limitation rule. First of all, in order to reduce the administrative and compliance burden, Member States may provide for a *de minimis* (safe harbour) rule by allowing deduction of exceeding borrowing costs up to EUR 3 million when this leads to a higher deduction than the EBITDA-based ratio. This threshold may be set lower, but not higher. In case an entity forms part of a group according to national tax law, be it on a tax-consolidated basis or otherwise, Member States shall choose to apply the threshold for the entire (domestic) group. The obvious background of this option is to avoid fragmentation, *i.e.*, to prevent taxpayers from splitting-up EUR 3 million+ exceeding borrowing costs between separate local group companies that, on a standalone basis, would all remain under the said threshold.

Secondly, standalone entities may be excluded from the scope of the interest limitation rule. A standalone entity is defined as a taxpayer that is not part of a consolidated group for financial accounting purposes and has no permanent establishment or associated enterprise (which somewhat misleadingly may under circumstances include individuals as well). The background of this exception is the idea that BEPS in principle takes place through excessive interest payments between associated enterprises. Standalone entities may thus be excluded given the limited risks of tax avoidance.[69]

Furthermore, in order to facilitate the transition to the new interest limitation rule, Member States may provide for a specific grandfathering clause with respect to loans which were concluded before 17 June 2016. This exclusion shall not extend, however, to any subsequent modification of such loans. In case of a subsequent increase in the amount or duration of the loan, the grandfathering clause would thus be limited to the original terms of the loan.[70]

Member States could also exclude exceeding borrowing costs incurred on loans used to fund long-term public infrastructure projects[71] considering that such financing arrangements present little or no BEPS risks. This option is without prejudice however, to the EU state aid rules.

68 See in the context of the Dutch loss carry-back rules in case of change of ownership: D.S. Smit & R.C. de Smit, 'The Credit Suisse Cases and Intra-Group Financing: Dutch Supreme Court Strikes a Balance between Tax Planning and Tax Avoidance', 19 *Derivs. & Fin. Instrums.* 6 (2017).

69 Recital 8 of Council Directive (EU) 2016/1164.

70 Recital 8 of Council Directive (EU) 2016/1164.

71 A long-term public infrastructure project means a project to provide, upgrade, operate and/or maintain a large-scale asset that is considered in the general public interest by a Member State.

Finally, a fixed ratio rule based on the taxpayer's EBITDA does not take into account the fact that groups in different sectors may be leveraged differently and, even without a sector bias, some groups are simply more highly leveraged.[72] To overcome this, the interest limitation rule provides for two optional, alternative group-escapes: an equity escape rule and a group ratio rule. Both escapes only come into play where the taxpayer is a member of a consolidated group for financial accounting purposes. Under the equity escape rule, the taxpayer may be given the right to fully deduct its exceeding borrowing costs if it can demonstrate that the ratio of its equity over its total assets is equal to or higher than the equivalent ratio of the group (a small margin of 2%-points is permitted), provided that all assets and liabilities are valued using the same method as in the consolidated financial statements (*i.e.* drawn up in accordance with the International Financial Reporting Standards or the national financial reporting system of a Member State):

$$\text{(1)} \quad \frac{\text{Equity}_{\text{taxpayer}}}{\text{Total assets}_{\text{taxpayer}}} \geq \frac{\text{Equity}_{\text{group}}}{\text{Total assets}_{\text{group}}}$$

Passing the equity escape means that all exceeding borrowing expenses become fully deductible. If the test is not passed, then the default interest limitation rule fully applies. The effect of the equity escape rule is that the interest limitation rule will, on balance, particularly hit entities that, from the perspective of the entire group, are excessively leveraged. At the same time, this implies that if the group as a whole is heavily leveraged as well, the taxpayer would be expected to pass the equity escape. BEPS-concerns may not be solved in such a case. The equity escape does not provide for specific rules to avoid, for example, a taxpayer to artificially increase its capital shortly before the equity escape is applied. Also the entire group is not prevented from artificially increasing its overall debt position. Again, to the extent such practices would not be governed by the GAAR under Article 6 ATAD, we assume that it is up to each individual Member State to take appropriate countermeasures against such practices.

Finally, under the second escape, the group ratio rule, one basically looks to what extent the taxpayer's EBITDA contributes to the overall EBITDA of the entire group. On the basis of this ratio, exceeding borrowing costs of the entire group vis-à-vis third party are subsequently allocated to the taxpayer:

$$\text{(2)} \quad \frac{\text{Third party interest}_{\text{group}}}{\text{EBITDA}_{\text{group}}} \times \text{EBITDA}_{\text{taxpayer}}$$

A proportionate link is thus made between third party excess borrowing expenses and the taxpayer's EBITDA. To the extent this allocation formula results in a higher amount of exceeding borrowing costs for the taxpayer compared to the actual amount of non-deductible exceeding borrowing costs calculated under the default interest limitation

72 OECD BEPS-4 Report, p. 57.

rule, the higher amount becomes deductible, up to the amount of the taxpayer's actual exceeding borrowing costs.

19.4.1.4 Compatibility with the TFEU Freedoms

Case law of the CJ demonstrates that interest limitation rules have to comply with the requirements imposed by the TFEU freedoms.[73] However, since the interest limitation under Article 4 ATAD rule applies generally to all taxpayers and all types of loans, both in domestic and cross-border situations, the rule seems non-discriminatory from a TFEU freedoms point of view. The question could be raised, however, whether the rule *de facto* disadvantages debt financing in cross-border situations compared to domestic situations, for example, as a result of the exclusion for standalone entities or as a result of the application of the EUR 3 million safe harbour.[74] In our view, the mere fact that in the majority of cases multinationals are affected by the rule should not be sufficient to accept the existence of a covert discrimination in the context of the TFEU freedoms. The view to the contrary would – in extreme consequence – imply that a Member State would be prevented from introducing a corporation tax if in that Member State more than 50% of active undertakings were foreign undertakings.[75] The fact that, more or less by chance, persons affected by the introduction of a tax originate to a large extent or even in their majority from other Member States cannot therefore constitute covert discrimination as such.[76] The Court decisions in *Tesco Global*[77] and *Vodafone*[78] support this view in the context of (steep) progressive taxation. In our view, however, the conclusion may be different where precisely due to the choice(s) that a Member State made for setting the parameters, multinational enterprises are affected purposefully and not as a random consequence while the chosen parameters are, seen from the perspective of the objective of the tax measure at stake, set in an inconsistent and non-systematic manner (*i.e.* the tax measure is manifestly inappropriate having regard to its objective).[79] See also, however, Section 12.3. This said, given the substantial financial interest that may be at stake in particular cases, the question of compatibility of the interest limitation rule with EU law will in all likelihood, sooner or later, be referred to the CJ, either on a standalone basis

73 See, for example, Case C-524/04, Test Claimants in the Thin Cap Group Litigation, EU:C:2007:161; Case C-324/00, Lankhorst-Hohorst, EU:C:2002:749; Case C-168/01, Bosal, EU:C:2003:479.

74 See A.P. Dourado, 'The Interest Limitation Rule in the Anti-Tax Avoidance Directive (ATAD) and the Net Taxation Principle, *EC Tax Review* 3 (2017).

75 To the same extent: Opinion Advocate General Kokott, Case C-233/16, Asociación Nacional de Grandes Empresas de Distribución (ANGED), EU:C:2017:852, point 35 and Opinion Advocate General Kokott, Case C-323/18, Tesco-Global Áruházak Zrt, ECLI:EU:C:2019:567, point 75.

76 *ibid.*

77 Case C-323/18, Tesco-Global Áruházak Zrt, ECLI:EU:C:2020:140.

78 Case C-75/18, Vodafone Magyarország Mobil Távközlési Zrt., ECLI:EU:C:2020:139.

79 See, by analogy, Opinion Advocate General Kokott, Case C-75/18, ECLI:EU:C:2019:492, point 117; Opinion Advocate General Kokott, Case C-562/19 P, European Commission v Republic of Poland, ECLI:EU:C:2020:834point 42 and, by analogy, Joined cases C-106/09 P and C-107/09 P, European Commission and Kingdom of Spain v Government of Gibraltar and United Kingdom of Great Britain and Northern Ireland, EU:C:2011:732, point 106.

or in combination with a domestic group taxation regime, such as a domestic group contribution scheme; see also Section 12.4.1.2.[80].

19.4.2 The Exit Tax and Tax Base Step-Up Rule

19.4.2.1 Introduction and Background

Business assets of a company may have a fair market value which is higher than their book value applied for tax purposes. Most Member States usually tax this difference between fair market and book value upon a realization basis instead of on an accruals basis.[81] Sometimes, for example in the context of business reorganizations within a group of companies, specific tax deferral facilities may even be available that seek to facilitate those business reorganizations through a roll-over mechanism, thus deferring taxation over capital gains realized upon the reorganization. In sharp contrast to the above, however, in situations where a company transfers its real seat abroad, most Member States usually switch-over to taxation on an accruals basis by deeming the business assets and liabilities to be disposed to the extent that they do not remain connected to a permanent establishment in the Member State from which the company's seat is transferred.[82] The same holds for situations where a company transfers assets or liabilities from its head office to its permanent establishment located abroad or *vice versa*.[83] Accordingly, any gains accrued while the assets or liabilities were effectively connected with the company resident in their territory are thus typically taxed immediately upon transfer of the assets in those cases, without being an actual disposal necessary. In an intra-EU/EEA context, however, the TFEU freedoms may restrain Member States in applying this type of "exit taxes".[84]

Although exit taxes are not part of the BEPS-package, the ATAD nonetheless explicitly addresses this issue. Article 5 ATAD contains two rules in this respect: an exit tax duty in a number of well-defined cases of cross-border corporate mobility to be imposed by the Member State of departure and a quasi-tax base step-up right for taxpayers in intra-EU/EEA situations to be granted by the Member State of destination. In addition, an option for deferred payment of the exit tax is offered, subject to several conditions. This option directly follows from *National Grid Indus*, as further refined in the CJ's subsequent case law on exit taxes.[85] The optional regime for deferred payments and perhaps also the (quasi) step-up right are one of the few examples of provisions included in the ATAD that

80 More indepth, for example, A.P. Dourado, 'The Interest Limitation Rule in the Anti-Tax Avoidance Directive (ATAD) and the Net Taxation Principle', *EC Tax Review* 3 (2017) and S.A Stevens, Evaluation of the Earnings Stripping Rules, *EC Tax Review* 29, No. 4 (2020), pp. 158-177.

81 See, for example, IFA, Cahiers de droit fiscal international, *Tax treatment of international acquisitions of businesses*, Vol. 90b (Amersfoort: Sdu Fiscale en Financiële Uitgevers, 2005).

82 Communication from the Commission to the Council, the European Parliament and the European Economic and Social Committee of 19 December 2006, 'Exit taxation and the need for co-ordination of Member States' tax policies', COM(2006) 825 final, p. 5-6.

83 *ibid.*

84 Case C-371/10, National Grid Indus, EU:C:2011:785; Case C-164/12. DMC, EU:C:2014:20; Case C-657/13, Verder LabTec, EU:C:2015:331.

85 Case C-371/10, National Grid Indus, EU:C:2011:785. See more elaborately: Chapter 20.

actually grant rights to taxpayers instead of imposing obligations on them. Presumably, both rights have direct effect.[86]

19.4.2.2 Exit Tax and Tax Base Step-Up, but Mutual Recognition of Market Value Bridge too Far

The exit tax rule and (quasi) step-up right are limited to the following four events listed in Article 5, paragraph 1 ATAD:

i. A taxpayer transfers its tax residence to another Member State or to a third country. An exception is made for those assets which remain effectively connected with a permanent establishment in the first Member State.
ii. A taxpayer transfers assets from its head office to its permanent establishment in another Member State or in a third country.
iii. A taxpayer transfers assets from its permanent establishment in a Member State to its head office or another permanent establishment in another Member State or in a third country.
iv. A taxpayer transfers the business carried on by its permanent establishment from a Member State to another Member State or to a third country.

In the last three situations (ii-iv), the mandatory exit tax only applies in so far as the Member State of departure has no longer the right to tax the transferred assets due to the transfer. From the ATAD's preamble one can infer that this exception was included to ensure the compatibility of the mandatory exit tax rule with the use by some Member States of the credit method.[87] Whether or not a Member State still has a right to tax must be determined at national level. By making the mandatory exit tax dependent on the national law of the Member States, its initial broad scope may thus potentially be reduced significantly.

In all cases, the difference between the market value of the business assets at the time of their "exit" and their value for tax purposes forms the basis of the mandatory exit tax. This means that, in line with *National Grid Indus*, but contrary to the *N.*-case, post emigration losses need not to be taken into account by the Member State of departure.[88] When the exit tax is imposed, the market value subsequently forms the basis for the tax base step-up to be granted by the Member State of destination. If Member States, however, disagree about the "right' market value, then the Member State of destination is not required to accept the value determined by the Member State of departure. Hence, despite that fact that Member States are encouraged to solve this conflict under existing dispute resolution mechanisms,[89] symmetry in fair market valuation is not guaranteed. Accepting the principle of mutual recognition when it comes to the valuation apparently was a bridge too far for Member States.

86 To the same extent M.F. de Wilde, De exitheffing in de Anti-ontgaansrichtlijn en zijn invloed op het Nederlandse belastingsysteem, *Fiscaal Tijdschrift FED* 2016/109.
87 Recital 10 of the preamble of Council Directive (EU) 2016/1164.
88 More elaborately Chapter 20.
89 Recital 10 of the preamble of Council Directive (EU) 2016/1164.

19.4.2.3 An Alarming Lack of Definitions and Over-and Under-Inclusiveness

Article 5 ATAD raises a couple of questions. First, the rule does not clearly tell us on the basis of which criteria and which law(s) it must be determined whether the tax residence of a company is transferred (Domestic law or tax treaty law?). As the rule is primarily directed to the Member State of departure, it would make sense to link-up with the domestic law of that State while taking the effects of a possible tax treaty into account as well. Similar questions arise with respect to the definition of the term permanent establishment (no definition included) and the methodology to attribute assets to that permanent establishment. For example, profit attribution methods may vary from Member State to Member State and from tax treaty to tax treaty. Based on Dutch (domestic) doctrine, to give just one example, a temporary transfer of fixed assets does not lead to an attribution of those assets to a foreign permanent establishment. Under the 2010 Authorized OECD Approach, by contrast, the place of use of these assets is, in principle, decisive. It is true that temporary transfers are excluded from the scope of Article 5, paragraph 7, ATAD, but only in very specific situations.[90] The ATAD does not make clear, however, which methodology has to be followed in other cases. Uniform interpretation throughout the EU is thus not guaranteed.

Secondly, Article 5 ATAD requires Member States to levy tax in one of the four specified cases of cross-border corporate mobility, but it does not make clear whether this obligation overrules domestic tax base exemptions, such as participation exemption regimes. Since the BEPS risk would be limited in such a case – any realized gain on participations would be tax-exempt anyway in purely domestic situations – it would appear a matter of over-inclusiveness – especially affecting holding jurisdictions within the EU – if accrued gains on otherwise tax-exempt participations would be taxed upon emigration.[91] Another peculiarity in this respect is that Article 5 ATAD only focuses on business assets. But what about the passive side of the taxpayer's balance sheet? Literally speaking, the Member State of departure is not required to tax, for example, technical reserves or to apply recaptures of previously allowed deductions or roll-over reliefs. And switching back to the active side of the balance sheet, it is even not beyond doubt whether accrued, non-capitalized goodwill is literally speaking caught by Article 5 ATAD. From the angle of the rule, this would all seem a matter of under-inclusiveness. In any case, as Article 5 ATAD provides for a minimum standard only, it is expected that Member States will take the passive side of the taxpayers' balance sheets and non-capitalized goodwill into account as well. Furthermore, other forms of cross border corporate mobility such as cross border conversions, mergers and divisions are not specifically covered by the exit tax and step-up rules. Also transfers of assets between a parent company and its subsidiaries explicitly fall outside the scope of the rule.[92] The question could be raised why these situations are

90 Article 5 ATAD shall not apply to asset transfers related to the financing of securities, assets posted as collateral or where the asset transfer takes place in order to meet prudential capital requirements or for the purpose of liquidity management, provided that the assets are set to revert to the Member State of the transferor within a period of 12 months.

91 To a similar extent: S. Peeters, 'Exit Taxation: From an Internal Market Barrier to a Tax Avoidance Prevention Tool', *EC Tax Review* 3 (2017).

92 Recital 10 of the preamble of Council Directive (EU) 2016/1164.

left untouched, since it may become relatively easy to circumvent the exit tax rule, for example, by choosing for a cross-border conversion instead of a corporate emigration. Again, since Article 5 ATAD provides for a minimum standard only, Member States are not refrained from extending the exit tax rule, as long as they respect the CJ case law in the field of corporate exit taxes. As an aside, as of the entry into force of the (civil law) Directive (EU) 2019/2121 (by 31 January 2023 at the latest), Member States may be required to deny a cross-border merger, conversion or division when there are serious doubts indicating that the cross-border operation is aimed at the circumvention of Union or national law. It seems to us that denying such a cross-border merger, conversion or division from a civil law perspective effectively comes close to a mandatory exit tax in case of tax avoidance.[93]

As observed earlier, three of the four mandatory exit tax rules are made dependent on the national law of the Member States. This implies that domestic case law in the field of exit taxes becomes relevant as well. The German Federal Finance Court in its decision of 28 October 2009 non-applied the German exit tax rules in a case where an entrepreneur moved his residence and his entire enterprise from Germany to Belgium. The Court decided that this emigration did not give rise to an exit tax under German domestic tax law since Germany would not lose its taxation rights after emigration. This was because any later realization of unrealized reserves would remain taxable in Germany if and to the extent that such reserves are attributable to the (former) permanent establishment in Germany. Germany was therefore allowed under the applicable tax treaty to tax in the future the gains accrued during the period the taxpayer was still a German resident.[94] A similar approach was followed by the Dutch Supreme Court in an *immigration* case that more or less mirrors the German case.[95] From this point of view, an immediate exit tax would not seem necessary, and in three of the four defined cases of corporate mobility even not required, since the emigration does not imply a loss of taxation rights under the applicable tax treaty.

Finally, the one-million-dollar question comes up as to how to determine the market value of the transferred business assets. The term 'market value' is defined in Article 5, paragraph 5, ATAD as the amount for which an asset can be exchanged or mutual obligations can be settled between willing unrelated buyers and sellers in a direct transaction. It follows that the market value must thus be determined based on the arm's length principle.[96] The question then comes up: which arm's length principle are we talking about: a domestic or a European one? As Article 5 ATAD provides for an autonomous definition, it seems reasonable to conclude that reference is made to a European arm's length standard. The case law in the context of the TFEU freedoms indeed supports the existence of a European arm's length standard the interpretation of which may deviate

93 Directive (EU) 2019/2121 of the European Parliament and of the Council of 27 November 2019 amending Directive (EU) 2017/1132 as regards cross-border conversions, mergers and divisions, OJ 2019 L 321, pp. 1–44.

94 German Federal Finance Court 28 October 2009, IR 99/08, *H&I* 2010/6.10.

95 Dutch Supreme Court 6 December 2013, No. 12/00252, *BNB* 2014/38.

96 As confirmed in recital 10 of the preamble of Council Directive (EU) 2016/1164.

from the domestic interpretation.[97] The ATAD is silent, however, on the question which transfer pricing methodologies may or may not be used when determining the market value (Direct or indirect methods? OECD or non-OECD methods? Etcetera). It is also not entirely clear what the nature of this European arm•s length standard is. From the TFEU freedoms cases *Thin Cap GLO*, *Lankhorst Hohorst* and *SGI* one can infer that the CJ attaches, in the context of the TFEU freedoms, an anti-tax avoidance and anti-base erosion nature to the arm's length standard. This also seems to be the position of the Commission in a number of state aid examinations with respect to individual tax rulings and ruling schemes in general. Essentially, the Commission seems not to accept a downward arm's length correction if such would not result in a corresponding taxation in another country. In other words, the Commission seems to require symmetry, which is precisely not guaranteed under Article 5 ATAD.[98] In the light of the above, it is remarkable that the Member States agreed to disagree about the market value in the context of the exit tax and step-up rule of Article 5 ATAD. By doing so, they deliberately accepted the risk of valuation mismatches leading to either (partial) double taxation or (partial) double non-taxation which, for their part, potentially may give rise to TFEU freedoms and state aid compatibility discussions.

19.4.2.4 The Intra-EU/EEA Option for Stagged Recovery: a Curse in Disguise?

As stated above, in intra-EU situations, an option for deferred payment of the exit tax is available in all four defined corporate mobility situations, meaning that the taxpayer can choose to pay the taxes due in instalments over five years ("stagged recovery").[99] The deferral option does not affect the taxpayer's tax base step-up right in the Member State of destination. If there is a demonstrable and actual risk of non-recovery, taxpayers may be required in such a case to provide a guarantee.[100] Furthermore, if a taxpayer chooses to defer payment, Member States may charge interest in accordance with their own legislation. Finally, from the ATAD's preamble one can infer that Member States may request the taxpayers concerned to include the necessary information in a declaration.[101] It becomes clear from these conditions that the choice for stagged recovery is not a free lunch. Rather, especially due to the possible duty to pay interest during the period of deferral, one may wonder whether taxpayers may under circumstances (e.g. where the

97 Case C-324/00, Lankhorst-Hohorst, EU:C:2002:749, points 37-38; Case C-524/04, Test Claimants in the Thin Cap Group Litigation, EU:C:2007:16, point 75; Case C-311/08, SGI, EU:C:2010:26, points 71-72; Case C-382/16 Hornbach, ECLI:EU:C:2018:366; Case C-484/19, Lexel AB v Skatteverket, ECLI:EU:C:2021:34.

98 Commission decision of 11 January 2016 on State Aid SA.37667 (2015/C) (ex 2015/NN) on the Excess Profit Exemption State aid Scheme implemented by Belgium, points 177-178; State aid SA.50400 (2019/C) (ex 2019/NN-2), Possible State aid in favour of Huhtamäki, Invitation to submit comments pursuant to Article 108(2) of the Treaty on the Functioning of the European Union, *OJ* 2019 C 161 pp. 3 *et seq*.

99 This period is probably derived from Case C-657/13, Verder LabTec, EU:C:2015:331.

100 This requirement is probably derived from Case C-164/12. DMC, EU:C:2014:20. This requirement does not apply where the legislation in the Member State involved provides for the possibility of recovery of the tax debt through another taxpayer which is member of the same group and is resident for tax purposes in that Member State.

101 Recital 10 of the preamble of Council Directive (EU) 2016/1164.

market interest rates are lower than the recovery interest) even simply be better off by paying the exit tax immediately.[102]

The option for deferred payment is also available in situations involving EEA Member States subject to the additional requirement that the EEA Member State has concluded an agreement with the Member State of the taxpayer or with the Union on the mutual assistance for the recovery of tax claims, equivalent to the mutual assistance provided for in Council Directive 2010/24/EU. How this equivalence test must be applied, however, remains unclear (Is it a static or dynamic test? Is equivalence required in all respects or only those aspects that are relevant in ensuring the collection of an exit tax? Is the mere existence of an equivalent agreement sufficient or should its application by a third country also be effective?).

In all cases, the deferral is discontinued immediately pursuant to Article 5, paragraph 4, ATAD in case of a number of specified "tainted" transactions which include situations of bankruptcy and liquidation, the disposal of assets, the subsequent transfer of assets or of the taxpayer's corporate residence to a third country, and failure by the taxpayer to comply with its obligations in relation to the instalments.

From the *Wächtler* case one could infer at first glance that the optional stagged recovery infringes the requirement of proportionality under the TFEU free movement provisions, particularly the freedom of establishment.[103] This would imply that recovery should be postponed until the moment of actual realization of the accrued gain. We do not, however, share this view. In brief, the *Wächtler* case concerned a (German) immediate exit tax upon the emigration of an individual majority shareholder to a third country (Switzerland). The Court saw this exit tax as a prohibited obstacle to the free movement of persons under the EU/Swiss Agreement on the free movement of persons.[104] That conclusion was not called into question by the fact that, in a situation where the immediate collection of the tax payable would have consequences that would be difficult for the taxpayer to bear, the German tax regime provided, subject to certain conditions, for the possibility of payment of that tax in instalments.[105] In our opinion, however, one should place this consideration in the context of the German scheme as a whole, leaving aside the fact that the Wächtler case involved an exit tax on accrued gains on shareholdings, whereas Article 5 ATAD is about exit taxation on accrued business profits (and the Court seems to take a more taxpayer friendly approach toward exit taxes imposed on individual majority shareholders).[106] In the case of emigration within the EU/EEA, payment was

102 To the same extent, *e.g.*, M.F. de Wilde, De exitheffing in de Anti-ontgaansrichtlijn en zijn invloed op het Nederlandse belastingsysteem, *Fiscaal Tijdschrift FED* 2016/109. During the pending ECJEU cases conference held at the WU Vienna in November 2015, Melchior Wathelet ironically paraphrased the CJEU case law on corporate exit taxes as essentially implying that taxpayers fortunately still have the right to pay tax immediately under the TFEU freedoms.

103 Case C-581/17, Wächtler, ECLI:EU:C:2019:138.

104 Agreement between the European Community and its Member States, of the one part, and the Swiss Confederation, of the other, on the free movement of persons, *OJ* 2002, L 114, pp. 6 et seq.

105 Case C-581/17, Wächtler, ECLI:EU:C:2019:138, point 68.

106 Compare Case C-470/04, N., ECLI:EU:C:2006:525 versus Case C-371/10, National Grid Indus, EU:C:2011:785.

always automatically deferred until the moment of actual realization. Apparently, in those cases the German legislator did not see any reason to impose further conditions on the deferral; these condition thus were only imposed vis-à-vis third country emigrations. If there would be a valid reason for the stagged recovery vis-à-vis Swiss emigrations, it had not been demonstrated why emigrations to Switzerland are so much different from emigrations within the EU/EEA from the perspective of recovery. Hence, assuming there would be any valid objective underlying the German exit tax, Germany did not achieve this objective in a consistent and systematic manner. As a result, Germany had so to speak "forfeited" its possibility of relying on the need to safeguard the effective recovery of taxes as a justification.[107] If, by contrast, Germany would have applied the same conditions for stagged recovery for EU/EEA and third country emigrations alike, or – reversely – if Germany would not have offered the possibility for stagged recovery for third country emigrations at all (*cf.* Article 5 ATAD), the *Wächtler* case would no longer be on point. To sum up, we do not see why the option for stagged recovery under Article 5 ATAD would infringe the freedom of establishment. The CJ's ruling in *Gallaher* has no bearing on this conclusion. In this case, the CJ only held that direct payment *without* the possibility for stagged recovery was compatible with the TFEU freedoms because of the fact that there was no liquidity problem for the taxpayer.[108] From this judgment one can not infer by analogy that the CJ would no longer allow a stagged recovery in case an exit tax would impose a liquidity problem for the taxpayer. This is without prejudice, however, that a more flexible approach could be desirable.[109] In our view, however, this would be up to the European legislator – and not the Court – to decide.

19.4.2.5 Valuation Mismatches: the Real BEPS-Issue Left Unsolved

From the perspective of the BEPS-package, Article 5 ATAD can be considered a bit of an outsider. On the one hand, it seeks to solve an issue that is not considered as problematic under the BEPS-package, *i.e.* the lack of corporate exit taxes in some Member States. However, by relying on the rather conservative case law of the CJ in the field of corporate exit taxes, the ATAD actually introduces an unnecessary obstacle for corporate mobility and could thus be seen as a step back in the process of creating an internal market.[110] On the other hand, by allowing the Member State of destination to contest the market value determined by the Member State of departure, Article 5 ATAD precisely permits what based on the BEPS rationale should be solved: valuation mismatches (lack of symmetry).

---

107 See in this sense also the opinion of Advocate General Wathelet, Case C-581/17, Wächtler, ECLI:EU:C:2018:779 point 92 *et seq.*

108 Case C-707/20, Gallaher, ECLI:EU:C:2023:101.

109 *Cf.*, for example, P.A. Hernández González-Barreda, Exit taxes: one size should not fit all, in: J.M. Almudí Cid & J.A. Ferreras Gutiérrez (eds), Combating tax avoidance in the EU: harmonization and cooperation in direct taxation, Alphen aan de Rijn: Kluwer Law International, 2019, pp. 191-226.

110 Also critical: P.A. Hernández González-Barreda, Exit taxes: one size should not fit all, in: J.M. Almudí Cid & J.A. Ferreras Gutiérrez (eds), Combating tax avoidance in the EU: harmonization and cooperation in direct taxation, Alphen aan de Rijn: Kluwer Law International, 2019, pp. 191-226. One could even wonder whether Article 115 TFEU actually provides a legal basis for such a step-back; see S.C.W. Douma, as cited by A. van der Kruk & D. Bodelier, 'Verslag van hét grote NOB Anti-BEPS Congres van 3 oktober 2016', *Weekblad Fiscaal Recht* 2017/7175.

As tool to combat BEPS, the suitability of Article 5 ATAD therefore could in our view be called into question.

19.4.3 *The CFC-Rule(s)*

19.4.3.1 *Introduction and Background*

Companies belonging to the same multinational group will typically be controlled by their ultimate parent company. In the area of corporate income taxation, these companies are often characterized by the term "Controlled Foreign Corporations" (CFCs). A substantial number of Member States have legislation in force that is specifically targeted at CFCs.[111] CFC legislation has been introduced for the purpose of countering the use of "base companies" in low-tax jurisdictions deriving income not directly relating to the exercise of commercial or industrial activities.[112] It aims at ensuring the taxable base of the affected states by avoiding profit shifting from high to low-tax jurisdictions.[113] Its application can – historically – be placed in the light of the underlying principle of capital export neutrality and the credit system as a method for the avoidance of double taxation connected there-with (as opposed to the principle of capital import neutrality and the exemption method connected therewith). It thus neutralizes the effect of tax deferral which is achieved in case profits made within a group are reallocated to foreign group companies rather than being distributed to the ultimate parent company.[114] The main characteristic of CFC rules is that income of such foreign companies is recognized at the level of the ultimate parent company immediately, without an actual distribution of profits being required ("piercing the corporate veil"), albeit the fiscal techniques through which this goal is achieved as well as the conditions under which these rules apply, may differ among States.[115] The OECD BEPS-3 recommendations provide for best practices to design effective CFC rules in the form of "building blocks" with respect to those elements that are necessary for effective CFC rules.[116] The recommendations are designed to ensure that jurisdictions that choose to implement them will have rules that effectively prevent taxpayers from shifting income into foreign subsidiaries.

The ATAD has followed-up on the OECD recommendations by including a mandatory CFC-rule. However, during the ATAD negotiations the inclusion of the CFC rule appeared to be a "hot potato". Some Member States feared that accepting the CFC rule would boil down to the introduction of minimum corporate tax rates within the Union through

111 See, for example, H-J. Aigner, U. Scheuerle & M. Stefaner, 'General Report', in *CFC Legislation, Tax Treaties and EC Law*, eds M Lang *et al.* (Alphen aan den Rijn: Kluwer Law International, 2004), p. 16.

112 G. Maisto & P. Pistone, 'A European Model for Member States' Legislation on the Taxation of Controlled Foreign Subsidiaries (CFCs) – Part 1', *European Taxation* 10 (2008), p. 505.

113 H-J. Aigner, U. Scheuerle & M. Stefaner, 'General Report', in *CFC Legislation, Tax Treaties and EC Law*, eds M Lang *et al.* (Alphen aan den Rijn: Kluwer Law International, 2004), p. 16.

114 *ibid.*

115 See, for example, G. Maisto & P. Pistone, 'A European Model for Member States Legislation on the Taxation of Controlled Foreign Subsidiaries (CFCs) – Part 2', *European Taxation* 11 (2008), p. 554-555.

116 OECD (2015), *Designing Effective Controlled Foreign Company Rules, Action 3 - 2015 Final Report*, OECD Publishing, Paris.

the backdoor. Another issue was how to ensure compatibility with the TFEU freedoms, especially the *Cadbury Schweppes* case law. Lastly, by their very nature, CFC-rules cannot be reconciled with the principle of capital import neutrality.[117] This was probably considered problematic by those Member States that actually pursue capital import neutrality as it could infringe their domestic tax policy framework. The proposed text of the CFC rule was therefore revised multiple times during the negotiations. Eventually, the Member States – like the OECD Members in the context of the BEPS-3 Action Plan – were unable to reach a common view on the CFC-provision. Therefore, they included two CFC-options, leaving the final choice to each Member State. In the meantime, the Pillar Two Directive that became effective as of 1 January 2024 demonstrates how quickly the international landscape has subsequently been changing in this respect. Under this Directive Member States are required to apply a minimum top-up tax on (mainly) residual profits of large multinational enterprises that have not been subject to an effective minimum tax rate of at least 15% abroad. This new Directive does not make, however, the CFC rule under the ATAD completely redundant given the substantial differences between the personal and substantive scope of both mechanisms. Thus, both systems can exist alongside each other, while the CFC-charge would effectively come first in cases of concurrence, at least as a main rule.

19.4.3.2 Three Cumulative Proxies: CFC, Effectively Low-Taxed, Bad Income

Article 7(1) read in conjunction with Article 7(2) ATAD formulates the three key criteria that all must be met for the CFC-rule to apply. Firstly, there must be a CFC. Secondly, the CFC's profits must effectively be lowly taxed. Thirdly, the CFC must receive "bad" or artificial income. The first two tests are discussed below. The third "bad income"-test is discussed in the next paragraph.

A CFC is defined as an entity in which the taxpayer holds itself or together with its associated enterprises, i) a direct or indirect participation of more than 50 percent of the voting rights, ii) owns directly or indirectly more than 50 percent of capital or iii) is entitled to receive more than 50 percent of the profits of that entity. Hence, in order to qualify as a CFC, majority is required – seen from the angle of the multinational group as a whole – either with respect to the voting rights, ownership or profit entitlement vis-à-vis the foreign company. In order to ensure a higher level of protection, Member States could reduce the control threshold.[118] In principle, a permanent establishment (PE) also qualifies as a (deemed) CFC.[119] It seems that only directly held PE's qualify and that PE's indirectly held by a foreign subsidiary remain outside the scope of the CFC-rule.

A CFC is considered to be lowly taxed in case the actual corporate tax paid on its profits is lower than 50% of the corporate tax that would have been charged on the CFC under the applicable corporate tax system in the Member State of the taxpayer (i.e. the parent

117 In the absence of full corporate tax harmonization.

118 Recital 12 of Council Directive (EU) 2016/1164.

119 Provided that its profits are not subject to tax or are exempt from tax in the Member State of the taxpayer (otherwise the foreign PE-income would be included in the domestic tax base of the Member State in any case).

or head-office state).[120] A comparison between effective tax rates must thus be made. In order to ensure a higher level of protection, Member States could employ a higher threshold in comparing the actual corporate tax paid with the corporate tax that would have been charged in the Member State of the taxpayer or use a sufficiently high tax rate fractional threshold.[121]

The effective tax rate test applies to all income of the CFC and not only to the "bad" or artificial income, although only the latter needs to be picked-up by the Member State. At least theoretically, this could lead to the somewhat unbalanced result that the CFC's high taxed "bad" income must be picked-up whereas taxation of the CFC's low taxed other income can be deferred. Furthermore, the effective tax rate test applies on a single entity (standalone) basis only. This means, for example, that the fact that the received CFC income (notably dividends and capital gains) may already have been highly taxed at the level of a lower-tier controlled subsidiary is irrelevant. This may boil down to overkill or, put more harshly, reduce the purpose of the CFC rule "to absurdity".[122]

On the other hand, the effective tax rate test implies that domestic tax base exemptions (e.g. a domestic participation exemption) or domestic downward transfer pricing adjustments in case of low-risk/routine activities can be taken into account as when assessing whether a CFC is lowly taxed according to the corporate tax standards of a Member State.[123] So, the more the features of a Member State's corporate tax regime (exemptions, credits, incentives...) are comparable to those included in the regime of the CFC's country, the sooner the CFC rule will remain inapplicable. Put more generally, as both the corporate tax bases and tax rates differ among Member States, a CFC can qualify as low-taxed according to the standards of one Member State whereas it does not do so under the standards of another Member State. To this extent, the ATAD's objective to avoid fragmentation within the internal market is not met and internationally operating companies could have an incentive to reallocate, for example, their European head-office to the Member State with the lowest effective tax rates, "the weakest link", in order to escape the CFC rule.

Finally, an optional *de minimis* rule applies under Article 7(4) ATAD for CFCs with accounting profits of no more than EUR 750 000 and non-trading income of no more than EUR 75 000, *i.e.*, low-profit CFCs. These entities may be excluded from the scope of the CFC-rule. The same holds for CFCs of which the accounting profits amount to no more than 10 percent of its operating costs, *i.e.*, low-profit margin CFCs.[124] In both cases, the BEPS-risk is considered remote.

120 The permanent establishment of a controlled foreign company that is not subject to tax or is exempt from tax in the jurisdiction of the controlled foreign company shall not be taken into account.

121 Recital 12 of Council Directive (EU) 2016/1164.

122 To this extent: J. Schönfeld, 'CFC Rules and Anti-Tax-Avoidance Directive', *EC Tax Review* 3 (2017), p. 145-152.

123 See J.W. Bellingwout, as cited by R. Gielen & C. Huisman, 'Verslag van het tweede grote NOB Anti-BEPS-richtlijn congres van 3 april 2017, *Weekblad Fiscaal Recht* 2017/7199.

124 Payments to associated enterprises and the cost of goods sold outside the CFC's state may not, however qualify as operating costs.

19.4.3.3 The Full-Fledged CFC-Rule and The Light (Quasi) CFC-Rule

If a low-taxed CFC is identified, the Member States must pick-up (part of) the CFC's non-distributed income in the tax period of the taxpayer in which the tax year of the CFC ends. The Member States can choose between two options in this respect: a full-fledged CFC-rule following the so-called entity based approach and a light (quasi) CFC-version following the so-called transactional based approach.

Under the full-fledged approach, all the CFC's "bad" income must be attributed to the parent or head-office State. Member States may decide, however, not to apply the CFC rule if one third or less of the CFC's income consists of "bad" income.[125] Also financial undertakings that predominantly deal with third parties may be left outside the scope of the CFC-rule.[126] Bad income is specifically defined as the non-distributed income of the CFC, or the income of the permanent establishment, which is derived from the following categories: (i) interest or any other income generated by financial assets; (ii) royalties or any other income generated from intellectual property; (iii) dividends and income from the disposal of shares; (iv) income from financial leasing; (v) income from insurance, banking and other financial activities; (vi) income from invoicing companies that earn sales and services income from goods and services purchased from and sold to associated enterprises, and add no or little economic value. It is not clear whether the "bad"-income test must be performed on a gross or net basis.

The light version of the CFC-rule takes a fundamentally different approach. It only requires allocation to the parent or head-office State to the extent the CFC's non-distributed income arises from non-genuine arrangements which have been put in place for the essential purpose of obtaining a tax advantage. An arrangement (or a series thereof) shall be regarded as non-genuine to the extent that the CFC would not own the assets or would not have undertaken the risks which generate all, or part of, its income if it were not controlled by a company where the significant people functions, which are relevant to those assets and risks, are carried out and are instrumental in generating the controlled company's income. Put differently, would the CFC have been able to generate the same income on its own strength, without assistance by its controlling parent?

It is observed that in both cases the CFC-rule only applies to non-distributed CFC income. This implies that the CFC rule could be easily circumvented, especially in Member States that have a liberal participation exemption regime. By distributing the CFC's "bad" or artificial income before year-end, the CFC-rule would not apply whereas the received income would be tax-exempt in the hands of the EU parent under the participation exemption. Hence, no taxable pick-up of foreign low-taxed income would take place. Under the Commission's proposal, this lacuna would not appear, or at least to a lesser extent, because of the proposed switch-over clause for distributed income from foreign, low-taxed shareholdings. This switch-over clause would thus overrule more liberal

125 Article 7, paragraph 3, ATAD.

126 Member States may furthermore choose not to treat financial undertakings as CFCs if one third or less of the entity's income from the above categories comes from transactions with the taxpayer or its associate enterprises.

participation exemption regimes. The switch-over rule was, however, eventually not adopted, whereas the CFC-rule was not amended correspondingly. Perhaps, the draftsmen simply overlooked this issue.

19.4.3.4 *The "Substance"-Escape under the Full-Fledged CFC-Rule*

From *Cadbury Schweppes* and *Test Claimants in the CFC and Dividend GLO* it follows that the application of CFC rules constitutes a restriction of the freedom of establishment which nevertheless can be justified by the need to combat tax avoidance. Whether or not abusive practices are at stake must be determined based on objective factors which are ascertainable by third parties with regard, in particular, to the extent to which the CFC physically exists in terms of premises, staff and equipment.[127] If checking those factors leads to the finding that the CFC is a fictitious establishment not carrying out any genuine economic activity in the territory of the host Member State, the creation of that CFC must be regarded as having the characteristics of a wholly artificial arrangement. That could be so in particular in the case of a 'letterbox' or 'front' subsidiary.[128] The parent company must be given an opportunity to produce evidence that the CFC is actually established and that its activities are genuine.[129]

Apparently, the draftsmen of the ATAD considered the full-fledged CFC-rule open to scrutiny under the freedom of establishment, at least in intra-EU/EEA situations. Therefore, in order to comply with the above CJ case law, a "substance" safe harbour has been included that is mandatory in intra-EU/EEA-situations and optional for non-EU CFCs. Based on Article 7, paragraph 2, sub a, ATAD, the CFC pick-up mechanism shall not apply where the CFC carries on a substantive economic activity supported by staff, equipment, assets and premises, as evidenced by relevant facts and circumstances. As this notion of substance still remains rather indefinite, the idea was suggested during the ATAD negotiations to leave it to the Member States – through the Code of Conduct group for Business Taxation – to make the concept of substance more operational. In the final stages of negotiations, however, this suggestion was waived.[130] The ATAD thus fails to tell us more concretely how the substance-test should be interpreted. How to distinguish fictitious from genuine establishments? As the safe harbour rule seeks to comply with the CJ's case law, it seems safe, particularly in the absence of other guidance, to adhere to the CJ's case law when interpreting the substance escape.[131] Hence, reliance on the

127 Case C-196/04, Cadbury Schweppes, EU:C:2006:544, point 67; Case C-201/05, Test Claimants in the CFC and Dividend GLO, EU:C:2008:239, point 79.

128 Case C-196/04, Cadbury Schweppes, EU:C:2006:544, point 68.

129 Case C-196/04, Cadbury Schweppes, EU:C:2006:544, point 70; Case C-201/05, Test Claimants in the CFC and Dividend GLO, EU:C:2008:239, point 82.

130 A couple of years earlier, the Council did issue some practical recommendations in its Council Resolution of 8 June 2010 on coordination of the controlled foreign corporation (CFC) and thin capitalisation rules within the European Union, 2010/C 156/01, *OJ* 20010 C 156, p. 1-2.

131 For details, *see* D.S. Smit, *EU Freedoms, Non-EU Countries and Company Taxation* (Kluwer Law International, 2012), p. 42 *et seq.*

substance requirements that exist in the Member State where the parent is located[132] or that apply in the Member State where the CFC is located,[133] although tempting from a practical perspective, does not, in our opinion, constitute the solution.

In this respect, as a point of departure, reference can be made to Advocate General Darmon in his Opinion in *Daily Mail*, who states that the concept of establishment is essentially an economic one and always implies a genuine economic link.[134] Establishment means integration in the national economy and involves two, closely connected factors: the exercise of an economic activity and a physical location, both on a permanent basis or at least on a durable one.[135] In our view, the following guidelines can be derived from the CJ case law that could further serve in distinguishing fictitious from genuine establishments in the context of the substance escape under the CFC-rule.

The mere fact that a CFC is established in a Member State where it benefits from a general low-or no-tax regime could be an indication for artificiality but does not, however, as such justify the application of CFC rules.[136] The same conclusion arguably holds if a CFC is located in a Member State where it benefits from a preferential tax regime.[137] Also the mere fact that the economic choices of a CFC are or can be controlled by its parent company established in another Member State is not enough to conclude that the CFC is merely fictitious or artificial.[138] However, it may be required that the essential decisions concerning the general management of the CFC must be adopted in the CFC's Member State of establishment and that the functions of the CFC's central administration must be carried out in the CFC's Member State as well.[139] This test therefore requires a series of factors to be taken into consideration, amongst which the CFC's registered office, the place of its central administration, the place where its directors meet and the place where the general policy of the CFC is determined. Other factors, such as the place of residence of the main directors, the place where general meetings are held, the place

132 To some different extent: M. Lang & S. Heidenbauer, 'Wholly Artificial Arrangements', in: *A Vision of Taxes within and outside European Borders*, Festschrift in honor of Prof. Dr. Frans Vanistendael, edited by L. Hinnekens & P. Hinnekens (Alphen aan den Rijn: Kluwer Law International), 2008, p. 603-604.

133 To some different extent: Opinion of Advocate General Mengozzi, Case C-298/05, *Columbus Container Services*, EU:C:2007:754, point 180.

134 Opinion of Advocate General Darmon in Case C-81/87, Daily Mail and General Trust PLC, EU:C:1988:456, points 3 and 5.

135 For details, *see* D.S. Smit, *EU Freedoms, Non-EU Countries and Company Taxation* (Alphen aan den Rijn: Kluwer Law International), 2012, p. 42 *et seq.*

136 Case C-294/97, Eurowings, EU:C:1999:524.

137 See Opinion of Advocate General Léger, Case Cadbury Schweppes, Case C-196/04, Cadbury Schweppes, EU:C:2006:544, points 55 *et seq.*; Opinion of Advocate General Mengozzi, Case C-298/05, *Columbus Container Services*, EU:C:2007:754, points 163 *et seq.*; Opinion of Advocate General Mazák, Case C-451/05, *ELISA*, EU:C:2007:594, points 114 *et seq.* Critical, however, P.J. Wattel, 'Beggar Thy Neighbour', *Weekblad Fiscaal Recht* 6208 (1996), p. 1854 *et seq.*

138 Case C-221/89, Factortame Ltd., EU:C:1991:320; Case C-341/04, Eurofood IFSC, EU:C:2006:281.

139 In the context of the VAT Directive, Case C-73/06, Planzer, EU:C:2007:397.

where administrative and accounting documents are kept, and the place where the CFC's financial transactions mainly take place, may also need to be taken into account.[140]

Furthermore, it may be required that a CFC has the necessary premises and equipment at its disposal in its Member State of establishment, and an adequate staff which performs the functions relevant to the activities carried out by the CFC in its Member State of establishment.[141] An office managed by the undertaking's own staff, but also by a person who is independent but authorized to act on a permanent basis for the undertaking may constitute an establishment.[142] The CFC may nonetheless be required to show a sufficient degree of permanence and a structure adequate, in terms of human and technical resources, to supply the services in question on an independent basis.[143] A business may not be considered to be independent where, for example, the (financial) situation of a company, as a whole, "makes inevitable the conclusion that it will very probably not be able to survive by its own means."[144] Also a property which does not have any human resource enabling it to act independently does not qualify.[145] A CFC that carries on activities that do not go beyond straightforward asset management probably does not qualify.[146] The same may be true where a CFC holds a fixed place for preparatory or auxiliary activities only.[147]

If the above substance requirements were not to be met, it nevertheless follows from the CJ's case law, such as the case *X GmbH*, that the parent must be given the opportunity to provide evidence of any commercial justification for the structure.[148] Where, for example, a CFC receives distributed profits that were already sufficiently taxed at the level of a lower-tier subsidiary, the interposition of the CFC might not necessarily have been motivated by tax considerations, even if the CFC lacks any substance. The ATAD does, however, not provide for a possibility to provide proof to the contrary in such a case.

As far as CFCs located in third countries are concerned, the substance test is optional. The question comes up, however, whether this test should also be applied in non-EU

140 By analogy, Case C-73/06, Planzer, EU:C:2007:397, points. 60-62 (the CJEU referring to *Cadbury Schweppes*) and Opinion of Advocate General Darmon in Case C-81/87, Case C-81/87, Daily Mail and General Trust PLC, EU:C:1988:456, point 8.

141 In the context of the freedom of establishment, Case C-33/78, Somafer, EU:C:1978:205; in the context of the VAT Directive, Case C-931/19, Titanium Ltd v Finanzamt Österreich, ECLI:EU:C:2021:446, point 40 *et seq.*

142 Case 205/84, Commission v. Federal Republic of Germany, EU:C:1986:463, point 21.

143 Case C-190/95, ARO Lease BV, EU:C:1997:374, point 16; in the context of the VAT Directive, Case C-931/19, Titanium Ltd v Finanzamt Österreich, ECLI:EU:C:2021:446, point 40 *et seq.*

144 In the context of the Merger Directive, Case C-43/00, Andersen og Jensen, EU:C:2002:15, point 37.

145 See, in the context of the free movement of capital, Case C-386/04, Stauffer, EU:C:2006:568 point 19 and, in the context of the VAT Directive, Case C-931/19, Titanium Ltd v Finanzamt Österreich, ECLI:EU:C:2021:446, point 44 *et seq.*

146 See, by analogy, in the context of the freedom of establishment, Case C-386/04, Stauffer, EU:C:2006:568, and, in the context of the VAT Directive, Case C-80/95, Harnas & Helm, EU:C:1997:56; Case C-77/01, EDM, EU:C:2004:243.

147 In the context of the VAT Directive, Case C-73/06, Planzer, EU:C:2007:397, point 56.

148 See, for example, Case C-135/17, X-GmbH v Finanzamt Stuttgart, ECLI:EU:C:2019:136, point 85; Case C-201/05, Test Claimants in the CFC and Dividend GLO, EU:C:2008:239 and, by analogy, Joined cases C-504/16 and C-613/16 (Deister Holding AG and Juhler Holding A/S), ECLI:EU:C:2017:1009.

situations based on the free movement of capital under Article 63 TFEU. From the CJ's case law it follows that CFC legislation must exclusively be examined in the light of the freedom of establishment to the extent this legislation is only targeted to situations involving definite investor influence.[149] Under Article 7 ATAD, majority is required – seen from the angle of the multinational group as a whole – either with respect to the voting rights, ownership or profit entitlement vis-à-vis the foreign company. This threshold would probably meet the definite investor influence test, although this is not beyond doubt. To the extent Member States would opt to introduce a lower threshold in their domestic laws (the threshold under Article 7 ATAD is a *de minimis* threshold), the free movement of capital nonetheless may become applicable, as can be inferred from the *X GmbH* case referred to above. In such a third country case, however, there may be more room to justify the application of the CFC-provision, irrespective of whether or not the CFC would meet the previously discussed substance test. Notably, the need for effective fiscal supervision,[150] the need to counteract harmful tax competition[151] and the need to combat tax havens[152] could be accepted as a valid justification in third country situations more easily. In the latter respect, it is observed that according to the ATAD's preamble, it should be acceptable that, in transposing CFC rules into their national law, Member States use white, grey or black lists of third countries.[153]

19.4.3.5 Income Attribution and Double Taxation Relief (Add-back & Credit)

Article 8 ATAD is concerned with the attribution of the CFC's bad or artificial income to the CFC's parent and with relief for double taxation. A distinction is made in this respect between the full-fledged and light CFC-rule. Under the full-fledged CFC-rule, the CFC's bad income must be attributed to the taxpayer in the tax period of the taxpayer in which the tax year of the CFC ends. In principle, this income allocation functions as an anti-deferral rule. That is to say, once the CFC distributes any profits to the taxpayer, an add-back mechanism applies to the extent the distributed profits are included in the taxable income of the taxpayer. Under this mechanism, the amounts of income previously included in the tax base pursuant to the CFC-rule must be deducted from the tax base

149 Case C-201/05, Test Claimants in the CFC and Dividend GLO, EU:C:2008:239, point 73 and, by analogy, Case C-196/04, Cadbury Schweppes and Cadbury Schweppes Overseas, EU:C:2006:544, point 33.

150 See, for example, Case C-135/17, X-GmbH v Finanzamt Stuttgart, ECLI:EU:C:2019:136, point 94; Case C-72/09, Établissements Rimbaud, EU:C:2010:645.

151 See for example M. Isenbaert, *EC law and the sovereignty of the member states in direct taxation* (Amsterdam: IBFD, 2010), p. 643; R. Lyal, 'Free Movement of Capital and non-Member Countries – Consequences for Direct Taxation', in *The Influence of European Law on Direct Taxation*, ed. D.M. Weber (Alphen aan den Rijn: Kluwer Law International, 2007), p. 25; D.J. Aigner & G.W. Kofler, Austria Clarifies Third-Country Impact of ECJ's Lenz Decision, *Tax Notes International* 5 (2004), p. 485. See, as regards the need to combat tax havens, Case C80/12, Felixstowe Dock and Railway Company Ltd and Others v The Commissioners for Her Majesty's Revenue & Customs, ECLI:EU:C:2014:200, point. 32; Joined Cases C-24/12 and C-27/12, X BV and TBG Limited, ECLI:EU:C:2014:1385, point 51 *et seq.*

152 Case C80/12, Felixstowe Dock and Railway Company Ltd and Others v The Commissioners for Her Majesty's Revenue & Customs, ECLI:EU:C:2014:200, point. 32; Joined Cases C-24/12 and C-27/12, X BV and TBG Limited, ECLI:EU:C:2014:1385, point 51 *et seq.*

153 Recital 12 of the preamble of Council Directive (EU) 2016/1164.

when calculating the amount of tax due on the distributed profits. By doing so, it should be ensured that the CFC's income is not taxed twice. The same mechanism applies in case the taxpayer disposes of its participation in the CFC.

The income to be included in the tax base of the taxpayer under the mandatory pick-up rule must be calculated in accordance with the corporate tax rules of the Member State where the taxpayer is resident. It is unclear whether the attributed income must be calculated on a gross or net basis and which expenses could be taken into account in case net calculation would be permitted. The question comes up whether the fact that the pick-up rule refers to domestic law would imply that domestic tax base exemptions, such as a participation exemption regime, may still be applied when attributing the CFC's income to the taxpayer. This question could be relevant since the low-tax test applies to the entire CFC while the mandatory attribution only applies to the CFC's bad income which may not necessarily be lowly taxed. The literal wording of Article 8 ATAD suggests a negative answer to this question, whereas the rationale of the CFC rule – without interposition of a CFC, the income would have been tax-exempt as well – suggests an answer in the positive.

Another question is how the income allocation rule has to be applied in case of an indirectly held CFC. From the CFC definition, as discussed previously, it becomes clear that also indirectly held participations in a company must be taken into account when determining whether the majority threshold of Article 7, paragraph 1, ATAD is exceeded. This is logical since the CFC-status could otherwise be easily circumvented, for example, by dividing a majority participation between different local associated enterprises. For income attribution purposes, however, the original Directive proposal only looked to direct participation relationships. More specifically, Article 9, paragraph 2, of the ATAD proposal stipulated that the income to be included in the tax base shall be calculated in proportion to the entitlement of the taxpayer to receive profits of the CFC. Hence, under the proposal, indirectly held participations were only relevant for determining whether or not a CFC exists, but income attribution would take place – on a pro rata basis – only in the direct participation relationships (*i.e.* in proportion to the taxpayer's profit entitlement in the CFC). During the final stage of negotiations, however, this pro rata approach was – without further explanation – waived through a seemingly innocent amendment of the wording of the income allocation rule. Based on the current wording of Article 8, paragraph 3, ATAD, the income to be included in the tax base shall be calculated in proportion to the taxpayer's participation in the entity (CFC) as defined in Article 7, paragraph 1, ATAD. As the taxpayer's participation as defined in this provision covers both direct and indirect participations, also income derived by indirectly held CFCs starts falling under the attribution rule. This implies that in case of an indirectly held CFC, the mandatory pick-up may need to take place twice, one time at the indirect relationship level of the top parent and one time at the intermediate, direct relationship level. This may result in significant cumulating effects. Similar concerns may come up where majority voting rights, ownership or profit entitlement are divided between three different entities. It is subsequently unclear how the add-back mechanism should apply in these cases. This is because the wording of the add-back mechanism links-up with CFC profit distributions (directly) made to the taxpayer and, hence, presupposes income attribution on the basis of a direct shareholder relationship only.

In case the mandatory pick-up rule applies, the Member State of the taxpayer must allow a deduction (credit) of the tax paid by the CFC from the taxpayer's own tax liability.[154] Hence, an indirect credit must be available. The calculation of the credit is left to national law. It is not fully clear whether withholding taxes levied by the CFC's country on payments from the CFC to the taxpayer shall be credited as well. Although these taxes are "paid by" the CFC, they are actually borne by the taxpayer. Finally, CFC losses shall not be picked-up, but may be carried forward and taken into account in subsequent tax periods.

Under the light CFC-rule, income allocation is limited to the amounts generated through assets and risks which are linked to significant people functions carried out by the controlling company. The attribution of controlled foreign company income shall be calculated in accordance with the arm's length principle. Profit attribution thus must take place based on a functional analysis following the at arm's length standard. Strictly speaking, however, one can wonder whether this option really adds something to the corporate tax rules of Member States that already include an arm's length standard. Also, for non-EU multinationals investing in the EU one could question the effectiveness of this rule if the significant people functions are predominantly carried on outside the Union. In the absence of an EU cake to be divided in such a case, there is nothing to (re-)allocate. Similar to the full-fledged CFC-rule, the same add-back and credit mechanism is available.

19.4.4 *The Hybrid Mismatch Rule*

19.4.4.1 *Introduction and Background*

The last specific anti avoidance rule of the ATAD consists of a number of specific neutralization rules for so-called hybrid mismatches. Loosely said, a hybrid mismatch can occur where two countries qualify a specific item of income differently or allocate a specific item of income to different entities. Overall, such a mismatch can result in either double taxation or double non-taxation and double deduction. Article 9 ATAD focusses on the second situation of non-taxation and double deduction. More specifically, Article 9 ATAD deals with the following categories of hybrid mismatches:
- Hybrid mismatches that result from payments under a financial instrument;
- Hybrid mismatches that are the consequence of differences in the allocation of payments made to a hybrid entity or permanent establishment, including as a result of payments to a so-called disregarded permanent establishment;
- Hybrid mismatches that result from payments made by a hybrid entity to its owner;
- Hybrid mismatches that result from deemed payments between the head office and permanent establishment or between two or more permanent establishments;
- Double deduction outcomes resulting from payments made by a hybrid entity or permanent establishment.

154 Article 8, paragraph 7, ATAD.

In addition, the ATAD contains specific anti avoidance rules for so-called reverse hybrid mismatches (Article 9a ATAD), dual residence mismatches (Article 9b ATAD) and hybrid transfers (e.g. resulting from sale and buy-back transactions or securities lending transactions). As a final "back-stop", the ATAD contains an anti-hybrid rule for so-called "imported mismatches" that seeks to avoid that the actual hybrid mismatch is shifted outside the EU while still "feeding" tax-deductible payments in a Member State. The personal scope of the anti-hybrid rule is restricted to situations involving associated enterprises, including head-office/permanent establishments relationships, and so-called structured arrangements.

The approach that the ATAD follows is based on the OECD recommendations under BEPS Action 2.[155] As a primary rule, the mismatch must be neutralized by one Member State - often the source state. If neutralization does not take place under the primary rule, for example since the source State is a non-EU country, then a defensive rule is triggered which in some cases requires, and in other cases only recommends, neutralization by the other Member State involved, often the taxpayer's state of residence. Especially as a result of the fact that the defensive rules are optional in some cases, hybrid mismatches are not categorically excluded under the ATAD. Also, hybrid mismatches resulting from conflicts other than those mentioned in the ATAD, such as tax rate mismatches and transfer pricing mismatches between associated enterprises, are not covered. Although (or perhaps: because) the hybrid mismatch provisions are designed in a rather straight-forward, no-nonsense style, their precise scope in concrete cases may be far from clear. In order to overcome this objection, the preamble states that the applicable explanations and examples in the OECD BEPS-2 Report should be used as a source of illustration or interpretation to the extent that they are consistent with the provisions of this Directive and with Union law.[156] As the OECD report contains more than 450 pages of which more than a half consists of detailed examples of hybrid mismatches that do and that do not fall under the scope of the BEPS 2 recommendations, it can be assumed that this report will indeed serve as an important reference in practice. The same presumably holds for the follow-up report from 2017 on Neutralising the Effects of Branch Mismatch Arrangements that expands the OECD recommendations to hybrid branch mismatches.[157]

19.4.4.2 Deduction without Inclusion (D/NI) Mismatches

The first type of situation that Article 9 ATAD seeks to address is that of a hybrid financing mismatch. This is the situation in which i) a payment under a financial instrument gives rise to a so-called deduction without inclusion outcome; ii) such payment is not taken into account as taxable income in the payee jurisdiction within a reasonable period of time;

155 OECD (2015), *Neutralising the Effects of Hybrid Mismatch Arrangements, Action 2 - 2015 Final Report*, OECD Publishing, Paris (OECD BEPS-2 Report (2015)).

156 Recital 28 of the preamble of Council Directive (EU) 2017/952.

157 OECD (2017), Neutralising the Effects of Branch Mismatch Arrangements, Action 2: Inclusive Framework on BEPS, OECD/G20 Base Erosion and Profit Shifting Project, OECD Publishing, Paris (OECD BEPS-2 Report (2017)).

and iii) the mismatch outcome is attributable to differences in the characterisation of the instrument or the payment made under it. One may think of the following situation:[158]

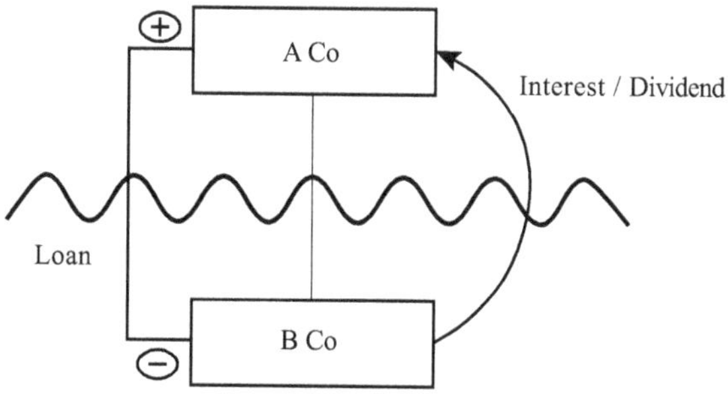

The primary neutralization rule under Article 9, paragraph 2, ATAD stipulates that to the extent that the hybrid mismatch results in a deduction at the level of B Co without inclusion at the level of A Co ("inclusion" means that the payment is taken into account as the taxable income under the laws of the payee jurisdiction) the deduction shall be denied in the Member State that is the payer jurisdiction (the country of B Co). Where the deduction is not denied in the payer jurisdiction (for example if that is a non-EU Member State), the non-optional defensive rule is triggered. In such case, the amount of the payment that would otherwise give rise to a mismatch outcome shall be included in the income in the Member State that is the payee jurisdiction (the country of A Co). In intra-EU situations that fall under the so-called "linking rule" of the Parent-Subsidiary Directive, the sole solution is mandatory taxation in the residence Member State of the parent, i.e., the payee jurisdiction, in order to neutralize a hybrid financing mismatch. In order to avoid a potential circular reasoning, it is stipulated that the linking-rule takes precedence over the ATAD in these cases.[159] Furthermore, from example 9.2 of the OECD BEPS-2 report one can infer that the defensive rule (taxation in the payee jurisdiction) probably also applies to situations where an interest deduction is denied in the payer country based on a general interest limitation rule, such as a thin capitalization rule. It is observed, however, that this approach seems to be in contradiction with the CJ's approach in the *Masco Denmark and Damixa* case.[160]

Comparable to the previous situation is the following situation of a deduction without inclusion involving a hybrid entity:[161]

158 Derived from example 1.1 of the OECD BEPS-2 report (2015).
159 Recital 30 of the preamble of Council Directive (EU) 2017/952.
160 Case C-593/14, Masco Denmark and Damixa, EU:C:2016:984.
161 Derived from example 2 of the ATAD 2 proposal.

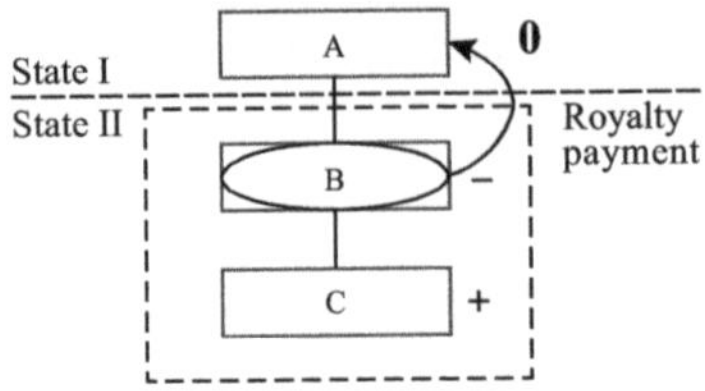

The approach to neutralize the mismatch (deduction by company B with no inclusion at the level of company A) in this case of a disregarded hybrid payment is comparable to the previous situation, although the escape that is available in the previous scenario if the payment is considered as taxable income within a reasonable period of time, does not apply here. Furthermore, an exception to the neutralization rule applies to the extent the double deduction can be off-set against so-called dual inclusion income, which is income that is included in the tax base of both countries. Hence, only the excess comes under the scope of this anti mismatch rule.

Comparable to the previous situation is the following example of a mismatch involving a deemed payment between a permanent establishment and its head-office (or another permanent establishment:[162]

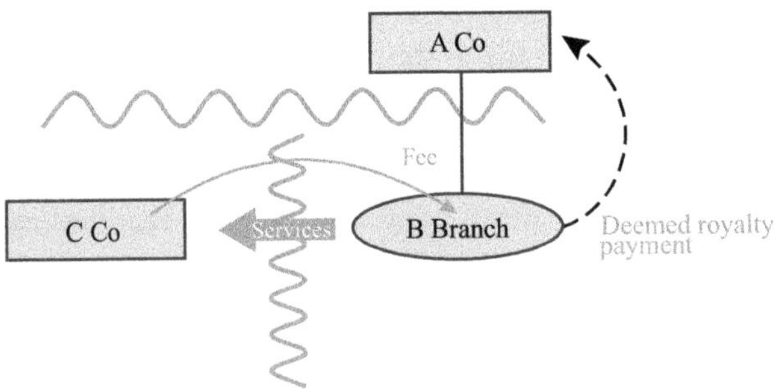

The approach to neutralize the mismatch (deduction at the level of B Branch with no inclusion at the level of A Co) in this case of a disregarded hybrid payment is comparable to the previous situation involving a hybrid entity.

A fourth example of a hybrid mismatch situation involving a so-called reverse hybrid entity can be depicted as follows:[163]

162 Derived from figure 3 of the OECD BEPS-2 Report (2017).
163 Derived from example 3 of the ATAD 2 proposal.

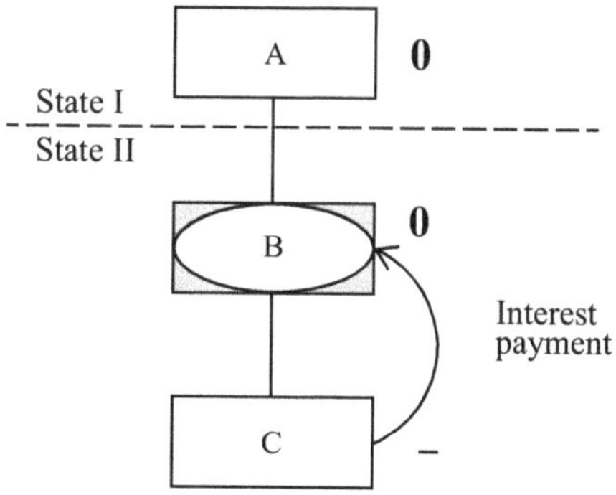

The solution, based on recommendation 5.2 of the OECD BEPS-2 report, is that the hybrid entity must be treated as a resident in the Member State where it is incorporated or established and shall be taxed by that Member State on its income to the extent that this income is not otherwise taxed under the laws of the Member State or any other jurisdiction (Article 9a ATAD). Hence, fiscal transparency of the hybrid entity must be ignored by the Member State concerned. In case of reverse hybrid situations that do not fall under the scope of this solution, the primary and defensive rule based of the previous situation could come into play again. In such a case, however, the defensive rule is – in line with the BEPS-2 recommendations – optional only.[164] It is observed that it is not entirely clear which country may apply the defensive rule: State II – by taxing the payment at the level of B – or State A, by taxing the payment at the level A?

A situation comparable to the previous example which is also covered by the ATAD 2 is the situation involving so-called diverted branch payments. Such a situation arises where a payment to an entity with one or more permanent establishments gives rise to a deduction without inclusion and that mismatch outcome is the result of differences in the allocation of payments between the head office and permanent establishment or between two or more permanent establishments of the same entity under the laws of the jurisdictions where the entity operates. One may think, for example, of the following situation:[165]

164 Article 9, paragraph 4, ATAD.
165 Derived from figure 2 of the OECD BEPS-2 Report (2017).

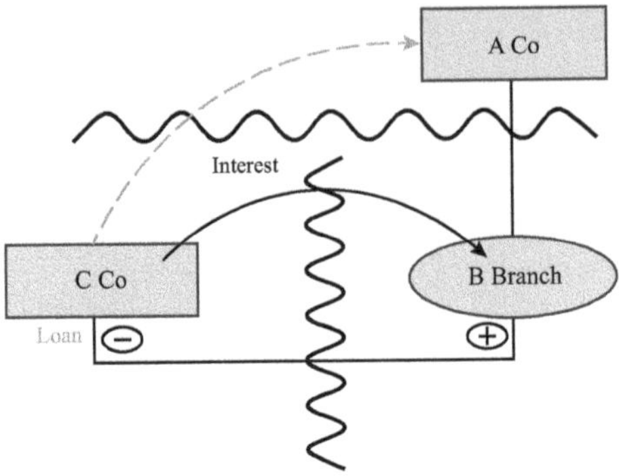

Again, the approach is that as a primary rule, the deduction should be denied by the Member State that is the payer jurisdiction (the country of C Co). Where the deduction is not denied in the payer jurisdiction (for example if that is a non-EU Member State), the optional defensive rule is triggered which says that the payment is to be taxed in the payee jurisdiction. Again, it is not entirely clear whether the defensive rule has to be applied by the State of B Branch or the State of A CO.

Closely related to the previous example is the situation of so-called disregarded branch mismatches. Such a situation arises in case of an arrangement that is treated as giving rise to a permanent establishment under the laws of the head office jurisdiction and is not treated as giving rise to a permanent establishment under the laws of the other jurisdiction. One may think of the following example:[166]

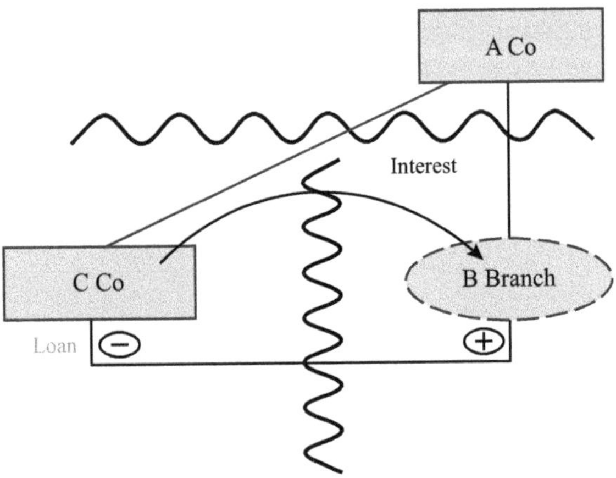

The primary rule in this situation differs from the previous case of diverted branch mismatches. Based on Article 9, paragraph 5, ATAD, the Member State of the taxpayer (in the example A Co) shall require the taxpayer to include the income that would otherwise

166 Derived from figure 1 of the OECD BEPS-2 Report (2017).

be attributed to the disregarded permanent establishment. In the relations with third countries, this requirement does not apply if the Member State is required to exempt the income under a double taxation treaty entered into by that Member State with the third country. From the preamble of ATAD 2, one can infer that this neutralization rule would function as a *lex specialis* in the sense that the other primary and defensive rule under Article 9, paragraph 2, ATAD do not come into play anymore in the above scenario (provided that neutralization takes place).[167] Interestingly, the original ATAD 2 proposal did not contain such a specific rule for disregarded branch mismatches.

19.4.4.3 Double Deduction (DD) Mismatches

A different category of hybrid mismatches is the situation where a payment, expense or loss is deducted twice (strictly speaking without being required that such a double deduction is due to a qualification or attribution conflict). One may think of the following situation where an interest expense is deducted in two different countries due to an attribution conflict:[168]

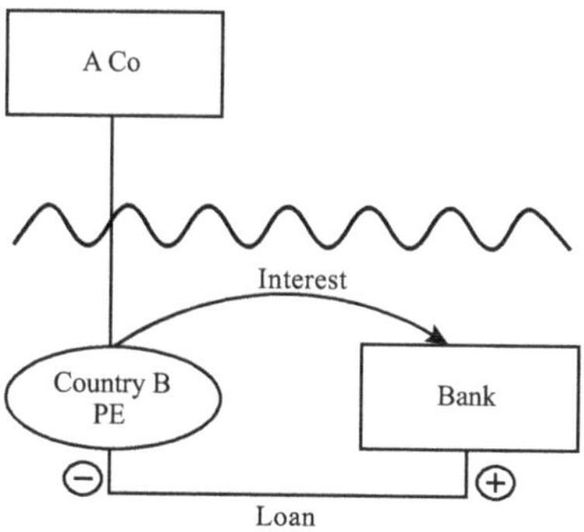

The approach to neutralize the double deduction outcome is reverse to the solutions in the previous cases: the primary rule requires the residence state of the investor to deny the deduction (in the example: the State of A Co). Where the deduction is not denied in this jurisdiction (for example if that is a non-EU Member State), the non-optional defensive rule requires the deduction to be denied in the payer jurisdiction, *i.e.*, the country where the permanent establishment is located (in the example: Country B). Both rules only apply to the extent the double loss deduction exceeds any dual inclusion income, *i.e.*, any income that is included in the tax base of both countries. The ATAD is silent on the question how to deal with so-called "stranded losses". The OECD approach is that in such case, the residence State of the investor may still allow deduction. This is in line with the Marks & Spencer case law.[169] On the other hand, the defensive rule seems to conflict with the approach in Philips Electronics, at least in intra-EU situations.[170]

167 Recital 28 of the preamble of Council Directive (EU) 2017/952.
168 Derived from example 6.2 of the OECD BEPS-2 report (2015).
169 Case C-446/03, Marks & Spencer, EU:C:2005:763.
170 Case C-18/11, Philips Electronics, EU:C:2012:532.

In the context of double deduction mismatches, the ATAD furthermore contains a specific rule for so-called dual resident mismatches in Article 9b ATAD. Such a mismatch can occur where a company is considered as a tax resident of two different countries with the result that, for example, a loss or payment can be deducted in both countries. The rule makes a distinction in this regard between intra-EU situations and situations involving non-EU countries. In the first situation, deduction shall be denied in the Member State where the company is not considered as a tax resident based on the tax treaty applicable between both Member States. Somewhat remarkably, it remains unclear how this rule should be applied if there is no tax treaty between both States. In situations involving non-EU countries, the deduction shall be denied in the Member State that considers the company as tax resident to the extent the loss exceeds any income that is included in the tax base of both countries. Strictly speaking, this dual inclusion exception does not seem to apply in intra-EU situations, although it is not very likely that this is what the Member States intended.

19.4.4.4 A Final Backstop against "Import of Mismatches"

As a final "back-stop", the ATAD contains a specific anti hybrid rule for so-called "imported mismatches". This rule seeks to prevent that the effects of an extra-EU mismatch are indirectly imported into the EU, although the rule could literally speaking also apply in pure intra-EU situations. The operation of this rule can be best explained through the following simplified example. Assume a parent company (A Co) located in non-EU country X provides a hybrid loan to its subsidiary (B Co) located in non-EU country Y. As a result of a qualification mismatch, the payment on the loan is tax-exempt at the level of A Co whereas the payment is tax-deductible at the level of B Co. Subsequently, B Co lends-on the funds received from its parent to an associated company (C Co) located in Member State Z through an ordinary (non-hybrid) loan. Consequently, C Co would typically be allowed to deduct the payments made on the loan to B Co. The overall effect is that a deduction is granted in Member State Z, while overall there is no corresponding pick-up; B Co will only be taxed for a small margin consisting of the difference between the interest received and the interest paid and the ultimate receipt of the payment by A Co will be tax-exempt. In such a case, the ATAD requires Member State Z to deny the deduction. Although the imported mismatch rule is understandable from the perspective to avoid that the neutralization rules could be easily circumvented, it creates at the same time a substantial source of potential discussion between taxpayers and tax authorities since each payment made from an EU Member State to a third country must be "traced" while going up in the corporate chain to the final recipient. That the application of this rule will not always be easy, is demonstrated by the detailed examples included in the OECD BEPS-2 report.

19.4.4.5 Tax Liability "Always Somewhere": Effective, but Questionable in the Light of Source Country Entitlement

Overall, the anti-hybrid provisions can be qualified as technically complex. In practice, they probably will mainly have a deterrent effect. We can imagine that, in practice, internationally operating enterprises will decide to leave the possibility to use hybrid mismatches as it is, and will start focussing on new forms of tax planning strategies that, from a BEPS-2 perspective, are more "neutral", for example by making use of tax rate differences and tax base reductions (e.g. tax incentives). As a final remark, it is recalled that the underlying guiding principle of the BEPS-package is that business profits should be taxed in the place where the economic activities generating these profits are performed and value is created. It is noted that this principle of source country entitlement is actually easily sacrificed under the anti-hybrid provisions in order to ensure that business profits are ultimately taxed once somewhere. It does not really seem to matter in which country. To that extent, the anti-hybrid provisions seem to be based on the idea of "always somewhere" rather than on the principle of source country entitlement.[171] To us, such an idea seems a rickety basis for creating or extending corporate tax liability.

19.5 The Mandatory General Anti-Tax Avoidance Rule (GAAR) for Corporate Taxation

19.5.1 Introduction and Background; a Single European Abuse of Law Concept

It is clear from the CJ's case law that taxpayers may choose to structure their business so as to limit their tax liability.[172] Nonetheless, tax mitigation must not turn into tax avoidance. In his Opinion in *Halifax*, Advocate General Maduro warned that "tax law should not become a sort of legal wild-west in which virtually every sort of opportunistic behaviour has to be tolerated so long as it conforms with a strict formalistic interpretation of the relevant tax provisions and the legislature has not expressly taken measures to prevent such behaviour."[173]

As follows from the previous sections, the ATAD contains four specific anti-avoidance measures. The Member States thought it useful to also include, by way of "backstop", a mandatory general anti-avoidance rule. Article 6, paragraph 1, ATAD therefore stipulates that for the purposes of calculating the corporate tax liability, Member States shall ignore an arrangement or a series of arrangements which, having been put into place for the main purpose or one of the main purposes of obtaining a tax advantage that defeats the object or purpose of the applicable tax law, are not genuine, having regard to all relevant facts and circumstances. It is often questioned in this respect whether Article 6 ATAD deviates from CJ case law in the field of abuse of law in that it would go beyond the scope of the Court's abuse doctrine. In our view, however, the CJ adheres to one single principle of abuse in the field of tax law, irrespective of whether the TFEU freedoms or

171 M.F. de Wilde, 'The ATAD's GAAR: A Pandora's Box?', eds P. Pistone & D.M. Weber (Amsterdam: IBFD, 2018), pp. 301-328; see also: D.S. Smit, *International Income Allocation Under EU Tax Law: Tinker, Tailor, Soldier, Sailor*, Inaugural address Tilburg University (Tilburg: Prismaprint, 2016).

172 For example, Case C-255/02, Halifax, EU:C:2006:121, point 73.

173 Opinion of Advocate General Maduro in Case C-255/02, Halifax, EU:C:2006:121, point 77.

the tax Directives or Regulations on agriculture are concerned.[174] For example, in *Kofoed*, the CJ explicitly held that the anti-abuse clause under Article 11 of the Merger Directive *"reflects the general Community law principle that abuse of rights is prohibited."*[175] To remove any confusion on this issue, the CJ confirmed in the more recent cases *Eqiom* and *Euro Park Service* that the objective of combating fraud and tax evasion, whether it is relied on in the context of the Parent-Subsidiary and Merger Directives or as justification for an exception to primary law, has the same scope.[176] Likewise, we expect the CJ to ignore (linguistic) differences between the CJ's abuse concept and the ATAD's GAAR and to give Article 6 ATAD an interpretation that is in conformity with the CJ's general abuse doctrine. See, for elaboration, Chapter 7.

19.5.2 Mandatory Harmonisation of National Corporate Taxation GAARs(?)

The ATAD's preamble suggests that the inclusion of the GAAR aims to fill gaps, which would imply that it should not affect the applicability of specific anti-abuse rules. Thus, application of the GAAR cannot be excluded by the fact that one of the SAARs is applicable: there seems to be room to apply the GAAR even if a SAAR specifically deals with a certain form of tax avoidance, but still leaves a loophole in that area. It should be noted that the CJ's case law seems to point in the opposite direction in this respect.[177]

Like the exit tax provision in Article 5 ATAD, the GAAR is not part of the BEPS-package. Although its inclusion may at first glance seem a logical and innocuous choice, a mandatory GAAR may have substantial impact on Member States' corporate tax systems.[178] It is true that *Kofoed* and *Italmoda* suggest that a similar obligation to fight abuse already exists on the basis of the loyalty principle of Article 4(3) TEU, which obligation was confirmed more explicitly in the cases *N Luxembourg* and *T Danmark*,[179] However, this obligation

174 In the same vein, *inter alia*,: P.J. Wattel, *Misbruik van Europees Recht*. Inaugural address Amsterdam (UvA) (Amsterdam: fed, 1993), p. 30-33; R. de la Feria, 'Prohibition of Abuse of (Community) Law: The Creation of a New General Principle of EC Law Through Tax', *Common Market Law Review* 45 (2008), p. 436 *et seq*. and, from the same author, EU General Anti-(Tax) Avoidance Mechanisms: From GAAP to GAAR, in: G Loutzenhiser and R de la Feria (eds), The Dynamics of Taxation (Oxford: Hart Publishing, 2020), pp. 155-183; B.J. Kiekebeld, 'Anti-abuse in the Field of Taxation: Is There One Overall Concept?', *EC Tax Review* 4 (2009), p. 145; F. Vanistendael, 'Halifax and Cadbury Schweppes: one single European theory of abuse in tax law?', *EC Tax Review* 4 (2006), p. 195.

175 Case C-321/05, Kofoed, EU:C:2007:408, point 38; Case C-251/16, Edward Cussens and Others, EU:C:2017:881, point 33.

176 Case C-14/16, Euro Park Service, EU:C:2017:177, point 69; Case C-6/16, Eqiom, EU:C:2017:641, point 64 and Joined cases C-504/16 and C-613/16, Deister Holding AG and Juhler Holding A/S, EU:C:2017:1009, point 97. See also Joined cases C116/16 and C117/16, T Danmark & Y Denmark, ECLI:EU:C:2019:135; Joined Cases C 115/16, C 118/16, C 119/16 and C 299/16, N Luxembourg 1 et al., ECLI:EU:C:2019:134.

177 See, e.g., Case C-2/94, Denkavit Internationaal and others, EU:C:1996:229, point 31 and Case C-39/16, Argenta Spaarbank NV (2), EU:C:2017:323.

178 To the same extent M.F. de Wilde, 'The ATAD's GAAR: A Pandora's Box?', in: *The Implementation of the Anti-BEPS in the European Union: A Comprehensive Study*, eds P. Pistone & D.M. Weber (Amsterdam: IBFD, forthcoming).

179 Joined cases C116/16 and C117/16, T Danmark & Y Denmark, ECLI:EU:C:2019:135; Joined Cases C 115/16, C 118/16, C 119/16 and C 299/16, N Luxembourg 1 et al., ECLI:EU:C:2019:134.

would only exist as regards the application of *EU* law.[180] By contrast, the *3 M Italia* case (involving the acceptance of an aggressive dividend-stripping transaction in the 1970s) shows that no general obligation for the Member States obtains to avoid abuse under domestic tax laws.[181] The EU abuse of law doctrine obviously does not apply beyond the scope of application of EU law itself; European law must thus be involved.[182] Leaving aside the question when this is the case, it is observed that Article 6 ATAD clearly overrules the *3 M Italia* decision. It introduces a general obligation for Member States to apply a GAAR domestically as regards corporate tax law. It is not restricted to intra-EU situations, but extends to situations involving non-EU Member States and to purely domestic situations, hence to situations that may have no (other) link with EU law at all.

The question then arises whether Article 6 ATAD should be interpreted as an implementation of the Court's EU abuse of rights doctrine which then effectively overrules any domestic GAAR in place, or whether Article 6 ATAD only requires Member States to have a domestic GAAR in place, while leaving the *interpretation* of that rule a domestic matter of the (local Courts of the) respective Member State. The latter view finds support by the literal wording of Article 6 ATAD, which refers to object and purpose of the applicable tax law (and not of EU law). This view is also supported in literature, where it is submitted that the transactions need to be in conflict with purpose and intent of the applicable *domestic* law.[183] This view would imply that the tests under Article 6 ATAD would coincide with the tests to be made for purposes of the domestic GAAR applicable in the respective Member State and that in the absence of any (other) link with EU law a separate assessment against the EU abuse of rights doctrine would consequently not need to be made. We expect the Court, however, if being asked, to take the first, divergent view, and to interpret Article 6 ATAD as a mere codification of its own EU abuse of rights doctrine, also because this would be more in line with the idea of introducing a minimum standard. This different view is (increasingly) supported in literature.[184] Several Advocates General also seem to take this position, albeit somewhat loosely and without considering the implications

180 Case C-321/05, Kofoed, EU:C:2007:408, point 41. In the same vein, H.W.M. van Kesteren, *Misbruik van recht in de omzetbelasting*. Inaugural address Tilburg (Kluwer, 2004), p. 14, and L. de Broe, *International Tax Planning and Prevention of Abuse* (Amsterdam: IBFD Publications, 2008), p. 833-834.

181 Case C-417/10, 3 M Italia, EU:C:2012:184, point 32.

182 E.g. Case C-417/10, 3 M Italia, EU:C:2012:184, point 32; Case C-363/20, Marcas MC Szolgáltató Zrt, ECLI:EU:C:2022:21, points 37 *et seq*.

183 In the context of the Dutch implementation law of ATAD in the Dutch Corporate Income Tax Act 1969, the Dutch legislator has taken this position, meaning that article 6 ATAD is correctly implemented through the existing national abuse of law doctrine (*fraus legis*). ....

184 For example, M.F. de Wilde, 'The ATAD's GAAR: A Pandora's Box?', in: The Implementation of the Anti-BEPS in the European Union: A Comprehensive Study, eds P. Pistone & D.M. Weber, ch. 14; J.J.A.M. Korving and C. Wisman, ATAD Implementation in the Netherlands, Intertax Volume 49; Issue 11; Pages 917-937, M.J. Velthoven, 'The general anti-abuse rule of article 6 of the EU Anti-Tax Avoidance Directive', thesis, University of Amsterdam, 2024, page 116, O.C.R. Marres, De anti-ontgaansrichtlijn, NTFR-B 2017/18, as well as De Broe and Beckers, The General Anti-Abuse Rule of the Anti-Tax Avoidance Directive: An Analysis Against the Wider Perspective of the European Court of Justice's Case Law on Abuse of EU Law, EC-Tax Review, 2017, Vol. 26, No. 3, pp. 133-144.

of this position.[185] We submit that this view could make the reference to the object or purpose of the applicable (domestic) tax law potentially obsolete (see also para. 19.5.3.3).

An important implication of the above conclusion is EU competence creep in tax matters: again, an area of formerly national sovereignty (the scope of domestic anti-abuse measures) seems to have come within EU (Court) scrutiny. If a local Court is not sure whether or not the GAAR should be applied in a specific case – be it cross-border or purely domestic – the CJ has become competent to give a final answer to that question and, if it is applicable, to decide on the substantive question of what 'abuse' is. The final say therefore would longer rest with the local Courts.

Up until the ATAD implementation date, the CJ typically only decided on the question whether domestic tax avoidance rules went beyond what was necessary to combat tax avoidance, leaving it for the referring domestic Court to decide whether or not tax avoidance was actually present in the case at hand. So far, the CJ essentially only needed to decide – in the abstract – whether a domestic anti-avoidance rule was incompatible with the EU abuse of law doctrine for being disproportionate, *i.e.*, whether there was impermissible *overkill*. The Court usually tried to stay far away from actually deciding the question of abuse in the concrete. However, given that the GAAR introduces an obligation to tax in cases of avoidance of domestic corporate taxes, the CJ may now also have to assess, in individual cases, whether a Member State should apply the GAAR, *i.e.*, whether there would otherwise be impermissible *underkill*. The CJ may thus be required to define more often and more precisely the effects of its abuse of law doctrine in concrete cases, both cross-border *and* domestic. Essentially, the mandatory GAAR thus boils down to harmonization of national GAARs in the field of corporate taxation, with potentially an important role being assigned to the CJ.

19.5.3 The GAAR tests

As stated above, Article 6, paragraph 1, ATAD stipulates that for the purposes of calculating the corporate tax liability, a Member State shall ignore an arrangement or a series of arrangements which, having been put into place for the main purpose or one of the main purposes of obtaining a tax advantage that defeats the object or purpose of the applicable tax law, are not genuine having regard to all relevant facts and circumstances. In essence, the GAAR entails three cumulative tests:

i. Artificiality;
ii. Motive; and
iii. Defeat of object and purpose of the applicable tax law.

185 Opinion of AG Kokott dated March 1, 2018, case C-115/16, N Luxembourg 1 vs. Skatteministeriet, point 101; Opinions of AG Pitruzzella dated 3 March 2022, Case C-98/21, W GmbH, point 80 and footnote 34 and dated 13 June 2019, Case C-75/18, Vodafone, point 88, footnote 48 and 49, as well as Opinion of AG Emiliou dated March 14, 2024, no. C-585/22, *X BV vs Staatssecretaris van Financiën*), point 82.

If all tests are met, the arrangements (or a series thereof) must be ignored. On that basis, the tax liability must subsequently be calculated in accordance with national law. The three tests are discussed separately (but non-exhaustively) in more detail below.

19.5.3.1 Artificiality

The artificiality test requires an arrangement or a series of arrangements which are not genuine having regard to all relevant facts and circumstances. Article 6(2) ATAD adds that an arrangement or a series thereof shall be regarded as non-genuine to the extent that they are not put into place for valid commercial reasons which reflect economic reality. The preamble of the ATAD clarifies that when evaluating whether an arrangement should be regarded as non-genuine, Member States may consider all valid economic reasons, including financial activities.[186] This clarification is in line with the CJ's case law to the effect that the assessment whether or not an arrangement is artificial must be based on objective factors, or indicators, which are ascertainable by third parties.[187]

The artificiality test resembles the notion of "wholly artificial arrangement" as developed by the CJ in its case law on abuse, that is to say, an arrangement which does not reflect economic reality and which has been set up with a view to escaping the tax normally due on the profits generated by activities carried out on the national territory of a Member State.[188] This test thus essentially reflects the idea of source country entitlement, meaning that business profits should be taxed in the jurisdiction in which the economic activities generating these profits are performed and value is created. Interpretation of the GAAR on that basis could, however, substantially challenge the Member States' corporate tax regimes which still take the legal reality as the starting for taxing multinational enterprises. Van Brunschot argued – only slightly exaggerating – that from an economic perspective, the establishment of subsidiaries in other countries always lacks real significance. In his view, one needs to determine in which place the activities take place and which value should be attributed to them, based on the arm's length standard."[189] If this would be the approach to be followed under the ATAD GAAR, that would imply a hidden standard of the "true" (mandatory) tax charge, based on economic analysis and irrespective of legal reality.[190] Obviously, this was probably not the Member States' intention. Nevertheless, the artificiality test implies at least to some extent a substance over form approach, as confirmed by the cases *N Luxembourg* and *T Danmark*[191], and it remains to be seen where the CJ will strike the balance in this respect.

186 Recital 3 of the preamble of Council Directive (EU) 2016/1164.

187 Case C-524/04, Test Claimants in the Thin Cap Group Litigation, EU:C:2007:161, point 74; Case C-425/06, Part Service, EU:C:2008:108, point 45; Case C-255/02, Halifax, EU:C:2006:121, point 81; Joined cases C116/16 and C117/16, T Danmark & Y Denmark, ECLI:EU:C:2019:135, point 97.

188 Case C-196/04, Cadbury Schweppes and Cadbury Schweppes Overseas, EU:C:2006:544, point 55.

189 F. van Brunschot in his case note to the decision by the Netherlands Supreme Court dated 15 October 1986, No. 23 702, *Beslissingen in Belastingzaken* 72 (1987).

190 By analogy, M.F. de Wilde, 'The ATAD's GAAR: A Pandora's Box?', in: *The Implementation of the Anti-BEPS in the European Union: A Comprehensive Study*, eds P. Pistone & D.M. Weber (Amsterdam: IBFD, forthcoming).

191 Joined cases C116/16 and C117/16, T Danmark & Y Denmark, ECLI:EU:C:2019:135; Joined Cases C 115/16, C 118/16, C 119/16 and C 299/16, N Luxembourg 1 et al., ECLI:EU:C:2019:134.

19.5.3.2 Motive

Secondly, the GAAR requires the non-genuine arrangement to have been put into place for the main purpose or one of the main purposes of obtaining a tax advantage. As taxpayers' motives are difficult to establish if one cannot be certain they are truthful about them, the CJ typically looks for objective factors which are ascertainable by third parties (e.g. absence of economic substance, derogation from the arm's length standard, a transaction result which is foreseeably negative but for the tax effects, *et cetera*) that can shed light on the taxpayer's (assumed) intention.[192] These factors typically also form part of the artificiality test. Motive is therefore mainly inferred from objective facts and circumstances which are difficult or impossible to explain if one ignores the tax effects. Where the taxpayer does not simply admit that its main driver was tax (arguing that nevertheless no abuse obtains because object and purpose of the law relied on have not been defeated), the motive test thus operates as a rebuttal possibility: if the fact pattern has the suspicious looks of a tax avoidance set up, the taxpayer may demonstrate otherwise by pointing out significant non-tax purposes. The significance of the motive test should, in our view, therefore not be overestimated. This said, the motive-test may give rise to multiple questions, three of which are addressed below.

A first question that has been discussed repeatedly in scholarly literature is whether under the CJ's case law in the field of abuse this test implies an "*essential* purpose"-test or an "*only* purpose"-test.[193] Some cases, such as *Tankreederei I* and *Jobra*, suggest that a sole purpose test must be applied. In the latter case, the CJ ruled that a restrictive tax measure can be justified "*where it specifically targets wholly artificial arrangements which do not reflect economic reality and whose only purpose is to obtain a tax advantage*".[194] By contrast, cases like *Part Service*, *Foggia* and *N Luxembourg* suggest that tax avoidance can already be established if the *essential* or *predominant aim*, or the *principal purpose or one of the principal purposes* of a (set of) transaction(s) is to obtain a tax advantage.[195] We believe the latter approach to be correct (see, for elaboration, Section 7.4), given that (i) the seminal non-tax abuse case *Emsland-Stärke*[196] is clear in that the 'essential aim' is sufficient, (ii) the Court uses both terms interchangeably in *Halifax*[197] ('solely' in point 68; 'essential' in point 75), and (iii) if any insignificant opportunist non-tax purpose would suffice to invalidate the GAAR (or the Court's unwritten anti-abuse doctrine in general), it would be

192 Case C-196/04, Cadbury Schweppes and Cadbury Schweppes Overseas, EU:C:2006:544, point 67; Case C-524/04, Test Claimants in the Thin Cap Group Litigation, EU:C:2007:161, paras 80 *et seq.*

193 See, for example, M. Tumpel, 'Konvergente Missbrauchsstandards bei direkten und indirekten steuern?, in *Europäisches Steuerrecht*, p. 904-905; B.J. Kiekebeld, 'Anti-abuse in the field of taxation: is there one overall concept', in *VAT in an EU and international perspective. Liber Amicorum Han Kogels*, eds. H.P.A. M. van Arendonk, S.J.J.M. Jansen & R.N.G. van der Paardt (Amsterdam: IBFD Publications, 2011), p. 239.

194 Case C-330/07, Jobra, EU:C:2008:685, point. 35; and Case C-287/10, Tankreederei I,: EU:C:2010:827, point 28; Joined Cases C 115/16, C 118/16, C 119/16 and C 299/16, N Luxembourg 1 et al., ECLI:EU:C:2019:134, point 100.

195 Case C-425/06, Part Service, EU:C:2008:108, point. 62, and Case C-126/10, Foggia, EU:C:2011:718, point. 49.

196 Case C-110/99, Emsland-Stärke, EU:C:2000:695.

197 Case C-255/02, Halifax, EU:C:2006:121, points 68 and 75.

meaningless.[198] Accordingly, the CJ held in *Foggia*, concerning the anti-abuse reservation of national competence in the Merger Directive, that by automatically accepting the non-tax reason stated for the merger at issue (some cost-saving) as a valid commercial reason, without taking account of the other objectives of the proposed operation, and particularly the tax advantages (carry-over of a substantial amount of tax losses), the anti-tax avoidance reservation of competence would be entirely deprived of its purpose.[199]

A second question is whether Article 6 ATAD also applies where withholding tax instead of corporation tax is circumvented. In scholarly literature, a positive answer is not ruled out.[200] The wording of Article 6 ATAD, however, suggests that its scope is restricted to corporate taxes. During the ATAD negotiations, extension of Article 6 ATAD was proposed to withholding taxes on interest, royalty and dividend payments to recipients in third countries. At a later stage, however, that proposal was withdrawn, but at the same time, a sentence was added in the preamble stating that where withholding taxes are part of the corporate taxation system of a Member State or involving a taxpayer subject to corporate taxation, the GAAR should also cover such taxes. Eventually, however, also this sentence was removed "as it was deemed to bring more confusion than clarity." In our view, withholding taxes are, in principle, not within the scope of Article 6 ATAD, as the taxable subject of a withholding tax is not the corporate entity paying the interest, royalty or dividend, but the recipient, which may well be an individual or a non-subject entity. Applying the GAAR also to withholding taxes would be tantamount to implementation of BEPS Action 6 through the backdoor of the ATAD. That said, from the case law of the CJ one can infer by analogy that the concept of "corporate tax" must be understood in a substantive rather than in a formal fashion. Regard must be paid in this respect to the objective characteristics by which a tax is levied, irrespective of its classification under national law.[201] Hence, the mere technique of a levy (distribution tax or yearly assessment tax) as such should in our view not be decisive.[202] For instance, Estonia levies its corporation tax in the form of a distribution tax, but that form does not change its essential character as a (belated) corporate income tax.

A final question that could be raised is whether the avoidance of corporation taxes of other States (EU or third) is covered as well. Does the term "tax advantage" refer to domestic corporation taxes only? The language of Article 6 GAAR does not exclude foreign taxes. Application of the GAAR to foreign corporation taxes would, however, dramatically expand its scope. Tax authorities of each Member State would be required to be the "tax police of the world". Given that neutralization by one Member State of the avoidance of corporate taxes in another State is likely to meet the proportionality test only by coincidence

198 Dissenting: Opinion of Advocate General Mengozzi in Case C-135/17, *X-GmbH v. Finanzamt Stuttgart – Körperschaften*, ECLI:EU:C:2018:389, point 90 (in particular footnote 48).

199 Case C-126/10, Foggia, EU:C:2011:718, point 49.

200 D.M. Weber, 'De algemene antimisbruikregel in de Anti-belastingontwijkingsrichtlijn', *Fiscaal Tijdschrift FED* 2016/110.

201 Case C-294/99, Athinaïki Zythopoiia, EU:C:2001:505, paras 26-29; Case C-284/06, Burda, EU:C:2008:365, point 52.

202 D.M. Weber, 'De algemene antimisbruikregel in de Anti-belastingontwijkingsrichtlijn', *Fiscaal Tijdschrift FED* 2016/110.

(typically, the compensatory taxation by the first Member State will not correspond to the taxes that are avoided abroad) and given that the test of suitability is not likely to be met either (typically, the Member State levying the abuse-neutralizing tax will not transfer the tax collected to the foreign State, so that the budgetary consequence of the abuse in the latter State will not be repaired), we conclude that the GAAR must be restricted to the avoidance of domestic corporate income taxes. Foreign tax motives could reinforce, however, the other found indicators for artificiality.[203]

19.5.3.3 Defeat of Object or Purpose of the Applicable Tax Law

Finally, Article 6 ATAD requires that obtaining the tax advantage defeats the object or purpose of the applicable tax law. In the Court's case law until now, the object and purpose of the domestic law effectively seems to coincide with the artificiality test. In Cadbury Schweppes, for example, the compatibility of the domestic UK CFC rules with the EU abuse of rights doctrine was tested in the light of the object and purpose of the freedom of establishment, requiring a genuine economic link ("economic substance") in the CFC Member State.[204] Assuming that Article 6 ATAD codifies the abuse of rights doctrine as developed by the Court (see Section 12.5.2), the reference to the object or purpose of the applicable (domestic) tax law therefore seems to have little autonomous meaning.

We furthermore assume that the mere use of mismatches between the corporate tax systems of different Member States does not satisfy this test. This is because the tax advantage is not attributable to the tax law of one single Member State in such a case. Typically, the corporate tax laws of both Member States are perfectly observed in case of a mismatch. It is only a disparity between the tax laws of the Member States involved which creates an overall tax benefit. Such a benefit can only be neutralized through specific tax avoidance rules (such as an anti-hybrid linking rule in Article 1(4) of the Parent-Subsidiary Directive). Also from the CJ's case law it follows that the fact that a taxpayer seeks to benefit from tax advantages in a Member State other than his state of residence does not, in itself, constitute tax avoidance. For example, *RBS Deutschland Holdings* concerned a typical VAT-mismatch: a deduction of input VAT in one Member State without corresponding VAT on the output transaction in the other Member State due to a different interpretation of the VAT Directive. The CJ held that a Member State cannot refuse to allow a taxable person to deduct input VAT paid on the acquisition of goods in that Member State, where those goods have been used for the purposes of leasing transactions carried out in another Member State, solely on the ground that the output transactions have not given rise to the payment of VAT in that other Member State.[205]

Also from *Cadbury Schweppes* it follows that the mere use of more favourable features of another Member State's tax regime does not constitute tax avoidance. The CJ held that "*it is settled case-law that any advantage resulting from the low taxation to which a subsidiary established in a Member State other than the one in which the parent company*

203 Joined cases C116/16 and C117/16, T Danmark & Y Denmark, ECLI:EU:C:2019:135, point 106.
204 Case C-196/04, Cadbury Schweppes and Cadbury Schweppes Overseas, EU:C:2006:544, points 52-54 and point 66.
205 Case C-277/09, RBS Deutschland Holdings GbmH, EU:C:2010:810, point 46.

was incorporated is subject cannot by itself authorise that Member State to offset that advantage by less favourable tax treatment of the parent company."[206] A low tax rate in another Member State cannot therefore justify, as such, the application of an anti-tax avoidance rule. As observed, that may pose problems for the ATAD's automatic CFC-rule providing that 50% of the domestic tax rate is too low, especially in the relations with non-EU CFCs.

19.5.3.4 The Burden of Proof

Article 6 ATAD is not concerned with the burden of proof. However, from the CJEU case law the following principles can be derived. See Section 15.6 for elaboration. An automatic reversal of proof is not permitted,[207] let alone automatic exclusion of proof.[208] In principle, in each case the tax authorities of the Member State concerned should prove that there is abuse.[209] The tax authorities may therefore not confine themselves to applying predetermined general criteria. Instead, they must subject each particular case to a general examination.[210] In any case, the taxpayer must at all times be given the opportunity, without being subject to undue administrative constraints, to provide evidence of any commercial justification.[211] General rules which automatically exclude certain categories of operations from a tax advantage, without the possibility for the taxpayer to provide proof to the contrary, are thus not permitted.[212]

19.5.4 Compatibility with the TFEU Freedoms

Finally, the question rises how the GAAR relates to the TFEU freedoms (see also Section 12.3). As stated above, the GAAR applies both in cross-border and domestic situations. In the ATAD's preamble it is stressed that it is important to ensure that the GAARs apply in domestic situations, within the Union and vis-à-vis third countries in a uniform manner, so that their scope and results of application in domestic and cross-border situations do not differ.[213] Apparently, the draftsmen were keen on making sure that the GAAR is effectively applied in a non-discriminatory manner.

19.6 Implementation and Temporal Scope

Pursuant to Article 12 ATAD, the Member States were required to implement the ATAD's provisions in their domestic laws by 31 December 2018 and to apply these provisions from 1 January 2019. However, the ATAD provides for a number of exceptions to this rule. First of all, for the exit tax provision, the implementation date in question is one year later, *i.e.*, 31 December 2019. The same holds for the anti-hybrid provision. For the specific anti-hybrid provision for reverse hybrid entities (Article 9a ATAD), the date in

206 Case C-196/04, Cadbury Schweppes and Cadbury Schweppes Overseas, EU:C:2006:544, point 49.
207 Case C-318/10, SIAT, EU:C:2012:415; Case C-6/16, Eqiom, EU:C:2017:641; Cases C-504/16 and C-613/16, Deister Holding and Juhler Holding, EU:C:2017:1009, point 62.
208 Case C-28/95, Leur-Bloem, EU:C:1997:369.
209 See Opinion of Advocate General Mazák, Case C-451/05, ELISA, EU:C:2007:594, point 102.
210 See, for example, Case C-14/16, Euro Park Services, EU:C:2017:177, point 55.
211 Case C-524/04, Test Claimants in the Thin Cap Group Litigation, EU:C:2007:161, point 82.
212 Case C-28/95, Leur-Bloem, EU:C:1997:369, point 44.
213 Recital 11 of the preamble of Council Directive (EU) 2016/1164.

question is 1 January 2022 and for the anti-hybrid financing rule for banks for specific instruments (contingent convertibles), the date in question is 1 January 2023. Finally, Member States which have national targeted rules for preventing BEPS risks at 8 August 2016, which are equally effective to the interest limitation rule set out in the ATAD, may apply these targeted rules until the end of the first full fiscal year following the date of publication of the agreement between the OECD members on the official website on a minimum standard with regard to BEPS Action 4, but at the latest until 1 January 2024. This exception was included during the final stage of negotiation upon specific request by Austria. Member States should have communicated to the Commission before 1 July 2017 all information necessary for evaluating the effectiveness of the national targeted rules for preventing base erosion and profit shifting risks (BEPS). Greece, France, Slovakia, Slovenia and Spain have successfully opted-in for this grandfathering clause.[214] To summarize:

- **1 January 2019**: Introduction of the interest limitation rule (with the exception of the Member States that opted for the grandfathering clause), the CFC-rule and the GAAR;
- **1 January 2020**: Introduction of the exit tax and step-up rule and the anti-hybrid rule, with the exception for the specific provision for reverse hybrids (Article 9a ATAD 2) and anti-hybrid financing rule for banks for some hybrid financing instruments (contingent convertibles);
- **1 January 2022**: Introduction of the specific anti-hybrid rule for reverse hybrid entities; (Article 9a ATAD 2);
- **1 January 2023**: Introduction of the anti-hybrid financing rule for banks; and
- **1 January 2024** (or earlier if agreement between the OECD members on a minimum standard with regard to BEPS Action 4 is reached and published): Introduction of interest limitation in the Member States that opted for the grandfathering clause.

Finally, it follows from the CJ's case law that, in the absence of a provision to the contrary, new Union rules apply immediately to the future effects of a situation which arose under the old rules.[215] Hence, absent specific transitional provisions, the ATAD provisions apply with immediate effect. This implies that, for example, the exit tax rule and CFC-rule apply without distinction as to whether gains or profits have been accrued or realized prior to the first date of application of the rules. Hence, no labelling between the taxpayer's "old" and "new" accrued gains and a CFC's "old" and "new" profits can be made.[216] An optional exception to the ATAD's immediate effect applies under the interest limitation rule; here a specific grandfathering clause is included for existing loans, *i.e.*, loans which were concluded before 17 June 2016, to the extent they are not modified afterwards.

214 See Commission Notice Measures considered equally effective to Article 4 of the Anti-Tax Avoidance Directive, OJ 7 December 2018, C 441, p. 1.

215 Case 270/84, Licata v. Economic and Social Committee, EU:C:1986:304, point 31; Case C-441/08, Elektrownia Pftnów, EU:C:2009:698, point 36; Case 278/84, Germany v. Commission, EU:C:1987:2, point 36; Case C-60/98, Butterfly Music, EU:C:1999:333, point 25.

216 Hence, there is no room for what is sometimes referred to as the "compartmentalization-doctrine". See also.by analogy, S. Shalhav, 'Interaction between the Participation Exemption and the Principle of Compartmentalization: Portfolio Investments in the New EU Accession Member States', *European Taxation* 2 (2005), p. 64-71.

19.7 A Final Chord?

Seen from a pre-BEPS world angle, where corporate tax harmonization within the Union used to be a taboo for many Member States, the adoption of the ATAD can be seen as a giant leap. Having a closer look, however, one can wonder whether the ATAD has fulfilled its promise. Its provisions contain over-but also under-inclusiveness, its implementation throughout the EU will eventually differ from Member State to Member State and the choices that the ATAD leaves to the Member States could give rise to tax competition practices. Eventually, the ATAD is only focusing on symptoms instead of the causes of BEPS. Like under the Member States' corporate tax regimes, it still takes legal reality, instead of the economic reality in which multinational enterprises operate, as the starting point, which essentially is the cause of BEPS. In our view, therefore, the ATAD should not be seen as the final chord, but as an upbeat to a more fundamental reform of the Member States' corporate tax systems in an international context.

CHAPTER 20

Tax Aspects of the European Economic Interest Grouping, the European Company and the European Cooperative Society

Peter Wattel

Update by Frederik Boulogne,[1] Mariken van Hilten[2] and Peter Wattel[3]

20.1 Introduction; European Legal Forms for Business: EEIG, SE, SCE (and SPE)

An internal market and a level playing field for economic operators presuppose the possibility of cross-border merging, cooperation, and relocation of the seat of undertakings as if national borders did not exist. Harmonization of national company laws in these fields has only partially been achieved, however. Disagreement remains, particularly on the questions of whether the legal personality and the legal regime of (national law) companies should be viewed on the basis of *siège réel* (central administration: place of mind and management) or *siège statutaire* (registered office: place of incorporation), whether a European Company (SE) should have a one-tier or a two-tier structure (a board and supervisors, or just one board), and to what extent employees should be represented on that board. Where sufficient harmonization of national company laws cannot be attained, another possibility is the parallel creation of an optional uniform legal form at EU level.

The first Union legal form for cooperation between undertakings or professionals of different Member States was introduced on 25 July 1985, in Council Regulation 2137/85/EEC on the European Economic Interest Grouping (the EEIG Regulation).[4] It is disappointing that it took until 1985 to create the first Union legal form ever, and it is even more disappointing that the EEIG was that first EU legal form. The need for a European Company (*Societas Europaea* or SE) was greater than the need for an EEIG, of which we heard little after its introduction. It took 34 years, from the first pre-draft in 1966 until 20 December 2000, to agree on a (watered down) Statute for a European Company, which became applicable

---

1 International Tax Partner, BDO; Lecturer, University of Amsterdam.

2 Professor of Indirect Taxes at the University of Amsterdam; vicepresident Supreme Court of the Netherlands.

3 Professor Emeritus of EU Tax Law, ACTL, University of Amsterdam; Advocate-General, Supreme Court of the Netherlands; State Councillor extraordinary, Netherlands Council of State.

4 O.J. No. L 199 of 31 July 1985, p. 1.

on 8 October 2004. The SE Statute consists of an SE Regulation[5] and an accompanying Directive on employee participation.[6] It applies not only for the EU Member States, but also for the EEA States (EU + Norway, Iceland, and Liechtenstein).

Furthermore, on 22 July 2003 a Statute for a European Cooperative Society (SCE for *Societas Cooperative Europaea*) was adopted, also consisting of a Regulation[7] and an accompanying Directive[8] on employee participation, opening the possibility of forming European cooperative societies as of 18 August 2006. The SCE Statute also applies for the EEA States.

Finally, in June 2008, under the slogans "Think Small First: a Small Business Act for Europe", and "Less Red Tape and More Red Carpet," the Commission tabled a proposal for a Small Business Act (SBA), introducing, *inter alia*, a new EU legal form for small and medium-sized businesses, which account for 67% of employment in the private sector: the European private company (*Societas Privata Europaea* or SPE).[9] That proposal for an SPE Regulation did not make any progress, however, and it was withdrawn as obsolete in 2014.[10]

The SE and the SCE are not – as initially envisaged – genuine *Union* legal forms independent from national law: for many issues the SE and SCE Regulations refer to national law of the State of the registered office. Nonetheless, the SE would seem more successful than the EEIG, the latter being largely non-existent in everyday legal and entrepreneurial practice in many Member States. The EEIG may have such modest spread because of its limited commercial possibilities. It does not have legal personality in all Member States, it can only have a limited number of employees, it may not issue shares to the public, its members have unlimited and joint liability for its (tax) obligations, and its activities must be ancillary to the activities of its members (see Section 20.2). The SE and SCE are not hampered by such limitations, but still have some limitations of their own impeding a true wide spread, such as (i) unclear interaction between the Regulation and national law, leading to legal uncertainty, (ii) costly, time-consuming and complex set-up procedures and (iii) unruly employee representation requirements in the accompanying Directives. A study by the European Trade Union Institute nonetheless shows that by 12 March 2018, 3000 SE's had been registered across all EU Member States except Croatia.[11] The vast majority, however, has been registered in just three Member States: the Czech Republic,

5 Council Regulation 2157/2001/EC of 8 October 2001 on the Statute for a European company (SE), O.J. No. L 294, of 10 November 2001, p. 1.
6 Council Directive 2001/86/EC of 8 October 2001 supplementing the Statute for a European company with regard to the involvement of employees, O.J. No. L 294 of 10 November 2001, p. 22.
7 Council Regulation 1435/2003/EC of 22 July 2003 on the Statute for a European Cooperative Society (SCE), O.J. No. L 207, of 18 August 2003, p. 1, to be applied as of 18 August 2006 (see Art. 80).
8 Council Directive 2003/72/EC of 22 July 2003 supplementing the Statute for a European Cooperative Society with regard to the involvement of employees, O.J. No. L 207 of 18 August 2003, p. 25, to be implemented by 18 August 2006.
9 Proposal for a Council Regulation on the Statute for a European private company, COM(2008) 396/3 (withdrawn in 2014; see next footnote).
10 See O.J. No. C153/3 of 21 May 2014.
11 See http://ecdb.worker-participation.eu.

Germany and Slovakia (2685 SE's in total). The disproportionate spread of SEs over just a few Member States appears to be driven by strict regulations on employee involvement that applies only to national legal forms.

We will not go into the SCE Regulation separately, as tax wise, there is little difference from the SE's tax position in the sense that neither Regulation provides for any tax statute for the SE or the SCE, meaning that national tax law and applicable bilateral tax treaties govern their tax position – except as regards the cross-border transfer of their seats, for which the Tax Merger Directive (see Chapter 17) provides deferral rules. Below, we will elaborate on the tax implications of this non-regulation for the SE and only very briefly touch upon the SCE.

The legal basis for the EEIG Regulation, the SE Regulation (and the accompanying Directive), and the SCE Regulation (and the accompanying Directive) is Article 352 TFEU (ex Article 308 of the EC Treaty; ex Article 235 of the EEC Treaty), providing for unanimous adoption of measures necessary to attain EU objectives where the EU Treaties have not otherwise provided the necessary powers to attain these objectives.

20.2 General Legal Aspects of the EEIG

The creation of the EEIG was inspired by the French *groupement d'intérêt économique*, a flexible legal form permitting undertakings and professional providers of services to join some of their economic activities while at the same time remaining independent.

Since the European Treaties did not provide the powers necessary to create legal instruments for the grouping of activities of undertakings, the EEIG Regulation was based on (now) Article 352 TFEU. The instrument of a regulation – instead of a directive – was chosen to ensure uniform application by the Member States and equal accessibility for participants throughout the EC.

The EEIG is intended to facilitate or develop the economic activities of its members and to improve or increase the results of their activities. It is not supposed to make a profit for itself: it is not an undertaking in its own right. An EEIG's activities should be ancillary to those of its members (Art. 3(1) of the EEIG Regulation). Accordingly, Articles 3(2) and 23 of the Regulation list a number of things an EEIG may not do, such as manage undertakings, hold shares in its members, employ more than 500 employees, be a member of another EEIG, or invite capital contributions by the public. Moreover, an EEIG is transparent for profit accounting purposes: the profits resulting from an EEIG's activities are not its own, but its members', to be apportioned among them in fractions they agreed upon in the contract establishing the EEIG or, in the absence of such agreement, in equal shares (Art. 21 of the EEIG Regulation). In the *EITO/EWI* case, the CJEU held that Article 5(a) of the EEIG Regulation must be interpreted as meaning that the business name of an EEIG must include the words `European Economic Interest Grouping' or the initials `EEIG'.[12]

---

12 Case C-402/96, *European Information Technology Observatory, Europäische Wirtschaftliche Interessenvereinigung*, EU:C:1997:634.

The above shows that an EEIG has only an auxiliary role. Its activities may be limited to cost pooling. This is not to say that its activities should be petty. One could imagine an EEIG serving as a vehicle for a consortium of independent companies to bid on an immense government contract. Most EEIGs registered, however, are contracts between providers of professional services (lawyers, tax consultants, architects, accountants, etc.) and between undertakings wishing to join purchasing, sale or import-export activities.

An EEIG must have at least two members from different Member States. They may be public or private corporations carrying on economic activities, or self-employed individuals, resident within the EU (Art. 4). The members of an EEIG are jointly and severally liable for its debts and other liabilities (Art. 24). An EEIG has full legal capacity, but whether it has legal personality (whether it is a separate legal entity), is dependent on the domestic law of its country of residence: Member States are free to choose whether they regard an EEIG as a body corporate or as a mere partnership (a contract).

20.3 Tax Aspects of the EEIG

20.3.1 Direct Taxes

Article 40 of the EEIG Regulation provides that the profits or losses resulting from the activities of an EEIG shall be taxable only in the hands of its members. This is a logical consequence of Article 21, providing that the profits of the EEIG are the profits of its members. The Preamble to the Regulation states that:

> 'it is understood that otherwise [that is, apart from Article 40; *authors*] national tax laws apply, particularly as regards the apportionment of profits, tax procedures and any obligation imposed by national tax law.'

This does not clarify matters very much. At first sight, it would seem that an EEIG is wholly transparent for tax purposes. If national law of the home State of the EEIG does not confer legal personality upon it, then it will not usually be liable to (corporate) income tax itself, either as a subject, or for its results. Even if from national tax law it would follow that an EEIG's results are subject to tax, this tax cannot legally be levied from the EEIG because of the superseding Article 40 of the EEIG Regulation. Therefore, for the purposes of taxation of its results, an EEIG is fiscally transparent. It follows that dividends received on shares held by an EEIG, or interest on debt-claims held by an EEIG, are taxed in the hands of its members, in proportion to their membership rights in the EEIG. The wording of Article 40 nonetheless suggests that the EEIG's results should be determined at EEIG level rather than for each member separately (which may lead to discrepancies if they are not subject to the same national tax regime, which must be the case for at least two of them).

However, notwithstanding Article 40 of the EEIG Regulation, an EEIG may qualify as an entity subject in principle to corporation tax under national tax law, particularly if national law endows it with legal personality. Indeed, Article 40 of the EEIG Regulation does not, in itself, seem to preclude *subjective* liability to corporation tax, because Article 40 only seems to address the question of *objective* liability to tax: the object of taxation (the EEIG's profit or loss) may be taxed only in the hands of its members, but this does not preclude Member States from listing an EEIG as a body subject to corporation tax, as long as they do not tax its profits in the hands of the EEIG itself. The matter is of some importance for the EEIG's position under bilateral tax treaties, because these treaties confer benefits only on 'residents' of the Contracting States, 'residents' being defined as, *inter alia*, persons *liable* to (corporate) income tax (see Art. 4(1) of the OECD Model Double Taxation Convention). Under national tax law a locally registered EEIG may in principle be liable to tax (and therefore a 'resident' for tax treaty purposes), but not effectively taxed on its profits because of the superseding Article 40 of the EEIG Regulation, a provision which is not, however, designed to affect the personal scope of bilateral tax treaties. It may therefore be argued that an EEIG qualifies as a 'resident' under an applicable tax treaty, and thus is entitled to the tax treaty benefits, such as reduction or refund of foreign withholding tax on dividends, interest and royalties received from abroad. If, on the other hand, the EEIG is not a resident for lack of subjection to corporation tax in its home State, it must be considered transparent for profits taxation purposes, and only its resident members may qualify for the benefits of the tax treaty with the source State, such as reduction or refund of foreign withholding taxes.

An EEIG must have at least two members from different Member States. Supposing that an EEIG can have its official address in only one State, it follows that an EEIG always has at least one nonresident member. The question arises whether being a member of an EEIG having its registered office in another Member State constitutes a permanent establishment of that EEIG member in that other Member State under Article 5 of the OECD Model Double Taxation Convention, and therefore under most bilateral tax treaties between Member States. Article 12 of the EEIG Regulation stipulates that the official address of an EEIG must be either where the EEIG itself has its central administration, or where one of its members has its principal administration or principal activity, provided that the EEIG carries on an activity there. We submit that a 'central administration' will probably constitute a permanent establishment for tax (treaty) purposes. 'An activity', on the other hand, does not necessarily constitute a permanent establishment, since an EEIG's activities must be 'ancillary', and Article 5(4)(e) and (f) of the OECD Model provides that the term 'permanent establishment' shall be deemed not to include a fixed place of business solely for the purpose of carrying on 'any other activity of a preparatory or auxiliary character'. However, Article 5 of the OECD Model presupposes that preparatory or auxiliary activities are performed for the benefit of only one enterprise (the head office), whereas the activities of an EEIG are by definition performed for the benefit of at least two members. We conclude that in many cases being a member of an EEIG having its official address in another State will constitute a permanent establishment of the EEIG member in that other State for tax (treaty) purposes. Consequently, a nonresident member of an EEIG will in principle be taxed in the source State (the EEIG's home State) for his or its share in the results of the EEIG. On the other hand, such a nonresident member is then also entitled to the prevention of international double taxation in his/its home State under the applicable tax treaty between that home State and the State of the EEIG.

Whether an EEIG which 'distributes' its profits, or which pays interest or royalties to its members, is subject to national withholding taxes on dividends, interest or royalties, is dependent on national tax law. We presume that, in general, without a specific domestic provision stipulating so, an EEIG is not subject to dividend withholding tax on profit remittances to its members, since it is not a capital company. It cannot be excluded that Member States may subject other payments than dividends to withholding taxes, in spite of an EEIG not having been granted legal personality.

In conclusion: the (international) direct tax (treaty) position of the EEIG has been left in the dark by the EEIG Regulation. This position is largely dependent on national tax law, and is characterized by uncertainties.

20.3.2 Indirect and Payroll Taxes

The EEIG Regulation contains no provisions on indirect and payroll taxes. Therefore, no transparency applies as regards indirect taxes, and national tax law is decisive (except where incompatible with directly applicable Union law, such as the VAT Directive (Directive 2006/112/EC)or the Directive on the general Arrangements for excise duty (EU/2020/262).

An EEIG hiring and paying employees will probably qualify in most Member States as an employer for national payroll tax purposes and, therefore, will be required to withhold payroll tax and social security contributions from the wages paid to its employees, and remit them to the local revenue service.

Article 2 of the recast Capital Duty Directive, does not seem to cover an EEIG, as it is not a capital company, nor does it otherwise qualify under that provision. We conclude, therefore, that an EEIG is not subject to capital duty.

An EEIG is, however, subject to taxes on transfer of immovable property and to VAT. As regards VAT, it is subject to tax in so far as it independently exercises an economic activity (Article 9 VAT Directive). Therefore, supplies and services between the EEIG and its members will generally be subject to VAT, except where the EEIG is a mere cost-pooling vehicle. Whether being a member of an EEIG having its official address in another Member State constitutes a permanent establishment for VAT purposes, can, as for direct taxation purposes, only be determined on a case-by-case basis.

On 15 March 2011 the Council adopted implementing Regulation (EU) No. 282/2011 laying down implementing measures for the VAT Directive. This recast Regulation replaces Regulation (EC) No. 1777/2005 laying down implementing measures for the Sixth Directive, which was the predecessor of the VAT Directive. Art. 5 of the Regulation clarifies the position of the EEIG as a taxable person in its own right.[13] According to the preamble:

> '(9) The further integration of the internal market has led to an increased need for co-operation by economic operators established in different Member States across internal

13 See also the questions regarding the EEIG raised in Case C-605/15, *Aviva*, EU:C:2017:718, which unfortunately were not answered.

borders and the development of European economic interest groupings (EEIGs), constituted in accordance with Council Regulation (EEC) No 2137/85 of 25 July 1985 on the European Economic Interest Grouping (EEIG). It should therefore be clarified that EEIGs are taxable persons where they supply goods or services for consideration.'

Art. 5 of the Regulation provides to that end:

> 'A European Economic Interest Grouping (EEIG), constituted in accordance with Regulation (EEC) No. 2137/85, which supplies goods or services for consideration to its members or to third parties shall be a taxable person within the meaning of Article 9(1) of Directive 2006/112/EC.'

20.4 General Legal Aspects of the Societas Europaea (SE)[14]

The *Societas Europaea* (SE) is a capital company limited by shares. Its capital is expressed in Euro. Its subscribed capital must be at least € 120 000. The SE has legal personality after it has been registered in the national company register of a Member State.[15] It cannot be registered as long as the matter of its employees' representation has not been settled (see *infra*). Its shareholders are not liable for more than the capital they subscribed. It must have its seat within the EU; its head office must be in the same Member State as its registered office. This means that for the SE, the Council adhered to the *siège réel* system (not the incorporation system), and that the SE is governed for a large part by the national law of the State of its head office/registration, not necessarily being the State of its incorporation.

The SE is not a uniform EU legal form. For many issues, the SE Regulation refers to the national law on public limited companies (plcs) of the Member State of incorporation, such as for shareholders' meetings, profit division and voting rights, issuance of shares or bonds, liquidation, insolvency, representation, liability of directors, etc. Only the essentials have been regulated at EU level, such as formation, legal personality, minimum capital, transformation, transfer of seat, dissolution, and management and supervision. The SE is a chameleon-like legal form, taking the colour of the national law of incorporation. As the 2010 Commission report on the SE (see Section 20.1) reports: there is not one, but there are 27 SEs: there are as many types of SE as there are Member States. The original idea of a uniform EU legal form has evaporated over the decades. During those decades, some parts of national company law have been harmonized, such as the rules on annual accounts, disclosure, capital protection and reliance by third parties on company information, reducing the need for exhaustive EU regulation.

The SE Statute, which entered into force in October 2004, addresses two needs of European industry in particular: (i) it makes possible a legal merger (into an SE) of companies of

14 See the special European Company website of the European Commission: https://europa.eu/youreurope/business/running-business/developing-business/setting-up-european-company/index_en.htm.

15 A of June 2017, business registers in all EU countries are interconnected through the "Business Registers Interconnection System", see Directive 2012/17/EU and Regulation (EU) 2015/884.

different Member States formed under different national laws of incorporation, and (ii) once the SE form has been adopted, a company may transfer its seat to another Member State without legal damage, such as the loss of legal personality (but not necessarily without fiscal damage; see Section 20.5).

An SE cannot be incorporated by individuals, only by entities. There are four possibilities:

i. a merger into an SE: two or more public limited companies (plcs) may merge into an SE, provided at least two of them are governed by the laws of different Member States. They either all cease to exist (merge into a new legal entity, the SE), or they merge into one of them, whose legal personality continues, but which becomes an SE (merger by acquisition);
ii. incorporation of a holding SE: two or more plcs, or private limited companies (Ltds) may incorporate a holding SE (of which they will be subsidiaries), provided at least two of them are governed by the laws of different Member States or have had for at least two years either a subsidiary company or a branch in another Member State;
iii. incorporation of a subsidiary SE: two or more companies or other entities addressed by Article 54 (2nd sentence) TFEU, created under the law of a Member State and having their registered office and central administration within the EU, may together incorporate a subsidiary SE by obtaining its shares, provided at least two of them are governed by the laws of different Member States or have had for at least two years either a subsidiary company or a branch in another Member State; or
iv. transformation (conversion): a national plc may be converted into an SE if it has had for at least two years either a subsidiary company or a branch in another Member State.

As the SE Regulation adheres to the *siège réel* principle, an SE must have its head office in the Member State of its registered office. However, its seat may be transferred to another Member State with retention of legal personality. If subsequently the central administration and the registered office do not territorially coincide anymore, the State of the registered office must enforce either the transfer of the registered office to the State of the central administration, or the relocation of the central administration to the State of the registered office.

The Articles of incorporation of an SE must choose between a one-tier management structure (one board of directors) or a two-tier structure (a board of directors and a board of supervisors[16]). This choice must also be respected if the national law of the Member State of its incorporation adheres to the management structure for which the SE does not opt. Member States therefore had to amend their national company laws to allow for the other choice. An SE may be transformed into a national plc two years after its incorporation and after approval of its first two annual accounts.

Employee representation must be negotiated between the participating companies and an employee committee representing their employees and the employees of their subsidiaries and branches. If no agreement on employee representation is reached within six months,

16 Such as the German *Aufsichtsrat* and the Netherlands *Raad van Commissarissen.*

or if the negotiators so agree, the matter of employee representation will be governed by rules of reference, to be enacted by the Member States on the basis of the Directive.

The SE is clearly a vehicle for intra-EU corporate restructuring. The most attractive features for European industry are understood to be the possibility of a transnational merger of companies of different Member States via an SE incorporation and the possibility of emigration of the SE with retention of legal personality. Since 15 December 2007 (the implementation deadline of Directive 2005/56/EC) cross-border merger of limited liability companies are also possible without using an SE[17] and as of 1 January 2023 cross-border divisions and cross-border conversions of limited liability company are possible across the EU (that date marks the implementation deadline of Directive (EU) 2019/2121[18]). Other positive drivers for the SE are its European image and its supranational character.

20.5 Tax Aspects of the *Societas Europaea*[19]

20.5.1 Direct Taxes

The SE Regulation does not contain a single provision on taxation, and neither does the accompanying Directive on employee representation. Possibly, it was felt it would not make sense to draw up a uniform tax Statute for the SE if the SE itself would for a large part be a construction of national (company) law, an EU-upgraded national public limited company, to be treated as if it were such national plc (Art. 10 of the SE Regulation). Also, a specific tax regime for the SE could discriminate against national legal forms, which is not likely to be acceptable for many Member States, and such regime might also be seen as a first step to comprehensive base harmonization of national corporation taxes, which probably did not rouse much enthusiasm either in many Member States. European industry had hoped for the SE to be subject to one single profits tax system, either 'common base taxation' or 'home State taxation', *i.e.* taxation under one single set of tax rules – common rules at EU level, or the tax legislation of the head office State, respectively – for the determination of the SE's tax base for its EU activities (see Chapter 15).[20] At least, it was hoped for that the SE would become the legal vehicle for the EU-wide cross-border set-off of losses within groups of companies; losses of the group in one Member State would then be offset against profits of the group in another Member State, reducing the group's overall tax exposure within the EU, and thus taking away a competitive disadvantage as compared to US, Japanese and Chinese industry. That hope was unrealistic, given the lack of progress of the proposal for a Directive on cross-border loss compensation (withdrawn in 2001; see Chapter 10). However, on this issue, the ECJ

17 Directive 2005/56/EC of the European Parliament and of the Council of 26 October 2005 on cross-border mergers of limited liability companies, O.J. L 310, 25.11.2005, p. 1.

18 Directive 2019/2121 of the European Parliament and of the Council of 27 November 2019 amending Directive (EU) 2017/1132 as regards cross-border conversions, mergers and divisions, O.J. L 321/2, 12.12.2019.

19 See the special issue 'Societas Europaea: Flagship for European Company Law – Catalyst for EC Tax Law?' 44 *European Taxation 1* (January 2004).

20 See Malcolm Gammie, 'Taxation Issues for the European Company,' *EC Tax Review* 1998/3, p. 159 ff, and Malcolm Gammie: 'EU Taxation and the Societas Europaea: Harmless Creature or Trojan Horse?' 44 *European Taxation* 1 (January 2004), p. 35-45.

modestly came to European business' help in Case C-446/03, *Marks & Spencer II* (see Section 10) by requiring the parent company State to set off *final* foreign subsidiary losses as if they were domestic subsidiary losses. On 2011, the Commission tabled a proposal for a common consolidated corporate tax base (CCCTB), which, after BEPS developments, was reviewed and retabled in 2016, only to be revamped in 2021 into a new proposal called "Business in Europe: Framework for Income Taxation" (BEFIT); see Chapter 25), but it may take some time before it is adopted, if even by an enhanced cooperation group of at least nine Member States (see Arts. 20 TEU and 326–334 TFEU).

Given the absence of tax provisions in the SE Statute and Article 10 of the SE Regulation requiring the SE to be treated as a public limited liability company under the national law of its State of registration, the direct-tax position of the SE is no different from the direct-tax position of a plc under national law, except for its inclusion in the Tax Merger Directive as regards corporate seat relocation.

Articles 12–14 of the Tax Merger Directive (see Chapter 17) defer capital gains tax upon the emigration of an SE, but do not defer taxation upon emigration of a company formed under internal law. We would qualify this as a discrimination against national legal forms, especially against the legal forms of Member States applying an incorporation system of company law (under such system, companies may transfer their effective management abroad without consequences as regards retention of legal personality and recognition).

Apart from the special seat transfer provisions in the Tax Merger Directive, the tax position of the SE, like the tax position of a national legal form, is entirely governed by (i) national tax law, (ii) regular international tax (treaty) law, (iii) general EU Treaty law, such as the freedom of establishment, and, since the SE is included in the list of legal forms to which these Directives apply, (iv) the Parent-Subsidiary Directive (see Chapter 16) and the Interest-Royalty Directive (see Chapter 18) and the general deferral rules of the Tax Merger Directive (see Chapter 17). Finally, also the rules in the Anti-Tax Avoidance Directives (ATAD) 1 and 2 apply to SEs when they are, as will commonly be the case, subject to corporate tax in a Member State.

This means that in principle, an SE is taxed as if it were a national public limited liability company of its State of incorporation (or its State of residence, if that is another State). It is subject, like any national law company, to national corporate income tax on its worldwide income in its State of residence (effective management), and on its sourced income in the State(s) in which it is not resident, but operates branches or agencies, with regular prevention of double taxation of the foreign branch/agency income. In the branch State, it is subject to tax on the income sourced there, in the same way as a company incorporated under the national law of its State of residence. It has access to tax schemes applicable to plcs resident in its State of residence, such as group income schemes, tax incentives, unilateral prevention of international double taxation, and tax treaties concluded by its State of residence. It is subject to national wage withholding tax on its payroll, to national dividend withholding tax on its profit distributions (except in so far as the Parent-Subsidiary Directive abolishes that tax within the EU), and possibly to national withholding taxes on interest and royalties in so far as these are levied in its State of residence and were not abolished by the Interest and Royalty Directive (see Chapter 18). It will have to pay capital duty on the raising of its capital, if such tax exists in its State of incorporation, and in so far as this is compatible with the capital duty Directive.

For the application of tax treaties an SE is resident in the State of its central management, which should coincide, according to the Regulation, with the State of its registered office. It thus has access to the tax treaties of that State. According to Case C-307/97, *Saint-Gobain*,[21] it also has indirect access to the benefits of the tax treaties concluded by the Member States in which it operates branches deriving third State income, as the branch State is required to grant the branch the same tax treatment as a resident taxpayer.

As observed, however, under the Tax Merger Directive the SE is in a different tax position from national public limited companies in one respect: where the central administration of an SE is transferred abroad, the SE is not required, given Articles 12–14 of the Tax Merger Directive, to settle its tax position in the State of departure in so far as a branch remains in that State. Although national tax law may provide for the same kind of tax deferral in case of emigration of a national legal form, the Tax Merger Directive does not require the Member States to provide for deferral for other legal forms than the SE (and the SCE). Therefore, corporate emigration of other legal forms than SEs (and SCEs) may entail taxation by the exit State of unrealized capital gains and fiscal provisions and reserves, and possibly the evaporation of unused losses. It follows, however, from the case-law starting with the *National Grid Indus BV*[22] case, that for all legal forms taxation must be refrained from in respect of a remaining branch. That case further provides for a choice between immediate payment and tax deferral upon corporate emigration as regards the assets and liabilities leaving the departure State (see Chapters 12 and 19). Thus, the discrimination against national legal forms appears to have been rectified. Moreover, as of 2019, Article 5 of the Anti Tax Avoidance Directive (ATAD; see Chapter 19) requires Member States to grant emigrating companies the right to defer payment of exit taxes (and to provide for a step up in tax value in the immigration State).

A merger of two companies of different Member States into an SE will typically not give rise to cross-border loss compensation: if company A in State A and company B in State B merge into an SE having its registered office (and central management) in State A, then the business of company B becomes a State B branch (permanent establishment) of the SE in State A. Thus, State B losses will be set off against State profits attributable to State B branch. If no branch remains in State B upon the merger of companies A and B into the SE, a 'final' loss of company B may be taken into account in State A.

If there is a loss in State A and a profit in State B, then no cross-border loss compensation is possible, as State B, in which the SE is not resident but merely has a branch (the former company B), taxes only the income sourced in State B (the income attributable to the permanent establishment in State B), see the *Futura* case.[23]

---

21 Case C-307/97, *Saint-Gobain ZN*, EU:C:1999:438, [1999] ECR I-6161.
22 Case C-371/10, *National Grid Indus BV*, EU:C:2011:785.
23 Case C-250/95, *Futura*, EU:C:1997:239.

Upon a transfer of seat of an SE or SCE to another Member State, neither the Tax Merger Directive (Article 13(2) only covers the carry-over of losses to a permanent establishment remaining in the Member State of departure) nor the fundamental freedoms require losses incurred in the Member State of departure to be allowed for offset by the Member State of arrival (see the *AURES Holdings* case).[24]

Incorporation of an SE by way of a merger does not trigger taxation of the unrealized capital gains and fiscal reserves of the merging companies, as the SE is on the list of qualifying legal forms under the Tax Merger Directive (see Section 17.6). Under Art. 2(a)(ii), in conjunction with Arts 4, 5 and 6 of that Directive, a merger of two existing companies of different Member States into a new company which they form, shall not give rise to any taxation on unrealized capital gains or fiscal reserves, provided that the new company (the SE) retains the book values and depreciation systems of the 'old' companies, and provided that the assets and liabilities of the merging State B company constitute a State B branch (permanent establishment) of the SE resident in State A, which will in general be the case. The tax claim on the unrealized gains among the assets of the disappearing companies is thus transferred to the SE. Under Art. 8 of the Tax Merger Directive, the shareholders of the disappearing companies must be granted deferral of capital gains tax on the substitution of shares. Likewise, in our opinion, the incorporation of a holding SE by two existing companies (which become subsidiaries of that holding SE) constitutes a share merger (exchange of shares) within the meaning of Art. 2(e) of the Tax Merger Directive if the two companies are from different Member States, and Art. 8 of the Tax Merger Directive provides for deferral of capital gains tax on the exchange.

20.5.2 Indirect Taxes

As for VAT, the SE is just another taxable person for VAT purposes, provided it carries out an economic activity as referred to in article 9 of the VAT Directive. Although there are no special provisions, it seems to be useful to analyse the VAT consequences of the incorporation of an SE.

The following stages are relevant:
(1) the pre-registration period;
(2) the creation of a new legal entity;
(3) the transformation into an SE;
(4) the transfer of the seat; and
(5) intra-company transactions.

(1) The Pre-Registration Period
According to Article 9(1) of the VAT Directive, 'any person' performing activities is a taxable person. When a one-person business or a partnership is brought into a public (or private) limited company, the result is a new taxable person, *e.g.* the plc (or ltd). However, when activities take place before the registration of the company, these are performed by a different person, namely the plc (or Ltd) 'in formation' (hereinafter 'i.f.'). From the various

24 Case C-405/18, *AURES Holdings*, EU:C:2020:127.

authentic languages of the VAT Directive, referring to 'quiconque', 'ieder', 'jeder', etc., it follows that '"any person" performing economic activities is a taxable person' should be read as '"any one" performing economic activities is a taxable person', *i.e.* even without having legal personality, such as an ltd i.f.

The consequence is that the plc or ltd, once registered, cannot claim deduction of the input VAT incurred by the ltd or plc i.f. during the pre-registration period.[25] This is different when a private limited company is transformed into a public limited company, or vice versa, since the person is not changing, but mainly the applicable corporate law.

In cases of incorporation of a holding SE, a subsidiary SE or an SE through a merger, by the formation of a new SE, the same rules apply regarding the formation of a plc or ltd, albeit by definition there is a cross-border dimension. Legal acts performed on behalf of the SE before registration are attributable to the SE i.f.; the SE cannot deduct the VAT incurred by the SE i.f.

According to Article 19 VAT Directive, in the event of a transfer, 'whether for consideration or not or as contribution to a company' of a totality of assets or part thereof, Member States may consider that no supply has taken place. (This applies in a like manner, according to Article 28 VAT Directive, to services.)[26] To our knowledge these provisions are applied in virtually all Member States. The result is that in the Member State where the SE is incorporated there are no VAT consequences regarding the change from an SE i.f. into an SE.[27] Neither should cross-border incorporation result in any VAT consequences.[28]

The question arises where the SE i.f., as separate 'anyone', must register. It seems to us in the Member State where the SE wants to have its registered office. This may, however, create some confusion when the central administration regarding the formation of the SE is conducted from another Member State.

(2) The Creation of a New Legal Entity

The creation of an SE either via a merger or by the formation of a new SE, via incorporation of a holding or subsidiary SE results in various VAT consequences for the incorporating parties and possibly for the new entity.

---

25 However, based on a *Polski Trawertyn* approach (see Case C-280/10, EU:C:2012:107), and on a *PPG Holdings* analysis (Case C-26/12, EU:C:2013:526), alternatively the SE should be able to deduct the VAT incurred by the SE i.f.

26 Note, that until Case C-137/02, *Faxworld*, EU:C:2004:267, [2004] ECR I-5547, was decided, it was unclear whether a transferring company could deduct VAT when from the outset, it did not intend to carry out any other output transactions than the transfer, when, in the Member State concerned, a transfer of a totality of assets is not deemed to be a supply of goods or services. See further Chapter 2 (par. 2.6.1 and 2.6.8) in the 2nd Volume of this book.

27 Although as mentioned the SE cannot deduct the pre-registration VAT incurred by the SE i.f. According to Article 19 VAT Directive, the SE may be treated as the successor of the transferor (the SE i.f.), especially with regard to adjustments.

28 Only, if tangible property is transferred to another Member State problems may arise, due to the application of the rules concerning intracommunity supplies and acquisitions. It is beyond the context of this book to discuss these rules.

When a subsidiary SE is incorporated, it seems to us that the *Cibo* principles apply, regarding the VAT charged on services purchased in the context of the acquisition of the shareholdings in subsidiaries. According to the ECJ, this expenditure forms part of the general costs and falls, if applicable, under the general pro-rata.[29]

It is also possible that the Member State where the SE has its seat applies Article 11 VAT Directive regarding VAT grouping. The subsidiary SE and the entities partaking in the incorporation of the SE, in so far as established within that Member State, can be treated as a single taxable person.

With regard to a holding SE it should be noted that according to the ECJ a pure holding company is to be treated as a non-taxable legal person.[30] Nevertheless the VAT Directive seems to allow VAT grouping incorporating a holding SE, in so far as they are established in the same Member State.[31] It should be noted, however, that some Member States do not allow a pure holding company – a non-taxable legal person – to be part of a VAT group. This is an issue that still has to be decided by the ECJ. VAT incurred on costs regarding their capital contribution form part of the general costs of the companies involved.

In so far as costs are attributable to the SE i.f., the above mentioned single taxable persons cannot deduct the VAT incurred in the pre-registration period. Once part of the VAT group, the input tax incurred by the SE follows the pro rata, if applicable, of the VAT group.

When an SE is incorporated via a merger, by the foundation of a new SE, the SE continues the economic activities of the merging entities. In the light of *Abbey National* deduction by the merging companies of the VAT on costs regarding the merger is possible, because in principle they form part of the overheads.[32] The ECJ held in *Abbey National:*

29 Case C-16/00, *Cibo*, EU:C:2001:495, [2001] ECR I-6663, and Joined Cases C-108/14 and C-109/14, *Larentia* and *Minerva*, EU:C:2015:496. The ECJ held that expenditure incurred by a holding company in respect of the various services which it purchased in connection with the acquisition of a shareholding in a subsidiary forms part of its general costs and therefore has, in principle, a direct and immediate link with its business as a whole. Thus, if the holding company carries out both transactions in respect of which VAT is deductible and transactions in respect of which it is not, it follows from Article 173 RVD that it may deduct only that proportion of the VAT which is attributable to the former. See also Chapter 2 (par. 2.12.) in the 2nd Volume of this book.

30 Case C-60/90, *Polysar*, EU:C:1991:268, [1991] ECR I-3111. See also Chapter 2 (par. 2.5.6) in the 2nd Volume of this book. In Case C-16/00, *Cibo* (see previous footnote), the ECJ held that the involvement of a holding company in the management of companies in which it has acquired a shareholding constitutes an economic activity within the meaning of Article 4(2) of the Sixth Directive (now Article 9(1) VAT Directive) where it entails carrying out transactions which are subject to VAT by virtue of Article 2 of that directive (now Article 2(1) VAT Directive), such as the supply by a holding company to its subsidiaries of administrative, financial, commercial and technical services. The involvement of a holding company in the management of companies in which it has acquired a shareholding constitutes an economic activity where it entails carrying out transactions which are subject to VAT, such as the supply by a holding company to its subsidiaries of administrative, financial, commercial and technical services.

31 E.g. Case C-85/11, Commission/Finland, EU:C:2013:217.

32 Case C-408/98, *Abbey National*, EU:C:2001:110, [2001] ECR I-01361. See also Section 26.6.

> '[If] the transfer of a totality of assets or part thereof is regarded as not being a supply of goods the costs incurred by the transferor for services acquired in order to effect that transfer form part of that taxable person's overheads and thus in principle have a direct and immediate link with the whole of his economic activity.'

However, if the various services acquired by the transferor in order to effect the transfer have a direct and immediate link with a clearly defined part of his economic activities, so that the costs of those services form part of the overheads of that part of the business, and all the transactions relating to that part of the business are subject to value added tax, he may deduct all the value added tax charged on his costs of acquiring those services.

(3) Transformation

In cases of incorporation of an SE by acquisition, or by transformation of a national plc into an SE, the SE Regulation stipulates for the latter *expressis verbis* that this does not result in the creation of a new legal person. The VAT consequences seem to be minimal: the same legal entity continues the activities. In the case of a merger by acquisition (the acquiring company takes the form of an SE), this seems to us to be no different from the transformation of a private limited company into a public one or vice versa. Thus, in contrast to the SE i.f., transactions performed in the preregistration period are attributable to the company that is transformed or the acquiring company taking the form of an SE.[33] With regard to the companies that are acquired we submit that the earlier-mentioned *Abbey National* principles apply. Deduction is allowed in accordance with the treatment of the overheads.

(4) Transfer of the Seat

The change of the statutory seat (and under the SE Regulation therefore of the central administration) results in the obligation to register in the new Member State. Since the SE retains its legal personality, there are no cross-border transactions for consideration. Only transfers of tangible property will result in fictitious intra-Community supplies and acquisitions. The SE Regulation does not allow a transfer of the registered office from one Member State to another, in case of the conversion of an existing plc into an SE, at the same time as the conversion is effected.

(5) Intra-Company Transactions

With regard to intra-company transactions within an SE, except for cross-border supplies of goods which are deemed intra-Community supplies, one of the attractive aspects of the SE is that intra-company services are not subject to VAT. Where services are rendered within the same legal entity (*e.g.* a service rendered by a head office to a branch), they are not considered to be supplies for purposes of the VAT Directive.[34] This is the case whether the establishments are within a single Member State or multiple countries. Services rendered for consideration between separate legal entities (*e.g.* head office and a wholly owned subsidiary) are taxable supplies.

---

33 Obviously the merging companies and the company to be transformed are jointly and severally liable if, after all, the SE will not be registered.

34 Case C-210/04, *FCE Bank plc*, [2006] ECR I-02803, EU:C:2006:196; see Chapter 2 (par.2.5.5 and 2.7.3) in the 2nd Volume of this book.

20.6 The European Cooperative Society

As the SE, the SCE is a capital company limited by shares, which makes it stand apart from many national cooperative forms, as these often do not have a capital divided into shares. It has legal personality after it has been registered in the national company register of a Member State. It cannot be registered as long as the matter of its employee's representation has not been settled. It is designed to contribute, by its activities, to the economic and social interests of its members. It may be formed, by both individuals and companies from different Member States, in several ways listed in the SCE Regulation, such as a merger or a transformation. Its subscribed capital must be at least € 30 000. Like the SE, the SCE is not only governed by the Regulation, but also by national law (on national cooperatives) of the Member State of its registered office (Art. 8 of the SCE Regulation). As observed, the SCE Statute, like the SE Statute, does not provide for any taxation rules. Art. 8 refers, for matters not governed by the SCE Regulation, to national law applicable to cooperatives. Therefore, for determination of the SCE's tax position, one needs to apply existing national tax law, in principle as if a national cooperative were at issue, and where applicable the (implementing) rules of EU tax law such as the VAT Directive and the Tax Merger Directive, much in the same way as succinctly shown above for the SE.

CHAPTER 21

The Settlement of Cross-Border Tax Disputes in the European Union

Pasquale Pistone[1]

21.1 Cross-border tax disputes: from none to up to four types of legal instruments for their settlement

Cross-border tax disputes create legal uncertainty, may increase the tax burden and result in undermining the exercise of activities across the borders, thus raising concern within the EU Internal Market.

Such disputes usually arise when taxpayers question whether the exercise of taxing powers by a State complies with the conditions that they have agreed in a public international law agreement. In most cases, these disputes relate to the interpretation and application of such agreement, namely of a double taxation convention, and result into forms of international double taxation that the States had not intended to produce.

EU Member States generally address international double taxation because of its negative repercussions on cross-border economic relations. However, sometimes they partly tolerate this phenomenon as the normal outcome of the exercise in parallel of their taxing jurisdiction and, some other times, they have not yet come to the point of concluding a double taxation convention. In such circumstances, international double taxation arises outside the framework of cross-border tax disputes. Consequently, it would be wrong to assume the existence of a cross-border tax dispute whenever there is an issue of international double taxation.

From a public international law perspective, cross-border tax disputes are essentially a matter of conflict between States as to how they exercise their respective sovereignty in tax matters. However, such disputes have an immediate impact on taxpayers, who suffer the implications of such disputes in their personal sphere.[2]

1 IBFD Academic Chairman. Holder of a Jean Monnet *ad Personam* Chair in European Tax Law and Policy at WU Vienna and Full Professor of Tax Law at the University of Salerno.

2 For a comprehensive analysis of such issues see Perrou, K., Taxpayer participation in tax treaty dispute resolution", 2014, IBFD Doctoral Series, volume 28; Kokott, J., Pistone, P., Taxpayers in International Law, Hart Publishing, 2022.

From the perspective of European tax law, such problems may dissuade cross-border economic relations within the internal market and therefore be at odds with the principles of supranational integration.[3]

For several decades in the 20th century, the absence of international legal mechanisms for settling cross-border disputes in tax matters has prevented States from reaching solutions to possible conflicts on the interpretation and application of tax treaties. In such circumstances, the affected taxpayers had no other option than undertaking domestic legal remedies in order to minimize the impact of such conflicts on their personal sphere, thus on the exercise of rights and freedoms within the internal market.

Much has changed ever since, and for the good, giving the affected taxpayer up to four options for requesting the settlement of cross-border tax disputes within the European Union.[4] Such options consist in administrative and legal remedies provided by public international law in tax treaties and by European Union law in order to obtain that States settle cross-border tax disputes. In particular, they are the dispute resolution mechanisms applicable under Article 25 of the OECD Model,[5] the ones included as minimum standard (Part V) and with optional nature (Part VI) in the BEPS Multilateral Instrument (hereinafter also: BEPS MLI),[6] the EU Multilateral Arbitration Convention signed on 23 July 1990[7] and the EU Tax Arbitration Directive of 10 October 2017.[8]

---

3 According to Kokott, J., Pistone, P., Taxpayers in International Law, cit., p. 62, then a taxpayers requests the initiation of MAP and arbitration under the Dispute Resolution Directive, he relies directly on EU law and the EU Charter of Fundamental Rights correspondingly applies to such situation.

4 Since 2011, Article 25 (alternative B) UN Model Convention also provides for settlement of tax treaty disputes through arbitration. Although the UN is currently particularly active in this domain, the absence of an immediate direct relevance of this provision in the current treaty relations between EU Member States and the focus of this textbook on European tax law issues have suggested to leave this legal instrument for settling tax treaty disputes out of the scope of this chapter. For a comprehensive overview of issues related to tax dispute settlement under the UN Model Convention see Turcan, L., Dispute Resolution, in Lang, M., Pistone, P., Rust, A., Schuch, J., Staringer, C. (eds.), The UN Model Convention and Its Relevance for the Global Tax Treaty Network, IBFD Publications, Amsterdam, 2017, pp. 261-318. Furthermore, dispute resolution mechanisms also exist under GATS, bilateral investment treaties and other international conventions, which may also apply to cross-border tax disputes on economic relations. See on these issues Pistone, P., General Report, in Lang, M., Owens, J., Pistone, P., Rust, A., Schuch, J., Staringer, C. (eds.), The Impact of Bilateral Investment Treaties on Taxation, IBFD Publications, Amsterdam, 2017, pp. 40-43 and the various national reports contained in the volume. See also van Weeghel, S., Tax and Investment Treaties: A Few Observations, in Thinker, Teacher, Traveler – Reimagining International Tax, Essays in Honor of H. David Rosenbloom, Kofler, G., Mason, R., Rust, A. (eds.), IBFD Publications, 2021.

5 OECD Model Tax Convention, Paris (2017). Of course, dispute settlement is possible also under Article 25 of the UN Model Tax Convention. However, this will not be separately addressed in this Chapter, as dispute settlement presents homogeneous features to those of the corresponding measure contained in the OECD Model.

6 Multilateral Convention to Implement Tax Treaty Related Measures to Prevent Base Erosion and Profit Shifting, signed in Paris on 7 June 2017 and entered into force on 1 July 2018.

7 Convention 90/436/EEC of 23 July 1990, on the elimination of double taxation in connection with the adjustment of profits of associated enterprises, in OJ L 225, 20 August 1990, p. 10.

8 Directive EU 2017/1852 of 10 October 2017 on tax dispute resolution mechanisms in the European Union, in OJ L 265, 14 October 2017, pp. 1-14.

States essentially use two mechanisms for settling cross-border tax disputes, which normally operate in the framework of a two-tier procedure. In particular, these mechanisms are the so-called mutual agreement procedure, which is an administrative procedure involving representatives from tax authorities, and the so-called tax arbitration.

The public international law nature of these disputes generally keeps taxpayers more as objects than as holders of actual rights in the framework of such procedures. However, the involvement of taxpayers in the procedures has grown over time. European Union law has further enhanced this trend, in order to secure actual legal remedies whenever supranational law grants a right with direct effect.

Although the focus of this chapter and textbook is on European tax law, our analysis cannot ignore the close connections between public international law and European Union law as to the settlement of cross-border tax disputes.[9] For this reason, this chapter will review the interpretation and application of the main legal instruments for settling cross-border tax disputes in the light of their implications for the internal market, but also single out the differences and common points to their operational mechanisms.

After a brief historical overview, this chapter will analyse the legal basis of the main legal instruments for settling cross-border tax disputes and their relations, before shifting the focus on the procedural issues. The analysis of the procedural issues will reflect the two-tier procedure, in which the mutual agreement procedure and arbitration (and, in the case of the EU Tax Arbitration Directive, also an alternative dispute resolution mechanism) are used for settling cross-border tax disputes within the European Union.

21.2 Brief historical overview

A short description of how the settling of cross-border tax disputes has evolved over the past half century is important in order to understand the object and purpose of the existing legal instruments, but also of their dynamics and functioning.

Although the 1927 League of Nations Model included a reference to alternative dispute resolution in its Article 14,[10] this had hardly any impact in the bilateral treaty practice for several decades.

9 However, the analysis of issues concerning international tax arbitration will not be comprehensive, taking into account the abundance of complex technical issues arising in this field, which will only be addressed hereby in function of their relevance for the EU internal market. Yet, numerous dissertations have provided a comprehensive analysis of the problems of cross-border tax dispute settlement, including the books by Züger, Z., Arbitration under tax treaties: improving legal protection in international tax law, IBFD Publications, 2001, and Altman, Z.D., Dispute resolution under tax treaties, IBFD Publications, 2005. Furthermore, the International Fiscal Association has repeatedly focused on such issues (namely in its 1951, 1956, 1960, 1973, 1981, 1987, 1993, 2011, 2012, 2016 and 2024 congresses) and there are additional notable in-depth works, including Pit, H.M., Dispute Resolution in the EU - The EU Arbitration Convention and the Dispute Resolution Directive, IBFD Doctoral Series, 2021.

10 See Pit, H.M., Arbitration under the OECD Model Convention: Follow-up under Double Taxation Conventions: An Evaluation, in 42 Intertax 2014/6-7, p. 445.

The main legal instruments for settling cross-border tax disputes present similar features, which include a two-tier procedure, consisting of mutual agreement and arbitration (and, in the case of the EU Tax Arbitration Directive, also of an alternative dispute resolution mechanism).

The introduction of mutual agreement procedures in Article 25 of the 1963 OECD Model marks the starting point of the evolution process for settling cross-border tax disputes, whose latest development in the European Union is the approval of the EU Tax Arbitration Directive 2017/1852 on 10 October 2017.

The object and purpose of mutual agreement procedures is to allow tax authorities to discuss the interpretation and application of tax treaties in respect of one specific case presented by the taxpayer (Article 25 (1) OECD MC), or difficulties and doubts directly raised by tax authorities (Article 25 (3) OECD MC).[11] Mutual agreement procedures operate as a technical framework between tax authorities and keep taxpayers completely out of the picture. When successful, such procedures allow tax authorities to reach common ground on an amicable basis and secure the settlement of an existing cross-border tax dispute.

Still today, mutual agreement procedures represent the starting point of all four legal instruments for settling cross-border tax treaty disputes and are included within the minimum standard of the BEPS project. Yet, their functioning over the past decades has revealed several shortcomings, which often undermine the effectiveness of such procedures in practice. Such problems include their duration, the lack of transparency, and the existence of wide discretionary powers attributed to tax authorities without an actual obligation to reach an agreement. Besides, they can produce an impact on the legal sphere of taxpayers without giving them an actual possibility to intervene after the moment in which they file the initial complaint, except of course for their right to reject a MAP.

In the absence of an international tax court, or of a single court with jurisdiction on cross-border tax disputes involving more than one country,[12] arbitration has gradually developed in several bilateral double taxation conventions as the natural solution to such problems.[13] It supplements mutual agreement procedures, by operating as an

11 Although only Article 25 (3) OECD MC refers to disputes on the interpretation and application of tax treaties, we consider that this is the object of the dialogue between competent tax authorities even when, as in the case of Article 25 (1) OECD MC, mutual agreement procedures have to exercise this activity in connection with a complaint raised by a taxpayer in respect of actions of one or both the contracting states that results or will result in taxation not in accordance with the provisions of the convention.

12 Under the double taxation convention between Austria and Germany, the CJEU has jurisdiction to operate as arbitration court. It was not until 2017 that the CJEU has decided the first case in such capacity. See Case C-648/15, Austria vs Germany, EU:C:2017:664 on the application of Article 11 of the double taxation convention to interest from a financial instrument sourced in Germany and paid to an Austrian resident.

13 The first arbitration clause operating in tax matters was introduced in the tax treaty signed in 1870 by Prussia and Saxony. Numerous tax treaties have included arbitration clauses, especially from the end of the 1980s'.

optional extension, usually upon request of the affected taxpayer (s),[14] and, also after the appointment of the arbitration panel (advisory commission), at certain conditions and for a limited period, preserves the right of tax authorities to achieve a settlement by mutual agreement.

Although arbitration in tax treaties essentially remains a mechanism for settling disputes between States, it sometimes allows an involvement of the affected person(s), i.e. the taxpayer(s), and generally give(s) such person(s) the opportunity to reject the outcome by not implementing it, or by pursuing an alternative solution, also based on national legal remedies.

The introduction of supranational law on the settlement of cross-border direct tax disputes in the European Union was prompted by the almost complete absence of international law instruments for mandatory binding settlement of such disputes within the European Union.

The approval of the EU Tax Arbitration Directive in 2017 completes a long process that had started over 40 years earlier, when the EU Commission first proposed the introduction of an EU Tax Arbitration Directive for the settlement of some cross-border tax disputes between related enterprises in the field of transfer pricing.[15]

With the 1976 Proposal for an EU Tax Arbitration Directive the EU Commission intended to establish an effective supranational legal remedy to solve the critical issues connected with the impact of transfer price adjustments and the possibly resulting double taxation on the establishment or functioning of the common market.[16]

However, in 1990 the Council then resolved to introduce a common regime on the mandatory binding settlement of such tax disputes by means of an instrument of ordinary public international law, namely a multilateral convention, whose *sui generis* legal status will be addressed later in this chapter.[17]

The Multilateral Arbitration Convention on the Settlement of Cross-border Tax Disputes Concerning Transfer Pricing between Associated Enterprises was signed by EU Member States on 23 July 1990 (hereinafter also: the EU Tax Arbitration Convention). The EU Tax

---

14 Nevertheless, several double taxation conventions, also within the European Union (namely Croatia-Italy, Croatia-Netherlands, Estonia-Netherlands, Italy-Slovenia, Latvia-Netherlands, Netherlands-Slovenia), restrict the right to submit the dispute for arbitration to the sole competent authorities, although generally requiring consent by the taxpayer.

15 Proposal for a Directive concerning the elimination of double taxation in connection with the adjustment of transfers of profits between associated enterprises (arbitration procedure), submitted to the Council on 29 November 1976, OJ C 304 of 21 December 1976, p. 4.

16 The EU Tax Arbitration proposed in 1976 was withdrawn by the EU Commission in 1996. See 20 November 1996, OJ C of 4 January 1997, p. 6.

17 See section 21.3.

Arbitration Convention entered into force on 1 January 1995,[18] expired on 31 December 1999,[19] was extended through a Protocol with retroactive effect,[20] and then acceded by Bulgaria and Romania,[21] and eventually also by Croatia.[22]

The actual usage of the EU Tax Arbitration Convention has been rather limited until recently. However, our major concern is that the actual functioning of arbitration under this legal instrument is surrounded by an aura of opacity. This opacity might be due to the need for preserving confidential information, but may not contribute to a correct exercise of discretionary powers by tax authorities in the framework of the mutual agreement procedure. In such context, preserving the right of taxpayers to access the relevant documents concerning the procedure might be the right way forward,[23] also considering that national Constitutions frequently allow for such right in domestic tax procedures.[24]

The 2008 Update to the OECD MC introduced an arbitration clause in Article 25 (5) OECD MC. The essential content of this clause is to supplement mutual agreement procedures, leaving wide discretionary powers to the Contracting States as to the actual regulation of how to settle the dispute.[25]

---

18 Article 17 and 18 EU Tax Arbitration Convention request the ratifications by national Parliaments and their deposits, the last of which (by Portugal) took place on 28 October 1994. The Convention on the accession of the Republic of Austria, the Republic of Finland and the Kingdom of Sweden was signed on 21 December 1995, O.J. No. C 26 of 31 January 1996, p. 1 ff, secured the entry into force (for the States having ratified it) three months after the three new Member States and at least one of the 'old' 12 Member States have ratified it, and that for the old Member states ratifying later, it will enter into force for them as well within three months after their individual ratification.

19 Article 20 EU Arbitration Convention contains the so-called sunset clause, which limited the validity of the convention to five years, unless expressly extended six months before the expiry of that period.

20 Although the Protocol was signed on 25 May 1999, the last ratification by Portugal occurred only in 2004 and from that moment the Convention retroactively applied to all disputes that had occurred between 2000 and 2004.

21 See Annex I to the Act concerning the conditions of accession of the Republic of Bulgaria and Romania and the adjustments to the Treaties on which the European Union is founded: List of conventions and protocols to which Bulgaria and Romania accede upon accession (referred to in Article 3(3) of the Act of Accession), O.J. L 157, 21 June 2005, p. 221-223, and Council Decision 2008/492/EC of 23 June 2008, concerning the accession of Bulgaria and Romania to the Convention of 23 July 1990 on the elimination of double taxation in connection with the adjustment of profits of associated enterprises, O.J. L 174, 03 July 2008, p. 1-5.

22 See Annex I to the Act concerning the accession of the Republic of Croatia to the European Union, O.J. L 112, 24 April 2012, p. 35 and Council Decision 2014/899/EU of 13 December 2014, concerning the accession of Croatia to the Convention of 23 July 1990 on the elimination of double taxation in connection with the adjustment of the profits of associated enterprises, O.J. L 358, p. 19-24.

23 In this sense see Kokott, J., Pistone, P., Taxpayers in international law, cit., p. 224.

24 See Belgian Council of State (9th Court Chamber on Administrative Law), judgment of 2 June 2020, X v Belgium, case A.224.757/IX-9262, judgment no 247.694, (2020) 23 part 2 International Tax Law Reports.

25 Besides the Commentary, Article 25 OECD MC contains an annex, namely the Sample Mutual Agreement, which provides for detailed rules that parties may use as standard for the agreement on the functioning of the procedure.

The introduction of secondary law on the settlement of cross-border tax dispute had to wait almost three more decades, namely until when the EU Council of Ministers approved the EU Directive on Tax Dispute Resolution Mechanisms (hereinafter also: the EU Tax Arbitration Directive) on 10 October 2017.[26]

2017 marks two important developments for the settlement of cross-border tax disputes, since almost 70 States signed the BEPS Multilateral Instrument on 7 June 2017 (hereinafter: the BEPS MLI)[27] and the Ecofin Council of Ministers has approved the EU Tax Arbitration Directive on 10 October 2017,[28] which EU Member States were obliged to implement by 30 June 2019.

The 2017 EU Tax Arbitration Directive does not repeal the EU Tax Arbitration Convention, but supplements it in a way that produces some partial overlaps – namely for cross-border transfer pricing disputes – and thus increases the complexity in the options available to the affected taxpayer(s). In areas falling within the scope of the EU Arbitration Convention and Directive, associated enterprises are free to choose between the two legal instruments and bear the consequences arising in connection with their decision.

Further overlaps arise with the two main public international law instruments for settling cross-border tax disputes and will now be addressed in a way that also takes into account their respective legal basis.

Finally, both the EU Tax Arbitration Convention and the EU Tax Arbitration Directive ceased to have their effects in the United Kingdom from 1 January 2021 as a consequence of the Withdrawal Act.[29]

21.3 Legal basis

The legal basis of the four main instruments for settling cross-border tax disputes varies in line with their respective function, object and purpose.

Two of them are pure instruments of public international law, namely the ones regulated by Article 25 of double taxation conventions following the OECD MC and the BEPS MLI.

26 Directive EU 2017/1852 of 10 October 2017 on tax dispute resolution mechanisms in the European Union, in OJ L 265, 14 October 2017, pp. 1-14.

27 The BEPS Multilateral Instrument supplements the functioning of double tax conventions by aligning their content and interpretation with a commonly agreed framework. In particular, Part V of the BEPS MLI forms part of its minimum content and includes two clauses (Articles 16 and 17) on improving dispute resolutions in the framework of administrative procedures. Furthermore, Part VI (which has an optional nature) contains several provisions that enhance the functioning of arbitration in double taxation conventions as a tool for settling cross-border tax disputes.

28 In particular, the Council has approved the final version of the document submitted on 2 October 2017, 9806/17 FISC 118 ECOFIN 472, interinstitutional file 2016/0338 CNS.

29 This means that, from that date onwards, no new MAP claims were accepted in the United Kingdom under either legal instrument.

The remaining two are only applicable to the settlement of cross-border tax disputes within the internal market. These instruments are the EU Tax Arbitration Convention and the 2017 EU Tax Arbitration Directive.

In particular, the legal basis of the two instruments of public international law is the double taxation convention that enshrines the two-tier procedures for the settlement of disputes on the interpretation and application of its clauses, as supplemented by the BEPS MLI, to the extent that the latter applies to the relations between the States involved in a given dispute.[30]

The EU Tax Arbitration Convention and Directive have a different legal basis.

The EU Tax Arbitration Convention is a multilateral convention signed by all EU Member States, whose original legal basis is in a provision of the EC Treaty – namely Article 220 (then 293) – lacking a direct effect[31] and no longer included in the TFEU. It represents the most important form of tax coordination within the European Union by means of an instrument of ordinary public international law, for which EU Member States did not need any actual EU law basis. It is, in fact, a *sui generis* legal status, which raises complex interpretation issues from the perspective of European Union law.

On the one hand, the EU Tax Arbitration Convention is not part of European Union law and therefore it neither confers jurisdiction upon the CJEU to interpret its provisions,[32] nor permits the Commission to initiate infringement procedures against a Member State's failure to comply with the Convention obligations or may otherwise be relevant for the EU Charter of Fundamental Rights.

On the other hand, it forms part of the *acquis* of the Union. Therefore, all its Contracting States are Member States of the European Union,[33] bound to loyally apply the Convention[34] under the principle of sincere cooperation (Article 4 TEU). As long as they remain Member

30 Article 26 BEPS MLI contains compatibility clauses, which bring together the multilateral instruments with the covered tax agreements.

31 In the Case C-336/96, *Gilly*, points 15-17, EU:C:1998:221 the CJEU held that Article 220 EC Treaty lacked a direct effect and merely defines a number of matters on which the Member States are to enter into negotiations with each other so far as is necessary. In our view, insofar as EU law conferred no right with direct effect based on such provision, also its removal from primary law of the European Union should have no consequences (see also Section 16.3.1).

32 We do not exclude that the Court might be competent to answer preliminary questions of a national civil court called upon by a taxpayer suing its Member State for wrongfully frustrating effective application of the Arbitration Convention. By contrast, it seems unlikely that the advisory commission may refer a case to the CJEU in the framework of a preliminary ruling procedure, since it should lack the independence required by European Union law to regard such body as exercising the judicial function.

33 Accordingly, its Contracting States must be Member States of the European Union.

34 This attitude is confirmed by the position taken by EU Member States in connection with the application of the OECD MC. In particular, OECD, Commentary on Article 25, para. 67 indicates that States, which are member of the European Union *must* coordinate the scope of paragraph 5 with their obligations under other legal instruments applicable to them.

States of the European Union, they may not unilaterally terminate their obligations connected with it.[35]

Unlike a Directive or a Regulation under Union law, a multilateral Convention under ordinary international public law does not have of itself direct effect in the national jurisdictions, nor priority over national law.[36] Furthermore, Article 15 EU Tax Arbitration Convention expressly indicates that the Convention does not prevent the fulfilment of wider obligations arising from existing and future conventions with respect of the elimination of double taxation.[37]

The legal basis of the EU Arbitration Directive is Article 115 TFEU. Therefore, its clauses with direct effect are expressions of secondary European Union law. The Directive was introduced by the Council, acting unanimously, after consulting the European Parliament and the Economic and Social Committee, in order to approximate national legislation on the settlement of cross-border disputes concerning the interpretation and application of double taxation conventions, as directly affects the establishment and functioning of the internal market.

The introduction of the Directive enhances the effective protection of rights in the framework of such disputes within the internal market, bringing it in line with the principles of European Union law, as enshrined in the EU Charter of Fundamental Rights, and under the judicial scrutiny and interpretation of the CJEU.[38]

21.4 The relations between the legal instruments

Although the EU Tax Arbitration Directive is secondary law of the European Union, it does not imply a complete shift of powers from EU Member States to the European Union, or establish an actual legal hierarchy among the four legal instruments that operate in this field within their respective scope. It neither prevents the application of the EU Tax

35 The Withdrawal Agreement of the United Kingdom from the European Union has allowed for the continuation of the application of the EU tax dispute settlement directive and of the EU Tax Arbitration Convention until the end of the transitional period. Consequently, mutual agreement procedures claims were no longer accepted under either instrument as of 1 January 2021.

36 Such direct effect and priority only exist if national constitutional law of the Member State(s) involved recognizes the possibility of self-executing provisions of international public law and the primacy of such international public law provisions over national law. Therefore, unlike the effectiveness of an EU Directive, the effectiveness of the Convention largely depends on national constitutional law.

37 Article 26 (3) BEPS MLI presents a largely similar wording, thus confirming that different legal instruments may provide the taxpayer with different legal tools for resolving cross-border tax disputes. Furthermore, OECD, Commentary on Article 25, para. 67 suggests that EU Member States include an additional paragraph in their double taxation convention in order to safeguard the wider obligation resulting from any other legal instrument applicable to the State in respect of unresolved issues.

38 In this sense also see Kokott, J., Pistone, P., Taxpayers in international law, cit., p. 62.

Arbitration Convention, which is an expression of the *acquis* of the Union, nor of the other tax[39] and non-tax instruments for settling cross-border tax disputes.[40]

In our view, this is due to the intention to preserve a wide range of solutions among which the affected taxpayer can choose the legal instrument that pursues the settlement of a given cross-border tax dispute.

Such differences affect taxpayers in connection with their decision to choose the applicable legal instrument for settling the cross-border tax dispute.

Although all such legal instruments allow for a settlement of cross-border tax disputes, only the EU Arbitration Directive gives the affected person(s) an actual legal remedy against all States involved in the cross-border tax dispute. This is because only the EU Arbitration Directive brings the protection of the rights and obligations of the affected person(s) within its scope and such protection is secured under the jurisdiction of the CJEU in line with the standards established by supranational law.

Yet there would be reasons to opt for the EU Tax Arbitration Convention. Its rules make it a more suitable instrument to pursue cross-border tax dispute settlement on technical matters falling within its scope, especially considering that it contains specific rules that conform to arm's length dealing and separate accounting,[41] and allow for mandatory arbitration without infringing the existing tax treaty obligations between EU Member States.

Since such instruments operate upon initiative of the affected person(s), such person(s) will therefore decide which one of them will govern the settlement of the cross-border tax disputes. All those instruments share the bulk of a two-tier procedure, the first of

39 Besides the combination of mutual agreement procedures with arbitration under Article 25 (5) OECD MC or part VI of the BEPS MLI, further bilateral tax treaties apply other types of arbitration clauses. The Austria-Germany double taxation convention allows for arbitration before the CJEU under Article 273 TFEU, thus in fact recognising the CJEU's jurisdiction over the interpretation and application of a double taxation convention that largely mirrors the OECD MC. In such legal framework, the CJEU (see Case C-648/15, *Austria vs. Germany*, EU:C:2017:664) has recently interpreted the dividend clause of such convention (Article 11) for aspects not reflecting the wording of the corresponding clause contained OECD MC. In this case, the CJEU concluded that the concept of debt-claims with participation of profits excluded from such provision certificates remunerated annually along a fixed percentage of their nominal value. Interestingly, both countries have accepted Part VI of the BEPS MLI, which in our view may imply the overriding of this clause.

40 Such as for instance the arbitration clauses, contained in bilateral investment treaties that do not carve out tax disputes from their scope.

41 Yet, the Convention does not specify to which arm's length method it adheres.

which has an administrative nature[42] and the second one a quasi-judicial one.[43] As for the first tier, insofar as the competent tax authorities cannot find a unilateral solution to the question in dispute, the procedure allows them to establish a dialogue in order to find a solution by mutual agreement. If that is not possible, the second tier makes the procedure evolve into a *sui generis* form of arbitration (or, in the case of the EU Arbitration Directive, also into the alternative dispute resolution mechanism), which supplements the administrative procedure and whose solution begets binding value unless competent authorities otherwise reach an agreement.[44]

The functioning of tax dispute settlement in connection with the mechanism of arbitration may raise critical issues of compatibility with EU law insofar as one considers that such issues could not be referred to the Court of Justice by the arbitration panel, which obviously lacks the typical features of a tribunal,[45]

Three further questions require analysis in connection with the two procedures, namely as to (i) whether the affected person(s) must identify the legal instrument at time of filing the complaint, (ii) whether a switch of legal instruments is possible during the procedure that settles the cross-border tax dispute, and (iii) whether the affected person(s) may simultaneously file several complaints under various legal instruments in respect of one and the same cross-border tax dispute.

The answer to the first question is that, for reasons of legal certainty, the affected person(s) must clearly identify the procedure to be used for settling the cross-border dispute. The need for adding this condition to the ones expressly indicated by the four legal instruments are simple. Since the starting phase of the procedure is in the hands of the affected person(s), the absence of such indication would undermine the compliance by tax authorities with the different requirements established by each of the legal instruments for settling the cross-border tax dispute.

Critical issues may arise when the affected person(s) do(es) not clearly identify such procedure or requests a procedure whose scope does not cover the scope of the cross-border tax dispute. In either case, good practice should be that tax authorities do not merely

42 As such, it may not depart from the principles that apply in any EU Member State to all administrative procedures in taxation matters. Moreover, insofar as there is a valid link with EU law, such as in the case of the EU Dispute Settlement Directive, the functioning of this procedure must comply with the standards of protection of taxpayers' rights that operate in the European Union.

43 Vandenberghe, L., The Limits to Arbitration Posed by the Natural Judge Theory (Due Process of Law) and Cross-Border Tax Disputes in Pistone, P. (ed.), Tax Procedures, IBFD Publications, 2020, p. 209 has pointed out that the non-final nature of the tax arbitration procedure and its structural features prevent such procedure from being equated to a judicial one and rather approximate it to those of an administrative procedure.

44 See OECD, Commentary on Article 25, para. 64.

45 In CJEU, 6 March 2018, C-264/16, Achmea, EU:C:2018:158, the Court of Justice has indicated that ad hoc arbitration panels are not compatible with EU law insofar as they lack a mechanism for activating the jurisdiction of the Court and thus prevent the correct interpretation and application of relevant EU law. In particular in connection with the EU Dispute Settlement Directive this might be particularly problematic.

regard the complaint as inadmissible, but rather become proactive in requesting the clarification or correction of the complaint, or the specification of the procedure under which the taxpayer has filed the complaint.[46]

However, in the case of the EU Tax Arbitration Directive, this conclusion can actually be derived from the wording of Article 3, which does not include such cases among those in which tax authorities may reject a complaint, and of Article 5. Furthermore, there may be situations in which tax authorities may have absolute certainty as to the legal instrument that should regulate a given cross-border tax dispute, since only one is applicable. This can occur in a transfer-pricing dispute between two EU Member States that have not yet concluded a double taxation convention.[47]

The second question raises issues that are more complex to address.

Preliminarily, we should exclude that tax authorities may switch, during the procedure, the legal instrument according to which the cross-border tax dispute is settled, since it is clear from the context that it is the affected taxpayer who has the ultimate power of making such selection.[48]

Seen from the perspective of whether the affected person(s) may do so, one may *prima facie* consider that there is no express prohibition in this respect. Furthermore, it could also be argued, that a shift towards the EU Tax Arbitration Directive should be accepted, since the settlement of a cross-border tax dispute under such legal instrument would increase the protection of rights secured to the affected person(s).

Yet, for various reasons we submit that any switch is hardly possible.

The procedure and legal implications under the four legal instruments are similar, but not identical. For instance, the EU Tax Arbitration Directive has a set of notification requirements that do not exist under other legal instruments and its remedies against possible violations are different from those applicable elsewhere. Therefore, a settlement of the dispute under the EU Tax Arbitration Directive requires compliance with such rule from the beginning to the end of the procedure. Furthermore, the participation of the affected person(s) is possible under the EU Tax Arbitration Directive, but not under the other instruments and significant differences also exist as to the rules for the establishment of the advisory commission when the States involved cannot reach an agreement.

46 Insofar as the taxpayer, not even after being prompted to do so by tax authorities, refuses to specify the procedure under which the complaint was filed, one could theoretically assume that the application of the EU Tax Arbitration Directive could be presumed within the European Union. This conclusion would secure the highest level of protection of the affected persons and still secure an effective tool for settling the cross-border tax dispute. However, it seems rather hard to derive such conclusion at the level of interpretation in the absence of a specific indication in this sense.

47 See further in section 21.5.3.

48 Yet, Article 25 (3) OECD MC would allow them to consult together for the elimination of double taxation, also in cases not provided for in the Convention. One can therefore not exclude a parallel running of one or more procedures initiated by the affected person(s) and of a similar or broader interpretative mutual agreement procedure initiated by the competent authorities.

Furthermore, any switch from one to the other legal instrument during the procedure may alter the effectiveness of legal protection and certainty in the applicable rules. This implies that when affected person(s) realise that the procedure initiated under the EU Tax Arbitration Convention or Article 25 OECD MC has reached stalemate, such persons may not request tax authorities to comply with the rights indicated under the EU Tax Arbitration Directive.

Likewise, if the affected person(s) starts the procedure under the EU Tax Arbitration Directive and intends to question the mutual agreement reached by tax authorities for not removing double taxation, such person(s) should not be allowed to invoke a continuation of the procedure under the EU Tax Arbitration Convention. Considering the duration of such procedures, we find it hard to imagine that the affected person(s), not accepting a given mutual agreement, would still be in time to file a second complaint for the same tax year and factual pattern, except insofar as such person(s) can prove that it was the mutual agreement itself to generate the problem.[49]

However, the conclusion needs not necessarily to be the same – and here we address the third question indicated earlier – if the affected person(s) may decide to file simultaneous or consecutive complaints under the same or various legal instruments in respect of the same cross-border tax dispute.

The BEPS MLI and the EU Arbitration Directive require filing the same complaint before the competent authorities of the States involved. Therefore, any parallel running of the same dispute is an intended feature of the unilateral phase within each legal instrument.[50]

The situation is different when the affected person(s) file(s) various complaints under various legal instruments in the same or different State(s). In principle, the four legal instruments include specific rules regulating the relations with domestic remedies, but do not exclude the filing of more complaints in the framework of international tax and non-tax procedures.

Despite the absence of a prohibition, we find it odd to justify an obligation for tax authorities to address the same factual pattern several times in the framework of different legal instruments for exactly the same purpose, namely of settling the same cross-border tax disputes. Besides, this situation can potentially generate mismatching solutions that undermine the correct functioning of such procedures. For such reasons, competent authorities should use their discretionary powers under the EU Tax Arbitration Convention, Article 25 OECD MC and the BEPS MLI to reject all but one complaints once they realise that the cross-border tax disputes in fact share the same legal and factual pattern and affect the same person(s). Since the three instruments contain no specific limitations as to how tax authorities should exercise such discretionary powers, one may not exclude

49 This could for instance be the case when the mutual agreement solves a problem of interpretation of the double taxation convention, but generates a new one.

50 Therefore, when the same situation occurs under Article 25 OECD MC and the EU Tax Arbitration Convention, there should be no problem even if taxpayers were not obliged to file two parallel complaints before the competent authorities of the States involved.

that tax authorities in such circumstances may freely decide according to which legal instrument the cross-border tax dispute may be settled.

The situation is more complex under the EU Tax Arbitration Directive, which does not include the parallel running of cross-border tax dispute settlement under various international legal instruments among the reasons for tax authorities to reject the complaint. In such circumstances, since tax authorities may request under Article 3 (3) (f) the affected person(s) to provide additional information, they could also request to indicate which procedure should govern the settling of the tax dispute. Our view is that, even if not specifically required under the other instruments, it constitutes good practice that tax authorities could follow under the other legal instruments also in cases not involving the settlement under the EU Tax Arbitration Directive. Among others, this would also prevent possible situations in which the affected person(s) rejects the implementation of the mutual agreement at the end of the procedure.[51]

21.5 Scope

21.5.1 General issues

The scope of the four legal instruments for settling cross-border tax disputes differs as to the personal entitlement (personal scope) to activate the procedure, the types of cross-border tax disputes (substantive scope) that can be settled, the taxes covered (objective scope) and the territorial issues (territorial scope).

Therefore, although all instruments share the two-tier procedure for settling cross-border tax disputes and make the access to the mutual agreement procedure subject to the initiative of the taxpayer, the various options are not equivalent.

Settling the dispute through the EU Tax Arbitration Directive brings the rights of the affected persons, i.e. the taxpayer(s), to a position of direct relevance within the cross-border tax dispute, which Article 1 explicitly acknowledges as part of the subject matter of the Directive, together with the solution to the dispute between the States involved. This may have several important implications for the affected persons, which range from a right of obtaining numerous notifications during the procedure to that of providing, throughout the entire procedure, information, evidence or documents that may be relevant for the decision. Furthermore, the Directive, on the one hand, opens up the enforcement through EU law instruments with the interpretative jurisdiction of the CJEU, even if, on the other hand, it may add one extra year of duration to the two-year term already set for the mutual agreement procedure by Article 7 of the EU Tax Arbitration Convention.

51 Under Article 25 (5) third sentence OECD MC, Article 19 (4) (b) (i) BEPS MLI, Article 15 (4) EU Arbitration Directive, the affected person(s) has/have no obligation to implement the agreement reached in the framework of arbitration. The EU Arbitration Convention does not specifically regulate such issue. However, it would be hard to believe that the procedure could automatically bind the affected person(s) without such right.

The experience with the EU Tax Arbitration Convention also shows that the time required for completing the arbitration procedure may in fact be much longer than that obtaining by summing up the maximum duration admissible for each of its phases. This is often due to problems concerning the appointment of arbitrators or other related situations in which the two States involved present different views.

Unlike all other instruments, the EU Tax Arbitration Convention specifically pursues the elimination of double taxation, which requires Contracting States to achieve this goal effectively. As indicated by Article 14 EU Tax Arbitration Convention, this occurs when the profits are either included in the computations of taxable profits in one state only, or addressed by means of a corresponding adjustment in the other State.

The formulation of the EU Tax Arbitration Directive is not so explicit about this goal, though still sets an obligation to resolve the question in dispute. By contrast, neither Article 25 OECD MC, nor the settlement of cross-border tax disputes under the BEPS MLI provide any guarantee of elimination of taxation not in accordance with the convention.

21.5.2 Personal scope

The entitlement to the two-tier procedure for the settlement of tax treaty disputes varies according to the applicable legal instrument.

Article 25 OECD Model, Articles 16 and 19 BEPS MLI and Article 1 EU Tax Arbitration Directive in fact come very close to sharing a common subjective entitlement to the procedure for settling the disputes.

In particular, the two public international law instruments define the subjective entitlement by reference to an interest in activating the procedure for having tax authorities addressing the problem of interpretation and application of the double taxation convention that affects a given person.

The 2017 Update to the OECD Model has removed the obligation to file the complaint in the State of residence (or, of nationality, for the cases falling under the scope of Article 24 (1) OECD MC). In such context, one may wonder whether the entitlement to activate the mutual agreement applies regardless of whether the person enjoys the personal entitlement to the benefits of a double taxation convention. The affirmative solution seems compatible with the current wording and context of such provision, as well as with that of Article 16 (1) BEPS MLI, which also does not contain any further specification in this respect.

The EU Tax Arbitration Directive defines the personal scope in a more precise way. Article 1 of the Directive links up the personal scope to the “affected persons” by a dispute, which Article 2 (1) (d) considers to be “any person, including an individual, that is a resident of a Member State for tax purposes, and whose taxation is directly affected by a question in dispute”. In such context, the EU Tax Arbitration Directive establishes in fact two conditions, namely (i) the residence in an EU Member State for tax purposes and (ii) the direct effect of the dispute on the taxation of such person, which can narrow down the personal scope as compared to what could otherwise apply under either international law instrument.

If one compares the personal scope of the EU Tax Arbitration Directive with that of the EU Tax Arbitration Convention, further differences arise.

The EU Tax Arbitration Convention restricts the personal entitlement to the enterprises of a Contracting State, thus excluding any other type of person from its scope. The term 'enterprise of a Contracting State' is not defined in the Convention, but it probably covers any company and any more or less permanent independent commercial activity carried on by a resident of a Contracting State for a profit (a business). Incorporation is not required. In line with Article 1 (2) EU Tax Arbitration Convention, the personal scope expressly covers a branch (permanent establishment) of an enterprise of one Member State in another Member State,[52] which in our view would not be entitled to the benefits of the EU Tax Arbitration Directive. Therefore, adjustments of transfer prices between head office and branch within one transnational enterprise certainly fall within the scope of the Convention, but it is doubtful whether they also do so under the Directive.

Furthermore, the EU Tax Arbitration Convention requires the involvement of associated enterprises, which its Article 4 defines along a similar wording to that contained in Article 9 OECD MC[53] and therefore in a way that resembles the personal scope of Article 17 BEPS MLI in respect of the application of the cross-border dispute settlement to corresponding adjustments.

21.5.3 Substantive scope

Differences can also be recorded across the types of cross-border tax disputes that can be arbitrated, which is the so-called substantive scope. In particular, the substantive scope of the EU Tax Arbitration Convention is, for some aspects, broader and, for others, narrower than that of all other instruments.

On the one hand, the EU Tax Arbitration Convention only covers cross-border tax disputes involving transfer-pricing adjustments between associated enterprises that arise when the profits of an enterprise of a Contracting State are also included in those of an associated enterprise of another Contracting State on the grounds of non-observation

52 In a joint declaration annexed to the Convention, the Contracting States agree that Article 4(1) also applies to transactions between an enterprise in one State and the branch in another State of an associated enterprise 'in a third country'. From the French text ('*dans un troisième État contractant*') it is clear this 'third country' is a third EU Member State, and not a non-EU Member State.

53 In particular, the criteria are direct or indirect participation by an enterprise of one Member State in the management, control or capital of an enterprise in another Member State (vertical affiliation), and direct or indirect participation by the same persons in the management, control or capital of an enterprise of one State and an enterprise of another State (horizontal affiliation).

of the arm's length principle.[54] For this reason, double taxation resulting from causes other than arm's length profit adjustments are in principle not covered by the EU Tax Arbitration Convention.[55]

On the other hand, the EU Tax Arbitration Convention includes within its scope disputes that do not involve double taxation conventions and those which arise in the absence of a double taxation convention.[56]

By contrast, Article 1 EU Arbitration Directive, Article 25 OECD MC and Parts V and VI of the BEPS MLI only cover disputes concerning the interpretation and application of double taxation conventions. The actual narrower boundaries of such instruments as compared to that of the EU Tax Arbitration Convention can also be perceived in the light of their objective scope.

21.5.4 Objective scope

The objective scope of the four legal instruments concerns the taxes that can be the object of the cross-border dispute settlement.

In particular, Article 1 EU Arbitration Directive, Article 25 OECD MC and Parts V and VI of the BEPS MLI only cover the settlement of tax treaty disputes connected with the elimination of double taxation of income and capital. By contrast, in line with the requirements indicated in Article 2, the EU Tax Arbitration Convention only applies to those taxes on income that are specifically indicated in Article 2 (2). The list contained in Article 2 (2) includes taxes on personal and corporate income by EU Member States, but also some additional types of taxes, such as business[57] and local taxes.[58]

Consequently, the EU Tax Arbitration Directive fully overlaps with the scope of the cross-border dispute settlement mechanisms provided by Article 25 OECD MC and the BEPS MLI, as well as partly with the EU Tax Arbitration Convention.

---

54 See Article 1 EU Tax Arbitration Convention. Furthermore, Article 1(3) ensures that the rules of the Convention also apply if, due to losses suffered by one or both of the associated enterprises (or by the branch or its head office), the disputed price adjustment has no current tax effect (but reduces future loss relief). Consequently, the Contracting States may not stall proceedings until the dispute produces current financial effects for the enterprises or branches involved. Likewise, the level of effective taxation is irrelevant: if an associated enterprise in State A enjoys a preferential tax treatment, Contracting State B may not challenge the applicability of the Convention for lack of benchmark taxation in State A.

55 Accordingly, the Convention offers no remedy for international double taxation as a result of mismatches between Member States in income classification, as a result of reclassification of income or costs by a national tax administration (e.g., a loan between a parent company and a subsidiary company may be reclassified as equity, and deduction of interest may be denied or reclassified as dividend if it is apparent that the subsidiary will never repay it), or as a result of disparities between Member States' profit determination rules.

56 As of 1.1.2025, only one bilateral relation within the European Union is not covered by a tax treaty, namely between Denmark and Spain, after Denmark terminated the old treaty.

57 As in the case of Germany, Italy and Luxembourg.

58 As in the case of Denmark, Finland, Italy, Portugal, Sweden.

Compared to this abundance of options for settling cross-border tax disputes within the internal market,[59] others entirely lack an effective settlement mechanism. This is particularly problematic and requires urgent attention for tax disputes in areas with limited or no harmonization, such as the ones concerning taxes on inheritances and gifts,[60] in order to overcome the existing problems of interpretation and application arising in such context. Such problems grow even further due to the existing disparities, not always addressed by the limited tax treaties existing in such context.[61] However, problems of cross-border double taxation with a potential impact on the Internal Market may also arise in the presence of harmonization, including VAT.[62] For this reason, a possible future extension of the EU Tax Arbitration Directive beyond its current boundaries may be advisable.

21.5.5 Territorial scope

The territorial scope varies according to the applicable legal instrument.

In particular, whilst the EU Tax Arbitration Directive applies within the European Union without exceptions, the EU Tax Arbitration Convention applies to its Contracting States, subject to the exceptions indicated by Article 16, namely the French Overseas Territories, the Faroe Islands and Greenland.

Also under the double taxation conventions following the OECD MC, the territorial scope is limited to the cross-border tax treaty disputes involving the two Contracting States. Their interaction with the BEPS MLI should take into account that the BEPS MLI does not automatically apply to all tax treaty disputes of those Contracting States, but also depends on whether such countries have included a reservation on its application and, in the case of arbitration, whether they have opted for being bound by it.[63]

21.5.6 Additional interpretative issues

The scope of the EU Arbitration Directive raises additional relevant interpretative issues.

59 In cases falling under the scope of the EU Arbitration Convention and involving the interpretation and application of tax treaties, the affected person can choose from up to four legal instruments for having the cross-border tax disputes settled.

60 The Expert Group Report on "Ways to tackle inheritance cross-border tax obstacles facing individuals within the EU", released by the EU Commission on 3 March 2016 (Publications Office of the European Union, Luxembourg, 2015) has stressed the importance of finding effective ways to address such problems, reiterating the conclusions of the Commission Recommendation regarding relief for double taxation of inheritance (2011/856/EU, published on 20 December 2011 in OJ L 366, p. 81).

61 See for instance the types of issues caused by the existence of disparities in Case C-67/08, *Block*, EU:C:2009:92.

62 A good example of this problem is the double taxation arising from the exercise of taxing jurisdiction by Hungary and Portugal on digital services in Case C-419/14, *WebMindLicences*. EU:C:2015:832.

63 See further on this the tables contained in Pit, H.M., Arbitration under the OECD Multilateral Instrument: Reservations, Options and Choices, in 71 Bulletin for International Taxation, cit., pp. 574, 578, 586 and 589-591.

A first issue arises in Article 1, as to the use of the expression "agreements", which precedes the reference to "conventions that provide for the elimination of double taxation...". In such context, one may wonder about the need for using the former expression, when the latter one already contains a clear reference to double tax conventions.

The literal interpretation of the two expressions in such context may lead to conclude that the reference to the elimination of double taxation applies to the conventions, but not to the agreements, or to the opposite result that it applies to both.

The former interpretation would notably broaden the scope of the Directive, allowing its use to arbitrate also disputes arising from the interpretation and application of public international law instruments others than the actual double taxation conventions. However, this consequence would be hard to reconcile with the object and purpose as resulting from its preamble. By contrast, it would perhaps be easier to justify the use of the EU Tax Arbitration Directive for the purpose of questioning the agreements reached by tax authorities in connection with interpretative mutual agreement procedures under Article 25 (3) OECD MC. Furthermore, still in line with this interpretation, one could argue that the EU Directive may have intended to refer to international agreements on income and capital other than the double taxation conventions, such as the Tax Information Exchange Agreements (TIEAs). Also, it could refer to the combination of the BEPS multilateral instrument as additional agreement applicable in combination with the double taxation conventions. Furthermore, from the perspective of literal interpretation, it would also be correct to hold that the reference to double taxation conventions already automatically absorbs the BEPS MLI, since the latter instruments flanks the interpretation and application of double taxation conventions at all times when the EU Contracting States have adopted it.

Insofar as one interprets the reference to the agreements as linked with the elimination of double taxation of income and capital, it could cover other public international law conventions applicable in the relations with the dependencies and territories of some Member States.[64]

Another more intricate interpretative issue concerns whether the EU Tax Arbitration Directive itself may settle problems of double taxation arising from the interpretation and application of the EU Tax Arbitration Convention. Such issue is separate from the one concerning the possibility of applying more than one legal instrument for settling cross-border tax disputes on income and capital. It involves whether an EU law instrument

64 In principle, this could be the case of the clauses on the elimination of double taxation in Article 4 of the agreements concluded by the Kingdom of the Netherlands in respect of Aruba with Sweden, or of the Netherlands Antilles with Denmark, Finland and Sweden on the promotion of economic activities. By contrast, the absence of a dispute between States (which constitutes an explicit requirement under Article 1) would prevent this interpretation from bringing under the scope of the Directive also the disputes arising on the interpretation of rules applicable in cross-border tax relations between a Member State and its dependency or overseas territory. The latter situation occurs for instance in the *regeling* of the Netherlands with Aruba and the BES islands, or the *conventions* of France with the French Polynesia, St. Martin and St. Pierre and Miquelon.

can intervene in the interpretation of an instrument, which forms part of the *acquis* of the Union, but in respect of which Member States have not agreed to have supranational law of the European Union, subject to the jurisdiction of the CJEU.

In principle, there is no doubt that the questions falling within the scope of the EU Tax Arbitration Convention are cross-border and on income, since the scope of the Convention relates to transfer pricing disputes that raise issues of economic double taxation on income between related enterprises. Such disputes occur when taxes are levied on income in a way that the profits of an associated enterprise (or permanent establishment) of a Contracting State are "included or likely to be included" in those of an associated enterprise (or permanent establishment) of another Contracting State, due to an adjustment geared at re-establishing the conditions applicable between independent enterprises.

Furthermore, the object and purpose of the EU Tax Arbitration Convention is to provide for the elimination of double taxation on income in respect of matters that fall within its scope, as confirmed by Article 14 of the Convention, which indicates the actual elimination of double taxation as the final point of the procedure.

In such circumstances, even if the EU Tax Arbitration Convention itself is an instrument for settling cross-border tax disputes, there may be problems that concern its interpretation and application that can block the effective functioning of its mechanisms and that can turn themselves into the source of an unsolved dispute between EU Member States.

Accordingly, the view may be held that, provided that the taxpayer is still in time to seek for protection under the EU Tax Arbitration Directive, in circumstances where the EU Tax Arbitration Convention is unable to reach a solution that eliminates double taxation. Insofar as one agrees with this view, in such circumstances, the case may also be given that the EU Tax Directive applies a dispute between two EU Member State that have not concluded a double taxation convention.

However, one may argue that the implications of this interpretation would be quite far-reaching, since it may indirectly lead to bring under the jurisdiction of the CJEU cross-border tax disputes that were initially to be arbitrated within the framework of the EU Tax Arbitration Convention.

We cannot entirely share this criticism. Just like it may occur when the EU Tax Arbitration Directive applies to cross-border double taxation arising from double taxation conventions on income and capital concluded by EU Member States, the CJEU does not actually interpret the EU Tax Arbitration Convention, but only those matters that are connected with the EU Tax Arbitration Directive.

Yet, if Member States do not implement the arbitration reached under the Convention and the taxpayer uses the EU Tax Arbitration Directive – under the scrutiny of the CJEU – for enforcement purposes, the issue would be whether this comes in line with the object and purpose of the Convention, which was not to arbitrate such dispute under a European law instrument.

21.6 The procedures

21.6.1 The mutual agreement procedure

21.6.1.1 General issues

In all the four legal instruments, arbitration operates as an extension of the mutual agreement procedure. For this reason, arbitration in cross-border tax disputes may only start after expiration of an initial period, during which tax authorities have the power of reaching common ground on the interpretation and application of the tax treaty in the framework of a mutual agreement procedure.[65]

Besides this common feature, significant differences exist as to the rights and obligations arising in connection with the affected person(s) during the mutual agreement procedure(s).

In particular, Article 25 OECD MC and Article 16 BEPS MLI regulate mutual agreement procedures as a matter between the two contracting States. This has various implications. The affected person(s) remain(s) to the side of such procedures, profiting from any solution reached in the framework of mutual agreement mainly in connection with an act of good tax governance, rather than as a consequence of an actual legal remedy. Furthermore, both instruments admit that mutual agreement procedures start through a complaint by the affected person(s), but also by initiative of tax authorities, which want to consult on problems concerning the interpretation and application of the convention, as well as on issues of double taxation not provided for in the Convention.[66]

By contrast, the EU Arbitration Convention and Directive conceive mutual agreement procedure as an instrument to address the actual cross-border tax dispute affecting one or more person(s) within the internal market. In such context, the mutual agreement procedure therefore constitutes the preliminary phase of a legal remedy for the affected person, on top of being a tool for good tax governance and a solution to a public international law dispute between States.

This has three main consequences. First, under the EU Arbitration Convention and Directive, mutual agreement procedures may only start upon initiative of the affected person(s). Second, the scope of such procedures is limited to the cases explicitly falling within the scope of the EU Arbitration Convention and, in the case of the EU Arbitration Directive, to the actual disputes involving the interpretation and application of a double taxation convention. Third, and most importantly, the EU Arbitration Convention, and,

65 See Article 7 (1) EU Arbitration Convention, Article 4 (1) EU Arbitration Directive, Article 25 (5) (b) OECD MC and Article 19 (1) (b) MLI.

66 See Article 25 (3), second sentence OECD MC and Article 16 (3), second sentence BEPS MLI. However, these forms of mutual agreement procedures do not involve the taxpayer and therefore may not evolve into arbitration.

even more, the EU Arbitration Directive establish actual rights and obligations for the affected person(s) throughout the mutual agreement procedure.[67]

We shall now more closely examine the functioning of mutual agreement procedures in all the four legal instruments and determine their implications for the access to arbitration and impact on the settlement of cross-border tax disputes.

Our analysis focuses on the four phases,[68] namely (i) the access to the mutual agreement procedure, (ii) the unilateral phase, (iii) the consultation phase and (iv) the final phase.

21.6.1.2 Access to the mutual agreement procedure

Article 25 OECD MC and Article 16 BEPS MLI allow mutual agreement procedures to start upon initiative of the affected person(s),[69] or of tax authorities.[70] By contrast, only the former option applies under Article 6 (1) EU Tax Arbitration Convention and Article 3 EU Tax Arbitration Directive.

In particular, under Article 25 (1) OECD MC as it stood until the 2017 update, the affected person(s) may file the complaint before the competent authority of the State of residence (or, in the case of discrimination falling under the scope of Article 24 (1), of nationality). The 2017 Update brings the access to the mutual agreement procedure in line with the conditions applicable under all other legal instruments, namely Article 6 (1) EU Tax Arbitration Convention, Article 16 (1), first sentence BEPS MLI, Article 3 (1), third sentence EU Tax Arbitration Directive.

All such instruments admit filing of the complaint (or include equivalent notification mechanisms) before all competent authorities of the States involved.[71] This mechanism enhances the functioning of the mutual procedure, since all relevant stakeholders are promptly informed about the existence of the cross-border tax problem raised by the affected person(s) and can indirectly discourage tax authorities from covering undue delays of the procedure.

---

67 Furthermore, Article 4 EU Tax Arbitration Convention anticipates such rights and obligations to the time of the adjustment that causes economic international double taxation.

68 For tax treaties that do not include the right for the taxpayer to request the settlement by arbitration or in cases when the taxpayer does not exercise such right, mutual agreement procedures may reach stalemate in either of the first three phases.

69 See Article 25 (1) OECD MC and Article 16 (1) BEPS MLI.

70 See Article 25 (3), second sentence OECD MC and Article 16 (3) BEPS MLI.

71 Article 6 (1), first sentence EU Tax Arbitration Convention requires the filing of the complaint before one single tax authority, namely the one of the EU Member State of the enterprise or of the permanent establishment. However, Article 6 (1), third sentence EU Tax Arbitration Convention establishes compulsory notification mechanisms, which secure an equivalent result to the one applicable under the requirements established by the corresponding provisions of the BEPS MLI and the EU Tax Arbitration Directive.

Nevertheless, a special simplified regime applies under Article 17 of the EU Tax Arbitration Directive, which allows individuals and smaller undertakings[72] to file the complaint and liaise only with the competent authority of the EU Member State of residence.[73]

The affected person(s) must file the complaint within a time limit of three years from the moment of the action that generates or will result in a cross-border tax problem. Whilst the EU Arbitration Convention characterizes such problem as double taxation,[74] the other three instruments merely refer to taxation not in accordance with the convention.

Furthermore, the EU Tax Arbitration Directive presents a significantly more regulated content,[75] which includes the minimum standard and content for the complaint filed by the affected person(s), thus securing a more expeditious and effective functioning of the procedure.[76] Also, it excludes that more than one mutual agreement procedure or dispute resolution procedure simultaneously take place in respect of the same question in dispute. In such circumstances, Article 16 (5) EU Tax Arbitration Directive indicates that any previous procedure ends from the date of the receipt of the new complaint.

21.6.1.3 The unilateral phase

The starting point of the mutual agreement procedure is the unilateral phase, in which the competent authority of either State evaluates whether the complaint is well founded, without involving competent authorities of other State(s).

---

72 According to Article 17 (b) EU Tax Arbitration Directive smaller undertakings are not large undertakings and not forming part of a large group, as defined by Directive 2013/34/EU. Consequently, this regime applies to entities that Article 3 of the latter Directive defines as micro-undertakings, small undertakings, medium-size undertakings and to small and medium-sized groups of companies by reference to criteria connected with their balance sheet total, net turnover and average number of employees, also taking into account the higher thresholds that Member States may define.

73 In such case, the competent authority of the EU Member State of residence operates as *trait-d'union* with those of all other States involved and be responsible for all required notifications, which must take place within two months from receipt of the communications from the individual or smaller undertaking.

74 See Article 6 EU Tax Arbitration Convention. Furthermore, Article 14 EU Tax Arbitration Convention allows for an autonomous reconstruction of the meaning of double taxation when profits are computed in more than one State or when the tax chargeable on profits in one State is not reduced by an equal amount in another State.

75 The Code of Conduct has partly overcome in practice the excessive discretionary powers of competent authorities under the mutual agreement. For instance, it has indicated detailed rules for avoiding that mutual agreement can lead to unreasonable or excessive cost for the taxpayer requesting it. The procedure must be transparent for the taxpayer (rules on communication are provided), and the competent authorities must exchange position papers, adjustment justifying documents, and preferred solutions; everything within time limits. The Code of Conduct recommends application of the same detailed rules in mutual agreement procedures under bilateral tax treaties.

76 Accordingly, Article 3 (1) fourth sentence EU Tax Arbitration Directive requires the submission of the complaint in at least an official language of each Member State concerned or any other language accepted by such State.

Out of the four instruments, only the EU Tax Arbitration Directive contains specific rules on the exercise of powers by the competent authorities, which reflect the object and purpose of reconciling the goal of settling cross-border tax disputes with that of securing an effective protection of rights of the affected person (s).

Various provisions contained in Articles 3 and 5 EU Tax Arbitration Directive confirm this in the framework of the unilateral phase of the mutual agreement procedure.

Article 3 (5) EU Tax Arbitration Directive sets a time limit of six months from submission or completion of information for tax authorities to handle the complaint. Furthermore, Article 3 contains other provisions contained that pursue a smooth functioning of the procedure,[77] limit the exercise of discretionary powers by the competent authorities[78] and establish rights and obligations for the affected person (s), in line with the object and purpose of the Directive.[79]

Article 5 EU Tax Arbitration Directive establishes specific requirements that secure an effective protection of the rights of the affected persons during the unilateral phase of mutual agreement procedures. Any failure by tax authorities to meet any of such requirements constitutes a possible breach in the implementation of European Union law, as such entitling the affected person(s) to protection in line with EU law principles as enshrined in the EU Charter of Fundamental Rights.

Article 5 (1) EU Tax Arbitration Directive lists three specific reasons for rejecting the complaint and sets obligations of motivation and notification to the affected person in case of rejection.

The wording suggests that the list of Article 5 (1) EU Tax Arbitration Directive is exhaustive. Such reasons narrow down any possible room for discretionary powers, since they relate to (i) insufficient information in respect of the specific points indicated under Article 3, (ii) the absence of a question in dispute and (iii) the late filing of the complaint. In this context, the EU Tax Arbitration Directive strives to prevent possible stalemate of the

77 In particular, Article 3 (2) EU Tax Arbitration Directive obliges tax authorities within two months from the receipt of the complaint to inform each other on the language or languages that they intend to use within the procedure. Furthermore, Article 3 (4) EU Tax Arbitration Directive sets specific time limits for authorities to request additional information and the affected persons to supply them.

78 As indicated by Article 3 (3) (f) EU Tax Arbitration Directive, competent authorities may request the affected person(s) to supply additional specific information insofar as this is necessary for allowing substantive consideration of the case. However, under Article 3 (4) they may only do so within three months from the receipt of the complaint. Since the second sentence of Article 3 (4) allows for additional requests, we understand from the context of this provision that this should be possible in a more limited number of cases.

79 Accordingly, Article 3 (2) EU Tax Arbitration Directive obliges competent authorities to acknowledge receipt of the complaint to inform other competent authorities within two months from the submission of the complaint. Furthermore, Article 3 (3) EU Tax Arbitration Directive sets the minimum content of the complaint, which constitutes a preliminary condition for tax authorities to accept the complaint.

procedure in its unilateral phase by either having complaints accepted or submitted to the bi-(or multi-) lateral consultative phase.

Article 5 (2) EU Tax Arbitration Directive deems acceptance of the complaint when tax authorities do not take a decision within six months from start of the procedure and Article 5 (3) states the right of affected persons to appeal before a national court against the rejection of the complaint by the competent authorities. The latter clause is an important innovation also for those Member States whose domestic law already includes a legal remedy against rejection of such complaint, since it brings this matter within the scope of the Directive.

Consequently, the appeal under Article 5 (3) EU Tax Arbitration Directive constitutes the object of implementation of EU law, which may trigger the application of protection under the EU Charter of Fundamental Rights.

Furthermore, Article 3 EU Tax Arbitration Directive secures an effective protection against the rejection of the complaint, by allowing the affected persons either to refer the case to a national court, or to activate the advisory commission.[80]

Article 5 (3) EU Tax Arbitration Directive characterizes the relations with domestic legal remedies as alternative to arbitration. On the one hand, its letters (a) and (b) freeze the access to arbitration throughout the duration of domestic legal remedies; on the other hand, its letter (c) excludes such access when national procedures do not admit for re-opening of matters that have been the object of a final judicial decision. Furthermore, it is the only one out of the four legal instruments, which requires implementation in domestic law.

This partly differs from the one contained in the other legal instruments, none of which expressly allows for domestic legal remedies against the rejection of the complaint, thus giving tax authorities in fact *carte blanche* as to whether considering such complaint as justified and well-founded.[81] This may in fact result in stranding the procedure during its unilateral phase, or keeping it on hold for an indefinite period.

Further differences arise in connection with the parallel running of mutual agreement and domestic judicial procedures.

Under Article 6 (1) EU Tax Arbitration Convention (*ius de non evocando*), submitting a complaint does not bar recourse to domestic legal remedies. *Vice versa*, the non-use of domestic legal remedy (making the adjustment decision final for domestic appeal purposes) does not prevent recourse to the Arbitration Convention procedures.[82]

In such circumstances, Article 7 (2) EU Tax Arbitration Convention keeps the right to access arbitration, but Article 7 (3) – similarly to what Article 5 (3) (c) EU Tax Arbitration Directive

80 Article 6 (1) (a) EU Tax Arbitration Directive.

81 Yet, this would not prevent judicial review of action undertaken in the framework of a mutual agreement, if domestic law of a State allows for it.

82 Article 13 EU Tax Arbitration Convention.

does – excludes it when domestic law of a Contracting State does not allow tax authorities to derogate from such judicial decision. By contrast, Article 25 (5) second sentence OECD MC only excludes the access to arbitration in the presence of final decisions rendered by a court or an administrative tribunal of a Contracting State. Furthermore, Article 19 (2) BEPS MLI allows tax authorities to suspend the mutual agreement procedure because a case is pending on the same issues before a national court or administrative tribunal and Article 19 (12) BEPS MLI admits the right of the Parties to bar access to arbitration in the presence of a court or administrative decision.

21.6.1.4 The consultation phase

The consultation phase gives tax authorities the opportunity to reach an agreement on an amicable basis, obliging them to endeavour to resolve the case, but without any actual obligation of result.

Although the consultation phase is the core part of mutual agreement procedure, it only operates with a subsidiary function within such procedure, since it presupposes the failure to resolve the problem of interpretation and application of the double taxation convention during the unilateral phase.

The consultation phase starts there where the unilateral ends, It generally runs until the final phase, in which either a mutual agreement is reached, or the case is referred to arbitration. However, in bilateral double taxation conventions lacking an option for arbitration, or when – despite the presence of such option – the taxpayer does not exercise such option, the consultation phase may continue open-ended, without excluding cases of mutual agreement procedures reaching stalemate.

All four tools include time limits for settling the dispute during the consultation phase, but differ as to the respectively applicable conditions, as well as to the implications arising when competent authorities fail to reach an agreement and the circumstances in which such failure occurs.

In principle, the second-tier mechanisms for the settlement of the cross-border tax dispute start once the time limits for the first-tier ones, namely the mutual agreement procedure, have expired. However, tax authorities may continue the consultation phase also after such moment. The EU Tax Arbitration Convention[83] and the EU Tax Arbitration Directive[84] expressly admit this within six months from the appointment of the advisory commission. This possibility also exists – even if halved to a period of three months – under the BEPS MLI.[85]

83 See Article 12 (1) EU Tax Arbitration Convention.
84 See Article 15 (1) EU Tax Arbitration Directive.
85 See Article 24 (2) BEPS MLI. Therefore, insofar as two States opt to be bound by Part VI of the BEPS MLI, this possibility will also apply to the interpretation and application of the clause reflecting Article 25 (5) OECD MC in the applicable bilateral double taxation convention.

In particular, Article 25 (5) OECD MC and the EU Tax Arbitration Convention set an overall time limit of two years for competent authorities to reach mutual agreement. The computation of this period starts from submission and therefore bundles together the unilateral and consultation phases in a way that any longer duration of either phase will correspondingly reduce that of the other.

Article 4 (1) second sentence EU Tax Arbitration Directive and Article 19 BEPS MLI admit further extensions of this period, thus in fact increasing the time for settling the cross-border tax dispute.[86]

The EU Tax Arbitration Directive caps such extension to one year and admits it upon request by each competent authority, subject to the presentation of written justification. Since no such extension operates under the EU Tax Arbitration Convention, Article 4 (1) second sentence EU Arbitration Directive constitutes a possible step back in the acquis of the Union established by the EU Arbitration Convention.[87] Furthermore, since the Directive does not specifically indicate the object of this written justification to request the extension, it establishes a rather discretionary framework within which competent authorities may obtain the extension.[88] For this reason, except for cases in which one of the involved competent authorities denies it, any effective protection before the CJEU against an undue extension of this period seem rather hard in practice. However, one may not exclude that the CJEU interprets the conditions for the extension in line with the object and purpose of the Directive and as an exceptional circumstance that should not unduly extend the time for settling the cross-border tax dispute.

Under Article 19 BEPS MLI the extension operates in four possible circumstances. First, Article 19 (1) (b) gives competent authorities the power to agree to a different time

86 In the absence of any specific provision, we consider that Article 25 (5) last sentence OECD MC allows for an extension of the time limit, insofar as tax authorities specifically include it when settling the mode of application of this paragraph. Furthermore, this may also be the consequence of the impact that either Article 19 (3) MLI, or the reservation contained in Article 19 (11) MLI have on the functioning of Article 25 (5) OECD MC.

87 Yet, practice shows that other problems may hamper the effectiveness of the EU Arbitration Convention, such as in the presence of divergent views between the States or difficulties concerning the appointment of arbitrators. However, when the affected person has activated a domestic legal remedy in any Contracting State, the EU Arbitration Convention requires its prior completion. Therefore, in such cases, under Article 7 second sentence EU Arbitration Convention, tax authorities compute the two-year deadline for the appointment of the advisory commission in charge of issuing the arbitration award from the moment of delivery of such judgment.

88 Article 14 (1) second sentence EU Tax Arbitration Directive raises a similar problem in connection with the 3-month extension of the time limit for the advisory commission and the alternative dispute resolution commission to deliver the opinion. The Directive does not indicate the circumstances in which such extension may be granted. Therefore, also in this case, it leaves ample discretionary powers to such bodies, which in our view could increase the time for justice and potentially worsen the time for settling the dispute as compared to the corresponding provisions contained in the EU Tax Arbitration Convention, which do not admit any extension of the period.

period with respect to a case.[89] Second, Article 19 (2) allows each competent authority to suspend the mutual agreement procedure when a case on one or more of the same issues is pending before a national administrative or judicial instance. In such circumstances, the period "will" (in our view automatically) stop running for as long as it is necessary to render a final decision, to suspend or withdraw the case. Third, Article 19 (2) allows the affected person and "a" competent authority to agree on the suspension of the mutual agreement procedure.[90] Fourth, Article 19 (3) MLI gives competent authorities the right and obligation ("shall") to extend such period when taxpayers fail to provide in a timely manner any information requested by the competent authorities. The latter clause operates upon agreement of the competent authorities involved and suspends the computation of the period until the taxpayer has provided such information. For how this mechanism secures the effective functioning of mutual agreement procedures against non-cooperative techniques of the affected persons, it leaves such persons without an actual legal remedy in the presence of non-cooperative attitude of the competent authorities pursuing an extension of the mutual agreement procedure.

The failure to reach an agreement in the framework of the consultation phase of mutual agreement procedure is a fact that results either from the absence of an agreement within the time limit indicated by each legal instrument for settling the dispute, or from a written acknowledgement of the competent authorities involved. The former alternative is incompatible with the wording of the EU Arbitration Directive, whose Article 4 (3) sets an obligation for the competent authorities to notify the affected person(s) about the failure to reach an agreement and the general reasons for it. In such circumstances, the absence of a validly notified information notice to the affected persons should be a specific ground for appeal before domestic Courts of the States involved, in line with the general right of appeal against the outcome of mutual agreement procedure, established by Article 5 (3) EU Arbitration Directive. Furthermore, such failure could constitute an infringement of secondary law of the European Union and the related obligation of public officials to execute its law, which could be sanctioned by the CJEU.[91]

Only the EU Arbitration Convention more precisely defines when a mutual agreement fails. In particular, Article 7 EU Arbitration Convention indicates that this occurs when such procedure does not eliminate double taxation, i.e. when neither the profits are included in the computation of taxable profits in one State only, nor the tax chargeable on such profits in one State is correspondingly reduced in another State.[92] Accordingly, in such context a mutual agreement may have failed even in circumstances where the competent

89 We concur with Govind,S., Turcan, L., Cross-Border Tax Dispute Resolution in the 21st century: A Comparative Study of Existing Bilateral and Multilateral Remedies, in 19 Derivative and Financial Instruments, 2017-5, sec. 2.1.2.2 in considering that this power of extension of the timeframe for mutual agreement procedure undermines the prophylactic effects of arbitration.

90 The wording of this provision suggests that the suspension may operate in the unilateral and consultation phases, in the latter one not being subject to the consent of all competent authorities involved in a given case.

91 See C-224/97, *Ciola*, EU:C:1999:212.

92 Article 14 EU Arbitration Convention.

authorities have reached a satisfactory agreement, which would constitute a successful conclusion of the first-tier procedure under Article 25 (5) OECD MC and the BEPS MLI.

The EU Arbitration Directive remains silent as to the factual circumstances in which an agreement is reached in the framework of the first-tier procedure for the settlement of cross-border tax disputes.[93] However, the interpretation of its clauses in the light of the object and purpose – as indicated in its Article 1 – should lead to conclude that mutual agreement procedures fail when they do not reach a common position as to the interpretation and application of the agreements and conventions that provide for the elimination of double taxation.[94]

21.6.1.5 The final phase

The final phase may either consist of the implementation of a mutual agreement, or mark the access to the second-tier mechanisms for settling the cross-border tax dispute when the competent authorities have failed to reach an agreement.

The implementation of a mutual agreement may be the immediate result of a common position reached by the competent authorities during the consultation phase, or the consequence of a second-tier mechanism, usually arbitration.

All four tools for settling cross-border tax disputes allow tax authorities to implement any agreement reached within the previous phases of mutual agreement procedures notwithstanding time limits applicable under domestic law of either State involved.[95] A similar regime applies to the implementation of the outcome of decisions reached in the framework of second-tier mechanisms, such as arbitration and, in the case of the EU Arbitration Directive, also the alternative dispute resolution.[96]

The EU Arbitration Directive strengthens the protection of the affected person(s), by giving actual remedies protected by supranational law of the European Union in order to enforce the solution to the cross-border tax dispute reached by the competent authorities.

In particular, according to Article 4 (2) EU Arbitration Directive, the final phase of mutual agreement starts with the obligation of each competent authority to notify, without delay,

---

93 Although Article 4 of the initial draft of the EU Arbitration Directive – COM (2016) 686 final of 25.10.2016 included a similar clause to Article 14 EU Arbitration Convention, no such provision was eventually included in the final version of the EU Arbitration Directive.

94 However, under Article 16 (7) EU Arbitration Directive, a Member State may deny access to the second-tier of the dispute resolution procedure when a question in dispute does not involve double taxation.

95 See Article 16 (2) second sentence and BEPS MLI, Article 25 (2) second sentence, Article 6 (2) second sentence EU Arbitration Convention and Article 4 (2) fourth sentence EU Arbitration Directive.

96 See Article 19 (4) (a) BEPS MLI, Article 25 (5) third sentence OECD MC, and Article 15 (4) third sentence EU Arbitration Directive. Although the EU Arbitration Convention does not contain a provision that specifically regulates this matter, its Article 6 (2) second sentence should be applicable to such situations.

the agreement to the affected person(s) and requires the acceptance by such person(s) in order to produce its effects.

Unlike in cases of rejection of the complaint during the unilateral phase, if an affected person does not accept the decision, Article 5 (3) EU Arbitration Directive does not apply, since its wording explicitly refers to cases of rejection of the complaint. Therefore, the EU Arbitration Directive gives the affected person(s) the right to enforce a decision that either competent authorities have reached by mutual agreement or that the advisory (or the alternative dispute resolution) commission has agreed, but not to force competent authorities to reconsider a mutual agreement and search for a new one.[97]

Whilst Article 7 (1) EU Tax Arbitration Convention explicitly indicates that the mutual agreement reached must eliminate double taxation,[98] all other tools, including the EU Arbitration Directive, remain silent, thus giving competent authorities full powers as to the content of the mutual agreement that determine how to resolve cases of taxation not in accordance with the convention.

Yet, just like all other tools for settling cross-border tax disputes, the EU Arbitration Directive does not deprive in such circumstances the affected person(s) of the right to activate domestic remedies (in either State involved), subject to the scrutiny of European Union law as to their effectiveness and equivalence with the ones applicable to purely domestic disputes.

Article 4 (2) EU Arbitration Directive regulates the relations with any pending remedy,[99] requiring their termination or completion as condition for implementing the mutual agreement, and obliges the affected person(s) to inform the competent authorities within 60 days from that of notification of the mutual agreement.

If the person complies with such conditions, Article 4 (3) obliges the competent authorities to implement the mutual agreement immediately, opening possible scenarios of breach of a right with direct effect established by secondary law in case the authorities do not comply with such obligation. In such circumstances, the affected persons can force the authorities to execute the agreement by using domestic administrative and judicial remedies, subject to the scrutiny of the EU Commission and the CJEU.

If the person does not comply with the conditions, the effects differ according to whether the person has given up the existing pending remedies. In the affirmative, any failure or

97 This will not prevent of course the affected person(s) from filing a new complaint in similar circumstances in the future.

98 As indicated by Article 14 EU Tax Arbitration Convention, this occurs in case of single taxation of cross-border profits or of a coordinated adjustment in the exercise of taxing powers between the Contracting States involved.

99 Since Article 4 (2) EU Arbitration Directive refers to "legal remedies" and "remedy" or "remedies" without further specifying, we believe that the wording of such provision should encompass both administrative and judicial remedies applicable under the law of a State. Furthermore, the absence of any specific reference to domestic remedies may lead to conclude that the wording of such provision covers non-domestic remedies, such as for instance arbitration under non-tax treaties.

irregularity as to the notification may deprive the affected person(s) of any right to have the authorities implementing the mutual agreement, leaving such person(s) without an actual legal protection as a consequence of the termination of the previously activated other remedies.[100] In the negative, the affected person(s) have the right to keep pursuing solutions in the framework of the other legal remedies.

When competent authorities fail to reach an agreement within the consultation phase of mutual agreement procedures, the access to the second-tier legal instruments for settling the cross-border tax dispute[101] operates differently under the four tools, also taking into account the factual framework in which the issues may arise.

In particular, Article 7 (1) EU Arbitration Convention automatically gives access to the second-tier mechanisms once the two years from the complaint have expired. By contrast, under all other tools the request by the person(s) constitutes a specific condition for the access to such mechanisms.[102]

Furthermore, Article 4 (3) EU Arbitration Directive protects the right of the affected person(s) to file such request, by establishing a specific obligation for the competent authorities to inform them about their failure of reaching mutual agreement during the consultation phase. This notification requirement may not only allow the person to request the activation of the procedure before the advisory commission, i.e. arbitration, but also to decide whether to file an appeal before a court or other judicial body of either State involved in the dispute.[103]

However, the right to access arbitration may be restricted under Article 16 (7) EU Arbitration Directive, when a Member State indicates that the question in dispute does not involve double taxation. Such factual framework should be interpreted in the light of the definition of double taxation contained in Article 2 (1) (c) of the EU Arbitration Directive. According to such provision, double taxation occurs when two or more Member States impose taxes covered by an international tax agreement or convention, or levy an additional charge, increase tax liability, or cancel or reduce losses that could be used to offset taxable profits.

100 This will of course not prevent tax authorities from voluntarily implementing the solution despite the absence of an actual obligation under European Union law to do so.

101 Whilst Article 25 (5) OECD MC and Article 19 BEPS MLI expressly use the expression "arbitration" to define this legal mechanism for settling the cross-border tax dispute, Article 6 EU Arbitration Directive and Article 7 EU Arbitration Convention indicate that the person may request the involvement of an "advisory commission", in fact implying a form of arbitration.

102 See Article 6 (1) EU Arbitration Directive, Article 25 (5) OECD MC (also interpreted in the light of para. 70 of the Commentary) and Article 19 (1) BEPS MLI.

103 Article 5 (3) EU Arbitration Directive. In case of appeal before a relevant court or other judicial body of an EU Member State involved in the dispute and throughout the duration of such appeal, the person(s) will be barred from requesting the activation of the second-tier mechanism for the settlement of such dispute, namely the dispute resolution by the Advisory Commission under Article 6 (1) of the EU Arbitration Directive.

21.6.2 Arbitration

21.6.2.1 Introductory remarks

Mutual agreement procedures do not imply an obligation for the competent authorities to reach an amicable settlement of the cross-border tax disputes. In the absence of an agreement, all four legal instruments allow the continuation of such procedures with a second tier before an independent body, namely advisory commission[104] or arbitration panel.[105]

Regardless of the formal denomination of such body, in all four legal instruments the second-tier procedure constitutes in fact a *sui generis* form of arbitration that the competent authorities access[106] when the affected person(s) so require(s) or, in the case of the EU Arbitration Convention, automatically.[107] However, Article 10 (1) EU Tax Arbitration Directive gives competent authorities the right to opt for an alternative dispute resolution mechanism.

Once established, the advisory commission/arbitration panel has an obligation to put forward a decision that achieves a common interpretation and application of the applicable cross-border tax provisions. However, such decision only binds the competent authorities insofar as they are unable to find an agreement that settles the dispute within the six months after the advisory commission has delivered its opinion, as indicated by the EU Tax Arbitration Convention and Directive[108] or, three months under the BEPS MLI.[109]

Although such procedure shares common features across the four legal instruments, its phases and issues require a more in-depth analysis. In general terms, Article 25 OECD MC leaves most matters of the procedure to the agreement of the parties, whilst the EU Directive contains the most detailed regulation of the procedure and also provides for a stronger set of legal remedies in case of failure to comply with the rules.

The analysis of such issues shall nevertheless be the object of separate subsections, focusing respectively on (i) the appointment and the composition of the commission, (ii) the rules of functioning, (iii) the involvement of the affected person(s), (iv) the protection of confidentiality, (v) the derogations, and (vi) other residual issues of relevance.

---

104 The EU Tax Arbitration Convention and Directive call this body "advisory commission".

105 The OECD MC and BEPS MLI expressly refer to arbitration in respect of the panel and procedure before the independent body.

106 See Article 6 (1) EU Tax Arbitration Directive, Article 25 (5) OECD MC and Article 19 (1) BEPS MLI.

107 See Article 7 (1) EU Tax Arbitration Convention.

108 See Article 12 (1) second sentence EU Tax Arbitration Convention, Article 15 (2) first sentence EU Tax Arbitration Convention.

109 See Article 24 (2) BEPS MLI.

21.6.2.2 The appointment and composition of the panel

The four legal instruments contain partly similar rules on the appointment and composition of the independent body for the settlement of the cross-border tax dispute, which aim at securing a speedy settlement of the dispute by an independent body, whilst preserving the right of the States to an active participation in the procedure.

The EU Tax Arbitration Directive and the BEPS MLI contain specific deadlines for speeding up the path of the procedure towards the settlement of the cross-border tax dispute.[110] Besides the deadlines for the appointment of arbitrators[111] – which is also included in Article 20 (2) (b) BEPS MLI[112] – Article 6 EU Tax Arbitration Directive also sets a deadline for filing the request to set up the advisory commission[113] and completion of the procedure.[114]

Neither the EU Tax Arbitration Convention, nor the BEPS MLI provide for remedies that effectively secure the compliance with such time limit in the absence of an agreement between tax authorities on the appointment and composition of the arbitration panel and the advisory commission.[115] By contrast, the EU Tax Arbitration Directive secures the effective functioning of the procedure by giving the affected person(s) the right to apply to a national court for the appointment of the advisory commission and its members.[116]

Several different rules reflect the priorities of each of the four legal instruments, such as for instance the subsidiary rules applicable under the BEPS MLI and the EU Tax Arbitration Directive when the States fail either to appoint members of the arbitration panel or to agree on the chairperson. In such circumstances, the BEPS MLI allows for the appointment of the highest-ranking official of the OECD Centre for Tax Policy and Administration,[117] whilst

---

110 Practice has shown that the rules on the appointment of the advisory commission under Articles 7 and 9 EU Tax Arbitration Convention present some difficulties, which prevent the procedure from its speedy functioning in the absence of an agreement by the tax authorities. Such problems also arise under Article 25 OECD MC.

111 Article 6 (1) fifth sentence EU Tax Arbitration Directive requires the appointment of the advisory committee within 120 days from the receipt of the request and establishes an obligation to promptly inform the affected person thereof.

112 Such provision requires each competent authority to appoint one panel member within 60 days from the request for arbitration and gives such members 60 additional days for the appointment of a third member who shall serve as chairperson of the arbitration panel. Furthermore.

113 According to Article 6 (1) fourth sentence EU Tax Arbitration Directive, the affected person shall request the set up of the advisory commission within 50 days from the date of receipt of the notification of the failure to settle the cross-border tax dispute. Such provision of the EU Tax Arbitration Convention also allows the affected person to request setting up the advisory commission when the unilateral phase of the first tier of the procedure for settling the cross-border procedure fails.

114 See further under 21.6.2.7.

115 Yet, legal remedies may apply under domestic law in order to secure the effective compliance with such rules.

116 Article 7 (1) EU Tax Arbitration Directive. When involved in the procedures for the appointment of the commission and its members, the national court has an obligation under Article 7 (3) EU Tax Arbitration Directive to notify all relevant decisions to the applicant in line with the applicable national procedural rules. Furthermore, Article 7 (3) fourth and fifth sentences EU Tax Arbitration Directive also admit possible appeals against such decisions.

117 See Article 20 (4) and (5) BEPS MLI.

the EU Tax Arbitration Directive relies on the appointment by the national courts.[118] In the case of the BEPS MLI, such rule is consistent with the characterization of the cross-border tax dispute as a matter between States, whilst the EU Tax Arbitration Directive seeks for mechanisms that more closely protect the rights of the affected persons.[119]

The composition of the arbitration panel varies according to the legal instrument. In particular, whilst Article 25 (5) OECD MC contains no specific rule in this respect, the composition of the panel varies from a minimum of three – under Article 20 (2) BEPS MLI,[120] which also expressly requires the expertise or experience of members in international tax matters – to a standard of five members under the EU Tax Arbitration Convention[121] and Directive.[122]

All legal instruments give competent authorities the power of appointing at least one member in the arbitration panel and the protection of independence and impartiality. The EU Tax Arbitration Convention and Directive secure the latter goal by requiring the

118 See Article 7 EU Tax Arbitration Directive. The appointment by the competent national court operates upon request of the affected person.

119 Accordingly, Article 8 (6) first sentence EU Tax Arbitration Directive requires the chairperson of the advisory commission to be selected among the independent persons of standing and the second sentence of such provision adds that it should be a judge, unless the competent authorities have otherwise agreed. Furthermore, when the members of the commission fail to reach an agreement, Article 7 (1) fourth sentence leaves the appointment of the chairperson up to independent persons of standing by drawing lots from the list of independent persons.

120 Article 20 (2) (a) BEPS MLI expressly indicates this number. However, the right of each competent authority to appoint one panel member (indicated in Article 20 (2) (b) BEPS MLI) can lead to increase the composition of the arbitration panel when more States are involved in the cross-border dispute.

121 According to Article 9 EU Tax Arbitration Convention, the advisory commission includes its chair, appointed among the persons of standing nominated by each Contracting State, two representatives of each competent authority and an even number of independent persons of standing. The appointment of the independent persons of standing takes place by mutual agreement between the authorities or, in the absence of an agreement, by drawing of lots. Furthermore, in the presence of a mutual agreement between competent authorities, such authorities may reduce the number of representatives to one per each Contracting State involved. The Code of Conduct has specified that the persons nominated do not need to be nationals of residents of the nominated State, but must be EU nationals and EU residents.

122 Article 8 (1) (b) EU Tax Arbitration Directive indicates that competent authorities may appoint one representative and one independent person of standing as members of the advisory committee. However, in the presence of an agreement between the competent authorities, this provision also allows in each of the two cases to double the number of such representatives in the advisory commission. In the absence of a specific indication, we believe that the list of independent persons of standing can be common to the EU Tax Arbitration Convention and Directive. However, if that were the case one may wonder whether the requirement of keeping the list up to date, contained in Article 10 EU Tax Arbitration Directive would be met by some Member States, which have not updated the list over almost one quarter of a century (and that even includes at least one deceased person). Furthermore, since the EU JTPF currently only functions in connection with the EU Tax Arbitration Convention, we believe that its indication as to the EU residence and nationality of the experts should not necessarily operate for the latter to operate in connection with the EU Tax Directive. Besides, the latter text does not include any specific requirement in this sense.

involvement of independent persons of standing in the advisory commission on top of the members appointed by competent authorities of the States involved.[123]

By contrast, the affected person(s) do(es) not have the power to appoint members of the arbitration panel. This does not constitute too much of a problem under Article 25 OECD MC and Article 20 BEPS MLI, since the affected person(s) enjoy hardly any rights in the framework of such procedures besides requesting arbitration and deciding whether to accept the decision. However, problems could arise under the EU Tax Arbitration Directive, since the rights and obligations of the affected persons fall within its scope. In such context, based on substantially similar criteria to the ones included in Article 9 (3) EU Tax Arbitration Convention, Article 8 (4) EU Tax Arbitration Directive allows competent authorities to object the appointment of any independent person of standing in specific situations that could undermine their impartiality and independence,[124] but gives no similar remedies to the affected person(s).

Article 9 (3) EU Tax Arbitration Directive further strengthens the protection of competent authorities, by giving them the power to inform the Commission about situations in which independent persons of standing lack the required independence and should therefore be removed from a national list.

21.6.2.3 The rules of functioning

All legal instruments but for the EU Tax Arbitration Directive scarcely regulate the matters connected with rules of functioning of the second-tier procedure for settling cross-border tax disputes, leaving broad discretionary powers to the arbitration panels.

The EU Tax Arbitration Directive contains a detailed regulation of the functioning of the procedure, which can be summarised in the four block of rules included in Article 11 and in the requirements on information, evidence and hearing contained in Article 13.

We shall now separately analyse those rules, starting by the four blocks contained in Article 11 and leaving the other provision to a separate section.[125]

---

123 The number of independent persons normally equals that of representatives of the competent authorities involved. Article 9 (4) EU Tax Arbitration Convention requires each Contracting State to nominate five persons and inform the Secretary-General of the EU Council thereof. Article 9 (1) EU Tax Arbitration Directive requires each Member State to appoint at least three individuals with technical competence and independence, who can act with impartiality and integrity. The Directive also obliges EU Member States to notify the names of such persons to the Commission (including their up-to-date information, possible conflicts of interest), indicate who may be appointed as chair, promptly inform the Commission about changes and remove the persons when ceasing to be independent.

124 From such perspective, the EU Tax Arbitration Directive and Convention secure a more effective remedy for competent authorities than that applicable under the BEPS MLI, which contains no right of objection in cases of arbitrators who lack the impartiality and independence required by Article 20 (2) (c) BEPS MLI.

125 On Article 13 EU Tax Arbitration Directive, see further under section 21.6.2.5.

First, Article 11 (1) EU Tax Arbitration Directive sets a notification requirement for the competent authorities to the affected person within the 120-day period. Such notification must contain rules of functioning, the date by which the opinion on the resolution of the question shall be adopted and the reference to the applicable rules to the dispute.

Second, Article 11 (2) EU Tax Arbitration Directive requires the competent authorities of the Member States involved in the dispute to sign the rules of functioning and indicates the minimum standard content of such rules. Such content consists of the following seven elements, namely (i) the description of the question in dispute, (ii) the agreed terms of reference for the settlement, (iii) the form of the resolution body,[126] (iv) the timeframe, (v) the information on the composition of the commission,[127] (vi) the procedural rules[128] and (vii) the logistical arrangements for delivering the opinion. However, for disputes on the rejection of the complaint during the unilateral phase only the first, fourth, fifth and sixth elements are necessary.

Third, Article 11 (3) EU Tax Arbitration Directive establishes an obligation for the advisory commission to establish rules reflecting the requirements of Article 11 (2), which apply insofar as the tax authorities have either not completely fulfilled such requirements or not (duly) notified them to the affected persons.

Fourth, Article 11 (4) sets a subsidiary obligation of notification for the advisory commission to the affected persons within two weeks from the appointment, which operates when tax authorities have not done so in line with the requirement of Article 11 (1) EU Tax Arbitration Directive. Furthermore, this clause contains one more legal remedy for the affected person(s), allowing such person(s) to apply to a national court for the implementation of the rules of functioning in case competent authorities and the advisory commission have failed to do so.

21.6.2.4 The modes of arbitration

The modes of arbitrating cross-border tax disputes vary according to the applicable legal instrument. Whilst Article 25 (5) OECD MC and the EU Tax Arbitration Convention do not specifically regulate this matter,[129] the BEPS MLI and the EU Tax Arbitration Directive indicate two possible modes for conducting this procedure, which operate in different contexts, but broadly share similar structural features. In particular, the EU Tax Arbitration Directive sets the independent opinion process before the advisory commission as

126 In case of alternative dispute resolution, also the type of process must be indicated.

127 According to Article 11 (2) (e), this information must include the full data of the members, including competence, qualification and disclosure of any conflict of interest.

128 According to Article 11 (2) (f) these rules concern the participation of the affected person(s) and third parties in the proceedings, exchange of memoranda, information and evidence, the costs, the type of dispute resolution process to be used and any other relevant procedural or organisational matter.

129 However, OECD, Commentary on Art. 25, paras. 86-87, indicates that States may agree on the use of mediation or, in the case of factual issues, refer the case to an expert. Furthermore, the current wording of the Commentary on Article 25 OECD also shows a strong inclination for settling disputes through baseball arbitration.

standard for arbitrating the cross-border tax dispute and admits an alternative dispute resolution, which operates upon agreement of the competent authorities of the Member States concerned.

Article 10 EU Tax Arbitration Directive does not indicate when exactly competent authorities may submit the settlement of the dispute to the alternative resolution commission,[130] but merely indicates that the alternative dispute resolution takes place before such commission, unless the competent authorities have agreed on the establishment of a standing committee.

In both cases, Article 10 allows competent authorities to agree on the rules of functioning[131] in accordance with the standard of Article 11 and provided that such bodies preserve the independence of its members in line with the requirements established by Article 8 (4) and (5). Among others, Article 10 (2) EU Tax Arbitration Directive expressly admits that competent authorities make use of the so-called 'final offer' or 'last-offer' arbitration, which can considerably facilitate and speed up the resolution of the cross-border tax dispute. This type of arbitration provides for various forms of accelerated procedures for arbitration, including the one known as baseball arbitration,[132] which restricts the authority of arbitrators by forcing them to endorse one of the two proposed solutions by the parties and, in such way, notably accelerates the path towards the settlement of the cross-border tax dispute. However, it may also create problems as to the right of the affected persons to have a transparent motivation on how the dispute settlement might impact their rights.

Article 23 BEPS MLI follows the opposite approach, since it adopts baseball arbitration as standard,[133] and admits the independent opinion process arbitration as the alternative solution applicable when the parties reserve the right not to apply the previous mode for arbitrating cross-border tax disputes.[134] In particular, under Article 23 (1) BEPS MLI

---

130 Article 6 (1) fourth and fifth sentence EU Tax Arbitration Directive establish precise deadlines for requesting and appointing the advisory commission. Once such commission is appointed, we believe that competent authorities no longer have the power of depriving such commission of the power to issue an opinion that settles the dispute and of appointing the alternative dispute resolution commission instead. However, in such circumstances Article 15 (2) EU Tax Arbitration Directive would still keep the power of competent authorities to take a decision that deviates from the opinion of the advisory commission.

131 According to Article 10 (4) EU Tax Arbitration Directive, the rules on cost of the proceedings, contained in Article 12, and the ones on information, evidence and hearing, contained in Article 13, apply when the competent authorities have otherwise agreed. Since the latter provision plays an important role in safeguarding the protection of the affected person(s) during the procedure, we submit that Article 10 (4) EU Tax Arbitration Directive does not give competent authorities full discretionary powers in this respect, but still requires its interpretation in line with the basic standards for protection of rights within the European Union.

132 See further under Petruzzi, R., Koch, P., Turcan, L., Baseball arbitration in comparison to other types of arbitration, in Lang, M., Owens, J., International Arbitration in Tax Matters, IBFD Publications, 2016, Chapter 6.

133 Article 23 (1) BEPS MLI.

134 Article 23 (2) BEPS MLI.

requires each competent authority to submit a proposed resolution before the arbitration panel, which shall select as its decision one of such proposals.[135]

In both modes of arbitration, Article 23 (1) (c) and (2) (c) BEPS MLI specifically indicate that the decision will be adopted by simple majority without a rationale or other explanation and that it shall not have precedential value. The intention of the Contracting Jurisdictions of the BEPS MLI is clear and precisely formulated. Furthermore, the absence of a motivation will structurally prevent the formation of any authority of precedent for the decisions of the arbitration panel. Yet, one may wonder whether it is possible to exclude any precedential value or more limited form of influence in respect of a public decision. The silence of Article 10 EU Tax Arbitration Directive on this matter will show what kind of impact the decisions of the alternative dispute resolution will in fact have. No doubt instead that the independent opinion based arbitration under the EU Tax Arbitration Directive will have an influence on the interpretation and application of tax treaties within the internal market.

21.6.2.5 *The involvement of the affected person(s) in the procedure*

The traditional characterization of cross-border tax disputes as controversies between States on the exercise of tax jurisdiction raises critical issues from the protection of the rights of persons affected by such disputes. Under Article 25 OECD MC and the BEPS MLI such persons are treated as mere object of a dispute on tax sovereignty without an international remedy that effectively protects their rights. The international coordination carried out in the framework of the BEPS project has rightly strengthened the interaction between tax authorities across the borders and their powers. We expect this situation to increase the exposure of cross-border situations to tax disputes involving more than one jurisdiction. For this reason, it is regrettable that the BEPS MLI has not correspondingly increased the international legal remedies for taxpayers in such circumstances, leaving the protection of their rights up to the remedies provided by domestic law in each Contracting State.[136] Even if the involvement of the national judiciaries is indispensable for securing an effective protection, the need to seek for protection of such rights in more than one legal system without an effective coordination is in our view as bad as the absence of a dialogue between tax authorities was before the introduction of the mutual agreement procedure.

From the perspective of European Union law there is yet one more reason to question this situation, especially if one takes into account that every EU national has the right to an

135 Under Article 23 (1) (b) BEPS MLI competent authorities may also submit a supporting position paper for consideration by the arbitration panel and, in such case, notify it to the other competent authority(ies), allowing in such case for a reply submission by such authority(ies).

136 See further on this in Baker, P., Pistone, P., BEPS Action 16: The Taxpayers' Right to an Effective Legal Remedy Under European Law in Cross-Border Situations, in EC Tax Review 2016-5-6, pp. 335 ff. In the same sense, also see Groen, G., The Nature and Scope of the Mandatory Arbitration Provision in the OECD Multilateral Convention (2016), in 71 Bulletin for International Taxation, 2017/11, p. 613. In particular, Groen regrets that the desire to attract as many states to sign up for mandatory arbitration as possible has in fact ended up in leaving too many escape clauses for the competent authorities to not fulfil their treaty obligations in bona fide cases.

immediate legal protection in respect of situations that are the object of provisions of EU law with direct effect. In such context, the wording of Article 10 EU Tax Arbitration Convention shows consideration for an involvement of the associated enterprises concerned, by allowing them to provide the advisory commission with any relevant information, evidence or documents. Likewise, Article 10 (2) EU Tax Arbitration Convention reflects the core values of the right to fair trial, by allowing each of the associated enterprises to appear or be represented before the advisory commission.[137]

However, in the absence of any obligation to inform the affected person(s) about the second-tier of the procedure for the settlement of the cross-border dispute, such remedies seem in fact deprived of their useful value and hard to exercise in practice. This may potentially undermine the participation of the associated enterprises to the procedure in line with the equality of arms. This is possibly due to the circumstance that the rights and obligations of such persons are not in fact directly relevant for the scope of the EU Tax Arbitration Convention.[138] Yet, this situation is potentially unsuitable to comply with the standards of legal protection within the EU legal system, as reflected in the EU Charter of Fundamental Rights.[139]

The EU Tax Arbitration Directive marks a step forward in the protection of the rights of the affected person(s) by a cross-border tax dispute, since it brings such rights directly within the scope of secondary EU legislation.

Two main factors have contributed to this improvement, namely the thorough system of notifications included in several provisions of the EU Tax Arbitration Directive – already addressed in other sections of this chapter – and Article 13, which regulates information, evidence and hearing within the procedure.

Although the wording of Article 13 (1) EU Tax Arbitration Directive largely reflects that of Article 10 (1) EU Tax Arbitration Convention, the context differs because of the existence of the notification requirements within the procedure set up by the former legal instrument.

By contrast, the comparison between the wording of Article 13 (2) EU Tax Arbitration Directive and Article 10 (2) EU Tax Arbitration Convention raises more complex issues, since the former provision subordinates the right of participation of the affected persons in the procedure to the consent of competent authorities.

Prima facie, this additional condition seems to worsen the legal framework for the protection of the right to fair trial. However, this provision must be interpreted in a way that neither generates clashes with relevant primary law of the European Union, as reflected in the EU Charter of Fundamental Rights, nor gives rise to a step back in the

137 Article 10 (2) EU Tax Arbitration Convention also gives the advisory commission the power to request that each of the associated enterprises shall appear or be represented before it.

138 However, some provisions contained in bilateral double taxation conventions, such as Article 41 of the between Germany and Sweden, openly state the right of persons to have the full right to be heard and to submit their own request.

139 See further on the potential friction with the *audi alteram partem* principle under section 4.3.5.

supranational integration as compared to Article 10 EU Tax Arbitration Convention, which constitutes an expression of the *acquis* of the Union. In such context, regardless of what the intention of the drafters may have been,[140] this condition – not originally included in the wording of the initial proposal of the Directive[141] – must be interpreted in a way that limits the right of competent authorities to object the exercise of the right of participation of the affected persons in the procedure. In our view, competent authorities should have the right to object the appearance of the affected person(s) when this could potentially undermine the confidentiality of information handled by the competent authorities and involving other taxpayers.

21.6.2.6 Confidentiality of the proceedings

The EU Tax Arbitration Convention and Directive, as well as the BEPS MLI contain specific provisions that secure an effective protection of confidentiality throughout the second tier of the procedure for settling cross-border tax disputes.[142]

For EU law purposes this is particularly important for complying with the requirements of the rights to privacy, enshrined in Article 7 EU Charter of Fundamental Rights, and data protection, addressed in Article 8 EU Charter of Fundamental Rights and regulated by the General Data Protection Regulation, signed on 8 April 2016 and in force since 25 May 2018.[143]

In particular, besides the general obligation for the competent authorities to preserve confidentiality on data concerning taxpayers, Article 9 (6) first sentence EU Tax Arbitration Convention, Article 13 (3) first to third sentence EU Tax Directive expressly oblige the members of the advisory commissions, arbitration panels and alternative dispute resolution commissions to do so. Furthermore, Member States are obliged to adopt appropriate sanctions in case of violation of such obligation, under Article 9 (6) second sentence EU Tax Arbitration Convention and Article 13 (3) fourth sentence.

Whilst Article 25 OECD MC remains silent on this matter,[144] Article 21 BEPS MLI provides with levels of protection of confidentiality that are substantially similar to the ones

---

140 Considering the absence of any similar provisions in Part VI of the BEPS MLI, which was in fact being drafted almost in parallel with the EU Tax Arbitration Directive, one may not exclude that EU Member States may have wanted to narrow down the differences between the two procedures. However, even if that were the case, the different context in which the clause of the EU Tax Arbitration Directive operates and the need to reconcile its interpretation with the principles and rules of supranational law requires limiting the possible consequences of the intention of the drafters.

141 See Article 12 (2) of COM (2016) 686 final of 25 October 2016.

142 Therefore, insofar as States opt to be bound by Part VI of the BEPS MLI, the protection of confidentiality will also affect the interpretation and application of Article 25 OECD MC in bilateral double taxation conventions, which can otherwise be regulated by reference to para. 8 of the sample agreement annexed to the Commentary on Article 25 OECD MC.

143 See further on this in Chapter 4, section 4.3.

144 However, the Sample Mutual Agreement in the OECD Commentary on Article 25 provides for a substantially homogeneous regulation to that which is currently included under Article 21 BEPS MLI.

secured by the EU Tax Arbitration Convention and Directive. In particular, this provision considers information handled between the arbitration panel and the competent authorities involved as equivalent to the one exchanged in the framework of mutual assistance under double taxation conventions. Accordingly, this information is entitled to the same level of protection than that indicated in Article 26 OECD MC and other equivalent provisions of international tax conventions.

Three additional measures further strengthen the protection of confidentiality. First, Article 21 (1) BEPS MLI expressly restricts the access to information object of the dispute settlement mechanism to a maximum of three persons per each members of the arbitration panel. This is in our view a good practice, which all States should consider to include in the rules of functioning of each mechanism for settling cross-border tax disputes. Second, Article 23 (5) BEPS MLI contains a confidentiality clause covering the relations between taxpayers and their advisors. The drafting of this clause allows covering with the privilege of confidentiality not only the relations with the lawyers, but also the ones with any other type of advisor involved in the case. Third, Article 13 (3) second and third sentence fills a gap of the EU Tax Arbitration Convention, by obliging the affected persons and, where applicable, their representatives to preserve confidentiality and to do so by means of a specific binding declaration. The BEPS MLI remains silent on this matter, perhaps based on the assumption that any confidential information exchanged in the framework of such procedure would not be disclosed to the taxpayers who have previously filed the complaint.

21.6.2.7 The decision

The decision by the independent body completes the second tier of the procedure and must settle the cross-border tax dispute.

The EU Tax Arbitration Convention and Directive require the delivery of the opinion within six months from the appointment of the advisory commission, alternative dispute resolution commission or arbitration panel.[145] However, unlike the EU Tax Arbitration Convention, Article 14 (1) second sentence gives the advisory commission and the alternative dispute resolution commission the power to extend such period by three months,[146] without indicating any criterion that may determine in what cases this is possible.

By contrast, Part VI of the BEPS MLI and Article 25 (5) OECD MC include no deadline for the arbitration panel to deliver its opinion.[147]

145 See Articles 6 (2) and 11 (1) EU Tax Arbitration Convention, and Article 14 (1) EU Tax Arbitration Directive. Article 18 (1) EU Tax Arbitration Directive requires the written form for the decision.

146 This constitutes a possible step back as compared to the EU Tax Arbitration Convention, since the EU Tax Arbitration Directive tolerates a longer time for achieving the settlement of the cross-border tax dispute.

147 However, the BEPS MLI sets baseball arbitration as standard mode for arbitrating cross-border tax treaty disputes, thus structurally promoting a speedy solution to such disputes.

Neither Article 25 OECD MC, nor the provisions contained in Part VI the BEPS MLI or the EU Tax Arbitration Directive more precisely define the content of the decision. However, in the light of the object and purpose of the cross-border tax dispute settlement that such instruments operate, it is reasonable to assume that such decision should reach an agreement as to how two or more States may exercise their rights in compliance with a correct interpretation and application of the applicable double tax convention in the specific case.

Unlike all other legal instruments, Article 12 (1) EU Tax Arbitration Convention expressly requires the elimination of double taxation. Article 14 EU Tax Arbitration Convention then adds that this is achieved once the profits are included in the computation of taxable profits in one State only or the tax chargeable on such profits in one State is reduced by that chargeable on the same profits in another State. Such requirement sets precise standards for the results of the advisory commission under the EU Tax Arbitration Convention.[148]

Under the BEPS MLI, the EU Tax Arbitration Convention and Directive, the final decision is adopted by simple majority of its members and communicated to the competent authorities.[149] Whilst the EU Tax Arbitration Convention allows for competent authorities to agree on additional rules of procedure, the EU Tax Arbitration Directive indicates that, when a majority cannot be reached, the vote of the chairperson shall be decisive.

The BEPS MLI[150] and the EU Tax Arbitration Directive exclude that the decision constitutes a precedent. However, one may wonder whether such decision could nevertheless have an indirect influence on the treaty practice and interpretation, especially in case where

148 Considering that the latter convention forms part of the acquis of the Union, it may also lead to wonder whether the EU Tax Arbitration Directive may reach a less ambitious result in respect of such situations. If that were the case, it would constitute a possible step back by the EU Tax Arbitration Directive as compared to the obligations arising in connection with the EU Tax Arbitration Convention, since the former instrument may tolerate forms of double taxation within the internal market, which the latter one does not.

149 In cases where the advisory commission decides on the rejection of the complaint in the unilateral phase of the first tier of the procedure, Article 6 (2) second sentence EU Tax Arbitration Directive requires its notification within 30 days from adoption thereof. Article 15 (3) EU Tax Arbitration Directive requires notification without delay, allowing the affected person to appeal before the national judicial authority of the State of residence in the absence of such notification, in order to obtain the final decision. Since Article 15 EU Tax Arbitration Directive has a general value for all decisions issued in the context of the settlement of cross-border tax disputes coming under the scope of the directive, we believe that also the failure to notify under Article 6 (2) EU Tax Arbitration may entitle the affected person(s) to the appeal before the national court.

150 Article 23 (1) (c) and (2) (c) BEPS MLI.

it is the outcome of an independent opinion process and it is published.[151] Furthermore, since the EU Tax Arbitration Directive in fact preserves the possibility for the affected persons to appeal against such decision before a national court[152] within 60 days from its notification, the disclosure of the decision is likely to occur before the national court also when the parties have not agreed to its publication.

Under the EU Tax Arbitration Convention and Directive, as well as under the BEPS MLI, the decision is, at time of its delivery, a mere opinion on how to settle the dispute. This is because competent authorities keep for a certain period – three months under the BEPS MLI[153] and six months under the EU Tax Arbitration Convention[154] and Directive[155] – the right to agree on a different resolution from that put forward by the independent body in charge of the settlement of the cross-border tax dispute.

Once that moment has expired the opinion begets binding value on tax authorities, but would still not bind the affected person(s). Such person(s) keep(s) the right to exercise their national judicial remedies and/or to refuse the implementation of the solution. However, there seems to be no right of the affected persons to have access to the grounds on which the case was settled. This makes it different for the affected person to decide whether to appeal. In the absence of such appeal within the time limits established by the applicable domestic law or an express rejection by the affected person(s), tax authorities may presume the acceptance of the opinion by the affected person(s), also considering their obligation to implement the opinion, notwithstanding any limits prescribed by national law.

In case of failure to do so, Article 15 (4) fourth sentence EU Tax Arbitration Directive gives yet one more legal remedy to the affected person in order to enforce the implementation of the decision of the advisory commission or alternative dispute resolution commission. This additional legal remedy secures a much high level of protection of the right of the affected person(s) as compared to the context that would otherwise occur in respect of cross-border tax disputes settled under the other legal instruments.

151 Article 12 (1) EU Tax Arbitration Convention and Article 18 (2) EU Tax Arbitration Directive allow for publication in the presence of an agreement between tax authorities and subject to consent of the enterprises concerned. Furthermore, Article 18 (3) third and fourth sentence EU Tax Arbitration Convention establish a procedure for competent authorities to notify the information to the affected person (s) before the publication takes place. This procedure gives the affected person the opportunity to prevent any publication that may harm any information that is to remain secret or contrary to public policy. When the competent authorities and the affected person(s) have not consented to the publication of the final decision, Article 18 (3) EU Tax Arbitration Directive requires a publication of the abstract of such decision, which shall contain the key elements of the facts of the dispute and a description of the final outcome, including the method of arbitration used.

152 Article 15 (4) EU Tax Arbitration Directive.

153 See Article 24 (2) BEPS MLI.

154 See Article 12 (1) EU Tax Arbitration Convention.

155 See Article 15 (1) and (2) first sentence EU Tax Arbitration Directive.

21.6.2.8 The derogations

By way of derogation from Article 6, the EU Tax Arbitration Directive restricts the access to the dispute resolution procedure in two cases, namely under Article 16 (6) for reasons connected with the liability of one or more affected persons for serious violation of tax rules and under Article 16 (7) for questions in disputes not involving double taxation.

The first case occurs in the presence of gross negligence, wilful default and tax fraud. In such situations, the offender goes way beyond the violation of tax rules and maintains a particularly dangerous conduct for the tax system, which is generally punishable with criminal sanctions. Gross negligence is essentially a form of voluntary act or omission in reckless disregard of a legal obligation. Wilful default is a conscious failure to comply with the law. Tax fraud is a form of tax evasion in which the offender intentionally fails to pay taxes and conceals the effects of such failure by producing false statements that hinder or make it more difficult for tax authorities to discover the crime. However, all such crimes may find a different and more nuanced legal definition across the national tax systems.

This case shares some broadly common features with the provisions that block access to the first tier of the procedure for settling cross-border tax treaty disputes under the BEPS MLI.[156]

The expressions used by the BEPS MLI and the EU Tax Arbitration Directive show the intention of the drafters to set a high threshold for derogating the right to request the settlement of cross-border tax disputes, such that neither the sole failure to pay taxes (tax evasion)[157] or their alleged circumvention (tax avoidance) would *per se* suffice.

Based on such considerations, we can consider that the BEPS MLI and the EU Tax Arbitration Directive in fact share some common ground also with the more vague expression "serious penalty" used in Article 8 (1) and (2) EU Tax Arbitration Convention.

Although the actual meaning of this expression is not entirely clear, we understand that the EU Tax Arbitration Convention blocks the access to the cross-border tax dispute settlement in cases in which domestic law applies a penalty and a serious one to any enterprise concerned. Taking into account the implications of the principle of proportionality, this should automatically lead to limit such consequence to the most dangerous forms of violations of tax rules, thus generally excluding at least cases of tax avoidance and aggressive tax planning.

---

156 Article 16 (5) (c) (ii) (A) and (B) BEPS MLI. The BEPS MLI also allows States to exclude further disputes from arbitration. However, being the emphasis of this chapter and book on EU law related issues, it is not necessary to address these situations more in detail.

157 French speakers should not be tempted to consider tax fraud as a synonym of *fraude fiscale*, expression, which in the French language indicates tax evasion. In this context, the wording clearly implies a more serious nature in the fraudulent conduct, since the drafters have decided not to use the expression "tax evasion", but "tax fraud" and to do so by combining it with "gross negligence" and "wilful default". However, the latter two expressions do not prevent the derogation from applying in cases of tax evasion where the author of the violation shows either of them.

The rather detailed unilateral declarations of several Member States to the EU Tax Arbitration Convention provide with further element for interpretation of this expression. In particular, such declarations consider that the term always includes situations liable to criminal sanctions and, in several States, also violations sanctioned by administrative penalties: sometimes even a simple administrative fine for not timely filing a return may bar access to the Convention procedures.[158] These national definitions have little in common and this total lack of coordination is in fact incompatible with an internal market,[159] as it leads to different treatment of similar transfer pricing disputes and may lead to arbitrary exclusion of groups of companies from arbitration.[160]

The second case in which the EU Tax Arbitration Directive derogated from Article 6 occurs in connection with cross-border disputes that do not involve double taxation, as defined by Article 2 (1) (c) EU Tax Arbitration Directive. In particular, double taxation is the levying by two or more Member States of taxes in respect of the same taxable income or capital, when it gives rise to an additional tax charge, an increase in tax liabilities or the cancellation or reduction of losses that could be used to offset taxable profits.

The rationale of Article 16 (7) EU Tax Arbitration Directive is in our view twofold. First, in the absence of double taxation, the settlement of the cross-border tax dispute usually generates obstacles that have more limited importance within the internal market and therefore may be addressed by other legal instruments. Second, in such circumstances the settlement of cross-border tax disputes may potentially generate an exposure to double non-taxation, which is potentially undesirable.

---

158 Most States refer to domestic legislation. Denmark, Estonia and the Netherlands (until the 2005 amendment) limit the application of the convention only in the presence of criminal sanctions. By contrast, over one-third of the Member States (namely Austria, Bulgaria, Croatia, Czech Republic, Finland, Germany, Greece (from the 2005 amendment onwards) Italy, Slovenia, Slovakia and Sweden) generally excludes the application of the convention also when administrative penalties are applicable. Other countries, such as Greece (until the 2005 amendment), Hungary and Portugal (until the 2005 amendment), apply this above the thresholds, or, as in the case of Belgium, Latvia and Spain, to forms of more serious administrative violations. Luxembourg follows the rule of the other State involved. Ireland and Romania determine the nature of serious penalty by reference to the type of tax violation. Cyprus, France, Ireland, Lithuania apply this also to cases of failures in the framework of tax inspections. Poland and Portugal (after the 2005 amendment) require evidence of the intention to defraud. France potentially considers the existence of a serious penalty in case of tax avoidance, since it expressly refers to the abuse of rights theory. Finally, Malta interprets the term in a very similar way to the wording currently used by the EU Tax Arbitration Directive and the BEPS MLI.

159 Besides, it is not self-evident that double taxation may be left unresolved if fraud or irregularities are suspected or even proven. Indeed, not eliminating the double taxation amounts to a double penalty for the same (suspected) offence, one through criminal prosecution or administrative fining, and another through the wilful maintaining of double taxation. We submit that fraud and irregularities should attract criminal or administrative sanctions, rather than arbitrary excessive taxation.

160 The JTPF has condemned this state of affairs and has undertaken to look at possibilities for coordination. See TPF Summary report on Penalties, Commission staff working document of 14 September 2009, SEC (2009) 1168 final.

21.6.2.9 *Cost of the proceedings*

The rules on the cost of the proceedings reflect the overall vision of each legal instrument for settling cross-border tax dispute, but also present some common features.

Since Article 25 OECD MC and the BEPS MLI treat the dispute as a matter for the sole Contracting Jurisdictions involved, the affected person(s) are excluded from any obligation to bear cost.

Although Article 25 OECD MC does not regulate this matter, it refers in the Commentary[161] to the conditions included in the sample agreement that the competent authorities may use as a basis for dispute settlement. Para. 13 of the sample agreement differentiates among five categories of cost, namely (i) cost for participation to the procedure, (ii) remuneration of arbitrators appointed by each State, (iii) remuneration and travel, communication and secretariat costs of other arbitrators, (iv) costs of the meetings of the arbitral panel and administrative personnel, and (v) all other cost of the procedure. The first two categories of cost are borne by each competent authority on a separate basis, whilst the remaining three are shared equally between them.

As for Article 25 BEPS MLI, the main criterion is that competent authorities settle the matter by mutual agreement, in the absence of which Contracting Jurisdictions to bear such cost in equal shares.

The regulation contained in the EU Tax Arbitration Convention and Directive also includes specific rules on cost borne by the affected person(s).

In particular, Article 11 (3) EU Tax Arbitration Convention always requires equal participation to all cost of the advisory commission procedure by the States involved, except for those incurred by the associated enterprises, which shall be borne by such enterprises.

Article 12 (1) EU Tax Arbitration Directive applies exactly the same criterion as under the BEPS MLI,[162] but further specifies that the affected person(s) will bear their own cost. Furthermore, Article 12 (2) obliges such person(s) to bear all cost of the dispute settlement procedure when such person(s) withdraw(s) the complaint or when the advisory commission confirms the rejection of the complaint that had been put forward by competent authorities during the unilateral phase. The rationale of this provision is to discourage taxpayers from filing complaints in situations where the existence of a cross-border tax problem connected with the interpretation and application of the convention is doubtful. Perhaps, it could also be fair to supplement such rule with an obligation for the competent authorities to bear in equal shares the cost incurred by the affected person(s) in cases where the complaint is well founded, as it often happens under various applicable domestic legal remedies for tax controversies within the European Union.

---

161 See OECD, Commentary on Art. 25, para. 85.

162 However, Article 12 (1) (b) EU Tax Arbitration Directive caps the expenses of the independent persons to EUR 1000 per person per day of meetings of the advisory commission or alternative dispute resolution commission.

21.7 The relations with domestic judicial procedures

Domestic judicial procedures have an impact on cross-border legal instruments for settling cross-border tax disputes, which differs according to the regulation contained in each applicable instrument.

In particular, differences arise as to the relations with pending domestic administrative and judicial procedures.

Article 25 (5) OECD MC gives the directly affected person the right to request arbitration in cases of taxation not in accordance with the convention that competent authorities of the two Contracting States have failed to solve within two years from the presentation of the case. However, under Article 25 (5) OECD MC, the existence of a decision by an administrative of judicial instance in either Contracting State blocks the access to arbitration.[163]

This type of safeguard clause also operates under Article 19 (12) (a) MLI upon application of a specific reservation. Article 25 (5) OECD MC says nothing in respect of cases in which a decision by a domestic court is rendered after parties have submitted the case to arbitration. Since the third sentence of Article 25 (5) OECD MC gives the affected person the right to reject the mutual agreement implementing the arbitration decision, we believe that tax authorities may not apply Article 25 OECD MC in a way that obliges the affected persons to have previously given up the exercise of domestic legal remedies. However, for tax treaties between States that have opted in Part VI of the BEPS Multilateral Instrument, Article 19 (12) (b) MLI allows in such circumstances the Contracting Jurisdictions the right to terminate the arbitration process in the presence of a decision rendered by a domestic court or administrative tribunal.

Article 7 EU Arbitration Convention presupposes the completion of domestic judicial remedies, since it requires a final judicial decision in case the affected persons have activated such remedies. In such circumstances, according to Article 7 second sentence EU Arbitration Convention, the deadline for setting up the advisory commission shall be computed from the date of the final judicial decision.

The interaction with domestic legal remedies is more complex under the EU Tax Arbitration Directive, since the latter allows for an interaction between mutual agreement and domestic procedures.

In particular, Article 5 (3) states that when all competent authorities reject a complaint, the affected person may file an appeal against the decision in accordance with national rules. According to Articles 5 (3) and 6 (1) second sentence, the appeal blocks the access to the advisory commission, i.e. to arbitration under the EU Directive, until a final judicial decision is rendered. Articles 6 (1) adds to such cases also that of a written declaration through which the affected person formally renounces the right of appeal. Furthermore,

163 See further on this OECD, Commentary on Art. 25, paras. 76-80 and 82.

Article 5 (3) (c) EU Tax Arbitration also excludes arbitration when national law does not allow derogating the decisions resulting from the appeal.

As Article 16 EU Tax Arbitration Directive specifically indicates, domestic legal remedies may apply in parallel with those provided by the Directive itself.

However, Article 16 (3) EU Tax Arbitration Directive adds that the terms of periods for the start (Article 3 (5) EU Tax Arbitration Directive) and completion (Article 4 (1) EU Tax Arbitration Directive) of the mutual agreement procedure are to be computed from the moment of a final judicial decision, of the equivalent conclusion of a judicial procedure or its suspension.

Furthermore, when national law of a Member State does not allow it to derogate from judicial decisions, Article 16 (4) EU Tax Arbitration Directive sets obligations of notification for competent authorities of that State to notify the existence of such decision. When this decision predates the moment of agreement in the framework of the mutual agreement procedure, or of the opinion of the advisory commission or alternative dispute resolution commission, such procedures must be terminated from the moment of the notification.

CHAPTER 22

The Pillar Two Directive

Daniël Smit[1]

22.1 Introduction

Under the heading of the ambitious Base Erosion and Profit Shifting (BEPS) project, countries worldwide have been working on a large scale since 2013 on the initiative of the OECD and the G-20 to reduce (aggressive) international tax planning by multinational companies. The premise is that corporate profits should always be taxed somewhere, preferably in the country where these profits are created. As a result, over the past decade, profit taxes have been further standardized globally in numerous ways both unilaterally and bi- or multilaterally, mainly through the introduction of specific and general anti-abuse provisions and by increasing existing standards against harmful tax competition. International exchange of information has also boomed, for example through the introduction of mandatory country-by-country reporting by large multinational companies (see section 28.3.2.4 25) and mandatory disclosure of (aggressive) tax planning schemes (see Chapter 29). This allows tax administrations to get the "bigger international tax picture" of these companies more quickly.

The BEPS project, however, looks at protecting countries' tax bases. It does not concern itself with the tax rates that countries subsequently apply to this base. As a result, internationally operating companies can (continue to) seek international mismatches in the form of tax rate advantages, for example by diverting or allocating corporate profits to no- or low-tax jurisdictions, or by transferring, without (exit) taxation, valuable assets (and the associated people functions) from no- or low-tax jurisdictions to high-tax countries.[2] Likewise, countries can still engage in international tax competition practices by offering favourable tax regimes that are generally applicable (e.g. a generally applicable low-tax rate regime). In this light, it does not come as a surprise that the OECD published a blueprint for a minimum rate tax for large multinationals in a follow-up initiative on October 14, 2020.[3] After all, tax base and rate are communicating vessels. The premise here is that corporate profits should not only always be taxed somewhere, but also sufficiently. This should

1 Professor (by special appointment) of Taxation of the Digital Economy, ACTL, University of Amsterdam; Head of the Scientific Tax Department of EY, Amsterdam.

2 Which countries also forego taxation to the extent that they assume that the profit does not "belong" in their jurisdiction because it predates the transfer. Over-valuation by the high-tax jurisdiction of the transferred assets may even increase this effect.

3 OECD (2020), Tax Challenges Arising from Digitalisation – Report on Pillar Two Blueprint: Inclusive Framework on BEPS, OECD/G20 Base Erosion and Profit Shifting Project, OECD Publishing, Paris, https://doi.org/10.1787/abb4c3d1-en.

put a floor on international tax competition and solve remaining BEPS-issues. Although international tax harmonization has long been politically taboo, political agreement on this blueprint was reached among 137 countries[4] worldwide in the fall of 2021 (shortly after the worldwide COVID-19 crisis with its massive budgetary consequences), resulting in the political adoption of the Pillar Two OECD Model Rules on 30 November 2021. This agreement means, in short, that while countries are not required to implement a global minimum tax, they should (for the sake of uniformity) follow these OECD Model Rules at the time they do implement. On 20 December 2021, the OECD officially published these Model Rules,[5] followed by an explanation (the Commentary) of these rules on 14 March 2022,[6] with multiple updates afterwards.

Within the European Union, the OECD Model Rules have been legally implemented through the Pillar Two Directive, which was adopted with the required unanimity by EU member states on 15 December 2022, after first Poland, and then Hungary hesitated for some time.[7] This EU Directive converts the legally non-binding OECD Model Rules within the EU into hard law, incidentally with some adjustments aimed primarily at preventing possible conflicts with primary EU law.

Hence, what seemed unthinkable for a long time recently became a reality. Starting in 2024, large multinationals – wherever head-quartered – operating within the European Union are required to pay at least an effective 15% annual profit tax in every country where they make excess profits. If this does not happen, EU member states where the multinational operates may have to levy a top-up tax to this minimum rate of 15%. In order to give business time to prepare for this new tax from an administrative point of view, various transitional arrangements (safe harbours) are provided for.

22.2 The Pillar Two Directive in a nutshell

In a nutshell, as stated before, the Pillar Two Directive has the effect that starting as of 2024, large domestic and multinational enterprises operating within the EU will have to pay annually at least an effective 15% profits tax on their excess (residual) profits in each country where they are operating. Excess profits typically include profits arising

4 These 137 countries thus consist of both OECD / G-20 / EU member countries and non-member countries, including a large number of developing countries, and together form part of the so-called "Inclusive Framework." Currently, the number of countries has reached 147 (status as of May 28, 2024).

5 OECD (2021), Tax Challenges Arising from the Digitalisation of the Economy – Global Anti-Base Erosion Model Rules (Pillar Two): Inclusive Framework on BEPS, OECD Publishing, Paris, https://doi.org/10.1787/782bac33-and. The OECD has updated and may continue to update this Guidance from time to time. The question of what the legal status of this Guidance is (including subsequent amendments) I leave unaddressed here.

6 OECD (2022), Tax Challenges Arising from the Digitalisation of the Economy – Guidance to the Global Anti-Base Erosion Model Rules (Pillar Two), First Edition: Inclusive Framework on BEPS, OECD Publishing, Paris, https://doi.org/10.1787/1e0e9cd8-en.

7 Council Directive (EU) 2022/2523 of 14 December 2022 on ensuring a global minimum level of taxation for multinational enterprise groups and large-scale domestic groups in the Union, OJ L 328, 22 December 2022, pp. 1-58.

from intangible assets – whether or not easily movable (such as trademark rights) – or profits arising from the presence of intra-group synergies. Thus, as a conceptual starting point, routine business profits are excluded from the minimum tax.

The crux is in the word "effectively". The fact that the statutory rate in a country is above 15% is thus not relevant. The effective tax burden (commonly referred to as the ETR; effective tax rate) must be determined, per country and per year. This effective tax burden is determined, on the one hand, according to an autonomous profit standard (the so-called "GloBE" income base) which primarily emerges from the commercial accounts of the large enterprise, subject to a number of adjustments that the Pillar Two Directive specifically provides for (the so-called denominator) and, on the other hand, by determining the amount of (covered) taxes (the so-called numerator). The ETR is calculated by dividing the amount of taxes by the amount of GloBE income per country and per year. The perhaps somewhat counter-intuitive consequence of the Pillar Two Directive's approach is that companies cannot simply assume that they will not encounter top-up taxation to the extent that they operate in a country with a high statutory tax rate. If a large enterprise, for example, avails itself of a particular tax facility in that high-tax country that is not grandfathered under the GloBE base (such as a tax facility to encourage research and development or a "green" tax incentive), this may result in a decrease in the effective rate. In particular, accumulation of (non-grandfathered) tax facilities may still put a company at risk. Conversely, a company operating in a non-taxing or low-taxing country will soon find itself "at risk", although the latter is not an automatism either.

If a large enterprise's profits are taxed below the 15% ETR-threshold in a given country in a given year, other EU member states in which the enterprise is active may have to levy a so-called "top-up tax" up to the minimum effective rate of 15%. A coordinated top-up tax mechanism has been created for this purpose. The country where the ultimate parent company is established is the first to apply the top-up tax under the so-called income inclusion rule (IIR, see section 22.7.1). If no or insufficient top-up tax is levied there, then – roughly speaking – the country or countries in which the subsidiaries and eventually, under the so-called undertaxed profit rule (UTPR, see section 22.7.2), the other operating companies of the multinational are established come next. Essentially, therefore, a top-up tax should be levied always somewhere, preferably at the top parent level, and otherwise elsewhere within the group.

Yet, countries that effectively tax below the 15% ETR-threshold, will first be allowed to apply a (domestic) top-up tax up to 15% themselves before the above top-up tax mechanism comes into play. It does not come as a surprise that many countries will do the latter. After all, few countries will want to become thieves of their own pockets. Therefore, top-up tax abroad will probably turn out to be the exception rather than the main rule, and (domestic) top-up tax in the low-tax country will turn out to be the main rule in practice. It is notable that both the OECD Model Rules and the Pillar Two Directive recognize this possibility of domestic top-up taxation, but have not elaborated on it further. The OECD, however, did publish a general framework within which countries wishing to introduce such a domestic top-up tax should move.[8] It expressly follows from this that countries should not adopt a different base for calculating such a tax. On the other hand, countries do have some manoeuvring space in the concrete interpretation of the domestic top-up tax base, as long as this base is not more favourable than the GloBE base.

To determine whether, and if so where, additional taxation should take place, there are essentially the following 5 steps to follow:
1. Does a large enterprise fall within the personal scope of the Piller Two Directive?
2. What is the amount of profit according to the GloBE base-standard per country and per year?
3. What is the amount of covered tax per country and per year?
4. Given the results under steps 2 and 3, is the effective tax rate in any country below 15% in a given year?
5. If yes, which Member State(s) should levy a top up tax?

Each step is briefly outlined below, with references to the relevant provisions of the Directive.

22.3 Personal scope of the Directive

22.3.1 *Only large domestic and multinational groups: the €750 threshold*

The top-up tax mechanism of the Pillar Two Directive is limited in terms of personal scope. First, there must be a domestic or multinational group with annual revenues of at least €750 million. Next in scope are the entities forming part of this group that are established in a Member State.

Conceptually, there is no immediate good reason to limit the scope of the Directive to very large companies. The limitation can mainly be explained by efficiency considerations. The additional administrative burden that the Pillar Two Directive would impose on smaller businesses and the tax authorities is probably disproportionate to the expected additional benefits. Moreover, the €750 million turnover threshold is aligned with the same threshold that already applies to mandatory country-by-country reporting for large multinational companies (see section 28.3.2.4). That group is considered best able to absorb the additional administrative burden.[9]

In assessing the €750 million turnover threshold, the consolidated financial statements of the ultimate parent entity are used. In order to avoid excessive shock effects in the event of annual revenue fluctuations, a 4-year look-back reference period applies. If the said threshold is exceeded in at least two of the four fiscal years immediately preceding the fiscal year tested, the turnover requirement is met. If an accounting year is shorter

8 OECD (2023), Tax Challenges Arising from the Digitalisation of the Economy – Administrative Guidance on the Global Anti-Base Erosion Model Rules (Pillar Two), OECD/G20 Inclusive Framework on BEPS, OECD, Paris, https://www.oecd.org/tax/beps/agreed-administrative-guidance-for-the-pillar-two-globe-rules.pdf.
9 *Cf.* OECD-Guidance (2022), para. 5, p. 14.

or longer than 12 months, the €750 million threshold is recalculated proportionally.[10] In the case of a new group, the turnover threshold can be met at the earliest in the third year after the creation of the group.[11] Furthermore, a specific approach applies to cases where a standalone entity becomes part of a group at some point.[12]

In determining the turnover threshold, minority shareholders in the group are not taken into account.[13] Furthermore, the turnover of exempt entities is included (assuming it is subject to the consolidated financial statements requirement). This approach was deliberately chosen to avoid complex allocation issues, among other things.[14]

22.3.2 Group entities (Constituent Entities)

As a main rule, only entities, including permanent establishments, that are part of a group (so-called constituent entities) are in scope of the top-up tax mechanism of the Pillar Two Directive. Whether this is the case must be determined on the basis of the applicable accounting standards of the ultimate parent company of the group, provided there is an accepted accounting standard, such as IFRS.[15] The determining factor thereby is, in principle, whether the results of a group entity must be included in the consolidated financial statements of the ultimate parent company (the so-called UPE; Ultimate Parent Entity). The degree of ownership and control is decisive. If the parent company does not prepare consolidated financial statements, or does not prepare accepted consolidated financial statements, the size of the group should be determined by applying an accepted accounting standard.[16] Entities that are exempt from the consolidation requirement under the applicable accounting standards still qualify as a group entity as long as there is control. This could include entities held for sale and entities that are exempt from consolidation due to a lack of materiality.[17] Finally, the term "ultimate parent" implies that the entity itself is not controlled by a (grand)parent that is subject to consolidated financial statements requirements. If the latter is the case, then that (grand)parent is the ultimate parent or, in turn, the parent of that (grand)parent, and so on.[18]

The Pillar Two Directive provides for some specific exceptions to the group entity concept. These include government entities, international organizations, non-profit organizations, pension funds and investment funds (including real estate vehicles) that are ultimate parent entities. To the extent that an entity falls into one of these categories, it is exempt from the group concept and thus from the personal scope of the Pillar Two Directive. Under certain conditions, entities that are held by one of the aforementioned categories of exempt entities are also exempt. It is stressed in this respect that the Pillar Two Directive

10 Article 2 paragraph 2 of the Directive.
11 *Cf.* OECD-Guidance (2022), para. 8, p. 15.
12 OECD-Guidance (2022), para. 7, p. 15.
13 OECD-Guidance (2022), para. 11, p. 15.
14 OECD-Guidance (2022), para. 12, p. 16.
15 Article 3 sub 3 of the Directive.
16 Article 3 sub 6 of the Directive.
17 Article 3 sub 3 of the Directive.
18 Article 3 sub 14 of the Directive.

provides an autonomous definition of the listed exempt entities. This means that the definition under domestic corporate tax law of, for example, the term (exempt) "pension fund" or "governmental entity" is not leading. Mismatches between the definition under the directive and national legislation are thus not fully excluded meaning that entities that are exempt under their local corporate tax rules could under circumstances still face top-up tax under the Directive.

22.3.3 *Place of residence of a group entity*

For purposes of the Pillar Two Directive, it is important to determine the place of residence of each individual group company for several reasons. First, the Directive applies only to group entities established in a Member State. Specifically, this means that the Directive's top-up tax mechanism is limited to group entities within the EU. In addition, the tax residency of each group entity (EU or non-EU) is important for the calculation of the local ETR of this entity. After all, the ETR is calculated on a per-country basis with no distinction being made between EU and non-EU group entities.

The foregoing raises the question of how to determine the tax residence of each individual group entity for purposes of the Pillar Two Directive. The starting point is that this has to be assessed under reference to the applicable (corporate) tax law of the relevant Member State. As a main rule, a group entity is established in the jurisdiction in which it is considered to be tax resident based on its place of management, place of incorporation, or similar criteria.[19] If this formula fails to identify the tax residency, the country under the law of which the relevant group entity is incorporated will be considered as the state of residence. A different approach applies to so-called flow-through entities.

Generally, the above formula will suffice to determine the tax residence of a group company. However, it may happen that a group entity is considered tax resident in two different Member States at the same time. For those cases, the Directive provides for a specific tie-breaker rule. The basic principle here is that the place of residence as it follows from the applicable tax treaty between the two countries is used.[20] If no tax treaty has been concluded, or if the tax treaty provides for a mutual agreement procedure to determine the treaty residence and no agreement on the treaty residence has been reached, the group entity will be deemed to be located in the country that has levied the highest amount of (covered) taxes in the relevant reporting year.[21] If this amount is equal or zero in two countries, the group entity will be deemed to be resident in the country with the highest amount of excluded income under the substance-based income exclusion (see section 22.6 below).[22] If this amount is again equal, or nil, in two countries, then the group entity is considered stateless, unless it is an ultimate parent. In the latter case, the residence is in principle determined by falling back on the country under which the

19 Article 4 paragraph 1 of the Directive.
20 Article 4 paragraph 4 of the Directive.
21 Article 4 paragraph 4 jo. paragraph 5 of the Directive.
22 Article 4 paragraph 5 of the Directive.

relevant ultimate parent company was incorporated.[23] Finally, changes of tax residence within an accounting year are ignored.[24]

It follows from the above that under certain circumstances a group entity can be considered stateless. The significance of this is, among other things, that the calculation of the effective tax rate in that case takes place exclusively at the level of this entity.[25] It is therefore not possible in that case to include income and taxes of other group entities established in the same country when determining the ETR for that (stateless) entity.

Finally, and in addition to the above, the place of residence of permanent establishments (which are also treated as group companies; see section 22.4.18) must also be determined. Specific rules apply here for, among other things, treaty and non-treaty situations.[26] A permanent establishment is considered stateless the moment there is a mismatch where, in brief, the residence country where the head office is located grants an exemption while the other country does not recognize a permanent establishment and thus does not levy a (corresponding) tax.

22.4 The GloBE base (the Denominator)

22.4.1 Introduction

The annual determination of the GloBE base is the backbone of the Pillar Two Directive. The Globe base forms, after all, the benchmark under reference to which the ETR is to be determined. This benchmark floats more or less between the methodologies for the accounting and tax calculation of profits. In practice, this means that both business and the authorities of each Member State (in particular the tax authorities and courts) have to deal with a whole new set of profit determination rules that must be interpreted and applied on top of the existing accounting and corporate income tax rules. From a practical perspective, it is not unimportant that this new set of rules presupposes the presence of certain data that traditionally are not included in the administration of large domestic and multinational companies. Since the GloBE base takes the accounting profit determination as its starting point, it should be clearly seen that to that extent the Pillar Two Directive should be regarded as supplementary law. It is basically only the derogations to the commercial profit determination under the applicable accounting standard that are regulated by the Directive. If a particular issue is not regulated in the Pillar Two Directive, then one falls entirely back on the applicable commercial accounting standards. Thus viewed, the Directive itself does not contain a fully autonomous profit standard. A sound knowledge of commercial accounting law is thus indispensable to arrive at a meaningful determination of the ETR.

23 Article 4 paragraph 5 of the Directive. An exception is provided for in paragraph 6.
24 Article 4 paragraph 9 of the Directive.
25 Article 26 paragraph 4 of the Directive.
26 Article 4 paragraph 3 of the Directive.

22.4.2 *Profit for accounting purposes as the starting point, subject to adjustments*

The starting point is formed by looking at the standalone commercial (net) profit per group entity, determined according to the (consolidated) accounting standards of the ultimate parent company (e.g. IFRS or another GAAP).[27] This is the standalone accounting of the relevant group entity prior to consolidation; intra-group transactions, for example, are not eliminated.[28] Using these (deconsolidated) accounts – and, for example, not the local accounts in the various jurisdictions – ensures maximum uniformity, avoids potential arbitrage and reduces implementation burdens.[29] Only under strict conditions – for example, in the case of a recent acquisition of a new group that historically applies a different accounting standard – may this be deviated from.[30] Minor differences between the local accounts and the accounts that serve as the basis for the group's consolidated financial statements may be disregarded. Any minority shareholders are not taken into account in the calculation, since they are already taken into account in the allocation under the income inclusion rule (see section 22.7, below). If the accounting of the relevant group entity as used to prepare the group's consolidated financial statements does not qualify as an accepted standard, then a recalculation must be made in accordance with a well-accepted standard.[31]

In many countries, commercial profit determination for accounting purposes may differ substantially from profit determination for corporate tax purposes. Without further adjustments, these (permanent) differences could inadvertently lead to mandatory top-up taxes. For example, many countries exempt benefits from a participation in a subsidiary (e.g. dividends and capital gains) from taxation when determining the corporate tax liability of the (corporate) parent company with the aim of avoiding economic double taxation of corporate profits. For accounting purposes, however, this income is in principle reported. Thus, without further adjustments, this difference could cause companies to quickly dip below the 15% ETR threshold. In this example, however, the tax policy objective of avoiding double taxation on corporate profits is respected under the Pillar Two Directive. This means that an adjustment is made to the commercial profit calculation for, among other things, participation dividends and capital gains.[32] Tax consolidation regimes (such as the Dutch fiscal unity) and shipping regimes ("tonnage regimes"), among others, are also respected. Conversely, adjustments are made for certain expenses that are not tax deductible but that are deductible for accounting purposes. These include, for example, fines and taxes. These expenses need, as a main rule, to be added back to the commercial result.

However, the chosen approach is not completely conclusive. There may still be (smaller or larger) differences between, for example, the participation exemption in the Pillar Two Directive and the participation exemption in the domestic corporate income tax laws of

27 Article 15 paragraph 1 of the Directive.
28 Article 15 paragraph 1 of the Directive.
29 OECD Guidance (2022), para. 7, p. 44.
30 *Cf.* OECD Guidance (2022), para. 13, p. 46.
31 Article 15 paragraph 2 of the Directive.
32 Article 16 paragraph 2 sub b and c of the Directive.

the various Member States. For example, the Netherlands allows, subject to conditions, deduction of losses incurred when liquidating a participation, which can lead to a reduction in the Dutch corporate tax liability. Under the Pillar Two Directive, however, such liquidation losses are exempt and therefore non-deductible. Thus, such permanent differences between commercial profit calculation and the tax profit calculation may still influence the ETR. Also, for example, domestic tonnage regimes may not always correspond exactly to the corresponding shipping income exclusion as included in the Pillar Two Directive itself.[33] Again, there may remain certain permanent differences that could affect the ETR. With respect to domestic shipping regimes, a (probably inadmissible) action has been lodged before the Court of Justice of the EU as to whether this is incompatible with primary EU law.[34] See also section 22.4.17.

Furthermore, there remains a category of tax facilities that are not recognized when calculating the GloBE base under the Pillar Two Directive. This category of permanent differences includes e.g. tax incentives for research and development and "green" tax incentives. This means that the benefits of those facilities could potentially (partly) be removed the moment a company falls below the 15% ETR threshold in the country in question, although the so-called substance-based income exclusion may still provide (some) relief in such a case (see section 22.6 below).

In addition to the above, the draftsmen of the Pillar Two rules have realized at some point in time that companies could try to shift profits from a low-tax to a high-tax jurisdiction for accounting purposes only, for example by using non-market intra-group transfer prices that are adjusted only for corporate tax purposes by the countries involved, or by creating intra-group debt for accounting purposes that is considered equity for tax purposes in both jurisdictions. In this way, the ETR in the low-tax jurisdiction could be inflated. This could lead to unintentional avoidance of top-up tax. To prevent this, and thus to protect the integrity of the Pillar Two Directive, the GloBE base determination rules contain a number of specific regulations that are similar to some anti-tax avoidance provisions as we are familiar with in the context of the BEPS project (see e.g. section 22.4.13). However, the Pillar Two Directive does not contain a general anti-abuse rule (GAAR) and the question is whether companies might still find ways to influence the GloBE base in their favour.

22.4.2.1 Net tax expenditures

First, an adjustment should be made to the commercial profit for net tax expenditures.[35] The background here is that such expenses will not usually not affect the amount of taxable profits. This means that taxes paid and any tax deferrals accrued in any year should be added-back to the commercial profit. On the other hand, deferred tax reductions, for example due to the presence of tax loss carry forwards, can be deducted from the commercial profit. The amount of taxes include those taxes to which the Pillar Two

33 Article 17 of the Directive.

34 Pending case C-146 P/24. See in more detail: D.S. Smit, in: CJEU - Recent Developments in Direct Taxation 2023 (eds M. Lang et al.), The Netherlands: Fugro (T-143/23) & ExxonMobil (T-802/22), Linde Verlag, 2024, blz. 19-29.

35 Article 16 paragraph 2, sub a of the Directive.

Directive applies, including top-up taxes and domestic top-up taxes, whether the latter two are paid or recognized as deferrals. Taxes related to income that is exempt under the GloBE base, such as income from a participation, are not deductible (i.e. must be added-back as well). Taxes that can be credited are also not deductible.[36]

22.4.2.2 Participation income

Second, an adjustment must be made for participation income reflected in the accounts of the local group entity.[37] For this purpose, the Directive distinguishes between two categories of income: dividend income and capital gains. Dividend income is exempt provided there is a participation interest of at least 10% (non-portfolio shareholding); if the interest is less than 10% (portfolio shareholding), dividend income is only exempt if this interest is held by the relevant entity for at least one year. Capital gains are exempt only if there is a participation interest of at least 10% (non-portfolio shareholding), but irrespective of the period of ownership. Commercial revaluation of a participation interest of at least 10% must be adjusted and previously exempt dividend income must be taken into account as well. The participation exemption is a gross exemption. This means that the deduction of costs related to the participation, such as financing costs, is not eliminated. Furthermore, the exemption applies not only to positive results, but also to losses incurred on a participation (i.e. losses are non-deductible).

22.4.3 Revaluation of certain tangible assets

Certain tangible assets are subject to a specific rule that aims to treat commercial revaluations of such assets symmetrically.[38]

22.4.4 Foreign exchange results

There is also a specific requirement for foreign exchange gains and losses to achieve symmetrical treatment between commercial and tax profit computation.[39]

22.4.5 Non-deductible fines, etc.

The Directive- further respects the fact that under the tax systems of many countries, fines, bribes and the like are not deductible. Indeed, such a deduction would be tantamount to the treasury co-paying for such payments. As a result, these deductions must be added-back to the commercial profit. There is a de minimis exception for fines up to €50,000 for practical reasons.[40]

36 OECD Guidance (2022), pp. 48-49.
37 Article 16 paragraph 2, sub b and sub c of the Directive.
38 Article 16 paragraph 2 sub b d of the Directive.
39 Article 16 paragraph 2 sub f of the Directive.
40 Article 16 paragraph 2 sub g of the Directive.

22.4.6 *Material changes for the purpose of balance sheet continuity*

Furthermore, the Directive contains a specific rule for (material) changes due to (i) previous errors in the financial statements of the relevant group entity and (ii) the application of a new method.[41]

22.4.7 *Employee stock options*

With respect to stock options in relation to stock-based compensation for employees, the Directive also intends to be consistent with the tax treatment in many countries. Whereas for accounting purposes the granting of employee stock options typically results in an expense at that time, for tax purposes the deduction is often only made at the time the option is exercised. Since the value at exercise will usually be higher than at grant, without further provision the ETR could drop in a certain year. In order to avoid this, also for GloBE base purposes, the choice is offered per country to match the timing by allowing a deduction no earlier than on the moment of exercise, provided that the option expense is attributable to the relevant group entity.[42] An election made applies for 5 years and to all group entities within the relevant jurisdiction. Some specific recapture provisions apply to avoid double counting.

22.4.8 *Pension contributions*

The Directive aims to be consistent with the tax treatment of pension liabilities in many countries. When determining the GloBE base, only contributions actually made to a pension fund, rather than the amount of pension expense included in determining the commercial profit in a reporting year, are taken into account in the year in which they are incurred.[43] This adjustment also eliminates differences in treatment under different accounting standards.

22.4.9 *At arm's length adjustments*

In determining the GloBE base, the prices used within the group may have to comply with the at arm's length principle.[44] This requirement is logical because otherwise the profits for commercial purposes within the group could easily be manipulated; for example, profits could be shifted from low-tax to high-tax countries for accounting purposes only. In principle, no adjustment needs to be made if the prices used for accounting purposes are considered at arm's length and thus followed for tax purposes as well. In that case, no mismatch arises between the tax and commercial profit calculation. However, adjustment may be necessary if there is a "mismatch" between the fiscal and accounting profit calculation in order to avoid double taxation or double non-taxation.

41 Article 16 paragraph 2 sub h of the Directive.
42 Article 16 paragraph 3 of the Directive.
43 Article 16 paragraph 2 sub i of the Directive.
44 Article 16 paragraph 4 of the Directive.

If the intra-group transactions take place within the same jurisdiction, there will not always be a need to adjust the prices charged on the basis of the at arm's length principle for tax purposes. After all, there will usually be a "zero sum game"; a downward profit adjustment in one group entity will be offset by an equally large upward profit adjustment in the other group entity within the same jurisdiction. From this perspective, there is in principle no reason to make an adjustment in the GloBE base if the commercially applied transfer price differs from the price applied for tax purposes; as long as the same price is used for the entities concerned. However, an exception is the situation in which a loss is created by non-business dealings within the group that can be deducted from the GloBE base; an arm's length adjustment will then have to be made within the GloBE base.[45]

22.4.10 *Qualifying tax credits*

Under conditions, in determining the GloBE base, certain qualifying credits are treated as direct subsidies. On the one hand, such credits increase the GloBE base. The latter is explicitly stipulated in the Directive, to the extent that this does not already follow from the applicable accounting standard.[46] On the other hand, however, these qualifying credits may be added to the amount of covered taxes to the extent that these credits were deducted from the (covered) taxes under the applicable accounting standard. On the other hand, non-qualifying credits are excluded from the GloBE base and reduce the amount of covered taxes.[47] In relative terms, therefore, qualifying tax credits decrease a group company's ETR less rigorously than other non-honoured tax incentives that do not qualify.

22.4.11 *Option for the realization principle*

An important difference between the determination of profit for accounting purposes on the one hand and for tax purposes on the other, is that hidden reserves (potential future profits) embedded in the assets and liabilities of a group entity typically need not be reported for tax purposes until realization; for accounting purposes, they may already be reported at the time the profit is accrued. This can create timing mismatches between commercial and tax profit calculations which may adversely impact the ETR in a given year. To avoid timing mismatches, group entities are permitted to opt to apply the realization principle on a country-by-country basis.[48] Such an election extends to a period of 5 years and applies in principle to all assets and liabilities of the group entities concerned, unless the election is limited to tangible assets. A specific recapture provision applies in cases where the 5-year period expires.

22.4.12 *Option for staggered backwards allocation of capital gains*

Similar to the previous regime, the Pillar Two Directive provides the option for a group entity to annually elect on a country-by-country basis to spread a capital gain on the transfer of tangible assets (real estate) to third parties (i.e., not within the group) over

45 Article 16, paragraph 4 of the Directive.
46 Article 16, paragraph 5 of the Directive.
47 Article 16, paragraph 5 of the Directive.
48 Article 16 paragraph 6 of the Directive.

the past 5-year period.[49] Again, the aim is to neutralize timing mismatches by allocating the capital gain as much as possible to the period in which it accrued. By doing so, reinvestment facilities provided for in the domestic corporate tax law of a Member State may – indirectly – be honoured (wholly or partly). The aggregate result per year is the starting point. This means in the first place that per year all capital gains are taken together. The positive surplus then qualifies for staggered carry-back allocation. There are detailed rules governing the allocation of this surplus to the past 5-year period the aim of which is to ensure that the surplus is first set off as far as possible against capital losses incurred in this period (a loss can only be utilized once). If after loss offsetting there is still a surplus of capital gains, this surplus is allocated pro rata to the past 5-year period. If staggered allocation is opted for, a corresponding adjustment must be made in the amount of taxes involved.

22.4.13 Intra-group financing mismatches

The Directive aims to neutralize mismatches with respect to intra-group financing. One example is hybrid financing where the financing instrument is regarded as debt capital for commercial purposes by both group entities involved, while this instrument is regarded as equity capital for tax purposes by both group entities involved. In this case, there may be a profit shift for accounting purposes that is not seen for tax purposes. In this way, the effective tax rate in a low-tax country could be inflated. To prevent this effect, a tax "pickup" of a payment on a financial instrument at the recipient is introduced as a condition for recognition of the deduction at the paying party for purposes calculating the GloBE basis.[50] It is noted that the provision is not limited to said hybrid forms of financing.

22.4.14 Tax consolidation regimes

The starting point in determining the GloBE base is the standalone accounts of each individual group entity. Some countries have tax consolidation regimes, such as the Dutch fiscal unity. A feature of these regimes is that they seek tax neutrality, e.g. by ignoring intra-group transactions and by allowing horizontal loss compensation for tax purposes. Without further provision, this premise of tax neutrality could under circumstances be jeopardized by the standalone (per-entity) approach that is to be followed when calculating the GloBE base in that country under the Directive. To avoid this, the relevant group entities are given the option per country to determine the GloBE base on a consolidated basis.[51] However, this option does not extend to transactions with third parties, i.e., counterparties that are not part of the tax group regime. In addition, the option is limited to intra-group transactions within the same jurisdictions. Thus, any cross-border benefits of such a tax consolidation regime are not recognized.

49 Article 16 paragraph 7 of the Directive.
50 Article 16 paragraph 8 of the Directive.
51 Article 16 paragraph 9 of the Directive.

22.4.15 Taxes on insurer's investment income

The Directive contains a specific provision for insurance companies.[52] This provision deals with the treatment of tax imposed on an insurer's investment income where that tax is passed on to the ultimate policyholders. Under circumstances, under the applicable accounting standard, the insurance company could report a (covered) tax – even though it is actually passed through – against which other low-taxed income could be offset. The latter is expressly prevented under the Pillar Two Directive.

22.4.16 Additional tier one capital

Another adjustment deals with the treatment of so-called additional tier one capital.[53] This is additional buffer capital that financial institutions, such as banks, are required to hold. Some countries treat this capital as debt for tax purposes, while it is classified as equity for accounting purposes. The Directive avoids this mismatch by requiring that increases or decreases in a group entity's equity attributable to distributions related to additional tier-one capital be treated as income or expense in the calculation of GloBE income. Equity changes attributable to the issuance or redemption of additional tier one capital are not included in the calculation of GloBE income.

22.4.17 Shipping regimes

Many maritime countries – both inside and outside the EU have special tax regimes for maritime transport income, such as a tonnage regime. The Pillar Two Directive recognizes the tax policy considerations underlying such regimes. To this end, it exempts income from international transport income (persons and goods) from the GloBE base, including income from ancillary activities.[54] However, the Directive contains an autonomous definition of such income based which is based on Article 8 of the OECD Model Convention. Thus, the Directive does not align 100% with the applicable national tax regimes. As a result, mismatches between the national and GloBE base are not fully avoided. A further requirement is that management with respect to the maritime fleet in question is actually exercised by a group entity from the relevant jurisdiction. In other words, a certain economic link with the country where the shipping company in question is based is required. Again, this substance requirement may not necessarily correspond with the substance requirement applicable under the local tax regime. A (probably inadmissible) action has been lodged before the Court of Justice of the EU as to whether this is incompatible with primary EU law.[55]

52 Article 16 paragraph 10 of the Directive.
53 Article 16 paragraph 11 of the Directive.
54 Article 17 of the Directive.
55 Pending case C-146 P/24. See in more detail: D.S. Smit, in: CJEU - Recent Developments in Direct Taxation 2023 (eds M. Lang et al.), The Netherlands: Fugro (T-143/23) & ExxonMobil (T-802/22), Linde Verlag, 2024, blz. 19-29.

22.4.18 Profit allocation in case of a permanent establishment

Since a permanent establishment is not an independent legal entity, the Directive provides for specific regulations that deal with the attribution of GloBE income to a permanent establishment, which is treated as a group entity.[56] The basic principle here is that there should be as little difference as possible from the profit allocation for tax purposes. GloBE income allocated to a permanent establishment is not again regarded as GloBE income of the head office. Furthermore, the Directive provides a specific regime for cases in which permanent establishment losses can also be deducted for tax purposes at the level of the head-office.

22.4.19 Transparent and hybrid entities

The Directive provides for specific rules with respect to group entities that qualify as transparent entity from a tax perspective. The background to this is that such entities will generally do account for their own result for commercial purposes. Because of the aforementioned tax transparency, however, no tax will be attributable to such result, as the result will be attributed to the underlying partners and taxed at that level. The result would be that the effective tax rate of such an entity would fall below 15%, despite the fact that there is taxation to the underlying partners. To avoid this effect, the commercial result can, under circumstances, be allocated to its participants.[57] The attributable profit is also reduced to the extent that this profit is attributable to entities that are not part of the group. The "look-through approach" does not apply to a transparent entity that qualifies as the ultimate parent. Indeed, in the latter case, attribution to the partners would result in no top-up tax being due at all. Reverse hybrid entities are also subject to an important exception in order to ensure single taxation.

22.5 Covered taxes (the Numerator)

22.5.1 Introduction

After having determined the GloBE base, the amount of taxes per country and per year should be determined for answering the question of whether at least 15% tax is effectively due in that country. As a rule of thumb, the higher the amount of taxes per year/per country, the sooner the group entity in question will be above the 15% ETR threshold and vice versa. Of course, this is not an irrefutable rule. For example, taxes on income that is exempt under the GloBE-base cannot be taken into account when calculating the total amount of taxes. Ultimately, therefore, an actual calculation will typically be required in each case.

The main questions here are which taxes may and may not be taken into account, to which year these taxes should be allocated and to which jurisdiction they should be allocated. The Directive elaborates these questions in more detail.

56 Article 18 of the Directive.
57 Article 19 of the Directive.

22.5.2 *Taxes on income or profits*

To answer the question of which taxes qualify, the principle is that they must be taxes on the income or profits of the relevant group entity and recognized in the financial statements of that group entity.[58] Not the formal heading, but the characteristics of the tax, in substance, is decisive. Payroll taxes, sales taxes, transfer taxes, capital taxes and excise taxes do not qualify.[59] Nor do fines and fees paid to the government in exchange for an individual service qualify. The same applies in principle to digital services taxes. A tax based purely on a gross basis – i.e. without deduction of costs etc. – also does not qualify in principle; an exception applies to, among others, withholding taxes. However, the fact that the tax base is determined on a flat-rate basis does not necessarily prevent it from being classified as a tax. Taxation on deemed income, as is the case for example with a CFC-legislation, does qualify as tax. Taxes levied in lieu of normal corporate income tax, such as a withholding tax on dividends, interest or royalty payments or a tax under a tonnage regime, in principle also qualify as tax, even if the basis differs from the normal corporate income tax base. Taxes on reserves and equity can also qualify. However, it is required that this tax cannot be seen as an independent tax in addition to the existing corporate income tax.

22.5.3 *Timing differences*

An important aspect in determining the covered taxes in a given year is timing differences between commercial and tax profit determination at the time income is recognized (temporary differences). For example, it is conceivable that for purposes of calculating the taxable profits, it is allowed under circumstances to deduct the purchase price of a certain asset from the taxable profits at once, whereas for accounting purposes this asset must be capitalized, after which it can then be depreciated annually. From a tax point of view, the deduction at once in the first year leads to an advantage in the form of a lower taxable profit in that year. However, this advantage is eventually neutralized in subsequent years by a correspondingly higher annual taxable profit (after all, no tax depreciation is possible in those years). The deduction of the purchase price in year 1 is thus offset by a deferred future tax liability in subsequent years. The question is how to deal with such timing mismatches when calculating the effective tax rate in the relevant years. Ignoring these timing differences entirely could result in a top-up tax becoming payable in certain shorter periods while, measured over a longer period, there is no effective tax rate below 15%. The Directive addresses this issue by taking into account deferred tax positions. The starting point chosen is that the Directive links up, as a main rule, with the treatment of deferred tax liabilities in the applied accounting standard. In practical terms, this means adhering to the method of deferred tax accounting.[60] Specifically, this means, among other things, that future taxes payable are, as it were, brought forward (spread) for the calculation of the effective tax rate. Conversely, the same applies to losses that can be carried forward.

58 Article 20 paragraph 1 of the Directive.
59 *Cf.* OECD-Guidance (2022), para. 36, p. 94.
60 Article 21 paragraph 1 sub b juncto Article 22 of the Directive.

However, the Pillar Two Directive provides for a number of important corrections to the aforementioned premise. For example, as a starting point, temporary differences that are not realized or settled within a 5-year period are not recognized, so that top-up can still arise.[61] There are a number of exceptions to this among others, with respect to tangible assets and research and development costs.[62] Furthermore, to protect the integrity of the GloBE rules, deferred taxes are taken into account at (a maximum of) 15% only and not at the possibly higher nominal rate. Timing mismatches are thus recognized, but not fully and also not in all cases. The foregoing concerns only temporary differences between the GloBE bases and the domestic tax base determination. Permanent differences are obviously not subject to further regulation.

22.5.4 *Specific adjustments*

22.5.4.1 Introduction

A number of specific adjustments must be made to the amount of covered taxes that emerge from the commercial accounts. These adjustments supplement the main rule set out above. Furthermore, one should keep in mind the interrelationship between the determination of the amount of taxes (the numerator) and the determination of GloBE income (the denominator) since taxes should be eliminated from this GloBE base.

22.5.4.2 Taxes on exempt GloBE income

Excluded from the amount of tax are first and foremost taxes related to income exempt under the GloBE base.[63] This could include participation dividends that are not exempt for tax purposes (e.g. dividends by foreign low-taxed and passive participations), but that are exempt for Pillar Two purposes, or income that is not exempt under a domestic tonnage regime but is exempt under the Pillar Two international shipping exclusion. In case income is partially exempt under the Pillar Two base, the corresponding tax is disregarded on a pro rata basis. Withholding taxes on (participation) dividends are not exempted from the amount of tax because they are considered a (second) additional tax compared to the corporate tax already levied.[64] The same applies to an additional tax under a CFC measure to the extent that this tax is allocated to the parent company under the Directive (see section 22.5.4.8 below).

22.5.4.3 Non-qualifying credits

A second adjustment must be made for non-qualifying credits.[65] On the one hand, these credits must be deducted from GloBE income. On the other hand, these credits reduce the amount of covered taxes payable. Tax credits or tax refunds must also be deducted from the amount of covered taxes due.

---

61 Article 22 paragraph 6 of the Directive.
62 Article 22 paragraph 8 of the Directive.
63 Article 21 paragraph 3 sub a of the Directive.
64 *Cf.* OECD-Guidance (2022), para. 11, p. 88.
65 Article 21 paragraph 3 sub b of the Directive.

22.5.4.4 *Uncertain tax positions*

Furthermore, an adjustment must be made for uncertain tax positions disclosed in the financial statements.[66] Precisely because of the nature of such positions – and presumably also the possible effect whereby overestimating (un)certainty could affect the timing of the effective tax burden – they should be eliminated from the amount of covered taxes involved.

22.5.4.5 *Unpaid taxes*

The same applies to the amount of taxes of the current tax year that are not expected to be paid within three years of the end of the reporting year.[67] Payments made after the expiration of this period will not be taken into account.[68] Certain advance payments of taxes are also not taken into account.[69]

22.5.4.6 *Top-up taxes*

Furthermore, expressly excluded from the definition of covered taxes are the top-up taxes resulting from the application of the Directive, as otherwise one would fall into circular reasoning. These are qualifying top-up taxes under the Directive, i.e. stemming from the income inclusion rule, the under-taxed profit rule or a (qualifying) domestic minimum top-up tax.[70] If there is a tax that does not qualify as such, it does count provided that it otherwise qualifies as a covered tax.

22.5.4.7 *Other*

Finally, a specific adjustment applies to the amount of taxes at insurers.[71]

22.5.4.8 *Allocation of covered taxes*

An important question is to which group entity the amount of the covered tax should be allocated. The starting point is the same as the allocation of GloBE income; in principle, the tax is allocated to the entity that for accounting purposes has recorded it as (qualifying) income tax, hence irrespective of the entity allocation for tax purposes. This general approach also applies to group entities that are considered stateless for the purposes of the Directive. This principle is departed from for a number of specific cross-border cases. For example, taxes arising from the application of a CFC regime are allocated to the country where the CFC is established in proportion to the interest in the income of the CFC.[72] This allocation is limited to prevent that a "high" amount of taxes in the CFC

66 Article 21 paragraph 3 sub d of the Directive.
67 Article 21 paragraph 3 sub e of the Directive.
68 Article 20 paragraph 2 sub d of the Directive.
69 Article 20 paragraph 2 sub d of the Directive.
70 Article 20 paragraph 2 sub a of the Directive.
71 Article 20 paragraph 2 sub e of the Directive.
72 Article 24 paragraph 3 of the Directive.

jurisdiction could be used to generate (additional) passive income without falling below the 15% ETR-threshold. In addition, withholding taxes on dividends are imputed to the country in which the paying entity is resident.[73] Finally, specific allocation provisions apply to, among others, permanent establishments, transparent entities and reverse hybrid entities.

22.5.4.9 Post-filing adjustments

It is conceivable that the calculation of the effective tax rate must be made at a time when no final assessment has yet been issued to the group entity in question. This means that the amount of tax due may ultimately be higher or lower than the amount initially assumed. The principle is that such changes are taken into account in the year in which the effective tax burden is calculated, and thus not in the earlier year to which the change relates, but only to the extent that the amount of tax is increased.[74] To the extent that the change results in a reduction in the amount of tax, a recalculation of the effective tax burden must be made in the year to which this reduction relates.

22.6 Calculation of the amount of up taxes

With the calculated GloBE profit base (A) and the calculated amount of taxes (B), the effective tax rate per country and per year can then easily be determined by dividing B by A. If in a given year there is a GloBE (net) loss, no calculation is made; however, top-up tax may still be due under specific circumstances.[75] To the extent this effective tax rate per country in a given year falls below 15%, top-up tax becomes due.[76] The rate of the top-up tax is determined by looking at the difference between the minimum rate of 15% and the effective tax rate: top-up tax percentage.[77] The calculated top-up tax percentage is then set against the GloBE profit base. However, two corrections first need to be made to this base at this stage. First, this has to do with the fact that the top-up tax is conceptually limited to excess profits. For this reason, a flat-rate deduction is allowed representing the normal return on investment in the country in question (the so-called substance-based income exclusion).

This deduction is determined – roughly speaking – by looking at the total amount of labour costs and the value of tangible assets in that country. Of both, 5% may (eventually, after expiry of a transition period)[78] be deducted from the GloBE base. In this way, the GloBE base ultimately approximates, more or less mathematically, the excess profit per country of the enterprise in question. Payroll expenses also include expenses paid to non-employees provided that these non-employees are subject to a specific instructional

73 Article 24 paragraph 5 of the Directive.
74 Article 25 paragraph 1 of the Directive.
75 Article 21 paragraph 5 of the Directive.
76 Mixing low-taxed profits from one country with high-taxed profits from another country is thus not possible.
77 Article 27 paragraph 2 of the Directive.
78 There is a 10-year "phase-in period" during which this rate is initially set higher (10% for labor costs and 8% for tangible assets, respectively) and then decreases annually to eventually 5%.

authority of the group entity. Labour costs are allocated to the country where the corresponding work is performed. A broad wage concept is assumed.[79] However, labour costs associated with activities exempted under the international shipping exemption of the Directive do not count. Regarding the determination of the value of tangible assets, it is the book value – as further defined – of tangible assets (property, plant, equipment) located in a jurisdiction, natural resources, the right to use tangible assets located in a jurisdiction, and a license or similar agreement by the government for the use of real estate or the exploitation of natural resources that involves a significant investment in tangible assets.[80] The premise is that the location of the relevant assets coincides with the location of the relevant group entity. Property held for sale, rental or investment (e.g. buildings and land) do not count. Finally, the Directive contains specific regulations and clarifications regarding the application of the substance carve-out at the level of permanent establishments and partnerships.

Second, any (domestic) top-up tax levied by the low-tax country itself must be deducted from the calculated top-up tax. This domestic top-up tax takes precedence over that levied by other countries. If an amount of top-up tax remains, this amount is then allocated to the group entities in the relevant country in proportion to their GloBE income.[81]

If an MNE makes only limited profits and sales in a particular country, the top up tax in that country is zero based on a de minimis provision. Furthermore, "new entrants" in the larger multinational business sector are temporarily generically exempt from top-up taxation under conditions. Finally top-up taxation is not triggered if GloBE income is negative in a given year in a given country.

22.7 The top-up tax mechanism

As noted earlier, the determination of low-taxed profits in one country (i.e. profit taxation below the 15% ETR-threshold) leads to top-up tax in (an)other country(ies). The compulsory top-up tax mechanism is thus the final element of the Directive. The rules surrounding this mechanism address the question of how and from whom to levy (which amount of) top-up tax. It should be emphasized once again that this top-up tax mechanism only comes into play if the low-tax country itself decides not to levy a (qualifying) domestic minimum top-up tax, which is precisely what many countries are expected to do.

22.7.1 Income inclusion rule (IIR)

The basic principle under the so-called income inclusion rule (IIR) is that top-up tax will primarily take place in the country where the ultimate parent company of the group in question is located. This means that, as a starting point, top-up tax must be levied at the

79 Article 28 paragraph 1 sub a and sub b of the Directive.
80 Article 28 paragraph 1 sub c of the Directive.
81 A domestic top-up tax can qualify as a safe harbor if it is labelled as "qualifying". In that case, no further allocation to other entities needs to be made; the (qualifying) domestic minimum top-up tax is final in that case.

level of the ultimate parent company up to the minimum rate of 15%.[82] The Directive then assumes what is known as a top-down approach. If in the country of the ultimate parent company no, or insufficient, top-up tax takes place (e.g. because that country has not implemented the GloBE rules), the obligation to impose a top-up tax – in accordance with the top-down approach – shifts to the subsidiary directly controlled by the ultimate parent company, then to the controlled lower-tier subsidiary, and so on.[83]

In order to prevent possible leakage, the Directive provides for a specific regime in the case of so-called partially owned parent entities established in the Union which are more than 20% owned by non-group stakeholders. In the case of such a partially held parent entity, top-up tax liability is shifted to this (intermediate) parent entity.[84] This ensures that the full top-up tax is taken into account within the group. Incidentally, this does not prevent top-up taxation also at the level of the ultimate parent company in proportion to its interest in the low-taxed group entity. In order to avoid double taxation, the Directive provides for a specific rule against overlapping in this case, whereby the country of residence of the ultimate parent company must allow a deduction from the top-up tax payable by the partially owned intermediate entity.[85] If, within the group, a partially owned entity is itself wholly owned by another partially owned entity, the obligation for top-up taxation shifts to the level of the latter entity.[86]

The top-up tax is subsequently allocated in proportion to the (ultimate) parent's interest in the GloBE income of the low-taxed group entity.[87] In the case of a 100% interest, the allocation ratio is always 1. In the case of a split shareholder interest, this is different; in that case, it must be determined what portion of the GloBE income of the low-taxed entity should be allocated to the other shareholder(s), including third parties (i.e. shareholders that are not part of the group).

Finally, intra-year purchases and acquisitions of low-taxed group entities do not affect the application of the top-up mechanism. Indeed, the shorter holding period is already taken into account when determining the GloBE base, following the applicable accounting standard. It is therefore sufficient for the top-up tax mechanism that at some point during the reporting year a (low-taxed) entity qualifies as a group entity.

22.7.2 Undertaxed profit rule (UTPR)

Should a residual top up tax remain uncollected after the top down approach has been exhausted, a secondary top up tax mechanism takes effect from 2025. On the basis of the so-called undertaxed profit rule (UTPR), top-up tax should be levied in the countries where the remaining (controlled) group entities are located. In that case, the remaining amount of top-up tax will be allocated half in proportion to the number of employees

82 Article 5 paragraph 1 of the Directive.
83 Article 5, paragraph 1 juncto paragraph 3 of the Directive.
84 Article 8 paragraph 1 and 2 of the Directive.
85 Article 10 of the Directive.
86 Art. 8 paragraph 3 of the Directive.
87 Art. 9 paragraph 2 of the Directive.

and half in proportion to the value of tangible assets in the respective countries. Thus, the degree of physical substance determines how much top-up tax is allocated to each Member State.

It is up to each country to decide exactly how to implement the UTPR, such as by eliminating cost deductions or loss relief. Because the UTPR acts as a "backstop" to the IIR, countries should make every effort to make it stand. For example, Member States may refuse the deduction of normally deductible payments or depreciation to the extent of the top-up tax due in that Member State. In addition to a deduction limitation, Member States can also opt for top-up taxation through, for example, a direct additional tax or a notional income imputation in the amount of the top-up tax due.[88] In any case, the requirement is that application of the UTPR directly results in an additional amount of tax to be paid. This means, for example, that a reduction of deductible losses in principle does not qualify if this reduction will (potentially) lead to a higher tax only in the future.[89] It may happen that a profit adjustment made does not ultimately result in full payment of the top-up tax due, for example, because there are few or no deductible expenses. If, as a result, the full top-up tax is not paid, a carry-forward mechanism is triggered.[90] The carried forward top-up tax claim will be preserved in the future, even if in any year the relevant group ceases to fall within the personal scope of the Directive or the relevant group entity is no longer part of the group. Member States may apply a final "exit charge" at the time when a group entity is liquidated.

Each Member State may decide to which group entity or entities within that Member State the top-up tax should be allocated, for example, to the ultimate parent company in that Member State. Allocation to a loss-making group entity is not allowed, as this does not ensure the effective payment of the top-up tax. The profit adjustment should be made in the relevant reporting year. If the relevant group entity in the Member State where the under-taxed profit rule applies has already filed the local corporate income tax return before the amount of the top-up tax has been declared, an opportunity to file a revised return should be provided.[91]

Finally, specific provisions apply to, among others, investment funds and transparent entities.

22.8 Safe harbours

Calculating the effective tax rate per country can quickly become a complex exercise. It is therefore not surprising that various stakeholders have advocated the introduction of so-called safe harbours. Based on certain indicators, top-up tax in a certain country could be excluded in advance, based on the idea that – given these indicators – the full application of the regular rules would probably result in little or no top-up tax. In this way, only the real weak links in the group structure would have to be subjected to a

88 *Cf.* OECD-Guidance (2022), para. 47, p. 32.
89 *Cf.* OECD-Guidance (2022), para. 49, p. 33.
90 Article 13 paragraph 2 of the Directive.
91 *Cf.* OECD-Guidance (2022), par 56, p. 34.

full ETR-calculation. Safe harbours could thus represent a significant simplification, especially if they were consistent with data that companies normally already have in their administration.

However, the question of which indicators could serve as generic safe harbours proves far from easy to answer. Indeed, simplification quickly comes into conflict with the effectiveness of the entire system. Hence, only administrative safe harbour rules have been agreed upon so far. First, under certain conditions, companies may temporarily (until 2027) use the profit calculation as reported under the aforementioned country-by-country reporting obligation (see also section 28.3.2.4), which in turn must be based on qualified accounting standards, as a benchmark (i.e. instead of the new GloBE benchmark). In addition, companies are allowed to use the amount of income taxes per country as included in the financial accounts of each group entity, with an adjustment only needing to be made for taxes under any uncertain tax positions. This safe harbour also applies to the calculation of any (qualifying) domestic top-up tax. Two further administrative safe harbours are provided for through a so-called routine profits test and a so-called de minimis profits test. Finally, probably under pressure from the side of the United States, at least until the end of 2026 a temporary safe harbour applies for the UTPR (although the Directive itself does not provide for this possibility) under the condition that profits are subject to a statutory rate of at least 20%, irrespective of the effective tax rate.

22.9 Final remarks

The introduction of a global effective minimum tax of 15% for large enterprises constitutes a fundamental policy step that fits well with developments within the international tax discourse over the past decade. It responds to society's call for large corporations to pay their fair share, although it is difficult to predict what the exact additional tax revenue for each country will be.

Yet there are also challenges, for example enforcement by the local tax authorities, especially in the light of the fact that the minimum tax rules as a whole are rather complex. In addition, the success of the minimum tax depends in part on the presence of sufficient critical mass. In other words, ultimately enough countries worldwide must participate, because countries will also not feel like pricing themselves out of the market relative to (a large part of) the rest of the world. Of note in this regard is that the United States is not willing to implement the OECD Model Rules and, even more, may impose countermeasures towards countries that will apply the UTPR in the future with respect to low-taxed US group entities. This could undermine the stability of the Pillar Two project as a whole. Also, uniform interpretation and implementation by all countries is important. Ultimately, there is no single overarching body to ensure this uniformity. Thus, the danger of implementation and interpretation conflicts between countries is present. A mechanism for international administrative dispute prevention and dispute resolution should overcome this danger, but an important question is how effective this mechanism will prove to be in practice. Moreover, in this light, one should also not underestimate the fact that the Directive contains hardly any uniform rules in the area of procedural tax law. Furthermore, it is noted that the Directive still contains a number of loose lends, despite the fact that the Directive has already been adopted. The mere fact that the Model Rules of 2021 have been supplemented multiple times afterwards through release of further administrative guidance from the OECD already says a lot. This posterior administrative guidance from the OECD raises legitimacy questions.

Furthermore, there are also more technical challenges. To what extent will companies be able to control the effective tax rate by means of tax planning strategies after all? To what extent might the additional tax run afoul of the existing international network of tax treaties?

Finally, countries may look for alternative incentives beyond the scope of the Pillar Two Directive, such as direct subsidies. But if exchanging tax incentives for direct subsidies allows countries to protect their own facilities from the top-up tax at all and hence would allow countries to continue (harmful) tax competition practices, what is then the remaining value of the Pillar Two system?

In short, it remains to be seen to what extent the Pillar Two Directive will deliver on its promise.

CHAPTER 23

Foreign Subsidies Regulation

Sjoerd Douma[1]

23.1 Introduction

On 12 July 2023, Regulation (EU) 2022/2560 of the European Parliament and the Council of 14 December 2022 on foreign subsidies distorting the internal market ("the Foreign Subsidies Regulation" or "FSR") started to apply.[2] According to its preamble, foreign subsidies can distort the internal market and undermine the level playing field for various economic activities in the Union. Foreign subsidies may be used, for instance, to finance economic activities in the internal market.[3] Before the FSR entered into force, no EU instruments addressed distortions caused by foreign subsidies, in particular when foreign subsidies take the form of subsidised investments, or when services and financial flows are concerned. For this reason, as the preamble explains, it was necessary to complement existing EU instruments with a new tool to effectively deal with distortions in the internal market caused by foreign subsidies. The FSR complements the EU State aid rules which deal with distortions in the internal market caused by Member State subsidies, whereas the FSR seeks to deal with such distortions caused by third countries.

The FSR contains four instruments for foreign subsidies review. Firstly, the Commission may on its own initiative examine information from any source, including Member States, a natural or legal person or an association, regarding alleged foreign subsidies distorting the internal market (*ex officio* review of foreign subsidies; Article 9 FSR). Secondly, the FSR introduces an obligation to notify in advance certain concentrations – mergers, take-overs and joint ventures – to the Commission in order to assess whether a foreign subsidy in a concentration distorts the internal market.[4] Thirdly, the FSR contains a notification requirement for foreign subsidies distorting the internal market in the context of public

1 Professor of International and European Procedural Tax Law, ACTL, University of Amsterdam; Partner, Lubbers, Boer & Douma, The Hague.

2 Article 53 FSR specifies that the Regulation shall apply to foreign subsidies granted in the five years prior to 12 July 2023 where such foreign subsidies distort the internal market after 12 July 2023. In case of foreign financial contributions granted to an undertaking notifying a concentration or notifying financial contributions in the context of a public procurement procedure, the Regulation shall apply to contributions granted in the three years prior to 12 July 2023.

3 Preamble FSR, at 2.

4 According to Article 20 FSR, a concentration needs to be notified if (a) at least one of the merging undertakings, the acquired undertaking or the joint venture is established in the Union and generates an aggregate turnover in the Union of at least EUR 500 million; and (b) more than EUR 50 million of aggregate foreign financial contributions were granted in the three years prior to the conclusion of the transaction. These conditions are cumulative.

procurement procedures.[5] Both of these notification requirements enable an *ex ante* review of the distortive effect of a foreign subsidy. Fourthly, the Commission may conduct a market investigation into a particular sector or economic activity or into the use of certain subsidy instruments, where there is a reasonable suspicion that foreign subsidies may distort the internal market (Article 36 FSR). In this context, the Commission may require undertakings to supply information and carry out inspections. The Commission may also request Member States or the third country concerned to supply information. The Commission shall, where relevant, publish a report on the results of its market investigation which may subsequently be used in the context of concrete situations.

Where the Commission finds that a foreign subsidy distorts the internal market, it may impose redressive measures in order to remedy the distortion in the internal market actually or potentially caused by a foreign subsidy, unless it has accepted commitments offered by the undertaking under investigation. Commitments or redressive measures shall be proportionate and fully and effectively remedy the distortion actually or potentially caused by the foreign subsidy in the internal market. They may consist, inter alia, of the repayment of the foreign subsidy (including interest), the reduction of capacity or market presence and the annulment of a concentration (Article 7 FSR).

The present chapter discusses the potential impact of the FSR on foreign subsidies in the context of tax measures. Section 23.2 contains a substantive evaluation of the notion of a foreign financial contribution. Section 23.3 discusses the balancing test which the Commission should carry out before drawing any conclusions around redressive measures. Section 23.4 provides an overview of the rules on procedure, enforcement and judicial review. Section 23.5 contains concluding remarks.

23.2 The notion of a foreign subsidy

23.2.1 Introduction

According to Article 3(1) FSR, a foreign subsidy shall be deemed to exist where a third country provides, directly or indirectly, a financial contribution which confers a benefit on an undertaking engaging in an economic activity in the internal market and which is limited, in law or in fact, to one or more undertakings or industries. Those conditions are cumulative.[6] They should be applied and interpreted in light of the relevant EU legislation, including that relating to State aid, mergers and public procurement.[7] Thus, it is clear that the case law of the Court of Justice of the European Union in the area of State aid and taxation is very relevant in the context of the FSR, just as the Commission's decision practice in this area.

5 According to Article 28 FSR, a foreign financial contribution in a public procurement procedure should be notified if: (a) its estimated value is equal to or greater than EUR 250 million; and (b) the economic operator was granted aggregate financial contributions in the three years prior to notification equal to or greater than EUR 4 million per third country. These conditions are cumulative.

6 Preamble to the FSR at 11.

7 Preamble to the FSR, at 9.

23.2.2 Undertaking

The notion of undertaking should be understood in the same way as in Article 107(1) TFEU. In this respect, we refer to section 15.2.2 of this book which clarifies, inter alia, that an undertaking may consist of a group of companies and may thus concern a multinational group as a whole. The FSR provides for one further element: the undertaking should be engaged in an economic activity in the internal market. The notion of economic activity is very broad, as we have shown in section 15.2.2. Further, it should be noted that it is irrelevant whether the undertaking is either headquartered within or outside the EU. What matters is whether the undertaking has any economic activity in the EU.

23.2.3 Imputability

A financial contribution should be attributable to a third country, which means that benefits arising from disparities between tax systems are out of scope (see section 15.2.3 of this book). If the central government of a third country has provided a financial contribution, there will be little discussion about imputability. This may be different if the financial contribution has been granted by other levels of government. In this respect, Article 3(2) stipulates that a financial contribution provided by a third country shall include contributions provided by public authorities at all other levels. The same is true for financial contributions by a foreign public entity whose actions can be attributed to the third country, taking into account elements such as the characteristics of the entity and the legal and economic environment prevailing in the State in which the entity operates, including the government's role in the economy. Finally, attribution of a financial contribution to a third country may also be warranted if that contribution has been provided by a private entity whose actions can be attributed to the third country, taking into account all relevant circumstances.

23.2.4 Financial contribution which confers a benefit

Article 3(2) FSR provides the following examples of a financial contribution:

a) the transfer of funds or liabilities, such as capital injections, grants, loans, loan guarantees, fiscal incentives, the setting off of operating losses, compensation for financial burdens imposed by public authorities, debt forgiveness, debt to equity swaps or rescheduling;
b) the foregoing of revenue that is otherwise due, such as tax exemptions or the granting of special or exclusive rights without adequate remuneration; or
c) the provision of goods or services or the purchase of goods or services.

This means that a financial contribution is a wide-reaching concept that can take a broad range of forms, including interest-free or low interest loans, tax incentives, capital injections and contributions in kind.

Such financial contributions are only in scope of the FSR if they also provide a benefit. This is the case if the contribution could not have been obtained under normal market conditions. According to the FSR's preamble, the existence of a benefit should be determined on the basis of comparative benchmarks, such as a comparable tax treatment. Specifically:

> "Transfer pricing in the context of goods and services exchanged within an undertaking can confer a benefit if that transfer pricing is not in line with normal market conditions. The benefit conferred by a financial contribution may be passed to an undertaking engaging in an economic activity in the Union."[8]

Thus, the notion of a benefit should be interpreted in the same manner as the notion of advantage, discussed in section 15.2.4. The identification of foreign subsidies within the tax system of a third country or through the concrete application thereof in specific taxpayer situations is a very sensitive exercise. After all, the third country concerned is, of course, best placed to explain its own tax system and the objectives underlying it. The third country is, however, not necessarily part of the procedure and dialogue. Moreover, it may be very difficult for a third country to accept, from a sovereignty perspective, that the Commission formulates a view on the 'correct' application of its tax system.

23.2.5 Selectivity

The benefit should be conferred on one or more undertakings or industries. The specificity of the foreign subsidy could be established by law or in fact.[9] This definition is sufficiently broad to incorporate the whole body of case law on selectivity in the context of Article 107(1) TFEU. In this respect, reference is made to section 15.2.5.

23.2.6 Distortions in the internal market

The Commission may impose redressive measures in order to remedy the distortion in the internal market actually or potentially caused by a foreign subsidy, unless it has accepted commitments offered by the undertaking under investigation (Article 7 FSR). This means that such a distortion has to be established first before any redressive measures can be imposed. According to Article 4(1) FSR, a distortion in the internal market shall be deemed to exist where a foreign subsidy is liable to improve the competitive position of an undertaking in the internal market and where, in doing so, that foreign subsidy actually or potentially negatively affects competition in the internal market. This definition of the term distortion is very broad, because the mere capacity of a foreign subsidy to negatively affect competition in the internal market suffices. Article 4(1) FSR further states that a distortion in the internal market shall be determined on the basis of indicators, which can include, in particular, the following:
a) the amount of the foreign subsidy;
b) the nature of the foreign subsidy;
c) the situation of the undertaking, including its size and the markets or sectors concerned;
d) the level and evolution of economic activity of the undertaking on the internal market;
e) the purpose and conditions attached to the foreign subsidy as well as its use on the internal market.

8 Preamble to the FSR, at 13.
9 Preamble to the FSR, at 14.

In our view, it follows from the FSR's preamble that the Commission must perform a detailed assessment in each case showing that a foreign subsidy leads to a distortion in the internal market.[10] To this extent, we expect that the Commission must perform a more in-depth analysis in comparison to Article 107(1) TFEU.[11] Article 4(2) FSR contains a *de minimis* rule: if a foreign subsidy to an undertaking does not exceed EUR 4 million over any consecutive period of three years, that foreign subsidy shall be considered unlikely to distort the internal market. Article 4(3) FSR extends the amounts of *de minimis* aid in an EU context to a third country as well: if the total amount of a foreign subsidy to an undertaking does not exceed € 200.000 *per third country* over any consecutive period of three years, that foreign subsidy shall not be considered to distort the internal market. Finally, a foreign subsidy may be considered not to distort the internal market to the extent that it is aimed at making good the damage caused by natural disasters or exceptional occurrences (Article 4(4) FSR).

There are certain categories of foreign subsidies that are deemed most likely to distort the internal market (Article 5(1) FSR). These include:
a) a foreign subsidy granted to an ailing undertaking, namely an undertaking which will likely go out of business in the short or medium term in the absence of any subsidy;
b) a foreign subsidy in the form of an unlimited guarantee for the debts or liabilities of the undertaking;
c) an export financing measure that is not in line with the OECD Arrangement on officially supported export credits;
d) a foreign subsidy directly facilitating a concentration;
e) a foreign subsidy enabling an undertaking to submit unduly advantageous tenders.

23.3 The balancing test

After the existence of a foreign subsidy and a distortion in the internal market have been established, there is a third test which needs to be performed before the Commission may impose redressive measures: a balancing test. The Commission may balance the negative effects of a foreign subsidy in terms of distortion in the internal market against the positive effects on the development of the relevant subsidised economic activity on the internal market, while considering other positive effects of the foreign subsidy such as the broader positive effects in relation to the relevant policy objectives, in particular those of the EU (Article 6(1) FSR).[12] After this balancing exercise has been performed, the Commission shall take a decision whether to impose redressive measures or to accept commitments by the undertaking, and the nature and level of those redressive measures or commitments (Article 6(2) FSR). In our view, this means that the Commission can

10 Preamble to the FSR, at 20. Note that Article 5 FSR lists a number of situations where the burden of proof is reversed (e.g. rescue aid without a restructuring plan, unlimited guarantees, direct support for concentrations and export subsidies beyond OECD guidelines).

11 Similarly, Wolfgang Weiß, *The Regulation on Foreign Subsidies Distorting the Internal Market A Path to a Level Playing Field?*, Springer 2024, p. 43.

12 According to Article 46 FSR, the Commission shall publish, at the latest on 12 January 2026, and shall regularly update thereafter, guidelines regarding the application of the balancing test in accordance with Article 6 FSR.

only take a decision on redress or acceptance of commitments after having balanced the positive and negative effects of the foreign subsidy. The balancing is inspired by Article 107(3) TFEU.

23.4 Procedure and enforcement

23.4.1 Introduction

As stated in the introduction to this chapter, the FSR contains four instruments for foreign subsidies review: i) the *ex officio* review of foreign subsidies, ii) an obligation to notify in advance certain concentrations to the Commission, iii) a notification requirement in the context of public procurement procedures and iv) a market investigation into a particular sector or economic activity or into the use of certain subsidy instruments. The present section discusses the procedural aspects of these instruments.

23.4.2 Ex officio review

The *ex officio* review supplements the notification-based tools for concentrations and public procurements. For the latter two tools certain high thresholds exist (EUR 500 million and EUR 250 million respectively; see sections 23.4.3 and 23.4.4). There is no threshold for the *ex officio* review. This means that this tool can be used not only outside the field of concentrations and public procurements, but also in that area below the mentioned thresholds.

Preliminary review
According to Article 9(1) FSR, the Commission may on its own initiative examine information from any source, including Member States, a natural or legal person or an association, regarding alleged foreign subsidies distorting the internal market. Indeed, as the FSR's preamble clarifies, Member States and any natural or legal person or association should be able to provide the Commission with information on alleged foreign subsidies distorting the internal market. The Commission could establish a contact point to facilitate the provision of such information in a confidential manner.[13] Article 10(1) FSR states that where the Commission considers that this information indicates the possibility that a foreign subsidy distorting the internal market exists, the Commission shall seek all the information it considers necessary to assess, on a preliminary basis, whether the financial contribution under examination constitutes a foreign subsidy and whether it distorts the internal market. To that end, the Commission may request information from the undertaking under investigation and other undertakings or associations of undertakings, taking due account of the principle of proportionality (Article 13 FSR). The Commission may, by decision, impose fines or periodic penalty payments where an undertaking or an association of undertakings, intentionally or negligently supplies incomplete, incorrect or misleading information in response to a request for information or does not supply the information within the prescribed time limit (Article 17(1) FSR). EU Member States are also under an obligation to respond to a request for information. The Commission may

13 Preamble to the FSR, at 27.

also ask third countries to provide information and interview natural and legal persons (with their consent; Article 13(6-7) FSR). In addition, the Commission may carry out inspections within the EU (Article 14 FSR) and in the territory of a third country with its consent (Article 15 FSR). If an undertaking under investigation or a third country that granted the foreign subsidy does not cooperate adequately, the Commission may take a decision on the basis of the facts available (Article 16 FSR). Where the Commission, in the course of a preliminary review, concludes that there are insufficient indications to initiate an in-depth investigation, either because there is no foreign subsidy or because there are insufficient indications of an actual or potential distortion in the internal market, it shall close the preliminary review (Article 10(4) FSR).

In-depth investigation
Where the Commission, based on the preliminary review, has sufficient indications that an undertaking has been granted a foreign subsidy that distorts the internal market, it shall adopt a decision to initiate an in-depth investigation ('decision to initiate the in-depth investigation') which summarises the relevant issues of fact and law and includes the preliminary assessment of the existence of a foreign subsidy and of the actual or potential distortion in the internal market. It shall inform the undertaking under investigation, the Member States and publish a notice in the Official Journal of the European Union inviting the submission of views in writing within a period of time prescribed by the Commission (Article 10(3) FSR; Article 40(1) FSR). During the in-depth investigation, the Commission shall further assess the foreign subsidy identified in the decision to initiate the in-depth investigation and seek all the information it considers necessary. Before adopting any decision, the Commission give the undertaking under investigation the opportunity to submit observations on the grounds on which the Commission intends to adopt its decision (Article 42(1) FSR). The Commission shall base its decision only on grounds on which the undertakings concerned have been given the opportunity to submit their observations (Article 42(3) FSR). In this process, the undertaking under investigation shall be entitled to have access to the case file (Article 42(4) FSR). A decision to initiate the in-depth investigation ends with one of three decisions:

i. A decision with redressive measures where the Commission finds that a foreign subsidy distorts the internal market,
ii. A decision with commitments where the Commission finds that a foreign subsidy distorts the internal market and the undertaking under investigation offers commitments which the Commission deems appropriate and sufficient to fully and effectively remedy the distortion, or
iii. A no objection decision where the Commission finds that: the preliminary assessment is not confirmed or a distortion in the internal market is outweighed by positive effects within the meaning of the balancing test.

If an undertaking under investigation or a third country that granted the foreign subsidy do not cooperate adequately, the Commission may take one of these decisions on the basis of the facts available (Article 16 FSR).

Interim measures
The Commission may adopt interim measures to preserve competition in the internal market and prevent irreparable damage when a foreign subsidy distorts the internal market (Article 12 FSR).

23.4.3 Concentrations

Introduction
Article 19 FSR states that when assessing whether a foreign subsidy in a concentration distorts the internal market that assessment shall be limited to the concentration concerned. Only foreign subsidies granted in the three years prior to the conclusion of the agreement, the announcement of the public bid, or the acquisition of a controlling interest shall be considered in the assessment. Article 20 FSR defines a concentration as a merger of two or more previously independent undertakings, an acquisition of direct or indirect control of one or more other undertakings, or the creation of a joint venture.[14]

Notification requirement
According to Article 20(4) FSR, a concentration needs to be notified to the Commission where:
a) at least one of the merging undertakings, the acquired undertaking or the joint venture is established in the Union and generates an aggregate turnover in the Union of at least EUR 500 million; and
b) the following undertakings were granted combined aggregate financial contributions of more than EUR 50 million from third countries in the three years preceding the conclusion of the agreement, the announcement of the public bid, or the acquisition of a controlling interest:
   i. in the case of an acquisition, the acquirer or acquirers and the acquired undertaking;
   ii. in the case of a merger, the merging undertakings;
   iii. in the case of a joint venture, the undertakings creating a joint venture and the joint venture. Article 22 FSR contains detailed rules on the calculation of turnover.[15]

In addition, the Commission may request the prior notification of any concentration at any time prior to its implementation where the Commission suspects that foreign subsidies may have been granted to the undertakings concerned in the three years prior to the concentration (Article 21(5) FSR). Concentrations should be notified prior to their implementation and following the conclusion of the agreement, the announcement of the public bid, or the acquisition of a controlling interest (Article 21 FSR). A notifiable concentration shall not be implemented before its notification (Article 24(1) FSR.

Procedure
After a complete notification, there is a waiting period of 25 working days before the concentration may be implemented. If the Commission initiates an in-depth investigation within that period, the concentration shall not be implemented for a period of 90 working

14 See Article 20(5) FSR for the definition of 'control'.
15 Article 22 FSR contains detailed rules on the calculation of turnover.

days after the opening of the in-depth investigation. The Commission may require a roll-back of the concentration if it finds that a notifiable concentration has already been implemented and that foreign subsidies in that concentration distort the internal market (Article 25(6) FSR). After the in-depth investigation, the Commission shall adopt an implementing act in the form of one of the following decisions:

a) a decision with commitments,
b) a no objection decision, or
c) a decision prohibiting a concentration, where the Commission finds that a foreign subsidy distorts the internal market.

A decision shall be adopted within 90 working days after the opening of the in-depth investigation. If the Commission does not adopt a decision within that time limit, the undertakings concerned shall be allowed to implement the concentration (Article 25(4) FSR. The above-discussed Articles 10, 11(1), (3) and (4), Articles 12 to 16 and 18 shall apply to notified concentrations as well (Article 25(1).

23.4.4 Public procurement

According to the FSR's preamble, the need to address foreign subsidies distorting the internal market – see Article 4 FSR – is especially salient in public procurement, given its economic significance in the internal market and the fact that it is financed by taxpayer funds. For this reason, the preamble states, the Commission should have the power, upon notification prior to the award of a contract, to examine information on foreign financial contributions to the participating economic operator in the context of a public procurement procedure.[16] The threshold for bids in public procurements is set at EUR 250 million for the value of the procurement and a three year foreign financial contribution of at least EUR 4 million per third country.[17] Prior notifications are mandatory above this threshold The notification procedure is described in Article 29 FSR, followed by the procedure on preliminary review and in-depth investigation in Article 30 FSR.

23.4.5 Market investigation

The Commission has the possibility to launch investigations regarding specific sectors of the economy, particular types of economic activity or the use of particular foreign subsidy instruments, in order to gather information on foreign subsidies.[18] Where the information available to the Commission substantiates a reasonable suspicion that foreign subsidies in a particular sector, for a particular type of economic activity or based on a particular subsidy instrument may distort the internal market, the Commission may conduct such a market investigation (Article 36(1) FSR). The Commission may require the undertakings or associations of undertakings concerned to supply the necessary information and may carry out the necessary inspections. The Commission may also request Member States or the third country concerned to supply information. According to Article 36(2) FSR, the

16 Preamble to the FSR, at 40.
17 See Article 28(1) FSR.
18 Preamble to the FSR, at 59.

Commission shall, where relevant, publish a report on the results of its market investigation into particular sectors, particular types of economic activity or particular subsidy instruments and seek comments. The Commission may use the information obtained from such market investigations in foreign subsidy investigations (Article 36(3) FSR).

23.4.6 *Commitments and redress*

According to Article 7(1) FSR, the Commission may impose redressive measures in order to remedy the distortion in the internal market actually or potentially caused by a foreign subsidy, unless it has accepted commitments offered by the undertaking under investigation.[19] As Article 7(2) FSR states, the Commission may accept commitments offered by the undertaking under investigation where such commitments fully and effectively remedy the distortion in the internal market. When accepting such commitments, the Commission shall make them binding on the undertaking under investigation in a decision with commitments. The undertaking's compliance with the commitments agreed upon shall, where appropriate, be monitored. Commitments or redressive measures shall be proportionate and fully and effectively remedy the distortion actually or potentially caused by the foreign subsidy in the internal market (Article 7(3) FSR). Under Article 7(4) FSR, commitments or redressive measures may consist, inter alia, of reducing capacity or market presence, refraining from certain investments, publication of results of research and development, divestment of certain assets, dissolving the concentration and repayment of the foreign subsidy with interest (Article 7(4) FSR). In case of a commitment to repay the foreign subsidy the repayment must be transparent, verifiable and effective, without a risk of circumvention (Article 7(6) FSR). The balancing test can help to determine the appropriate nature and level of the commitments or redressive measures.[20] If an undertaking does not comply with a decision with commitments, a decision with redressive measures, or a decision ordering interim measures, the Commission may impose fines or periodic penalty payments (Article 17(5) FSR).[21] For reasons of legal certainty the period within which it is possible for the Commission to investigate a foreign subsidy is limited to 10 years from the date of granting that foreign subsidy (Article 38 FSR); the start of a preliminary investigation, request for information or inspection interrupts the limitation period and EU court proceedings suspend it.[22] A foreign subsidy should be considered granted from the moment the beneficiary obtains an entitlement to receive the foreign subsidy. The actual disbursement of the foreign subsidy is not a necessary condition for a foreign subsidy to fall within the scope of the FSR.[23]

19 Article 44(9) FSR prevents redress if this would run counter to the EU's obligations under international agreements.

20 Preamble to the FSR, at 21.

21 Preamble to the FSR, at 32. Before any penalty will be adopted, the undertaking under investigation has the opportunity to submit observations (Article 42(1) FSR).

22 Preamble to the FSR, at 61.

23 Preamble to the FSR, at 15.

23.4.7 *Revocation*

If a Commission decision was based on incomplete, incorrect or misleading information, where an undertaking acts contrary to its commitments or the redressive measures imposed, or where the commitments or redressive measures were not effective, the Commission may revoke the decision and adopt a new one (Article 18 FSR).[24]

23.4.8 *Judicial appeal*

Acts of the Commission under the FSR are subject to review by the Court of Justice of the European Union in accordance with Article 263 TFEU.[25] According to Article 256 TFEU, the General Court shall have jurisdiction to hear and determine at first instance actions or proceedings referred to in Article 263 TFEU. Decisions given by the General Court may be subject to a right of appeal to the Court of Justice on points of law only, under the conditions and within the limits laid down by the Statute of the Court of Justice of the European Union. Article 263 TFEU grants a right of appeal to, inter alia, EU Member States and to any natural or legal person against an act addressed to that person. The proceedings shall be instituted within two months of the publication of the measure (Article 40 FSR), or of its notification to the plaintiff, or, in the absence thereof, of the day on which it came to the knowledge of the latter, as the case may be. Since a decision with commitments or redress will be addressed to the undertaking concerned (Article 41 FSR), it will have a right to lodge an appeal.

23.5 Concluding remarks

The present chapter has discussed the impact of foreign subsidies review in the area of taxation. This impact can be quite substantial and raises questions with respect to the sovereignty of third countries to design their tax systems in the way they see fit and to determine the normal tax regime applicable there. Undertakings which will be confronted with redressive measures may find it difficult to understand why the application of the tax system of a third country to their specific situation may lead to an obligation to repay a benefit to that country. Practically, this may even be impossible. It will be very interesting to see how the Commission's practice will develop in the future.

---

24 Preamble to the FSR, at 33.

25 Preamble to the FSR, at 72. Its jurisdiction is unlimited in respect of fines or periodic penalty payments. It may cancel, reduce or increase the fine or periodic penalty payment imposed (Article 45 FSR).

CHAPTER 24

The FASTER Directive

Maarten de Wilde[1]

24.1 Introduction

On 10 December 2024, the Council of the European Union (Council) adopted the so-called FASTER Directive, i.e., the EU Directive on a Faster and Safer Relief of Excess Withholding Taxes.[2] The European Commission published its proposal for the Directive on 19 June 2023.[3] The European Parliament advised positively on 28 February 2024.[4]

On 14 May 2024, a compromise proposal was politically agreed upon in the Council.[5] The modifications made to the original Directive proposal at the Council level – including the introduction of the so-called market capitalisation ratio, see Section 6 below, as well as the postponement of the entry into force of the measures from 1 January 2027 to 1

1 Maarten de Wilde is affiliated with the Erasmus School of Law (ESL) of Erasmus University Rotterdam, the Netherlands, and PwC, Rotterdam, the Netherlands. This chapter draws from and builds on commentaries (in Dutch) of the author in Nederlands Tijdschrift voor Fiscaal Recht (NTFR), a Dutch weekly on tax developments.

2 See Council Directive (EU) 2025/50 of 10 December 2024 on faster and safer relief of excess withholding taxes (hereinafter: FASTER Directive). For some further reading and analyses, see Katherina Konstantinou and Melina Konstantinou, 'Modernization and Digitalization of the EU Withholding Tax Procedure: Opportunities Offered by the FASTER Initiative', (2023), 32, *EC Tax Review*, Issue 6, pp. 274-278, Melina Konstantinou and Katherina Konstantinou, 'Balancing Digitalization and Proportionality: The Progress of the FASTER Initiative', (2024), 33, EC Tax Review, Issue 5, pp. 208-214, Paul Radcliffe and Reinhart Devisscher, 'FASTER – A European Withholding Tax Directive to Remove Obstacles to Cross-Border Investment While Combating Tax Fraud and Abuse', *European Taxation*, 2024 (Volume 64), No. 8, Paul Radcliffe and Reinhart Devisscher, 'FASTER: The European Commission Publishes a Proposed Council Directive Aimed at Improving the Withholding Tax Process within the European Union', *European Taxation*, 2023 (Volume 63), No. 8, Jasper Korving, '"BEFIT and HOT: FASTER and SAFE!" EU Law or Slogan for Slimming Pills?', *European Taxation*, 2023 (Volume 63), No. 12, as well as, for instance, R.P.C. Adema, 'Snellere en veiligere terugvordering van bronbelasting – Een verbetering van de mobiliteit van kapitaal?! (deel I)', *MBB Belasting Beschouwingen* 2024/36, and R.P.C. Adema, 'Snellere en veiligere terugvordering van bronbelasting – Een verbetering van de mobiliteit van kapitaal?! (deel II)', *MBB Belasting Beschouwingen* 2024/39 (hereinafter Adema 2024).

3 See Proposal for a Council Directive on Faster and Safer Relief of Excess Withholding Taxes, COM(2023) 324 final, 2023/0187(CNS), Brussels, 19 June 2023 (hereinafter original Directive proposal).

4 See European Parliament legislative resolution of 28 February 2024 on the proposal for a Council directive on Faster and Safer Relief of Excess Withholding Taxes, COM(2023)0324, C9-0204/2023, 2023/0187(CNS).

5 See Council Directive on Faster and Safer Relief of Excess Withholding Taxes, 9925/24, FISC 115, ECOFIN 577, 2023/0187(CNS), Brussels, 14 May 2024.

January 2030, amongst others – necessitated a renewed consultation by the European Parliament, before the Council could formally adopt the Directive. On 14 November 2024, the European Parliament issued a positive opinion on the compromise Directive proposal.[6] Now that the Directive has been adopted by the Council, EU Member States have until 31 December 2028 at the latest to transpose the directive into national law.[7] The measures apply from 1 January 2030.[8]

This Chapter reflects on some of the issues and backgrounds involving the FASTER Directive initiative, and elaborates on the various administrative obligations and procedural aspects involving the technical operation of the relief mechanisms as available to taxpayers under the Directive.

24.2 Streamlining procedures

Addressing the EU Member States,[9] the FASTER Directive introduces an EU-wide coordinated regulatory and governance mechanism around the administrative measures in place in the various EU Member States for the reduction or refund of withholding taxes on proceeds from listed securities investments.[10] More specifically, the matter concerns withholding taxes withheld by EU Member States on dividend payments and interest payments on publicly traded shares and bonds held by individuals, companies, collective investment undertakings, and institutional investors such as pension funds and insurance companies.[11] The Directive primarily seeks to address withholding taxes withheld in relation to publicly traded shares, while allowing the EU Member States to extend the scope of the measures to include withholding taxes on interest payments on publicly traded bonds.[12]

The administrative arrangements for withholding tax reduction or refund in the FASTER Directive take precedence over the equivalent administrative mechanisms that the EU Member States have put in place on a unilateral basis.[13] Where the provisions of the Directive do not apply, it is possible to resort to the national rules. The Directive does not change substantive claims for withholding tax relief based on, for example, the national withholding tax legislation of the EU Member States or their double tax treaty networks. Substantive tax law is not harmonized here. This means that any issues of a substantive nature, for instance EU treaty freedoms issues such as the gross/net issue are also not

6 See European Parliament legislative resolution of 14 November 2024 on the draft Council directive on Faster and Safer Relief of Excess Withholding Taxes, 09925/2024, C10-0002/2024, 2023/0187(CNS).
7 See Article 25 (Transposition) FASTER Directive. The Directive's entry into force is organised in Article 26 FASTER Directive.
8 See Article 25 FASTER Directive.
9 See Article 27 (Adressees) FASTER Directive.
10 See Articles 1 and 2 (Chapter I General provisions) FASTER Directive. Notably, Article 3 FASTER Directive provides a list of definitions of terms used in the Directive.
11 See Articles 1 and 2 FASTER Directive.
12 See Articles 1 and 2 FASTER Directive.
13 See, e.g., Article 17 (Standard refund system) FASTER Directive in conjunction with observations (4), (5) and (17) in the Preamble to the FASTER Directive.

addressed.[14] The same applies to the proportionality test under the operation of the anti-abuse doctrine in EU law.[15] For example, there are no possibilities made available under the provisions in the Directive to refute any suspected tax abuse.

The EU Member States are seeking to achieve several objectives with the FASTER Directive.[16] A general aim is to avoid double taxation (withholding tax withheld from the payor, income tax or corporation tax levied from the payee) that still exists for bureaucratic reasons like inefficient and disproportionately burdensome procedures to relieve excess source taxes despite the existence of double tax treaties and national tax reclaim rules.[17] In addition, the EU Member States aim to reduce administrative burdens with the Directive while also mitigating tax abuse and tax fraud risks.[18] All this is to contribute to the removal of investment barriers on the capital markets of the EU Member States and thus bring the envisaged European capital markets union a step closer.[19] By removing these obstacles, the Directive should contribute to increasing the capital availability needed to meet future political and economic challenges.[20] This includes financing the implementation of the energy transition, the development of emerging high-quality and cutting-edge innovative technologies, and the modernisation of infrastructure works within the internal market.

24.3 Years of discussion and debate

The FASTER Directive is the result of years of discussion and debate on measures to simplify the procedures for reducing or refunding withholding taxes and at the same time addressing any associated tax avoidance and fraud risks. The procedures in place in the different EU Member States are widely seen as slow-moving, fragmented, outdated, unfocused, complex, inefficient and non-abuse-proof. Illustrative is the May 2032 study by Better Finance entitled 'Withholding taxes on dividends in the European Union: An uphill battle for individual shareholders'.[21] This study also evokes an image of costly red tape and susceptibility to fraud. Worthy of note perhaps, is that in the current book chapter author's home country, the Netherlands, the Dutch government positively endorsed the Directive proposal, while – interestingly perhaps – noting in its communications on the merits of

14 See on this matter, for instance, recently, Court of Justice, 7 November 2024, case C-782/22 (*XX*).

15 See on this matter, for instance, and, Court of Justice, 26 February 2019, joined cases C-115/16 (*N Luxembourg 1*), C-118/16 (*X Denmark*), C-119/16 (*C Danmark I*) and C 299/16 (*Z Denmark*), as well as Court of Justice, 26 February 2019, joined cases C-116/16 (*T Danmark*) and C-117/16 (*Y Denmark*) (hereinafter Danish Cases). See also Court of Justice, 12 September 2006, case C-196/04 (*Cadbury Schweppes*), and, recently, Court of Justice, 4 October 2024, case C-585/22 (*X BV*).

16 See, e.g., observations (1) and (2) in the Preamble to the FASTER Directive.

17 *Ibidem.*

18 *Ibidem.*

19 *Ibidem.*

20 *Ibidem*, and see, for a comparison, e.g., European Commission, Communication from the Commission to the European Parliament, the European Council, the Council, the European Economic and Social Committee and the Committee of the Regions, A Green Deal Industrial Plan for the Net-Zero Age, COM(2023) 62 final, Brussels, 1 February 2023.

21 See Christiane Hölz and Martin Molko (Better Finance; the European Federation of Investors and Financial Services Users), Withholding taxes on dividends in the European Union: An uphill battle for individual shareholders, A Better Finance & DSW fact-checking report, May 2023, available on https://betterfinance.eu/publication/report-withholding-taxes-EU-dividends-shareholders-2023/.

the proposal to Dutch Parliament that the administrative procedures and regulations for withholding tax reclaims in the Netherlands already function very efficiently so that the impact of the proposals when adopted seem limited, at least as regards the case of the Netherlands.[22] The bottlenecks accordingly lie elsewhere in the internal market it seems.

In 2009, the European Commission published a recommendation to the EU Member States aimed at simplifying withholding tax reduction procedures.[23] At the beginning of 2013, the OECD introduced the so-called 'Treaty Relief and Compliance Enhancement (TRACE) implementation package'.[24] In 2017, the European Commission published a non-binding and voluntary-based code of conduct, the so-called Code of conduct on withholding tax, with a compilation of approaches based on best practices.[25] This, with the aim of achieving a more efficient coordination of withholding tax refund procedures within the EU. In the Tax Package of 15 July 2020,[26] the European Commission announced that it would introduce hard-law measures, followed by several rounds of consultations and then, mid-2023, the proposed Directive that has now been adopted in December 2024.

The FASTER Directive is intended to cut back on bureaucracy and provide investors with cost savings of €5.17 billion.[27] In addition, the directive aims to address a staggering amount of €150 billion in tax revenue lost through so-called dividend arbitrage and dividend stripping transactions (Cum/Ex, Cum/Cum).[28] As regards to the current author's home country, – again, interestingly perhaps – it has been estimated that the Dutch treasury may have been disadvantaged by €27 billion during 2000-2020.[29] The terms Cum/Ex and Cum/Cum, notably, refer to the trading of shares with dividend (cum) or without (ex)

22 See the letter of the Dutch Minister of Foreign Affairs of 18 August 2023, No. BZ-DOC-1942494997-30, and the attachment thereto, containing an assessment made by the Dutch cabinet of the original Directive proposal.

23 See Commission Recommendation of 19.10.2009 on withholding tax relief procedures, C(2009)7924 final, Brussels, 19 October 2009.

24 See OECD, 'TRACE implementation package for the adoption of the authorized intermediary system; a standardised system for effective withholding tax relief procedures for cross-border portfolio income', OECD, Paris, 2013. The document was approved by the OECD Committee on Fiscal Affairs on 23 January 2013.

25 See European Commission, Code of Conduct on Withholding Tax European Union, 2017.

26 See European Commission, Communication from the Commission to the European Parliament and the Council, An action plan for fair and simple taxation supporting the recovery strategy, COM(2020) 312 final, 15 July 2020.

27 See European Commission, FASTER initiative on withholding tax to boost cross-border investment and help fight tax fraud, Press release, IP/24/2607, Brussels, 14 May 2024, and see Commission Staff Working Document, Impact Assessment Report, SWD(2023) 216 final, Brussels, 19 June 2023.

28 See European Commission, FASTER initiative on withholding tax to boost cross-border investment and help fight tax fraud, Press release, IP/24/2607, Brussels, 14 May 2024, and see Commission Staff Working Document, Impact Assessment Report, SWD(2023) 216 final, Brussels, 19 June 2023.

29 See TaxLive, Raming: gederfde belastinginkomsten in Nederland door dividendstripping 27 miljard euro, 21 October 2021, available at https://www.taxlive.nl/nl/documenten/nieuws/raming-gederfde-belastinginkomsten-in-nederland-door-dividendstripping-27-miljard-euro/, referencing to the studies of the University of Mannheim and the international investigative initiative 'The CumEx Files' to support the claim, including links to the underlying research documents and, amongst others, a link to a clip on YouTube addressing matters in terms of the 'biggest tax robbery in the history of the Netherlands' ("De grootste belastingroof in de Nederlandse geschiedenis").

dividend. As regards Cum/Ex arbitrage or stripping, dividend taxes are reclaimed while no dividends have been paid, or dividend taxes are reclaimed several times while the tax has only been paid once. Cum/Cum arbitrage or stripping occurs when a shareholder has paid dividend tax, and is not entitled to a tax refund on the basis of the tax laws involved, and in view of this trades its dividend entitlement through a transaction or an arrangement or set of transactions or arrangements with another party, which is entitled to a tax refund, that is, to effectively create and collect said tax refund to the benefit of said shareholder by embedding it in the transaction price under the arrangement with said other party. Please note that the terms dividend arbitrage and dividend stripping are allotted a broad meaning here. It concerns the entire spectrum of identified undesirable situations: from the tax-avoiding arrangements that we know around the term 'beneficial owner' and general anti-abuse doctrines in the area of withholding and dividend tax legislation in the EU Member States, primary and secondary EU law, as well as the double tax treaties (beneficial ownership, principal purposes tests), on the one hand, to those tax fraudulent behaviours at the other end of the spectrum, where different parties present themselves simultaneously to different tax authorities for the same withholding taxes as being entitled to tax refunds or tax reliefs and then run off with the tax booty.[30]

24.4 Authorised-intermediary system

24.4.1 Regulation and governance

The FASTER Directive seeks to solve the identified bottlenecks in tax regulation and governance. This, through the introduction of a so-called authorised-intermediary system.[31] The Directive is addressed, basically, to the shareholder or bondholder (natural person, legal entity), the payee that is, resident in an EU Member State that is the beneficial owner of the dividend or interest payments involved, which are taxed by the local tax authorities in the other EU Member State of source, i.e., at the level of the payor of the dividend or interest.[32] For the withholding taxes to which these security holders are subject, the Directive provides for a streamlining of tax reduction and tax refund procedures. This is the case where tax is withheld at a higher national rate than is permitted under the applicable double tax treaties and the taxpayer must be repaid the excess part on that basis. Notably, also third country shareholders and third country bondholders that

30 See, e.g., observation (22) in the Preamble to the FASTER Directive, saying: *"It is acknowledged that financial arrangements can be used to shift the ownership, in whole or in part, of a security or relevant investment risks. It is also the case that such arrangements have been used in dividend arbitrage and dividend stripping schemes, such as the Cum/Ex and Cum/Cum schemes, with the sole purpose to obtain refunds in cases where there was no entitlement thereto or to increase the amount of refund to which an investor was entitled. It should be possible to consider arrangements such as futures contracts, repurchase transactions, securities lending and securities borrowing, buy-sell back transactions or sell-buy back transactions, derivatives, margin lending transactions and contracts for difference as financial arrangements in cases where they imply a temporary or permanent split between the natural person or entity bearing the economic risks of the investment and the legal owner of the share or underlying rights. Those examples are not exhaustive."*

31 See Chapter III Withholding tax relief procedure FASTER Directive.

32 See Article 1 FASTER Directive.

beneficially own the income items involved and that are subject to withholding taxation in the EU are eligible to invoke the benefits of the Directive.

The Directive organises the procedural streamlining in the hands of the financial service providers where the securities holders, taxpayers that is, have placed their securities accounts.[33] Under the new rules, requests for *ex ante* withholding tax relief or *ex post* withholding tax refunds can in principle only be submitted by so-called 'Certified Financial Intermediaries' (CFIs).[34] These are the financial institutions (large banks, clearing banks, investment platforms, central custodians, payment offices, etc.) where securities owners hold their securities accounts. To this end, the Directive refers to the financial institution that is most directly involved in a customer relationship with the shareholder or bondholder involved that is entitled to the respective proceeds and subject to taxation on these.[35]

In practice, securities owners often hold their investment portfolios with financial institutions, rather than holding their portfolio holdings in companies directly. This makes it possible for the EU legislator to delegate the necessary administrative obligations and responsibilities to these intermediaries. At the same time, this opens the possibility of offering security holders an accelerated relief or refund procedure, the so-called fast-track procedure.[36] This, in addition to and in priority over the existing regulations that apply in the various EU Member States on a unilateral basis. Note that the EU Member States are required to safeguard the interests of those in scope of the Directive's operation with regards to their personal data protection rights.[37]

24.4.2 *Certification*

Certified financial intermediaries (CFIs) are assigned an essential role and responsibility.[38] They are subject to standardised reporting, verification and due diligence obligations.[39] The Commission Staff has estimated the associated implementation costs for these intermediaries at €75.9 million.[40]

In order to be recognised or certified as a certified financial intermediary, the financial institution concerned will first have to register itself.[41] This, in publicly accessible national

33 See Chapter III FASTER Directive.
34 See Article 5 FASTER Directive.
35 See observation (20) in the Preamble to the FASTER Directive, saying: *"the obligation should be understood in the sense that the closest certified financial intermediary to the investor, its client, should take reasonable measures ...".*
36 See observation (17) in the Preamble to the FASTER Directive.
37 See Article23 (Personal data protection) FASTER Directive.
38 See Chapter III Withholding tax relief procedure, Section 1 Certified Financial Intermediaries, FASTER Directive.
39 See Chapter III, Section 1 Certified Financial Intermediaries, Section 2 Reporting, Section 3 Systems of Relief, FASTER Directive.
40 See Commission Staff Working Document, Impact Assessment Report, SWD(2023) 216 final, Brussels, 19 June 2023.
41 See Articles 5-9 FASTER Directive.

registers to be set up and kept up to date by the individual EU Member States.[42] The Directive specifies the criteria and conditions, including linking provisions to existing mandatory regulatory rules for financial institutions, that must be met in order to be eligible for registration under the Directive provisions.[43] For reasons of simplicity, the registers of the EU Member States are made accessible via a central EU website set up by the European Commission, the so-called 'European Certified Financial Intermediary Portal'.[44]

Certified financial intermediaries should be entered in the register of each EU Member State in which they wish to submit applications for withholding tax relief or refund on behalf of their clients, the respective security holders.[45] The registration does not operarte as a European passport, as is the case with a banking or investment institution licence for instance.[46] However, an institution that is registered in one of the registers of one of the EU Member States will be recognised as a certified financial intermediary in the other EU Member States.[47] Large financial institutions are required to register.[48] Smaller financial institutions can do this voluntarily, if they meet certain conditions.[49] For example, they must also be declared compliant with anti-money laundering regulations. Financial institutions established outside the EU can only register if they are subject to appropriate supervisory rules in their country of tax residence and this country is also a qualifying third country.[50] Third countries qualify if they are not on the blacklist of non-cooperative jurisdictions or the EU anti-money laundering list.[51] This makes it more difficult for intermediaries from non-qualifying countries to enter the European capital markets.

The Directive also provides for required guarantees in appropriate cases, grounds for refusal of registration, deregistration/removals, liabilities, and frameworks for fines and other sanctions in the event of violations.[52]

24.4.3 Reporting obligation

Certified financial intermediaries throughout the payment chain are required to collect, store and report relevant information and identity data (name, address, place of residence, etc.) about the parties involved in the dividends and/or interests flows (payer, recipient, data-supplying party or parties in the payment chain).[53] The intermediary's reporting

42 See Article 5 (National register of certified financial intermediaries) FASTER Directive.
43 See Article 7 (Requirement to register as a certified financial intermediary) in conjunction with Article 24 (Notification) FASTER Directive.
44 See Article 6 (Development and operation of the European Certified Financial Intermediary Portal) FASTER Directive.
45 See Article 8 (Registration procedure) FASTER Directive.
46 This has also been observed in literature, see, for instance, Adema 2024, *supra note* 2.
47 See Articles 5-9 FASTER Directive.
48 See Article 7 FASTER Directive.
49 See Article 8 FASTER Directive.
50 *Ibidem.*
51 *Ibidem.*
52 See Articles 9 (Removal from the national register), 18 (Liability) and 19 (Penalties) FASTER Directive.
53 See Chapter III Withholding tax relief procedure, Section 2 Reporting, Article 10 Obligation to report, FASTER Directive.

obligation is addressed to the local authority that maintains the register in the EU Member State from which the relevant payments subject to withholding taxation arise (e.g. the tax authorities, or some other authority the respective EU Member State delegates such tasks thereto).[54] In the case of dividends, information must also be provided on the application, where appropriate, of domestic anti-abuse measures.[55] Authorities may request specific information, for example on recent underlying securities transactions, or when it comes to payments on share certificates such as so-called depository receipts.[56]

Each certified financial intermediary reports the piece of information to the relevant authority from the payment chain that they have access to (partial reporting). This is the so-called direct reporting to the relevant EU source Member State.[57] EU Member States can also opt for so-called indirect reporting.[58] In that case, the withholding agent or a designated certified financial intermediary will compile the partial reports of the different intermediaries in the payment chain and report them to the local authorities of the relevant EU source Member State. In that case, it seems, the successive intermediaries in the payment chain exchange their partial reports with each other.

The obligations are aimed at every payment flow, regardless of its size. There is no lower limit. The original proposal for a directive, for reasons of efficiency, still provided for less stringent obligations for dividend payments per share class up to €1,000 (efficiency threshold).[59] The threshold, however, was taken out during the negotiation stage within the Council. In order to guarantee an efficient flow and handling of information flows, conditions apply to formats to be used (xml) and reporting and retention periods apply.[60]

---

54 See Article 10 FASTER Directive.

55 See Article 10 in conjunction with Annex II FASTER Directive.

56 *Ibidem*. A depositary receipt may be described as a negotiable financial instrument that is issued by a financial institution such as a bank to represent a foreign company's publicly traded shares and other securities. Depository receipts are traded on a local stock exchange, and facilitate the trade in shares in foreign companies as these shares involved do not leave, c.q. do not have to leave, the home country of the company's whose shares are traded. The Directive (Article 3) similarly defines a depositary receipt as a 'financial instrument which is negotiable on the capital market of a Member State or a third country and which represent ownership of the securities of an issuer within the Union while being traded on a trading venue in a Member State or a third country and traded independently of the securities of the issuer'.

57 See Article 10 FASTER Directive, and, e.g., Observation (13) in the Preamble to the FASTER Directive, excplicating: *"Two reporting options should be provided for in this Directive: direct and indirect reporting"*.

58 *Ibidem*.

59 See Articles 9 and 12 original Directive proposal and see the Explanatory Memorandum to the original proposal: *"In addition, for the sake of simplification and bringing lighter requirements to the WHT procedures for small investors, a de minimis rule has been introduced for the reporting obligations and due diligence procedure. It consists of not requesting information about financial arrangements or minimum holding period to investors with dividend payments below a threshold of EUR 1000."*

60 See Articles 10 and 17 in conjunction with Annex II FASTER Directive.

24.4.4 Verification obligation

Certified financial intermediaries who wish to apply for a reduction or refund of withholding tax on behalf of their investing clients are required to first verify the accuracy of the information to be reported to the authorities.[61] The relevant security owner, the registered owner (natural person, legal entity), is obliged to declare to his intermediary in writing that he is the beneficial owner of the dividend or interest under national law or a double tax treaty and is entitled to a withholding tax reduction or refund up to the treaty rate.[62] The security holder must also declare that he is not involved in dividend stripping or arbitrage transactions, and that he will inform the intermediary of any relevant change in circumstances.[63] This is the so-called self-declaration. The EU Member States, in their capacity as source Member States, are free to make this declaration recur annually.[64]

The intermediary must investigate the correctness of the entitlement claimed by his trading account holder and verify that there are no fraud or abuse risks (customer due diligence).[65] For example, the intermediary must verify the tax residence (including residence certificate, see next section) and beneficial ownership of his client, his withholding tax reduction or refund entitlement, and that there is no question of dividend stripping or dividend arbitrage.[66] The verification is carried out on the basis of the information available to the intermediary, inter alia, pursuant to the obligations arising from the anti-money laundering rules and the internal control mechanisms that the intermediary must have implemented in its systems on this basis ('know-your-customer', KYC).[67] The EU Member States, in their capacity as source Member States, are free to have this due diligence take place annually.[68] The EU Member States, accordingly, seem to consider financial institutions sufficiently equipped to perform the tax-technical analyses involving their clients' tax treaty entitlements, c.q. have these performed by their tax-specialist consultants, or at least bear the legal responsibilities for such analyses that is. Matters are not without risk here for the intermediaries involved, for these being subject to liability in the event of loss of withholding taxes and the imposition of effective, proportionate and dissuasive penalties.[69] It will be interesting to see how dynamics will flesh-out here.

24.4.5 Certificate of residence

The FASTER Directive introduces a uniformed and automated digital tax residence certificate (eTRC).[70] This certificate of residence will be issued by the EU Member State where the

61 See Article 11 (Request for relief at source or quick refund) in conjunction with Article 12 (Due diligence of the registered owner's eligibility) FASTER Directive.
62 See Article 12 FASTER Directive.
63 *Ibidem.*
64 *Ibidem.*
65 *Ibidem.*
66 *Ibidem.*
67 *Ibidem.*
68 *Ibidem.*
69 *Ibidem* and see Observation (27) in the Preamble to the FASTER Directive.
70 See Article 4 (Chapter II Digital tax residence certificate) in conjunction with Annex I FASTER Directive.

taxpayer in question is a registered owner of securities and is resident for tax purposes.[71] On this basis, security holders can prove their tax residence to the source Member State as the basis for the withholding tax reduction or refund under the fast-track procedure. The certificate of residence can be applied for online, by the taxpayer himself or by his certified financial intermediary (who will need to be authorised for such by the taxpayer/investor involved). The European Commission has a delegated power to organise the online forms and additional technical matters, in order to ensure the recognisability and uniformity of the residence certificates.[72]

The residence certificate is issued by the Member State of residence and is valid in the source Member State as proof of the taxpayer's place of residence.[73] The certificate provides information about the taxpayer's tax residency, tax number and identity details, the date of issue of the statement, the period of validity (maximum one year), the declaring tax authority and which tax treaties the statement relates to.[74] After the request has been submitted, the Member State of residence issues the declaration within two weeks (initial Directive proposal: automatically, within one working day).[75] The Member State of residence shall inform the applicant in due time of any delays in the processing time.[76]

The tax authority of the Member State of residence may invalidate the declaration if information emerges that would show a different place of residence.[77] Other EU Member States will continue to have the opportunity to make a plausible case that the person concerned resides there.[78] The Directive does not provide an explicit basis for the source Member State to challenge the validity of a certificate of residence issued by a fellow EU Member State. In third-country situations, the source Member State seems to have more room for maneuver here: 'proof of tax residence ... deemed appropriate by the source member state'.[79] At the same time, the Directive is about procedures and not about the substantive application of tax law. This seems to make the legal status of the statement somewhat ambiguous. Notably, the source Member State can continue to play the abuse card regardless. It should be noted that the preamble states that the certificate of residence may have a broader scope than just the procedures for reducing or refunding withholding taxes.[80] The author of the current chapter does not know what that means exactly. Here too, it will be interesting to see how dynamics will flesh-out in this area.

---

71 See Article 4(1) FASTER Directive.

72 See, e.g., Article 20 FASTER Directive. The Commission will be assisted by a Committee (Article 21 FASTER Directive (Committee procedure).

73 See Article 4(5) FASTER Directive.

74 See Article 4(2) FASTER Directive.

75 See Article 4(2) FASTER Directive.

76 See Article 4(4) FASTER Directive.

77 See Article 4(5) FASTER Directive.

78 See Article 4(5)FASTER Directive.

79 See Article 12(2)(a) FASTER Directive.

80 See observation (9) in the in the Preamble to the FASTER Directive, saying: "*While primarily intended for the implementation of the withholding tax procedures, the eTRC could also have a wider scope of application and serve for proving the residence for tax purposes beyond withholding tax procedures.*"

24.5 Fast-track procedure

The withholding tax reduction or refund will be made available to the registered owners of the securities concerned according to the so-called fast-track procedure.[81] This procedure comes in two variants, respectively: (i) the 'relief-at-source system', or; (ii) the 'quick refund system' (within 60 calendar days, and if not met refund carries interest where national rules so provide).[82] EU Member States can choose which variant they want to apply.[83] The EU Member States can also introduce both procedures.[84] This, for example, by using profiling for abuse or fraud risks in the event of minor risks at source to reduce it to the treaty rate and to divert to the refund procedures where these risks are less low. Where the risk of abuse or fraud is higher, the Directive allows the EU Member States not to apply the fast-track procedure. This can be the case, for example, with large amounts in certain cases, with changes of ownership shortly before the ex-dividend date and with non-certified intermediary(s) in the payment chain.[85] Then, national procedural rules apply.[86] It will be interesting to see how the mutual interactions between domestic law, international tax treaty law, and primary and secondary EU law will play-out here.

The request for the application of the fast-track procedure is submitted by the certified financial intermediary of the registered owner concerned, i.e. the intermediary where he holds his securities account and who has authorised the intermediary to represent him for tax purposes here.[87] The fast-track procedure starts if the intermediary submits the information prescribed for this purpose with the request and does so in a timely manner.[88] The dossier needs to be in order and should also be submitted on time. Otherwise, the fast-track procedure cannot be applied and the national procedural rules for reduction or refund must be used.

In the relief-at-source procedure, the intermediary submits the aforementioned certificate of residence and the applicable reduced withholding tax rate to the withholding agent prior to the withholding tax payment of dividends or interest.[89] The withholding agent

81 See Articles 11 and 12 in conjunction with Articles 13 and 14 FASTER Directive in conjunction with Observation (16) in the Preamble to the FASTER Directive.
82 See Article 11 in conjunction with Articles 13, 14, and 16 FASTER Directive.
83 *Ibidem.*
84 *Ibidem.*
85 *Ibidem.*
86 See, e.g., observation (25) in the Preamble to the FASTER Directive, saying: "*Nevertheless, there are cases where taxpayers could claim the reduced withholding tax rate based on Union legal acts implemented by national rules. This would typically be the case where national rules ensure that freedom of establishment or free movement of capital is equally granted in domestic and non-domestic comparable situations, or in the case where a directive is transposed. Such cases can require verifications to be carried out, especially to assess the comparability of situations and the applicability of national law to cross-border cases. Where such verifications are required, it should be possible for Member States to deal with those cases under their existing national relief-at-source systems, thus leading to relief of excess withholding tax in the fastest and safest manner.*"
87 See Article 11 in conjunction with Articles 13 and 14 FASTER Directive.
88 See Article 11 in conjunction with Articles 13 and 14 FASTER Directive.
89 See Article 13 FASTER Directive.

then withholds withholding tax and applies the reduced rate.[90] In the case of the quick refund system, the intermediary submits the documents to the tax authorities of the source Member State 'within the second month following the month of the payment date of the dividend or interest' (after which the 60-calendar day period for refund starts to run).[91] The documents to be submitted concern the identity details of the registered owner, including the verification code of the electronic residence certificate, the relevant information about the dividend or interest payment in question, the legal basis for the refund of excess withholding tax, including the amount of this amount, and the aforementioned self-declaration of the registered owner.[92] The authorities also have the information shared with them on the basis of the aforementioned reporting obligations.

The EU Member States may exclude the use of the fast-track procedure in appropriate cases.[93] The Directive says that this is the case, for example, in scenarios where a request is made not for a withholding tax reduction but for the application of a withholding exemption, or when a request is made for the application of a special rate that is based on other grounds than the relevant double tax treaty.[94] This gives EU Member States room to unilaterally steer the scope of the Directive for their jurisdictions, for example by basing their rate reductions in national legislation or by transforming their refund mechanisms into exemption mechanisms.[95] In practice, it has been noted that this limitation in the scope of the FASTER Directive will likely make it more difficult for pension funds, for instance, to make use of the benefits of the Directive, as they often make use of exemptions or rate reductions based on national law (i.e., since treaty benefits may not be available as the exemptions pension funds may typically make use of under domestic law render these institutions to not be considered a resident under the treaties involved, that is, for these institutions not being fully liable to tax on the basis of which treaty benefits would otherwise be made available).

It should be noted that some additional measures have been incorporated into the original Directive proposal allowing the application of fast-track procedures when security holders invest through a collective investment undertaking (undertakings for collective investment in transferable securities (UCITS) or alternative investment funds (AIF)).[96] Otherwise, things could go wrong in some cases, for example if the registered owner and the beneficial owner entitled to the reduced rate were not the same person (investment institution versus underlying investor), leaving the benefits of the Directive unavailable. The Directive allows the certified financial intermediary to apply for a reduction or refund on behalf of the investment institution or the underlying investor in the relevant case at hand.[97]

90 See Article 14 FASTER Directive.
91 See Article 14(1) FASTER Directive.
92 See Article 14 FASTER Directive.
93 See Articles 13 and 14 in conjunction with Articles 11 and 12 FASTER Directive.
94 *Ibidem.*
95 This has also been observed in literature, see, e.g., Adema 2024, *supra note* 2.
96 See Article 15 (Special provisions for indirect investments) FASTER Directive.
97 *Ibidem.*

24.6 Opting-out

The FASTER Directive offers EU Member States an opt-out, dependent on whether some eligibility requirements are met.[98] An EU Member State does not need to introduce the authorised-intermediary system under the Directive, if it has a domestic stock market of a relatively small size and the EU Member State concerned already has a 'comprehensive' withholding tax reduction procedure in place that is equivalent to the Directive.[99] A stock market is of a relatively small size with a so-called market capitalisation ratio lower than 1.5% (in at least 1 of 4 consecutive years).[100] This ratio will be tracked and published by the European Securities and Markets Authority (ESMA) from 2026 onwards.[101] The idea is that setting up the governance mechanism under the Directive for these EU Member States will bring more administrative costs than administrative benefits. The Directive becomes mandatory for EU Member States as soon as they exceed the market capitalisation ratio for 4 consecutive years.[102] These EU Member States will then have 5 years to transpose the Directive obligations into national law.[103] The original proposal for a Directive did not provide for such an opt-out option. The author of the current book chapter was honestly wondering for a moment which of the EU Member States have a small stock market and at the same time a comprehensive withholding tax reduction procedure with regards to publicly traded shares and bonds.

24.7 Final remarks

Will the FASTER Directive live up to its promise? It is interesting to see how a substantive matter – the legal question of whether the recipient of the income is the beneficial owner of the income and entitled to a treaty refund or reduction of withholding tax – is addressed with new supranational procedural rules in addition to existing national procedural rules and an efficiency-promise. But then again, on some closer merit such an approach may not be that unusual. We oftentimes see compliance-oriented solutions for substantive issues. An example may be the self-declaration in the context of the Pillar Two Global Minimum Tax peer review process, on the basis of which countries self-assess their alternative minimum tax systems (a new business tax system in addition to the existing business tax system) as qualifying, whereas other countries accept all of this without questions or initiate discussion and without these other countries moving to levying additional taxes themselves.

Matters may appeal to those who find reassurance in checklists. The point, however, the author of the current book chapter ponders, is that when it comes to determining the substantive tax position, it is sometimes quite difficult – at least in the author's experience – to get the tax residence or place of business firmly determined, for example, and

98 See Observation (3) in the Preamble to the FASTER Directive in conjunction with Articles 2 and 3 and in conjunction with Article 20 FASTER Directive.
99 *Ibidem.*
100 *Ibidem.*
101 *Ibidem.*
102 *Ibidem.*
103 *Ibidem.*

then also in such a way that everyone agrees with each other. The author thinks the same applies to the question of whether there is beneficial ownership and treaty entitlement,[104] and whether or not there is an abuse of rights.[105] As far as the author knows, decades of legal developments – national, international, and at the EU levels also – has not yet led to an unambiguous answer to all these legal questions. The author is a bit afraid that a procedure and a checklist perhaps may not change that much, not even if it is called FASTER and arriving in 2030.

This raises the question of what will happen when things get tense and when FASTER will be actually tested – where the rubber hits the road. Financial institutions will of course all be very diligent and compliant (read: not liable). Residence certificates are issued automatically by EU Member States of residence with a high processing time. Of course, source Member States will not query or even challenge the accuracy of this (after all, A1 certificates in the European social security coordination domain do not lead to any discussion either, isn't it?). Taxpayers will all be self-declared beneficial owners. The European Commission will find that the EU legislator has made a nice EU legislative instrument and that the procedures are in order whereas CFI-compliance can be even better than it already is – should it come to a Directive evaluation in 2032, that is.[106] Those involved will, of course, all have fulfilled their formal duties and responsibilities in quite an appropriate manner. In the meantime, the author estimates that we will mainly collect a lot of data while we will have to keep increasingly scarce financials and IT people enthusiastic in the meanwhile about a career in the business of forms, administrative procedures and online tooling. Are we going to look, substantively that is, and actually, at some point in time at the data in our water-cooled and electric energy slurping data centers? Maybe artificial intelligence will solve matters for us; although the author wonders whether we will find in the forms and declarations and data the circumstances that will provide us the clarifying answer to the aforementioned legal questions.

It concerns, as it has been estimated, around €150 billion worth of Cum/Ex and Cum/Cum stripped tax revenue. The stress test will, the author thinks, inevitably come, sooner or later. The author of the current chapter is curious whether formal-procedural and substantive-actual realities will then turn-out to coincide. Are we going to be in shock and awe, or is all going to be well? If things go wrong, and it turns out that we have been stripping through regardless, who are we going to hold responsible? If we start squeezing, which of the parties at the table is going to squeak? Are the financial institutions going to say that they were diligent and compliant, and – of course – vigilant but also dependent on the information provided by taxpayers? Are the tax authorities

104 See, e.g., Tax Court of Canada 24 February 2004, Velcro Canada Inc. v. The Queen, 2012 TCC 57, Tax Court of Canada 22 April 2008, Prévost Car Inc. v. The Queen, 2008 TCC 231, England and Wales Court of Appeal, 2 March 2006, Indofood International Finance Ltd v JP Morgan Chase Bank NA London Branch, and the Supreme Court of the Netherlands, 19 January 2024, case 20/01884, ECLI:NL:HR:2024:49.

105 See for a comparison Danish Cases, *supra note* 14, Cadbury Schweppes, *supra note* 14, and X BV, *supra note* 14.
Danish Cases).

106 See Article 22 FASTER Directive.

going to say that no legitimate expectations could be derived from the certificates of residence issued?[107] Is the Commission going to say that the evaluations were merely focused on the administrative procedures and formal procedures instead of substantive matters and circumstances? Are the taxpayers going to say in court that they have acted in accordance with the spirit of the law? (Or will the non-tax-paying birds have flown?). Or will it be not too bad at all? The government of the Netherlands, as noted above, has communicated to Dutch Parliament that the numbers of tax reclaim requests are expected to increase only slightly in the Netherlands. This is because the procedures already work very efficiently, the Dutch cabinet has said. This in turn raises the question of what the problem exactly is that we are solving together, starting from 2030. But then again, this makes it a bit difficult to place the aforementioned €27 billion Dutch treasury loss, or the €150 billion for that matter.

We will have to be patient. Whatever the billions in losses, capital markets union ambitions and political-economic challenges, we will have to wait another half a decade before the new rules apply. In the meantime, perhaps we can think about simplifying substantive tax law, decluttering as it is called. Is the glass half full or half empty? We will have to see.

107 See for a comparison, Supreme Court of the Netherlands, 1 December 2023, case 21/05174, ECLI:NL:HR:2023:1675, in which the Dutch Supreme Court held that an administrative declaration issued by the Dutch tax authorities on the existence of a fiscal unity for purposes of Dutch corporate income taxation, a tax consolidation of a group of affiliated corporate taxpayers, does not establish, in substance that is, a fiscal unity for purposes of Dutch corporate income taxation, i.e., if the eligibility criteria for such under the provisions in the Dutch corporate income tax legislation have not substantially been met; an approach where the substance of the matter prevails over formalities and administrative matters.

CHAPTER 25

Company tax proposals and tax policy initiatives

Maarten de Wilde[1]

25.1 Introduction

In this chapter, we discuss the European Commission's tax policy agenda in business income taxation and the ongoing legislative initiatives in this regard as per early 2025. The focus and starting point of the current analysis is on the Commission Communication titled 'Business Taxation for the 21st Century' of 18 May 2021 and the legislative initiatives that have resulted from it, such as the Commission proposal of 12 September 2023 for a Business in Europe: Framework for Income Taxation (BEFIT).[2] The key to the current chapter is that we observe that the European Commission is consistently utilizing political developments and momentum in the international tax policy debate as a driver to further a decades-old ambition of a European Union wide harmonised unitary company taxation system in combination with a tax base distribution key based on a formulaic approach, i.e., instead of the at arm's length principle, together with a furthering of some evolving ambitions to boost the EU's own resources to help financing EU expenditure initiatives.

Worthy of note at this place is that former Italian Prime Minister and former EU Central Bank President Draghi published a report on 9 September 2024 titled 'The future of European competitiveness' outlining an economic strategy for Europe for the years to come.[3] The message of the report is clear. The EU needs to be pulled out of the doldrums and catch up with its rivals – The United States of America and China that is – or face 'slow agony', and that requires, amongst others, spending of a lot of public money the report says. The report calls to prevent the EU from putting itself at a disadvantage both competitively and geopolitically by not following suit. European business communities have been raising similar concerns, and increasingly call for action from the EU and its institutions to boost EU competitiveness via fiscal interventions and by creating efficiency

1 Maarten de Wilde is affiliated with the Erasmus School of Law (ESL) of Erasmus University Rotterdam, the Netherlands, and PwC, Rotterdam, the Netherlands. This chapter draws from and builds on commentaries (in Dutch) of the author in Nederlands Tijdschrift voor Fiscaal Recht (NTFR), a Dutch weekly on tax developments.

2 See European Commission, Proposal for a Council Directive on Business in Europe: Framework for Income Taxation (BEFIT), COM(2023) 532 final, 2023/0321(CNS), Strasbourg, 12.9.2023.

3 The report is available at https://commission.europa.eu/topics/strengthening-european-competitiveness/eu-competitiveness-looking-ahead_en#paragraph_47059.

gains via a decluttering of the overlays of increasingly complex tax mechanisms that have been put into place over the past recent years.

The Draghi report talks about tax incentives as well. This too is considered a necessary component to further an achieving of the major strategic policy goals in the area of, for example, the environment and the energy transition, but also when it comes to building innovative and technological strength to further the economic power and strategic independence and resilience of the EU Member States in concert. High-tech companies and their investments, in the EU of course, play a pivotal role in the pursuit of such aims. All is about innovation, R&D, technology and tech companies, about digitalisation, artificial intelligence, and how all this may be cranked-up to promote European prosperity.

Upon its publication, the Draghi report and its messages have gained some significant momentum within the EU institutions. Although the report has not yet led to some concrete outcomes at the time of writing of the current chapter, early 2025, at least not in terms of some releases of some legislative initiatives in the tax domain that is, the author of the current chapter would not be surprised if we will see the European Commission to start moving at some point in the not-too-distant future to further concretize matters.

25.2 Commission Communication 'Business Taxation for the 21st Century'

25.2.1 General remarks

On 18 May 2021, the European Commission published its Communication 'Business Taxation for the 21st Century'.[4] In this Communication, the Commission presented an ambitious tax policy agenda with measures for the short term and longer term in the area of business taxation. The Commission aims to develop an efficient and fair, sustainable and future-proof, job-creating and growth-friendly tax framework for the internal market, which is suitable for generating lasting tax revenues in a globalising and digitalising economy, which helps co-finance the NextGenerationEU Recovery Package[5] and that supports the digital transition and greening of Member States' economies.

In its Communication, the Commission set out its intention to act swiftly on the EU-wide implementation of the global company tax reform commitments of 1 July 2021 and 8 October 2021 on a redistribution of tax bases to market jurisdictions (Pillar One) and an establishment of a minimum global level of taxation of business profits (Pillar Two).

4 See Communication from the Commission to the European Parliament and the Council, 'Business Taxation for the 21st Century', COM(2021) 251 final, Brussels, 18.5.2021.

5 See Council Regulation (EU) 2020/2094 of 14 December 2020 establishing a European Union Recovery Instrument to support the recovery in the aftermath of the COVID-19 crisis.

Box 1

OECD/G20 IF Two-pillar solution – global company tax reform proposals (BEPS 2.0)

On 8 October 2021, around 140 countries within the OECD/G20 Inclusive Framework on Base Erosion and Profit Shifting (IF) reached a political agreement on a reform of the international business taxation system, an implementation plan, and a concrete timetable.[6] On 1 July 2021, 130 IF countries already reached a political agreement on the new global company tax framework.

On the basis of two pillars, the aim is to find a global solution to the challenges that the digitalising economy poses in relation to the taxation of multinationals. Pillar One is about a tax base redistribution towards sales jurisdictions. More specifically, it concerns the adjustment of the rules on taxable presence and profit allocation, which allows countries where a multinational has customers to levy company taxes, even if this multinational company is not physically present in that country. Pillar Two aims to ensure that large multinationals worldwide always pay at least a minimum level of profit tax of 15%. The countries that have joined the political agreement on the two-pillar solution have agreed on a rollback of unilateral digital services taxes and any corresponding trade sanctions until year-end 2024. It is yet to be seen how developments will evolve during 2025 and the years to come.

6 See https://www.oecd.org/tax/beps/.

<table>
<tr><th>Pillar One</th><th>Pillar Two</th></tr>
<tr><td>Pillar One relates to the allocation of part of the (adjusted) consolidated commercial profit of the multinationals concerned to sales jurisdictions for company tax purposes.
The system establishes a formulary-based allocation of tax base to market countries, i.e., 25% of commercial profit, insofar as this amount exceeds an amount equal to 10% of the turnover ('Amount A'). Pillar One applies to the approximately top 100 largest multinationals worldwide: companies with a profitability of more than 10% (profit before tax/revenue) and a worldwide annual turnover of more than 20 billion euros. The measures do not apply to the extraction of natural resources and regulated financial services. It has been estimated that every year, 150 billion US dollars in taxable profit would be redistributed on the basis of this new tax base division system.</td><td>Pillar Two seeks to establish a minimum level of business taxation of 15% and accompanying additional taxation, top-up taxation that is, by countries up to that level – predominantly those jurisdictions where the companies headquarters are based, that is where other countries do not conform to the new minimum tax standard. The top-up tax applies under a so-called income inclusion rule (IIR), and a backstop top-up tax is envisaged under a so-called undertaxed profits rule (UTPR). Countries are eligible to top-up tax domestic low-taxed profits on the basis of a so-called qualified domestic minimum top-up tax (QDMTT). The aim is to establish a floor in the possibilities for countries to compete for corporate investment with each other in the field of corporate income taxation. Pillar Two applies to multinationals with an annual turnover of 750 million euros or more. Among other things, investment and pension funds are excluded from the scope of application and the same applies to 'international shipping income'. The system also provides for carve-outs in the form of an additional tax-free amount, in the base determination that is, on which any top-up taxation is determined.
It has been estimated that the reform would produce a worldwide additional tax revenue of 200 billion US dollars annually. Countries have agreed that if they actually take measures, they will do so along the policies established within the Inclusive Framework (common approach).</td></tr>
<tr><td colspan="2">The implementation timeline of the two-pillar solution has been, and still is, ambitious and has aimed to enter into force in 2023. And indeed, Pillar Two has been effectuated as per year-end 2023, at least in a range of countries, including the EU Member States via the EU Pillar Two Directive of 14 December 2022.[1] Pillar One, however, has not yet come to fruition. Political discussions are still ongoing at the time the current chapter was finalized. As far as Pillar One is concerned, the intention has been, and indeed still is, to transpose the political outcomes into EU legislation someday.</td></tr>
</table>

1 See Council Directive (EU) 2022/2523 of 14 December 2022 on ensuring a global minimum level of taxation for multinational enterprise groups and large-scale domestic groups in the Union.

The Commission also presented practical measures in its Communication of 18 May 2021 for the upcoming two years (2021-2023) to address identified immediate challenges. These include transparency measures aimed at publishing effective tax rates in countries along the lines of envisaged Pillar Two measures (2022), measures to tackle tax avoidance and tax evasion with letterbox companies (Unshell: 2021), introduction of a so-called 'debt equity bias reduction allowance' (DEBRA: 2022) and a recommendation for vertical loss relief. The Commission also presented a plan for an EU-wide holistic business taxation framework for the coming decades. To this end, by 2023, the European Commission said that it will launch its 'Business in Europe: Framework for Income Taxation' (BEFIT), a proposal for a common consolidated business income tax base to be divided among Member States on the basis of a formulaic approach. This, while withdrawing the proposals for Directives from the Corporate Tax Reform Package of 25 October 2016 for a Common (Consolidated) Corporate Tax Base (C(C)CTB). The Commission delivered, and Unshell, DEBRA, as well as BEFIT were launched in follow-up to the communication. The proposals are pending at the time of writing of the current chapter, and will be discussed in some detail in the sections below.

The Commission built in its Communication on an earlier Communication, the so-called Tax Package that it presented on 15 July 2020,[7] which is also part of the broader tax reform agenda for the coming years. In late 2021, the European Commission also proposed a digital levy, inspired by the Pillar One plans, as an own resource that is, lifted from the Pillar One plans, to help co-finance the NextGenerationEU recovery package – see further section 25.3.1 below. The proposals for Directives from the Digital Tax Package of 21 March 2018 for a digital permanent establishment ('Digital PE') and a turnover-oriented digital services tax ('Digital Services Tax'; 'DST') were withdrawn. Furthermore, in the summer of 2021, as part of the Fit for 55 package to support established climate objectives, the Commission also launched proposals for, inter alia, the revision of the Energy Taxation Directive and the introduction of a carbon border adjustment mechanism (CBAM) – see further section 25.3.1 below for some general remarks on the initiatives. The Commission noted that it will present proposals for other own resources in the form of, for example, a Financial Transaction Tax (FTT) and an own resource linked to the corporate sector soon. The developments are part of a broader rethinking of the future of taxation in the EU that should culminate in a 'Tax Symposium' in 2022 on the 'EU tax mix on the road to 2050'. Many of the plans crystallized into legislative initiatives of which a number have been adopted at the time of writing of the current chapter and of which some are still pending before the Council – see Section 25.3 below for some further details.

25.2.2 International developments as a driving force for advancing the EU agenda

The Commission Communication is an interesting policy document. On the one hand, the Commission paraded some old ideas as new ones. On the other hand, the Communication is a very cleverly conceived and, in many ways, a rather timeless document, also

---

7 See Communication from the Commission to the European Parliament and the Council, 'An Action Plan for Fair and Simple Taxation Supporting the Recovery Strategy', COM(2020) 312 final, Brussels, 15.7.2020.

looking at the timing of it, the way in which the Commission formulated its ambitions, the political acumen, the deft packaging and skillful pressurizing, as well as the strategic roll-out of plans and proposals. The communication, also at the time of writing of the current chapter, early 2025, is a centerpiece document bringing together the blueprints of Commission policies in company taxation for the internal market for years to come.

The Commission has been utilizing international societal and political attention and senses of urgency to act when it comes to the taxation of profits of international business enterprises, the momentum in the various international tax policy arenas (Base Erosion and Profit Shifting; BEPS 2.0), covid recovery financing issues as a driving force to bring forward its, actually, traditional EU company tax integration agenda; much like the 2024 Draghi report is doing when it comes with a view to geopolitical and economic dynamics that we have seen over the recent years. The Commission has already engaged into similar strategies before, with its 'Action Plan on Corporate Taxation' of 17 June 2015, for example, when the Commission used the, then, forthcoming BEPS-2015 outcomes to relaunch the CCCTB in phases. The Anti-Avoidance Directives of 2016 and 2017 (ATAD1 and ATAD2) are only partly about addressing BEPS and mainly concern the transposition into the tax systems of the EU Member States of the 'international aspects of the CCCTB'. With its 18 May 2021 Communication the Commission has done the same thing again and has since then been instrumentalising BEPS 2.0 developments and the covid pandemic of 2021 and 2022 to further its agenda with the ultimate goal of achieving unitary taxation in the internal market: BEFIT. And BEFIT at the end of the day is not much more than a rebranding and, allright then, an updating of the CCCTB proposals of 2011 and 2016 – possibly, perhaps, if we read it correctly, with the base determination conforming to that for Pillar Two purposes.

At the time of writing this chapter, at the beginning of 2025, the European effective minimum business tax rate has arrived. The Digital Tax Package of 2018 had done its political pressure work, the United States came back (back; see box 2 below) at the policy discussion tables within the Inclusive Framework of the OECD/G20 in 2021, and the Council has committed itself to a digital levy, as a 'coexistent' own resource in addition to whatever will come out from the OECD sleeves. The Commission Communication of 18 May 2021 can therefore be seen as a stone casted in the pond, and the policies outlined in the document are here to stay it seems.

25.2.3 *Megatrends desire comprehensive EU agenda*

The Commission highlights megatrends such as demographic change (ageing), climate change and environmental degradation, globalisation and the digitalisation of our economy, and the covid pandemic as an accelerator of the latter. According to the Commission, there is a consensus that the concepts of country of residence and country of source as accustomed in international tax law have become obsolete and are no longer equipped to deal with societal and economic realities of today in an appropriate way; tax -wise that is. The Commission draws attention to the Pillar One and Pillar Two discussions and political developments in the United States (see box 2 below) and indicated that regardless of how matters turn out, the envisaged pillars will continue to shape the tax policy agenda in the EU in the coming years.

For the Commission, these trends call for a comprehensive agenda that focuses on a balanced tax mix and a tax system based on the principles of fairness, neutrality and simplicity. EU Member States remain autonomous in setting their rates above the minimum and on focusing on process-efficiency in the administrative assessment and collection of tax debts, supported where appropriate by grants to that end from the EU recovery package. Moreover, there is a question of autonomy here, on which several of the parliaments of the Member States have drawn yellow cards in the past, for instance in the context of company tax integration initiatives under the C(C)CTB proposals in 2011 and 2016. When it comes to incentive regimes the Commission sees for itself, where appropriate, an 'agenda-shaping role'. This does mean, however, that targeted carve-outs will have to be provided for in the Pillar Two context to create the necessary policy instrumentation space, or the EU minimum rate will have to be set at a higher level than the global minimum rate. Otherwise, EU Member States run the risk that the benefit of an EU tax incentive will be taxed away abroad under a Pillar-Two-oriented top-up tax charge. The Commission will therefore also have to take this agenda-shaping role internationally. The same issue also applies to the DEBRA initiative. That initiative, may narrow EU company tax bases vis-à-vis the Pillar Two benchmark tax base too, creating effective tax rate decreases for Pillar Two purposes and potentially leading to additional taxation under Pillar Two top-up tax charge mechanisms operative in third countries abroad. This agenda-shaping role, however, has not been explicated, at least not yet, at the time of writing this chapter – see further paragraph 2.2.3.2 for some details. Please note that the OECD reportedly has been working on frameworks within which countries can or cannot compete with each other via their tax systems without falling foul under the Pillar Two global minimum tax rules.

25.2.4 Pillar One and Pillar Two measures sort for unitary taxation and minimum rate harmonisation

The Commission expressed in its Communication of 18 May 2021 that it supports the international discussions on base redistribution (Pillar One) and minimum profit taxation (Pillar Two). The Commission also indicated that it intends to implement the Pillars in the EU through EU Directives, with adjustments where necessary for instance to conform to primary EU law parameters and requirements.

The Commission considers Pillar One and Pillar Two to be in line with the EU agenda, or rather, the Commission sees them as an ideal steppingstone for further EU company tax reforms. Pillar One is seen by the Commission as a steppingstone towards unitary taxation (unitary combination, formula apportionment) and this is in line with the Commission's decades-long-cherished ambition to achieve this for the internal market, the CCCTB (that has been rebranded into BEFIT). Pillar Two is seen by the Commission as a steppingstone towards minimum rate harmonisation and curbing tax competition within the internal market. We also saw this ambition before, for example during the discussions in 2016 on the switch-over measure and in particular the 'subject to an effective tax rate test' in the Anti-Tax Avoidance Package in 2016 from which the Anti-Tax Avoidance Directive originated later that year, and also within the context of the C(C)CTB where political discussions on minimum rates and/or rate bandwidths emerged too. And we have seen the same in the discussions before that, since 2011, on a 'subject to an effective tax' requirement for with-holding tax exemption under the Interest and Royalty Directive ('IRR') ('minimum effective taxation'; 'MET'). Furthermore, we must not forget the 'fair taxation' desire expressed by the Commission to broaden the gateway criterion from the Code of Conduct on Business Taxation with a minimum effective tax rate test and thus to broaden the mandate of the Code of Conduct group when blacklisting non-cooperative jurisdictions. Agreement on Pillars One and Two would offer excellent opportunities to make progress within the EU on all these dossiers with the stroke of a pen.

25.2.5 Commission's ambitions extend further

'Going beyond the OECD agreement'
The Commission's ambitions go beyond just keeping up with international developments. The Commission therefore presented initiatives for both the short term (2021-2023) and the long term (period thereafter).

Short term
In the short term, the Commission first and foremost announced transparency measures for 2022. The methodology in the Pillar Two proposal to calculate the jurisdictional effective tax rate (ETR) in countries offers, it seems, a convenient tool to give existing transparency and reporting ambitions in this area some extra momentum. For reasons of transparency, the Commission Communication announced a proposal for a Directive that will do something similar as the measures adopted on public country-by-country reporting,[8] but then devised along Pillar Two-ETR lines. The Communication is silent on the possible interaction of any envisaged Pillar Two derived public transparency measures with existing public country-by-country reporting rules.

Secondly, the Commission announced a proposal to combat aggressive tax planning with the use of shell companies for the fourth quarter of 2021. This measure, initially referred to as 'ATAD3' and later, upon its release on 22 December 2022, 'Unshell' (as the Directive proposal published that day actually is not a modification of ATAD but a stand-alone Directive proposal), introduces a reporting obligation for multinationals with business activities within the EU. These should enable the relevant tax authorities to assess the extent to which there are actual business activities undertaken within the taxable corporate entities involved in their jurisdictions (substance); and then, in the absence thereof, of the relevant minimum substance that is – or in the presence of 'abusive shell companies' – to deny the companies involved any related tax advantages under for instance intra-EU tax treaties and/or EU Directives such as the Parent Subsidiary

8 See Directive (EU) 2021/2101 of the European Parliament and of the Council of 24 November 2021 amending Directive 2013/34/EU as regards disclosure of income tax information by certain undertakings and branches.

Directive[9] and the Interest and Royalty Directive[10]. The Commission did not speak in its Communication in terms of harmonising substance requirements as such, or as to what exactly these conditions would or should look like (the Commission nevertheless later did upon the launch of the Directive proposal on 22 December 2022 – see further section 25.3.2 below). At the time of writing of the current chapter, the Unshell proposal is still pending. The Communication stated en passant that the Commission also intends to take further steps to prevent outgoing interest and royalty payments from leaving the EU without taxation ('double non-taxation'). The narrative here feels a bit 'EU-wide-source-tax-ish' and we will have to wait and see what this will be about when concrete measures are to be brought forward at some point.

Thirdly, the Commission announced for 2022 a proposal for a capital deduction mechanism to mitigate the financing discrimination problem, called DEBRA, the so-called 'debt equity bias reduction allowance'. The corporate tax systems of most Member States use the nominal return on equity as a taxable income concept for company tax purposes. This means that capital costs are not deductible, while interest costs are deductible (in principle that is, save for the application of any interest deductibility mechanisms put in place in the country's business income tax system involved). This leads to a differential tax treatment of equity financing (no deduction of cost component equity financing) compared to debt financing (deduction of cost component debt financing), and thereby creating a relative tax subsidy for debt financing – a 'financing discrimination' that is, in taxation. The Commission considers this problematic, especially now that companies are facing sizeable debt burdens due to the economic crisis caused by the covid pandemic and the putting in place of lockdown response measures in responses to that in countries worldwide during 2020-2021, the Commission says. DEBRA aims to reduce this inequality in tax treatment. Anti-abuse measures should prevent unwanted use of the allowance. Upon the release of the DEBRA proposal on 11 May 2022,[11] it became clear that he intended capital deduction will be linked to a percentage of the equity change (i.e., the so-called 'Soft ACE') rather than a percentage of the invested equity (i.e., the so-called 'Hard Allowance for Corporate Equity', 'Hard ACE').

The idea, notably, to mitigate financing discrimination issues in taxation with an equity allowance is not new. An Italian-style soft ACE mechanism ('Aiuto alla crescita economica'; 'Aid to Economic Growth') was included in the CCTB Directive proposal of 2016: the so-called 'Allowance for Growth and Investment' (AGI). It is worth noting that the GloBE tax base in the Pillar Two system, the basis against which the 15% minimum tax standard is assessed that is, incidentally, does not have a capital deduction and hence, too, embeds the financing discrimination issue the Commission now seeks to address with DEBRA. In order to absorb the base-narrowing effect of DEBRA vis-à-vis the Pillar

9 See Council Directive 2011/96/EU of 30 November 2011 on the common system of taxation applicable in the case of parent companies and subsidiaries of different Member States (recast).

10 See Council Directive 2003/49/EC of 3 June 2003 on a common system of taxation applicable to interest and royalty payments made between associated companies of different Member States.

11 See European Commission, Proposal for a Council Directive on laying down rules on a debt-equity bias reduction allowance and on limiting the deductibility of interest for corporate income tax purposes, COM(2022) 216 final, 2022/0154(CNS), Brussels, 11.5.2022.

Two's GloBE tax base – or to prevent DEBRA from becoming Pillar Two incompatible – this means that either Pillar Two will have to provide for a carve-out, or the EU minimum rate will have to be set at a higher level than the global minimum rate. A similar point applies to above-mentioned ETR-reducing incentive regimes. At the time of writing of the current chapter, the DEBRA Directive proposal is still pending, while the Pillar Two Directive does not provide a carve-out to this end and sets the minimum rate at the internationally agreed 15%.

Fourthly, in addition to its Communication, the Commission published a Recommendation on the tax treatment of losses during the COVID-19 crisis.[12] The Commission recommends that Member States provide for vertical loss relief (carry back loss-offset). This, in order to assist companies that were profitable prior to corona and paying tax and then, in 2020 and 2021, found themselves ending up in a loss-making position due to the lockdown measures that were put in place in countries worldwide. Vertical loss relief in this way reduces a liquidity disadvantage. En passant, the Commission Communication indicated that the Commission services will examine in a more general sense the merits of a coordinated opening of cross-border loss relief to SMEs and enterprises 'in the initial stages of their European expansion'. Loss import and ensuing market distortion issues have been on the Commission's tax policy agenda for years.

Longer term: EU-wide company tax system

For the longer term (2023 and forward), the Commission presented plans for an EU-wide holistic company tax framework for the coming decades, BEFIT that is: a common consolidated business income tax base allocated to Member States for company tax purposes on the basis of a formula. This was (CCCTB) and is (BEFIT) the final destination: an EU-wide company tax system. The Commission still sees this as the comprehensive solution for Member States' internal market-distorting corporate taxes. BEFIT aims to simplify and fairer taxation of profits in the EU, reduce red tape and compliance costs, combat tax avoidance, facilitate job creation, growth and investment, and generate tax revenues for Member States in a sustainable manner. BEFIT will be developed in cooperation with Member States, in consultation with industry and civil society groups, and the vision of the European Parliament will also be taken into account, the communication says. In the design, attention will be paid to the weighting of the formula factors, to an appropriate arrangement of the factor 'labour' and to the inclusion of 'intangibles' in the factor 'assets'. 'Digital' should also be reflected appropriately in the new distribution key to be developed. The BEFIT Directive proposal was launched on 12 September 2023,[13] and has been pending before the Council since.

And furthermore

The Commission indicated that the principles of fairness, neutrality and simplicity also apply to the system of own resources to finance the EU budget. In line with the Council's mandate thereto, the Commission announced to present proposals for, among other

12 See Commission Recommendation (EU) 2021/801 of 18 May 2021 on the tax treatment of losses during the COVID-19 crisis.

13 See European Commission, Proposal for a Council Directive on Business in Europe: Framework for Income Taxation (BEFIT), COM(2023) 532 final, 2023/0321(CNS), Strasbourg, 12.9.2023.

things, a digital levy. The Commission stated that '[d]igital companies tend to pay less taxes than other companies and the taxes they pay do not always benefit the countries where their activities take place'. The digital levy would allow these companies to contribute fairly to the recovery package and to the building of society in a broad sense. The Commission said the levy will be in line with World Trade Organization (WTO) rules and international agreements. In any case, the 'EU digital levy' will not be incompatible with the tax treaties, since the EU is not a party to these treaties. Furthermore, the FTT is back on the table, now as an own resource or the EU budget. In 2011, a tax on financial transactions was already proposed, and the proposal was later withdrawn in 2016. Also the own resource linked to the corporate sector' was mentioned in the Communication.

Decision making via qualified majority voting
It is noteworthy that the Commission did not address in its Communication the pending political debate on qualified majority voting in tax matters, rather than the current veto.[14] For some years now, the Commission has been in favour of abolishing unanimous decision-making within the Council in tax matters. This has met some resistance from the Member States here and there for some countries considering such a move to encroach upon their sovereignty as a nation state. On previous occasions, the Commission has indicated its willingness to invoke Article 116 TFEU if necessary and to take qualified majority voting on this legal basis also in tax matters under the ordinary legislative procedure,[15] a step that – if such were to be taken at some point in time – would be unprecedented. Perhaps this discussion will come up again some next time.

25.3 Developments in follow-up to the Communication 'Business Taxation for the 21st Century'

25.3.1 European Commission proposals for Directives Unshell and Pillar Two and Own Resources Package

General
Developments did not end with the Commission's tax policy document of 18 May 2021. On the contrary. On 22 December 2021, the European Commission published a comprehensive package of tax measures following-up on its plans launched with the release of its tax agenda earlier that year on May 18, 2021.

The package consists of:
a proposal for a Directive on the EU implementation of the global 15% minimum business income tax level for large multinationals (Pillar Two);[16]

14 See Articles 113 and 115 TFEU.

15 See Communication from the Commission to the European Parliament, the European Council and the Council, 'Towards a more efficient and democratic decision making in EU tax policy', COM(2019) 8 final, Strasbourg, 15.1.2019, and Communication from the Commission to the European Parliament and the Council, An Action Plan for Fair and Simple Taxation Supporting the Recovery Strategy', COM(2020) 312 final, Brussels, 15.7.2020.

16 See Proposal for a Council Directive on ensuring a global minimum level of taxation for multi-national groups in the Union, COM(2021) 823 final, 2021/0433(CNS), Brussels, 22.12.2021.

a proposal for a Directive to address the improper use of so-called shell entities within the EU (Unshell),[17] and;
the 'Next generation of EU own resources' package (Own Resources Package).[18]

Ad (i). Pillar Two implementation EU
With the Pillar Two Directive proposal the Commission delivered on the envisaged EU-wide implementation of the 15% minimum business income tax level for large multinationals along the lines of the global political agreement of 1 July 2021 and its update of 8 October 2021 on the developing new global company tax framework (BEPS 2.0, Pillar Two). The proposed Directive was adopted on 14 December 2022, and achieves – in close alignment with the Model Rules that the OECD Secretariat published on 20 December 2021: (i) a minimum level of business taxation within the internal market of 15%, and; (ii) accompanying additional taxation by Member States up to that level where other countries do not adhere to the minimum standard. The intended entry into force of the original Pillar Two Directive was 1 January 2023 (income inclusion rule, IIR) and 1 January 2024 (undertaxed profits (until 2022: payments) rule, UTPR). Under the later compromise texts published by the French Presidency in March and April 2022 the implementation date was postponed with a year to year-end 2023 and 2024 respectively. The Pillar Two Directive is discussed on a stand-alone basis in depth in Chapter [XX], to which is referred to at this place. For some general policy related aspects see section 25.3.2 below.

Ad (ii). Unshell
The Unshell Directive proposal introduces a governance, levying and sanctioning mechanism for entities established within the EU, which, according to the European Commission, are at risk of being used by companies or wealthy individuals as a so-called shell entity (letterbox company) for tax avoidance and/or tax evasion purposes. To this end, the Directive on Administrative Cooperation (Directive on Administrative Cooperation; DAC)[19] will be amended as well. The intended implementation date and date of entry into force of the Unshell Directive, upon their launched, are 30 June 2023 and 1 January 2024 respectively. The Directive proposal is pending at the time of writing of the current chapter. For some details, see section 25.3.3 below.

Ad (iii). Own Resources Package
With the Own Resources Package, the Commission is launching three proposals for new own resources to help co-finance, inter alia, the NextGenerationEU recovery package. To this end, the Commission is linking up with:
the expanding European Emissions Trading System (EU ETS);
the carbon border adjustment mechanism (CBAM) introduced in mid-2021, and;

17 See European Commission, Proposal for a Council Directive laying down rules to prevent the misuse of shell entities for tax purposes and amending Directive 2011/16/EU, COM(2021) 565 final, 2021/0434 (CNS), Brussels, 22.12.2021.
18 See European Commission – Press release, 'The Commission proposes the next generation of EU own resources Brussels', IP/21/7025, 22 December 2021, and underlying documents.
19 See Council Directive 2011/16/EU of 15 February 2011 on administrative cooperation in the field of taxation and repealing Directive 77/799/EEC.

the Pillar One measures on tax base redistribution for the very largest multinationals from the above-mentioned global political agreement on company tax reform of 1 July 2021.

The Commission aimed to phase in the own resources package gradually from 1 January 2023 and to publish the necessary EU legislative proposals during the first half of 2022. The own resources package should generate an average of around €17 billion per year in revenue for the EU budget in the coming years (period 2026-2030). For some details, see section 25.3.4 below. The Commission completed its proposal for a next generation of own resources on 20 June 2023.[20]

Following-up on 18 May 2021 Communication, and more
With these measures, the European Commission, as said, gave a first follow-up to the measures announced in its Communication 'Business Taxation for the 21st Century' of 18 May 2021.

In addition to this, the Commission also is further consolidating its own dominant political position, for example with regard to the instruments that have been rolled-out to finance NextGenerationEU and the accompanying expansion of the long-term EU budget (Multiannual Financial Framework 2021-2027, MFF).[21] Moreover, the Commission now also scheduled in its package the transparency measures mentioned also in the Communication aimed at publishing effective tax rates in countries along Pillar Two measures (2022), the introduction of a Debt Equity Bias Reduction Allowance (DEBRA; 2022), the seventh modification to the Administrative Cooperation Directive on cryptocurrency information exchange (DAC8; 2022), as well as the Pillar One Directive proposal (originally scheduled for 27 July 2022). The Commission also announced an initiative for 2022 to address the challenges posed by shell entities established outside the EU. Furthermore, the Commission announced a second round of new own resources by the end of 2023, which will build on the envisaged Business in Europe: Framework for Income Taxation (BEFIT), which, as said, includes a proposal for a common consolidated profit tax base allocated to Member States on the basis of a formula. The Commission delivered on 12 September 2023, launching the BEFIT proposal that is currently pending. The Commission also once more referred to the Communication on other own resources to be presented in the form of above-mentioned Financial Transaction Tax; 'FTT') together with the noted own resource linked to the corporate sector.[22]

Whatever the merits, a certain degree of political dexterity cannot be denied the Commission here, especially when it comes to way in which Pillar One was quite surreptitiously wheeled-into the debate on a digital levy as an own resource for the EU budget – more on that below.

20 See for some information https://commission.europa.eu/strategy-and-policy/eu-budget/long-term-eu-budget/2021-2027/revenue/next-generation-eu-own-resources_en.
21 See Council Regulation (EU, Euratom) 2020/2093 of 17 December 2020 laying down the multiannual financial framework for the years 2021 to 2027.
22 See Communication from the Commission to the European Parliament and the Council, the European Economic and Social Committee and the Committee of the Regions, 'The next generation of own resources for the EU Budget', COM(2021) 566 final, Brussels, 22.12.2021.

Let's take a closer look at the developments.

25.3.2 Pillar Two

Expeditious EU-wide implementation Pillar Two
With the Pillar Two Directive proposal, the first component of the package of 22 December 2021, the European Commission had made the announced opening move for a dynamic EU-wide implementation of the global 15% minimum business tax standard for large multinationals (annual turnover more than €750 million). The proposed Directive closely follows the Model Rules that were published by the OECD on 20 December 2021, and so does the Pillar Two Directive as it was ultimately adopted on 14 December 2022. In adherence to the ambitions expressed within the Inclusive Framework to this end, the measures apply from 31 December 2023 (income inclusion rule; original proposal: 1 January 2023) and 31 December 2024 (undertaxed payments rule; original proposal: 1 January 2024).

When it came to the chances of success, back in December 2021, it should be noted that the Commission had stated on its website that: "It is important to note that EU members of the OECD Inclusive Framework are already supporting the global agreement that the Commission proposal is implementing. The only EU Member State that is not a member of the Inclusive Framework, and as such has not formally committed to the agreement, is Cyprus. However, we expect Cyprus to support the Directive".[23] The pressure on the Member States to transform the political commitment of 8 October 2021 into a real legal commitment, in other words, was being stepped up considerably already as of the launch of the Directive proposal on 22 December 2021.

The adoption of the Directive did not come without some turmoil. Despite the French Presidency's aims to reach a political agreement on the Directive proposal at the ECOFIN Council of 5 April 2022, the presidency did not manage to get the Directive proposal adopted that day, because of a veto of Poland being the last Member State not willing to lift its reservations. Earlier, on 12 March 2022, the Presidency published a compromise proposal on which no agreement was reached at the ECOFIN Council of 15 March 2022.[24] Poland, Estonia, Sweden and Malta hesitated and maintained their reservations. Poland took the position that Pillar One and Pillar Two should be adopted as a package deal.

The French Presidency's compromise proposal of 12 March 2022 amended the original Directive proposal in some respects. A striking modification was the postponement of the implementation date, which was adjourned by one year, to year-end 2023 for the income-inclusion rule and to year-end 2024 for the undertaxed payments/profits rule. Furthermore, the power to judge non-EU-country top-up tax systems as a qualifying top-up tax under the Pillar Two Directive measure was shifted from the European Commission

23 See European Commission – Questions and answers, 'Questions and Answers on Minimum corporate taxation Brussels', QANDA/21/6967, 22 December 2021.

24 See Council of the European Union, Draft Council Directive on ensuring a global minimum level of taxation for multinational groups in the Union - Compromise text, 6975/22, FISC 61, ECOFIN 199, Brussels, 12 March 2022 (Compromise proposal).

to the Council, whereby the Council takes a decision to that effect by unanimity. The compromise proposal also provided for a transitional arrangement for Member States with 10 or fewer ultimate parent entities of in-scope multinationals established within their territory.[25] These Member States may choose not to apply the IIR and UTPR for the first three years after the implementation date. The other Member States will respect this and, where appropriate, set their UTPR at nil. Furthermore, some technical changes were made which remain undiscussed.

A second compromise text was prepared and published by the French Presidency on 2 April 2022 to deal with the reservations from Sweden, Malta, Estonia and Poland.[26] The compromise extended the transitional arrangement for EU Member States from 10 to 12 or fewer ultimate parent entities of in-scope multinationals. Together with the compromise text a draft Council statement was prepared in which the Council would reiterate its political commitment to bringing both pillars into existence. For Estonia, Malta and Sweden these modifications were sufficient to lift their initial reservations. However, this was not the case for Poland that stood by its position of not being able to waive its opposition on the basis of this compromise for not having any legal assurance of the two-pillar solution to come to fruition as a package deal.

A third compromise text was prepared and published by the French Presidency on 16 June 2022 to deal with the reservations from Poland.[27] The compromise proposal, again, postponed the introduction of the measures by one year to year-end 2023, allotted the power to assess non-EU-country top-up tax systems as a qualifying top-up tax under the Pillar Two Directive measure to the Council, extended the transitional arrangement for Member States to 12 or fewer ultimate parent entities of in-scope multinationals, and introduced some administrative and technical elements that are not further discussed at this here. This led Poland to agree in June 2022. Hungary, however, withdrew the previously expressed support. The move from Hungary did not allow unanimity to be reached in the summer of 2022. This led to all kinds of discussions, especially towards Poland and Hungary, about the backgrounds and considerations for withdrawing or expressing reservations and the usefulness and necessity of whether to move towards EU-decision-making via qualified majority voting (QMV) instead of unanimity voting.

On 9 September 2022, France, Germany, Italy, the Netherlands, and Spain, issued a joint statement underlining the desire for an agreement in the Council and the commitment to implement Pillar Two in 2023.[28] The ministers of these EU Member States devised the statement in the margins of the informal ECOFIN that took place in Prague, Czech

25 See Article 47a Compromise proposal.

26 See Council of the European Union, Directive on ensuring a global minimum level of taxation for multinational groups in the Union General approach, 7709/22, FISC 86, ECOFIN 284, Brussels, 2 April 2022.

27 See Council of the European Union, Draft Council Directive on ensuring a global minimum level of taxation for multinational groups in the Union - Presidency compromise text and draft Council statement, 10497/22, FISC 143, ECOFIN 647, Brussels, 21 June 2022.

28 See statement is available at, e.g., the website of the Finance Ministry of France: https://presse.economie.gouv.fr/09-09-2022-joint-statement-by-france-germany-italy-netherlands-and-spain/.

Republic on 9-10 September 2022. The statement said the following: "As inflation hits heavily the spending power of our fellow citizens, companies must pay their fair share of the burden to alleviate the impact of the global energy crisis. This is why we reaffirm today our strengthened commitment to swiftly implement the global minimum effective corporate taxation. It is a key lever for further tax justice through a more efficient fight against tax optimisation and evasion. At the June 2022 Ecofin, 26 out of 27 EU Member States expressed their willingness to implement this important step towards tax justice, and our first goal remains to gather a consensus. Should unanimity not be reached in the next weeks, our governments are fully determined to follow through on our commitment. We stand ready to implement the global minimum effective taxation in 2023 and by any possible legal means. We are also fully committed to complete the work on the better reallocation of taxing rights from huge global multinationals' profits with the objective of signing a multilateral convention by mid-2023."

Finally, on 15 December 2022, under the Czech Presidency a political agreement was reached within the Council on the proposal for a Directive on Pillar Two.[29] All in all, it took the EU Member States one year to translate the political agreement on Pillar Two within the Inclusive Framework into a hard-law EU legislative instrument. It was a major political achievement. The European Council conclusions of 15 December 2022 include some lines to provide sufficient comfort to all Member States on progress on both Pillar One and Pillar Two (see also Article 57 of the Pillar Two Directive).[30] Following a consultation with the Committee of Permanent Representatives (Comité des représentants permanents: COREPER) the night before, it became clear that an agreement on the proposed directive was imminent. All that was left was a written procedure before the agreement could be definitively ratified. This procedure was completed on 15 December 2022. Until the last moment, allegedly, all kinds of political prickliness had to be overcome, including the establishment of political connections with funds for Ukraine and resources for Hungary and conditions set by the EU institutions in that regard. Hungary eventually abstained from voting, but this did not prevent the adoption of the Pillar Two Directive (Article 235 TFEU).[31]

Underlying objective?

As to the merits of the Directive proposal it is interesting to observe the continuing search for the underlying objectives of the project and thus the justification for the intended measures. Is Pillar Two about tackling tax avoidance through anti-abuse measures or is Pillar Two about tackling tax competition through tax harmonisation?

29 The final compromise proposal was Council of the European Union, Council Directive on ensuring a global minimum level of taxation for multinational enterprise groups and large-scale domestic groups in the Union, 8778/22, FISC 106, ECOFIN 396, Brussels, 25 November 2022, available at https://data.consilium.europa.eu/doc/document/ST-8778-2022-INIT/en/pdf.

30 European Council, European Council meeting (15 December 2022) – Conclusions, EUCO 34/22, CO EUR 29, CONCL 7, Brussels, 15 December 2022, available at https://www.consilium.europa.eu/media/60872/2022-12-15-euco-conclusions-en.pdf.

31 See for some information https://www.consilium.europa.eu/en/press/press-releases/2022/12/16/outcome-of-written-procedure-on-aid-to-ukraine-minimum-tax-hungary-s-recovery-plan-and-the-conditionality-mechanism/.

The same thing may be observed in the Commission's press release, where Executive Vice-President for an Economy that Works for People, Valdis Dombrovskis, speaks in terms of 'fighting tax avoidance and evasion while preventing a 'race to the bottom' with unhealthy tax competition between countries', as well as Commissioner for Economy, Paolo Gentiloni, who speaks of 'to put an end to the tax race to the bottom that harms the European Union and its economies.'[32] The preamble to the Directive text states that 'this major reform aims to put a floor on competition over corporate income tax rates through the establishment of a global minimum level of taxation.' That, in turn, seems to be about tackling tax competition via a bottom-up harmonisation of company tax systems. At the same time, the Preamble says that 'it is necessary to ensure that tax avoidance practices are discouraged'. So tackling tax avoidance.

The observation of the author of the current chapter here would be that some of the ambiguity in the objectives underlying Pillar Two could continue coming back on the table again, in due course, should the Court of Justice (CJEU) be asked to rule on the (in) compatibility of the measures with the EU treaty freedoms, especially considering that the top-up tax system from Pillar Two also moves away from the idea that emerged from the BEPS project the outcomes of which were launched back in 2015 that taxation should take place at the location of value creation, considering that a similar concept has reflected in the CJEU's interpretation of the EU treaty freedoms, under the wording of the territoriality principle basically saying that the EU Member States should be able and enabled to subject income sourced within their territories to direct taxation, while leaving effectively untaxed income sourced and taxed in territories abroad – though in an efficient non-distortive way.

Implications of EU law

The (in)compatibility of Pillar Two with Union law is and has remained a difficult issue to this day. At the heart of the tensions lies the reality that Pillar Two has been built on the notion of jurisdictional blending, of countries and borders, a per-country approach that is, while the internal market without frontiers has been built on the notion of an economic region and the creation of a single market where production factors and goods and services can flow unhindered, a regionally blended orientation that is. Any top-up taxation, e.g., due to the per-country approach adopted in the Pillar Two Directive (e.g., no inter-EU Member State ETR-pooling), while no top-up taxation would be due by reference to an internal market oriented regional approach (inter-EU Member State ETR-pooling), immediately triggers tensions with the fundamental freedoms, accordingly initiating potential conflicts of the Directive with primary EU law.

In seeking to avoid tensions with primary EU law, the proposed Directive was extended in scope, by way of derogation from the OECD's Model Rules, to large companies operating purely domestically, including top-up taxation in the hands of the parent company on low-taxed domestic income produced by a domestic subsidiary. Use was also made of the

32 See European Commission – Press release, 'Fair Taxation: Commission proposes swift transposition of the international agreement on minimum taxation of multinationals', IP/21/7028, Brussels, 22 December 2021.

opening created in the OECD Model Rules to provide Member States with the possibility of introducing a so-called 'Qualified Domestic Minimum Top-Up Tax', a local alternative minimum tax that is, that allows Member States that do not meet the minimum tax standard under their local corporate taxation to first levy the top-up tax themselves under the alternative minimum tax to thereby adhere to the global minimum rate ensuring that tax revenues would not in consequence flow to foreign treasuries.

These adjustments, notably, are in fact diversions in the sense that these do not make the EU freedoms analysis any different than it already was. Even without such a Qualified Domestic Minimum Top-Up Tax, Member States can increase their corporate tax rates to the minimum level to avoid additional taxation abroad. It is the extraterritorial additional levy, the top-up tax on foreign low-taxed operational income, as such that makes the system in the view of the current chapter's author vulnerable from a primary EU law perspective, and this holds with or without any intermediate local additional levy or alternative domestic minimum tax variants, and with or without any extension of the measures to domestic situations. This is because – when we shift the perspective from the home jurisdiction of the parent entity to the perspective of the investment jurisdiction of the operational group entity – we have to conclude that additional taxation on foreign income prevents economic operators in investment jurisdictions from using rate differences between Member States under the protection of the fundamental freedoms surrounding their investment decisions, which, except in abusive situations (anti-tax avoidance, not: anti-tax competition) has been consistently held contrary to the freedom of movement by the CJEU; see for instance and for a comparison the CJEU judgments in the *Cadbury Schweppes* and *Eurowings* cases.[33]

The 'Questions and answers' document of the Commission states that 'there is thus no difference in treatment, all are taxed at 15%' and the Preamble states that 'in this way, the legal framework would be designed to avoid any risk of discrimination between cross-border and domestic situations'.[34] Both describe here the quasi-export neutrality-promoting characteristics of the top-up tax measure. That may be the case, but that does not detract from the EU tension here. The additional levy continues to hinder the influx of factors of production into the tax-competing Member State of investment, even in the current variant. Extraterritorial top-up taxation is not promoting production factor neutrality, on the contrary, it is hindering capital import neutrality (of course, import neutrality promoting tax systems actually foster tax competitive responses and ensuing race to the bottom issues, but that is not the argument here, at least if matters are considered from the starting position of a fragmentation of tax systems in the internal market). The idea that export neutrality in relation to non-repatriated business profits produced abroad creates tension with EU law freedoms, notably, is not new. Klaus Vogel wrote about this two decades ago in Bulletin for International Fiscal Documentation.[35]

33 See Court of Justice, 12 September 2006, Case C-196/04 (*Cadbury Schweppes and Cadbury Schweppes Overseas*), and Court of Justice, 26 October 1999, Case C-294/97 (*Eurowings Luftverkehr*).

34 See European Commission – Questions and answers, 'Questions and Answers on Minimum corporate taxation Brussels', QANDA/21/6967, 22 December 2021.

35 See Klaus Vogel, 'Which method should the European Community adopt for the avoidance of double taxation?', Bulletin for International Fiscal Documentation, Vol. 56, No. 1, p. 4-10.

As primary EU law currently stands, any issues involving Pillar Two in this regard seem in fact unsolvable in this respect. The only thing the EU Member States can do here is to embrace capital export neutrality through the proposed EU Pillar Two Directive and then to entrust that the CJEU will follow them in this, also because the CJEU usually seems a little more reluctant when it comes to reviewing Directives against primary EU law c.q. limiting itself to a review of manifest errors of assessment in such cases, or at least a review outside some discretionary room for the EU-legislator. The EU compatibility, perhaps, may then be based on the argument that the Pillar Two Directive created a new reality in which the company taxation of big multinationals that is (i.e., those multinational firms producing an annual turnover in excess of 750 million euros) has (exhaustively) been harmonised in the internal market in order to address any tax competition issues and responses within the EU, the race to the bottom that is. As an alternative, perhaps, though analytically somewhat more ambiguous, the latter, the anti-tax competition argument that is, may perhaps also serve as a newly introduced justification ground under the rule of reason test. The first has now happened, the Directive is there. The second, the assessment of its compatibility or incompatibility with primary EU law that is, that will be a matter on which we will have to wait and see as that is ultimately up to the CJEU to decide on. Perhaps it may then, too, become clear as a corollary what Pillar Two is really trying to achieve at the end of the day: (i) an anti-tax abuse mechanism or (ii) a corporate tax harmonisation system – our bet would be on the latter.

Legitimacy

The proposed Directive closely follows the OECD Pillar Two Model Rules of 20 December 2021. The Preamble says that 'it is necessary to implement the GloBE Model Rules agreed by the Member States in a way that it remains as close as possible to the global agreement'. The Explanatory Memorandum says that 'the EU would have no policy options to choose from as key elements of the framework, such as the scope or tax rates and base, have already been prescribed and agreed on.' To say now that the EU would not be in a position here on the substance of the matter, we think, to be honest, goes a bit far, at least from a rule of law perspective. The political agreement of October and July 2021 concerns a political commitment in the form of a 'common approach'. IF countries that would decide to take measures have committed themselves, politically that is, to do so along the lines rolled out in the agreement. The agreement however is not a legally binding agreement of public international law, like a ratified treaty that the members of the parliaments of the contracting states concerned have been able to consider and to decide on in a democratically legitimised manner. This state of affairs accordingly may be considered somewhat atypical, to say the least, from a rule of law perspective, because it actually marginalises the role of the representatives of the people of the EU Member States in the process even further. This is because the ball in the EU legislative process lies in the corner of the Commission (right of initiative) and the Council (the ministers responsible for the file deciding on any adoption of an EU legislative instrument on the basis of unanimity) and not primarily with the parliaments of the EU Member States. This, while these should ultimately be in position here, as, after all, company tax reform is about legislation to which the primacy rests – or is supposed to rest – in the hands of the peoples representatives, parliament that is.

Since the adoption of the Directive tension has grown subsequent to the releases by the IF of various batches of administrative guidances, introducing various safe harbours, and white lists of qualifying jurisdictions, thereby changing the rules as we go, at least in a number of instances, while the Directive has not been amended to cater for any of these. Various rounds of releases of such informal guidance documents, peer review outcomes, et cetera, from the Inclusive Framework are anticipated in the future as well. This raises the fundamental question as to the legal status of all these documents for EU law purposes, i.e., regardless of some political statements that have been issued in the meanwhile by the European Commission and Council, such as the Statements of the Council and the European Commission of 9 November 2023, and the letters from the Cypriot government on the operation of the IF-devised safe harbours under the acquis communautaire ex Article 21 EU Directive Pillar Two.[36] The same holds as to any potential unilateral or even bilateral releases of some government interpretative documents, tax authority position statements, tax rulings, et cetera. It seems that nothing of such sort of documentation will have any standing under EU law, i.e., if in contradict with the Directive provisions or primary EU law, and in any case not unless the Court of Justice of the EU would rule otherwise at some point in time (which we, to be honest, do not anticipate as such would initiate a decentralisation of judiciary powers from the Court of Justice to the Member States, or the OECD or Inclusive Framework for that matter).

DEBRA, incentives?

In the Pillar Two Directive, we see nothing in relation to the envisaged debt equity bias reduction allowance (DEBRA) that the Commission announced in its Communication of 18 May 2021, and which was released on 11 May 2022. We also see nothing (at least for the time being) in relation to the agenda-shaping role that the Commission sees for itself when it comes to incentive regimes. The same holds as to the incentives that the Draghi report of 9 September 2024 seems to envisage. In order to create the necessary policy instrumental space, as said, the Pillar Two political tax deal would need to be revisited to provide for some targeted carve-outs for this purpose (or the EU minimum rate will have to be set at a higher level than the global minimum rate to secure that the 15% level in the global tax deal is adhered to). This is because the EU Member States otherwise run the risk that the economic benefits of an EU-wide capital deduction allowance or a tax incentive regime will be taxed away abroad under a Pillar-Two-oriented top-up tax in place there. Now that both routes have been closed with the Pillar Two Directive, something else will have to be thought of.

As far as any addressing of financing discrimination issues concerned, the only route that currently seems left to be open is to broaden the base – i.e., instead of narrowing it down via a capital cost deduction – via furthering the limitation of interest deductibility (comprehensive business income tax; CBIT), or, alternatively, by letting the while DEBRA initiative be for what it is. A CBIT measure to that end, however, is known to push marginal

36 These documents are available on the website of the European Commission on the minimum tax, see https://taxation-customs.ec.europa.eu/taxation/business-taxation/minimum-corporate-taxation_en. Note that none of these documents have been based on any formal EU legislative or otherwise rulemaking procedures.

effective tax rates upwards to infinite levels and thus slow down marginal investment decisions and impeding economic growth by inference. Notably, if the measure were to evolve into a CBIT-like mechanism, the acronym DEBRA needs to be changed as well since a base expansion mechanism cannot really be referred to as a an 'allowance'; perhaps something like DEBBIE ('debt equity bias income base expansion' – well, we will have to see on that. DEBRA, as said, was launched on 11 May 2022, and things have turned rather quiet since then. With regard to the incentive regimes for, for example, research and development (R&D) that we saw in the proposals for the Directives for a Common Corporate Tax Base (CCTB) and a Common Consolidated Corporate Tax Base (CCCTB), the option remains to pursue and arrange matters EU-wide, for example, through a direct EU-harmonised subsidisation of certain sectors and industries. Within Pillar Two there seems to be some room to model any envisaged EU coordinated incentives into something called a 'qualified refundable tax credit' (QRTC), a levy rebate, that is, in combination with a refund or subsidy mechanism that the Pillar Two rules consider income rather than a negative tax for purposes of calculating the effective tax rate for Pillar Two purposes. Perhaps we will see something about this in due course, for example in the context of the envisaged own resources discussion in connection with BEFIT, and perhaps even in combination with some further EU budget expansions in due course. Or, perhaps, we will see something evolving in the context of EU-integration in the area of wage tax incentives – then, EU tax integration would start addressing personal income taxation matters as well.

It is also worth noting that the Explanatory Memorandum accompanying the original Pillar Two Directive proposal points to the ongoing discussions on the question of compatibility of the US GILTI rules with the Pillar Two measures. The proposal for a Directive provides for a mechanism under which the European Commission can assess foreign systems as a qualifying additional levy mechanism for the application of the Pillar Two Directive measure and to include them in a list annexed to the Directive. This further increases the pressure from the EU on progress in the United States in the ongoing GILTI legislative amendment process. The compromise proposal under the French Presidency, notably, shifts this delegated power (back) to the Council. In February 2023 the Inclusive Framework issued some administrative guidance saying that US GILTI rules should be seen as a CFC-regime,[37] initiating some discussions as to the compatibility of the administrative guidance document of the Inclusive Framework to this end with the Pillar Two Directive.[38]

37 See OECD (2023), Tax Challenges Arising from the Digitalisation of the Economy – Administrative Guidance on the Global Anti-Base Erosion Model Rules (Pillar Two), OECD/G20 Inclusive Framework on BEPS, OECD, Paris.

38 See, e.g., the study of the Brussels-based Centre for European Policy Studies (CEPS): Thomadakis, A. (2023), EU corporate taxation in the digital era – The road to a new international order, CEPS-ECMI Task Force Report, Centre for European Policy Studies, 18 September 2023, available at https://www.ceps.eu/.

Box 2

OECD/G20 IF Two-pillar solution – Context and background

The Pillar One plans, stemming from BEPS Action 1, initially focused on measures specific to certain types of internet companies, including platform companies. In 2015, the OECD wrote that the 'digital economy' cannot be separated – ring-fenced that is in OECD terminology – from the rest of the economy and it is therefore more appropriate to talk about the 'digitalising economy'. In that light, it is perhaps remarkable that the subsequent plans for tax measures developed within the OECD framework under the developing name Pillar One since 2018 did exactly this: tax-ringfencing.
This led to difficult demarcation discussions about 'tech' versus 'non-tech', and ensuing terminologies devised for that purpose such as 'consumer facing businesses' (CFB) and 'automated digital services' (ADS) as the tax measures originally developed were aimed at large companies (with an annual turnover of more than €750 million) operating such consumer facing business models or companies that provide auto-mated digital services. The tricky thing there was that nobody really knew exactly what those were at the end of the day, for reasons much similar to the arguments forwarded earlier on the basis of which it was said that the digital economy cannot be separated from the rest of the economy. Moreover, some countries, notably the United States, found that such sector-related demarcations, tech versus non-tech that is, tax-discriminated to the detriment of the large (read: US) platform companies and other internet companies.
For the United States, the discriminatory demarcation lines drawn for tax purposes between tech and non-tech were a reason to put any political endeavors on this dossier on the back burner for some time. Only in April 2021, after the American presidential elections, did the United States return to the negotiating table within the Inclusive Framework after an intervention by the United States government in April 2021. The aim of that was to reduce the proliferation of unilateral measures against United States' tech companies (rollback workstream) with proposals to limit down the scope of the measures under Pillar One to only the approximately 100 large multi-nationals and then regardless of whether they are internet companies or other types of companies. At the same time, on the other hand, the United States government was committed to embracing the Pillar Two global minimum tax level, at a level of (initially) 21%. "Multilateralism" under the Presidency of Biden, as a counterpart that is to the "America First" under the Presidency under Trump. In reality, the current United States presidency under Biden wants to invest large-scale public in infrastructure (American Jobs Plan) in fulfillment of campaign promises (Build Back Better) and finance this with tax burden increases in the American corporate tax system (Made in America Tax Plan). In order not to put too much pressure on the relative competitive position of the United States and to give the plans a political chance of success, this can only be implemented if the rest of the world moves with the American company tax increases. It should be noted that under the Trump administration, the United States introduced a measure in

2018 that can be seen as a more flexible variant of Pillar Two, the so-called GILTI legislation, on which proposals at the time of writing of the current chapter have been made to tighten it up and where achieving progress is a politically thorny issue we understand. The international commitment of the United States is to get the American legislation labelled as Pillar-Two-compliant, or otherwise as a local ETR increasing CFC-equivalent.

The Pillar Two plans for a 15%-minimum level of business taxation emerged under the heading 'addressing the remaining BEPS issues', inspired by or following the GILTI-regime introduced in the United States in 2018 and accompanying tax measures. The plans appeared in 2019 in the Inclusive Framework's policy note, the public consultation, and the subsequent programme of work. The precise policy objectives under Pillar Two remained ambiguous for quite a long time, see also above. Is it tackling harmful tax competition and aggressive tax planning with letterbox companies, or is it addressing all forms of country tax competition and company strategisation on tax costs, and thus all types of tax-induced investment location decisions? The reality is that if the whole world devises and implements an agreement on a minimum company tax level, business income taxation will be harmonised globally on a bottom-up basis. Assuming that the race-to-the-bottom hypothesis is correct, this means that countries will continue to compete to the newly established bottom rate, that is a race-to-the-minimum. The result would be that countries worldwide would use the same company tax system and can no longer compete with each other via corporate income taxation (global company tax convergence). Countries would then effectively no longer be autonomous on that part of their tax mix. The desirability of this outcome of course is a political matter. It has been reported that this implication initially formed a reason for EU Member State Ireland, for instance, not to join in on the global tax deal in July 2021, but in October 2021, after some discussions, Ireland, Estonia and Hungary also declared themselves politically willing and agreed to the political tax deal. With the OECD press release of 8 October 2021 at the launch of the October update of the Statement, we read for the first time explicitly about the rationale under Pillar Two: "The global minimum tax agreement does not seek to eliminate tax competition, but puts multilaterally agreed limitations on it...". It is therefore (after all) about tackling tax competition through global minimum level company tax harmonisation and not, or no longer only, about base erosion and profit shifting BEPS that is.

25.3.3 Unshell

7- step filtering process set up along substance indicators

The Unshell Directive proposal, the second part of the package of 22 December 2021 and which is pending at the time of writing of the current chapter, introduces a governance, levying and sanctioning mechanism set up along substance indicators for entities and legal forms ('undertakings' in the language of the proposed Directive) established within the EU, which, according to the European Commission, run the risk of being used by companies or wealthy individuals as so-called shell entity (letterbox company) for tax avoidance and tax evasion purposes ('entities at risk to be shell and misused for tax purposes, such as tax evasion and avoidance, as confirmed by recent massive media revelations'). The measure aims to discourage the use of shell entities and thus to contribute to the reduction of tax avoidance and tax evasion issues via the utilisation of these. To this end, the Directive proposal provides for a substance test according to a 7-step filtering process to be completed with substantive and formal legal consequences attached to it. The 7-step process under the original proposal looks like this.

Step 1: Gateway
The Directive proposal seeks to apply to all entities and legal forms established within the EU for tax purposes. The first step identifies the group of entities at risk of being deployed as a shell using so-called gateway criteria.

These are three conditions that must be met cumulatively:
the income of the entity concerned is mainly passive (75% or more);
the activities of the entity concerned are in particular cross-border (60% or more), and;
the management and administration of the entity concerned has been outsourced to third parties (outsourcing).

Specific carve-outs apply to entities that are considered to be low-risk, for example because there is some government regulation of the entities involved, or because the activities in question are carried out purely domestically. The question, notably, of how the latter distinction relates to the principle of equal treatment under primary EU law remains undiscussed here. In short, this includes listed entities, banks, investment institutions, insurers, domestic holding structures, and entities with more than 5 FTEs active staff. For these undertakings, there is no need to assess whether the gateway criteria have been met. It is worth noting, perhaps, that the Directive indicates that, for reasons of equal treatment, it does not opt for an approach on the basis of which, for example, only large companies would be affected by the rules, for example on the basis of a turnover threshold such as that applicable to Pillar Two. This raises the question on what about the Pillar Two Directive in that regard, since that Directive, on the contrary, indeed does make such a distinction between smaller and larger companies.

Step 2: Reporting obligation
Subsequently, a reporting obligation applies to entities that have been identified as being at risk under the gateway criteria. They must report in their annual tax return whether they meet the following three so-called indicators of minimum substance:
exclusive availability of office space in the EU;
at least one active own bank account in the EU, and;
(a) at least one equipped and dedicated director whose place of residence is sufficiently nearby the place of business of the entity concerned for this director to perform his or hers duties involved, *or*;
(b) a majority of qualifying employees whose place of residence is sufficiently nearby the place of business of the entity concerned for these workers to perform their duties.

The entity concerned is required to substantiate the reporting with evidence to enable the relevant tax authorities to verify the presence of these substance indicators.

Step 3: Assumption shell/non-shell
If it follows from the reporting and its substantiation that the minimum substance indicators are met, then the assumption follows that the entity involved is not a shell entity for Directive purposes. Nevertheless, the tax authorities of the Member States may take the position that the entity concerned is not sufficiently economically active under the domestic tax laws of the Member State concerned or does not qualify as a beneficial owner in respect of the income stream at hand. The authorities can also challenge the above-mentioned substantiation in relation to the sufficient presence, or absence thereof, substance indicators. If the minimum subsidy indicators are not met, it follows that there is an assumption that there is a shell for Directive purposes, i.e., a substance-less or substance-light entity being misused for tax purposes.

Step 4: Proof to the contrary
Entities which do not comply with the minimum substance indicators and are therefore presumed to be misused for tax purposes for the purposes of the Directive shall be given the opportunity to provide evidence to the contrary to the tax authorities in the Member State of residence, i.e., on substance presence or at least that the entity or arrangement involved it is not being misused here for tax purposes. The counter-evidence mechanism makes it possible to take into account any specific facts and circumstances of the specific case at hand. The counter-evidence to be provided addresses at least the commercial (i.e. non-tax) considerations for deploying the entity, as well any present staff profiles, as well as the geographic location where relevant decision-making takes place. The counter-evidence is also deemed to have been provided if it is proved that 'the undertaking has performed and continuously had control over, and borne the risks of, the business activities that generated the relevant income or, in the absence of income, the undertaking's assets,' something that appears to us as a transfer pricing (TP) analysis or TP-safe harbour for Unshell Directive application purposes. If the entity concerned succeeds in providing such counter-evidence, the relevant tax authority validates and certifies such for the current year with the possibility of granting an extension (under the condition of the same facts and circumstances) for a subsequent period of up to 5 years (i.e. a total of 6 years). The Directive is silent on the legal standing of such a certificate, for instance in other Member States.

Step 5: Exemption
Entities identified as being at risk are given the opportunity to request the tax authorities in the Member State of residence to be exempted from the Directive obligations. This, on the basis that the deployment or inter-positioning of the entity in the group structuring concerned has not led to a tax cost savings for the ultimate beneficial owner (UBO) involved. The tax cost saving is determined by making a comparison of case at hand to the situation without the use of this entity in the group structuring. The evidence to be provided for this purpose (e.g. information on the group structure, etc.) should make it possible to make the comparison on this point. If the entity concerned succeeds in providing evidence in this regard, the relevant tax authority shall validate and certify

this in the same way as under the counter-evidence mechanism as mentioned in the previous paragraph.

Step 6: Tax consequences
Entities that do not meet the minimum substance indicators and are not able to shake-off the resulting assumption of being misused for tax purposes by showing proof to the contrary are faced with tax consequences as specified in the Directive. Here is the overview.

In the first place, these entities are denied the application of tax advantages, such as those resulting from applicable tax treaties and EU Directives (Parent Subsidiary Directive and Interest and Royalty Directive). Secondly, in their Member State of residence, these entities are no longer eligible for a certificate of residence to be issued by the tax authorities, or such a certificate is accompanied by a warning. Next, thirdly, the Directive regulates the way in which the Member States concerned imposes taxes in such a situation.

First, the Member State of residence of the shell entity concerned remains free to continue to tax it under domestic tax law, at least as it appears at first sight. In the view of the author of the current chapter some uncertainty seems to exist as to whether the Member State of the shell entity may grant economic double tax relief under a mechanism put in place for that purpose in relation to any shareholding proceeds derived from the corporate shareholding relationship in the underlying entity. The reason for this is that such a mechanism can potentially be seen as a benefit of the Parent Subsidiary Directive begging the question as to how such relates to the requirement not to provide the benefits of that directive for anti-tax avoidance reasons under Unshell in connection with the communication of such under the certificate issued by the Member State of the shell entity involved.[39]

Secondly, the Member State of residence of the shareholder(s) in the shell entity taxes the income in question from the shell entity, as if it had flowed directly to the shareholder(s) concerned. This, taking into account any underlying tax paid by the shell entity for credit purposes; a CFC-like look-through approach, therefore. Here, too, at least in the view of the current chapter's author, rises the question as to how to deal exactly with underlying taxes levied, and – to the extent applied – any implications of, say, the application of participation exemption regimes at the level of the shell entity involved. Should that be appreciated or should such perhaps be considered as a catering for, indirectly that is, the application of benefits under for instance the Parent Subsidiary Directive and with that a fostering of tax avoidance?

Thirdly, the Member State of residence of the payer(s) to the shell entity subjects the income flows concerned to a source tax under domestic law; it should be noted immediately at this place that the Explanatory Memorandum and Preamble seem to seek to deny source tax rights in intra-EU scenarios ("EU source/payer: it will not have a right

39 The author of the current chapter wishes to thank Ms. Ciska Wisman (University of Amsterdam, the Netherlands, EY, Rotterdam, the Netherlands) for the insightful tax-technical input and discussions in this regard. The author, however, bears full responsibility for the content of these lines.

to tax…"). However, this, as it seems, cannot be directly inferred from the text and literal wording of the provisions in the proposed Directive. The text of the Directive proposal takes out tax treaty and Directive benefits, but not, at least not according to the literal wording of the Directive text, any charges to tax as created under the domestic tax laws in this context in the Member States concerned. The text of the directive then introduces, again according to the text and its wording, for third-country scenarios, and only for third country scenarios that is, a source tax in accordance with national law, while respecting the treaty obligations with any relevant third country shareholder jurisdiction. As a result, according to the literal wording of the Directive text, but probably perhaps unintentionally, any source tax jurisdiction and Member State tax levy eligibilities in this regard remains untouched in intra-EU matters, or at least unaddressed.

In third country situations, any tax treaties in place between any source Member State and shell entity shareholder State and any shell entity shareholder Member State and source state are respected under Unshell (i.e., a look-through approach).

Step 7: Administrative cooperation
With regard to entities identified as at risk, the proposed Directive provides for an automatic exchange of information and mutual assistance mechanism to support any administrative cooperation in this regard between the tax authorities of the EU Member States involved. To this end, the logistics that have been rolled out around the transparency measures in the Directive on Administrative Cooperation in relation to rulings issued by the tax authorities (DAC3) and in the Directive on Administrative Cooperation in relation to tax intermediaries and their reporting obligations (DAC6) will be used. The Directive provides for a tax audit request for any cases where the aforementioned validation/certification procedures in one Member States is doubted by any one of the other Member States concerned. Finally, the Directive provides for a penalty mechanism in the event of non-compliance with the introduced reporting obligations. Member States are free to organise the imposition of fines, while fines must be effective, proportionate and dissuasive and these fines should be set at least at an amount equal to 5% of the turnover of the non-compliant entity concerned.

We see all kinds of things coming back
We see all kinds of EU law related matters being transposed into the context of the proposed Directive, from the substance indicators in the CJEU judgments in the Danish cases,[40] the taking into account of the specific facts and circumstances of the case at hand from the CJEU judgment in Deister and Juhler[41] and the TP-safe harbour from the CJEU judgment in Lexel[42] to the logistical connections made with existing transparency measures in the Directive on Administrative Cooperation involving rulings and tax intermediaries.

40 See Court of Justice, 26 February 2019, joined cases C-115/16 (*N Luxembourg 1*), C-118/16 (*X Denmark*), C-119/16 (*C Danmark I*) and C-299/16 (*Z Denmark*), involving the interest and Royalty Directive, and see Court of Justice, 26 February 2019, joined cases C-116/16 (*T Danmark*) and C-117/16 (*Y Denmark*), involving the Parent Subsidiary Directive.

41 See Court of Justice, 20 December 2017, case C-504/16 (*Deister Holding AG and Juhler Holding A/S v Bundeszentralamt für Steuern*).

42 See Court of Justice, 20 January 2021, case C-484/19 (Lexel).

It should be noted however that the Unshell Directive proposal, at the end of the day, does not do much in terms of substantive content when it comes to the interpretation of the doctrine of tax abuse under primary EU law. The Directive for instance does not elaborate on the object and purpose of the 'law' that is assessed and that is subject to interpretation, nevertheless an essential element in the EU doctrine on tax abuse. The Explanatory Memorandum occasionally refers to an '... act against the actual purpose of tax law...' and further keeps quiet at this point.

In the application of the Directive, we nevertheless do see some elements of the tax-abuse doctrine appearing in some of the Directive provisions. Some of these elements surface when the Directive text refers on ways and means to substantiate any demonstrating by the economic operators involved of their intentions in structuring their business operations and the artificiality, or lack thereof, in relation to the transactions and arrangements entered into in this regard. Perhaps at some point the approach adopted in the Directive may reflect back at some point to the interpretation of the anti-tax abuse doctrine in primary EU law by the CJEU.

Box 3

Tax Abuse Doctrine CJEU

According to consistent case law of the CJEU, abuse of EU law plays a role in cases where the granting of an advantage or benefit under EU law would entail that the objective pursued by an act of law would not be achieved despite any formal fulfilment of conditions and requirements involved (the so-called objective element), and whereby the economic operator, the taxpayer, concerned intended, having had as a purpose that is, to obtain the anticipated advantage or benefit by artificially creating the conditions under which the right to that advantage or benefit arises (the so-called subjective element). In that subjective element there is a subtest of a more subjective nature (i.e., the taxpayer's motive; its intention to avoid the respective tax charge involved) and a subtest of a more objective nature (i.e., the artificiality of the transaction or structure involved, such as the deployment of a letterbox company or a shell entity).

Legitimacy

The lack of direction when it comes to the substantive interpretation of the EU law tax-abuse doctrine, in particular with regard to the 'object and purpose of the law', seems quite explainable in the light of the Directive's objective of discouraging the use of shell entities by in fact attaching an increased price tag to any tax-induced deployment of these entities. This, by further limiting the tax attractiveness of steering or directing flows of funds through a jurisdiction unrelated to the conducting of substantial economic activities in that jurisdiction. The Directive accordingly moves towards an increasing of transaction costs in this regard, i.e., by means of requiring more transparency, by means of exchanging more information and by means of strengthening the supervision and enforcement in relation to any such activity, instead of – for example – moving towards a clarifying of the manner in which multinational firms (or the entities that make them up), in accordance with the object and purpose of the tax law should be subject to taxation on their investment returns (who to tax, what to tax, where to tax, how much to tax; the building blocks of company tax legislation that is).

However, we do wonder what the thinking is underlying the tax charging mechanism in the Unshell Directive proposal. The proposal is silent here. Looking at what the charging mechanism achieves, we see the Unshell Directive proposal moving towards source EU Member State taxation (EU withholding taxation) in inbound scenarios, i.e., where a non-EU investor invests in an EU Member State via an EU shell entity. In outbound scenarios, i.e., where an EU investor invests in a non-EU Member State via an EU shell entity, we see the Unshell Directive proposal moving towards EU investor resident Member State taxation (EU CFC taxation). In intra-EU-scenarios, i.e., where an EU investor invests in an EU Member State via an EU shell entity, we see the Unshell Directive proposal, so at least it seems, moving towards a more or less exclusive EU investor resident Member State taxation. In scenarios where the EU itself is used as a hubjurisdiction, i.e., where a non-EU investor invests in a non-EU Member State via an EU shell entity the proposed Directive in fact does nothing really. When it comes to explaining the underlying intent of Unshell in terms of tax charging, to be honest, we don't get much further than 'EU (big) countries First'. Perhaps the announced initiative to address the challenges of shell entities established outside the EU will give a little more direction at some point. And otherwise, perhaps, the CJEU in due course, if it were asked at some point to consider the merits under EU law of the distinction made in the Directive between cross-border and domestic situations.

In view of the lack of direction when it comes to the substantive interpretation of the EU law tax-abuse doctrine under Unshell, it is important to see the following. In concrete terms this means that any substance-less or substance-light entities that fail to provide evidence to the contrary as to those parts required under the application of the directive (i.e. about their non-fiscal motives or their substance presence) and is charged to tax by its tax authorities in consequence of this may still litigate their case through the court system in their Member State concerned, and the CJEU in ultimo, for a plea with their interpretation of the object and purpose of the tax law at hand with which their actions would correspond. This said, of course, we can however imagine that the approach taken under the Directive proposal to disincentivise shell entity utilisation, i.e., by putting a price tag increase on the deployment of these, creates a barrier against this. In concrete terms this also means that the tax authorities of the Member States charging entities to tax, including those substance-sufficient entities who succeed in providing evidence about their substance-sufficientness under the Directive provisions, may still litigate their case through the court system in their Member State concerned, and the CJEU in ultimo, for a plea with their interpretation of the object and purpose of the tax law at hand with which the deployment of these entities would not correspond. This said, of course, we can however imagine that the de facto safe-harbour approach taken under the Directive proposal in relation to substance-sufficient entities creates a barrier against this. This also means that, for example, the ongoing discussion on the relation between the Danish cases (no substance safe harbour in EU tax abuse doctrine) and the ruling of the CJEU in Lexel (substance (TP) safe harbour in EU tax abuse doctrine) has not been settled with the current Directive proposal, and that the chance of this being settled by the CJEU any time soon will probably not increase if this Directive in its current form sees the light of day.

This also means that the Directive proposal also does not do anything with the underlying perhaps a somewhat more legal philosophical question as to whether it is, or actually should be, up the (European Union's) court to reform the business taxation framework into a direction that is or could be perceived to be more fair c.q. in line and in accordance with the apparent intention and object and purpose of the 'law'. Such an allocation of tasks to the judiciary to this end seems to be in trend now. Or is it, or perhaps should it be, ultimately a task that should be reserved for the legislator, and therefore the people's representatives to reform taxation systems? That is, because that is where the primacy rests (or perhaps at least should rest) under the rule of law. This raises the somewhat more philosophical follow-up question, at least for us, of whether the EU legislative intervention here, the Unshell Directive proposal that is, actually is the most appropriate instrument to be pushed forward here to address the implications of an outdated and failing company tax framework.

As an alternative to moving to a putting of a price tag increase to curb any unwanted effects of the existing company tax system and its operation would be to create some thoughts on how the company taxation framework involving multinational business enterprises should be systemically organised in an equitable and efficient manner. Then, the search for a fair business taxation framework would focus on the development of a system that would not create the incentive for any tax-induced utilisation of letterbox companies in the first place. Perhaps the BEFIT initiative at some will provide us any answers and findings to this.

Status of Unshell?
As from its launch it became immediately clear that it would become an uphill battle to achieve political consensus on Unshell. Simultaneously much has remained a bit in the unclear. Since its launch the EU working party on tax questions has been discussing various practical implications of the approaches taken in the proposal. The scope of the proposal has been discussed, the risk hallmarks, substance tests, reporting requirements, the exchange of information, as well as the tax consequences. The objectives sought by the Unshell Directive proposal are supported by most of the EU Member States' delegations. Discussions, however, have remained outstanding, though.[43] On 25 November 2024, Bloomberg Tax reported that several EU countries and businesses question the need for

43 See for some insights, for instance, Council of the European Union, Draft Ecofin report to the European Council on tax issues – Approval, 10594/24, LIMITE, FISC 125, ECOFIN 626, Brussels, 14 June 2024, and Council of the European Union, Ecofin report to the European Council on tax issues, 16673/24, FISC 267, ECOFIN 1481, Brussels, 10 December 2024, both under the header 'Misuse of shell entities'.

the Unshell Directive proposal.[44] It was reported that in a compromise proposal, dating 20 November 2024, the section dealing with the abovementioned tax consequences was removed. The compromise proposal would allow the EU Member States to decide for themselves what they would do, if anything. The compromise proposal would also drop the economic substance test that was included in the initial Directive proposal to determine if an entity is a shell. As far as the author of the current chapter knows, the compromise proposal is not publicly available at the time the drafting of the chapter was finalised.

25.3.4 Own resources

Next generation of EU own resources
With the Own Resources Package, the third part of the package of 22 December 2021, the Commission has launched three proposals for own resources to help co-finance the NextGenerationEU recovery package and the Social Climate Fund[45] proposed on 14 July 2021 as part of the Fit for 55 package. The Commission completed its proposal for a next generation of own resources on 20 June 2023, adding, amongst others, a statistical own resource linked to the corporate sector to the basket of proposed own resources.[46] Discussions are currently pending before the EU institutions. The European Commission says on its website that these resources will not create new taxes, thereby fully respecting national fiscal sovereignty of the Member States.[47] The revenues, as the Commission nevertheless puts it, are meant to provide the European Union the means for its ambitions, "a climate neutral, digital, just, inclusive and resilient society for all Europeans".[48] Below an overview of the proposed package of 22 December 2021, as completed in 2023.

The Own Resources Package of 22 December 2021 proposed to amend the Own Resources Decision.[49] Under this framework decision, the EU budget is now financed almost entirely from four own resources:
customs duties, i.e., the traditional own resource (Member States retain 25% of customs duties collected);
a VAT-based own resource on the basis of which Member States each pay 0.3% of a national VAT base;
a uniform call rate on the weight of non-recycled plastic packaging waste generated in each Member State (€0,80/kg) (since 1 January 2021), and;

44 Saim Saeed, 'EU Countries, Business Question Need for Shell Companies Bill', Bloomberg Tax, Nov. 25, 2024.
45 See European Commission, Proposal for a Regulation of the European Parliament and of the Council establishing a Social Climate Fund, COM(2021) 568 final, 2021/0206(COD), Brussels, 14.7.2021.
46 See for some information https://commission.europa.eu/strategy-and-policy/eu-budget/long-term-eu-budget/2021-2027/revenue/next-generation-eu-own-resources_en.
47 See https://commission.europa.eu/strategy-and-policy/eu-budget/long-term-eu-budget/2021-2027/revenue/next-generation-eu-own-resources_en.
48 *Ibidem.*
49 See Council Decision (EU, Euratom) 2020/2053 of 14 December 2020 on the system of own resources of the European Union and repealing Decision 2014/335/EU, Euratom.

GNI-payments; Member States contribute a fixed percentage of their gross national income (GNI) directly to the EU budget.[50]

Adaptation of the Own Resources Decision requires unanimity within the Council. The European Parliament shall be consulted.

The NextGenerationEU Recovery Fund[51] allowed the European Commission for the first time to raise €750 billion in capital markets for EU investments and to finance the borrowings for this purpose out of the long-term EU budget. On 16 December 2020, the European Parliament, the Council and the Commission agreed to accompany NextGenerationEU with a roadmap towards the introduction of new own resources. In doing so, these institutions agreed that the financing of the recovery package (i.e. the repayment in the coming decades of the debts incurred by the Commission for this purpose) should not give rise to cuts in other MFF investments. In addition, GNI remittance increases had to be mitigated as well. Thus, not only is it now proposed to add the new own resources to the Own Resources Decision, but at the same time it is proposed to increase the EU budget (MFF), the ceiling, annually (proposal: by 2024) with the revenues from these new own resources in the previous year (capped at €15 billion per year; 2018 prices). Adaptation of the MFF requires the consent of the European Parliament and unanimity within the Council.

Emissions Trading System (2021 proposal: 25%, 2023 proposal: 30%)
The first proposed own resource is aimed at the European CO2 Emissions Trading System (EU ETS),[52] i.e., the trading system designed to help cut greenhouse gas emissions and that is seen as the flagship of European climate policy, providing for a diversion of 30% (2023 proposal; 25%: 2021 proposal) of revenues from the Member States' EU-coordinated allowance allocation and auctioning system (where these revenues currently go) to the European Union. In addition, a 'temporary solidarity adjustment mechanism' is provided that limits the contribution of 'low-income' and 'carbon-intensive' Member States and ensures a fair contribution from 'higher-income' Member States with a 'low carbon intensity'. The new own resource should enter into force when the scope of the emissions trading system has been extended to the built environment (real estate, transport sector). The scope extension to these sectors has been proposed in the context of the Fit for 55 package in support of climate objective).[53] The planned own resource should generate €12 billion annually for the EU budget.

50 See European Commission – Questions and answers, 'The next generation of EU own resources: Questions and Answers. Brussels', QANDA/21/7026, 22 December 2021.

51 See Council Regulation (EU) 2020/2094 of 14 December 2020 establishing a European Union Recovery Instrument to support the recovery in the aftermath of the COVID-19 crisis.

52 See Directive 2003/87/EC of the European Parliament and of the Council of 13 October 2003 establishing a scheme for greenhouse gas emission allowance trading within the Community and amending Council Directive 96/61/EC.

53 See Proposal for a Directive of the European Parliament and of the Council amending Directive 2003/87/EC establishing a system for greenhouse gas emission allowance trading within the Union, Decision (EU) 2015/1814 concerning the establishment and operation of a market stability reserve for the Union greenhouse gas emission trading scheme and Regulation (EU) 2015/757, COM(2021) 551 final, 2021/0211 (COD), Brussels, 14.7.2021.

Carbon Border Adjustment Mechanism (75%)
The second proposed own resource addresses the Carbon Border Adjustment Mechanism (CBAM) introduced by the Commission as part of the Fit for 55 package.[54] In short, CBAM is a CO2 pricing equivalent to the EU ETS and actually a levy on the import of certain goods produced abroad (currently iron, steel, aluminum, cement, manure, electricity) in the form of a certificate system (importers must purchase CBAM certificates). The levy aims to create a level playing field vis-à-vis European producers of these goods that are subject to CO2 pricing via the EU ETS. The proposal provides for 75% of the revenue from this levy to flow to the EU budget instead of that of the Member States. The planned own resource should generate €1 billion annually for the EU budget.

Pillar One (15%)
The third proposed own resource ties in with the Pillar One measures on tax base redistribution for the approximately top 100 largest multinationals worldwide from the above-mentioned global political agreement of 1 July 2021 on company tax reform. It is proposed to channel 15% of the company tax base to be allocated to EU Member States under the envisaged Pillar One measures into the EU budget as own resources. Pillar One is aimed at multinationals with a profitability of more than 10% (profit before tax/ revenue) and a worldwide annual turnover of more than 20 billion euros. Pillar One, as noted, relates to the allocation of part of the (adjusted) consolidated commercial profit of the multinationals concerned to sales jurisdictions for company tax purposes. Pillar One establishes a formulary-based allocation of tax base to market countries, i.e., 25% of commercial profit, insofar as this amount exceeds an amount equal to 10% of the turnover ('Amount A'). A proposal for a directive to implement Pillar One EU-wide was initially scheduled for 27 July 2022. The envisaged own resource will enter into force as soon as Pillar One becomes a reality. The planned own resource should generate between €2.5 and €4 billion annually for the EU budget.

Temporary statistical based own resource on company profits
The 2023 completion of the 2021 Own Resources Package concretised the additional own resource linked to the corporate sector that was already mentioned in the Commission Communication 'Business Taxation for the 21st Century of 18 May 2021. The addition to the basket of proposed own resources involves a temporary statistical based own resource on company profits, calculated as 0.5% of the notional EU company profit base. The EU company profit base is an indicator of profit base as calculated by Eurostat by reference to national accounts statistics. The own resource would be temporary, and is envisaged to be replaced by a possible contribution from the envisaged EU-wide company tax system, i.e., the Business in Europe: Framework for Income Taxation (BEFIT) as proposed by the Commission on 12 September 2023.

---

54 See European Commission, Proposal for a Regulation of the European Parliament and of the Council establishing a carbon border adjustment mechanism, COM(2021) 564 final, 2021/0214(COD), Brussels, 14.7.2021.

Observations
With NextGenerationEU, that the Commission itself had initiated,[55] the Commission has been empowered by the EU-institutions to borrow money from the capital markets, to spend these borrowings under the recovery fund, and to finance such expenditures from the long-term EU budget. The EU institutions did not want to cut back on other expenditure within the MFF. Nor did they want to increase the own contributions financed from their national budgets. The funds to enable a repay of the borrowed amounts must therefore come from somewhere else, i.e., the market, the European economy that is, by means of a package of additional own resources for the EU budget, and then be added to the EU budget ceiling. The EU ETS, CBAM and Pillar One were chosen because "[t]hese initiatives require EU action, and therefore constitute an appropriate base for EU own resources".[56] This passage is interesting, because if an own resource turns out to be eligible to be successfully linked on this basis to an EU Directive in the field of corporate taxation, direct taxation that is, we can imagine that we may perhaps encounter these types of maneuverers and developments more often in the future. And maybe even faster than we might think at this point. It has already been announced, after all, that the second basket of own resources will build on BEFIT, as mentioned above.

The Commission writes that these new own resources are not European taxes. Whatever the correctness of this, we do see that with these proposals additional resources are aimed to be shifted from operators on the European markets towards the EU budget. The desirability of this is a political question. It can be said, however, that the Commission is manoeuvring quite deftly here, for example if you look at how Pillar One is wheeled-in into the 'digital as an own resource discussion'. The originally planned EU digital levy, it seems, eventually had to be given up for political reasons. It is known that the United States sees in unilaterally imposed digital services taxes mainly discriminatory levies at the expense of American tech companies. On 21 October 2021, the United States, Austria, France, Italy, Spain and the United Kingdom presented a joint statement on the rollback of unilateral taxes and countervailing trade sanctions in the interim period up to Pillar One. The fate of the European digital levy had yet to be decided at that time. In mid-December 2021, the digital levy was removed from the EU legislative agenda. So now a newly devised Pillar-One-skimming-own-resource-mechanism has come in its place, a sharp move. It will be difficult for the United States to counter this measure as discriminatory, since the Pillar One system as it currently stands came from the sleeve of the United States government to redress such, in April 2021, in the wings of the Made in America Tax Plan of the Biden administration. It is reported that the political discussion on Pillar One in the United States is even more complicated than that on Pillar Two, also because it has been made clear for the implementation of Pillar One that the treaty networks must be adapted for this purpose and treaty adjustment in the United States requires a 'super

55 See Communication from the Commission to the European Parliament, the European Council, the Council, the European Economic and Social Committee and the Committee of the Regions, 'Europe's moment: Repair and Prepare for the Next Generation', COM(2020) 456 final, Brussels, 27.5.2020.

56 See Communication from the Commission to the European Parliament, the Council, the European Economic and Social Committee and the Committee of the Regions, 'The next generation of own resources for the EU Budget', COM(2021) 566 final, Brussels, 22.12.2021.

majority' in parliament (two-thirds majority in the U.S. Senate that is). Also interesting, perhaps, in Tax Notes International we read that the companies that would fall within the scope of the measures would be about 50% American, 22% would have a G7 origin and 8% would be of Chinese origin.[57] Then it is immediately clear where that 2.5 to € 4 billion will have to come from mostly. We will have to see what comes out. We can imagine that the EU institutions will not make the financing of the EU budget dependent on the outcome of political decision-making processes on the other side of the Atlantic. In any case, a proprietary resource for the EU budget derived from Pillar One will not be able to conflict with the tax treaties, as the EU is not a party to these treaties.

25.3.5 European Commission proposals for DEBRA Directive

General

In follow-up to the Commission Communication 'Business Taxation for the 21st Century of 18 May 2021, the European Commission published its DEBRA Directive proposal on 11 May 2022. DEBRA introduces a capital cost deduction, the so-called Debt Equity Bias Reduction Allowance. The allowance is combined with a deduction-limitation, the so-called Interest Limitation Rule, for exceeding borrowing costs. The interest limitation rule applies in addition to the interest deduction limitation mechanism already in place under the ATAD Directive.

The proposed measures are aimed at entities that are subject to corporate tax in one or more EU Member States as resident or non-resident taxpayers. The measures do not apply to financial undertakings, as defined in the proposal. The envisaged Directive implementation date and date of entry into force, at the time the proposal was launched that is, are 31 December 2023 and 1 January 2024 respectively. EU Member States with corporate tax systems that already include a capital cost deduction mechanism (Belgium, Cyprus, Malta, Poland, Portugal, Italy) may postpone the implementation of the measures for a period of 10 years, or as much shorter as the applicable period for applying the capital deduction under national tax law. The DEBRA Directive proposal is pending at the time the current chapter was finalized.

In its communication on Business Taxation for the 21st Century, the Commission already announced its plans to mitigate the financing discrimination problem by means of a capital deduction. The somewhat surprising interest deduction limiting measure has its origins in a consultation round launched by the European Commission's Directorate-General for Taxation and Customs Union (TAXUD) in mid-2021 on possible measures to be introduced for this purpose. DEBRA, too, is part of the Commission's ambitions to develop an efficient and fair, sustainable and future-proof, job-creating and growth-friendly tax framework for the Single Market, which is fit for the continued generation of tax revenues in a globalising and digitalising economy, helps finance needed expenditure, supports the digital transition and greening of our economies, and contributes to the further unification of the Capital Markets Union.

57 See Kartikeya Singh, 'Amount A: The G-20 is Calling the Tune, And U.S. Multinationals Will Pay the Piper', Tax Notes International, August 2021.

Debt-equity bias
The debt-equity bias is a classic design flaw in the traditional approaches that most countries, EU Member States as well as third countries, resort to as the basis for their domestic business taxation systems. In essence, the determination of the corporate income tax base is linked to the nominal return to the equity as invested by the taxpayer. As a result, typical corporation taxes distort financing decisions, especially at the margin. In addition to the degree of financial leverage, the way corporate income taxes typically operate encourage taxpayers to finance their investments with debt, especially at the margin. The costs of debt financing, interest, are allowed to be deducted (in principle). The cost of equity financing is not. Viz., tax subsidisation of debt financing therefore and tax discrimination of equity financing: the debt-equity bias. This can give rise to tax-induced excessive debt financing. In this light, at the time the DEBRA initiative was launched the European Commission pointed to, among other things, the debt financing of post-covid recovery investments that it has observed among European businesses and linked up with this to address matters on the basis of the proposed measure.

Matters in this respect may also be referred to in terms of an inequitable tax treatment of equity financing (no deduction of cost of equity capital) compared to debt financing (deduction of cost of debt capital), financing discrimination. This is because in an analytical sense no hard distinction can be made between the two forms of financing. The differences made are of a tax-legal nature. Economically, there is only a gradual difference between equity and debt in terms of economic risks and investment return expectations. The creditor has more certainty than the shareholder that the funds provided will be repaid and the provision of monetary resources will yield a return. On the other hand, the expected return for the creditor is lower than for the shareholder, i.e., considering the relative differences in risks incurred. Both capital providers share a return expectation and a willingness to provide risk-bearing monetary resources in exchange for a higher or lower remuneration appropriate to the risk profile. The lack of a distinctive element explains the typical struggle in international company taxation to accurately delineate financing transactions, when it comes to establishing a non-arbitrary dividing line between debt and equity for corporate tax purposes. The problem arises in the taxation of both internationally operating businesses and national small and medium-sized enterprises, despite all of the (re)qualifications in relation to hybrid financing arrangements and interest deduction limitation measures typically found in company tax systems throughout the world.

DEBRA proposal; mitigating debt-equity bias (and EU company tax integration)

Capital deduction and interest deduction limitation
The Directive proposal can be seen as an attempt to achieve an EU-wide harmonised corporate tax system optimisation, or at least a relative improvement of it: a step in the search for a financing-neutral taxable base in the company taxes of the EU Member States. To this end, the proposal introduces an intervention in the tax systems of the Member States on two sides. On the one hand, the proposal introduces a flat-rate deduction that focuses on the costs of equity financing, a so-called 'allowance on equity': a measure that narrows the tax base. On the other hand, the proposal introduces a deduction limitation

that focuses on the costs of debt financing, a so-called 'interest limitation rule': a measure that broadens the tax base. The proposal can – and should – be seen as a stepping-stone towards a European corporate tax, Business in Europe: Framework for Income Taxation (BEFIT) that is, which we already saw earlier in 2011 and later again in 2016 as the Common Consolidated Corporation Tax Base (CCCTB). The plans are not new. A variant of the now proposed DEBRA measure – which we have gotten acquainted with on a more conceptual basis in literature as a 'soft allowance for corporate equity' (soft-ACE) or also 'incremental ACE' – was previously seen in the 2016 EU Directive proposal for a Common Corporate Tax Base (CCTB), then under the name 'Allowance for Growth and Investment' ('AGI'). And the AGI in the CCTB? This in turn was based on the Italian 'Aiuto alla crescita economica' ('Aid to Economic Growth').

Capital deduction: allowance on equity

Firstly, the capital deduction, the allowance on equity. The proposal allows taxpayers to pay for each additional positive change in capital in a fiscal year (new equity) annually, i.e. in the relevant fiscal year (Tax Year; TY) and the subsequent 9 fiscal years (TY+9), to deduct a flat-rate amount from the taxable profit. The same applies to a capital increase in a subsequent year. a capital deduction also applies to this that year (TY+1) and the following 9 fiscal years (TY+10). The deductible amount is determined by multiplying the basis established for this purpose, the 'allowance base' by a notional interest rate, the 'notional interest rate'('NIR'), i.e.: allowance on equity = allowance base * NIR. Negative capital movements lead to tax base additions, along the same lines 'and up to the total increase of net equity for which such allowance has been obtained'. This is unless the taxpayer can demonstrate that the downward movement is the result of commercial losses or a legal obligation to reduce capital.

The allowance base and the notional interest rate are determined as follows. The allowance base is set at an amount equal to the difference between the equity of the taxpayer concerned at the end of the tax year and the equity of this taxpayer at the end of the previous tax year, the so-called 'year-on-year increase in equity'. Equity is made up of the sum of paid-up capital, share premium, revaluation reserve and reserves and profits and losses carried forward, with reference to the Accounting Directive (Directive 2013/34/EU). In order to avoid double counting in the capital deduction calculation, the tax book value of its participations in the capital of associated enterprises is deducted from this, in order to arrive at the so-called 'net equity' of the taxpayer. The notional interest rate is a flat-rate imitation of the cost component of equity and is set at an amount equal to a risk-free interest rate and a risk premium (NIR = Risk Free Rate + Risk Premium). To this end, the proposed Directive is based on the risk-free interest rate for a 10-year bond in the exchange rate of the taxpayer claiming the capital deduction with a risk premium of 1% on top of that (and 1.5% for small and medium-sized enterprises considered to be more risky for this purpose; small and medium sized enterprises; SMEs), with reference to Directive 2009/138/EC (Solvency II).

For anti-abuse reasons, the capital deduction is limited to 30% of taxpayers' EBITDA (earnings before interest, tax, depreciation and amortisation) for tax purposes in a fiscal year. An unlimited carry-forward applies to non-cashable capital deduction if and insofar as the capital deduction exceeds the taxable profit. Unused capital deduction capacity eligibility, if and to the extent that the capital deduction exceeds the ceiling of 30% of the taxable EBITDA, can be carried forward for 5 years. It is not entirely clear to the current author how exactly these two components relate to each other. Further anti-abuse measures focus on artificial increases in taxpayers' equity for tax reasons, through certain cash carrousels or round-tripping exercises within a group, contributions of non-business-related assets, contributions of funds from jurisdictions with which no transparency agreements have been made and transactions in which existing equity within the group is converted into new equity ('re-categorisation of old capital as new capital'). These anti-abuse measures are inspired by the 'Guidance on notional interest deduction regimes' from the Code of Conduct Group in 2019.[58] However, a safeguard clause applies, a rebuttal rule that allows the taxpayer to demonstrate business motives and that there is no double capital deduction. If the taxpayer succeeds in this, the capital increase will be included in the capital deduction. The EU abuse doctrine and all related CJEU case law and discussions also resonate directly in the DEBRA Directive proposal.

Interest limitation rule

Secondly, the interest deduction limiting measure, the interest limitation rule. The Directive proposal further restricts taxpayers in the possibilities of deducting exceeding borrowing costs. Matters concern the deductibility of the on-balance amount of interest paid and received, as defined in the earnings stripping measure in Article 4 of the Anti-Tax Avoidance Directive (ATAD 1). The deduction limitation will be applied under the proposal in terms of a sequencing to the earnings-stripping measure. The deductibility of the balance of interest will be limited to 85%. In concrete terms, this means that for every euro, 100 euro cents, on balance interest paid, 15 euro cents will not be deductible and 85 euro cents will be deductible. For the non-deductible interest of 15 euro cents under the interest limitation rule, no carry-forward or roll-back is available. In concurrence with the interest deduction-limiting earnings-stripping measure, the most deduction-limiting measure will take precedence. In concrete terms, this means that if the deductible amount of interest is 85 euro cents for the application of the interest limitation rule and for the application of the earnings-stripping measure, for example, 80 euro cents, the latter amount, i.e. 80 euro cents, is deductible for tax purposes. The remaining 5 euro cents of non-deductible interest will be carried forward/ backward, if and to the extent that it such is made available under the national legislation in the EU Member State concerned that has transposed the Directive provisions in domestic law.

Observations

Both better and worse

The DEBRA Directive proposal introduces a narrowing of the tax base (capital deduction) on the one hand and a broadening of the tax base (interest deduction limitation) on the other. Both measures are portrayed as financing discrimination-mitigating. The combination of the two measures is interesting. The proposal mixes elements of an ACE with elements

58 See Council of theEuropean Union, Code of Conduct Group (Business Taxation) - Report to the Council = Endorsement, 14114/19, FISC 444, ECOFIN 1005, Brussels, 25 November 2019.

of a CBIT, the comprehensive business income tax that does not allow interest deduction across the board, either intra-group or external interests paid that is. An ACE is moving towards a tax base aimed at taxing economic profit, especially in the case of a full-ACE that provides capital deduction on the total invested equity, rather than the soft ACE does – such as DEBRA – that only includes any changes in equity in the tax mechanism. An ACE creates a tax model where the effective marginal tax rate (where marginal returns and costs are equal) is zero. This leaves financing decisions at the margins unimpeded regarding both capital and debt-financed investment, which is good for the economy. A soft-ACE does the same, but only partially, as it only includes new equity in the capital deduction mechanism. A CBIT moves towards a tax base aimed at taxing EBIT. A CBIT creates a tax model where the effective marginal tax rate (where marginal returns and costs are equal) in debt-financed marginal investments is infinitely high. The sought financing tax parity is then exchanged for a tax-impediment at the margin, which is less good for the economy. It is important to note that the earnings stripping measure from ATAD 1 functions as a CBIT insofar as it limits the deduction of third-party interest. This is the case where the national legislation of the EU Member State transposing ATAD 1 involved does not provide for an additional group ratio rule along EBITDA lines, or an equity escape that ties in with the ratio between equity and total assets of the group involved, i.e., in addition to the fixed ratio up to 30% of gross profit (tax EBITDA / adjusted profit). We will leave aside the franchise of up to €3 million here, and the same applies to other permitted scope exceptions (on the earnings stripping measure from ATAD 1). The further deduction limitation of 15% of the balance of interest that has now been introduced on top of this will exacerbates the effect of this. The proposal can therefore be seen as both system-improving and system-deteriorating at the same time. To mitigate this adverse effect on the economy, our suggestion to the EU Member States would be to consider or perhaps reconsider utilising the option in ATAD 1 of a group ratio, i.e., to the extent not already put in place by the respective individual EU Member State concerned.

Mismatches and other things

The DEBRA Directive proposal introduces something new into the company taxation systems in most countries, and where some novel items are introduced into existing tax systems market distortions may arise in consequence of mutual tax system interactions due to disparities and mismatches. This will also be the case with the DEBRA measure, especially in the interaction between the corporate income tax systems of the EU Member States and those in countries that are not members of the EU. In fact, these are the same issues and complexities that the Code of Conduct Group has already looked into in the past and which resulted in the guidance and recommendations mentioned above in 2019. Countries outside the EU could consider the European capital deduction and its use by European operators to be something improper (unfair tax competition, aggressive tax planning) which could then give rise to the application, for example, of all kinds of additional anti-abuse measures, for example in the context of the operation of domestic participation exemption regimes. In addition, the Pillar Two system, i.e. the envisaged global 15% global minimum tax for large multinationals that is to be c.q. has been transposed into the company tax systems of the EU Member States based on the Pillar Two Directive does not take into account any of the DEBRA measures when determining the basis on which the 15% rate is calculated. The application of the base-broadening interest deduction limitation will push up the Jurisdictional Effective Tax Rate (ETR) for Pillar Two purposes (except to the extent that the aforementioned carry forward entitlements are included in the deferred tax position in the financial statements, which in turn are included in the ETR calculation for Pillar Two purposes). The application of the tax base narrowing capital deduction will actually lower the effective rate for Pillar Two purposes. The EU Member States therefore run the risk that the anticipated effect of an EU capital deduction will soon be taxed away with a Pillar Two top-up tax abroad. We can imagine that under the operation of the DEBRA measures, if effectuated as proposed, companies may have to re-examine their financing arrangements at some point in time to avoid surprises afterwards.

25.3.6 European Commission proposal for BEFIT Directive (co-author: Dafnomilis)[59]

General

On 12 September 2023, the European Commission published a Proposal for a Council Directive on Business in Europe: Framework for Income Taxation (BEFIT).[60] The BEFIT proposal introduces a common company tax base for large European companies (annual turnover of more than €750 million). BEFIT replaces the 2016 Directive proposals for a Common Corporate Tax Base (CCTB)[61] and a Common Consolidated Corporate Tax Base (CCCTB)[62]. Groups with an annual turnover below the €750 million threshold and that draw up consolidated financial statements can opt for the application of the new rules. The envisaged implementation date of the BEFIT Directive is 1 January 2028, after which the Directive is anticipated to become applicable as of 1 July 2028.

The BEFIT proposal, too, builds on, inter alia, the Commission Communication 'Business Taxation for the 21st Century' of 18 May 2021[63] and fleshes out the Commission's existing tax reform agenda for the coming years. The BEFIT proposal is accompanied by a proposal for a Directive on transfer pricing.[64] The EU TP Directive proposal harmonises the at arm's length standard within the internal market. On the same day, the European Commission

59 The current section is a republication in a single part of the diptych piece prepared by the author of the current chapter, as a co-author together with Vassilis Dafnomilis (University of Amsterdam, PwC, who kindly permitted), titled 'BEFIT: A Company Tax System Layering Exercise for the Internal Market', published in the Kluwer International Tax Blog (kluwertaxblog.com) on 28 (Part 1) and 29 December 2023 (Part 2).

60 See European Commission, Proposal for a Council Directive on Business in Europe: Framework for Income Taxation (BEFIT), COM(2023) 532 final, 2023/0321(CNS), Strasbourg, 12.9.2023.

61 See European Commission, Proposal for a Council Directive on a Common Corporate Tax Base, COM(2016) 685 final, 25 October 2016 (withdrawn).

62 See European Commission, Proposal for a Council Directive on a Common Consolidated Corporate Tax Base, COM(2016) 683 final, 25 October 2016 (withdrawn).

63 See BEFIT proposal, page 3; European Commission, Communication from the Commision to the European Parliament and the Council, Business Taxation for the 21st Century, COM(2021) 251 final, 18 May 2021 (available at https://taxation-customs.ec.europa.eu/communication-business-taxation-21st-century_en).

64 See European Commission, Proposal for a Council Directive on Transfer Pricing, COM(2023) 529 final, 12 September 2023 (available at https://eur-lex.europa.eu/resource.html?uri=cellar:35311f2e-5210-11ee-9220-01aa75ed71a1.0001.02/DOC_1&format=PDF).

published a proposal for a Directive for a Head Office Tax system for micro, small and medium sized enterprises. The HOTS Directive proposal introduces the possibility for small and medium-sized enterprises to calculate profits of permanent establishments within the EU according to the corporate income tax base determination rules in the Member State of the company's head office.[65] The TP and HOTS Directive proposals are further discussed in section 25.3.7 below.

With the release of the BEFIT proposal, the EU Member States were set to engage in discussions in the upcoming periods. The adoption of the proposal, like all Directive proposals, hinges on securing a unanimous vote from all EU Member States. Many anticipate that the deliberations surrounding BEFIT will extend over several years, given its introduction at a time when EU Member States are grappling with the implementation of their Pillar Two rules, and everything that comes with it. Adding to the complexity, the BEFIT proposal introduces a wholly new company tax system. Notably, Finland[66], Sweden[67], and the Netherlands[68] amongst others have articulated their perspectives on BEFIT. The potential success of the proposal mostly is a political matter. Whether the proposal will gain any traction and support remains a significant aspect that may influence the ongoing discussions.

How would BEFIT operate?

Who to tax, what to tax, where to tax, and how to tax
The BEFIT proposal introduces an aggregated common company tax base for so-called BEFIT groups, a *single tax base*, which is distributed among the EU Member States for the further application of their domestic corporate income tax rules on the basis of a 7-year transitional distribution mechanism. The following is a brief explanation of the personal scope *(who to tax)*, substantive scope (*what to tax*) and geographical scope (*where to tax*) of the BEFIT proposal, accompanied by some comments on the operation of the proposal of an administrative nature (*how to tax*).

Who does BEFIT tax?
The BEFIT proposal affects EU subsets of groups with a combined annual turnover of €750 million or more and includes the entities whose ultimate parent entity holds an interest in terms of ownership rights or profit rights of 75% or more.[69] For groups with an ultimate parent entity established outside the EU, an additional criterion is that the annual turnover within the EU, in the last 4 years prior to the year in which the Directive first becomes applicable to the group concerned, must be €50 million or more and this annual turnover must represent at least 5% of the total annual turnover of the group

65 See European Commission, Proposal for a Council Directive establishing a Head Office Tax system for micro, small and medium sized enterprises, and amending Directive 2011/16/EU, COM(2023) 528 final, 12 September 2023.

66 See https://valtioneuvosto.fi/-/10623/hallitus-suhtautuu-varauksella-yritysten-tuloverotusta-eu-roopassa-koskevaan-befit-kehykseen (Finnish).

67 See https://www.regeringen.se/faktapromemoria/2023/10/202324fpm9/ (Swedish).

68 See https://open.overheid.nl/documenten/e0787088-e0c7-428f-a932-0aa7f58cadf6/file (Dutch).

69 See Article 2, par. 1, and Article 5 BEFIT proposal.

concerned.[70][71] (materiality requirement). For companies with an annual turnover below the €750 million threshold and which draw up consolidated financial statements, the BEFIT regime is available for an optional five-year period in each case.[72] The rules will apply to the intra-EU part of the groups concerned, i.e., their EU subsets. These are the group entities established within the EU and the permanent establishments located within the EU of non-EU group entities established outside the EU.

What does BEFIT tax?
The single tax base in the BEFIT proposal is derived from the financial reporting standard used by the ultimate parent entity in the preparation of the consolidated financial statements (e.g. IFRS).[73] As with the Pillar Two Directive, the starting point of the provisional BEFIT tax basis calculation is the result based on an accepted accounting standard. A number of fixed adjustments are then made. These adjustments differ from those used under Pillar Two to calculate the GLoBE income for Pillar Two purposes.[74]

The proposal also introduces a regime for revaluations of qualifying participations. It is worth mentioning that the BEFIT proposal introduces a harmonised generic interest deduction limitation mechanism, based on the EBITDA deduction limitation laid down in the Anti-Tax Avoidance Directive (ATAD1) of 2016.[75] Excessive interest as determined according to the ATAD-EBITDA rule and paid by the relevant BEFIT group entity to group entities that are not part of the EU subset of the group shall not be deductible for BEFIT base determination purposes. It also stipulates that shipping income and income items covered by a tonnage tax regime in the EU Member States are not part of the BEFIT base.[76] A roll-over relief measure applies to reinvestments.[77] BEFIT also provides adjustments that follow from a tax regime for, for example, real estate and intangible assets. Subsidies for the acquisition, construction and improvement costs of fixed assets that are depreciable are exempt from the BEFIT basis.[78] If the BEFIT basis is negative, such is carried forward and offset against the next year in which the BEFIT basis is positive.[79]

70 For companies with an annual turnover below the €750 million threshold and which draw up consolidated financial statements, the BEFIT regime is available for an optional five-year period in each case. See article 2, par. 7 BEFIT proposal.
71 See Article 2, par. 2, BEFIT proposal. It is important to note meeting just one of the conditions, according to the literal wording of the provision as it currently reads, is sufficient to be excluded from the scope, without the requirement of meeting both conditions simultaneously.
72 See Article 2, par. 7, BEFIT proposal.
73 See Article 7 BEFIT proposal.
74 For example, a 95% participation exemption regime applies that deviates from the participation exemption in Pillar Two, the double tax relief system in the Parent-Subsidiary Directive as well as the various participation exemption regimes in the domestic company tax systems of the EU Member States. See Article 8, and Article 9 BEFIT proposal.
75 See Article 13 BEFIT proposal.
76 See Article 15 BEFIT proposal.
77 See Article 18 BEFIT proposal.
78 See Article 19 BEFIT proposal.
79 See Article 42, par. 2, BEFIT proposal.

Where does BEFIT tax?

The single tax base accordingly established is determined at BEFIT group entity level (separate accounting).[80] More specifically, the common basis of individual BEFIT group entities is aggregated at BEFIT group level, and also across the national borders of the EU Member States. This creates a cross-border EU taxable profit pooling regime (loss imports; no fiscal consolidation).

In Pillar Two terms, the intra-EU netting of business income essentially leads to regional blending, contrasting with the jurisdictional blending approach in the Pillar Two system. It is worth mentioning that, due to the regional blending à la BEFIT, the jurisdictional effective tax rate in an EU Member State for Pillar Two purposes may fall below 15%. See below for some further elaboration of this implication together with a detailed numerical example on the concurrence of BEFIT with Pillar Two.

A positive BEFIT company tax base is distributed among the EU Member States through a transitional distribution mechanism.[81] This mechanism applies for a transitional period of 7 years, specifically for fiscal years between 1 July 2028 and 30 June 2035.[82] Before the end of the third year after the entry into force of the Directive, the European Commission may propose another attribution mechanism.[83] If this does not happen, or if this proposal is not adopted before the end of the transitional regime, the transitional regime will become final.

After the end of the 7-year transition period, the idea is that a switch will be made to a permanent distribution key to be developed by the European Commission which can be based on a formula (formulary apportionment).[84] It is reported that the European Commission is putting its formula ideas on hold in order to get the EU Member States on board. The argument would then be that the proposed transitional distribution mechanism doesn't differ significantly in terms of tax revenues from the current rules. Moreover, EU Member States with Pillar Two have already committed to base coordination. Notably, the EU Member States may not apply withhold taxes on transactions between the BEFIT group entities.[85]

Following the application of the apportionment mechanism, EU Member States will be able to apply their national corporate income tax rules to their allocated part of the single tax base, such as national deduction limitations and/or base-narrowing measures such as investment allowances and patent box regimes.[86] EU Member States can also apply their tax grouping regimes at this stage. In doing so, BEFIT harmonises part of the taxable base within the EU and thus pushes variants of the concept of profit for individual EU Member State corporate tax purposes further into the background. EU Member States then apply their national rates. Of course, the 15% minimum rate under the Pillar Two system will

80 See Article 42 BEFIT proposal.
81 See Article 45 BEFIT proposal.
82 See Article 45, par. 1, BEFIT proposal.
83 See Article 45, par. 9, BEFIT proposal.
84 See BEFIT proposal, Explanatory Memorandum, Sec. 5, page 15.
85 See Article 43 BEFIT proposal.
86 See Article 45, par. 2, BEFIT proposal.

have to be taken into account, at least if and to the extent that these EU Member States wish to avoid any Pillar Two top-up taxation.

How does BEFIT tax?
The BEFIT proposal provides for a 'one-stop-shop' tax administration system.[87] A BEFIT information return is provided. The system is to some extent similar to that of the GloBE Information Return in the Pillar Two system, as well as the EU-variant thereof, the Top-up tax information return, under the eighth amendment to the Directive on Administrative Cooperation (DAC9) that the European Commission proposed on 28 October 2024 (see Section 25.3.8 below). The ultimate parent entity of the BEFIT group, i.e., the (ultimate) parent entity, is designated as the primary BEFIT information declaration submitting group entity.[88] This is when this ultimate parent entity is established in the EU. If the ultimate parent entity is not established in the EU, the BEFIT group may designate an EU group entity for that purpose.[89] The BEFIT information return will be submitted to the tax authorities of the EU Member State of establishment, which will then ensure the further dissemination of the information declaration to the EU Member States where the group in question operates.[90]

It follows from the BEFIT proposal that it should be possible to amend a tax assessment without a time limit if a tax authority or court in another EU Member State issues a ruling that (indirectly) also affects the corporate income tax basis of one of the EU Member States concerned.[91] This raises the question of whether and to what extent this could in practice lead to a tax assessment in a Member State not being irrevocably established. If this is the consequence, it will be at odds with the notion of formal legal effect of government decisions and thus the legal certainty and legitimacy of government interventions towards taxpayers. The formalisation process, in addition, will continue to be in the hands of the individual EU Member States at a decentralised level. The same applies to any tax-administrative procedures or any tax litigation appeal proceedings.

The BEFIT proposal also indicates that a BEFIT team should be installed: a team of tax officials that is from the various EU Member States in which the group involved is active.[92] Such a BEFIT team would be equipped with an online collaborative tool and would mutually exchange relevant tax information and would also provide advance legal certainty in relation to certain elements of BEFIT's legal operation.[93] The BEFIT team will have to be sufficiently equipped to resolve any disputes between tax authorities on the tax base.

For the sake of administrative simplicity, a so-called 'traffic light system' will be introduced for the arm's length pricing of affiliated transactions with group entities outside the BEFIT group.[94] The envisaged traffic light system is a risk analysis system for the tax authorities

87 See Article 57 BEFIT proposal.
88 See Article 3, par. 10, BEFIT proposal.
89 See Article 56 BEFIT proposal.
90 See Article 57 BEFIT proposal.
91 See Article 64 BEFIT proposal.
92 See Article 60 BEFIT proposal.
93 See Article 61 BEFIT proposal.
94 See BEFIT proposal, chapter IV.

of the EU Member States to assess the pricing of so-called low-risk activities (distribution activities by low-risk distributors, manufacturing activities by contract manufacturers) on the basis of a public benchmark (based on the transactional net margin method; TNMM) on their arm's length nature and, depending on the position of the transfer price employed in the interquartile range, to place them in one of three risk zones (low/medium/high). The tax authorities will then be able to tailor their efforts to the sub-population of the transactions in question that is considered to be the riskiest. Moreover, the administrative transfer pricing traffic light system is separate from the substantive transfer pricing application.

Observations

Focusing on four elements
It could be said from the outset that any ambitions to strengthen the EU internal market and the competitiveness of the EU deserve support providing that the harmonizing rules achieve a robust, efficient and fair company tax system for all European companies. The same applies to achieving a level playing field within the EU for the mitigation of tax competition between the EU Member States. Our observations focus on the following four elements: (i) administrative burden for companies, (ii). legal certainty for companies, (iii), simplicity of the tax system in the EU, and; (iv) aggregation into a single BEFIT tax base.

Administrative burden for companies
A harmonised company tax system within the EU could allow companies to directly enjoy the benefits of the internal market without incurring an unnecessary additional administrative burden which is inherent when a multinational enterprise deals with different tax systems, as is currently the case. Therefore, BEFIT seems to ease the administrative burden and compliance for EU and non-EU headquartered multinational enterprises given that the EU Member States would need to apply common rules for the determination of the BEFIT tax base of each BEFIT group member.

Although the BEFIT tax base of each BEFIT group member will be calculated based on harmonised rules, the compliance required from the BEFIT group should not be neglected. Groups will need to file the BEFIT return and continue to file tax returns locally so that post-allocation the tax authorities can ensure that adjustments to the BEFIT tax base have been applied correctly. From a compliance perspective it is doubtful whether BEFIT will in essence reduce the tax compliance and administrative burdens faced by groups.[95]

Legal certainty for companies
A standardised tax system has the potential to significantly improve legal certainty for companies when doing business in the EU. Specifically, a harmonised tax base aligned with accounting standards could be seen as a progressive stride towards achieving legal certainty, especially in light of the concurrent Pillar Two system, which uses accounting standards as well as a starting point.

95 According to the EC, however, these compliance costs are estimated to be outweighed by compliance cost savings as well as simplified administrative procedures and in the long run, the improved allocation of resources by businesses and tax administrations. See BEFIT proposal, Explanatory Memorandum, Sec. 2, page 6.

The emerging disparities between BEFIT and Pillar Two, particularly in the adjustments to financial accounting profits and losses, will undoubtedly present challenges for EU and non-EU groups. This discrepancy hampers, in our view, the pursuit of legal certainty in the EU: compliance with Pillar Two does not inherently also ensure compliance with BEFIT and vice versa. In essence, the calculations under Pillar Two occur independently from those under BEFIT. This disconnection does not assure a cohesive tax system in the EU, even when considering the distinct objectives between BEFIT and Pillar Two.

Furthermore, due to differences in the distribution of the tax base, BEFIT base allocation may give rise to Pillar Two top-up taxation.[96] The Dutch government has acknowledged this effect and outlined it as follows (author's translation): *"Under the Pillar Two rules, top-up taxation might occur based on the commercial results within that year. As BEFIT's recognised profit relies on results from the previous three years, an undesired discrepancy might arise. For instance, if losses were incurred in the past three years and a commercial profit is gained in the present year. This scenario could lead to BEFIT showing a loss for the tax year, despite the commercial profit, thus resulting in no tax liability. However, according to Pillar Two rules, top-up taxation will be applicable in that year. The situation becomes more intricate with the potential offsetting of losses against profits in another Member State."* The Dutch government explains the effect with a numerical example, which we include in full below for the sake of convenience.

Box 1. Numerical example concurrence Pillar Two rules with BEFIT

Multinational group ABC falls within the scope of both BEFIT and Pillar Two. ABC has three entities (A, B and C) that are established in EU Member States A, B and C. For the sake of convenience, the differences between BEFIT and Pillar Two have been abstracted for purposes of the income calculations. In Member State A, the income is €200, in Member State B it is €150, and in Member State C there is a loss of €50. The statutory tax rate in Member State A is 20%, and in EU Member States B and C it is 15%.

Under Pillar Two, a top-up tax should be levied up to 15% if the effective tax rate in a jurisdiction is less than 15%. In the situation where BEFIT is not yet applicable, there is no low-tax jurisdiction and no Pillar Two top-up tax will take place. The effective tax rate ('ETR') of the group is 20.8%. In the scenario where BEFIT does apply, Pillar Two seems to result in top-up taxation. This can be illustrated as follows. The BEFIT basis is the aggregate result of the three BEFIT entities and is €300 (€200 + €150 – €50). The results of the three group entities in the three previous years were the same, which means that the basis is distributed equally. €100 will be allocated to each BEFIT group entity. This amount is subject to the BEFIT levy. Based on the above-mentioned statutory tax rates, this means that €20 (20% of 100) will be paid in Member State A. In EU Member States B and C, €15 is paid.

96 This effect has already been observed in practice (see e.g., Stephanie Soong, 'Slow EU Pillar Two Adoption Is a Challenge, Says EU Official', Tax Notes International, 19 September 2023).

Pillar Two seems to be based on income and not on the BEFIT allocation. As a result, the ETR in EU Member States A and B is 10%, i.e., lower than the minimum of 15%. Due to the concurrence with BEFIT, it seems that under Pillar Two in EU Member States A and B an additional €10 and €7.5 respectively will have to be levied. This is despite the fact that without the application of BEFIT, there is no Pillar Two top-up tax. As a result, the group's ETR increases from 16.7% to 22.5%.

	Member State A	**Member State B**	**Member State C**	**Total**	**ETR Group**
Income*	200	150	-50	300	
Tax rate	20%	15%	15%		
Pillar Two (without BEFIT)					
National tax	40	22.5	-7.5	55	
Effective rate	20%	15%	0%		
Pillar Two minimum %	15%	15%	15%		
Pillar Two additional levy %	0%	0%	0%		
Pillar Two additional levy	-	-	-		
	40.0	22.5	-	62.5	20.8%***
Pillar Two (with BEFIT)					
BEFIT attribution **	100	100	100		
BEFIT levy	20	15	15	50	16.7%
Effective rate ***	10%	10%	0%		
Pillar Two minimum %	15%	15%	15%		
Pillar Two additional levy %	5%	5%	0%		
Pillar Two additional levy	10	7.5	-	17.5	
				67.5	22.5%

* It is assumed that Pillar Two income and BEFIT income (for the application of the formula) are the same.
**It is assumed that countries have contributed equally over the past 3 years.
*** Loss relief rules, and related deferred tax liabilities, have been abstracted under Pillar Two.

> *Source:* Fact sheet 3 Working Group on the Assessment of New Commission Proposals (werkgroep Beoordeling Nieuwe Commissie voorstellen (BNC)): Business in Europe Directive: Framework for income taxation, annex to Letter from the Minister of Foreign Affairs, 6 October 2023 (BZDOC-1953107355-69).

Simplicity of the tax system in the EU
A harmonised tax system holds the potential to ensure a simpler tax system within the EU. In this scenario, national corporate income tax laws would not be the starting point, but rather the accounting standards. This means that MNEs would not have to navigate through different tax systems and tax administrations, thus contributing to a simpler tax system.

The implementation of BEFIT and its EU-wide tax base results in a significant revamp of the current company tax systems across individual EU Member States. BEFIT introduces multiple parallel company tax systems within the EU Member States, encompassing diverse taxable profit structures relating to BEFIT, corporate income taxation[97] (post-BEFIT allocation) and Pillar Two (post-BEFIT allocation). The option for smaller groups to choose BEFIT introduces potential transitional challenges, such as how to handle losses both during and after the designated "BEFIT period".

In addition, the concurrence with Pillar Two, the Pillar One initiative, the EU TP Proposal[98] and the HOTS Proposal[99], to be discussed in the following section below, seems to make things complex and far-reaching from the outset. Besides affecting financial reporting, BEFIT introduces a fourth accounting system for companies. Its implementation is likely to have far-reaching consequences for the tax authorities of EU Member States, impacting areas like automation, enforcement, service provision, communication, international collaboration, and potentially necessitating capacity expansions. EU and non-EU groups can expect a similar scenario, and it might take time for the new system to solidify in practice. The unanimity requirement for decision-making in the EU could pose challenges in adapting to future developments.

Aggregation into a single BEFIT tax base
The aggregation of results across the borders of the EU Member States brings an advantage to taxpayers compared to the current company tax systems in the EU. The current reality of a netting of corporate income basis within national borders, territoriality, or jurisdictional blending in Pillar Two terminology, creates a lock-in effect for company tax purposes. This is the case as such (i.e., a tax-netting of domestic investment returns) favors investments in jurisdictions in which the market operator is already operative over investments across national borders in other jurisdictions (i.e., by not allowing a

97 Or even personal income tax system (PIT), that is, when the corporate income tax legislation of the country concerned refers directly to personal income tax rules of that country for the definition of certain concepts.
98 See Council Directive on Transfer Pricing, COM(2023) 529 final.
99 See Council Directive establishing a Head Office Tax system for micro, small and medium sized enterprises, and amending Directive 2011/16/EU, COM(2023) 528 final.

tax-netting of cross-border investment returns). Within the scope of EU law, this goes against the idea of an internal market without internal borders for groups. Hence the regional blending in BEFIT is a renewed expression of the Commission's long-cherished wish for intra-EU netting of taxable bases.

The aggregation of BEFIT results may be offset by the Pillar Two system. When BEFIT results are combined, the effects could be nullified by the Pillar Two system. Offsetting losses against profits in another EU Member State might reduce the Effective Tax Rate (ETR) of the group in an EU Member State to below 15%, potentially triggering a top-up tax under the Pillar Two rules. For further details, including a numerical example, please refer to section 3.2 of this article.

Will BEFIT be adopted?
It seems too early to say whether BEFIT will be adopted, whether at all or in its current form. Some EU Member States, inter alia, the Netherlands[100] and Finland[101] have announced that they are supportive of the BEFIT but that they nevertheless have serious reservations. Both countries, for instance, are referring to unpredictable tax bases.

The Netherlands government, for instance, largely supports BEFIT but seeks a closer link to the Pillar Two tax base, preferring to gain experience with Pillar Two before transitioning to a harmonised tax base. It anticipates significant challenges dealing with four different tax systems, expresses concerns about unpredictability in tax base allocation, and doubts the reduction of compliance costs. Recently, the Dutch parliament requested its government to convey its disapproval of the proposal to the European Commission. Before the government can give approval, the parliament wants to make clear arrangements on how it will be informed about the negotiations of the proposal.

Finland, for example, supports BEFIT but has concerns. The government doubts whether the administrative burden will decrease and emphasises the need for attention during legislation. Additionally, Finland is apprehensive about the transfer of taxing powers to the national level, highlighting significant harmonisation challenges and uncertainties in tax revenue, coupled with demanding implementation deadlines in the evolving international corporate taxation landscape.

Whatever the case, the BEFIT proposal brings a new dynamic to the debate on the taxation of multinational business profits within the internal market. The arguments for or against BEFIT are to some extent similar to those that also played a role in the context of Pillar Two. Pillar Two is now a reality, at least within the EU.

So how will BEFIT fare? The EU Member States still have their own tax policies. On the one hand, BEFIT is about strengthening the internal market and the EU's competitive position. A harmonised tax base can contribute to this. BEFIT, on the other hand, is about a cumulation of tax legislation and a possible coexistence of parallel company tax systems

100 See https://open.overheid.nl/documenten/e0787088-e0c7-428f-a932-0aa7f58cadf6/file (Dutch).
101 See https://valtioneuvosto.fi/-/10623/hallitus-suhtautuu-varauksella-yritysten-tuloverotusta-eu-roopassa-koskevaan-befit-kehykseen (Finnish).

(company taxation, Pillar Two, BEFIT). The proposed transitional distribution mechanism will result in a tax netting for businesses within the internal market and a more volatile treasury revenue for EU Member States. The suggestion to limit the EU Member States' room for maneuver and at the same time to promote it represents a trade-off in terms of the administrative simplification sought, amongst others. Furthermore, the European Commission reminds the public that '[i]n 2020, the Council, Parliament and the European Commission agreed that a common corporate tax base could be the basis for a new own resource that the European Commission will propose'.[102]

Looking at the experiences in the past within the Council with the EU directive proposals for a CC(C)TB of 2011 and 2016, the BEFIT proposal may very well also give rise to complex political discussions. At the same time, times have changed. After Pillar Two, EU Member States will no longer be able to play the autonomy card nearly as firmly as they did in the earlier days with the CCCTB.

25.3.7 European Commission proposals for Transfer Pricing and HOTS Directives

General

In addition to the BEFIT Directive proposal discussed in the above section, the European Commission published on 12 September 2023 an accompanying proposal for a Directive on transfer pricing,[103] as well as a proposal for a Directive for a Head Office Tax system for micro, small and medium sized enterprises.[104] The EU TP Directive proposal harmonises the at arm's length standard within the internal market. The HOTS Directive proposal introduces the possibility for small and medium-sized enterprises to calculate profits of permanent establishments within the EU according to the corporate income tax base determination rules in the Member State of the company's head office. The EU TP Directive proposal and HOTS Directive proposal are scheduled to enter into force on 1 January 2026. The TP Directive and HOTS proposals, too, build on, inter alia, the EC's Communication 'Business Taxation for the 21st Century' of 18 May 2021.[105] Moreover, the HOTS Directive proposal concretises the SME Relief Package announced by Commission President von der Leyen in her 2022 State of the Union address. Since their launch, the proposals and HOTS particularly have been struggling to gain political momentum. The Directive proposals are discussed in this section on a more high-level basis.

102 BEFIT proposal, Explanatory Memorandum, Sec. 1, pages 1-2.

103 See European Commission, Proposal for a Council Directive on Transfer Pricing, COM(2023) 529 final, 12 September 2023 (available at https://eur-lex.europa.eu/resource.html?uri=cellar:35311f2e-5210-11ee-9220-01aa75ed71a1.0001.02/DOC_1&format=PDF).

104 See European Commission, Proposal for a Council Directive establishing a Head Office Tax system for micro, small and medium sized enterprises, and amending Directive 2011/16/EU, COM(2023) 528 final, 12 September 2023.

105 See BEFIT proposal, page 3; European Commission, Communication from the Commision to the European Parliament and the Council, Business Taxation for the 21st Century, COM(2021) 251 final, 18 May 2021 (available at https://taxation-customs.ec.europa.eu/communication-business-taxation-21st-century_en).

EU Transfer pricing

The Transfer Pricing Directive proposal focuses on an EU-wide harmonisation of transfer pricing rules and accompanying administrative rules (transfer pricing documentation) for entities resident for tax purposes within the EU and for permanent establishments located within the EU of entities resident outside the EU for tax purposes. The proposal establishes a common approach to the at arm's length standard and its core elements. In fact, the proposal introduces an EU-variant of the at arm's length standard for the internal market, i.e., as the European Commission previously envisioned in the context of the state aid procedures that the Commission has initiated over the years against various EU Member States that, in the Commission's view, would favour large companies through transfer pricing rulings. It is now becoming increasingly clear that the reference framework in the field of state aid is really determined by the EU Member States themselves and not by the European Commission.[106] The European Commission now seems to be looking for the institutional basis for transfer pricing harmonisation in a proposal for a Directive. The Directive proposal aims to bring legal certainty to businesses and reduce the risks of tax litigation and double taxation. The proposal should also further curb opportunities for aggressive tax planning in the field of transfer pricing. It is worth noting that the CCTB also included an arm's length determination. The CCCTB also contained an arm's length provision for the pricing of transactions with group members beyond the EU's external borders, the so-called 'water's edge'.

It is particularly noteworthy that it is proposed in the TP Directive proposal to elevate the latest version of the OECD Transfer Pricing Guidelines to supranational EU law. Confidence in the OECD is high, it seems, at least from the European Commission. The proposed Transfer Pricing Directive even requires the EU Member States to embrace future versions of the OECD Transfer Pricing Guidelines as a legally binding framework. In order to ensure compliance by the EU Member States, it is proposed that the Council, on a proposal from the Commission, will decide within the context of decision-making within the OECD on a position at hand on behalf of the European Union. This, on the basis of Article 218(9) TFEU, and considering that the OECD Transfer Pricing Guidelines, with their anticipated decisive influence on the content of EU law in this regard under the Directive, are adopted within the OECD whereas the Council must therefore establish the position of the EU Member States within the OECD decision-making framework. In order to continue to ensure alignment with future versions of the OECD Transfer Pricing Guidelines, the EU Transfer Pricing Directive will be further amended where necessary in the future. It is also proposed that further regulations on Safe Harbours and on specific transactions in areas such as intangible assets, corporate restructurings, financing, marketing and distribution activities and cost contribution arrangements should be adopted. This is envisaged to be done on the basis of implementing acts, to be adopted by the Council on a proposal from the Commission. Implementing powers to take decisions on the basis of the Directive should also be conferred on the Council, acting on a proposal from the

106 See, for example, Court of Justice, 8 November 2022, Joined Cases C 885/19 P and C 898/19 P (*Fiat Chrysler Finance Europe v Commission*), and see Court of Justice, 14 December 2023, Case C-457/21 P (*Commission v Amazon.com and Others*). Notably, also see Court of Justice, 10 September 2024, Case C-465/20 P (*Commission v Ireland and Others*). The latter mentioned case was decided on formal grounds (res judicata).

Commission, i.e., in the light of the sensitivities arising from the fiscal autonomy of the EU Member States in the field of direct taxation. As said, the Directive proposal so far has gained little political traction.

Head Office Tax System (HOTS)
The HOTS Directive proposal concretises, as said, parts of the SME Relief Package announced by Commission President von der Leyen in her 2022 State of the Union address. The SME Relief Package concerns a basket of measures that would encourage small and medium-sized enterprises (SMEs) in operating cross-border business enterprises in the internal market. The proposed HOTS Directive introduces the possibility for non-resident taxpayers that operate a small and medium-sized business via local permanent establishment to opt for taxable profit determination in the jurisdiction of that permanent establishment by reference to the corporate tax base calculation rules of the EU Member State where they are resident for company tax purposes, the EU Member State where their head office is situated that is. The HOTS Directive proposal also introduces a supporting tax administration system for this purpose, whereby the EU Member State where the taxpayer's head office is located collects the relevant corporate taxes due and then transfers the relevant tax revenues to the respective EU Member States in which the permanent establishments of the taxpayers involved are situated, thus a one-stop-shop.

The scope of the proposal may be considered somewhat limited perhaps. The proposed Directive only applies to so-called 'standalone SMEs' with permanent establishments in other EU Member States. Standalone SMEs are corporate entities that are not part of a consolidated group for accounting purposes. The definition of SME is based on Directive 2013/34/EU of 26 June 2013. This Directive, for instance, defines medium-sized enterprises as enterprises that are not micro-enterprises or small enterprises and which, at the balance sheet date, do not exceed the thresholds for at least two of the following three criteria: (a) balance sheet total: €20 million; (b) net turnover: €40 million; (c) average number of employees during the financial year: 250. The application of the HOTS mechanism is also subject to the condition that during the past two fiscal years: (i) the combined turnover of the permanent establishments does not exceed twice the turnover generated from the head office; (ii) the entity concerned is resident for tax purposes in the said principal Member State of origin, the jurisdiction in which the head office is located, and; (iii) the body concerned qualifies as an SME for the purposes of Directive 2013/23EU. Companies that make use of tonnage tax rules are not eligible for application of the HOTS mechanism. SMEs that opt in for the HOTS mechanism are bound by the HOTS rules for a 5-year period, after which they can opt for an extension for another 5-year period. To prevent abuse of the HOTS mechanism, SMEs are excluded from when the tax residence is transferred. HOTS, in other words, provides an unconditional residence trap (which notably immediately begs the question as to its proportionality). The mechanism also ceases to apply as soon as the turnover achieved with the permanent establishments exceeds three times the turnover generated from the head office. The attribution of profit to the permanent establishments involved is not regulated by the Directive proposal. Such is envisaged to be based on the (EU) arm's length principle. Notably, the tax rates are also set by the respective EU Member States themselves.

Although the scope of the HOTS Directive proposal may be somewhat limited, this does not alter the fact that the envisaged mechanism has some interesting elements in an analytical sense. It is interesting to observe that it the proposal envisages that the tax rules in place in one EU Member State will be adhered to when establishing the tax implications in another EU Member State. As a phenomenon, this is not new in itself within EU law and also has a name: mutual recognition. Nevertheless, the introduction of the concept of mutual recognition in taxation would indeed be something new. Mutual recognition of each other's tax rules does place some pressure on the tax systems of the EU Member States however, as such would accelerate the process towards the application of the most favourable tax rules within the European Union. We saw this, for example, in the past, where mutual recognition in the company law domain heralded the reform and flexibilisation of company laws throughout the European Union for reasons of competition, particularly with regard to capital protection rules. A recognition of the tax rules in the EU Member State in which the head office is located for taxable profit determination purposes in the EU Member State of the permanent establishment incentives, ceteris paribus, a shifting of the company tax residence to the EU Member State with the most favourable tax rules, a concept something called *corporate inversion*, for instance in the United States, and thus fuels tax competition and with that the race to the bottom. Perhaps such explains the scope of the proposal being kept rather limited. The proposed Directive also puts some pressure because of the distinction that is being created under the Directive proposal between permanent establishments on the one hand and subsidiaries on the other. Unlike in the case of permanent establishments and head offices, the taxable profits of subsidiaries in the EU Member State in which these subsidiaries are established may not be determined according to the taxable profit calculation rules applicable in the hands of the parent company in the EU Member State in which the partent company involved has its tax place of residence. Such a difference in treatment is discriminatory and if the EU Member States do so unilaterally, such would very likely be incompatible with primary EU law, as we have known since the first judgment of the ECJ in the field of direct taxation in *Avoir Fiscal*.[107] We also know that Directives must also comply with primary EU law and otherwise be invalid.[108] Furthermore, it may be questioned whether the aforementioned unconditional residence trap in the HOTS mechanism and the resulting lock-in effect is proportionate from an internal market proportionality perspective. We will have to see whether secondary EU law will stand the test of primary EU law criticism when asked. Perhaps we will never know, as, as said, the HOTS Directive proposal, too, has gained rather little political traction as of its release.

107 See Court of Justice, 28 January 1986, case 270/83 (*Avoir Fiscal*).

108 See, for example, CJEU 8 December 2022, case C694/20 (*Orde van Vlaamse Balies and Others*).

25.3.8 European Commission proposal for DAC 9 (Pillar Two)

General

On 28 October 2024, the European Commission published a proposal submitting an eighth amendment to the Directive on Administrative Cooperation (DAC[109]; DAC 9[110]), introducing an EU-wide Top-up tax information return obligation for multinational companies. The information return seeks to support the administrative operation of the 15% Global Minimum Tax in the European Union under the Pillar Two Directive[111]. If adopted by the Council – in the usual way, unanimously that is and after obtaining the opinion of the European Parliament – as proposed by the Commission the EU Member States will have until 31 December 2025 time to transpose the Directive into their domestic law. The first Top-up tax information returns are subsequently anticipated to be submitted by the relevant in-scope multinational enterprises to their respective tax authorities (reporting) before 30 June 2026 upon which the returns are anticipated to be mutually exchanged by the relevant tax authorities (automatic exchange of information) before 31 December 2026.

At the heart of the Directive proposal lies the Top-up tax information return, the GloBE Information Return (GIR) as it is referred to in international Pillar Two terms within the context if the OECD's Inclusive Framework. The information return is a standardised administrative form developed within the context of the Inclusive Framework that in-scope multinational enterprises must complete and provide to the tax authorities. The tax authorities, the thinking goes, then exchange the data among themselves on the basis of a multilateral information exchange framework.

The proposed Directive aims to establish the GIR of the Inclusive Framework in a coordinated and consistent manner within the European Union. The Top-up tax return provides for this purpose an information collection framework as a basis for tax authorities to be able to verify Pillar Two calculations provided, to determine Pillar Two top-up tax obligations and to perform appropriate risk analyses. The idea is thus to facilitate the reporting obligation for businesses and the exchange of information between tax authorities on Pillar Two. The European Commission considers the proposal proportionate and in line with the principle of subsidiarity and the EU Charter.

Standardised and centralised Top-up tax information return desk

The proposed Directive opens the possibility for groups that fall within the scope of the EU Pillar Two Directive to submit their information return in a standardised manner within the EU, and in a centralised manner instead of per individual EU Member State. The Directive allows companies to file their Top-up tax information return in a single EU Member State (central filing), i.e. the EU Member State where the ultimate parent entity

109 See Council Directive 2011/16/EU on administrative cooperation in the field of taxation.

110 See European Commission, Proposal for a Council Directive amending Directive 2011/16/EU on administrative cooperation in the field of taxation, COM(2024) 497 final, 2024/0276(CNS), Brussels, 28.10.2024.

111 See Council Directive (EU) 2022/2523 of 14 December 2022 on ensuring a global minimum level of taxation for multinational enterprise groups and large-scale domestic groups in the Union.

is established, or the designated EU Member State (i.e. the EU Member State in which a constituent entity is established and which designates the company in question as a supplementary top-up tax information return filing group entity). This is instead of in all EU Member States separately where the multinational group in question has established group entities (local filing). The basis for this has already been laid down in the EU Pillar Two Directive.[112] The EU Member States then exchange the information provided through the return. This is done within 3 months of the submission of the Top-up tax information return by the group entity concerned (6 months in the first round of tax returns) and on the basis of a standardised digital form to be developed by the European Commission. The proposal provides for possibilities for EU Member States to make follow-up information requests. This, for example, if EU Member States believe that additions are needed after verification of the information provided.[113] The requested EU Member State must then contact the relevant group entity with the relevant further requests, in order to share the further information subsequently collected with the requesting Member State. This, of course, if the Directive is adopted as currently proposed.

In addition to an EU information exchange framework, the proposed Directive introduces further rules and guidance on the form and content of the Top-up tax information return, the manner in which it is submitted and the data and information to be provided (see the annex to the proposed Directive). This should be made mandatory within the EU by the format developed for this purpose within the OECD/Inclusive Framework and published on 17 July 2023,[114] and, perhaps, the additional batch of documentation published by the OECD/Inclusive Framework on 15 January 2025.[115] The proposed Directive also incorporates the so-called Transitional Simplified Jurisdictional Reporting Framework from the OECD/ Inclusive Framework document of 17 July 2023, a temporarily applicable simplified information collection framework that is. For the sake of flexibility, the proposal gives the European Commission a regulatory power to update the format where necessary. This is to keep things in line with international agreements and work that has been done within the Inclusive Framework to further facilitate the administrative processes surrounding the information return and the exchange of information.

The envisaged implementation date of the amending Directive is 31 December 2025. The first Top-up tax information returns must be submitted by 30 June 2026 at the latest. Under the DAC9 Directive proposal, the exchange of information on the information return

112 See Article 44 EU Pillar Two Directive in conjunction with Article 8ae DAC9 Directive proposal.
113 See Article 9a DAC9 Directive proposal.
114 See OECD (2023), Tax Challenges Arising from the Digitalisation of the Economy – GloBE Information Return (Pillar Two), OECD Publishing, Paris.
115 See OECD (2025), Tax Challenges Arising from the Digitalisation of the Economy – GloBE Information Return (January 2025): Inclusive Framework on BEPS, OECD/G20 Base Erosion and Profit Shifting Project, OECD Publishing, Paris, OECD (2025), Tax Challenges Arising from the Digitalisation of the Economy – Administrative Guidance on Article 8.1.4 and 8.1.5 of the Global Anti-Base Erosion Model Rules (January 2025), OECD/G20 Inclusive Framework on BEPS, OECD, Paris, OECD (2025), Tax Challenges Arising from the Digitalisation of the Economy – Multilateral Competent Authority Agreement on the Exchange of GloBE Information (January 2025), OECD/G20 Inclusive Framework on BEPS, OECD, Paris, and OECD (2025), GloBE Information Return (Pillar Two) XML Schema: User Guide for Tax Administrations, OECD Publishing, Paris.

between the tax authorities of the EU Member States will take place by 31 December 2026. For EU Member States that have opted to defer Pillar Two implementation on the basis of Article 50 of the EU Pillar Two Directive (Estonia, Latvia, Lithuania, Malta, Slovakia), the application of the measures set out in the Directive proposal will be postponed accordingly.

Observations

EU one-stop-shop for intra-EU activities
The DAC9 Directive proposal introduces an EU-wide one-stop-shop mechanism for the filing of the information return, derived from the template of the Inclusive Framework. The basic principle of the EU Pillar Two Directive is that constituent entities each have a separate Top-up tax information return obligation in the (Member) State in which they are located for Pillar Two purposes, i.e., their jurisdiction of tax residence. If there are several constituent entities located within the same (Member) State, the Top-up tax information return can be filed on behalf of the other local constituent entities by the local entity that has been appointed by the group to do so. This is only different, and that is the exception, if the return is filed by the ultimate parent entity or the so-called designated filing entity, i.e., an entity from another jurisdiction that has been appointed by the group to fulfil the filing obligations. As a requirement a designated filing entity should be located – i.e., having its tax place of residence – in a jurisdiction with which qualifying information exchange agreements have been made in the form of a competent authority agreement for Pillar Two purposes. If the return is filed by a constituent entity in such a qualifying jurisdiction, then there is no need to file a return locally as well. In that case, a notification is sufficient, so that the tax authorities are aware that an information return is coming their way from abroad. Incidentally, it seems to us that it is ultimately up to the CJEU to assess information exchange agreements as to the question of whether or not these qualify for Pillar Two purposes.

The DAC9 Directive proposal does not provide for an information exchange framework in relation to third countries. The Inclusive Framework is anticipated to produce a Multilateral Competent Authority Agreement (MCAA) similar to DAC9 but then regulated under international public law, which the EU Member States can join. It is expected that countries that do not implement Pillar Two (e.g., the United States) can also join an MCAA. The preamble to the DAC9 Directive proposal indicates that qualifying agreements must be made in relation to third countries to ensure that groups with constituent entities located in the EU can also use the envisaged one-stop-shop for their activities outside the EU. After all, if groups file Pillar Two related information returns in countries with which no qualifying agreements have been made, they will continue to have to file Top-up tax information returns in the EU under DAC9.

Top-up tax information return is not a formalisation of Pillar Two tax liability
Of relevance to note is that the Top-up tax information return is to be seen as separate from the formalisation of any substantive top-up tax liabilities and any related Pillar Two tax-filing obligations. The Top-up tax information return is not a tax return. The formalisation of Pillar Two top-up taxation is a matter for the individual EU Member States to arrange for. The information return also is not to be seen as a replacement of any existing

or any newly to be developed tax enforcement mechanisms, or any related competences of the tax authorities for that matter, in those jurisdictions that have implemented Pillar Two into their domestic tax systems. Subject to domestic administrative regulations, local tax authorities will be able to continue querying and subjecting local constituent entities to any enforcement proceedings with regard to the monitoring of any Pillar Two compliant behaviours. In alignment with the dissemination approach developed within the Inclusive Framework, which is also incorporated in the DAC9 Directive proposal, any EU Member States where the Top-up tax information return is filed will only share any information or data with any other jurisdictions that is of relevance – or that they consider of relevance – for the determination of any top-up taxing rights of those jurisdictions.

Time will tell whether tax authorities will be satisfied with the information made available by the jurisdiction of the relevant constituent entity that is filing the information return, i.e., to determine their top-up taxing rights on this basis. Or perhaps they will, in addition to this, divert to any other administrative enforcement possibilities and powers available under domestic procedural law for the collection of data to determine their Pillar Two related taxing rights on that basis. The future will have to show to what extent things will proceed in an orderly manner or will give rise to discussions, disputes and controversy. The DAC9 proposal opens possibilities for the EU Member States to proceed to subsequent information requests, for example for verification purposes (which seems to us to imply that these Member States will then have to obtain the information from somewhere else in order to be able to verify the information provided to them under the DAC9 framework). Perhaps the EU Member States will be reluctant to do this, perhaps not. Perhaps, the Dispute Resolution Directive may provide some scope for settling any disputes involving the application of the Pillar Two rules within the internal market, perhaps not. The MCAA, as to be put in place within the context of the Inclusive Framework is also envisaged to provide some instrumentation for dispute resolution. But to this day, an MCAA and dispute resolution mechanisms are not there yet, and as far as we know there also is no glimmer on the horizon, at least not at the time the drafting of the current chapter was finalized.

Complex

We would like to leave it to the enthusiast to take a look at the information return related documents, both those from the EU institutions as well as the Inclusive Framework, for an idea of the proportions of the administrative requirements that have been arrived at for information return purposes. Since the rounds of public consultations on the GloBE Information Return, and now the arrival of the DAC9 Directive proposal and its appendix in 2024, we have been enabled to get used to what Pillar Two brings about in terms of compliance and administrative burdens, both for taxpayers as well as for tax authorities. Still, the multitude of requested information and data points is still a bit overwhelming, at least for us. In addition, the Pillar Two rules, including those of an administrative nature, are constantly changing and evolving, whereby the rules are being changed as we go. This makes it a bit difficult to organize and manage the administrative work properly. How will countries for instance proceed to (dis)qualify each other's information exchange frameworks in due course? In any case, the DAC9 Directive proposal indicates that it considers itself an 'appropriate' international agreement for the exchange of Pillar Two related information with third country jurisdictions.

This said, the European Commission has been the first institution to introduce a hard-law based one-stop shop mechanism for the filing of the envisaged Pillar information return. We will have to see to which extent other countries and regions will follow suit. So far, internationally, no framework on the exchange of information and the settlement of disputes in relation to Pillar Two has been put in place. The formalisation of any substantive top-up tax liabilities is and will remain up to the individual countries to organise and cater for themselves. The same holds for the availability and utilisation of any legal remedies. Disputes with the tax authorities need to be litigated via domestic judicial systems, and within the EU with the Court of Justice as the judiciary with the final say in matters. There is no instrument for addressing disparities and also the settling of international disputes seems a long way off for the time being.

It will be interesting to see which of the available jurisdiction(s) the international business community will favor for the filing of the Top-up tax information return(s). Whose counter will be preferred? Will countries move to compete and/or (dis)qualify each other on this as well? We will see.

25.4 Final remarks

Much work has been done and also remains to be done to make the European Commission's reform proposals and ambitions a reality. When preparing the update of this chapter in early 2025, international tax-political processes and discussions had begone to blend, or perhaps clutter, with processes and discussions of a more tax-technical nature, initiating a new and interesting stage in the EU company tax reform process.

We see the European Commission's undercurrent ambitions for further EU integration in the field of company taxation and corporate tax reform increasingly coming to the surface. It is fascinating to see how the Commission pulls out all the stops to keep things together. We see references in the proposals and explanatory memoranda to policy documents dating back to the 1960s, which of course refers to the famous Neumark report from 1963,[116] and reports delivered afterwards, including those by Segre[117], Van den Tempel[118], and Ruding.[119] And of course, the Bolkestein report from 2001 from which the CCCTB proposal arose should not go unnoticed either.[120]

The BEFIT proposal of 12 September 2023, perhaps, is a nice example of the envisioned culmination of matters. We see how the international developments on Pillar One and

116 The Neumark report is available at https://koflerge.files.wordpress.com/2019/01/neumark.pdf.
117 The Segre report is available at http://aei.pitt.edu/31823/1/Dev_Eur_Cap_Mkt_1966.pdf.
118 The Van den Tempel report is available at https://aei.pitt.edu/40293/1/A4688.pdf.
119 The Ruding report is available at https://op.europa.eu/en/publication-detail/-/publication/0044caf0-58ff-4be6-bc06-be2af6610870.
120 See the 2001 Commission titled 'Towards an Internal Market without tax obstacles' (COM(2001) 582 final).

Pillar Two form the stepping-stone for the far-reaching EU tax reform proposals that have been presented over the recent years. We see how transfer pricing harmonisation is being diverted, now that attempts to achieve this through negative integration via the state aid angle seem to be stagnating. We read about how BEFIT, which may not be called a CCCTB, provides the old CCCTB with a new branding and how the plans have been presented to us for the third time in slightly different segments. We even see the old idea of Home State Taxation echoing, in the earlier days one of the variants from which the CCCTB was later chosen, as an inspiration for the HOTS Directive proposal. All would fit well with other currently pending measures of course, at least according to the EU institutions, such as DEBRA and Unshell, together with already existing measures such as the Parent-Subsidiary Directive, the Interest Royalty Directive, the Mergers Directive, the Anti-Tax Avoidance Directive, the Administrative Cooperation Directive, the Dispute Resolution Directive, the EU Arbitration Convention and of course the Pillar Two Directive. Simultaneously, we see various references in the documents on the own resources ambitions – not EU taxes of course – of the EU institutions. And indeed, assessing all together it is quite a lot.

At the same time, it is also interesting to see the functioning of decision-making processes surrounding all these international tax harmonisation ambitions and the concretisation thereof, i.e., from a rule of law perspective. This, for example, when it comes to the marginalisation, in fact, of the role of domestic parliaments in company tax reform, particularly in the context of Pillar Two, where much – if not all – of the action comes from Paris, the Inclusive Framework and OECD that is, rather than from the Commission and the Council in Brussels, or the individual EU Member States for that matter.

Tax policy to an ever-greater extent is not being discussed any more at the levels of the individual EU Member States' domestic parliaments. At the same time, the international and EU company tax debate is about the very foundations of our tax systems in the field of company taxation. For some time now, it has not been about the approach to tax avoidance and letterbox companies and conduits only. The subject matter on the table today is fundamental corporate tax reform.

Whether such is something good or something bad is a political discussion of course. Whatever the matter, there seems sufficient reason for a substantive discussion on the future of company taxation in the European Union, the curbing of the increasing administrative burdens for both companies and tax authorities, or perhaps a decluttering of tax rules, and the commitment of the EU Member States as to their policy autonomy in this regard, as well as the legitimacy of decision making in the company tax domain, by unanimity or perhaps at some point in time via qualified majority voting. And what about the legal status, for instance, from an EU law perspective that is, of all that what comes from the Inclusive Framework and the OECD? Nobody seems to know really. Challenge is coming, it seems.

Whatever the chances of success of the European Commission's proposals and ambitions, the international and EU tax-debate on how those multinational enterprises should be taxed on their investment returns does not seem to be muted for the time being. And if developments unfold as intended, it will quite likely remain busy times in corporate taxation upcoming years.

CHAPTER 26

Harmful Tax Competition and the Code of Conduct for Business Taxation

Servaas van Thiel[1]

26.1 Introduction

Harmful tax competition can be understood in a wide sense as comprising all tax measures of one state that contribute to the erosion of the tax base of another state and, as such, public sector harmful tax measures facilitate private sector aggressive tax planning and tax avoidance. It may be clear, therefore, that certain measures against tax avoidance, such as increasing corporate reporting obligations, facilitating exchange of information or adopting a minimum corporate income tax rate, greatly reduce the scope for harmful tax competition. This chapter should thus be read together with the chapters that discuss different aspects of the fight tax against tax avoidance (see inter alia chapter 19).

The European chapter on harmful tax competition starts with the November 1992 ECOFIN Council conclusions on the Ruding Committee report, which essentially rejected far reaching proposals for tax harmonization in the EU, but instead called for stepping up the fight against tax avoidance and harmful tax competition.[2] In 1996, Commissioner Mario Monti wrote to the informal ECOFIN[3] in Verona that excessive tax competition and a 'race to the bottom' were causing erosion of national tax bases (first Monti paper).[4] After further consultations between the Commissioner and Member States, ECOFIN adopted

---

1 Prof van Thiel is Emeritus Professor at the Brussels School of Governance/Institute for European Studies of the Free University Brussels (VUB) and Guest Professor at the Institute for International and European Tax Law at the Vienna University of Business and Economics (WU). He is an expert judge in the Tax Chamber of the Regional Court of Appeal of Den Bosch, Netherlands. From 2004 to 2010 he was Head of the Tax unit of the EU Council of Ministers and in this capacity acted as the Secretary to the Code of Conduct Group. Comments are welcome at: servaasvanthiel@hotmail.com.

2 The Council, amongst others: 'endorses the concern expressed by the Commission and the Ruding Committee about the effects of special tax arrangements designed to attract internationally mobile capital and other tax incentives where these tax arrangements of incentives result in loss of revenue to other Member States and unfair competition; believes that consideration is urgently needed of possible remedies to this problem in general', 1621st Council meeting Economic and Financial Questions, 23 November 1992, 10088/92 (Presse 216), available at: https://koflerge.org/wp-content/uploads/2019/01/ruding_council.pdf

3 The Council of Ministers of the European Union meets in different compositions and the 'ECOFIN' Council consists of Ministers of the EU Member States that are responsible for economic affairs and finance.

4 Taxation in the European Union, Discussion paper for the informal meeting of the ECOFIN (Economy and Finance) Council, SEC(96) 487 final of 20 March 1996, Page 11.

a tax package in December 1997, that included a 'Resolution on a Code of Conduct for Business taxation' (Code) which provided for a collective review of potentially harmful business tax measures and an invitation to the Commission to clarify how the EU State aid prohibition should be understood and applied in the area of direct business taxation.[5] In 2022, ECOFIN revised the Code Resolution (effective as from 1 January 2023)[6] and rephrased the scope of the Code's review process to cover not only potentially harmful 'preferential tax measures' but also potentially harmful 'tax features of general application'.[7] In spite of extensive discussions from the outset, the Code only applies to business taxation and not to personal taxation which may, however, also contain measures that may distort the location of business activity in the Union.[8]

Since 2023, the Code applies to (potentially and/or actually harmful) 'preferential tax measures' and to 'tax features of general application', which affect, or may affect, in a significant way the location of business activity in the Community' (point A of the Code). Potentially harmful preferential tax measures are those that provide for a significantly lower effective level of taxation than the general tax level in a member state (Point B 1), and potentially harmful tax features of general application are those which create opportunities for double non-taxation or that can lead to the double or multiple use of tax benefits, in connection with the same expenses, amount of income or chain of transactions (Point B 2).[9] The Code provides for different criteria to assess whether potentially harmful tax measures are actually harmful (see 23.3 and 23.4.5).

The Code is a 'gentlemen's agreement' between EU Member States to tackle harmful tax competition by means of a collective review process, accompanied by a political commitment to phase out existing harmful tax measures (roll-back) and not to introduce

---

5 1 December 1997 ECOFIN Conclusions, with Annex 1 'Resolution on a Code of Conduct for business taxation'. https://eur-lex.europa.eu/legal-content/EN/TXT/?uri=CELEX%3A31998Y0106%2801%29. The 1997 Resolution was replaced in 2022 by the 8 November 2022 Council conclusions on the reform of the Code of Conduct for Business Taxation at: https://www.consilium.europa.eu/media/59966/st14452-en22.pdf. See also Official Journal of the EU, nr C 433/01 of 15 November 2022 at 1 to 5.

6 See the 8 November 2022 Council conclusions on the reform of the Code of Conduct for Business Taxation at: https://www.consilium.europa.eu/media/59966/st14452-en22.pdf published in the Official Journal of the EU, nr C 433/01 of 15 November 2022 at 1 to 5. The revised Code applied as from 1 January 2023 but 'general features' could be notified and assessed only as from January 2024 and only to the extent adopted or modified after 1 January 2023 (point P of the Code).

7 The Code of Conduct uses different terminology including 'harmful tax measures' (Seventh Preambular paragraph to and point M of the 1997 Code; Seventh Preambular para of the 2022 Code), "business taxation tax measures' (first line of the 1997 Code), measures' (Point A the 1997 Code), 'tax measures' (points A to C, E to H, and J of the 1997 Code; Seventh Preambular para of the 2022 Code and points A and following of the 2022 Code), and 'preferential tax measures (2022 Code). This Chapter uses the term (potentially or actually) harmful tax measures to cover both 'preferential tax measures' and 'features of general application' (cf. Point A of the 2022 Code).

8 See for instance European Parliament (2022): Harmful Practices and Competition in the Area of Personal Income and Wealth Taxation', available at: https://www.europarl.europa.eu/RegData/etudes/IDAN/2022/703343/IPOL_IDA(2022)703343_EN.pdf.

9 See the 8 November 2022 Council conclusions on the reform of the Code of Conduct for Business Taxation at: https://www.consilium.europa.eu/media/59966/st14452-en22.pdf published in the Official Journal of the EU, nr C 433/01 of 15 November 2022 at 1 to 5.

new ones (stand-still).[10] The Code is thus an early example of what the European Council in March 2000 would call the 'Open Method of Coordination (OMC)', a non-regulated form of political (diplomatic) cooperation and coordination between Member States on the basis of best practices.[11]

To carry out the collective review process, the Council created the 'Code of Conduct Group' in 1998,[12] consisting of representatives of all Member States and the Commission, and served by the Council Secretariat. It reports to the ECOFIN and its meetings and documents were initially, confidential, but many of its reports and meeting documents have now been made public,[13] in particular since the Council, in its conclusions of 8 December 2015, agreed "that its results, in particular its 6-monthly reports, are systematically made available to the public" (paragraph 16).[14] Important for a good understanding of the work of the Code Group is the 'Guidance' that has been agreed throughout the years on a large number of topics and the publication of which is regularly updated (lastly in November 2024).[15]

Initially, the Group focused on phasing out harmful tax measures of single EU Member States and their overseas territories and on monitoring their respective standstill and roll back commitments, but gradually the Group also started reviewing popular tax measures applied by several Member States, such as patent boxes, zero/10 regimes, special economic zones, and notional interest deductions (see 23.3). Moreover, it began formulating coordinated policy responses to cross-border tax issues or tax measures with multi-jurisdictional effects, such as rulings, EU inbound profit transfers and mismatches between tax systems. This again prompted the 2022 extension of the scope of the Code to 'features of general application' (see 23.4). From the outset, the Group has also tackled third country issues to ensure a level playing field between economic operators of the

10 The Preamble to the Code emphasises 'that the Code of Conduct is a political commitment and does not affect the Member States' rights and obligations or the respective spheres of competence of the Member States and the Community resulting from the Treaty'.

11 Point 37 of the Lisbon European Council Conclusions reads: 'Implementation of the strategic goal will be facilitated by applying a new open method of coordination as the means of spreading best practice and achieving greater convergence towards the main EU goals.' Point 37 mentions 'fixing guidelines combined with specific timetables', 'translating these European guidelines into national and regional policies' and 'periodic monitoring, evaluation and peer review organised as mutual learning processes. (available at: https://www.europarl.europa.eu/summits/lis1_en.htm).

12 See 1998 'Council Conclusions concerning the establishment of the Code of conduct Group (Business Taxation)', OJ C 99/1 of 9 March 1998.

13 Progress reports and meeting documents are available at http://www.consilium.europa.eu/en/council-eu/preparatory-bodies/code-conduct-group/, and *room*-and *working documents* and *informal meeting minutes* are partly available at: https://circabc.europa.eu/faces/jsp/extension/wai/navigation/container.jsp). Access to a non-public COC document may be requested from the Council under the EU Transparency Regulation (EC) No. 1049/2001.

14 See Council Document ST 15148/15.

15 Whenever reference is made in this Chapter to guidance agreed by the Code Group, the text can be found in: 'Agreed guidance by the Code of Conduct Group (business taxation): 1998- 2024, Council Document 5814/7/18 REV 7 of 14 November 2024 at 102 (Available at: https://data.consilium.europa.eu/doc/document/ST-5814-2018-REV-7/en/pdf).

EU and third countries (see 23.5), and, after more than 25 years, the conclusion must be that the Code Group has been rather successful in its work (see 23.6).[16]

26.2 How the Code works in practice: criteria and review process

26.2.1 The Code criteria

The Code contains a number of criteria to determine whether preferential tax measures (point B 1) and tax features of general application (point B 2) are harmful and thus need to be rolled-back.

A preferential tax measure is considered *potentially harmful* by the Code Group if it provides for a significantly lower effective level of taxation than the general level of taxation in the Member State concerned (i.e. when it departs from the benchmark tax system), so that it affects or may affect in a significant way the location of business activity in the Community. This 'gateway criterion' was important because competitive *general features* of a tax system, including a zero-rate corporate income tax, were not considered problematic at that time.[17]

To assess whether potentially harmful preferential tax measures are *actually harmful* the Code Group tests them against the following non-exhaustive list of criteria:

- Ring-fencing: tax advantages are ring-fenced de facto or de jure from the domestic market, e.g., they are accorded only to non-residents or in respect of transactions carried out with non-residents (Ring-fencing 1: off-shore characteristics), or they do not affect the national tax base but rather tax bases of other member states (Ring-fencing 2: beggar thy neighbour);
- Lack of substance: tax advantages are granted even without any real economic activity and substantial economic presence within the Member State offering such tax advantages,
- Lack of arm's length dealing: rules for profit determination in respect of activities within a multinational group of companies depart from internationally accepted principles, notably the rules agreed upon within the OECD,
- Non-transparency: tax measures lack transparency, including where legal provisions are relaxed at administrative level in a non-transparent way.

---

16 See also Court of Auditors (2024): 'Special Report 27/2024: Combatting harmful tax regimes and corporate tax avoidance – The EU has established a first line of defence, but there are shortcomings in the way measures are implemented and monitored', points 67 ff. Available at: https://www.eca.europa.eu/en/publications/SR-2024-27.

17 This changed when the Code's scope was extended to cover also 'tax features of general application of a Member State, which create opportunities for double non-taxation or that can lead to the double or multiple use of tax benefits'. To be noted, also, that in October 2021, 137 jurisdictions participating in OECD/G20 Inclusive Framework, agreed on a 15% minimum tax on profits of multinational enterprises (Pillar 2), and that the European Commission followed up with a proposal for an EU wide minimum corporate income tax. Com 2021 (823) final, Proposal for a Council Directive on ensuring a global minimum level of taxation for multinational groups in the Union. (https://ec.europa.eu/taxation_customs/system/files/2021-12/COM_2021_823_1_EN_ACT_part1_v11.pdf).

In principle therefore, a preferential tax measure that departs from the benchmark risks to be harmful if discriminatory (i.e. if only benefitting -transactions with-non-residents or eroding the tax base of other Member States), if not based on substance (no real economic activity; no real presence; non arm's length) or if non-transparent (e.g. no provided for by law but by discretionary decisions; not subject to exchange of information). Interestingly, these broad criteria partly overlap with the State aid criteria (non-benchmark tax measure that provides a selective advantage and is thus discriminatory) (see Chapter 15). This is probably why Member States, when embarking on the Code process, requested the Commission to clarify its policy on State aid and tax measures, which resulted in a 1998 Commission Notice.[18] Nevertheless, the exact demarcation line between harmful tax measures and prohibited State aid measures has remained blurred (see also point J of the Code). In fact, an intended tax measure allowed by the Commission under the State aid rules is not automatically an acceptable measure under the Code, and vice versa, and a further complication is that a contested tax measure may constitute both a State aid ad a harmful tax measure, as well as a discrimination contrary to the Treaty Freedoms.[19]

Tax features of general application (point B2) are considered potentially harmful by the Code Group if they create opportunities for double non-taxation or if they can lead to the double or multiple use of tax benefits, in connection with the same expenses, amount of income or chain of transactions (thus leading to a lower-than-normal tax liability or to deferred taxation). To determine whether potentially harmful tax features of general application are actually harmful, the Code Group considers the following cumulative criteria and the existence of a direct causal link between them:

- the tax feature of general application is not accompanied by appropriate anti-abuse provisions or other adequate safeguards and as a result, leads to double non-taxation or allows the double or multiple use of tax benefits in connection with the same expenses, amount of income or chain of transactions; and
- the tax feature of general application affects in a significant way the location of business activity in the Union, taking into account the fact that the location of business activity can also be influenced by circumstances other than tax features.

26.2.2 The Code's review process

The Code's review process takes place in a number of steps set out in points E to H of the 2022 Code. First, tax measures that are potentially within the scope of the Code are notified by the Member State concerned, by another Member State or by the Commission

18 European Commission: Notice on the application of the State aid rules to measures relating to direct business taxation, *OJ C 384, 10.12.1998, p. 3–9. For a good insight into the parallel processes on harmful tax competition and State aid see*: Edoardo Traversa and Alessandra Flamini (2015): Fighting Harmful Tax Competition through EU State Aid Law: will the hardening of soft law suffice?'. European State Aid Law Quarterly, Vol. 14, No. 3 (2015), pp. 323-331.

19 Case C-478/98, *Commission v. Belgium*, EU:C:2000:497, [2000] ECR I-7587 concerned a Belgian interest withholding tax exemption upon the issuing of Belgian State bonds on the euro-bond market, but with a prohibition for Belgian residents to buy the bonds, which the Court considered to be incompatible with the free movement of capital.

(point E and 2024 Guidance[20]). Second, once a notification is received, the Commission and the Member State concerned enter into consultations so as to arrive at an agreed description of the measure (points F1 and I and 2016 Guidance[21]). Third, that agreed description of the tax measure is subsequently submitted to the Code Group, together with the Commission's initial assessment of its harmfulness (point I). Fourth, the Group discusses the tax measure and makes a collective assessment of whether it is harmful or not (points F and G of the 2022 Code). Fifth, the findings of the Group are presented to the Council, in a report that records the position of the Group while reflecting any dissenting views of individual Member States in footnotes (point H). Sixth, once the Council endorses the Report, Member States are politically committed to a stand-still, i.e. no new applications of the tax measure concerned and no introduction of similar harmful measures (point C) and a roll back, i.e. abolition or phase out of the measure or removal of its harmful effects, generally, within a period of two years, or the introduction of anti-abuse measures or other safeguards (point D).[22] Seventh, the Group monitors the standstill and roll back on a regular basis.

In practice, the assessment of specific tax measures has proven to be more of a political-than an academic or judicial exercise, because Member States inevitably took different views on the interpretation of the assessment criteria and their application in practice. In spite of this, at least three factors have helped to ensure the workability and even the success of the exercise.

First, a dominant role was played in the review process by the European Commission. It not only drafted the initial lists of potentially harmful measures, with summary descriptions and initial assessments, but when dissenting Member States risked jeopardising the progress, the Commission would sometimes resort to its State aid powers whether at the explicit invitation of the Council or not (see, for instance, the 15 investigations initiated in 2001).[23]

20 'Procedural issues: Guidance on the notification of preferential tax measures under para E of the Cocde' (Pages 84-96 of Council Document 5814/7/18 REV 7, supra footnote 16). The guidance concerns: the annual timetable for the notification of tax measures; the identification of measures that should be notified to other Member States; the identification of in which year a measure should be notified, and the content of notifications.

21 Procedural issues: Guidance on the provision of information in the review process. (Pages 97-99 of Council Document 5814/7/18 REV 7, supra footnote 16).

22 For agreed guidance on standstill and roll-back see Pages 4- 10 of Council Document 5814/7/18 REV 7, supra footnote 16.

23 See Commission Press Release IP 01/981 of 11 July 2001: The Commission launches large scale State aid investigation into business taxation schemes, available at: file:///Users/servaasvanthiel/Downloads/Commission_launches_large_scale_state_aid_investigation_ into_business_taxation_schemes.pdf. The investigation concerned 15 tax provisions in 12 Member States and focused on preferential tax arrangements granted to multinational companies or to companies active in the insurance and financial sector. The regimes concerned coordination centres in Belgium, Germany, Luxembourg and Spain; Headquarters and Logistics Centres in France; taxation of foreign income/companies in Ireland and Greece; Finance companies in Luxembourg and the Netherlands; Insurance in Finland and Sweden; offshore Companies in Gibraltar; Trieste tax incentives in Italy.

Second, as provided for in point L of the Code, the Group has regularly agreed guidance on implementation of the Code, including on the assessment criteria and their application to specific types of tax measures (such as interest and royalty regimes, holding companies and special economic zones), and on procedural issues, mismatches and third country issues. In addition, Member States agreed to collectively monitor their implementation of agreed Guidance and to rollback incompatible measures within two years (similar to the implementation period of an EU Directive). The Group files specific reports on this monitoring exercise to the Council.[24]

Third, the Group used an interesting decision-making procedure that in a way abandoned the traditional unanimity rule that guides tax related conclusions and decisions of the Council. Member States had agreed 'that the Reports of the Group forwarded to the Council will reflect either the unanimous opinion of its members or the various opinions expressed in the course of the discussions'.[25] But a practice developed under which the Code Group would report to the Council that it had come to a broad 'consensus' on a measure, even if there was no unanimous opinion amongst its members. In that case, the broad consensus conclusion of 'the Group' would be recorded in the Report and the dissenting opinions of one or two Member States, would be recorded in a footnote. In most cases, the Council would subsequently endorse the Report, so that the broad consensus conclusion of 'the Group' would stand and the political stand-still and roll-back commitments would kick in.[26]

Even so, the road has been bumpy by times, as illustrated for instance by the fact that the tax package as a whole, was agreed by Council only in June 2003,[27] and by the crisis which unfolded in 2005 when five Member States objected against qualifying the Hungarian royalty box as a harmful tax measure, and refused to endorse the report of the Group at Council level. This incident caused considerable discussions in the Group which resulted in a 2008 agreed Guidance on the way conclusions are reached in the Code of Conduct Group. In this context, it was agreed that any Code Group reports to ECOFIN can still use the terms ' the Group' and 'broad consensus', in the case that all Member States (minus the one Member State concerned) share an opinion, as well as in other cases where Member States, other than the Member State concerned, have a dissenting opinion, and none of these Member States oppose the use of the wording 'the Group' and 'broad consensus' (e.g. in case Member States might technically object to an evaluation of a measure but do not politically object to the end result of the Group at ECOFIN level).[28]

24 Pages 107-111 and 129-131 of Council Document 5814/7/18 REV 7, supra footnote 16.

25 Para 14 of the 1998 'Council Conclusions concerning the establishment of the Code of Conduct Group (Business Taxation)', OJ C 99/1 of 9 March 1998.

26 See also para 30 of the first Report of the Group. Report of the Code of Conduct Group of 28 November 1999, Council Doc. SN 4901/99, available at: https://ec.europa.eu/taxation_customs/system/files/2016-09/primarolo_en.pdf (accessed 15 February 2022).

27 The agreement on the tax package was complicated by a conditioning request by Italy concerning fines imposed on its farmers for exceeding their milk production quota. See 'Agence Europe' Daily Bulletin 8475, of 4 June 2003, at https://agenceurope.eu/aewebsite_dev/en/bulletin/article/8475/11.

28 Page 14-20 of Council Document 5814/7/18 REV 7, supra footnote 16.

26.3 Outcome on preferential tax measures

26.3.1 *Harmful preferential tax measures of Member States and their territories*

By adopting the Code, Member States committed themselves not to introduce new harmful tax measures (stand-still),[29] and to amend existing laws and practices to the extent necessary to eliminate any harmful measures (roll-back).[30] The review process of the Code Group initially focused on screening the tax measures of the 15 Member States and territories (1999) and the 10 acceding States (2003-2004), after which standstill and roll back became routine items on the Code Group's agenda.

As regards the 15 EU Member States and their associated territories,[31] the November 1999 Report of the Code of Conduct Group to the ECOFIN Council listed 271 tax measures that were examined by the group. Of these, around 70 tax measures were considered harmful and grouped in the following 6 categories:

First, under the heading: *financial services, group financing measures and royalty payments*, 8 financial services measures were considered harmful because they provided no or low tax levels. In addition, 6 group financing measures were considered harmful because of low or no tax levels resulting from a formulaic, non-arm's length, profit apportionment between head office and branch, from excess reserve allowances or from fixed profit margins. Finally, 2 royalty measures were considered harmful because of low or no tax levels resulting from reduced nominal tax rates or fixed profit margins.

Second, under the heading *Insurance, reinsurance and captive insurance*, 10 measures were considered harmful because of low or no tax levels due to excessive tax-free reserves, long deferrals, broad exemptions, reduced tax rates or fixed tax bases.

Third, under *intra-group services*, 13 measures were considered harmful, essentially, because of low or no tax levels due to non-arm's length transfer pricing rulings that were

29 The Code clarifies in C that Member States will therefore respect the principles underlying the code when determining future policy and will have due regard for the review process (referred to in paragraphs E to I of the Code) in assessing whether any new tax measure is harmful.

30 The Code clarifies in D: Member States commit themselves to re-examining their existing laws and established practices, having regard to the principles underlying the code and to the review process outlined in paragraphs E to I. Member States will amend such laws and practices as necessary with a view to eliminating any harmful measures as soon as possible taking into account the Council's discussions following the review process.

31 The Group found 26 harmful tax measures in Aruba (4), Netherlands Antilles (3), Jersey (4), Guernsey (5), Isle of Man (6), British Virgin Islands (1) and Gibraltar (3) after examination of 85 tax measures of Gibraltar, Greenland, Faroe Islands, New Caledonia, French Polynesia, Wallis and Futuna Islands, French Southern & Antarctic Territories, Mayotte, Saint-Pierre and Miquelon, Netherlands Antilles, Aruba, East Timor, Macao, Anguilla, Guernsey, Jersey, Isle of Man, Bermuda, British Antarctic Territory, British Indian Ocean Territory, British Virgin Islands, Cayman Islands, Falkland Islands, Montserrat, Pitcairn Island, St Helena and dependencies, South Georgia & South Sandwich Islands, Turks and Caicos Islands, UK Sovereign Base Areas in Cyprus. See pages 26 to 28 and 255 to 299 of Council Doc. SN 4901/99, available at: https://ec.europa.eu/taxation_customs/system/files/2016-09/primarolo_en.pdf (accessed 15 February 2022).

based on the cost-plus or resale-minus methods. The use of such methods was considered harmful in particular when a comparable uncontrolled price might reasonably be obtained, or when there was no individual examination of the underlying facts of the particular case or no regular review of the mark-up or margin against normal commercial criteria. They were also considered harmful if a reduction in the expense base was allowed for the purposes of determining the taxable income, such as in the case of Belgian coordination centres and Belgian and Dutch US foreign sales company rulings.

Fourth, under *Holding companies*, 7 measures were considered harmful mainly because of low or no tax levels due to participation exemptions granted in respect of dividends from none or low taxed profits. But asymmetrical measures under which holding companies were allowed to exempt their capital gains from the tax base while being able to include their capital losses as tax deductible costs, were also considered harmful.

Fifth, under *Exempt and Offshore Companies*, 8 tax exemptions and 7 offshore company measures were considered harmful if they were restricted to companies with non-resident shareholders, or if businesses with local residents did not qualify, or if the measure was targeted at mobile capital.

Sixth, 9 *Miscellaneous measures* were considered harmful including notional capital cost deductions (2), reduced rates applicable in free zones (2) or to certain activities (2), and significant tax base reductions (3) (paragraphs 54 to 59).

Even though the rollback of these harmful tax measures was formally agreed only in June 2003,[32] the ECOFIN Council agreed on 27 November 2000 to phase out headquarters-, finance-and holding companies within a period of 2 to 5 years and invited the Commission to take State aid action on other measures. The phase out was realised in the agreed time-frame and the Commission initiated fifteen State aid procedures against non-benchmark tax advantages for financial-, co-ordination-, headquarters-, insurance-and offshore activities. Thirteen of these measures had also figured on the 1999 list of potentially harmful national tax measures. They were abandoned, adapted or taken to the European Court, which, however, did not uphold their substance (merely concluding insufficient transitional provisions in some cases).[33]

With regard to the ten States that acceded to the EU in 2004,[34] the Council Working Party on Enlargement (Tax Experts) reviewed 52 potentially harmful tax measures, and established a list of 30 measures that were found harmful under the Code, while

32 For an analysis of the emerging consensus on the 'tax package' see: European Commission, Taxation and customs union, Taxation, Working Paper 10 (2006): A history of the "tax package" The principles and issues underlying the community approach'. The tax package is contained as an annex to Council Doc 13898/00 FISC 207 and was approved by Council on 27 and 28 November 2000, but not made public.

33 See: Case T-348/03, *Koninklijke Friesland Foods v. Commission*, EU:T:2007:256, [2007] ECR II-101, and Joined cases C-182/03 and C-217/03, *Belgium and Forum 187 v. Commission*, EU:C:2006:416, [2006] ECR I-3875.

34 Estonia, Latvia, Lithuania, Poland, Hungary, Czechia, Slovakia, Slovenia, Cyprus and Malta.

simultaneously agreeing on the rollback measures envisaged or already undertaken for 27 of these measures, including 9 from Cyprus, 7 from Malta and 5 from Slovakia.[35]

Since 2004, the Group continuously assesses newly notified tax measures and monitors the implementation of 'standstill' (to ensure that no new harmful tax measures are introduced) and 'rollback' commitments (to ensure that measures which were found to constitute harmful tax competition are discontinued and not reintroduced). For details on the concrete measures examined by the group, reference is made to the addenda to the twice-yearly progress reports to the ECOFIN, which are made available on the web site of the Council.[36] In 2024 the Council also published an updated overview of EU Member States' preferential tax regimes examined by the Code of Conduct Group (Business Taxation) since its creation in March 1998 (doc. 8602/8/20 REV 8).[37]

26.3.2 *From review of individual tax measures to multi-country policy-making*

Interestingly, the routine monitoring of potentially harmful tax measures over the years, has given rise to a number of more horizontal policy outcomes that affect more than one particular country, including, for instance, on patent boxes, zero/10 regimes, special economic zones, and notional interest deductions.

First, as regards patent boxes, the Group had approved a French 19% reduced tax rate for royalty income (which was lower than the 33 1/3% benchmark rate), provided it was available regardless of the place of residence of the payer of the royalties,[38] an approach that was also approved by the European Commission under the State aid rules.[39] This green light for the French measure resulted in a proliferation of patent boxes in EU Member States (and third countries),[40] but in 2016 the Group agreed to tighten the rules by requiring that all regimes should comply with the OECD modified nexus approach

35 Council Document 13213/03 ELARG 94 FISC 138 available at: https://data.consilium.europa.eu/doc/document/ST-13213-2003-INIT/en/pdf.

36 Available on the web site of the Council at: https://www.consilium.europa.eu/en/documents-publications/public-register/ccg-reports/.

37 Council Document ST-8602-2020-REV-8, of 9 December 2024, available at: https://data.consilium.europa.eu/doc/document/ST-8602-2020-REV-8/en/pdf.

38 See Progress report of 23 November 1999, doc. no. 4901/99 (available at: https://ec.europa.eu/taxation_customs/system/files/2016-09/primarolo_en.pdf accessed 15 February 2022), p. 13 and Progress report of 6 March 2003, doc. no. 7018/1/03 REV 1 (available at: https://data.consilium.europa.eu/doc/document/ST-7018-2003-REV-1/en/pdf accessed 15 February 2022), p. 23.

39 See: Commission State aid decision B 480/07 of 13 February 2008, O.J. C80, on the Spanish patent box regime.

40 According to the Tax Foundation, 14 of the 27 EU member States had a patent box regime in place in July 2021, including Belgium, Cyprus, France, Hungary, Ireland, Italy, Lithuania, Luxembourg, Malta, Netherlands, Poland, Portugal, Slovakia, and Spain (federal, Basque Country, and Navarra). Five Non-EU European countries also had a patent box, including Andorra, San Marino, Switzerland, Turkey, and the United Kingdom. The reduced tax rates provided under patent box regimes range from 0 percent in San Marino to 13.91 percent in Italy. See Ele Asen (2021): Patent Box Regimes in Europe, Tax Foundation post of 9 September 2021, published at: https://taxfoundation.org/patent-box-regimes-europe-2021/(accessed 23 March 2022).

(BEPS Action 5).[41] It subsequently assessed the patent boxes of Belgium, Cyprus, Hungary, Ireland, Italy, Portugal, the UK and the Netherlands as not being harmful,[42] while urging France to adapt its rules.[43]

A second multi-country issue, was the Group's evaluation of the 'zero/ten' regimes introduced in 2008 by Jersey, Guernsey and the Isle of Man. These regimes provided for a mainstream tax rate of 0% for business profits at company level, combined with deemed distribution provisions at shareholder level.[44] This cleverly designed combination of corporate and individual income tax measures thus ensured that only resident individual shareholders would be taxed on distributed and undistributed profits (ring-fencing). Though there was a discussion on whether the regimes were within the scope of the Code (which applies to business taxes, but not to individual income taxes), the Group did confirm the Commission's draft assessment,[45] which considered these regimes as effectively granting a tax exemption for business profits of foreign investors, and it qualified them as harmful.[46]

A third issue, concerned tax incentives in specific regional areas. With the particular situation of the outermost regions and small islands in mind, the Code had allowed tax incentives for regional development if in proportion to, and targeted at, the aims sought.[47] In June 2017, however, the Council nevertheless agreed Guidance that those tax incentives could be harmful, for instance if the zone favoured foreign investors or transactions with non-residents (ring-fencing) or if an economic presence or real economic activity was not required (no economic substance). Moreover, tax privileges could also be harmful if

---

41 A first 'Guidance on the modified nexus approach for IP regimes' was endorsed by the Council on 11 December 2014 (doc. 16553/1/14 REV 1 Annex 1). Pages 56-58 of Council Document 5814/7/18 REV 7, supra footnote 16. To prevent tax avoidance, the modified nexus approach requires a strong territorial connection between the R&D costs incurred to develop a patent or know-how and the profits made on the basis of that patent or know-how to which the patent box regime may be applied.

42 See e.g. progress report of 12 June 2017, doc. no. 10047/17, p. 9. Available at: https://data.consilium.europa.eu/doc/document/ST-10047-2017-INIT/en/pdf.

43 France initially considered that no adjustments to its regime were necessary on the ground that its patent box tax rate of 15% would 'not affect in a significant way the location of business activities', taking into account the effective tax levels in other Member States. The Group disagreed and reported to ECOFIN Council that France was in contravention of the agreement to start the legislative process necessary to bring its patent box in line with the modified nexus approach. See: progress report of 3 November 2016, doc. no. 13924/16 available at: https://data.consilium.europa.eu/doc/document/ST-13924-2016-INIT/en/pdf.

44 For a description of these regimes, see: room document #1 of 23 September 2010 (Jersey), room document #2 of 20 October 2010 (Guernsey) and room document #2 of 23 September 2010 (Isle of Man).

45 See: room document #1 of 19 November 2010 (Jersey); room document #2 of 19 November 2010 (Isle of Man) and room document #8 of 17 April 2012 (Guernsey).

46 For the Group's assessment of the regimes of Jersey and Isle of Man in 2011, see: informal meeting minutes of 17 February 2011 and progress report of 27 May 2011, doc. no. 10857/11, p. 5. For the assessment of the Guernsey regime in 2012, see: informal meeting minutes of 17 April 2012 and progress report of 11 June 2012, do. No. 10903/12, p. 4-5. Available at: https://data.consilium.europa.eu/doc/document/ST-10903-2012-INIT/en/pdf.

47 Para G of the Code of Conduct.

access criteria and procedures were not defined or published (lack of transparency) or in the absence of sun-set clauses and regular tax audits and reviews.[48] At its meeting of 23 November 2022, the Group concluded, on the basis of the results of a questionnaire, that all Member States are compliant with the Guidance, but that the measures in five Member States shall be "under particular scrutiny" with regard to highly mobile activities carried out in the SEZ. The Group agreed that a new monitoring of all the SEZ regimes in force at that point in time should take place in the future (e.g. 2027).[49]

A fourth issue concerned the notional interest deductions applied by several Member States. In 2019 Guidance, the Group agreed that NID regimes should be limited in scope to ensure they are focused on incentivizing the creation of additional equity. As such, a NID regime should be limited to new equity created after the starting date of the regime, while excluding own shares (to prevent a company to increase its equity and simultaneously subscribe the new shares), and shares held in other resident and non-resident legal persons (to avoid cascading of the NID through chains of equity injection). In addition, the application of the NID should neither create nor increase tax losses (and thus not generate a loss carry forward) and it should exclude assets not necessary for conducting business (e.g. luxury goods, artwork, etc.). Finally, there should be no deduction for capital which is allocated to a permanent establishment if the profits attributable to the permanent establishment are tax exempt.

26.4 The work of the Group on horizontal issues and tax features of general application

26.4.1 *Broadening the scope of the work of the Code Group*

In addition to assessing specific tax regimes introduced by one or several Member States, the Group also developed common policies on horizontal tax competition issues (i.e. targeting measures affecting more than one Member State) such as cross-border tax rulings, EU-inbound and outbound profit transfers and hybrid mismatches. Interestingly, this work of the Group sometimes served as a forerunner of legally binding measures. For example, the common policies agreed by the Group on exchange of information on tax rulings and on international hybrid mismatches were turned into hard law, i.e. into Article 8a of the DAC Directive (see Chapter 25) and Article 9 of the ATAD Directive (see Chapter 19). This work of the Group also prompted discussions on a possible extension of the Code Group's mandate which resulted in the 2022 revised Code of Conduct that applies also to 'tax features of general application' that create opportunities for double non-taxation or that can lead to the double or multiple use of tax benefits (see 23.4.5).

48 2017 'Guidance on Tax Privileges related to Special Economic Zones'. Pages 102-106 of Council Document 5814/7/18 REV 7, supra footnote 16.

49 See Report of the Code of Conduct Group of 24 November 2022 paragraph V and ADD 10. Council Document 14674/22, available at: https://data.consilium.europa.eu/doc/document/ST-14674-2022-INIT/en/pdf.

26.4.2 Cross border Tax Rulings and APA

Tax rulings and Advance Pricing Arrangements (APA)[50] have been at the centre of the Code Group's work from the outset, and in a first step, the Group agreed in June 2003, *to improve transparency of tax rulings*.[51] More in particular, it was agreed that the tax administration involved in the APA should notify the Member State affected by the APA as swiftly as possible, and that it should, upon request, provide all the further relevant information about the transactions covered by the APA.[52] To further increase transparency, the Group agreed in 2010 that domestic procedures on rulings and individual rulings suitable for horizontal application, should be published, notified to the Code Group and shared spontaneously with the other Member States concerned (specific reference was made to rulings on the existence of a PE or elements of its tax base; on the tax status of a hybrid entity; the tax value of assets acquired from another group member).[53] In 2014 the Group followed up by agreeing a detailed 'model instruction' for that spontaneous exchange of information concerning both the way in which that information should be exchanged (i.e. on the basis of a standard electronic form using the common communication network (CCN) between the competent authorities), the content of that information (at least a short summary in English or in a bilaterally agreed language) and on the need to provide feed-back if requested and to provide statistics for monitoring the use of cross border rulings and APA.[54]

Following the LuxLeaks scandal and the OECD BEPS initiative, the transparency guidelines were turned into hard law, when, on 6 October 2016, ECOFIN adopted a Commission proposal to amend the DAC Directive. As a result, from 1 January 2017 onwards, Member States are now legally required to automatically exchange specific information on cross-border rulings without the possibility of refusing on grounds of protection of business secrets (Article 8a(6)(b) DAC) (see Chapter 25).

In a second step, the Group decided to increase its own *scrutiny of tax rulings*. On 20 March 2013,[55] it agreed that Regimes providing advance certainty to intermediary financing or

50 A cross border tax ruling is a ruling in which a Member State provides advance interpretation or application of a legal provision for a cross-border situation or transaction of an individual taxpayer (hereafter: cross-border ruling), which is likely to be relevant for the tax authorities of another Member State. Advance Transfer Pricing Agreements are a specific type of cross border ruling relating to transfer pricing. See 2014 Model instruction for the spontaneous exchange of information on advance interpretations of legal provisions in cross border situations ("rulings"). Council Doc. 10608/14. Pages 29-38 of Council Document 5814/7/18 REV 7, supra footnote 16.

51 Pages 11-13 of Council Document 5814/7/18 REV 7, supra footnote 16.

52 Information should be provided on the basis of either Directive 77/799/EEC on Mutual Assistance, or a Double Taxation Convention, or national law, if it provides for a more extensive exchange of information).

53 Spontaneous exchange of information as foreseen in Arts 9 and 10 of Council Directive 2011/16/EU. (see Chapter 25). Page 22 of Council Document 5814/7/18 REV 7, supra footnote 16.

54 Pages 29-38 of Council Document 5814/7/18 REV 7, supra footnote 16.

55 Pages 27-28 of Council Document 5814/7/18 REV 7, supra footnote 16.

licensing activities, would be the object of particular scrutiny by the Code Group, if one or more of the following circumstances apply:

- The regime provides for a standard approach including fixed spreads for intermediary type companies rather than relying on a case-by-case approach taking account of all the facts and circumstances involved with particular regard to the functions performed and risks assumed;
- Advance certainty provided by a tax administration concerning the profits reported by an intermediary company does not comply with the OECD Transfer Pricing Guidelines throughout the period to which it relates including the use of an inappropriate transfer pricing methodology.
- Advance certainty provided by a tax administration is granted de jure or de facto without any terminal date or with automatic renewal. Similarly, if a renewal were granted on application, it would be potentially harmful if such cases were not periodically reviewed by the tax authority to ensure an individual examination of the underlying facts and to check that the conditions are at arm's length.
- The regulations covering the conditions for granting advance certainty for intermediary companies are not publicly available;
- The regulations covering the conditions for granting advance certainty for intermediary companies do not ensure effective exchange of information of the methodology applied and of the arm's length profit agreed with other concerned MS.
- The regime is not equally available (whether on a de jure or de facto basis) to domestic commercial activities or requires no substantial domestic presence.

Third, in 2016, the Group agreed to *common procedural requirements* applying to the issuance, monitoring and review of tax rulings.[56] These are partly based on BEPS Action 5 deliverables, and concern issues such as the process of granting a ruling, the term of the ruling and subsequent checks and revisions, and the exchange of information on and publication of rulings. As regards the granting of rulings, it was agreed that official rules and administrative procedures for rulings should be published (transparency requirement), that applications for rulings should be in writing and accompanied by a detailed ruling file (documentation requirement) and that the tax ruling itself should also be in writing, granted only by the competent authority and involving at least two officials (4 eyes requirement), who should check precedent (consistency requirement). As regards the terms of the ruling, it was agreed that tax rulings should be binding on the tax authority, that APAs should be granted only for a fixed period of time (sunset requirement) and should be subject to review before extension or in case of a change in the underlying facts or circumstances (review requirement). The ruling should be revised or cancelled if based on an incorrect application or a change of laws or circumstances.

Finally, the Code Group, with the support of the European Commission and the EU Joint Transfer Pricing Forum (JTPF) has been working on common policies in the area of transfer

56 Pages 80-83 of Council Document 5814/7/18 REV 7, supra footnote 16.

pricing, including common standards for the alignment of transfer prices to actual value creation and to standards for transfer pricing documentation, in line with BEPS.[57]

26.4.3 EU-inbound and outbound profit transfers

In the early years, between 1998 and 2003, the Group reviewed the participation exemption for intra-group dividends applied by several Member States, and discussed the problem of double non-taxation of dividends paid by low-or non-taxed third-country subsidiaries to EU companies established in Member States applying a participation exemption to such inbound dividend flows. Multinationals of EU Member States that did not apply a participation exemption were likely to channel third country group dividends through a sub-holding in a Member State that did apply a participation exemption (i.e. the cheapest EU entry point), thus avoiding the tax that would have been payable, had the dividends been paid directly to the (ultimate) parent company in non-participation exemption Member States. Once within the EU, the group dividends could flow tax-free from the sub-holding to the ultimate EU parent company, under the EU Parent-Subsidiary Directive (see Chapter 16). This made it pointless for any Member State to try to tax third country subsidiary dividends if any other Member State did not tax them.

The Code Group Report of 23 November 1999 therefore required participation exemption regimes to contain either a subject-to-tax clause as regards the profits of the third-country subsidiary, or 'appropriate CFC-legislation'.[58] The 'interim report' of 27 November 2000 clarified once again that Member States should ensure that their participation exemption regimes should be equipped with 'effective anti-abuse or countermeasures'.[59] As a result, some Member States, such as Denmark and the Netherlands, had to change their participation exemption regimes.

In 2010, the Group agreed that Member States that applied participation exemptions should enact effective anti-abuse provisions in the form of either a switch-over clause (i.e. switching from a tax exemption for dividends from low taxed third-country subsidiaries, to a direct foreign tax credit, i.e. the inclusion of the dividends from low taxed third-country subsidiaries into the recipient's tax base while allowing the recipient a credit for foreign tax paid) *or* CFC-rules (taxing the low-taxed subsidiary profits in the hands of the EU parent company as if it were a branch or as if it had distributed its profits

57 See Council Conclusions of 8 December 2015, doc. no. 15150/15, par. 24, p. 5: "(...).INVITES the Code of Conduct Group to assess the opportunity, in the light of the fourth criterion, of developing EU guidance for implementing OECD BEPS conclusions on Actions 8-9-10 (aligning transfer pricing outcomes with value creation) and on Action 13 (Guidance on transfer pricing Documentation), with the support of the Commission and its advisory bodies, notably the EU Joint Transfer Pricing Forum; (...)".

58 Progress report of 23 November 1999, doc. no. 4901/99, available at: https://ec.europa.eu/taxation_customs/system/files/2016-09/primarolo_en.pdf (accessed 15 February 2022).

59 Progress report of 20 November 2001, doc. no. 13563/00, available at: https://data.consilium.europa.eu/doc/document/ST-15434-2005-INIT/en/pdf (accessed 15 February 2022).

to the EU parent).[60] In 2016, the Commission suggested to improve the effectiveness of the Member States' switch-over clauses and/or CFC provisions, but the Group noted that the CFC-provisions in the ATAD would render the Group's work on this issue obsolete.[61]

A similar problem arises for EU outbound profit transfers. Third country multinationals are likely to channel these outbound transfers through the cheapest exit, i.e. through a sub-holding in a Member States with the lowest withholding tax on outbound dividends (whether based on a tax treaty or national law). To the extent, one Member State has concluded a zero withholding tax agreement with a third country, it makes little sense for other Member States to try to impose a withholding tax on the outbound dividends to that third country. This issue came up in the case law of the European Court, which can be summarised as follows: first, the benefits of the parent-subsidiary directive can, in principle, not be refused in respect of dividends paid from one Member State company to another Member State company, even if that other company has third country shareholders.[62] Second, and exceptionally, however, the benefits of the parent-subsidiary directive can, and indeed must, be refused in respect of dividends paid from one Member State company to an intermediate company established in another Member State by its third country shareholders, if that intermediate company constitutes an abuse of law (see Section 16.8).[63] Moreover, the EU law-maker included a general anti-avoidance rule (GAAR) in the Parent-Subsidiary Directive (see Chapter 16) and OECD countries adopted the OECD BEPS Action 6 on treaty-abuse.[64]

26.4.4 Cross border mismatches

Hybrid entities or situations can give rise to mismatches between two tax jurisdictions that can be exploited by taxpayers to reduce their overall tax burden, and they arise in particular if the same event gets a different legal qualification in different tax jurisdictions.

60 See Council Doc 5814/2018 Rev 6 available at: http://www.consilium.europa.eu/en/council-eu/preparatory-bodies/code-conduct-group/.

61 See: progress report of 28 November 2016, doc. no. 14750/16, p. 6-7 (available at: https://data.consilium.europa.eu/doc/document/ST-14750-2016-INIT/en/pdf). To be noted, however, that the switch-over clause did not make it into the ATAD, but it returned in the Commission's 2016 proposal for a CCCTB (see Section 11.6.2).

62 In Joined Cases C-504/16 Deister Holding and C613/16 Juhler Holding (ECLI: EU:C:2017:1009, available at: https://curia.europa.eu/juris/liste.jsf?language=en&num=C-504/16), the Court considered it incompatible with the parent subsidiary Directive and the freedom of establishment, for Germany to refuse, on grounds of combating tax avoidance, to exempt from withholding tax the outbound dividends paid to a parent company in another Member State, because that parent company was controlled by third country shareholders. The Court reached the same conclusion, as regards French anti-avoidance legislation, in case C6/16 *Eqiom and Enka* (ECLI:EU:C:2017:641, available at: https://curia.europa.eu/juris/liste.jsf?td=ALL&language=en&jur=C,T,F&num=c-6/16).

63 In Case C-116/16 T Danmark (ECLI:EU:C:2019:135, available at: https://curia.europa.eu/juris/liste.jsf?num=C-116/16), the Court held that the advantages of the parent subsidiary Directive (e.g. exemption from withholding tax) must be refused by Member States in the case of an abuse of law, i.e. when dividends are paid from an EU company to another EU company that has no economic substance and re-distributes those dividends almost immediately to its third country shareholders/beneficial owners.

64 See OECD BEPS Action 6 Prevention of Tax Treaty Abuse, at https://www.oecd.org/tax/beps/beps-actions/action6/.

One example of a hybrid situation is the profit participating loan, which may cause a mismatch when the Member State of the corporate taxpayer paying interest allows deduction of the interest from its tax base, whereas the Member State of the corporate taxpayer which receives the income considers it as a tax-exempt dividend income. In 2010 the Code Group agreed that, if payments under a hybrid loan arrangement are qualified as a tax-deductible expense for the debtor, Member States shall not exempt such payments as profit distributions under a participation exemption.[65]

A second example concerns hybrid entities that are considered tax transparent in one tax jurisdiction but not in another, which may give rise to double non-taxation mismatches as a result of a double deduction (tax relief is given in each of two Member States for the same payment, expense or loss) or a deduction without inclusion (tax relief is given in one of the two Member States but the amount is not included in taxable income in the other Member State). In 2014, the Group agreed that a double deduction should be avoided, by providing that the two Member States concerned should treat that entity as not being transparent, and that a deduction without inclusion should be avoided, by providing that the two Member States concerned should treat that entity as being transparent.[66]

A third example concerns hybrid permanent establishments (PE), i.e. activities of an enterprise that are considered a PE in one State but not in another, which may give rise to double non-taxation mismatches as a result of a double deduction (tax relief is given in each of two Member States for the same payment, expense or loss) or a non-taxation (in the source State where the activities are not considered a PE) without inclusion (in the other State where the income is exempt as attributable to a PE). In 2015, the Group agreed that the two Member States should prevent non-taxation without inclusion by treating the business activities concerned as if they were not being carried on through a permanent establishment, and to prevent a double deduction by treating the business activities concerned as if they were not being carried on through a permanent establishment.[67]

The Group's work on mismatches was partly overtaken by legislation, in particular the 2015 Anti-Tax Avoidance Directive (ATAD; see Chapter 19), which also includes a provision on exit taxation of companies, and an ever-expanding mandatory automatic exchange of tax information laid down in an ever-expanding Directive on administrative cooperation (DAC; see Chapter 25). Whereas ATAD 1 tackled intra-EU mismatches, the 2017 ATAD 2 tackled EU-Third Country mismatches.[68]

---

65 See Council Doc 5814/2018 Rev 6 available at: http://www.consilium.europa.eu/en/council-eu/preparatory-bodies/code-conduct-group/.

66 Guidance on hybrid entity mismatches concerning two member states. Pages 39-47 of Council Document 5814/7/18 REV 7, supra footnote 16).

67 Guidance on hybrid permanent establishment mismatches concerning two member states. Pages 48-55 of Council Document 5814/7/18 REV 7, supra footnote 16).

68 Council Directive (EU) 2017/952 of 29 May 2017 amending Directive (EU) 2016/1164 as regards hybrid mismatches with third countries, available at: https://eur-lex.europa.eu/legal-content/en/ALL/?uri=CELEX%3A32017L0952.

26.4.5 Tax features of general application

Even though the Code Group already examined double non-taxation and mismatches between tax systems (see 23.4.3. and 23.4.4.), it can be expected to do so more systematically under its new 2023 mandate which considers 'tax features of general application' potentially harmful if they create opportunities for double non-taxation or lead to the double or multiple use of tax benefits (in connection with the same expenses, amount of income or chain of transactions). Such effects may occur by virtue of any relevant feature of a Member State national tax system that leads to lower tax liability, including no tax liability, other than the nominal tax rate or deferred taxation as a feature of a distribution tax system (point B2).

When determining whether features of general application are actually harmful, the Code Group considers cumulatively whether they are not accompanied by appropriate anti-abuse provisions or other adequate safeguards while affecting in a significant way the location of business activity in the Union (need for a direct causal link).

26.5 Third Country Issues

Para M of the Code provides that it is advisable 'that principles aimed at abolishing harmful tax measures should be adopted on as broad a geographical basis as possible' and Member States committed themselves 'to promoting their adoption in third countries'. Since 2008 different efforts have been undertaken to export Union standards on transparency and fair tax competition, including by means of general good governance clauses to be included in trade, partnership and cooperation agreements with third countries, by means of negotiations with Switzerland on corporate income taxation and, since 2016, by means of the EU listing exercise of non-cooperative tax jurisdictions.[69]

As regards 'good governance', ECOFIN agreed in 2008[70] on the need to implement on as broad a geographical basis as possible, the "principles of good governance in the tax area, i.e., the principles of transparency, exchange of information and fair tax competition" and it, more specifically, recognised the need to include general good governance clauses in relevant agreements with third countries.[71] Subsequent negotiations with third countries, however, showed a mixed response, with some being outright hostile to the idea of such a reference in their agreement with the EU.[72]

69 Communication from the Commission to the European Parliament and the Council on an External Strategy for Effective Taxation. COM(2016) 24 final.

70 Conclusions of the ECOFIN Council of 14 May 2008, available at http://www.consilium.europa.eu.

71 "With a view to strengthening and developing economic activities while taking into account the need to develop an appropriate regulatory framework, the Parties recognise and commit themselves to implement the principles of good governance in the tax area, as subscribed to by Member States at Community level. To that effect, without prejudice to Community and Member States competences, the Parties will improve international cooperation in the tax area, facilitate the collection of legitimate tax revenues, and develop measures for the effective implementation of the above-mentioned principles" (point 4 of the Conclusions).

72 See Communication from the Commission to the European Parliament and the Council on an External Strategy for Effective Taxation, Brussels, COM(2016) 24 final of 28.1.2016, at point 3.1.

In 2012 the Commission recommended measures to encourage third countries to apply minimum standards of good governance in tax matters[73] and ECOFIN confirmed in its May 2013 Conclusions (points 19-21) that it wished 'to promote the principles of good governance in the tax area (transparency, exchange of information and fair tax competition) amongst third countries'. Almost as a side remark, however, it also 'invited consideration of whether developing a European list of third country non-cooperative jurisdictions' was appropriate. In this respect it supported the ongoing work of the Code of Conduct Group on Business Taxation and encouraged the Member States and the Commission to work closely with the OECD and the Global Forum on Transparency and Exchange of Information for tax purposes, 'to devise action plans aimed at combating lack of transparency and harmful tax practices in third countries'.

In 2014 an important positive result was achieved with the EU-Switzerland Joint Statement[74] on the abolition of special company tax regimes (such as the *Zug* and *Schwyz* regimes for management companies, mixed companies and holding companies). The agreement was, no doubt, helped by the fact that the Commission had adopted a 2007 Decision[75] based on the Article 23 prohibition of State aid of the 1972 EEC Trade Agreement with Switzerland.[76] In 2016, the Swiss federal parliament approved a wide-ranging tax reform that should have replaced these regimes, but in a 2017 referendum Swiss citizens and Swiss cantons rejected the reform. A new CIT Reform was adopted by referendum in 2019: it abolishes cantonal tax privileges for holding, domicile and mixed companies as of January 1, 2020, and introduces a combined federal, Cantonal and municipal corporate income tax rate of between 11.9% and 21.6%.[77]

In its 2016 Communication on an external tax strategy, the Commission followed up on the Council's 2013 suggestion to consider listing non-cooperative jurisdictions, with detailed suggestions for an EU process for assessing and listing third countries.[78] The Group screened almost 100 jurisdictions against three key criteria: tax transparency, fair taxation and the implementation of the OECD Base Erosion and Profit Shifting (BEPS) minimum standards. Under fair taxation, it assessed the harmfulness of tax measures on

73 Commission Recommendation of 6.12.2012 regarding measures intended to encourage third countries to apply minimum standards of good governance in tax matters, Council Doc. 17669/12 of 12 December 2012. See also: Commission Communication (2009): "Promoting good governance in tax matters", COM(2009) 201 final, Council Document 9281/09 of 29 April 2009. Communication from the Commission to the European Parliament, the Council and the European Economic and Social Committee - Tax and Development Cooperating with Developing Countries on Promoting Good Governance in Tax Matters SEC(2010)426 COM/2010/0163 final of 21 April 2010.

74 See: report of 1 October 2014, doc. no. 13759/14. The Statement has also been published on the Swiss federal government website (see: www.news.admin.ch).

75 Décision de la Commission du 13-II-2007 concernant l'incompatibilité de certains régimes suisses d'imposition des sociétés avec l'accord entre la Communauté économique européenne et la Confédération Suisse du 22 juillet 1972, C(2007) 411 final.

76 O.J. L 300 of 31 December 1972, p. 189–280.

77 See Grunblatt et.al. (2019): 'Swiss Tax Reform - Passed by the People's referendum', at: https://www.homburger.ch/en/insights/swiss-tax-reform-passed-by-the-peoples-referendum (accessed 21.2.1922).

78 See Communication from the Commission to the European Parliament and the Council on an External Strategy for Effective Taxation, Brussels, COM(2016) 24 final of 28.1.2016, at point 5.

the basis of previously agreed criteria (essentially the Code Criteria applied by analogy). In December 2017 the Council listed 17 non-EU countries or territories, that had not made sufficient commitments in response to the EU's concerns (Annex I), and noted that the other jurisdictions had responded with sufficient commitments, and needed to take effective action by the end of 2018 or 2019, to avoid being listed in the future (Annex II).[79]

The Code Group continued to monitor potentially harmful third country tax measures and in 2023, the Council published an updated overview of third country jurisdictions' preferential tax regimes and other measures examined by the Code of Conduct Group under EU listing criteria 2.1 and 2.2 (doc. 6430/23).[80]

Moreover, the Code Group revises the list of non-cooperative jurisdictions on an annual basis, lastly in October 2024.[81] The ongoing monitoring process of third country tax measures and regular revision of the black list takes place on the basis of a cooperative effort between different players including the Code Group Chair (who sends a letter to a third country if a potentially harmful tax measure has been identified within its jurisdiction), the European Commission (which sends a questionnaire to the jurisdiction concerned in order to come to an agreed description of the tax measure in question), the Code Group (which assesses the harmfulness of the tax measure concerned and, if applicable, prepares letters to be send letters to jurisdictions to invite them to repeal or amend their harmful measures) and the third country jurisdiction concerned (which initially shares information on its tax measures and subsequently commits to amend or repeal them if found harmful by the Code Group). In general, this process yields surprisingly positive results perhaps also because of the risk of EU member states taking counter measures if a third country jurisdiction refuses to cooperate or to amend its harmful tax measures.

Possible countermeasures (including of a non-tax nature[82]) against uncooperative jurisdictions were explored by the Code Group, and, in 2017 and 2019 Guidance,[83] Member

79 Council Doc 15429/17 FISC 345 ECOFIN 1088 of 5 December 2017, available at: https://data.consilium.europa.eu/doc/document/ST-15429-2017-INIT/en/pdf.

80 Council Document ST-6430-2023 of 17 February 2023, available at https://data.consilium.europa.eu/doc/document/ST-6430-2023-INIT/en/pdf.

81 The updated list contains the following 11 uncooperative jurisdictions: American Samoa, Anguilla, Fiji, Guam, Palau, Panama, Russian Federation, Samoa, Trinidad and Tobago, US Virgin Islands, and Vanuatu. Official Journal of the EU, OJ C 2024/6322 of 18 October 2024, pages 1-4, available at: https://eur-lex.europa.eu/legal-content/EN/TXT/PDF/?uri=CELEX:52024XG06322.

82 Non tax measures include Article 22 of Regulation (EU) 2017/1601 of the European Parliament and of the Council of 26 September 2017 establishing the European Fund for Sustainable Development (EFSD), the EFSD Guarantee and the EFSD Guarantee Fund, which contains a link to the EU list of non-cooperative jurisdictions. Furthermore, a link with the EU list of non-cooperative jurisdictions for tax purposes in other EU legislative acts would also be considered as a part of the defensive measures. Overall effects on the compliance by the jurisdictions with the Criteria as a result of such measures should be monitored by the Code of Conduct Group, as well as by the HLWP in the context of implementation of the EU external strategy on taxation.

83 Pages 100-101, 112-117 and 174-184 of Council Document 5814/7/18 REV 7 supra foornote 16.

States were invited to apply, as of 1 January 2021, at least one of the following defensive legislative measures against non-cooperative jurisdictions:

- Reinforced monitoring of certain transactions and increased audit risks for taxpayers benefiting from the regimes at stake or using structures or arrangements involving these jurisdictions.
- Non-deductibility of costs and payments directed to entities or persons in listed jurisdictions (for example interest, royalties and other concessions on intellectual property assets and service fees).
- Controlled Foreign Company (CFC) Rules (including the income of an entity in a listed jurisdiction, in the tax base of the taxpayer, in accordance with to the rules laid down in Articles 7 and 8 of the Anti-Tax Avoidance Directive (EU) 2016/1164).
- Withholding tax measures (withholding tax on interest, royalties, service fees or remuneration, when these payments are treated as received in listed jurisdictions)
- Limiting the participation exemption for dividends received from a listed jurisdiction.
- Switch-over rules;
- Reversal of the burden of proof;
- Special documentation requirements to reinforce the effect of any of the defensive measures;
- Mandatory disclosure by tax intermediaries of specific tax schemes with respect to cross-border arrangements.

In 2021, the Code Group published an overview of the defensive measures taken thus far, which revealed that all Member States had increased monitoring and auditing of transactions/taxpayers and that 17 Member States applied CFC rules, 16 the non-deductibility of costs, 11 a withholding tax, and 11 a limitation to the participation exemption. In addition, 3 Member States had reversed the burden of proof (1 in combination with special documentation requirements).[84]

Finally, the Code Group has also started working on potentially harmful tax regimes applied by more than one single third country jurisdiction. As regards foreign income exemption regimes, for instance, it was agreed in 2019 Guidance (revised in 2022)[85] that, though recommendable to prevent double taxation, these regimes may create situations of double-non taxation, for instance if passive income (including dividends, interest, royalties, and capital gains) is tax exempt without any conditions (e.g. an explicit link to some real activity in the jurisdiction) or if active income is exempt on the basis of a nexus definition that is non-compliant with the definition of a permanent establishment in the OECD Model. Third country jurisdictions could thus be invited to tax passive income, or implement adequate substance requirements to the entities concerned, have robust anti-abuse rules in place and remove any administrative discretion in determining the income to be excluded from taxation. They can also be asked to ensure the application

84 See November 2021 Progress Report of the Code Group. Council 14230/21, Annex at pages 18 to 43. https://data.consilium.europa.eu/doc/document/ST-14230-2021-INIT/en/pdf (accessed 16.2.2022).

85 Guidance on foreign source income exemption regime. Pages 161-164 of Council Document 5814/7/18 REV 7 supra footnote 16.

of internationally accepted principles in relation to the taxation of foreign source active income (notably the OECD definition of permanent establishment).

26.6 Conclusions

On *substance*, the Code Group's work has been rather successful in creating more transparency on Member States' tax systems and, together with the Commission's ongoing action on State aid, in weeding out the more obvious harmful measures that caused distortions on the internal market and resulted in the poaching by Member States of each other's tax base.

Since its establishment, the Group has reviewed over around 700 individual tax measures of Member States and third countries, and it has labelled around 200 of these as harmful. A wide variety of regimes has been reviewed, and more horizontal approaches have been formulated on special regimes such as interest and intellectual property boxes, insurance and re-insurance companies, group coordination, activities holding companies, finance-and conduit companies, finance branches, informal capital, as well as participation exemption regimes, tax-free zones, shipping regimes, ruling practices, and even generic corporate tax regimes which – due to their design – effectively tax certain (passive) income at a level lower than the normal effective level of taxation in the Member State concerned.

The Group's conclusions and the repeal of many national tax base reduction regimes had a converging effect on national corporate tax base definitions and may have increased the chances for a common corporate tax base (see Chapter 11 on CCCTB and Chapter 22 on BEFIT). At the same time, this shifted the focus from tax base competition to tax rate competition, with many Member States lowering their corporate income tax rates (while simultaneously broadening their tax bases and, where necessary for compensation, increasing consumption and environmental taxes). The minimum corporate income tax rate of 15% for large groups, which went into effect in 2024, has put a welcome first floor in this tax *rate* race to the bottom.[86] Tax competition between EU Member States has also shifted towards other aspects of the tax system. Interesting in this respect is that the old question of whether the scope of the Code of Conduct should be extended to personal income taxes, has come back to the forefront. In fact, preferential tax treatment of high income and wealth individuals has become a popular way to attract the mobile rich and whereas, in 1994, there were only five preferential personal income tax regimes in the European Union, in 2020, there were 28.[87] In this light it is perhaps a missed opportunity

86 In October 2021, the 137 jurisdictions participating in OECD/G20 Inclusive Framework, agreed on a 15% minimum tax on profits of multinational enterprises (Pillar 2). The European Commission followed up with a proposal for a minimum corporate income tax. (Com 2021 (823) final, Proposal for a Council Directive on ensuring a global minimum level of taxation for multinational groups in the Union), which was adopted in 2022 and applies as from 1 January 2024. (https://taxation-customs.ec.europa.eu/taxation/business-taxation/minimum-corporate-taxation_en).

87 Rita Szudoczky and Camilo Rodríguez Peña (2024): Preferential Personal Income Tax Regimes in the European Union: A New Form of Permitted (Harmful) Tax Competition?, World Tax Journal of May 2024 at 245 -288.

that the 2022 review of the mandate of the Code of Conduct Group did not extend the group's work to this new area of taks competition.

As regards the *method of work of the Code Group*, it is rather astonishing to note that in 25 years, it moved from the starting point of a voluntary exercise based on non-legally binding political commitments of the Member States working together in the framework of the Council, to a method that has gradually gathered features that make it more of a hybrid between the open method of coordination in which Member States work together and coordinate policies on the basis of best practices, and the traditional Community method of harmonisation, in which the Council and European Parliament, as EU institutions, adopt binding legislation on the basis of a Commission proposal. Four aspects of this movement are worth mentioning.

First, the examination by the Group of new tax measures or tax measures of new Member States has become so routine, that it can hardly be seen as a voluntary exercise anymore. In fact, a common spotlight has been placed on the adoption of new national tax measures which almost automatically makes any possible tax competition visible and thereby subject to a collective screening process that works on a 'broad consensus' rather than a unanimity basis.

Second, the Group moved from a case-by-case examination of national tax measures, to a much more horizontal approach in which it examines broad solutions to types of measures that are possibly harmful (such as non-arms-length rulings, tax incentives in economic zones), thus creating what literature has come to call 'quasi-legislation'.[88]

Third, in particular in the last 10 years, this more horizontal work has, in an increasing number of cases, indeed been translated in binding EU secondary legislation. ATAD 1, for instance, tackled intra-EU mismatches, and ATAD 2 tackled EU-Third Country mismatches, which had both been discussed in the Code Group. Likewise, the Group's guidance on transparency on tax rulings, was incorporated in the DAC Directives which provide for the automatic exchange of specific information on cross-border rulings. As such the Code Group's horizontal work is more and more a precursor for EU legislation.

Fourth, the work of the Group on third country situations has given rise to legally binding commitments that are included in good tax governance clauses in trade and cooperation agreements and sometimes even in broad changes in the national legislation of third countries (e.g. Switzerland CIT).

As regards the *future of the Code and the work of the Code Group*, it is important to note that discussions on renewing the mandate were successfully completed, but that other aspects of the 2020 Commission proposal to modernise the Code,[89] remain open (e.g. the proposed switch to qualified majority decision making and the possibility of considering

88 See: Martijn Nouwen (2021): 'Inside the European Code of Conduct Group: 20 years of tackling harmful tax competition', IBFD Doctoral Series, Amsterdam.

89 Communication from the Commission to the European Parliament and the Council on Tax Good Governance in the EU and beyond, COM(2020) 313 final of 15.7.2020.

effective consequences for non-complying Member States). As noted above, it is also regrettable that the mandate was not extended to certain aspects of personal income taxes.

A *final observation* concerns the remarkable shift in the willingness of Member States to take action on tax issues at EU level. In the first 40 years of the European integration process the underlying political narrative for taking legislative action has often been the need for neutrality on the internal market, but this narrative clearly failed to appeal to national Ministries of Finance, whose overriding objective of maximising tax revenue may have been the reason why the many Commission proposals for direct tax harmonisation were unsuccessful. The 1997 ECOFIN Council conclusions were perhaps an early indication that the narrative of harmful tax competition and erosion of tax bases could be more successful and the remarkable work of the Code Group, not only in rolling back harmful tax measures but also in tackling disparities and convincing third countries, illustrated an unexpected readiness of Finance Ministries to pool their sovereignty in an attempt to protect their respective tax bases. When the (public sector) tax competition narrative was subsequently linked to the (private sector) tax avoidance and evasion narrative, Member States suddenly proved to be fully on board to exercise their collective legislative powers and they have adopted a record of 14 EU instruments in the last 10 years.[90] The last of these is a Directive providing for a minimum corporate income tax rate of 15%, a substantive harmonisation measure that had been repeatedly proposed in the past, but that had been qualified as 'unrealistic' by many. It may be clear that a rate harmonisation makes little sense without some minimum base harmonisation and it would be in the logic of developments for member States to make that further step in the future, meaning that many years of principled and sovereignty-based opposition to direct tax harmonisation may have finally given way to the more reasonable position that pooling sovereignty may actually be in the common interest, also in the direct tax area.

90 For a broad overview see Dirk Verbeken (2021) General Tax Policy, Facts sheets on the European Union, at: https://www.europarl.europa.eu/factsheets/en/sheet/92/general-tax-policy.

PART 4 EXCHANGE OF INFORMATION AND RECOVERY ASSISTANCE

CHAPTER 27

Exchange of Information and Recovery Assistance: Background, History and Legal Basis

Sigrid Hemels[1]

27.1 Introduction

Exchange of information and – to a lesser extent – recovery assistance have been very much in focus since the 2007-2009 global financial and economic crisis.[2] The Directive on Administrative Cooperation 2011/16/ EU[3] (DAC) has been changed so many times that the Luxembourg Minister of Finance joked in 2020: "We have a new DAC every year, it seems to be like wine."[4] As a result of these developments, the editors of this book decided to dedicate a specific section to this topic, that is divided into five chapters. In this Chapter 27, the background, history and legal basis of exchange of information and recovery assistance are discussed. Chapter 28 discusses the DAC, with a separate Chapter 29 on DAC6 (mandatory disclosure). Chapter 30 focusses on the Recovery Assistance Directive. Chapter 31 concludes this part with a discussion of concurrence rules.

27.2 The Need for Cross-Border Administrative Cooperation in Tax Matters

Most States tax their residents, whether legal or natural persons, on their worldwide income, and tax nonresidents on their domestic-source income. The competence to inspect

1 Professor of Tax Law, Erasmus University Rotterdam School of Law and affiliated to Lund University School of Economics and Management; State Councillor in the Advisory Division of the Dutch Council of State.

2 The European Association of Tax Law Professors dedicated its 2009 congress to 'Mutual Assistance and Information Exchange', presenting a general report, section reports, country reports and statistics; EATLP International Tax Series, Vol. 8, IBFD 2010. In 2014 the congress theme was 'New Exchange of Information versus Tax Solutions of Equivalent Effect', the book of this conference was published in EATLP International Tax Series, Vol. 13, IBFD 2016. The 2018 congress had 'Tax Transparency' as its theme. The book of this conference was published in EATLP International Tax Series, Vol. 17, IBFD 2019. See also Xavier Oberson, *International Exchange of Information in Tax Matters. Towards Global Transparency* Cheltemham/Northampton, Edward Elgar 2023 and M. Serrat Romaní, J. J. A. M. Korving & M. Eliantonio, *Exchange of information in the EU : taxpayers' rights, transparency and effectiveness*. Edward Elgar 2024.

3 Council Directive 2011/16/EU of 15 February 2011 on administrative cooperation in the field of taxation and repealing Directive 77/799/EEC, O.J. 11 March 2011, L 064.

4 Elodie Lamer, EU Sees Stars Aligning on Digital Taxation, *Tax Notes International*, 7 December 2020, p. 1362.

accounts, gather tax information and, if need be, attach property for unpaid tax claims, however, stops at the border. Seer and Gabert[5] and Bal[6] refer in this respect to the public international law principle of formal territoriality. This entails that a State's sovereignty does not extend beyond its territorial limits. It thus prohibits States from performing field audits or other investigations or to collect tax claims in other States as sovereign acts may not be carried out on foreign national territory. Therefore, transnational tax cooperation is necessary to be able to effectively tax worldwide income. As Stewart observes, such cooperation has a long history.[7] In a globalising economy, such tax cooperation became even more important.

This is even more so for the EU. Free movement of goods, services, persons and especially of capital and payments entails opportunities not only for cross-border trade and investment, but also for transfer-pricing irregularities, tax evasion and tax avoidance. International tax avoidance and fraud and the nonpayment of legitimate tax claims distort conditions of competition, as they cause overall budget losses and territorial revenue shifts, violate inter-taxpayer equity (compliant taxpayers will have to pay more), and frustrate economically rational allocation of capital. With the growth of the internal market and of cross-border economic activity, the Member States needed more cooperation in the field of assessment and collection of national taxes. Preamble 1 of the DAC speaks of 'a tremendous development of the mobility of taxpayers, of the number of cross-border transactions, and of the internationalization of financial instruments, which makes it difficult for Member States to assess taxes due properly'. A major drawback of the success of free movement and the euro is that it provides opportunities for tax evasion (fraud) and tax avoidance. The European Commission appreciates that it is difficult to conclusively quantify the scale of tax evasion and avoidance, but according to the Commission there is a general consensus that it is substantial, with tens of billions of euro lost each year.[8] Member States cannot manage their domestic tax systems without information and assistance from other Member States, given also the Treaty Freedom's prohibition on restrictive tax measures which distinguish between cross-border movement and payment and domestic movement and payment.

The EU Member States are not alone in their need of information and assistance in tax matters. Exchange of tax information has always been important for, *inter alia*, checking the acceptability of intra-group transfer prices, establishment of the fiscal residence of (legal) persons (necessary for, notably, withholding tax reduction under tax treaties) and checking deduction of cross-border payments. Therefore, not only on an EU scale, but also on a global scale, coordinated by the Organisation for Economic Co-operation and Development (OECD), initiatives have been taken to enhance tax transparency and

5 Roman Seer and Isabel Gabert, European and International Tax Cooperation: Legal Basis, Practice, Burden of Proof, Legal Protection and Requirements, *Bulletin for International Taxation*, February 2011, pp. 88-98, p. 88.

6 Aleksandra Bal, Extraterritorial Enforcement of Tax Claims, *Bulletin for International Taxation*, October 2011, pp. 598-602, p. 598.

7 Miranda Stewart, Transnational Tax Information Exchange Network: Steps towards a Globalized, Legitimate Tax Administration, *World Tax Journal*, June 2012, pp. 152-179, p. 154.

8 European Commission, *Tax Policies in the European Union, 2016 Survey*, 2016, p. 15.

cooperation in tax matters. In this regard, the global financial crisis which started in 2007 was an important accelerator both in the EU and globally, especially for the automatic exchange of information. Somare and Wöhrer characterise this new global standard as 'unprecedented global solidarity'.[9]

27.3 OECD Initiatives before the Financial Crisis

Bilateral tax treaties traditionally contain an information exchange provision. It is often patterned after Art. 26 OECD Model Convention (OECD-MC). Until 1975 the provision was usually limited to information necessary for the application of the provisions of the tax treaty itself. With internationalisation and increasing mobility, the object and purpose of tax treaties evolved from mainly prevention of double taxation to also cover prevention of tax avoidance and fraud. In addition, a need was felt to be able to request information on taxes not covered by the treaty, such as sales taxes. Therefore, since 2000, Art. 26(1) OECD-MC does not only include the exchange of information foreseeably relevant for carrying out the provisions of the treaty, but also for the enforcement of domestic laws 'concerning taxes of every kind and description' insofar as the taxation thereunder is not contrary to the treaty. As paragraph 2 of the Commentary on Article 26 OECD-MC points out, the exchange of information is explicitly not restricted by Articles 1 and 2 OECD-MC, so that the information may include particulars about non-residents and may relate to the administration or enforcement of taxes not referred to in Article 2. However, in paragraph 10.1 of the Commentary on Article 26 OECD-MC it is pointed out that contracting States are free to restrict the scope to the taxes covered by the tax treaty.

In 1987, a Committee of Experts of the Council of Europe (CoE) and the Committee on Fiscal Affairs of the OECD jointly drew up the Multilateral Convention on Mutual Administrative Assistance in Tax Matters (MCMAATM), covering not only assessment assistance, but also recovery assistance, service of documents and initiation of criminal prosecution of tax offences. It was opened for signature to the Member States of the OECD and the CoE as of 25 January 1988. It is in force since 1 April 1995 among the States that have ratified it. The OECD website provides for an overview of countries where the MCMAATM is in force, countries that have signed it and countries that have been requested to join.[10]

In 2002, the OECD Global Forum Working Group on Effective Exchange of Information published a Model Agreement on Exchange of Information on Tax Matters (TIEA: tax information exchange agreement), to back up the initiative[11] of the G20 and the OECD against unfair tax competition – especially against uncooperative jurisdictions (tax havens). Its main feature was transparency, with a special focus on the abolition of banking secrecy in tax matters.

9 Maryte Somare and Viktoria Wöhrer, Automatic Exchange of Financial Information under the Directive on Administrative Cooperation in the Light of the Global Movement towards Transparency, *Intertax*, 2015 no. 12, pp. 804-815, p. 804.
10 https://www1.compareyourcountry.org/tax-cooperation/en/1/623/default.
11 Initiated with the OECD Report of 1998 'Harmful Tax Competition: An Emerging Global Issue'.

In 2003, the OECD added Art. 27 (Assistance in the collection of taxes) to the OECD-MC, covering mutual assistance in the recovery of tax claims. However, this Article is not included in many tax treaties and it is regarded as ineffective and slow.[12] In footnote 1 to article 27 in the OECD-MC it is noted that in some countries, national law, policy or administrative considerations may not allow or justify this type of assistance or may require that it is restricted, e.g. to countries that have similar tax systems or tax administrations or as to the taxes covered. Paragraph 1 of the Commentary on Article 27 OECD-MC further elaborates on the reasons not to (fully) implement this article. Parker observed that States are hesitant in implementing provisions on recovery assistance, even though it would seem to be a potent weapon against tax evasion.[13] De Troyer summarised various reasons why many States are reluctant to grant recovery assistance. These include political reasons but also practical reasons such as that the administrative burden and costs of providing assistance and the belief that the amounts recovered through international assistance are relatively low.[14] Parker discusses both internal and external limitations to the effectiveness of tax collection assistance and observes that it remains unclear whether provisions on tax collection assistance are really rewarding in practice.[15] She suggests that exchange of information may be more effective in curbing tax avoidance.

27.4 EU Mutual Assistance Initiatives before the Financial Crisis

The OECD solutions did not solve all problems the EU faced. Not all bilateral relations between the EU Member States were covered by tax treaties, and not all existing treaties lived up to the latest OECD standard. Even if they did, some forms of tax avoidance or evasion, of double taxation or of nonpayment escaped bilateral solutions because of their multinational character. Also, a bilateral approach leads to fragmentation as it does not provide for automatic EU-wide reciprocity, or for common and hard time limits, common standard forms and procedures, common competences, rights and obligations, and a common (electronic) format of exchange.

In 1977, the European Council adopted the 'Directive Concerning Mutual Assistance by the Competent Authorities of the Member States in the Field of Direct Taxation',[16] which required Member States to exchange '... any information that may enable them to effect a correct assessment of taxes (...)' (Art. 1(1)). The implementation deadline was 1 January 1979. The Directive only covered assessment assistance. It recognised banking secrecy as a reason not to provide information.

12 Philip Baker, Ernst Czakert, Arie van Eijsden, Maria Amparo Grau Ruiz and Liselotte Kana, International Assistance in the Collection of Taxes, *Bulletin for International taxation*, April/May 2011, pp. 281-287, p. 283 and Ilse De Troyer, Tax Recovery Assistance in the EU: Analysis of Directive 2010/24/EU, *EC Tax Review*, 2014, No. 3, pp. 135-148, p. 135-136.

13 Louise Parker, Mutual Assistance in the Collection of Taxes, *Bulletin for International Taxation*, 2017, No. 9, Section 1.

14 Ilse De Troyer, Implementation of Agreements on International Assistance in Tax Collection: Avoiding the Complexity of a "Mirror" Approach, *Bulletin for International Taxation*, August 2017, pp. 424-429, Section 1.1.

15 Louise Parker, Mutual Assistance in the Collection of Taxes, *Bulletin for International Taxation*, 2017, No. 9.

16 Council Directive 77/799/EEC of 19 December 1977, O.J. No. L 336 of 27 December 1977, p. 15.

Originally, the Directive covered direct taxes on income and capital and VAT (from 1979 to 2003)[17] and was later extended to excise duties (from 1992 to 2004).[18] However, the Directive did not work very well for VAT and excises. Furthermore, as of 1992 two parallel but different instruments had to be applied for VAT as VAT information exchange was co-based on Regulation (EEC) No. 218/92, which provided for a VAT Information Exchange System (VIES), involving a common database on intra-Community supplies and acquisitions. This was complex and inefficient. Therefore, a new environment for administrative cooperation for VAT and excise duties was created. On 7 October 2003, the 1992 Regulation was replaced by Council Regulation (EC) No. 1798/2003 'on administrative cooperation in the field of value added tax and repealing Regulation (EEC) No. 218/92' (which, in turn, was replaced by Regulation (EU) No. 904/2010). On that occasion (2003), the Assessment Assistance Directive was amended to delete VAT from its scope.[19]. Upon the request of a number of Member States, the amendment of October 2003, deleting VAT, was also used to extend the scope of the Directive to taxes on insurance premiums, and to widen the permissible use of the information exchanged.

In 2004, the Assessment Assistance Directive was amended[20] in order to 'improve, expand and modernize' it. To speed up the exchange of information, a new provision specified that the requested State was required to gather the requested information as if it needed it for itself or for a domestic authority (principle of equivalence). Further, two new provisions were inserted on (i) notification of documents to the taxpayer and (ii) simultaneous controls in different Member States, to cope with the ever-increasing cross-border economic activity and technological possibilities which had led to increasing difficulties in detecting tax fraud and transfer-pricing irregularities (over invoicing and under invoicing). The limitations on the use of the information obtained were relaxed. It could also be used in public hearings and judgments, and for the recovery of tax claims.

Initially, the Assessment Assistance Directive proposal was coupled with a proposal for a Directive on arbitration in cases of double taxation due to profit adjustments of associated enterprises in different Member States. This Arbitration Directive proposal was never adopted. It was withdrawn when the Member States instead agreed on a multilateral Convention on Arbitration, signed in 1990, which came into force 16 years later (see Chapter 21.6.2). With ongoing internationalisation, the need for mutual assistance in the collection of tax claims was also felt. In 2001, therefore, direct taxes were included in the

17 Council Directive 79/1070/EEC of 6 December 1979, O.J. No. L 331 of 27 December 1979, p. 8 extended the scope of the Assessment Assistance Directive to cover VAT, not just because VAT involves huge revenue and is vulnerable to cross-border evasion schemes, but also because a considerable part of the Union's own resources consists of a percentage of the VAT base.

18 The – now replaced – Horizontal Excises Directive of 1992 (further) extended the scope of the Directive to excise duties on tobacco, alcohol and mineral oils, but when the Council adopted, on 16 November 2004, Regulation (EC) No. 2073/2004 on administrative cooperation in the field of excise duties, it also adopted Directive 2004/106/EC in order to remove excise duties from the scope of the Assessment Assistance Directive.

19 Council Directive 2003/93/EC of 7 October 2003, O.J. No. L 264 of 15 October 2003, pp. 23-24.

20 Council Directive 2004/56/EC of 21 April 2004 amending Directive 77/799/EEC, O.J. No. L 127 of 29 April 2004, pp. 70-72. The Council changed the legal basis proposed by the Commission (Art. 95 EC Treaty; qualified majority) to Arts. 93 and 94 EC Treaty (unanimity).

scope of an already existing Directive on mutual assistance in the recovery of certain EU law-based claims.[21] This Directive was repealed as of 29 June 2008 by Council Directive 2008/55/EC.[22]

27.5 Poor Results, Failing the OECD Standard; Revised Directives on Recovery Assistance (2012) and Administrative Cooperation (2013)[23]

Even after amendments, neither the Assessment Assistance Directive nor the Recovery Assistance Directive was sufficiently effective. In several respects, these Directives did not meet the cooperation standard of Arts. 26 and 27 OECD-MC after the 2005 amendments to that model (i.e., introducing 'foreseeably relevant' instead of 'necessary', adding 'enforcement' to 'administration', and prohibiting banking secrecy and lack-of-own-interest as refusal grounds). The EU Directives did not cover all national taxes, and as regards assessment assistance, exchange of information was slow and inefficient. It was even nonexistent where banking secrecy stood in the way. Automatic exchange was left to bilateral negotiations. The only common system of automatic exchange was based on the Savings Directive,[24] which provided for mandatory automatic exchange of information on interest payments to individuals. Even that system showed gaps as some Member States could still apply banking secrecy, and because of the rather easy escape from the scope of that Directive. As regards recovery assistance, only 5% of the tax claims for which assistance was requested was actually recovered.[25]

The worldwide financial crisis that started in 2007 and became a severe economic crisis, the resulting ensuing steeply climbing national budget deficits and sovereign debts from 2008 onward, and the G20 and OECD initiatives against uncooperative tax havens and banking secrecy, provided the momentum for a thorough revamp of the EU tax cooperation instruments in order to (i) broaden their scopes, (ii) make them more practicable and efficient, and (iii) provide for more mutual confidence, balance and reciprocity. All taxes except the separately regulated VAT and excise duties were included, banking secrecy exceptions eliminated, the possible use of the information obtained was broadened, the scope of mandatory automatic exchange of information was broadened, hard time limits, standard forms and a common (electronic) exchange platform were introduced and the rules for admission of foreign tax officials and for simultaneous controls were simplified.

---

21 Council Directive 76/308/EEC of 15 March 1976 on mutual assistance for the recovery of claims resulting from operations forming part of the system of financing the European Agricultural Guidance and Guarantee Fund, and of the agricultural levies and customs duties, O.J. 19 March 1976, L 064, p. 18.

22 Council Directive 2008/55/EC of 26 May 2008 on mutual assistance for the recovery of claims relating to certain levies, duties, taxes and other measures, O.J. 10 June 2008, L 150, p. 28.

23 For an extensive discussion see Roman Seer, Recent Development in Exchange of Information within the EU for Tax Matters, *EC Tax Review*, 2013 no. 2, pp. 66-77.

24 Council Directive 2003/48/EC of 3 June 2003 on taxation of savings income in the form of interest payments, O.J. 26 June 2003, L 157, p. 38.

25 For the difficulties the Member States faced as regards tax recovery in cross-border situations see Ilse De Troyer, 'A European Perspective on Tax Recovery in Cross-Border Situations', *EC Tax Review* 2009/5, pp. 211-220.

The revamp also brought the EU Directives up to – and above – the OECD standard for tax transparency,[26] which may be summarised as follows: (i) exchange – at any rate upon request – of tax information relevant for the administration and enforcement of all national tax laws; (ii) domestic availability of reliable information and of the competence to obtain it; (iii) refusal cannot be based on the facts that the information rests with a financial institution (no banking secrecy), or is not relevant for the requested State itself; (iv) no fishing expeditions: requests must be specific; (v) respect for the rights of the taxpayer, and (vi) confidentiality of the information obtained.

The Case Law of the CJEU was another reason for improving the effectiveness of fiscal administrative cooperation. Protecting national tax systems against artificial profit shifts by measures which distinguish between domestic and cross-border situations, may be held disproportionately restrictive – even though they may be justified by the need to safeguard the balanced allocation of taxing rights between the Member States – if the information needed was obtainable under the Assessment Assistance Directive,[27] or if the recovery of tax claims may be enforced using the Recovery Assistance Directive.[28] In other words: the CJEU forced the Member States to actually use their mutual assistance instruments. The application of the Treaty Freedoms by the Court shifted the tax risk of lack of information to a certain extent from the taxpayers to the tax administrations.

Consequently, in March 2010, the Council adopted a revised Directive on recovery assistance (RAD),[29] which had to be implemented before 1 January 2012. That directive is discussed in Chapter 30. Subsequently, in February 2011 a revised Directive on administrative co-operation[30] was adopted. The DAC had to be implemented before 1 January 2013 and is discussed in Chapter 28. Administrative cooperation concerning VAT and excise duties is not dealt with in this volume, but in chapter 4 of volume 2.[31]

27.6 Influence of BEPS on the DAC

Brodzka characterised exchange of tax information as a non-fiscal measure aimed at curbing tax base erosion.[32] The OECD/G20 Base Erosion and Profit Shifting (BEPS) Project was a direct result of the credit crunch and the ensuing successive financial and economic crises

26 For a comparison of the Commission proposals for the two directives with the relevant OECD Model provisions, see Andres Caram, 'Enhancing International Cooperation among Tax Authorities in the Assessment and the Recovery of Taxes: The Proposals for New European Directives,' 37 *Intertax* 11 (2009), pp. 630-646.

27 See, for instance, Case C-204/90, *Bachmann*, EU:C:1992:35, and Case C-55/98, *Vestergaard*, EU:C:1999:533.

28 See, for instance, Case C-470/04, *N*, EU:C:2006:525.

29 Council Directive 2010/24/EU of 16 March 2010 concerning mutual assistance for the recovery of claims relating to taxes, duties and other measures, O.J. of 31 March 2010, L 084, p. 1.

30 Council Directive 2011/16/EU of 15 February 2011 on administrative cooperation in the field of taxation and repealing Directive 77/799/EEC, O.J. of 11 March 2011, L 064, p. 1.

31 Marie Lamensch and Madeleine Merkx, Administrative Cooperation in the field of indirect taxes in M. Lamensch and M. Merkx (ed.) Terra/Wattel *European Tax Law. Volume 2 – Indirect Taxation*, Deventer: Wolters Kluwer 2021.

32 Alicja Brodzka, Automatic Exchange of Tax Information in the European Union – The Standard for the Future, *European Taxation*, January 2016, pp. 26-33, p. 26.

which had strengthening effects on the wish for increased transparency and exchange of information.[33] In 2009, the Global Forum on Transparency and Exchange of Information for Tax Purposes was established to ensure a consistent and effective implementation of international transparency standards. In the same year, the European Commission started a 'good governance' offensive, which in the tax area focused on the principles of transparency, exchange of information and fair tax competition.[34] In 2010, the US introduced FATCA to enforce filing of foreign accounts by putting information obligations on foreign financial institutions and certain other non-financial foreign entities.[35] Subsequently, the G20 mandated the OECD to develop a single global standard for the automatic exchange of financial account information in tax matters.

On 6 December 2012, the Commission published an Action Plan with concrete proposals to strengthen the fight against tax fraud and tax evasion.[36] The Commission highlighted the need to promote vigorously the automatic exchange of information as the future European and international standard for transparency and exchange of information in tax matters. At the same time, the OECD developed, at the request of the G20, an Action Plan to tackle BEPS in a comprehensive manner. The BEPS Action Plan was published on 19 July 2013. It included 15 Actions to equip governments with domestic and international instruments to address tax avoidance. Four of these actions regarded administrative cooperation, more specifically enhancing tax transparency and information exchange. First of all, Action 5 'Countering harmful tax practices more effectively, taking into account transparency and substance' aimed, among others, to revamp the work on harmful tax practices with a focus on improving transparency, including compulsory spontaneous exchange on rulings. This eventually led to a change in the DAC, which had to be applied as of 1 January 2017 (see Chapter 28.3.2.3). Second, Action 12 'Mandatory disclosure rules' regarding recommendations on the design of mandatory disclosure rules for aggressive tax planning schemes. Taking the momentum after scandals regarding tax evasion, such as the Lux Leaks and the Panama Papers, this led to DAC6 with an original effective date of 1 July 2020 (which could be postponed due to the Covid-19 crisis). DAC6 is discussed separately in Chapter 29. Third, Action 13 'Transfer pricing documentation and country-by-country reporting' aimed to enhance transparency by revised guidance on transfer-pricing documentation, including country-by-country reporting. This led to

33 See also Nana Ama Sarfo, Grace Perez-Navarro, - A Champion Of Transparency and Inclusion, *Tax Notes International*, 19December 2022, p. 1499-1506 and Nana Ama Sarfo, Achim Pross: Taking the Long Gamble on Tax Multilateralism, *Tax Notes International*, 16 December 2024, p. 1669-1677.

34 Communication from the Commission to the Council, the EP and the ESC of 28 April 2009, 'Promoting Good Governance in Tax Matters', COM(2009) 201 final. See, on the global and EU tax governance movement, Gemma Martinez Bárbara, 'The Role of Good Governance in the Tax Systems of the European Union', 4/5 *Bulletin for International Fiscal Documentation* 65, 2011.

35 See for an extensive discussion of FATCA and its background, Luzius Cavelti, Automatic Information Exchange versus the Withholding Tax Regime Globalization and Increasing Sovereignty Conflicts in International Taxation, *World Tax Journal*, June 2013, pp. 172-214.

36 Communication from the Commission to the European Parliament and the Council. An Action Plan to strengthen the fight against tax fraud and tax evasion, COM/2012/0722 final. See for an extensive discussion: Mirugia Richardson, Fighting Tax Fraud and Tax Evasion in the EU: The 2012 Action Plan, *EC Tax Review* 2015, no. 4, pp. 220-231.

DAC4 which had to be applied as of 5 June 2017 (see Chapter 28.3.2.4). Fourth was Action 15 'Developing a multilateral instrument to modify bilateral tax treaties'.

The Multilateral Convention to Implement Tax Treaty Related Measures to Prevent Base Erosion and Profit Shifting (Multilateral Instrument or MLI)[37] which was open for signing as of 7 June 2017, implements the BEPS measures which require changes to tax treaties (BEPS Actions 2, 6, 7 and 14) and was as such included in BEPS Action 15.[38] The MLI modifies bilateral tax treaties in the following way. Signatories of the MLI may choose which bilateral tax treaties they would like to modify using the MLI (the so-called 'covered tax treaties'). If the other party to the treaty also lists it as a covered treaty, it is, after ratification by both countries changed by the MLI in so far as both countries have made the same choices regarding the options and application of the provisions in the MLI.[39] Based on Art. 6(3) of the MLI, countries may opt for the following addition to the preamble if such wording is not yet included: "Desiring to further develop their economic relationship and to enhance their cooperation in tax matters."

On 18 March 2015, the European Commission published a Communication on the fight against tax fraud and tax evasion.[40] It included a Tax Transparency Package which set out a number of measures to enhance tax transparency, among others the automatic exchange of tax rulings and the repeal of the Savings Directive. The Savings Directive[41] was repealed on 1 January 2016.[42] It became redundant after the DAC as of the same date obliged Member States to implement the global standard for automatic exchange of financial account information in tax matters mentioned above (DAC2, see Chapter 28.3.2.2).

27.7 Legal Basis: 'Internal Market' or 'Fiscal'?[43]

The Commission had based its 2003 proposal to amend Directive 77/799/EEC on Art. 95(1) of the EC Treaty (now Art. 114(1) TFEU) concerning the establishment and the functioning of the internal market. This required qualified majority voting instead of the unanimity requirement for tax measures (see Arts. 113 and 114 TFEU). Although Art. 114(2) excludes 'fiscal provisions' from the scope of Art. 114(1), the Commission considered that 'fiscal provisions (do not) constitute the main purpose of the proposed measure', since 'the regulation is confined to building bridges between tax administrations'. The Council, however, designated Arts. (now) 113 TFEU (for indirect taxes) and 115 TFEU (for direct taxes) to be the legal basis for the amending measures. Based on Art. 115 TFEU, the Council may unanimously adopt directives for the approximation of legislation, regulations or

37 https://www.oecd.org/en/topics/beps-multilateral-instrument.html.

38 OECD, *Action 15: A Mandate for the Development of a Multilateral Instrument on Tax Treaty Measures to Tackle BEPS*, 2015.

39 The OECD has developed a 'BEPS MLI Matching Database': https://www.oecd.org/en/data/tools/beps-mli-matching-database.html.

40 COM(2015) 136 final.

41 Council Directive 2003/48/EC of 3 June 2003 on taxation of savings income in the form of interest payments, O.J. 26 June 2003, L 157, p. 38.

42 Council Directive (EU) 2015/2060 of 10 November 2015 repealing Directive 2003/48/EC on taxation of savings income in the form of interest payments, O.J. 18 November 2015, L 301, p. 1.

43 See for a general discussion on the different legislative procedures Chapter 2.3.1.

administrative provisions of the Member States that directly affect the establishment or functioning of the internal market.

Subsequent CJEU case law on the question of whether the Assessment Assistance Directive applied in Gibraltar would seem to support the Commission's position that the Directive concerns 'provisions (...) which have as their object the establishment and the functioning of the internal market' as referred to in (now) Art. 114(1) TFEU (qualified majority), rather than 'fiscal provisions' within the meaning of Arts. 113 and 114(2) TFEU (unanimity). The Court considered in point 44 of the the *Gibraltar* Case[44] that provisions which merely require cooperation between the Member States, leaving each of them to use their own methods of enquiry and communication of information, cannot be regarded as "acts on the harmonisation of legislation of Member States concerning turnover taxes".

However, earlier Case C-338/01, *Commission v. Council*,[45] confirmed the Council's view that both the Assessment Assistance Directive and the Recovery Assistance Directive contain 'fiscal provisions' even though they only concern administrative cooperation and do not seek to harmonise national substantive tax law or tax procedure. The case concerned the legal basis of the Recovery Assistance Directive. The Commission chose Art. 95(1) EC Treaty (qualified majority); the Council wanted Arts. 93 and 94 EC Treaty (unanimity). The Court agreed with the Council and decided (point 63-67) that "fiscal provisions" does not only cover the provisions determining taxable persons, taxable transactions, the basis of imposition, and rates of and exemptions from direct and indirect taxes, but also arrangements for the collection of such taxes. In other words: all aspects of taxation, whether material rules or procedural rules.

It may be argued that not only provisions on recovery assistance, but also the rules on assessment assistance, are 'fiscal provisions' in the meaning of Art. 114(2) TFEU, implying that all EU legislation affecting them must be adopted unanimously. Even though the later *Gibraltar* Case supported the Commission's view, the Commission has apparently given up its efforts to bring administrative cooperation under qualified majority voting, as both the DAC and the RAD,[46] discussed below, are based on Arts. 113 and 115 TFEU (unanimity). Also later amendments to the DAC are based on Art. 115 TFEU. In the Proposal to introduce mandatory disclosure (DAC6)[47] the Commission observed under 'legal basis' that a lack of transparency may lead to a shift of profits to low tax jurisdictions, tax base erosion and unfair tax competition against businesses that do not evade taxes, which would distort the operation of the internal market. The Commission is of the opinion that such a situation can only be tackled through a uniform approach aimed to improve the functioning of the internal market, as prescribed in Art. 115 TFEU. In the DAC9 proposal introducing a framework for filing and exchanging the pillar 2 top-up

44 Case C-349/03, *Commission v. UK (Gibraltar)*, EU:C:2005:488.

45 Case C-338/01, *Commission v. Council*, EU:C:2004:253.

46 Directive 2010/24/EU of 16 March 2010 concerning mutual assistance for the recovery of claims relating to taxes, duties and other measures, O.J. No. L 84, of 31 March 2010, p. 1.

47 Proposal for a Council Directive amending Directive 2011/16/EU as regards mandatory automatic exchange of information in the field of taxation in relation to reportable cross-border arrangements, 21 June 2017, COM(2017) 335 final, hereinafter: the Proposal.

tax return, the Commission held that although no explicit reference to taxation is made, Art. 115 can be used for the approximation of national laws and administrative practices that directly affect the establishment or functioning of the single market in the field of direct taxation.[48] Thus, the Commission now also regards this Article as the legal basis for amendments to the DAC.

This seems to be reflected in the fact that the obligation of public country by country reporting (CbCR, see Chapter 28.3.2.4) was not included in an amendment of the DAC, but as an amendment of the Accounting Directive[49] on the basis of Art. 50(1) TFEU pertaining to the right of establishment and more specifically to the protection of the interests of members of companies and others. This meant that the amending Directive[50] could be adopted by qualified majority vote under the ordinary legislative procedure. This is another indication that the Commission is of the opinion that the DAC can only be changed by unanimity voting under the special legislative procedure of Art. 115. Various Member States objected against the legal basis for public CbCR. In 2016, the Council Legal Service was requested to give a written opinion[51] on the legal basis, more specifically whether it had to be adopted on the same legal basis as the introduction of CbCR in the DAC (DAC4, see Chapter 28.3.2.4), namely Arts. 113 and/or 115 TFEU, rather than on the basis of Art. 50(1) TFEU. According to the Council Legal Service it was apparent that the objective of the measure was to deter tax avoidance. It was of the opinion that Art. 50(1) TFEU was not an appropriate basis. It considered Art. 115 TFEU as the appropriate legal basis since both the aim and the content of the proposal related to 'fiscal provisions'. Subsequently, some changes were made to the preamble putting the focus on corporate transparency. Preamble 22 states that given that the Directive only concerns obligations to publish reports on income tax information, and does not concern the harmonization of taxes, Art. 50(1) TFEU constitutes the appropriate legal basis.

This did not convince all Member States. In September 2021, Sweden and Cyprus voted against the proposal and the Czech Republic, Ireland, Luxembourg, and Malta abstained from voting. Cyprus, the Czech Republic, Ireland, Luxembourg, Malta and Sweden made a statement that notwithstanding their general support for tax transparency, they had ongoing concerns regarding the legal basis repeating the formula of the 2016 Legal Services Opinion that the basis should be Art. 115 TFEU since both the aim and content relate to 'fiscal provisions' and rejected the appropriateness of Art. 50(1) TFEU as the legal basis. Croatia made a similar statement and added that this should not become precedent for a qualified majority voting in the future decision-making process in regard to tax matters.[52]

48 Proposal of 28 October 2024 for a Council Directive amending Directive 2011/16/EU on administrative cooperation in the field of taxation, COM(2024) 497 final.

49 Directive 2013/34/EU of 26 June 2013 on the annual financial statements, consolidated financial statements and related reports of certain types of undertakings, amending Directive 2006/43/ EC of the European Parliament and of the Council and repealing Council Directives 78/660/EEC and 83/349/EEC.

50 Directive 2021/2101 of 24 November 2021 amending Directive 2013/34/EU as regards disclosure of income tax information by certain undertakings and branches.

51 Opinion of the Council Legal Service of 11 November 2016, 2016/0107/(COD), FISC 194.

52 Both statements are included in Item Note 2016/0107 (COD) FISC 143 of 20 September 2021.

Notwithstanding this opposition, because of the qualified majority voting procedure, the proposal was adopted. On 21 December 2021, the Public CbCR Directive entered into force.

On a more general level, Stöber questioned whether the reporting obligation of DAC6 has a direct effect on the functioning of the internal market, and thus whether it met the requirement of Art. 115 TFEU.[53] He observed that according to preamble 2, DAC6 is intended to enable Member States' tax authorities to react promptly against harmful tax practices to counteract the considerable reductions in tax revenues. In his view, the reporting obligation only directly serves the purpose of securing the tax revenue of individual Member States which, in his opinion, has no relation with the internal market. Therefore, he came to the conclusion that the EU lacks regulatory competence for DAC6. If his view would be correct, this would also have impact on other parts of the DAC. However, in the ECJ jurisprudence on DAC6 (see Chapter 29), this question was not raised and thus not answered. Also, the older case law of the ECJ on the old administrative assistance directive does not seem to indicate that the ECJ would support this view.

53 Michael Stöber, The charter of fundamental rights and EU tax directives, *EC Tax Review*, 2023-5, p. 203-213, Section 5.2.

CHAPTER 28

The Directive on Administrative Cooperation

Sigrid Hemels[1]

28.1 Introduction

With effect from 1 January 2013 the 'old' Directive on Mutual Assistance 77/799/EEC was repealed by Art. 28 of the Directive on Administrative Cooperation 2011/16/EU (DAC) and, at the same time, Member States had to have implemented the DAC (Art. 29).

Mid 2025, the DAC had already been amended six times – not counting the language corrections and the COVID-19 extension of DAC6[2] – with a seventh amendment (DAC8) to be implemented on 31 December 2025,[3] an eight amendment (DAC9) just adopted with also an implementation date of 31 December 2025,[4] a change proposed in 2021 through the so called 'Unshell' Directive[5] (also known as ATAD3; see Chapter 25.3.3), and a (new) codification proposal being announced[6] which is expected to include changes following from the assessment of the earlier DACs[7] and maybe even integrate Unshell[8] and which is expected to be proposed under the name of DAC10[9] in 2026.[10]

1 Professor of Tax Law, Erasmus University Rotterdam School of Law and affiliated to Lund University School of Economics and Management; State Councillor in the Advisory Division of the Dutch Council of State.

2 Council Directive 2020/876 of 24 June 2020 amending Directive 2011/16/EU to address the urgent need to defer certain time limits for the filing and exchange of information in the field of taxation because of the COVID-19 pandemic, O.J. 26 July 2020, L 204, p. 46.

3 Council Directive 2023/2226 of 17 October 2023 amending Directive 2011/16/EU on administrative cooperation in the field of taxation.

4 Council Directive (EU) 2025/872 of 14 April 2025 amending Directive 2011/16/EU on administrative cooperation in the field of taxation.

5 Proposal of 21 December 2021 for a Council Directive laying down rules to prevent the misuse of shell entities for tax purposes and amending Directive 2011/16/EU, COM(2021) 565 final.

6 Annex IV to the Commission work programme 2025, COM(2025) 45 final, p. 23.

7 Elodie Lamer, What We Know So Far About the Upcoming DAC10, *Tax Notes International* 6 June 2025.

8 Elodie Lamer, Unshell's assimilation in DAC6 Appears to Have Member States' OK, *Tax Notes International* 28 May 2025, pp. 1143-1144 and Sophie Petitjean, EU Commission Lacks Clear Signal on Unshell's Inclusion in DAC6, *Tax Notes International* 4 June.

9 Elodie Lamer and Sophie Petitjean, EU Commission Confirms Completion Date for ATAD Evaluation, *Tax Notes International* 2 June 2025, p. 1389.

10 See also the European Commission's main page on the DAC: https://taxation-customs.ec.europa.eu/taxation/tax-transparency-cooperation/administrative-co-operation-and-mutual-assistance/directive-administrative-cooperation-dac_en.

On 12 February 2020 , the European Commission already published a proposal for a codification of the DAC.[11] According to preamble 4 of that 2020 proposal it would fully preserve the content of the DAC and would not do more than bringing the various amendments together with only such formal amendments as are required by the codification exercise itself. Such codification would be welcome, as because of the expansion of automatic exchange of information, the numbering of the DAC, especially in the language versions based on the French numbering (8 bis, 8 bis bis, 8 bis ter, 8 bis quarter, 8 ter), has become rather complex. But as the DAC was changed many times again after this proposal was adopted, the Commission deemed that this codification was obsolete.[12] For that reason, this proposal was withdrawn, but at the same time, the Commission announced it will, also as part of its decluttering agenda, propose a new codified proposal. This proposal, which is for the moment being called DAC10 and expected in 2026, is expected to be more than the mere reordering of the DAC which was proposed in 2020. It is also supposed to reduce the administrative and compliance burden for Member States' administrations and taxpayers, for example regarding DAC6 obligations.[13] Until that future codification we will have to make do with the complex numbering[14] and the consolidated versions of the DAC which are published on EUR-Lex.[15]

The original DAC without amendments is commonly referred to as DAC1. The subsequent (proposed) amendments of the DAC are – state of affairs mid 2025 – numbered from 2 to 9.[16] The first change which introduced Common Reporting Standards is known as DAC2.[17] The second change, requiring automatic exchange of cross-border rulings, is called DAC3.[18] The third change, introducing Country by Country Reporting is known as DAC4.[19] The fourth change, regarding access to anti-money-laundering information by tax authorities

11 Proposal for a Council Directive on administrative cooperation in the field of taxation (codification), COM(2020) 49 final.

12 Annex IV to the Commission work programme 2025, COM(2025) 45 final, p. 23.

13 Council Conclusions on a tax decluttering and simplification agenda which contributes to the EU's competitiveness, 11 March 2025, 6748/25. See on this decluttering initiative, also in relation to DAC6 Georg Kofler, The 'Decluttering'of EU Direct Tax Law, *EC Tax Review* 2025-1, pp. 2-7.

14 The numbering is a little less complex (8a, 8aa, 8ab, 8ac, 8b) in the English language version used in this chapter than in the French version. For clarity's sake it would be desirable that if changes are made in a future codified new DAC, only one kind of sub numbering is used, preferably the English numbering which is more comprehensible.

15 https://eur-lex.europa.eu/legal-content/EN/ALL/?uri=CELEX:32011L0016.

16 It seems that even the Commission itself is confused every now and then by the numbering: the Commission website on DAC8 (https://taxation-customs.ec.europa.eu/taxation/tax-transparency-cooperation/administrative-co-operation-and-mutual-assistance/directive-administrative-co-operation-dac/dac8_en) calls DAC8 the eighth amendment of the DAC, whereas it is 'only' the seventh.

17 Council Directive 2014/107/EU of 9 December 2014 amending Directive 2011/16/EU as regards mandatory automatic exchange of information in the field of taxation, O.J. 16 December 2014, L 359, p. 1.

18 Council Directive 2015/2376/EU of 8 December 2015 amending Directive 2011/16/EU as regards mandatory automatic exchange of information in the field of taxation, O.J. 18 December 2015, L 332, p. 1.

19 Council Directive 2016/881/EU of 25 May 2016 amending Directive 2011/16/EU as regards mandatory automatic exchange of information in the field of taxation, O.J. 3 June 2016, L 146, p. 8.

is called DAC5.[20] The fifth, and probably most well-known, change is the introduction of mandatory disclosure on tax arrangements: DAC6.[21] This will be discussed separately in Chapter 29. The sixth change, DAC7[22] included both changes to various provisions of the DAC and introduced mandatory disclosure for platform operators. DAC8, the seventh change, provides for automatic exchange of information on crypto-assets between EU Member States.[23] DAC9,[24] which is the eight change, is closely linked with the 2022 Pillar 2 Directive (P2D)[25] and introduces a standard form, in line with that developed by the Inclusive Framework of the OECD and the G20, to report information with respect to the Pillar 2 top-up tax information returns. The Unshell amendments were envisaged to have an application date of 1 January 2024, but by mid 2025, the Member States could still not agree on this proposal. Because of these amendments, it is important to always consult the updated consolidated version of the DAC.[26]

28.2 General Provisions; Minimum Standard; Language, Scope and Organisation

The DAC lays down rules and procedures under which the Member States must cooperate in the exchange of information which is 'foreseeably relevant' to the administration and enforcement of Member States' domestic tax laws (Art. 1(1), see Section 28.2.3). Within the context of exchange of information, the State or authority that makes a request for assistance, is referred to as the 'requesting State' or 'requesting authority', the authority that receives a request for assistance, is referred to as the 'requested State' or 'requested authority'.[27] This terminology is also used in this book.

Art. 3 point 9, second subparagraph provides for rules on where to find the definitions of capitalized terms that are used in the DAC. Definitions are not only included in Art. 3, but also, regarding specific articles, in specific annexes to the DAC and, in case of DAC9, also in another directive, the P2D.

20 Council Directive 2016/2258/EU of 6 December 2016 amending Directive 2011/16/EU as regards access to anti-money-laundering information by tax authorities, O.J. 16 December 2016, L 342, p. 1.

21 Council Directive 2018/822 of 25 May 2018 amending Directive 2011/16/EU as regards mandatory automatic exchange of information in the field of taxation in relation to reportable cross-border arrangements, O.J. 5 July 2018, L 139, p. 1.

22 Council Directive 2021/514 of 22 March 2021 amending Directive 2011/16/EU on administrative cooperation in the field of taxation, O.J. 25 March 2021, L 104, p. 1.

23 Council Directive 2023/2226 of 17 October 2023 amending Directive 2011/16/EU on administrative cooperation in the field of taxation.

24 Council Directive (EU) 2025/872 of 14 April 2025 amending Directive 2011/16/EU on administrative cooperation in the field of taxation.

25 Council Directive (EU) 2022/2523 of 14 December 2022 on ensuring a global minimum level of taxation for multinational enterprise groups and large-scale domestic groups in the Union.

26 A helpful reference point is the Document Information tab on the DAC EUR-Lex internet page which, among others, includes information on amendments, available consolidated versions, national transposition measures and case law of the CJEU on this Directive: EUR-Lex 32011L0016, https://eur-lex.europa.eu/legal-content/EN/ALL/?uri=CELEX:32011L0016. Please note that amendments will only be included in the consolidated version from the date these must be applied by the Member States. This means, for example, that the DAC8 amendments will only be included as of 1 January 2026.

27 Arts. 3(5) and 3(6) DAC and Joined Cases C245/19 and C246/19, *B and others*, EU:C:2020:795, point 109.

Unlike the old Directive, the DAC is not confined to assistance as regards assessment (determination of the tax liability) but calls for cooperation in all respects of application ('administration and enforcement') of national tax law, therefore including the recovery of tax, the service of documents and the (administrative) punishment of tax irregularities. The DAC also includes provisions for electronic exchange of information (Art. 1(2)). Preamble 9 of the DAC states that the procedural requirements of Art. 20 must be interpreted liberally in order not to frustrate the effective exchange of information.

The DAC provides for common minimum rules (see preamble 21). Consequently, Member States may agree to cooperate on a wider scale. However, if two or more Member States bilaterally or multilaterally negotiate automatic exchange of information on other categories of income or capital than those listed in Art. 8(1) (see Section 28.3.2.1), they must send their agreement to the Commission, which will make it available to the other Member States (Art. 8(8)). Furthermore, the DAC does not affect the application of rules on mutual assistance in criminal matters and it does not in any way limit Member State commitments to wider cooperation ensuing from other legal instruments (Art. 1(3)). The purpose of the DAC is to extend and improve administrative cooperation rather than to limit any existing obligations and possibilities.

Requests and attached documents may be submitted in any language agreed between the requesting and the requested authorities. A translation of the request in the official language of the requested State is only necessary 'in special cases' in which the requested authority gives reasons for requiring a translation (Art. 21(4)).

The DAC contains an explicit most-favoured nation clause (Union preference): if a Member State agrees with a non-Member State on wider cooperation than that provided for by the DAC, it may not refuse to provide the same wider cooperation to any other Member State wishing to enter into such mutual wider cooperation with it (Art. 19). For example, preamble 8 of amending Directive 2014/107/EU[28] (introduction of the CRS, see Section 28.3.2.2), stated that Member States which had concluded an Intergovernmental Agreement (IGA)[29] relating to FATCA with the US were providing for wider cooperation within the meaning of Art. 19 and were thus under an obligation to provide such wider cooperation to other Member States as well. Apparently, this Union preference clause does not apply within the EU. If Member States A and B decide to cooperate more closely than the DAC calls for, apparently Member State C cannot oblige Member State A or B to enter into the same wider mutual cooperation with Member State C.

The DAC contains a number of provisions which provide for evaluations and offer flexibility as regards allowing future extension and improvement, especially:

- the possibility of wider bilateral and multilateral arrangements (Arts. 1(3) and 8(8)),

28 Council Directive 2014/107/EU of 9 December 2014 amending Directive 2011/16/EU as regards mandatory automatic exchange of information in the field of taxation, O.J. 16 December 2014, L 359, p. 1.

29 See for an extensive discussion on the implementation of IGAs in the EU: Leopoldo Parada, Intergovernmental Agreements and the implementation of FATCA in Europe, *World Tax Journal*, June 2015, pp. 201-240.

- annual provision by the Member States of the European Commission with statistics on the volume of automatic exchanges and with information on the administrative and other relevant costs and benefits relating to exchanges that have taken place and any potential changes, for both tax administrations and third parties (Art. 8b).
- the sharing of best practices and experience (Art. 15),
- evaluation and yearly effectiveness reports on the automatic exchange of information (Art. 23), and
- the adoption of implementation measures, practical arrangements for standard forms, computerised formats, feedback, evaluation, and the use of the Common Communication Network (CCN) by 'comitology'[30] procedure (. This implies that as regards certain implementation measures, Commission proposals are adopted by qualified majority in a Committee (see Art. 26) functioning on the basis of the Comitology Regulation (EU) No. 182/2011. Like the Recovery Assistance Directive[31] (RAD) (see Chapter 230), the DAC thus provides for a 'light' delegated qualified majority decision-making in tax matters. The use, as much as possible, of the CCN for all communications based on the DAC reflects the Commission's intentions to get all tax systems using the same channel. The CCN is also used for value added tax (VAT) and excises.

28.2.1 Taxes Covered; Not Just Direct Taxes

Art. 2, which defines which taxes are covered, takes its lead from the 1987 Joint Council of Europe/OECD Convention on Mutual Administrative Assistance in Tax Matters (see Chapter 31). In principle, the DAC applies to all taxes (Art. 2(1): 'all taxes of any kind'), including regional and local taxes. In principle, indirect taxes are included as well, which means that, for example, inheritance taxes, gift taxes,[32] real estate transfer taxes, car taxes and environmental taxes are covered. However, VAT, customs duties and excise duties covered by other Union legislation on administrative cooperation are explicitly excluded (Art. 2(2)).[33] In this respect, it is noted that Art. 8ac(2)(f) obliges to report the VAT identification number of reportable sellers. In addition, Art. 16(1) states that information exchanged under the DAC may be used for the assessment, administration and enforcement of both taxes referred to in Art. 2 as well as VAT and other indirect taxes. According to preamble 30 of DAC7, this is just a clarification as the use of information for VAT was not precluded so far. The same applies, according to preamble 35 of DAC8, to the inclusion of customs duties, anti-money laundering and combating the financing of terrorism to Art. 16(1) as of 2026.

---

30 See Chapter 3.

31 Council Directive 2010/24/EU of 16 March 2010 concerning mutual assistance for the recovery of claims relating to taxes, duties and other measures.

32 AG Kokott explicitly mentioned in para 61 of her opinion delivered on 2 October 2014 in Case C 133/13, *Q (Bean House)*, EU:C:2014:2255 (a request for a preliminary ruling from the Raad van State of the Kingdom of the Netherlands regarding the application of a Dutch gift tax exemption on the Bean House, an estate in the United Kingdom) that, given the fact that the DAC applies to all taxes according to Art. 2(1) and as gift tax is not among the taxes that are excluded from its scope in Art. 2.2, the DAC applies to gift tax.

33 See on administrative cooperation and VAT and the problems resulting from the separation of the direct tax system: Giorgio Beretta, VAT and Administrative Cooperation in the EU, *Tax Notes International* 5 October 2020, pp. 71-79.

Art. 2(2) also excludes compulsory social security contributions. The concept of 'taxes' refers, in this respect, to general levies (funding general public means), not to fees for specific public services such as for certificates or other documents issued by public authorities or to contractual remunerations such as considerations for public utilities (Art. 2(3)). Given the broad scope of the DAC the demarcation vis-à-vis mandatory social security contributions (not covered) and the question of how wide the term 'all taxes of any kind' is, are of relevance. This is especially the case for levies which are not fees for public services, but not really general taxes either, as their proceeds are earmarked for a specific spending. There may be in-between cases, but the general tone of the Preambles to the DAC is that as wide a scope as possible was envisaged.

28.2.2 *Personal Scope; Anyone or Anything Subject to Tax*

No limitations exist as regards nationality or residence of the taxpayer(s) involved, or on their legal status (individual, corporate or anything in between). Information on both residents and nonresidents may be exchanged, even on nonresidents who are neither nationals nor residents of any of the Member States, as long as the information is 'foreseeably relevant' in the administration or enforcement of any of the Member States' taxes covered. Art. 3(11) defines 'person' in a very wide sense in order to also catch partnerships, trusts, foundations, investment funds and any other 'legal arrangement' which owns or manages assets which, including the income derived therefrom, are subject to any of the taxes covered.

28.2.3 *Objective Scope: 'Foreseeably Relevant' Information*

Cooperation is obligatory if the information requested is 'foreseeably relevant' to the administration and enforcement of domestic tax law (Art. 1). The term 'foreseeably relevant' is also used in Art. 26 OECD-MC, in which the term 'necessary' was changed into 'foreseeably relevant' in 2005.

Until the adoption of DAC7, the DAC did not define what 'foreseeably relevant' meant. The European Court of Justice (ECJ) was called upon to interpret the term in the *Berlioz* Case,[34] the *B and others* Case (also known as the *Shakira* Case)[35] and the *L* Case.[36] In the *Berlioz* Case[37] the Court held that the words 'foreseeably relevant' describe a necessary characteristic of the requested information (*Berlioz* points 63 and 64). It observed that the concept of foreseeable relevance in the DAC reflects that of the OECD-MC.[38] The reasons are the similarity between the concepts used, and the reference to the OECD-MC

34 Case C-682/15, *Berlioz*, EU:C:2017:373.
35 Joined Cases C-245/19 and C-246/19, *B and others*, EU:C:2020:795.
36 Case C-437/19, *L.*, EU:C:2021:953.
37 Case C-682/15, *Berlioz*, EU:C:2017:373.
38 See also C. Öner, An Analysis of the "Foreseeable Relevance" Standard and the International Exchange of Tax Information: Are the European Union and the OECD in Agreement?, 77 *Bulletin of International Taxation* 6 2023.

in the explanatory memorandum to the proposal[39] which led to the adoption of the DAC. In addition, the Court referred to the Commentary on Art. 26 of the OECD-MC (*Berlioz* point 67). In the *L* Case (point 69-70) the Court also held that the interpretation of the provisions of the DAC corresponds to that of the concept of 'foreseeable relevance' of Art. 26(1) OECD-MC and refers to point 67 of the *Berlioz* Case. Furthermore, in point 71 of the *L* Case, the Court directly referred to paragraphs 5.1 and 5.2 of the Commentary on the OECD-MC.

Preamble 3 of DAC7 states that to ensure the effectiveness of the exchanges of information and to prevent unjustified refusals of requests as well as to provide legal certainty for both tax administrations and taxpayers, 'the internationally agreed standard of foreseeably relevance' should be clearly delineated and codified. For that reason, Art. 5a was inserted in the DAC.

Art.5a(1) states that information is foreseeably relevant where, at the time the request is made, the requesting authority considers that, in accordance with its national law, there is a reasonable possibility that the requested information will be relevant to the tax affairs of one or several taxpayers and that it must be justified for the purposes of the investigation. This is in line with paragraph 5 of the Commentary on Art. 26 OECD-MC and with the case law of the Court. Paragraph 5 of the Commentary to Art. 26 of the OECD-MC states that the test must be done at the time the request is made and adds that whether the information, once provided, actually proves to be relevant, is immaterial. In *Berlioz* (points 70, 71 and 76) the Court held that the 'foreseeable relevance' of a request must be assessed by the requesting Member State implying little scope for review of the requested Member State. According to the Court, the requested authority must, in principle, start from the premise that the request complies with the domestic law of the requesting authority and that the information is necessary for the purposes of its investigation. The requested authority cannot substitute its own assessment of the possible usefulness of the information for that of the requesting authority (*Berlioz*, point 77). However, the requesting authority cannot request information that is of no relevance to the investigation concerned (*Berlioz* point 71). The requested authority must verify whether the information is not devoid of any foreseeable relevance to the investigation being carried out by the requesting authority (*Berlioz* point 78). Art. 5a(2) DAC helps the requested authority by requiring that the requesting authority must at least provide the following information to demonstrate the foreseeable relevance of the requested information: (i) the tax purpose for which the information is sought, and (ii) a specification of the information required for the administration or enforcement of its national law. The Court included similar requirements in *Berlioz* (point 80).

Both in the Commentary on Art. 26 OECD-MC and in the case law of the ECJ, an important border which the requesting State cannot cross is 'fishing expeditions'. Paragraph 5 of the Commentary on Art. 26 of the OECD-MC states that the requested State does not have to provide information in response to requests that are fishing expeditions which the

39 Proposal for a Council Directive COM(2009) 29 final of 2 February 2009 on administrative cooperation in the field of taxation.

Commentary defines as 'speculative requests that have no apparent nexus to an open inquiry or investigation.' According to Preamble 9 of the DAC, the standard of 'foreseeable relevance' is intended to provide for exchange of information in tax matters to the widest possible extent, but Member States are not at liberty to engage in – or obliged to assist in – 'fishing expeditions' or to request information that is unlikely to be relevant to the tax affairs of a given taxpayer. In point 68 of the *Berlioz* Case, the Court observed, with a reference to the Commentary on the OECD-MC, that the aim of the concept of foreseeable relevance according to Preamble 9 of the DAC is to enable the requesting authority to obtain any information that seems to it to be justified for the purpose of its investigation, while not authorising it manifestly to exceed the parameters of that investigation or to place an excessive burden on the requested authority. In the *Shakira* Case the Court also had to decide on what is and what is not a fishing expedition and more specifically, what information and persons must be identified by the requesting State. The Court held that a request relating to contracts, invoices and payments which, although not specifically identified, are defined by criteria relating, first, to the fact that they were concluded or carried out by the person holding the information, secondly, to the fact that they took place during the period covered by that investigation and, thirdly, to their connection with the taxpayer concerned, is not manifestly devoid of any foreseeable relevance where it states the identity of the person holding the information in question, that of the taxpayer concerned by the investigation giving rise to the request for exchange of information, and the period covered by that investigation.[40] In the *L* Case[41] the Court observed that the risk of a 'fishing expedition' is particularly high where the request for information relates to a group of taxpayers who are not identified individually and by name (point 64). However, with reference to paragraphs 5.1 and 5.2 of the Commentary on the OECD-MC regarding the concept of a 'fishing expedition' (point 71), the Court held that a request for information must be regarded as relating to information which does not appear to be manifestly devoid of any foreseeable relevance, where persons are not identified individually and by name but the requesting authority provides a clear and sufficient explanation that it is conducting a targeted investigation into a limited group of persons, justified by reasonable suspicions of non-compliance with a specific legal obligation (point 72).

In this respect, Art. 5a aims to provide a clear legal framework for so called group requests, request for information that concern groups of taxpayers who cannot be identified individually and in which cases the foreseeable relevance of the requested information can only be described on the basis of a common set of characteristics (preamble 4 of DAC7). In her opinion on the *L* Case,[42] AG Kokott held that it follows from this preamble 4 that this is a declaratory amendment to the directive and that group requests were also permissible previously. In her opinion, the amendment was made for reasons of legal certainty and legal clarity, both for persons required to pay taxes and provide information and for the tax administrations.

40 Joined Cases C245/19 and C246/19, *B and others*, EU:C:2020:795, point 124.
41 Case C-437/19, *L.*, EU:C:2021:953.
42 Case C-437/19, *L.*, EU:C:2021:450, point 72.

In Art. 5a(1) it is made clear that the one or several taxpayers for whose tax affairs the information must be foreseeably relevant may be identified by name or otherwise. Art. 5a(3) requires that if a request relates to a group of taxpayers who cannot be identified individually, the requesting authority must provide the requested authority at least with the following information: (a) a detailed description of the group, (b) an explanation of the applicable law and of the facts based on which there is reason to believe that the taxpayers in the group have not complied with the applicable law, (c) an explanation how the requested information would assist in determining compliance by the taxpayers in the group, and (d) where relevant, facts and circumstances related to the involvement of a third party that actively contributed to the potential non-compliance with the applicable law of the taxpayers in the group.

In the *Bean House* Case[43] Germany argued that the DAC does not apply to administrative proceedings which precede taxation, such as a declaratory procedure on the tax status of an asset. Advocate General (AG) Kokott did not agree. According to her the scope of the DAC is broad and includes all information that is 'foreseeably relevant' to the administration and enforcement of the domestic laws concerning taxes. If a binding declaration can affect the determination of a tax within the scope of the DAC, information regarding that declaration is, in her view, also foreseeably relevant to taxation. On the other hand, she observes in point 63 that the monitoring of compliance with conditions for a waiver of inheritance tax (the inheritance tax assessment would not be collected if certain conditions were met for a long period of time), does not fall under the scope of the DAC because as regards conditions of recovery of tax, the RAD (See Chapter 30) applies instead of the DAC. The Court did not touch upon this question.[44]

Some (older) bilateral tax treaties contain restrictions as to the nature or the availability of the data requested. Under those treaties, no obligation exists to supply information which is not readily available, or which is held by banks or insurance companies. The DAC recognises no such restrictions. Art. 6 explicitly requires Member States to carry out administrative enquiries in order to obtain the information requested by the other Member State.[45] The concept of administrative enquiries is defined in Art. 3(7). It means 'all controls, checks and other action taken by Member States in the performance of their duties with a view to ensuring the proper application of tax legislation'. According to AG Kokott in point 67 of her opinion in the *Bean House* case (C-133/13), this is a broad definition which easily includes on-site controls, as the requested authority is to carry out 'any ... enquiries necessary to obtain the information'. The requested authority must follow the same procedures as it would when acting on its own initiative (Art. 6(3)).

The opinion of the AG illustrates the wide scope of the Directive. However, there are still some limitations on the obligation to cooperate, which are discussed in Section 28.10.

43 Opinion of AG Kokott of 2 October 2014 in Case C-133/13, Q *(Bean House)*, EU:C:2014:2255.
44 Opinion of AG Kokott of 2 October 2014 in Case C-133/13, Q *(Bean House)*, EU:C:2014:2255.
45 With DAC7, 'a specific administrative enquiry' was replaced by 'an administrative enquiry' in Art. 6(2), first sentence.

28.2.4 *Channel of Exchange*

Art. 4 describes how the Member States must organise the administrative cooperation. It draws on the organisation of tasks contained in the VAT Regulation on administrative cooperation with the necessary adaptations. The general idea is that, in order to avoid inefficiency and under-use of instruments, exchange of information should take place as much as possible through direct contact between Member States' officials in charge of cooperation. Communication between national liaison offices should be the rule. To that end, every Member State must not only designate a competent authority (Art. 4(1)), but also a single central liaison office (Art. 4(2)). It may further designate competent liaison departments or competent officials to directly exchange information. The central liaison office is responsible for keeping the list of these departments and persons up to date and to make them available to the central offices of other Member States and to the Commission (Arts. 4(3) and (4) *juncto* Arts. 3(3) and (4)). These delegated departments and officials may therefore directly call or email their counterparts in other Member States. Arts. 1(2) and 21 provide that as far as possible, exchange of information should take place by electronic means, using the CCN.

Art. 22 specifically points out to the Member States that they must ensure that their part of the common cooperation system actually works in all respects: effective internal coordination of the liaison organisation, direct contact with the officials of other Member States and smooth operation of all cooperation modalities.

28.2.5 *Temporal Scope*

For the largest part the DAC had immediate effect as from 1 January 2013. As it concerns procedural issues as regards administrative cooperation, immediate effect does not imply any retroactive taxation effect. In the *Sabou* Case[46] the Court observed in point 3 that if a case refers to facts which date from before the repeal of the old Directive, such proceedings are still governed by Directive 77/799. Furthermore, in the *Sparkasse Allgäu* Case,[47] the Court held that for a fundamental freedoms analysis, if facts occurred before the entry into force of a specific provision in the Directive, a later provision cannot retroactively restrict Member States in ensuring the effectiveness of fiscal supervision before the entry into force of the later provision.

Art. 18(3) allows Member States to refuse cooperation as regards requests for information concerning taxable periods prior to 2011 where Art. 8(1) of Directive 77/799/EEC would have allowed them to refuse cooperation before 2011. This Article provided that a requested State was not obliged to furnish information if it would be prevented by its laws or administrative practices from carrying out these enquiries or from collecting or using this information for its own purposes. In practice, Art. 18(3) has the effect that Austria, Luxembourg and Belgium may continue to decline requests concerning bank account information on tax years before 2011.

46 Case C-276/12, *Sabou*, EU:C:2013:678.
47 Case C-522/14, *Sparkasse Allgäu*, EU:C:2016:253.

28.3 Three Types of Exchange of Information

Chapter II of the DAC distinguishes in three separate sections three ways in which information may be exchanged: on request (Section I: Arts. 5, 5a, 6, 7), automatically (Section II: Arts. 8, 8a, 8aa, 8ab, 8ac, 8b (and, as of 1 January 2026 (DAC8), Art. 8adand Art. 8ae) or spontaneously (Section III: Arts. 9, 10). Where the section on exchange on request was changed for the first time with DAC7 and the section on spontaneous exchange has not changed since the DAC was adopted, the section on automatic exchange of information has been amended significantly and regularly. Below, the three types of exchange of information are discussed.

28.3.1 Mandatory Exchange upon Request

Subject to the (few) exceptions discussed in Section 28.10, a requested State is required to supply the information requested by the applying State (Art. 5). However, the obligation to cooperate does not extend to information that is not considered to be 'foreseeably relevant' (see Section 28.2.3).

The requesting State must provide at least the identity of the person under scrutiny (in the case of group requests (see Section 28.2.3): a detailed description of the group) and the tax purpose for which it requests the information (Art. 20(2)). If the information is not available, the requested State must carry out the necessary administrative enquiries to get it (Art. 6(1)). Art. 3(7) defines 'administrative enquiries' as all controls, checks and other actions taken by Member States in the performance of their duties with a view to ensuring the proper application of tax legislation. This includes on-site controls.[48] Furthermore, these administrative enquiries outside offices may be carried out in the whole territory of the requested Member State, according to AG Kokott and the Commission.[49]

A State must conduct administrative enquiries for the requiring authority as if it were enquiring for its own taxation purposes or upon the request of a domestic authority instead of a foreign authority ('national treatment' of foreign requests; Art. 6(3)), even if the information is irrelevant for its own tax purposes (Art. 18(1)).

In the *Berlioz* Case[50] the Court observed that in order to ensure that the DAC has practical effect, the measures to obtain the requested information must include arrangements which ensure that there is sufficient incentive for the relevant person to respond to tax authorities' requests, and thereby enable the requested authority to fulfil its obligations towards the requesting authority. Even though the DAC at that time did not explicitly mention pecuniary penalties,[51] these can be encompassed under 'measures aimed at gathering information' (Art. 18) and under the 'necessary measures to ensure the smooth operation of the administrative cooperation arrangements' (Art. 22(1)(c)). It is irrelevant

48 Opinion of AG Kokott of 2 October 2014 in Case C-133/13, *Q (Bean House)*, EU:C:2014:2255, para 67.
49 Opinion of AG Kokott of 2 October 2014 in Case C-133/13, *Q (Bean House)*, EU:C:2014:2255, para 67.
50 Case C-682/15, *Berlioz*, EU:C:2017:373, point 38.
51 As of 5 June 2017, the DAC includes Art. 25a on penalties; however, this only refers to Arts. 8aa, 8ab, and 8ac (see Section 28.11).

that the national provision in which the penalty is included was not adopted specifically to transpose the Directive, as long as it enables the Member State to comply with the DAC and can thus be regarded as implementing the DAC (*Berlioz* points 37-41).

The requesting State may ask for an administrative enquiry in the requested State, but it has to state reasons for that. If the requested authority considers such enquiry unnecessary, it must 'immediately' inform the requesting authority of its reasons (Art. 6(2)). If specifically asked for, the requested authority is obligated to supply original documents, unless that is contrary to the requested State's provisions (Art. 6(4)).

The information must be provided as soon as possible, at any rate within three[52] months; if no enquiries are necessary (*i.e.* the information is available) within two months (Art. 7(1)). If the requested authority is unable to respond to the request by the three month time limit, it must inform the requesting authority immediately – at any rate within three months after the request was made – stating reasons for its failure, and the date by which it considers it might be able to respond. The time limit may not be longer than six months from the date of the receipt of the request (7(1)). By way of exception, other time limits may be agreed upon (Art. 7(2)). The receipt of the request must be confirmed immediately, preferably electronically (Art. 7(3)). If there are deficiencies in the request, the requested State must notify the applying State immediately – in any case within a month – also of the need for any additional background information (Art. 7(4)). If the requested State does not have the information and is unable to get it or refuses to respond on the grounds provided for in Art. 17, it must relate the reasons thereof immediately and in any case within a month of receipt of the request (Art. 7(6)).

All communications on requests must, as far as possible, be sent using a standard form (Art. 20(1)) and, as far as possible, by electronic means, using the CCN (Art. 21). Feedback motivates officials in the field to make better use of the various forms of information exchange. Therefore, if the supplying State asks for feedback, the requesting State must provide it as soon as possible and no later than three months after the outcome of the use of the information is known, but respecting its national provisions on tax secrecy and data protection (Art. 14(1)). Art. 20(3) requires the use of a standard form, developed by the European Commission in a comitology procedure, to ask and provide this feedback.

28.3.2 Mandatory Automatic Exchange

The preambles to the DAC recognise that mandatory automatic exchange of information without preconditions by all Member States alike is the most effective means of enhancing correct assessments and fighting fraud in cross-border situations. Automatic exchange of information is also regarded an important instrument to fight base erosion and profit shifting (BEPS). For that reason, automatic exchange has been extended significantly. In addition to the already existing automatic exchange on available information on specific categories of income and capital in Art. 8(1) (see Section 28.3.2.1), provisions were included in Art. 8(3a) with DAC2 regarding automatic exchange of information obtained

52 Based on DAC7. Before 2024 it was six months.

from financial institutions under the Common Reporting Standard (CRS) (see Section 28.3.2.2), in Art. 8a with DAC3 regarding the automatic exchange of advance cross-border rulings and advance pricing agreements (see Section 28.3.2.3), in Art. 8aa with DAC4 on the automatic exchange of information on country-by-country reports of multinational entities (see Section 28.3.2.4), in Art. 8ab with DAC6 on mandatory automatic exchange of information on reportable cross-border arrangements (see Chapter 29) and, with DAC7, in Art. 8ac on mandatory exchange of information reported by platform operators (see Section 28.3.2.5). As of 2026, Art. 8ad further expands the automatic exchange with information on crypto-assets (see Section 28.3.2.6), and Art. 8ae results in a further expansion with information on Pillar 2 top-up tax information returns (see Section 28.3.2.7).

Art. 3(9) provides for three definitions of 'automatic exchange'. For the Arts. 8(1), and 8a to 8ac (as of 2026 based on DAC8 and DAC9: 8a to 8ae) it means the systematic communication of predefined information to another Member State, without prior request, at pre-established regular intervals (Art. 3(9)(a)). For Art. 8(3a) it means the systematic communication of predefined information on residents of other Member States to the relevant Member State of residence, without prior request, at pre-established regular intervals (Art. 3(9)(b)). For the purposes of other provisions than those mentioned before, it means the systematic communication of predefined information mentioned in Art. 3(9)(a) and 3(9)(b) (Art. 3(9)(c)).

Once a year, Member States must send each other feedback on the automatic exchange of information, in accordance with practical arrangements agreed upon bilaterally (Art. 14(2)). This feedback must be provided through a standard form, developed by the European Commission in a comitology procedure (Art. 20(3)).

28.3.2.1 Available Information on Specific Categories of Income and Capital (Art. 8(1))

Art. 8(1)) provides for the automatic exchange of six[53] categories of all[54] available information on: (a) employment income; (b) directors' fees; (c) life insurance products not covered by other exchange instruments; (d) pensions; (e) ownership and income from real estate; and (f) royalties. Based on DAC8, as of 2026, a seventh category is added: (g) non-custodial dividend income[55] other than income from dividends exempt from corporate income tax pursuant to Arts. 4, 5 or 6 of the Parent Subsidiary Directive.[56]

The information must be exchanged at least once a year, within six months following the end of the tax year of the Member State during which the information became available (Art. 8(6)(a)). If the tax year and the calendar year coincide, this means that the information must be exchanged before 1 July of the following year. Art. 3(9)(a) (second sentence) clarifies that for the purposes of Art. 8(1), reference to available information relates to information in the tax files of the Member State communicating the information, which

53 Before 2024, it was five, DAC7 added royalties as of that date.
54 The word 'all' was introduced by DAC7 in 2024.
55 As defined in Art. 3, point 28 that is added by DAC8.
56 Council Directive 2011/96/EU of 30 November 2011 on the common system of taxation applicable in the case of parent companies and subsidiaries of different Member States.

is retrievable in accordance with the procedures for gathering and processing information in that Member State. For taxable periods starting on or after 1 January 2024, Member States must endeavor to include the Tax Identification Number (TIN) of residents that is issued by the Member State of residence.[57]

The condition that only 'available' information is automatically exchanged may lead to imbalances of exchange content between different Member States. Therefore, Member States must annually inform the Commission of at least two categories with regard to which they communicate information concerning residents of another Member State (Art. 8(1) last sentence). In addition, Art. 8(2) required Member States to inform the Commission before 1 January 2024 of at least four categories on which they would automatically exchange information concerning taxable periods starting on or after 1 January 2025. DAC8 added the requirement to Art. 8(2) that before 1 January 2026, Member States must inform the Commission of at least five categories on which they will automatically exchange information concerning taxable periods starting on or after 1 January 2026.

Member States may indicate to other Member States that they do not wish to receive information on one or several of the listed categories of income and capital and must inform the Commission thereof (Art. 8(3)). The idea is to provide each other with useful information, not to be snowed under bulk information. The format of this automatic exchange is a standard computerised format adopted by the Commission in a comitology procedure (Art. 20(4) *juncto* Art. 26(2)).

Both the European Commission[58] and the European Court of Auditors evaluated the exchange of information under Art. 8(1) in 2019 and 2021 respectively. The European Court of Auditors came to the conclusion that there are weaknesses related to the timeliness and accuracy: the data exchanged is not always complete and information is sometimes shared late.[59] In 2024, the European Commission started a second evaluation, which covered the years 2018 to 2022 (DAC1-DAC6). At the time of writing, the results of this evaluation had not yet been published.

28.3.2.2 *The Common Reporting Standard (CRS): Information on Foreign Account Holders and Their Accounts to be reported by Financial Institutions (DAC2)*[60]

All over the world, tax evasion by not including (income on) foreign accounts and other assets in one's tax return has been regarded problematic for years. In 2010, the US forced

57 Added to art. 8(1) by DAC7.

58 Commission staff working document. Evaluation of the Council Directive 2011/16/EU on administrative cooperation in the field of taxation and repealing Directive 77/799/EEC {SWD(2019) 328 final, https://ec.europa.eu/taxation_customs/system/files/2019-09/2019_staff_working_document_evaluation_on_dac.pdf.

59 European Court of Auditors, *Exchanging tax information in the EU: solid foundation, cracks in the implementation*, 2021, p. 24, https://www.eca.europa.eu/lists/ecadocuments/sr21_03/sr_exchange_tax_inform_en.pdf.

60 For an extensive discussion I refer to Maryte Somare and Viktoria Wöhrer, Automatic Exchange of Financial Information under the Directive on Administrative Cooperation in the Light of the Global Movement towards Transparency, *Intertax*, 2015 no. 12, pp. 804-815.

a breakthrough by introducing an unconventional measure which led to the end of bank secrecy in third States such as, notably Switzerland, but also in all EU Member States, as the old DAC contained a Union preference clause requiring Member States to share information with other Member States at least at the same level as they share information with any third State. The US Foreign Account Tax Compliance Act (FATCA) aimed at enforcing the filing of foreign accounts by requiring foreign financial institutions and certain other non-financial foreign entities to either report foreign assets held by their US account holders or face a 30% withholding tax on all of their US income. To reduce the administrative burden on their financial institutions, various countries, including all Member States, have negotiated bilateral automatic exchange agreements with the US to implement FATCA.

Following this development, the G20 mandated the OECD to build on these intergovernmental agreements (IGAs) to develop a single global standard for automatic exchange of financial account information in tax matters.[61] This global standard was released in 2014 in the form of a package: a Model Competent Authority Agreement, a Common Reporting Standard (CRS), Commentaries on the Model Competent Authority Agreement and Common Reporting Standard and the Information Technology Modalities for implementing the global standard.[62] The influence of FATCA is clear: even though there are differences (most importantly, FATCA's 30% withholding tax obligation is not included), FATCA and the CRS are very similar.[63]

In 2014, the OECD's Multilateral Competent Authority Agreement for the Common Reporting Standard (CRS MCAA)[64] to automatically exchange foreign account information was opened for signing. This agreement specifies the details of what information will be exchanged and when, as set out in the Standard. The CRS MCAA is based on Art. 6 of the Multilateral Convention on Mutual Administrative Assistance in Tax Matters (see Chapter 28). A total of 106 jurisdictions had signed the agreement on 7 November 2024.[65] The US is not one of them as it relies on FATCA and its bilateral IGAs.[66]

Subsequently, DAC2 extended the scope of Art. 8 DAC to include the same information covered by the OECD Model Competent Authority Agreement and Common Reporting

61 See also Nana Ama Sarfo, Achim Pross: Taking the Long Gamble on Tax Multilateralism, *Tax Notes International*, 16 December 2024, pp. 1669-1677.

62 https://web-archive.oecd.org/tax/automatic-exchange/common-reporting-standard/index.htm.

63 For an overview of the differences between the FATCA Model 1 IGA and the CRS, see OECD, Standard for Automatic Exchange of Financial Information in Tax Matters, Implementation Handbook, second edition (2018), Part III: The Standard Compared with FATCA Model 1 IGA, pp. 127-144, https://web-archive.oecd.org/temp/2020-02-05/369593-implementation-handbook-standard-for-automatic-exchange-of-financial-account-information-in-tax-matters.htm.

64 https://web-archive.oecd.org/2020-05-29/385805-cbc-mcaa.pdf.

65 https://www.oecd.org/tax/automatic-exchange/about-automatic-exchange/CbC-MCAA-Signatories.pdf.

66 See also Robert, Goulder, Can FATCA Serve Two Masters? The Swedish Experience, *Tax Notes International*, 23 December 2024, pp. 1993-1996.

Standard.[67] These extensive measures are included in Art. 8(3a), (6), and (7a) and in Annexes I and II and had to be implemented before 1 January 2016 (for Austria: 1 January 2017). According to preamble 13 to DAC2, the OECD Commentaries on the Model Competent Authority Agreement and Common Reporting Standard are a source of illustration or interpretation of the Directive. Given the much wider scope of the obligations under the DAC, the EU Savings Directive became obsolete and was repealed as of 1 January 2016.[68]

As of 2016, financial institutions must report certain information on their non-resident account holders and their accounts to the tax authorities in the financial institution's Member State of residence. The residence of a financial institution is, in general, in the Member State that is able to enforce reporting (Annex II Art. 3). Special rules apply for trusts and financial institutions without a tax residence, *e.g.* because they are tax transparent.

Financial institutions must establish the tax residence of their account holders. This might not always be straightforward. In order to facilitate this, Section VI of Annex I obliges financial institutions to obtain a self-certification by new clients enabling financial institutions to determine the client's tax residence. Financial institutions may use their own templates. However, they may not rely on self-certifications and documentary evidence if they know or have reason to know that it is incorrect or unreliable. In these and some other cases the special due diligence rules of Section VII of Annex I apply.[69] Annex II provides for some complementary due diligence rules.

The scope of the reporting obligation is broad. First of all, 'financial institution' means a custodial institution, a depository institution, an investment entity, or a specified insurance company (all terms are defined in Section VIII A of Annex I of the Directive). However, not all financial institutions have to report under the CRS, as certain exemptions apply for institutions which are regarded to be low risk, such as governmental entities, certain pension funds and certain investment vehicles (Section VIII B of Annex I of the Directive; again, all terms used are defined there).

Second, 'financial account' is broadly defined in Section VIII C of Annex I. It does not only include depository accounts and custodial accounts, but also certain equity or debt interests in a financial institution and cash value insurance contracts and annuity insurance contracts (all terms used are defined in Section VIII C of Annex I).[70]

---

67 Council Directive 2014/107/EU of 9 December 2014 amending Directive 2011/16/EU as regards mandatory automatic exchange of information in the field of taxation, O.J. 16 December 2014, L 359, p. 1 (DAC2).

68 Council Directive 2015/2060 of 10 November 2015 repealing Directive 2003/48/EC on taxation of savings income in the form of interest payments, O.J. 18 November 2015, L 301, p. 1.

69 For accounts existing before 31 December 2015, separate due diligence rules applied, which, among others, exempted from the identification and reporting requirements all accounts with a balance below USD 250,000 (Section V of Annex I).

70 See on the similar CRS definitions of 'financial account' and 'investment entity' Grahame Jackson & Harriet Brown, 'The Common Reporting Standard, the "Managed By" Entity and the Purpose Test', 62 *European Taxation* 2 2022.

Third, the reporting obligations of the financial institutions have a broad scope. It includes information on the holder of the account, on the account or its value, and the interest, dividends and other income which were received in relation to the account (Section I of Annex I). The Member State must electronically (Art. 20(4), using the CCN), annually (Art. 8(6)(b)) and automatically exchange this information with the tax administration of the residence country of the account holder (Art. 8(3a)) within nine months following the end of the calendar year or other appropriate reporting period to which the information relates (Art. 8(6)(b)). In this regard it is important to notice that the condition that automatic exchange may be subject to the availability of the information requested as provided for in Art. 8(1) does not apply to the obligations under Art. 8(3a) (preamble 14 to DAC2). Section IX of Annex I obliges Member States to have rules and administrative procedures in place to ensure effective implementation of, and compliance of financial institutions with, the reporting and due diligence procedures. These include (1) rules to prevent financial institutions, persons or intermediaries from adopting practices intended to circumvent the reporting and due diligence procedures, (2) rules requiring financial institutions to keep records on these procedures, (3) administrative procedures to verify compliance with the reporting and due diligence procedures and to follow up with a financial institution when undocumented accounts are reported, (4) administrative procedures to ensure that the non-reporting financial institutions and excluded accounts continue to have a low risk of being used to evade tax, and (5) effective enforcement provisions to address non-compliance. The latter may include financial penalties.

The Directive only has regard to the exchange of financial account information between Member States. However, the EU has also signed agreements on the automatic exchange of financial account information with Switzerland,[71] Liechtenstein,[72] San Marino,[73] Andorra,[74] Monaco[75] and Saint-Barthélemy.[76] These provide for the implementation of the OECD global standard for automatic exchange of financial account information and include provisions similar to those in the DAC. These jurisdictions automatically exchange the information listed in Section I of Annex I to the DAC. The jurisdictions with which such

71 Amending Protocol to the Agreement between the European Community and the Swiss Confederation providing for measures equivalent to those laid down in Council Directive 2003/48/EC on taxation of savings income in the form of interest payments, O.J. 19 December 2015, L 333, p. 12.

72 Amending Protocol to the Agreement between the European Community and the Principality of Liechtenstein providing for measures equivalent to those laid down in Council Directive 2003/48/EC on taxation of savings income in the form of interest payments, O.J. 24 December 2015, L 339, p. 3.

73 Amending Protocol to the Agreement between the European Community and the Republic of San Marino providing for measures equivalent to those laid down in Council Directive 2003/48/ EC on taxation of savings income in the form of interest payments, O.J. 31 December 2015, L 346, p. 3.

74 Amending Protocol to the Agreement between the European Community and the Principality of Andorra providing for measures equivalent to those laid down in Council Directive 2003/48/EC on taxation of savings income in the form of interest payments, O.J. 1 October 2016, L 268, p. 40.

75 Amending Protocol to the Agreement between the European Community and the Principality of Monaco providing for measures equivalent to those laid down in Council Directive 2003/48/EC, O.J. 19 August 2016, L 225, p. 3.

76 Agreement between the European Union and the French Republic concerning the application to the collectivity of Saint-Barthélemy of Union legislation on the taxation of savings and administrative cooperation in the field of taxation, O.J. 15 November 2014, L 330, p. 12.

agreement is in place are included in the definition of 'participating jurisdiction' of Annex I, Section VIII(D) (4)(c) of the DAC if they are identified in a list published by the European Commission. In 2024, the EU started negotiations with Switzerland, Liechtenstein, San Marino, Andorra and Monaco to update these agreements[77] to include the OECD's crypto-asset reporting framework (CARF, see Section 28.3.2.6) and changes to the CRS and to make them compliant with the General Data Protection Regulation[78] (GDPR).

For the purposes of data protection (see also Section 28.14), reporting financial institutions and the competent authorities are 'data controllers' (Art. 25(3)). This means that certain data protection obligations are imposed on financial institutions. Member States must ensure that financial institutions inform their clients that their information is collected and transferred in accordance with the DAC and provide to their clients all the information they are entitled to in sufficient time for the client to exercise his data protection rights, in any case before the information is reported (Art. 25(4)). Just as is the case for any information exchanged under the DAC, financial institutions and Member States may not retain the information on the foreign account holders and their accounts for longer than necessary to achieve the purposes of the DAC and, in any case, must act in accordance with each data controller's domestic rules on statute of limitations (Art. 25(5)). A breach of security must be reported to each individual person whose personal data this concerns if that breach is likely to adversely affect the protection of his personal data or privacy (Art. 21(2), third paragraph).

Both the European Commission[79] and the European Court of Auditors evaluated the exchange of information under Art. 8(3a) in 2019 and 2021, respectively. The European Court of Auditors came to the conclusion that DAC2 information exchange functions generally on time, but still lacks in data quality and completeness.[80] In 2024, the European Commission started a second evaluation, which covered the years 2018 to 2022 (DAC1-DAC6). At the time of writing, the results of this evaluation had not yet been published.

On 8 June 2023, the OECD published an update to the CRS with amendments to the CRS rules and related commentary and an addendum to the CRS MCAA and related commentary.[81] This was developed alongside the Crypto-Asset Reporting Framework (CARF, see

77 Elodie Lamer, EU Seeks GDPR-Compliant EOI Agreement Updates With Five Countries, *Tax Notes International*, 20 May 2024.

78 Regulation (EU) 2016/679 of the European Parliament and of the Council of 27 April 2016 on the protection of natural persons with regard to the processing of personal data and on the free movement of such data, and repealing Directive 95/46/EC (General Data Protection Regulation) O.J. No. L 119 of 4 May2016, p. 1.

79 Commission staff working document. Evaluation of the Council Directive 2011/16/EU on administrative cooperation in the field of taxation and repealing Directive 77/799/EEC {SWD(2019) 328 final, https://ec.europa.eu/taxation_customs/system/files/2019-09/2019_staff_working_document_evaluation_on_dac.pdf.

80 European Court of Auditors, *Exchanging tax information in the EU: solid foundation, cracks in the implementation*, 2021, p. 27, https://www.eca.europa.eu/Lists/ECADocuments/SR21_03/SR_Exchange_tax_inform_EN.pdf.

81 OECD (2023), International Standards for Automatic Exchange of Information in Tax Matters: Crypto-Asset Reporting Framework and 2023 update to the Common Reporting Standard, OECD Publishing, Paris, https://doi.org/10.1787/896d79d1-en.

Section 28.3.2.6) and brought new financial assets, products, and intermediaries within the scope of CRS, because they are potential alternatives to traditional financial products. This alignment was meant to avoid duplicative reporting with that foreseen in the CARF. In addition, to enhance the reporting outcomes under the CRS, it included more detailed reporting requirements, the strengthening of the due diligence procedures, the introduction of a new, optional non-reporting financial institution category for investment entities that are genuine non-profit organisations and the creation of a new excluded account category for capital contribution accounts.

DAC8[82] integrated, amongst others, these amendments to the CRS in the DAC, including the integration of e-money and central bank digital currency provisions, set out in Part II of the CARF. This leads, amongst others to changes of Annex I of the DAC as of 2026. Preamble 26 of DAC8 repeated that in implementing the CRS amendments Member States should use the commentaries on the CRS MCAA and CRS as sources of illustration or interpretation.

28.3.2.3 Mandatory Automatic Exchange of Information on Advance Cross-Border Rulings and Advance Pricing Arrangements (DAC3)

Under OECD BEPS Action 5 on countering harmful tax practices, a framework was agreed for the compulsory spontaneous exchange of information on rulings that could give rise to BEPS concerns in the absence of such exchange.[83] The fight against cross-border tax avoidance, aggressive tax planning and harmful tax competition also inspired the introduction of Art. 8a on the automatic exchange of information on Advance Cross-Border Rulings (ACRs) and Advance Pricing Arrangements (APAs) through DAC3.[84] Member States had to implement the provisions on this form of automatic exchange of information before 1 January 2017.

Before 2017, information on rulings could also be exchanged based on Art. 1(1) in combination with Art. 5, but this only covered exchange on request. Tax administrations are not always aware of foreign rulings and thus will not actively request information on such rulings. Rulings may also fall under the scope of spontaneous exchange of information under Art. 9, but the initiative to exchange rulings under this Article lies with the Member State which would have to exchange the information (similarly: preamble 4 of DAC3), and this might not have a high priority for that Member State. The Member States had agreed on spontaneous exchange of rulings within the Code of Conduct Group (see Chapter 23), but this soft law agreement was not very effective.

---

82 Council Directive (EU) 2023/2226 of 17 October 2023 amending Directive 2011/16/EU on administrative cooperation in the field of taxation.

83 OECD, Countering Harmful Tax Practices More Effectively, Taking into Account Transparency and Substance, Action 5 - 2015 Final Report, 5 October 2015.

84 Council Directive 2015/2376/EU of 8 December 2015 amending Directive 2011/16/EU as regards mandatory automatic exchange of information in the field of taxation, O.J. 18 December 2015, L 332, p. 1.

Preamble 1 of DAC3 observes that rulings concerning tax-driven structures have, in certain cases, led to a low level of taxation of artificially high amounts of income in the country issuing, amending or renewing the advance ruling and left artificially low amounts of income to be taxed in any other countries involved. According to this preamble, an increase in transparency was urgently required. It has to be mentioned that the preamble appreciates that the common practice of the issuance of advance tax rulings facilitates the consistent and transparent application of the law, providing certainty, and can thus encourage investment and compliance with the law and therefore be conducive to the objective of further developing the single market. Rulings are, therefore, not necessarily bad according to the preambles. The amendments to the DAC are not aimed at prohibiting rulings, but at increasing transparency. Nevertheless, the new rules seem to have had a negative effect on the appetite to request a ruling in some jurisdictions.

Member States must automatically exchange information on cross-border tax rulings and transfer-pricing arrangements with other EU Member States (Art. 8a(1)). The scope of this automatic exchange is very broad. This is intended as, according to preamble 6, the scope has to be sufficiently broad to cover a wide range of situations.

'ACR' and 'APA' are defined broadly and in general terms and not limited to what certain jurisdictions might use the word 'ruling' for. In addition, the definitions are broader than the more precise ones used in the BEPS Action 5 report. In para 95 (p. 47) of that report rulings are defined as "any advice, information or undertaking provided by a tax authority to a specific taxpayer or group of taxpayers concerning their tax situation and on which they are entitled to rely". Furthermore, the report includes specific definitions of advance tax rulings and APAs. The latter is derived from the OECD Transfer Pricing Guidelines. Because of the difference in definitions, more information must be exchanged under the DAC than under BEPS Action 5.

'Advance cross-border ruling' means (Art. 3(14)) any agreement, communication, or any other instrument or action with similar effects, including one issued, amended or renewed in the context of a tax audit, and which meets the following conditions: it (a) is issued, amended or renewed by or on behalf of the government of the tax authority of the Member State, irrespective of whether it is effectively used; (b) is issued, amended or renewed to a particular person or a group of persons (this includes natural persons, legal persons, association of persons recognised as having the capacity to perform legal acts and any other legal arrangement, regardless of whether it has legal personality, owning or managing assets, which, including income derived therefrom, are subject to any of the taxes covered by the DAC (Art. 3(11)), and upon which that person or a group of persons is entitled to rely; (c) concerns the interpretation or application of a legal or administrative provision on the administration or enforcement of tax legislation (including local tax legislation); (d) relates to a cross-border transaction or to the question of whether or not activities carried on by a person in another jurisdiction create a permanent establishment (as of 2026, DAC8 adds 'or to the question of whether or not a natural person is resident for tax purposes in the Member State issuing the ruling'); and (e) is made in advance of: (i) the cross-border transaction; (ii) the activities potentially creating a permanent establishment; or (iii) the filing of a tax return covering the period in which the transaction or series of transactions or activities took place.

In this respect, 'cross-border transaction' means that not all of the parties to the transaction or series of transactions are resident in the Member State issuing the ruling; or that any of the parties to the transactions or series of transactions is simultaneously resident in more than one jurisdiction; or that one of the parties to the transactions or series of transactions carries on business in another jurisdiction through a permanent establishment; or that the transactions or series of transactions have a cross-border impact (Art. 3(16)). The cross-border transaction may involve, but is not restricted to, the making of investments, the provision of goods, services, finance or the use of tangible or intangible assets and does not have to directly involve the person receiving the advance cross-border ruling.

'Advance pricing arrangement' is defined in Art. 3(15) as any agreement, communication or any other instrument or action with similar effects, including one issued, amended or renewed in the context of a tax audit which: (a) is issued, amended or renewed by or on behalf of the government of the tax authority of the Member State, irrespective of whether it is effectively used; (b) is issued, amended or renewed to a person or a group of persons, and upon which that person or a group of persons is entitled to rely; and (c) determines in advance of cross-border transactions between related entities an appropriate set of criteria for the determination of the transfer pricing for those transactions or determines the attribution of profits to a permanent establishment.

Here, 'cross-border transaction' means that not all of the related entities to the transactions or series of transactions are resident in the territory of a single jurisdiction, or that the transaction or series of transactions have a cross-border impact (Art. 3(16) (last sentence)). Entities are deemed related where one entity participates directly or indirectly in the management, control or capital of another entity or the same persons participate directly or indirectly in the management, control or capital of the entities (Art. 3(15) (penultimate sentence)). Transfer prices are the prices at which an entity transfers physical goods and intangible property or provides services to related entities (Art. 3(15) (last sentence).

It is important to note that not the ACRs and APAs themselves are automatically exchanged, but only summary information on these ACRs and APAs. Exchange of the full text of the ACRs and APAs is, as before, possible upon request, but now the requesting Member State will have more information to assess the 'foreseeable relevance' of a request. The following information on ACRs and APAs must be exchanged automatically with other EU Member States (Art. 8a(6)): (a) the identification of the person, other than a natural person (based on DAC8, as of 2026, an exception applies to ACRs concerning natural persons on which information must be exchanged[85]), and where appropriate the group of persons to which it belongs; (b) a summary of the ACR or APA, including a description of the relevant business activities or transaction or series of transactions provided and any

85 See also Vassilis Dafnomilis, DAC8: Exchange of HNWI Cross-border Rulings, *Kluwer International Tax Blog*, 16 January 2023, https://kluwertaxblog.com/2023/01/16/dac8-exchange-of-hnwi-cross-border-rulings/.

other information that could assist the competent authority in assessing a potential tax risk without leading to the disclosure of a commercial, industrial or professional secret or of information the disclosure of which would be contrary to public policy; (c) the dates of issuance, amendment or renewal of the ACR or APA; (d) the start date of the period of validity of the ACR or APA, if specified; (e) the end date of the period of validity of the ACR or APA, if specified; (f) the type of ACR or APA; (g) the amount of the transaction or series of transactions of the ACR or APA if such amount is referred to in the advance cross-border ruling or advance pricing arrangement; (h) the description of the set of criteria used for the determination of the ACR or APA itself in the case of an transfer-pricing arrangement; (i) the identification of the method used for determination of the transfer pricing or the transfer price itself in the case of an transfer pricing arrangement; (j) the identification of the other Member States, if any, likely to be concerned by the ACR or APA; (k) the identification of any person, other than a natural person (based on DAC8, as of 2026, an exception applies to ACRs concerning natural persons on which information must be exchanged), in the other Member States, if any, likely to be affected by the ACR or APA (indicating to which Member States the affected persons are linked); and (l) an indication of whether the information communicated is based upon the ACR or APA itself or upon a request to conclude a multilateral or bilateral transfer-pricing arrangement with a third country if this transfer-pricing arrangement may not be disclosed to third parties.

The exchange takes place through standard forms in a secure Member State central directory on administrative cooperation in the field of taxation (Arts. 20(5) and 21(5)). The competent authorities of all Member States have access to the information recorded in that directory. The European Commission also has access, except for the information under (a), (b), (h) and (k) (Art. 8a(8)). The necessary practical arrangements are adopted by comitology procedure, as referred to in Art. 26(2).

The information on ACRs or APAs issued, amended or renewed after 31 December 2016, must be exchanged without delay after the ACRs or APAs have been issued, amended or renewed and at the latest three months following the end of the half of the calendar year during which the ACRs or APAs were issued, amended or renewed (Arts. 8a(1), 8a(5)(a)).[86] If an ACR or APA exclusively concerns and involves the tax affairs of one or more natural persons, no information is exchanged until 2026 (Art. 8a(4)). As of 2026, DAC8 introduces an exception in Art. 8(4) for certain ACRs regarding natural persons that were issued, amended or renewed after 1 January 2026. Information must be exchanged if the amount of the transaction(s) exceeds EUR 1,5 million or if the ACR determines whether a person is or is not resident for tax purposes in the Member State issuing the ruling (except for rulings on taxation at source with regard to non-residents' income from employment, director's fees or pensions if the threshold of 1,5 million euro is not exceeded).

86 Information on rulings which were issued, amended or renewed on or after 1 January 2012 and before 1 January 2017 had to be exchanged before 1 January 2018 (Arts. 8a(1), 8a(5)(b)). No information is automatically exchanged on rulings which were no longer valid on 1 January 2014 (Art. 8a(2)). Furthermore, no information is exchanged on rulings issued, amended or renewed before 1 April 2016 to a particular person or a group of persons, excluding those conducting mainly financial or investment activities, with a group-wide annual net turnover of less than EUR 40 million (Art. 8a(2)).

Bilateral or multilateral advance pricing arrangements with third countries are excluded where the international tax agreement under which the advance pricing arrangement was negotiated does not permit its disclosure to third parties. These APAs will be exchanged under Art. 9, where the international tax agreement under which the APA was negotiated permits its disclosure, and the competent authority of the third country gives permission for the information to be disclosed (Art. 8a(3)).

Both the European Commission and the European Court of Auditors evaluated the exchange of information under Art. 8a in 2019 and 2021, respectively. The European Commission found that a few countries did not share any rulings and that no information is available on the actual use of DAC3 information and that information exchanged (especially, the summary of the ruling) is often too brief to be usable.[87] The European Court of Auditors came to the conclusion that information in the EU's DAC3 directory is mostly complete, but little used by Member States.[88] In 2024, the European Commission started a second evaluation, which covered the years 2018 to 2022 (DAC1-DAC6). At the time of writing, the results of this evaluation had not yet been published.

28.3.2.4 Country-by-Country Reporting (DAC4)[89]

One of the problems for tax administrations is that when companies which are part of one multinational group trade with each other, this is not a regular market transaction. For that reason, the price agreed on by the two companies (the 'transfer price') might not resemble the market price which would have been agreed on by two unrelated companies. This transfer-pricing problem (see also Chapter 21) has been dealt with in international tax law by the so-called "at arm's length principle", which is endorsed by the OECD. This principle entails that any related party transaction or dealing is treated for tax purposes as if such transaction or dealing was agreed under the same terms and conditions as third party transactions or dealings would have been. However, establishing that internal cross-border transactions have taken place and whether a correct at arm's length price has been used can be difficult for tax administrations. This leaves room for base erosion and profit shifting by multinational enterprises (MNEs).

---

87 Commission staff working document. Evaluation of the Council Directive 2011/16/EU on administrative cooperation in the field of taxation and repealing Directive 77/799/EEC {SWD(2019) 328 final, p. 21, https://ec.europa.eu/taxation_customs/system/files/2019-09/2019_staff_working_document_evaluation_on_dac.pdf.

88 European Court of Auditors, *Exchanging tax information in the EU: solid foundation, cracks in the implementation*, 2021, p. 33, https://www.eca.europa.eu/Lists/ECADocuments/SR21_03/SR_Exchange_tax_inform_EN.pdf.

89 See for an extensive discussion: Roman Seer and Anna Lena Wilms, Tax Transparency in the European Union Regarding Country by Country Reporting (BEPS Action 13), *EC Tax Review*, 2016 no. 5/6, pp. 325-334 and Raphael Müller, Miles Schoenrock and Christoph Spengel, How to Move Forward with Country-by-Country Reporting? A Qualitative Content Analysis of the Stakeholders' Comments in the OECD 2020 Review, 14 *World Tax Journal* 2022 no. 2, pp. 261-284.

In the BEPS Action 13 Report[90] it was suggested to tackle BEPS by enhancing transparency for tax administrations by revised standards for transfer-pricing documentation and a template for country-by-country (CbC) reporting of income, taxes paid and certain measures of economic activity.[91] It provided for a three-tiered standardised approach to transfer-pricing documentation which obliges MNEs to provide for (1) a master file with high-level information on their global business operations and transfer-pricing policies which has to be available to all relevant tax administrations; (2) a local file with detailed transactional transfer-pricing documentation specific to a country; and for large MNEs (3) a CbC Report that provides annually and for each tax jurisdiction in which they do business for certain information. The CbC reports must be filed in the residence country of the ultimate parent and be shared between countries through automatic exchange of information. The aim of these three documents is to require taxpayers to articulate consistent transfer-pricing positions and to provide tax administrations with useful information to assess transfer-pricing risks.

The 2006 Code of Conduct on transfer pricing documentation in the EU (EU TPD),[92] initiated by the EU Joint Transfer Pricing forum, already set out an EU-wide common approach to transfer pricing documentation requirements. The EU TPD includes a master file available to all Member States involved and a local file available to the specific Member State concerned. The EU TPD is soft law which does not impose obligations on Member States. At the time the Commission felt that transfer pricing was not an area in which it had a clear mandate to present more than soft-law initiatives.[93] The EU TPD did not provide for a mechanism for the provision of a CbC report.

One of the elements of the January 2016 Anti-Tax Avoidance Package[94] regarded a revision of the DAC to include country-by-country reporting. DAC4[95] introduced this CbC report of BEPS Action 13 and the mandatory automatic exchange thereof as hard law in the DAC (most importantly: Art. 8aa and Annex III). The CbC provisions had to be implemented by 4 June 2017 and apply as of 5 June 2017. The first CbC report had to be filed over fiscal years starting on or after 1 January 2016.[96]. The EU CbC provisions closely follow the standards

90 OECD, *Transfer Pricing Documentation and Country-by-Country Reporting, Action 13 – 2015 Final Report*, 5 October 2015.

91 See also on CbC: Annet Wanyana Oguttu, Curtailing BEPS through Enforcing Corporate Transparency: The Challenges of Implementing Country-by-Country Reporting in Developing Countries and the Case for Making Public Country-by-Country Reporting Mandatory, 12 *World Tax Journal* 2020 no. 12.

92 Resolution of the Council and of the representatives of the governments of the Member States, meeting within the Council, of 27 June 2006 on a code of conduct on transfer pricing documentation for associated enterprises in the European Union (EU TPD), O.J. 28 July 2006, C 176, p. 1.

93 European Commission, Code of Conduct on transfer pricing documentation in the EU – Frequently Asked Questions, MEMO/05/414, 10 November 2005.

94 Communication from the Commission to the European Parliament and the Council, Anti-Tax Avoidance Package: Next steps towards delivering effective taxation and greater tax transparency in the EU, 28 January 2016, COM(2016) 23 final.

95 Council Directive 2016/88/EU of 25 May 2016 amending Directive 2011/16/EU as regards mandatory automatic exchange of information in the field of taxation, O.J. 3 June 2016, L 146, p. 8.

96 Member States were allowed to postpone this to 1 January 2017 (Art. 2(1) third paragraph of Annex III).

developed by the OECD in Action 13 in order to minimise costs and administrative burdens both for tax administrations and for MNE groups (preamble 13 and 14 of DAC4). Preamble 17 of DAC4 holds that to ensure a consistent implementation in the EU, Member States must use the 2015 Action 13 Report as a source of illustration or interpretation when implementing the Directive. This means that the Action 13 Report is an important source of information when interpreting the EU CbC rules.

Preamble 3 of DAC4 emphasises the need for Member States' tax authorities to have comprehensive and relevant information on MNE Groups regarding their structure, transfer-pricing policy and internal transactions in and outside the EU in order to react on harmful practices by making changes in legislation, undertaking risk assessments and tax audits and to identify whether companies have artificially shifted profits to low tax countries. Furthermore, the idea is that increased tax transparency could induce MNEs to abandon BEPS practices (preamble 4). The amendments to the DAC both included the inclusion of filing rules for groups of MNEs in Annex III of the Directive, the introduction of mandatory automatic exchange of information on the CbC report in Art. 8aa and Art. 25a (See Section 28.11) on penalties for MNEs failing to comply with the CbC reporting obligations.

Art. 8aa(1) requires Member States to take the necessary measures to require an MNE group's ultimate parent (as defined in Art. 1(7) of Annex III) that is tax resident in their territory to file a CbC report within 12 months after the end of the fiscal year. Section I of Annex III defines the terms used in this regard. In this respect, 'Group' means a collection of enterprises related through ownership or control such that it is either required to prepare consolidated financial statements for financial reporting purposes under applicable accounting principles or would be so required if equity interests in any of the enterprises were traded on a public securities exchange (Art. 1(1) of Annex III). Art. 1(3) defines an 'MNE group' as any group of companies that includes two or more enterprises with tax residence in different jurisdictions, or that includes an enterprise that is tax resident in one jurisdiction and has a permanent establishment taxed in another jurisdiction. A group which, based on its consolidated financial statements, has a total consolidated group revenue of less than EUR 750 million during the preceding fiscal year is exempt from the CbC reporting obligation (Art. 1(4) of Annex III). If the ultimate parent entity is not obliged to file a CbC report in its tax residence jurisdiction or if this report is or cannot be exchanged,[97] each entity which is tax resident in a Member State must, in principle, file the CbC report in its tax jurisdiction (Art. 2(1) of Annex III). This could, for example, be the case if the ultimate parent company is tax resident outside the EU in a tax haven. When there are more entities tax resident in the EU, the MNE group may designate one of those entities to file the CbC report (Art. 2(1) (fifth paragraph) of Annex III). If the MNE group has appointed a 'surrogate parent entity' (as defined in Art. 1(8) of Annex III) which files the CbC report in its jurisdiction of tax residence on behalf of the MNE group, the other entities do not have to file a CbC report. The surrogate parent

97 For example, because there is no agreement with the country of the ultimate parent based on which this is possible (this would not apply to EU Member States) or that country has systematically failed to provide CbC reports.

entity may be deemed a resident of a non-EU Member State if its country of residence requires the filing of CbC reports, information can be exchanged with this jurisdiction, the country does not systematically fail to do so and if notification requirements have been met (Art. 2(2) of Annex III).

Art. 8aa(3) states which information the CbC report must provide for. It must contain aggregate information relating to the amount of revenue, profit or loss before income tax, income tax paid, income tax accrued, stated capital, accumulated earnings, number of employees, and tangible assets other than cash or cash equivalents with regard to each jurisdiction in which the MNE group operates. Furthermore, it must identify each entity of the group: the jurisdiction of tax residence and, where different from such jurisdiction, the jurisdiction under the laws of which it is organised and the nature of the main business activity or activities of such entities. Section III (A) of Annex III provides for a template for the CbC report which consists of three tables. Table 1 gives an overview of allocation of income, taxes and business activities by tax jurisdiction. Table 2 lists all entities and table 3 must include any further brief information or explanation which is considered necessary or that would facilitate the understanding of the compulsory information provided in the CbC report. Section III(B) and (C) of Annex III provide for general and specific (for each column of the template) instructions for filling in the CbC report.

The Member State which receives the CbC report from the ultimate parent entity or any other reporting entity must communicate this by way of automatic exchange to any other Member State in which, on the basis of the information in the CbC report, one or more entities of the MNE group are tax resident or subject to tax with respect to a business carried out through a permanent establishment (Art. 8aa(2)). The information must be provided by electronic means, using the CCN (Arts 20(6) and 21(6)). This has to take place within 15 months after the fiscal year to which the CbC report relates (Art. 8aa(4)). As the reporting entity must file the report within 12 months (Art. 8aa(1)), the minimum period a Member State has to automatically exchange the information is three months.

Receiving tax administrations may use CbC reports for purposes of assessing high-level transfer pricing and other BEPS-related risks, including assessing the risk of non-compliance with transfer-pricing rules and, where appropriate, for economic and statistical analysis (Art. 16(6)). However, transfer-pricing adjustments may not be based on the CbC report, although the receiving tax administration may use the information as a basis for making further enquiries into the MNE Group's transfer-pricing arrangements or into other tax matters in the course of a tax audit, and, as a result, may make appropriate adjustments to the taxable income of an entity (Art. 16(6) (last two sentences)). The exchange of information under Art. 8aa has been evaluated, both by the European Commission[98] and the European Court of Auditors, in 2019 and 2021, respectively. The European Court of

98 Commission staff working document. Evaluation of the Council Directive 2011/16/EU on administrative cooperation in the field of taxation and repealing Directive 77/799/EEC {SWD(2019) 328 final, https://ec.europa.eu/taxation_customs/system/files/2019-09/2019_staff_working_document_evaluation_on_dac.pdf.

Auditors came to the conclusion that DAC4 information is greatly under-used.[99] It will be interesting to see if the public CbC reporting obligation that was introduced in 2025 (see Section 28.3.2.4.1), has an effect on the use of CbC information by Member States. In 2024, the European Commission started a second evaluation, which covered the years 2018 to 2022 (DAC1-DAC6). At the time of writing, the results of this evaluation had not yet been published.

28.3.2.4.1 Public Country-by-Country Reporting[100]

The OECD and the G20 did not promote public CbC reporting. However, the European Parliament was very much in favour of such tax transparency measure. According to Velte, the main goal of public CbC reporting is to increase transparency regarding the tax policies of multinational corporations which may lead to an incentive to managers to abandon unethical and unsustainable legal tax practices.[101] He questions whether the power of national regimes should be complemented by an additional monitoring channel of stakeholder pressure. For certain financial institutions[102] and firms in de commodities sector,[103] public CbC already applied. In 2016, the Commission published a proposal (COM 2016 (198))[104] for public CbC reporting, which was debated fiercely both in the Council and in the European Parliament (for the debate on the legal basis I refer to Chapter 27.7).[105]

Some Member States feared that such obligation would lead to a competitive disadvantage of European companies vis a vi US and Chinese companies that do not have such obligation. In November 2019, the required majority was not obtained in the Council. In 2021, a compromise was found and a sufficient majority was reached in the Council. Although European Parliament Members would have preferred more far reaching public CbC reporting obligations,[106] they also adopted the compromise. On 24 November 2021,

99 European Court of Auditors, *Exchanging tax information in the EU: solid foundation, cracks in the implementation*, 2021, p. 38, https://www.eca.europa.eu/Lists/ECADocuments/SR21_03/SR_Exchange_tax_inform_EN.pdf.

100 See also S. Verloove, P. Hoving & R. Aviles Gutierrez, EU Public Country-by-Country Reporting, 29 *International Transfer Pricing Journal* 3 2022.

101 P. Velte, The New European Public Country-by-Country-Reporting Requirement, 62 *European Taxation* 4 2022.

102 Directive 2013/36/EU of the European Parliament and of the Council of 26 June 2013 on access to the activity of credit institutions and the prudential supervision of credit institutions and investment firms, amending Directive 2002/87/EC and repealing Directives 2006/48/EC and 2006/49/EC (CRD IV).

103 Directive 2013/34/EU of the European Parliament and of the Council of 26 June 2013 on the annual financial statements, consolidated financial statements and related reports of certain types of undertakings, amending Directive 2006/43/EC of the European Parliament and of the Council and repealing Council Directives 78/660/EEC and 83/349/EEC.

104 https://eur-lex.europa.eu/legal-content/EN/TXT/?uri=CELEX:52016PC0198.

105 See also: Vikram Chand and Serena Picariello, The Revamping of Public CbCR in Europe: much ado about nothing? *Kluwer International Tax Blog*, 1 June 2021, http://kluwertaxblog.com/2021/06/01/the-revamping-of-public-cbcr-in-europe-much-ado-about-nothing/.

106 European Parliament, Corporate tax transparency: MEPs okay new country-by-country reporting rules, Press release 11 November 2021, ref.: 20211108IPR16839, https://www.europarl.europa.eu/news/en/press-room/20211108IPR16839/corporate-tax-transparency-meps-okay-new-country-by-country-reporting-rules.

the amendment[107] of the Accounting Directive (AD)[108] was adopted and it was published in the Official Journal on 1 December 2021.

In short,[109] Members States are required to oblige ultimate parent undertakings and stand-alone undertakings governed by their national laws with a consolidated revenue exceeding EUR 750 million for each of the last two consecutive years to draw up, publish and make accessible a report on income tax information (with the content required by Art. 48c AD) as regards the latter of those two consecutive financial years (Art. 48b(1) AD). This obligation does not apply to standalone undertakings or groups that are established within the territory of a single Member State and no other tax jurisdiction. The information must be published and made publicly accessible (for free) on a website of the entity to which the public CbC reporting obligation applies. This must be done in at least one of the official languages of the EU and within twelve months after the financial year (Art. 48d AD). The Member States must make the members of the administrative management and supervisory bodies of the company that has the reporting obligation responsible for meeting the public CbC reporting obligation (Art. 48e AD). Member States must apply the public CbC reporting obligations at the latest from the commencement date of the first financial year starting on or after 22 June 2024 (Art. 48g AD).

On 29 November 2024, the European Commission adopted an implementing regulation that standardised the presentation of income tax information for public CbCR.[110] It introduced a common template and electronic formats for public CbC reports, specifications for financial data, requirements for report filing and a taxonomy defining the reportable data. It came into effect for financial years starting on or after 1 January 2025.

Some companies already voluntary started to make tax information public, as part of their ESG (Environment, Social, Governance) policy. For example, since the financial year 2018, Shell publishes a yearly Tax Contribution Report, and also reports on this in its yearly Sustainability Report.[111]

Art. 48h AD obliges the Commission to submit a report by 22 June 2027 on compliance with, and the impact of the public CbC reporting obligations. In addition, the Commission

107 Directive 2021/2101 of 24 November 2021 amending Directive 2013/34/EU as regards disclosure of income tax information by certain undertakings and branches.

108 Directive 2013/34/EU of 26 June 2013 on the annual financial statements, consolidated financial statements and related reports of certain types of undertakings, amending Directive 2006/43/ EC of the European Parliament and of the Council and repealing Council Directives 78/660/EEC and 83/349/EEC.

109 For a more elaborate discussion I refer to Manuel Campos Loureiro, The Shortcomings of the EU Public Country-by-Country Reporting Directive, *EC Tax Review* 2022, no. 3, pp 115-123; Willemien Netjes and Dominik Freyer, Tax Transparency Is Here to Stay: An Analysis of the Public CbCR Directive, *Intertax*, 2022 no. 8/9, pp. 1-7.

110 Commission Implementing Regulation (EU) 2024/2952 of 29 November 2024 laying down a common template and electronic reporting formats for the application of Directive 2013/34/EU of the European Parliament and of the Council as regards the information to be presented in reports on income tax information.

111 https://reports.shell.com/report-home/2020/.

must review and asses whether it would be appropriate to extend the obligation to other companies and to extend the content of the report. In this assessment it must take into account the situation at OECD level, the need to ensure that there is a sufficient level of transparency and the need to preserve and ensure a competitive environment for undertakings and private investment.

28.3.2.5 Reporting Obligations for Digital Platforms (DAC7)[112]

DAC7[113] introduced a new category of information that must be collected and automatically exchanged and it made various changes to other provisions in the DAC. The latter changes are not discussed in this section, but in the sections on those provisions.[114]

The tax transparency requirements for digital platforms included in DAC7 are part of the Tax Package the European Commission launched on 15 July 2020 to support economic recovery and growth.[115] Again, the EU initiative cannot be seen separate from OECD developments. On 3 June 2020 the OECD published its report Model Rules for Reporting by Platform Operators with respect to Sellers in the Sharing and Gig Economy (OECD Model Rules), followed, on 22 June 2021 by the report Model Reporting Rules for Digital Platforms: International Exchange Framework and Optional Module for Sale of Goods.[116] The OECD reports provide for more guidance than DAC7.

There are clear similarities. For example, the definitions of platform and platform operator are similar as is the information the platform operator is required to report. However, there are also differences: the OECD allows to exclude smaller platform operators (sales less than EUR 1 million) and platform operators that do not make a profit, where DAC7 does not include such options. Also, the scope of activities is more limited in the OECD report and the OECD does not apply to non-resident platform operators.[117]

---

112 See, in addition to the other references in this section, also S.A. Stevens and J.T. van Wamelen, The DAC7 Proposal and Reporting Obligation for Online Platforms, *EC Tax Review* 2021, no. 1, pp. 24-30.

113 Council Directive 2021/514 of 22 March 2021 amending Directive 2011/16/EU on administrative cooperation in the field of taxation, O.J. 25 March 2021, L 104, p. 1.

114 See on these provisions also: Ana Paula Dourado, 'Editorial: The European Commission Tax Package: The Condition of Foreseeable Relevance, Group Requests and Data Breaches ', 2020, 48, *Intertax*, Issue 11, pp. 949-952 and M. Manca, EU DAC7 Proposal Further Strengthens EU Tax Administrative Cooperation, Even in Respect of Digital Platforms, 61 *European Taxation* 4 2021.

115 https://ec.europa.eu/taxation_customs/package-fair-and-simple-taxation_en.

116 https://www.oecd.org/ctp/exchange-of-tax-information/model-rules-for-reporting-by-platform-operators-with-respect-to-sellers-in-the-sharing-and-gig-economy.htm.

117 See for a comprehensive comparison between the OECD June 2020 report and the proposal for DAC7: Giorgio Beretta, The New Rules for Reporting by Sharing and Gig Economy Platforms Under the OECD and EU Initiatives, (2021), 30, *EC Tax Review*, Issue 1, pp. 31-38, Giorgio Beretta, The EU Proposal for Tax Information Reporting by Sharing and Gig Economy Platforms, *Kluwer International Tax Blog*, 21 December 2020 http://kluwertaxblog.com/2020/12/21/the-eu-proposal-for-tax-information-reporting-by-sharing-and-gig-economy-platforms/ and G. Zilli, The OECD Model Rules and DAC7: a critical assessment of selected design and enforcement issues, 62 *European Taxation* 2022, pp. 521-536.

Various EU Member States, for example France, Belgium, Italy, Latvia and Spain already obliged platform operators to submit certain information on traders using their platform. Cases were brought before the ECJ on the question on whether the Italian and Belgian national obligations on providers such as Airbnb to collect information on short-term rental agreements concluded through them and to provide that information to the tax authority for the purpose of collecting taxes payable by the users of the service, are, amongst others, in line with the freedom to provide services (Art. 56 TFEU). In the Belgian case[118] the ECJ held that such requirement to provide information falls within the field of taxation which is expressly excluded from the scope of the Directive on electronic commerce[119] and is not precluded by Art. 56 TFEU. In the Italian case, the ECJ also held that Art. 56 does not preclude the obligation to collect and transmit information or to withhold tax, but that an obligation to appoint a tax representative constitutes a disproportionate restriction.[120]

The ECJ also decided on an obligation Latvia imposed on a provider of online advertisement services to forward data on second-hand car advertisements to ensure that the taxes on the sale of cars were properly collected.[121] This is in line with the GDPR provided that the data requested are necessary for the specific purposes for which they are collected and that the period during which the data are collected is no longer than strictly necessary to accomplish the objective of general interest (point 85 of *'SS' SIA*).

There is a certain overlap of the DAC7 requirements with the VAT rules for e-commerce that entered into force on 1 July 2021. To allow the control of the (Import) One Stop Shop (OSS/IOSS) VAT returns, traders are required to report certain information in a standard form to provide the records of their transactions declared under the OSS/IOSS schemes.[122] This information is subsequently exchanged by use of the CCN network. Some of this information is also exchanged based on DAC7. The same applies to the legislative package adopted on 18 February 2020 which, in order to prevent VAT fraud, obliges payment service providers to transmit, as of 1 January 2024, certain information on cross-border payments originating from Member States and on the beneficiary of these cross-border payments.[123] This information is centralised in the Central Electronic System of Payment information (CESOP) where it is stored, aggregated and cross-checked with other European databases and then made available to anti-fraud experts of Member States via the Eurofisc network. Beretta notes that an important flaw common to the OECD and EU initiatives relates to the lack of coordination with other instruments for collection and exchange of

118 Case C-674/20, *Airbnb Ireland UC v Région de Bruxelles-Capitale*, EU:C:2022:303.

119 Directive 2000/31/EC of 8 June 2000 on certain legal aspects of information society services, in particular electronic commerce, in the Internal Market.

120 Case C-83/21, *Airbnb Ireland UC, Airbnb Payments UK Ltd v Agenzia delle Entrate*, EU:C:2022:1018.

121 Case C-175/20, *'SS' SIA* EU:C:2022:124.

122 Commission Implementing Regulation (EU) 2021/965 of 9 June 2021 amending Implementing Regulation 2020/194 as regards the exchange of records held by taxable persons or their intermediaries and the designation of competent authorities responsible for coordinating administrative enquiries, O.J. 17 June 2021, L 214, p. 1.

123 Directive 2020/284 of 18 February 2020 amending Directive 2006/112/EC as regards introducing certain requirements for payment service providers O.J. 2 March 2020, L 62, p. 7 and Regulation 2020/283 of 18 February 2020 amending Regulation No 904/2010 as regards measures to strengthen administrative cooperation in order to combat VAT fraud, 2 March 2020, L 62, p. 1.

information already available to tax administrations (e.g. information exchanged with tax authorities by means of electronic invoicing or due to anti-money laundering (AML)/ know your customer (KYC) reporting).[124]

The DAC7 reporting obligation for digital platforms seems to build on the reporting obligations for tax intermediaries which were introduced in DAC6 (see Chapter 29). Again, it is an intermediary that has to collect and report the information in order to enable tax administrations to assess whether taxpayers (here: sellers on digital platforms) fulfilled their tax obligations. However, unlike DAC6, the DAC7 obligation covers both cross-border and non-cross-border activities in order to ensure the effectiveness of the reporting rules, the proper functioning of the internal market, a level playing field and the principle of non-discrimination and to reduce the administrative burden on digital platforms (preamble 10 DAC7). The reason to introduce these obligations is to increase tax compliance, reduce and detect tax fraud, tax evasion and tax avoidance (both regarding income taxes and VAT) and to introduce a standardized reporting requirement in the EU instead of unilateral, diverging reporting obligations (preambles 6-8 DAC 7).

DAC7 introduced Art. 8ac which obliges Member States to require so called reporting platform operators to carry out the due diligence procedures and fulfil reporting obligations that are included in Annex V to the DAC (Art. 8ac(1)). This Annex contains an extensive Section I with definitions, a Section II with the due diligence procedures, a Section III with reporting requirements and a Section IV with rules and administrative procedures Member States have to implement.

Platform operators are entities (broadly defined in Annex V(I)(C)(1)) that contract with sellers to make available a platform (Annex V(I)(A)(2)).[125] The reporting obligation applies regardless of the legal nature of the seller as this term encompasses both individuals and entities (Annex V(I)(B)(1)). The latter term includes not only legal entities, such as corporations and foundations but also legal arrangements such as partnerships and trusts (Annex V(I) (C)(1)). However, governmental entities are excluded as sellers on whom platforms have to report as are entities of which the stock is regularly traded on an established securities market or a related entity thereof (Annex V(I)(B)(4) and (I)(C)(2)).

Sellers must be registered on the platform and carry out an activity for consideration that entails any of the following (Annex V(I)(A)(8)): (a) rental of immovable property; (b)

---

124 Giorgio Beretta, The New Rules for Reporting by Sharing and Gig Economy Platforms Under the OECD and EU Initiatives, (2021), 30, *EC Tax Review*, Issue 1, p. 38. A proposal for more alignment was also included in M. Merkx, A. Janssen & M. Leenders, Platforms, a convenient source of information under DAC 7 and the VAT Directive: a proposal for more alignment and efficiency, 31 *EC Tax Review* 2022, pp. 202-218.

125 See for a critical discussion on the broad scope of DAC7 in respect of the definition of platform operators: Alessio Persiani, DAC7: Some thoughts on the Different roles of platform operators and the appropriate definition of the scope of reporting obligations, *EC Tax Review*, 2023-4, pp. 163-171 and Nathalie Bravo, The meaning of Platform under DAC7: more clarity needed, 27 June 2023, *Kluwer International Tax Blog*, https://kluwertaxblog.com/2023/06/27/the-meaning-of-platform-under-dac7-more-clarity-needed/.

personal service (defined in Annex V(I)(A)(11) as a service[126] involving time-or task based work performed, upon request of a user, by one or more individuals independently or on behalf of an entity either online or physically after having been facilitated by a platform); (c) the sale of goods (tangible property (Annex V(I)(C)(9)). Activities carried out by a seller acting as employee of the platform operator do not fall withing the scope of reporting.

A platform is any software (including websites and apps) accessible by users and allowing sellers to be connected to users to carry out one of the activities mentioned above. This includes any arrangements for the collection and payment of the consideration for these activities (Annex V(I)(A)(1)).[127] It excludes software that without any further intervention allows (a) processing of payments for such activities, (b) users to list or advertise such activity, redirecting or transferring users to a platform.

Platforms must either be resident in a Member State, be incorporated in a Member State, have their place of management in a Member State, have a permanent establishment in a Member State or facilitate the carrying out of an in-scope activity by a seller that is resident in a Member State or a rental of immovable property located in a Member State (Annex V(I)(A)(4)). The reason for this broad scope is ensuring a level playing field and prevent unfair competition (preamble 14 DAC7). Platforms resident in third countries that have an agreement with all Member States that requires the automatic exchange of equivalent information are excluded from the reporting obligations (Annex V(I)(A)(4)-(7), the so called 'switch-off' mechanism). The OECD Model Rules mentioned before are expected to provide for the reporting of equivalent information in relation to relevant activities that are in scope of both the DAC and the OECD Model Rules, even though the latter are not identical to the DAC in terms of the in-scope sellers and platforms (preamble 16). The Commission determines whether information is equivalent. Such determination can upon request of a Member State take place before an agreement is concluded with a third country. Art. 8ac(7) gives the procedure for such decision (and the decision that information is no longer equivalent). In its decision, the Commission has to take into account definitions of reporting platform operators, reportable sellers and relevant activities, due diligence procedures, reporting requirements and administrative procedures to ensure effective implementation and compliance with the due diligence procedures and reporting requirement in the third country.[128] The equivalence regime is rather tight, as European Commission Regulation 2023/823 of 13 April 2023 closely

126 See on the definition of sellers in relation to digital content creators such as influencers: Felix Desmyttere and Juan Manuel Vázquez, DAC7 and Digital Content Creators: Opaque transparency for influencers, streamers and other content creators? 6 February 2024 *Kluwer International Tax Blog*, https://kluwertaxblog.com/2024/02/06/dac7-and-digital-content-creators-opaque-transparency-for-influencers-streamers-and-other-content-creators/.

127 See on the broad scope F. Desmyttere, Digital Platform Reporting (DAC7): Fundamental Considerations Regarding the Notion of "Relevant Activity" – A Belgian Case Study, 63 *European Taxation* 11 (2023).

128 See for a discussion on a third country regime L. Ateş, Tax Cooperation between the EU Member States and Türkiye Regarding Automatic Exchange of Information on Income Collected by Digital Platform Operators, 63 *European Taxation* 11 (2023).

matches the DAC 7 provisions, also where they go beyond those of the OECD.[129] In 2023 and 2024, the European Commission adopted determinations of equivalence for the United Kingdom,[130] New Zealand,[131] and Canada.[132] However, as the switch-off mechanism only takes effect after all EU Member States have activated their automatic exchange of information relationships with these countries and many Member States have not yet activated these,[133] it was by mid 2025 not in effect yet for any of these countries.

Platforms must collect and report a range of information on sellers, including, amongst others, address, TIN, and VAT number (Annex V(II)(B)) and addresses of immovable property rented out (Annex V(II)(E)). In addition, they must verify whether the information is reliable (Annex V(II)(C)). They must do this by 31 December of the calendar year (Annex V(II)(F)). They are allowed to rely on third party service providers to fulfil the due diligence obligations, but they remain responsible for this themselves (Annex V(II)(H)). If a seller does not provide the information required for the due diligence after two reminders of the platform, the platform must close the account of the seller and prevent it from re-registering or withhold payments to the seller as long as it does not provide the information.[134]

The information on the seller (which includes the income they earned through the digital platform) must be reported no later than 31 January of the year following the calendar year in which the seller is identified as being in scope (Annex V(III)(A)). The platform operator must both report information on itself (including name address, TIN) and information on the sellers (including the due diligence information) (Annex V(III)(B)). Members States must require platform operators to register themselves as such in the EU. Registration in one EU Member State must be allowed (Art. 8ac(4)).

---

129 Alessio Persiani, DAC7: Some thoughts on the Different roles of platform operators and the appropriate definition of the scope of reporting obligations, *EC Tax Review*, 2023-4, p. 163-171 and Elodie Lamer, EU Commission adopts tight DAC7 equivalence regime, *Tax Notes International*, 24 April 2023, pp. 520-521 and Elodie Lamer, OECD Official sees practical issues with DAC8 equivalence, *Tax Notes International*, 3 April 2023, pp. 101-102.

130 Commission Implementing Regulation (EU) 2023/2389 of 29 September 2023 determining that the information to be automatically exchanged pursuant to the agreement to be concluded between the competent authorities of Finland and the United Kingdom is equivalent to the information specified in certain provisions of Council Directive 2011/16/EU.

131 Commission Implementing Regulation (EU) 2023/2693 of 30 November 2023 determining that the information to be automatically exchanged pursuant to the agreement signed by the competent authorities of New Zealand and certain Member States is equivalent to the information specified in certain provisions of Council Directive 2011/16/EU.

132 Commission Implementing Regulation (EU) 2024/432 of 2 February 2024 determining that the information to be automatically exchanged pursuant to the agreement signed by the competent authorities of Canada and certain Member States is equivalent to the information specified in certain provisions of Council Directive 2011/16/EU. The links to all determinations of equivalence can be found on https://taxation-customs.ec.europa.eu/taxation/tax-transparency-cooperation/administrative-co-operation-and-mutual-assistance/dac7_en#equivalence-mechanism.

133 See for an overview: https://taxation-customs.ec.europa.eu/taxation/tax-transparency-cooperation/administrative-co-operation-and-mutual-assistance/dac7_en.

134 See also K. Perrou, Sanctions Imposed on Digital Platforms under DAC7 and the Freedom to Conduct Business, 63 *European Taxation* 5 (2023).

Member States must automatically exchange the information reported by the platforms and that is listed in Art. 8ac (2) within two months after the end of the calendar year (Art. 8ac(3)) to the Member State in which the seller is resident and where it provides immovable property rental services to the Member State where it is located (Art. 8ac(2)). The automatic exchange of this information must be carried out electronically through the CCN (Art. 20(4) and preamble 29 of DAC7).

The information is recorded in a central register established by the European Commission that is available to all Member States. Member States had to apply these provisions from 1 January 2023 (Art. 2(1) DAC7).

DAC7 is not included the second DAC evaluation the European Commission started in 2024. However, several stakeholders used the public consultation for that evaluation to share some issues they encounter when applying DAC7. They are of the opinion that its scope is too broad as it includes information on many private platform users that are unlikely to incur any tax liabilities from their platform activities on the one hand and on business-to-business transactions on the other hand. In addition, they experienced reluctance of users to provide their Tax Identification Numbers to platform operators. Furthermore, they identified overlaps with other pieces of EU legislation such as the AMLD and Digital Services Act that also require the collection of some seller information and suggest aligning data collection and verification requirements to minimize data collection in line with data protection rules, reduce mistrust of sellers and the compliance burden on platform operators and tax authorities.[135] In a study requested by the European Parliament Committee on the Internal Market and Consumer Protection, it was found that the DAC7 reporting requirements pose considerable challenges for small and medium-size enterprises in the accommodations sector.[136] The obligation to regularly report seller data and transaction specifics to tax authorities can be both resource-intensive and complex, adding an extra layer of administrative tasks which is further complicated by varying interpretations and implementations of the DAC by Member States. According to the report, this significantly increases the workload and operating costs of businesses in the accommodation sector and comes on top of an 'already demanding regulatory environment.'

28.3.2.6 *Information on Crypto-assets (DAC8)*

After the implementation of FATCA, CRS and DAC2, crypto-assets became an alternative for tax evaders who could no longer count on bank secrecy to hide their assets from tax administrations. Most crypto-assets were not covered under CRS or DAC2 as they do not constitute money held in depository accounts nor in financial assets. In addition,

135 Elodie Lamer, Used-Goods Sales Platforms Challenge DAC7 Reporting Rules, *Tax Notes International*, 5 August 2024, pp. 929-930.

136 European Parliament: Directorate-General for Internal Policies of the Union, Rzepecka, J., Fuksiewicz, A., Squillante, F., Alijošius, L. et al., *The impact of EU legislation in the area of digital and green transition, particularly on SMEs*, Publications Office of the European Union, 2024, https://data.europa.eu/doi/10.2861/5296842, p. 49.

crypto-asset service providers and crypto-asset operators were often not covered by the definition of financial institution and thus out of scope of the reporting requirements.[137]

On 26 August 2022, the OECD approved the Crypto-Asset Reporting Framework (CARF) and on 8 June 2023 the CARF and amendments to the CRS with associated commentaries were published.[138] CARF provides for the reporting of tax information on transactions in crypto-assets in a standardised manner, with a view to automatically exchanging such information.

CARF consists of three distinct components. The first component consists of the rules and related commentary that can be transposed into domestic law to collect information from reporting crypto-asset service providers with a relevant nexus to the jurisdiction implementing the CARF. These were designed around four key building blocks: i) the scope of crypto-assets to be covered; ii) the entities and individuals subject to data collection and reporting requirements; iii) the transactions subject to reporting and the information to be reported; and iv) the due diligence procedures to identify crypto-asset users and controlling persons and to determine the relevant tax jurisdictions for reporting and exchange purposes. The second component is a Multilateral Competent Authority Agreement on Automatic Exchange of Information pursuant to the CARF (CARF MCAA) and related commentary (or bilateral agreements or arrangements). On 13 March 2025, 50 jurisdictions had signed the CARF MCAA.[139] These include all 27 EU Member States. The third component is an electronic format (XML schema) to be used for exchanging the CARF information, and by reporting crypto-asset service providers to report CARF information to tax administrations.

In the meantime, some EU Member States imposed or were planning to impose reporting obligations on crypto-assets and e-money service providers to safeguard national tax rules on income derived from crypto-asset transactions. However, the decentralised nature of crypto-assets made it difficult for Member States' tax administrations to ensure tax compliance (preamble 6 to DAC8). As part of the Tax Package for Fair and Simple Taxation of 15 July 2020,[140] the European Commission announced that it would expand the DAC

137 See also Marwan Ahmed, Cryptocurrency Tax Compliance in the European Union: Reality or Mirage?, 61 *European Taxation* 11 2021.

138 OECD (2023), International Standards for Automatic Exchange of Information in Tax Matters: Crypto-Asset Reporting Framework and 2023 update to the Common Reporting Standard, OECD Publishing, Paris, https://doi.org/10.1787/896d79d1-en. See for a discussion of CARF series of the five articles of Paul Foster Millen and Peter A. Cotorceanu, Old tricks for new dogs, *Tax Notes International* 16 October 2023, pp. 345-351; 8 April 2024, pp. 203-209; 30 september 2024, pp. 2153-2159; 4 November 2024, pp. 801-806; 9 December 2024, pp. 1517-1521.

139 https://www.oecd.org/content/dam/oecd/en/topics/policy-issues/tax-transparency-and-international-co-operation/carf-mcaa-signatories.pdf/_jcr_content/renditions/original./carf-mcaa-signatories.pdf.

140 https://ec.europa.eu/taxation_customs/package-fair-and-simple-taxation_en.

to cover crypto-assets and e-money,[141] just as the 5th Anti-Money Laundering Directive (AMLD5)[142] extended the 4th Anti-Money Laundering Directive (AMLD4) obligations (including due diligence obligations and the obligation to report suspicious activities) to crypto-currency exchange providers and custodian wallet providers. The 2023 Markets in Crypto-Assets Regulation (MiCAR)[143] extended the EU financial regulatory framework to issues of crypto-assets and crypto-asset service providers. The scope of entities subject to EU anti-money laundering and countering the financing of terrorism framework rules was extended to crypto-asset service providers regulated by MiCAR, and Regulation (EU) 2023/1113[144] obliged crypto-asset service providers to accompany transfers of funds with information on the payer and the payee to ensure the traceability of transfers of crypto-assets.

In order to address the challenges arising from the growing use of alternative means of payment and investment and the associated risks of tax evasion, it was decided that the DAC should cover crypto-assets and their users (preamble 11 of DAC8). On 17 October 2023, DAC8[145] was adopted. DAC8 adds a new Art. 8ad and a new Annex VI to the DAC. Member States must, for the largest part, implement it on 31 December 2025 at the latest and apply it as of 1 January 2026.[146] DAC8 includes other amendments to the DAC as well, such as the inclusion of non-custodial dividend income to Art. 8(a),[147] an amendment to Art. 8ab to reflect the case law of the ECJ on the legal professional privilege in relation to the DAC6 notification obligations on intermediaries,[148] and a new Art. 27c on reporting and communication of the TIN,[149] but these are not discussed in this section.

Reporting crypto-asset service providers must report information on themselves, their reportable users and reportable crypto-assets to the Member State that granted them authorisation under MiCAR, or, in case of crypto-asset operators that are not regulated by MICAR, the Member State where they are registered. Reportable users are crypto-asset

141 For an exploration of the problems DAC8 will attempt to address, I refer to Marwan Ahmed, Cryptocurrency Tax Compliance in the European Union: Reality or Mirage? 61 *European Taxation* 11 2021. He discusses the cryptocurrency stakeholders (users, miners, exchange platforms, trading platforms and wallet providers), cryptocurrency taxable events and tax compliance challenges and solutions.

142 Directive 2018/843 of 30 May 2018 amending Directive (EU) 2015/849 on the prevention of the use of the financial system for the purposes of money laundering or terrorist financing, and amending Directives 2009/138/EC and 2013/36/EU, O.J. of 19 June 2018, L 156, p. 43.

143 Regulation (EU) 2023/1114 of the European Parliament and of the Council of 31 May 2023 on markets in crypto-assets, and amending Regulations (EU) No 1093/2010 and (EU) No 1095/2010 and Directives 2013/36/EU and (EU) 2019/1937.

144 Regulation (EU) 2023/1113 of the European Parliament and of the Council of 31 May 2023 on information accompanying transfers of funds and certain crypto-assets and amending Directive (EU) 2015/849.

145 Council Directive (EU) 2023/2226 of 17 October 2023 amending Directive 2011/16/EU on administrative cooperation in the field of taxation.

146 See alsof or an overview of DAC8 M. Bernt, DAC8: Commentary on the European Union's New Crypto Tax Reporting Regime, 63 *European Taxation* 9 (2023).

147 See Section 28.3.2.1.

148 Chapter 29.5.

149 See Section 28.12.

users that are a reportable person resident in a Member State (Annex VI(IV)(D). To enable tax administrations to analyse and use the information they receive, for example for matching of information and valuation of assets and capital gains, the information reported and exchanged per crypto-asset user must be subdivided per crypto-asset with respect to which he made transactions. Reportable transactions are exchange transactions and transfers of reportable crypto-assets (Annex VI(IV)(C). Exchange transactions include crypto-to-fiat and crypto-to-crypto transactions. Also, the transfer of reportable crypto-assets in consideration of goods or services for a value exceeding USD 50 000 must be reported (reportable retail payment transactions). The reporting obligation covers both cross-border and domestic transactions in order to ensure the effectiveness of the reporting rules, the proper functioning of the internal market, a level playing field and respect of the principle of non-discrimination (preamble 13). Annex VI, Section I provides that a reporting crypto-asset service provider is subject to the reporting and due diligence requirements in a Member State, if (1) it is an entity authorised by a Member State in accordance with Art. 63 MiCAR or a financial entity allowed to provide crypto-asset services in accordance with Art. 60 MiCAR; or (2) it is an entity that does not meet the requirements under (1) and that is (a) an entity or individual resident for tax purposes in a Member State; (b) an entity that is incorporated or organised under the laws of a Member State and either has legal personality in a Member State or has an obligation to file tax returns or tax information returns to the tax authorities in a Member State with respect to the income of the entity; (c) an entity managed from a Member State; or (d) an entity or individual that has a regular place of business in a Member State. To avoid duplicative reporting, reporting takes place in the Member State with the strongest nexus.

Non-EU crypto-asset operators are allowed to solely report information on EU resident crypto-asset users to the tax authorities of a third country insofar as the reported information corresponds to the DAC8 information and insofar as there is an effective qualifying competent authority agreement in place with such jurisdiction. The third country must in turn communicate such information to the tax administrations of the Member States where the crypto-asset users are resident. This mechanism should prevent information from being reported and transmitted more than once.

The European Commission determines either on its own initiative or upon request of a Member State whether information automatically exchanged pursuant to an agreement between competent authorities of a Member State and a third country corresponds to that specified in Annex VI (Art. 8ad(11). The Commission must exercise those powers in accordance with Regulation (EU) No 182/2011.[150] The Commission must specifically take into account definitions of reporting crypto-asset service provider, reportable user, and reportable transaction, procedures to identify reportable users, reporting requirements and rules and administrative procedures to ensure effective implementation and compliance with the due diligence procedures and reporting requirements in the third country. Such Commission decision is not required if an international standard on the reporting and

150 Regulation (EU) No 182/2011 of the European Parliament and of the Council of 16 February 2011 laying down the rules and general principles concerning mechanisms for control by Member States of the Commission's exercise of implementing powers.

automatic exchange of information on crypto-assets (such as CARF) is determined to be a minimum standard or equivalent. That information is deemed to correspond to the DAC8 information if there is an agreement between all Member States concerned and the third country that requires the automatic exchange of information on customers of a reporting crypto-asset service provider (Art. 8ad(12)).

Preamble 25 explicitly states that the exemption from reporting obligations provided for in DAC8, which is dependent upon the determination of corresponding reporting and exchange mechanisms, apply only in the area of taxation, and in particular for the purposes of DAC8, and should not be considered as a basis for recognising correspondence in other areas of EU law.

DAC8 is largely based on the OECD CARF,[151] although there are some differences.[152] Preamble 9 of DAC8 observes that Union rules should take into account the CARF to increase the effectiveness of the exchange of information and to reduce the administrative burden. Furthermore, the preamble states that Member States must use the Commentaries on the CARF MCAA and the CARF as sources of illustration or interpretation and in order to ensure consistency in application across Member States. This alignment of DAC8 with CARF is clearly visible from DAC8.

Art. 8ad and Annex VI are also aligned with and refer to the definitions laid out in the MiCAR and take into account the authorisation requirement for crypto-asset service providers under MiCAR.[153] Preamble 7 of DAC8 observes that this was done to minimise the administrative burden for crypto-asset service providers. Preamble 23 states that DAC8 does not substitute any wider obligations arising from MiCAR.

The term reporting crypto-asset service providers is defined in Section IV(B), point 3 of Annex VI and includes both crypto-asset service providers as defined in the MiCAR (Section IV(B), point 1 of Annex VI) and other providers of crypto-asset services (these are defined as crypto-asset operators in Section IV(B), point 2 of Annex VI). This means that both service providers that are regulated and authorized under the MiCAR and those that are not, are in scope of DAC8. Art. 3(1), point (15) MiCAR defines crypto-asset service provider as a legal person or other undertaking whose occupation or business is the provision of one or more crypto-asset services to clients on a professional basis, and that is allowed to provide crypto-asset services in accordance with Art. 59 MiCAR. Crypto-asset service providers covered by the MiCAR may exercise their activity in the EU through passporting once they have received their authorisation in a Member State. The European Securities and Markets Authority (ESMA) holds a register with authorised crypto-asset

151 See also A.M.L. Gorissen and Y. Uslu, Investing in Crypto-Assets: Council Adoption of DAC8, 24 *Finance & Capital Markets* 3 2023.

152 Elodie Lamer, Stakeholders note DAC8's deviations from OECD cryptoasset framework, *Tax Notes International* 10 April 2023, pp. 245-247 and Claudio Cipollini, DAC8 and Extraterritoriality: How to Enforce Compliance for non-EU Operators, 33 *EC Tax Review* 1 2024, pp. 19-32.

153 See also A. Corruchaga Frago, Hans van der Leeden, Mahir Budak and Nico Salemans, Understanding the Role of DAC8 and MiCAR in the European Union's Efforts towards Tax Harmonization, 24 *Finance & Capital Markets* 1 2023.

service providers and maintains a blacklist of operators that require an authorisation under MiCAR. To comply with their reporting obligations, crypto-asset operators (not regulated under the MiCAR) must register with one single Member State which gives them an individual identification number (Art. 8ad(7)). The European Commission will establish a crypto-asset operator register (Art. 8ad(10)). If a registration is revoked, the crypto-asset operator may only register again if it provides appropriate assurance as regards its commitment to comply with the reporting requirements, including any outstanding unfulfilled reporting requirements (Art. 8ad(7) last section).

A broad scope of crypto-assets is covered (preamble 14).[154] Section IV(A), point 1 of Annex VI refers to Art. 3(1), point (15) MiCAR for the definition of crypto-asset, which definition is refined to reportable crypto assets in Section IV(A), point 4 of Annex VI. All crypto-assets that can be used for payment or investment purposes are reportable. This includes crypto-assets that have been issued in a decentralised manner, as well as stablecoins, including e-money tokens as defined in MiCAR and certain non-fungible tokens (NFTs). Crypto-asset service providers must consider on a case-by-case basis whether crypto-assets can be used for payment and investment purposes, taking into account the exemptions provided for the MiCAR, in particular in relation to a limited network and certain utility tokens (preamble 14). Russo et. al. warned that adopting an excessively broad interpretation of reportable crypto-asset definition (which they especially linked to the inclusion of NFTs) may lead to the imposition of unnecessary obligations on reporting crypto-assets service providers to provide tax administrations with largely irrelevant information.[155]

Art. 8ad includes the scope and conditions of mandatory automatic exchange of information reported by crypto-asset service providers. Annex VI lays down the reporting requirements (Section II), due diligence procedures (Section III) and other rules to be applied by the reporting crypto-asset service providers to enable Member States to communicate the information referred to in Art. 8ad. The Annex also lays down the rules and administrative procedures that Member States must have in place to ensure the effective implementation of, and compliance with, the reporting requirements and the due diligence procedures (Section V).

Section I clarifies when reporting crypto-asset service providers are subject to the reporting and due diligence requirements and when they are not. Section IV includes an extensive list of defined terms with a subdivision in definitions consisting of (A) reportable crypto-asset; (B) reporting crypto-asset service provider; (C) reportable transaction; (D)

154 See also Dennis Post and Claudio Cipollini, The DAC8 Proposal and the Future of Crypto-Asset Reporting: Some Preliminary Thoughts, *Kluwer International Tax Blog*, 9 January 2023, https://kluwertaxblog.com/2023/01/09/the-dac8-proposal-and-the-future-of-crypto-asset-reporting-some-preliminary-thoughts/ and Šime Jozipović, Marko Perkušić and Stjepan Gadžo, Tax Compliance in the Era of Cryptocurrencies and CBDCs: The End of the Right to Privacy or No Reason for Concern?, *EC Tax Review*, 2022-1, pp. 16-29.

155 Raffaele Russo, Tiziana Ventrella, and Marco Gesualdi, The EU DAC8: Tax transparency in sight for cryptoassets, *Tax Notes International* 10 July 2023, pp. 153-160, p. 156.

reportable user; (E) excluded person; and (F) miscellaneous. The definition categories A-D reflect the four building blocks of the CARF model rules.

Member States must exchange the information automatically though a standard computerised form referred to in Art. 20(5) within 9 months of the reporting year (Art 8ad(6)). The calendar year or other appropriate reporting period as from 1 January 2026 is the first period over which information must be exchanged (Art 8ad(6)). Therefore, the exchanges relating to the first reporting year will take place by 30 September 2027. The Commission does not have access to the identification information of Reportable Persons (Art. 8ad(5).

To ensure uniform conditions for implementation, the European Commission may adopt practical arrangements in implementing acts in accordance with the comitology procedure, as referred to in Art. 26(2). This includes measures to standardise the communication of the information as part of the procedure for establishing the standard computerised form provided for in Art. 20(5) (Art. 8ad(4)) and the practical and technical arrangements necessary for the registration and identification of crypto-asset operators (Art. 8ad(9)).

28.3.2.7 Exchange of Pillar 2 Information (DAC9)

On 28 October 2024, the European Commission published a proposal for an eight amendment to the DAC, DAC9.[156] The proposal was adopted by the Council on 14 April 2025.[157] Again, this amendment to the DAC built upon work done by the OECD/G20, in this case the Global Anti-Base Erosion (GloBE) (or Pillar 2) rules that were designed to ensure that large MNEs pay a minimum tax rate of 15% on the income arising in each jurisdiction where they operate.[158] The Pillar 2 Directive (P2D, See Chapter 22)[159] required the implementation of those rules by the EU Member States. Art. 44 of the P2D requires the filing of a top-up tax information return using a standard template and broadly sets out the basic rules for this filing and the information categories that must be reported. Based on Art. 44(2) of the P2D, each constituent entity must file its top-up tax information return in the Member State where it is located. However, Art. 44(3) provides for a derogation from this local filing requirement if the ultimate parent entity (UPE) or a designated filing entity has filed the return on behalf of the entire MNE. This is only allowed if, for the reporting fiscal year, arrangements to exchange information are in place between the Member State of the UPE or a designated filing entity and the Member States of the other constituent entities. DAC9 creates such framework to exchange Pillar 2 information between Member States and to enable MNEs to switch from filing in each jurisdiction where they are based (local filing) to central filing through the ultimate parent entity or designated filing entity. In line with the OECD framework it uses a dissemination

156 Proposal of 28 October 2024 for a Council Directive amending Directive 2011/16/EU on administrative cooperation in the field of taxation, COM(2024) 497 final.

157 Council Directive (EU) 2025/872 of 14 April 2025 amending Directive 2011/16/EU on administrative cooperation in the field of taxation.

158 https://www.oecd.org/en/topics/sub-issues/global-minimum-tax/global-anti-base-erosion-model-rules-pillar-two.html.

159 Council Directive (EU) 2022/2523 of 14 December 2022 on ensuring a global minimum level of taxation for multinational enterprise groups and large-scale domestic groups in the Union.

approach which ensures that all relevant jurisdictions receive the information they need. Furthermore, DAC9 designates the GloBE Information Return (GIR),[160] the standard template developed by the OECD/G20 Inclusive Framework (IF) to fulfill the filing obligations, as the top-up tax information return standard template of Art. 44(5) of the P2D and thus and transposes the GIR into EU law. The OECD/G20 IF instructions for the filling of the GIR are, according to preamble 16 to DAC9, a useful source of interpretation for MNEs to file the top-up tax information return.

This results, amongst others, in DAC9 inserting a new Art. 8ae, Art. 9a and Annex VII in the DAC. Preamble 15 to DAC9 states that both the DAC and Annex VII must be read together with the P2D and that the terms in the DAC that are also found in the P2D have the same meaning as in the P2D. Art. 8ae includes the obligation for Member States to require MNEs to use the standard template for the filing of the top-up tax information return (Art. 8ae(1)) and sets out the framework for the exchange of top-up tax information returns.

DAC9 does not apply to exchange of information with third countries. For this, Member States must sign appropriate international agreements, such as bilateral agreements or the Multilateral Competent Authority Agreement on the Exchange of GloBE Information (GIR MCAA)[161] that the OECD published on 15 January 2025 and that is based on Art. 6 of the MCMAATM. Preamble 16 requires that in implementing DAC9, Member States must use the GIR MCAA and its commentary, the Pillar 2 OECD Model Rules and commentary and updates thereto as source of illustration and interpretation to the extent that these are consistent with DAC9, the P2D and Union Law.

Annex VII gives definitions (Section I), describes the filing requirements (Section II), and includes (Section III) the form for the top-up tax information return, the data points that must be reported. This top-up tax information return is fully in line with the GIR developed by the OECD and aligns it with the P2D. MNEs must include information on their constituent entities, corporate structure, and data necessary to calculate constituent entities' effective tax rate, the top-up tax, and allocations in their information return.

The Pillar 2 project seems to remain a moving target for a while. The OECD will probably keep updating the GIR template and the XML schema that sets out the format for that information to be exchanged between tax administrations. The original DAC9 proposal[162] included an Art. 21(9) that would have allowed the Commission to amend the top-up tax information return by delegated acts in accordance with Art. 290 TFEU to reflect updates agreed at the international level and an Art. 26a that would have provided for rules on the exercise of the delegation. Such delegated acts would have allowed to swiftly amend the top-up tax information return standard template that is included in Annex VII, section 3 of DAC9. However, this delegation led to discussions in the Council, because it would

160 OECD (2023), Tax Challenges Arising from the Digitalisation of the Economy – GloBE Information Return (Pillar Two), OECD Publishing, Paris, https://doi.org/10.1787/91a49ec3-en.

161 https://www.oecd.org/content/dam/oecd/en/topics/policy-sub-issues/global-minimum-tax/multilateral-competent-authority-agreement-exchange-of-globe-information.pdf.

162 Proposal of 28 October 2024 for a Council Directive amending Directive 2011/16/EU on administrative cooperation in the field of taxation, COM(2024) 497 final.

mean that the Member States would not be involved in these changes. In the end it was decided to omit the delegating powers to the European Commission. The consequence is that the standard form of the top-up tax information return must be amended through a Council directive under the special legislative procedure requiring unanimity.[163]

Preamble 17 to DAC9 states that a standardized information return does not preclude a tax administration from requesting supporting information in follow-up requests to verify compliance with the P2D, but that Member States should generally refrain from requiring additional data points beyond the top-up tax information return as part of their routine tax return and payment requirements. Any such information should, according to preamble 17 of DAC9, relate, for instance, to liability, timing and method of payment or identification of the taxpayer and contact details rather than the calculation of the constituent entity's top-up tax liability.

The Member State that receives the information is responsible for the automatic exchange through a standard computerised form referred to in Art. 20(4) which is developed by the Commission by means of implementation acts adopted in accordance with the comitology procedure of Art. 26(2) (Art. 8ae(5)). The Member States must exchange the information as soon as possible through the CCN network, but no later than three months after the filing deadline for the reporting year (Art. 8ae(3)). This filing deadline is, based on Art. 44(7) P2D, 15 months after the last day of the reporting fiscal year.[164]

For the exchange of information the following dissemination approach approved by the OECD/G20 IF is used (Art. 8ae(2)). The UPE Member State receives the full top-up tax information return. All Member States that implemented a qualified income inclusion rule (IIR) and/or qualified under-taxed profit rule (UTPR) (so called implementing member states (Annex VII(I)(1))) receive the full general section (as defined in Annex VII(I)(4)) of the top-up tax information return if constituent entities of the MNE are located there. Member States with a UTPR of zero will only be provided with the portion of the top-up tax information return that contains information on the attribution of top-up tax under the UTPR in respect of that jurisdiction (i.e. an excerpt of Section 3.4.3). The implementing Member State in which the ultimate parent entity is located must be provided with all jurisdictional sections (as defined in Annex VII(I)(5)). Member States that only have a qualified domestic top-up tax and where constituent entities of the MNE are located, receive the general section without the high-level summary information of section 1.4. Member States with taxing rights under the P2D receive specific jurisdictional sections.

163 See for an elaborate discussion: Sigrid Hemels, National constitutions and EU primary law limits in the case of the implementation of the Pillar 2 Directive: the legality principle and Pillar 2. In: Pasquale Pistone, Menita de Flora and Alessia Tomo (eds.), The Common Constitutional Tradition of the European Union and Its Impact on Tax Law, IBFD GREIT series (forthcoming).

164 For the first reporting year (2024), Art. 51 P2D sets this deadline at 18 months after the last day of the reporting fiscal year. Art. 27d(3) subsequently sets the deadline for exchanging the information at six months after this filing deadline to accommodate any delays in the new system of exchange.

The new Art. 9a includes provisions on collaboration between Member States on corrections, compliance and enforcement with respect to the top-up tax information returns. A Member State that, through automatic exchange, received a top-up tax information return and after verification has reason to believe that it requires corrections, must notify the sending Member State (Art. 9a(1)). If the latter agrees that corrections are needed, it must, without delay, take appropriate measures to obtain the corrected information from the filing entity and exchange it with all relevant Member States. Art. 9a(2) obliges Member States that received a notification from one or more constituent entities that the top-up tax information return would be filed centrally, but did not receive the information through automatic exchange within the deadlines of Art. 8ae(3), to notify the other Member State that they did not receive the information. That other Member State must without delay determine the reason for not exchanging the information and inform the Member State that notified the missing exchange within one month, including, where relevant, the new expected date for the exchange. If, and only if, the top-up tax information return has not been received within three months of the new expected filing date, local filing requirements may be imposed on the constituent entities of the MNE.

Member States have until 31 December 2025 to implement DAC9. This is a very tight deadline, but based on the P2D the first top-up tax returns (over the reporting period as from 1 Januari 2024) are due by 30 June 2026 (Art. 51 P2D). DAC9 requires the exchange of this information by 31 December 2026 (Art. 27d(3)). For the Member States that, based on Art. 50(1) P2D have elected for a delayed application of the IIR and the UTPR, the application of DAC9 is also postponed (Art. 27d(2) and Art. 2(3) DAC9).

28.3.2.8 Proposal for Exchange of Information on Entities in Scope of the Unshell Directive (ATAD3)

On 22 December 2021, the European Commission launched the proposal for the so called 'Unshell' (also known as ATAD3) Directive[165] on shell companies. This Proposal is discussed in Chapter 25.3.3.[166] It would apply to undertakings that cross three so called gateways, in short: (1) more than 75% passive income; (2) more than 60% of assets cross border or more than 60% of income earned or paid out was cross border; and (3) outsourced management and administration). If an entity crosses all three gateways, it would be required to report information in its tax return. These so called "substance indicators" include information on its premises in the Member State, its bank accounts, the tax residency of its directors and that of its employees. The declarations would have to be accompanied by supporting evidence. If an entity fails at least one of the substance indicators, it would be presumed to be a 'shell'. This would be a rebuttable presumption.

Unshell proposed to include an Art. 8ad in the DAC. If the Unshell proposal would be adopted including this provision, this article must be renumbered, as 8ad is by now

165 Proposal of 21 December 2021 for a Council Directive laying down rules to prevent the misuse of shell entities for tax purposes and amending Directive 2011/16/EU, COM(2021) 565 final.

166 See also O. Popa Proposal for an EU Directive Laying Down Rules to Prevent the Misuse of Shell Entities for Tax Purposes (Unshell): Seven Steps towards Disgrace or Redemption, 62 *European Taxation* 4, 2022.

used in DAC8. However, in the remainder of this section the numbering of the Unshell proposal will be used. Based on the proposed Art. 8ad DAC, Member States would have to automatically exchange the information on these substance indicators. They would have to do this within 30 days from receipt of that information through the CCN network (Art. 8ad(1)). If an undertaking rebutted the presumption, or if it is exempt from the reporting of the substance indicators, the Member State would also have to communicate that information within 30 days through the CCN network (Art. 8ad(2)). The same would apply to the conclusion that an undertaking does not meet the substance indicators (Art. 8ad(3)). The Dutch Ministry of Finance noted that the 30 days term is difficult to meet and aimed for an extension.[167]

The information that would have to be communicated included the TIN, VAT number, identification of shareholders and beneficial owners, Member States likely to be concerned and any person in the other member states likely to be affected by the reporting, the declaration on the substance indicators and the evidence provided (Art. 8ad(4)). Certification of rebuttal or exemption and a summary of the evidence relevant for that certification (Art. 8ad(5)) and, if available, an audit report (Art. 8ad(6)) would have to be communicated as well through the CCN. The information would be retained for 5 years and no longer than necessary to achieve the purposes of the DAC (Art. 8ad(9)). Art. 8ad(11) would provide that in the event of unauthorized disclosure of information on the substance indicators, Member States may suspend the exchange of information with the Member State where the unauthorized disclosure occurred. The Unshell Directive Proposal includes its own provision for penalties (Art. 14 Unshell, unlike Art. 25a DAC, this defines a minimum penalty), requests for tax audits (Art. 15 Unshell) and monitoring (Art. 16 Unshell). Preamble 14 of the proposed Unshell Directive explicitly states that where necessary, the stage of mandatory automatic exchange of information can be followed by exchange on request, based on Art. 5 DAC.

The Unshell amendments were envisaged to have an application date of 1 January 2024, but at the end of May 2025, there was still no agreement on the proposal.[168] Furthermore, in May 2025, EU Member States seemed to be in support of integrating the economic substance hallmarks of the Unshell Proposal into the DAC and dropping the Unshell Proposal.[169]

28.3.3 *Spontaneous Exchange*

In the context of the DAC, 'spontaneous' does not mean 'voluntary', but merely without prior request (*ex officio*). Spontaneous exchange of information may, therefore, be either

167 Tweede Kamer, 2021–2022, 22112, no. 3349, and https://www.rijksoverheid.nl/documenten/kamerstukken/2022/05/06/antwoorden-op-kamervragen-over-bnc-fiche-tegengaan-misbruik-doorstroomvennootschappen.

168 See also Elodie Lamer, EU Countries Doubt Value of Watered-Down Unshell Proposal, *Tax Notes International*, 9 December 2024, p. 1599.

169 Elodie Lamer, Unshell's assimilation in DAC6 Appears to Have Member States' OK, *Tax Notes International* 28 May 2025, pp. 1143-1144 and Elodie Lamer, EU Commission open to trading Unshell Proposal for DAC6 Overhaul, *Tax Notes International* 26 May 2025, pp. 1231-1232.

mandatory (Art. 9(1)) or voluntary (Art. 9(2)). A Member State is obliged to forward information of which it has knowledge in five cases (Art. 9(1)):

- a possible loss of tax in another Member State. Such loss does not need to be certain or proven; a reasonable expectation is enough; the obligation exists where a Member State has reason to believe that without the information, an unjustified saving in tax, whatever its amount, may ensue in the other Member State;[170]
- a taxpayer obtains a tax reduction or exemption which should be followed by a corresponding tax liability or increase in another Member State. For instance: a taxpayer resident in country A receiving dividends from country B, and who is subject to country B withholding tax, credits that withholding tax against his country A income tax, but later, *e.g.* after litigation, obtains a refund in country B. In such a case, country B should forward the information to country A in order to enable the latter to undo the credit;
- taxpayers in two different Member States conduct business dealings through one or more countries in a way liable to reduce tax in a Member State (tax avoidance through conduit structures);
- a possible loss of tax as a result of 'artificial transfers of profits' within a multinational group of enterprises (*e.g.* transfer pricing not at arm's length);
- *do ut des:* where Member State A obtains information from Member State B which enables State A to get hold of new information possibly relevant to tax liability in State B, State A must return the favour by forwarding that new information on to State B.

In all other cases, Member States may forward information of which they are aware and which may be useful to another Member State (Art. 9(2)).

Art. 10(1) lays down a time limit for forwarding the information referred to in Art. 9(1). This must be forwarded as quickly as possible and no later than one month after it has become available. The receiving State must immediately confirm, if possible by electronic means, the receipt of the information and in any event within seven working days (Art. 10(2)).

If the supplying State asks for feedback on the information it provided under Art. 9, the requesting State must provide this as soon as possible and no later than three months after the outcome of the use of the information is known, respecting its national provisions on tax secrecy and data protection (Art. 14(1)).

Art. 20(3) requires the use of a standard form, developed by the European Commission in a comitology procedure, for providing spontaneous information, acknowledging its receipt and for asking and providing feedback.

28.4 Admission of Foreign Officials

It may be very efficient and effective to have tax officials of the requesting State present in the requested State during the investigation instituted by the requested State in order to comply with the request for information. This is especially the case where a person's premises or possessions must be inspected, where individuals must be interviewed or

170 Case C-420/98, *W.N.*, EU:C:2000:209.

where books must be examined. Art. 11(1) provides that the competent authority of one Member State may request the competent authority of another Member State that officials of the requesting State may be present in the offices of the requested State's tax administration (Art. 11(1)(a)), as well as during administrative enquiries in the requested State's territory (Art. 11(1)(b)) and may participate in the administrative enquiries by the requested Member State through the use of electronic means of communication, where appropriate (Art. 11(1)(c)). The requested authority must respond to a request within 60 days to confirm its agreement or to communicate its reasoned refusal (Art. 11(1), second paragraph). The officials of the requesting State must be given copies of documents available to the requested State's authorities which contain the requested information (Art. 11(1), third paragraph).

Where officials of the requesting authority are present during administrative enquiries or participate in them through means of electronic communication, they may interview individuals and examine records subject to procedural arrangements laid down by the requested Member State (Art. 11(2)). Preamble 22 to DAC7 states that this provision makes it clear that the foreign officials are subject to the procedural arrangements of the requested state to directly interview individuals and examine records. Sanctions on a refusal to cooperate by the persons inspected must be applied as if the refusal was committed against the national authorities (national treatment of refusals, Art. 11(2) second subparagraph).

The difficulty with admitting foreign tax officials to domestic tax offices and to domestic enquiries, and to have them interview people and check books, is that this may render meaningless the inspected person's or the taxpayer's rights under domestic law to apply for an injunction or to contest the intended exchange of information in Court prior to disclosure to the foreign authorities. If the foreign officials already know what they wanted to know from being present during the audit, or from interviewing individuals, it is of little use to file for an injunction or to litigate against the planned forwarding of information already known to the foreign officials. However, tax courts or criminal courts of the applying State may consider the information inadmissible as evidence if a court of the requested State *a posteriori* holds the information not to have been eligible for exchange. Also, the requested State may be liable for damages if the information already found its way across the border before the interested parties were able to raise legal objections and it is later established that national law was violated or overstepped, or that the taxpayer was right in objecting against the exchange of the information.

28.5 Simultaneous Controls

Art. 12 provides for simultaneous controls by two or more Member States, each in their own territory, of one or more persons of common or complementary interest with a view to exchanging the information so obtained. The Member States remain sovereign in their territories. They can only invite each other to join a simultaneous international tax audit where this appears to be more efficient than separate controls, by suggesting to each other cases and, persons and time spans within which to strike, and by giving reasons for these suggestions (Art. 12(2)). Member States are free to decide whether or not to participate, but if they refuse, they must give reasons for not obliging (Art. 12(3)). This communication must be made within 60 days of receiving the proposal. All States involved in a joint operation must appoint a supervisor/coordinator for the operation (Art. 12(4)).

28.6 Joint Audits

In a joint audit, tax administrations cooperate in a tax audit of one or more taxpayers with cross-border activities. Čičin-Šain and English observed that joint audits enable national tax administrations to collect and analyse information more rapidly, more targeted and more comprehensively and in closer cooperation with their counterparts in other countries.[171] A benefit for tax payers is that joint audits can serve as a dispute prevention tool, because these can solve complex cross-border situations at an early stage, allow taxpayers to present the relevant facts and explain their legal position to all tax administrations involved and thus mitigate the risk of double taxation.[172]

In recent years, some EU Member States started pilot projects on joint audits with the support of the Fiscalis 2020 programme which allows developing and operating major trans-European IT systems together, as well as establishing networks by bringing together national tax administration officials from across Europe to create and exchange information and expertise.[173] These joint audits were usually based on Art. 11(2) on participation by foreign officials (see Section 28.4) occasionally combined with Art. 12 (simultaneous controls, see Section 28.5) Čičin-Šain and English noted, however, that the effective use of joint audits was hampered by a lack of clarity, even regarding the relevant legal basis.[174] This also lead to uncertainty as to the nature of public powers exercised by foreign officials and the applicable procedural law. Some Member States even doubted as to whether joint audits, were allowed at all under the DAC.

171 Nevia Čičin-Šain and Joachim English, DAC 7: an entire new framework for joint audits in the EU: how do the taxpayers fare? *Intertax* vol. 50(1) 2022, pp. 7-27.

172 OECD Forum on Tax Administration, *Joint Audit 2019 -Enhancing Tax Co-operation and Improving Tax Certainty* OECD 2019 https://www.oecd.org/tax/joint-audit-2019-enhancing-tax-co-operation-and-improving-tax-certainty-17bfa30d-en.htm and preamble 25 of DAC7.

173 Regulation (EU) 2021/847 of the European Parliament and of the Council of 20 May 2021 establishing the 'Fiscalis' programme for cooperation in the field of taxation and repealing Regulation (EU) No 1286/2013, O.J. of 28 May 2021, L 188, p. 1.

174 Nevia Čičin-Šain and Joachim English, Joint audits under the new DAC 7, *Kluwer International Tax Blog*, 22 March 2021, http://kluwertaxblog.com/2021/03/22/joint-audits-under-the-new-dac-7/.

Because of the benefits of coordinated controls[175] and to ensure legal certainty (preamble 24 of DAC7), DAC7 introduced a separate section in the DAC, Section IIa, on joint audits. This section, that consists of Art. 12a, provides a legal framework for these audits, including the initiation of joint audits, procedural aspects and the applicable national law. It had to be implemented by 31 December 2023 and apply from 1 January 2024 at the latest (Art. 2(2) DAC7). For some Member States, joint audits were difficult to accept, which resulted in a watering down of the original proposal on joint audits. For example, Art. 12a does not give the taxpayer the right to request a joint audit in its final form.[176] Čičin-Šain and English note that there is still ample room for improvement as joint audits are still governed by domestic procedural rules, especially regarding taxpayer rights, which creates complexities and ambiguities.[177]

Art. 3(26) defines a joint audit as an administrative enquiry jointly conducted by the competent authorities of two or more Member States and linked to one or more persons of common or complementary interest to the competent authorities of those Member States. Member States may request one or more other Member States to conduct a joint audit (Art. 12a(1)). The requested Member State(s) must respond withing 60 days and may reject the request on justified grounds (Art. 12a(1)). It is not specified what would constitute justified grounds. Čičin-Šain and English question specifically whether 'justified grounds' includes the lack of administrative capacity of the requested tax administration.[178]

Joint audits must be conducted in a pre-agreed and coordinated manner, including linguistic arrangements and in accordance with the laws and procedural requirements of the Member State where the activities of the joint audit take place. In addition, officials of the other Member State may not exercise any powers that they could not exercise under the laws of their own Member State. Therefore, the foreign officials are bound to the stricter rules of either the host State or the sending State. Each Member State where

175 See for an extensive discussion on joint tax audits, the advantages and obstacles to conducting joint tax audits, measuring their possible impact and their beneficial effects Irene J.J. Burgers and Dana Criclivaia, Joint Tax Audits: Which Countries May Benefit Most? *World Tax Journal* October 2016, pp. 306-355. Other literature on this topic includes Nevia Čičin-Šain, Tina Ehrke-Rabel and Joachim Englisch, Joint Audits: Applicable Law and Taxpayer Rights, *World Tax Journal*, no. 4, 18, November 2018; N. Čičin-Šain, Joint and Simultaneous Audits, in P. Pistone ed. *Tax Procedure*, IBFD 2020; N. Čičin-Šain, Joint Audits, in: G. Kofler et al. eds. *CJEU, Recent Developments in Value Added Tax 2019*, Linde 2020; D. Criclivaia, Joint Audits – Ten Years of Experience: A Literature Review, 12 *World Tax Journal* 2020, Nevia Čičin-Šain and Joachim English, DAC 7: an entire new framework for joint audits in the EU: how do the taxpayers fare? *Intertax* vol. 50(1) 2022, pp. 7-27, Isabella Zimmerl, Reaching Cross-Border Tax Certainty With Joint Audits, (2022), 31, *EC Tax Review*, Issue 6, pp. 300-311.

176 See for a more elaborate discussion: Nevia Čičin-Šain and Joachim English, DAC 7: an entire new framework for joint audits in the EU: how do the taxpayers fare? *Intertax* vol. 50(1) 2022, pp. 7-27, section 4.1.

177 Nevia Čičin-Šain and Joachim English, DAC 7: an entire new framework for joint audits in the EU: how do the taxpayers fare? *Intertax* vol. 50(1) 2022, pp. 7-27 and Nevia Čičin-Šain and Joachim English, Joint audits under the new DAC 7, *Kluwer International Tax Blog*, 22 March 2021, http://kluwertaxblog.com/2021/03/22/joint-audits-under-the-new-dac-7/.

178 Nevia Čičin-Šain and Joachim English, Joint audits under the new DAC 7, *Kluwer International Tax Blog*, 22 March 2021, http://kluwertaxblog.com/2021/03/22/joint-audits-under-the-new-dac-7/.

the activities of a joint audit take place, must appoint a representative responsible for supervision and coordination of the joint audit in that Member State (Art. 12a(2)).

Member State(s) where the activities of a joint audit take place must (a) permit that officials of other Member States interview individuals and examine records together with the officials of the Member State where the joint audit activities take place, (b) ensure that evidence collected during the joint audit can be assessed (which includes in a process of complaint, review or appeal), including on its admissibility, under the same legal conditions as would be the case for a regular audit in that Member State, and (c) ensure that the person(s) subject to a joint audit or affected by it enjoy the same rights and have the same obligations as would be the case in a regular audit in that Member State (Art. 12a(3)).

The competent authorities must endeavour to agree on the facts, circumstances relevant to the joint audit and to reach an agreement on the tax position of the audited person(s) based on the results of the joint audit. The findings must be incorporated in a final report which reflects the issues on which competent authorities agree. Those issues must be taken into account in the relevant instruments issued by the competent authorities issued following the joint audit. Where the original proposal for DAC7 included obligations to make the findings of the audit legally binding for the follow-up national instruments, this is not the case in the current Art. 12a. The actions following the joint audit and any further processes in a Member State, such as decisions, appeal and settlements, must take place in accordance with the national law of that Member State (Art. 12a(4)).

The audited person(s) must be informed of the outcome of the joint audit, This includes receiving a copy of the final report within 60 days of its issuance (Art. 12a(5)).

28.7 Notification of Foreign Decisions and Instruments

In various Member States, national law requires the tax authorities to notify taxpayers within a specific span of time of any decision or instrument concerning their tax position, such as assessments, interest or penalty decisions, decisions on objections, enforcement orders, writs, summons, etc. As taxpayers become increasingly internationally mobile, it is becoming more difficult for Member States to comply with such requirement. In order to obviate this bureaucratic difficulty as regards taxpayers who relocated to another Member State, Art. 13 requires national treatment of foreign instruments and decisions relating to taxes covered by the DAC.

Member States are required, upon request of another Member State, to notify to addressees within their territory any decision or instrument of the tax authorities of the requesting Member State as if it were their own similar decision or instrument (Art. 13(1)). The request for notification must indicate the instrument or decision to be notified and must include the name and address of the addressee together with other information which may facilitate identification of the addressee. Standard forms are used for the exchange of this information (Art. 20(3)). The DAC contains a limiting provision (Art. 13(4)), stating that (i) notification requests shall only be made if it is impossible or disproportionally difficult for the requesting State to notify according to its own rules, and (ii) competent authorities of a Member State may notify documents directly to addressees in another Member State by registered mail or electronically.

28.8 Access to Anti-Money-Laundering Information, Including Information on Ultimate Beneficial Owners (DAC5)

As was discussed in Section 28.3.2.2, Art. 8(3a) provides for automatic exchange of information on foreign account holders and their accounts provided for by financial institutions under the CRS. If the account holder is an intermediary structure, the financial institution must look through that structure and identify and report on its beneficial owners (Section VIII(E)(1) of Annex I). This element of the customer due-diligence procedure relies on anti-money laundering (AML) information obtained pursuant to the 4th Anti-Money Laundering Directive (AMLD4)[179] for the identification of beneficial owners.

In order for Member States to monitor, confirm and audit that financial institutions apply their CRS obligations properly by correctly identifying and reporting on the beneficial owners of intermediary structures, Member States need to have access to the AML information (preamble 2 to Directive DAC5[180]). This may also be the case for other forms of administrative cooperation and the monitoring thereof.

For that reason, Art. 22(1a) DAC obliges Member States to provide for access by tax authorities to certain personal data referred to in AMLD4. In order to comply with the privacy requirements of Art. 8(2) of the European Convention on Human Rights (ECHR) and of the EU Charter of Fundamental Rights of the European Union, access to the information must be provided for by law. This law must be clear and precise and its application must be clear and foreseeable to persons subject to it in order to comply with the case law of the Court of Justice and the European Court of Human Rights (ECtHR).

The information tax authorities must have access to based on Art. 22(1a), includes the mechanisms, procedures, documents and information referred to in Arts. 13 AMLD4 (customer due diligence procedures), 30 AMLD4 (UBO register for corporate and other legal entities), 31 AMLD4 (UBO register for trusts) 32a AMLD4 (centralised automated mechanisms allowing the identification of persons holding or controlling payment accounts and bank accounts and safe-deposit boxes), and 40 AMLD4 (documents necessary to comply with the customers due diligence requirements and supporting evidence and records of transactions which are necessary to identify transactions). These provisions had to be applied as of 1 January 2018.

---

179 Council Directive 2015/849/EU of 20 May 2015 on the prevention of the use of the financial system for the purposes of money laundering or terrorist financing, amending Regulation (EU) No. 648/2012 of the European Parliament and of the Council, and repealing Directive 2005/60/ EC of the European Parliament and of the Council and Commission Directive 2006/70/EC, O.J. 5 June 2015, L 141, p. 73.

180 Council Directive 2016/2258/EU of 6 December 2016 amending Directive 2011/16/EU as regards access to anti-money-laundering information by tax authorities, O.J. 16 December 2016, L 342, p. 1.

28.9 Disclosure, Use and Forwarding of Information Obtained

Information obtained under the DAC is covered by the obligation for official secrecy and must enjoy the same protection in the receiving State as similar information received under its domestic legislation (national confidentiality treatment (Art. 16(1)). In the *Berlioz* Case,[181] the Court held that such secrecy is accounted for by the discretion which the requesting authority must normally display at the information-gathering stage and which it is entitled to expect of the requested authority if the effectiveness of its investigation is to avoid jeopardy. Consequently, the Court held that anyone can be barred from having access to a request for information, *i.e.* the Competent Authority Letter, in an investigation on account of the fact that it is secret. This also applies to the person involved. In order for that person to be given a full hearing of his case in relation to the lack of any foreseeable relevance of the requested information, the Court deems it sufficient that he is given the information which should at least be included on the standard form for a request for information: the identity of the taxpayer concerned and the tax purpose for which the information is sought (DAC7 included this in Art. 20(2)). If the requested Member State asks for additional information, that additional information must be provided as well, while taking due account of the possible confidentiality of some of that information.

The information obtained may be used for (Arts. 16(1)-(3) and 24(2)):

- the 'assessment, administration and enforcement' of the domestic laws on taxes referred to in Art. 2 as well as VAT and other indirect taxes (Art. 16(1) first subparagraph). DAC7 explicitly inserted in the first subparagraph of Art. 16(1) that the information may be used for VAT and other indirect taxes. According to preamble 30 of DAC7 this is a clarification. The same applies to the insertion of customs duties, anti-money laundering and combating the financing of terrorism as of 2026 (preamble 35 of DAC8);
- the 'assessment and enforcement' of other taxes and duties covered by Art. 2 of the RAD (Art. 16(1) second subparagraph);
- the assessment and enforcement of compulsory social security contributions, even though the exchange itself for that purpose is outside the scope of the DAC (Art. 2(3)). (Art. 16(1) second subparagraph);
- judicial and administrative proceedings which may involve penalties and which are initiated because of tax law infringements, provided the rights of defendants and witnesses in such proceedings are respected (therefore, the right not to incriminate oneself and the other fair hearing requirements ex Art. 6 ECHR and the EU Charter of Fundamental Rights must be respected); this means that the information may also be used in criminal proceedings against tax offenders, provided their defense rights are respected (Art. 16(1) third subparagraph);
- with the permission of the supplying State, any other purpose for which the use of the information is legally permitted in the receiving Member State. The supplying State is obliged to grant such permission if the envisaged use is legally permitted within its own jurisdiction (Art. 16(2) first subparagraph). Art. 16(2) second subparagraph provides that each Member State may communicate to all other Member States a list of purposes, other than those mentioned in Art. 16(1), for which, in accordance with

181 Case C682/15, *Berlioz*, EU:C:2017:373, paras 94 and 95 and 100-101.

its national law, information and documents may be used. For such use the receiving Member State does not need a specific permission. The list must be communicated using the standard forms adopted by the Commission in accordance with the comitology procedure of Art. 26(2) (Art. 20(3)(3)). DAC8 inserts a new subparagraph in Art. 16(2): as of 2026 the receiving Member State may also use the information without permission for any purpose that is covered by an act based on Art. 215 TFEU regarding restrictive measures and share them for such purpose with the competent authority in charge of restrictive measures in the Member State concerned. According to preamble 36 of DAC8, information exchanged under the DAC can be relevant for the detection of violation or circumvention of restrictive measures and, in return, any potential breaches of restrictive measures will be relevant for tax purposes, since avoidance of restrictive measures will in most cases also amount to tax avoidance in relation to the assets concerned;

- forwarding to a third Member State, if such forwarding accords with the rules and procedures of the directive. The Member State of origin must be informed beforehand and may oppose the sharing of the information within ten working days (as of 2026 based on DAC8: 15 calendar days) (Art. 16(3)). Art. 20(4) requires that these communications are done using the standard forms adopted by the Commission in accordance with the comitology procedure of Art. 26(2); and
- forwarding to a non-Member State, provided (i) the supplying Member State consents, and (ii) the non-Member State has given an undertaking to cooperate in combating tax avoidance and fraud (the OECD minimum standard) (Art. 24(2)).

Art. 16(5) provides that any information, report, statement, document or certified copy or extract thereof provided by the authorities of the requested State according to the DAC may be relied on as evidence by the competent bodies of the receiving State on the same basis as similar evidence provided by a domestic authority. Art. 16(6) limits the purposes for which the CbC information may be used (see Section 28.3.2.4).

28.10 Grounds for Refusal of Cooperation

Art. 17 contains five narrowly defined limitations on Member States' obligation to exchange information upon request: (i) the requesting authority has not exhausted the usual sources of information which it could have used in the circumstances for obtaining the information requested, without running the risk of jeopardising the achievement of its objectives; (ii) it would be contrary to the legislation of the requested Member State to conduct the requested enquiries or to collect the information requested for its own purposes; (iii) the requesting Member State is unable, for legal reasons, to provide similar information; (iv) the provision of the requested information would lead to the disclosure of a commercial, industrial or professional secret or of a commercial process; and (v) the disclosure of the requested information would be contrary to public policy. These categories will be discussed in the next subsections.

These limitations largely coincide with those set out in Art. 26(2) of the OECD-MC. In the *Berlioz* Case,[182] the Court held that some of the limits included in Art. 17(1) could be taken into account when determining the legality of a request for information, but that these would not have any bearing on a review of the foreseeable relevance of that information. In the *Établissements Rimbaud* Case[183] the court held that the predecessor of Art. 17 in the old Directive only provided for exceptions to the exchange of information by way of derogation. It thus has to be narrowly construed and, by virtue of the principle of sincere cooperation (now Art. 4(3) TEU), the Member States are required to engage fully in the exchange of information provided for under the Directive. I agree with AG Kokott in her opinion in the *Bean House* Case[184] that this case law also applies to the current Directive.

Evidently, a general ground for refusal may be that the information requested lies outside the scope of the DAC (*e.g.* social security contributions or fees for public services rather than taxes). If a requested Member State refuses cooperation, it must inform the requesting State of its ground(s) for refusal (Art. 17(5)). A Member State cannot refuse to cooperate on the ground(s) that it has no domestic interest in the information requested (Art. 18(1)).

28.10.1 Non-Exhaustion of Appropriate Domestic Means

Art. 17(1) allows the requested State to refuse a request for information where the applying State has not exhausted the usual sources of information which it could have used in the circumstances without jeopardising the result sought. A requested State can hardly verify whether this requirement is met. In practice, requested States content themselves with a statement of the applying State that domestic means were used, but did not produce the result desired.

28.10.2 Lack of Domestic Legal Basis

The requested State is not required to carry out enquiries or to communicate information if it would be contrary to its own laws to carry out such enquiries or to collect the information for its own purposes (Art. 17(2)). Under Art. 8(1) of the old Directive, this limitation stopped requests for information resting with Luxembourg and Austrian banks. However, the DAC explicitly precludes Member States from relying on national rules on banking secrecy or ownership secrecy in order to decline information requests as regards bank information (Art. 18(2)). Thus, banking secrecy is done away with, albeit only with prospective effect: Art. 18(3) provides that bank information may still be refused if the request concerns tax years prior to 2011.

The DAC only recognises limitations in national statutory law; it does not recognise limitations imposed by national 'administrative practices', as was the case under Art. 8(1) of the old Directive.

182 Case C-682/15, *Berlioz*, EU:C:2017:373, para 88.
183 Case C-72/09, *Établissements Rimbaud*, EU:C:2010:645, para 48.
184 Opinion of AG Kokott of 2 October 2014 in Case C-133/13, *Q (Bean House)*, EU:C:2014:2255, para 70.

The lack of a legal basis clause also has the effect of allowing a Member State to exclude from the benefits of its tax treaties nonresident companies which in their State of residence are not required to provide tax information to their tax administration. This follows from the *ELISA* Case[185] concerning the French-Luxembourg tax treaty. That treaty excluded (participants in) a Luxembourg 'Société Holding 1929' because these were exempt from tax and they were not required to provide any information for Luxembourg income taxation purposes.

The wording of Art. 17(2) does not seem to allow a Member State to refuse communicating information which it would not be competent to collect, but which it nonetheless has readily available. Indeed, if it is unnecessary 'to conduct enquiries' or 'to collect the information requested for its own purposes' because it is already there, then Art. 17(2) does not seem to provide any ground for refusal. The fact that a tax administration would not have been competent to require certain information does not exclude that it nevertheless legally comes across such information. For example, the microfiches containing data on KB Lux bank accounts were found by the Belgian judicial authorities in the course of a house search. They were transmitted to the Belgian tax authorities. Under the (old) Directive, the Belgian tax authorities forwarded copies of the fiches to the Netherlands tax authorities. Another example is the CD-ROM containing bank account information which Germany bought from an ex-employee of a Liechtenstein bank and which was shared with other Member States in so far as relevant for them.[186]

AG Kokott in her opinion in the *Bean House* Case[187] did not see a justification in Art. 17(2) to refuse to monitor public access to an immovable property without prior notice as the information concerned was publicly available and obtaining it would not require the exercise of sovereignty. However, should it transpire that, by reason of a corresponding prohibition in its procedural law, the requested Member State would, in fact, be prevented from monitoring public access to an immovable property without prior notice, she was of the opinion that the requesting State could still carry out the necessary controls as regards public access to the immovable property on the basis of pre-announced on-site checks and additional evidence, such as witness statements.

28.10.3 *Lack of Reciprocity*

Where the applying State is legally unable itself to provide similar information upon request in the inverse situation, the requested State is under no obligation to comply (Art. 17(3)). A Member State thus cannot take advantage of the tax information system of another Member State which offers wider possibilities than its own system. This means

185 Case C-451/05, *ELISA*, EU:C:2007:594.

186 The legitimacy of the initial obtaining of the information is less clear in the last example (is this not sovereign fencing?), but the Member States to which the information was forwarded did nothing wrong, and in any case the purpose of the fencing provisions in criminal codes is not to protect tax fraudsters.

187 Opinion of AG Kokott of 2 October 2014 in Case C-133/13, Q (*Bean House*), EU:C:2014:2255, paras 71-72.

that no Member State is obliged to provide banking information to Luxembourg and Austria concerning tax years prior to 2011.

Refusal is, unlike as was the case in the old Directive, not allowed if the applying State for reasons of fact is unable itself to provide similar information. Apparently, such limitation hinders exchange, as Member State A would probably not be enthusiastic about conducting investigations for the benefit of Member State B which, in the inverse position, replies that it does not have the resources to comply. In any case, Member State B is not allowed to reply in that way; even if it were true that its competent authority does not have the necessary possibilities, that is no excuse: it should bring its administration up to standard.

28.10.4 Protection of Commercial Secrets

Member States may refuse to provide information if it would mean disclosing a commercial, industrial or professional secret or a commercial process (Art. 17(4)). This exception is aimed at protecting the legitimate competitive interests of the undertakings concerned, but also at protecting Member States' economies against economic espionage. By way of endorsement, Art. 18(2) explicitly provides that banking secrets and ownership secrets are not commercial or industrial secrets. This refusal ground cannot be relied on to refuse automatic exchange of ruling information (see Section 28.3.2.3). However, it can be used to refuse a request to exchange the full text of a ruling.

28.10.5 Protection of the Ordre Public

Member States may refuse to exchange information if that would be contrary to public policy *(ordre public)* (Art.17(4)). An example might be a Member State requesting another Member State with which it has concluded a bilateral tax treaty for information which the applying State intends to use for applying a treaty override in its domestic legislation, precisely to override the treaty with the requested State. The requested State can hardly be expected to assist its tax treaty partner in frustrating or even violating its tax treaty obligations as regards the requested State.

28.11 Penalties

Art. 25a obliges Member States to provide for penalties for non-compliance in order to ensure the timely compliance with the CbC reporting obligations (Art. 8aa), the mandatory disclosure obligations (Art. 8ab), the reporting obligations for digital platforms (Art. 8ac), and, as of 2026 obligations for reportable crypto-asset service providers (Art. 8ad, DAC8) and filing obligations regarding the top-up tax information return (Art. 8ae, DAC9),. The DAC does not give any specifications regarding these penalties, other than that these must be effective, proportionate and dissuasive (Art. 25a, last sentence).

The choice of penalties thus remains within the discretion of the Member States. Member States can incorporate these in the national system for tax penalties. This has led to substantial differences between Member States. From a May 2020 overview of penalties made by TaxModel International[188] it became clear that the range of penalties varied enormously between Member States. In 2020, Poland had the highest maximum penalty (€ 5.5 million), followed by the Netherlands (€ 870,000), Luxembourg (€ 250,000) and Slovenia (€ 150.000). Of the other Member States, 3 applied a maximum penalty between € 50,000 and € 100,000; 13 between €10,000 and € 50,000 and 6 had a penalty of at most € 10,000. The median maximum penalty was € 26,100. A report commissioned in 2022 by the European Parliament's subcommittee on tax matters stated that the range of penalties for DAC6 violations across EU countries varied between €3,000 and €4.7 million.[189] In 2024, the Dutch Association of Tax Advisers said in its response to the public consultation for the DAC1-6 evaluation that where the penalties are as little as EUR 500 per day in Ireland, the Netherlands may impose a penalty up to a total amount of EUR 1,030,000 and Poland may even impose penalties up to an amount of PLN 25,000,000 (approximately EUR 5,300,000).[190]

These differences might induce certain companies to structure themselves such that the reporting entity is tax resident in a country with a low penalty. This is especially easy for companies with an ultimate parent outside the EU. Thus, this penalty freedom of the DAC might distort competition in the internal market. The DAC includes the requirements of 'effectiveness' and 'dissuasiveness' to curtail Member States in this respect, but it remains to be seen how the European Court of Justice will apply these requirements. The same applies for the protection of taxpayers by the proportionality requirement which taxpayers can invoke when a Member State has imposed a penalty for non-compliance.

The DAC8 proposal included a harmonized minimum level of penalties, but this was removed by the Council.[191] Gorissen and Uslu were of the opinion that limiting the Directive to the generic Art. 25a is a missed opportunity for the European Union to harmonize the minimum penalties and improve overall compliance with the DAC.[192] The failure to harmonise penalties is DAC8 has not, however, ended the plea for more harmonization of penalties.[193]

188 Hank Moonen, Overview of the penalties for non-compliance DAC6, TaxModel International, 7 May 2022, https://tax-model.com/resources/blog/dac6-penalties/.

189 Werner Haslehner and Katerina Pantazatou, Assessment of recent anti-tax avoidance and evasion measures (ATAD & DAC 6), Policy Department for Economic, Scientific and Quality of Life Policies, p. 33.

190 Nederlandse Orde van Belastingadviseurs Response public consultation "Administrative Cooperation on direct taxation – evaluation", 29 July 2024, p. 5, https://www.nob.net/wp-content/uploads/2024/07/NOB-response-DAC6-evaluation-for-EC.pdf.

191 See also M. Bernt, DAC8: Commentary on the European Union's New Crypto Tax Reporting Regime, 63 *European Taxation* 9, 2023, section 7.

192 A.M.L. Gorissen and Y. Uslu, Investing in Crypto-Assets: Council Adoption of DAC8, 24 *Finance & Capital Markets* 3 (2023).

193 See for example Robert Attard, Tax penalty regimes, a call for harmonisation, *EC Review*, 2023, Claudio Cipollini, DAC8 and Extraterritoriality: How to Enforce Compliance for non-EU Operators', *EC Tax Review*, 2024-1, pp. 19-32 and Nederlandse Orde van Belastingadviseurs, *Response public consultation "Administrative Cooperation on direct taxation – evaluation"*, 29 July 2024, p. 5, https://www.nob.net/wp-content/uploads/2024/07/NOB-response-DAC6-evaluation-for-EC.pdf.

28.12 Tax Information Number

From the first evaluations of the DAC, it became clear that it was not always possible to match information exchanged under the DAC to individual taxpayers and data available in national databases. The Tax Information Number (TIN) is essential for this matching but was not always available. This made the DAC less effective. For that reason, DAC8[194] added Art. 27c to the DAC on the inclusion of the TIN of reported individuals and entities in the reporting and communication of information in the context of exchanges related to certain categories of income and capital subject to the mandatory automatic exchange of information, financial accounts, ACRs and APAs, country-by-country reports, reportable cross-border arrangements, and information on sellers on digital platforms and crypto-assets. For the categories of income mentioned in Art. 27c(2) and 27c(3) it is recognised, by using the words 'where possible', that there may be situations where it is not possible to collect and report the TIN, including where, despite best efforts, the reporting entity or the reporting individual was not able to collect the TIN or where a TIN has not been issued to the taxpayer. According to preamble 30 tot DAC8, these are 'rare' situations.

The date as of which the TIN must be reported and exchanged, depends on the category. For the categories of income and capital included in Art. 8(1), points (a), (b) and (d), Art. 27c(2) requires, where possible, reporting of the TIN to the extent that those are categories of income and capital on which information would have been communicated even if the TIN was not available. This must be the required for taxable periods starting on or after 1 January 2030.

For the information referred to in Art. 8a(6), points (a) and (k) in relation to ACRs and APAs, and information on reported individuals and entities as referred to in Art. 8aa(3), point (b) (regarding CbCR), and in Art. 8ab(14), point (h) (DAC6), the TIN must be reported, where possible, and -if the TIN is obtained – exchanged, for taxable periods starting on or after 1 January 2028 (Art. 27c(3) and 27c(4)).

In addition to the introduction of Art. 27c DAC8 also introduces a new Art. 21(8) that obliges the European Commission to provide Member States with a tool allowing an electronic and automated verification of the correctness of the TIN provided by a reporting entity or a taxpayer for the purposes of the automatic exchange of information. The Commission must develop the technical parameters of this tool through implementing acts that are to be adopted in accordance with the comitology procedure of Art. 26(2). The IT tool is intended to help increase the matching rates for tax administrations and improve the quality of the exchanged information in general (preamble 39 of DAC8).

Art. 22(4) that is applicable as of 2026 based on DAC8, requires Member States to endeavour to ensure that a reporting entity is allowed to obtain confirmation by electronic means of the validity of the information on the TIN of any taxpayer subject to the exchange of information under Arts. 8 to 8ae. The confirmation of the information on the TIN may

194 Council Directive (EU) 2023/2226 of 17 October 2023 amending Directive 2011/16/EU on administrative cooperation in the field of taxation.

be requested only for the purposes of validation of the correctness of data referred to in Arts. 8(1), 8(3a), 8a(6), 8aa(3), 8ab(14), 8ac(2) and 8ad(3).

28.13 Taxpayers' Judicial Protection

The DAC does not provide for judicial protection other than the official secrecy obligation Art. 16(1) imposes on the Member States, and the referral in the third subparagraph of 16(1) to 'the general rules and provisions governing the rights of defendants and witnesses' in proceedings initiated as a result of tax law infringements. Giusy De Flora observed that European (just as international) legislation on the exchange of information does not have a specific provision governing the relations between taxpayers and tax authorities.[195] Persons (potentially) affected by an exchange of tax information can thus rely only on domestic legislation for:

i. a possible right to be notified prior to an intended transmission of information;
ii. a right to be heard before information is transmitted (consultation right); in such case the decision to transmit information remains at the discretion of the requested tax authority;
iii. a possible injunction against an intention to transmit information (intervention right), which gives the taxpayer the right to block the transmission of the information in cases where there are formal or substantive defects; and
iv. a possible claim of damages in the event of unlawful exchange of information or violation of confidentiality or data protection.

Only if taxpayers are informed in advance, legal protection can be effective. However, this might delay the transmission of information or make it ineffective. The level of domestic legal protection varies considerably between Member States, especially as regards prior notification and the possibilities for (timely) obtaining judicial interim decisions such as a provisional injunction.[196] Therefore, Giusy De Flora is of the opinion that referral to the domestic legislation of the Member States is not sufficient to achieve a full balance between the interests of the requesting State and those of the taxpayer.[197] Furthermore, according to her, this legislation has limited or no consideration of the legal position of the taxpayer. In her view States are more interested in obtaining the required information rather than ensuring the procedural rights of taxpayers in the phase of exchange of information. Also, other authors have argued that more attention to taxpayer's rights is needed due to the increase of automatic exchange of information, which may lead to less control over the accuracy and use of the information by the requesting and the

195 Menita Giusy De Flora, Protection of the Taxpayer in the Information Exchange Procedure, *Intertax*, 2017, no. 6/7, pp. 447-460.

196 See Roman Seer and Isabel Gabert, 'European and International Tax Cooperation: Legal Basis, Practice, Burden of Proof, Legal Protection and Requirements', *Bulletin for International Taxation* February 2011, pp. 88-98, p. 96.

197 Menita Giusy De Flora, Protection of the Taxpayer in the Information Exchange Procedure, *Intertax*, 2017, no. 6/7, pp. 447-460.

requested States.[198], Zagà adds that also the protection of third parties, which includes the holders of tax information and parties affected by information obtained by information requests, is at issue.[199]

28.13.1 No Right to Be Involved

In the *WebMindLicenses* Case,[200] the Court held that tax authorities may use evidence obtained without the taxable person's knowledge in the context of a parallel criminal procedure, in order to establish the existence of an abusive VAT practice, as long as the obtaining of that evidence in the context of the criminal procedure and its use in the context of the administrative procedure do not infringe any rights guaranteed by EU law. The national court had to assess whether the use by the tax authorities of the evidence obtained by those means was also authorised by law and necessary. Furthermore, it had to assess whether, in accordance with the general principle of observance of the rights of the defense, the taxable person had the opportunity, in the context of the administrative procedure, to gain access to that evidence and to be heard concerning it. The Court observed that if a Directive includes a duty to cooperate, a request for information may prove expedient or even necessary. This is in particular the case where the tax authorities of a Member State know or should reasonably know that the tax authorities of another Member State have information which is useful, or even essential, for determining the tax liability in the first Member State. Taxpayers will probably not find much argument in this case law to require involvement in the exchange of information (except in relation to the rights of defense at a later stage).[201]

198 For example: Giuseppe Marino, General Report, in: Giuseppe Marino (ed.) *New exchange of information versus tax solutions of equivalent effect*, IBFD 2015, pp. 3-46, pp. 45-46, F. Alfredo García Prats, The Legitimacy of AEOI and measures other than AEOI, in: Giuseppe Marino (ed.) *New exchange of information versus tax solutions of equivalent effect*, IBFD 2015, pp. 133-162, Giuseppe Melis, AEOI and Protection of Taxpayers' Procedural Rights, in: Giuseppe Marino (ed.) *New exchange of information versus tax solutions of equivalent effect*, IBFD 2015, pp. 3-46, pp. 45-46, Niels Diepvens, Filip Debelva, The Evolution of the Exchange of Information in Direct Tax Matters: The Taxpayer's Rights under Pressure, *EC Tax Review*, 2015, no. 4, pp. 210-219; Marcel Schaper, Data Protection Rights and Tax Information Exchange in the European Union: An Uneasy Combination, *Maastricht Journal of European and Comparative Law*, 2016, 23(3), pp. 514-530; Saturnina Moreno González, The Automatic Exchange of Tax Information and the Protection of Personal Data in the European Union: Reflections on the Latest Jurisprudential and Normative Advances, *EC Tax Review*, 2016, no. 3, pp. 146-161; Filip Debelva and Irma Mosquera, Privacy and Confidentiality in Exchange of Information Procedures: Some Uncertainties, many Issues, but few Solutions, *Intertax* 2017, no. 5, pp. 362-381, which Article includes a wealth of references to other literature on this topic, V. Wöhrer, *Data Protection and Taxpayers' Rights: Challenges Created by Automatic Exchange of Information*, IBFD 2018, P. Baker, CRS/DAC, FATCA and the GDPR, *British Tax Review* 3, p. 252 2016, C.E. Weffe, Highlights and Trends in Global Taxpayers' Rights 2020, 75 *Bulletin for International Taxation* 7 2021, and Ana Paula Dourado, 'Editorial: Fake Tax Transparency? Leaks and Taxpayer Rights', *Intertax* 2018, vol. 46, no. 2, pp. 100-103.

199 Stefano Zagà, 'The protection of individual taxpayer rights regarding exchange of information on request in the European Union' 62 *European Taxation* 2/3 2022.

200 Case C-419/14, *WebMindLicenses*, EU:C:2015:832.

201 See for an extensive discussion of both cases in relation to exchange of information: Ine Lejeune and Liesbeth Vermeire, The Influence of the EU Charter of Fundamental Rights on ECJ Case Law on the International exchange of Information, 57 *European Taxation* 4 2017.

In the *Sabou* Case,[202] the Court had to answer the question whether the old Directive 77/799/ EEC did provide rights to taxpayers to be involved in the exchange of information. The Court held that it had jurisdiction to interpret the Directive and that it could impose obligations on Member States. A Member State is not obliged to submit a request (paras 33, 36), but where it decides to make use of that assistance, it must comply with the rules laid down in the Directive (point 26). This does not differ under the DAC. The Court made clear that the rights of the defense do not give a taxpayer a right to participate in the exchange of information between the competent authorities. In this respect the court distinguished in point 40 the investigation stage, during which information is collected, and which includes the request for information by one tax authority to another, from the contentious stage, between the tax authorities and the taxpayer, which begins when the taxpayer is sent the proposed adjustment. The rights of the defense have to be respected in the latter stage. Where the authorities gather information, including by making a request for assistance, they are, however, not required to notify the taxpayer or to obtain his point of view, as this is not part of the contentious stage. Thus, a taxpayer does not have the right to be informed of a request for assistance, to take part in formulating the request, or to take part in an examination of witnesses organised by the requested Member State. However, Member States are allowed (but not obliged) to extend the right to be heard to other parts of the investigation stage by involving the taxpayer in various stages of the gathering of information, in particular the examination of witnesses (point 45). Furthermore, it is up to domestic legislation whether or not the taxpayer may challenge the accuracy of the information conveyed by the requested Member State, as the old Directive did not address such right of the taxpayer. The same applies regarding obligations with regard to the content of the information conveyed, such as the sources of information or how it was gathered (points 47-50). In the *Berlioz* Case[203] the Court made clear that the same applies under the current Directive.

The ECtHR decided in the 2015 *Othymia Investments* Case that the transfer of information pursuant to the old Directive without a prior notification did not interfere with the company's right to private life of Art. 8 ECHR.[204] The Court observed that as the Directive was transposed into domestic law, there was an adequate statutory basis for this interference. Furthermore, this interference was found to be necessary, in which reasoning the Court relied on the *Sabou* Case. In this respect the Court did not deem it of relevance that the focus of the *Sabou* Case was on the taxpayer, whereas the *Othymia Investments* Case was on a third party. The Court referred to its case law in the context of 'the interests of national security', 'public safety' and 'the prevention of crime' in which it held that investigative methods may have to be used covertly even against persons who are not themselves objects of investigation or surveillance. It considered that the same applies in matters of taxation. It is not a requirement of Art. 8 that prior notice of lawful

202 Case C-276/12, *Sabou*, EU:C:2013:678. See for an extensive discussion of this case: José Manuel Calderón Carrero and Alberto Quintas Seara, The Taxpayer's Right of Defence in Cross-Border Exchange-of-Information Procedures, *Bulletin for International Taxation* September 2014, pp. 498-507.

203 Case C-682/15, *Berlioz*, EU:C:2017:373, paras 46-47.

204 Application No. 75292/10, *Othymia Investments*, CE:ECHR:2015:0616DEC007529210.

tax investigations or exchanges of tax-related information must be given to all persons potentially implicated (point 44).

Even though exchange of information is an interference with Art. 8, it is justified if it is (i) in accordance with the law (which will be the case if the DAC has been implemented in national legislation correctly); (ii) in the interest of the economic well-being of the country (which requirement will usually be met as well); and (3) necessary in a democratic society to achieve that aim (a criterion met based on the reasoning of the *Sabou* Case). Thus, the Convention also does not give a right to prior notification or other involvement.

28.13.2 Right to Legal Remedy

In the *Berlioz* Case[205] (points 48-52) the Court made it clear that if a penalty is imposed in relation to the DAC, the right to an effective remedy and to a fair trial under Art. 47 of the EU Charter of Fundamental Rights (Charter) applies. In this case a penalty was imposed, because Berlioz did not provide all the information Luxembourg needed to comply with a French request for information based on the DAC. The Court observed that penalties can be encompassed under 'measures aimed at gathering information' (Art. 18) and 'necessary measures to ensure the smooth operation of the administrative cooperation arrangements', and that the Luxembourg penalty was thus an implementation of EU law, more specifically the DAC, in the meaning of Art. 51(1) of the Charter. It was not deemed relevant that the Luxembourg provision on the penalty was not adopted to transpose the DAC, as it enabled the Member State to comply with the DAC and could thus be regarded as implementing the DAC (points 37-41). This means that the Charter is applicable and that in cases in which a penalty is imposed in order to ensure that a Member State can fulfil the obligations it has under the Directive, the safeguards of the DAC apply, including the right to a remedy of Art. 47. This protection can be invoked by a relevant person in respect of a measure adversely affecting him. Such measures include an information order and a penalty. Thus, through the Charter some legal protection is obtained regarding measures stemming from the Directive. In the *L* Case.[206] (point 89) the Court repeated the right of an effective legal remedy for the person on whom a penalty is imposed for failing to comply with an order to provide information in the context of the DAC.

However, the Court makes clear in the *Berlioz* Case that under the DAC a taxpayer who is the subject of a request for information as between national tax administrations does not have a right to be heard or to participate in that process. The legal protection in *Berlioz* has regard to the right of a person on whom a penalty has been imposed to challenge the legality of that decision. An argument to challenge an information order can be that the information requested by the other Member State is not 'foreseeably relevant', which means that the requested Member State would not have to comply with the request (point 74). However, as was discussed in Section 28.2.3, the courts' review

205 Case C-682/15, *Berlioz*, EU:C:2017:373, paras 46-47.

206 Case C-437/19, *L*, EU:C:2021:953. See also on this case G.W. Kofler et al., Opinion Statement ECJ-TF 1/2022 on the ECJ Decision of 25 November 2021 in État Luxembourgeois v. L (Case C-437/19) on the Conditions for Information Requests and Taxpayer Remedies, 62 European Taxation 5 (2022).

of the foreseeable relevance of the requested information is limited to verification that the requested information manifestly has no such relevance.

In the *Shakira* Case[207] the Court went further and made it clear that a person cannot be forced to incur a penalty in order to obtain an effective legal remedy. It observed that Art. 47 of the Charter, the right to an effective remedy, also applies to legislation implementing the DAC in particular where that legislation provides for the possibility, for the competent authority, of taking a decision that obliges a person holding information to provide it with that information (point 46 and 54). In order to have access to a court, a person cannot be compelled to infringe a legal rule or obligation or to be subject to the penalty attached to that offence (point 66). A person who is obliged to provide information, but who is of the opinion that the decision ordering him to provide that information is arbitrary or disproportionate should have a legal remedy without being forced to refuse to comply to the order upon which a penalty is imposed for which a legal remedy does exist (point 68). Legislation, which excludes the possibility for a person holding information of bringing a direct action against an order to provide that information does not respect the essence of the right to an effective remedy guaranteed by Art. 47 of the Charter (point 69). In the *L* Case[208] the Court repeated the right of an effective legal remedy for the person who has received an order to provide information (point 88). In addition, it made clear that if the legality of the order to provide information is upheld, the person must be given the opportunity to comply with that order within the time limit initially prescribed by national law as of the moment of which the order was upheld. Only if the information is not provided within that time limit after the order has been upheld, a penalty would legitimately become payable (point 98-99).

The taxpayer whom the information concerns, but who is not ordered to provide information himself does not have that right to a legal remedy (*Shakira* Case point 93) and the same applies to third parties whom the information may concern, but who are not required to provide information themselves (point 102). So only the person, may it be the taxpayer or another person, who is under the legal obligation to provide information, must have the right to a legal remedy.

Furthermore, the right does not go further than necessary to provide a legal remedy. Thus, even though the court reviewing the case must have access to the request for information, the relevant person does not have a right of access to the whole of the request (*Berlioz* point 101, *L* point 91). This request is to remain a secret document in accordance with Art. 16 DAC. In order to give the relevant person a full hearing in relation to possible lack of foreseeable relevance, it is sufficient, in principle, that he is informed of the identity of the person under examination or investigation and of the tax purpose for which the information is sought (the minimum information referred to in Art. 20(2)). If the court reviewing the case considers that that minimum is not sufficient and therefore asks the requested authority for additional information which it may have obtained from

207 Joined Cases C245/19 and C246/19, *B and others*, EU:C:2020:795. See also for an elaborate discussion: Stefano Zagà, 'The protection of individual taxpayer rights regarding exchange of information on request in the European Union' 62 *European Taxation* 2/3 2022.

208 Case C-437/19, *L.*, EU:C:2021:953.

the requesting authority and which may be necessary to rule out the possibility of a manifest lack of foreseeable relevance, it must forward that additional information to the relevant person, while taking due account of the possible confidentiality of some of that information.

However, in the *L* Case, the court made it clear that the person concerned must be able to ascertain the reasons upon which an information order is based so that he can decide whether or not to challenge it.[209]

28.13.3 Legal Professional Privilege

In a string of case law in the years 2022-2024, the ECJ has clarified the role of the legal professional privilege in relation to the DAC.

First, in *Orde van Vlaamse balies*[210] the ECJ held that the obligation of Art. 8ab(5) DAC (see Chapter 29) was invalid in the light of Art. 7 of the Charter of Fundamental Rights of the European Union insofar as it required a lawyer acting as an intermediary to notify without delay any other intermediary who is not his client of that intermediary's reporting obligations, if that lawyer is exempt from the DAC6 reporting obligation on account of the legal professional privilege. Art. 7 of the Charter recognises that everyone has the right to respect for his private and family life, home and communications. This provision corresponds to Art. 8(1) ECHR. The ECJ observed that it is apparent from the case-law of the ECtHR that Art. 8(1) ECHR protects the confidentiality of all correspondence between individuals and affords strengthened protection to exchanges between lawyers and their clients[211] and that the protection also covers legal advice. The ECJ held that Art. 7 of the Charter necessarily guarantees the secrecy of that legal consultation, both with regard to its content and to its existence. Individuals who consult a lawyer can reasonably expect that their communication is private and confidential.[212] Therefore, other than in exceptional situations, those persons must have a legitimate expectation that their lawyer will not disclose to anyone, without their consent, that they are consulting him.

The ECJ held that the specific protection which Art. 7 of the Charter and Art. 8(1) ECHR afford to lawyers' legal professional privilege, is justified by the fact that lawyers are assigned a fundamental role in a democratic society, that of defending litigants.[213] The obligation for a lawyer-intermediary to notify without delay other intermediaries who are not his clients entails the consequence that those other intermediaries become aware of the identity of the notifying lawyer-intermediary, of his assessment that the arrangement at issue is reportable and of the lawyer having been consulted in connection with the

209 Case C-437/19, *L.*, EU:C:2021:953, point 92 and 93.
210 Case C-694/20, *Orde van Vlaamse Balies*, EU:C:2022:963.
211 The ECJ referred in para 27 to ECtHR, judgment of 6 December 2012, *Michaud v. France*, CE:ECHR:2012:1206JUD001232311, §§ 117 and 118.
212 The ECJ referred to ECtHR, judgment of 9 April 2019, *Altay v. Turkey (No 2)*, CE:ECHR:2019:0409JUD001123609, § 49.
213 The ECJ referred to ECtHR, judgment of 6 December 2012, *Michaud v. France*, CE:ECHR:2012:1206JUD001232311, §§ 118 and 119.

arrangement. This entails an interference with the right to respect for communications between lawyers and their clients, guaranteed in Art. 7 of the Charter. The ECJ observed that combating aggressive tax planning and preventing the risk of tax avoidance and evasion constitute objectives of general interest capable of enabling a limitation to be placed on the exercise of the rights guaranteed by Art. 7 of the Charter. However, the ECJ held that the notification obligation cannot be regarded as being strictly necessary in order to attain those objectives and, in particular, to ensure that the information concerning the reportable cross-border arrangements is filed with the competent authorities. The DAC6 directive ensures that information is provided to the tax authorities, without the disclosure to them of the identity of the lawyer-intermediary and of his having been consulted being necessary for that purpose. Art. 8ab was changed by DAC8 (see Chapter 29), but the question remained who was to be regarded as having a legal professional privilege.

In *Belgian Association of Tax Lawyers*,[214] in which various questions on the validity of Art. 8ab were answered (see Chapter 29), the ECJ gave a further clarification on the legal professional privilege in the context of the DAC, especially regarding intermediaries who are not lawyers but who are bound by legal professional privilege under national law. The ECJ observed that a literal interpretation of Art. 8ab(5) does not make it possible to determine the scope of the professions that may be concerned, as the language versions of that provision diverged in this respect. The ECJ, therefore, applied a contextual analysis. The ECJ observed, amongst others that the OECD Model Rules that inspired the wording of DAC6 as regards the reporting obligation and the obligation to notify, sought, in essence, to protect professional secrecy only for lawyers and other professionals who, like lawyers, are legally authorised to ensure legal representation. Also, the ECJ held that while it is justified, for the Member States to have a measure of discretion to allow them to take account of professions, other than lawyers, which they authorise to ensure legal representation, that discretion is not intended to allow those Member States to extend the benefit of that substitution of obligations to professions which do not ensure such representation. This would, in the view of the ECJ, risk creating distortions between Member States since a broad exercise of that power by some of them could lead to the relocation of potentially aggressive tax-planning activities in their territory, thereby undermining the effectiveness and the uniformity, at EU level, of the fight against tax avoidance and evasion in the internal market. Therefore, the ECJ came to the conclusion that that the power of the Member States to substitute the obligation to notify for the reporting obligation was given only in respect of professionals who, like lawyers, are authorised under national law to ensure legal representation.

The ECJ held that the confidentiality of the relationship between a lawyer and his client enjoys very specific protection, which relates to the special position occupied by a lawyer in the judicial organisation of the Member States and to the fundamental task entrusted to him and which is recognised by all the Member States and that it was in that light that the Court held in *Orde van Vlaamse Balies* that the obligation to notify, when it is imposed on the lawyer, infringes Art. 7 of the Charter. For this reason, this can extend only to persons pursuing their professional activities under one of the professional

214 Case C-623/22, *Belgian Association of Tax Lawyers*, EU:C:2024:639.

titles referred to in Art. 1(2)(a) of Directive 98/5 on the profession of lawyers.[215] For the purposes of that Directive 'lawyer` means any person who is a national of a Member State and who is authorised to pursue his professional activities under one of the professional titles included in the table of Art. 1(2)(a). Other professionals who, although authorised, by the Member States to ensure legal representation, do not meet the abovementioned characteristics according to the ECJ.

This case law still left the question unanswered whether all persons pursuing their professional activities under one of the professional titles referred to in Art. 1(2)(a) of Directive 98/5 were within scope, or only a specific sub section of those lawyers. In *Ordre des avocats du barreau de Luxembourg*[216] the ECJ answered this question in the context of Art.17(1) and (4) DAC on the conditions governing administrative cooperation and Art.18(1) DAC on obligations. Following up on a request of Spain, Luxembourg required a Luxembourg law firm to provide all available documents it created on a corporate investment structure for a Spanish client. The law firm refused under reference to the legal professional privilege. However, under Luxembourg law advice and representation by a lawyer in tax matters did not enjoy – except where there was a risk of criminal prosecution against the client – the strengthened protection of communications between lawyers and clients guaranteed by Art. 7 of the Charter. The ECJ clarified, however, that whatever the area of law to which it relates, legal advice given by a lawyer enjoys the strengthened protection guaranteed by Art. 7 of the Charter to communications between lawyers and their clients. A decision requiring a lawyer to provide the authorities of the requested Member State – for the purposes of an exchange of information on request in accordance with the DAC – with all the documentation and information relating to his relations with his client, concerning such legal advice, constitutes, therefore, an interference with the right to respect for communications between lawyers and their clients guaranteed by that article.

The result seems to be that all persons that meet the definition of lawyers of Art. 1(2)(a) of Directive 98/5 can refuse to provide information that is requested with reference to the DAC, but that all other persons that have legal professional privilege under national law, cannot. It is not clear how this relates to a level playing field between professions that might have very similar activities, such as tax lawyers that meet the definition of Art. 1(2)(a) of Directive 98/5 providing tax advice and other legal professionals providing exactly the same tax advice.

In *Ordre des avocats du barreau de Luxembourg*[217] the ECJ also made clear that for the purposes of the exchange of information on request the EU legislature has merely determined in Art. 17 and Art. 18 DAC the obligations that the Member States have towards each other, while authorising them not to comply with a request for information if that would be contrary to their legislation. Thus, the EU legislature has left it to the Member

215 Directive 98/5/EC of the European Parliament and of the Council of 16 February 1998 to facilitate practice of the profession of lawyer on a permanent basis in a Member State other than that in which the qualification was obtained.

216 Case C-432/23, *Ordre des avocats du barreau de Luxembourg*, EU:C:2024:791.

217 Case C-432/23, *Ordre des avocats du barreau de Luxembourg*, EU:C:2024:791.

States to ensure that their national procedures for gathering information for the purposes of this exchange comply with the Charter, and in particular Art. 7 thereof.

The ECJ observed that the system for exchange of information on request does not include provisions relating to the protection of the confidentiality of communications between lawyers and their clients. In the context of the information gathering that is the responsibility of the requested Member State. The ECJ held that this does not mean that the DAC infringes Arts. 7 and 52(1) of the Charter. In accordance with Art. 51(1) of the Charter it is for each Member State to guarantee, in the context of the national procedures implemented for the purposes of that information gathering, the strengthened protection of communications between lawyers and their clients guaranteed by Art. 7 of the Charter. Thus, each Member State must ensure that any limitation on the exercise of the rights guaranteed by Art.7 arising from those national procedures is 'provided for by law' within the meaning of Art. 52(1) of the Charter.

28.14 Data Protection[218]

Schapers observed that three developments imply that greater scrutiny must be paid to data protection in relation to exchange of information: (i) the shift from exchange on request of specific information to automatic exchange of bulk information; (ii) the increase in the scope of information that must be exchanged automatically; and (iii) the need to provide a counterbalance to the measures against tax underreporting by ensuring the protection of private rights of taxpayers in a State governed by the rule of law: as the scope of anti-avoidance and anti-evasion measures expands, the scope of taxpayer rights, such as data protection rights, should be reassessed accordingly.[219] Other authors also voiced data protection concerns in relation to exchange of information.[220]

218 See for an extensive discussion of data protection in relation to the DAC: Saturnina Moreno González, The Automatic Exchange of Tax Information and the Protection of Personal Data in the European Union: Reflections on the Latest Jurisprudential and Normative Advances, *EC Tax Review*, 2016, no. 3, pp. 146-161 and Belisa Ferreira Liotti, Taxpayers' Data Protection: Do International, Regional, and Domestic Instruments Guarantee Adequate Rights in Tax (A)EoI?, *Intertax*, 2022, no. 2, pp. 138-158.

219 Marcel Schaper, Data Protection Rights and Tax Information Exchange in the European Union: An Uneasy Combination, *Maastricht Journal of European and Comparative Law*, 2016 23(3), pp. 514-530.

220 See for example: Stefano Maria Ronco S.M, Data Protection in Direct Tax Matters and Developments from the EU Standpoint: The Case of Automatic Exchange of Information, *International Tax Studies* 4 2020 and Gianmaria Alberto Carlo Favaloro, The Exchange of Tax Information between EU Member States and Third Countries: Privacy and Data Protection Concerns, 61 *European Taxation* 4 2021.

Art. 25(1) DAC brings all information exchanged under the data protection provided by the (national implementation of) the General Data Protection Regulation[221] (GDPR).[222]

The DAC explicitly requires the Member States to restrict their data protection, based on the exception provided for in Art. 23(1)(e) GDPR (Art. 25(1)). This exception includes important economic or financial interests of a Member State or of the EU, including monetary, budgetary and taxation matters and public health and social security. The exception applies to the extent necessary to safeguard the protection of national tax revenue and to effectively fight fraud (preamble 27 DAC). As the DAC requires Member States to implement this exception in national law, this meets the requirement of the Court of Justice that restrictions of data protection rights must be based on legislative measures and must be appropriate and necessary for the purpose of attaining the objectives pursued (see, for example the *Puškár* Case).[223]

The exception restricts the obligations and rights of the so-called data subject (Art. 4(1) GDPR). In the context of the DAC the data subject would usually be the person on whom information is being exchanged. The rights which are restricted are the following:
- Art. 13 GDPR, concerning the information which must be given to the data subject in case of data collection from the data subject;
- Art. 14(1) GDPR, concerning the information which must be given to the data subject in cases of data collection from another person than the data subject; and
- Art. 15 GDPR, concerning the right of access of the data subject;

In the *Smaranda Bara* Case,[224] concerning the implementation of the Data Protection Directive (DPD),[225] the predecessor of the GDPR, the Court held that a public administrative body may not transfer personal data to another public administrative body without informing the data subjects on the transfer or processing. This case concerned data

221 Regulation (EU) 2016/679 of the European Parliament and of the Council of 27 April 2016 on the protection of natural persons with regard to the processing of personal data and on the free movement of such data, and repealing Directive 95/46/EC (General Data Protection Regulation) O.J. No. L 119 of 4 May 2016, p. 1.

222 Until DAC7 Art. 25(1) made reference to Directive 95/46/EC of the European Parliament and of the Council of 24 October 1995 on the protection of individuals with regard to the processing of personal data and on the free movement of such data, O.J. No. L 281 of 23 November 1995, p. 31. This Data Protection Directive (DPD) was replaced by Directive (EU) 2016/680 of the European Parliament and of the Council of 27 April 2016 on the protection of natural persons with regard to the processing of personal data by competent authorities for the purposes of the prevention, investigation, detection or prosecution of criminal offences or the execution of criminal penalties, and on the free movement of such data, and repealing Council Framework Decision 2008/977/JHA, O.J. No. L 119 of 4 May 2016, p. 89 and the GDPR on 25 May 2018 (Art. 94(2) GDPR). Art. 94 (2) GDPR provides that references to the repealed DPD must be construed as references to the GDPR. For that reason, I will only refer to the equivalent provisions in the GDPR, even though the DAC before DAC7 still refers to the DPD-provisions.

223 Case C-73/16, *Puškár*, EU:C:2017:725, paras 96 and 116.

224 Case C-201/14, *Smaranda Bara*, EU:C:2015:638.

225 Directive 95/46/EC of the European Parliament and of the Council of 24 October 1995 on the protection of individuals with regard to the processing of personal data and on the free movement of such data, O.J. No. L 281 of 23 November 1995, p. 31.

necessary to certify that the person concerned qualified for health insurance. It seems that the relevance of this judgment is rather limited for information that is exchanged based on the DAC, as Art. 23(1)(e) GDPR restricts the right to be informed if this is necessary to safeguard, among others, taxation matters. Giusy De Flora observed that the protection of personal data can hardly be relied on as an effective limit to the exchange of information, given the major significance of the financial interests of the State aimed at safeguarding the proper and equitable distribution of the tax burden among taxpayers.[226] Goulder observed that it is an unsettled concern whether modern automatic exchange of information (AEOI) practices can coexist with the full expression of taxpayer rights and other recognized safeguards such as the GDPR.[227]

Art. 25(2) DAC[228] ensures that Regulation (EU) 2018/1725[229] applies to any processing of personal data under the DAC by the EU institutions, bodies, offices and agencies. This Regulation includes the European Data Protection Supervisor (EDPS), the authority responsible for monitoring the application of the data protection rules by EU institutions and bodies. It also sets out the rules to ensure that personal data managed by EU institutions and bodies is protected and defines citizens' rights in this respect.

The rights provided for in the following provisions of this Regulation are restricted to the extent required to safeguard objectives of general public interests of the EU or a Member State, amongst others, an important economic or financial interest, including monetary, budgetary and taxation matters, public health and social security (as referred to in Art. 25(1) (c) of the Regulation):
- Art. 15 concerning information which must be given to the data subject if the data have been obtained from the data subject;
- Art. 16(1) concerning information which must be given to the data subject if the data have not been obtained from the data subject;
- Art. 17 concerning right of access of the data subject to the data;
- Art. 18 concerning the right to rectification;
- Art. 19 concerning the right to be forgotten;
- Art. 20 concerning the right to restriction of processing, and
- Art. 21 concerning the obligation for the data controller to notify any rectification or erasure of personal data or restriction of processing to each recipient to whom personal data have been disclosed and informing the data subject about this if he requests it.

226 Menita Giusy De Flora, Protection of the Taxpayer in the Information Exchange Procedure, *Intertax*, 2017, no. 6/7, pp. 447-460.

227 Robert Goulder, Can FATCA Serve Two Masters? The Swedish Experience, *Tax Notes International*, 23 December 2024, pp. 1993-1996, p. 1993.

228 Until DA7: Art. 25(1a) with a reference to Regulation (EC) No. 45/2001 of the European Parliament and of the Council of 18 December 2000 on the protection of individuals with regard to the processing of personal data by the institutions and bodies of the Community and on the free movement of such data, O.J. 12 January 2001, L008, p. 1.

229 Regulation (EU) 2018/1725 of the European Parliament and of the Council of 23 October 2018 on the protection of natural persons with regard to the processing of personal data by the Union institutions, bodies, offices and agencies and on the free movement of such data, and repealing Regulation (EC) No 45/2001 and Decision No 1247/2002/EC, O.J. 21 November 2018, L295, p. 39.

Arts. 25(3) and (4) impose data protection obligations on financial institutions with reporting obligations on foreign account holders and their accounts (DAC2, see Section 28.3.2.2), on intermediaries (DAC6, See Chapter 29), on reporting platform operators (DAC7, see Section 28.3.2.5) and, as of 2026, on reporting crypto-asset service providers (DAC8, see Section 28.3.2.6). This includes informing individuals that information will be collected and transferred in accordance with the DAC and providing all information he is entitled to in sufficient time to exercise his data protection rights and, in any case, before the information is reported. Each Member State must lay down rules obliging platform operators to inform sellers of the reported consideration.

Preamble 41 to DAC8 observes that reporting financial institutions, intermediaries, reporting platform operators, reporting crypto-asset service providers or competent authorities of Member States are data controllers within the meaning of the GDPR. Where two or more of those controllers jointly determine the purposes and means of processing of personal data, they are considered to be joint controllers. Preamble 41 gives as an example that competent authorities of Member States are joint controllers of the central directory, having jointly agreed on the personal data to be processed and the manner of processing.

As of 2026, Art. 25(3) will, based on DAC8, also provide that the European Commission is considered to process the personal data on behalf of the controllers when processing personal data for the purposes of the DAC. The Commission must in such case comply with the requirements for processors set out in the GDPR.

Information processed in accordance with the DAC may not be retained for any longer than necessary to achieve the purposes of the Directive, and in any case in accordance with each data controller's domestic rules on statute of limitations (Art. 25(5)). As of 2026, DAC8 introduces a new Art. 22(3) that requires that Member States retain the records of the information received through the automatic exchange of information pursuant to Arts. 8 to 8ae for no longer than necessary but in any event not shorter than five years from its date of receipt. According to preamble 40 of DAC8, Member States should not retain information longer than necessary to achieve the purposes of this Directive. The preamble does not clarify how the minimum term of retention of Art. 22(3) relates to that general requirement and the requirement of Art. 25(5).

Because of the broadening scope of the DAC and the increase in information that is automatically exchanged, data protection became an even more pressing issue. This is even more so given all the data leaks which have already happened. If more information is available in more places, this might increase the risk of such data leaks. These concerns were partly addressed by DAC7 by inserting procedures in the event of data breaches in Art. 25(6). A Member State where a data breach occurred is obliged to report the data breach and any subsequent remedial action to the Commission without delay which is subsequently reported to all Member States. Each Member State may suspend, with immediate effect, the exchange of information to the Member State(s) where the data breach occurred by giving notice to the Commission and the Member State concerned. The Member State where the data breach occurred must investigate, contain and remedy the data breach and by giving notice to the Commission request the suspension of CCN access for the purposes of the DAC if the data breach cannot be contained immediately and appropriately. If the Member State reports that the data breach has been remedied, the Commission will give CCN access again. If one or Member States asked the Commission to verify whether the remediation of the data breach was successful, CCN access is only resumed upon such verification.

If the data breach occurs to the CCN and exchanges through the CCN can potentially be affected, the Commission must inform the Member States of the data breach and any remedial actions taken without undue delay. These may include suspending access to the CCN for purposes of the DAC until the data breach is remedied.

Art. 25(7) stipulates that Member States, assisted by the Commission, must agree on the practical arrangements for the implementation of Art. 25, including data breach management processes which are aligned with internationally recognized good practices and where appropriate a joint data controller agreement, a data processor-data controller agreement or models thereof. Preamble 32 makes clear that only persons duly accredited by the Security Accreditation Authority of the Commission may have access to the information communicated pursuant to the DAC and provided by the CCN and only in so far as it is necessary for the care, maintenance and development of the central directory and the CCN. The Commission is responsible for ensuring the security of the central directory and the CCN.

28.15 Confidentiality Obligation of the European Commission

Art. 23a imposes a confidentially obligation on the European Commission regarding information communicated to the Commission pursuant to the DAC. The Commission may not use this information for any purposes other than those required to determine whether and to what extent Member States comply with the DAC (Art. 23a(1)).

Information sent to the Commission for evaluation purposes under Art. 23 and reports produced by the Commission using such information may be transmitted to other Member States, but it is covered by the obligation of official secrecy and is protected in the same way as similar information under the national law of the receiving Member State (Art. 23a(2), first subparagraph). Member States may only use these reports for analytical purposes, and they may not be published or made available to any other person or body without the express agreement of the European Commission (Art. 23a(2), second subparagraph).

The third subparagraph of Art. 23a(2) allows the Commission to annually publish anonymised summaries of the statistical data that Member States communicate in accordance with the obligation in Art. 23(4) to provide the Commission with data for evaluation purposes as defined in Art. 23.

28.16 Information Overload?

In 2001, Vording and Caminada suggested that "Meaningful international tax cooperation may well require that in the near future, a substantial part of national tax administrations' efforts is to provide services to other national tax administrations."[230] The subsequent (and envisaged) amendments to the DAC have definitely increased the obligations on Member States' tax administrations to collect information and make it available to other Member States. In January 2017, the Dutch tax administration reported that the obligation to exchange rulings had imposed a large administrative burden on the tax administration which means that these resources could not be used for regular checks and audits.[231] As a result, the tax administration shifted part of the administrative burden to the taxpayer. The CbC obligation imposes a heavy burden on tax administrations and companies as well, as do the CRS, DAC6, DAC7 and DAC8 obligations. In a reply to questions of the German Parliament, the German government stated that in the period from 1 July 2020-31 March 2023, Germany received a total of 26,921 DAC6 notifications, and downloaded 1,967 notifications of other Member States that regarded German tax payers.[232] Out of the notifications, the German tax administration identified 206 tax structuring models.[233] On 24 cross border tax structuring models (that came out of 4 268 notifications) legal action was deemed necessary.[234] The DAC6 costs for Germany amounted to € 44.5 million between 2019-2022.[235] Stöber regarded these figures as a confirmation of his point that the suitability of the DAC6 reporting obligation to achieve its purpose of enabling the tax authorities to take counter measures against aggressive tax planning is more than doubtful as intermediaries would in case of doubt op for disclosure to avoid penalties, with the consequence that tax administrations would be overwhelmed by a flood of reports in which the real cases of aggressive tax planning would be lost.[236] In his view it would be better to direct resources to hiring better or additional staff to prevent tax loopholes from arising through more careful tax legislation and to identify and close loopholes.

Information exchange should not be a purpose in itself, but a means to improve tax compliance. As Steward observed: "obtaining tax information is only one step towards the real goal of collection of adequate tax revenues and effective and fair division of the global tax base."[237] For that purpose, tax administrations must have enough human and ICT resources to handle big data and to perform effective searches. Brodzka observes that the main barriers to the effective functioning of the EU system of tax information exchange seem to be the capabilities and resources required to handle the process of data exchange for tax purposes.[238] If Member States get snowed under by both the information

230 H. Vording and K. Caminada, 'Tax co-ordination: crossing the Rubicon?' in: D.A. Albregtse, A.L. Bovenberg en L.G.M. Stevens (red.) *Er zal geheven worden!, Opstellen aangeboden aan Prof. dr. S. Cnossen*, Kluwer, Deventer 2001, pp. 335-345, p. 345.

231 State Secretary of Finance, letter of 11 January 2017, no. 2017-0000005643.

232 Deutscher Bundestag, 20. Wahlperiode Drucksache 20/6734, 8 May 2023, answer to question 1.

233 Deutscher Bundestag, 20. Wahlperiode Drucksache 20/6734, 8 May 2023, answer to question 15.

234 Deutscher Bundestag, 20. Wahlperiode Drucksache 20/6734, 8 May 2023, answer to question 6 and 7.

235 Deutscher Bundestag, 20. Wahlperiode Drucksache 20/6734, 8 May 2023, answer to question 12.

236 Michael Stöber, The charter of fundamental rights and EU tax directives, *EC Tax Review*, 2023-5, pp. 203-213, Section 5.3.3.

237 Miranda Stewart, Transnational Tax Information Exchange Network: Steps towards a Globalized, Legitimate Tax Administration, *World Tax Journal*, June 2012, pp. 152-179, p. 179.

238 Alicja Brodzka, Automatic Exchange of Tax Information in the European Union – The Standard for the Future, 56 *European Taxation* 1 2015, p. 30.

gathered by them to exchange and the information exchanged to them, there may not be enough resources left to effectively analyse the information received and to put it into use.

The effective use of the information exchanged should, therefore, be carefully monitored in order to avoid huge efforts being wasted on sending out bulk information not being effectively used at the other end. As Mariano observed: "behind DAC implementation in each Member State, there are going to be huge investments in information technology, the costs of which will probably be shifted to society".[239]

It is worrying that the focus in the past years and for the near future seems to have been and to remain on expanding (automatic) exchange of information under the DAC (quantity) instead of on its effectiveness (quality). In 2021, the European Court of Auditors concluded that the system for exchange of tax information has been well established, but that more needs to be done in terms of monitoring, ensuring data quality and using the information received. It reproached the European Commission for not proactively providing guidance and insufficiently measuring the outcomes and impact of the use of the information exchanged. It observed that the information collected by Member States lacks in quality, completeness and accuracy. and that although Member States identify the relevant taxpayers, information exchanged automatically is under-used.[240] The question is, therefore, whether Member States and their taxpayers get enough value for the money the public and private sector invest in DAC-exchange of information obligations.

As of 2026, based on DAC8 Art. 18(4) requires that the competent authority of each Member State puts in place an effective mechanism to ensure the use of information acquired through the reporting or the exchange of information under Arts. 8 to 8ae. This is easily put on paper but will not always be easy to execute for tax administrations, because of a lack of resources, including human resources. It may be problematic if requirements like these force tax authorities to reprioritise and to shift resources from more effective and efficient instruments for enforcing compliance and filling the public purse. However, based on preamble 37 of DAC8 the requirement of Art. 18(4) might not be too burdensome as such use of information can include, for instance, voluntary compliance programs, notifications to generate disclosure, awareness campaigns, prefilling tax returns, risk assessments, limited audits, general audits, tax coding, tax estimation, assimilation into domestic systems and other tax-related measures. Most Member States will already have implemented one or more of such measures. In that case this provision will not really improve the use of the information, and the question remains why it was inserted.

239 Giuseppe Marino, General Report, in: Giuseppe Marino (ed.) *New exchange of information versus tax solutions of equivalent effect*, IBFD 2015, p. 14.

240 European Court of Auditors, *Exchanging tax information in the EU: solid foundation, cracks in the implementation*, 2021, pp. 4-5, https://www.eca.europa.eu/Lists/ECADocuments/SR21_03/SR_Exchange_tax_inform_EN.pdf.

CHAPTER 29

Mandatory Disclosure: the Contribution of DAC6 to the Common EU System of Mutual Assistance in Tax Matters

Pasquale Pistone[1]

29.1 Introduction

Mandatory disclosure establishes a reporting obligation for private parties to public authorities in respect of transactions that present potentially harmful features. Such reporting obligation enhances risk assessment, using indicators created by law and mechanisms, which might operate in different contexts, but present essentially uniform features that are suitable for a joint analysis.

In principle, the validity of mandatory disclosure rules relies, on the one hand, on the capacity of their indicators to nudge a quality detection of harmful transactions and, on the other hand, on the accuracy of reporting. In practice, a balanced assessment of how mandatory disclosure operates concretely depends on how the legislation shapes either of such elements. Accordingly, also when targeting indicators that per se would be suitable, mandatory disclosure could create real threats to legal certainty when such indicators overlap. Moreover, for how it might be desirable to effectively react against harmful tax practices, the dramatic increase of formal obligations often connected with mandatory disclosure might create more problems than it solves. These preliminary caveats also characterise the analysis of mandatory disclosure in European tax law contained in this Chapter, which stresses the importance of a balanced approach to harmful practices in line with the Rule of Law and the protection of fundamental rights of taxpayers and other private parties.[2]

European Union law applies mandatory disclosure not only in connection with aggressive tax planning schemes, but also in the fight against money laundering. Both contexts share the common core of potentially harmful features. However, such contexts notably differ as to the size of their threats to the legal system.

---

1 Academic Chairman, IBFD, Professor of European Tax Law and Policy, WU Vienna, Full Professor of Tax Law at the University of Salerno.

2 See further on this in Chapter 4 of this book.

Money laundering is an extremely serious crime, often directly connected with funding terrorism. This scenario certainly justifies the incumbency of reporting obligations. By contrast, aggressive tax planning concerns the circumvention of tax law, which the system should neutralise in order to preserve the effective and consistent levying of taxes. In the latter context, one may wonder whether the reporting burden on intermediaries – substantially similar to that connected with the fight against money laundering – in fact complies with the requirements of the principle of proportionality.

Mandatory disclosure is not new to international tax law and has already applied in some domestic legislation for several years – such as in particular in the United States[3] and United Kingdom -[4] before being introduced into EU tax law. Conveyed through the findings of BEPS Action 12, the national rules on mandatory disclosure of those two countries have served as models for the ones that the Directive 2018/822,[5] also known as DAC6, brought into the system of cross-border mutual assistance within the European Union.

The analysis of such issues will address, on the one hand, the auxiliary role of mandatory disclosure in the European Union secondary legislation to the functioning of administrative cooperation in tax matters and, on the other hand, the need to interpret and apply the said rules in compliance with the general principles of EU law. Such principles obviously operate under EU law regardless of whether they are specifically recalled by the DAC system.[6]

The influence of the EU legal system on DAC6 prevents the latter from being regarded as a legal instrument to implement its external models into EU law. Such models may be no more than a source of inspiration for DAC6. However, they do not play a decisive role in interpreting the rules that this Directive introduced into the DAC system.[7] Moreover, the EU chose to partly deviate from such models, bundling them together in a combination with its own distinctive features, as reflected in the numerous general and specific hallmarks regulated by DAC6.[8]

3 See sections 6011, 6111, 6112, 6707, 6707A, 6662A, and 6708 of the US Internal Revenue Code.

4 This type of legislation is known in the UK as DoTaS, which is the acronym for "Disclosure of Tax Avoidance Schemes". See further on this in www.gov.uk/government/publications/disclosure-of-tax-avoidance-schemes-guidance.

5 Council Directive (EU) 2018/822 of 25 May 2018 amending Directive 2011/16/EU as regards mandatory automatic exchange of information in the field of taxation in relation to reportable cross-border arrangements, OJ L 139/1 of 5 June 2018.

6 This consequence may be drawn in the light of judicial interpretation of the EU DAC system in CJEU, 16 May 2017, Case C-682/15, Berlioz Investment Fund, EU:C:2017:373. In such judgment, the Court admitted that the need to secure an effective judicial remedy in respect of penalties gave third parties holders of tax relevant information legal standing to verify, with the intervention of the judiciary, that tax authorities operated mutual assistance in conformity with the Rule of Law.

7 The technical meaning of the expression "implementation" under EU law suggests to refrain from using it in this context. This will, however, not prevent taking the models of DAC6 into consideration, when reconstructing the technical meaning of its rules.

8 For instance, mandatory disclosure follows in the US a transaction-based approach and in the UK a promoter-based approach. By contrast, DAC6 combines both approaches and also adds a subsidiary disclosure obligation for taxpayers, which in fact ends up forcing the latter ones to request a kind of preliminary authorisation for the right to organise their affairs.

The main criterion to follow when interpreting the content of DAC6 is that mandatory disclosure of potential aggressive tax planning schemes applies as an integral part of the EU cross-border tax system of mutual assistance. Therefore, all the clauses introduced by DAC6 (i.e. Directive 2018/822) into the DAC system will have to be interpreted and applied in line with the object and purpose of this system and the content of all the clauses that are contained in the consolidated EU Directive.[9]

There are several important innovations introduced by DAC6 into the EU system of cross-border mutual assistance in tax matters.

First, DAC6 reflects the dynamics of risk assessment, using indicators, which hint at the possible existence of aggressive tax planning, but do not necessarily prove it. Accordingly, it helps steering mutual assistance towards tainted cases, replacing random action with a qualitative selection of the cases that might require tax auditing. The flip side of the coin is that it requires coordination with both secondary, notably ATAD, and primary law, including in particular fundamental freedoms, fundamental rights and the underlying principles of EU law.

Second, DAC6 establishes an outsourcing mechanism of fact finding on private parties, which notably increases the formal obligations of intermediaries (with no remuneration) and of taxpayers. Intermediaries are exposed to penalties for the failure to comply with their obligations,[10] but do not get any remuneration for reporting. Moreover, it is still unclear whether the DAC6 rules – including their possible overimplementation by certain EU Member States – could, directly or indirectly, prompt mandatory disclosure of information covered by the client-attorney privilege[11] and thus generate a disproportionate violation of the right to defence. The impact of DAC6 on taxpayers' rights is very far reaching, as the indicators reverse the burden of proof and set very low thresholds for flagging with practices that might constitute tax avoidance, creating a relevant degree of legal uncertainty. In principle, the desirable goal of countering tax avoidance may justify these rules; in practice, the existence of numerous indicators, as well as their interpretation and application, might undermine the right of taxpayers to minimise taxes also in genuine situations, creating in practice procedural obstacles that could make such right more burdensome and even a problem of self-incrimination.[12]

Third, DAC6 stretches the timeframe of cross-border mutual assistance in tax matters. The reporting obligation starts from before the transaction takes place and can operative in a prospective way, generating automatic exchange of information at regular intervals,[13] which are likely to produce large volumes of reportable schemes (and also overreporting)

9 See Chapters 24 and 25.
10 In such circumstances, intermediaries might therefore be indirectly induced to overreport in order to limit their exposure to penalties. However, overreporting is not desirable from the perspective of a balanced approach to tax avoidance, as it produces a structural unnecessary burden on taxpayers. See further on this in sec. 26.3.
11 See further on this in sec. 26.5.
12 See further on this in sec. 26.3.
13 See Art. 3 (9) (a) Directive 2011/16/EU, as amended by Directive 2018/822/EU.

for the reasons that will be indicated below.[14] Flooding of data might prevent tax authorities from duly processing the information.[15] In such circumstances, mandatory disclosure would neither be effective, nor proportionate, especially if one considers the notable reporting burden on private parties.

Fourth, insofar as DAC6 feeds mutual assistance with the mandatory reporting by intermediaries and taxpayers, the obligation to do so in respect of years that predate its entry into force[16] can potentially raise critical issues of retroactive application,[17] whose compatibility with the principles of EU law could be questioned.[18]

29.2 The Objective Scope

Being fully integrated into the DAC system, the objective scope of DAC6 requires that mandatorily reported transactions trigger automatic exchange of information.[19]

The core of this mechanism lies in reportable cross-border arrangements, which DAC6 determines by means of a three-step procedure. Such procedure starts with (1) the prior identification of arrangements, i.e. of the relevant transactions or series of transactions, continues with (2) the conditions for identifying cross-border arrangements and ends with (3) the selection of the ones that are to be reported within the framework of mandatory disclosure, i.e. the reportable cross-border arrangements.

14 See further on this in sec. 26.2.
15 This situation may be worsened by the additional reporting obligations that apply under DAC7 and that might be introduced by further secondary EU legislation in tax matters, such as for instance the Proposal for a Council Directive laying down rules to prevent the misuse of shell entities for tax purposes and amending Directive 2011/16/EU, COM(2021) 565 final – 2021/0434 (CNS) of 22 December 2021. See Chapter 25.3.2.5.
16 The entry into force of this Directive was initially planned by 1 July 2020, but Council Directive (EU) 2020/876 of 24 June 2020 amending Directive 2011/16/EU to address the urgent need to defer certain time limits for the filing and exchange of information in the field of taxation because of the COVID-19 pandemic, OJ L 204/46 of 26 June 2020 allowed Member States to postpone the period for filing information on reportable cross-border arrangements.
17 Article 8 ab (12) of Directive 2018/822/EU set the starting date for obligation to report cross-border arrangements to the moment in which DAC6 entered into force, thus predating the moment in which it became applicable. These effects create a *sui generis* kind of retroactivity, which can be questioned in the light of the general principles of law, considering that such obligation predates the moment in which the Directive could produce its effects. See further on this Čičin-Šain, N., New Mandatory Disclosure Rules for Tax Intermediaries and Taxpayers in the European Union, in (11) World Tax Journal, 2019, pp. 79-90. Similar issues then were added in connection with the right for some Member States to postpone the application of the Directive in connection with the COVID crisis. See further on this the wording of Art. 27a, inserted by Directive 2020/876 into Directive 2011/16/EU.
18 See Kokott, J., Pistone, P., Taxpayers in international law, Hart Publishing, 2022, p. 439.
19 See Art. 8 ab Directive 2011/16/EU, as amended by Directive 2018/822/EU.

DAC6 does not define the concept of arrangement. Therefore, the reconstruction of such concept at the level of interpretation will have to take into account the criteria established by the Court of Justice when addressing cases of tax avoidance.[20]

When a transaction, or series of transactions, constitute(s) an arrangement, the conditions introduced by DAC6 into Art. 3 (18) of the Directive 2011/16/EU will allow identifying the cross-border arrangements, which will then have to be mandatorily reported insofar as they contain at least one of the indicators, i.e. the hallmarks, contained in Annex IV.

In particular, according to Art. 3 (18) the arrangement is cross-border when it involves (a) at least two participants that are tax residents of two different jurisdictions,[21] (b) (one or more) dual (or multiple) tax residents, (c) (one or more) participants carrying on business with a permanent establishment forming part of the arrangement, (d) (one or more) participants carrying out an activity without a permanent establishment, or (e) when having a possible impact on automatic exchange of information or the identification of beneficial ownership.

The list of conditions included in Art. 3 (18) of Directive 2011/16/EU essentially leaves out only purely internal arrangements, showing an inclination to be as comprehensive as possible and to expand automatic exchange of information to the maximum possible extent. If one then considers that these five conditions also operate on a standalone basis, the obvious consequence is that DAC6 creates a structural exposure to flooding of information and overreporting.

These effects are partly mitigated by the third step, which uses a system of hallmarks for singling out reportable cross-border arrangements. However, the numerous (generic and specific) hallmarks contained in Annex IV significantly increase the complexity of reporting, also requiring a delicate technical assessment as to whether a given transaction meets any of such hallmarks.[22]

29.3 The Subjective Scope

The subjective scope of DAC6 concerns the addressees of the obligation of mandatory disclosure. It includes two categories of persons, namely intermediaries and taxpayers.

20 Art. 6 (1) ATAD uses the expression "arrangement" in the context of tax avoidance too. This expression is defined by Art. 6 (2) ATAD. The latter definition expressly indicates that it applies to paragraph 1, thus preventing the application of such definition to other secondary EU law in tax matters. However, the content of this definition in fact largely reflects the criteria used by the Court of Justice to identify the existence of tax arrangements as expressions of abusive transactions.

21 Even though Article 3 (18) (a) does not contain a more precise indication, its object and purpose, on the one hand, do not prevent an application to cases involving a tax resident in a non-EU jurisdiction and, on the other hand, presuppose that at least one participant to the arrangement is a tax resident of an EU Member State.

22 See further in sec. 26.4.

Intermediaries are the primary addressees of the reporting obligation. Taking into account the disfavour towards cross-border arrangements, this non-remunerated extra burden for intermediaries operates as a way to safeguard the interest to tax collection. This obligation arises in connection with their involvement in the cross-border arrangement, which may relate to designing, marketing, organising, implementing it, or facilitating or managing such implementation.[23] Considering that such functions might be performed by different persons, the subjective scope of DAC6 does not exclude multiple reporting by different intermediaries,[24] even though DAC6 contains specific rules to avoid it[25] and to exclude multiple reporting by one intermediary in different EU Member States.[26]

DAC6 allows Member States to waive intermediaries from the reporting obligations only for preserving the legal professional privilege.[27]

23 See Art. 3 (21) of Directive 2011/16/EU, as amended by DAC6.

24 Kokott, J., Pistone, P., cit., p. 441 suggest amending the existing secondary legislation to overcome such issues.

25 In principle, Art. 8 ab (9) and (10) of Directive 2011/16/EU, as amended by DAC6, waive intermediaries from this obligation when they can give evidence that there has already been a reporting of the cross-border arrangement by another intermediary. In practice, this mechanism tolerates multiple reporting by different intermediaries, especially if one considers that not all intermediaries have the opportunity to give such evidence, or would necessarily know the situation involving reporting by the other intermediaries. If, on the one hand, this mechanism aims at avoiding non-reporting, on the other hand, it generates overreporting, which can contribute to flooding tax authorities with information and increase the compliance burden in a way that is possibly disproportionate. Moreover, insofar as some intermediaries may have a limited knowledge of the entire arrangement, they might be inclined to overreporting in order to avoid their liability to the penalties that would apply under Article 25a of Directive 2011/16/EU, as amended by DAC6. In this sense also see Kokott, J., Pistone, P., cit., p. 440 and, in economic literature Casi-Eberhard, E., Mardan, M., Muddasani R.R., The ability of mandatory disclosure regimes to crack down on offshore tax evasion, Working Paper, Norges Handelshøyskole & Wirtschaftsuniversität Wien, 2022.

26 Art. 8 ab (3) and (7) of Directive 2011/16/EU, as amended by DAC6, express the obligation of single reporting and include specific criteria for determining the country in which respectively intermediaries and relevant taxpayers have to report. Such criteria are partly common – namely (a) their EU Member State of residence, (b) the EU Member State of the permanent establishment (which has provided the services or has benefited from the arrangement) - and partly different. For the intermediaries. the latter criteria are (c) the EU Member State in which the intermediary is incorporated in or governed by the laws of, and (d) the EU Member State of professional registration. By contrast, for the relevant taxpayers, such criteria are (c) the EU Member State where the taxpayer receives income or generates profits, and (d) the EU Member State where the taxpayer carries on an activity. Despite such precise list and order of priority, different interpretation and implementations of such criteria may not be entirely excluded and are such that disparities could still produce situations of legal uncertainty and the exposure to an obligation of double reporting by the same intermediary or taxpayer.

27 Art. 8 ab (5) of Directive 2011/16/EU, as amended by DAC6. The CJEU (case C-623/22, Belgian Association of Tax Lawyers, ECLI:EU:C:2024:639; case C-432/23, Ordre des avocats du Barreau de Luxembourg, ECLI:EU:C:2024:791 case C-623/22, Belgian Association of Tax Lawyers, ECLI:EU:C:2024:639; case C-432/23, Ordre des avocats du Barreau de Luxembourg, ECLI:EU:C:2024:791) regarded this provision as partly infringing the client-attorney privilege and thus data protection, as enshrined by Art. 7 EU Charter. See further on this in sec. 29.5.

Not all intermediaries involved in cross-border arrangements fall within the subjective scope of DAC6, but only those who meet one of the following four additional conditions in an EU Member State, namely (a) be a resident for tax purposes, (b) have a permanent establishment through which the services are delivered, (c) be incorporated or governed by the law of that State, (d) be registered for professional purpose as legal, tax advisor or consultant.[28] These criteria leave out of the subjective scope all intermediaries not established in the European Union and only occasionally operating on its territory.

Taxpayers have a subsidiary reporting obligation, which operates in at least three group of situations. The first situation occurs when the intermediary is waived from the reporting obligation in connection with the legal privilege and no other intermediary established in the European Union has an obligation to report the arrangement.[29] The absence of intermediaries in the European Union with a reporting obligation also operates as a (second and) standalone reason to activate the one of the relevant taxpayers.[30] The third situation concerns the case of intermediaries who do have a reporting obligation, but have failed to fulfil it.

The subsidiary reporting obligation of the relevant taxpayers might raise critical issues at least in the second and third situations indicated above. Unlike in the first situation, where a professional intermediary prompts the relevant taxpayers to report, in the other two the latter persons are exposed to an obligation, which presupposes a tax technical knowledge that such persons do not necessarily have. In such circumstances, this reporting obligation could turn into a kind of objective liability for the failure to report the cross-border arrangements, which could limit fundamental freedoms and would have to be addressed at the level of justifications. In principle, the need for securing an effective reaction to tax avoidance is understandable, but, in practice, the reasonableness and proportionality of this obligation could be questioned for its implications on legal certainty and the right of such persons to minimise the tax burden in genuine cases.

Two examples can prove this type of problems more clearly. The first example concerns taxpayers entering transactions with the involvement of an intermediary established in the European Union, who might erroneously indicate that such transactions do not trigger the hallmarks of Annex IV. In such circumstances, it is unlikely that such taxpayers, who might perhaps have no technical knowledge of complex tax technical matters, could overrule the intermediary, whom they might fully trust. Leaving aside the implications

28 See Art. 3 (21) of Directive 2011/16/EU, as amended by DAC6.

29 Art. 8 ab (6) of Directive 2011/16/EU, as amended by DAC6, indicates that if an EU intermediary other than the one entitled to waiver from the reporting obligation is involved in the arrangement, the latter obligation arises on such intermediary and not directly on the relevant taxpayer. The compatibility of this indirect disclosure, on which see further in para. 5 of this Chapter, was rejected by the Court of Justice in (C-694/20, *Orde van Vlaamse Balies*, EU:C:2020:372; followed by various other judgments), due to the conflict with the fundamental right to private life, enshrined in Article 7 EU Charter.

30 Art. 8 ab (6) of Directive 2011/16/EU, as amended by DAC6.

that could arise for the intermediary in terms of penalties,[31] the nature of subsidiary reporting obligation under DAC6 makes it difficult for the taxpayers to exclude any responsibility for the failure to comply with such obligation. The second example may arise in connection with an investment that either involves one or more intermediaries not established in the European Union, or no intermediary at all. No matter how frequently these situations might in practice occur, the point is – in both the latter circumstances – that the obligation to know about the requirements established by DAC6 turns into a condition for exercising the rights to invest capital. Even if there may be less doubts of legitimacy for this type of conditions in cases clearly tainted of tax avoidance, the existence of numerous hallmarks and their complexity lead to question whether this type of mechanisms is in fact proportionate, or whether it exposes the relevant transactions to a limbo of legal uncertainty[32] for the fact of being reportable cross-border tax arrangements that a person not necessarily familiar with tax technicalities, such as the taxpayer may be, has failed to declare.

Moreover, it can clash with the privilege against self-incrimination.[33] In principle, tax-payers may not invoke such privilege to abstain from engaging in loyal cooperation with tax authorities. Accordingly, they are obliged to file returns and submit all tax relevant documentation, including books that are necessary to determine taxable income. However, this disclosure obligation presents a different substance and is tantamount to obliging the taxpayers to inform tax authorities of an arrangement that may give rise to tax avoidance. Also considering that automatic exchange of information is already fully operational within the European Union, one may wonder whether this obligation, even though subsidiary, for the taxpayer is a truly proportionate mechanism to pursue an otherwise legitimate goal of effective fight against tax avoidance.

29.4 The Hallmarks

The hallmarks are the most distinctive feature of DAC6 and their central role within the mandatory reporting system basically affects any operational aspect of how such system screens cross-border tax arrangements in the European Union for the purposes of automatic exchange of information.

The validity of DAC6 hallmarks relies on their ability to detect a potential risk of tax avoidance. They are in essence indicators of the tax avoidance that is intrinsic in the cross-border arrangements that DAC6 obliges intermediaries and taxpayers to report

---

31 In such circumstances, Article 25 a of Directive 2011/16/EU, as amended by DAC6 leaves it up to the Member States to apply penalties and secure their implementation, indicating that such penalties shall be "effective, proportionate and dissuasive". This formula is often used in connection by secondary law with tax penalties. However, it brings together criteria that are not necessarily easy to reconcile with each other. In particular, when the dissuasive nature of a penalty is combined with its effectiveness, it is often hard to comply with the requirement of proportionality. It can be interesting to note that the maximum applicable penalty is in Poland as high as the equivalent of EUR 5.8 million.

32 In this sense, see Kokott, J., Pistone, P., Taxpayers in international law, cit., p. 439.

33 See Kokott, J., Pistone, P., ibidem.

to tax authorities.[34] The character of hallmarks as indicators implies that they are not per se sufficient to prove the existence of tax avoidance, especially when operating on a standalone basis.[35], DAC6 expressly admits their use for flagging out situations with a higher risk of the occurrence of tax avoidance, even when the arrangement only contains one hallmark.[36]

The thorough understanding of the implications of hallmarks within DAC6 and the high level of detail in their regulation within Annex IV requires a more granular analysis in order to give a more specific overview of the actual cross-border reportable arrangements and to clarify the reasons for which they constitute a major source of legal uncertainty for taxpayers and of overreporting by intermediaries. This line of reasoning does not ignore the importance of an effective framework of transparency for fighting tax avoidance, but stresses the need for doing that in a way that balances out such needs with the protection of the rights of private parties to exercise their rights in genuine situations without procedural burden.[37] Because of the great number of hallmarks, their multiple and usually low thresholds for flagging out tainted situations, concerns do arise as to whether DAC6 truly constitutes a balanced secondary legislation of the European Union in tax matters.[38]

The starting point is the difference between generic and specific hallmarks. This difference reflects the one between general and specific anti-avoidance clauses, except for the fact that such clauses are used to prove the existence of tax avoidance and that the hallmarks instead only indicate the situations in which tax avoidance might occur.

General hallmarks are contained in Part II, letter A of Annex IV. Specific hallmarks are the object of letters B to E of Annex IV. There is no order of priority between them. Therefore,

---

34 In this sense, see the definition contained in Art. 3 (20) of Directive 2011/16/EU, as amended by DAC6, which includes an express reference to Annex IV, where all hallmarks and their specific effects are specifically regulated.

35 The Court of Justice had various occasions to express its view on the use of indicators in the context of countering abusive tax practices. Perhaps the most interesting judicial precedent is represented by the (almost) twin decisions on the Danish beneficial ownership cases (CJEU, 26 February 2019, joined cases C-115/16, C-118/16, C-119/16 and C-299/16, N Luxembourg et al., para.140, ECLI:EU:C:2019:134; and CJEU, 26 February 2019, joined cases C-116/16 and C-117/16, T Danmark et al., para. 114, ECLI: EU:C:2019:135), where the Court acknowledged that "the presence of a certain number of indications may demonstrate that there is an abuse of rights, insofar as those indications are objective and consistent" and accepted the validity of the ones concerning conduit companies, the purely formal nature of the structure of the group of companies, the financial arrangements and the loans lacking a valid economic substance. This line of reasoning is certainly compatible with the use of indicators in the fight against tax avoidance, as long as they are duly backed up by a reasonable capacity of detecting such phenomenon and accordingly reverse the burden of proof. However, the Court was not yet given the opportunity to clarify whether one single indicator is sufficient for that purpose. Until then it is reasonable to express concerns as to the legitimacy of reversing the burden of proof in the presence of a single indicator. This argument could lead to question the overall validity of the architecture of DAC6 in terms of proof, despite accepting its underlying concept of flagging suspicious transactions in the context of automatic exchange of information.

36 See Art. 3 (19) of Directive 2011/16/EU, as amended by DAC6.

37 See on this Kokott, J., Pistone, P., cit., p. 440 f.

38 See Kokott, J., Pistone, P., cit., p. 439 ff.

the obligation to report a cross-border arrangement can be triggered by either of them and such obligation can arise also in case one arrangement meets one, but not the other hallmarks.

All general hallmarks and some specific hallmarks[39] only operate in combination with the main benefit test. This also means that such hallmarks at least share partially common conditions for determining what arrangements must be reported and that not meeting the main benefit test is enough to automatically block the reporting obligations, due to the absence of a high risk of tax avoidance.

The main benefit test is formulated in a way that can apply to both taxpayers and intermediaries, creating an obligation to report in different contexts, when either of them may reasonably expect to derive a tax advantage from the implementation of the cross-border tax arrangement.

Even though the existence of tax avoidance does not constitute a condition for triggering the obligation to report the cross-border arrangements, the actual content of the hallmarks and their combination with the main benefit test is capable of addressing the typical framework within which taxpayers conduct such arrangements. This confirms the validity of the assumption underlying such hallmarks, used in combination with the main benefit test, and the appropriateness of reporting such arrangements.

The three general hallmarks contained in letter A) relate to (1) the existence of a confidentiality clause concerning the content of the arrangement as opposed to other intermediaries or tax authorities;[40] (2) the agreement of a success fee giving the intermediary (a) the entitlement to a remuneration determined by reference to the tax advantage,[41] or (b) the obligation for the intermediary to repay in part or full the fees in case of failure to achieve the tax advantage pursued by the arrangement;[42] and (3) the standard nature or documentation of the tax saving arrangement.[43]

The overall validity of such indicators is hard to deny, considering their frequent recurrence in tax avoidance schemes. However, there may be specific problems, such as for instance the fact that the tax advantage may not necessarily give rise to a situation of tax avoidance, or the fact that the confidentiality operates against other intermediaries, but not against tax authorities. In both groups of cases, the wording of the generic hallmarks could be rather broadly drafted, thus giving rise to a potential problem of proportionality between the reporting obligation and the goals that it pursues.

The specific hallmarks operating in combination with the main benefit test are included in letter B), as well as in points (b) (i), (c) and (d) of paragraph 1 of letter C) of Annex IV.

---

39 Namely, the ones indicated in Part II under letter B, and under points (b)(i), (c) and (d) of paragraph 1 of letter C of Annex IV.
40 See Annex IV, Part II, letter A), point 1.
41 See Annex IV, Part II, letter A), point 2 (a).
42 See Annex IV, Part II, letter A), point 2 (b).
43 See Annex IV, Part II, letter A), point 3.

The ones listed in letter B) represent well-known tax avoidance schemes, such as (1) the acquisition of loss-making company with the discontinuation of its main activity and the transfer of losses to another jurisdiction or the accelerated use of those losses; (2) the conversion of income into capital, gifts or revenue taxed at a lower level or exempted from tax; (3) self-cancelling circular transactions involving interposed entities without a main commercial function. Unlike in the general hallmarks, in the specific ones listed in letter B) the main benefit test is almost intrinsic in the type of the arrangements that such hallmarks target, thus suggesting their strong capacity of detecting a possible tax avoidance scheme at an early stage and making it difficult to argue that in fact such arrangements do not give rise to such phenomenon.

The specific hallmarks listed under letter C) relate to cross-border transactions. The ones operating with the main benefit test concern respectively the ones involving deductible payments to a recipient who is resident for tax purposes in a jurisdiction, that, in the case listed under (1) (b) (i), either does not impose any corporate tax, or does so at a(n almost) zero rate; in the case listed under (c), exempts such payment from tax; and, in the case listed under (d), taxes it at a preferential rate. Also for those specific hallmarks, the link with the main benefit test has a strong validity, which could allow to alert tax authorities of potential issues that could trigger the application of anti-avoidance rule and thus steer tax audits towards a more targeted approach.

All other specific hallmarks operate without requiring the main benefit test.

The two other hallmarks listed under letter C) relate to a recipient that – in the case under (1) (a) – is not a tax resident of any jurisdiction, or – in the case under (1) (b) (ii) – is a resident of a non-cooperative jurisdiction.[44] The first of such cases could be the outcome of the failure to disclose the tax residence of the recipient, who might for instance be in the situation of the second case, or of the willingness to avoid tracking of transactions. The presence of those specific hallmarks is important in order to protect the correct functioning of the reporting obligations under DAC6 and avoid creating loopholes that could undermine the overall consistency of the reporting network.

Letter D) lists several specific hallmarks concerning automatic exchange of information (under 1) and beneficial ownership (under 2).

The first set of specific hallmarks essentially protects automatic exchange of information, including the one implementing FATCA, and includes six types of specific arrangements that could undermine these mechanisms of global tax transparency. All such hallmarks expand the boundaries of mandatory reporting and create an alert system that increases the complexity of the formal obligations for intermediaries and taxpayers themselves. Once again, it is more difficult to justify the proportionality of such measures for taxpayers in the critical examples already outlined earlier in this paragraph, especially if one takes

44 Interestingly, this specific hallmarks expressly refers to the OECD list of non-cooperative jurisdictions, thus depriving the EU list of non-cooperative jurisdictions (on which see https://www.consilium.europa.eu/en/policies/eu-list-of-non-cooperative-jurisdictions/, updated latest on 24 February 2022) of any relevance for this purpose. Moreover, the two lists are not identical.

into account that taxpayers are neither obliged to have tax technical knowledge, nor are necessarily always aware of detailed information concerning those arrangements. For such reason, the point can be made that the failure by taxpayers to meet the subsidiary obligation to report could in some cases raise problems as to the legitimacy of applying penalties, including especially when the taxpayers prove that they did not have technical knowledge of such matters. This justification will of course not apply to intermediaries, for whom this set of specific hallmarks will anyway create an obligation to enact a mechanism to avoid triggering their application.

The second set of specific hallmarks listed under letter D) is generally known for targeting arrangements that do not involve the beneficial owners. In fact, these specific hallmarks present a complex structure, which targets intermediate entities, including the relevant arrangements that involve them, and bundles one general and three specific requirements, which contribute to create conditions of legal uncertainty and overreporting. The general part of the specific hallmarks contained in letter D) refers to "a non-transparent legal or beneficial ownership chain", but does not define any of such expressions directly. Nevertheless, relevant elements for interpretation can be found in letter (c), which refers to cases in which the beneficial ownership are unidentifiable, and defines the concept of beneficial owner by reference to the anti-money laundering Directive[45] This means that such concept indicates in this context the so-called ultimate owner, implying on turn that all payments to other recipient of the payments must reported when they are not tracked. The fact that such payments can involve several countries and intermediaries shows by itself that different interpretations and knowledge of relevant information, not always available to all intermediaries and the taxpayer produce in this context a stronger likelihood of triggering the application of this hallmark.

More critical issues arise in connection with the application of the other two specific requirements. In particular, letter (a) requires the lack of a "substantive economic activity supported by adequate staff, equipment, assets and premises". The coordination of this condition with CJEU case law on abusive practices might be problematic, because it adds an express reference to assets, included in ATAD,[46] but not mentioned in the standard interpretative formula derived from the Cadbury Schweppes case.[47] Moreover, the standard of "substantive economic activity" is very subjective and, as such, unsuitable to operate in a proportionate way without a connection with the main benefit test. In such circumstances, it might lead to legal uncertainty and create further exposure to overreporting, as already described earlier in this Chapter. Letter (b) refers the second condition of the hallmark to situations of incorporation, management, residence, control or establishment in a different jurisdiction from that of one or more of the beneficial owners. Obviously, meeting at least one of these conditions in cross-border tax situations is extremely easy. As indicated earlier, letter (c) requires traceability of the arrangements down to the ultimate (i.e. beneficial) owners, thus indicating that the intermediaries either keep track of all steps, or have to report. This conclusion is strengthened by the consideration

45 Directive 2015/849/EU.

46 Art. 7 (2) ATAD, on which see further in Chapter 19 of this book.

47 See further on this in Chapter 7 of this book.

that also the other two steps bundled together in these specific hallmarks are easily met. From the perspective of proportionality, and also taking into account the view held by the Court of Justice in the so-called Danish beneficial ownership cases, one may wonder whether, in a context – such as that of the European Union – where automatic exchange of information is fully operational, it is really reasonable and proportionate to flag out such transactions by obliging intermediaries to mandatorily report them. A different view might be perhaps be more reasonable in case of situations involving non-cooperative non-EU jurisdictions.[48]

Finally, letter E) lists three specific hallmarks concerning transfer pricing, which operate on a standalone basis and, as already indicated, without the application of the main benefit test. In particular, point 1 refers to arrangements that use unilateral safe harbour rules, point 2 to the hard-to-value intangibles,[49] and point 3 to the cross-border transfer of functions, risk or assets when it has a relevant impact on the projected annual earnings before interest and taxes (EBIT). For at least two reasons, also these specific hallmarks generate a potential for legal uncertainty and overreporting. First, even though most EU countries are completely aligned with the OECD Transfer Pricing Guidelines, differences can still be recorded across them. Second, the very subjective nature of transfer pricing frequently creates hard-to-value intangibles.

This comprehensive and detailed analysis of the content of the hallmarks and their implications has provided various specific arguments to put forward the view that DAC6, as an amendment to mutual assistance that pursues the goal of fighting tax avoidance, produces a structural negative impact on legal certainty and a strong potential of overreporting. From a policy perspective, especially if tax authorities are flooded with information, even in a highly digitalised environment, one may question whether the potential for an overwhelmingly abundant information can in fact be swiftly handled by tax authorities. Such doubts further increase if one considers that DAC7 further feeds this trend for online platforms. Perhaps, the creation of safe harbour rules could be a reasonable compromise to streamline the boundaries within which taxpayers can legitimately exercise their right to minimise the tax burden.

29.5 The Legal Professional Privilege

Art. 8 ab (5) of the Directive establishes the "legal professional privilege" (also known as the client-attorney privilege) as the only ground for waiving the obligations of EU established intermediaries to report cross-border tax arrangements. This is an extremely delicate domain, due to the presence of two potentially conflicting elements, such as the protection of confidentiality in the communication of taxpayers with their legal advisers and the assumption of DAC6 that the latter category is actively involved in the reportable cross-border arrangements producing tax avoidance.

48 Interestingly, this type of situations is targeted by the specific hallmark listed under letter C) (1) (b) (ii) only in respect of cross-border deductible payments.
49 Letter E) (2) provides for a specific definition of the hard-to-value intangibles.

This clause of the Directive includes an express reference to domestic law, which makes the actual boundaries of the waiver depending on the dimension that the legal professional privilege has in each EU Member State. This solution preserves full consistency with such rules, but creates notable differences across EU Member States, since the privilege in some countries covers both attorneys and other tax advisors, and in others only includes the first category of persons. In the latter type of situations, tax advisors other than lawyers are, therefore, obliged to reveal confidential information concerning the taxpayers, which lawyers are instead entitled not to disclose.

The indirect disclosure of information covered by the legal professional privilege in fact frustrates the object and purpose of such privilege. In other words, it circumvents its essence and gives rise to a situation that is equivalent to having no confidentiality at all. However, indirect disclosure does not seem to be problematic under the Directive, which obliges the persons entitled to the legal professional privilege to share information covered by the privilege with the other intermediaries established in the European Union. The Court of Justice has rejected the compatibility of such rules with private life.[50] See Chapter 28.13.3 for an elaborate discussion on these and other cases regarding the legal professional privilege.

Only when no such intermediary exists, the legal professional waived from mandatory disclosure has the obligation to prompt the taxpayer to communicate the arrangement to tax authorities. In such circumstances, also considering the numerous hallmarks and the very low threshold for creating the obligation of disclosure, there might be a problem of self-incrimination.[51]

50 See Case C-694/20, Orde van Vlaamse Balies, EU:C:2020:372; followed by other judgments in the same vein (case C-623/22, Belgian Association of Tax Lawyers, ECLI:EU:C:2024:639; case C-432/23, Ordre des avocats du Barreau de Luxembourg, ECLI:EU:C:2024:791).

51 See further on this in sec. 4.3.

CHAPTER 30

The Recovery Assistance Directive (RAD)

Pasquale Pistone[1]

30.1 Introduction

Administrative cooperation between tax authorities within the European Union includes three pillars. Two of them focus on mutual assistance (essentially on exchange of information and recovery of claims) and the third one, added at a much later moment, on dispute settlement.[2]

The two directives on mutual assistance pursue fully complementary functions, which characterize the recovery of claims at a logical later moment than fact finding, the latter being regulated under what has now become the so-called DAC system.[3]

Both Mutual Assistance Directives share the need for having common rules that allow tax authorities to exercise their functions across the borders within the European Union[4] and do so in the framework of a common regime.

However, the two mutual assistance Directives have not developed in an entirely parallel manner across the years. For this reason, their scope is not identical and their content presents overlaps. Accordingly, the recovery assistance directive (hereinafter also: RAD) can, on the one hand, be used for assistance on recovery of more claims than the ones related to taxes and, on the other hand, it also includes in its scope rules on exchange of information, which are not entirely identical to the ones contained in the DAC system. Moreover, the RAD does not apply to VAT, which is regulated instead within the framework of a dedicated regulation.

---

1 Academic Chairman, IBFD, Professor of European Tax Law and Policy, WU Vienna, Full Professor of Tax Law at the University of Salerno.
2 See further on this in Chapter 21 of this book.
3 See further on this in Chapters 27, 28 and 29 of this book.
4 Even though the geographical scope of these Directives is entirely internal to the European Union, European international agreements are now being concluded to extend the scope of these Directives to third countries. In particular, an agreement on combating fraud and allowing for the recovery of VAT has been concluded with Norway. This agreement entered into force on 1 September 2018.

After an overview of the historical developments (27.2) of mutual assistance in the recovery of claims, this Chapter will focus (27.3) on the scope and mechanisms of the RAD, the types of assistance in the recovery of claims (27.4) and on the remaining rules (27.5).

30.2 History

In 1972, the European Commission submitted a Proposal for a first Directive on tax recovery assistance,[5] but only in 1976 the Directive on the recovery of claims in relation to the agricultural sector and customs duties was adopted,[6] covering only the recovery of the traditional own resources of the Union, such as agricultural subsidies, agricultural levies and customs duties. This regime was extended first, in 1979, to cover VAT,[7] in 1992 to harmonised excise duties[8] and in 2001 to taxes on income and capital and on insurance premiums.[9] In 2008, this Directive and its amendments were codified to make it more accessible.[10] Detailed implementation rules were laid down at first in a Commission Directive of 9 December 2002[11] and later, after the 2008 recasting, in a Commission Regulation.[12] The detailed implementation arrangements concern, *inter alia*, the electronic communication system, deadlines for responses, administrative procedures, and reimbursement arrangements for costs connected to the recovery of debts.

Still, the Directive proved to be insufficient to meet the needs emanating from greater taxpayer and capital mobility. Only 5% of the requests for recovery actually led to recovery. Fraud and budgetary losses were soaring. Important adaptations were needed, both extending the scope of the Directive and making recovery assistance more practicable,

5 COM(72) 1578 final of 15 December 1972.

6 Council Directive 76/308/EEC of 15 March 1976 on mutual assistance for the recovery of claims resulting from operations forming part of the system of financing the European Agricultural Guidance and Guarantee Fund, and of agricultural levies and customs duties, O.J. No. L 73 of 19 March 1976, p. 18.

7 Council Directive 79/1071/EEC of 6 December 1979 amending Directive 76/308/EEC on mutual assistance for the recovery of claims relating to certain levies, duties, taxes and other measures, O.J. No. L 331 of 27 December 1979, p. 10.

8 Council Directive 92/108/EEC of 14 December 1992 amending Directive 92/12/EEC on the general arrangements for products subject to excise duty and on the holding, movement and monitoring of such products and amending Directive 92/81/EEC, O.J. No. L 390 of 31 December 1992, p. 124.

9 Council Directive 2001/44/EC of 15 June 2001 amending Directive 76/308/EEC on mutual assistance for the recovery of claims resulting from operations forming part of the system of financing the European Agricultural Guidance and Guarantee Fund, and of agricultural levies and customs duties and in respect of value added tax and certain excise duties, O.J. No. L 175 of 28 June 2001, pp. 17-20.

10 Council Directive 2008/55/EC of 26 May 2008 on mutual assistance for the recovery of claims relating to certain levies, duties, taxes and other measures (Codified version), O.J. No. L 150, of 10 June 2008, p. 28.

11 Commission Directive 2002/94/EC of 9 December 2002 laying down detailed rules for implementing certain provision of Council Directive 76/308/EEC on mutual assistance for the recovery of claims relating to certain levies, duties, taxes and other measures, O.J. No. L 337, pp. 41-45.

12 Commission Regulation (EC) No. 1179/2008 of 28 November 2008 laying down detailed rules for implementing certain provisions of Council Directive 2008/55/EC on mutual assistance for the recovery of claims relating to certain levies, duties, taxes and other measures, O.J. No. L 319, of 29 November 2008, p. 21.

effective and efficient. This called for a new Directive rather than for amending the existing one.

On 16 March 2010, the Council agreed on this Recovery Assistance Directive (RAD),[13] which had to be implemented by 31 December 2011 and applied as of 1 January 2012. Unlike the DAC, the RAD has not been changed or amended since its entry into force (except for some linguistic corrections in the Romanian, Greek and French versions), nor has it given rise to much case law until recently.[14]

30.3 Scope and Mechanisms

The RAD applies to three categories of claims, only the first one of which relates to taxes (and duties) of all kinds[15]. The broad language used by Art. 2 (1) (a) of the RAD reflects the goal of a comprehensive coverage, which could also bring within the scope of the Directive the ones that are not nominally indicated as taxes and levies, but in fact share their substance and typical features. The express reference to the Union also allows to use this Directive for the recovery of present and future supranational claims.

The second and third categories of claims reflect the history of this Directive, making it applicable (b) to EU agricultural refunds and funding measures connected with that system, as well as to (c) duties on sugar.

Article 2 continues with (2) an extension of the scope and (3) with the grounds for exclusions from the obligation to assist in the collection of taxes.

Not surprisingly the first list includes (a) administrative penalties, (b) fees and (c) interest connected with claims. The wording means to include all liability claims regarding taxes, not only those of the principal (co-)debtor, but also of all other persons liable for the settlement of the taxes.[16] The RAD only applies to *recovery* claims, as AG Kokott pointed out in her opinion in the *Bean House* Case.[17]

The second list expressly carves out four groups of measures.

13 Council Directive 2010/24/EU of 16 March 2010 concerning mutual assistance for the recovery of claims relating to taxes, duties and other measures, O.J. No. L 84, of 31 March 2010, p. 1.

14 The first relevant case on the assistance in the recovery of taxes (concerning Directive 76/308) was *Kyrian*, C 233/08, EU:C:2010:11. In Case C-133/13, *Q (Bean House)*, ECLI:EU:C:2014:2460, the Directive was included in the questions referred and addressed in the opinion of AG Kokott of 2 October 2014, EU:C:2014:2255, but not in the judgment of the Court of 18 December 2014, EU:C:2014:2460. More recently, the Court of Justice has stated on three sets of issues connected with the application of the Recovery Assistance Directive in the cases C-34/17, *Donnellan*, ECLI:EU:C:2018:282; C-19/19, *Pantochim*, ECLI:EU:C:2020:456; and C-420/19, *Heavyinstall*, ECLI:EU:C:2021:33.

15 See Art. 2 (1) (a) RAD.

16 Art. 3(2)(b) Commission Implementing Regulation (EU) No. 1189/2011 of 18 November 2011 laying down detailed rules in relation to certain provisions of Council Directive 2010/24/EU concerning mutual assistance for the recovery of claims relating to taxes, duties and other measures, O.J. No. L 302, of 19 November 2011, p. 16. Baler, P., Pistone, P., Perrou, K., Third-Party Liability for the Payment of Taxes and Their Fundamental Rights, in 15 World Tax Journal 1 (2023), p. 94 ff. doubt that the involvement of third parties without their specific involvement in a scheme of tax avoidance or evasion is in line with the standards of protection of fundamental rights of private parties in tax matters. This argument is held also considering the impact of such liability on the right to property of such third parties.

17 Opinion of AG Kokott of 2 October 2014 in Case C-133/13, *Q (Bean House)*, EU:C:2014:2255, para 59.

Just like the DAC, Art. 2 (3) (a) of the RAD indicates that mutual assistance does not apply to the recovery of claims concerning (i) compulsory social security contributions and (ii) other fees than those referred to in paragraph 2.

The exclusion of Art. 2 (3) (b) applicable to fees other than the ones referred in para. 2 indicates the strict interpretation of the latter list.

Art. 2 (3) (c) carves out dues of a contractual nature, strengthening the assumption that for the recovery of any claim other than taxes, an express indication is strictly necessary. This may raise problematic issues for payments due in consideration of the use of public utilities that lack an authoritative element.

The most problematic exclusion is the one of Art. 2 (3) (d) concerning criminal penalties. In principle, its scope is defined by reference to the ones that do not fall under Article 2 (2) (a). The line of demarcation between the two categories is clearly drawn. However, various issues may arise in practice, such as in respect of administrative penalties that are equivalent to the criminal ones for meeting the *Engel* criteria.[18] In such circumstances, it is rather difficult to understand whether the characterization of a sanction as an administrative penalty under the law of the EU Member State requesting assistance will per se prevent the requested State from objecting that the essence of such sanction makes it equivalent to the criminal ones and thus not eligible to assistance in the recovery of the claim.[19]

The existence of a specific list of situations that are carved out from the scope of the Directive also raises the issues as to whether it has an exhaustive nature.

The negative answer is prompted by the absence of a specific indication of such nature, as well as by the existence of grounds, regulated elsewhere in the RAD, which exclude the obligation to provide assistance. This is for instance the case of the *de minimis* rule contained in Art. 18(3). According to such rule, the requested State is not obliged to grant assistance if the amount of the claim requested is below EUR 1,500. Moreover, the RAD also contains in Art. 9 (2) the legal basis for direct notification, by registered mail or electronically, of documents to persons in other Member States, and rules to prevent Member States from excessively outsourcing their tax collection on other States,[20] including the subsidiary nature of the recovery of the claim by the requested EU jurisdiction.[21]

18 See further on this in Chapter 4.

19 Pistone, P., Lazarov, I., The Fundamental Right to Fair and Equitable Treatment in the Cross-Border Recovery of Taxes within the EU: A Need for a Common Minimum Standard, in 15 World Tax Journal 1 (2023), p. 122 ff. argue that both the requesting State and the requested State are exercising their powers on the basis of the Directive. Therefore, the exercise of such powers has a clear link to EU law and should be subject to the scrutiny of the CJEU also from the perspective of fundamental rights.

20 See for instance Art. 8 (2), Art. 9 (2) and Art. 18 (2) of the RAD on the recovery of final claims and Art. 18 (1) on the precautionary recovery.

21 See Art. 11 (2) of the RAD.

However, the RAD does not exclude mutual assistance in the recovery of final claims involving a disproportionate administrative burden.[22]

A more complex issue arises as to whether the obligation to provide assistance in the recovery of tax may be excluded on the basis of grounds that are not specifically indicated in the RAD itself. This type of issues is an expression of the more general problem of the extent to which the rules of secondary law of the European Union have to be interpreted and applied in line with the general principles of EU law and its primary law.[23] Leaving aside the obvious fact that secondary law may not determine a blatant clash of primary law, the more difficult situations arise in understanding how much such general principles may integrate the actual rules of the RAD.

The Court of Justice has provided very useful input on these matters in its case law on the RAD about the single enforcement instrument, which allow the latter to operate in line with the EU legal framework.

The single enforcement instrument is the EU uniform instrument, drafted in several languages, which has validity throughout the European Union and operates as the sole basis for recovery and precautionary measures in the requested State under Article 12 (1). It allows by itself the enforcement without any need for recognition or replacement procedures, or for translations, thus avoiding unnecessary delays.[24]

In particular, in the *Donnellan* case the Court of Justice recalled that the principle of mutual trust influences the RAD and requires that the uniform instrument can operate without any need for acts of recognition or integration.[25] In the *Heavyinstall* case it followed the same reasoning and added a reference to the principle of mutual recognition, concluding that the requested State may not make the assistance conditional upon a check of compatibility with the Rule of Law, whenever this has already been done by the judiciary in the requesting State.[26]

---

22 As in the case of precautionary measures and, in general, for mutual assistance in the recovery of VAT under Art. 54 (1) of the VAT RAC. In her Opinion on the *Q Bean Case*, AG Kokott (Opinion of AG Kokott of 2 October 2014 in Case C-133/13, *Q (Bean House)*, EU:C:2014:2255, para 76.) indicated that in exceptional cases there may be problems with the lack of proportionality. However, this would not occur, in principle, even in the case of extensive investigations are reasonable, because cooperation between Member States' tax administrations is on a reciprocal basis. However, in the light of the principle of sincere cooperation pursuant to Art. 4(3) TEU, the requesting Member State must not demand more frequent or intensive controls by the requested Member State than it would carry out itself.

23 De Troyer, I., Default Interest in the Event of Late Payment of Taxes, in 15 World Tax Journal 1 (2023), p. 46 elaborates on the importance of applying general principles in respect of matters covered by the Directive on the Recovery of Tax Claims. In the same vein, Attard, R., Weffe, C.E., Towards a Taxpayers' Rights-Compliant Cross-Border Recovery of Tax Sanctions, in 15 World Tax Journal 1 (2023), p. 74 ff. reconstruct the specific legal framework in which the directive should operate in a way to comply with the protection of fundamental rights of taxpayers.

24 Interestingly, no similar mechanism exists under the DAC system, not even in the case of joint audits. Consequently, in the latter cases, an additional notice will have to follow the one concerning the joint activity in order to produce the binding effects in each State involved in such procedures.

25 See *Donnellan*, cit., paras. 40-42.

26 See *Heavyinstall*, cit., para. 41. Fritz, C., Kargitta, S., Seer, R., Recovery of Disputed Tax Claims, in 15 World Tax Journal 1 (2023), p. indicate that effective tax collection should be conducted in line with the requirements of the rule of law, p. 24 f.

This line of interpretation shows that, just like for the DAC system, also the operational mode of the RAD admits limits that are not regulated by the Directive, requiring its interpretation and application in line with the general principles of EU law. Consequently, developments concerning the protection of taxpayers' rights may be expected as soon as the CJEU will be given the opportunity to address them in specific cases.

As for the subjective scope, this time in line with the rules contained in the DAC system, the RAD introduces a very wide definition of 'person', including trusts, foundations, investment funds, contractual partnerships and other 'legal arrangements' owning or managing assets, which, including the income therefrom, are subject to any of the taxes covered[27].

Common elements may be recorded between the two blocks of Directives, such as the ones concerning the direct contact between competent officials in different Member States (designation of competent authorities, central liaison offices, liaison departments and liaison officers; Art. 4) and creating electronic standard forms (Art. 21). And like the DAC, it permits a wider use of the information obtained under the Directive, *e.g.* also for the assessment or enforcement of compulsory social security contributions, for any other use which would be legal in the requested State, as evidence in proceedings, and for forwarding to a third Member State (Art. 23). Furthermore, like the DAC, the RAD prohibits banking secrecy to be used as a ground for refusal to assist (Art. 5(3).

The main difference with the DAC is that the RAD can activate its rules only from the moment in which there is an instrument permitting enforcement in a Member State[28] and when such instrument is no longer contested.[29] The exception to this principle occurs in the case of precautionary recovery of taxes, which allow for recovery in line with the requirements established in Articles 16 and 17.

30.4 Types of Recovery Assistance

The RAD provides for four main types of mutual assistance for the recovery of (tax) claims, namely (a) exchange of information, (b) notification of documents, (c) recovery upon request and (d) precautionary measures. The flexible language requirements, especially as regards documents to be notified (Art. 22(2)) facilitate the functioning of mutual assistance.

Rules on exchange of information do not entirely match the ones contained in the DAC system, but largely share a common core.

Accordingly, also the RAD applies the standard of foreseeable relevance[30] and the grounds for exclusion.[31] However, it includes a more specific condition as to the obligation of the requested authority to conduct any administrative enquiry that is necessary to provide the information. According to AG Kokott,[32] such enquiries include on-site investigations.

27 Art. 3(c).
28 If the laws of both States allow enforcement even at a time in which the tax claim is contested, Art. 14 (4) 3rd indent of the RAD allows for the recovery, subject to the obligation of the requesting State to pay all damages and refunds if the debtor's objection is successful.
29 See Art. 11 of the RAD.
30 See Art. 5 (1) of the RAD.
31 See Art. 5 (2) of the RAD.
32 Opinion of AG Kokott of 2 October 2014 in Case C-133/13, Q *(Bean House)*, C:2014:2255, para 74.

The request for information under the RAD may relate to the (co)-debtor, another person who is held liable for the claim and any third party holding assets belonging to or having debts towards the (co-)debtor or a liable person[33] implementing Regulation 1189/2011).

The wording used by Article 6 of the RAD for spontaneous exchange of information is broader than the one applicable under the DAC system, but includes a carve-out for VAT.

Within the rules governing exchange of information, the RAD also includes Article 7. This clause regulates the presence of officials in the administrative offices and their participation in administrative enquiries. In essence, such rules implement joint audits, which is in fact a different form of mutual assistance from the one concerning exchange of information. Unlike the latter, the former also allows for the presence of foreign officials during tax audits, which is more than obtaining information by mutual assistance. Also on matters of joint audits differences can be recorded with the corresponding rules contained in the DAC system.

The second form of assistance in the recovery of taxes concerns the notification upon request by the applicant Member State of all documents relating to the tax claim or its recovery,[34] such as (additional) assessments, distress warrants, judgments, court orders, writs of attachment, etc.[35], in accordance with the national notification rules in force in the requested State[36]; the request must be accompanied by a standard form[37].

The third form of assistance is the recovery upon request, *i.e.* collection and enforcement by the requested State[38], as if it were collecting its own similar claims[39]. Interestingly, even if Article 13 (1) of the RAD expressly states the obligation to grant national treatment, the Court of Justice has ruled that such type of clause does not imply for the State providing assistance to grant the same order of priority as the one that would apply on its territory in respect of its own claims,[40] unless where so agreed or unilaterally provided.[41] However, the national treatment implies, as indicated by the CJEU's *Pusa* judgment[42] that a Member State, taking into account domestic tax liabilities in calculating the attachment-free amount of income of a defaulting loan debtor, must take equal account, with equal privileges, of foreign (EU) tax on that income under Art. 21 TFEU.

Finally, the fourth form of assistance concerns the precautionary measures, i.e. the ones concerning a claim or enforcement instrument that is contested by the debtor in the applying State, or where there is no enforcement instrument yet (Art. 16 and 17). Even though the wording of Art. 16 allows assistance in respect of precautionary measures only in two situations, such as (i) litigation against the (domestic) recovery title, and (ii) in the absence as yet of a domestic recovery title, Art. 13 (1) also gives the requested

33 Art. 3(2).
34 See, C 233/08, Kyrian, ECLI:EU:C:2010:11, para. 57.
35 Art. 8.
36 Art. 9.
37 Art. 8.
38 Arts 10-15.
39 Art. 13(1).
40 See *Pantochim*, cit.
41 If that were the case, Art. 13 (1) 3rd indent requires the State to grant the same preferences to similar claims from other Member States, implying in fact the application of the most-favoured-nation treatment.
42 Case 224/02, *Pusa*, EU:C:2004:273.

Member State the power to freeze assets in cases other than those referred to in Art. 16 and with a function that is in fact equivalent to it.

30.5 Other Rules

A number of further rules contained in the RAD essentially resemble the ones that regulate mutual assistance in the DAC system. Such rules will not be the object of specific analysis, but some of them are worth a brief mention hereby, such as the ones on (i) the cost of recovery, (ii) the applicable legislation, (iii) disputes, (iv) statute-on-limitation require and (v) the relations with other legal instruments.

According to Article 20 of the RAD, the requested State will seek to recover cost from the debtor applying similar rules to the one that operate in respect of its own tax debts without charging the requesting State for a reimbursement, except where the two States have otherwise agreed in respect of cases that involve extraordinary difficulties, very high costs or connected with organised crime[43]. If, in retrospect, the tax claim or the enforcement instrument proves to be legally defective, the applying State is liable for costs and losses resulting from actions thus held to be unfounded[44].

In principle, the execution of the request, the charging of interest and the granting of payment in instalments takes place according to the legislation of the requested State, and in its currency[45].

Disputes regarding the validity of the (tax) claim, of the initial enforcement instrument, of the uniform EU enforcement instrument and of a notification made by the requesting authority itself, must be brought before the courts of the requesting State (Art. 14 (1)). Disputes on the enforcement measures taken by the requested State and on the validity of notifications made by the requesting State must in principle be brought before the courts of the latter[46].

Therefore, the requested authority may not question the validity or enforceability of the measure or the decision of which notification is sought and that, in principle, the courts of the requested State have no jurisdiction to hear disputes on the validity of the claim or the instrument permitting enforcement. However, as indicated by CJEU in the *Kyrian* Case,[47] in exceptional cases, the courts of the requested State are competent to review whether the enforcement of the instrument is contrary to the public policy of that State and, where appropriate, to refuse to grant assistance or to make it subject to fulfilling certain conditions. The CJEU excluded that those circumstances were met in the *Donnellan* case, but the wording of this judgment clearly indicates that the scope of the RAD has to be read in light of the EU Charter.[48]

43 Art. 20 (2).
44 Art. 20 (3).
45 Arts. 13(1), (3) and (4).
46 Art. 14 (2).
47 Case C-233/08, *Kyrian*, EU:C:2010:11.
48 See in particular *Donnellan*, para. 58 and the ruling. In this sense, Vandenberghe, L., Fairness in International Tax Recovery Assistance: The European Court of Justice as a Driving Force for the Respect of Fundamental Tax Debtor Rights, in 15 World Tax Journal 1, 2023, 9 ff., stresses the importance of fairness in the recovery of taxes under the EU Directive.

If a claim or enforcement instrument is being contested in the requesting State after the requested State has already initiated recovery measures, the former must inform the latter, and the latter must suspend recovery, unless the former is pressing forward and is prepared to carry the risk of having to pay refunds and damages if it loses the litigation[49].

Art. 19 (1) of the RAD indicates that the statute of limitation rules are solely governed by the law of the requesting Member State. However, suspension, interruption or prolongation of that period is in principle determined by the law of the requested State, unless that law does not provide for suspension, interruption or prolongation. In that case the steps taken in the requested State are deemed to have been taken in the requesting State in so far as they would produce suspension, interruption or prolongation under the law of the requesting State[50]. This rule serves to avoid that no request is made for fear of losing suspension, interruption or prolongation possibilities.

Finally, just like in the case of the DAC, also the RAD explicitly states that its application does not limit in any way the possibilities for mutual assistance under other legal instruments, existing or future[51]. This means concretely that the recovery of taxes may be secured also by means of the applicable tax treaties. However, in such circumstances the absence of a link with EU law might give rise to a different legal framework with repercussions also for the rights of the affected persons.

49 Arts. 13 (3) and (4)(1st indent).
50 Art. 19 (2).
51 Art. 24 (1).

CHAPTER 31

Concurrence Rules

Sigrid Hemels[1]

31.1 Introduction

There are other international bodies than the EU producing rules on cross-border administrative cooperation in tax matters, such as the OECD. Furthermore, many countries have domestic provisions for administrative cooperation. Thus, in many Member States at least four levels of rules regarding cross-border cooperation in tax matters exist: (1) domestic law, (2) bilateral tax treaty provisions (Arts. 26 and 27 OECD-MC), (3) the Multilateral Convention on Mutual Administrative Assistance in Tax Matters (MCMAATM),[2] and (4) the EU level with the DAC, the RAD and indirect taxes Regulations. This chapter discusses the relationship between these four levels in cases of overlapping or incompatible provisions, which includes overlaps between EU rules.

31.2 DAC and RAD

Since the DAC and the RAD both cover exchange of recovery information, these Directives overlap in this respect. Art. 1(3) DAC declares itself to be without prejudice to wider administrative cooperation ensuing from other legal instruments, which would seem to include the RAD. Art. 24(1) RAD, however, only refers to wider bilateral or multilateral agreements. I would submit that the widest competence/obligation on recovery assistance contained in the two directives is decisive.

31.3 MCMAATM Convention and EU Rules

In the 1980s, the Committee of Experts of the Council of Europe (CoE) and the Committee on Fiscal Affairs of the OECD jointly drew up the MCMAATM, which was opened for signature to the Member States of the OECD and of the CoE as of 25 January 1988. Since 1 April 1995, the MCMAATM has been in force between the States that have ratified it.

Among the international instruments of administrative cooperation and recovery assistance in tax matters, the MCMAATM was the first comprehensive one. In 1987, it

1 Professor of Tax Law, Erasmus University Rotterdam School of Law, affiliated to Lund University School of Economics and Management; State Councillor in the Advisory Division of the Dutch Council of State.

2 http://www.oecd-ilibrary.org/taxation/the-multilateral-convention-on-mutual-administrative-assistance-in-tax-matters_9789264115606-en.

provided for the widest assistance. Apart from exchange of information foreseeably relevant for the assessment of domestic taxes, it covered:

- exchange of information foreseeably relevant to the prosecution before an administrative authority or to the initiation of criminal prosecution (Art. 4(1)(b));
- mutual assistance in the recovery of tax claims, which may involve measures of conservancy and enforcement, such as seizure of property (Arts. 11-16); and
- mutual assistance in the service of documents (Art. 17).

In 2010, an amending Protocol was opened for signing, bringing the MCMAATM, which was initially the most far-reaching cooperation instrument, up to the international (OECD and Global Transparency Forum) standard. The main features of that Protocol are (i) the deletion of banking secrecy, essential national interests, and lack of domestic relevance as justifications for refusing cooperation, and (ii) the opening up of the MCMAATM to States which are a member of neither OECD nor CoE (*i.e.* for the whole world). This became feasible after the Global Forum on Transparency and Exchange of Information (counting more than a hundred States among its members), the G20 and the Committee of Experts on International Cooperation on Tax Matters (responsible for the UN Model Tax Treaty) all adhered to the OECD standard of transparency and cooperation (and after the successive global credit, bank, and budget crises). The Protocol entered into force on 1 June 2011. The amended Convention provides for all possible forms of administrative cooperation between States in the assessment and collection of all kinds of taxes, in particular with a view to combating tax avoidance and evasion. This cooperation ranges from exchange of information, including automatic exchange, to the recovery of foreign tax claims. Since the addition of the Protocol in 2010, the MCMAATM thus covers more or less the combined scopes of the 2013 DAC and the 2012 RAD (see Chapters 28 and 30).

On 3 December 2024, 149 jurisdictions participated in the convention.[3] These include all G20 countries, all BRICS, all OECD countries, major financial centres and an increasing number of developing countries.[4]

However, acceding States may make reservations as to the scope of the Convention within their jurisdiction (Art. 30). These reservations may exclude:

- assistance concerning taxes not on income or on capital;
- assistance in the recovery of tax claims or of administrative fines; and
- assistance in the service of documents.

Many signatories, including Brazil, the US, Japan and the UK have made reservations, in particular regarding recovery assistance, or added declarations.[5] Evidently, a State making reservations cannot require another Contracting State, not having made such reservation, to assist in a matter for which the requesting State itself reserved its rights (reciprocity principle). Notwithstanding these reservations, the OECD regarded the MCMAATM as the

3 https://www.oecd.org/ctp/exchange-of-tax-information/Status_of_convention.pdf.

4 https://www.oecd.org/tax/exchange-of-tax-information/convention-on-mutual-administrative-assistance-in-tax-matters.htm.

5 Reservations and Declarations for Treaty No.127 - Convention on Mutual Administrative Assistance in Tax Matters (ETS No. 127), https://www.coe.int/en/web/conventions/full-list?module=declarations-by-treaty&numSte=127&codeNature=0.

most comprehensive multilateral instrument available for all forms of tax cooperation to tackle tax evasion and avoidance.[6]

As regards taxpayer protection, the MCMAATM refers to domestic law (Art. 21(1)). The Convention contains more grounds for refusal of cooperation than the DAC, *e.g.* essential national interests, violation of generally accepted taxation principles or of a bilateral treaty between the applying and the requested State, discrimination against nationals of the requested State as compared to nationals of the applying State in the same circumstances, and disproportionate administrative burdens (Art. 21(2)).

For EU Member States, the MCMAATM rules and the EU rules may overlap *(i.e.* for the subjects covered by the DAC, the RAD and the EU regulations on administrative cooperation in the field of indirect taxes and the VAT information exchange system). In such case, only the EU rules apply so as to avoid differences between different bilateral relationships between EU Members (Union preference, see Section 28.2). Art. 27(2) of the MCMAATM allows Member States to do so by providing that Member States of the EU can apply the possibilities of assistance provided for in the MCMAATM in so far as they allow a wider cooperation than the possibilities offered by the applicable EU rules. Therefore, for the exchange of tax information and for the recovery assistance within the Union, the MCMAATM only applies where the Directives do not provide common rules. As the current cooperation rules in the EU have a very wide scope, there is very little scope left for the MCMAATM for EU Member States in their mutual relations.

31.4 Domestic Law, Bilateral or Multilateral (Tax) Treaties and EU Rules

Between EU Member States (at the interstate level), EU Directives and Regulations take priority over domestic law and over bilateral or multilateral (tax) treaties between them, whether anterior or posterior to the Directive or Regulation.[7] Therefore, at the level of State obligations (horizontal obligations), for EU Member States the Directives and Regulations apply exclusively, unless any other rule (such as a bilateral treaty provision or a provision in the MCMAATM) would provide for a wider obligation to cooperate (see Art. 1(3) of the DAC and Art. 24(1) of the RAD). In short, between EU Member States, the most effective rule (from the point of view of the tax authorities) applies, whether domestic, EU-law-based, bilateral or multilateral; the common EU rules are the minimum level of cooperation.

Between a Member State and a taxpayer, however (vertical relation), things are different. As Directives are addressed to the Member States rather than to their residents, they cannot of themselves directly impose obligations on individuals and undertakings.[8] If a Member State has failed to transpose a Directive into national law, it cannot rely on its provisions against economic operators. Consequently, neither the DAC nor the RAD lends legal basis to Member States wishing to compel individuals or undertakings to cooperate in fiscal enquiries or in the collection of tax instituted at the request of another Member

6 https://www.oecd.org/tax/exchange-of-tax-information/convention-on-mutual-administrative-assistance-in-tax-matters.htm.

7 See Art. 5 TEU, and Case 6/64, *Costa v. ENEL*, EU:C:1964:66, Case 106/77, *Simmenthal*, EU:C:1978:49, and Case 235/87, *Annunziata Mateucci*, EU:C:1988:460.

8 See, for example, Case 152/84, *Marshall*, EU:C:1986:84, Case 80/86, *Kolpinghuis*, EU:C:1987:431, and Case C-168/95, *Arcaro*, EU:C:1996:363.

State. For that, they need legal basis in domestic (implementation) law.[9] Reversely, given Art. 1(3) of the DAC (delimitation clause), individuals and undertakings cannot rely on the Directive in order to limit the scope of other, wider, legal instruments requiring them to cooperate. Depending on the constitutional system of the State concerned, an individual or an undertaking may in some States, however, in order to escape from a domestic law obligation, rely on a provision in a bilateral or multilateral treaty prohibiting the exchange of information, provided this provision of international law is self-executing (clear and unconditional enough to be applied directly by a Court in concrete cases). Usually, however, bilateral tax treaties do not contain such self-executing prohibitions on the exchange of information. It is true that older tax treaties sometimes contain rather limited cooperation provisions (*e.g.* only in so far as necessary to apply the treaty itself), and do not usually envisage any use of the information for other than assessment purposes, nor for the passing on to third States, but these older limitations do not prohibit the wider exchange of information either. They merely grant the Contracting States the discretionary choice to comply or not to comply with a request for such information. The States remain entirely free to furnish the information sought anyway if that is what they consider expedient in the given circumstances (and if domestic law allows). In other words, these old limitations do not confer any rights on individuals.

In conclusion, between EU Member States (horizontally) the EU Directives prevail, unless a further-reaching obligation to exchange information or assist in recovery exists between them, in which case that further-reaching provision must (also) be applied. The only other cases in which other instruments than the Directives may apply between EU Member States, are the cases in which the Directives are silent on the subject. Such a case is hard to find after 2013. Between a Member State and its subjects (vertically), on the other hand, in principle only domestic (implementation) law applies. However, an individual may rely on directly effective Directive provisions where these protect him better than domestic law. Only Arts. 16(1) and 25 of the DAC, concerning confidentiality and data protection, and Arts. 11 and 23(1) of the RAD, concerning a prohibition on recovery requests in certain circumstances and confidentiality, may possibly have such protective direct effect, but the right to confidentiality usually already exists under national law. Art. 17 DAC and Art. 18 RAD (limitations on the obligation to cooperate) have no direct effect, since they merely grant discretionary refusal grounds to Member States, rather than conferring rights on individuals. Possibly, depending on the constitutional system of the Member State concerned, an individual may also rely on self-executing provisions in bilateral or multilateral tax treaties. However, Arts. 26 and 27 OECD-MC do not seem to confer any (confidentiality or limitation) rights on taxpayers they do not already enjoy under domestic law either, at least not self-executing.

9 Possibly, under some constitutional systems a bilateral treaty provision (*cf.* Arts. 26 and 27 of the OECD Model Tax Treaty) may also suffice.

INDEX

TABLE OF CASES

Court of Justice of the EU

Case	**Name**	**Reported**	**Reference**
26/62	*Van Gend & Loos*	EU:C:1963:1	3.5.1, 3.5.4.1
25/62	*Plaumann v. Commission*	EU:C:1963:17	15.4.5
23529	*Costa v. ENEL*	EU:C:1964:66	3.5.1, 3.5.4.1, 31.4
57/65	*Lutticke*	EU:C:1966:34	2.3.2
24/68	*Commission v. Italy*	EU:C:1969:29	2.3.2, 3.2.1.2
25873	*Internationale Handels-gesellschaft*	EU:C:1970:114	2.2.2.4, 4.1
22/70	*Commission v. Council*	EU:C:1971:32	5.5.1
26755	*Nold*	EU:C:1974:51	2.2.2.4
173/73	*Italy v. Commission ('Italian textiles')*	EU:C:1974:71	3.3, 15.1
27242	*Dassonville*	EU:C:1974:82	3.2.1.2
33/74	*Van Binsbergen*	EU:C:1974:131	7.4
33/76	*Rewe*	EU:C:1976:188	3.4, 3.5.2.1, 16.8.7
45/76	*Comet*	EU:C:1976:191	3.4, 3.5.2.1, 3.5.3.1
74/76	*Ianelli v. Meroni*	EU:C:1977:51	15.3.2
28338	*Sagulo*	EU:C:1977:131	19.1
106/77	*Simmenthal*	EU:C:1978:49	3.5.4.1, 31.4
33/78	*Somafer*	EU:C:1978:205	19.4.3.4
115/78	*Knoors*	EU:C:1979:31	7.4
120/78	*Rewe Zentrale AG v. Bundesmonopolverwaltung fur Branntwein*	EU:C:1979:42	3.2.1.2, 3.2.5, 6.5.2, 7.6
44/79	*Hauer*	EU:C:1979:290	2.2.2.4
C-157/79	*Pieck [1980]*	ECR 2171	12.1.1
61/79	*Denkavit italiana*	EU:C:1980:100	15.2.5
46/80	*SpA Vinal v. SpA Orbat*	EU:C:1981:4	3.1.0
29799	*Ursula Becker v. Finanzamt Munster-Innenstadt*	EU:C:1982:7	3.5.1
15/81	*Gaston Schul I*	EU:C:1982:135	3.1.0, 3.1.1, 3.2.1.2
283/81	*CILFIT*	EU:C:1982:335	3.5.4.4
249/81	*Commission v. Ireland*	EU:C:1982:402	3.2.1.2
199/82	*San Giorgio*	EU:C:1983:318	3.4, 16.8.7
14/83	*Von Colson and Kamann*	EU:C:1984:153	3.4, 3.5.1
107/83	*Klopp*	EU:C:1984:270	3.2.1.1
229/83	*Leclerc v. Au ble vert*	EU:C:1985:1	7.4
18/84	*Commission v. France (Tax advantages for newspaper publishers)*	EU:C:1985:175	3.2.3
112/84	*Michel Humblot v. Directeur des services fiscaux*	EU:C:1985:185	3.1.0
270/83	*Commission v. France (Avoir Fiscal)*	EU:C:1986:37	3.2.2, 3.2.7.1, 6.5.4, 7.1, 8.3.5, 9.2, 11.2, 11.5.1, 13.4.2, 16.3.1, 16.4.1, 19.1
169/84	*Cofaz*	EU:C:1986:42	15.4.5
152/84	*Marshall*	EU:C:1986:84	28.3.3, 31.4

Case	Name	Reported	Reference
294/83	*Les Verts*	EU:C:1986:166	2.2.6
270/84	*Licata v. Economic and Social Committee*	EU:C:1986:304	19.6
79/85	*Segers*	EU:C:1986:308	7.4
201/85 and 202/85	*Klensch and others*	EU:C:1986:439	2.2.2.4
205/84	*Commission v. Federal Republic of Germany*	EU:C:1986:463	19.4.3.4
278/84	*Germany v. Commission*	EU:C:1987:2	19.6
80/86	*Kolpinghuis Nijmegen*	EU:C:1987:431	3.4, 3.5.1, 19.2.3, 31.4
222/86	*Heylens*	EU:C:1987:442	3.5.2.1
81/87	*Daily Mail*	1988 ECR 5483	12.1
292/86	*Claude Gullung*	EU:C:1988:15	7.4
299/86	*Drexl*	EU:C:1988:103	3.1.0
C-376/96	*Kefalas*	EU:C:1988:222	7.1, 7.4
39/86	*Sylvie Lair*	EU:C:1988:322	7.4
240/87	*Deville v. Administration des impots*	EU:C:1988:349	3.4
143/87	*Stanton*	EU:C:1988:378	3.2.7.1
286/86	*Gerard Deserbais*	EU:C:1988:434	5.5.2, 21.4.2
81/87	*Daily Mail and General Trust PLC*	EU:C:1988:456	3.2.7.1, 7.4.3, 19.4.3.4, 20.1, 20.3
235/87	*Annunziata Mateucci*	EU:C:1988:460	5.5.2, 8.3.4, 21.4.2, 31.4
249/86	*Commission v. Germany*	[1989] ECR 1263	12.1
186/87	*Cowan*	EU:C:1989:47	3.2.4
305/87	*Commission v. Greece*	EU:C:1989:218	3.1.3.1
32264	*Wachauf*	EU:C:1989:321	2.2.2.4
322/88	*Grimaldi*	EU:C:1989:646	2.2.5.1
132/88	*Commission v. Hellenic Republic*	EU:C:1990:165	3.1.0
175/88	*Biehl*	EU:C:1990:186	20.1, 21.2, 21.3
C-213/89	*Factortame I*	EU:C:1990:257	3.2.2, 3.5.2.1, 3.5.4.1
32629	*Commission v. Germany*	EU:C:1990:320	15.4.4
C-106/89	*Marleasing*	EU:C:1990:395	3.4, 3.5.1, 16.8.6, 19.2.3
69/88	*H. Krantz GmbH & Co. v. Ontvanger der directe belastingen*	EU:C:1990:97	3.2.3
47/88	*Commission v. Denmark*	EU:C:1990:449	3.1.0
C-376/89	*Giagounidis*	*[1991] ECR I-1069*	*12.1*
C-10/90	*Masgio*	EU:C:1991:107	3.2.7.1
C-340/89	*Vlassopoupou*	EU:C:1991:193	3.2.5, 14.5.2
C-260/89	*ERT*	EU:C:1991:254	2.2.2.4
C-90/90 and C-91/90	*Jean Neu and others*	EU:C:1991:303	2.2.6
C-87/90, C-88/90 and C-89/90	*Verholen and others*	EU:C:1991:314	3.5.2.1
C-221/89	*Factortame II*	EU:C:1991:320	15.4, 19.4.3.4
C-208/90	*Emmott*	EU:C:1991:333	3.4, 3.5.2.1, 3.5.3.1
C-6/90 and C-9/90	*Francovich v. Italy and Bonifaci v. Italy*	EU:C:1991:428	3.4, 3.5.4.1, 16.9
C-204/90	*Hans Martin Bachmann v. Belgium*	EU:C:1992:35	3.2.2, 3.2.4, 3.2.7.1, 5.2.4, 6.4.2, 7.5, 7.6, 7.8.1, 8.3.5, 13.0.4, 13.4.2 18.7, 20.1, 20.2, 20.3

Case	Name	Reported	Reference
C-300/90	*Commission v. Belgium*	EU:C:1992:37	20.1, 20.2
C-260/90	*Leplat*	EU:C:1992:66	5.3
C-357/89	*Raulin*	EU:C:1992:87	7.4
C-370/90	*Surinder Singh*	EU:C:1992:296	7.4
C-163/90	*Legros a.o.*	EU:C:1992:326	5.3
C-97/91	*Oleificio Borelli Spa v. Commission*	EU:C:1992:491	3.5.2.1
C-17/91	*Lornoy v. Belgium*	EU:C:1992:514	2.3.2
C-112/91	*Hans Werner v. Finanzamt Aachen-Innenstadt*	EU:C:1993:27	20.1
opinion 2/91	*(external treaty – making power)*	EU:C:1993:106	5.5.1
C-90/92	*Dr Tretter*	EU:C:1993:264	2.2.6
C-330/91	*The Queen v. Inland Revenue Commissioners, ex parte Commerzbank AG*	EU:C:1993:303	3.2.2, 3.5.2.1, 6.5.4, 9.2
C-266/91	*Celulosa Beira Industrial (CELBI)*	EU:C:1993:334	2.3.2
C-271/91	*Marshall/Southampton and South West Hampshire Area Health Authority*	EU:C:1993:335	16.9
C-276/91	*Commission v. France*	EU:C:1993:336	3.1.0
C-93/92	*CMC Motorradcenter*	EU:C:1993:838	3.2.1.2
C-338/91	*Steenhorst-Neerings*	EU:C:1993:857	3.5.3.1
C-334/92	*Wagner Miret*	EU:C:1993:945	3.5.1
C-1/93	*Halliburton Services BV*	EU:C:1994:127	3.1.3.1, 3.2.7.4, 21.4.2
C-91/92	*Faccini Dori*	EU:C:1994:292	3.5.1
C-379/92	*Criminal proceedings against Matteo Peralta*	EU:C:1994:296	3.2.7.2
C-44/93	*Namur-Les assurances du credit*	EU:C:1994:311	15.4.3
C-363/93, 407/93, 408/93, 409/93, 410/93, and 411/93	*Rene Lancry*	EU:C:1994:315	5.3
C-23/93	*TV 10*	EU:C:1994:362	7.4
C-151/93	*Criminal proceedings against Voogd Vleesimport en-export*	EU:C:1994:365	3.5.3.2
opinion 2/92	*(external treaty – making power)*	EU:C:1994:384	5.5.1
C-279/93	*Schumacker*	EU:C:1995:31	2.1, 3.2.7.1, 3.2.7.3, 6.4.2, 13.4.2, 21.3, 21.4.1
C-358/93 and C-416/93	*Bordessa*	EU:C:1995:54	5.2.2
opinion 1/94	*(external treaty – making power)*	EU:C:1995:83	5.5.1
C-384/93	*Alpine Investments*	EU:C:1995:126	3.2.1.1
C-135/93	*Spain v. Commission*	EU:C:1995:201	2.2.6
C-80/94	*Wielockx*	EU:C:1995:271	3.2.7.1, 8.3.5, 13.4.1, 20.2, 21.6
C-151/94	*Commission v. Luxembourg ('Biehl II')*	EU:C:1995:357	13.2, 21.3
C-484/93	*Peter Svensson and Lena Gustavsson*	EU:C:1995:379	3.2.4, 21.7

Case	Name	Reported	Reference
C-55/94	*Reinhard Gebhard*	EU:C:1995:411	3.2.2, 3.2.7.1
C-430/93 and C-431/93	*Van Schijndel/Stichting Pensioenfonds voor Fysiotherapeuten and van Veen*	EU:C:1995:441	3.5.2.3, 6.8.7
C-163/94, C-165/94 and C-250/94	*Sanz de Lera and others*	EU:C:1995:451	3.2.6, 5.2.2
C-415/93	*VZW Koninklijke Belgische Voetbalbond and others v. Jean-Marc Bosman*	EU:C:1995:463	3.2.1.1, 3.2.7.1
C-177/94	*Criminal proceedings against Gianfranco Perfili*	EU:C:1996:24	3.2.7.2
C-197/94 and C-252/94	*Bautiaa en Societe francaise maritime/Directeurs des services fiscaux des Landes en du Finistere and Societe francaise maritime*	EU:C:1996:47	16.8.6
C-46/93 and C-48/93	*Brasserie du Pecheur SA and Factortame Ltd and others*	EU:C:1996:79	3.5.4.1, 16.9
C-392/93	*The Queen/H.M. Treasury, ex parte British Telecommunications*	EU:C:1996:131	3.5.4.1, 6.9
C-5/94	*Hedley Lomas*	EU:C:1996:205	3.5.4.2
C-2/94	*Denkavit Internationaal and others*	EU:C:1996:229	19.5.2
C-107/94	*Asscher v. Staatssecretaris van Financien*	EU:C:1996:251	3.2.7.1, 6.4.5.4, 13.2, 13.4.1, 13.4.4
C-241/94	*France v. Commission ('Kimberly Clark')*	EU:C:1996:353	15.2.5
C-168/95	*Arcaro*	EU:C:1996:363	31.4
C-283/94, C-291/94 and C-292/94	*Denkavit Internationaal BV, VITIC Amsterdam BV and Voormeer BV*	EU:C:1996:387	3.5.4.2, 10.3.2.2, 16.3.1, 16.3.2
C-72/95	*Kraaijeveld a.o.*	EU:C:1996:404	16.9
C-84/94	*United Kingdom v. Council (Working Time Directive)*	EU:C:1996:431	2.1
C-267 and 268/91	*Criminal Proceedings against Keck and Mithouard*	EU:C:1996:905	3.2.1.2, 7.8.2, 15.1
C-169/95	*Spain v. Commission*	EU:C:1997:10	25.4.4
C-80/95	*Harnas & Helm*	EU:C:1997:56	19.4.3.4
C-264/96	*ICI v. Colmer*	EU:C:1997:182	15.4
C-250/95	*Futura Participations SA and Singer v. Administration des contributions*	EU:C:1997:239	3.2.1.2, 3.2.2, 3.2.7.3, 6.3, 6.4.2, 6.5.2, 9.2, 15.6, 18.4
C-299/95	*Kremzow*	EU:C:1997:254	3.1.4
C-368/95	*Familiapress Zeitungsverlags*	EU:C:1997:325	2.2.2.4
C-28/95	*Leur-Bloem v. Inspecteur*	EU:C:1997:369	4.2.1.1, 7.13.2, 19.5.3.3
C-190/95	*ARO Lease BV*	EU:C:1997:374	19.4.3.4
C-347/95	*Fazenda Publica v. UCAL*	EU:C:1997:411	2.3.2
C-28/96	*Fazenda Publica v. Fricarnes*	EU:C:1997:412	2.3.2
C-375/95	*Commission v. Hellenic Republic*	EU:C:1997:505	3.1.0
C-309/96	*Annibaldi*	EU:C:1997:631	3.1.4
C-118/96	*Jessica Safir*	EU:C:1998:170	3.2.4, 13.6, 14.3, 16.4.1, 20.2

Case	Name	Reported	Reference
C-336/96	*Gilly*	EU:C:1998:221	3.1.3.2, 8.1.1, 8.1.2, 8.2.5, 8.3, 8.3.1, 8.3.3, 13.4.4, 14.5.3, 16.4.3, 18.5
C-264/96	*ICI v. Colmer*	EU:C:1998:370	6.5.2, 10.4, 20.1
C-231/96	*Edis*	EU:C:1998:401	3.5.2.1
C-260/96	*Spac*	EU:C:1998:402	3.5.2.1
C-228/96	*Aprile*	EU:C:1998:544	3.5.2.1
C-326/96	*Levez v. Jennings Ltd*	EU:C:1998:577	3.5.3.1
C-18/95	*Terhoeve*	EU:C:1999:22	21.4.2
C-212/97	*Centros*	EU:C:1999:126	3.1.3.3, 7.4, 7.5.1, 19.3, 20.3
C-311/97	*Royal Bank of Scotland*	EU:C:1999:216	3.1.3.1, 3.2.7.1, 6.4.2, 9.2
C-126/97	*Eco Swiss China Time*	EU:C:1999:269	3.5.2.3
C-302/97	*Konle*	EU:C:1999:271	5.2.3
C-166/98	*Socridis*	EU:C:1999:316	2.2.6
C-60/98	*Butterfly Music*	EU:C:1999:333	19.6
C-391/97	*Gschwind*	EU:C:1999:409	13.4.1, 13.4.4
C-307/97	*Compagnie de Saint-Gobain*	EU:C:1999:438	6.4.2, 8.3.4, 8.3.5, 9.2, 13.4.2, 16.3.1
C-294/97	*EUrowings Luftverkehrs AG*	EU:C:1999:524	3.2.4, 6.5.2, 7.4, 7.13.6, 8.2.5, 19.4.3.4, 20.1
C-55/98	*Skatteministeriet v. Bent Vestergaard*	EU:C:1999:533	7.6, 13.0.4, 13.4.2, 19.5
C-200/98	*X AB & Y AB*	EU:C:1999:566	9.4
C-83/98	*Ladbroke Racing*	EU:C:1999:577	15.4.4
C-34/98	*Commission v. France*	EU:C:2000:84	20.1
C-292/97	*Karlsson*	EU:C:2000:202	2.2.2.4
C-251/98	*Baars v. Inspecteur der belastingen*	EU:C:2000:205	3.2.5
C-420/98	*W.N.*	EU:C:2000:209	28.3.3
C-87/99	*Zurstrassen*	EU:C:2000:251	20.1
C-35/98	*Staatssecretaris van Financien v. B.G.M. Verkooijen*	EU:C:2000:294	11.2, 11.4.1, 13.7, 20.1
C-375/98	*Ministerio Publico Fazenda Publica v. Epson EUrope BV*	EU:C:2000:302	10.6.1.1, 16.3.1, 16.6.3, 16.8.6
C-156/98	*Germany v. Commission*	EU:C:2000:467	3.3, 25.3.2
C-478/98	*Commission v. Belgium*	EU:C:2000:497	26.2.3
C-15/98 and C-105/99	*Sardegna Lines*	EU:C:2000:570	15.4.5
C-110/99	*Emsland-Starke*	EU:C:2000:695	7.1, 7.4, 19.5.3.2
C-141/99	*AMID v. Belgium*	EU:C:2000:696	10.5
C-226/99	*Siples Sri v. Ministero delle Finanze c.s.*	EU:C:2001:14	3.5.2.1
C-150/99	*Stockholm Lindopark*	EU:C:2001:34	3.5.4.2
C-397/98 and C-410/98	*Metallgesellschaft and Hoechst*	EU:C:2001:134	3.5.4.3, 6.5.2, 17.4, 20.1
C-265/99	*Commission v. France*	EU:C:2001:169	3.1.0
C-157/99	*Smits and Peerbooms*	EU:C:2001:404	25.2.5
C-16/00	*Cibo*	EU:C:2001:495	20.5.2
C-294/99	*Athinaiki Zythopoiia AE v. Elliniko Dimosio*	EU:C:2001:505	10.6.1.1, 11.3, 16.5.1, 16.6.3, 19.5.3.2
C-377/98	*Netherlands v. EUropean Parliament and Council (Biotechnology Directive)*	EU:C:2001:523	2.1
C-143/99	*Adria-Wien Pipeline GmbH*	EU:C:2001:598	3.3, 25.2.4, 25.3.1

Case	Name	Reported	Reference
C-451/98	*Antillean Rice Mills v. Council*	EU:C:2001:622	15.4.5
C-43/00	*Andersen og Jensen ApS v. Skatteministeriet*	EU:C:2002:15	17.4.1, 17.4.2, 19.4.3.4
C-55/00	*Gottardo*	EU:C:2002:16	5.5.2, 16.3.4
C-310/99	*Italy v. Commission*	EU:C:2002:143	25.4.4
C-234/99	*Nygard*	EU:C:2002:244	3.1.0, 3.2.7.1
C-482/99	*France v. Commission (Stardust)*	EU:C:2002:294	25.2.3
C-430/99 and C-431/99	*Sea-Land Service*	EU:C:2002:364	3.2.7.1
C-313/99	*Mulligan*	EU:C:2002:386	2.2.2.4
C-224/98	*Marie Nathalie D'Hoop*	EU:C:2002:432	7.8.3
C-60/00	*Carpenter*	EU:C:2002:434	2.2.2.4
C-62/00	*Marks & Spencer I*	EU:C:2002:435	3.4, 3.5.2.2
C-431/01	*Mertens v. Belgium*	EU:C:2002:492	10.5
C-413/99	*Baumbast*	EU:C:2002:493	3.1.3.1
C-101/00	*Tulliasiamies and Siilin*	EU:C:2002:505	3.1.0
C-255/00	*Grundig Italiana*	EU:C:2002:525	3.5.3.1
C-136/00	*Rolf Dieter Danner*	EU:C:2002:558	3.2.4, 13.4.2, 13.6 15.8.1, 20.2
C-94/00	*Roquette Freres*	EU:C:2002:603	4.2.3
C-446-469/98, C-471-472/98, C-475-476/98	*Commission v. UK, Denmark, Sweden, Finland, Belgium, Luxembourg, Austria and Germany*	EU:C:2002:624-631	5.5.1, 13.4.2, 16.3.4
C-208/00	*Uberseering*	EU:C:2002:632	3.2.1.2, 3.2.5, 7.4.3, 14.5.2, 20.3
C-436/00	*X & Y v. Riksskatteverket*	EU:C:2002:704	8.3.5, 20.1, 20.2
C-491/01	*British American Tobacco*	EU:C:2002:741	2.1
C-324/00	*Lankhorst-Hohorst GmbH*	EU:C:2002:749	6.5.2, 10.2.4.3, 16.5.1, 17.6, 19.4.1.4, 19.4.2.3
C-385/00	*De Groot v. Inspecteur van belastingen*	EU:C:2002:750	3.1.2, 3.2.7.3, 6.3, 6.5.1, 6.5.4, 8.3.5, 13.4.5, 16.1.2
C-388/01	*Commission v. Italy*	EU:C:2003:30	3.2.4
C-327/00	*Santex Spa*	EU:C:2003:109	3.5.3.1
C-187/00	*Kutz-Bauer v. Hamburg*	EU:C:2003:168	3.5.2.1
C-462/99	*Connect Austria GmbH*	EU:C:2003:297	3.5.2.1
C-234/01	*Arnoud Gerritse*	EU:C:2003:340	11.5.1, 13.2, 13.3, 13.4.1
C-385/99	*Muiller-Faure and van Riet*	EU:C:2003:370	15.8.3
C-404/00	*Commission v. Spain*	EU:C:2003:373	25.4.4
C-422/01	*Forsakringsaktiebolaget Skandia, Ola Ramstedt v. Riksskatteverket*	EU:C:2003:380	3.2.4, 20.2
C-168/01	*Bosal Holding BV v. Staatssecretaris van Financien*	EU:C:2003:479	2.2.6, 3.2.7.3, 3.2.7.3, 6.4.1, 6.4.1, 6.5.1, 6.5.3, 7.2, 7.8.2, 18.5, 19.3, 19.4.1.4
C-308/01	*GIL Insurance*	EU:C:2003:481	25.2.4
C-30/01	*Commission v. United Kingdom*	EU:C:2003:489	19.2.5
C-58/01	*Oce van der Grinten*	EU:C:2003:495	2.3.1, 8.3.5, 16.5.1, 16.6.3

Case	Name	Reported	Reference
C-167/01	*Inspire Art*	EU:C:2003:512	20.3
C-224/01	*Kobler v. Austria*	EU:C:2003:513	3.5.4.4, 6.9
C-261/01 and C-262/01	*Van Calster*	EU:C:2003:571	15.3.2
C-42/02	*Diana Elisabeth Lindman*	EU:C:2003:613	3.2.2
C-296/01	*Commission of the European Communities v. French Republic*	EU:C:2003:626	16.8.6
C-278/01	*Commission v. Spain*	EU:C:2003:635	3.5.4.5
C-129/00	*Commission v. Italy*	EU:C:2003:656	3.4, 3.5.2.2, 3.5.4.4
C-364/01	*Barbier*	EU:C:2003:665	14.1, 14.4.3
C-201/02	*the Queen, ex parte Delena Wells*	EU:C:2004:12	3.5.1
C-453/00	*Kuhne & Heitz NV v. Productschap voor pluimvee en eieren*	EU:C:2004:17	3.5.3.2
C-334/02	*Commission v. France (fixed levy)*	EU:C:2004:129	11.4.1, 20.1, 21.4.2
C-9/02	*Hughes de Lasteyrie de Saillant*	EU:C:2004:138	4.3.5, 7.5, 20.1, 20.2, 20.3, 20.4,
C-77/01	*EDM*	EU:C:2004:243	19.4.3.4, 25.2.2
C-338/01	*Commission v. Council*	EU:C:2004:253	2.3.2, 2.3.3, 27.7
C-387/01	*Weigel*	EU:C:2004:256	6.4.1
C-224/02	*Heikki Antero Pusa*	EU:C:2004:273	3.1.3.2
C-30/02	*Recheio Cash & Carry*	EU:C:2004:373	3.5.3.1
C-169/03	*Florian W. Wallentin v. Riksskatteverket*	EU:C:2004:403	3.2.5, 21.4.1
C-501/00	*Spain v. Commission*	EU:C:2004:438	2.1
C-315/02	*Lenz*	EU:C:2004:446	11.2, 11.4.1, 20.1
C-365/02	*Lindfors*	EU:C:2004:449	3.1.3.2, 3.2.7.1, 3.2.7.3, 8.3.3, 17.3
C-242/03	*Jean-Claude Weidert, Elisabeth Paulus*	EU:C:2004:465	19.2, 21.7
C-319/02	*Manninen*	EU:C:2004:484	6.4.2, 11.1.5, 11.2, 11.4.1, 18.5
C-397/01 to C-403/01	*Pfeiffer a.o.*	EU:C:2004:584	3.5.1
C-442/02	*CaixaBanque France*	EU:C:2004:586	3.2.1.1, 3.2.5, 6.5.2
C-222/02	*Peter Paul a.o. v. Germany*	EU:C:2004:606	3.5.4.1
C-304/02	*Commission v. France*	[2005] ECR I-6263	3.5.4.5
C-174/02	*Streekgewest*	EU:C:2005:10	15.2.4
C-172/03	*Heiser*	EU:C:2005:130	15.2.5, 25.2.6
C-39/04	*Laboratoires Fournier*	EU:C:2005:161	15.2.5, 15.2.7
C-255/02	*Halifax a.o.*	EU:C:2005:200	15.4
C-376/02	*Goed Wonen*	EU:C:2005:251	3.1.4
C-376/03	*D. v. Inspecteur*	EU:C:2005:424	3.2.7.1, 5.2.5, 5.5.2, 8.3.4
C-403/03	*Schempp*	EU:C:2005:446	3.1.3.2, 3.2.7.1, 3.2.7.2, 3.2.7.3, 6.4.1, 8.3.3, 9.3
C-154/04 and C-155/04	*Alliance for Natural Health*	EU:C:2005:449	2.1, 3.2.1.1, 15.3
C-349/03	*Commission v. United Kingdom*	EU:C:2005:488	19.2.5, 27.7
C-544/03 and C-545/03	*Mobistar and Belgacom Mobile*	EU:C:2005:518	3.2.7.1
C-204/03	*Commission v. Spain*	EU:C:2005:588	3.5.3.2

Case	Name	Reported	Reference
C-291/03	*MyTravel*	EU:C:2005:591	2.2.2.4
C-293/02	*Jersey Produce Marketing Organisation*	EU:C:2005:664	5.4
C-144/04	*Werner Mangold*	EU:C:2005:709	3.5.1
C-411/03	*SEVIC Systems Aktiengesell-schaft*	EU:C:2005:762	5.2.4, 17.4.3, 20.3
C-446/03	*Marks & Spencer II*	EU:C:2005:763	2.1, 3.2.2, 3.2.7.1, 3.2.7.3, 6.1, 6.3, 6.4.2, 6.5.1, 7.5, 9.4, 10.1.3, 18.1, 19.4.4.3, 20.1
C-148/04	*Unicredito Italiano*	EU:C:2005:774	15.4.4
C-222/04	*Cassa di Risparmio di Firenze*	EU:C:2006:8	15.2.2, 15.2.6
C-265/04	*Bouanich*	EU:C:2006:51	8.3.2, 11.5.1, 16.3.5, 19.2
C-452/04	*Fidium Finanz*	EU:C:2006:72	3.2.6, 5.2.4
C-255/02	*Halifax*	EU:C:2006:121	2.2.2.4, 19.5.1, 19.5.3.1, 19.5.3.2
C-152/03	*Ritter-Coulais*	EU:C:2006:123	3.2.7.3, 10.4, 21.2, 21.4.3
C-253/03	*CLT-UFA SA*	EU:C:2006:129	9.2
C-513/03	*Van Hilten-van der Heijden v. Inspecteur*	EU:C:2006:131	3.2.6, 6.2, 6.4.5, 6.5.3, 7.5, 16.1.1, 16.2.5, 16.3.5, 20.2, 21.5
C-471/04	*Keller Holding*	EU:C:2006:143	2.2.6
C-234/04	*Rosmarie Kapferer*	EU:C:2006:178	3.5.3.2
C-341/04	*EUrofood IFSC*	EU:C:2006:281	19.4.3.4
C-442/03 and C-471/03	*P&O EUropean Ferries*	EU:C:2006:356	15.4.4
C-517/04	*Koornstra*	EU:C:2006:375	2.3.2, 3.1.0, 3.2.7.1
C-173/03	*Traghetti del Mediterraneo Spa*	EU:C:2006:391	3.5.4.4
C-28/05	*Dokter*	EU:C:2006:408	3.5.2.1, 4.3.5
C-182/03 and C-217/03	*Belgium and Forum 187 v. Commission*	EU:C:2006:416	15.2.7, 26.2.3
C-524/05	*Test Claimants in the Thin Cap Group Litigation*	EU:C:2006:436	7.7
C-524/04	*Thin Cap GLO*	EU:C:2006:436	15.8.1
C-524/05	*Test Claimants in the Thin Cap Group Litigation*	EU:C:2006:436	7.4
C-212/04	*Konstantinos Adeneler and Others v. Ellinikos Organis-mos Galaktos (ELOG)*	EU:C:2006:443	3.5.1, 16.8.6, 19.2.3
C-346/04	*Conijn*	EU:C:2006:445	3.5.2.1, 21.4.1
C-88/03	*Portugal v. Commission ('Azores')*	EU:C:2006:511	15.2.4, 15.2.5
C-470/04	*N v. Inspecteur van de Belastingdienst*	EU:C:2006:525	3.1.3.2, 3.2.2, 3.2.7.3, 6.4.2, 6.5.1, 7.8.2, 8.3.5, 13.0.4, 20.2, 20.3, 20.4, 21.6
C-526/04	*Laboratoires Boiron*	EU:C:2006:528	15.2.4

Case	Name	Reported	Reference
C-196/04	*Cadbury Schweppes*	EU:C:2006:544	2.1, 3.1.3.3, 3.2.2, 3.2.6, 5.2.4, 6.4.2, 7.4, 7.6, 9.5, 11.3, 16.2.4, 16.3.4, 19.3, 19.4.3.4, 19.5.3.1, 19.5.3.3, 20.3, 26.2.3
C-181-183/04	*Elmeka*	EU:C:2006:563	15.4.4
C-386/04	*Stauffer*	EU:C:2006:568	19.4.3.4
C-392/04 and C-422/04	*Arcor and i-21*	EU:C:2006:586	3.5.3.1, 3.5.3.2
C-290/04	*FKP Scorpio Konzertproduktionen GmbH*	EU:C:2006:630	3.2.2, 7.6, 11.5.1, 21.3
C-368/04	*Transalpine Olleitung*	EU:C:2006:644	15.4.4
C-290/05 and C-333/05	*Nadasdi and Nemeth*	EU:C:2006:652	3.1.0
C-436/05	*De Graaf en Daniels*	EU:C:2006:656	20.2
C-168/05	*Mostaza Claro*	EU:C:2006:675	3.5.2.3
C-345/05	*Commission v. Portugal*	EU:C:2006:685	21.7
C-520/04	*Pirkko Marjatta Turpeinen*	EU:C:2006:703	3.1.3.2, 11.5.1, 21.2
C-513/04	*Kerckhaert and Morres*	EU:C:2006:713	3.1.2, 3.1.3.2, 3.2.7.1, 4.3.2, 7.8.2, 8.1.2, 8.2.5, 8.3.5, 11.2, 11.4.2, 13.5, 20.2, 25.2.7
C-374/04	*Test Claimants in Class IV of the ACT Group Litigation*	EU:C:2006:773	3.2.7.1, 3.2.7.3, 5.5.2, 6.4.2, 11.2, 11.5.1
C-446/04	*Test Claimants in the FII Group Litigation*	EU:C:2006:774	2.2.6, 3.2.7.1, 3.5.4.2, 3.5.4.3, 5.2.3, 5.2.4, 6.5.3, 8.2.4, 8.2.5, 9.5, 11.2, 11.4.1, 11.4.3, 16.4.1, 16.4.5, 16.8.7, 19.3
C-170/05	*Denkavit International BV and Sarl, Denkavit France*	EU:C:2006:783	6.4.2, 6.5.4, 8.3.2, 11.2, 11.5.1, 20.1, 20.2
C-104/06	*Commission v. Sweden*	EU:C:2007:40	21.7
C-329/05	*Meindl*	EU:C:2007:57	21.4.1
C-150/04	*Commission v. Denmark*	EU:C:2007:69	20.2, 21.6
C-292/04	*Meilicke a.o.*	EU:C:2007:132	11.2, 11.4.1
C-524/04	*Test Claimants in the Thin Cap Group Litigation*	EU:C:2007:161	3.1.2, 3.2.6, 5.2.4, 7.5, 9.6 19.3, 19.4.1.4, 19.4.2.3, 19.5.3.1, 19.5.3.2, 19.5.3.3
C-432/05	*Unibet v. Justitiekanslern*	EU:C:2007:163	3.5
C-35/05	*Reemtsma*	EU:C:2007:167	2.2.2.4
C-383/05	*Talotta v. Belgium*	EU:C:2007:181	6.4.2, 9.2
C-347/04	*Rewe Zentralfinanz eG*	EU:C:2007:194	7.8.3, 9.3, 20.1
C-492/04	*Lasertec*	EU:C:2007:273	3.2.6, 5.2.4, 19.3
C-102/05	*(order) Skatteverket v. A and B*	EU:C:2007:275	5.2.4
C-157/05	*Winfried Holbock*	EU:C:2007:297	3.2.6, 5.2.3, 5.2.4

Case	Name	Reported	Reference
C-222/05 through C-225/05	*Van der Weerd a.o.*	EU:C:2007:318	3.5.2.3
C-73/06	*Planzer*	EU:C:2007:397	19.4.3.4
C-522/04	*Commission v. Belgium*	EU:C:2007:405	
C-321/05	*Hans Markus Kofoed v. Skatteministeriet*	EU:C:2007:408	2.2.2.4, 7.4, 16.8.3, 16.8.7, 17.5, 19.5.1
C-119/05	*Lucchini Siderurgica Spa*	EU:C:2007:434	3.5.3.2
C-2/08	*Fallimento Olimpiclub*	EU:C:2007:434	3.5.3.2
C-231/05	*Oy AA*	EU:C:2007:439	3.2.2, 6.5.2, 7.5, 7.8.3, 14.4.2, 18.5
C-182/06	*Lakebrink and Peters-Lakebrink*	EU:C:2007:452	3.2.7.3, 8.3.5, 13.2, 13.4.3, 13.4.6, 18.1
C-74/06	*Commission v. Hellenic Republic*	EU:C:2007:534	3.1.0
C-409/04	*Teleos*	EU:C:2007:548	2.2.2.4
C-185/05	*Twoh International BV v. Staatssecretaris van Financien*	EU:C:2007:550	15.6
C-451/05	*ELISA*	EU:C:2007:594	9.2, 19.4.3.4, 19.5.3.3, 28.10.2
C-427/05	*Porto Antico di Genova*	EU:C:2007:630	25.2.5
C-464/05	*Geurts*	EU:C:2007:631	14.1, 14.3.1, 14.3.4, 14.4.6
C-415/06	*Stahlwerk Ergste Westig*	EU:C:2007:651	10.1.3, 19.3
C-379/05	*Amurta*	EU:C:2007:655	3.1.2, 3.2.7.1, 6.5.4, 7.8.3, 8.3.2, 11.2, 11.5.1, 16.3.5, 20.2
C-260/05	*Sniace*	EU:C:2007:700	15.4.5
C-298/05	*Columbus Container Services*	EU:C:2007:754	3.1.3.2, 3.2.6, 3.2.7.1, 3.2.7.3, 5.2.4, 6.5.2, 8.2.5, 8.3.3, 8.3.6, 9.3, 9.5, 9.6, 18.5, 18.7, 19.4.3.4,
C-101/05	*Skatteverket v. A*	EU:C:2007:804	3.2.6, 5.2.2, 19.3
C-345/04	*Centro Equestre da Leziria Grande*	EU:C:2007:96	19.5.1, 21.3
C-152/05	*Commission v. Germany (Eigenheimzulage)*	EU:C:2008:17	13.7
C-256/06	*Jager*	EU:C:2008:20	14.1, 14.3.1, 14.3.3, 14.4.4
C-105/07	*Lammers & Van Cleeff*	EU:C:2008:24	9.6
C-199/06	*CELF*	EU:C:2008:79	15.4.4
C-138/07	*Belgische Staat v. Cobelfret NV*	EU:C:2009:82	16.4.2.1, 16.4.2.2.2, 16.9
C-67/08	*Block*	EU:C:2009:92	3.1.3.2, 3.2.7.1, 4.3.2, 8.1.2, 8.2.5, 13.4.5, 13.5, 17.6, 18.7,
C-425/06	*Part Service Srl*	EU:C:2008:108	2.2.2.4, 15.4, 19.5.3.1, 19.5.3.2,
C-293/06	*Deutsche Shell*	EU:C:2008:129	3.2.7.3, 6.3, 6.5.1, 6.5.4, 18.5, 18.7
C-212/06	*Gouvernement de la Communaute francaise et Gouvernement wallon*	EU:C:2008:178	16.4.1, 21.4.2
C-27/07	*Banque Federative du Credit Mutuel*	EU:C:2008:195	16.4.7
C-309/06	*Marks & Spencer*	EU:C:2008:211	2.2.2.4

Case	Name	Reported	Reference
C-201/05	*Test Claimants in the CFC and Dividend GLO*	EU:C:2008:239	19.4.3.4
C-414/06	*Lidl Belgium GmbH & Co. KG v. Finanzamt Heilbronn*	EU:C:2008:278	3.2.7.3, 6.2, 6.3, 6.4.2, 7.8.3, 8.2.5, 10.1.3, 10.2.2, 10.3.1, 18.2
C-194/06	*Orange EUropean Smallcap Fund*	EU:C:2008:289	3.2.2, 11.2, 11.4.2, 16.3.1
C-284/06	*Burda*	EU:C:2008:365	5.2.4, 6.5.3, 6.6.3 11.2, 19.5.3.2
C-333/07	*Regie Networks*	EU:C:2008:371	15.4.5
C-25/07	*Sosnowska*	EU:C:2008:395	2.2.2.4
C-402/05 P and C-415/05	*P Kadi and Al Barakaat Foundation*	EU:C:2008:461	3.1.4, 4.1
C-11/07	*Eckelkamp*	EU:C:2008:489	14.1, 14.3.3, 14.4.3
C-43/07	*Arens-Sikken*	EU:C:2008:490	6.5.3, 6.5.4, 14.1, 14.3.3, 14.4.3
C-527/06	*Renneberg*	EU:C:2008:566	3.2.5, 3.2.7.3, 6.3, 8.3.2, 8.3.5, 13.2, 13.4.6, 18.1
C-157/07	*Krankenheim Ruhesitz am Wannsee-Seniorenheimstatt*	EU:C:2008:588	3.2.2, 3.2.7.3, 6.4.1, 6.4.2, 7.5, 7.8.1, 8.2.5, 10.3.1, 18.2, 18.5, 18.7
C-214/07	*Commission v. France*	EU:C:2008:619	25.4.5
C-455/06	*Heemskerk en Schaap*	EU:C:2008:650	3.5.2.3
C-418/07	*Papillon*	EU:C:2008:659	7.8.1
C-330/07	*Jobra*	EU:C:2008:685	19.5.3.2
C-285/07	*A.T. AG v. Finanzamt Stuttgart-Korperschafien*	EU:C:2008:705	17.8.5
C-210/06	*Cartesio*	EU:C:2008:723	3.2.5, 6.5.2, 7.4.3, 20.3
C-349/07	*Soprope v. Fazenda Publica*	EU:C:2008:746	3.1.4, 3.5.2.1, 4.1, 4.2.1.1, 4.3.5, 4.3.7, 11.7.3
C-487/06	*British Aggregates*	EU:C:2008:757	15.2.5, 25.4.5
C-48/07	*Les Vergers du Vieux Tauves SA*	EU:C:2008:758	16.3.2
C-282/07	*Truck Center*	EU:C:2008:762	3.2.2, 3.2.7.1, 6.4.2, 11.2, 11.5.1
C-377/07	*STEKO Industriemontage*	EU:C:2009:29	5.2.2
C-318/07	*Persche*	EU:C:2009:33	6.4.2, 21.1
C-110/05	*Commission v. Italy*	EU:C:2009:66	3.2.1.1, 3.2.5, 14.5.2
C-406/07	*Commission v. Greece*	EU:C:2009:251	11.4.1
C-460/07	*Puffer*	EU:C:2009:254	2.2.2.4, 25.2.3
C-544/07	*Uwe Ruffler*	EU:C:2009:258	20.2, 21.1
C-439/07and C-499/07	*KBC Bank*	EU:C:2009:339	5.2.4, 6.4.5
C-429/07	*X BV v. Inspecteur*	EU:C:2009:359	3.4, 25.4.4
C-521/07	*Commission v. the Netherlands*	EU:C:2009:360	5.2.2, 6.3.2, 11.5.1
C-155/08 and C-157/08	*X. and Passenheim-Van Schoot*	EU:C:2009:368	3.2.2, 3.2.7.1, 11.7.3
C-303/07	*Aberdeen property Fininvest Alpha Oy*	EU:C:2009:377	5.2.4, 6.3.1, 7.8.3, 11.2, 11.5.1
C-169/08	*Presidente del Consiglio dei Ministri v. Regione autonoma della Sardegna*	EU:C:2009:420	25.2.5

Case	Name	Reported	Reference
C-128/08	*Damseaux*	EU:C:2009:471	3.1.3.2, 3.2.7.1, 4.3.2, 8.1.2, 8.3.6, 11.2, 11.4.2, 13.4.5, 13.5, 14.4.1, 18.7
C-250/95	*Futura Participations SA*	EU:C:2009:479	7.8.2, 15.8.2
C-269/07	*Commission v. Germany*	EU:C:2009:527	20.2
C-201/08	*Plantanol*	EU:C:2009:539	2.2.2.4
C-519/07	*Koninklijke FrieslandCampina*	EU:C:2009:556	25.4.4, 25.4.5
C-182/08	*Glaxo Wellcome*	EU:C:2009:559	5.2.4
C-247/08	*Gaz de France v. Berliner Investissement*	EU:C:2009:600	3.2.2, 6.3.1, 6.8.6, 17.7
C-40/08	*Asturcom Telecomuni-caciones*	EU:C:2009:615	3.5.2.3
C-35/08	*Busley and Cibrian*	EU:C:2009:625	10.1.3
C-101/08	*Audiolux*	EU:C:2009:626	2.2.2.4
C-63/08	*Pontin*	EU:C:2009:666	3.5.2.1
C-174/08	*NCC Construction*	EU:C:2009:669	2.2.2.4
C-441/08	*Elektrownia Pţtnow*	EU:C:2009:698	19.6
C-540/07	*Commission v. Italy*	EU:C:2009:717	5.2.2, 6.3.2, 6.5.4, 11.1.5, 11.5.1
C-311/08	*Societe de Gestion Industrielle (SGI)*	EU:C:2010:26	6.2, 6.4.2, 7.5, 8.2.4, 8.2.5, 17.6, 19.4.2.3
C-406/08	*Uniplex*	EU:C:2010:45	3.5.3.1
C-337/08	*X Holding BV*	EU:C:2010:89	6.4.2, 17.3, 17.4.2, 18.5
C-317-320/08	*Alassini a.o. v. Telecom Italia Spa a.o.*	EU:C:2010:146	3.5.2.1
C-440/08	*Gielen*	EU:C:2010:148	6.3, 13.2, 13.5
C-542/08	*Barth*	EU:C:2010:193	3.5.3.2
C-510/08	*Mattner*	EU:C:2010:216	14.1, 14.2, 14.3.3, 14.4.1
C-352/08	*Modehuis A. Zwijnenburg*	EU:C:2010:282	17.13.1
C-56/09	*Zanotti*	EU:C:2010:288	21.1
C-487/08	*Commission v. Spain*	EU:C:2010:310	11.5.1, 16.3.2
C-58/08	*Vodafone*	EU:C:2010:321	2.1
C-105/08	*Commission v. Portugal*	EU:C:2010:345	21.4.1
C-188 and 189/10	*Melki and Abdeli*	EU:C:2010:363	3.5.2.1
C-338/08 and C-339/08	*P. Ferrero e C. and General Beverage EUrope BV*	EU:C:2010:364	16.5.1, 16.6.3
C-118/08	*Transportes Urbanos*	EU:C:2010:39	3.5.3.2
C-35/09	*Paolo Speranza*	EU:C:2010:393	3.5.2.2
C-246/09	*Susanne Bulicke*	EU:C:2010:418	3.5.3.1
C-173/09	*Elchinov*	EU:C:2010:581	3.5.2.1
C-400/10	*PPU J. McB. v. L.E.*	EU:C:2010:582	3.1.4
C-97/09	*Ingrid Schmelz*	EU:C:2010:632	3.2.1.1, 15.3
C-103/09	*HMRC v. Weald Leasing Ltd*	EU:C:2010:633	7.4, 7.5, 15.7
C-72/09	*Etablissements Rimbaud*	EU:C:2010:645	5.2.2, 19.3, 19.4.3.4, 28.10
C-199/10	*Secilpar Sociedade Unipes-soal SL*	EU:C:2010:706	6.5.4, 11.2, 11.5.1
C-108/09	*Ker-Optika*	EU:C:2010:725	3.2.1.2, 3.2.5, 6.5.2
C-277/09	*RBS Deutschland Holdings GbmH*	EU:C:2010:810	19.5.3.3
C-279/09	*DEB GmbH v. Bundesrepu-blik Deutschland*	EU:C:2010:811	3.1.4
C-287/10	*Tankreederei I*	EU:C:2010:827	19.5.3.2

Case	Name	Reported	Reference
C-436/08 and 437/08	*Haribo Lakritzen Hans Riegel and Osterreichische Salinen*	EU:C:2011:61 and EU:C:2009:17	3.2.7.1, 5.2.2, 6.4.2, 6.5.3, 7.5, 7.6, 8.2.5, 11.2, 11.4.2, 11.4.3, 16.4.1, 16.4.3, 16.8.7
C-25/10	*Missionswerk Werner*	EU:C:2011:65	14.1, 14.3.3, 14.4.5
C-407/09	*Commission v. Greece*	EU:C:2011:196	3.5.4.5
C-384/09	*Prunus*	EU:C:2011:276	5.3
C-83/09	*Kronoply and Kronotex*	EU:C:2011:341	15.4.5
C-262/09	*Meilicke II*	EU:C:2011:438	3.5.2.1, 6.4.2, 6.5.2, 11.2
C-4/10 and C-27/10	*Bureau national interprofes-sionnel du Cognac*	EU:C:2011:484	2.2.3
C-397/09	*Scheuten Solar Technology*	EU:C:2011:499	10.6.1.2, 16.5.1
C-403/10	*Mediaset*	EU:C:2011:533	15.2.2, 15.2.4
C-398/09	*Lady & Kid A/S a.o.*	EU:C:2011:540	3.5.2.2
C-78/08 to C-80/08	*Paint Graphos*	EU:C:2011:550	25.2.5, 25.2.7, 25.4.3
C-310/09	*Accor SA*	EU:C:2011:581	3.5.2.2, 6.4.1, 11.2, 11.3, 11.4.2, 11.4.3
C-132/10	*Halley*	EU:C:2011:586	14.1, 14.3.1, 14.3.3, 14.4.4
C-284/09	*Commission v. Germany*	EU:C:2011:670	11.4.2, 16.3.2, 19.2
C-126/10	*Foggia – Sociedade Gestora de Participacoes Sociais SA v. Secretario de Estado dos Assuntos Fiscais*	EU:C:2011:718	7.13.6, 15.4, 16.8.3, 19.5.3.2,
C-106/09 and C-107/09	*Commission and Spain v. Gibraltar and UK*	EU:C:2011:732	15.2.3, 15.2.5
C-371/10	*National Grid Indus BV*	EU:C:2011:785	3.2.2, 6.4.2, 7.5, 7.8.1, 7.8.2, 13.2.1, 19.4.2.1, 20.4
C-411/10	*N.S.*	EU:C:2011:865	4.2.3
C-424/10 and C-425/10	*Ziolkowski and Szeja*	EU:C:2011:866	7.8.3
C-417/10	*3M Italia*	EU:C:2012:184	2.1, 3.5.2.1, 19.5.2, 25.2.4, 25.2.5, 25.2.7
C-500/10	*Belvedere Costruzioni*	EU:C:2012:186	4.3.5
C-338/11	*Santander Asset Manage-ment*	EU:C:2012:286	7.8.3, 11.2
C-318/10	*Societe d'investissement pour l'agriculture tropicale SA (SIAT)*	EU:C:2012:415	7.6, 16.8.7, 17.6, 19.5.3.3
C-269/09	*Commission v. Spain (individuals)*	EU:C:2012:439	20.1, 20.3, 20.4
C-250/95 and C-378/10	*VALE Epitesi kft*	EU:C:2012:440	17.4.3, 20.3
C-31/11	*Scheunemann*	EU:C:2012:481	14.1, 14.3.1
C-48/11	*Veronsaajien oikeudenval-vontayksikko v. A Oy*	EU:C:2012:485	17.1
C-38/10	*Commission v. Portugal*	EU:C:2012:521	20.3
C-18/11	*Philips Electronics*	EU:C:2012:532	10.1.3, 10.6, 19.4.4.3
C-249/11	*Byankov*	EU:C:2012:608	3.5.3.2
C-498/10	*X NV*	EU:C:2012:635	11.5.1

Case	Name	Reported	Reference
C-371/11	*Punch Graphix Prepress Belgium N.V. v. Belgische Staat*	EU:C:2012:647	16.5.1
C-342/10	*Commission v. Finland*	EU:C:2012:688	19.5.1
C-35/11	*Test Claimants in the FII Group Litigation 2*	EU:C:2012:707	5.2.4, 6.4.1, 6.4.5, 8.2.5, 11.2, 11.4.3, 11.5.1, 19.3
C-224/11	*BGŻ Leasing*	EU:C:2013:15	18.2.3
C-301/11	*Commission v. the Netherlands (companies and unincorporated businesses)*	EU:C:2013:47	20.3
C-123/11	*A Oy*	EU:C:2013:84	10.1.3, 10.2.3, 10.3.2, 17.8.2
C-617/10	*Akerberg Fransson*	EU:C:2013:105	3.1.4, 4.2.1.1, 4.3.9
C-399/11	*Melloni*	EU:C:2013:107	4.1, 4.2.1.2
C-168/11	*Manfred Beker & Christa Beker*	EU:C:2013:117	7.8.3
C-85/11	*Commission/Finland*	EU:C:2013:217	20.5.2
C-565/11	*Irimie*	EU:C:2013:250	3.5.2.1
C-64/11	*Commission v. Spain (companies and asset relocation)*	EU:C:2013:264	20.3
C-653/11	*Newey*	EU:C:2013:409	7.4
C-259/12	*Rodopi*	EU:C:2013:414	4.3.8
C-350/11	*Argenta Spaarbank NV I*	EU:C:2013:477	7.8.3
C-261/11	*Commission v. Denmark (transfer of assets)*	EU:C:2013:480	20.3
C-426/11	*Alemo Herron*	EU:C:2013:521	4.2.1.1
C-6/12	*P Oy*	EU:C:2013:525	15.2.5, 25.4.3
C-49/12	*HMRC v. Sunico ApS a.o.*	EU:C:2013:545	3.5.4.1
C-282/12	*ITELCAR and Fazenda Publica*	EU:C:2013:629	7.4, 17.6
C-181/12	*Welte*	EU:C:2013:662	14.1.2, 14.3.1, 14.3.3, 14.4.1
C-181/12	*Welte*	EU:C:2013:662	5.2.3
C-276/12	*Sabou*	EU:C:2013:678	4.3.1, 4.3.5, 28.2.5, 28.19.1
C-322/11	*K.*	EU:C:2013:716	3.2.7.3, 7.8.1, 10.1.3, 10.1.4, 10.2, 10.3, 10.7
C-303/12	*Imfeldt and Garcet*	EU:C:2013:822	7.8.3
C-164/12	*DMC Beteiligungs-gesellschaft mbH*	EU:C:2014:20	3.2.2, 7.8.2, 19.4.2.1, 20.3
C-296/12	*Commission v. Belgium*	EU:C:2014:24	20.2
C-385/12	*Hervis Sport*	EU:C:2014:47	19.4.1.4
C-18/13	*Maks Pen OEED*	EU:C:2014:49	3.5.2.3
C-155/13	*SICES*	EU:C:2014:145	7.4
C-138/02	*Collins*	EU:C:2014:172	7.8.3
C-80/12	*Felixstowe Dock and Railway Company Ltd a.o.*	EU:C:2014:200	3.2.2, 15.5
C-190/12	*Emerging Markets Series*	EU:C:2014:249	5.2.2
C-209/13	*UK v. Council*	EU:C:2014:283	2.3.3
C-24/12 en C-27/12	*X and TBG Ltd*	EU:C:2014:1385	5.3
C-39/13 to C-41/13	*SCA, X AG MSA*	EU:C:2014:1758	9.3
C-129/13 and 130/13	*Kamino and Datema Hellman*	EU:C:2014:2041	3.5.2.1, 4.1, 4.3.5, 4.3.7
C-198/13	*Hernandez*	EU:C:2014:2055	4.2.1.1
C-48/13	*Nordea Bank Danmark A/S*	EU:C:2014:2087	10.1.3, 10.3.2, 10.6
C-58/13	*Torresi*	EU:C:2014:2088	15.4

Case	Name	Reported	Reference
C-227/12	*Commission v. Spain*	EU:C:2014:2130	14.1
C-589/12	*GMAC UK plc*	EU:C:2014:2131	3.5.1
C-211/13	*Commission v. Germany*	EU:C:2014:2148	14.1
C-47/12	*Kronos International*	EU:C:2014:2200	19.3
C-133/13	*Q (Bean House)*	EU:C:2014:2255	14.1, 14.3.2, 14.3.3, 14.4.2, 28.2.1, 28.2.3, 28.10, 28.10.2
C-333/13	*Dano*	EU:C:2014:2358	7.8.3
C-112/14	*Commission v. UK*	EU:C:2014:2369	5.2.4
C-202/13	*Mc Carthy*	EU:C:2014:2450	7.4
C-131/13, C-163/16 and C-164/16	*Italmoda a.o.*	EU:C:2014:2455	3.5.1, 19.2.3
C-640/13	*Commission v. UK*	EU:C:2014:2457	3.5.2.2
C-172/13	*Commission v. UK ('Marks & Spencer III')*	EU:C:2015:50	3.2.7.3, 10.1, 10.2.2, 10.2.3, 10.2.4, 10.3, 15.8.2
C-512/13	*Sopora*	EU:C:2015:108	3.2.2, 8.3.4, 17.5
C-591/13	*Commission v. Germany*	EU:C:2015:230	7.8.2, 20.4
C-66/14	*Finanzamt Linz*	EU:C:2015:242	9.3
C-497/14	*Burzio*	EU:C:2015:251	4.2.1.1
C-657/13	*Verder LabTec GmbH & Co. KG*	EU:C:2015:331	7.4, 7.8.2, 19.4.2.1, 19.4.2.4, 20.3
C-560/13	*Wagner-Raith*	EU:C:2015:347	5.2.3, 5.2.4, 19.2
C-15/14	*Commission v. MOL*	EU:C:2015:362	15.2.5
C-686/13	*X AB v. Skatteverket*	EU:C:2015:375	6.5.1
C-29/14	*EUropean Commission v. Republic of Poland*	EU:C:2015:379	6.8.6
C-98/14	*Berlington Hungary*	EU:C:2015:386	4.2.3
C-508/13	*Estonia/European Parlement*	EU:C:2015:403	2.3.1
C-9/14	*Kieback*	EU:C:2015:406	3.2.7.3, 7.5.1, 21.4.8
C-108/14 and C-109/14	*Larentia and Minerva*	EU:C:2015:496	20.5.2
C-386/14	*Groupe Steria SCA*	EU:C:2015:524	2.2.6, 6.5.1, 9.3, 9.4.3, 11.4.1, 16.4.7
C-105/14	*Taricco et aa.*	EU:C:2015:555	3.5.2.1, 4.2.1.1, 4.2.3, 4.3.8, 4.3.9
C-160/14	*Ferreira da Silva e Brito a.o.*	EU:C:2015:565	3.5.4.4
C-10/14, C-14/14 and C-17/14	*Miljoen, X and Societe Generale*	EU:C:2015:608	6.5.4, 11.2, 11.4.2, 11.5.1, 16.3.2
C-201/14	*Smaranda Bara et aa.*	EU:C:2015:638	4.2.2, 4.3.1, 28.13
C-362/14	*Schrems*	EU:C:2015:650	4.2.3, 4.3.1
C-198/14	*Visnapuu*	EU:C:2015:751	19.3
C-632/13	*Hirvonen*	EU:C:2015:765	6.3, 21.2, 21.5
C-388/14	*Timac Agro Deutschland GmbH*	EU:C:2015:829	3.2.2, 3.2.7.1, 3.2.7.3, 6.3, 6.4.2, 7.5, 7.8.1, 8.2.5, 9.3, 9.4.2, 10.1.3, 10.2.2, 10.3.1, 10.3.2, 18.1, 18.2, 18.7, 21.4.6
C-419/14	*WebMindLicences*	EU:C:2015:832	4.2.1.1, 4.2.3, 4.3.5, 4.3.7, 15.4, 28.19.1
C-194/15	*Baudinet*	EU:C:2016:81	4.3.2
C-299/14	*Vestische Arbeit Jobcenter Kreis Recklinghausen*	EU:C:2016:114	7.8.3

Case	Name	Reported	Reference
C-522/14	*Sparkasse Allgau*	EU:C:2016:253	28.2.5
C-100/15	*Netherlands Maritime Technology Association*	EU:C:2016:254	15.2.7
C-244/15	*Commission v. Greece*	EU:C:2016:359	14.1, 14.3.3, 14.4.2
C-252/14	*Pensioenfonds Metaal en Techniek v. Skatteverket*	EU:C:2016:402	11.1.5, 11.2, 11.5.1, 20.2
C-479/14	*Hunnebeck*	EU:C:2016:412	14.1, 14.2, 14.3.3, 14.4.1
C-176/15	*Riskin and Timmermans*	EU:C:2016:488	5.2.5, 9.5
C-123/15	*Max-Heinz Feilen vs Finanzamt Fulda*	EU:C:2016:496	7.8.1, 14.1, 14.3.1, 14.3.2, 14.3.3, 14.4.8
C-18/15	*Brisal and KBC Finance Ireland*	EU:C:2016:549	11.2, 11.5.1, 13.4.1, 21.3
C-423/15	*Kratzer*	EU:C:2016:604	7.4
C-576/15	*Maya Marinova*	EU:C:2016:740	4.3.8
C-24/15	*Plockl*	EU:C:2016:791	4.3.8
C-449/14	*DTS*	EU:C:2016:848	15.2.4
C-464/14	*SECIL v. Fazenda Publica*	EU:C:2016:896	5.2.2
C-503/14	*EUropean Commission v. Portuguese Republic*	EU:C:2016:979	3.2.2, 6.5.1, 7.10, 20.4, 21.6
C-20/15 and C-21/15	*World Duty Free*	EU:C:2016:981	15.2.5
C-593/14	*Masco Denmark ApS and Damixa ApS v. Skatteministeriet*	EU:C:2016:984	9.6, 11.2, 11.4.1
C-164/15	*Aer Lingus*	EU:C:2016:990	25.2.7, 25.4.4
C-189/15	*IRCCS - Fondazione Santa Lucia*	EU:C:2017:1	15.2.3
C-283/15	*X v. Staatssecretaris*	EU:C:2017:102	3.2.7.3, 6.5.1, 13.1, 13.2, 13.4.2, 13.4.6, 13.4.8
C-317/15	*X v. Staatssecretaris*	EU:C:2017:119	3.2.6, 5.2.3
C-390/15	*Rzecznik Praw Obywatelskich (RPO)*	EU:C:2017:174	2.2.6, 2.3.1, 19.3
C-14/16	*EUro Park Service*	EU:C:2017:177	3.2.1.1, 7.4, 7.13.1, 18.2.4.3 19.3, 19.5.1, 19.5.3.3
C-448/15	*Belgische Staat v. Wereldhave Belgium*	EU:C:2017:180	7.7, 16.3.1, 18.3.1, 19.2.4
C-217/15 and C-350/15	*Orsi and Baldetti*	EU:C:2017:264	4.2.1.1, 4.2.3, 4.3.9
C-98/16	*Commission v. Greece*	EU:C:2017:346	14.1, 14.3.3, 14.4.5
C-59/16	*The Shirtmakers*	EU:C:2017:362	18.2.3
C-682/15	*Berlioz*	EU:C:2017:373	4.1, 4.2.1.1, 4.2.3, 4.3.5, 4.3.6, 28.2.3, 28.3.1, 28.9, 28.10, 28.19.1, 28.19.2
C-365/16	*Association francaise des entreprises privees (AFEP) a.o.*	EU:C:2017:378	6.4.7, 16.4.2.1
C-68/15	*X v. Ministerraad*	EU:C:2017:379	16.4.2.1, 16.4.7, 16.6.3
C-580/15	*Van der Weegen a.o. v. Belgium*	EU:C:2017:429	3.2.1.1, 21.7
C-591/15	*The Gibraltar Betting and Gaming Association Limited*	EU:C:2017:449	5.3
C-20/16	*Bechtel*	EU:C:2017:488	3.2.7.3

Case	Name	Reported	Reference
C-74/16	*Congregacion de Escuelas Pias Provincia Betania*	EU:C:2017:496	15.2.2, 15.4.3
C-6/16	*Eqiom SAS/Enka former Holcim France SAS*	EU:C:2017:641	5.5.2, 6.8.7, 7.2, 7.4, 7.5, 7.6, 9.5, 9.6, 18.2.4.3, 19.3, 19.5.1, 19.5.3.3
C-648/15	*Austria v. Germany*	EU:C:2017:664	8.2, 8.4, 16.3.5, 18.2.3, 21.2
C-524/15	*Menci*	EU:C:2017:667	4.3.9
C-537/16	*Garlsson Real Estate*	EU:C:2017:668	3.1.4, 4.2.1.2, 4.3.9
C-646/15	*Trustees of the P Panayi Accumulation & Maintenance Settlements*	EU:C:2017:682	7.8.2, 20.1, 20.3
C-628/15	*The Trustees of BT Pension Scheme*	EU:C:2017:687	5.2.4
C-300/16	*Frucona*	EU:C:2017:706	15.2.4, 15.2.7
C-73/16	*Puškar*	EU:C:2017:725	28.13
C-192/16	*Stephen Fischer et al*	EU:C:2017:762	5.3
C-522/16	*A.*	EU:C:2017:778	7.4
C-106/16	*Polbud*	EU:C:2017:804	20.3
C-39/16	*Argenta Spaarbank NV v. Belgium II*	EU:C:2017:813	7.2, 7.4, 7.13.1, 16.3.2, 16.4.1, 16.4.7, 16.8.7, 19.5.2
C-306/16	*Marques da Rosa*	EU:C:2017:844	18.2.3
C-233/16	*Asociacion Nacional de Grandes Empresas de Distribucion (ANGED)*	EU:C:2017:852	19.4.1
C-236/16 and C-237/16	*ANGED*	EU:C:2017:854	15.2.4, 15.2.5
C-251/16	*Edward Cussens and Others*	EU:C:2017:881	15.4, 15.7, 19.5.1
C-292/16	*A Oy*	EU:C:2017:888	9.3, 20.1, 20.3
C-510/16	*Carrefour Hypermarches*	EU:C:2017:929	25.4.3
C-382/16	*Hornbach-Baumarkt AG*	EU:C:2017:974 (pending)	3.2.1.1, 3.2.2, 3.2.7.1, 6.3, 6.4.1, 6.4.2, 7.8.2, 11.4.2
C-504/16 and C 613/16	*Deister Holding AG and Juhler Holding A/S*	EU:C:2017:1009	5.5.2, 6.8.7, 6.8.7, 7.1, 7.2, 7.5, 7.6, 7.8.3, 9.5, 9.6, 18.2.4.3, 19.4.3.4, 19.5.1, 19.5.3.3
C-398/16 and C-399/16	*X BV and X NV*	EU:C:2018:110	9.4.2
C-327/16 and C-421/16	*Jacob and Lassus pending*		20.3
C-355/16	*(Picart)*	EU:C:2018:184	13.7
C-110/17	*(Commission v. Belgium)*	EU:C:2018:250	13.1
C-650/16	*A/S Bevola, Jens W. Trock ApS v. Skateministeriet*	EU:C:2018:424	9.3, 9.4.2 10.1, 10.2.2, 10.3.1, 10.3.2
C-602/17	*(Sauvage)*	EU:C:2018:856	13.4.2, 13.6
C-697/17	*Huijbrechts*	EU:C:2018:940	14.1, 14.3.2, 14.3.3, 14.4.2
C-575/17	*Sofina and Others*	EU:C:2018:943	6.5.2, 7.8.2, 9.4.2, 11.5.2, 13.3
C-480/17	*(Montag)*	EU:C:2018:987	13.6
C-272/17	*(Zyla)*	EU:C:2019:49	13.4.10

Case	Name	Reported	Reference
C-115/16, C-118/16, C-119/16 and C-299/16	*N Luxembourg 1, X Denmark A/S, C Danmark I and Z Denmark ApS*	EU:C:2019:134	2.2.3.1, 7.4, 18.2.3, 18.3.1, 18.3.4, 18.7.1
C-116/16 and C-117/16	*T Danmark and Y Denmark ApS*	EU:C:2019:135	2.2.3.1, 18.2.3, 18.3.4, 18.7.1
C-135/17	*X GmbH v. Finanzamt Stuttgart*	EU:C:2019:136	5.2.3, 7.4, 7.6, 9.5
C-607/17	*Skatteverket v. Memira Holding AB*	EU:C:2019:510	10.1.3, 10.2.3, 10.2.4, 10.3.2
C-608/17	*Holmen AB*	EU:C:2019:511	
C-641/17	*College Pension Plan of British Columbia*	EU:C:2019:960	5.2.3, 11.1.5, 11.2, 21.4.1
C-416/17	*Commission v. France*		11.1.5
C-482/17	*Czech Republic v. EU Parliament and Council*	EU:C:2019:1035	2.2.6
C-389/18	*Brussels Securities SA*	EU:C:2019:1132	16.4.2.1
C-156/17	*Köln-Aktienfonds Deka*	EU:C:2020:51	3.2.1.1, 6.5.2
C-480/19	*E or Veronsaajien oikeuden-valvontayksikkö*	EU:C:2020:94	11.2
C-788/18	*(Stanleyparma and Stanleybet)*	EU:C:2020:110	11.2
C-405/18	*AURES*	EU:C:2020:127	10.1.3
C-749/18	*B and Others*	EU:C:2020:370	9.3
C-667/18	*Orde van Vlaamse Balies*	EU:C:2020:372	4.2.2
C-245/19 and C-246/19	*B and others (Shakira)*	EU:C:2020:795	28.2.3, 28.19.2
C-558/19	*Impresa Pizzarotti & C SPA Italia Sucursala Cluj*	EU:C:2020:806	9.6
C-626/18	*Poland v. EU Parliament and Council*	EU:C:2020:1000	2.2.6
C-420/19	*Heavyinstall*	EU:C:2021:33	6.5.2
C-484/19	*Lexel AB*	EU:C:2021:34	7.5, 9.4, 11.5.2
C-403/19	*Société Générale*	EU:C:2021:136	11.2
C-388/19	*MK*	EU:C:2021:212	13.5
C-449/20	*Real Vida Seguros SA*	EU:C:2021:721	13.7
C-437/19	*L*	EU:C:2021:953	28.2.3, 28.19.2
C-478/19 and C-479/19	*UBS Real Estate*	EU:C:2021:1015	11.1.5
C-394/20	*XY*	EU:C:2021:1044	7.8.1, 14.1, 14.2, 14.3.3, 14.4.1, 14.4.3
C-181/20	*VYSOCINA WIND*	EU:C:2022:51	2.3.1
C-788/19	*EUropean Commission v. Kingdom of Spain*	EU:C:2022:55	5.2.4
C-175/20	*'SS' SIA*	EU:C:2022:124	28.3.2.5
C-657/20	*'Viva Telecom Bulgaria' EOOD*	EU:C:2022:125	9.6, 16.5, 18.1.1, 18.2.1, 18.2.4.1, 18.2.4.3, 18.5.2, 18.6.1.2
C-52/21	*Pharmacie populaire*	EU:C:2022:127	9.5, 9.6
C-545/19	*AllianzGI-Fonds*	EU:C:2022:193	11.1.5, 11.2, 11.5.2
C-342/20	*A SCPI*	EU:C:2022:276	9.3, 9.6, 11.1.5, 11.2
C-674/20	*Airbnb Ireland UC v. Region de Bruxelles-Capitale*	EU:C:2022:303	28.3.2.5
C-556/20	*Schneider Electric SA a.o.*	EU:C:2022:378	11.3, 16.4.1, 16.4.2.1
C-572/20	*ACC Silicones*	EU:C:2022:469	11.2

Case	Name	Reported	Reference
C-278/20	*Commission v Spain (Violation du droit de l'Union par le législateur)*	EU:C:2022:503	3.5.4.1
C-538/20	*W AG*	EU:C:2022:717	6.4.2
C-431/21	*X GmbH & Co. KG*	EU:C:2022:792	9.5, 9.6
C-295/21	*Allianz Benelux SA*	EU:C:2022:812	16.4.2.1
C-435/22	*PPU, Generalstaats-anwaltschaft München*	EU:C:2022:852	19.2.3
C-885/19 P & C-898/19 P	*Fiat Chrysler Finance Europe*	EU:C:2022:859	2.2.3.1, 6.5.3, 15.2.7
C-203/21	*Delta Story 2003*	EU:C:2022:865	4.3.6
C-37/20 and C-601/20	*WM*	EU:C:2022:912	2.3.1
C-694/20	*Orde van Vlaamse Balies*	EU:C:2022:963	2.2.6
C-340/22	*Cofidis*	EU:C:2023	9.3
C-649/20, C-658/20 and C-662/20	*Spain v Commission*	EU:C:2023:60	15.2.5
C-707/20	*Gallaher*	EU:C:2023:101	5.2.4
C-537/20	*L Fund*	EU:C:2023:339	11.1.6
C-827/21	*(Banca A v Agenția Națională de Administrare Fiscală (ANAF), Președintele ANAF)*	EU:C:2023:355	17.12.3
C-407/22 and C-408/22	*Manitou and Bricolage*	EU:C:2023:392	9.4.3
C-105/22	*P.M.*	EU:C:2023:414	3.1.0
C-258/22	*H Lebensversicherung*	EU:C:2023:506	11.2
C-461/21	*Cartrans Preda*	EU:C:2023:632	11.3, 11.4.2, 13.4.1
C-312/22	*FL*	EU:C:2023:771	13.1
C-472/22	*NO*	EU:C:2023:880	13.1
C-318/22	*(GE Infrastructure Hungary Holding Kft. v Nemzeti Adó – és Vámhivatal Fellebbviteli Igazgatósága)*	EU:C:2023:890	17.12.3
C-451/21	*Luxembourg v Commission (Engie)*	EU:C:2023:948	15.3.2
C-457/21	*Commission v Amazon.com and Others*	EU:C:2023:985	15.2.7
C-627/22	*AB*	EU:C:2024:431	13.2, 13.3
C-420/23	*Faurécia*	EU:C:2024:534	9.2, 11.5.2
C-184/23	*Finanzamt T/S*	EU:C:2024:599	2.2.5.1
C-623/22	*Belgian Association of Tax Lawyers*	EU:C:2024:639	2.2.6, 6.5.4, 19.3, 19.5.2
C-39/23	*Keva*	EU:C:2024:648	6.5.3, 11.1.5, 11.2, 11.5.2
C-465/20	*Commission v Ireland and Others*	EU:C:2024:724	15.2.7
C-555/22, C-556/22 and C-564/22	*United Kingdom v Commission and Others*	EU:C:2024:763	15.2.4, 15.2.7
C-432/23	*F SCS/Ordre des avocats du Barreau de Luxembourg*	EU:C:2024:791	2.2.6, 4.2.2
C-585/22	*X BV*	EU:C:2024:822	7.1, 7.5, 7.6, 7.7, 9.6, 11.5.2, 19.5.2
C-782/22	*XX*	EU:C:2024:932	11.1.6, 13.4.1
C-336/24	*Sinhren Invest*	EU:C:2024:982	4.3.6
C-436/23	*Volvo Group Belgium*	EU:C:2024:1023	3.2.2

Case	Name	Reported	Reference
C-601/23	*Credit Suisse Securities*	EU:C:2024:1048	6.5.2, 7.8.2, 9.4.2, 10.1.2, 10.14, 10.4, 11.5.2
C-18/23	*Dyrektor Krajowej Informacji Skarbowej (Mode de gestion d'un OPC)*	EU:C:2025:119	3.2.1.1
C-135/24	*John Cockerill SA*	EU:C:2025:176	16.4.1, 16.4.2.1
C-92/24 and C-94/24	*Banca Mediolanum a.o.*	EU:C:2025:223	16.4.2.1
C-228/24	*'Nordcurrent group' UAB*	EU:C:2025:239	16.8.1, 16.8.2, 16.8.3, 16.8.4, 16.8.5, 16.8.6
T-143/23	*Fugro*	EU:T:2023:873	2.2.6
C-83/21	*Airbnb Ireland UC, Airbnb Payments UK Ltd v. Agenzia delle Entrate*	pending	28.3.2.5
C-597/16	*Consob v. Zecca*	pending	4.2.1.2, 4.3.9
C-828/2	*Erdrich Umformtechnik GmbH*	pending	18.6.2.2
C-685/16	*EV v. Finanzamt Lippstadt*	pending	5.2.3
C-188/92	*TWD Textilwerke Deggendorf*	pending	15.4.5
C-538/20	*W AG*	Pending	10.1.3, 10.1.4, 10.2.2, 10.2.4, 10.3.1, 10.3.2

EFTA Court

Case	Name	Reporte	Reference
E-1/04	*Fokus Bank ASA v. The Norwegian State*	EFTA Court Report 2004 p 11; OJ C 45 of 23 February 2006	11.1.5, 11.2
E-7/07	*Seabrokers*	EFTA Court Report 2008	9.6
E-3/13 and E-20/13	*Fred. Olsen and Others v. the Norwegian State*		9.5
E-15/16	*Yara International*		10.1.3, 10.2.2, 10.2.4
E-3/21	*RA Group*	Europe SA EFTA Court 1 June 2022	19.1.4.2
E-7/23	*ExxonMobil*	EFTA Court, 24 May 2024	10.1.3, 10.2.2, 10.2.4
E-3/21	*PRA Holding SA*	pending	9.6

European Court of Human Rights

Case	Name	Reported	Reference
5100/71, 5101/71, 5102/71, 53454/72	*Engel v. Netherlands*	CE:ECHR:1976:1123JUD000510071	4.3.9
9248/81	*Leander v. Sweden*	CEECHR:1987:0326JUD000924881	4.3.1
13972/88	*Imbrioscia*	CEECHR:1993:1124JUD001397288	4.3.5
18731/91	*Murray v. United Kingdom*	CEECHR:1996:0208JUD001873191	4.3.6
19187/91	*Saunders v. United Kingdom*	CEECHR:1996:1217JUD001918791	4.3.6
27798/95	*Amann v. Switzerland*	CEECHR:2000:0216JUD002779895	4.3.1
28341/95	*Rotaru v. Romania*	CEECHR:2000:0504JUD002834195	4.3.1
31827/96	*J.B. v. Switzerland*	CEECHR:2001:0503JUD003182796	4.3.6
44759/98	*Ferrazzini v. Italy (Grand Chamber)*	CEECHR:2001:0712JUD004475998	4.2.1.1
34619/97	*Janosevic v. Sweden*	CEECHR:2002:0723JUD003461997	4.3.2, 4.3.5
36677/97	*Dangeville v. France*	CEECHR:2002:0416JUD003667797	4.2.3

Case	Name	Reported	Reference
44759/98	*Ferrazzini v. Italy*		3.1.4, 4.3.2
45036/98	*Bosphorus Hava Yollari Turizm*	CEECHR:2005:0630JUD004503698	4.2.3
49429/99	*Capital Bank AD v. Bulgaria Case*	CEECHR:2005:1124JUD004942999	4.3.2
73053/01	*Jussila v. Finland*	CEECHR:2006:1123JUD007305301	4.3.2, 4.3.5, 4.3.9
14939/03	*Sergey Zolotukhin v. Russia*	CEECHR:2009:0210JUD001493903	4.3.9
18497/03	*Ravon*	CEECHR:2008:0221JUD001849703	4.3.5
30562/04 and 30566/04	*S. and Marper v. The United Kingdom*	CEECHR:2008:1204JUD003056204	4.3.1
30696/09	*M.S.S. v. Belgium and Greece*	CEECHR:2011:0121JUD003069609	4.2.3
8319/07 and 11449/07	*Sufi and Elmi v. United Kingdom*	CEECHR:2011:0628JUD000831907	4.2.3
16188/07	*Khelili v. Switzerland*	CEECHR:2011:1018JUD001618807	4.3.1
11663/04	*Chambaz v. Switzerland*	CEECHR:2012:0405JUD001166304	4.3.6
24029/07	*M.M. v. The United Kingdom*	CEECHR:2012:1113JUD002402907	4.3.1
12323/11	*Michaud v. France*	CEECHR:2012:1206JUD001232311	4.2.3
57665/12 and 57657/12	*Koufaki and ADEDY v. Greece*	CEECHR:2013:0507DEC005766512	4.3.2
66529/11	*N.K.M. v. Hungary*	CEECHR:2013:0514JUD006652911	4.3.2
49570/11	*Gall v. Hungary*	CEECHR:2013:0625JUD004957011	3.2.1.1, 4.3.2
41838/11	*R.Sz. v. Hungary*	CEECHR:2013:0702JUD004183811	3.2.1.1
11082/06 and 13772/05	*Khodorkovskiy and Lebedev v. Russia [Yukos] case*	CEECHR:2013:0725JUD001108206	4.3.8
62235/12 and 57725/12	*Da Conceicao Mateus v. Portugal*	CEECHR:2013:1008DEC006223512	4.3.2
75292/10	*Othymia Investments*	CEECHR:2015:0616DEC007529210	28.12.1
17502/07	*Avotins v. Latvia*	CEECHR:2016:0523JUD001750207	4.2.3
24130/11 and 29758/11	*A. and B. v. Norway*	CEECHR:2016:1115JUD002413011	3.1.4, 4.2.1.2, 4.3.9
66529/11	*N.K.M. v. Hungary*	CEECHR:2017:1114DEC004618416	3.2.1.1
13341/14	*Da Silva Carvalho Rico v. Portugal*	CEECHR:2015:0901DEC001334114	4.3.2

National Courts:

Conseil d'État (France)

Case	Name	Reported	Reference
249047	*SarL Coreal Gestion*	ECLI:FR:CESEC:2003:24904720031230	9.6

Case	Name	Reported	Reference
2010/ AR/2449			18.6.2.2

Bundesfinanzhof (Germany) and Reichsfinanzhof (predecessor of Bundesfinanzhof)

Case	Name	Reported	Reference
VI A 414/35	*10.3.1*		
I R 59/71	*10.3.1*		
I R 116/04	*10.3.1*		
I R 207/09	*10.2.4*		
I R 48/11	*10.3.1*		

Case	Name	Reported	Reference
I R 2/15	*10.3.2*		
I R 32/18	*10.1.4, 10.2.4, 10.3.1, 10.3.2*		

Verwaltungsgerichtshof (Austria)

Case	Name	Reported	Reference
85/14/0001			10.3.1
99/14/0217			10.3.2
Ro 2015/15/0004			10.3.2

Hof van Cassatie (Belgium)

Case	Name	Reported	Reference
F.15.0102.N			11.4.2

Hoge Raad (Netherlands Supreme Court)

Case	Name	Reported	Reference
27 252		*BNB 1992/379*	6.3.1
14/00521			14.4.3

Tribunal de première instance Arlon (Belgium)

Case	Name	Reported	Reference
	SA NWB v. Etat belge	Tijdschrift voor Fiscaal Recht June 2014 p 553-556	18.7.2

US Supreme Court

Case	Name	Reported	Reference
13-485	*Comptroller (Maryland) v. Wynne*		

www.ingramcontent.com/pod-product-compliance
Ingram Content Group UK Ltd.
Pitfield, Milton Keynes, MK11 3LW, UK
UKHW020256051026
15470UKWH00020B/349

9 789403 541457